# Anthology of
# Modern American Poetry

# Editorial Advisory Board

# Anthology of
# Modern American Poetry

EDITED BY CARY NELSON

NEW YORK    OXFORD
**OXFORD UNIVERSITY PRESS**
2000

OXFORD UNIVERSITY PRESS

Oxford     New York
Athens  Auckland  Bangkok  Bogotá  Buenos Aires  Calcutta
Cape Town  Chennai  Dar es Salaam  Delhi  Florence  Hong Kong  Istanbul
Karachi  Kuala Lumpur  Madrid  Melbourne  Mexico City  Mumbai
Nairobi  Paris  São Paulo  Singapore  Taipei  Tokyo  Toronto  Warsaw
*and associated companies in*
Berlin  Ibadan

Published by Oxford University Press, Inc.,
198 Madison Avenue, New York, New York, 10016
http://www.oup-usa.org

Oxford is a registered trademark of Oxford University Press

*Anthology of Modern American Poetry* incorporates selected notes from *American
Literature: A Prentice Hall Anthology (1991)* edited by Emory Elliott (general Editor),
Linda K. Kerber, A. Walton Litz, and Terence Martin

Library of Congress Cataloging-in-Publication Data

Anthology of modern American poetry / edited by Cary Nelson.
    p.  cm.
  Includes index.
  ISBN 0-19-512271-2 (paper : acid-free paper)
  1. American poetry—20th century.  I. Nelson, Cary.
PS613 .A54 1999
811.008—dc21
                                                    99-16339
                                                    CIP
                                                    Rev.


Printing (last digit): 9 8 7 6 5 4 3 2 1


Printed in the United States of America
on acid-free paper

# Contents

# Preface

This is an anthology with a special claim on readers' attention. The claim is unashamedly grandiose—that modern American poetry is one of the major achievements of human culture. Now, with the twentieth century only recently come to an end, we can for the first time see that achievement in its entirety. With perhaps as much catholicity of taste as one editor can muster, I have tried to present twentieth-century American poetry in its astonishing and endlessly energetic variety. There are omissions, to be sure. Like any editor I would readily trade my kingdom for another hundred pages. If I had them, my first addition would be a full and fair representation of American song. Unable to do the tradition justice, I chose not to do it at all. Are there other poets I would love to add? Certainly. Are there a few who would have a slightly more generous selection if their publishers did not demand such exorbitant reprint fees? To be sure. But overall I believe this anthology more than fulfills its aims.

It includes many familiar poets and poems, among them poems reprinted in anthology after anthology with good reason. In some cases this anthology urges a major reassessment. This is the first comprehensive anthology to give sufficiently full and diverse coverage to Langston Hughes to show he ranks with our most accomplished poets. In other cases I include poets who will be unknown to many readers. From time to time a poet appears here with a single poem, not to signal a distinguished career but rather to honor one poem that has proven to be one of the highlights of a major literary movement. It was not just important individual careers I decided to include, therefore, but also notable individual poems.

Even with unquestionably talented writers, however, a basic decision had to be made—whether to choose representative poems from a poet's entire career or to focus on one decisive moment of creativity. I made this decision for each writer individually. With Randall Jarrell I chose the World War II poems, which I believe are his most distinctive contribution to American poetry.

With William Carlos Williams, Theodore Roethke, and Gwendolyn Brooks I tried to represent entire careers. With Robert Frost and Wallace Stevens I emphasized the early work but added selections from other periods as well. Most poets' work is presented chronologically, but I diverged from chronology when it made for a more coherent selection. Thus I follow Wallace Stevens' own lead—as evidenced by the contents of *Harmonium*—and open his section with some of his short lyrics rather than with the earlier "Sunday Morning." Here and there I invent chronologies. For the Japanese American concentration camp poems, I create a miniature narrative by selecting and arranging these wartime Haikus in a particular order.

There are other sorts of chronologies and compelling thematic groupings that can only be discovered by reading the book. The long American poetic dialogue about race that began with the nineteenth-century Abolitionist movement becomes a powerful feature of twentieth-century poetry. White poets, black poets, Asian poets, Chicano poets, and Native American poets take up race here, reflecting on our history, interrogating both whiteness and blackness, and producing searing statements of astonishing condensation to be found nowhere else in our literature, perhaps nowhere else in our culture. I offer these reflections on race as an end-of-the-century version of William Carlos Williams' observation that people die every day for lack of the knowledge available in poems. A comparable debate about religion runs through the book, ranging from T. S. Eliot to William Everson, Amiri Baraka, Carolyn Rodgers, and Lucille Clifton.

In some cases the groupings are less conflictual. You can read Marianne Moore, Robert Lowell, Denise Levertov, Mona Van Duyn, Gregory Corso, and Ai about marriage. You can read love poems by Amy Lowell, William Carlos Williams, E. E. Cummings, and Kenneth Rexroth. You can gather together poems by Joseph Freeman, Kenneth Fearing, John Beecher, Joseph Kalar, Richard Wright, Edwin Rolfe, Sol Funaroff, Muriel Rukeyser, Genevieve Taggard, and Tillie Olsen to revisit the political 1930s. You can read poems about Helen of Troy by H.D. and Laura Riding, poems about Cassandra by Robinson Jeffers and Louise Bogan. Holocaust poems come from Randall Jarrell, Muriel Rukeyser, Charles Reznikoff, Anthony Hecht, and Robert Pinsky.

This is also the first anthology to give full coverage to the central American tradition of long poems and poem sequences. Although we could not obtain permission to reprint Hart Crane's *The Bridge* in its entirety, we do publish an unusually large number of long poems or poem sequences in complete form: Gertrude Stein's "Patriarchal Poetry," William Carlos Williams' *The Descent of Winter*, T. S. Eliot's *The Waste Land*, Edna St. Vincent Millay's "Sonnets from an Ungrafted Tree," Melvin Tolson's *Libretto for the Republic of Liberia*, Kenneth Rexroth's "The Love Poems of Marichiko," Theodore Roethke's "North American Sequence," Muriel Rukeyser's "The Book of the Dead," Denise Levertov's "Olga Poems," Allen Ginsberg's "Howl" and "Wichita Vortex Sutra," Adrienne Rich's "Twenty-one Love Poems," and Sylvia Plath's bee poems. Book-length poem sequences like Ezra Pound's *Cantos* and Charles Reznikoff's *Testimony* receive substantial selections.

I have tried to provide throughout more detailed annotation than any comprehensive American poetry anthology has offered before. Many of these poems deal with historical themes and readers will benefit, I believe, from having basic information ready-to-hand. Although the selections and headnotes are all by me, some of the notes were done by others and some were collaborative. Edward Brunner did the notes for Melvin Tolson's *Libretto for the Republic of Liberia*, notes that are a major scholarly achievement. The notes for

Muriel Rukeyser's "Book of the Dead" are by Michael Thurston, the notes for Gwendolyn Brooks' "Gay Chaps at the Bar" by Karen Ford, and for Lawson Inada's "Listening Images" by Edward Brunner. The notes for Dickinson's poems 341 and 754, for Sandburg's "Grass," Stevens' "Sunday Morning," Pound's "Portrait d'une Femme," Canto I and LXXXI, H.D.'s "Helen," Eliot's "The Love Song of J. Alfred Prufrock," *The Waste Land*, and "Journey of the Magi," Crane's "To Brooklyn Bridge" and "The River," Lowell's "Man and Wife," Merrill's "The Broken Home," Ginsberg's "Howl," Ashbery's "Farm Implements and Rutabagas in a Landscape," Plath's "Daddy," and Pinsky's "The Unseen" are partly by me and partly by the editors of Prentice-Hall's *American Literature*. Since we did not consult, all additions and judgments are my responsibility. The notes for Dickinson's 585 and 1072, Robinson's "Minniver Cheevy" and "Mr. Flood's Party," Frost's "Home Burial" and "The Wood-Pile" "The Oven Bird" and "The Need of Being Versed in Country Things," Sandburg's "Cool Tombs," Stevens' "Thirteen Ways of Looking at a Blackbird," "Disillusionment of Ten O'clock," "The Emperor of Ice-Cream," "The Idea of Order at Key West," "Mozart, 1935," "A Postcard from the Volcano," "Study of Two Pears," Williams's "The Young Housewife," "Portrait of a Lady," "The Yachts," and "Landscape with the Fall of Icarus," Moore's "Poetry," "A Grave," and "Silence," Crane's "Chaplinesque," Winters' "Sir Gawain and the Green Knight," Hughes's "The Negro Speaks of Rivers" and "The Weary Blues," Roethke's "The Flight" and "I Knew a Woman," Bishop's "In the Waiting Room," Hayden's "Runagate Runagate," Jarrell's "The Death of the Ball Turret Gunner," Berryman's 14th, 29th, and 40th *Dream Songs*, Lowell's "Memories of West Street and Lepke," "Skunk Hour," "For the Union Dead," "The Mouth of the Hudson," Ammons's "Coon Song," Wright's "Autumn Begins in Martins Ferry Ohio," Sexton's "Her Kind," and Plath's "Tulips," "The Bee Meeting," "Ariel," and "Lady Lazarus" are taken unchanged from the Prentice-Hall anthology. All other notes are by me. Recognizing the increasing availability of bibliographic information electronically, we have used the space traditionally given to lists of publications to print additional poems. The "Acknowledgments," section, which is arranged alphabetically and gives poets separate entries, does, however, list key texts for further reading, which often includes a selected or collected poems.

Along the way, many friends have offered advice. These include Julianna Chang, Alan Golding, Jefferson Hendricks, Walter Kalaidjian, William Maxwell, Tim Newcomb, Lori Newcomb, Paula Treichler, and Alan Wald. The Advisory Board was very much a working group, commenting on the contents, tolerating many phone conversations, suggesting additions and deletions. The people at Oxford have been a genuine pleasure to work with; these include my editor Tony English, his assistant Ruth Levine, and my production editor Benjamin Clark. The result of all this is an anthology that returns the last 100 years of our poetic heritage to us in a uniquely rich and provocative form.

Critical commentary or historical background on many of these poems may be found on our web site:

http://www.english.uiuc.edu/maps

The web site is edited by Cary Nelson and designed by Matthew Hurt.

# Acknowledgments

Pages xxxiii–xli constitute an extension of the copyright page.

Ai "The German Army in Russia 1943" from *Killing Floor* copyright 1979, Houghton Mifflin. Reprinted by permission of the author. "The Priest's Confession," copyright © 1986 by Ai, "The Testimony of J. Robert Oppenheimer," copyright © 1986 by Ai, "Twenty Year Marriage," copyright © 1973 by Ai, from *Vice: New and Selected Poems by Ai*. Reprinted by permission of W. W. Norton & Company, Inc.

Sherman Alexie "Indian Boy Love Song," "Evolution" from *The Business of Fancydancing*, Hanging Loose Press 1992; "No. 9" and "Scalp Dance by Spokane Indians" from *First Indian on the Moon*, Hanging Loose Press 1993; "How to Write the Great American Indian Novel" and "Tourists" from *The Summer of Black Widows*, Hanging Loose Press 1996. Reprinted by permission of the publisher.

A. R. Ammons "Corsons Inlet," copyright © 1963 by A. R. Ammons, "Gravelly Run," copyright © 1987, 1977, 1975, 1974, 1972, 1971, 1966, 1965, 1964, 1955 by A. R. Ammons, from *The Selected Poems, Expanded Edition* by A. R. Ammons. "Coon Song" from *Collected Poems 1951–1971* by A. R. Ammons. Copyright © 1972 by A. R. Ammons. Reprinted by permission of W. W. Norton Company, Inc.

Angel Island: Poems by Chinese Immigrants No. 9: ("As a traveller in wind and dust"), No. 8: ("Instead of remaining a citizen of China"), No. 47: ("I am distressed that we Chinese are detained"), No. 22: ("America has power, but not justice"), No. 46: ("The low building with three beams"), No. 42: ("The dragon out of water is humiliated by ants"), No. 27: ("The silvery red shirt is half covered with dust"), No. 27: "Poem by One Named Xu, from Xiangshan, Consoling Himself," No. 35: "Leaving Behind My Writing Brush" from *Poetry and History of Chinese Immigrants on Angel Island, 1910–1940* ed. by Him Mark Lai, Genny Lim, and Judy Yung, University of Washington Press 1980. Reprinted by permission of the University of Washington Press.

John Ashbery "They Dream Only of America" from *The Tennis Court Oath* © 1962 by John Ashbery, Wesleyan University Press by permission of University Press of New England. "Mixed Feelings," copyright © 1975 by John Ashbery, "Hop o' My Thumb," copyright © 1975 by John Ashbery, from *Self-Portrait in a Convex Mirror* by John Ashbery. Used by permission of Viking Penguin, a division of Penguin Putnam, Inc. "Farm Implements and Rutabagas in a Landscape" from *The Double Dream of Spring* (New York: Dutton, 1970). Copyright © 1970, 1969, 1968, 1967, 1966, by John Ashbery. Reprinted by permission of Georges Borchardt, Inc. "Street Musicians," "Syringa," and "Daffy Duck in Hollywood" from *Houseboat Days* (New York: Viking, 1977). Copyright © 1975, 1976, 1977, by John Ashbery. Reprinted by Permission of Georges Borchardt, Inc. "Paradoxes and Oxymorons" from *Shadow Train* (New York: Viking, 1981). Copyright © 1980, 1981 by John Ashbery. Reprinted by permission of Georges Borchardt, Inc.

Jimmy Santiago Baca "Mi Tio Baca El Poeta de Socorro" from *Black Mesa Poems*. Copyright © 1989 by Jimmy Santiago Baca. Reprinted by permission of New Directions Publishing Corp.

Amiri Baraka (Leroi Jones) "SOS" from *Black Magic Poetry*. Reprinted by permission of Sterling Lord Literistic, Inc. Copyright © 1969 by Amiri Baraka. "Black Art" (1969) and "When We'll Worship Jesus" (1972) from *Transbluesency: Selected Poems 1961–1995*, Marsilio Publishers, 1995. Reprinted by permission of the publisher.

Ray A. Young Bear "In Viewpoint: Poem for 14 Catfish and the Town of Tama, Iowa" and "It Is The Fish-faced Boy Who Struggles" from *The Winter of the Salamander,* Harper & Row, 1980. Reprinted by permission of the author.

John Berryman Dream songs #1, #4, #5, #14, #22 ("Of 1826"), #29, #40, #45, #46, #55, #76 ("Henry's Confessions"), #382, and #384 from *The Dream Songs* by John Berryman. Reprinted by permission of Farrar, Strauss & Giroux, Inc.

Elizabeth Bishop "The Fish," "The Man-Moth," "At the Fishhouses," "Filling Station," "Questions of Travel," "The Armadillo," "In the Waiting Room," "Crusoe in England," "One Art," and "Pink Dog" from *The Complete Poems 1927–1979* by Elizabeth Bishop. Reprinted by permission of Farrar, Strauss & Giroux, Inc.

Paul Blackburn "At the Well" from *The Selected Poems of Paul Blackburn.* Copyright © 1985 by Joan Blackburn. Reprinted by permission of Persea Books, Inc.

Robert Bly "Looking at New Fallen Snow from a Train" and "Counting Small-Boned Bodies" from *The Light Around My Body.* Copyright © 1967 by Robert Bly. Reprinted by permission of HarperCollins Publishers, Inc. "The Dead Seal Near McClure's Beach" from *Eating the Honey of Words: New and Selected Poems* by Robert Bly, HarperCollins 1999. Reprinted by permission of the author.

Louise Bogan "Cassandra" and "The Dragonfly" from *The Blue Estuaries* by Louise Bogan. Reprinted by permission of Farrar, Strauss & Giroux, Inc.

Arna Bontemps "A Black Man Talks of Reaping" and "Southern Mansion." Reprinted by permission of Harold Ober Associates Incorporated. Copyright © 1963 by Arna Bontemps.

Kay Boyle "A Communication to Nancy Cunard" from *Collected Poems* 1962. Reprinted by permission of the estate of Kay Boyle and the Watkins/Loomis Agency.

William Bronk "At Tikal," "The Mayan Glyphs Unread," "I Thought It was Harry," and "Where It Ends" from *Life Supports: New and Collected Poems* Talisman House. Reprinted by permission of the author.

Gwendolyn Brooks "Gay Chaps at the Bar," "Of De Witt Williams on His Way to Lincoln Cemetery," "A song in the Front Yard," "We Real Cool," "The Ballad of Rudolph Reed," "The Blackstone Rangers," "To the Diaspora," "To Those of My Sisters Who Kept Their Naturals," "The Boy Died in My Alley," and "Young Africans" from *Blacks* 1991 by Gwendolyn Brooks. Reprinted by permission of the author.

Sterling A. Brown "Rent Day Blues," "Old Lem," "Sharecroppers," "Southern Cop," "Choices," "Scotty Has His Say," "Memphis Blues," and "Slim in Hell" from *The Collected Poems of Sterling A. Brown* edited by Michael S. Harper. Copyright © 1980 by Sterling A. Brown. "Slim in Atlanta" from *Southern Road* by Sterling A. Brown. Included in *The Collected Poems of Sterling A. Brown* selected by Michael S. Harper. Copyright 1980 © 1980 by Sterling A. Brown. Reprinted by permission of Harper-Collins Publishers, Inc.

Ana Castillo "Seduced by Natassja Kinski" from the forthcoming *I Ask the Impossible.* Copyright © 1998 by Ana Castillo. To be published in English. Reprinted by permission of Susan Bergholz Literary Services, New York. All rights reserved.

Marilyn Chin "How I Got that Name" was published in *The Phoenix Gone, The Terrace Empty* by Marilyn Chin (Milkweed Editions, 1994). Copyright © 1994 by Marilyn Chin. Reprinted with permission from Milkweed editions.

Sandra Cisneros "Little Clown, My Heart" from *Loose Woman.* Copyright © 1994 by Sandra Cisneros. Published by Vintage Books, a division of Random House, Inc., and originally in hardcover by Alfred A. Knopf, Inc. Reprinted by permission of Susan Bergholz Literary Services, New York. All rights reserved.

Lucille Clifton "the message of crazy horse" copyright © 1987 by Lucille Clifton. Reprinted from *Next: New Poems.* "I am accused of tending to the past," "at the cemetery, walnut grove plantation, south carolina 1989," "reply," "poem to my uterus," and "to my last period," copyright © 1991 by Lucille Clifton, Reprinted from *Quilting: Poems 1987–1990,* with permission of BOA Editions, Ltd., 260 East Ave., Rochester, NY 14604. "brothers" from *The Book of Light* © 1993 by Lucille Clifton. Reprinted by permission of Copper Canyon Press, Post Office Box 271, Port Townsend, WA 98368

Gregory Corso "Marriage" and "Bomb" from *The Happy Birthday of Death.* copyright © 1960 by New Directions Publishing Corp. Reprinted by permission of New Directions Publishing Corp.

Jane Cortez "Do You Think?" and "I am New York City." Copyright 1998 by Jane Cortez. Reprinted by permission of the author.

Hart Crane "October–November," "Black Tambourine," "Chaplinesque," "Porphyro in Akron," "Voyages I," "Episode of Hands," "The Mango Tree," "To Brooklyn Bridge," "Ave Maria," "The River," "Cape Hatteras," and "Atlantis" from *Complete Poems of Hart Crane* by Marc Simon, editor. Copyright 1933, © 1958, 1966 by Liveright Publishing Corporation. Copyright © by Marc Simon. Reprinted by permission of Liveright Publishing Corporation.

Robert Creeley "I Know a Man," "After Lorca," "The Flower," "For Love," and "America" from *Collected Poems of Robert Creeley.* Copyright © 1983 The Regents of the University of California. "Age" from *Selected Poems.* Copyright © 1991 The Regents of the University of California. Reprinted by permission of the University of California Press and the Regents of the University of California.

Countee Cullen "Incident," "For A Lady I Know," "Yet Do I Marvel," "Near White," "Tableau," and "Heritage," from *Color* by Countee Cullen. Copyright © 1925 by Harper and Brothers; copyright renewed 1953 by Ida M. Cullen. "From the Dark Tower" from *Copper Sun* by Countee Cullen. Copyright © 1927 by Harper & Brothers; copyright renewed 1955 by Ida M. Cullen. Reprinted by permission of GRM Associates, Inc., Agents for the Estate of Ida M. Cullen.

E. E. Cummings "next to of course god america i," "my sweet old etcetera," "i sing of olaf glad and big," "Space being(don't forget ro remember)Curved," "r-p-o-p-h-e-s-s-a-g-r," "anyone lived in a pretty town," and "what if a much of a which of a wind" from *Complete Poems: 1904–1962* by E. E. Cummings, Edited by George J. Firmage. Copyright 1923, 1925, 1926, 1931, 1935, 1938, 1940, 1944, 1945, 1946, 1947, 1948, 1949, 1950, 1951, 1952, 1953, 1954, © 1995, 1956, 1957, 1958, 1959, 1960, 1961, 1962, 1963, 1966, 1967, 1968, 1972, 1973, 1974, 1975, 1976, 1977, 1978, 1980, 1981, 1982, 1983, 1984, 1985, 1986, 1987, 1988, 1989, 1990, 1991 by the Trustees of the e. e. cummings Trust. Copyright © 1973, 1976, 1978, 1979, 1981, 1983, 1985, 1991 by George James Firmage. Reprinted by permission of Liveright Publishing Corporation.

Joy Davidman "This Woman" from *Letter to a Comrade,* Yale University Press 1938. Reprinted by permission of the publisher. "For the Nazis" from *Seven Poets in Search of and Answer* ed. by Thomas Yoseoff, Bernard Ackerman 1944. Reprinted by permission of Douglas Gresham and David Gresham.

James Dickey "The Sheep Child" and "Falling" from *The Whole Motion: Collected Poems 1945–1992* © 1992 by James Dickey, Wesleyan University Press by permission of University Press of New England.

Emily Dickinson #258, 280, 303, 341, 465, 508, 520, 585, 601, 613, 657, 712, 754, 1072, 1129, 1705 from *The Poems of Emily Dickinson.* Reprinted by permission of the publishers and Trustees of Amherst College from *The Poems of Emily Dickinson,* Thomas H. Johnson, ed. Cambridge, Mass.: The Belknap Press of Harvard University Press, Copyright © 1951, 1955, 1979, 1983 by the President and Fellows of Harvard College.

H.D. (Hilda Doolittle) "The Walls Do Not Fall 1 and 6" from *Collected Poems 1912–1944.* Copyright © 1982 by the Estate of Hilda Doolittle. Reprinted by permission of New Directions Publishing Corp.

Mark Doty "Homo Will Not Inherit" from *Atlantis* by Mark Doty. Copyright © 1995 by Mark Doty. Reprinted by permission of HarperCollins Publishers, Inc.

Rita Dove "Parsley" from *Museum,* © 1983 by Rita Dove. Carnegie-Mellon University Press, Pittsburgh 1983. Reprinted by permission of the author.

Henry Dumas "Son of Msippi," "Kef 24," Kef 16," "Fish," "Knees of a Natural Man," "Low Down Dog Blues," "Black Star Line" from the book *Knees of a Natural Man: The Selected Poetry of Henry Dumas* edited by Eugene B. Redmond. Copyright © 1989 by Loretta Dumas and Eugene B. Redmond. Appears by permission of the publisher, Thunder's Mouth Press

Robert Duncan "Often I am Permitted to Return to a Meadow" from *The Opening of the Field.* Copyright © 1960 by Robert Duncan. "My Mother Would Be a Falconress," "The Torso," and "Up Rising" from *Bending the Bow.* Copyright © 1968 by Robert Duncan. Reprinted by permission of New Directions Publishing Corp.

T. S. Eliot "The Hollow Men" and "The Journey of the Magi" from *Collected Poems 1909–1962* by T. S. Eliot, copyright 1936 by Harcourt Brace & Company, copyright 1964, 1963 by T. S. Eliot, reprinted by permission of the publisher. "Burnt Norton" from *Four Quartets,* copyright 1943 by T. S. Eliot and renewed 1971 by Esme Valerie Eliot, reprinted by permission of Harcourt Brace & Company.

Anita Endrezze "Birdwatching at Fan Lake" and "Return of the Wolves" from *Harper's Anthology of 20th Century Native American Poetry,* HarperCollins 1988. Reprinted by permission of the author

Louise Erdrich "Indian Boarding School: The Runaways" and "Dear John Wayne" from *Jacklight* by Louise Erdrich, © 1984 by Louise Erdrich. Reprinted by permission of Henry Holt and Company, Inc.

Martín Espada "Bully," "Federico's Ghost," and "The Saint Vincent de Paul Food Pantry Stomp" from *Rebellion Is the Circle of a Lover's Hands* by Martín Espada (Curbstone Press, 1990). Reprinted with permission of Curbstone Press. Distributed by Consortium. "Imagine the Angels of Bread," from *Imagine the Angels of Bread* by Martín Espada. Copyright © 1996 by Martín Espada. Reprinted by permission of W. W. Norton & Company, Inc. "The Lover of a Subversive Is Also a Subversive," "The Skull Beneath the Skin of the Mango," and "Fidel in Ohio," from *City of Coughing and Dead Radiators* by Martín Espada. Copyright © 1993 by Martín Espada. Reprinted by permission of W. W. Norton & Company, Inc.

William Everson "A Canticle to Waterbirds." Copyright © 1978 by William Everson. Reprinted from *The Veritable Years: poems 1949–1966* with the permission of Black Sparrow Press.

Kenneth Fearing "Dear Beatrice Fairfax," "$2.50," "Dirge," and "Denoument" from *Kenneth Fearing: Complete Poems* edited by Robert M. Ryley, National Poetry Foundation 1994. Published by permission of the National poetry Foundation.

Carolyn Forché "The Colonel" from *The Country Between Us* by Carolyn Forche. Copyright © 1981 by Carolyn Forché. Originally appeared in *Women's International Resource Exchange.* Reprinted by permission of HarperCollins Publishers, Inc.

Charles Henri Ford "Plaint" and "Flag of Ecstasy" from *Out of the Labyrinth: Selected Poems* by Charles Henri Ford. Copyright © 1991 by Charles Henri Ford. Reprinted by permission of City Lights Books.

Sesshu Foster "I try to pee but I can't," "Life Magazine, December 1941," "We're caffinated by rain inside concrete underpasses," "The Japanese man would not appear riding a horse," "I'm always grateful no one hears this terrible racket," "Look and look again, will he glance up all of a sudden" and "You'll be fucked up" from *City Terrace Field Manual* Kaya Productions 1996. Reprinted by permission of Kaya, New York.

Robert Frost "Desert Places," "Two Tramps in Mud Time," "Neither out Far Nor in Deep," "Never Again Would Birds' Song Be the Same," and "The Gift Ouright" from *The Poetry of Robert Frost,* edited by Edward Connery Lathem, Copyright 1936, 1942, 1956 by Robert Frost, Copyright 1964, © 1970, 1974 by Lesley Frost Ballantine, Copyright 1928, 1947, © 1969 by Henry Holt & Company. Reprinted by permission of Henry Holt & Company, Inc.

Allen Ginsberg "Howl" copyright © 1955 by Allen Ginsberg, "Love Poem on a Theme by Whitman" copyright © 1978 by Allen Ginsberg, "Wichita Vortex Sutra" copyright © 1966 by Allen Ginsberg, and "Father Death Blues" copyright © 1984 by Allen Ginsburg from *Collected Poems 1947–1980* by Allen Ginsberg. Reprinted by permission of HarperCollins Publishers, Inc.

Louise Glück "Penelope's Song," "Quiet Evening," "Parable of the King," "Parable of the Hostages," "Circe's Power," "Circe's Grief," and "Reunions" from *Meadowlands* by Louise Glück. Copyright © 1996 by Louise Glück. Reprinted by permission of The Ecco Press.

Judy Grahn "I have come to claim," "Vietnamese woman speaking," "Carol, in the park, chewing on straws," "Plainsong: From a younger woman to an older woman," and "The women whose head is on fire" from *The Work of A Common Woman: The Collected Poetry of Judy Grahn 1964–1977*, Diana Press 1978, St. Martin's Press 1981, 1982, the Crossing Press 1984, 1986. Reprinted by permission of Judy Grahn.

Robert Hass "Rusia en 1931" and "A Story About the Body" from *Human Wishes* by Robert Hass. Copyright © 1989 by Robert Haas. Reprinted by permission of The Ecco Press.

Jessica Hagedorn "Ming the Merciless," from *Danger and Beauty* by Jessica Hagedorn. Copyright © 1993 by Jessica Hagedorn. Used by permission of Viking Penguin, a division of Penguin Putnam Inc.

Michael S. Harper "Song: I Want a Witness," "Blue Ruth: America," "Brother John," "American History," "We Assume: On the Death of Our Son, Reuben Masai Harper," "Reuben, Reuben," "Deathwatch," and "Dear John, Dear Coltrane" from *Images of Kin: New and Selected Poems*. Copyright 1977 by Michael S. Harper. Used with the permission of the poet and the University of Illinois Press.

Robert Hayden "Middle Passage," copyright © 1962, 1966 by Robert Hayden. "Runagate Runagate," copyright 1966 by Robert Hayden. "A Letter from Phillis Wheatley," copyright © 1978 by Robert Hayden. "Night, Death, Mississippi," copyright © 1962, 1966 by Robert Hayden. "Aunt Jemima of the Ocean Waves," copyright © 1985 by Emma Hayden. "Elegies for Paradise Valley," copyright © 1978 by Robert Hayden. "The Dogwood Trees," copyright © 1985 by Emma Hayden. "O Daedalus, Fly Away Home," copyright © 1966 by Robert Hayden. From *Collected Poems of Robert Hayden* by Frederick Glaysher, editor. Reprinted by permission of Liveright Publishing Corporation.

Anthony Hecht "More Light! More Light!" and "A Hill" from *Collected Earlier Poems* by Anthony Hecht. Copyright © 1990 by Anthony E. Hecht. Reprinted by permission of Alfred A. Knopf, Inc.

Garrett Hongo "Ancestral Graves, Kahuku" from *The River of Heaven* by Garrett Hongo. Copyright © 1988 by Garrett Hongo. Reprinted by permission of Alfred A. Knopf, Inc.

Susan Howe "The Falls Flight" and "Hope Atherton's Wanderings" from *Singularities* © 1990 by Susan Howe, Wesleyan University Press, by permission of University Press of New England.

Langston Hughes "The Weary Blues," "The Cat and the Saxophone (2 a.m.)," "To the Dark Mercedes of El Palacio de Amor," "Mulatto," "Fire," "House in the World," "Silhouette," "Flight," "Lynching Song," "Ballad of Roosevelt," "Park Bench," "Let America Be America Again," "The Bitter River," "Ku Klux," "Shakespeare in Harlem," "Ballad of the Landlord," "Madam and the Phone Bill," "Dream Deferred (Harlem)," "Late Corner," "Dinner Guest: Me," "The Backlash Blues," and "Bombings in Dixie" from *Collected Poems* by Langston Hughes. Copyright © 1994 by the Estate of Langston Hughes. Reprinted by permission of Alfred A. Knopf.

Lawson Fusao Inada "Listening Images" is from *Legends From Camp* by Lawson Fusao Inada, Coffee House Press, 1993. Used by permission of the publisher. Copyright © 1993 by Lawson Fusao Inada.

Laura (Riding) Jackson "Helen's Burning" and "Elegy in A Spider's Web" from *The Poems of Laura Riding* by Laura (Riding) Jackson. Copyright © 1991 by The Board of Literary Management of the late Laura (Riding) Jackson. "The Wind Suffers" from *Selected Poems in Five Sets* by Laura (Riding) Jackson. Copyright © by the Board of Literary Management of the late Laura (Riding) Jackson. Reprinted by permission of Persea Books, Inc. In conformity with the late author's wish, her Board of Literary Management asks us to record that, in 1941, Laura (Riding) Jackson renounced, on grounds of linguistic principle, the writing of poetry: she had come to hold that "poetry obstructs general attainment to something better in our linguistic way-of-life than we have."

Japanese Haiku "Being arrested" Shido Okamoto; "Hand-cuffed and taken away" Sadayo Taniguchi; "Lingering summer heat," "Passed guard tower," "Want to be with children" Kyotaro Komuro; "In the shade of the summer sun" Shiho Okamoto; "Young Grass red and shriveled," "Released seagull," "Even the croaking frogs" Hakuro Wado; "Dandelion has bloomed" Hyakuissei Okamoto; "On Certain Days" Shizuku Uyemaruko; "Sprinkling water outside" Ryokuin Matsui; "Sentry at the main gate" Hangetsu Tsunekawa; "Thin shadow at tule reed" Wakoshi Saga; "Looking at summer moon," "Early moon has set" Tokuji Hirai; "Moon shadows on internment camp" Suzuki; "Rain shower from mountain," "Oh shells" Suiko Matsushita; "Desert rain falling" Neiji Ozawa; "Frosty morning," "Winter wind" Senbinshi Takaoka; "Black clouds instantly shroud" Jyosha Yamada; "Doll without a head" Hekisamei Matsuda; "Suddenly awakened" Sei Sagara; "Jeep patrolling slowly" Hyakuissei Okamoto; "Grieving within" Shizuku Uyemaruko; "In the sage brush" Okamoto. From *May Sky: There Is Always Tomorrow* by Violet Kazue de Cristoforo, ed. and trans. © 1997 by Violet Kazue de Cristoforo (Los Angeles: Sun & Moon Press, 1997), pages 145, 175, 103, 147, 261, 271, 275, 269, 273, 133, 105, 273, 177, 255, 239, 261, 247, 221, 167, 183, 241, 257, 251, 277, 151, 245. Reprinted by permission of the publisher

Randall Jarrell "Death of the Ball Turret Gunner," "A Front," "Losses," "Second Air Force," and "Protocols" from *The Complete Poems* by Randall Jarrell. Copyright © 1969 by Mrs. Randall Jarrell. Reprinted by permission of Farrar, Strauss & Giroux, Inc.

Robinson Jeffers "Shine, Perishing Republic," copyright © 1925 and renewed 1953 by Robinson Jeffers; "Hurt Hawks," copyright 1928 and renewed 1956 by Robinson Jeffers; "The Purse-Seine," copyright © 1937 and renewed 1965 by Donnan Jeffers and Garth Jeffers; "Cassandra," copyright 1971 by Hardstick Press, copyright 1944 by Oscar Williams; "Vulture," copyright 1963 by Garth Jeffers and Donnan Jeffers; "Birds and Fishes," copyright 1963 by Steuben Glass. All from *Selected Poems* by Robinson Jeffers. Reprinted by permission of Random House, Inc. "November Surf" and "Fantasy" reprinted from *The Collected Poetry of Robinson Jeffers, Three Volumes* edited by Tim Hunt with the permission of the publishers, Stanford University Press. © 1995 by the Board of Trustees of the Leland Stanford Junior University.

Bob Kaufman "The Biggest Fisherman," "Crootey Songo," and "No More Jazz at Alcatraz" from *Cranial Guitar* by Bob Kaufman, Coffee House Press, 1996. Reprinted by permission of Coffee House Press.

Weldon Kees "Travels in North America" reprinted from *The Collected Poems of Weldon Kees,* edited by Donald Justice, by permission of the University of Nebraska Press. Copyright 1965, by the University of Nebraska Press.

Galway Kinnell "The Porcupine" and "The Bear," from *Three Books* by Galway Kinnell. Copyright © 1993 by Galway Kinnell. Previously published in *Body Rags* (1965, 1966, 1967). Reprinted by permission of Houghton Mifflin Company. All rights reserved.

Etheridge Knight "Haiku," "Hard Rock Returns to Prison from the Hospital for the Criminal Insane," "The Idea of Ancestry," "A Poem for Myself," "For Malcolm, a Year After," "Television Speaks," and "For Black Poets Who Think of Suicide" from *The Essential Etheridge Knight* by Etheridge Knight, © 1986. Reprinted by Permission of the University of Pittsburgh Press.

Yusef Komunyakaa "Tu Do Street," "Prisoners," "Communique," "The Dog Act," "The Nazi Doll" "Fog Galleon," and "Work" from *Neon Vernacular: New and Selected Poems* © 1993, originally published in *Dien Cai Dau* © 1988 by Yusef Komunyakaa, Wesleyan University Press by permission of the University Press of New England.

Maxine Kumin "Voices from Kansas" and "Saga: Four Variants on the Sonnet," from *Looking for Luck* by Maxine Kumin. Copyright © 1992 by Maxine Kumin. Reprinted by permission of W. W. Norton Company, Inc.

Stanley Kunitz "The Wellfleet Whale," copyright © 1985 by Stanley Kunitz; "The Snakes of September," copyright © 1985 by Stanley Kunitz, from *Passing Through: The Later Poems New and Selected* by Stanley Kunitz. Reprinted by permission of W. W. Norton & Company, Inc.

Denise Levertov "Life at War," "The Ache of Marriage," "Olga Poems," and "What Were They Like" from *Poems 1960–1967*. Copyright © 1966 by Denise Levertov. Reprinted by permission of New Directions Publishing Corp.

Philip Levine "The Horse," "Animals Are Passing from Our Lives," "Belle Isle, 1949," "They Feed the Lion," and "Francisco, I'll Bring You Red Carnations" from *New Selected Poems* by Philip Levine Copyright © 1991 by Philip Levine. Reprinted by Permission of Alfred A. Knopf, Inc. "Fear and Fame" from *What Work Is* by Philip Levine Copyright © 1991 by Philip Levine. Reprinted by permission of Alfred A. Knopf, Inc. "On the Meeting of García Lorca and Hart Crane" from *The Simple Truth* by Philip Levine Copyright © 1994 by Philip Levine. Reprinted by permission of Alfred A. Knopf, Inc.

Vachel Lindsay "The Child-Heart in the Mountains" (1925) and "Celestial Flowers on Glacier Park" (1925) from *The Poetry of Vachel Lindsay,* Spoon River Press. Reprinted by permission of the publisher.

Audrey Lorde "Coal" copyright © 1968, 1970, 1973 by Audrey Lorde. "Sisters in Arms" copyright © 1986, by Audrey Lorde. "Outlines" copyright © 1986 by Audrey Lorde. "Call" copyright © 1986 by Audrey Lorde. From *Collected Poems* by Audrey Lorde. Reprinted by permission of W. W. Norton & Company, Inc.

Adrian C. Louis "Dust World" and "Coyote Night" from *Among the Dog Eaters* 1992, published by permission of West End Press. "Wakinyan" from *Fire Water World* 1989, published by permission of West End Press. "How Verdell and Dr. Zhivago Disassembled the Soviet Union," "Wanbli Gleska Win" and "Looking for Judas" from Adrian Louis, *Vortex of Indian Fevers,* Northwestern University Press/TriQuarterly Books 1995 by Adrian Louis, published by permission of Northwestern University Press. "Petroglyphs of Serena" and "A Colossal American Copulation" from *Ceremonies of the Damned* by Adrian C. Louis. Copyright © 1997 by Adrian C. Louis. Reprinted with the permission of the University of Nevada Press.

Amy Lowell "The Sisters" and "New Heavens for Old" from *The Complete Poetical Works of Amy Lowell.* Copyright © 1955 by Houghton Mifflin Company, © renewed by Houghton Mifflin Company, Brinton P. Roberts, and G. D'Andelot Belin, Esq. Reprinted by permission of Houghton Mifflin Co. All rights reserved.

Robert Lowell "Inauguration Day: January 1953," "A Mad Negro Soldier Confined at Munich," "Commander Lowell," "Man and Wife," "Memories of West Street and Lepke," "To Speak of Woe That Is In Marriage," and "Skunk Hour" from *Life Studies* by Robert Lowell. Copyright © 1959 by Robert Lowell. Renewed copyright © 1987 by Harriett Lowell, Caroline Lowell, and Sheridan Lowell. "For the Union Dead," "The Mouth of the Hudson," and "July in Washington" from *For the Union Dead* by Robert Lowell. Copyright © 1959 by Robert Lowell. Renewed copyright © 1987 by Harriet Lowell, Caroline Lowell, and Sheridan Lowell. "Central Park" from *Near the Ocean* by Robert Lowell. Copyright © 1967 by Robert Lowell. "The March I" and "The March II" from *Notebook* by Robert Lowell. Copyright © 1969 by Robert Lowell. Reprinted by permission of Farrar, Strauss & Giroux, Inc.

Archibald MacLeish "The End of the World" and "Ars Poetica" from *Collected Poems 1917–1982* by Archibald MacLeish. Copyright © 1955 by the Estate of Archibald MacLeish. Reprinted by permission of Houghton Mifflin Co. All rights reserved.

Thomas McGrath "Deep South," "Ars Poetica: or: Who Lives in the Ivory Tower?," "A Little Song About Charity," "Ode for the American Dead in Asia," and "Against the False Magicians" from *Selected Poems: 1938–1988* © 1998 by Thomas McGrath. Reprinted by permission of Copper Canyon Press, Post Office Box 271, Port Townsend, WA 98368. "Crash Report," "First Book of Genesis/ According to the Diplomats," and "After the Beat Generation" from *The Movie at the End of the World: Collected Poems* by Thomas McGrath (Ohio University Press/Swallow Press 1972). Reprinted with the permission of Ohio University Press, Athens, Ohio.

James Merrill "An Urban Convalescence," "The Broken Home," "Willowware Cup," and "Lost in Translation" from *Selected Poems 1946–1985* by James Merrill. Copyright © 1992 by James Merrill. Reprinted by permission of Alfred A. Knopf, Inc.

W. S. Merwin "The Drunk in the Furnace" from *The Drunk in the Furnace* (The Macmillan Company, New York, 1960) Copyright © 1956, 1957, 1958, 1959, 1960 by W. S. Merwin. "It is March," "Caesar," "The Room," "December Among the Vanished," "For the Anniversary of My Death," "When the War is Over," "The Asians Dying," "For a Coming Extinction," and "Looking for Mushrooms at Sunrise" from *The Lice* (Atheneum, New York, 1970) Copyright © 1963, 1964, 1965, 1966, 1967 by W. S. Merwin. "The Gardens of Zuni" and "Beginning" from *The Carrier of Ladders* (Atheneum, New York, 1970) Copyright © 1967, 1968, 1969, 1970 by W. S. Merwin. "The Horse" from *The Compass Flower* (Atheneum, New York, 1977) Copyright 1977 by W. S. Merwin. "Sun and Rain" and "Berryman" from *Opening the Hand* (Atheneum, New York, 1983) Copyright © 1983 by W. S. Merwin. Reprinted by permission of Georges Borchardt, Inc., for W. S. Merwin.

Edna St. Vincent Millay Sonnet XLVII ("Well, I have lost you; and I lost you fairly") and Sonnet XXX ("Love is not all; it is not meat nor drink") of *Fatal Interview,* "Justice Denied in Massachusetts," "Say that We Saw Spain Die," and "I Forgot for a Moment." From *Collected Poems,* HarperCollins. Copyright © 1928, 1931, 1939, 1940, 1955, 1958, 1967, 1968 by Edna St. Vincent Millay and Norma Millay Ellis. All rights reserved. Reprinted by permission of Elizabeth Barnett, literary executor.

N. Scott Momaday "Plainview: 3," "Buteo Regalis," "Crows in a Winter Composition," "Carriers of the Dream Wheel," "Rings of Bone," "The Stalker," "Purple (from "The Colors of Night")," "The Burning," "December 29, 1890," and "The Shield That Came Back (from "In the Presence of the Sun: A Gathering of Shields")" from *In the Presence of the Sun: Stories and Poems 1961–1991* by N. Scott Momaday. Copyright © 1992 by N. Scott Momaday. Reprinted by permission of St. Martin's Press, Incorporated.

Marianne Moore "No Swan So Fine" from *The Collected Poems of Marianne Moore.* Copyright 1935 by Marianne Moore; copyright renewed © 1963 by Marianne Moore and T. S. Eliot. "The Pangolin," "Bird-Witted," "The Paper Nautilus," and "Spenser's Ireland" from *The Collected Poems of Marianne Moore.* Copyright 1941 by Marianne Moore; copyright renewed 1969 by Marianne Moore. Reprinted with the permission of Simon & Schuster

Thylias Moss "Fullness" and "There Will Be Animals" from *Small Congregations: New and Selected Poems* by Thylias Moss. Reprinted by permission of The Ecco Press. "Ambition" and "Crystals" from *Last Chance for the Tarzan Holler* by Thylias Moss. Copyright © 1998 by Thylias Moss. Reprinted by permission of Persea Books, Inc.

Harryette Mullen Six untitled prose poems on pages 45, 49, 52, 53, 63, & 65 of *Trimmings* by Harryette Mullen (1991). Six untitled prose poems from *S\*PeRM\*\*K\*T* by Harryette Mullen (1992): "Aren't you glad you use petroleum," "Kills bug dead," "A daughter turned against the grain," "Off the pig," "Ad infinitum perpetual infants goo," and "Flies in buttermilk." Reprinted by permission of the author.

Lorine Niedecker "Paean to Place" and "Poet's work" from *The Granite Pail: Selected Poems* (North Point, 1985). Reprinted by permission of Cid Corman, Executor of the Estate of Lorine Niedecker.

Frank O'Hara "Poem" (The eager note on my door) and "On Seeing Larry Rivers" from *Meditations in an Emergency.* Copyright © 1957 by Frank O'Hara. Used by permission of Grove/Atlantic, Inc. "A Step Away from Them" and "The Day Lady Died" from *Lunch Poems,* copyright © 1964 by Frank O'Hara. Reprinted by permission of City Lights Books. "Why I Am Not a Painter" from *Collected Poems* by Frank O'Hara. Copyright © 1958 by Maureen Granville-Smith, Administratrix of the Estate of Frank O'Hara. Reprinted by permission of Alfred A. Knopf, Inc. "A True Account of Talking to the Sun at Fire Island" from *Collected Poems.* Copyright © 1968 by Maureen Granville-Smith. Reprinted by permission of Alfred A. Knopf, Inc. "Thinking of James Dean" from *Collected Poems.* Copyright © 1971 by Maureen Granville-Smith. Reprinted by permission of Alfred A. Knopf, Inc.

Sharon Olds "Ideographs," "Photograph of the Girl," and "Things That Are Worse Than Death" from *The Dead and the Living* by Sharon Olds. Copyright © 1983 by Sharon Olds. Reprinted by permission of Alfred A. Knopf, Inc. "The Waiting" from *The Father* by Sharon Olds. Copyright © 1992 by Sharon Olds. Reprinted by permission of Alfred A. Knopf, Inc. "His Father's Cadaver" from *The Wellspring* by Sharon Olds. Copyright © 1996 by Sharon Olds. Reprinted by permission of Alfred A. Knopf, Inc.

Mary Oliver "The Lilies Break Open Over the Dark Water" from *House of Light* by Mary Oliver. Copyright © 1990 by Mary Oliver. Reprinted by permission of Beacon Press, Boston. "Black Snake This Time" from *West Wind* by Mary Oliver. Copyright © 1997 by Mary Oliver. Reprinted by permission of Houghton Mifflin Company. All rights reserved.

Charles Olson "Cole's Island" and "Variations Done for Gerald De Wiele" from *Collected Poems of Charles Olson—excluding Maximus Poems,* translated/edited by George Butterick. Copyright © 1987 Estate of Charles Olson. Reprinted by permission of the University of California Press.

George Oppen "Image of the Engine," "Exodus," and "No. 5 (In Alsace)" from *Collected Poems.* Copyright © 1975 by George Oppen. Reprinted by permission of New Directions Publishing Corp.

Michael Palmer "Song of the Round Man," "All those words we . . . ," "I have answers to all of your questions," and "Fifth Prose" reprinted by permission of Michael Palmer. All rights reserved. "Autobiography" from *The Lion Bridge: Selected Poems 1972–1995*. Copyright © 1998 by Michael Palmer. Reprinted by permission of New Directions Publishing Corp.

Dorothy Parker "Unfortunate Coincidence" by Dorothy Parker, copyright 1926, © renewed 1954 by Dorothy Parker, "Resume," by Dorothy Parker, copyright 1926, 1928, renewed 1954, © 1956 by Dorothy Parker, "One Perfect Rose" by Dorothy Parker, copyright 1926, renewed © 1954 by Dortohy Parker, from *The Portable Dorothy Parker* by Dorothy Parker, Introduction by Brendan Gill. Used by permission of Viking Penguin, a division of Penguin Putnam Inc.

Robert Pinsky "The Unseen" from *The Figured Wheel: New and Collected Poems 1966–1996* by Robert Pinsky. Copyright © 1996 by Robert Pinsky. Reprinted by permission of Farrar, Strauss & Giroux, Inc. "The Shirt" from *The Want Bone*. Copyright © by Robert Pinsky. Reprinted by permission of The Ecco Press.

Sylvia Plath "Black Rook in Rainy Weather" from *Crossing the Water* by Sylvia Plath. Copyright © 1960 by Ted Hughes. "Tulips" from *Ariel* by Sylvia Plath. Copyright © 1962 by Ted Hughes. "The Bee Meeting" from *Ariel* by Silvia Plath. Copyright © 1963 by Ted Hughes. "The Arrival of the Bee Box" from *Ariel* by Sylvia Plath. Copyright © 1963 by Ted Hughes. Copyright renewed. "Stings" from *Ariel* by Sylvia Plath. Copyright © 1963 by Ted Hughes. Copyright renewed. "The Swarm" from *Ariel* by Sylvia Plath. Copyright © 1963 by Ted Hughes. "Wintering" from *Ariel* by Sylvia Plath. Copyright © 1963 by Ted Hughes. "Daddy" from *Ariel* by Sylvia Plath. Copyright © 1963 by Ted Hughes. Copyright renewed. "Ariel" from *Ariel* by Sylvia Plath. Copyright © 1965 by Ted Hughes. Copyright renewed. "Lady Lazarus" from *Ariel* by Sylvia Plath. Copyright © 1963 by Ted Hughes. Copyright renewed. Reprinted by permission of HarperCollins Publishers, Inc. "The Colossus" from *The Colossus and Other Poems* by Sylvia Plath. Copyright © 1961 by Sylvia Plath. Reprinted by permission of Alfred A. Knopf, Inc.

Ezra Pound "Canto I," "Canto IX," "Canto XLV," "Canto LXXXI," "Canto CXVI," and Notes to "Canto CXVII" from *The Cantos of Ezra Pound*. Copyright © 1934, 38, 48 by Ezra Pound. Reprinted by permission of New Directions Publishing Corp.

Carl Rakosi "The Menage" from *The Collected Poems of Carl Rakosi* (Orono, Maine, The National Poetry Foundation, 1986). Reprinted by permission of the National Poetry Foundation.

Dudley Randall "Ballad of Birmingham" from *Poem Counterpoem* by Margaret Danner and Dudley Randall, Broadside Press 1966. Reprinted by permission of Dudley Randall.

John Crowe Ransom "Dead Boy" from *Selected Poems* by John Crowe Ransom. Copyright 1927 by Alfred Knopf, Inc. and renewed 1955 by John Crowe Ransom. Reprinted by permission of Alfred A. Knopf, Inc.

Ishmael Reed "I am a cowboy in the boat of Ra" from *New and Collected Poems* (Atheneum, 1989). Reprinted by permission of Lowenstein Associates, Inc.

Kenneth Rexroth "Love Poems of Marichiko" from *Flower Wreath Hill*. Copyright © 1979 by Kenneth Rexroth. Reprinted by permission of New Directions Publishing Corp.

Charles Reznikoff Poems by Charles Reznikoff Copyright © 1978 by Marie Syrkin Reznikoff. Reprinted from *Testimony Volume I: The United States (1885–1915) Recitative* with the permission of Black Sparrow Press. Poems by Charles Reznikoff Copyright © 1979 by Marie Syrkin Reznikoff. Reprinted from *Testimony Volume II: The United States (1885–1915) Recitative* with the permission of Black Sparrow Press. "Massacres" Copyright © 1975 by Charles Reznikoff. Reprinted from *Holocaust* with the permission of Black Swallow Press.

Adrienne Rich "Aunt Jennifer's Tigers," "Shooting Script," "Trying to Talk with a Man," "Diving into the Wreck," "Twenty-one Love poems," and "Power" from *The Fact of a Doorframe: Poems Selected and New 1950–1984* by Adrienne Rich. Copyright © 1984 by Adrienne Rich. Copyright © 1975, 1978 by W. W. Norton & Company, Inc. Copyright © 1981 by Adrienne Rich. Reprinted by permission of the author and W. W. Norton & Company, Inc. "Part XIII (Dedications)" from "An Atlas of the Difficult World," from *An Atlas of the Difficult World: Poems 1988–1991* by Adrienne Rich. Copyright © 1991 by Adrienne Rich. Reprinted by permission of the author and W. W. Norton & Company, Inc.

Carolyn M. Rodgers "how I got ovah," "And When the Revolution Came," and "Mama's God" from *How I Got Ovah* by Carolyn M. Rodgers. Copyright © 1968, 1970, 1971, 1972, 1973, 1975 by Carolyn M. Rodgers. Used by permission of Doubleday, a division of Bantam Doubleday Dell Publishing Group.

Theodore Roethke "Cuttings" copyright 1948 by Theodore Roethke, "Cuttings (*later*)" copyright 1948 by Theodore Roethke, "Frau Bauman, Frau Schmidt, and Frau Schwartze" copyright 1952 by Theodore Roethke, "The Lost Son (The Flight)" copyright 1947 by Theodore Roethke, "I Knew a Woman" copyright 1954 by Theodore Roethke, "North American Sequence" copyright © 1962 by Beatrice Roethke, Administratrix of the Estate of Theodore Roethke. From *Collected Poems of Theodore Roethke* by Theodore Roethke. Used by permission of Doubleday, a division of Bantam Doubleday Dell Publishing Group.

Edwin Rolfe "Asbestos," "Season of Death," "First Love," "Elegia," "A Letter to the Denouncers," "Are You Now Or Have You Ever Been," "A Poem to Delight My Friends Who Laugh at Science-Fiction," "In Praise of," and "Little Ballad for Americans-1954" reprinted with permission from Edwin Rolfe, *Collected Poems*, ed. Cary Nelson and Jefferson Hendricks (University of Illinois Press, 1993). Copyright 1993 by the Board of Trustees of the University of Illinois.

Wendy Rose "Truganinny" from Wendy Rose *The Halfbreed Chronicles and Other Poems*, Northwestern University Press.

Muriel Rukeyser "The Book of the Dead," "The Minotaur," and "Rite" from *Out of Silence: Selected Poems* by Muriel Rukeyser, 1992, TriQuarterly Books, Evanston, IL, © William L. Rukeyser. From

Paul Violi "Index" from *Splurge* SUN, 1982. Reprinted by permission of the author.

Margaret Walker "For My People" (1937), from *This Is My Country,* University of Georgia Press, 1989. Reprinted by permission of the publisher.

Robert Penn Warren "Bearded Oaks," "Evening Hawk," and "Heart of Autumn" from *Robert Penn Warren: New and Selected Poems 1923–1985* Random House, 1985. Reprinted by permission of the William Morris Agency.

John Wheelwright "Plantation Drouth" from *Collected Poems of John Wheelwright.* Copyright © 1971 by Louise Wheelwright Damon. Reprinted by permission of New Directions Publishing Corp.

Richard Wilbur "A Baroque Wall Fountain in the Villa Sciarra" from *Things of This World,* copyright © 1955 and renewed 1983 by Richard Wilbur. "Love Calls Us to the Things of this World" from *Things of This World,* copyright © 1956 and renewed 1984 by Richard Wilbur. "Advice to a Prophet" from *Advice to a Prophet and Other Poems,* copyright 1959 and renewed 1987 by Richard Wilbur. Reprinted by permission of Harcourt Brace & Company.

William Carlos Williams "Young Sycamore," "This Is Just to Say," "Proletarian Portrait," and "The Yachts" from *Collected Poems; 1909–1939,* Volume I. Copyright © 1938 by New Directions Publishing Corp. *The Descent of Winter,* "The Descent," "Asphodel, That Greeney Flower, Book I," and "Landscape With Fall of Icarus" from *Collected Poems 1939–1962,* Volme II. Copyright © 1944, 1962 by William Carlos Williams. Reprinted by permission of New Directions Publishing Corp.

Yvor Winters "Sir Gawain and the Green Knight" from *Poems of Yvor Winters.* Copyright © 1971 by New Directions Publishing Corp. Reprinted by permission of New Directions Publishing Corp.

C. D. Wright "Obedience of the Corpse" from *Terrorism,* Lost Roads Publishers, 1979. Reprinted by permission of the author. "Song of the Gourd" from *Tremble* by C. D. Wright. Copyright © 1996 by C. D. Wright. Reprinted by permission of The Ecco Press. The prose passage on p. 42 of *Just Whistle* beginning "Over everything . . . " and concluding, "On the eigth day . . . " owes syntactic structure and glossary to John Hersey's *Hiroshima* (Bantam Pathfinder ed., 1966, © John Hersey 1946). Reprinted by permission of Kelsey St. Press.

Charles Wright "Homage to Paul Cezanne" from *The World of Ten Thousand Things: Poems 1980–1990* by Charles Wright. Copyright © 1990 by Charles Wright. Reprinted by permission of Farrar, Strauss & Giroux, Inc.

James Wright "Saint Judas," "A Blessing," "Autumn Begins in Martins Ferry, Ohio," "A Centenary Ode: Inscribed to Little Crow, Leader of the Sioux Rebellion in Minnesota, 1862," and "Lying in a Hammock at William Duffy's Farm in Pine Island, Minnesota" from *Collected Poems* © by James Wright, Wesleyan University Press by permission of the University Press of New England.

Richard Wright "We of the Streets," copyright © 1937 by Richard Wright. Reprinted by permission of John Hawkins & Associates, Inc.

Louis Zukofsky No. 22 ("To my washstand"), "Mantis," "A Song for the Year's End," No. 3 ("Because Tarzan triumphs"), and "Non Ti Fidar" from *Complete Short Poetry* pp. 52-3, 65-6, 111-13, 115-16, 123-24, © Louis Zukofsky. Johns Hopkins University Press, 1997. Reprinted by permission of Johns Hopkins University Press.

# Anthology of
# Modern American Poetry

# Walt Whitman (1819–1892)

It has been said repeatedly, with some considerable justice, that much of twentieth-century American poetry is a dialogue with Walt Whitman. Sometimes the dialogue takes place through resistance, especially among those who reject his open forms, his prophetic stance, his long lines and broad cultural ambitions, his frank sexuality, his incantatory lists, and his search for a representative and unifying American selfhood. But often as not, as readers of this collection will recognize, the relationship is enacted by poets who adapt Whitman's expansive techniques to new historical contexts. We begin with Whitman because he should always be kept in mind when reading the poetry of our own time.

He was born on Long Island in New York and raised in Brooklyn. He quit school when he was but eleven, working as an office boy, a printer's apprentice, and an itinerant teacher, finally becoming a journalist for the New York press. *Leaves of Grass,* his poetic masterpiece, was first published in 1855, but it went through several editions. A watershed experience came in 1862, when Whitman spent several months nursing wounded veterans of the American Civil War. After the war he became a clerk in the Indian Bureau of the Department of the Interior, but was soon dismissed as the author of the immoral *Leaves of Grass.* In 1873, he suffered a stroke and moved to Camden, New Jersey, for the last 19 years of his life.

## One's-Self I Sing

One's-Self I sing, a simple separate person,
Yet utter the word Democratic, the word En-Masse.

Of physiology from top to toe I sing,
Not physiognomy alone nor brain alone is worthy for the Muse, I
say the Form complete is worthier far,
5    The Female equally with the Male I sing.

Of Life immense in passion, pulse, and power,
Cheerful, for freest action form'd under the laws divine,
The Modern Man I sing.

1867

## I Hear America Singing

I hear America singing, the varied carols I hear,
Those of mechanics, each one singing his as it should be blithe
    and strong,
The carpenter singing his as he measures his plank or beam,
The mason singing his as he makes ready for work, or leaves off
    work,
5      The boatman singing what belongs to him in his boat, the deck-
    hand singing on the steamboat deck,
The shoemaker singing as he sits on his bench, the hatter singing
    as he stands,
The wood-cutter's song, the ploughboy's on his way in the morning,
    or at noon intermission or at sundown,
The delicious singing of the mother, or of the young wife at work,
    or of the girl sewing or washing,
Each singing what belongs to him or her and to none else,
10     The day what belongs to the day—at night the party of young fel-
    lows, robust, friendly,
Singing with open mouths their strong melodious songs.

*1867*

## As Adam Early in the Morning

As Adam early in the morning,
Walking forth from the bower refresh'd with sleep,
Behold me where I pass, hear my voice, approach,
Touch me, touch the palm of your hand to my body as I pass,
5     Be not afraid of my body.

*1861, 1867*

## For You O Democracy

Come, I will make the continent indissoluble,
I will make the most splendid race the sun ever shone upon,
I will make divine magnetic lands,
        With the love of comrades,
5            With the life-long love of comrades.

I will plant companionship thick as trees along all the rivers of
    America, and along the shores of the great lakes, and all over
    the prairies,
I will make inseparable cities with their arms about each other's
    necks,
        By the love of comrades,
10          By the manly love of comrades.

For you these from me, O Democracy, to serve you ma femme!
For you, for you I am trilling these songs.

*1860, 1881*

## I Hear It Was Charged Against Me

I hear it was charged against me that I sought to destroy institu-
    tions,
But really I am neither for nor against institutions,
(What indeed have I in common with them? or what with the
    destruction of them?)
Only I will establish in the Mannahatta and in every city of these
    States inland and seaboard,
5    And in the fields and woods, and above every keel little or large
    that dents the water,
Without edifices or rules or trustees or any argument,
The institution of the dear love of comrades.

*1860*

## A Glimpse

A glimpse through an interstice caught,
Of a crowd of workmen and drivers in a bar-room around the stove
    late of a winter night, and I unremark'd seated in a corner,
Of a youth who loves me and whom I love, silently approaching
    and seating himself near, that he may hold me by the hand,
A long while amid the noises of coming and going, of drinking and
    oath and smutty jest,
5    There we two, content, happy in being together, speaking little,
    perhaps not a word.

*1860, 1867*

## Vigil Strange I Kept on the Field One Night

Vigil strange I kept on the field one night;
When you my son and my comrade dropt at my side that day,
One look I but gave which your dear eyes return'd with a look I
    shall never forget,
One touch of your hand to mine O boy, reach'd up as you lay on
    the ground,
5    Then onward I sped in the battle, the even-contested battle,
Till late in the night reliev'd to the place at last again I made my
    way,
Found you in death so cold dear comrade, found your body son of
    responding kisses, (never again on earth responding,)
Bared your face in the starlight, curious the scene, cool blew the
    moderate night-wind,
Long there and then in vigil I stood, dimly around me the battle-
    field spreading,
10    Vigil wondrous and vigil sweet there in the fragrant silent night,
But not a tear fell, not even a long-drawn sigh, long, long I gazed,
Then on the earth partially reclining sat by your side leaning my
    chin in my hands,
Passing sweet hours, immortal and mystic hours with you dearest
    comrade—not a tear, not a word,

Vigil of silence, love and death, vigil for you my son and my sol-
dier,
15 As onward silently stars aloft, eastward new ones upward stole,
Vigil final for you brave boy, (I could not save you, swift was your
death,
I faithfully loved you and cared for you living, I think we shall
surely meet again,)
Till at latest lingering of the night, indeed just as the dawn ap-
pear'd,
My comrade I wrapt in his blanket, envelop'd well his form,
20 Folded the blanket well, tucking it carefully over head and carefully
under feet,
And there and then and bathed by the rising sun, my son in his
grave, in his rude-dug grave I deposited,
Ending my vigil strange with that, vigil of night and battle-field
dim,
Vigil for boy of responding kisses, (never again on earth respond-
ing,)
Vigil for comrade swiftly slain, vigil I never forget, how as day
brighten'd,
25 I rose from the chill ground and folded my soldier well in his
blanket,
And buried him where he fell.

1865

## Out of the Cradle Endlessly Rocking

Out of the cradle endlessly rocking,
Out of the mocking-bird's throat, the musical shuttle,
Out of the Ninth-month midnight,
Over the sterile sands and the fields beyond, where the child leav-
ing his bed wander'd alone, bareheaded, barefoot,
5 Down from the shower'd halo,
Up from the mystic play of shadows twining and twisting as if they
were alive,
Out from the patches of briers and blackberries,
From the memories of the bird that chanted to me,
From your memories sad brother, from the fitful risings and fallings
I heard,
10 From under that yellow half-moon late-risen and swollen as if with
tears,
From those beginning notes of yearning and love there in the mist,
From the thousand responses of my heart never to cease,
From the myriad thence-arous'd words,
From the word stronger and more delicious than any,
15 From such as now they start the scene revisiting,
As a flock, twittering, rising, or overhead passing,
Borne hither, ere all eludes me, hurriedly,
A man, yet by these tears a little boy again,
Throwing myself on the sand, confronting the waves,
20 I, chanter of pains and joys, uniter of here and hereafter,
Taking all hints to use them, but swiftly leaping beyond them,
A reminiscence sing.

Once Paumanok,°
When the lilac-scent was in the air and Fifth-month grass was
    growing,
25   Up this seashore in some briers,
Two feather'd guests from Alabama, two together,
And their nest, and four light-green eggs spotted with brown,
And every day the he-bird to and fro near at hand,
And every day the she-bird crouch'd on her nest, silent, with bright
    eyes,
30   And every day I, a curious boy, never too close, never disturbing
    them,
Cautiously peering, absorbing, translating.

*Shine! shine! shine!*
*Pour down your warmth, great sun!*
*While we bask, we two together.*

35   *Two together!*
*Winds blow south, or winds blow north,*
*Day come white, or night come black,*
*Home, or rivers and mountains from home,*
*Singing all time, minding no time,*
40   *While we two keep together.*

Till of a sudden,
May-be kill'd, unknown to her mate,
One forenoon the she-bird crouch'd not on the nest,
Nor return'd that afternoon, nor the next,
45   Nor ever appear'd again.

And thenceforward all summer in the sound of the sea,
And at night under the full of the moon in calmer weather,
Over the hoarse surging of the sea,
Or flitting from brier to brier by day,
50   I saw, I heard at intervals the remaining one, the he-bird,
The solitary guest from Alabama.

*Blow! blow! blow!*
*Blow up sea-winds along Paumanok's shore;*
*I wait and I wait till you blow my mate to me.*

55   Yes, when the stars glisten'd,
All night long on the prong of a moss-scallop'd stake,
Down almost amid the slapping waves,
Sat the lone singer wonderful causing tears.

He call'd on his mate,
60   He pour'd forth the meanings which I of all men know.

---

23 *Paumanok*: Native American name for Long Island, New York.

Yes my brother I know,
The rest might not, but I have treasur'd every note,
For more than once dimly down to the beach gliding,
Silent, avoiding the moonbeams, blending myself with the shadow,
65 Recalling now the obscure shapes, the echoes, the sounds and
    sights after their sorts,
The white arms out in the breakers tirelessly tossing,
I, with bare feet, a child, the wind wafting my hair,
Listen'd long and long.

Listen'd to keep, to sing, now translating the notes,
70 Following you my brother,

*Soothe! soothe! soothe!*
*Close on its wave soothes the wave behind,*
*And again another behind embracing and lapping, every one close,*
*But my love soothes not me, not me.*

75 *Low hangs the moon, it rose late,*
*It is lagging—O I think it is heavy with love, with love.*

*O madly the sea pushes upon the land,*
*With love, with love.*

*O night! do I not see my love fluttering out among the breakers?*
80 *What is that little black thing I see there in the white?*

*Loud! loud! loud!*
*Loud I call to you, my love!*

*High and clear I shoot my voice over the waves,*
*Surely you must know who is here, is here,*
85 *You must know who I am, my love.*

*Low-hanging moon!*
*What is that dusky spot in your brown yellow?*
*O it is the shape, the shape of my mate!*
*O moon do not keep her from me any longer.*

90 *Land! land! O land!*
*Whichever way I turn, O I think you could give me my mate back*
    *again if you only would,*
*For I am almost sure I see her dimly whichever way I look.*

*O rising stars!*
*Perhaps the one I want so much will rise, will rise with some of you.*

95 *O throat! O trembling throat!*
*Sound clearer through the atmosphere!*
*Pierce the woods, the earth,*
*Somewhere listening to catch you must be the one I want.*

*Shake out carols!*
100 *Solitary here, the night's carols!*
*Carols of lonesome love! death's carols!*
*Carols under that lagging, yellow, waning moon!*
*O under that moon where she droops almost down into the sea!*
*O reckless despairing carols.*

105 *But soft! sink low!*
*Soft! let me just murmur,*
*And do you wait a moment you husky-nois'd sea,*
*For somewhere I believe I heard my mate responding to me,*
*So faint, I must be still, be still to listen,*
110 *But not altogether still, for then she might not come immediately to me.*

*Hither my love!*
*Here I am! here!*
*With this just-sustain'd note I announce myself to you,*
*This gentle call is for you my love, for you.*

115 *Do not be decoy'd elsewhere,*
*That is the whistle of the wind, it is not my voice,*
*That is the fluttering, the fluttering of the spray,*
*Those are the shadows of leaves.*

*O darkness! O in vain!*
120 *O I am very sick and sorrowful.*

*O brown halo in the sky near the moon, drooping upon the sea!*
*O troubled reflection in the sea!*
*O throat! O throbbing heart!*
*And I singing uselessly, uselessly all the night.*

125 *O past! O happy life! O songs of joy!*
*In the air, in the woods, over fields,*
*Loved! loved! loved! loved! loved!*
*But my mate no more, no more with me!*
*We two together no more.*

130 The aria sinking,
All else continuing, the stars shining,
The winds blowing, the notes of the bird continuous echoing,
With angry moans the fierce old mother incessantly moaning,
On the sands of Paumanok's shore gray and rustling,
135 The yellow half-moon enlarged, sagging down, drooping, the face of
    the sea almost touching,
The boy ecstatic, with his bare feet the waves, with his hair the
    atmosphere dallying,
The love in the heart long pent, now loose, now at last tumultuously
    bursting,
The aria's meaning, the ears, the soul, swiftly depositing,
The strange tears down the cheeks coursing,
140 The colloquy there, the trio, each uttering,
The undertone, the savage old mother incessantly crying,
To the boy's soul's questions sullenly timing, some drown'd secret
    hissing,
To the outsetting bard.

Demon or bird! (said the boy's soul,)
145    Is it indeed toward your mate you sing? or is it really to me?
For I, that was a child, my tongue's use sleeping, now I have heard
       you,
Now in a moment I know what I am for, I awake,
And already a thousand singers, a thousand songs, clearer, louder
       and more sorrowful than yours,
A thousand warbling echoes have started to life within me, never to
       die.

150    O you singer solitary, singing by yourself, projecting me,
O solitary me listening, never more shall I cease perpetuating you,
Never more shall I escape, never more the reverberations,
Never more the cries of unsatisfied love be absent from me,
Never again leave me to be the peaceful child I was before what
       there in the night,
155    By the sea under the yellow and sagging moon,
The messenger there arous'd, the fire, the sweet hell within,
The unknown want, the destiny of me.

O give me the clew! (it lurks in the night here somewhere,)
O if I am to have so much, let me have more!

160    A word then, (for I will conquer it,)
The word final, superior to all,
Subtle, sent up—what is it?—I listen;
Are you whispering it, and have been all the time, you sea-waves?
Is that it from your liquid rims, and wet sands?

165    Whereto answering, the sea,
Delaying not, hurrying not,
Whisper'd me through the night, and very plainly before day-break,
Lisp'd to me the low and delicious word death,
And again death, death, death, death,
170    Hissing melodious, neither like the bird nor like my arous'd child's
       heart,
But edging near as privately for me rustling at my feet,
Creeping thence steadily up to my ears and laving me softly all
       over,
Death, death, death, death, death.

Which I do not forget,
175    But fuse the song of my dusky demon and brother,
That he sang to me in the moonlight on Paumanok's gray beach,
With the thousand responsive songs at random,
My own songs awaked from that hour,
And with them the key, the word up from the waves,
180    The word of the sweetest song and all songs,
That strong and delicious word which, creeping to my feet,
(Or like some old crone rocking the cradle, swathed in sweet gar-
       ments, bending aside,)
The sea whisper'd me.

                                                            *1859*

# Emily Dickinson (1830–1886)

Born in Amherst, Massachusetts, to a well-known family—her father was a lawyer—Dickinson was educated at Amherst Academy and enrolled in what was then Mount Holyoke Female Seminary, but she returned home after a year. Settling in her family home in 1848, she became uneasy in public places and thus rarely went out. Visitors were also uncommon. But her creative life was unfailingly intense, and she maintained contact with others in letters that are so crafted, many consider them prose poems. Little about her imagination was typical of her time, though she did adapt the meters of hymns and the stanzas of ballads for her intricately nuanced, variously skeptical or ecstatic poems. The cultural environment was fervently religious, but Dickinson instead gradually chose irony as her way of viewing the world. She is thus, in an uncanny and symbolic way, the precursor to everything in modern poetry that is condensed, elliptical, and disjunctive, rather than being expansively Whitmanesque. Yet only half a dozen of her ambiguous and witty poems were published in her lifetime, all without her permission. Her substantial output of over one thousand poems, her large body of letters, would have to wait for an audience. Several volumes of her poems were issued in the 1890s, after her death, but the editors normalized her deliberately unconventional punctuation and made bad decisions about how to display the poems on the page. When additional volumes of her poems were issued in 1914, 1929, 1930, 1936, and 1945—with a true collected poems not appearing until 1955—it was repeatedly as if a new poet was being introduced to readers.

## 258

There's a certain Slant of light,
Winter Afternoons—
That oppresses, like the Heft°
Of Cathedral Tunes—

5 Heavenly Hurt, it gives us—
We can find no scar,
But internal difference,
Where the Meanings, are—

---

3 *Heft*: weight.

None may teach it—Any—
10      'Tis the Seal Despair—
An imperial affliction
Sent us of the Air—

When it comes, the Landscape listens—
Shadows—hold their breath—
15      When it goes, 'tis like the Distance
On the look of Death—

*c. 1861*

## 280

I felt a Funeral, in my Brain,
And Mourners to and fro
Kept treading—treading—till it seemed
That Sense was breaking through°—

5      And when they all were seated,
A Service, like a Drum—
Kept beating—beating—till I thought
My Mind was going numb—

And then I heard them lift a Box
10      And creak across my Soul
With those same Boots of Lead, again,
Then Space—began to toll,

As° all the Heavens were a Bell,
And Being, but an Ear,
15      And I, and Silence, some strange Race
Wrecked, solitary, here—

And then a Plank in Reason, broke,
And I dropped down, and down—
And hit a World, at every plunge,
20      And Finished knowing—then—

*c. 1861*

## 303

The Soul selects her own Society—
Then—shuts the Door—
To her divine Majority—
Present no more—

---

4 *breaking through:* giving way.
13 *As:* as if.

5    Unmoved—she notes the Chariots—pausing—
     At her low Gate—
     Unmoved—an Emperor be kneeling
     Upon her Mat—

     I've known her—from an ample nation—
10   Choose One—
     Then—close the Valves of her attention—
     Like Stone—

                                        *c. 1862*

## 341

     After great pain, a formal feeling comes—
     The Nerves sit ceremonious, like Tombs—
     The stiff Heart questions was it He, that bore,
     And Yesterday, or Centuries before?

5    The Feet, mechanical, go round—
     Of Ground, or Air, or Ought°—
     A Wooden way
     Regardless grown,°
     A Quartz contentment, like a stone—

10   This is the Hour of Lead—
     Remembered, if outlived,
     As Freezing persons, recollect the Snow—
     First—Chill—then Stupor—then the letting go—

                                        *c. 1862*

## 465

     I heard a Fly buzz—when I died—
     The Stillness in the Room
     Was like the Stillness in the Air—
     Between the Heaves of Storm—

5    The Eyes around—had wrung them dry—
     And Breaths were gathering firm
     For that last Onset—when the King
     Be witnessed—in the Room—

     I willed my Keepsakes—Signed away
10   What portion of me be
     Assignable—and then it was
     There interposed a Fly—

---

6 *Ought*: a double meaning: anything (from Dickinson's spelling of "aught"), and obliga-
tion (the feet do what they are obliged to do, mechanically).
8 *Regardless grown*: having stopped noticing.

With Blue—uncertain stumbling Buzz—
Between the light—and me—
15   And then the Windows failed—and then
I could not see to see—

*c. 1862*


## 508

I'm ceded—I've stopped being Theirs—
The name They dropped upon my face
With water, in the country church
Is finished using, now,
5   And They can put it with my Dolls,
My childhood, and the string of spools,
I've finished threading—too—

Baptized, before, without the choice,
But this time, consciously, of Grace—
10   Unto supremest name—
Called to my Full—The Crescent dropped—
Existence's whole Arc, filled up,
With one small Diadem.

My second Rank—too small the first—
15   Crowned—Crowing—on my Father's breast—
A half unconscious Queen—
But this time—Adequate—Erect,
With Will to choose, or to reject,
And I choose, just a Crown—

*c. 1862*


## 520

I started Early—Took my Dog—
And visited the Sea—
The Mermaids in the Basement
Came out to look at me—

5   And Frigates—in the Upper Floor
Extended Hempen Hands°—
Presuming Me to be a Mouse—
Aground—upon the Sands—

But no Man moved Me—till the Tide
10   Went past my simple Shoe—
And past my Apron—and my Belt
And past my Bodice°—too—

---

6 *Hands:* rope.
12 *Bodice:* a stiffened woman's garment worn like a vest.

And made as He would eat me up—
As wholly as a Dew
Upon a Dandelion's Sleeve—
And then—I started—too—

And He—He followed—close behind—
I felt His Silver Heel
Upon my Ankle—Then my Shoes
Would overflow with Pearl—

Until We met the Solid Town—
No One He seemed to know—
And bowing—with a Mighty look—
At me—The Sea withdrew—

*c. 1862*

## 585

I like to see it lap the Miles—
And lick the Valleys up—
And stop to feed itself at Tanks—
And then—prodigious step

Around a Pile of Mountains—
And supercilious peer
In Shanties—by the sides of Roads—
And then a Quarry pare

To fit its Ribs
And crawl between
Complaining all the while
In horrid—hooting stanza—
Then chase itself down Hill—

And neigh like Boanerges°—
Then—punctual as a Star
Stop—docile and omnipotent
At its own stable door—

*c. 1862*

## 601

A still—Volcano—Life—
That flickered in the night—
When it was dark enough to do
Without erasing sight—

---

14 *Boanerges:* (Greek) "Sons of Thunder," here a loud preacher or orator; originally a term describing the active evangelizing of the Apostles John and James.

5  A quiet—Earthquake Style—
   Too subtle to suspect
   By natures this side Naples—
   The North cannot detect

   The Solemn—Torrid—Symbol—
10 The lips that never lie—
   Whose hissing Corals part—and shut—
   And Cities—ooze away—

                                              *c. 1862*

## 613

   They shut me up in Prose—
   As when a little Girl
   They put me in the Closet—
   Because they liked me "still"—

5  Still! Could themself have peeped—
   And seen my Brain—go round—
   They might as wise have lodged a Bird
   For Treason—in the Pound°—

   Himself has but to will
10 And easy as a Star
   Look down upon Captivity—
   And laugh—No more have I°—

                                              *c. 1862*

## 657

   I dwell in Possibility—
   A fairer House than Prose—
   More numerous of Windows—
   Superior—for Doors—

5  Of Chambers as the Cedars—
   Impregnable of Eye°—
   And for an Everlasting Roof
   The Gambrels° of the Sky—

   Of Visitors—the fairest—
10 For Occupation—This—
   The spreading wide my narrow Hands
   To gather Paradise—

                                              *c. 1862*

---

8 *Pound*: a roofless enclosure for livestock.
12 *I*: to escape my captivity, I need only do what the bird does.
6 *Eye*: impossible to see through, like a dense stand of cedar trees.
8 *gambrels*: ridged roofs with two slopes per side; the lower slope has a steeper pitch.

### 712

Because I could not stop for Death—
He kindly stopped for me—

The Carriage held but just Ourselves—
And Immortality.

5      We slowly drove—He knew no haste
And I had put away
My labor and my leisure too,
For His Civility—

We passed the School, where Children strove
10     At Recess—in the Ring—
We passed the Fields of Gazing Grain—
We passed the Setting Sun—

Or rather—He passed Us—
The Dews drew quivering and chill—
15     For only Gossamer,° my Gown—
My Tippet°—only Tulle°—

We paused before a House that seemed
A Swelling of the Ground—
The Roof was scarcely visible—
20     The Cornice—in the Ground—

Since then—'tis Centuries—and yet
Feels shorter than the Day
I first surmised the Horses' Heads
Were toward Eternity—

*c. 1863*

### 754

My Life had stood—a Loaded Gun—
In Corners—till a Day
The Owner passed—identified—
And carried Me away—

5      And now We roam in Sovereign Woods—
And now We hunt the Doe—
And every time I speak for Him—
The Mountains straight reply—

---

15 *Gossamer:* extremely fine fabric.
16 *Tippet:* shoulder cape or scarf.
16 *Tulle:* thin netlike silk fabric.

And do I smile, such cordial light
10　　Upon the Valley glow—
It is as a Vesuvian° face
Had let its pleasure through—

And when at Night—Our good Day done—
I guard My Master's Head—
15　　'Tis better than the Eider-Duck's
Deep° Pillow—to have shared—

To foe of His—I'm deadly foe—
None stir the second time—
On whom I lay a Yellow Eye°—
20　　Or an emphatic Thumb°—

Though I than He—may longer live
He longer must—than I—
For I have but the power to kill,
Without—the power to die—

　　　　　　　　　　　　　　　　　　*c. 1863*


## 1072

Title divine—is mine!
The Wife—without the Sign!
Acute Degree—conferred on me—
Empress of Calvary!°
5　　Royal—all but the Crown!
Betrothed—without the swoon
God sends us Women—
When you—hold—Garnet to Garnet—
Gold—to Gold—
10　　Born—Bridalled—Shrouded—
In a Day—
Tri Victory
"My Husband"—women say—
Stroking the Melody—
15　　Is *this*—the way?

　　　　　　　　　　　　　　　　　　*c. 1862*

---

11 *Vesuvian:* capable of erupting, like Italy's volcano Mt. Vesuvias, of bursting forth with destructive fire and light.
16 *Deep:* downy.
19 *Yellow Eye:* like a hunter's deadly eye.
20 *Thumb:* as in a thumb that rubs things out.
4 *Calvary:* The hill near Jerusalem on which Christ was crucified. Dickinson evokes the idea of suffering in a situation that yields the closeness but not the fact of marriage.

### 1129

Tell all the Truth but tell it slant—
Success in Circuit lies
Too bright for our infirm Delight
The Truth's superb surprise
5   As Lightning to the Children eased
With explanation kind
The Truth must dazzle gradually
Or every man be blind—

*c. 1868*

### 1705

Volcanoes be in Sicily
And South America
I judge from my Geography
Volcanoes nearer here
5   A Lava step at any time
Am I inclined to climb
A Crater I may contemplate
Vesuvius° at Home

---

8 *Vesuvius:* Mt. Vesuvius, a potent active volcano in Italy.

# Edwin Markham (1852–1940)

Charles Edward Anson Markham was born in Oregon City, in the Oregon Territory, but his mother took him to a farm at Suisun, California, in 1856. The farm was halfway between Sacramento and San Francisco; Markham lived in California, where he became a schoolteacher, until moving to New York's Staten Island at the turn of the century, and publishing a number of volumes of poetry thereafter. "The Man With the Hoe" (1899) was reprinted repeatedly across the country; it galvanized farmers' awareness of the economic grievances they had against banking and industry, and became one of the signature poems of the labor movement. It would eventually appear in 10,000 newspapers in more than forty languages. His poem "Lincoln, the Man of the People" was published in almost every American newspaper in 1900. The late Victorian illustrated version of "The Man With the Hoe" included in the appendix was published as a special supplement to the *San Francisco Examiner,* the place the poem first appeared, after it became famous. The original is in the editor's collection.

Prior to issuing "The Man With the Hoe," Markham had published "Song of the Workers" in William Morris's (1834–1896) London journal *Commonweal,* and had written a number of conventionally romantic poems. But he was also reading Karl Marx (1818–1883) and other socialist writers and becoming radicalized. "The Man With the Hoe" is an explicit response to an oil painting by the French artist Jean François Millet (1814–1875), one of several paintings on contemporary agricultural, working-class subjects Millet produced at the middle of the nineteenth century. It depicts a rough-shod farmer or agricultural worker, probably exhausted and certainly leaning forward on his hoe, in a flat scrub landscape as yet untamed and unplowed. Markham's poetic response is effective in marshalling moral outrage and linking it to literariness on workers' behalf. Its indictment of the ravages wrought by those in power was decisive for its time, in part because Markham treated exploitation as a violation of God's will. The poem is equally effective in issuing a broad revolutionary warning to capitalists and politicians. The version printed here was slightly revised by Markham in 1920.

# The Man With the Hoe

*(Written after seeing Millet's world-famous painting)*

Bowed by the weight of centuries he leans
Upon his hoe and gazes on the ground,
The emptiness of ages in his face,
And on his back the burden of the world.
5    Who made him dead to rapture and despair,
A thing that grieves not and that never hopes,
Stolid and stunned, a brother to the ox?
Who loosened and let down this brutal jaw?
Whose was the hand that slanted back this brow?
10   Whose breath blew out the light within this brain?

Is this the Thing the Lord God made and gave
To have dominion over sea and land;
To trace the stars and search the heavens for power;
To feel the passion of Eternity?
15   Is this the dream He dreamed who shaped the suns
And marked their ways upon the ancient deep?
Down all the caverns of Hell to their last gulf
There is no shape more terrible than this—
More tongued with censure of the world's blind greed—
20   More filled with signs and portents for the soul—
More packt with danger to the universe.

What gulfs between him and the seraphim!
Slave of the wheel of labor, what to him
Are Plato and the swing of Pleiades?
25   What the long reaches of the peaks of song,
The rift of dawn, the reddening of the rose?
Through this dread shape the suffering ages look;
Time's tragedy is in that aching stoop;
Through this dread shape humanity betrayed,
30   Plundered, profaned, and disinherited,
Cries protest to the Judges of the World,
A protest that is also prophecy.

O masters, lords and rulers in all lands,
Is this the handiwork you give to God,
35   This monstrous thing distorted and soul-quenched?
How will you ever straighten up this shape;
Touch it again with immortality;
Give back the upward looking and the light;
Rebuild in it the music and the dream;
40   Make right the immemorial infamies,
Perfidious wrongs, immedicable woes?

O masters, lords and rulers in all lands,
How will the Future reckon with this man?
How answer his brute question in that hour
45   When whirlwinds of rebellion shake all shores?
How will it be with kingdoms and with kings—
With those who shaped him to the thing he is—
When this dumb terror shall rise to judge the world,
After the silence of the centuries?

*1899, 1920*

# Sadakichi Hartmann (1867–1944)

Hartmann was born on an island in Nagasaki Harbor in Japan, of a Japanese mother and German father. His father sent him to the U. S. in 1882, and he was naturalized in 1894. His *Conversations with Walt Whitman* (1895) apparently grows out of meetings they had late in Whitman's life. Hartmann wrote a number of verse and prose plays, as well as numerous poems that helped shape the imagist movement.

## Cyanogen Seas Are Surging

Cyanogen° seas are surging
On fierce cinnabarine° strands,
Where white Amazons are marching,
Through the radiance of the sands.

5      Oh, could only lambent love-flame
Be like the surging sea,
Deluge the red of the desert
And drown the white virgins in me!

*1892*

## Tanka I

Winter? Spring! Who knows!
   White buds from the plumtrees wing
And mingle with the snows.
   No blue skies these flowers bring,
   Yet their fragrance augurs Spring.

*1920*

## Tanka III

Moon, somnolent, white,
   Mirrored in a waveless sea,
What fickle mood of night
   Urged thee from heaven to flee
   And live in the dawnlit sea!

*1920*

---

1 *cyanogen:* a colorless, flammable poisonous gas, with an odor similar to that of peach leaves.
2 *cinnabarine:* brilliant red, like crystals of cinnabar (mercuric sulfide).

# Edgar Lee Masters (1868–1950)

With its concise and telling graveyard epitaphs, Masters' 1915 collection *Spoon River Anthology* established his reputation and remains his best-known work. Born and raised in a small town in Illinois, his first and last volumes of poetry focus on the life of his native Midwest. Yet he also took up other subjects, and used a variety of verse forms in the course of his career, meanwhile working as a lawyer and writing biographies of Vachel Lindsay, Walt Whitman, and Mark Twain. See especially *Spoon River Antholoy: An Annotated Edition* (1992).

## Lucinda Matlock°

I went to the dances at Chandlerville,
And played snap-out at Winchester.
One time we changed partners,
Driving home in the moonlight of middle June,
5    And then I found Davis.
We were married and lived together for seventy years,
Enjoying, working, raising the twelve children,
Eight of whom we lost
Ere I had reached the age of sixty.
10   I spun, I wove, I kept the house, I nursed the sick,
I made the garden, and for holiday
Rambled over the fields where sang the larks,
And by Spoon River gathering many a shell,
And many a flower and medicinal weed—
15   Shouting to the wooded hills, singing to the green valleys.
At ninety-six I had lived enough, that is all,
And passed to a sweet repose.
What is this I hear of sorrow and weariness,
Anger, discontent and drooping hopes?
20   Degenerate sons and daughters,
Life is too strong for you—
It takes life to love Life.

*1915*

---

**poem title:** Masters indicated that the poem was based on his paternal grandmother.

## Petit, the Poet°

Seeds in a dry pod, tick, tick, tick,
Tick, tick, tick, like mites in a quarrel—
Faint iambics that the full breeze wakens—
But the pine tree makes a symphony thereof.
5   Triolets, villanelles, rondels, rondeaus,
Ballades by the score with the same old thought:
The snows and the roses of yesterday are vanished;°
And what is love but a rose that fades?
Life all around me here in the village:
10   Tragedy, comedy, valor and truth,
Courage, constancy, heroism, failure—
All in the loom, and oh what patterns!
Woodlands, meadows, streams and rivers—
Blind to all of it all my life long.
15   Triolets, villanelles, rondels, rondeaus,
Seeds in a dry pod, tick, tick, tick,
Tick, tick, tick, what little iambics,
While Homer and Whitman roared in the pines?

*1915*

## Seth Compton

When I died, the circulating library
Which I built up for Spoon River,
And managed for the good of inquiring minds,
Was sold at auction on the public square,
5   As if to destroy the last vestige
Of my memory and influence.
For those of you who could not see the virtue
Of knowing Volney's "Ruins" as well as Butler's "Analogy"
And "Faust" as well as "Evangeline,"°
10   Were really the power in the village,
And often you asked me,
"What is the use of knowing the evil in the world?"
I am out of your way now, Spoon River,
Choose your own good and call it good.
15   For I could never make you see
That no one knows what is good
Who knows not what is evil;
And no one knows what is true
Who knows not what is false.

*1915*

---

**poem title:** Masters suggested he had the minor poet Ernest McGaffey in mind, but the poem is also substantially autobiographical.
7 snows . . . vanished: the line echoes Rossetti's translation of the refrain of François Villon's (c. 1431–1463) "Ballade of Dead Ladies": "Where are the snows of yesteryear?"
9 "Evangeline": John Hallwas offers the following gloss: "Volney's *Ruins* (1791) is a famous skeptical work, whereas Joseph Butler's *Analogy of Religion* (1736) is a work of religious apologetics; Goethe's *Faust* (1808, 1832) is a tragedy about enormous passion and a relentless quest for self-fulfillment, whereas Henry Wadsworth Longfellow's *Evangeline* (1847) is a sentimental narrative poem about a thwarted love relationship."

## Trainor, the Druggist

Only the chemist can tell, and not always the chemist,
What will result from compounding
Fluids or solids.
And who can tell
5   How men and women will interact
On each other, or what children will result?
There were Benjamin Pantier and his wife,
Good in themselves, but evil toward each other:
He oxygen, she hydrogen,
10  Their son, a devastating fire.
I Trainor, the druggist, a mixer of chemicals,
Killed while making an experiment,
Lived unwedded.

*1915*

## Cleanthus Trilling

The urge of the seed: the germ.
The urge of the germ: the stalk.
The urge of the stalk: leaves.
The urge of leaves: the blossom.
5   The urge of the blossom: to scatter pollen.
The urge of the pollen: the imagined dream of life.
The urge of life: longing for to-morrow.
The urge of to-morrow: Pain.
The urge of Pain: God.

*1924*

# Edwin Arlington Robinson (1869–1935)

Although much of Robinson's work was done before American modernism's heyday, in several respects his poetry heralds elements of what was to come. Best known for his portraits of individuals, portraits often comparable to those done by Edgar Lee Masters, he is actually more versatile, writing dramatic monologues and blank-verse narratives of considerable length. If his use of the vernacular and the absence of sentimentality in some of his portraits helps usher in modernism, so does a quality of indirection and irresolution in other poems. Born in Head Tide, Maine, and raised in nearby Gardiner, the model for his fictional "Tilbury Town," Robinson enrolled at Harvard but had to leave after two years when the family's income fell when his father died. For several years, Robinson was thoroughly impoverished as he struggled to become a poet. He moved to New York in 1899 and early on he worked there inspecting subways under construction and then in the Customs House, a job obtained in 1904 with assistance from President Theodore Roosevelt, who admired his work. By the 1920s, he would become one of the country's most widely read poets. His characters were often failed but learned figures, and he urged on his readers a certain stoicism in the face of difficulty.

## The House on the Hill

They are all gone away,
    The House is shut and still,
There is nothing more to say.

Through broken walls and gray
5      The winds blow bleak and shrill:
They are all gone away.

Nor is there one to-day
    To speak them good or ill:
There is nothing more to say.

10  Why is it then we stray
    Around the sunken sill?
They are all gone away,

And our poor fancy-play
    For them is wasted skill:
15  There is nothing more to say.

> There is ruin and decay
>    In the House on the Hill:
> They are all gone away,
> There is nothing more to say.

*1897*

## Richard Cory

Whenever Richard Cory went down town,
We people on the pavement looked at him:
He was a gentleman from sole to crown,
Clean favored, and imperially slim.

5   And he was always quietly arrayed,
And he was always human when he talked;
But still he fluttered pulses when he said,
"Good-morning," and he glittered when he walked.

And he was rich—yes, richer than a king—
10  And admirably schooled in every grace:
In fine, we thought that he was everything
To make us wish that we were in his place.

So on we worked, and waited for the light,
And went without the meat, and cursed the bread;
15  And Richard Cory, one calm summer night,
Went home and put a bullet through his head.

*1897*

## The Clerks

I did not think that I should find them there
When I came back again; but there they stood,
As in the days they dreamed of when young blood
Was in their cheeks and women called them fair.
5   Be sure, they met me with an ancient air,—
And yes, there was a shop-worn brotherhood
About them; but the men were just as good,
And just as human as they ever were.

And you that ache so much to be sublime,
10  And you that feed yourselves with your descent,
What comes of all your visions and your fears?
Poets and kings are but the clerks of Time,
Tiering the same dull webs of discontent,
Clipping the same sad alnage° of the years.

*1897*

---

14 *alnage*: as in the measurement of cloth (in Old English law) in units of about forty-five inches, its value affirmed by affixing a leaden seal.

# Miniver Cheevy

Miniver Cheevy, child of scorn,
    Grew lean while he assailed the seasons;
He wept that he was ever born,
    And he had reasons.

5    Miniver loved the days of old
    When swords were bright and steeds were prancing;
The vision of a warrior bold
    Would set him dancing.

Miniver sighed for what was not,
10    And dreamed, and rested from his labors;
He dreamed of Thebes° and Camelot,
    And Priam's° neighbors.

Miniver mourned the ripe renown
    That made so many a name so fragrant;
15    He mourned Romance, now on the town,
    And Art, a vagrant.

Miniver loved the Medici,°
    Albeit he had never seen one;
He would have sinned incessantly
20    Could he have been one.

Miniver cursed the commonplace
    And eyed a khaki suit with loathing;
He missed the mediæval grace
    Of iron clothing.

25    Miniver scorned the gold he sought,
    But sore annoyed was he without it;
Miniver thought, and thought, and thought,
    And thought about it.

Miniver Cheevy, born too late,
30    Scratched his head and kept on thinking;
Miniver coughed, and called it fate,
    And kept on drinking.

*1910*

---

11 *Thebes:* an ancient Greek city that rivaled Athens and Sparta and provided the setting
for Sophocles's tragic legend of King Oedipus; Camelot: the legendary city of King Arthur's
court.
12 *Priam:* king of Troy, the city destroyed during the Trojan War in Homer's *Iliad*.
17 *Medici:* the Florentine family of merchant-statesmen known for their political power
and cruelty, and celebrated for their patronage of the arts during the Renaissance.

## The Mill

The miller's wife had waited long,
   The tea was cold, the fire was dead;
And there might yet be nothing wrong
   In how he went and what he said:
5   "There are no millers any more,"
   Was all that she had heard him say;
And he had lingered at the door
   So long that it seemed yesterday.

Sick with a fear that had no form
10   She knew that she was there at last;
And in the mill there was a warm
   And mealy fragrance of the past.
What else there was would only seem
   To say again what he had meant;
15   And what was hanging from a beam
   Would not have heeded where she went.

And if she thought it followed her,
   She may have reasoned in the dark
That one way of the few there were
20   Would hide her and would leave no mark.
Black water, smooth above the weir°
   Like starry velvet in the night,
Though ruffled once, would soon appear
   The same as ever to the sight.

*1920*

## Mr. Flood's Party

Old Eben Flood, climbing alone one night
Over the hill between the town below
And the forsaken upland hermitage
That held as much as he should ever know
5   On earth again of home, paused warily.
The road was his with not a native near;
And Eben, having leisure, said aloud,
For no man else in Tilbury Town° to hear:

---

21 *weir:* the dam regulating water flow to the mill.
8 *Tilbury Town:* a fictitious town modeled after Robinson's hometown, Gardiner, Maine.

"Well, Mr. Flood, we have the harvest moon
10      Again, and we may not have many more;
The bird is on the wing,° the poet says,
And you and I have said it here before.
Drink to the bird." He raised up to the light
The jug that he had gone so far to fill,
15      And answered huskily: "Well, Mr. Flood,
Since you propose it, I believe I will."

Alone, as if enduring to the end
A valiant armor of scarred hopes outworn,
He stood there in the middle of the road
20      Like Roland's ghost winding a silent horn.°
Below him, in the town among the trees,
Where friends of other days had honored him,
A phantom salutation of the dead
Rang thinly till old Eben's eyes were dim.

25      Then, as a mother lays her sleeping child
Down tenderly, fearing it may awake,
He set the jug down slowly at his feet
With trembling care, knowing that most things break;
And only when assured that on firm earth
30      It stood, as the uncertain lives of men
Assuredly did not, he paced away,
And with his hand extended paused again:

"Well, Mr. Flood, we have not met like this
In a long time; and many a change has come
35      To both of us, I fear, since last it was
We had a drop together. Welcome home!"
Convivially returning with himself,
Again he raised the jug up to the light;
And with an acquiescent quaver said:
40      "Well, Mr. Flood, if you insist, I might.

"Only a very little, Mr. Flood—
For auld lang syne.° No more, sir; that will do."
So, for the time, apparently it did,
And Eben evidently thought so too;

---

11 *"the bird is on the wing"*: a quotation from and paraphrase of Edward Fitzgerald's very
free 1859 translation of the eleventh-century Persian poem *The Rubáiyat of Omar Khayyám*
(25–28): "Come, fill the Cup, and in the Fire of Spring / Your Winter Garment of Repen-
tance fling: / The Bird of Time has but a little way / To fly—and Lo! the Bird is on the
Wing."
20 *horn*: at the battle of Roncesvalles in A.D. 778, Roland (later, hero of the medieval
French poem *Chanson de Roland*, or *Song of Roland*, 1000?) blows his horn for help just
before he dies.
42 *auld lang syne*: Scottish dialect for "days long gone," from a song attributed to Robert
Burns (1759–1796).

45      For soon amid the silver loneliness
        Of night he lifted up his voice and sang,
        Secure, with only two moons listening,
        Until the whole harmonious landscape rang—

        "For auld lang syne." The weary throat gave out,
50      The last word wavered, and the song was done.
        He raised again the jug regretfully
        And shook his head, and was again alone.
        There was not much that was ahead of him,
        And there was nothing in the town below—
55      Where strangers would have shut the many doors
        That many friends had opened long ago.

                                                            *1921*


## The Tree in Pamela's Garden

        Pamela was too gentle to deceive
        Her roses. "Let the men stay where they are,"
        She said, "and if Apollo's avatar
        Be one of them, I shall not have to grieve."
5       And so she made all Tilbury Town believe
        She sighed a little more for the North Star
        Than over men, and only in so far
        As she was in a garden was like Eve.

        Her neighbors—doing all that neighbors can
10      To make romance of reticence meanwhile—
        Seeing that she had never loved a man,
        Wished Pamela had a cat, or a small bird,
        And only would have wondered at her smile
        Could they have seen that she had overheard.

                                                            *1921*

# James Weldon Johnson (1871–1938)

Johnson's work and multiple careers defy easy characterization. He was born and grew up in Jacksonville, Florida, where his grandfather had moved after a hurricane destroyed his business in the Bahamas. Johnson graduated from Atlanta University and then studied for the law, serving simultaneously as principal of the Stanton School. But he also began writing poems, which served as the lyrics for songs his brother John, a trained musician, had begun composing. At the turn of the century, both brothers were in New York composing songs for Broadway musicals. One earlier composition, "Lift Every Voice and Sing," was called the Negro National Anthem by the National Association for the Advancement of Colored People. From 1906 to 1909, Johnson served as Washington's ambassador to Venezuela. On his return he wrote his novel *The Autobiography of an Ex-Colored Man* (1912). He would later become a key organizing figure in the Harlem Renaissance of the 1920s, editing ground-breaking collections of poetry and spirituals, writing his autobiography, and collecting a series of biblical stories in verse, including "The Creation," in *God's Trombones: Seven Negro Sermons in Verse* (1927).

## O Black and Unknown Bards

O black and unknown bards of long ago,
How came your lips to touch the sacred fire?
How, in your darkness, did you come to know
The power and beauty of the minstrel's lyre?
5    Who first from midst his bonds lifted his eyes?
Who first from out the still watch, lone and long,
Feeling the ancient faith of prophets rise
Within his dark-kept soul, burst into song?

Heart of what slave poured out such melody
10   As "Steal away to Jesus"? On its strains
His spirit must have nightly floated free,
Though still about his hands he felt his chains.
Who heard great "Jordan roll"? Whose starward eye
Saw chariot "swing low"? And who was he
15   That breathed that comforting, melodic sigh,
"Nobody knows de trouble I see"?°

---

16 *see:* "Steal Away to Jesus," "Roll Jordan, Roll" (referring to the Jordan River in Palestine), "Swing Low, Sweet Chariot," and "Nobody knows de trouble I see" are all Negro spirituals.

What merely living clod, what captive thing,
Could up toward God through all its darkness grope,
And find within its deadened heart to sing
20     These songs of sorrow, love and faith, and hope?
How did it catch that subtle undertone,
That note in music heard not with the ears?
How sound the elusive reed so seldom blown,
Which stirs the soul or melts the heart to tears.

25     Not that great German master in his dream
Of harmonies that thundered amongst the stars
At the creation, ever heard a theme
Nobler than "Go down, Moses." Mark its bars
How like a mighty trumpet-call they stir
30     The blood. Such are the notes that men have sung
Going to valorous deeds; such tones there were
That helped make history when Time was young.

There is a wide, wide wonder in it all,
That from degraded rest and servile toil
35     The fiery spirit of the seer should call
These simple children of the sun and soil.
O black slave singers, gone, forgot, unfamed,
You—you alone, of all the long, long line
Of those who've sung untaught, unknown, unnamed,
40     Have stretched out upward, seeking the divine.

You sang not deeds of heroes or of kings;
No chant of bloody war, no exulting paean
Of arms-won triumphs; but your humble strings
You touched in chord with music empyrean.
45     You sang far better than you knew; the songs
That for your listeners' hungry hearts sufficed
Still live,—but more than this to you belongs:
You sang a race from wood and stone to Christ.

                                                    *1908*


# The Creation

And God stepped out on space,
And he looked around and said:
I'm lonely—
I'll make me a world.

5     And far as the eye of God could see
Darkness covered everything,
Blacker than a hundred midnights
Down in a cypress swamp.

Then God smiled,
10    And the light broke,
And the darkness rolled up on one side,
And the light stood shining on the other,
And God said: That's good!

Then God reached out and took the light in his hands,
15    And God rolled the light around in his hands
Until he made the sun;
And he set that sun a-blazing in the heavens.
And the light that was left from making the sun
God gathered it up in a shining ball
20    And flung it against the darkness,
Spangling the night with the moon and stars.
Then down between
The darkness and the light
He hurled the world;
25    And God said: That's good!

Then God himself stepped down—
And the sun was on his right hand,
And the moon was on his left;
The stars were clustered about his head,
30    And the earth was under his feet.
And God walked, and where he trod
His footsteps hollowed the valleys out
And bulged the mountains up.

Then he stopped and looked and saw
35    That the earth was hot and barren.
So God stepped over to the edge of the world
And he spat out the seven seas—
He batted his eyes, and the lightnings flashed—
He clapped his hands, and the thunders rolled—
40    And the waters above the earth came down,
The cooling waters came down.

Then the green grass sprouted,
And the little red flowers blossomed,
The pine tree pointed his finger to the sky,
45    And the oak spread out his arms,
The lakes cuddled down in the hollows of the ground,
And the rivers ran down to the sea;
And God smiled again,
And the rainbow appeared,
50    And curled itself around his shoulder.

Then God raised his arm and he waved his hand
Over the sea and over the land,
And he said: Bring forth! Bring forth!
And quicker than God could drop his hand,
55    Fishes and fowls

And beasts and birds
Swam the rivers and the seas,
Roamed the forests and the woods,
And split the air with their wings.
60      And God said: That's good!

Then God walked around,
And God looked around
On all that he had made.
He looked at his sun,
65      And he looked at his moon,
And he looked at his little stars;
He looked on his world
With all its living things,
And God said: I'm lonely still.

70      Then God sat down—
On the side of a hill where he could think;
By a deep, wide river he sat down;
With his head in his hands,
God thought and thought,
75      Till he thought: I'll make me a man!

Up from the bed of the river
God scooped the clay;
And by the bank of the river
He kneeled him down;
80      And there the great God Almighty
Who lit the sun and fixed it in the sky,
Who flung the stars to the most far corner of the night,
Who rounded the earth in the middle of his hand;
This Great God,
85      Like a mammy bending over her baby,
Kneeled down in the dust
Toiling over a lump of clay
Till he shaped it in his own image;

Then into it he blew the breath of life,
90      And man became a living soul.
Amen. Amen.

                                                    *1920*


## The White Witch

O brothers mine, take care! Take care!
The great white witch rides out tonight,
Trust not your prowess nor your strength;
Your only safety lies in flight;
5      For in her glance there is a snare,
And in her smile there is a blight.

The great white witch you have not seen?
Then, younger brothers mine, forsooth,
Like nursery children you have looked
For ancient hag and snaggle-tooth;
But no, not so; the witch appears
In all the glowing charms of youth.

Her lips are like carnations red,
Her face like new-born lilies fair,
Her eyes like ocean waters blue,
She moves with subtle grace and air,
And all about her head there floats
The golden glory of her hair.

But though she always thus appears
In form of youth and mood of mirth,
Unnumbered centuries are hers,
The infant planets saw her birth;
The child of throbbing Life is she,
Twin sister to the greedy earth.

And back behind those smiling lips,
And down within those laughing eyes,
And underneath the soft caress
Of hand and voice and purring sighs,
The shadow of the panther lurks,
The spirit of the vampire lies.

For I have seen the great white witch,
And she has led me to her lair,
And I have kissed her red, red lips
And cruel face so white and fair;
Around me she has twined her arms,
And bound me with her yellow hair.

I felt those red lips burn and sear
My body like a living coal;
Obeyed the power of those eyes
As the needle trembles to the pole;
And did not care although I felt
The strength go ebbing from my soul.

Oh! she has seen your strong young limbs,
And heard your laughter loud and gay,
And in your voices she has caught
The echo of a far-off day,
When man was closer to the earth;
And she has marked you for her prey.

She feels the old Antæan strength
50      In you, the great dynamic beat
Of primal passions, and she sees
In you the last besieged retreat
Of love relentless, lusty, fierce,
Love pain-ecstatic, cruel-sweet.

55      O, brothers mine, take care! Take care!
The great white witch rides out tonight.
O, younger brothers mine, beware!
Look not upon her beauty bright;
For in her glance there is a snare,
60      And in her smile there is a blight.

1922

## Paul Laurence Dunbar (1872–1906)

The son of former slaves, Dunbar was born and grew up in Dayton, Ohio. His father had escaped from Kentucky to serve in a Massachusetts regiment during the Civil War. He began writing poetry in high school and eventually acquired a large multiracial audience. By late nineteenth-century standards, Dunbar's work was steadfast both in its black pride and its rejection of racism. Yet during the Harlem Renaissance his dialect poetry would win praise from Langston Hughes and Sterling Brown, while meeting severe criticism from James Weldon Johnson and others. The question was whether the dialect poetry gave voice to authentic black folk traditions or unintentionally collaborated in the racist tradition of white writers who employed black dialect to suggest slaves were happy under their masters. Yet Dunbar actually experimented with Irish-American and German-American dialects as well, and wrote many poems in standard English. Moreover, in his own lifetime the poems in black dialect were published in heavily illustrated volumes whose realist photographs of rural blacks effectively undercut any possibility for reading condescension or stereotyping into the poems themselves. Unfortunately, the illustrations have never been reprinted.

## We Wear the Mask

We wear the mask that grins and lies,
It hides our cheeks and shades our eyes,—
This debt we pay to human guile;
With torn and bleeding hearts we smile,
5    And mouth with myriad subtleties.

Why should the world be overwise,
In counting all our tears and sighs?
Nay, let them only see us, while
    We wear the mask.

10    We smile, but, O great Christ, our cries
To Thee from tortured souls arise.
We sing, but oh, the clay is vile
Beneath our feet, and long the mile;
But let the world dream otherwise,
    We wear the mask.

*1895*

# When Malindy Sings

G'way an' quit dat noise, Miss Lucy—
  Put dat music book away;
What's de use to keep on tryin'?
  Ef you practise twell° you're gray,

5   You cain't sta't no notes a-flyin'
  Lak de ones dat rants and rings
F'om de kitchen to de big woods
  When Malindy sings.

You ain't got de nachel o'gans°

10  Fu' to make de soun' come right,
You ain't got de tu'ns° an' twistin's
  Fu' to make it sweet an' light.
Tell you one thing now, Miss Lucy,
  An' I'm tellin' you fu' true,

15  When hit comes to raal° right singin',
  'T ain't no easy thing to do.

Easy 'nough fu' folks to hollah,
  Lookin' at de lines an' dots,
When dey ain't no one kin sence° it,

20    An' de chune comes in, in spots;
But fu' real melojous music,
  Dat jes' strikes you' hea't° and clings,
Jes' you stan' an' listen wif me
  When Malindy sings.

25  Ain't you nevah hyeahd° Malindy?
  Blessed soul, tek up de cross!
Look hyeah, ain't you jokin', honey?
  Well, you don't know whut you los'.
Y' ought to hyeah dat gal a-wa'blin',°

30    Robins, la'ks, an' all dem things,
Heish dey moufs° an' hides dey faces
  When Malindy sings.

Fiddlin' man jes' stop his fiddlin',
  Lay his fiddle on de she'f;

35  Mockin'-bird quit tryin' to whistle,
  'Cause he jes' so shamed hisse'f.
Folks a-playin' on de banjo
  Draps dey fingahs on de strings—
Bless yo' soul—fu'gits to move 'em,

40    When Malindy sings.

---

4 *twell:* until.
9 *nachel o'gans:* natural organs.
11 *tu'ns:* turns.
15 *raal:* real.
19 *kin sence:* can sense.
22 *hea't:* heart.
25 *hyeahd:* heard.
29 *wa'blin:* warbling.
31 *Heish dey moufs:* Hush their mouths.

She jes' spreads huh mouf and hollahs,
    "Come to Jesus,"° twell you hyeah
Sinnahs' tremblin' steps and voices,
    Timid-lak a-drawin' neah;
45  Den she tu'ns to "Rock of Ages,"°
    Simply to de cross she clings,
An' you fin' yo' teahs a-drappin'°
    When Malindy sings.

Who dat says dat humble praises
    Wif de Master° nevah counts?
50  Heish yo' mouf, I hyeah dat music,
    Ez hit rises up an' mounts—

Floatin' by de hills an' valleys,
    Way above dis buryin' sod,
55  Ez hit makes its way in glory
    To de very gates of God!

Oh, hit's sweetah dan de music
    Of an edicated band;
An' hit's dearah dan de battle's
60    Song o' triumph in de lan'.
It seems holier dan evenin'
    When de solemn chu'ch bell rings,
Ez I sit an' ca'mly listen
    While Malindy sings.

65  Towsah, stop dat ba'kin', hyeah me!
    Mandy, mek dat chile keep still;
Don't you hyeah de echoes callin'
    F'om de valley to de hill?
Let me listen, I can hyeah it,
70    Th'oo de bresh of angels' wings,
Sof' an' sweet, "Swing Low, Sweet Chariot,"°
    Ez Malindy sings.

*1895*

# Sympathy

I know what the caged bird feels, alas!
    When the sun is bright on the upland slopes;
When the wind stirs soft through the springing grass,
And when the river flows like a stream of glass;
5    When the first bird sings and the first bud opes,°
And the faint perfume from its chalice° steals—
I know what the caged bird feels!

---

42 *"Come to Jesus"*: popular hymn.
45 *"Rock of Ages"*: popular hymn.
47 *teahs a-drappin'*: tears a-dropping.
50 *Master*: God.
71 *"Swing Low, Sweet Chariot"*: popular hymn.
5 *opes*: opens.
6 *chalice*: a flower shaped like a cup or glass.

I know why the caged bird beats his wing
   Till its blood is red on the cruel bars;
10   For he must fly back to his perch and cling
   When he fain would be° on the bough a-swing;
     And a pain still throbs in the old, old scars
   And they pulse again with a keener sting—
   I know why he beats his wing!

15   I know why the caged bird sings, ah me,
     When his wing is bruised and his bosom sore,—
   When he beats his bars and he would be free;

It is not a carol of joy or glee,
     But a prayer that he sends from his heart's core,
20   But a plea, that upward to Heaven he flings—
   I know why the caged bird sings!

                            *1899*

## The Haunted Oak

Pray why are you so bare, so bare,
   Oh, bough of the old oak-tree;
And why, when I go through the shade you throw,
   Runs a shudder over me?

5   My leaves were green as the best, I trow,°
   And sap ran free in my veins,
But I saw in the moonlight dim and weird
   A guiltless victim's pains.

I bent me down to hear his sigh;
10   I shook with his gurgling moan,
And I trembled sore when they rode away,
   And left him here alone.

They'd charged him with the old, old crime,
   And set him fast in jail:
15   Oh, why does the dog howl all night long,
   And why does the night wind wail?

He prayed his prayer and he swore his oath,
   And he raised his hand to the sky;
But the beat of hoofs smote on his ear,
20   And the steady tread drew nigh.

Who is it rides by night, by night,
   Over the moonlit road?
And what is the spur that keeps the pace,
   What is the galling goad?

---

11 *fain would be:* would like to be.
5 *trow:* believe.

25　And now they beat at the prison door,
　　　　"Ho, keeper, do not stay!
　　We are friends of him whom you hold within,
　　　　And we fain would take him away

　　"From those who ride fast on our heels
30　　　　With mind to do him wrong;
　　They have no care for his innocence,
　　　　And the rope they bear is long."

　　They have fooled the jailer with lying words,
　　　　They have fooled the man with lies;
35　The bolts unbar, the locks are drawn,
　　　　And the great door open flies.

　　Now they have taken him from the jail,
　　　　And hard and fast they ride,
　　And the leader laughs low down in his throat,
40　　　　As they halt my trunk beside.

　　Oh, the judge, he wore a mask of black,
　　　　And the doctor one of white,
　　And the minister, with his oldest son,
　　　　Was curiously bedight.°

45　Oh, foolish man, why weep you now?
　　　　'Tis but a little space,
　　And the time will come when these shall dread
　　　　The mem'ry of your face.

　　I feel the rope against my bark,
50　　　　And the weight of him in my grain,
　　I feel in the throe of his final woe
　　　　The touch of my own last pain.

　　And never more shall leaves come forth
　　　　On a bough that bears the ban;
55　I am burned with dread, I am dried and dead,
　　　　From the curse of a guiltless man.

　　And ever the judge rides by, rides by,
　　　　And goes to hunt the deer,
　　And ever another rides his soul
60　　　　In the guise of a mortal fear.

　　And ever the man he rides me hard,
　　　　And never a night stays he;
　　For I feel his curse as a haunted bough
　　　　On the trunk of a haunted tree.

*1903*

---

44 *bedight:* dressed.

## Lola Ridge (1873–1941)

Born Rose Emily Ridge in Dublin, Ireland, Ridge was taken by her mother to New Zealand when she was thirteen. After a failed marriage, Ridge herself moved to Sydney, New South Wales, where she enrolled at Trinity College and studied painting at the Académie Julienne. Meanwhile she was writing poems. She arrived in San Francisco in 1907, renaming herself Lola Ridge; the following year she was in New York. In Greenwich Village her radical sentiments and sympathies for the poor found expression in her poetry. She published in Emma Goldman's radical magazine *Mother Earth* and issued *The Ghetto, and Other Poems* in 1918, meanwhile surviving by writing advertising copy, publishing stories, and being employed as a factory worker, artist's model, and illustrator. She began to publish in both well-known and experimental magazines, becoming associate editor of *Others* and American editor of *Broom*. *New Masses* made her a contributing editor in 1926, and the following year she was arrested while protesting the execution of Sacco and Vanzetti, events which later inspired her *Dance of Fire* (1935).

### Stone Face

They have carved you into a stone face, Tom Mooney,°
You, there lifted high in California
Over the salt wash of the Pacific,
With your eyes . . . crying in many tongues,
5    Goading, innumerable eyes of the multitudes,
Holding in them all hopes, fears, persecutions,
Forever straining one way.

Even in the Sunday papers,
    and your face tight-bitten like a pierced fist,
10   The eyes have a transfixed gleam
    as they have glimpsed some vision and there hung
Impaled as on a bright lance.

---

1 *Tom Mooney:* (1892–1942), labor leader who was falsely accused of planting a bomb that killed ten people at a 1916 parade in San Francisco. With perjured testimony, he was convicted of murder, despite the fact that he was nowhere near the scene when the bomb was planted. A federal commission later found that Mooney was indicted only because he was an effective labor organizer whom conservatives wanted to eliminate. The judge and jury publicly admitted the verdict was an error. Under the circumstances, President Woodrow Wilson made a plea for mercy, and Mooney's death sentence was commuted to life, but he remained in jail for twenty-three years, from 1916–1939.

Too much lip-foam has dripped on you, too many
And disparate signatures are scrawled on your stone face
15       that all
Have set some finger on, to say who made you for the
    years
To mouth as waves mouth rock . . . you, a rough man,
Rude-nurtured, casually shouldering
20 Through a May-day crowd in San Francisco,
To be cast up out of the dark mass—terribly gestating,
    swarming without feature,
And raised with torsion to identity.

Now they—who wrote you plain, with Sacco° and the fish-
25     monger,
High on the scroll of the Republic—
Look up with a muddled irritation at your clenched face,
It set up in full sight under the long
Gaze of the generations—to be there
30 Haggard in the sunrise, when San Quentin
Prison shall be caved in and its steel ribs
Food for the ant-rust . . . and Governor Rolph°
A fleck of dust among the archives.

                              *1935*

## *from* Ice Heart

What if the heat of this enormous hive
Plotted and combed with fire, shall not suffice
To stay the bleak offensive of the ice,
Advancing in its old insensate drive
5 Over the loving and the agile quick,
Over the spawning rivers and the wires,
Constrained in dark adhesions to the brick;
Until no thing shall move beneath the spires—
Each sunk in clotted silver like a lance
10 Held fast in a dead side—but the bright hail,
The hail to join the blizzard in its dance
Tip-toe upon the chastened mouths that lie
Entranced in crystal, in the frozen mail
Yet shapen to the pure, the final cry?

                              *1935*

---

24 *Sacco:* See p. 328.
32 *Rolph:* James Rolph, the California Governor who refused to pardon Mooney. He also
offered to pardon anyone convicted of the crime of lynching.

# Amy Lowell (1874–1925)

Lowell was born in Brookline, Massachusetts, of a family long influential in New England commerce, history, and culture. Her ancestors founded Lowell, Massachusetts; George Washington had appointed one a judge; others founded the Lowell textile mills. But the family lineage also included scholars and educators and the poet James Russell Lowell. Largely self-educated and more than slightly self-assured, Amy Lowell turned to writing poetry seriously in her thirties, publishing her first book in 1912. Inspired by H.D.'s poetry, she took up the imagist banner, editing anthologies and publishing related criticism. All this infuriated Ezra Pound, who thought he owned the movement, but in fact it was Lowell who opened and lengthened the imagist line and helped make it integral to modernist poetry.

Among the poems published here are a group of intensely lyrical love poems written to her longtime companion Ada Dwyer Russell, but no brief selection can represent Lowell's full range. She excelled at free verse and in the use of traditional forms, in compressed imagistic poems and in longer historical and political narratives. Her massive *Collected Poems*, regrettably long out of print, includes experiments in numerous other styles as well. Her publications include a biography of John Keats and a series of experiments in "polyphonic prose" that embodied several features of poetic language.

## September, 1918°

This afternoon was the colour of water falling through sunlight;
The trees glittered with the tumbling of leaves;
The sidewalks shone like alleys of dropped maple leaves;
And the houses ran along them laughing out of square, open
    windows.
5    Under a tree in the park,
Two little boys, lying flat on their faces,
Were carefully gathering red berries
To put in a pasteboard box.

---

**poem title:** the summer and fall of 1918 saw major battles as the First World War drew to a close. American forces had played an important military role in June; then in July they participated in the second battle of the Marne. August saw the second battle of the Somme; toward the end of September the battles of the Argonne and of Ypres began. Hostilities would not cease on the western front until November 11.

10 Some day there will be no war.
Then I shall take out this afternoon
And turn it in my fingers,
And remark the sweet taste of it upon my palate,
And note the crisp variety of its flights of leaves.
15 To-day I can only gather it
And put it into my lunch-box,
For I have time for nothing
But the endeavour to balance myself
Upon a broken world.

                                                    1919


# The Letter

Little cramped words scrawling all over the paper
Like draggled fly's legs,
What can you tell of the flaring moon
Through the oak leaves?
5 Or of my uncurtained window and the bare floor
Spattered with moonlight?
Your silly quirks and twists have nothing in them
Of blossoming hawthorns,
And this paper is dull, crisp, smooth, virgin of loveliness
10 Beneath my hand.

I am tired, Beloved,° of chafing my heart against
The want of you;
Of squeezing it into little inkdrops,
And posting° it.
15 And I scald alone, here, under the fire
Of the great moon.

                                                    1919


# Venus Transiens°

Tell me,
Was Venus more beautiful
Than you are,
When she topped
5 The crinkled waves,
Drifting shoreward
On her plaited shell?
Was Botticelli's vision°
Fairer than mine;

---

11 *Beloved:* many of Lowell's love poems were inspired by her relationship with the actress
Ada Dwyer Russell, Lowell's partner from 1912 until her death.
14 *posting:* mailing.
**poem title:** (Latin) "Venus Passing Over"; Venus is the Greek goddess of love.
8 *Botticelli:* Italian Renaissance painter Sandro Botticelli (1444–1510), whose most famous
painting is *The Birth of Venus* (c. 1485), in which Venus rises from the ocean astride a
large scalloped seashell; roses are scattered around her.

10    And were the painted rosebuds
He tossed his lady,
Of better worth
Than the words I blow about you
To cover your too great loveliness
15    As with a gauze
Of misted silver?

For me,
You stand poised
In the blue and buoyant air,
20    Cinctured by bright winds,
Treading the sunlight.
And the waves which precede you
Ripple and stir
The sands at my feet.

*1919*

## Madonna of the Evening Flowers°

All day long I have been working,
Now I am tired.
I call: "Where are you?"
But there is only the oak-tree rustling in the wind.
5    The house is very quiet,
The sun shines in on your books,
On your scissors and thimble just put down,
But you are not there.
Suddenly I am lonely:
10    Where are you?
I go about searching.

Then I see you,
Standing under a spire of pale blue larkspur,
With a basket of roses on your arm.
15    You are cool, like silver,
And you smile.
I think the Canterbury bells° are playing little tunes.

You tell me that the peonies need spraying,
That the columbines have overrun all bounds,

20    That the pyrus japonica should be cut back and rounded.
You tell me these things.
But I look at you, heart of silver,
White heart-flame of polished silver,
Burning beneath the blue steeples of the larkspur,

---

**poem title:** Madonna ("my lady"); the phrase is often applied to the Virgin Mary.
17 *Canterbury bells:* a pun, referring at once to the blue, bell-shaped flowers (on long spikes) of a popular ornamental plant and to the famous bells of Canterbury Cathedral in England.

25    And I long to kneel instantly at your feet,
      While all about us peal the loud, sweet Te Deums° of the
          Canterbury bells.

                                                      *1919*

## The Weather-Cock Points South°

      I put your leaves aside,
      One by one:
      The stiff, broad outer leaves;
      The smaller ones,
5     Pleasant to touch, veined with purple;
      The glazed inner leaves.
      One by one
      I parted you from your leaves,
      Until you stood up like a white flower
10    Swaying slightly in the evening wind.

      White flower,
      Flower of wax, of jade, of unstreaked agate;°
      Flower with surfaces of ice,
      With shadows faintly crimson.
15    Where in all the garden is there such a flower?
      The stars crowd through the lilac leaves
      To look at you.
      The low moon brightens you with silver.

      The bud is more than the calyx.°
20    There is nothing to equal a white bud,
      Of no colour, and of all,
      Burnished by moonlight,
      Thrust upon by a softly-swinging wind.

                                                      *1919*

## Opal

      You are ice and fire,
      The touch of you burns my hands like snow.
      You are cold and flame.
      You are the crimson of amaryllis,
5     The silver of moon-touched magnolias.
      When I am with you,
      My heart is a frozen pond
      Gleaming with agitated torches.

                                                      *1919*

---

26 *Te Deums:* from an ancient Latin hymn, *Te Deum laudamus,* "We praise thee, Lord,"
the Roman Catholic daily morning prayer.
**poem title:** weather-cock, a weather vane, sometimes in the form of a rooster; the word
also suggests changeability or fickleness, but here the direction seems sure.
12 *unstreaked agate:* a stone that is most often streaked or clouded.
19 *calyx:* both the sepals of a flower and the cuplike divisions of the human pelvis. Through-
out the poem Lowell's flower images double as descriptions, often vaginal, of a woman's
body; they also link sensuality and spirituality.

## Wakefulness

Jolt of market-carts;
Steady drip of horses' hoofs on hard pavement;
A black sky lacquered over with blueness,
And the lights of Battersea° Bridge
5    Pricking pale in the dawn.
The beautiful hours are passing
And still you sleep!
Tired heart of my joy,
Incurved upon your dreams,
10    Will the day come before you have opened to me?

1919

## Grotesque

Why do the lilies goggle their tongues at me
When I pluck them;
And writhe, and twist,
And strangle themselves against my fingers,
5    So that I can hardly weave the garland
For your hair?
Why do they shriek your name
And spit at me
When I would cluster them?
10    Must I kill them
To make them lie still,
And send you a wreath of lolling corpses
To turn putrid and soft
On your forehead
15    While you dance?

1919

## The Sisters

Taking us by and large, we're a queer lot
We women who write poetry. And when you think
How few of us there've been, it's queerer still.
I wonder what it is that makes us do it,
5    Singles us out to scribble down, man-wise,
The fragments of ourselves. Why are we
Already mother-creatures, double-bearing,
With matrices in body and in brain?
I rather think that there is just the reason

───────────────

4 *Battersea:* a borough of London, England.

10    We are so sparse a kind of human being;  
The strength of forty thousand Atlases°  
Is needed for our every-day concerns.  
There's Sapho, now I wonder what was Sapho.°  
I know a single slender thing about her:  
15    That, loving, she was like a burning birch tree  
All tall and glittering fire, and that she wrote  
Like the same fire caught up to Heaven and held there,  
A frozen blaze before it broke and fell.  
Ah, me! I wish I could have talked to Sapho,  
20    Surprised her reticences by flinging mine  
Into the wind. This tossing off of garments  
Which cloud the soul is none too easy doing  
With us to-day. But still I think with Sapho  
One might accomplish it, were she in the mood  
25    To bare her loveliness of words and tell  
The reasons, as she possibly conceived them,  
Of why they are so lovely. Just to know  
How she came at them, just to watch  
The crisp sea sunshine playing on her hair,  
30    And listen, thinking all the while 'twas she  
Who spoke and that we two were sisters  
Of a strange, isolated little family.  
And she is Sapho—Sapho—not Miss or Mrs.,  
A leaping fire we call so for convenience;  
35    But Mrs. Browning°—who would ever think  
Of such presumption as to call her "Ba."  
Which draws the perfect line between sea-cliffs  
And a close-shuttered room in Wimpole Street.  
Sapho could fly her impulses like bright  
40    Balloons tip-tilting to a morning air  
And write about it. Mrs. Browning's heart  
Was squeezed in stiff conventions. So she lay  
Stretched out upon a sofa, reading Greek  
And speculating, as I must suppose,  
45    In just this way on Sapho; all the need,  
The huge, imperious need of loving, crushed  
Within the body she believed so sick.  
And it was sick, poor lady, because words  
Are merely simulacra after deeds  
50    Have wrought a pattern; when they take the place  
Of actions they breed a poisonous miasma  
Which, though it leave the brain, eats up the body.  
So Mrs. Browning, aloof and delicate,  
Lay still upon her sofa, all her strength  

---

11 *Atlases:* in Greek mythology, Atlas was a giant responsible for holding up the earth; he was a member of the race of Titans.

13 *Sapho:* the legendary Greek poet (born c. 612 B.C.) who was the major figure among a group of women held together both by their erotic passion for one another and by their devotion to poetry; most of her poems survive only as luminous fragments.

35 *Mrs. Browning:* British poet Elizabeth Barrett Browning (1806–1861), who lived in her family house as an invalid after a riding accident, until she met and married poet Robert Browning (1812–1889) in 1845. Elizabeth and Robert Browning lived in Italy until her death.

55      Going to uphold her over-topping brain.
        It seems miraculous, but she escaped
        To freedom and another motherhood
        Than that of poems. She was a very° woman
        And needed both.
60                      If I had gone to call,
        Would Wimpole Street have been the kindlier place,
        Or Casa Guidi° in which to have met her?
        I am a little doubtful of that meeting,
        For Queen Victoria was very young and strong
65      And all-pervading in her apogee
        At just that time. If we had stuck to poetry,
        Sternly refusing to be drawn off by mesmerism°
        Or Roman revolutions,° it might have done.
        For, after all, she is another sister,
70      But always, I rather think, an older sister
        And not herself so curious a technician
        As to admit newfangled modes of writing—
        "Except, of course, in Robert, and that is neither
        Here nor there for Robert is a genius."
75      I do not like the turn this dream is taking,
        Since I am very fond of Mrs. Browning
        And very much indeed should like to hear her
        Graciously asking me to call her "Ba."
        But then the Devil of Verisimilitude
80      Creeps in and forces me to know she wouldn't.
        Convention again, and how it chafes my nerves,
        For we are such a little family
        Of singing sisters, and as if I didn't know
        What those years felt like tied down to the sofa.
85      Confounded Victoria,° and the slimy inhibitions
        She loosed on all us Anglo-Saxon creatures!
        Suppose there hadn't been a Robert Browning,
        No "Sonnets from the Portuguese"° would have been written.
        They are the first of all her poems to be,

---

58 *very*: true.
62 *Casa Guidi:* the Florence home of Elizabeth and Robert Browning; one of her books is
*The Casa Guidi Windows, A Poem* (1851).
67 *mesmerism:* after Austrian physician Franz Anton Mesmer (1734–1815) who argued that
a force he called "animal magnetism" could be invoked at séances and used to cure dis-
eases.
68 *Roman revolutions:* the Brownings lived in Italy at a time of violent historical change.
There was a revolt in Rome in 1848, and the papal premier was assassinated; the follow-
ing year Rome was declared a republic, but the French occupied the city and restored
Pope Pius IX. At the end of the next decade Giuseppi Garibaldi (1807–1882) joined Italy's
war of liberation and sought to unify the country under one leader. Elizabeth Browning
praised the *Risorgimento* ("rebirth," Italian), the whole nineteenth-century movement by
which Italy achieved unity and nationhood, in her 1860 volume *Poems before Congress.*
85 *Victoria:* Alexandrina Victoria (1819–1901) was queen of Great Britain and Ireland from
1837 to 1901.
88 *Sonnets from the Portuguese:* a sequence of 44 love poems, begun before her marriage,
that is considered Elizabeth Browning's masterpiece.

90  One might say, fertilized. For, after all,
    A poet is flesh and blood as well as brain
    And Mrs. Browning, as I said before,
    Was very, very woman. Well, there are two
    Of us, and vastly unlike that's for certain.
95  Unlike at least until we tear the veils
    Away which commonly gird souls. I scarcely think
    Mrs. Browning would have approved the process
    In spite of what had surely been relief;
    For speaking souls must always want to speak
100 Even when bat-eyed, narrow-minded Queens
    Set prudishness to keep the keys of impulse.
    Then do the frowning Gods invent new banes
    And make the need of sofas. But Sapho was dead
    And I, and others, not yet peeped above
105 The edge of possibility. So that's an end
    To speculating over tea-time talks
    Beyond the movement of pentameters
    With Mrs. Browning.

                        But I go dreaming on,
110 In love with these my spiritual relations.
    I rather think I see myself walk up
    A flight of wooden steps and ring a bell
    And send a card in to Miss Dickinson.°
    Yet that's a very silly way to do.
115 I should have taken the dream twist-ends about
    And climbed over the fence and found her deep
    Engrossed in the doing of a humming bird
    Among nasturtiums. Not having expected strangers,
    She might forget to think me one, and holding up
120 A finger say quite casually: "Take care.
    Don't frighten him, he's only just begun."
    "Now this," I well believe I should have thought,
    "Is even better than Sapho. With Emily
    You're really here, or never anywhere at all
125 In range of mind." Wherefore, having begun
    In the strict centre, we could slowly progress
    To various circumferences, as we pleased.
    We could, but should we? That would quite depend
    On Emily. I think she'd be exacting,
130 Without intention possibly, and ask
    A thousand tight-rope tricks of understanding.
    But, bless you, I would somersault all day
    If by so doing I might stay with her.
    I hardly think that we should mention souls

---

113 *Miss Dickinson:* American poet Emily Dickinson (1830–1866).

135    Although they might just round the corner from us
       In some half-quizzical, half-wistful metaphor.
       I'm very sure that I should never seek
       To turn her parables to stated fact.
       Sapho would speak, I think, quite openly,
140    And Mrs. Browning guard a careful silence,
       But Emily would set doors ajar and slam them
       And love you for your speed of observation.

       Strange trio of my sisters, most diverse,
       And how extraordinarily unlike
145    Each is to me, and which way shall I go?
       Sapho spent and gained; and Mrs. Browning,
       After a miser girlhood, cut the strings
       Which tied her money-bags and let them run;
       But Emily hoarded—hoarded—only giving
150    Herself to cold, white paper. Starved and tortured,
       She cheated her despair with games of patience°
       And fooled herself by winning. Frail little elf,
       The lonely brain-child of a gaunt maturity,
       She hung her womanhood upon a bough
155    And played ball with the stars—too long—too long—
       The garment of herself hung on a tree
       Until at last she lost even the desire
       To take it down. Whose fault? Why let us say,
       To be consistent, Queen Victoria's.
160    But really, not to over-rate the queen,
       I feel obliged to mention Martin Luther,°
       And behind him the long line of Church Fathers
       Who draped their prurience like a dirty cloth
       About the naked majesty of God.
165    Good-bye, my sisters, all of you are great,
       And all of you are marvellously strange,
       And none of you has any word for me.
       I cannot write like you, I cannot think
       In terms of Pagan or of Christian now.
170    I only hope that possibly some day
       Some other woman with an itch for writing
       May turn to me as I have turned to you
       And chat with me a brief few minutes. How
       We lie, we poets! It is three good hours
175    I have been dreaming. Has it seemed so long
       To you? And yet I thank you for the time
       Although you leave me sad and self-distrustful,
       For older sisters are very sobering things.
       Put on your cloaks, my dears, the motor's waiting.

---

151 *games of patience:* card games (solitaire).
161 *Martin Luther:* (1483–1546), German religious reformer who founded the Protestant church.

180   No, you have not seemed strange to me, but near,
    Frightfully near, and rather terrifying.
    I understand you all, for in myself—
    Is that presumption? Yet indeed it's true—
    We are one family. And still my answer
185   Will not be any one of yours, I see.
    Well, never mind that now. Good night! Good night!

*1925*

## New Heavens for Old

    I am useless,
    What I do is nothing.
    What I think has no savour.
    There is an almanac between the windows:
5   It is of the year when I was born.

    My fellows call to me to join them,
    They shout for me,
    Passing the house in a great wind of vermillion banners.
    They are fresh and fulminant,
10   They are indecent and strut with the thought of it.
    They laugh, and curse, and brawl,
    And cheer a holocaust of "Who comes Firsts!" at the iron fronts of
      the houses at the two edges of the street.
    Young men with naked hearts jeering between iron house-fronts,
    Young men with naked bodies beneath their clothes
15   Passionately conscious of them,
    Ready to strip off their clothes,
    Ready to strip off their customs, their usual routine,
    Clamouring for the rawness of life,
    In love with appetite,
20   Proclaiming it as a creed,
    Worshipping youth,
    Worshipping themselves.
    They call for the women and the women come,
    They bare the whiteness of their lusts to the dead gaze of the old
      house-fronts,
25   They roar down the street like flame,
    They explode upon the dead houses like new, sharp fire.

    But I—
    I arrange three roses in a Chinese vase:
    A pink one,
30   A red one,
    A yellow one.
    I fuss over their arrangement.
    Then I sit in a South window
    And sip pale wine with a touch of hemlock in it,
35   And think of Winter nights,
    And field-mice crossing and re-crossing
    The spot which will be my grave.

*1927*

# Gertrude Stein (1874–1946)

Born in Allegheny, Pennsylvania, Stein and her six siblings were left alone when her mother died in 1888 and her father died in 1891. Stein and her brother Leo moved to live with her mother's sister. Meanwhile, an older brother helped to secure an independent income for them. She then followed Leo to Harvard, studying at the Annex that would later become Radcliffe, and spent two years with him at Johns Hopkins studying medicine. By then Leo was in Paris studying art, and Stein had become a writer and an active lesbian; she made her way to Paris in 1902 after some months in London and New York. They established what would become a famous Paris salon, and Stein entertained the literary and artistic avant garde. By the end of the decade, Stein had met her lifelong companion and collaborator, fellow American expatriate Alice B. Toklas (1877–1967).

Increasingly influenced by the visual arts and by experimental modernism, Stein wrote both recognizable narratives like *Three Lives* (1909) and playful experimental texts like *Tender Buttons* (1914). In her experimental mode she was arguably the most radical and forward looking of all modernists. "Patriarchal Poetry" is a 1927 prose poem that did not make its way into print until decades later. Yet it may be the only fully realized and rigorous deconstructive poem in American modernism. Can the poem, the title implicitly asks, be *about* patriarchal poetry, or is it to be an instance *of* patriarchal poetry? The parameters of that question are immediately ruptured. For the "poetry" referred to here is not just a literary genre but rather the poetics of everyday thought. "Patriarchal Poetry" is the metaphoric logic ruling the meanings that make our culture what it is. The ambiguity of the title thus reflects Stein's judgment that everything one writes will be in some ways patriarchal. A critique of patriarchal poetry cannot be mounted from a position outside it. The only strategy for demolition is a defamiliarizing burlesque from within: "Patriarchal Poetry in pieces."

Using witty and strategically staged repetition, variation, and rhyme, Stein exposes hierarchical and gendered biases built into the most unassuming usages. Repetition short circuits the expectation that words and phrases can function as neutral syntactic units and frees us to recognize patterns of semantic association that all language carries with it in use: "They said they said they said when they said men. / Men many men many how many many many men men men said many here" (p. 280). "Men," we hear here is always a statement, always an assertion, always a cultural imprimatur. In patriarchal poetics "they said" always means "men said." Patriarchy's differences are really the repetition of the same: the honorific imposition of the law of male priority, "patriarchal poetry as signed."

Repetition and variation let Stein place a variety of words, phrases, and concepts under philosophical and cultural pressure, so that all the components of a statement are shown to be permeated with the assumptions of patriarchal poetry. This technique also isolates and decontextualizes words and phrases, seeming at first to turn them into unstable echolalic nonsense, but thereby severing them from their syntactical functionalism and making it possible to see them as counters in a very different semantic game. On the other side of nonsense is the world view that patriarchal poetics continually reinforces: "Patriarchal poetry makes no mistake"; "Patriarchal poetry is the same as Patriotic Poetry."

Patriarchal poetry is the poetics of unreflective reason and order, of officious segmentation and classification—often to comic effect: "Patriarchal poetry and not meat on Monday patriarchal poetry and meat on Tuesday. Patriarchal poetry and venison on Wednesday Patriarchal poetry and fish on Friday Patriarchal poetry and birds on Sunday." Patriarchal poetry is therefore a poetics of marching: "One Patriarchal Poetry. / Two Patriarchal Poetry. / Three Patriarchal Poetry." It is the signature of the authority of the nation-state and of the corollary authority of the individual male person: "signed by them. / Signed by him."

Stein's poem does not proceed in a linear way; that would be to adopt the armature she wants to disavow. So she works by indirection. But the poem does have signal moments of disruption and revelation. The first of these occurs as a serial eruption of the phrases "Let her be," "Let her try," and "Let her be shy." These are pleas for space for women's freedom and commands disseminating women's differences through the language. "Let her be" is also the letter "b," whose additive and secondary character Stein offers in place of patriarchal claims for priority, origin, and power.

## Patriarchal Poetry

As long as it took fasten it back to a place where after all he would be carried away, he would be carried away as long as it took fasten it back to a place where he would be carried away as long as it took.

For before let it before to be before spell to be before to be before to have to be to be for before to be tell to be to having held to be to be for before to call to be for to be before to till until to be till before to be for before to be until to be for before to for to be for before will for before to be shall to be to be for to be for to be before still to be will before to be before for to be to be for before to be before such to be for to be much before to be for before will be for to be for before to be well to be well before to be before for before might while to be might before to be might while to be might before while to be might to be while before for might to be for before to for while to be while for before while before to for which as for before had for before had for before to for to before.

Hire hire let it have to have to hire representative to hire to representative to representative hire to representative to hire wire to representative to hire representative to hire.

There never was a mistake in addition.

Ought ought my prize my ought ought prize with a denies with a denies to be ought ought to denies with a to ought to ought ought with a denies plainly detained practically to be next. With a with a would it last with a with a have it passed come to be with this and theirs there is a million of it shares and stairs and stairs to right about. How can you change from their to be sad to sat. Coming again yesterday.

Once to be when once to be when once to be having an advantage all the time.

Little pieces of their leaving which makes it put it there to be theirs for the beginning of left altogether practically for the sake of relieving it partly.

As your as to your as to your able to be told too much as to your as to as able to receive their measure of rather whether intermediary and left to the might it be letting having when win. When win makes it dark when win makes it dark to held to beheld behold be as particularly in respect to not letting half of it be by. Be by in this away.

To lay when in please and letting it be known to be come to this not in not in not in nightingale in which is not in land in hand there is it leaving light out out in this or this or this beside which may it for it to be in it lest and louder louder to be known which is could might this near special have near nearly reconcile oblige and indestructible and mainly in this use.

Mainly will fill remaining sad had which is to be following duke-dome duke in their use say to amount with a part let it go as if with should it might my makes it a leader.

Feels which is there.

To change a boy with a cross from there to there.

Let him have him have him heard let him have him heard him third let him have him have him intend let him have him have him defend let him have him have him third let him have him have him heard let him have him have him occurred let him have him have him third.

Forty-nine Clive as well forty-nine Clive as well forty-nine sixty-nine seventy-nine eighty-nine one hundred and nine Clive as well forty-nine Clive as well which is that it presses it to be or to be stay or to be twenty a day or to be next to be or to be twenty to stay or to be which never separates two more two women.

Fairly letting it see that the change is as to be did Nelly and Lily love to be did Nelly and Lily went to see and to see which is if could it be that so little is known was known if so little was known shone stone come bestow bestown so little as was known could which that for them recognisably.

Wishing for Patriarchal Poetry.

Once threes letting two sees letting two three threes letting it be after these two these threes can be two near threes in threes twos letting two in two twos slower twos choose twos threes never came twos two twos relieve threes twos threes. Threes twos relieves twos to twos to twos to twos relieve to twos to relieve two threes to relieves two relieves threes twos two to relieve threes relieves threes relieve twos relieves threes two twos slowly twos relieve threes threes to twos relieve relieve two to relieve threes twos twos relieves twos threes threes relieves twos two relieve twos relieves relieve twos relieves threes relieve twos slowly twos to relieves relieve threes relieve threes twos two relieve twos threes relieves relieve relieves twos two twos threes relieves threes two twos relieve relieves relieves threes relieve relieves threes relieves as two so threes twos relieves twos relieve.

Who hears whom once once to snow they might if they trained fruit-trees they might if they leaned over there they might look like it which when it could if it as if when it left to them to their use of pansies and daisies use of them use of them of use of pansies and daisies use of pansies and daisies use of them use of them of use use of pansies and use of pansies and use of pansies and use use of them use of pansies and daisies use of use of them which is what they which is what they they do they which is what they do there out and out and leave it to the meaning of their by their with their allowance making allowed what is it.

They have it with it reconsider it with it they with it reconsider it with it they have it with it reconsider it have it they with it reconsider it they have it they with it reconsider it they with it they reconsider it have it they have it reconsider it with it have it reconsider it have it with it. She said an older sister not an older sister she said an older sister not an older sister she said an older sister have it with it reconsider it with it reconsider it have it an older sister have it with it. She said she had followed flowers she had said she had said she had followed she had said she had said she had followed she had said with it have it reconsider it have it with it she had said have followed have said have had have followed have said followed had followed had said followed flowers which she had had will it reconsider it with it have it had said followed had followed had followed flowers had said had with it had followed flowers had have had with it had said had have had with it.

Is no gain.

Is no gain.

To is no gain.

Is to to is no gain.

Is to is to to is no gain.

Is to is no is to is no gain.

Is no gain.

Is to is no gain.

Is to is to is no gain.

Is no gain.

Is to is no gain.

With it which it as it if it is to be to be to come to in which to do in that place.

As much as if it was like as if might be coming to see me.

What comes to be the same as lilies. An ostrich egg and their after lines.

It made that be alike and with it an indefinable reconciliation with roads and better to be not as much as felt to be as well very well as the looking like not only little pieces there. Comparing with it.

Not easily very much very easily, wish to be wish to be rest to be like not easily rest to be not like not like rest to be not like it rest to not like rest to be not like it.

How is it to be rest to be receiving rest to be how like it rest to be receiving to be like it. Compare something else to something else. To be rose.

Such a pretty bird.

Not to such a pretty bird. Not to not to not to not to such a pretty bird.

Not to such a pretty bird.

Not to such a pretty bird.

As to as such a pretty bird. As to as to as such a pretty bird.
To and such a pretty bird.
And to and such a pretty bird.
And to as to not to as to and such a pretty bird.
As to and to not to as to and such a pretty bird and to as such a
pretty bird and to not to as such a pretty bird and to as to not to and
to and such a pretty bird as to and such a pretty bird and to and such
a pretty bird not to and to as such a pretty bird as to as such a pretty
bird and to as such a pretty bird and to as to and to not to and to as
to as such a pretty bird and to as such a pretty bird and to as to not
to as to and to and such a pretty bird and to and such a pretty bird as
to and such a pretty bird not to and such a pretty bird not to and such
a pretty bird as to and such a pretty bird and to and such a pretty bird
as to and to and such a pretty bird not to as to and such a pretty bird
and to not as to and to not to as such a pretty bird and such a pretty
bird not to and such a pretty bird as to and such a pretty bird as such
a pretty bird and to as such a pretty bird and to and such a pretty bird
not to and such a pretty bird as to and such a pretty bird not to as
such a pretty bird not to and such a pretty bird as to and such a pretty
bird not to as to and to not to as such a pretty bird and to not to and
to and such a pretty bird as to and such a pretty bird and to as such
a pretty bird as to as such a pretty bird not to and to as to and such a
pretty bird as to and to and to as to as such a pretty bird as such a
pretty bird and to as such a pretty bird and to and such a pretty bird
and to and such and to and to and such a pretty bird and to and to
and such a pretty bird and to and such a pretty bird and to and such
a pretty bird and to and such a pretty bird and to and such a pretty
bird and to as to and to and such a pretty bird and to as to as such a
pretty bird and to and to and such a pretty bird and such a pretty bird
and to and such a pretty bird and to and to and such a pretty bird and
to and such a pretty bird.
Was it a fish was heard was it a bird was it a cow was stirred was
it a third was it a cow was stirred was it a third was it a bird was heard
was it a third was it a fish was heard was it a third. Fishes a bird cows
were stirred a bird fishes were heard a bird cows were stirred a third.
A third is all. Come too.
Patriarchal means suppose patriarchal means and close patriarchal
means and chose chose Monday Patriarchal means in close some day
patriarchal means and chose chose Sunday patriarchal means and
chose chose one day patriarchal means and close close Tuesday. Tues-
day is around Friday and welcomes as welcomes not only a cow but
introductory. This always patriarchal as sweet.
Patriarchal make it ready.
Patriarchal in investigation and renewing of an intermediate recti-
fication of the initial boundary between cows and fishes. Both are ad-
mittedly not inferior in which case they may be obtained as the result
of organisation industry concentration assistance and matter of fact
and by this this is their chance and to appear and to reunite as to their
date and their estate. They have been in no need of stretches stretches
of their especial and apart and here now.
Favored by the by favored by let it by the by favored by the by. Pa-
triarchal poetry and not meat on Monday patriarchal poetry and meat
on Tuesday. Patriarchal poetry and venison on Wednesday Patriarchal

poetry and fish on Friday Patriarchal poetry and birds on Sunday Patriarchal poetry and chickens on Tuesday patriarchal poetry and beef on Thursday. Patriarchal poetry and ham on Monday patriarchal poetry and pork on Thursday patriarchal poetry and beef on Tuesday patriarchal poetry and fish on Wednesday Patriarchal poetry and eggs on Thursday patriarchal poetry and carrots on Friday patriarchal poetry and extras on Saturday patriarchal poetry and venison on Sunday Patriarchal poetry and lamb on Tuesday patriarchal poetry and jellies on Friday patriarchal poetry and turkeys on Tuesday.

They made hitherto be by and by.

It can easily be returned ten when this, two might it be too just inside, not as if chosen that not as if chosen, withal if it had been known to be going to be here and this needed to be as as green. This is what has been brought here.

Once or two makes that be not at all practically their choice practically their choice.

Might a bit of it be all the would be might be if a bit of it be all they would be if it if it would be all be if it would be a bit of all of it would be, a very great difference between making money peaceably and making money peaceably a great difference between making money making money peaceably making money peaceably making money peaceably.

Reject rejoice rejuvenate rejuvenate rejoice reject rejoice rejuvenate reject rejuvenate reject rejoice. Not as if it was tried. How kindly they receive the the then there this at all.

In change.

Might it be while it is not as it is undid undone to be theirs awhile yet. Not in their mistake which is why it is not after or not further in at all to their cause. Patriarchal poetry partly. In an as much to be in exactly their measure. Patriarchal poetry partly.

Made to be precisely this which is as she is to be connectedly leave it when it is to be admittedly continued to be which is which is to be that it is which it is as she connectedly to be which is as she continued as to this to be continuously not to be connected to be which to be admittedly continued to be which is which is which it is to be. They might change it as it can be made to be which is which is the next left out of it in this and this occasionally settled to the same as the left of it to the undertaking of the regular regulation of it which is which which is which is which is what it is when it is needed to be left about to this when to this and they have been undetermined and as likely as it is which it is which it is which is it which is it not as in time and at a time when it is not to be certain certain makes it to be makes it to be makes it to be makes it to be makes it to be that there is not in that in consideration of the preparation of the change which is their chance inestimably.

Let it be as likely why that they have it as they try to manage. Follow. If any one decides that a year is a year beginning and end if any one decides that a year is a year beginning if any one decides that a year is a year if any one decides that a year simultaneously recognised. In recognition.

Once when if the land was there beside once when if the land was there beside.

Once when if the land was there beside.

Once when if the land was there beside.

If any one decided that a year was a year when once if any one de-
cided that a year was a year if when once if once if any one when once
if any one decided that a year was a year beside.

Patriarchal poetry includes when it is Wednesday and patriarchal
includes when it is Wednesday and patriarchal poetry includes when
it is Wednesday.

Never like to bother to be sure never like to bother to be sure never
like to bother to be sure never like never like to never like to bother
to be sure never like to bother never like to bother to be sure.

Three things which are when they are prepared. Three things which
are when they are prepared. Let it alone to be let it alone to be let it
alone to be to be sure. Let it alone to be sure.

Three things which are when they had had this to their best arrange-
ment meaning never having had it here as soon.

She might be let it be let it be here as soon. She might be let it be
let it be let it be here as soon. She might be let it be here as soon. She
might be let it be let it be she might be she might be let it be she might
be let it be she might be let it be here as soon. Theirs which way mar-
guerites. Theirs might be let it there as soon.

When is and thank and is and and and is when is when is and
when thank when is and when and thank. When is and when is and
thank. This when is and when thank and thank. When is and when
thank and this when is and thank.

Have hear which have hear which have hear which leave and leave
her have hear which have hear which leave her hear which leave her
hear she leave her hear which. They might by by they might by by
which might by which they might by which they by which they might
which they might by which they by which they might by which. In face
of it.

Let it be which is it be which is it be which is it let it let it which
is it let it which let it which is it let it be which is it be which let it be
which let it which is it which is it let it let it which is it let it. Near
which with it which with near which with which with near which with
near which with near which with it near which near which with near
which near which with which with it.

Leave it with it let it go able to be shiny so with it can be is it near
let it have it as it may come well be. This is why after all at a time that
is which is why after all at the time this is why it is after all at the time
this is why this is why this is after all after why this is after all at the
time. This is why this is why this is after all this is why this is after all
at the time.

Not a piece of which is why a wedding left have wedding left which
is why which is why not which is why not a piece of why a a wedding
having why a wedding left. Which is what is why is why is why which
is what is why is why is why a wedding left.

Leaving left which is why they might be here be here be here. Be
here be here. Which is why is why is why is why is which is why is
why is why which is here. Not commence to to to be to leave to come
to see to let it be to be to be at once mind it mind timely always change
timely to kindly kindly to timely timely to kindly timely to kindly al-
ways to change kindly to timely kindly to timely always to change timely
to kindly.

If he is not used to it he is not used to it, this is the beginning of their singling singling makes Africa shortly if he is not used to it he is not used to it this makes oriole shortly if he is not used to it if he is not used to it if he is not used to it if he is not used if he is not used to it if he is not used to it if he is not used to it he if he is not used to it he is not used to it and this makes an after either after it. She might be likely as to renew prune and see prune. This is what order does.

Next to vast which is which is it.

Next to vast which is why do I be behind the chair because of a chimney fire and higher why do I beside belie what is it when is it which is it well all to be tell all to be well all to be never do do the difference between effort and be in be in within be mine be in be within be within in.

To be we to be to be we to be to be to be to be we to be we to be to be to be to be to be to be to be to be we we to be to be to be we to be. Once. To be we to be to be to be we to be. Once. To be to be to be to be to be we to be. Once. To be we to be to be to be.

We to be. Once. We to be. Once. We to be be to be we to be. Once. We to be.

Once. We to be we to be. Once. To be. Once. We to be. Once. To be. Once. To be we to be. Once. To be. Once. To be we to be. We to be. Once. To be. We to be. Once.

To be we to be. Once. To be. Once. To be. Once. To be. Once. To be. Once. We to be. To be we to be. We to be. To be we to be. We to be. Once. To be to be to be. We to be. We to be. To be. Once. We to be.

Once. We to be.

Once. We to be. We to be. Once. To be we to be. Once. To be. Once. To be we to be. Once. We to be. To be. We to be. Once. Once. To be. Once. To be. Once. We to be. Once. We to be. We to be. Once. To be. Once. We to be. We to be. We to be. To be. Once. To be. We to be.

Their origin and their history patriarchal poetry their origin and their history patriarchal poetry their origin and their history.

Patriarchal Poetry.

Their origin and their history.

Patriarchal Poetry their origin and their history their history patriarchal poetry their origin patriarchal poetry their history their origin patriarchal poetry their history patriarchal poetry their origin patriarchal poetry their history their origin.

That is one case.

Able sweet and in a seat.

Patriarchal poetry their origin their history their origin. Patriarchal poetry their history their origin.

Two make it do three make it five four make it more five make it arrive and sundries.

Letters and leaves tables and plainly restive and recover and bide away, away to say regularly.

Never to mention patriarchal poetry altogether.

Two two two occasionally two two as you say two two two not in their explanation two two must you be very well apprised that it had had such an effect that only one out of a great many and there were a great many believe in three relatively and moreover were you aware of the fact that interchangeable and interchangeable was it while they were if not avoided. She knew that is to say she had really informed herself. Patriarchal poetry makes no mistake.

Never to have followed farther there and knitting, is knitting knitting if it is only what is described as called that they should not come to say and how do you do every new year Saturday. Every new year Saturday is likely to bring pleasure is likely to give pleasure is likely to bring pleasure every new year Saturday is likely to bring pleasure.

Day which is what is which is what is day which is what is day which is which is what is which is what is day.

I double you, of course you do. You double me, very likely to be. You double I double I double you double. I double you double me I double you you double me.

When this you see remarkably.

Patriarchal poetry needs rectification and there about it.

Come to a distance and it still bears their name.

Prosperity and theirs prosperity left to it.

To be told to be harsh to be told to be harsh to be to them.

One.

To be told to be harsh to be told to be harsh to them.

None.

To be told to be harsh to be told to be harsh to them.

When.

To be told to be harsh to be told to be harsh to them.

Then.

What is the result.

The result is that they know the difference between instead and instead and made and made and said and said.

The result is that they might be as very well two and as soon three and to be sure, four and which is why they might not be.

Elegant replaced by delicate and tender, delicate and tender replaced by one from there instead of five from there, there is not there this is what has happened evidently.

Why while while why while why why identity identity why while while why. Why while while while while identity.

Patriarchal poetry is the same as Patriotic poetry is the same as patriarchal poetry is the same as Patriotic poetry is the same as patriarchal poetry is the same.

Patriarchal poetry is the same.

If in in crossing there is a if in crossing if in in crossing nearly there is a distance if in crossing there is a distance between measurement and exact if in in crossing if in in crossing there is a measurement between and in in exact she says I must be careful and I will.

If in in crossing there is an opportunity not only but also and in in looking in looking in regarding if in in looking if in in regarding if in in regarding there is an opportunity if in in looking there is an opportunity if in in regarding there is an opportunity to verify verify sometimes as more sometimes as more sometimes as more.

Fish eggs commonly fish eggs. Architects commonly fortunately indicatively architects indicatively architects. Elaborated at a time with it with it at a time with it at a time attentively today.

Does she know how to ask her brother is there any difference between turning it again again and again and again or turning it again and again. In resembling two brothers.

That makes patriarchal poetry apart.

Intermediate or patriarchal poetry.

If at once sixty-five have come one by one if at once sixty-five have come one by one if at once sixty-five have come one by one. This took two and two have been added to by Jenny. Never to name Jenny. Have been added to by two. Never have named Helen Jenny never have named Agnes Helen never have named Helen Jenny. There is no difference between having been born in Brittany and having been born in Algeria.

These words containing as they do neither reproaches nor satisfaction may be finally very nearly rearranged and why, because they mean to be partly left alone. Patriarchal poetry and kindly, it would be very kind in him in him of him of him to be as much obliged as that. Patriotic poetry. It would be as plainly an advantage if not only but altogether repeatedly it should be left not only to them but for them but for them. Explain to them by for them. Explain shall it be explain will it be explain can it be explain as it is to be explain letting it be had as if he had had more than wishes. More than wishes.

Patriarchal poetry more than wishes.

Assigned to Patriarchal poetry.

Assigned to patriarchal poetry too sue sue sue sue shall sue sell and magnificent can as coming let the same shall shall shall shall let it share is share is share shall shall shall shall shell shell shall share is share shell can shell be shell be shell moving in in in inner moving move inner in in inner in meant meant might might may collect collected recollected to refuse what it is is it.

Having started at once at once.

Put it with it with it and it and it come to ten.

Put it with it with it and it and it for it for it made to be extra.

With it put it put it prepare it prepare it add it add it or it or it would it would it and make it all at once.

Put it with it with it and it and it in it in it add it add it at it at it with it with it put it put it to this to understand.

Put it with it with it add it add it at it at it or it or it to be placed intend.

Put it with it with it in it in it at it at it at it add it add it or it or it letting it be while it is left as it might could do their danger.

Could it with it with it put it put it place it place it stand it stand it two doors or two doors two tables or two tables two let two let two let two to be sure.

Put it with it with it and it and it in it in it add it add it or it or it to it to be added to it.

There is no doubt about it.

Actually.

To be sure.

Left to the rest if to be sure that to be sent come to be had in to be known or to be liked and to be to be to be to be to be mine.

It always can be one two three it can be always can can always be one two three. It can always be one two three.

It is very trying to have him have it have it have him. Have it as she said the last was very very much and very much to distance to distance them.

Every time there is a wish wish it. Every time there is a wish wish it. Every time there is a wish wish it.

Every time there is a wish wish it.

Dedicated to all the way through. Dedicated to all the way through. Dedicated too all the way through. Dedicated too all the way through.

Apples and fishes day-light and wishes apples and fishes day-light and wishes day-light at seven.

All the way through dedicated to you.

Day-light and wishes apples and fishes, dedicated to you all the way through day-light and fishes apples and wishes dedicated to all the way through dedicated to you dedicated to you all the way through day-light and fishes apples and fishes day-light and wishes apples and fishes dedicated to you all the way through day-light and fishes apples and wishes apples and fishes day-light and wishes dedicated to dedicated through all the way through dedicated to.

Not at once Tuesday.

They might be finally their name name same came came came came or share sharer article entreat coming in letting this be there letting this be there.

Patriarchal poetry come too.

When with patriarchal poetry when with patriarchal poetry come too.

There must be more french in France there must be more French in France patriarchal poetry come too.

Patriarchal poetry come too there must be more french in France patriarchal come too there must be more french in France.

Patriarchal Poetry come to.

There must be more french in France.

Helen greatly relieves Alice patriarchal poetry come too there must be patriarchal poetry come too.

In a way second first in a way first second in a way in a way first second in a way.

Rearrangement is nearly rearrangement. Finally nearly rearrangement is finally nearly rearrangement nearly not now finally nearly nearly finally rearrangement nearly rearrangement and not now how nearly finally rearrangement. If two tables are near together finally nearly not now.

Finally nearly not now.

Able able nearly nearly nearly nearly able able finally nearly able nearly not now finally finally nearly able.

They make it be very well three or nearly three at a time.

Splendid confidence in the one addressed and equal distrust of the one who has done everything that is necessary. Finally nearly able not now able finally nearly not now.

Rearrangement is a rearrangement a rearrangement is widely known a rearrangement is widely known. A rearrangement is widely known. As a rearrangement is widely known.

As a rearrangement is widely known.

So can a rearrangement which is widely known be a rearrangement which is widely known which is widely known.

Let her be to be to be to be let her be to be to be let her to be let her to be let her be to be when is it that they are shy.

Very well to try.

Let her be that is to be let her be that is to be let her be let her try.

Let her be let her be let her be to be to be shy let her be to be let her be to be let her try.

Let her try.

Let her be let her be let her be let her be to be to be let her be let her try.

To be shy.

Let her be.

Let her try.

Let her be let her let her let her be let her be let her be let her be shy let her be let her be let her try.

Let her try.

Let her be.

Let her be shy.

Let her be.

Let her be let her be let her let her try.

Let her try to be let her try to be let her be shy let her try to be let her try to be let her be let her be let her try.

Let her be shy.

Let her try.

Let her try.

Let her be

Let her let her be shy.

Let her try.

Let her be.

Let her let her be shy.

Let her be let her let her be shy

Let her let her let her let her try.

Let her try.

Let her try.

Let her try.

Let her be.

Let her be let her

Let her try.

Let her be let her.

Let her be let her let her try.

Let her try.

Let her

Let her try.

Let her be shy.

Let her

Let her

Let her be.

Let her be shy.

Let her be let her try.

Let her try.

Let her try.

Let her try.

Let her let her try

Let her be shy.

Let her try

Let her let her try to be let her try.
Let her try.
Just let her try.
Let her try.
Never to be what he said.
Never to be what he said.
Never to be what he said.
Let her to be what he said.
Let her to be what he said.
Not to let her to be what he said not to let her to be what he said.
Never to be let her to be never let her to be what he said. Never let her to be what he said.
Never to let her to be what he said. Never to let her to be let her to be let her to be let her what he said.
Near near near nearly pink near nearly pink nearly near near nearly pink. Wet inside and pink outside. Pink outside and wet inside wet inside and pink outside latterly nearly near near pink near near nearly three three pink two gentle one strong three pink all medium medium as medium as medium sized as sized. One as one not mistaken but interrupted. One regularly better adapted if readily readily to-day. This is this this readily. Thursday.
This part the part the part of it.
And let to be coming to have it known.
As a difference.
By two by one by and by.
A hyacinth resembles a rose. A rose resembles a blossom a blossom resembles a calla lily a calla lily resembles a jonquil and a jonquil resembles a marguerite a marguerite resembles a rose in bloom a rose in bloom resembles a lily of the valley a lily of the valley resembles a violet and a violet resembles a bird.
What is the difference between right away and a pearl there is this difference between right away and a pearl a pearl is milk white and right away is at once. This is indeed an explanation.
Patriarchal poetry or indeed an explanation.
Try to be at night try to be to be at night try to be at night try to be at night try to be to try to be to try to be to try to be at night.
Never which when where to be sent to be sent to be sent to be never which when where never to be sent to be sent to be sent never which when where to be sent never to be sent never to be sent never which when where to be sent never to be sent never to be sent which when where never to be sent which when where never which when where never which when where to be sent never which when where to be sent never which when where to be sent which when where to be sent never to be sent never which when where to be sent never which when which when where to be sent never which when where never which when where which when where never to be sent which when where.
Never to be sent which when where.
As fair as fair to them.
It was not without some difficulty.
Five thousand every year.
Three thousand divided by five three thousand divided as five.
Happily very happily.

They happily very happily.
Happily very happily.
In consequence consequently.
Extra extremely additionally.
Intend or intend or intend or intend or intend additionally.
Returning retaining relatively.
This makes no difference between to be told so admittedly.
Patriarchal Poetry connectedly.
Sentence sent once patriarchal poetry sentence sent once.
Patriarchal poetry sentence sent once.
Patriarchal Poetry.
Patriarchal Poetry sentence sent once.
Patriarchal Poetry is used with a spoon.
Patriarchal poetry is used with a spoon with a spoon.
Patriarchal poetry is used with a spoon.
Patriarchal poetry used with a spoon.
Patriarchal poetry in and for the relating of now and ably.
Patriarchal poetry in preferring needless needless needlessly patriarchal poetry precluding needlessly but it can.
How often do we tell tell tell tale tell tale tell tale tell tale might be tell tale.
Supposing never never never never supposing never never in supposed widening.
Remember all of it too.
Patriarchal poetry reasonably.
Patriarchal poetry administratedly.
Patriarchal poetry with them too.
Patriarchal poetry as to mind.
Patriarchal poetry reserved.
Patriarchal poetry interdiminished.
Patriarchal poetry in regular places largely in regular places placed regularly as if it were as if it were placed regularly.
Patriarchal poetry in regular places placed regularly as if it were placed regularly regularly placed regularly as if it were.
Patriarchal poetry every little while. Not once twenty-five not once twenty-five not once slower not once twenty not once twenty-five. Patriarchal poetry every little while not every little while once every little while once every little while once every twenty once every little while once every twenty-five once every little while once every little while every once twenty-five once.
Make it a mistake.
Patriarchal she said what is it I know what it is it is I know I know so that I know what it is I know so I know so I know so I know what it is. Very slowly. I know what it is it is on the one side a to be her to be his to be their to be in an and to be I know what it is it is he who was an known not known was he was at first it was the grandfather then it was not that in that the father not of that grandfather and then she to be to be sure to be sure to be I know to be sure to be I know to be sure to be not as good as that. To be sure not to be sure to be sure correctly saying to be sure to be that. It was that. She was right. It was that.
Patriarchal Poetry.

## A Sonnet

To the wife of my bosom
All happiness from everything
And her husband.
May he be good and considerate
Gay and cheerful and restful.
And make her the best wife
In the world
The happiest and the most content
With reason.
To the wife of my bosom
Whose transcendent virtues
Are those to be most admired
Loved and adored and indeed
Her virtues are all inclusive
Her virtues her beauty and her beauties
Her charms her qualities her joyous nature
All of it makes of her husband
A proud and happy man.

Patriarchal poetry makes no mistake makes no mistake in estimating the value to be placed upon the best and most arranged of considerations of this in as apt to be not only to be partially and as cautiously considered as in allowance which is one at a time. At a chance at a chance encounter it can be very well as appointed as appointed not only considerately but as it as use.

Patriarchal poetry to be sure to be sure to be sure candidly candidly and aroused patriarchal to be sure and candidly and aroused once in a while and as a circumstance within that arranged within that arranged to be not only not only not only not not secretive but as one at a time not in not to include cautiously cautiously cautiously at one in not to be finally prepared. Patriarchal poetry may be mistaken may be undivided may be usefully to be sure settled and they would be after a while as establish in relatively understanding a promise of not in time but at a time wholly reconciled to feel that as well by an instance of escaped and interrelated choice. That makes it even.

Patriarchal poetry may seem misplaced at one time.

Patriarchal poetry might be what they wanted.

Patriarchal poetry shall be as much as if it was counted from one to one hundred.

From one to one hundred.

From one to one hundred.

From one to one hundred.

Counted from one to one hundred.

Nobody says soften as often.

From one to one hundred.

Has to say happen as often.

Laying while it was while it was while it was. While it was.

Patriarchal poetry while it was just as close as when they were then being used not only in here but also out there which is what was the thing that was not only requested but also desired which when there is not as much as if they could be while it can shall have and this was what was all when it was not used just for that but simply can be not what is it like when they use it.

As much as that patriarchal poetry as much as that.

Patriarchal poetry as much as that.

To like patriarchal poetry as much as that.

To like patriarchal poetry as much as that is what she did.

Patriarchal poetry usually.

In finally finding this out out and out out and about to find it out when it is neither there nor by that time by the time it is not why they had it.

Why they had it.

What is the difference between a glass pen and a pen what is the difference between a glass pen and a pen what is the difference between a glass pen and a pen to smile at the difference between a glass pen and a pen.

To smile at the difference between a glass pen and a pen is what he did.

Patriarchal poetry makes it as usual.

Patriarchal poetry one two three.

Patriarchal poetry accountably.

Patriarchal poetry as much.

Patriarchal Poetry reasonably.

Patriarchal poetry which is what they did.

One Patriarchal Poetry.

Two Patriarchal Poetry.

Three Patriarchal Poetry.

One two three.

One two three.

One Patriarchal Poetry.

Two Patriarchal Poetry.

Three Patriarchal Poetry.

When she might be what it was to be left to be what they had as they could.

Patriarchal Poetry as if as if it made it be a choice beside.

The Patriarchal Poetry.

At the time that they were sure surely certain certainly aroused arousing laid lessening let letting be it as if it as if it were to be to be as if it were to be letting let it nearly all it could be not be nearly should be which is there which is it there.

Once more a sign.

Signed by them.

Signed by him.

Signed it.

Signed it as it was.

Patriarchal Poetry and rushing Patriarchal Poetry and rushing.

Having had having had having had who having had who had having having had and not five not four not three not one not three not two not four not one not one done.

Patriarchal poetry recollected.

Putting three together all the time two together all the time two together all the time two together two together two together all the time putting five together three together all the time. Never to think of Patriarchal Poetry at one time.

Patriarchal poetry at one time.

Allowed allowed allowed makes it be theirs once once as they had had it have having have have having having is the same.

Patriarchal Poetry is the same.

Patriarchal Poetry.

It is very well and nicely done in Patriarchal Poetry which is be-
gun to be begun and this was why if when if when when did they please
themselves indeed. When he did not say leave it to that but rather in-
deed as it might be that it was not expressed simultaneously was ex-
pressed to be no more as it is very well to trouble him. He will attend
to it in time. Be very well accustomed to this in that and plan. There
is not only no accounting for tastes but very well identified extra com-
ing out very well identified as repeated verdure and so established as
more than for it.

She asked as she came down should she and at that moment there
was no answer but if leaving it alone meant all by it out of it all by it
very truly and could be used to plainly plainly expressed. She will be
determined determined not by but on account of implication implica-
tion re-entered which means entered again and upon.

This could be illustrated and is and is and is. There makes more
than contain contained mine too. Very well to please please.

Once in a while.

Patriarchal poetry once in a while.

Patriarchal Poetry out of pink once in a while.

Patriarchal Poetry out of pink to be bird once in a while.

Patriarchal Poetry out of pink to be bird left and three once in a
while.

Patriarchal Poetry handles once in a while.

Patriarchal Poetry once in a while.

Patriarchal Poetry once in a while.

Patriarchal Poetry to be added.

Patriarchal Poetry reconciled.

Patriarchal Poetry left alone.

Patriarchal Poetry and left of it left of it Patriarchal Poetry
left of it Patriarchal Poetry left of it as many twice as many patriarchal
poetry left to it twice as many once as it was once it was once every
once in a while patriarchal poetry every once in a while.

Patriarchal Poetry might have been in two. Patriarchal Poetry added
to added to to once to be once in two Patriarchal poetry to be added
to once to add to to add to patriarchal poetry to add to to be to be to
add to to add to patriarchal poetry to add to.

One little two little one little two little one little at one time one
little one little two little two little two little at one at a time.

One little one little two little two little one little two little as to two
little as to two little as to one little as to one two little as to two two
little two. Two little two little two little one little two one two one two
little two. One little one little one little two little two little one little
two one little two.

Need which need which as it is need which need which as it is very
need which need which it is very warm here is it.

Need which need which need need in need need which need which
is it need in need which need which need which is it.

Need in need need which is it.

What is the difference between a fig and an apple. One comes be-
fore the other. What is the difference between a fig and an apple one
comes before the other what is the difference between a fig and an ap-
ple one comes before the other.

When they are here they are here too here too they are here too. When they are here they are here too when they are here they are here too.

As out in it there.

As not out not out in it there as out in it out in it there as out in it there as not out in it there as out in as out in it as out in it there.

Next to next next to Saturday next to next next to Saturday next to next next to Saturday.

This shows it all.

This shows it all next to next next to Saturday this shows it all.

Once or twice or once or twice once or twice or once or twice this shows it all or next to next this shows it all or once or twice or once or twice or once or twice this shows it all or next to next this shows it all or next to next or Saturday or next to next this shows it all or next to next or next to next or Saturday or next to next or once or twice this shows it all or next to next or once or twice this shows it all or Saturday or next to next this shows it all or once or twice this shows it all or Saturday or next to next or once or twice this shows it all or once or twice this shows it all or next to next this shows it all or once or twice this shows it all or next to next or once or twice or once or twice this shows it all or next to next this shows it all or once or twice this shows it all or next to next or once or twice this shows it all or next to next or next to next or next to next or once or twice or once or twice or next to next or next to next or once or twice this shows it all this shows it all or once or twice or next to next this shows it all or next to next this shows it all or next to next this shows it all or next to next this shows it all or next to next this shows it all or once or twice or once or twice this shows it all or once or twice or next to next this shows it all this shows it all or next to next or shows it all or once or twice this shows it all or shows it all or next to next or once or twice or shows it all or once or twice or next to next or next to next or once or twice or next to next or next to next or shows it all or shows it all or next to next or once or twice or shows it all or next to next or shows it all or next to next or shows it all or once or twice or next to next or next to next or next to next or next or next or next or shows it all or next or next or next to next or shows it all or next to next to next to next to next.

Not needed near nearest.

Settle it pink with pink.

Pinkily.

Find it a time at most.

Time it at most at most.

Every differs from Avery Avery differs from every within.

As it is as it is as it is as it is in line as it is in line with it.

Next to be with it next to be with it with it with with with it next to it with it with it. Return with it.

Even if it did not touch it would you like to give it would you like to give it give me my even if it did not touch it would you like to give me my. Even if you like to give it if you did not touch it would you like to give me my.

One divided into into what what is it.

As left to left left to it here left to it here which is not queer which is not queer where when when most when most and best what is the difference between breakfast lunch supper and dinner what is the difference between breakfast and lunch and supper and dinner.

She had it here who to who to she had it here who to she had it here who to she had it here who to she had it here who to who to she had it here who to. Who to she had it here who to.

Not and is added added is and not added added is not and added added is and not added added added is not and added added not and is added added is and is added added and is not and added added and is not and added added is and is not added added is and not and added added is and not and added.

Let leave it out be out let leave it out be out be out let leave it out be out let leave it out be out. Let leave it out be out let leave it out be out. Let leave it out be out. Let leave it out. Let leave it out. Let. Let leave it out. Let leave it out. Let leave it out.

Eighty eighty one which is why to be after one one two Seattle blue and feathers they change which is why to blame it once or twice singly to be sure.

A day as to say a day two to say to say a day a day to say to say to say a day as to-day to say as to say to-day. To dates dates different from here and there from here and there.

Let it be arranged for them.

What is the difference between Elizabeth and Edith. She knows. There is no difference between Elizabeth and Edith that she knows. What is the difference. She knows. There is no difference as she knows. What is the difference between Elizabeth and Edith that she knows. There is the difference between Elizabeth and Edith which she knows. There is she knows a difference between Elizabeth and Edith which she knows. Elizabeth and Edith as she knows.

Contained in time forty makes forty-nine. Contained in time as forty makes forty-nine contained in time contained in time as forty makes forty-nine contained in time as forty makes forty-nine.

Forty-nine more or at the door.

Forty-nine or more or as before. Forty-nine or forty-nine or forty-nine.

I wish to sit with Elizabeth who is sitting. I wish to sit with Elizabeth who is sitting I wish to sit with Elizabeth who is sitting. I wish to sit with Elizabeth who is sitting.

Forty-nine or four attached to them more more than they were as well as they were as often as they are once or twice before.

As peculiarly mine in time.

Reform the past and not the future this is what the past can teach her reform the past and not the future which can be left to be here now here now as it is made to be made to be here now here now.

Reform the future not the past as fast as last as first as third as had as hand it as it happened to be why they did. Did two too two were sent one at once and one afterwards.

Afterwards.

How can patriarchal poetry be often praised often praised.

To get away from me.

She came in.

Wishes.

She went in.

Fishes.

She sat in the room

Yes she did.

Patriarchal poetry.

She was where they had it be nearly as nicely in arrangement.

In arrangement.

To be sure.

What is the difference between ardent and ardently.

Leave it alone.

If one does not care to eat if one does not care to eat oysters one has no interest in lambs.

That is as usual.

Everything described as in a way in a way in a way gradually.

Likes to be having it come.

Likes to be.

Having it come.

Have not had that.

Around.

One two three one two three one two three one two three four.

Find it again.

When you said when.

When you said

When you said

When you said when.

Find it again.

Find it again

When you said when.

They said they said.

They said they said they said when they said men.

Men many men many how many many many many men men men said many here.

Many here said many many said many which frequently allowed later in recollection many many said when as naturally to be sure.

Very many as to that which which which one which which which which one.

Patriarchal poetry relined.

It is at least last let letting letting letting letting it be theirs.

Theirs at least letting at least letting it be theirs.

Letting it be at least be letting it be theirs.

Letting it be theirs at least letting it be theirs.

When she was as was she was as was she was not yet neither pronounced so and tempted.

Not this this is the way that they make it theirs not they.

Not they.

Patriarchal Poetry makes mistakes.

One two one two my baby is who one two one two one two my baby or two one two. One two one one or two one one one one one one one one one one or two. Are to.

It is very nearly a pleasure to be warm.

It is very nearly a pleasure to be warm.

It is very nearly a pleasure to be warm.

A line a day book.

One which is mine.

Two in time

Let it alone

Theirs as well

Having it now
Letting it be their share.
Settled it at once.
Liking it or not
How do you do.
It.
Very well very well seriously.
Patriarchal Poetry defined.
Patriarchal Poetry should be this without which and organisation. It should be defined as once leaving once leaving it here having been placed in that way at once letting this be with them after all. Patriarchal Poetry makes it a master piece like this makes it which which alone makes like it like it previously to know that it that that might that might be all very well patriarchal poetry might be resumed.
How do you do it.
Patriarchal Poetry might be withstood.
Patriarchal Poetry at peace.
Patriarchal Poetry a piece.
Patriarchal Poetry in peace.
Patriarchal Poetry in pieces.
Patriarchal Poetry as peace to return to Patriarchal Poetry at peace.
Patriarchal Poetry or peace to return to Patriarchal Poetry or pieces of Patriarchal Poetry.
Very pretty very prettily very prettily very pretty very prettily.
To never blame them for the mischance of eradicating this and that by then.
Not at the time not at that time not in time to do it. Not a time to do it. Patriarchal Poetry or not a time to do it.
Patriarchal Poetry or made a way patriarchal Poetry tenderly.
Patriarchal Poetry or made a way patriarchal poetry or made a way patriarchal poetry as well as even seen even seen clearly even seen clearly and under and over overtake overtaken by it now. Patriarchal Poetry and replace. Patriarchal Poetry and enough. Patriarchal Poetry and at pains to allow them this and that that it would be plentifully as aroused and leaving leaving it exactly as they might with it all be be careful carefully in that and arranging arrangement adapted adapting in regulating regulate and see seat seating send sent by nearly as withstand precluded in this instance veritably in reunion reunion attached to intermediate remarked remarking plentiful and theirs at once. Patriarchal Poetry has that return.
Patriarchal Poetry might be what is left.
Indifferently.
In differently undertaking their being there there to them there to them with them with their pleasure pleasurable recondite and really really relieve relieving remain remade to be sure certainly and in and and on on account account to be nestled and nestling as understood which with regard to it if when and more leave leaving lying where it was as when when in in this this to be in finally to see so so that that should always be refused refusing refusing makes it have have it having having hinted hindered and implicated resist resist was to be exchanged as to be for for it in never having as there can be shared sharing letting it land lie lie to adjacent to see me. When it goes quickly they must choose Patriarchal Poetry originally originate as originating

believe believing repudiate repudiating an impulse. It is not left to right
to-day to stay. When this you see remember me should never be added
to that.

Patriarchal Poetry and remind reminding clearly come came and
left instantly with their entire consenting to be enclosed within what
is exacting which might and might and partaking of mentioning much
of it to be to be this is mine left to them in place of how very nicely
it can be planted so as to be productive even if necessarily there is no
effort left to them by their having previously made it be nearly able to
be found finding where where it is when it is very likely to be this in
the demand of remaining. Patriarchal Poetry intimately and intimating
that it is to be so as plead. Plead can have to do with room. Room
noon and nicely.

Even what was gay.

Easier in left.

Easier in an left.

Easier an left

Easier in an left.

Horticulturally.

Easier in august.

Easier an august.

Easier an in august

Howard.

Easier how housed.

Ivory

Ivoried.

Less

Lest.

Like it can be used in joining gs.

By principally.

Led

Leaden haul

Leaden haul if it hails

Let them you see

Useful makes buttercup buttercup hyacinth too makes it be lilied
by water and you.

That is the way they ended.

It.

It was was it.

You jump in the dark, when it is very bright very bright very bright
now.

Very bright now.

Might might tell me.

Withstand.

In second second time time to be next next which is not convinc-
ing convincing inhabitable that much that much there.

As one to go.

Letting it letting it letting it alone.

Finally as to be sure.

Selecting that that to that selecting that to that to that all that. All
and and and and and and it it is very well thought out.

What is it.

Aim less.

What is it.
Aim less.
Sword less.
What is it
Sword less
What is it
Aim less
What is it.
What is it aim less what is it.
It did so.
It did so.
Said so
Said it did so.
Said it did so did so said so said it did so just as any one might.
Said it did so just as any one might said it did so said so just as
any one might.
If water is softened who softened water.
Patriarchal Poetry means in return for that.
Patriarchal poetry means in return.
Nettles nettles her.
Nettle nettle her.
Nettle nettle nettle her nettles nettles nettles her nettle nettle net-
tle her nettles nettles nettles her. It nettles her to nettle her to nettle
her exchange it nettles her exchange to nettle her exchange it nettles
her.
Made a mark remarkable made a remarkable interpretation made
a remarkable made a remarkable made a remarkable interpretation
made a remarkable interpretation now and made a remarkable made a
remarkable interpretation made a mark made a remarkable made a re-
markable interpretation made a remarkable interpretation now and here
here out here out here. The more to change. Hours and hours. The
more to change hours and hours the more to change hours and hours.
It was a pleasant hour however however it was a pleasant hour it
was a pleasant hour however it was a pleasant hour resemble hour how-
ever it was a pleasant however it was a pleasant hour resemble hour
assemble however hour it was a pleasant hour however.
Patriarchal Poetry in assemble.
Assemble Patriarchal Poetry in assemble it would be assemble as-
semble Patriarchal Poetry in assemble.
It would be Patriarchal Poetry in assemble.
Assemble Patriarchal Poetry resign resign Patriarchal Poetry to be-
lieve in trees.
Early trees.
Assemble moss roses and to try.
Assemble Patriarchal Poetry moss roses resemble Patriarchal po-
etry assign assign to it assemble Patriarchal Poetry resemble moss roses
to try.
Patriarchal Poetry resemble to try.
Moss roses assemble Patriarchal Poetry resign lost a lost to try. Re-
semble Patriarchal Poetry to love to.
To wish to does.
Patriarchal Poetry to why.
Patriarchal Poetry ally.

Patriarchal Poetry with to try to all ally to ally to wish to why to. Why did it seem originally look as well as very nearly pronounceably satisfy lining.

To by to by that by by a while any any stay stationary.

Stationary has been invalidated.

And not as surprised.

Patriarchal Poetry surprised supposed.

Patriarchal Poetry she did she did.

Did she Patriarchal Poetry.

Is to be periwinkle which she met which is when it is astounded and come yet as she did with this in this and this let in their to be sure it wishes it for them an instance in this as this allows allows it to to be sure now when it is as well as it is and has ever been outlined.

There are three things that are different pillow pleasure prepare and after while. There are two things that they prepare maidenly see it and ask it as it if has been where they went. There are enough to go. One thing altogether altogether as he might. Might he.

Never to do never to do never to do to do to do never to do never to do never to do to do to do to do never to do never never to do to do it as if it were an anemone an anemone an anemone to be an anemone to be to be certain to let to let it to let it alone.

What is the difference between two spoonfuls and three. None.

Patriarchal Poetry as signed.

Patriarchal Poetry might which it is very well very well leave it to me very well patriarchal poetry leave it to me leave it to me leave it to leave it to me naturally to see the second and third first naturally first naturally to see naturally to first see the second and third first to see to see the second and third to see the second and third naturally to see it first.

Not as well said as she said regret that regret that not as well said as she said Patriarchal Poetry as well said as she said it Patriarchal Poetry untied. Patriarchal Poetry.

Do we.

What is the difference between Mary and May. What is the difference between May and day. What is the difference between day and daughter what is the difference between daughter and there what is the difference between there and day-light what is the difference between day-light and let what is the difference between let and letting what is the difference between letting and to see what is the difference between to see immediately patriarchal poetry and rejoice.

Patriarchal Poetry made and made.

Patriarchal Poetry makes a land a lamb. There is no use at all in reorganising in reorganising. There is no use at all in reorganising chocolate as a dainty.

Patriarchal Poetry reheard.

Patriarchal Poetry to be filled to be filled to be filled to be filled to method method who hears method method who hears who hears who hears method method method who hears who hears who hears and method and method and method and who hears and who who hears and method method is delightful and who and who who hears method is method is method is delightful is who hears is delightful who hears method is who hears method is method is method is delightful is delightful who hears who hears of of delightful who hears of method of

delightful who of whom of whom of of who hears of method method
is delightful. Unified in their expanse. Unified in letting there there
there one two one two three there in a chain a chain how do you lat-
erally in relation to auditors and obliged obliged currently.

Patriarchal Poetry is the same.
Patriarchal Poetry thirteen.
With or with willing with willing mean.
I mean I mean.
Patriarchal Poetry connected with mean.
Queen with willing.
With willing.
Patriarchal Poetry obtained with seize.
Willing.
Patriarchal Poetry in chance to be found.
Patriarchal Poetry obliged as mint to be mint to be mint to be
obliged as mint to be.
Mint may be come to be as well as cloud and best.
Patriarchal Poetry deny why.
Patriarchal Poetry come by the way to go.
Patriarchal Poetry interdicted.
Patriarchal Poetry at best.
Best and Most.
Long and Short.
Left and Right.
There and More.
Near and Far.
Gone and Come.
Light and Fair.
Here and There.
This and Now.
Felt and How
Next and Near.
In and On.
New and Try
In and This.
Which and Felt.
Come and Leave.
By and Well.
Returned.
Patriarchal Poetry indeed.
Patriarchal Poetry which is let it be come from having a mild and
came and same and with it all.
Near.
To be shelled from almond.
Return Patriarchal Poetry at this time.
Begin with a little ruff a little ruffle.
Return with all that.
Returned with all that four and all that returned with four with all
that.
How many daisies are there in it.
How many daisies are there in it.
How many daisies are there in it.
How many daisies are there in it.

A line a day book.
How many daisies are there in it.
Patriarchal Poetry a line a day book.
Patriarchal Poetry.
A line a day book.
Patriarchal Poetry.
When there is in it.
When there is in it.
A line a day book.
When there is in it.
Patriarchal Poetry a line a day book when there is in it.
By that time lands lands there.
By that time lands there a line a day book when there is that in it.

Patriarchal Poetry reclaimed renamed replaced and gathered together as they went in and left it more where it is in when it pleased when it was pleased when it can be pleased to be gone over carefully and letting it be a chance for them to lead to lead to lead not only by left but by leaves.

They made it be obstinately in their change and with it with it let it let it leave it in the opportunity. Who comes to be with a glance with a glance at it at it in palms and palms too orderly to orderly in changes of plates and places and beguiled beguiled with a restless impression of having come to be all of it as might as might as might and she encouraged. Patriarchal Poetry might be as useless. With a with a with a won and delay. With a with a with a won and delay.

He might object to it not being there as they were left to them all around. As we went out by the same way we came back again after a detour.

That is one account on one account.

Having found anemones and a very few different shelves we were for a long time just staying by the time that it could have been as desirable. Desirable makes it be left to them.

Patriarchal Poetry includes not being received.
Patriarchal Poetry comes suddenly as around.
And now.
There is no difference between spring and summer none at all.
And wishes.
Patriarchal Poetry there is no difference between spring and summer not at all and wishes.
There is no difference between spring and summer not at all and wishes.
There is no difference not at all between spring and summer not at all and wishes.
Yes as well.
And how many times.
Yes as well and how many times yes as well.
How many times yes as well ordinarily.
Having marked yes as well ordinarily having marked yes as well.
It was to be which is theirs left in this which can have all their thinking it as fine.
It was to be which is theirs left in this which is which is which can which can which may which may which will which will which in which in which are they know they know to care for it having come back with-

out and it would be better if there had not been any at all to find to
find to find. It is not desirable to mix what he did with adding adding
to choose to choose. Very well part of her part of her very well part of
her. Very well part of her. Patriarchal Poetry in pears. There is no
choice of cherries.

Will he do.

Patriarchal Poetry in coins.

Not what it is.

Patriarchal Poetry net in it pleases. Patriarchal Poetry surplus if
rather admittedly in repercussion instance and glance separating let-
ting dwindling be in knife to be which is not wound wound entirely as
white wool white will white change white see white settle white un-
derstand white in the way white be lighten lighten let letting bear this
neatly nearly made in vain.

Patriarchal Poetry who seats seasons patriarchal poetry in gather
meanders patriarchal poetry engaging this in their place their place
their allow. Patriarchal Poetry. If he has no farther no farther no far-
ther to no farther to no farther to no no to farther to not to be right
to be known to be even as a chance. Is it best to support Allan Allan
will Allan Allan is it best to support Allan Allan patriarchal poetry pa-
triarchal poetry is it best to support Allan Allan will Allan best to sup-
port Allan will patriarchal poetry Allan will patriarchal poetry Allan will
patriarchal poetry is it best to support Allan patriarchal poetry Allan
will is it best Allan will is it best to support Allan patriarchal poetry Al-
lan will best to support patriarchal poetry Allan will is it best Allan will
to support patriarchal poetry patriarchal poetry Allan will patriarchal
poetry Allan will.

Is it best to support patriarchal poetry Allan will patriarchal poetry.

Patriarchal Poetry makes it incumbent to know on what day races
will take place and where otherwise there would be much inconve-
nience everywhere.

Patriarchal Poetry erases what is eventually their purpose and their
inclination and their reception and their without their being beset. Pa-
triarchal poetry an entity.

What is the difference between their charm and to charm.

Patriarchal Poetry in negligence.

Patriarchal Poetry they do not follow that they do not follow that
this does not follow that this does not follow that theirs does not fol-
low that theirs does not follow that the not following that the not fol-
lowing that having decided not to abandon a sister for another. This
makes patriarchal poetry in their place in their places in their places
in the place in the place of is it in the next to it as much as aroused
feeling so feeling it feeling at once to be in the wish and what is it of
theirs. Suspiciously. Patriarchal poetry for instance. Patriarchal poetry
not minded not minded it. In now. Patriarchal poetry left to renown.
Renown.

It is very certainly better not to be what is it when it is in the af-
ternoon.

Patriarchal poetry which is it. Which is it after it is after it is after
it is after before soon when it is by the time that when they make let
it be not only because why should why should why should it all be fine.

Patriarchal poetry they do not do it right.

Patriarchal poetry letting it be alright.

Patriarchal Poetry having it placed where it is.

Patriarchal Poetry might have it.

Might have it.

Patriarchal Poetry a choice.

Patriarchal poetry because of it.

Patriarchal Poetry replaced.

Patriarchal Poetry withstood and placated.

Patriarchal Poetry in arrangement.

Patriarchal Poetry that day.

Patriarchal Poetry might it be very likely which is it as it can be very precisely unified as tries.

Patriarchal poetry with them lest they be stated.

Patriarchal poetry. He might be he might he he might be he might be.

Patriarchal poetry a while a way.

Patriarchal poetry if patriarchal poetry is what you say why do you delight in never having positively made it choose.

Patriarchal poetry never linking patriarchal poetry.

Sometime not a thing.

Patriarchal Poetry sometimes not anything.

Patriarchal Poetry which which which which is it.

Patriarchal Poetry left to them.

Patriarchal poetry left together.

Patriarchal Poetry does not like to be allowed after a while to be what is more formidably forget me nots anemones china lilies plants articles chances printing pears and likely meant very likely meant to be given to him.

Patriarchal Poetry would concern itself with when it is in their happening to be left about left about now.

There is no interest in resemblances.

Patriarchal poetry one at a time.

This can be so.

To by any way.

Patriarchal poetry in requesting in request in request best patriarchal poetry leave that alone.

Patriarchal poetry noise noiselessly.

Patriarchal poetry not in fact in fact.

After patriarchal poetry.

I defy any one to turn a better heel than that while reading.

Patriarchal poetry reminded.

Patriarchal poetry reminded of it.

Patriarchal Poetry reminded of it too.

Patriarchal Poetry reminded of it too to be sure.

Patriarchal Poetry reminded of it too to be sure really. Really left.

Patriarchal Poetry and crackers in that case.

Patriarchal Poetry and left bread in that case.

Patriarchal Poetry and might in that case.

Patriarchal Poetry connected in that case with it.

Patriarchal Poetry make it do a day.

Is he fond of him.

If he is fond of him if he is fond of him is he fond of his birthday the next day. If he is fond of his birthday the next day is he fond of the birthday trimming if he is fond of the birthday the day is he fond

of the day before the day before the day of the day before the birth-
day. Every day is a birthday the day before. Patriarchal Poetry the day
before.

Patriarchal Poetry the day that it might.

Patriarchal Poetry does not make it never made it will not have
been making it be that way in their behalf.

Patriarchal Poetry insistance.

Insist.

Patriarchal Poetry insist insistance.

Patriarchal Poetry which is which is it.

Patriarchal Poetry and left it left it by left it by left it. Patriarchal
Poetry what is the difference Patriarchal Poetry.

Patriarchal Poetry.

Not patriarchal poetry all at a time.

To find patriarchal poetry about.

Patriarchal Poetry is named patriarchal poetry.

If patriarchal poetry is nearly by nearly means it to be to be so.

Patriarchal Poetry and for them then.

Patriarchal Poetry did he leave his son.

Patriarchal Poetry Gabrielle did her share.

Patriarchal poetry it is curious.

Patriarchal poetry please place better.

Patriarchal poetry in come I mean I mean.

Patriarchal poetry they do their best at once more once more once
more once more to do to do would it be left to advise advise realise re-
alise dismay dismay delighted with her pleasure.

Patriarchal poetry left to inundate them.

Patriarchal Poetry in pieces. Pieces which have left it as names
which have left it as names to to all said all said as delight.

Patriarchal poetry the difference.

Patriarchal poetry needed with weeded with seeded with payed it
with left it without it with me. When this you see give it to me.

Patriarchal poetry makes it be have you it here.

Patriarchal Poetry twice.

Patriarchal Poetry in time.

It should be left.

Patriarchal Poetry with him.

Patriarchal Poetry.

Patriarchal Poetry at a time.

Patriarchal Poetry not patriarchal poetry.

Patriarchal Poetry as wishes.

Patriarchal poetry might be found here.

Patriarchal poetry interested as that.

Patriarchal Poetry left.

Patriarchal Poetry left left.

Patriarchal poetry left left left right left.

Patriarchal poetry in justice.

Patriarchal poetry in sight.

Patriarchal poetry in what is what is what is what is what.

Patriarchal poetry might to-morrow.

Patriarchal Poetry might be finished to-morrow.

Dinky pinky dinky pinky dinky pinky dinky pinky once and try. Dinky
pinky dinky pinky dinky pinky lullaby. Once sleepy one once does not
once need a lullaby. Not to try.

Patriarchal Poetry not to try. Patriarchal Poetry and lullaby. Patriarchal Poetry not to try Patriarchal poetry at once and why patriarchal poetry at once and by by and by Patriarchal poetry has to be which is best for them at three which is best and will be be and why why patriarchal poetry is not to try try twice.

Patriarchal Poetry having patriarchal poetry. Having patriarchal poetry having patriarchal poetry. Having patriarchal poetry. Having patriarchal poetry and twice, patriarchal poetry.

He might have met.

Patriarchal poetry and twice patriarchal poetry.

1927

# Robert Frost (1874–1963)

Frost was born and spent his first eleven years in San Francisco. At that point his father, a journalist, died and the family moved to New England. Frost was educated at Dartmouth and Harvard and for a time made an effort to run a poultry farm in New Hampshire. But in 1912 he went to England, where he published his first book, *A Boy's Will*, the following year. With Ezra Pound's help he was able to publish his next volume in the United States, after which he returned and made another New Hampshire farm his home, supporting himself by regular college teaching. Increasingly successful as a poet, his family life was nonetheless often bitter. His son Carol took his own life in 1940, and a daughter Irma suffered a severe mental breakdown and was institutionalized. These disasters followed upon the death of his daughter Marjorie in 1934; she contracted a fever after giving birth and died slowly.

Frost cultivated the public image of a New England sage, and the poems, read carelessly in search of platitudes, often seem to support that view. In American high schools, Frost's poems continue to be misread as teaching little moral lessons that the poems themselves actually decisively undercut. "Take the road less traveled by," students are urged, in a sentimentalized promotion of individual initiative; or, even more crudely, "don't turn like most toward sin or self-gratification; take the road less traveled by." About the only certainty "The Road Not Taken" may be said to offer is that of self-deception.

In fact the poems can be corrosively sardonic, offering a menacing nature or human cruelty as the only alternative to emptiness. That the voice is so crisp, folksy, and pithy only adds to the underlying sense of terror. Over and over again the poems drain human choices of any meaning, yet they do so in straightforward images, colloquial diction, and rhythms that mimic natural speech.

## Mending Wall

Something there is that doesn't love a wall,
That sends the frozen-ground-swell under it,
And spills the upper boulders in the sun;
And makes gaps even two can pass abreast.
5   The work of hunters is another thing:
I have come after them and made repair
Where they have left not one stone on a stone,
But they would have the rabbit out of hiding,
To please the yelping dogs. The gaps I mean,
10   No one has seen them made or heard them made,
But at spring mending-time we find them there.

I let my neighbor know beyond the hill;
And on a day we meet to walk the line
And set the wall between us once again.
15 We keep the wall between us as we go.
To each the boulders that have fallen to each.
And some are loaves and some so nearly balls
We have to use a spell to make them balance:
"Stay where you are until our backs are turned!"
20 We wear our fingers rough with handling them.
Oh, just another kind of outdoor game,
One on a side. It comes to little more:
There where it is we do not need the wall:
He is all pine and I am apple orchard.
25 My apple trees will never get across
And eat the cones under his pines, I tell him.
He only says, "Good fences make good neighbors."
Spring is the mischief in me, and I wonder
If I could put a notion in his head:
30 "*Why* do they make good neighbors? Isn't it
Where there are cows? But here there are no cows.
Before I built a wall I'd ask to know
What I was walling in or walling out,
And to whom I was like to give offense.
35 Something there is that doesn't love a wall,
That wants it down." I could say "Elves" to him,
But it's not elves exactly, and I'd rather
He said it for himself. I see him there
Bringing a stone grasped firmly by the top
40 In each hand, like an old-stone savage armed.
He moves in darkness as it seems to me,
Not of woods only and the shade of trees.
He will not go behind his father's saying,
And he likes having thought of it so well
45 He says again, "Good fences make good neighbors."

*1914*

# Home Burial

He saw her from the bottom of the stairs
Before she saw him. She was starting down,
Looking back over her shoulder at some fear.
She took a doubtful step and then undid it
5 To raise herself and look again. He spoke
Advancing toward her: "What is it you see
From up there always—for I want to know."
She turned and sank upon her skirts at that,
And her face changed from terrified to dull.
10 He said to gain time: "What is it you see,"
Mounting until she cowered under him.
"I will find out now—you must tell me, dear."
She, in her place, refused him any help
With the least stiffening of her neck and silence.

15    She let him look, sure that he wouldn't see,
      Blind creature; and awhile he didn't see.
      But at last he murmured, "Oh," and again, "Oh."

      "What is it—what?" she said.

                          "Just that I see."

      "You don't," she challenged. "Tell me what it is."

20    "The wonder is I didn't see at once.
      I never noticed it from here before.
      I must be wonted° to it—that's the reason.
      The little graveyard where my people are!
      So small the window frames the whole of it.
25    Not so much larger than a bedroom, is it?
      There are three stones of slate and one of marble,
      Broad-shouldered little slabs there in the sunlight
      On the sidehill. We haven't to mind *those*.
      But I understand: it is not the stones,
      But the child's mound—"

30                    "Don't, don't, don't, don't," she cried.

      She withdrew, shrinking from beneath his arm
      That rested on the bannister, and slid downstairs;
      And turned on him with such a daunting look,
      He said twice over before he knew himself:
35    "Can't a man speak of his own child he's lost?"

      "Not you! Oh, where's my hat? Oh, I don't need it!
      I must get out of here. I must get air.
      I don't know rightly whether any man can."

      "Amy! Don't go to someone else this time.
40    Listen to me. I won't come down the stairs."
      He sat and fixed his chin between his fists.
      "There's something I should like to ask you, dear."

      "You don't know how to ask it."

                          "Help me, then."

      Her fingers moved the latch for all reply.

45    "My words are nearly always an offense.
      I don't know how to speak of anything
      So as to please you. But I might be taught
      I should suppose. I can't say I see how.
      A man must partly give up being a man
50    With women-folk. We could have some arrangement
      By which I'd bind myself to keep hands off

---

22 *wonted*: accustomed.

Anything special you're a-mind to name.
Though I don't like such things 'twixt those that love.
Two that don't love can't live together without them.
55      But two that do can't live together with them."
She moved the latch a little. "Don't—don't go.
Don't carry it to someone else this time.
Tell me about it if it's something human.
Let me into your grief. I'm not so much
60      Unlike other folks as your standing there
Apart would make me out. Give me my chance.
I do think, though, you overdo it a little.
What was it brought you up to think it the thing
To take your mother-loss of a first child
65      So inconsolably—in the face of love.
You'd think his memory might be satisfied—"

"There you go sneering now!"

                         "I'm not, I'm not!
You make me angry. I'll come down to you.
God, what a woman! And it's come to this,
70      A man can't speak of his own child that's dead."

"You can't because you don't know how to speak.
If you had any feelings, you that dug
With your own hand—how could you?—his little grave;
I saw you from that very window there,
75      Making the gravel leap and leap in air,
Leap up, like that, like that, and land so lightly
And roll back down the mound beside the hole.
I thought, Who is that man? I didn't know you.
And I crept down the stairs and up the stairs
80      To look again, and still your spade kept lifting.
Then you came in. I heard your rumbling voice
Out in the kitchen, and I don't know why,
But I went near to see with my own eyes.
You could sit there with the stains on your shoes
85      Of the fresh earth from your own baby's grave
And talk about your everyday concerns.
You had stood the spade up against the wall
Outside there in the entry, for I saw it."

"I shall laugh the worst laugh I ever laughed.
90      I'm cursed. God, if I don't believe I'm cursed."

"I can repeat the very words you were saying.
'Three foggy mornings and one rainy day
Will rot the best birch fence a man can build.'
Think of it, talk like that at such a time!
95      What had how long it takes a birch to rot
To do with what was in the darkened parlor.
You *couldn't* care! The nearest friends can go

With anyone to death, comes so far short
They might as well not try to go at all.
100    No, from the time when one is sick to death,
One is alone, and he dies more alone.
Friends make pretense of following to the grave,
But before one is in it, their minds are turned
And making the best of their way back to life
105    And living people, and things they understand.
But the world's evil. I won't have grief so
If I can change it. Oh, I won't, I won't!"

"There, you have said it all and you feel better.
You won't go now. You're crying. Close the door.
110    The heart's gone out of it: why keep it up.
Amy! There's someone coming down the road!"

"You—oh, you think the talk is all. I must go—
Somewhere out of this house. How can I make you—"

"If—you—do!" She was opening the door wider.
115    "Where do you mean to go? First tell me that.
I'll follow and bring you back by force. I *will!*—"

*1914*

## After Apple-Picking

My long two-pointed ladder's sticking through a tree
Toward heaven still,
And there's a barrel that I didn't fill
Beside it, and there may be two or three
5    Apples I didn't pick upon some bough.
But I am done with apple-picking now.
Essence of winter sleep is on the night,
The scent of apples: I am drowsing off.
I cannot rub the strangeness from my sight
10    I got from looking through a pane of glass
I skimmed this morning from the drinking trough
And held against the world of hoary grass.
It melted, and I let it fall and break.
But I was well
15    Upon my way to sleep before it fell,
And I could tell
What form my dreaming was about to take.
Magnified apples appear and disappear,
Stem end and blossom end,
20    And every fleck of russet showing clear.
My instep arch not only keeps the ache,
It keeps the pressure of a ladder-round.
I feel the ladder sway as the boughs bend.
And I keep hearing from the cellar bin

25 The rumbling sound
Of load on load of apples coming in.
For I have had too much
Of apple-picking: I am overtired
Of the great harvest I myself desired.
30 There were ten thousand thousand fruit to touch,
Cherish in hand, lift down, and not let fall.
For all
That struck the earth,
No matter if not bruised or spiked with stubble,
35 Went surely to the cider-apple heap
As of no worth.
One can see what will trouble
This sleep of mine, whatever sleep it is.
Were he not gone,
40 The woodchuck could say whether it's like his
Long sleep, as I describe its coming on,
Or just some human sleep.

*1914*

## The Wood-Pile

Out walking in the frozen swamp one gray day,
I paused and said, "I will turn back from here.
No, I will go on farther—and we shall see."
The hard snow held me, save where now and then
5 One foot went through. The view was all in lines
Straight up and down of tall slim trees
Too much alike to mark or name a place by
So as to say for certain I was here
Or somewhere else: I was just far from home.
10 A small bird flew before me. He was careful
To put a tree between us when he lighted,
And say no word to tell me who he was
Who was so foolish as to think what *he* thought.
He thought that I was after him for a feather—
15 The white one in his tail; like one who takes
Everything said as personal to himself.
One flight out sideways would have undeceived him.
And then there was a pile of wood for which
I forgot him and let his little fear
20 Carry him off the way I might have gone,
Without so much as wishing him good-night.
He went behind it to make his last stand.
It was a cord of maple, cut and split
And piled—and measured, four by four by eight.
25 And not another like it could I see.
No runner tracks in this year's snow looped near it.
And it was older sure than this year's cutting,
Or even last year's or the year's before.
The wood was gray and the bark warping off it

30          And the pile somewhat sunken. Clematis°
            Had wound strings round and round it like a bundle.
            What held it though on one side was a tree
            Still growing, and on one a stake and prop,
            These latter about to fall. I thought that only
35          Someone who lived in turning to fresh tasks
            Could so forget his handiwork on which
            He spent himself, the labor of his ax,
            And leave it there far from a useful fireplace
            To warm the frozen swamp as best it could
40          With the slow smokeless burning of decay.

                                                              *1914*


## The Road Not Taken

            Two roads diverged in a yellow wood,
            And sorry I could not travel both
            And be one traveler, long I stood
            And looked down one as far as I could
5           To where it bent in the undergrowth;

            Then took the other, as just as fair,
            And having perhaps the better claim,
            Because it was grassy and wanted wear;
            Though as for that the passing there
10          Had worn them really about the same,

            And both that morning equally lay
            In leaves no step had trodden black.
            Oh, I kept the first for another day!
            Yet knowing how way leads on to way,
15          I doubted if I should ever come back.

            I shall be telling this with a sigh
            Somewhere ages and ages hence:
            Two roads diverged in a wood, and I—
            I took the one less traveled by,
20          And that has made all the difference.

                                                              *1915*


## Birches

            When I see birches bend to left and right
            Across the lines of straighter darker trees,
            I like to think some boy's been swinging them.
            But swinging doesn't bend them down to stay
5           As ice-storms do. Often you must have seen them
            Loaded with ice a sunny winter morning

---

30 *Clematis*: flowering vine.

After a rain. They click upon themselves
As the breeze rises, and turn many-colored
As the stir cracks and crazes their enamel.
10    Soon the sun's warmth makes them shed crystal shells
Shattering and avalanching on the snow-crust—
Such heaps of broken glass to sweep away
You'd think the inner dome of heaven had fallen.
They are dragged to the withered bracken by the load,
And they seem not to break; though once they are bowed
So low for long, they never right themselves:
You may see their trunks arching in the woods
Years afterwards, trailing their leaves on the ground
Like girls on hands and knees that throw their hair
20    Before them over their heads to dry in the sun.
But I was going to say when Truth broke in
With all her matter-of-fact about the ice-storm
I should prefer to have some boy bend them
As he went out and in to fetch the cows—
25    Some boy too far from town to learn baseball,
Whose only play was what he found himself,
Summer or winter, and could play alone.
One by one he subdued his father's trees
By riding them down over and over again
30    Until he took the stiffness out of them,
And not one but hung limp, not one was left
For him to conquer. He learned all there was
To learn about not launching out too soon
And so not carrying the tree away
35    Clear to the ground. He always kept his poise
To the top branches, climbing carefully
With the same pains you use to fill a cup
Up to the brim, and even above the brim.
Then he flung outward, feet first, with a swish,
40    Kicking his way down through the air to the ground.
So was I once myself a swinger of birches.
And so I dream of going back to be.
It's when I'm weary of considerations,
And life is too much like a pathless wood
45    Where your face burns and tickles with the cobwebs
Broken across it, and one eye is weeping
From a twig's having lashed across it open.
I'd like to get away from earth awhile
And then come back to it and begin over.
50    May no fate willfully misunderstand me
And half grant what I wish and snatch me away
Not to return. Earth's the right place for love:
I don't know where it's likely to go better.
I'd like to go by climbing a birch tree,
55    And climb black branches up a snow-white trunk
*Toward* heaven, till the tree could bear no more,
But dipped its top and set me down again.
That would be good both going and coming back.
One could do worse than be a swinger of birches.

1915

## The Oven Bird°

There is a singer everyone has heard,
Loud, a mid-summer and a mid-wood bird,
Who makes the solid tree trunks sound again.
He says that leaves are old and that for flowers
5          Mid-summer is to spring as one to ten.
He says the early petal-fall is past
When pear and cherry bloom went down in showers
On sunny days a moment overcast;
And comes that other fall we name the fall.
10          He says the highway dust is over all.
The bird would cease and be as other birds
But that he knows in singing not to sing.
The question that he frames in all but words
Is what to make of a diminished thing.

*1916*

## An Old Man's Winter Night

All out-of-doors looked darkly in at him
Through the thin frost, almost in separate stars,
That gathers on the pane in empty rooms.
What kept his eyes from giving back the gaze
5          Was the lamp tilted near them in his hand.
What kept him from remembering what it was
That brought him to that creaking room was age.
He stood with barrels round him—at a loss.
And having scared the cellar under him
10          In clomping here, he scared it once again
In clomping off;—and scared the outer night,
Which has its sounds, familiar, like the roar
Of trees and crack of branches, common things,
But nothing so like beating on a box.
15          A light he was to no one but himself
Where now he sat, concerned with he knew what,
A quiet light, and then not even that.
He consigned to the moon, such as she was,
So late-arising, to the broken moon
20          As better than the sun in any case
For such a charge, his snow upon the roof,
His icicles along the wall to keep;
And slept. The log that shifted with a jolt
Once in the stove, disturbed him and he shifted,
25          And eased his heavy breathing, but still slept.
One aged man—one man—can't keep a house,
A farm, a countryside, or if he can,
It's thus he does it of a winter night.

*1916*

---

**poem title:** an American warbler, which builds a dome-shaped nest on the ground.

# The Hill Wife

### LONELINESS

#### *Her Word*

One ought not to have to care
    So much as you and I
Care when the birds come round the house
    To seem to say good-by;

5    Or care so much when they come back
    With whatever it is they sing;
The truth being we are as much
    Too glad for the one thing

As we are too sad for the other here—
10    With birds that fill their breasts
But with each other and themselves
    And their built or driven nests.

### HOUSE FEAR

Always—I tell you this they learned—
Always at night when they returned
To the lonely house from far away
To lamps unlighted and fire gone gray,
5    They learned to rattle the lock and key
To give whatever might chance to be
Warning and time to be off in flight:
And preferring the out- to the in-door night,
They learned to leave the house-door wide
10    Until they had lit the lamp inside.

### THE SMILE

#### *Her Word*

I didn't like the way he went away.
That smile! It never came of being gay.
Still he smiled—did you see him?—I was sure!
Perhaps because we gave him only bread
5    And the wretch knew from that that we were poor.
Perhaps because he let us give instead
Of seizing from us as he might have seized.
Perhaps he mocked at us for being wed,
Or being very young (and he was pleased
10    To have a vision of us old and dead).
I wonder how far down the road he's got.
He's watching from the woods as like as not.

### THE OFT-REPEATED DREAM

She had no saying dark enough
    For the dark pine that kept
Forever trying the window-latch
    Of the room where they slept.

The tireless but ineffectual hands
    That with every futile pass
Made the great tree seem as a little bird
    Before the mystery of glass!

It never had been inside the room,
    And only one of the two
Was afraid in an oft-repeated dream
    Of what the tree might do.

### THE IMPULSE

It was too lonely for her there,
    And too wild,
And since there were but two of them,
    And no child,

And work was little in the house,
    She was free,
And followed where he furrowed field,
    Or felled tree.

She rested on a log and tossed
    The fresh chips,
With a song only to herself
    On her lips.

And once she went to break a bough
    Of black alder.
She strayed so far she scarcely heard
    When he called her—

And didn't answer—didn't speak—
    Or return.
She stood, and then she ran and hid
    In the fern.

He never found her, though he looked
    Everywhere,
And he asked at her mother's house
    Was she there.

Sudden and swift and light as that
    The ties gave,
And he learned of finalities
    Besides the grave.

*1916*

# Fire and Ice

Some say the world will end in fire,
Some say in ice.
From what I've tasted of desire
I hold with those who favor fire.
5    But if it had to perish twice,
I think I know enough of hate
To say that for destruction ice
Is also great
And would suffice.

*1920*

# Good-by and Keep Cold

This saying good-by on the edge of the dark
And the cold to an orchard so young in the bark
Reminds me of all that can happen to harm
An orchard away at the end of the farm
5    All winter, cut off by a hill from the house.
I don't want it girdled by rabbit and mouse,
I don't want it dreamily nibbled for browse
By deer, and I don't want it budded by grouse.
(If certain it wouldn't be idle to call
10   I'd summon grouse, rabbit, and deer to the wall
And warn them away with a stick for a gun.)
I don't want it stirred by the heat of the sun.
(We made it secure against being, I hope,
By setting it out on a northerly slope.)
15   No orchard's the worse for the wintriest storm;
But one thing about it, it mustn't get warm.
"How often already you've had to be told,
Keep cold, young orchard. Good-by and keep cold.
Dread fifty above more than fifty below."
20   I have to be gone for a season or so.
My business awhile is with different trees,
Less carefully nurtured, less fruitful than these,
And such as is done to their wood with an ax—
Maples and birches and tamaracks.
25   I wish I could promise to lie in the night
And think of an orchard's arboreal plight
When slowly (and nobody comes with a light)
Its heart sinks lower under the sod.
But something has to be left to God.

*1920*

# The Need of Being Versed in Country Things

The house had gone to bring again
To the midnight sky a sunset glow.
Now the chimney was all of the house that stood,
Like a pistil after the petals go.

5     The barn opposed across the way,
      That would have joined the house in flame
      Had it been the will of the wind, was left
      To bear forsaken the place's name.

      No more it opened with all one end
10    For teams that came by the stony road
      To drum on the floor with scurrying hoofs
      And brush the mow with the summer load.

      The birds that came to it through the air
      At broken windows flew out and in,
15    Their murmur more like the sigh we sigh
      From too much dwelling on what has been.

      Yet for them the lilac renewed its leaf,
      And the aged elm, though touched with fire;
      And the dry pump flung up an awkward arm;
20    And the fence post carried a strand of wire.

      For them there was really nothing sad.
      But though they rejoiced in the nest they kept,
      One had to be versed in country things
      Not to believe the phoebes° wept.

                                                    *1920*


## Design

      I found a dimpled spider, fat and white,
      On a white heal-all,° holding up a moth
      Like a white piece of rigid satin cloth—
      Assorted characters of death and blight
5     Mixed ready to begin the morning right,
      Like the ingredients of a witches' broth—
      A snow-drop spider, a flower like a froth,
      And dead wings carried like a paper kite.

      What had that flower to do with being white,
10    The wayside blue and innocent heal-all?
      What brought the kindred spider to that height,
      Then steered the white moth thither in the night?
      What but design of darkness to appall?°—
      If design govern in a thing so small.

                                                    *1922*

---

24 *phoebes*: American flycatchers, birds named after the Greek moon goddess.
2 *heal-all*: or self-heal, plants reputed to have healing powers, especially one in the mint family with deep violet-blue flowers.
13 *appall*: to make pale.

# The Witch of Coös°

I stayed the night for shelter at a farm
Behind the mountain, with a mother and son,
Two old-believers. They did all the talking.

MOTHER.   Folks think a witch who has familiar spirits
5    She could call up to pass a winter evening,
But won't, should be burned at the stake or something.
Summoning spirits isn't "Button, button,
Who's got the button," I would have them know.

SON.   Mother can make a common table rear
10   And kick with two legs like an army mule.

MOTHER.   And when I've done it, what good have I done?
Rather than tip a table for you, let me
Tell you what Ralle the Sioux Control° once told me.
He said the dead had souls, but when I asked him
15   How could that be—I thought the dead were souls,
He broke my trance. Don't that make you suspicious
That there's something the dead are keeping back?
Yes, there's something the dead are keeping back.

SON.   You wouldn't want to tell him what we have
Up attic, mother?

20   MOTHER.   Bones—a skeleton.

SON.   But the headboard of mother's bed is pushed
Against the attic door: the door is nailed.
It's harmless. Mother hears it in the night
Halting perplexed behind the barrier
25   Of door and headboard. Where it wants to get
Is back into the cellar where it came from.

MOTHER.   We'll never let them, will we, son! We'll never!

SON.   It left the cellar forty years ago
And carried itself like a pile of dishes
30   Up one flight from the cellar to the kitchen,
Another from the kitchen to the bedroom,
Another from the bedroom to the attic,
Right past both father and mother, and neither stopped it.
Father had gone upstairs; mother was downstairs.
35   I was a baby: I don't know where I was.

---

**poem title:** Coös, a county in New Hampshire.
13 *Control*: a spirit presumed to speak or act through a medium in a séance; the dead
speak to the medium through the control.

MOTHER.   The only fault my husband found with me—
I went to sleep before I went to bed,
Especially in winter when the bed
Might just as well be ice and the clothes snow.
40   The night the bones came up the cellar-stairs
Toffile had gone to bed alone and left me,
But left an open door to cool the room off
So as to sort of turn me out of it.
I was just coming to myself enough
45   To wonder where the cold was coming from,
When I heard Toffile upstairs in the bedroom
And thought I heard him downstairs in the cellar.
The board we had laid down to walk dry-shod on
When there was water in the cellar in spring
50   Struck the hard cellar bottom. And then someone
Began the stairs, two footsteps for each step,
The way a man with one leg and a crutch,
Or a little child, comes up. It wasn't Toffile:
It wasn't anyone who could be there.
55   The bulkhead double-doors were double-locked
And swollen tight and buried under snow.
The cellar windows were banked up with sawdust
And swollen tight and buried under snow.
It was the bones. I knew them—and good reason.
60   My first impulse was to get to the knob
And hold the door. But the bones didn't try
The door; they halted helpless on the landing,
Waiting for things to happen in their favor.
The faintest restless rustling ran all through them.
65   I never could have done the thing I did
If the wish hadn't been too strong in me
To see how they were mounted for this walk.
I had a vision of them put together
Not like a man, but like a chandelier.
70   So suddenly I flung the door wide on him.
A moment he stood balancing with emotion,
And all but lost himself. (A tongue of fire
Flashed out and licked along his upper teeth.
Smoke rolled inside the sockets of his eyes.)
75   Then he came at me with one hand outstretched,
The way he did in life once; but this time
I struck the hand off brittle on the floor,
And fell back from him on the floor myself.
The finger-pieces slid in all directions.
80   (Where did I see one of those pieces lately?
Hand me my button-box—it must be there.)
I sat up on the floor and shouted, "Toffile,
It's coming up to you." It had its choice
Of the door to the cellar or the hall.
85   It took the hall door for the novelty,
And set off briskly for so slow a thing,
Still going every which way in the joints, though,
So that it looked like lightning or a scribble,

From the slap I had just now given its hand.
90  I listened till it almost climbed the stairs
From the hall to the only finished bedroom,
Before I got up to do anything;
Then ran and shouted, "Shut the bedroom door,
Toffile, for my sake!" "Company?" he said,
95  "Don't make me get up; I'm too warm in bed."
So lying forward weakly on the handrail
I pushed myself upstairs, and in the light
(The kitchen had been dark) I had to own
I could see nothing. "Toffile, I don't see it.
100  It's with us in the room though. It's the bones."
"What bones?" "The cellar bones—out of the grave."
That made him throw his bare legs out of bed
And sit up by me and take hold of me.
I wanted to put out the light and see
105  If I could see it, or else mow the room,
With our arms at the level of our knees,
And bring the chalk-pile down. "I'll tell you what—
It's looking for another door to try.
The uncommonly deep snow has made him think
110  Of his old song, 'The Wild Colonial Boy,'
He always used to sing along the tote road.
He's after an open door to get outdoors.
Let's trap him with an open door up attic."
Toffile agreed to that, and sure enough,
115  Almost the moment he was given an opening,
The steps began to climb the attic stairs.
I heard them. Toffile didn't seem to hear them.
"Quick!" I slammed to the door and held the knob.
"Toffile, get nails." I made him nail the door shut
120  And push the headboard of the bed against it.
Then we asked was there anything
Up attic that we'd ever want again.
The attic was less to us than the cellar.
If the bones liked the attic, let them have it.
125  Let them stay in the attic. When they sometimes
Come down the stairs at night and stand perplexed
Behind the door and headboard of the bed,
Brushing their chalky skull with chalky fingers,
With sounds like the dry rattling of a shutter,
130  That's what I sit up in the dark to say—
To no one anymore since Toffile died.
Let them stay in the attic since they went there.
I promised Toffile to be cruel to them
For helping them be cruel once to him.

135  SON.   We think they had a grave down in the cellar.

MOTHER.   We know they had a grave down in the cellar.

SON.   We never could find out whose bones they were.

MOTHER.   Yes, we could too, son. Tell the truth for once.
They were a man's his father killed for me.
140    I mean a man he killed instead of me.
The least I could do was help dig their grave.
We were about it one night in the cellar.
Son knows the story: but 'twas not for him
To tell the truth, suppose the time had come.
145    Son looks surprised to see me end a lie
We'd kept all these years between ourselves
So as to have it ready for outsiders.
But tonight I don't care enough to lie—
I don't remember why I ever cared.
150    Toffile, if he were here, I don't believe
Could tell you why he ever cared himself. . . .

She hadn't found the finger-bone she wanted
Among the buttons poured out in her lap.
I verified the name next morning: Toffile.
155    The rural letter box said Toffile Lajway.

                                                        *1922*

# Stopping by Woods on a Snowy Evening

Whose woods these are I think I know.
His house is in the village though;
He will not see me stopping here
To watch his woods fill up with snow.

5       My little horse must think it queer
To stop without a farmhouse near
Between the woods and frozen lake
The darkest evening of the year.

He gives his harness bells a shake
10      To ask if there is some mistake.
The only other sound's the sweep
Of easy wind and downy flake.

The woods are lovely, dark and deep,
But I have promises to keep,
15      And miles to go before I sleep,
And miles to go before I sleep.

                                                        *1923*

# Gathering Leaves

Spades take up leaves
No better than spoons,
And bags full of leaves
Are light as balloons.

5      I make a great noise
       Of rustling all day
       Like rabbit and deer
       Running away.

       But the mountains I raise
10     Elude my embrace,
       Flowing over my arms
       And into my face.

       I may load and unload
       Again and again
15     Till I fill the whole shed,
       And what have I then?

       Next to nothing for weight,
       And since they grew duller
       From contact with earth,
20     Next to nothing for color.

       Next to nothing for use.
       But a crop is a crop,
       And who's to say where
       The harvest shall stop?

*1923*

## In a Disused Graveyard

The living come with grassy tread
To read the gravestones on the hill;
The graveyard draws the living still,
But never anymore the dead.

5      The verses in it say and say:
       "The ones who living come today
       To read the stones and go away
       Tomorrow dead will come to stay."

       So sure of death the marbles rhyme,
10     Yet can't help marking all the time
       How no one dead will seem to come.
       What is it men are shrinking from?

       It would be easy to be clever
       And tell the stones: Men hate to die
15     And have stopped dying now forever.
       I think they would believe the lie.

*1923*

## Nothing Gold Can Stay

Nature's first green is gold,
Her hardest hue to hold.
Her early leaf's a flower;
But only so an hour.
5      Then leaf subsides to leaf.
So Eden sank to grief,
So dawn goes down to day.
Nothing gold can stay.

                       *1923*

## Desert Places

Snow falling and night falling fast, oh, fast
In a field I looked into going past,
And the ground almost covered smooth in snow,
But a few weeds and stubble showing last.

5      The woods around it have it—it is theirs.
All animals are smothered in their lairs.
I am too absent-spirited to count;
The loneliness includes me unawares.

And lonely as it is that loneliness
10     Will be more lonely ere it will be less—
A blanker whiteness of benighted° snow
With no expression, nothing to express.

They cannot scare me with their empty spaces
Between stars—on stars where no human race is.
15     I have it in me so much nearer home
To scare myself with my own desert places.

                       *1934*

## Two Tramps in Mud Time

Out of the mud two strangers came
And caught me splitting wood in the yard.
And one of them put me off my aim
By hailing cheerily "Hit them hard!"
5      I knew pretty well why he dropped behind
And let the other go on a way.
I knew pretty well what he had in mind:
He wanted to take my job for pay.

---

11 *benighted*: unenlightened, overtaken by darkness.

Good blocks of oak it was I split,
10  As large around as the chopping block;
And every piece I squarely hit
Fell splinterless as a cloven rock.
The blows that a life of self-control
Spares to strike for the common good
15  That day, giving a loose to my soul,
I spent on the unimportant wood.

The sun was warm but the wind was chill.
You know how it is with an April day
When the sun is out and the wind is still,
20  You're one month on in the middle of May.
But if you so much as dare to speak,
A cloud comes over the sunlit arch,
A wind comes off a frozen peak,
And you're two months back in the middle of March.

25  A bluebird comes tenderly up to alight
And turns to the wind to unruffle a plume
His song so pitched as not to excite
A single flower as yet to bloom.
It is snowing a flake: and he half knew
30  Winter was only playing possum.
Except in color he isn't blue,
But he wouldn't advise a thing to blossom.

The water for which we may have to look
In summertime with a witching-wand,
35  In every wheelrut's now a brook,
In every print of a hoof a pond.
Be glad of water, but don't forget
The lurking frost in the earth beneath
That will steal forth after the sun is set
40  And show on the water its crystal teeth.

The time when most I loved my task
These two must make me love it more
By coming with what they came to ask.
You'd think I never had felt before
45  The weight of an ax-head poised aloft,
The grip on earth of outspread feet,
The life of muscles rocking soft
And smooth and moist in vernal heat.

Out of the woods two hulking tramps
50  (From sleeping God knows where last night,
But not long since in the lumber camps).
They thought all chopping was theirs of right.
Men of the woods and lumberjacks,
They judged me by their appropriate tool.
55  Except as a fellow handled an ax,
They had no way of knowing a fool.

Nothing on either side was said.
They knew they had but to stay their stay
And all their logic would fill my head:
60 As that I had no right to play
With what was another man's work for gain.
My right might be love but theirs was need.
And where the two exist in twain
Theirs was the better right—agreed.

65 But yield who will to their separation,
My object in living is to unite
My avocation and my vocation
As my two eyes make one in sight.
Only where love and need are one,
70 And the work is play for mortal stakes,
Is the deed ever really done
For Heaven and the future's sakes.

1934

## Neither Out Far Nor In Deep

The people along the sand
All turn and look one way.
They turn their back on the land.
They look at the sea all day.

5 As long as it takes to pass
A ship keeps raising its hull;
The wetter ground like glass
Reflects a standing gull.

The land may vary more;
10 But wherever the truth may be—
The water comes ashore,
And the people look at the sea.

They cannot look out far.
They cannot look in deep.
15 But when was that ever a bar
To any watch they keep?

1934

## Never Again Would Birds' Song Be the Same

He would declare and could himself believe
That the birds there in all the garden round
From having heard the daylong voice of Eve
Had added to their own an oversound,
5 Her tone of meaning but without the words.
Admittedly an eloquence so soft

Could only have had an influence on birds
When call or laughter carried it aloft.
Be that as may be, she was in their song.
10  Moreover her voice upon their voices crossed
Had now persisted in the woods so long
That probably it never would be lost.
Never again would birds' song be the same.
And to do that to birds was why she came.

1942


## The Gift Outright

The land was ours before we were the land's.
She was our land more than a hundred years
Before we were her people. She was ours
In Massachusetts, in Virginia,
5  But we were England's, still colonials,
Possessing what we still were unpossessed by,
Possessed by what we now no more possessed.
Something we were withholding made us weak
Until we found out that it was ourselves
10  We were withholding from our land of living,
And forthwith found salvation in surrender.
Such as we were we gave ourselves outright
(The deed of gift was many deeds of war)
To the land vaguely realizing westward,
15  But still unstoried, artless, unenhanced,
Such as she was, such as she would become.

1942

# Alice Dunbar-Nelson (1875–1935)

Born in New Orleans, of mixed African American, Native American, and European ancestry, Dunbar-Nelson was educated at Straight College. A 1898–1902 marriage to poet Paul Laurence Dunbar is the source of her hyphenated name. She is known not only for her poetry but also for her short stories and posthumously published diary. She worked repeatedly for social justice for women and minorities and was a noted public speaker.

## I Sit and Sew

I sit and sew—a useless task it seems,
My hands grown tired, my head weighed down with dreams—
The panoply of war, the martial tread of men,
Grim-faced, stern-eyed, gazing beyond the ken
5    Of lesser souls, whose eyes have not seen Death
Nor learned to hold their lives but as a breath—
But—I must sit and sew.

I sit and sew—my heart aches with desire—
That pageant terrible, that fiercely pouring fire
10   On wasted fields, and writhing grotesque things
Once men. My soul in pity flings
Appealing cries, yearning only to go
There in that holocaust of hell, those fields of woe—
But—I must sit and sew.—

15   The little useless seam, the idle patch;
Why dream I here beneath my homely thatch,
When there they lie in sodden mud and rain,
Pitifully calling me, the quick° ones and the slain?
You need, me, Christ! It is no roseate seam
20   That beckons me—this pretty futile seam,
It stifles me—God, must I sit and sew?

*1920*

---

18 *quick*: live.

# Carl Sandburg (1878–1967)

Born in Galesburg, Illinois, and educated at Lombard College, Sandburg for many years was drawn both to America's most radical union, the Industrial Workers of the World, and also to international socialism. The great poems of his first volume, *Chicago Poems* (1914), and of the next several years, some of them uncollected or unpublished, reflect his deep commitment to working people and his strong left politics, including his initial opposition to U.S. involvement in World War I and his interest in African American culture. His portraits of black life mix stereotypical elements with moments of real power. Sandburg would later travel the country collecting American folk songs, and compile a massive biography of Abraham Lincoln. One of the most popular poets of his time, his full canon, only now coming into print, shows him to be a much tougher and more challenging poet than his posthumous critical reception would suggest. Readers interested in Sandburg should consult not only his *Complete Poems*, a misleadingly titled volume, but also the series of supplementary books currently being published. Among the poems here, "Planked Whitefish" and "Elizabeth Umpstead" are not in his collected poems, and "Man, the Man-Hunter" is there only in a less aggressive version.

## Chicago

Hog Butcher for the World,
Tool Maker, Stacker of Wheat,
Player with Railroads and the Nation's Freight Handler;
Stormy, husky, brawling,
5      City of the Big Shoulders:

They tell me you are wicked and I believe them, for I have seen
your painted women under the gas lamps luring the farm boys.
And they tell me you are crooked and I answer: Yes, it is true I
have seen the gunman kill and go free to kill again.
And they tell me you are brutal and my reply is: On the faces of
women and children I have seen the marks of wanton hunger.
And having answered so I turn once more to those who sneer at
this my city, and I give them back the sneer and say to them:
10     Come and show me another city with lifted head singing so proud
to be alive and coarse and strong and cunning.
Flinging magnetic curses amid the toil of piling job on job, here is
a tall bold slugger set vivid against the little soft cities;

Fierce as a dog with tongue lapping for action, cunning as a savage
    pitted against the wilderness,
Bareheaded,
Shoveling,
15   Wrecking,
Planning,
Building, breaking, rebuilding,
Under the smoke, dust all over his mouth, laughing with white teeth,
Under the terrible burden of destiny laughing as a young man laughs,
20   Laughing even as an ignorant fighter laughs who has never lost a
    battle,
Bragging and laughing that under his wrist is the pulse, and under
    his ribs the heart of the people,
        Laughing!
Laughing the stormy, husky, brawling laughter of Youth, half-
    naked, sweating, proud to be Hog Butcher, Tool Maker, Stacker
    of Wheat, Player with Railroads and Freight Handler to the
    Nation.

                                                            *1916*

# Subway

Down between the walls of shadow
Where the iron laws insist,
    The hunger voices mock.
The worn wayfaring men
5   With the hunched and humble shoulders,
    Throw their laughter into toil.

                                                            *1916*

# Muckers

Twenty men stand watching the muckers.
    Stabbing the sides of the ditch
    Where clay gleams yellow,
    Driving the blades of their shovels
5   Deeper and deeper for the new gas mains,
    Wiping sweat off their faces
        With red bandanas.

The muckers work on . . . pausing . . . to pull
Their boots out of suckholes where they slosh.

10      Of the twenty looking on
    Ten murmur, "O, it's a hell of a job,"
    Ten others, "Jesus, I wish I had the job."

                                                            *1916*

## Child of the Romans

The dago shovelman sits by the railroad track
Eating a noon meal of bread and bologna.
    A train whirls by, and men and women at tables
    Alive with red roses and yellow jonquils,
5       Eat steaks running with brown gravy,
      Strawberries and cream, eclairs and coffee.
The dago shovelman finishes the dry bread and bologna,
Washes it down with a dipper from the water-boy,
And goes back to the second half of a ten-hour day's work
10 Keeping the road-bed so the roses and jonquils
Shake hardly at all in the cut glass vases
Standing slender on the tables in the dining cars.

*1916*

## Nigger

I am the nigger.
Singer of songs,
Dancer . . .
Softer than fluff of cotton . . .
5 Harder than dark earth
Roads beaten in the sun
By the bare feet of slaves . . .
Foam of teeth . . . breaking crash of laughter . . .
Red love of the blood of woman,
10 White love of the tumbling pickaninnies . . .
Lazy love of the banjo thrum . . .
Sweated and driven for the harvest-wage,
Loud laughter with hands like hams,
Fists toughened on the handles,
15 Smiling the slumber dreams of old jungles,
Crazy as the sun and dew and dripping, heaving life of the jungle,

Brooding and muttering with memories of shackles:
    I am the nigger.
    Look at me.
    I am the nigger.

*1916*

## Buttons

I have been watching the war map slammed up for advertising in
    front of the newspaper office.
Buttons—red and yellow buttons—blue and black buttons—are
    shoved back and forth across the map.

A laughing young man, sunny with freckles,
Climbs a ladder, yells a joke to somebody in the crowd,
5 And then fixes a yellow button one inch west
And follows the yellow button with a black button one inch west.

(Ten thousand men and boys twist on their bodies in a red soak
    along a river edge,
Gasping of wounds, calling for water, some rattling death in their
    throats.)
Who would guess what it cost to move two buttons one inch on
    the war map here in front of the newspaper office where the
    freckle-faced young man is laughing to us?

*1915*

# Planked Whitefish

(*"I'm a going to live anyhow until I die."*
—MODERN RAGTIME SONG)

Over an order of planked whitefish at a downtown club,
Horace Wild, the demon driver who hurled the first aeroplane
    that ever crossed the air over Chicago,
Told Charley Cutler, the famous rassler who never touches booze,
And Carl Sandburg, the distinguished poet now out of jail,
5    He saw near Ypres a Canadian soldier fastened on a barn door
    with bayonets pinning the hands and feet
And the arms and ankles arranged like Jesus at Golgotha 2,000
    years before
Only in northern France he saw
The genital organ of the victim amputated and placed between
    the lips of the dead man's mouth,
And Horace Wild, eating whitefish, looked us straight in the
    eyes,
10    And piled up circumstantial detail of what he saw one night
    running a truck pulling ambulances out of the mud near
    Ypres in November, 1915:
A box car next to a field hospital operating room . . . filled
    with sawed-off arms and legs . . .
Faces in the gray and the dark on the mud flats, white faces
    gibbering and loose convulsive arms making useless gestures,
And Horace Wild, the demon driver who loves fighting and can
    whip his weight in wildcats,
Pointed at a blue button in the lapel of his coat, "P-e-a-c-e"
    spelled in white letters, and he blurted:
15    "I don't care who the hell calls me a pacifist. I don't care who
    the hell calls me yellow. I say war is the game of a lot of
    God-damned fools."

*c. 1916*

## Cool Tombs

When Abraham Lincoln was shoveled into the tombs, he forgot the
    copperheads° and the assassin° . . . in the dust, in the cool
    tombs.

And Ulysses Grant° lost all thought of con men and Wall Street,
    cash and collateral turned ashes . . . in the dust, in the cool
    tombs.

Pocahontas' body, lovely as a poplar, sweet as a red haw° in No-
    vember or a pawpaw° in May, did she wonder? does she remem-
    ber? . . . in the dust, in the cool tombs?

Take any streetful of people buying clothes and groceries, cheering
    a hero or throwing confetti and blowing tin horns . . . tell me if
    the lovers are losers . . . tell me if any get more than the lovers
    . . . in the dust . . . in the cool tombs.

*1918*

## Grass

Pile the bodies high at Austerlitz° and Waterloo.°
Shovel them under and let me work—
                I am the grass; I cover all.

And pile them high at Gettysburg°
5    And pile them high at Ypres and Verdun.°
Shovel them under and let me work.
Two years, ten years, and passengers ask the conductor:
                What place is this?
                Where are we now?

10              I am the grass.
                Let me work.

*1918*

---

1 *copperheads*: Southern sympathizers in the North during the American Civil War.
1 *assassin*: John Wilkes Booth (1838–1865).
2 *Grant*: Civil War General and U.S. President, whose second administration was notori-
ously corrupt; he went bankrupt after leaving office.
3 *red haw*: hawthorn berry.
3 *pawpaw*: fruit of the pawpaw tree.
1 *Austerlitz*: the December 1805 site (in Moravia) of one of Napoleon's great victories.
Napoléon Bonaparte (1769–1821), French general and Emperor, a titanic figure in Euro-
pean history.
1 *Waterloo*: the battle at Waterloo, Belgium, where Napoleon was defeated in June of 1815.
4 *Gettysburg*: the July 1863 Pennsylvania site of a major defeat for the Confederacy in the
American Civil War.
5 *Ypres and Verdun*: major battles with considerable casualties in 1914, 1915, and 1917 (Ypres,
Belgium) and 1916 (Verdun, France) during World War I. The third battle near Ypres in
particular is considered a massive and fruitless loss of life. It lasted for months and was
fought in deep mud, into which men and horses sank without a trace.

## Fog

The fog comes
on little cat feet.

It sits looking
over harbor and city
5      on silent haunches
and then moves on.

*1916*

## Elizabeth Umpstead

I am Elizabeth Umpstead, dead at seventy-five years of age, and they
are taking me in a polished and silver-plated box today, and an under-
taker, assured of cash for his work, will supply straps to let the box
down the lean dirt walls, while a quartet of singers—assured of cash
for their work, sing "Nearer My God to Thee," and a clergyman, also
assured of cash for his services—will pronounce the words: "Dust to
dust and ashes to ashes."

I am gone from among the two-legged moving figures on top the
earth now, and nobody will say my heart is someway wrong when I as-
sert, I was the most beautiful nigger girl in northern Indiana; and men
wanted my beauty, white men and black men—they wanted to take it
and crush it and taste it—and I learned what they wanted and I traded
on it; I schemed and haggled to get all I could for it—and so, I am one
nigger girl who today has a grand funeral with all the servitors paid in
spot cash.

I learned early, away back in short dresses, when a lawyer took me
and used me the same as a brass cuspidor or a new horse and buggy
or a swivel chair or anything that gives more life-ease for spot cash—
he paid $600 cash to me for the keep of the child of my womb and his
loins. And then he went to a revival, sang "Jesus Knows All about Our
Troubles," moaned he was a sinner and wanted Jesus to wash his sins
away. He joined the church and stood up one night before hundreds
of people and blabbed to them how he used me, had a child by me,
and paid me $600 cash. And I waited till one night I saw him in the
public square and I slashed his face with a leather horsewhip, calling
all the wild crazy names that came to my tongue to damn him and
damn him and damn him, for a sneak in the face of God and man.

*c. 1919*

## Man, the Man-Hunter

I saw Man, the man-hunter,
Hunting with a torch in one hand
And a kerosene can in the other,
Hunting with guns, ropes, shackles.

5              I listened
               And the high cry rang.
        The high cry of Man, the man-hunter:
        We'll get you yet,   you   Son of a Bitch!


               I listened later,
10             The high cry rang:
        Kill him! kill him!   the Judean equivalent   the Son of a Bitch!


        In the morning the sun saw
        Two butts of something, a smoking rump,
        And a warning in charred wood:
15                    Well, we got him,
                      the   Son of a Bitch.

                                                        *c. 1919*


# Two Humpties

        They tried to hand it to us on a platter,
        Us hit in the eyes with marconigrams from moon dancers—
        And the bubble busted, went flooey, on a thumb touch.


            So this time again, Humpty,
5       We cork our laughs behind solemn phizzogs,
        Sweep the floor with the rim of our hats
        And say good-a-by and good-a-by, just like that.


            Tomorrow maybe they will be hit
            in the eyes with marconigrams
10          From moon dancers.
        Good-a-by, our hats and all of us say good-a-by.

                                                        *1922*

# Vachel Lindsay (1879–1931)

Lindsay was born in the family home in Springfield, Illinois, delivered by his physician father. The house, which once belonged to Abraham Lincoln's sister-in-law, was across the street from the Illinois governor's mansion; it had been the site of a send-off party for Lincoln after he was elected president. Lindsay spent nearly three years at Hiram College trying to fulfill his father's ambition that he become a doctor, but then convinced his parents that art was his real mission. He enrolled at the Chicago Art Institute in 1901. Two years later he transferred to the New York School of Art, but he was already spending a good deal of time writing poems. On a visit home in 1904, he had the first of many visions; one of the results was a large pen-and-ink drawing of his personal mythology, "The Map of the Universe." He began to issue illustrated poetry broadsides and taught art appreciation at New York's West Side YMCA. In 1906, he joined a friend on a tramp steamer to Florida. Lindsay decided to see America on the way home; walking 600 miles and begging a few train rides, he made his way north to Kentucky. He continued walking on to Indiana. It was the first of several major walks, though on the later trips Lindsay brought books, illustrated poetry broadsides, and pamphlets with him to exchange for room and board. *Rhymes to be Traded for Bread* accompanied him on his 1912 trek along the Santa Fe trail to Colorado and New Mexico. He took a train to Los Angeles, then hiked north to San Francisco. Meanwhile he was giving away poems and writing new ones. Earlier he had walked his native Midwest, giving away poems; no other American poet, before or since, has done anything quite like this.

In 1914, Lindsay wrote "The Congo," which would win admirers and detractors and haunt him for the rest of his life. It would be attacked in the black magazine *Opportunity*, yet anthologized by Langston Hughes. Sterling Brown would later write a poem in answer to Lindsay. Some would point out that Lindsay knew precious little about Africa, yet it is not clear he intended the poem to be representational. He had a continuing interest in vaudeville and performed the poem out loud in the most histrionic style possible. When race riots had broken out in Illinois in 1908 and several Springfield blacks were killed, Lindsay gave a public lecture titled "The Negro. His Native Genius:— Sorrow Songs; Folk Lore; Oratory; Sense of the Picturesque; Minstrelsy." Then he contrasted these talents with the depressing opportunities for blacks in contemporary Springfield. Unquestionably offensive in many respects, "The Congo" also aims for minstrel effects, itself a tradition with mixed racist and satiric impact. In any case, any collection aiming to document the dialogue over race in American poetry needs to give "The Congo" its place.

On demand as a performer over the next decade and more, his "Evening of Higher Vaudeville and Orthodox Verse" always met with demands for "The

Congo." Yet Lindsay was moving into more visionary poetry. He spent the summer of 1921 hiking in Glacier National Park in northern Montana, an experience that produced the poems of *Going-to-the-Sun* (1923), illustrated in a style influenced by his study of Egyptian hieroglyphics. The poems are hymns to a mythologized nature and to a cultural zone, half material and half otherworldly, that Lindsay offered as an antidote to war and social misery. The public was uninterested. Meanwhile Lindsay had met and impulsively married Elizabeth Conner in 1925. His new work ignored, his marriage in difficulty, Lindsay took his own life in December, 1931, by drinking a bottle of lye.

## The Congo

### A Study of the Negro Race

(Being a memorial to Ray Eldred, a Disciple missionary of
the Congo River)

#### I. THEIR BASIC SAVAGERY

Fat black bucks in a wine-barrel room,      *A deep rolling*
Barrel-house kings, with feet unstable,      *bass.*
Sagged and reeled and pounded on the table,
Pounded on the table,
5    Beat an empty barrel with the handle of a broom,
Hard as they were able,
Boom, boom, BOOM,
With a silk umbrella and the handle of a broom,
Boomlay, boomlay, boomlay, BOOM.
10   THEN I had religion, THEN I had a vision.
I could not turn from their revel in derision.
THEN I SAW THE CONGO, CREEPING      *More deliberate.*
   THROUGH THE BLACK,      *Solemnly*
CUTTING THROUGH THE FOREST WITH      *chanted.*
   A GOLDEN TRACK.
Then along that riverbank
15   A thousand miles
Tattooed cannibals danced in files;
Then I heard the boom of the blood-lust song
And a thigh-bone beating on a tin-pan gong.      *A rapidly*
And "BLOOD" screamed the whistles and the      *piling*
   fifes of the warriors,      *climax*
"BLOOD" screamed the skull-faced, lean witch-      *of speed and*
20   doctors,      *racket.*
"Whirl ye the deadly voo-doo rattle,
Harry the uplands,
Steal all the cattle,
Rattle-rattle, rattle-rattle,
25   Bing.
Boomlay, boomlay, boomlay, BOOM,
A roaring, epic, rag-time tune      *With a philo-*
From the mouth of the Congo      *sophic pause.*
To the Mountains of the Moon.

<table>
<tr><td>30</td><td>Death is an Elephant,</td><td></td></tr>
</table>

30    Death is an Elephant,
      Torch-eyed and horrible,                    *Shrilly and*
      Foam-flanked and terrible.                  *with a heavily*
      BOOM, steal the pygmies,                    *accented metre.*
      BOOM, kill the Arabs,
36    BOOM, kill the white men,
      HOO, HOO, HOO.
      Listen to the yell of Leopold's ghost       *Like the wind*
      Burning in Hell for his hand-maimed host.   *in the chimney.*
      Hear how the demons chuckle and yell
40    Cutting his hands off, down in Hell.
      Listen to the creepy proclamation,
      Blown through the lairs of the forest-nation,
      Blown past the white-ants' hill of clay,
      Blown past the marsh where the butterflies
          play:—
45    "Be careful what you do,                     *All the "o"*
      Or Mumbo-Jumbo, God of the Congo,           *sounds very*
      And all of the other                        *golden. Heavy*
      Gods of the Congo,                          *accents very*
      Mumbo-Jumbo will hoo-doo you,               *heavy. Light*
50    Mumbo-Jumbo will hoo-doo you,               *accents very*
      Mumbo-Jumbo will hoo-doo you."              *light. Last line*
                                                  *whispered.*

### II. Their Irrepressible High Spirits

      Wild crap-shooters with a whoop and a call  *Rather shrill*
      Danced the juba in their gambling hall      *and high.*
      And laughed fit to kill, and shook the town,
55    And guyed the policemen and laughed them
          down
      With a boomlay, boomlay, boomlay, BOOM.
      THEN I SAW THE CONGO, CREEPING             *Read exactly as*
          THROUGH THE BLACK,                     *in first section.*
      CUTTING THROUGH THE FOREST WITH A
          GOLDEN TRACK.
      A negro fairyland swung into view,          *Lay emphasis*
60    A minstrel river                            *on the delicate*
      Where dreams come true.                     *ideas. Keep as*
      The ebony palace soared on high             *light-footed as*
      Through the blossoming trees to the evening sky.  *possible.*
      The inlaid porches and casements shone
65    With gold and ivory and elephant-bone.
      And the black crowd laughed till their sides were
          sore
      At the baboon butler in the agate door,
      And the well-known tunes of the parrot band
      That trilled on the bushes of that magic land.

70    A troupe of skull-faced witch-men came     *With*
      Through the agate doorway in suits of flame,  *pomposity.*
      Yea, long-tailed coats with a gold-leaf crust

And hats that were covered with diamond-dust.
And the crowd in the court gave a whoop and a call
75 And danced the juba from wall to wall.
But the witch-men suddenly stilled the throng    *With a great*
With a stern cold glare, and a stern old song:—    *deliberation*
"Mumbo-Jumbo will hoo-doo you." . . .    *and ghostliness.*
Just then from the doorway, as fat as shotes,    *With over-*
80 Came the cake-walk princes in their long red coats *whelming as-*
Canes with a brilliant lacquer shine,    *surance, good*
And tall silk hats that were red as wine.    *cheer, and pomp.*
And they pranced with their butterfly partners
   there,
Coal-black maidens with pearls in their hair,    *With growing*
85 Knee-skirts trimmed with the jassamine sweet,    *speed and*
And bells on their ankles and little black feet.    *sharply marked*
And the couples railed at the chant and the frown *dance-rhythm.*
Of the witch-men lean, and laughed them down.
(Oh, rare was the revel, and well worth while
90 That made those glowering witch-men smile.)

The cake-walk royalty then began
To walk for a cake that was tall as a man
To the tune of "Boomlay, boomlay, BOOM,"
While the witch-men laughed, with a sinister air,    *With a touch*
95 And sang with the scalawags prancing there:—    *of negro dia-*
"Walk with care, walk with care,    *lect, and*
Or Mumbo-Jumbo, God of the Congo,    *as rapidly as*
And all of the other Gods of the Congo,    *possible toward*
Mumbo-Jumbo will hoo-doo you.    *the end.*
100 Beware, beware, walk with care,
Boomlay, boomlay, boomlay, boom.
Boomlay, boomlay, boomlay, boom.
Boomlay, boomlay, boomlay, boom.
Boomlay, boomlay, boomlay,
105 BOOM."
(Oh, rare was the revel, and well worth while    *Slow philo-*
That made those glowering witch-men smile.)    *sophic calm.*

### III. The Hope of Their Religion

A good old negro in the slums of the town    *Heavy bass.*
Preached at a sister for her velvet gown.    *With a literal*
110 Howled at a brother for his low-down ways,    *imitation of*
His prowling, guzzling, sneak-thief days.    *camp-meeting*
Beat on the Bible till he wore it out    *racket, and*
Starting the jubilee revival shout.    *trance.*
And some had visions, as they stood on chairs,
115 And sang of Jacob, and the golden stairs,
And they all repented, a thousand strong
From their stupor and savagery and sin and wrong
And slammed with their hymn books till they shook
   the room
With "glory, glory, glory,"

120 And "Boom, boom, BOOM."
THEN I SAW THE CONGO, CREEPING
  THROUGH THE BLACK,
CUTTING THROUGH THE JUNGLE WITH
  A GOLDEN TRACK.
And the gray sky opened like a new-rent veil
And showed the Apostles with their coats of
  mail.
125 In bright white steel they were seated round
And their fire-eyes watched where the Congo
  wound.
And the twelve Apostles, from their thrones on
  high
Thrilled all the forest with their heavenly cry:—
"Mumbo-Jumbo will die in the jungle;
130 Never again will he hoo-doo you,
Never again will he hoo-doo you."

Then along that river, a thousand miles
The vine-snared trees fell down in files.
Pioneer angels cleared the way
135 For a Congo paradise, for babes at play,
For sacred capitals, for temples clean.
Gone were the skull-faced witch-men lean.
There, where the wild ghost-gods had wailed
A million boats of the angels sailed
140 With oars of silver, and prows of blue
And silken pennants that the sun shone through.
'Twas a land transfigured, 'twas a new creation.
Oh, a singing wind swept the negro nation
And on through the backwoods clearing flew:—
145 "Mumbo-Jumbo is dead in the jungle.
Never again will he hoo-doo you.
Never again will he hoo-doo you."

Redeemed were the forests, the beasts and the
  men,
And only the vulture dared again
150 By the far, lone mountains of the moon
To cry, in the silence, the Congo tune:—
"Mumbo-Jumbo will hoo-doo you,
Mumbo-Jumbo will hoo-doo you.
Mumbo . . . Jumbo . . . will . . . hoo-doo . . . you."

*Exactly as in*
*the first section.*
*Begin with*
*terror and*
*power, end*
*with joy.*

*Sung to the*
*tune of "Hark,*
*ten thousand*
*harps and*
*voices."*

*With growing*
*deliberation*
*and joy.*

*In a rather*
*high key—as*
*delicately as*
*possible.*

*To the tune of*
*"Hark, ten*
*thousand harps*
*and voices."*

*Dying down*
*into a pene-*
*trating,*
*terrified*
*whisper.*

1913

## The Child-Heart in the Mountains

On Rising Wolf Peak
Is a canyon of snow
Heart-shaped and
Strange and wild.
5   The pilgrim
Who climbs
To the canyon of snow
Returns
With the heart of a child.

*1925*

## Celestial Flowers of Glacier Park

*A Song with Hieroglyphs*

Celestial flowers spring up in Glacier Park.
Invisible to all but faithful eyes.
Those who are wise
See each flower springing with its aureole.
5   Every dawning brings one more surprise,
Shining in heaven between them and the sun,
Or nodding where the cold fountains run,
Or hovering over granite, shale, and snow,
The ghostly flowers like rainbows come and go.

I

10   These are the flowers: Lettuce for the Deer,
The Bee's Book, The Clouds Appear,
The Angel's Puff Ball, The Chipmunk's Big Salt Cellar,
A Daisy Gone Wrong, The Sparrow's Fortune Teller,
The Fountain of Feathers, Idle Hours,—
15   These are the flowers.

II

These are the flowers: The Bear's Bridal Wreath,
The Glacier's Dance, The Summer Storm's White Teeth,
The Frost's Temple, The Icicle's Dream,
Going Toward the Rainbow, Sunlight on the Stream,
20   The Mountain Carpet, The Red Ant's Towers,
These are the flowers.

III

These are the flowers: Wall Paper for the Sky,
The Eaglet, The East Wind's Eye,
The South Wind's Lady, The Amazing Dawn,
25   The West Wind, The Vision of the Fawn,
The Companion of the Fern, The Dragon-Fly Lowers,
These are the flowers.

### IV

These are the flowers: Going-to-the-Stars,°
Going-on-Vacation, The Moth's Train of Cars,
30    Going-to-the-West, Going-to-the-Snow,
Going-to-the-Honey, The Indian's Bow,
Going-to-the-Moon, The Perfumed Bowers,
These are the flowers.

### V

These are the flowers: The Flapper's Pride,
35    Ribbon for Your Hat, The Lover's Guide,
The Golden Garter, The Sheik's Plume,
Clocks for Your Stockings, Torch for the Gloom,
The Mirror of Fashion, The Crab-Apple Sours,
These are the flowers.

### VI

40    These are the flowers: Romeo's Cap,
Kisses on the Mountain-Top, Diana's Lap,
A Thought from the Waterfall, Juliet's Bed,
The Midnight Wind, The Robin's Head,
The Breasts of Pocahontas, The Shadowy Powers,
45    These are the flowers.

### VII

These are the flowers: The Sugar Candy Bun,
The Mohawk Fantasy, Singing-to-the-Sun,
Going-to-the-Stream, The Cricket from the Sea,
The Outdoor Corsage, The Baby Peach Tree,
50    Going-to-the-Winds, The June Time Showers,
These are the flowers, these are the dream flowers.

*1925*

## The Virginians Are Coming Again

*This song is to be chanted to your own unwritten
troubadour chant invented by yourself after reading
it many times yourself aloud out-of-doors.*

### I

Babbitt, your tribe is passing away.
This is the end of your infamous day.
The Virginians are coming again.

---

28 *Stars:* Going-to-the-Sun Road is the famous road that bisects Glacier National Park. It
rises to high alpine meadows.

5     With your neat little safety-vault boxes,
        With your faces like geese and foxes,
        You
        Short-legged, short-armed, short-minded men,
        Your short-sighted days are over,
        Your habits of strutting through clover,

10     Your movie-thugs, killing off souls and dreams,
        Your magazines, drying up healing streams,
        Your newspapers, blasting truth and splendor,
        Your shysters, ruining progress and glory,

15     Babbitt, your story is passing away.
        The Virginians are coming again.

        All set for the victory, calling the raid
        I see them, the next generation,
        Gentlemen, hard-riding, long-legged men,
        With horse-whip, dog-whip, gauntlet and braid,
20     Mutineers, musketeers,
        In command
        Unafraid:

        Great-grandsons of tidewater, and the bark-cabins,
        Bards of the Blue-ridge, in buckskin and boots,
25     Up from the proudest war-path we have known
        The Virginians are coming again.

        The sons of ward-heelers
        Threw out the ward-heelers,
        The sons of bartenders
30     Threw out the bartenders,
        And made our streets trick-boxes all in a day,
        Kicked out the old pests in a virtuous way.

        The new tribe sold kerosene, gasoline, paraffine.
        Babbitt sold Judas, Babbitt sold Christ,
30     Babbitt sold everything under the sun.
        The Moon-Proud consider a trader a hog.
        The Moon-Proud are coming again.

        Bartenders were gnomes,
        Foreigners, tyrants, hairy babboons.
40     But you are no better with saxophone tunes,
        Phonograph tunes, radio tunes,
        Water-power tunes, gasoline tunes, dynamo tunes,
        And pitiful souls like your pitiful tunes,
        And crawling old insolence blocking the road,

45     So, Babbitt, your racket is passing away.
        Your sons will be changelings, and burn down your world.
        Fire-eaters, troubadours, conquistadors.

Your sons will be born, refusing your load,
Thin-skinned scholars, hard-riding men,
50     Poets unharnessed, the moon their abode,
With the statesmen's code, the gentlemen's code,
With Jefferson's code, Washington's code,
With Powhatan's° code!
From your own loins, for your fearful defeat
55     The Virginians are coming again.

## II

Our first Virginians were peasants' children,
But the Power of Powhatan reddened their blood,
Up from the sod came splendor and flood.
Eating the maize made them more than men,
60     Potomac fountains made gods of men.

## III

In your tottering age, not so long from you now,
The terror will blast, the armies will whirl,
Cavalier boy beside cavalier girl!
In the glory of pride, not the pride of the rich,
65     In the glory of statesmanship, not of the ditch.
The old grand manner, lost no longer:

Exquisite art born with heart-bleeding song
Will make you die horribly raving at wrong.
You will not know your sons who are true to this soil,

70     For Babbitt° could never count much beyond ten,
For Babbitt could never quite comprehend men.
You will die in your shame, understanding not day.

Out of your loins, to your utmost confusion
The Virginians are coming again.

75     Do you think boys and girls that I pass on the street,
More strong than their fathers, more fair than their fathers,
More clean than their fathers, more wild than their fathers,
More in love than their fathers, deep in thought not their fathers',
Are meat for your schemes diabolically neat?

80     Do you think that all youth is but grist to your mill
And what you dare plan for them, boys will fulfill?
The next generation is free. You are gone.
Out of your loins, to your utmost confusion
The Virginians are coming again.

---

53 *Powhatan:* American Indian chief who founded the Powhatan Confederacy of Indian tribes in Virginia.
70 *Babbitt:* the narrow-minded, self-congratulatory businessman typified in Sinclair Lewis' 1922 novel *Babbitt.*

## IV

85     *Rouse the reader to read it right,*
       *Find a good hill by the full-moon light,*
       *Gather the boys and chant all night:—*
       *"The Virginians are coming again."*

       *Put in rhetoric, whisper and hint,*
90     *Put in shadow, murmur and glint;*
       *Jingle and jangle this song like a spur.*
       *Sweep over each tottering bridge with a whirr,*
       *Clearer and faster up main street and pike*
       *Till sparks flare up from the flints that strike.*

95     *Leap metrical ditches with bridle let loose.*
       *This song is a war, with an iron-shod use.*

       *Let no musician, with blotter and pad*
       *Scribble his pot-hooks to make the song sad.*
       *Find*
100    *Your own rhythms*
       *When Robert E. Lee°*
       *Gallops once more to the plain from the sea.*
       *Give the rebel yell every river they gain.*

       *Hear Lee's light cavalry rhyme with rain.*
105    *In the star-proud, natural fury of men*
       *The Virginians are coming again.*

                                                        *1928*

---

101 *Lee:* Robert E. Lee (1807–1870) American soldier, one of the greatest of the confeder-
ate generals in the American Civil War.

# Wallace Stevens (1879–1955)

Had Wallace Stevens not existed—a lifelong insurance executive writing some of his country's most insistently metaphysical poetry—it would hardly have been plausible to invent him. Yet Stevens had actually committed himself to writing poetry before taking a position with the Hartford Accident and Indemnity Company; the job was a way to earn a living. He was born and grew up in Reading, Pennsylvania, and was educated at Harvard and at the New York University Law School. He began publishing poems in magazines in 1914, but his first book, *Harmonium*, did not appear until 1923.

The book was organized to open with a number of his short, exquisite lyrics, rather than with the longer and more abstract poems that have become the focus of extended critical analysis. We follow the same strategy here, taking the liberty of using lyrics from both the first and second (1931) edition of *Harmonium* to introduce readers to his work and lead up to longer poems like "Sunday Morning." Although Stevens lived and worked in Connecticut, a number of his poems drew on the Florida landscape he saw on regular business trips. Indeed the sheer riotous excess and profusion of Florida's flora and fauna often gave him a perfect analogue for the mental life he used nature to evoke. The poems are thus at once referential and devoted to elaborate rhetorical invention that creates a world of its own. In comments in letters that are less than fully trustworthy or definitive, Stevens sometimes denied the poems this double life, but readers should judge for themselves.

The poems are so captivating in their rhetorical inventiveness—the play of words deployed for their sound, the almost palimpsestic thickness of imagery, the wit—that one can easily miss Stevens' regular (if abstract) engagement with the issues of his day, but it is nonetheless a continual feature of his work. Debates both with the world of public events and between contrasting philosophical or cultural positions occur throughout the poems. In "Sunday Morning" a woman wonders whether her sensual pleasures amount to a belief system comparable to Christianity's obsession with mortality.

To some degree, such philosophical issues crowd out the sensuous surfaces and the rich music in his later poems. Some critics also find many of the late lyrics too similar to one another. Yet their obsessive circling around related themes of emptiness is a large part of their interest. They form a single, driven project that anticipates postmodern work like W.S. Merwin's poetry of Vietnam war despair.

# Sea Surface Full of Clouds

## I

In that November off Tehuantepec,°
The slopping of the sea grew still one night
And in the morning summer hued the deck

5    And made one think of rosy chocolate
And gilt umbrellas. Paradisal green
Gave suavity to the perplexed machine

Of ocean, which like limpid water lay.
Who, then, in that ambrosial latitude
Out of the light evolved the moving blooms,

10   Who, then, evolved the sea-blooms from the clouds
Diffusing balm in that Pacific calm?
*C'était mon enfant, mon bijou, mon âme.*°

The sea-clouds whitened far below the calm
And moved, as blooms move, in the swimming green
15   And in its watery radiance, while the hue

Of heaven in an antique reflection rolled
Round those flotillas. And sometimes the sea
Poured brilliant iris on the glistening blue.

## II

In that November off Tehuantepec
20   The slopping of the sea grew still one night.
At breakfast jelly yellow streaked the deck

And made one think of chop-house chocolate
And sham umbrellas. And a sham-like green
Capped summer-seeming on the tense machine

25   Of ocean, which in sinister flatness lay.
Who, then, beheld the rising of the clouds
That strode submerged in that malevolent sheen,

Who saw the mortal massives of the blooms
Of water moving on the water-floor?
30   *C'était mon frère du ciel, ma vie, mon or.*°

---

1 *Tehuantepec:* the Gulf of Tehuantepec is by an isthmus that forms the narrowest part of Mexico. The poem memorializes a cruise that Stevens took with his wife, Elsie, in October–November 1923, when they sailed from New York to California via the Panama Canal. It was the single extended holiday the Stevenses had taken together since their marriage fourteen years earlier. The following August their child Holly was born, about nine months after "that November off Tehuantepec."
12 . . . *mon âme:* (French) That was my child, my jewel (also a term of endearment: pretty baby), my soul.
30 . . . *mon or:* (French) That was my sky-brother (like a divine other self), my life, my treasure.

The gongs rang loudly as the windy booms
Hoo-hooed it in the darkened ocean-blooms.
The gongs grew still. And then blue heaven spread

Its crystalline pendentives on the sea
35       And the macabre of the water-glooms
In an enormous undulation fled.

### III

In that November off Tehuantepec,
The slopping of the sea grew still one night
And a pale silver patterned on the deck

40       And made one think of porcelain chocolate
And pied umbrellas. An uncertain green,
Piano-polished, held the tranced machine

Of ocean, as a prelude holds and holds.
Who, seeing silver petals of white blooms
45       Unfolding in the water, feeling sure

Of the milk within the saltiest spurge, heard, then,
The sea unfolding in the sunken clouds?
Oh! *C'était mon extase et mon amour.*°

So deeply sunken were they that the shrouds,
50       The shrouding shadows, made the petals black
Until the rolling heaven made them blue,

A blue beyond the rainy hyacinth,
And smiting the crevasses of the leaves
Deluged the ocean with a sapphire blue.

### IV

55       In that November off Tehuantepec
The night-long slopping of the sea grew still.
A mallow morning dozed upon the deck

And made one think of musky chocolate
And frail umbrellas. A too-fluent green
60       Suggested malice in the dry machine

Of ocean, pondering dank stratagem.
Who then beheld the figures of the clouds
Like blooms secluded in the thick marine?

Like blooms? Like damasks that were shaken off
65       From the loosed girdles in the spangling must.
*C'était ma foi, la nonchalance divine.*°

---

48 . . . *mon amour:* (French) That was my ecstasy and my love.
66 . . . *divine:* (French) That was my faith, my divine nonchalance.

The nakedness would rise and suddenly turn
Salt masks of beard and mouths of bellowing,
Would—But more suddenly the heaven rolled

70    Its bluest sea-clouds in the thinking green,
And the nakedness became the broadest blooms,
Mile-mallows that a mallow sun cajoled.

V

In that November off Tekuantepec
Night stilled the slopping of the sea. The day
75    Came, bowing and voluble, upon the deck,

Good clown. . . . One thought of Chinese chocolate
And large umbrellas. And a motley green
Followed the drift of the obese machine

Of ocean, perfected in indolence.
80    What pistache one, ingenious and droll,
Beheld the sovereign clouds as jugglery

And the sea as turquoise-turbaned Sambo, neat
At tossing saucers—cloudy-conjuring sea?
*C'était mon esprit bâtard, l'ignominie.*°

85    The sovereign clouds came clustering. The conch
Of loyal conjuration trumped. The wind
Of green blooms turning crisped the motley hue

To clearing opalescence. Then the sea
And heaven rolled as one and from the two
Came fresh transfigurings of freshest blue.

*1924*

## Thirteen Ways of Looking at a Blackbird

I

Among twenty snowy mountains,
The only moving thing
Was the eye of the blackbird.

II

I was of three minds,
5    Like a tree
In which there are three blackbirds.

---

84 . . . *l'ignominie:* (French) That was my bastard spirit, shame.

### III

The blackbird whirled in the autumn winds.
It was a small part of the pantomime.

### IV

A man and a woman
10      Are one.
A man and a woman and a blackbird
Are one.

### V

I do not know which to prefer,
The beauty of inflections
15      Or the beauty of innuendoes,
The blackbird whistling
Or just after.

### VI

Icicles filled the long window
With barbaric glass.
20      The shadow of the blackbird
Crossed it, to and fro.
The mood
Traced in the shadow
An indecipherable cause.

### VII

25      O thin men of Haddam,°
Why do you imagine golden birds?
Do you not see how the blackbird
Walks around the feet
Of the women about you?

### VIII

30      I know noble accents
And lucid, inescapable rhythms;
But I know, too,
That the blackbird is involved
In what I know.

### IX

35      When the blackbird flew out of sight,
It marked the edge
Of one of many circles.

---

25 *Haddam*: town in Connecticut.

## X

At the sight of blackbirds
Flying in a green light,
40   Even the bawds of euphony
Would cry out sharply.

## XI

He rode over Connecticut
In a glass coach.
Once, a fear pierced him,
45   In that he mistook
The shadow of his equipage
For blackbirds.

## XII

The river is moving.
The blackbird must be flying.

## XIII

50   It was evening all afternoon.
It was snowing
And it was going to snow.
The blackbird sat
In the cedar-limbs.

*1917*

# Tea at the Palaz of Hoon

Not less because in purple I descended
The western day through what you called
The loneliest air, not less was I myself.

What was the ointment sprinkled on my beard?
5   What were the hymns that buzzed beside my ears?
What was the sea whose tide swept through me there?

Out of my mind the golden ointment rained,
And my ears made the blowing hymns they heard.
I was myself the compass of that sea:

10   I was the world in which I walked, and what I saw
Or heard or felt came not but from myself;
And there I found myself more truly and more strange.

*1921*

## Floral Decorations for Bananas

Well, nuncle, this plainly won't do.
These insolent, linear peels
And sullen, hurricane shapes

Won't do with your eglantine.
5   They require something serpentine.
Blunt yellow in such a room!

You should have had plums tonight,
In an eighteenth-century dish,
And pettifogging buds,
10  For the women of primrose and purl,
Each one in her decent curl.
Good God! What a precious light!

But bananas hacked and hunched . . .
The table was set by an ogre,
15  His eye on an outdoor gloom
And a stiff and noxious place.
Pile the bananas on planks.
The women will be all shanks
And bangles and slatted eyes.

20  And deck the bananas in leaves
Plucked from the Carib trees,
Fibrous and dangling down,
Oozing cantankerous gum
Out of their purple maws,
25  Darting out of their purple craws
Their musky and tingling tongues.

1922

## Anecdote of the Jar

I placed a jar in Tennessee,
And round it was, upon a hill.
It made the slovenly wilderness
Surround that hill.

5   The wilderness rose up to it,
And sprawled around, no longer wild.
The jar was round upon the ground
And tall and of a port in air.

It took dominion everywhere.
10  The jar was gray and bare.
It did not give of bird or bush,
Like nothing else in Tennessee.

1919

## Disillusionment of Ten O'clock

The houses are haunted
By white night-gowns.
None are green,
Or purple with green rings,
5      Or green with yellow rings,
Or yellow with blue rings.
None of them are strange,
With socks of lace
And beaded ceintures.°
10    People are not going
To dream of baboons and periwinkles.
Only, here and there, an old sailor,
Drunk and asleep in his boots,
Catches tigers
In red weather.

1915

## A High-Toned Old Christian Woman

Poetry is the supreme fiction, madame.
Take the moral law and make a nave of it
And from the nave build haunted heaven. Thus,
The conscience is converted into palms,
5     Like windy citherns° hankering for hymns.
We agree in principle. That's clear. But take
The opposing law and make a peristyle,°
And from the peristyle project a masque
Beyond the planets. Thus, our bawdiness,
10    Unpurged by epitaph, indulged at last,
Is equally converted into palms,
Squiggling like saxophones. And palm for palm,
Madame, we are where we began. Allow,
Therefore, that in the planetary scene
15    Your disaffected flagellants,° well-stuffed,
Smacking their muzzy bellies in parade,
Proud of such novelties of the sublime,
Such tink and tank and tunk-a-tunk-tunk,
May, merely may, madame, whip from themselves
20    A jovial hullabaloo among the spheres.
This will make widows wince. But fictive things
Wink as they will. Wink most when widows wince.

1922

---

9 *ceintures*: belts.
5 *citherns*: (also cittern), a sixteenth-century guitar with a flat, pear-shaped body.
7 *peristyle*: either an architectural space enclosed by columns or a roof supported by them.
15 *flagellants*: people who whip themselves as part of their religious discipline.

# The Snow Man

One must have a mind of winter
To regard the frost and the boughs
Of the pine-trees crusted with snow;

And have been cold a long time
5      To behold the junipers shagged with ice,
The spruces rough in the distant glitter

Of the January sun; and not to think
Of any misery in the sound of the wind,
In the sound of a few leaves,

10     Which is the sound of the land
Full of the same wind
That is blowing in the same bare place

For the listener, who listens in the snow,
And, nothing himself, beholds
Nothing that is not there and the nothing that is.

                                                                        *1921*


# The Emperor of Ice-Cream

Call the roller of big cigars,
The muscular one, and bid him whip
In kitchen cups concupiscent curds.
Let the wenches dawdle in such dress
5      As they are used to wear, and let the boys
Bring flowers in last month's newspapers.
Let be be finale of seem.
The only emperor is the emperor of ice-cream.

Take from the dresser of deal.°
10     Lacking the three glass knobs, that sheet
On which she embroidered fantails° once
And spread it so as to cover her face.
If her horny feet protrude, they come
To show how cold she is, and dumb.
15     Let the lamp affix its beam.
The only emperor is the emperor of ice-cream.

                                                                        *1922*

---

9 *deal*: cheap wood.
11 *fantails*: fantail pigeons.

# Peter Quince at the Clavier°

## I

Just as my fingers on these keys
Make music, so the selfsame sounds
On my spirit make a music, too.

Music is feeling, then, not sound;
5      And thus it is that what I feel,
Here in this room, desiring you,

Thinking of your blue-shadowed silk,
Is music. It is like the strain
Waked in the elders by Susanna.°

10      Of a green evening, clear and warm,
She bathed in her still garden, while
The red-eyed elders watching, felt

The basses of their beings throb
In witching chords, and their thin blood
15      Pulse pizzicati° of Hosanna.°

## II

In the green water, clear and warm,
Susanna lay.
She searched
The touch of springs,
20      And found
Concealed imaginings.
She sighed,
For so much melody.

Upon the bank, she stood
25      In the cool
Of spent emotions.
She felt, among the leaves,
The dew
Of old devotions.

---

**poem title:** Peter Quince appears in Shakespeare's *A Midsummer Nights Dream* as one of the primitive actors who perform a "tragedy." *clavier:* an early form of piano; also, the keyboard of a stringed instrument, including the piano and the harpsichord.
9 *Susanna:* in Daniel 13 in the Apocrapha, Susanna is falsely accused of an illicit relationship with a young man after she refuses the advances of two elders; Daniel prevents her from being punished.
15 *pizzicati:* notes produced by plucking a stringed instrument.
15 *Hosanna:* a cry expressing praise or adoration of God.

30      She walked upon the grass,
        Still quavering.
        The winds were like her maids,
        On timid feet,
        Fetching her woven scarves,
35      Yet wavering.

        A breath upon her hand
        Muted the night.
        She turned—
        A cymbal crashed,
40      And roaring horns.

### III

        Soon, with a noise like tambourines,
        Came her attendant Byzantines.°

        They wondered why Susanna cried
        Against the elders by her side;

45      And as they whispered, the refrain
        Was like a willow swept by rain.

        Anon, their lamps' uplifted flame
        Revealed Susanna and her shame.

        And then, the simpering Byzantines
50      Fled, with a noise like tambourines.

### IV

        Beauty is momentary in the mind—
        The fitful tracing of a portal;
        But in the flesh it is immortal.
        The body dies; the body's beauty lives.
55      So evenings die, in their green going,
        A wave, interminably flowing.
        So gardens die, their meek breath scenting
        The cowl of winter, done repenting.
        So maidens die, to the auroral
60      Celebration of a maiden's choral.
        Susanna's music touched the bawdy strings
        Of those white elders; but, escaping,
        Left only Death's ironic scraping.
        Now, in its immortality, it plays
65      On the clear viol of her memory,
        And makes a constant sacrament of praise.

                                        *1915*

---

42 *Byzantines*: natives of Byzantium, an ancient city on the site of present-day Istanbul, Turkey.

# Sunday Morning

## I

Complacencies of the peignoir, and late
Coffee and oranges in a sunny chair,
And the green freedom of a cockatoo
Upon a rug mingle to dissipate
5    The holy hush of ancient sacrifice.
She dreams a little, and she feels the dark
Encroachment of that old catastrophe,
As a calm darkens among water-lights.
The pungent oranges and bright, green wings
10   Seem things in some procession of the dead,
Winding across wide water, without sound.
The day is like wide water, without sound,
Stilled for the passing of her dreaming feet
Over the seas, to silent Palestine,
15   Dominion of the blood and sepulchre.°

## II

Why should she give her bounty to the dead?
What is divinity if it can come
Only in silent shadows and in dreams?
Shall she not find in comforts of the sun,
20   In pungent fruit and bright, green wings, or else
In any balm or beauty of the earth,
Things to be cherished like the thought of heaven?
Divinity must live within herself:
Passions of rain, or moods in falling snow;
25   Grievings in loneliness, or unsubdued
Elations when the forest blooms; gusty
Emotions on wet roads on autumn nights;
All pleasures and all pains, remembering
The bough of summer and the winter branch.
30   These are the measures destined for her soul.

## III

Jove° in the clouds had his inhuman birth.
No mother suckled him, no sweet land gave
Large-mannered motions to his mythy mind
He moved among us, as a muttering king,
35   Magnificent, would move among his hinds,°
Until our blood, commingling, virginal,
With heaven, brought such requital to desire

---

15 *sepulchre*: as in the holy sepulcher, the Jerusalem cave in which Jesus was entombed; the bloody medieval crusades sought to gain control over such holy sites.
31 *Jove*: according to Roman myth, Jupiter, the supreme god.
35 *hinds*: farm hands, but perhaps the line also alludes to the shepherds who saw the star of Bethlehem, which marked the birth of Jesus.

The very hinds discerned it, in a star.
Shall our blood fail? Or shall it come to be
40    The blood of paradise? And shall the earth
Seem all of paradise that we shall know?
The sky will be much friendlier then than now,
A part of labor and a part of pain,
And next in glory to enduring love,
45    Not this dividing and indifferent blue.

### IV

She says, "I am content when wakened birds,
Before they fly, test the reality
Of misty fields, by their sweet questionings;
But when the birds are gone, and their warm fields
50    Return no more, where, then, is paradise?"
There is not any haunt of prophecy,
Nor any old chimera° of the grave,
Neither the golden underground,° nor isle
Melodious, where spirits gat them home,
55    Nor visionary south, nor cloudy palm
Remote on heaven's hill, that has endured
As April's green endures; or will endure
Like her remembrance of awakened birds,
Or her desire for June and evening, tipped
60    By the consummation of the swallow's wings.

### V

She says, "But in contentment I still feel
The need of some imperishable bliss."
Death is the mother of beauty; hence from her,
Alone, shall come fulfilment to our dreams
65    And our desires. Although she strews the leaves
Of sure obliteration on our paths,
The path sick sorrow took, the many paths
Where triumph rang its brassy phrase, or love
Whispered a little out of tenderness,
70    She makes the willow shiver in the sun
For maidens who were wont to sit and gaze
Upon the grass, relinquished to their feet.
She causes boys to pile new plums and pears
On disregarded plate.° The maidens taste
75    And stray impassioned in the littering leaves.

---

52 *chimera*: in Greek myth, a fire-breathing monster; also a hallucination.
53 *golden underground*: in Greek myth, Elysium, resting place of the virtuous.
74 *plate*: Stevens' note: "plate is used in the sense of so-called family plate. Disregarded refers to the disuse into which things fall that have been possessed for a long time. I mean, therefore, that death releases and renews. What the old have come to disregard, the young inherit and make use of" (*Letters*).

## VI

Is there no change of death in paradise?
Does ripe fruit never fall? Or do the boughs
Hang always heavy in that perfect sky,
Unchanging, yet so like our perishing earth,
80     With rivers like our own that seek for seas
They never find, the same receding shores
That never touch with inarticulate pang?
Why set the pear upon those river-banks
Or spice the shores with odors of the plum?
85     Alas, that they should wear our colors there,
The silken weavings of our afternoons,
And pick the strings of our insipid lutes!
Death is the mother of beauty, mystical,
Within whose burning bosom we devise
90     Our earthly mothers waiting, sleeplessly.

## VII

Supple and turbulent, a ring of men
Shall chant in orgy on a summer morn
Their boisterous devotion to the sun,
Not as a god, but as a god might be,
95     Naked among them, like a savage source.
Their chant shall be a chant of paradise,
Out of their blood, returning to the sky;
And in their chant shall enter, voice by voice,
The windy lake wherein their lord delights,
100    The trees, like serafin,° and echoing hills,
That choir among themselves long afterward.
They shall know well the heavenly fellowship
Of men that perish and of summer morn.
And whence they came and whither they shall go
105    The dew upon their feet shall manifest.°

## VIII

She hears, upon that water without sound,
A voice that cries, "The tomb in Palestine
Is not the porch of spirits lingering.
It is the grave of Jesus, where he lay."
110    We live in an old chaos of the sun,
Or old dependency of day and night,
Or island solitude, unsponsored, free,
Of that wide water, inescapable.
Deer walk upon our mountains, and the quail
115    Whistle about us their spontaneous cries;

---

100 *serafin*: seraphim, the highest order of angels.
105 *manifest*: Stevens' note: "Life is as fugitive as dew upon the feet of men dancing in dew. Men do not either come from any direction or disappear in any direction. Life is as meaningless as dew. Now these ideas are not bad in a poem. But they are a frightful bore when converted as above" (*Letters*).

Sweet berries ripen in the wilderness;
And, in the isolation of the sky,
At evening, casual flocks of pigeons make
Ambiguous undulations as they sink,
120        Downward to darkness, on extended wings.

                                                        *1915*


## The Death of a Soldier

Life contracts and death is expected,
As in a season of autumn.
The soldier falls.

He does not become a three-days personage,
5        Imposing his separation,
Calling for pomp.

Death is absolute and without memorial,
As in a season of autumn,
When the wind stops,

10        When the wind stops and, over the heavens,
The clouds go, nevertheless,
In their direction.

                                                        *1918*


## The Idea of Order at Key West

She sang beyond the genius of the sea.
The water never formed to mind or voice,
Like a body wholly body, fluttering
Its empty sleeves; and yet its mimic motion
5        Made constant cry, caused constantly a cry,
That was not ours although we understood,
Inhuman, of the veritable ocean.

The sea was not a mask. No more was she.
The song and water were not medleyed sound
10        Even if what she sang was what she heard,
Since what she sang was uttered word by word.
It may be that in all her phrases stirred
The grinding water and the gasping wind;
But it was she and not the sea we heard.

15        For she was the maker of the song she sang.
The ever-hooded, tragic-gestured sea
Was merely a place by which she walked to sing.
Whose spirit is this? we said, because we knew
It was the spirit that we sought and knew
20        That we should ask this often as she sang.

If it was only the dark voice of the sea
That rose, or even colored by many waves;
If it was only the outer voice of sky
And cloud, of the sunken coral water-walled,
25    However clear, it would have been deep air,
The heaving speech of air, a summer sound
Repeated in a summer without end
And sound alone. But it was more than that,
More even than her voice, and ours, among
30    The meaningless plungings of water and the wind,
Theatrical distances, bronze shadows heaped
On high horizons, mountainous atmospheres
Of sky and sea.
                        It was her voice that made
35    The sky acutest at its vanishing.
She measured to the hour its solitude.
She was the single artificer of the world
In which she sang. And when she sang, the sea,
Whatever self it had, became the self
40    That was her song, for she was the maker. Then we,
As we beheld her striding there alone,
Knew that there never was a world for her
Except the one she sang and, singing, made.

Ramon Fernandez,° tell me, if you know,
45    Why, when the singing ended and we turned
Toward the town, tell why the glassy lights,
The lights in the fishing boats at anchor there,
As the night descended, tilting in the air,
Mastered the night and portioned out the sea,
50    Fixing emblazoned zones and fiery poles,
Arranging, deepening, enchanting night.

Oh! Blessed rage for order, pale Ramon,
The maker's rage to order words of the sea,
Words of the fragrant portals, dimly-starred,
55    And of ourselves and of our origins,
In ghostlier demarcations, keener sounds.

*1934*

## Mozart, 1935

Poet, be seated at the piano.
Play the present, its hoo-hoo-hoo,
Its shoo-shoo-shoo, its ric-a-nic,
Its envious cachinnation.°

---

44 *Fernandez*: a French literary critic (1894–1944), but Stevens repeatedly denied that he
was thinking of any real person and had just picked names at random.
4 *cachinnation*: loud laughter.

5      If they throw stones upon the roof
       While you practice arpeggios,
       It is because they carry down the stairs
       A body in rags.
       Be seated at the piano.

10     That lucid souvenir of the past,
       The divertimento;
       That airy dream of the future,
       The unclouded concerto . . .
       The snow is falling.
15     Strike the piercing chord.

       Be thou the voice,
       Not you. Be thou, be thou
       The voice of angry fear,
       The voice of this besieging pain.

20     Be thou that wintry sound
       As of the great wind howling,
       By which sorrow is released,
       Dismissed, absolved
       In a starry placating.

25     We may return to Mozart.
       He was young, and we, we are old.
       The snow is falling
       And the streets are full of cries.
       Be seated, thou.

                                                    *1935*

## A Postcard from the Volcano

       Children picking up our bones
       Will never know that these were once
       As quick as foxes on the hill;

       And that in autumn, when the grapes
5      Made sharp air sharper by their smell
       These had a being, breathing frost;

       And least will guess that with our bones
       We left much more, left what still is
       The look of things, left what we felt

10     At what we saw. The spring clouds blow
       Above the shuttered mansion-house,
       Beyond our gate and the windy sky

       Cries out a literate despair.
       We knew for long the mansion's look
15     And what we said of it became

A part of what it is . . . Children,
Still weaving budded aureoles,°
Will speak our speech and never know,

Will say of the mansion that it seems
20      As if he that lived there left behind
A spirit storming in blank walls,

A dirty house in a gutted world,
A tatter of shadows peaked to white,
Smeared with the gold of the opulent sun.

1936

## Study of Two Pears

### I

Opusculum paedagogum.°
The pears are not viols,°
Nudes or bottles.
They resemble nothing else.

### II

5       They are yellow forms
Composed of curves
Bulging toward the base.
They are touched red.

### III

They are not flat surfaces
10      Having curved outlines.
They are round
Tapering toward the top.

### IV

In the way they are modelled
There are bits of blue.
15      A hard dry leaf hangs
From the stem.

### V

The yellow glistens.
It glistens with various yellows,

---

17 *aureoles*: halos.
1 *Opusculum paedagogum*: (Latin), a small opus for study.
2 *viols*: fiddles.

20          Citrons, oranges and greens
            Flowering over the skin.

                         VI

            The shadows of the pears
            Are blobs on the green cloth.
            The pears are not seen
            As the observer wills.

                                                    *1938*


## Of Modern Poetry

            The poem of the mind in the act of finding
            What will suffice. It has not always had
            To find: the scene was set; it repeated what
            Was in the script.
5                          Then the theatre was changed
            To something else. Its past was a souvenir.
            It has to be living, to learn the speech of the place.
            It has to face the men of the time and to meet
            The women of the time. It has to think about war
10          And it has to find what will suffice. It has
            To construct a new stage. It has to be on that stage
            And, like an insatiable actor, slowly and
            With meditation, speak words that in the ear,
            In the delicatest ear of the mind, repeat,
15          Exactly, that which it wants to hear, at the sound
            Of which, an invisible audience listens,
            Not to the play, but to itself, expressed
            In an emotion as of two people, as of two
            Emotions becoming one. The actor is
20          A metaphysician in the dark, twanging
            An instrument, twanging a wiry string that gives
            Sounds passing through sudden rightnesses, wholly
            Containing the mind, below which it cannot descend,
            Beyond which it has no will to rise.
25                                         It must
            Be the finding of a satisfaction, and may
            Be of a man skating, a woman dancing, a woman
            Combing. The poem of the act of the mind.

                                                    *1940*


## The Course of a Particular

            Today the leaves cry, hanging on branches swept by wind,
            Yet the nothingness of winter becomes a little less.
            It is still full of icy shades and shapen snow.

            The leaves cry . . . One holds off and merely hears the cry.
5           It is a busy cry, concerning someone else.
            And though one says that one is part of everything,

There is a conflict, there is a resistance involved;
And being part is an exertion that declines:
One feels the life of that which gives life as it is.

10      The leaves cry. It is not a cry of divine attention,
Nor the smoke-drift of puffed-out heroes, nor human cry.
It is the cry of leaves that do not transcend themselves,

In the absence of fantasia, without meaning more
Than they are in the final finding of the ear, in the thing
Itself, until, at last, the cry concerns no one at all.

*1950*

## The Plain Sense of Things

After the leaves have fallen, we return
To a plain sense of things. It is as if
We had come to an end of the imagination,
Inanimate in an inert savoir.°

5      It is difficult even to choose the adjective
For this blank cold, this sadness without cause.
The great structure has become a minor house.
No turban walks across the lessened floors.

The greenhouse never so badly needed paint.
10     The chimney is fifty years old and slants to one side.
A fantastic effort has failed, a repetition
In a repetitiousness of men and flies.

Yet the absence of the imagination had
Itself to be imagined. The great pond,
15     The plain sense of it, without reflections, leaves,
Mud, water like dirty glass, expressing silence

Of a sort, silence of a rat come out to see,
The great pond and its waste of the lilies, all this
Had to be imagined as an inevitable knowledge,
Required, as a necessity requires.

*1952*

## As You Leave the Room

*You speak. You say*: Today's character is not
A skeleton out of its cabinet. Nor am I.

That poem about the pineapple, the one
About the mind as never satisfied,

5     The one about the credible hero, the one
About summer, are not what skeletons think about.

---

4 *savoir*: knowledge.

I wonder, have I lived a skeleton's life,
As a disbeliever in reality,

A countryman of all the bones in the world?
10        Now, here, the snow I had forgotten becomes

Part of a major reality, part of
An appreciation of a reality

And thus an elevation, as if I left
With something I could touch, touch every way.

15        And yet nothing has been changed except what is
Unreal, as if nothing had been changed at all.

*1954*


## A Clear Day and No Memories

No soldiers in the scenery,
No thoughts of people now dead,
As they were fifty years ago:
Young and living in a live air,
5        Young and walking in the sunshine,
Bending in blue dresses to touch something—
Today the mind is not part of the weather.

Today the air is clear of everything.
It has no knowledge except of nothingness
10        And it flows over us without meanings,
As if none of us had ever been here before
And are not now: in this shallow spectacle,
This invisible activity, this sense.

*1954*


## Of Mere Being

The palm at the end of the mind,
Beyond the last thought, rises
In the bronze decor,

A gold-feathered bird
15        Sings in the palm, without human meaning,
Without human feeling, a foreign song.

You know then that it is not the reason
That makes us happy or unhappy.
The bird sings. Its feathers shine.

10        The palm stands on the edge of space.
The wind moves slowly in the branches.
The bird's fire-fangled feathers dangle down.

*1955*

# Angelina Weld Grimké (1880–1958)

Grimké's troubled family history almost willfully theatricalizes key themes of America's racial history. Her father, Archibald, was the child of a South Carolina slaveholder and a slave on his plantation. Her great aunts on her father's side were southern white abolitionists. Grimké's father married a white Bostonian, but the marriage disintegrated soon after Angelina's birth, and she never saw her mother again. She was educated at Cushing and Carleton academies and became interested in dramatizing the country's racial conflicts. A successful 1916 play, *Rachel*, was her first major work, after which she published a small number of distinctive and haunting lyrics in several Harlem Renaissance anthologies, including love poems addressed to other women. She was something of a recluse after 1930. "Fragment" was an untitled manuscript in her papers. Also see *Selected Works of Angelina Weld Grimké* (1993).

## The Black Finger

I have just seen a most beautiful thing:
Slim and still,
Against a gold, gold sky,
A straight, black cypress
Sensitive
Exquisite
A black finger
Pointing upwards.
Why, beautiful still finger, are you black?
And why are you pointing upwards?

5

10

1923

## Tenebris°

There is a tree by day
That at night
Has a shadow,
A hand huge and black,
With fingers long and black.
 All through the dark,
Against the white man's house,
 In the little wind,

5

---

**poem title:** (Latin) in darkness.

The black hand plucks and plucks
10        At the bricks.
The bricks are the color of blood and very small.
    Is it a black hand,
    Or is it a shadow?

1927

# A Mona Lisa

### I.

I should like to creep
Through the long brown grasses
    That are your lashes;
I should like to poise
5        On the very brink
Of the leaf-brown pools
    That are your shadowed eyes;
I should like to cleave
    Without sound,
10   Their glimmering waters,
    Their unrippled waters;
I should like to sink down
    And down
        And down . . .
15            And deeply drown.

### II.

Would I be more than a bubble breaking?
    Or an ever-widening circle
    Ceasing at the marge?
Would my white bones
20        Be the only white bones
Wavering back and forth, back and forth
    In their depths?

1927

# Fragment

I am the woman with the black black skin
I am the laughing woman with the black black face
I am living in the cellars and in every crowded place
    I am toiling just to eat
    In the cold and in the heat
        And I laugh
I am the laughing woman who's forgotten how to weep
I am the laughing woman who's afraid to go to sleep

*c. 1930*

# Georgia Douglas Johnson (1880–1966)

Born in Atlanta, Georgia, Johnson spent much of her adult life at 1461 S Street NW in Washington, D.C., which she turned into one of the most famous literary salons of the 1920s. She moved to Washington with her husband after graduating from Atlanta University, but he died in 1925, after which she struggled to earn enough to support herself and her children. She became the most celebrated female poet of the Harlem Renaissance, publishing stories, writing plays, issuing a newspaper column, and publishing four books of poetry. In the midst of the Great Depression, this prolific writer lost her job at the Labor Department, and then had to survive on temporary positions. Her time to write was thus cut back still further. A number of her unpublished stories and plays have never been recovered.

## The Heart of a Woman

The heart of a woman goes forth with the dawn
As a lone bird, soft winging, so restlessly on;
Afar o'er life's turrets and vales does it roam
In the wake of those echoes the heart calls home.

5  The heart of a woman falls back with the night,
And enters some alien cage in its plight,
And tires to forget it has dreamed of the stars
While it breaks, breaks, breaks on the sheltering bars.

*1918*

## Common Dust

And who shall separate the dust
What later we shall be:
Whose keen discerning eye will scan
And solve the mystery?

5  The high, the low, the rich, the poor,
The black, the white, the red,
And all the chromatique between,
Of whom shall it be said:

Here lies the dust of Africa;
10    Here are the sons of Rome;
Here lies the one unlabelled,
The world at large his home!

Can one then separate the dust?
Will mankind lie apart,
15    When life has settled back again
The same as from the start?

1922

## Motherhood

Don't knock on my door, little child,
I cannot let you in;
You know not what a world this is
Of cruelty and sin
5    Wait in the still eternity
Until I come to you,
The world is cruel, cruel, child,
I cannot let you through.

Don't knock at my heart, little one,
10    I cannot bear the pain
Of turning deaf ears to your call,
Time and time again.
You do not know the monster men
Inhabiting the earth.
15    Be still, be still, my precious child,
I cannot give you birth.

1922

# Mina Loy (1882–1966)

Born in England, Loy studied art in Germany, France, and Britain, and continued to paint thereafter. She moved to Florence and became deeply involved with the futurist movement, though she gave its politics and cultural ambitions a feminist inflection, as her 1919 "Aphorisms on Futurism" suggests. Eventually she abandoned the movement as its patriarchal bias evolved into an emergent sympathy for fascism. Although she did not move permanently to the United States until 1936—first living in New York and then in Aspen, Colorado—and take up U.S. citizenship until late in her life, her work is often considered part of American modernism because some of her most important work was written while she was here for several years in the second decade of the century and because it was often American journals that published and championed her poetry.

In her "Feminist Manifesto," unpublished but probably written shortly before the 1915–1917 "Songs to Joannes," Loy argues that "woman must destroy in herself the desire to be loved" and urges that "honor, grief, sentimentality, pride and consequently jealousy must be detached from sex." The "Songs" accomplish that and more. Loy concludes that all the values embedded in masculinity and femininity are perilous and destructive. Idealization of female purity and virtue, for example, is "the principle instrument of her subjugation."

The "Songs" display only elliptical and minimalist vestiges of narrative. As it begins, the speaker has already failed at conventional romance—steeped in all the drama of stereotyped emotions—and opts instead not for unreflective animal sexuality but for something like a verbally inventive biological union. The sequence repeatedly offers up the illusory dramas of gender ("I am the jealous store-house of the candle-ends / That lit your adolescent learning") only to reject them; repeatedly, in their place, Loy offers us versions of intercourse that invent figures for bodily fluids and anatomy: "laughing honey," "spermatozoa . . . in the milk of the Moon," "Shuttle-cock and battle-door." Some critics have concluded that these are images of degraded lust; they seem instead to be antiromantic but celebratory. Moreover, their variety and surprising capacity to recode the rhetoric of romance ("honey," "the milk of the Moon," "pink-love," and "feathers" above all reposition romance tropes) demonstrate that a degendered human sexuality—one freed of cultural clichés about men and women—need not be impoverished. Published in the American journal *Others*, "Songs to Joannes" is a major contribution to experimental modernism. Readers interested in Loy should be sure to consult *The Lost Lunar Baedeker* (1996), which is the only accurate edition of her poems.

# Songs to Joannes°

## I

Spawn   of   Fantasies
Silting the appraisable
Pig Cupid°   his rosy snout
Rooting erotic garbage
5      "Once upon a time"
Pulls a weed   white star-topped
Among wild oats   sown in mucous-membrane

I would   an   eye in a Bengal light°
Eternity in a sky-rocket°
10      Constellations in an ocean
Whose rivers run no fresher
Than a trickle of saliva

These   are suspect places

I must live in my lantern
15      Trimming subliminal flicker
Virginal   to the bellows
Of Experience
               Coloured   glass

## II

        The skin-sack°
20      In which a wanton duality
Packed
All the completion of my infructuous° impulses
Something the shape of a man
To the casual vulgarity of the merely observant
25      More of a clock-work mechanism
Running down against time
To which I am not paced
       My finger-tips are numb from fretting your hair
A God's door-mat°
30                On the threshold of your mind

---

**poem title:** "Joannes" simultaneously identifies and disguises the name of Giovanni Papini (1881–1956), the Italian writer with whom Loy had a difficult relationship, but memories of other lovers are no doubt woven into the dedication as well.

3 *Cupid:* the Roman god of love, depicted as a naked winged boy with bow and arrows; here he is a "Pig Cupid," a mortal with animal instincts burrowing in the body's erotic sites.

8 *Bengal light:* blue flare used for signaling or illumination.

9 *sky-rocket:* partly an orgiastic image.

19 *skin-sack . . . shape of a man:* a reference to male genitals, to the entire body, and to the principle of masculinity.

22 *infructuous:* fruitless, unfruitful.

29 *God's door-mat:* the hair fretted in the previous line.

### III

We might have coupled
In the bed-ridden monopoly of a moment
Or broken flesh with one another
At the profane communion table
35   Where wine is spill'd on promiscuous lips

We might have given birth to a butterfly
With the daily news
Printed in blood on its wings

### IV

Once in a mezzanino°
40   The starry ceiling
Vaulted an unimaginable family
Bird-like abortions
With human throats
And Wisdom's eyes
45   Who wore lamp-shade red dresses
And woolen hair

One bore a baby
In a padded porte-enfant°
Tied with a sarsenet° ribbon
50   To her goose's wings

But for the abominable shadows
I would have lived
Among their fearful furniture
To teach them to tell me their secrets
55   Before I guessed
—Sweeping the brood clean out

### V

Midnight empties the street
Of all but us
Three
60   I am undecided which way back
              To the left a boy
—One wing has been washed in the rain
       The other will never be clean any more—
Pulling door-bells to remind
65   Those that are snug
              To the right a haloed ascetic
              Threading houses
Probes wounds for souls

---

39 *mezzanino:* (Italian) an apartment one-half story up from the ground floor.
48 *porte-enfant:* (French) "baby carriage."
49 *sarsenet:* soft, thin, Oriental silk.

—The poor can't wash in hot water—
70        And I don't know which turning to take
Since you got home to yourself—first

## VI

I know the Wire-Puller° intimately
And if it were not for the people
On whom you keep one eye
75        You could look straight at me
And Time would be set back

## VII

My pair of feet
Smack the flag-stones
That are something left over from your walking
80        The wind stuffs the scum of the white street
Into my lungs and my nostrils
Exhilarated birds
Prolonging flight into the night
Never reaching— — — — — —

## VIII

85        I am the jealous store-house of the candle-ends
That lit your adolescent learning
— — — — — — — — —
Behind God's eyes
There might
Be other lights

## IX

90        When we lifted
Our eye-lids on Love
A cosmos
Of coloured voices
And laughing honey

95        And spermatozoa
At the core of Nothing
In the milk of the Moon

---

72 *Wire-Puller:* one who uses secret or underhanded means to influence a person's or an
institution's actions.

## X

Shuttle-cock and battle-door°
A little pink-love
100    And feathers are strewn

## XI

Dear one   at your mercy
Our Universe
Is only
A colorless onion
105    You derobe
Sheath by sheath
            Remaining
A disheartening odour
About your nervy hands

## XII

110    Voices break on the confines of passion
Desire   Suspicion   Man   Woman
Solve in the humid carnage°

Flesh from flesh
Draws the inseparable delight
115    Kissing at gasps   to catch it

Is it true
That I have set you apart
Inviolate in an utter crystallization
Of all   the jolting of the crowd
120    Taught me willingly to live to share

Or are you
Only the other half
Of an ego's necessity
Scourging pride with compassion
125    To the shallow sound of dissonance
And boom of escaping breath

---

98 *Shuttle-cock and battle-door:* the male and female genitals in sexual intercourse; Loy
has adapted the name of a game that evolved into badminton (battledore and shuttlecock),
where the *battledore* is the paddle that strikes the *shuttlecock*, to refer to sexual foreplay,
contest, and intercourse. In badminton the shuttlecock is a ball with feathers attached
that is batted back and forth across a net; Loy's "feathers are strewn" carries the shuttle-
cock/sexuality analogy along by suggesting pillow feathers, hair, and clothes.
112 *humid carnage:* as Loy's biographer Carolyn Burke points out, both an image of sex
and an allusion to the large-scale slaughter of World War I.

## XIII

Come to me   There is something
I have got to tell you   and I can't tell
Something taking shape
130   Something that has a new name
A new dimension
A new use
A new illusion

It is ambient        And it is in your eyes
135   Something shiny    Something only for you
                     Something that I must not see

It is in my ears      Something very resonant
Something that you must not hear
                     Something only for me

Let us be very jealous
140   Very suspicious
Very conservative
Very cruel
Or we might make an end of the jostling of aspirations
Disorb° inviolate egos

145   Where two or three are welded together
They shall become god
— — — — — — —
Oh that's right
Keep away from me   Please give me a push
Don't let me understand you   Don't realise me
150   Or we might tumble together
Depersonalized
Identical
Into the terrific Nirvana°
Me you — you — me

## XIV

155   Today
Everlasting   passing   apparent   imperceptible
To you
I bring the nascent° virginity of
—Myself   for the moment
160   No love   or the other thing
Only the impact of lighted bodies
Knocking sparks off each other
In chaos

---

144 *disorb*: to throw something out of its normal orbit; sometimes applied to a comet, which connotation continues the cosmic metaphors of sections IX and XI.
153 *Nirvana*: in Hinduism, the extinction of all attachment; in Buddhism, the ultimate state of disinterested wisdom and compassion; more generally, an ideal of bliss and harmony.
158 *nascent*: emergent, coming into existence.

### XV

Seldom   Trying for Love

165    Fantasy dealt them out as gods

Two or three men   looked only human

But you alone

Superhuman   apparently

I had to be caught in the weak eddy

170    Of your drivelling humanity

To love you most

### XVI

We might have lived together

In the lights of the Arno°

Or gone apple stealing under the sea

175    Or played

Hide and seek in love and cob-webs

And a lullaby on a tin-pan

And   talked till there were no more tongues

To talk with

180    And never have known any better

### XVII

I don't care

Where the legs of the legs of the furniture are walking to

Or what is hidden in the shadows they stride

Or what would look at me

185    If the shutters were not shut

Red   a warm colour on the battle-field°

Heavy on my knees as a counterpane

Count counter

I counted   the fringe of the towel

190    Till two tassels clinging together

Let the square room fall away

From a round vacuum

Dilating with my breath

### XVIII

Out of the severing

195    Of hill from hill

The interim

Of star from star

The nascent

Static

200    Of night

---

173 *Arno*: river of central Italy.
186 *Red . . . battle-field*: both love and war are invoked.

## XIX

Nothing so conserving
As cool cleaving
Note of the Q H U°
Clear carving
205  Breath-giving
Pollen smelling
Space

White telling
Of slaking
210  Drinkable
Through fingers
Running water
Grass haulms°
Grow to
215  Leading astray
Of fireflies
Aerial quadrille°
Bouncing
Off one another
220  Again conjoining
In recaptured pulses
Of light

You too
Had something
225  At that time
Of a green-lit glow-worm
— — — — — —
Yet slowly drenched
To raylessness
In rain

## XX

230  Let Joy go solace-winged
To flutter whom she may concern

## XXI

I store up nights against you
Heavy with shut-flower's nightmares
— — — — — — — —
Stack noons
235  Curled to the solitaire
Core of the
Sun

---

203 *QHU:* unidentified reference.
213 *haulms:* the stalks or stems of cultivated plants.
217 *quadrille:* patterned group dancing.

## XXII

Green things grow
Salads
240 For the cerebral
Forager's revival
Upon bossed° bellies
Of mountains
Rolling in the sun
245 And flowered flummery°
Breaks
To my silly shoes

In ways without you
I go
250 Gracelessly
As things go

## XXIII

Laughter in solution
Stars in a stare
Irredeemable pledges
255 Of pubescent consummations
Rot
To the recurrent moon
Bleach
To the pure white
260 Wickedness of pain

## XXIV

The procreative truth of Me
Petered out
In pestilent
Tear drops
265 Little lusts and lucidities
And prayerful lies
Muddled with the heinous acerbity°
Of your street-corner smile

## XXV

Licking the Arno
270 The little rosy
Tongue of Dawn
Interferes with our eyelashes

———————

We twiddle to it

---

242 *bossed*: carries the sense of both rounded and ornamented.
245 *flummery*: an empty compliment; also a sweet dessert.
267 *heinous acerbity*: hateful sharpness of manner.

Round and round
275   Faster
And turn into machines

Till the sun
Subsides in shining
Melts some of us
280   Into abysmal pigeon-holes
Passion has bored
In warmth

Some few of us
Grow to the level of cool plains
285   Cutting our foot-hold
With steel eyes

### XXVI

Shedding our petty pruderies
From slit eyes

We sidle up
290   To Nature
— — — that irate pornographist

### XXVII

Nucleus   Nothing
Inconceivable concept

Insentient repose
295   The hands of races
Drop off from
Immodifiable plastic

The contents
Of our ephemeral conjunction
300   In aloofness from Much
Flowed to approachment of — — — —
NOTHING
There was a man and a woman
In the way
305   While the Irresolvable
Rubbed with our daily deaths
Impossible eyes

### XXVIII

The steps go up for ever
And they are white
310   And the first step   is the last white
Forever
Coloured   conclusions

Smelt    to synthetic
Whiteness
315    Of my
Emergence
And I am burnt quite white
In the climacteric
Withdrawal of your sun
320    And wills and words all white
Suffuse
Illimitable monotone

White   where there is nothing to see
But a white towel
325    Wipes the cymophanous° sweat
      —Mist rise of living—
From your
Etiolate° body
And the white dawn
330    Of your   New Day
Shuts down on me

Unthinkable   that white over there
— — — Is smoke from your house

### XXIX

Evolution    fall foul of
335    Sexual equality
Prettily miscalculate
Similitude

Unnatural selection
Breed such sons and daughters
340    As shall jibber° at each other
Uninterpretable cryptonyms°
Under the moon

Give them some way of braying brassily
For caressive calling
345    Or to homophonous° hiccoughs
Transpose the laugh
Let them suppose that tears
Are snowdrops or molasses
Or anything

---

325 *cymophanous*: displaying a wavy, floating light; opalescent.
328 *etiolate*: colorless, pale.
340 *jibber*: to speak rapidly and unintelligibly.
341 *cryptonyms*: secret names.
345 *homophonous*: having the same sound.

350    Than human insufficiencies
       Begging dorsal vertebrae°
       Let meeting be the turning
       To the antipodean°
       And Form    a blurr
355    Anything

       Than seduce them
       To the one
       As simple satisfaction
       For the other

360    Let them clash together
       From their incognitoes
       In seismic orgasm

       For far further
       Differentiation
365    Rather than watch
       Own-self distortion
       Wince in the alien ego

XXX

       In some
       Prenatal plagiarism
370    Fœtal buffoons
       Caught tricks
       — — — — —

       From archetypal pantomime
       Stringing emotions
       Looped aloft
       — — — —

375    For the blind eyes
       That Nature knows us with
       And the most of Nature   is green
       — — — — — — — — —

       What guaranty
       For the proto-form
380    We fumble
       Our souvenir ethics to
       — — — — — —

---

351 *dorsal vertebrae:* those situated between the cervical (neck) and lumbar (above the pelvis) vertebrae.
353 *antipodean:* diametrically opposite, opposed.

## XXXI

Crucifixion
Of a busy-body
Longing to interfere so
385    With the intimacies
Of your insolent isolation

Crucifixion
Of an illegal ego's
Eclosion°
390    On your equilibrium
Caryatid°   of an idea

Crucifixion
Wracked arms
Index extremities
395    In vacuum
To the unbroken fall

## XXXII

The moon is cold
Joannes
Where the Mediterranean° — — — —

## XXXIII

400    The prig of passion — — — —
To your professorial paucity

Proto-plasm was raving mad
Evolving us — — —

## XXXIV

Love — — — the preeminent litterateur°

                                             *1915–1917*

---

389 *eclosion:* hatching out, as in hatching out of an egg or emerging (like an insect) from a pupus.

391 *caryatid:* a supporting column sculpted in the form of a draped female figure. Virginia Kouidis cites a line from French critic Rémy de Gourmont's (1858–1915) "Women and Language" (1901): "The role of women in the work of civilization is so great that it would scarcely be an exaggeration to say that the structure is built on the shoulders of these frail caryatids."

399 *Mediterranean:* the inland sea surrounded by Europe, the Middle East, and Africa; also the region surrounding the sea.

404 *litterateur:* (French) "author," "man of letters."

# Anne Spencer (1882–1975)

Born Annie Bethel Bannister on a Virginia plantation of racially diverse parentage—her father was of African American, white, and Native American heritage, while her mother was the child of a slaveholder and a slave—Spencer herself was carefully prepared for the black middle class. To this complex background was added the political education she received from James Weldon Johnson, whom she first met when he was field secretary for the NAACP in 1918. She had begun writing poetry in 1896, but in the 1920s took on modernist techniques and a more pointed politics, though she addressed women's issues more frequently than racial ones. Many of her poems were about nature, and they were often enigmatic and ironic. Meanwhile she organized the Lynchburg, Virginia, NAACP chapter, and wrote editorials attacking the fiction of white supremacy. Yet she also loved the solitude of her garden and spent much time away from the world in a cabin there. A large quantity of her unpublished work was destroyed after her death.

## White Things

Most things are colorful things—the sky, earth, and sea.
   Black men are most men; but the white are free!
White things are rare things; so rare, so rare
They stole from out a silvered world—somewhere.
5   Finding earth-plains fair plains, save greenly grassed,
They strewed white feathers of cowardice, as they passed;
   The golden stars with lances fine,
   The hills all red and darkened pine,
They blanched with their wand of power;
10  And turned the blood in a ruby rose
To a poor white poppy-flower.

They pyred a race of black, black men,
And burned them to ashes white; then,
Laughing, a young one claimed a skull,
15  For the skull of a black is white, not dull,
   But a glistening awful thing
   Made, it seems, for this ghoul to swing
In the face of God with all his might,
And swear by the hell that sired him:
   "Man-maker, make white!"

*1923*

## Lady, Lady

Lady, Lady, I saw your face,
Dark as night withholding a star . . .
The chisel fell, or it might have been
You had borne so long the yoke of men.
5      Lady, Lady, I saw your hands,
Twisted, awry, like crumpled roots,
Bleached poor white in a sudsy tub,
Wrinkled and drawn from your rub-a-dub.
Lady, Lady, I saw your heart,
10     And altared° there in its darksome place
Were the tongues of flames the ancients knew,
Where the good God sits to spangle through.

*1925*

## (God never planted a garden)

God never planted a garden
But He placed a keeper there
And the keeper ever razed the ground
And built a city where
5      God cannot walk at the eve of day,
Nor take the morning air.

*n.d.*

---

10 *altared:* enshrined, placed on an altar.

# William Carlos Williams (1883–1963)

Born in Rutherford, New Jersey, a town near the city of Paterson, Williams made the city his home for most of his life. He would mix cosmopolitan experience with a commitment to local American life. His father, of British birth and West Indies upbringing, was a perfume company salesman; his mother, of mixed Spanish, French, Dutch, and Jewish ancestry, was born in Puerto Rico and had studied art in Paris. After two years of study in Switzerland and Paris, Williams returned to earn an M.D. at the University of Pennsylvania. From then on, he would maintain a remarkable dual career. One of the most prolific and versatile writers of the period, he was also a full-time doctor serving poor and middle-class patients in northern New Jersey, delivering over a thousand of their babies in the course of his career.

From his medical practice, Williams would draw characters who appeared in his fiction and poetry; he would also remain deeply committed to their lives, to the struggles they underwent, and to their sustaining humor. His class sympathy helped him understand the relationship between radical artistic innovation and radical politics in the 1920s and 1930s. As a result, for decades he was a fellow traveler on the Left, publishing in communist journals, supporting the Spanish Republic, and earning enough of a progressive reputation to be turned down for a position as poetry consultant at the Library of Congress a year after the anticommunist witch hunts started in 1947. Many literary scholars during the McCarthy period of the next decade avoided Williams out of fear of his politics and revulsion at his conversational idiom and working-class commitments. But Williams had been immensely influential for other poets all along, and scholars would finally rediscover him in the 1960s and 1970s. To think of American modernism now without him would be unimaginable.

Williams had met Pound and H.D. at Penn; he would later become friends with Moore and Stevens and a number of avant garde painters based in New York. His first poems were somewhat derivatively romantic, but by 1916 he was writing short lyrics in a decidedly American idiom that drew on several modernist impulses. They remain among his masterpieces. *Spring and All* (1923) and *The Descent of Winter* (1928) were breakthrough volumes, radical collages of poetry and prose that mix flawless, crafted, and rather minimalist texts with passages of almost automatic writing. These rich books remain infinitely interpretable. A highly poetic prose meditation on American myth, character, and history, *In the American Grain* (1925), would come from the same time; it is an enterprise of vision and critique that anyone interested in American literature should read.

Beginning in the 1930s, Williams would write a number of novels and short stories. In the 1940s, he would begin publishing portions of his book-length poetic epic, *Paterson*. It was the fulfillment of his impassioned sense of place, of a commitment to American culture that was never merely celebratory but rather the witness of a devoted and attentive critic, a critic seeking a redemptive idiom amidst crass materialism and violence. *Paterson* was also the culmination of his lifelong rejection of the Eliot/Pound expatriate impulse, and its mix of letters, documents, and lyrics was a further realization of the collage experiments of the 1920s. In his last years he devised a triadic, or step-down, form that he called a "variable foot." It is employed in "Asphodel, That Greeny Flower," a three-part love poem to his wife Florence.

## The Young Housewife°

At ten A.M. the young housewife
moves about in negligee behind
the wooden walls of her husband's house.
I pass solitary in my car.

5    Then again she comes to the curb
to call the ice-man, fish-man, and stands
shy, uncorseted, tucking in
stray ends of hair, and I compare her
to a fallen leaf.

10   The noiseless wheels of my car
rush with a crackling sound over
dried leaves as I bow and pass smiling.

*1916*

## Portrait of a Lady

Your thighs are appletrees
whose blossoms touch the sky.
Which sky? The sky
where Watteau° hung a lady's
5    slipper. Your knees
are a southern breeze—or
a gust of snow. Agh! what
sort of man was Fragonard?
—as if that answered
10  anything. Ah, yes—below
the knees, since the tune
drops that way, it is
one of those white summer days,
the tall grass of your ankles
15  flickers upon the shore—
Which shore?—
the sand clings to my lips—

---

**poem title:** Williams' note: "Whenever a man sees a beautiful woman it's an occasion for poetry—compensating beauty with beauty."
4 *Watteau:* Jean Antoine Watteau (1684–1721), and Jean Honoré Fragonard (1732–1806), both French painters. The painting described is actually Fragonard's "The Swing."

Which shore?
Agh, petals maybe. How
20      should I know?
Which shore? Which shore?
I said petals from an appletree.

*1920*

## Queen-Anne's-Lace°

Her body is not so white as
anemone petals nor so smooth—nor
so remote a thing. It is a field
of the wild carrot taking
5       the field by force; the grass
does not raise above it.
Here is no question of whiteness,
white as can be, with a purple mole
at the center of each flower.
10      Each flower is a hand's span
of her whiteness. Wherever
his hand has lain there is
a tiny purple blemish. Each part
is a blossom under his touch
15      to which the fibres of her being
stem one by one, each to its end,
until the whole field is a
white desire, empty, a single stem,
a cluster, flower by flower,
20      a pious wish to whiteness gone over—
or nothing.

*1921*

## The Widow's Lament in Springtime

Sorrow is my own yard
where the new grass
flames as it has flamed
often before but not
5       with the cold fire
that closes round me this year.
Thirtyfive years
I lived with my husband.
The plumtree is white today
10      with masses of flowers.
Masses of flowers
load the cherry branches
and color some bushes
yellow and some red

---

**poem title:** a common white field flower.

15  but the grief in my heart
is stronger than they
for though they were my joy
formerly, today I notice them
and turn away forgetting.
20  Today my son told me
that in the meadows,
at the edge of the heavy woods
in the distance, he saw
trees of white flowers.
25  I feel that I would like
to go there
and fall into those flowers
and sink into the marsh near them.

*1921*

## The Great Figure

Among the rain
and lights
I saw the figure 5
in gold
5  on a red
firetruck
moving
tense
unheeded
10  to gong clangs
siren howls
and wheels rumbling
through the dark city.

*1921*

## Spring and All

By the road to the contagious hospital
under the surge of the blue
mottled clouds driven from the
northeast—a cold wind. Beyond, the
5  waste of broad, muddy fields
brown with dried weeds, standing and fallen

patches of standing water
the scattering of tall trees

All along the road the reddish
10  purplish, forked, upstanding, twiggy
stuff of bushes and small trees
with dead, brown leaves under them
leafless vines—

15    Lifeless in appearance, sluggish
dazed spring approaches—

They enter the new world naked,
cold, uncertain of all
save that they enter. All about them
the cold, familiar wind—

20    Now the grass, tomorrow
the stiff curl of wildcarrot leaf

One by one objects are defined—
It quickens: clarity, outline of leaf

But now the stark dignity of
25    entrance—Still, the profound change
has come upon them: rooted, they
grip down and begin to awaken

*1923*

## To Elsie°

The pure products of America
go crazy—
mountain folk from Kentucky

or the ribbed north end of
5    Jersey
with its isolate lakes and

valleys, its deaf-mutes, thieves
old names
and promiscuity between

10    devil-may-care men who have taken
to railroading
out of sheer lust of adventure—

and young slatterns, bathed
in filth
15    from Monday to Saturday

to be tricked out that night
with gauds
from imaginations which have no

peasant traditions to give them
20    character
but flutter and flaunt

---

**poem title:** Elsie was a nursemaid from the state orphanage who worked for the Williams family.

sheer rags—succumbing without
emotion
save numbed terror

25        under some hedge of choke-cherry
or viburnum—
which they cannot express—

Unless it be that marriage
perhaps
30        with a dash of Indian blood

will throw up a girl so desolate
so hemmed round
with disease or murder

that she'll be rescued by an
35        agent—
reared by the state and

sent out at fifteen to work in
some hard-pressed
house in the suburbs—

40        some doctor's family, some Elsie—
voluptuous water
expressing with broken

brain the truth about us—
her great
45        ungainly hips and flopping breasts

addressed to cheap
jewelry
and rich young men with fine eyes

as if the earth under our feet
50        were
an excrement of some sky

and we degraded prisoners
destined
to hunger until we eat filth

55        while the imagination strains
after deer
going by fields of goldenrod in

the stifling heat of September
Somehow
60        it seems to destroy us

It is only in isolate flecks that
something
is given off

No one
to witness
and adjust, no one to drive the car

65

1923

## The Red Wheelbarrow

so much depends
upon

a red wheel
barrow

glazed with rain
water

5

beside the white
chickens

1923

## Young Sycamore

I must tell you
this young tree
whose round and firm trunk
between the wet

pavement and the gutter
(where water
is trickling) rises
bodily

5

into the air with
one undulant
thrust half its height—
and then

10

dividing and waning
sending out
young branches on
all sides—

15

hung with cocoons—
it thins
till nothing is left of it
but two

20

eccentric knotted
twigs
bending forward
hornlike at the top

1927

## *The Descent of Winter*

9/27

"*What are these elations I have*
*at my own underwear?*

*I touch it and it is strange*
*upon a strange thigh.*"

• • •

9/29

My bed is narrow
in a small room
at sea

The numbers are on
the wall
Arabic 1

Berth No. 2
was empty above me
the steward

took it apart
and removed
it

only the number
remains
• 2 •

on an oval disc
of celluloid
tacked

to the white-enameled
woodwork
with

two bright nails
like stars
beside

the moon

9/30

There are no perfect waves—
Your writings are a sea
full of misspellings and
faulty sentences. Level. Troubled.

A center distant from the land
touched by the wings
35          of nearly silent birds
that never seem to rest—

This is the sadness of the sea—
waves like words, all broken—
a sameness of lifting and falling mood.

40          I lean watching the detail
of brittle crest, the delicate
imperfect foam, yellow weed
one piece like another—

There is no hope—if not a coral
45          island slowly forming
to wait for birds to drop
the seeds will make it habitable

10/9

and there's a little blackboy
in a doorway
50          scratching his wrists

The cap on his head
is red and blue
with a broad peak to it

and his mouth
55          is open, his tongue
between his teeth—

10/10

Monday
          the canna° flaunts
its crimson head

60          crimson lying folded
crisply down upon
                              the invisible
darkly crimson heart
of this poor yard

65          the grass is long
                              October tenth
1927

10/13
a beard . . . not of stone but particular hairs purpleblack . . .
lies upon his stale breast

---

58 *canna:* a tropical flowering plant with large, broad leaves.

10/21

In the dead weeds a rubbish heap
aflame: the orange flames
70       stream horizontal, windblown
they parallel the ground
waving up and down
the flamepoints alternating
the body streaked with loops
75       and purple stains while
the pale smoke, above
steadily continues eastward—

What chance have the old?
There are no duties for them
80       no places where they may sit
their knowledge is laughed at
they cannot see, they cannot hear.
A small bundle on the shoulders
weighs them down
85       one hand is put back under it
to hold it steady.
Their feet hurt, they are weak
they should not have to suffer
as younger people must and do
90       there should be a truce for them

10/22

that brilliant field
of rainwet orange
blanketed

by the red grass
95       and oilgreen bayberry

the last yarrow°
on the gutter
white by the sandy
rainwater

100     and a white birch
with yellow leaves
and few
and loosely hung

and a young dog
105     jumped out
of the old barrel

10/23

I will make a big, serious portrait of my time. The brown and
creamwhite block of Mexican onyx has a poorly executed replica of the

---

96 *yarrow:* an herb that grows wild in North America, strong scented with small white or
pink flowers.

Aztec calendar on one of its dicefacets the central circle being a broad-
nosed face with projected hanging tongue the sun perhaps though why
the tongue is out I do not know unless to taste or gasp in the heat, its
own heat, to say it's hot and is the sun. Puebla, Mexico, Calendario
Azteca, four words are roughly engraved in the four corners where the
circle leaves spaces on the square diceface this is America some years
after the original, the art of writing is to do work so excellent that by
its excellence it repels all idiots but idiots are like leaves and excellence
of any sort is a tree when the leaves fall the tree is naked and the wind
thrashes it till it howls it cannot get a book published it can only get
poems into certain magazines that are suppressed because because wav-
ing waving waving waving waving waving tic tack tic tock tadick there
is not excellence without the vibrant rhythm of a poem and poems are
small and tied and gasping, they eat gasoline, they all ate gasoline and
died, they died of—there is a hole in the wood and all I say brings to
mind the rock shingles of Cherbourg, on the new houses they have put
cheap tile which overlaps but the old roofs had flat stone sides steep
but of stones fitted together and that is love there is no portrait with-
out that has not turned to prose love is my hero who does not live, a
man, but speaks of it every day

### 1. Continued (The Great Law)

What is he saying? That love was never made for man and woman
to crack between them and so he loves and loves his sons and loves as
he pleases. But there is a great law over him which—is as it is. The
wind blowing, the mud spots on the polished surface, the face reflected
in the glass which as you advance the features disappear leaving only
the hat and as you draw back the features return, the tip of the nose,
the projection over the eyebrows, the cheek bones and the bulge of the
lips the chin last.

### 2

I remember, she said, we had little silver plaques with a chain on
it to hang over the necks of the bottles, whiskey, brandy or whatever
it was. And a box of some kind of wood, not for the kitchen but a pretty
box. Inside it was lined with something like yes, pewter, all inside and
there was a cover of metal too with a little knob on it, all inside the
wooden box. You would open the outer cover and inside was the lid.
When you would take that off you would see the tea with a silver spoon
for taking it out. But now, here are the roses—three opening. Out of
love. For she loves them and so they are there. They are not a picture.
Holbein° never saw pink thorns in such a light. Nor did Masaccio.°
The petals are delicate, it is a question if they will open at all and not
drop, loosing at one edge and falling tomorrow all in a heap. All around
the roses there is today, machinery leaning upon the stem, an aero-
plane is upon one leaf where a worm lies curled. Soppy it seems and
enormous, it seems to hold up the sky for it has no size at all. We eat
beside it—beside the three roses that she loves. And an oak tree grows

---

145 *Holbein:* Hans Holbein (1497–1543), German painter reknowned for his portraits.
146 *Masaccio:* (1401–1428), Florentine painter and pioneer of the Renaissance, known for
increasing the drama and figurative force of Biblical subjects.

out of my shoulders. Its roots are my arms and my legs. The air is a field. Yellow and red grass are writing their signature everywhere.

10/27

And Coolidge° said let there be imitation brass filigree fire fenders behind insured plateglass windows and yellow pine booths with the molasses-candygrain in the wood instead of the oldtime cake-like whitepine boards always cut thick their faces! the white porcelain trough is no doubt made of some certain blanched clay baked and glazed but how they do it, how they shape it soft and have it hold its shape for the oven I don't know nor how the cloth is woven, the grey and the black with the orange and green strips wound together diagonally across the grain artificial pneumothorax their faces! the stripe of shadow along the pavement edge, the brownstone steeple low among the office buildings dark windows with a white wooden cross upon them, lights like fuchsias, lights like bleeding hearts lights like columbines, cherry-red danger and applegreen safety. Any hat in this window $2.00 barred windows, wavy opaque glass, a block of brownstone at the edge of the sidewalk crudely stippled on top for a footstep to a carriage, lights with sharp bright spikes, stick out round them their faces! STOP in black letters surrounded by a red glow, letters with each bulb a seed in the shaft of the L of the A lights on the river streaking the restless water lights upon pools of rainwater by the roadside a great pool of light full of overhanging sparks into whose lower edge a house looms its center marked by one yellow window-bright their faces!

10/28

born, September 15, 1927, 2nd child, wt. 6 lbs. 2 ozs. The hero is Dolores Marie Pischak, the place Fairfield, in my own state, my own county, its largest city, my own time. This is her portrait: O future worlds, this is her portrait—order be God damned. Fairfield is the place where the October marigolds go over into the empty lot with dead grass like Polish children's hair and the nauseous, the stupefying monotony of decency is dead, unkindled even by art or anything—dead: by God because Fairfield is alive, coming strong. Oh blessed love you are here in this golden air, this honey and dew sunshine, ambering the houses to jewels. Order—is dead. Here a goose flaps his wings by a fence, a white goose, women talk from second-story windows to a neighbor on the ground, the tops of the straggling backyard poplars have been left with a tail of twigs and on the bare trunk a pulley with a line in it is tied. A cop whizzes by on his sidecar cycle, the bank to the river is cinders where dry leaves drift. The cinders are eating forward over the green grass below, closer and closer to the river bank, children are in the gutters violently at play over a dam of mud, old women with seamed faces lean on the crooked front gates. Where is Pischak's place? I don't know. I tink it's up there at the corner. What you want?—

Here one drinks good beer. Don't tell my husband. I stopped there yesterday, really good. I was practically alone, yes.

Some streets paved, some dirt down the center. A Jew has a clothing store and looks at you wondering what he can sell. And you feel

155 *Coolidge:* Calvin Coolidge (1872–1933), 30th president of the U.S. (1923–1929).

he has these people sized up. A nasty feeling. Unattached. When he gets his he'll burn it up and clear out in a day. And they do not suspect how nicely he has measured them. They need stuff. He sells it. Who's that guy I wonder. Never seen him around here before. Looks like a doctor.

That's the feeling of Fairfield. An old farm house in long tangled trees, leaning over it. A dell with a pretty stream in it below the little garden and fifty feet beyond, the board fence of the Ajax Aniline Dye Works with red and purple refuse dribbling out ragged and oily under the lower fence boards. No house is like another. Small, wooden, a garden at the back, all ruined by the year. Man leaning smoking from a window. And the dirt, dry dust. No grass, or grass in patches, hedged with sticks and a line of cord or wire or grass, a jewel, a garden embanked, all in a twenty-foot square, crowded with incident, a small terrace of begonias, a sanded path, pinks, roses in a dozen rococo beds.

Knock and walk in: The bar. Not a soul. In the back room the kitchen. Immaculate, the enameled table featured. The mother nursing her from a nearly empty breast. She lies and sucks. Black hair, penciled down the top flat and silky smooth, the palmsized face asleep, the mother at a point of vantage where under an inside window raised two inches she can govern the street entrance.

Who's that?
A woman. Oh that old woman from next door.

The father, young, energetic, enormous. Unsmiling, big headed, a nervous twitch to his head and a momentary intense squint to his eyes. She watches the door. He is in shirt sleeves. Restless, goes in and out. Talks fast, manages the old woman begging help for a bruised hand. A man who might be a general or president of a corporation, or president of the states. Runs a bootleg saloon. Great!

This is the world. Here one breathes and the dignity of man holds on. "Here I shall live. Why not now? Why do I wait?"

Katharin, 9, sheepish, shy—adoring in response to gentleness so that her eyes almost weep for sentimental gratitude, has jaundice, leans on his knee. Follows him with her eyes. Her hair is straight and blond.
On the main river road, a grey board fence over which a grove of trees stick up. Oaks, maples, poplars and old fruit trees. Belmont Park, Magyar Home. For rent for picnics. Peace is here—rest, assurance, life hangs on.
Oh, blessed love, among insults, brawls, yelling, kicks, brutality— here the old dignity of life holds on—defying the law, defying monotony.

She lies in her mother's arms and sucks. The dream passes over her, dirt streets, a white goose flapping its wings and passes. Boys, wrestling, kicking a half-inflated football. A grey motheaten squirrel pauses at a picket fence where tomato vines, almost spent, hang on stakes.

Oh, blessed love—the dream engulfs her. She opens her eyes on the troubled bosom of the mother who is nursing the babe and watching the door. And watching the eye of the man. Talking English, a stream of Magyar, Polish what? to the tall man coming and going.

Oh, blessed love where are you there, pleasure driven out, order triumphant, one house like another, grass cut to pay lovelessly. Bored we turn to cars to take us to "the country" to "nature" to breathe her good air. Jesus Christ. To nature. It's about time, for most of us. She is holding the baby. Her eye under the window, watching. Her hair is bobbed halfshort. It stands straight down about her ears. You, you sit and have it waved and ordered. Fine. I'm glad of it. And nothing to do but play cards and whisper. Jesus Christ. Whisper of the high-school girl that had a baby and how smart her mama was to pretend in a flash of genius that it was hers. Jesus Christ. Or let us take a run up to the White Mountains or Lake Mohonk. Not Bethlehem (New Hampshire) any more, the Jews have ruined that like lice all over the lawns. Horrible to see. The dirty things. Eating everywhere. Parasites.

And so order, seclusion, the good of it all.

But in Fairfield men are peaceful and do as they please—and learn the necessity and the profit of order—and Dolores Marie Pischak was born.

    10/28

On hot days
the sewing machine
    whirling

110            in the next room
in the kitchen

and men at the bar
talking of the strike
and cash

    10/28
a flash of juncos° in the field of grey locust saplings with a white sun powdery upon them and a large rusty can wedged in the crotch of one of them, for the winter, human fruit, and on the polished straws of the dead grass a scroll of crimson paper—not yet rained on

    10/28
115            in this strong light
the leafless beechtree
shines like a cloud

it seems to glow
of itself
120            with a soft stript light
of love
over the brittle
grass

But there are
125            on second look
a few yellow leaves
still shaking

---

271 *juncos:* small American finches, often having a pink bill, a gray head, reddish brown or gray body, and white tail feathers.

                              far apart

                         just one here one there
130                      trembling vividly

      10/29
                         The justice of poverty
                              its shame its dirt
                         are one with the meanness
                              of love

135                      its organ in a tarpaulin
                              the green birds
                         the fat sleepy horse
                              the old men

                         the grinder sourfaced
140                           hat over eyes
                         the beggar smiling all open
                              the lantern out

                         and the popular tunes—
                              sold to the least bidder
145                      for a nickel
                              two cents or

                         nothing at all or even
                              against the desire
                         forced on us

      10/30
150                      To freight cars in the air

                         all the slow
                              clank, clank
                              clank, clank
                         moving above the treetops

155                      the
                              wha,   wha
                         of the hoarse whistle

                              pah,   pah,   pah
                         pah, pah, pah, pah, pah

160                           piece and piece
                              piece and piece
                         moving still trippingly
                         through the morningmist

                         long after the engine
165                      has fought by
                                   and disappeared

in silence
> to the left

11/1

Introduction

in almost all verse you read, mine or anybody's else, the figures used
and the general impression of the things spoken of is vague "you could
say it better in prose" especially good prose, say the prose of Heming-
way.° The truth of the object is somehow hazed over, dulled. So no-
body would go to see a play in verse if

the salvias, the rusty hydrangeas, the ragged cannas

there's too often no observation in it, in poetry. It is a soft second light
of dreaming. The sagas were not like that they seem to have been made
on the spot. The little Greek I have read—and in translation—is not
like that. Marlowe, Chaucer, el Cid, Shakespeare° where he is homely,
uncultured, a shrewd guesser is not like that. Where he puts it over
about some woman he knew or a prince or Falstaff.° The good poetry
is where the vividness comes up "true" like in prose but better. That's
poetry. Dante was wrestling with Italian, his vividness comes from his
escape from Latin. Don Quixote.° I don't know about the Russians or
the French.

and the late, high growing red rose
170            it is their time
of a small garden

poetry should strive for nothing else, this vividness alone, *per se*, for it-
self. The realization of this has its own internal fire that is "like" noth-
ing. Therefore the bastardy of the simile. That thing, the vividness
which is poetry by itself, makes the poem. There is no need to explain
or compare. Make it and it *is* a poem. This is modern, not the saga.
There are no sagas—only trees now, animals, engines: There's that.

11/1

I won't have to powder my nose tonight 'cause Billie's gonna take me
home in his car—

The moon, the dried weeds
and the Pleiades°—

---

335 *Hemingway:* Ernest Hemingway (1899–1961), American novelist.
342 *Shakespeare:* Christopher Marlowe (1564–1593), English dramatist; Geoffrey Chaucer
(c. 1345–1400), English poet; el Cid (c. 1043–1099), Spanish warrior hero who captured Va-
lencia and became its ruler (*El Cid,* "the lord"); William Shakespeare (1564–1616), Eng-
land's greatest dramatist.
344 *Falstaff:* Sir John Falstaff, a character in Shakespeare's *Henry the Fourth,* Parts One
and Two (1597–1598). A friend of Prince Hal, he is repudiated when Hal comes to the
throne.
347 *Don Quixote:* the title character of *Don Quixote de la Mancha* (1615) by Miguel de
Cervantes (1547–1616).
360 *Pleiades:* Williams has woven echoes of a fragment by the Greek lyric poet Sappho
(born c. 612 B.C.) into this poem: "The moon has gone down, the Pleiades have set; it is
the middle of the night, and I lie here alone." The Pleiades are seven stars in the con-
stellation Taurus.

                    Seven feet tall
                    the dark, dried weedstalks
175                 make a part of the night
                    a red lace
                    on the blue milky sky

                    Write—
                    by a small lamp

180                 the Pleiades are almost
                    nameless

                    and the moon is tilted
                    and halfgone

                    And in runningpants and
189                 with ecstatic, æsthetic faces
                    on the illumined
                    signboard are leaping
                    over printed hurdles and
                    "¼ of their energy comes from bread"

190                 two
                    gigantic highschool boys
                    ten feet tall

        11/2
                    Dahlias—
                    What a red
195                     and yellow and white
                    mirror to the sun, round
                            and petaled
                        is this she holds?
                        with a red face
200                 all in black
                            and grey hair
                        sticking out
                    from under the bonnet brim
                    Is this Washington Avenue Mr. please
205                     or do I have to
                        cross the track?
        11/2

                    A MORNING IMAGINATION OF RUSSIA

            The earth and the sky were very close
            When the sun rose it rose in his heart
            It bathed the red cold world of
300         the dawn so that the chill was his own
            The mists were sleep and sleep began
            to fade from his eyes, below him in the
            garden a few flowers were lying forward
            on the intense green grass where

305    in the opalescent shadows oak leaves
were pressed hard down upon it in patches
by the night rain. There were no cities
between him and his desires
his hatreds and his loves were without walls

310    without rooms, without elevators
without files, delays of veiled murderers
muffled thieves, the tailings of
tedious, dead pavements, the walls
against desire save only for him who can pay

315    high, there were no cities—he was
without money—

                Cities had faded richly
into foreign countries, stolen from Russia—
the richness of her cities—

320    Scattered wealth was close to his heart
he felt it uncertainly beating at
that moment in his wrists, scattered
wealth—but there was not much at hand

Cities are full of light, fine clothes
325    delicacies for the table, variety,
novelty—fashion: all spent for this.
Never to be like that again:
the frame that was. It tickled his
imagination. But it passed in a rising calm

330    Tan dar a dei! Tan dar a dei!

He was singing. Two miserable peasants
very lazy and foolish
seemed to have walked out from his own
feet and were walking away with wooden rakes

335    under the six nearly bare poplars, up the hill

There go my feet.

He stood still in the window forgetting
to shave—

The very old past was refound
340    redirected. It had wandered into himself
The world was himself, these were
his own eyes that were seeing, his own mind
that was straining to comprehend, his own
hands that would be touching other hands

345    They were his own!
His own, feeble, uncertain. He would go
out to pick herbs, he graduate of
the old university. He would go out
and ask that old woman, in the little

350   village by the lake, to show him wild
ginger. He himself would not know the plant.

A horse was stepping up the dirt road
under his window

He decided not to shave. Like those two
355   that he knew now, as he had never
known them formerly. A city, fashion
had been between—

Nothing between now.

He would go to the soviet° unshaven. This
360   was the day—and listen. Listen. That
was all he did, listen to them, weigh
for them. He was turning into
a pair of scales, the scales in the
zodiac.

365       But closer, he was himself
the scales. The local soviet. They could
weigh. If it was not too late. He felt
uncertain many days. But all were uncertain
together and he must weigh for them out
370   of himself.

He took a small pair of scissors
from the shelf and clipped his nails
carefully. He himself served the fire.

We have cut out the cancer but
375   who knows? perhaps the patient will die.
The patient is anybody, anything
worthless that I desire, my hands
to have it—instead of the feeling
that there is a piece of glazed paper
380   between me and the paper—invisible
but tough running through the legal
processes of possession—a city, that
we could possess—

It's in art, it's in
385   the French school.

What we lacked was
everything. It is the middle of
everything. Not to have.

---

459 *soviet:* local, elected organizational unit in communist countries, like a committee or
council, often concerned with public health, education, and new construction.

              We have little now but
390       we have that. We are convalescents. Very
          feeble. Our hands shake. We need a
          transfusion. No one will give it to us,
          they are afraid of infection. I do not
          blame them. We have paid heavily. But we
395       have gotten—touch. The eyes and the ears
          down on it. Close.


      11/6
Russia is every country, here he must live, this for that, loss for gain.
Dolores Marie Pischak. "New York is a blight on my heart, lost, a street
full of lights fading to a bonfire—in order to see their hats of wool on
their heads, their lips to open and a word to come out. To open my
mouth and a word to come out, my word. Grown like grass, to be like
a stone. I pick it. It is poor. It must be so. There are no rich. The rich-
ness is everywhere, belongs to everyone and it is hard to get. And loss,
loss, loss. Cut off from my kind—if any exist. To get that, everything
is lost. So he carries them and gets—himself and has nothing to do
with himself. He also gets their lice.

      Romance, decoration, fullness—are lost in touch, sight, a word, to
bite an apple. Henry Ford° has asked Chas. Sheeler° to go to Detroit
and photograph everything. Carte blanche. Sheeler! That's rich. Shake-
speare had that mean ability to fuse himself with everyone which no-
bodies have, to be anything at any time, fluid, a nameless fellow whom
nobody noticed—much, and *that* is what made him the great drama-
tist. Because he was nobody and was fluid and accessible. He took the
print and reversed the film, as it went in so it came out. Certainly he
never repeated himself since he did nothing but repeat what he heard
and nobody ever hears the same words twice the same. Homekeeping
youth had ever homely wit, Sheeler and Shakespeare should be on this
Soviet. Mediæval England, Soviet Russia.

      It is a pure literary adjustment. The supremacy of England is purely
a matter of style. Officially they are realists, such as the treaty with Italy
to divide Abyssinia. Realists—it is the tactical spread of realism that is
the Soviets. Imperial Russia was romanticist, strabismic,° atavistic.
Style. He does not blame the other countries. They fear what he sees.
He sees tribes of lawyers tripping each other up entirely off the ground
and falling on pillows full of softly jumbled words from goose backs.

      I know a good print when I see it. I know when it is good and why
it is good. It is the neck of a man, the nose of a woman. It is the same
Shakespeare. It is a photograph by Sheeler. It is. It is the thing where
it is. So. That's the mine out of which riches have always been drawn.
The kings come and beg for it. But it is too simple. In the complexity,
when we try to enrich ourselves—the richness is lost. Loss and gain

---

508 *Ford:* Henry Ford (1863–1947), American automobile engineer and manufacturer.
508 *Sheeler:* Charles Sheeler (1883–1965), American painter and photographer who was
one of Williams' friends. In 1927, he was commissioned by Henry Ford to record the build-
ing of the Ford Motor installation at River Rouge, Michigan.
522 *strabismic:* failing to perceive clearly or accurately.

go hand in hand. And hand in hand means my hand in a hand which is in it: a child's hand soft skinned, small, a little fist to hold gently, a woman's hand, a certain woman's hand, a man's hand. Thus hand in hand means several classes of things. But loss is one thing. It is lost. It is one big thing that is an orchestra playing. Time, that's what it buys. But the gain is scattered. It is everywhere but there is not much in any place. A city is merely a relocation of metals in a certain place.— He feels the richness, but a distressing feeling of loss is close upon it. He knows he must coordinate the villages for effectiveness in a flood, a famine.

The United States should be, in effect, a Soviet State. It is a Soviet State decayed away in a misconception of richness. The states, counties, cities, are anemic Soviets. As rabbits are cottontailed the office-workers in cotton running pants get in a hot car, ride in a hot tunnel and confine themselves in a hot office—to sell asphalt, the trade in tanned leather. The trade in everything. Things they've never seen, will never own and can never name. Not even an analogous name do they know. As a carter, knowing the parts of a wagon will know, know, touch, the parts of—a woman. Maybe typists have some special skill. The long legged down east boys make good stage dancers and acrobats. But when most of them are drunk nothing comes off but— "Nevada" had a line of cowboy songs.

11/7

We must listen. Before
she died she told them—
I always liked to be well dressed
400        I wanted to look nice—

So she asked them to dress
her well. They curled her hair . . .

Now she fought
She didn't want to go
405        She didn't want to!

The perfect type of the man of action is the suicide.

11/8

O river of my heart polluted
and defamed I have compared you
to that other lying in
410        the red November grass
beginning to be cleaned now
from factory pollution

Though at night a watchman
must still prowl lest some paid hand
415        open the waste sluices—
That river will be clean
before ever you will be

11/8

Out of her childhood she remembered, as one might remember Charlie Wordsworth's print shop in the rear of Bagellons, the hinged paperknife, the colored posters of horses (I'll bet it was for the races at Clifton where the High School now stands). Once Pop made a big kite, five feet tall maybe, with the horses' heads in the middle and it flew and I couldn't hold it without help. They fastened it to a post of the back porch at nightfall, real rope they had on it, and in the morning it was still there. She remembered the day the old man painted the mirror back of the bar: He took off his coat and laid the brushes and pans from his bag on one of the barroom tables. No one else was there but Jake who sat with his head in his hands except when someone came in for something or to telephone. Then he'd unlock the inside door and sit down again watching the old man. It was a big mirror. First he painted in a river coming in over from the door and curving down greenywhite nearly the whole length of it and very wide to fall in a falls into the edge of another river that ran all along the bottom all the way across, only a little of the water to be seen. Then he put in a blue sky all across the top with white clouds in it and under them a row of brown hills coming down to the upper river banks. Green trees he made with a big brush, just daubing it on, some of it even up top over the hills on the clouds, the trunks of the trees to be put in later. But down below, under the top river and all down the right side where it curved down to the falls he painted in the trunks first like narrow dark brown bottles. Then he drew in the houses, with white sides, three of them near the falls. "A good place to fish," Jake said. The roofs were red. On the other side of the falls, between the two rivers, the houses were brown, two of them on brown hills with trees all among them. Then, after the paint of the rivers was dry, he began to paint in little boats, above and below—She never saw the work finished, for the saloon had been sold and they moved away. The last thing she saw him do was paint in the boats, "Look out that boat up there don't go over those falls," Jake said. The rivers were painted flat on the glass, wonderful rivers where she wanted to be. Some day she wanted to go to that place and see it. Like the song she remembered in school and she always wanted them to sing when you could ask what song you wanted sung, "Come again soon and you shall hear sung the tale of those green little islands." She always wanted to hear the rest of it but there was never any more. They moved away.

11/10

          The shell flowers
          the wax grapes and peaches
420       the fancy oak or mahogany tables
          the highbacked baronial hall chairs.

          Or the girls' legs
          agile stanchions
          the breasts
425       the pinheads—

          —Wore my bathing suit
          wet
          four hours after sundown.
          That's how. Yea?
430       Easy to get
          hard to get rid of.

Then unexpectedly
a small house with a soaring oak
leafless above it

435          Someone should summarize these things
in the interest of local
government or how
a spotted dog goes up a gutter—

and in chalk crudely
440          upon the railroad bridge support
a woman rampant
brandishing two rolling pins

11/11

A cat licking herself solves most of the problems of infection. We wash
too much and finally it kills us.

11/13

SHAKESPEARE

By writing he escaped from the world into the natural world of his
mind. The unemployable world of his fine head was unnaturally use-
less in the gross exterior of his day—or any day. By writing he made
this active. He melted himself into that grossness, and colored it with
his powers. The proof that he was right and they passing, being that
he continues always and naturally while their artificiality destroyed
them. A man unable to employ himself in his world.

Therefore his seriousness and his accuracies, because it was not
his play but the drama of his life. It is his anonymity that is baffling
to nit-wits and so they want to find an involved explanation—to defeat
the plainness of the evidence.

When he speaks of fools he is one; when of kings he is one, dou-
bly so in misfortune.

He is a woman, a pimp, a prince Hal°—

Such a man is a prime borrower and standardizer—No inventor.
He lives because he sinks back, does not go forward, sinks back into
the mass—

He is Hamlet plainer than a theory—and in everything.

You can't buy a life again after it's gone, that's the way I mean.

He drinks awful bad and he beat me up every single month while
I was carrying this baby, pretty nearly every week.

(Shakespeare) a man stirred alive, all round *not* minus the intelli-
gence but the intelligence subjugated—by misfortune in this case

---

655 *Prince Hal:* from Shakespeare's *Henry the Fourth*, Parts One and Two. After a playful
youth, he matures, kills the rebel Hotspur, and finally repudiates the wild friends of his
youth when he becomes King Henry V.

maybe—subjugated to the instinctive whole as it must be, but not minus it as in almost everything—not by cupidity that blights an island literature—but round, round, a round world *E pur si muove.*° *That* has never sunk into literature as it has into geography, cosmology. Literature is still mediæval, formal, dogmatic, the scholars, the obstinate rationalists—

These things are easy and obvious but it is not easy to formulate them, and it is still harder to put them down briefly. Yet it must be possible since I have done it here and there.

Such must be the future: penetrant and simple—minus the scaffolding of the academic, which is a "lie" in that it is inessential to the purpose as to the design.

This will do away with the stupidity of little children at school, which is the incubus of modern life—and the defense of the economists and modern rationalists of literature. To keep them drilled.

The difficulty of modern styles is made by the fragmentary stupidity of modern life, its lacunæ of sense, loops, perversions of instinct, blankets, amputations, fulsomeness of instruction and multiplications of inanity. To avoid this, accuracy is driven to a hard road. To be plain is to be subverted since every term must be forged new, every word is tricked out of meaning, hanging with as many cheap traps as an altar.

The only human value of anything, writing included, is intense vision of the facts, add to that by saying the truth and action upon them,—clear into the machine of absurdity to a core that is covered.

God—Sure if it means sense. "God" is poetic for the unobtainable. Sense is hard to get but it can be got. Certainly that destroys "God," it destroys everything that interferes with simple clarity of apprehension.

11/16

The art of writing is all but lost (not the science which comes afterward and depends completely on the first) it is to make the stores of the mind available to the pen—Wide! That which locks up the mind is vicious.

Mr. Seraphim: They hate me. Police Protection. She was a flaming type of stupidity and its resourceful manner under Police Protection—the only normal: a type. One of the few places where the truth (demeaned) clings on.

11/16

TRAVELLING IN FAST COMPANY

As the ferry came into the slip there was a pause then a young fellow on a motorcycle shot out of the exit, looked right and left, sighted the hill, opened her up and took the grade at top speed. Right behind him came three others bunched and went roaring by, and behind them was a youngster travelling in fast company his eyes fastened on the others, and behind him an older guy sitting firm and with a face on

---

667 . . . *muove:* (Italian) "and then he moves it."

him like a piece of wood ripped by without a quiver. And that brings
it all up—Shakespeare—plays.

. . . Its hands stuck up in the air like prongs. Just sticking up in
the air, fingers spread apart.

                                        Goethe° was a rotten
dramatist . . .

11/20

445                        Even idiots grow old
                               in a cap with the peak
                           over his right ear
                               cross-eyed
                           shamble-footed
                               minding the three goats
                           behind the firehouse
450                            his face is deeper lined
                           than last year
                               and the rain comes down
                           in gusts suddenly

11/22

                           and hunters still return
455                        even through the city
                           with their guns slung
                           openly from the shoulder
                           emptyhanded howbeit
                           for the most part
460                                    but aloof
                           as if from and truly from
                           another older world

11/24

If genius is profuse, never ending—stuck in the middle of a work is—
the wrong track. Genius is the track, seen. Once seen it is impossible
to keep from it. The superficial definitions, such as "genius is indus-
try, genius is hard work, etc." are nonsense. It is to see the track, to
smell it out, to know it inevitable—sense sticking out all round feel-
ing, feeling, seeing—hearing touching. The rest is pure gravity (the
earth pull).

Creations:—they are situations of the soul (Lear, Harpagon, Œdi-
pus Rex, Electra)° but so closely (subjectively) identified with life that

---

710 *Goethe:* Johann Wolfgang von Goethe (1749–1832), German poet, dramatist, scientist,
and court official, author of *Faust* (1808, 1832).
741 *Electra: Lear:* the title character in Shakespeare's tragedy *King Lear* (1605) who pro-
vokes a series of disasters by dividing his kingdom among his daughters; Harpagon: a char-
acter from Molière's *The Miser* (1668) whose greed fatally infects all around him; Oedipus
Rex: title character of *Oedipus Tyrannus* (c. 429 B.C.) and *Oedipus at Colonus* (401 B.C.)
by Greek dramatist Sophocles (c. 496–c. 406 B.C.) who cannot escape a prophecy that he
will kill his father and lie with his mother; Electra: title character of *Electra* (413 B.C.) by
Greek dramatist Euripides (c. 485–c. 406 B.C.); the daughter of Agamemnon and
Clytemnestra, she plots the murder of her mother in revenge for her mother's murder of
Agamemnon.

they become people. They are offshoots of an intensely simple mind. It is no matter what we think, no matter what we are.

The drama is the identification of the character with the man himself (Shakespeare—and his sphere of knowledge, close to him). As it flares in himself the drama is completed and the back kick of it is the other characters, created as the reflex of the first, so the dramatist "lives," himself in his world. A poem is a soliloquy without the "living" in the world. So the dramatist "lives" the character. But to labor over the "construction" over the "technique" is to defeat, to tie up the drama itself. One cannot live after a prearranged pattern, it is all simply dead.

This is the thing (obvious and simple) that except through genius makes the theater a corpse. To intensely realize identity makes it live (borrowing stealing the form by feeling it—as an uninformed man must). A play is this primary realization coming up to intensity and then fading (futilely) in self. This *is* the technique, the unlearnable, it is the *natural* drama, which can't imagine situations in any other way than in association with the flesh—till it becomes living, it is so personal to a nothing, a nobody.

The painfully scrupulous verisimilitude which honesty affects— drill, discipline defeats its own ends in—

To be nothing and unaffected by the results, to unlock, and to flow (They believe that when they have the mold of technique made perfect without a leak in it that the mind will be *drilled* to flow there whereas the mind is locked the more tightly the more perfect the technique is forged) (or it may flow, disencumbered by what it has learned, become unconscious, provided the technique becomes mechanical, goes out of the mind and so the mind (now it has been cut for life in this pattern)) can devote itself to that just as if it had learned it imitatively or not at all.

To be nothing and unaffected by the results, to unlock and flow, uncolored, smooth, carelessly—not cling to the unsolvable lumps of personality (yourself and your concessions, poems) concretions—

11/28

465

I make really very little money.
What of it?
I prefer the grass with the rain on it
the short grass before my headlights
when I am turning the car—
a degenerate trait, no doubt.
It would ruin England.

12/2

The first snow was a white sand that made the white rocks seem red.

The police are "the soldiers of the Duke." The great old names: Gaynor, Healy—°

---

785 *Healy:* William Gaynor (1849–1913), mayor of New York 1903–1913; Timothy Michael Healy (1855–1931), Irish Nationalist leader who was first governor-general of the Irish Free State (1922–1928).

12/9

Imagine a family of four grown men, one in bed with a sore throat, one with fresh plaster dust on his pants, one who played baseball all last summer and one holding the basin, four young men and no women but the mother with smallpox scars marring the bridge and the end of her nose and dinner on the table, oil and meat bits and cuts of green peppers, the range giving out a heat for coats on the backs of the chairs to dry in.

Fairfield: Peoples Loan and Service, Money to Loan: and a young man carrying a bowling ball in a khaki canvas case. The Midland and a fern in the window before the inner oak and cut-glass screen. House and sign painting in all its branches. Fairfield Bowling and Billiard Academy. Architect John Gabrone Architect, U.S. Post Office, Fairfield, N.J. Branch. Commercial Barber Shop. The New Cigarette Three Castles. Real Estate and Insurance. Motor Vehicle Agency. Commercial Lunch. Fairfield Home Laundry, soft water washing.

12/15

470        What an image in the face of Almighty God is she
           her hands in her slicker pockets, head bowed,
           Tam pulled down, flat-backed, lanky-legged,
           loose feet kicking the pebbles as she goes

12/18

Here by the watertank and the stone, mottled granite, big as a rhinocerous head—cracked on one side—Damn families. My grandfather was a business man, you know. He kept the ice house in Mayaguez. They imported the ice. He kept it and sold it. My grandmother, my mother's mother, would make syrups, strawberry and like that. He would sell them also. But his half-brother Henriquez, there's plenty of that in my family, would go there, to the ice house, and drink all day long without paying anything, until the man my grandfather had there complained. "You know Henriquez comes and drinks five or six glasses of syrup and never pays anything." He did that. Just drank, lived at the house, took anything he pleased. That's how, as my mother says, she came to know Manuel Henriquez, her half-cousin, better than she did her own brother who was away much of the time studying. Henriquez would never work, help or do anything until my grandfather had to tell him to stop. It was at about this time my grandfather died and this is how my mother came to distrust and hate the Germans. All my grandfather's friends were German, all but a few. "It was a man named Krug. I suppose he may have been father's partner anyhow he was his best friend, I don't know. When my father died, Krug came to my mother and asked her if she had anything because my father owed some money. She had an *hacienda*° in the country that she had had since before she was married, her own. She gave that. Then Krug came and said it was all gone, that there was nothing left. After that, he turned his back on the family (The skunk). It was the Spanish druggist Mestre who lent my mother the money to buy a few things and sell them to make a little business. He was a Catalan—they can't say Pepe, like a Castilian

---

826 *hacienda*: (Spanish) "country estate with a large house."

but he would call his wife, Papeeta. My mother would send to Paris
for a half dozen fine shirts, but fine, fine shirts and a few things like
that. My brother was in Paris studying. When Krug told my mother she
must send for him, that there was nothing left, she wrote. He answered
her that he would sweep the streets of Paris rather than leave. She
would send him money she made on her little business. Sometimes, he
told us afterward, he would keep a sou in his pocket two weeks so as
not to say he hadn't any money. The students helped each other. Bar-
clay, an Englishman, was one of his best friends. He helped him."

That's why my own mother's education ended abruptly. Sometimes
she would copy out letters for my grandmother, child that she was, to
send to Paris. When her brother returned a doctor he himself sent her
to Paris to study painting. But he married and he began to have chil-
dren and he never collected any money—he had a wife too. So finally
he sent for my mother to go back to Santo Domingo where they were
living then. Mother cried for three days then she had to go and leave
it all. When she got there her brother told her about his friend, Black-
well. A fine fellow, the best in the world *"pero no es musicante."*° Black-
well was in the States at the time of my mother's return from Paris
having his teeth fixed.

When a little child would be bothersome they would tell her to go
ask the maid for a little piece of *ten te aya.*°

When my brother was happy he would sing, walking up and down
kicking out his feet: *Si j'étais roi de Bayaussi-e, tu serais reine-e par ma
foi!*° You made me think right away of him.

*1928*

# This is Just to Say

I have eaten
the plums
that were in
the icebox

5         and which
you were probably
saving
for breakfast

Forgive me
10        they were delicious
so sweet
and so cold

*1934*

---

849 *musicante*: (Spanish), "However, he's no musician." Williams may be misremember-
ing the Spanish word *musico*.
853 *ten te aya*: (Spanish) "keep you there," a direction to the maid to keep a child occupied.
856 . . . *foi!*: (French) "If I were king of [Bayeux], you would be queen, by God [literally,
by my fate]."

## Proletarian Portrait

A big young bareheaded woman
in an apron

Her hair slicked back standing
on the street

5      One stockinged food toeing
the sidewalk

Her shoe in her hand. Looking
intently into it

She pulls out the paper insole
10     to find the nail

That has been hurting her

1935

## The Yachts°

contend in a sea which the land partly encloses
shielding them from the too-heavy blows
of an ungoverned ocean which when it chooses

tortures the biggest hulls, the best man knows
5      to pit against its beatings, and sinks them pitilessly
Mothlike in mists, scintillant° in the minute

brilliance of cloudless days, with broad bellying sails
they glide to the wind tossing green water
from their sharp prows while over them the crew crawls

10     ant-like, solicitously grooming them, releasing,
making fast as they turn, lean far over and having
caught the wind again, side by side, head for the mark.

In a well guarded arena of open water surrounded by
lesser and greater craft which, sycophant, lumbering
15     and flittering follow them, they appear youthful, rare

as the light of a happy eye, live with the grace
of all that in the mind is fleckless, free and
naturally to be desired. Now the sea which holds them

---

**poem title:** Williams' notes: "A *very* vague imitation of Dante. I was quickly carried away by my own feelings." "The yachts do not sink but go on with the race while only *in the imagination* are they seen to flounder. It is a false situation which the yachts typify with the beauty of their movements while the real situation (of the poor) is desperate while 'the skillful yachts pass over.'"
6 *scintillant:* sparkling, brilliant.

is moody, lapping their glossy sides, as if feeling
20    for some slightest flaw but fails completely.
Today no race. Then the wind comes again. The yachts

move, jockeying for a start, the signal is set and they
are off. Now the waves strike at them but they are too
well made, they slip through, though they take in canvas.

25    Arms with hands grasping seek to clutch at the prows.
Bodies thrown recklessly in the way are cut aside.
It is a sea of faces about them in agony, in despair

until the horror of the race dawns staggering the mind,
the whole sea become an entanglement of watery bodies
30    lost to the world bearing what they cannot hold. Broken,

beaten, desolate, reaching from the dead to be taken up
they cry out, failing, failing! their cries rising
in waves still as the skillful yachts pass over.

1935


# The Descent

The descent beckons
          as the ascent beckoned.
                    Memory is a kind
of accomplishment,
5              a sort of renewal
                    even
an initiation, since the spaces it opens are new places
          inhabited by hordes
                    heretofore unrealized,
10    of new kinds—
          since their movements
                    are toward new objectives
(even though formerly they were abandoned).

No defeat is made up entirely of defeat—since
15    the world it opens is always a place
                    formerly
                              unsuspected. A
world lost,
          a world unsuspected,
20                    beckons to new places
and no whiteness (lost) is so white as the memory
of whiteness   .

With evening, love wakens
          though its shadows
25                    which are alive by reason
of the sun shining—
          grow sleepy now and drop away
                    from desire   .

<blockquote>
Love without shadows stirs now
<br>    beginning to awaken
<br>       as night
<br>advances.
</blockquote>

30

<blockquote>
The descent
<br>    made up of despairs
<br>       and without accomplishment
<br>realizes a new awakening:
<br>      which is a reversal
<br>of despair.
<br>    For what we cannot accomplish, what
<br>is denied to love,
<br>    what we have lost in the anticipation—
<br>      a descent follows,
<br>endless and indestructible    .
</blockquote>

35

40

1954

## Asphodel, That Greeny Flower

### Book I

Of asphodel, that greeny flower,
<br>    like a buttercup
<br>      upon its branching stem—
<br>save that it's green and wooden—
<br>    I come, my sweet,
<br>      to sing to you.
<br>We lived long together
<br>    a life filled,
<br>      if you will,
<br>with flowers. So that
<br>    I was cheered
<br>      when I came first to know
<br>that there were flowers also
<br>    in hell.
<br>      Today
<br>I'm filled with the fading memory of those flowers
<br>    that we both loved,
<br>      even to this poor
<br>colorless thing—
<br>    I saw it
<br>      when I was a child—
<br>little prized among the living
<br>    but the dead see,
<br>      asking among themselves:
<br>What do I remember
<br>    that was shaped
<br>      as this thing is shaped?
<br>while our eyes fill
<br>    with tears.
<br>      Of love, abiding love

5

10

15

20

25

30

it will be telling
        though too weak a wash of crimson
                colors it
to make it wholly credible.
35              There is something
                    something urgent
I have to say to you
        and you alone
                but it must wait
40      while I drink in
            the joy of your approach,
                    perhaps for the last time.
And so
        with fear in my heart
                I drag it out
45  and keep on talking
        for I dare not stop.
                Listen while I talk on
against time.
50              It will not be
                    for long.
I have forgot
        and yet I see clearly enough
                something
55  central to the sky
        which ranges round it.
                An odor
springs from it!
        A sweetest odor!
60              Honeysuckle! And now
there comes the buzzing of a bee!
        and a whole flood
                of sister memories!
Only give me time,
65          time to recall them
                before I shall speak out.
Give me time,
        time.
When I was a boy
70          I kept a book
                to which, from time
to time,
        I added pressed flowers
                until, after a time,
75  I had a good collection.
        The asphodel,
                forebodingly,
among them.
        I bring you,
80              reawakened,
a memory of those flowers.
        They were sweet
                when I pressed them

and retained
85          something of their sweetness
                    a long time.
It is a curious odor,
          a moral odor,
                    that brings me
90     near to you.
               The color
                    was the first to go.
There had come to me
          a challenge,
95                    your dear self,
     mortal as I was,
          the lily's throat
                    to the hummingbird!
Endless wealth,
100          I thought,
                    held out its arms to me.
A thousand tropics
          in an apple blossom.
                    The generous earth itself
105     gave us lief.
          The whole world
                    became my garden!
But the sea
          which no one tends
110                    is also a garden
when the sun strikes it
          and the waves
                    are wakened.
I have seen it
115          and so have you
                    when it puts all flowers
to shame.
          Too, there are the starfish
                    stiffened by the sun
120     and other sea wrack
          and weeds. We knew that
                    along with the rest of it
for we were born by the sea,
          knew its rose hedges
125                    to the very water's brink.
There the pink mallow grows
          and in their season
                    strawberries
and there, later,
130          we went to gather
                    the wild plum.
I cannot say
          that I have gone to hell
                    for your love
135     but often
          found myself there
                    in your pursuit.

I do not like it
            and wanted to be
140                    in heaven. Hear me out.
Do not turn away.
I have learned much in my life
            from books
                    and out of them
145    about love.
            Death
                    is not the end of it.
There is a hierarchy
            which can be attained,
150                    I think,
in its service.
            Its guerdon
                    is a fairy flower;
a cat of twenty lives.
155            If no one came to try it
                    the world
would be the loser.
            It has been
                    for you and me
160    as one who watches a storm
            come in over the water.
                    We have stood
from year to year
            before the spectacle of our lives
165                    with joined hands.
The storm unfolds.
            Lightning
                    plays about the edges of the clouds.
The sky to the north
170            is placid,
                    blue in the afterglow
as the storm piles up.
            It is a flower
                    that will soon reach
175    the apex of its bloom.
            We danced,
                    in our minds,
and read a book together.
            You remember?
180                    It was a serious book.
And so books
            entered our lives.
The sea! The sea!
            Always
185                    when I think of the sea
there comes to mind
            the *Iliad*
                    and Helen's public fault
that bred it.
190            Were it not for that
                    there would have been

no poem but the world
    if we had remembered,
        those crimson petals
195    spilled among the stones,
      would have called it simply
         murder.
The sexual orchid that bloomed then
    sending so many
200         disinterested
men to their graves
    has left its memory
      to a race of fools
or heroes
205    if silence is a virtue.
        The sea alone
with its multiplicity
    holds any hope.
        The storm
210    has proven abortive
    but we remain
      after the thoughts it roused
to
    re-cement our lives.
215        It is the mind
the mind
    that must be cured
      short of death's
intervention,
220    and the will becomes again
      a garden. The poem
is complex and the place made
    in our lives
      for the poem.
225    Silence can be complex too,
    but you do not get far
      with silence.
Begin again.
    It is like Homer's
230        catalogue of ships:
it fills up the time.
    I speak in figures,
      well enough, the dresses
you wear are figures also,
235    we could not meet
      otherwise. When I speak
of flowers
    it is to recall
      that at one time
240    we were young.
    All women are not Helen,
      I know that,
but have Helen in their hearts.
    My sweet,
245        you have it also, therefore

I love you
                and could not love you otherwise.
                                Imagine you saw
a field made up of women
250                 all silver-white.
                                What should you do
but love them?
                The storm bursts
                        or fades! it is not
255     the end of the world.
                        Love is something else,
                                or so I thought it,
a garden which expands,
                though I knew you as a woman
260                         and never thought otherwise,
until the whole sea
                has been taken up
                        and all its gardens.
It was the love of love,
265                 the love that swallows up all else,
                                a grateful love,
a love of nature, of people,
                animals,
                        a love engendering
270     gentleness and goodness
                that moved me
                        and *that* I saw in you.
I should have known,
                though I did not,
275                         that the lily-of-the-valley
is a flower makes many ill
                who whiff it.
                        We had our children,
rivals in the general onslaught.
280                 I put them aside
                        though I cared for them
as well as any man
                could care for his children
                        according to my lights.
285     You understand
                I had to meet you
                        after the event
and have still to meet you.
                Love
290                         to which you too shall bow
along with me—
                a flower
                        a weakest flower
shall be our trust
295             and not because
                        we are too feeble
to do otherwise
                but because
                        at the height of my power

300 I risked what I had to do,
              therefore to prove
                    that we love each other
      while my very bones sweated
              that I could not cry to you
305                 in the act.
      Of asphodel, that greeny flower,
              I come, my sweet,
                    to sing to you!
      My heart rouses
310               thinking to bring you news
                    of something
      that concerns you
              and concerns many men. Look at
                    what passes for the new.
315 You will not find it there but in
              despised poems.
                    It is difficult
      to get the news from poems
              yet men die miserably every day
320                 for lack
      of what is found there. 
              Hear me out
                    for I too am concerned
      and every man
325               who wants to die at peace in his bed
                    besides.

*1955*

## Landscape with the Fall of Icarus°

According to Brueghel°
when Icarus fell
it was spring

a farmer was ploughing
5   his field
the whole pageantry

of the year was
awake tingling
near

---

**poem title:** *Icarus:* according to Greek myth, Icarus was a young man whose father, Daedalus, made wings for him, attached by wax. Icarus flew too near the sun; the wax melted, and he fell into the sea and drowned. The story is often taken to symbolize arrogance or over-reaching.
1 *Brueghel:* Pieter Brueghel the Elder (1525?–1569), a Flemish painter. In a corner of his painting "Landscape with the Fall of Icarus" (1555?), Icarus's leg protrudes from the sea; a farmer ploughing and a delicate sailing ship nearby are unconcerned by his fall.

10        the edge of the sea
          concerned
          with itself

          sweating in the sun
          that melted
15        the wings' wax

          unsignificantly
          off the coast
          there was

          a splash quite unnoticed
20        this was
          Icarus drowning

                                      1962

# Ezra Pound (1885–1972)

Perhaps no other major, modern American poet's work is so deeply and irreducibly conflicted. Pound was at once the impresario of high modernism—promoting the work of those contemporaries he admired, among them H.D., Marianne Moore, and James Joyce; editing T.S. Eliot's *The Waste Land* so drastically he is almost its coauthor; defining the imagist movement and making metrical innovation and metaphoric concision central to modernist poetics—and its most tragic figure, undermined by his own arrogance and eventually allied with the worst political impulses of the century. One may compare two early poems in this selection, "Portrait d'une Femme" and "The River-Merchant's Wife: A Letter," to get a glimpse of how divided his impulses can be; the first is arguably misogynist, the second almost a sympathetic interior portrait. Decades later he would leave officially unfinished, but for all practical purposes complete, a major poem sequence torn between utopianism and bestiality.

Born in Idaho and raised in Pennsylvania, he would earn an M.A. in Romance Languages at the University of Pennsylvania, teach briefly, and then depart for Europe. But he remained interested in America for years and put himself in direct conflict with his country during World War II.

Pound's major poetic achievement, and the focus of decades of his life, is *The Cantos*, a book-length sequence of 116 poems that is unquestionably at once one of the most influential and most controversial documents of twentieth-century literature. The poem's learning and system of unexplained references are immense; like all passionate learning it is also periodically idiosyncratic. No one save Pound himself is likely to have ready to hand both the range of classical references and the unconventional economic and cultural theories he cites. Pound himself is effectively the only reader fully prepared to read his poem. Unlike Eliot or Tolson, moreover, he published no notes with *The Cantos*, though when he read Canto XLVI over shortwave radio from Mussolini's Italy in World War II, he did preface it with some glosses, so he was clearly aware that the ordinary reader would either need a course of study or a handbook. Pound scholars have now done that for us, most notably in Carroll F. Terrell's *A Companion to the Cantos of Ezra Pound*, but also in continuing work by many others. We have tried to provide sufficient notes here to make these Cantos accessible, but still more annotation would be possible. Indeed, Pound pioneered the distribution of what one critic liked to call "radiant gist" throughout *The Cantos*, brief allusions that are designed to invoke a whole historical and emotional context for the reader; in such cases, just glossing the name cited will hardly suffice, so here and there we have chosen representative references for more detailed commentary.

Pound himself called *The Cantos* "a poem containing history," and in that deceptively neutral, if potentially grandiose, formulation inheres the poem's great challenge. For *The Cantos* is history as Pound saw it; to some degree the poem sequence is also history as he participated in it, albeit in a modest but unforgettable way. Some critics have tried to separate Pound's political views from his art—among them those who supported his receipt of the first Bollingen prize for his "Pisan Cantos" in 1949, an award that sparked a firestorm of debate at the time—but only a casual or self-deceptive reader of *The Cantos* can manage that trick. The poems are replete with Pound's enthusiasm for and defense of the nightmare of European fascism; over fifty million people died in the Second World War, and Pound believed the wrong side won. Moreover, as Pound looked over history he decided that all the arts were at their best when allied with absolute political power. He made such an alliance himself in Italy, and *The Cantos* repeatedly urges it on us as one route to a new Golden Age. None of this makes the poems easier to deal with, but none of it makes them less interesting either. The relationship between poetry and power receives in *The Cantos* its most compromising realization, as one of our most accomplished poets decides the century's most evil means served glorious ends.

Pound was initially contemptuous of Germany's dictator, Adolf Hitler; Mussolini was his contemporary hero. Yet Pound gradually became an admirer of the Nazis, and in a wartime radio broadcast from Rome announced that in *Mein Kampf* (1925), Hitler's anti-Semitic and megalomaniac manifesto, history is "keenly analyzed." Certainly Pound's racial theories found more reinforcement in Hitler than in Mussolini. Yet Pound's anti-Semitism was firmly in place early on; as early as his 1914 *Blast* poem "Salutation the Third," Pound had written, "Let us be done with Jews and Jobbery,/Let us SPIT upon those who fawn on the JEWS for their money." Pound's decades-long jeremiad against usury, or money lending (see Canto XLV here) was for him also a denunciation of world Jewry. In his 1941–1943 wartime radio broadcasts, published as *"Ezra Pound Speaking": Radio Speeches of World War II* (1978), he rails against the Jews unceasingly, against them and their fantasized allies, "Jews, Jews-playfellows, and the bedfellows of Jews and of Jewesses" (113). "The danger to the United States as a system of government is NOT from Japan, but from Jewry" (86):

> As to the Hitler program, it was (what we ALL knew, and did nothing about, namely) that the breedin' of human beings deserves MORE care and attention than the breedin' of horses and wiffetts, or even the breedin' of sheep, goat, and the larger livestock. That is point ONE of the NAZI program. Breed GOOD, and preserve the race. Breed thorough, that is for thoroughbreds, conserve the BEST of the race. Conserve the best elements. That means EUGENICS; as opposed to race suicide. And it did not and does NOT please the Talmudic Jews who want to kill off ALL the other races whom they can not subjugate (140).

President Franklin D. Roosevelt he sometimes called "Rosenfeld," to suggest his fantasy dominance by Jewish interests. In Canto LXXIII, published in an Italian military journal in 1945, Pound calls Roosevelt and Churchill "bastards and small Jews." He warned us in the radio broadcasts that "any man who submits to Roosevelt's treason to the Republic commits breach of citizen's duty" (104). Meanwhile, from time to time he tried to persuade American troops they would lose the war. For an American citizen to give aid and comfort to the enemy in the midst of a declared war is a capital offense. When Pound was cap-

tured by American troops in 1945 he was headed toward a U.S. trial for trea-
son; government agencies had recorded his broadcasts. The likely verdict was
not in doubt, but a group of friends intervened and had him declared insane.
It was a ruse, since he was no more insane than some millions of Germans
who shared his beliefs, but it kept him alive. The price he paid was to be con-
fined to St. Elizabeth's Hospital in Washington, D.C. from 1946 to 1958.

Despite this anguished history, *The Cantos* remains the primary model for
an ambitious American poem based on collage and historical and literary ci-
tation. Poets at the opposite end of the political spectrum from Pound, in-
cluding Charles Olson and Robert Duncan, were deeply influenced by Pound's
technique. And *The Cantos* themselves are richly conflicted texts—at once lyri-
cal and polemical, visionary and demonic—that well reward the investment
required to read them carefully. To that end we present here something like
the spine of the sequence, a selection that highlights the entanglement of aes-
thetics and politics, that emphasizes the compromised ambitions that make
the poem compelling reading. Canto I gives us Pound's epic ambitions at their
most pure. Canto IX presents the fatal allure of aestheticized power that would
haunt Pound for the rest of his life. Canto XLV is his towering brief against
usury. Canto LXXXI juxtaposes apologies for fascism with lyrical invocations
of nature; for a moment he verges on humility, then rejects it and denies that
vanity defined either his ambitions or Mussolini's. Finally, in a mixture of mul-
tilinguistic collage and counterpointed arguments, Canto CXVI and the un-
finished fragments give us the competing tensions in Pound's life and work in
their most condensed form.

## A Pact

    I make a pact with you, Walt Whitman—
    I have detested you long enough.
    I come to you as a grown child
    Who has had a pig-headed father;
5    I am old enough now to make friends.
    It was you that broke the new wood,
    Now is a time for carving.
    We have one sap and one root—
    Let there be commerce between us.

*1913*

## In a Station of the Metro°

The apparition of these faces in the crowd;
Petals on a wet, black bough.

*1913*

---

**poem title:** *Metro:* the Paris subway. In *Gaudier-Brzeska* (1916) Pound describes seeing
a series of lovely faces one day on the Metro. He attempted to find language "as worthy,
or as lovely as that sudden emotion. And that evening . . . I found, suddenly, the expres-
sion. I do not mean that I found words, but there came an equation . . . in little splotches
of color. . . . The 'one-image poem' is a form of super-position . . . one idea set on top of
another. I found it useful in getting out of the impasse in which I had been left by my
metro emotion. I wrote a thirty-line poem, and destroyed it. . . . Six months later I made
the following *hokku*-like sentence."

# Portrait d'une Femme°

Your mind and you are our Sargasso Sea,°
London has swept about you this score years
And bright ships left you this or that in fee:
Ideas, old gossip, oddments of all things,
5    Strange spars of knowledge and dimmed wares of price.
Great minds have sought you—lacking someone else.
You have been second always. Tragical?
No. You preferred it to the usual thing:
One dull man, dulling and uxorious,
10    One average mind—with one thought less, each year.
Oh, you are patient, I have seen you sit
Hours, where something might have floated up.
And now you pay one. Yes, you richly pay.
You are a person of some interest, one comes to you
15    And takes strange gain away:
Trophies fished up; some curious suggestion;
Fact that leads nowhere; and a tale or two,
Pregnant with mandrakes,° or with something else
That might prove useful and yet never proves,
20    That never fits a corner or shows use,
Or finds its hour upon the loom of days:
The tarnished, gaudy, wonderful old work;
Idols and ambergris° and rare inlays,
These are your riches, your great store; and yet
25    For all this sea-hoard of deciduous things,
Strange woods half sodden, and new brighter stuff:
In the slow float of differing light and deep,
No! there is nothing! In the whole and all,
Nothing that's quite your own.
        Yet this is you.

*1912*

# The River-Merchant's Wife: A Letter°

While my hair was still cut straight across my forehead°
I played about the front gate, pulling flowers.
You came by on bamboo stilts, playing horse,
You walked about my seat, playing with blue plums.

---

poem title: Portrait d'une Femme (French): Portrait of a Lady.
1 *Sargasso Sea*: a relatively calm portion of the North Atlantic sea named for its abundant seaweed, thought to entrap ships.
18 *mandrakes*: the forked root of the mandrake, a plant in the nightshade family, roughly shaped like a human body; it was thought to cry when pinched and to promote conception.
23 *ambergris*: a waxy substance, from the intestines of sperm whales, that is used in perfumes.
poem title: "The River-Merchant's Wife: A Letter," translated and adapted from a Chinese poem by Li Po (701–762).
1 *forehead*: in other words, while I was a child.

5      And we went on living in the village of Chokan:°
       Two small people, without dislike or suspicion.

       At fourteen I married My Lord you.
       I never laughed, being bashful.
       Lowering my head, I looked at the wall.
10     Called to, a thousand times, I never looked back.

       At fifteen I stopped scowling,
       I desired my dust to be mingled with yours
       Forever and forever and forever.
       Why should I climb the look out?

15     At sixteen you departed,
       You went into far Ku-to-yen,° by the river of swirling eddies,
       And you have been gone five months.
       The monkeys make sorrowful noise overhead.

       You dragged your feet when you went out.
20     By the gate now, the moss is grown, the different mosses,
       Too deep to clear them away!
       The leaves fall early this autumn, in wind.
       The paired butterflies are already yellow with August
       Over the grass in the West garden;
25     They hurt me. I grow older.
       If you are coming down through the narrows of the river
            Kiang,°
       Please let me know beforehand,
       And I will come out to meet you
30                As far as Cho-fu-Sa.°

                                                    *By Rihaku*°
                                                    *1915*


from

## The Cantos

### I°

       And then went down to the ship,
       Set keel to breakers, forth on the godly sea, and
       We° set up mast and sail on that swart ship,
       Bore sheep aboard her, and our bodies also
5      Heavy with weeping, and winds from sternward

---

5 *Chokan*: Ch'ang-kan, a suburb of Nanking.
16 *Ku-to-en*: Yen-yu-tui, an island in the dangerous river Ch'u-t'ang.
27 *Kiang*: the river Ch'u-t'ang.
30 *Cho-fu-Sa*: Ch'ang-feng-sha, several hundred miles up river from Nanking.
31 *Rihaku*: the Japanese name of Li Po.
**poem title:** to begin his *Cantos*, Pound adapts what he thought to be the oldest section of Homer's *Odyssey* (Book XI), Odysseus's visit to Hades (the Underworld of the dead); most of the names Pound cites are featured in Greek myth.
3 *We*: Odysseus and his men.

Bore us out onward with bellying canvas,
Circe's° this craft, the trim-coifed goddess.
Then sat we amidships, wind jamming the tiller,
Thus with stretched sail, we went over sea till day's end.
10 Sun to his slumber, shadows o'er all the ocean,
Came we then to the bounds of deepest water,
To the Kimmerian lands,° and peopled cities
Covered with close-webbed mist, unpierced ever
With glitter of sun-rays
15 Nor with stars stretched, nor looking back from heaven
Swartest night stretched over wretched men there.
The ocean flowing backward, came we then to the place
Aforesaid by Circe.
Here did they rites, Perimedes and Eurylochus,°
20 And drawing sword from my hip
I dug the ell-square pitkin;°
Poured we libations unto each the dead,
First mead° and then sweet wine, water mixed with white flour.
Then prayed I many a prayer to the sickly death's-heads;
25 As set in Ithaca,° sterile bulls of the best
For sacrifice, heaping the pyre with goods,
A sheep to Tiresias only, black and a bell-sheep.°
Dark blood flowed in the fosse,°
Souls out of Erebus,° cadaverous dead, of brides
30 Of youths and of the old who had borne much;
Souls stained with recent tears, girls tender,
Men many, mauled with bronze lance heads,
Battle spoil, bearing yet dreory° arms,
These many crowded about me; with shouting,
35 Pallor upon me, cried to my men for more beasts;
Slaughtered the herds, sheep slain of bronze;
Poured ointment, cried to the gods,
To Pluto° the strong, and praised Proserpine;°
Unsheathed the narrow sword,

---

7 *Circe*: according to Greek myth, a sorceress who detained Odysseus for a year; here, she has directed him to Hades to seek instructions from the Theban seer, Tiresias, on how to sail home, and gives him a favoring wind.

12 *Kimmerian lands*: lands of perpetual darkness, shrouded in mist, at the edge of the world; the Kimmerians were the mythical people who lived there.

19 *Perimedes/Eurylochus*: two of Odysseus' crew members; Eurylochus was chief mate.

21 *pitkin*: a square pit, measuring an arm's length (one-el, or forty-five inches) on each side.

23 *mead*: alcoholic drink derived from fermented honey.

25 *Ithaca*: Odysseus's island home, off the coast of Greece.

27 *bell-sheep*: a sheep wearing a bell that leads the flock.

28 *fosse*: ditch.

29 *Erebus*: a dark place through which souls passed on their way to Hades.

33 *dreory*: dripping with blood; from the Old English word "dreorig."

38 *Pluto*: according to Roman myth, the god who ruled Hades; in Greek myth, the god was himself Hades.

38 *Proserpine*: goddess of regeneration abducted by Pluto to become his wife; in Greek myth, Persephone.

40       I sat to keep off the impetuous impotent dead,
         Till I should hear Tiresias.
         But first Elpenor came, our friend Elpenor,°
         Unburied, cast on the wide earth,
         Limbs that we left in the house of Circe,
45       Unwept, unwrapped in sepulchre, since toils urged other.
         Pitiful spirit. And I cried in hurried speech:
         "Elpenor, how art thou come to this dark coast?
         "Cam'st thou afoot, outstripping seamen?"
                   And he in heavy speech:
50       "Ill fate and abundant wine. I slept in Circe's ingle.°
         "Going down the long ladder unguarded,
         "I fell against the buttress,
         "Shattered the nape-nerve,° the soul sought Avernus.°
         "But thou, O King, I bid remember me, unwept, unburied,
55       "Heap up mine arms, be tomb by sea-bord, and inscribed:
         *"A man of no fortune, and with a name to come.*
         "And set my oar up, that I swung mid fellows."

         And Anticlea° came, whom I beat off, and then Tiresias Theban,
         Holding his golden wand, knew me, and spoke first:
60       "A second time?° why? man of ill star,
         "Facing the sunless dead and this joyless region?
         "Stand from the fosse, leave me my bloody bever°
         "For soothsay."
                   And I stepped back,
65       And he strong with the blood, said then: "Odysseus
         "Shalt return through spiteful Neptune,° over dark seas,
         "Lose all companions." And then Anticlea came.
         Lie quiet Divus. I mean, that is Andreas Divus,°
         In officina Wecheli,° 1538, out of Homer.
70       And he sailed, by Sirens and thence outward and away
         And unto Circe.
                   Venerandam,°

---

42 *Elpenor*: crew member who drunkenly fell and broke his neck while on Circe's island, when he awoke to hear his companions leaving.
50 *ingle*: corner, house.
53 *nape-nerve*: neck nerve.
53 *Avernus*: lake near Naples thought to be the entrance to Hades.
58 *Anticlea*: Odysseus's mother, who died during his voyage. In Homer's *Odyssey*, Odysseus weeps when he sees her, but Circe has instructed him not to speak to anyone until Tiresias has drunken blood and spoken.
60 *second time*: Tiresias and Odysseus had met once previously on earth.
62 *bever*: drink.
66 *Neptune*: according to Roman myth, the sea god; in Greek myth, Poseidon, whose son (Cyclops) Odysseus had blinded. Neptune will delay Odysseus's return home.
68 *Divus*: Latin translator whose version of Homer's *Odyssey* (1538) Pound used for this canto.
69 *Wecheli*: (Latin) "at the workshop of Wechel" in Paris where Divus translated Homer; the phrase is printed on the title page of Divus's *Odyssey*.
72 *Venerandum*: (Latin) "venerable," "worthy of adoration," from the Latin translation of the second Homeric hymn to Aphrodite.

In the Cretan's° phrase, with the golden crown, Aphrodite,°
Cypri munimenta sortita est,° mirthful, orichalchi, with golden
75 Girdles and breast bands, thou with dark eyelids
Bearing the golden bough of Argicida.° So that:°

                                                                *1915/1925*


# IX°


One year° floods rose,
One year they fought in the snows,
One year hail fell, breaking the trees and walls.

---

73 *Cretan*: Georgius Dartona Cretensis, Latin translator of the Homeric hymns.
73 *Aphrodite*: Greek goddess of love.
74 *Cypri . . . est*: (Latin) "Held dominion over the Cyprian heights"; orichalchi: (Greek)
Aphrodite's earrings "of copper," a gift presented to her in the second Homeric hymn.
76 *Argicida*: (Latin) "Slayer of Argos." According to Greek myth, the god Hermes slew the
hundred-eyed Argus; with his golden staff, Hermes led the souls of the dead to Hades.
The golden bough gives Aeneas access to the Underworld; he offered it to Persephone be-
fore descending.
76 *so that*: the Canto ends with the colon, leading the reader directly into Canto II.
**poem title:** This is the second of the four Malatesta Cantos (VIII–XI). They concern
Sigismundo Pandolfo Malatesta (1417–1468), a famous condottiere (Italian leader of mer-
cenary soldiers), military engineer, and patron of the arts. Pound's Cantos follow on two
earlier efforts to rescue Malatesta's reputation from the highly critical account offered by
one of the condottiere's chief enemies, Pope Pius II, in his *Commentaries*. Malatesta grew
up in the age when Italian city states, formally subservient to the Pope, actually enjoyed
considerable autonomy, but the families that controlled the cities warred with one another
(and amongst themselves) and competed for power and papal recognition. In 1429, when
he was barely 13 years old, Malatesta commanded a small force that repelled papal troops
attempting to occupy Rimini. Malatesta became Lord of Rimini, Fano, and Cesena at age
15, but he would have to defend his domain for the rest of his days, and his means were
sometimes ruthless. Yet he also patronized poets and painters (who often took Malatesta
himself as their subject) and employed the greatest artists of his day (Leon Battista Al-
berti, Matteo da Pasti, Simone Ferucci, Agostino di Duccio) to design and build a temple
at Rimini. The Tempio, honoring Malatesta and perhaps his mistress Isotta, was to con-
tain fourteen sarcophagi for the remains of artists and philosophers, in addition to Malat-
esta's ancestors. It was never quite finished and thus remained in part a "monumental fail-
ure." For Pound, these aesthetic ends justify Malatesta's sometimes murderous means. He
is the prototype for Pound of a leader who kills with warrant in the service of a purported
ideal of achievement; Mussolini for Pound would be a contemporary Malatesta. As Pound
will note in Canto LXXX, Malatesta's Tempio was damaged by World War II allied bombers
in the effort to "cwuth Mutholini" (crush Mussolini). Toward the end of the war Pound
thought the Tempio had been entirely destroyed; hence the cry in the first of the two long-
suppressed Italian cantos (LXXII and LXXIII, published separately in Italy but until re-
cently excluded from *The Cantos*): "Rimini is burned down . . . Fallen are the arches, the
walls are burned / Of the divine Ixotta's mystic bed" (Massimo Bacigalupo's translation
from Pound's Italian). In response to this wartime message the speaker gasps, "Are you
Sigismundo?" Pound has his symbolic revenge in Canto LXXIII, when an Italian woman
tricks a group of British soldiers into crossing a minefield in front of the Tempio; twenty
of them die. In the end, *The Cantos* becomes Pound's unfinished, ruined Tempio.
1 *one year . . .* : the opening stanzas sketch a series of events in Malatesta's life. In 1440,
Rimini was beset with floods; four years later Malatesta started a military campaign in a
snowstorm; in 1442, Rimini was beset with a damaging hailstorm. Malatesta stood in wa-
ter up to his neck to escape pursuing hounds when he was ambushed crossing the terri-
tory of Astorre Manfredi (line 10), Lord of Faenza and a hereditary enemy of the Malat-
esta family. For information here and throughout the notes to Canto IX, I am indebted to
Carroll F. Terrell's *A Companion to the Cantos of Ezra Pound*.

Down here in the marsh they trapped him
5                in one year,
And he stood in the water up to his neck
           to keep the hounds off him,
And he floundered about in the marsh
           and came in after three days,
10    That was Astorre Manfredi of Faenza
           who worked the ambush
           and set the dogs off to find him,
In the marsh, down here under Mantua,
And he fought in Fano,° in a street fight,
           and that was nearly the end of him;
And the Emperor° came down and knighted us,
And they had a wooden castle° set up for fiesta,
And one year Basinio° went out into the courtyard
           Where the lists were, and the palisades
20           had been set for the tourneys,
And he talked down the anti-Hellene,
           And there was an heir male to the seignor,
           And Madame Ginevra° died.
And he, Sigismundo, was Capitan for the Venetians.°
25    And he had sold off small castles
           and built the great Rocca° to his plan,
And he fought like ten devils at Monteluro°
           and got nothing but the victory
And old Sforza° bitched us at Pesaro;
30           (*sic*) March the 16th:
           "that Messire Alessandro Sforza
           is become lord of Pesaro

---

14 *Fano*: town in the marshes of central Italy, part of the hereditary domain of the Malat-
estas, but Sigismundo Malatesta had to fight the town's inhabitants in the streets to as-
sert his dominance.
16 *Emperor*: Sigismund V (1368–1437), Holy Roman Emperor of the House of Luxembourg;
he knighted Malatesta in Rimini in 1433 on the way back from being crowned emperor in
Rome by the pope. A Piero della Francesca fresco in Malatesta's Tempio illustrates the
knighting ceremony.
17 *wooden castle*: designed by Malatesta for fiesta celebrating his 1433 marriage.
18 *Basinio*: Basinio de Basini (1425–1457), Italian poet; Malatesta was his patron. Basinio's
*L-Isottaeus* is devoted to Malatesta's love for Isotta degli Atti. Challenged to a debate by
rival court poet, Porcellio Pandone (1405–1485), they argued over whether it is possible to
write good Latin poetry without knowing Greek. Basinio won by demonstrating Latin lit-
erature's dependence on Greek, a view Pound supports. The debate took place in a fortress
Malatesta had designed. Basinio was later interred near the Tempio.
23 *Madame Ginevra*: Malatesta's first wife, who died at age 22; Pius II claimed Malatesta
poisoned her.
24 *Venetians*: Malatesta was more than once employed as a mercenary by other cities.
26 *Rocca*: a fortress at Rimini that Malatesta designed, considered one of Italy's marvels
at the time.
27 *Monteluro*: site of a 1444 battle that Malatesta won for his father-in-law Francesco
Sforza; they soon broke when Sforza, who had purchased Pèsaro from Malatesta's cousin
Galeazzo, then sold the town to his (Sforza's) brother Alessandro on March 16, 1445.
29 *Sforza*: Francesco Sforza (1401–1466), a peasant turned condottieri who became Duke
of Milan. The Medici family supported him as a way of balancing the power of Venice.
His successes contrast with Malatesta's struggles throughout this sequence of Cantos.

through the wangle of the Illus. Sgr. Mr. Fedricho d'Orbino°
Who worked the wangle with Galeaz
35        through the wiggling of Messer Francesco,
Who waggled it so that Galeaz should sell Pesaro
        to Alex and Fossembrone to Feddy;
and he hadn't the right to sell.
And this he did *bestialmente*; that is Sforza did *bestialmente*°
40   as he had promised him, Sigismundo, *per capitoli*°
        to see that he, Malatesta, should have Pesaro"
And this cut us off from our south half
        and finished our game, thus, in the beginning,
And he, Sigismundo, spoke his mind to Francesco
45        and we drove them out of the Marches.°

And the King o' Ragona,° Alphonse le roy d'Aragon,
        was the next nail in our coffin,
And all you can say is, anyway,
        that he Sigismundo called a town council
50   And Valturio° said "as well for a sheep as a lamb"
        and this change-over *(hæc traditio)*°
As old bladder° said *"rem eorum saluavit"*°
Saved the Florentine state; and that, maybe, was something.
And "Florence our natural ally" as they said in the meeting
55        for whatever that was worth afterward.
And he began building the TEMPIO,
        and Polixena,° his second wife, died.
And the Venetians sent down an ambassador

---

33 *d'Orbino*: (1422–1482), first Duke of Urbino, another condottiere and arts patron; in an astonishing moment of identification—one that illuminates Pound's view of literary struggles and his own wars of position—he described Federigo as Malatesta's "Amy Lowell" in *Guide to Kulchur*. Pound is referring to his belief that Lowell stole imagism from him and degraded it.

39 *bestialmente*: (Italian) "bestially, meanly," Pound's judgment about the injustice of the sale of Pèsaro; the same word was used in an account by Caspare Broglio, a Malatesta comrade, but one may well be at a loss to sort out ethical rights among a group of murderous competitors.

40 *per capitoli*: (Italian) "by agreement."

45 *Marches*: Malatesta joined an alliance against Sforza and harried him from the Marches of Ancona in a two-year military campaign.

46 *Ragona*: Malatesta had signed on as a mercenary in 1447 to help the king of Naples, Alphonso of Aragon, take power over Milan; despite having been paid more than two-thirds of his fee, he accepted a counter-offer from the Florentines. For this treachery Alphonso hated him thereafter.

50 *Valturio*: Roberto Valturio (1414?–1489), engineer and author of *De Re Militari*, adviser to Malatesta; he recommended keeping Alphonso's money and accepting the Florentine offer.

51 *hæc traditio*: (Latin) "this treachery," which Pound in the preceding phrase translates as "this change-over."

52 *old bladder*: Pius II, who suffered from gallstones.

52 *saluavit*: (Latin) "saved their cause," from Pius II's *Commentaries*: "There is no doubt that Sigismundo's treachery saved the Florentine Cause."

57 *Polixena*: Francesco Sforza's illegitimate daughter, whom Malatesta married in exchange for her father's promise to help him regain Pèsaro. After their young son died, Malatesta transferred his interest to mistresses, first Vanetta Toschi and then Isotta degli Atti. When bubonic plague struck Rimini in 1449, Polixena escaped to a convent, but she soon died there, perhaps of the plague. Pius II would later say Malatesta strangled her.

And said "speak humanely,
60       But tell him it's no time for raising his pay."
And the Venetians sent down an ambassador
         with three pages of secret instructions
To the effect: Did he think the campaign was a joy-ride?
And old Wattle-wattle° slipped into Milan
65       But he couldn't stand Sidg° being so high with the Venetians
And he talked it over with Feddy; and Feddy° said "Pesaro"
And old Foscari° wrote *"Caro mio°*
"If we split with Francesco you can have it
"And we'll help you in every way possible."
70              But Feddy offered it sooner.
And Sigismundo got up a few arches,
And stole that marble in Classe,° "stole" that is,
*Casus est talis:*
         *Foscari doge*, to the prefect of Ravenna
75       "Why, what, which, thunder, damnation????"

*Casus est talis:°*
         Filippo,° commendatary of the abbazia
Of Sant Apollinaire, Classe, Cardinal of Bologna
That he did one night (*quadam nocte*)° sell to the
80       Ill<sup>mo</sup> D°, D° Sigismund Malatesta
Lord of Arimininum, marble, porphyry, serpentine,°
Whose men, Sigismundo's, came with more than an hundred
two wheeled ox carts and deported, for the beautifying
of the *tempio* where was Santa Maria in Trivio°

---

64 *Wattle-wattle*: Francesco Sforza when he became Duke of Milan in 1450.
65 *Sidg*: Malatesta, still in the service of the Venetians.
66 *Feddy*: Federigo d'Urbino, who cooperated with Sforza in a later plot against Malatesta.
67 *Foscari*: Francesco Foscari (1372?–1457), Doge of Venice (1423–1457).
67 *Caro mio*: (Italian) "my dear man," Foscari addressing Malatesta, trying to keep him loyal to the Venetians by offering help in recapturing Pèsaro.
72 *Classe*: the magnificent basilica of S. Apollinare in Classe, Ravenna, the most notable Byzantine church in Italy. Malatesta removed its marble ornaments and placed them in his Tempio. Terrell suggests that Malatesta's effort "to avail himself of the treasures of the basilica" amounted to treating the church "as though it were a stone quarry."
76 *Casus est talis*: (Latin) "That's the way it is," Malatesta justifying himself to Foscari. Ravenna's residents were angry at Malatesta's plundering and protested to Venice, one of whose magistrates was responsible for Ravenna's legal matters. Malatesta paid a fine, but this was only one of his efforts to strip the basilica of its art.
77 *Filippo*: Filippo Calandrini, Cardinal Bishop of Bologna, who had authority over the Abbey of S. Apollinare. Pound claims Malatesta bribed him with four hundred ducats for the right to carry off the art of the basilica; according to Terrell, there is no supporting evidence for this claim.
79 *quadam nocte*: (Latin) "on a certain night."
81 *marble, porphyry, serpentine*: the spoils of the basilica.
84 *Santa Maria in Trivio*: an older church replaced by the Tempio Malatestiano. Terrell writes, "The great Renaissance architect, Leon Battista Alberti, had decided not to destroy the older church with the tombs of Sigismundo's ancestors but to superimpose the Tempio upon it, so showing a respect for earlier achievements obviously missing in Sigismundo. Thus the Tempio incorporates cultural layers from various periods (the Gothic church, the Renaissance shell, the Byzantine marbles) as Pound does in *The Cantos*. Pound's defense of Sigismundo from the charge of stealing is therefore not devoid of a self-serving element."

85 Where the same are now on the walls. Four hundred
   ducats to be paid back to the *abbazia* by the said swindling
   Cardinal or his heirs.
                 grnnh! rrnnh, pthg.
   wheels, plaustra,° oxen under night-shield,
90 And on the 13th of August: Aloysius Purtheo,°
   The next abbot, to Sigismundo, receipt for 200 ducats
   Corn-salve° for the damage done in that scurry.


   And there was the row about that German-Burgundian female°
   And it was his messianic year, Poliorcetes,°
95               but he was being a bit too POLUMETIS°
   And the Venetians wouldn't give him six months vacation.


   And he went down to the old brick heap of Pesaro
               and waited for Feddy
   And Feddy finally said "I am coming! . . .
100          . . . to help Alessandro."
   And he said: "This time Mister Feddy has done it."
   He said: "Broglio, I'm the goat. This time
               Mr. Feddy has done it (*m'l'ha calata*)."°
   And he'd lost his job with the Venetians,
105 And the stone didn't come in from Istria:°
   And we sent men to the silk war;°
   And Wattle never paid up on the nail
               Though we signed on with Milan and Florence;
   And he set up the bombards° in muck down by Vada°
110            where nobody else could have set 'em
               and he took the wood out of the bombs
               and made 'em of two scoops of metal

---

89 *plaustra*: (Latin) "wagons, carts."
90 *Aloysius Purtheo*: the next abbot of S. Apollinare.
92 *corn-salve*: recompense for crop damage done by the nighttime raid on the basilica; we
are to agree that Malatesta was quite a responsible fellow.
93 *German-Burgundian female*: unsubstantiated charges by Pius II that Malatesta assaulted
a woman traveling from Germany to Rome.
94 *Poliorcetes*: (Greek) "Taker of cities," epithet associated with an ancient king of Mace-
donia and part of the motto inscribed on medallions of Malatesta.
95 *Polumetis*: (Greek) "many-minded," Homeric epithet for Ulysses, here characterizing
Malatesta.
103 *m'l'ha calata*: (Italian) "he's tricked me."
105 *Istria*: peninsula that was a source of marble ordered for Malatesta's Tempio; delivery
was delayed.
106 *silk war*: Venice and Ragusa (now Dubrovnik) were rivals in the silk trade.
109 *bombards*: late medieval cannons that hurled large stone balls.
109 *Vada*: fortress taken by Malatesta's forces in 1453.

And the jobs getting smaller and smaller,
                    Until he signed on with Siena;°
115            And that time they grabbed his post-bag.
And what was it, anyhow?
              Pitigliano, a man with a ten acre lot,
Two lumps of tufa,
              and they'd taken his pasture land from him,
120   And Sidg had got back their horses,
              and he had two big lumps of tufa
              with six hundred pigs in the basements.
And the poor devils were dying of cold.
And this is what they found in the post-bag:
125                    *Ex Arimino die xxii Decembris*
          *"Magnifice ac potens domine, mi singularissime°*
"I advise yr. Lordship how
"I have been with master Alwidge who
"has shown me the design of the nave that goes in the middle,
130   "of the church and the design for the roof and . . ."
"JHesus,
"*Magnifico exso.* Signor Mio°
"Sence to-day I am recommanded that I have to tel you my
"father's opinium that he has shode to Mr. Genare about the
135   "valts of the cherch . . . etc . . .
          "Giovane of Master alwise P. S. I think it advisabl that
"I shud go to rome to talk to mister Albert so as I can no
"what he thinks about it rite.
"Sagramoro . . ."
140   "*Illustre signor mio,*° Messire Battista . . ."
"First: Ten slabs best red, seven by 15, by one third,

---

114 *Siena*: In 1454, Malatesta was contracted by Siena to attack the holdings of the Count of Pitigliano, including the castle of Sorano. Malatesta considered it a minor campaign (merely "two big lumps of tufa"), but, after a prolonged siege, Venice added an army and Siena hired a second condottiere. This divided command produced intensifying suspicions. When Malatesta breached the castle wall, he offered a truce to the count, at which point the Sienese decided he was dealing against their interests and behind their backs. They tried to arrest him, but he escaped, leaving behind a postbag with some 50 letters he had received over the preceding months. Four centuries later they were found in the Sienese archives. Pound quotes excerpts from them, designed to show us that, even while fighting for hire, Malatesta is concerned to receive reports on the welfare of his children and the progress on the Tempio.
126 *Ex . . . singularissime*: (medieval Latin) "From Rimini, 22 December 1454, Magnificent and powerful master to me most extraordinary." The letter is from Matteo Nuto of Fano, who was employed to explain the architectural plans Alberti had left in Rimini when he was recalled to Rome. Alwidge: Luigi Alvise, supervisor of carpenters and Masons building the Tempio.
132 *Magnifico . . . Mio*: (Italian) "Magnificent Excellency, My Lord." Alvise's son Giovane writes a letter dictated by his father. Genare: Pietro di Genari, Malatesta's chancellor. Albert: Leon Battista Alberti (1404–1472), a master architect, under the patronage of Pope Nicholas V, from whom Malatesta had obtained his services. Alberti was also a poet, sculptor, painter, inventor, musician, philosopher, and astronomer, one of the brilliant figures of the Renaissance. Sagramoro: Jacopo S. da Soncino, Malatesta's secretary and counselor, whose postscript testifies that he examined the work.
140 *Illustre . . . mio*: (Italian) "My dear sir." December 21, 1454, letter from Genari and Matteo da Pasti, addressed to Alberti and identifying materials needed for the Tempio.

"Eight ditto, good red, 15 by three by one,
"Six of same, 15 by one by one.
"Eight columns 15 by three and one third
145              etc . . . with carriage, danars 151
"MONSEIGNEUR:°
"Madame Isotta has had me write today about Sr. Galeazzo's
"daughter. The man who said young pullets make thin
"soup, knew what he was talking about. We went to see the
150  "girl the other day, for all the good that did, and she denied
"the whole matter and kept her end up without losing her
"temper. I think Madame Ixotta very nearly exhausted the
"matter. *Mi pare che avea decto hogni chossia.* All the
"children are well. Where you are everyone is pleased and
155  "happy because of your taking the chateau here we are the
"reverse as you might say drifting without a rudder. Madame
"Lucrezia has probably, or should have, written to you, I
"suppose you have the letter by now. Everyone wants to be
"remembered to you.                    21 Dec. D. de M."

160  ". . . *sagramoro* to put up the derricks. There is a supply of
"beams at . . ."


"MAGNIFICENT LORD° WITH DUE REVERENCE:
"Messire Malatesta is well and asks for you every day. He
"is so much pleased with his pony, It wd. take me a month
165  "to write you all the fun he gets out of that pony. I want to
"again remind you to write to Georgio Rambottom or to his
"boss to fix up that wall to the little garden that madame Isotta
"uses, for it is all flat on the ground now as I have already told
"him a lot of times, for all the good that does, so I am writing
170  to your lordship in the matter I have done all that I can, for
"all the good that does as noboddy hear can do anything
"without you.
            "your faithful
                        LUNARDA DA PALLA.
175                      20 DEC. 1454."


" . . .gone over it with all the foremen and engineers. And
"about the silver for the small medal . . ."


"*Magnifice ac potens* . . .°
            "because the walls of . . ."

---

146 *Monseigneur:* December 21, 1454, letter to Malatesta reporting on a visit by Malatesta's
mistress Isotta (later his wife) to a young girl with whom he may have had an affair. *Mi
pare . . . chossia:* (Italian), translated by the previous sentence. Lucrezia: one of at least
seven of Malatesta's illegitimate children; Lucrezia had been made legitimate the year be-
fore by the pope.
162 *Magnificent Lord:* letter from Lunarda da Palla, tutor to Malatesta's son Sallustio ("Mes-
sire Malatesta," 1448–1470). Georgio Rambottom: a stonemason. Sallustio was later mur-
dered by his half-brother, Roberto, either directly or at his instigation.
178 *Magnifice ac potens:* (medieval Latin) "to the magnificent and powerful."

180     "Malatesta de Malatestis ad Magnificum Dominum Patremque
        "suum.°

        "Ex^so D^no et D^no sin D^no Sigismundum Pandolfi Filium
        "Malatestis Capitan General

        "Magnificent and Exalted Lord and Father in especial my
185     "lord with due recommendation: your letter has been pre-
        "sented to me by Gentilino da Gradara and with it the bay
        "pony (ronzino baiectino) the which you have sent me, and
        "which appears in my eyes a fine caparison'd charger, upon
        "which I intend to learn all there is to know about riding, in
190     "consideration of yr. paternal affection for which I thank
        "your excellency thus briefly and pray you continue to hold
        "me in this esteem notifying you by the bearer of this that
        "we are all in good health, as I hope and desire your Ex^ct
        "Lordship is also: with continued remembrance I remain
195          "Your son and servant
                 MALATESTA DE MALATESTIS.
             *Given in Rimini, this the 22nd day of December*
                     *anno domini 1454*"
                 (*in the sixth year of his age*)

200     "ILLUSTRIOUS PRINCE:
           "Unfitting as it is that I should offer counsels to Hannibal . . ."°
        "*Magnifice ac potens domine, domine mi singularissime,*
        "*humili recomendatione premissa*° etc. This to advise your
        "M^gt Ld^shp how the second load of Veronese marble has
205     "finally got here, after being held up at Ferrara with no end
        "of fuss and botheration, the whole of it having been there
        "unloaded.
           "I learned how it happened, and it has cost a few florins to
        "get back the said load which had been seized for the skipper's

---

181 *Malatesta de . . . suum*: (medieval Latin) "from Malatesta of Malatestis to his magnifi-
cent Lord and father," from a December 22, 1454, letter from six-year-old Sallustio to his
father. *Ex . . . Capitan General*: (medieval Latin) "Excellent Lord, my Lord, and also Lord
Sigismundo Pandolpho of the Malatesti, Captain General," inscription on the outside of
Sallustio's letter, the text of which follows in translation. *Gentilio de Gradara*: a Malatesta
employee.
201 *Hannibal*: (247–187 B.C.) Carthaginian soldier who defeated the Gauls, crossed the
Alps in fifteen days with his elephants, against almost insuperable odds, defeated the Tau-
rini, and then turned his forces against the Roman empire, destroying several Roman
armies. Malatesta claimed to have descended from Hannibal and used elephants as his
emblem.
203 *Magnifice . . . premissa*: (medieval Latin) "Magnificent and powerful Lord, my most par-
ticular Lord, I send you my most humble greetings," December 18, 1454, letter from Piero
di Genari to Malatesta, announcing delivery of marble and reporting progress on the Tem-
pio and La Rocca. *defalcation*: embezzlement; *aliofants*: elephants, namely sculptured ele-
phants that support the columns of the Tempio; *Antonio*: Antonio degli Atti, Isotta's
brother, knighted by Emperor Sigismund along with Malatesta; *Ottavian*: Ottaviano, a
painter hired to illustrate the papal bull permitting Malatesta to construct an altar; *Agostino*:
Agustino di Duccio (1418–1481), Florentine sculptor who worked on the Tempio.

210 "debt and defalcation; he having fled when the lighter was
"seized. But that Y^r M^gt Ld^shp may not lose the moneys
"paid out on his account I have had the lighter brought here
"and am holding it, against his arrival. If not we still have
"the lighter.

215 "As soon as the Xmas fêtes are over I will have the stone
"floor laid in the sacresty, for which the stone is already cut.
"The wall of the building is finished and I shall now get the
"roof on.

"We have not begun putting new stone into the martyr
220 "chapel; first because the heavy frosts wd. certainly spoil
"the job; secondly because the aliofants aren't yet here and
"one can't get the measurements for the cornice to the columns
"that are to rest on the aliofants.

"They are doing the stairs to your room in the castle ... I
225 "have had Messire Antonio degli Atti's court paved and the
"stone benches put in it.

"Ottavian is illuminating the bull. I mean the bull for
"the chapel. All the stone-cutters are waiting for spring
"weather to start work again.

230 "The tomb is all done except part of the lid, and as soon as
"Messire Agostino gets back from Cesena I will see that he
"finishes it, ever recommending me to y^r M^gt Ld^shp

> "believe me y^r faithful
> PETRUS GENARIIS."

235 That's what they found in the post-bag
And some more of it to the effect that
> he "lived and ruled"

*"et amava perdutamente Ixotta degli Atti"*
e *"ne fu degna"*
240 *"constans in proposito*
*"Placuit oculis principis"*
*"pulchra aspectu"*
*"populo grata (Italiaeque decus)"*°
"and built a temple so full of pagan works"°
245 i. e. Sigismund
and in the style "Past ruin'd Latium"°
The filigree hiding the gothic,
> with a touch of rhetoric in the whole
And the old sarcophagi,
250 such as lie, smothered in grass, by San Vitale.°

> *1923*

---

243 *et amava . . . decus*: (medieval Latin) "And he loved Isotta degli Atti to distraction / and she was worthy of it/ constant in purpose / She delighted the eye of the prince / lovely to look at / pleasing to the people (and the ornament of Italy." Pound's tribute to Isotta mixes Italian with American sources, including Pius II's *Commentaries*, Horace's *Odes* III, and *The Diary of John Quincy Adams* ("constant in purpose, just and enduring").
244 *so full of pagan works*: from Pius II's *Commentaries*.
246 *Past Ruin'd Latium"*: As Terrell writes, "an echo of the line 'Past ruined Ilion Helen lives,' from the poem 'To Ianthe,' by W. S. Landor, which Pound quotes to align Isotta with the archetypal Helen."
250 *San Vitale*: A Byzantine church in Ravenna from the sixth century.

# XLV

With *Usura*°

With usura hath no man a house of good stone
each block cut smooth and well fitting
that design might cover their face,
5      with usura
hath no man a painted paradise on his church wall
*harpes et luz*°
or where virgin receiveth message
and halo projects from incision,
10      with usura
seeth no man Gonzaga° his heirs and his concubines
no picture is made to endure nor to live with
but it is made to sell and sell quickly
with usura, sin against nature,
15      is thy bread ever more of stale rags
is thy bread° dry as paper,
with no mountain wheat, no strong flour
with usura the line grows thick°
with usura is no clear demarcation
20      and no man can find site for his dwelling.
Stonecutter is kept from his stone
weaver is kept from his loom
WITH USURA
wool comes not to market
25      sheep bringeth no gain with usura
Usura is a murrain,° usura

---

1 *Usura*: Latin for usury, lending money at interest. Money lending underlies the modern banking system that Pound despises, a banking system foreshadowed by the Medici bank operated in Florence by the Medici family for most of the fifteenth century. Usury was outlawed by the Catholic Church until the Reformation, when French Protestant theologian and reformer John Calvin (1509–1564) legalized the practice. For Pound, usury underlies all the evils of the modern world; it corrupts all exchanges and degrades both the nature of human labor and all its products. It is thus the power that keeps us from creating a paradise on earth; indeed it inhibits our even having a vision of such a paradise. See Pound's definition at the end of the poem.

7 *luz*: (Latin) "harps and lutes." Angels commonly play these instruments in religious paintings. Taken from line 896 of "Ballade pour Prier Notre Dame" from *Testament* (1461) by French poet François Villon (1431–?); here Villon's mother speaks of seeing paradise painted.

11 *Gonzaga*: Pound incorporates the full title of the painting "Gonzaga, His Heirs and His Concubines" by Andrea Mantegna (1431–1506). Luigi Gonzaga (1267–1360) was one of the great patron lords of the Italian city of Mantua; he founded a dynasty that ruled the city for centuries.

16 *thy bread*: a complaint against the adulteration and degradation of this most basic food, inherent for Pound in mass production by companies financed with borrowed money; in Canto LXXX Pound observes that Spanish bread used to be "made out of grain." Pound may also have known that Mussolini wrote and circulated a poem praising the purity of bread.

18 *the line grows thick*: in *Guide to Kulchur* Pound wrote, "I suggest that finer and future critics of art will be able to tell from the quality of a painting the degree of tolerance or intolerance of usury extant in the age and milieu that produced it."

26 *murrain*: plague.

blunteth the needle in the maid's hand
and stoppeth the spinner's cunning. Pietro Lombardo°
came not by usura
30    Duccio° came not by usura
nor Pier della Francesca; Zuan Bellin'° not by usura
nor was 'La Calunnia'° painted.
Came not by usura Angelico; came not Ambrogio Praedis,°
Came no church of cut stone signed: *Adamo me fecit.*°
35    Not by usura St Trophime
Not by usura Saint Hilaire,°
Usura rusteth the chisel
It rusteth the craft and the craftsman
It gnaweth the thread in the loom
40    None learneth to weave gold in her pattern;
Azure hath a canker by usura; cramoisi° is unbroidered
Emerald findeth no Memling°
Usura slayeth the child in the womb
It stayeth the young man's courting
45    It hath brought palsey to bed, lyeth
between the young bride and her bridegroom
                    CONTRA NATURAM°
They have brought whores for Eleusis°
Corpses are set to banquet
50    at behest of usura.°

                                                    *1936*

---

28 *Lombardo*: (1435–1515), Italian architect and sculptor who designed Dante's tomb at Ravenna. There follows a list of Renaissance artists who were likely to be supported by patrons, not financed by borrowed money ("not by usura").

30 *Duccio*: Agostino di Duccio (1418?–1481), Italian sculptor.

31 *Bellin'*: Piero della Francesa (1420–1492) and Giovanni Bellini (1430–1516), Italian painters from Florence and Venice.

32 *"La Calunnia"*: (Italian) "Calumny, rumor," a painting by Sandro Botticelli (1444–1510), a major painter of the Italian Renaissance.

33 *Praedis*: Fra Angelico (1387–1455) and Ambrogio Praedis (1455?–1506), Italian painters from Florence and Milan.

34 *fecit*: (Latin) "Adam made me," from a phrase carved into a pillar of the church of San Zeno Maggiore in Verona, Italy; the full inscription is "*Adaminus Desco Georgio me fecit,*" which effectively signs the artist's name to his work, a sign for Pound of his pride in singular creation, in contrast to mass production financed with borrowed money.

36 *Hilaire*: St. Trophine is a medieval church in Arles, France, noted for its cloistered courtyard, while Saint Hilaire is in Poitiers.

41 *cramoisi*: (French) "crimson cloth."

42 *Memling*: Hans Memling (1430?–1495), Flemish painter of religious subjects and portraits.

47 *CONTRA NATURUM*: (Latin) "Against nature," a phrase Aristotle applies to usury in his *Politics*.

48 *Eleusis*: town in ancient Greece, near Athens, where priestesses celebrated spring rites in honor of the goddess of fertility; now, in the time of usury, the priestesses are replaced by whores. Usury debauches the sacred.

50 *usura*: Pound adds a note of definition at the end of the canto—"N.B. Usury: A charge for the use of purchasing power, levied without regard to production; often without regard to the possibilities of production. (Hence the failure of the Medici bank.)" Shortly before his death Pound had second thoughts about his lifelong obsession with usury: "I was out of focus, taking a symptom for a cause. The cause is AVARICE."

# LXXXI°

Zeus lies in Ceres'° bosom
Taishan° is attended of loves
　　　　　　under Cythera,° before sunrise
and he said: "Hay aquí mucho catolicismo—(sounded

5　　　　　　　　　　　　　catoli*th*ismo)
　　y muy poco reli*H*ion"°
and he said: "Yo creo que los reyes desaparecen"°
(Kings will, I think, disappear)
That was Padre José Elizondo°

10　　　　　　　　in 1906 and in 1917
or about 1917
　　　　　　and Dolores said: "Come pan, niño," eat bread, me lad°
Sargent° had painted her
　　　　　　before he descended

15　　(i.e. if he descended°
　　　　　　but in those days he did thumb sketches,
impressions of the Velázquez° in the Museo del Prado
and books cost a peseta,°
　　　　　　brass candlesticks in proportion,

20　hot wind came from the marshes
　　and death-chill from the mountains.
And later Bowers° wrote: "but such hatred,
　　I had never conceived such"

---

**poem title:** perhaps the most lyrical of the *Pisan Cantos* (LXXIV–LXXXIV, published in 1948), the collection based on Pound's imprisonment in a military camp near Pisa, Italy, after American soldiers landed in Italy during World War II. Pound was wanted for treason because of the extensive radio broadcasts he had made on behalf of Mussolini and fascist Italy. The ellipses are Pound's. As Ronald Bush points out, Pound included passages in the sequence that he had written earlier; some of the fascist references are relatively late additions and thus amount to a willful reassertion of Pound's belief in Hitler and Mussolini.

1 *Zeus / Ceres:* the supreme Greek god and the Roman goddess of agriculture and fertility.

2 *Taishan:* Mount Taishan, a sacred mountain in China; Pound was reminded of it by a mountain that he could see from the Disciplinary Training Camp in Pisa.

3 *Cythera:* Aphrodite (Greek) or Venus (Roman), the goddess of love.

6 *Hay . . . reliHion:* (Spanish) "Here is much Catholicism and very little religion."

7 *Yo . . . desaparecen:* (Spanish), translated in the following line.

9 *Elizondo:* José Maria de Elizondo, the Spanish priest who helped Pound obtain a copy of a poetry manuscript by Guido Cavalcanti (1250?–1300).

12 *lad:* the phrase translates the preceding Spanish phrase.

13 *Sargent:* the American artist John Singer Sargent (1856–1925); he traveled to Spain in 1880 and copied paintings in the Prado.

15 *descended:* deteriorated artistically.

17 *Velazquez:* the Spanish painter Diego Rodríguez de Silva y Velazquez (1599–1660) in the Prado, the great national art museum in Madrid.

18 *peseta:* small Spanish monetary unit.

22 *Bowers:* Claude Bowers (1879–1958), American historian and ambassador to Spain (1933–1939) with whom Pound corresponded in the 1930s.

and the London reds° wouldn't show up his friends
25          (i.e. friends of Franco°
working in London) and in Alcázar°
forty years gone,° they said: go back to the station to eat
you can sleep here for a peseta"
          goat bells tinkled all night
30          and the hostess grinned: Eso es luto, *haw*!
mi marido es muerto°
          (it is mourning, my husband is dead)
when she gave me paper to write on
with a black border half an inch or more deep,
35     say 5/8ths, of the locanda°
"We call *all* foreigners frenchies"
and the egg broke in Cabranez'° pocket,
          thus making history. Basil° says
they beat drums for three days
40     till all the drumheads were busted
          (simple village fiesta)
and as for his life in the Canaries . . . °

---

24 *the London reds*: the communists were key supporters and organizers of the antifascist
Popular Front movement throughout the West that began in the mid-1930s; Pound's im-
plicit assumption that they were *all* communists echoes Francoist propaganda from the
1930s and since. Pound was passionately anticommunist; moreover, he saw communist and
Jewish intellectuals as part of the same worldwide conspiracy. In *Guide to Kulchur* (1937)
Communism is "barbarous and Hebrew." In the radio broadcasts Communism and Marx-
ism are the instruments of "Judah."
25 *Franco*: Francisco Franco (1892–1975), reactionary general who led conservative forces
in overthrowing the elected Spanish government and establishing a brutal fascist dicta-
torship from 1939–1975. Although Pound initially expressed indifference to the Spanish
Civil War, Mussolini's intervention on Franco's side—the Italian dictator supplied both
men and equipment—helped shape Pound's view once he integrated references to it in
*The Cantos*.
26 *Alcázar*: this is a reference to two different events in 1936, in the opening months of
the Spanish Civil War, both of which were widely publicized in the foreign press and both
of which became potent political symbols for Franco's sympathizers (including Pound)
worldwide. Alcázar de San Juan is a small town in the province just south of Toledo, which
Pound visited in 1906. In the opening days of the war small groups of government sup-
porters, on their own initiative, committed several atrocities there, among them killing the
local Bishop. Near the same time, the Alcázar fortress, the Spanish Army's school for in-
fantry officers in Toledo (a city about twenty-five miles from Madrid) was placed under
seige by government forces (from July until September). By resisting the seige for months,
the defenders of the Alcázar become heroes of the Nationalist (or fascist) cause.
27 *forty years gone*: depending on the date Pound is invoking, he may be referring to the
way Spain was weakened and discredited by the Spanish-American War (1898) or to the
Barcelona general strike (1909) and the brief period of liberal rule in Spain (1910–1913).
31 *es muerto*: translated from the Spanish in the next line.
35 *locanda*: (Italian) "inn."
37 *Cabranez*: probably Augustin Cabanes (1900–1985), historian and sexual researcher.
38 *Basil*: Basil Bunting (1900–1985), an English poet and friend of Pound. The "fiesta"
refers to a village ceremony recognizing the three days between Christ's crucifixion and
resurrection, when Christ was harrowing Hell. The villagers beat drums day and night un-
til their hands were bloodied.
42 *Canaries*: the Canary Islands of Spain, off northwest Africa; Basil Bunting lived there
from 1933-1936, but found the food unpleasant and the people cruel; Bunting has sug-
gested Pound may have found the sexual mores in the islands unacceptable.

Possum° observed that the local portagoose° folk dance
was danced by the same dancers in divers localities
45                    in political welcome . . .
the technique of demonstration
          Cole° studied that (not G.D.H., Horace)
"You will find" said old André Spire,°
that every man on that board (Crédit Agricole)
50      has a brother-in-law
                    "You the one, I the few"
                    said John Adams°
speaking of fears in the abstract
          to his volatile friend Mr Jefferson.
55      (To break the pentameter, that was the first heave°)
or as Jo Bard° says: they never speak to each other,
if it is baker and concierge° visibly
          it is La Rouchefoucauld and de Maintenon° audibly.
"Te cavero le budella"
60                    "La corata a te"°
In less than a geological epoch
                    said Henry Mencken°

---

43 *Possum*: Pound's affectionate name for T.S. Eliot.

43 *portagoose*: Portuguese.

47 *Cole*: Horace de Vere Cole (1874-1935), an English economist who mounted a demonstration at the time of Italy's entrance in World War I. G.D.H. Cole (1880–1959) was an English economist and novelist who was a leader of one of the factions of the English Guild Socialists; it was the other faction, dominated by A. R. Orage, editor of *New Age*, that helped shape Pound's view of economics. Orage's concept of the organization was anti-democratic, neo-feudalist, and hierarchical, which Pound found appealing. For Pound to write "not G.D.H.," therefore, is to recall that earlier controversy.

48 *Spire*: (1868–1966), a French poet; Pound quotes his derisive estimate of the directors of France's Agricultural Bank (Crédit Agricole). In a 1920 piece in *The Dial*, Pound commented, "Spire is a poet, however much time he may spend in being a Zionist."

52 *Adams*: in a letter to Thomas Jefferson (third U.S. president), John Adams (second U.S. president) noted that Jefferson feared a powerful president could destroy democracy; Adams saw the danger as coming from the rich and influential upper class. Adams said Jefferson feared a monarchy, while he feared an aristocracy. In the radio broadcasts, Pound claims that Italy and Germany "make EFFECTIVE what had been INTENDED in the United States by Adams and Jefferson" p. 112; this from a man who supported Mussolini's supression of free speech.

55 *first heave*: the first job of poets was to stop using traditional pentameter verse, which Pound felt was artificial.

56 *Bard*: Joseph Bard (1892–1975), English critic and essayist.

57 *concierge*: in France, a doorkeeper at an apartment house; also, a hotel employee who assists guests with travel and other arrangements.

58 *Maintenon*: Francois Alexandre Frederic (1613–1680), Duc de la Rochefoucauld, a French politician and writer; Françoise d'Aubigné (1635–1719), Marquise de Maintenon, the mistress and later second wife of King Louis XIV of France and the author of a famous series of letters. Both were elegant prose stylists. Pound is protesting the poetic practice of making ordinary people (like bakers and innkeepers) sound like people of wit and learning.

60 *corata*: (Italian) "I'll cut your guts out" / "I'll cut out yours." In Canto X this exchange occurs between Pound's hero Sigismundo Malatesta and his enemy Federigo d'Urbino.

62 *Mencken*: H.L. Mencken (1880–1956), a celebrated American journalist, author, and critic with whom Pound had an extensive correspondence. The line refers to a passage from one of Mencken's letters to Pound: "I believe that all schemes of monetary reform collide inevitably with the nature of man in the mass. He can't be convinced in anything less than a geological epoch," quoted in Pound's *Guide to Kulchur*.

> "Some cook, some do not cook°
>     some things cannot be altered"
> 65 Ἰυγξ . . . . . ʼεμὸν ποτί δῶμα τὸν ἄνδρα°
> What counts is the cultural level,
>         thank Benin° for this table ex packing box
> "doan yu tell no one I made it"
>                 from a mask fine as any in Frankfurt°
> 70 "It'll get you offn th' groun"
>             Light as the branch of Kuanon°
> And at first disappointed with shoddy
>     the bare ram-shackle quais,° but then saw the
> high buggy wheels
> 75             and was reconciled,
> George Santayana° arriving in the port of Boston
> and kept to the end of his life that faint *thethear*°
> of the Spaniard
>             as a grace quasi imperceptible
> 80 as did Muss° the *v* for *u* of Romagna
> and said the grief was a full act
>             repeated for each new condoleress
> working up to a climax.
>     and George Horace° said he wd/ "get Beveridge"° (Senator)
> 85 Beveridge wouldn't talk and he wouldn't write for the papers
> but George got him by campin' in his hotel
> and assailin' him at lunch breakfast an' dinner
>             three articles
> and my ole man went on hoein' corn

---

63 *cook*: Pound's wife, Dorothy Shakespear, declined to cook for the family.

65 *ándra*: " 'Little wheel . . . ' [Bring that] man [back] to my house," from the second *Idyll* of Theocritus (third century B.C.), in which a young woman uses a magical charm to attract her lover.

67 *Benin*: a fellow prisoner of Pound's in Pisa, who built him a writing table. Pound calls him Benin because the black man's face resembled the masks made by the Benin tribe of Nigeria.

69 *Frankfurt*: German city, site of the Frobenius Institute, where Pound had seen the Benin masks.

71 *Kuanon*: according to Chinese myth, Kuan-yin, the goddess of mercy.

73 *quais*: (French, "quays") "wharves."

76 *Santayana*: (1863–1952) a Spanish-born American philosopher and poet who taught at Harvard and then lived in Italy. Pound met him in 1939 and the two subsequently corresponded. Pound hoped that he could give guidance to the then-projected Paradise section of *The Cantos*.

77 *thethear*: pronouncing *th* for *c* in certain words.

80 *Muss*: Pound's fond nickname for Benito Mussolini (1883–1945), fascist dictator of Italy from 1922-1945 and ally of Adolf Hitler in World War II. Mussolini's accent identified his birthplace, the province of Romagna in northern Italy. In the previous Canto (LXXX) Pound writes of "poor old Benito" who was betrayed by those around him.

84 *Horace*: George Horace Lorimer (1868–1937), an American journalist, editor of the *Saturday Evening Post*, and a neighbor of the Pound family in Wyncote, Pennsylvania.

84 *Beveridge*: Albert Jeremiah Beveridge (1862–1927), U.S. senator from Indiana (1899–1911). He wrote a series of imperialistic articles for Lorimer about the 1899 U.S. conquest of the Philippines, which immediately followed the Spanish-American War.

90          while George was a-tellin' him,
       come across a vacant lot
              where you'd occasionally see a wild rabbit
       or mebbe only a loose one
              AOI!°
95          a leaf in the current
                     at my grates no Althea°

-------

*libretto*°

Yet
Ere the season died a-cold
Borne upon a zephyr's° shoulder
100   I rose through the aureate sky
              *Lawes°* and *Jenkyns guard thy rest*
              *Dolmetsch°* ever be thy guest,
       Has he tempered the viol's wood
       To enforce   both the grave   and the acute?
105   Has he curved us the bowl of the lute?
              *Lawes and Jenkyns guard thy rest*
              *Dolmetsch ever be thy guest*
       Hast 'ou fashioned so airy a mood
       To draw up leaf from the root?
110   Hast 'ou found   a cloud   so light
       As seemed neither mist nor shade?

              Then resolve me, tell me aright
              If Waller° sang or Dowland played.

       Your eyen two wol sleye me sodenly
115          I may the beauté of hem nat susteyne°

And for 180 years almost nothing.

Ed ascoltando al leggier mormorio°
       there came new subtlety of eyes into my tent,
       whether of spirit or hypostasis,°

-------

94 *AOI!*: cry of lamentation.
96 *Althea*: "To Althea, from Prison," by the English poet Richard Lovelace (1618–1658); in the prison camp at Pisa, Pound found the poem in Morris Speare's *The Pocket Book of Verse* (1940). Unlike the speaker in the Lovelace poem, Pound is not visited in prison by such a person as Althea.
*libretto*: a book or words of an opera; as Carroll Terrell writes, "the climactic pages of Canto LXXXI are given a musical label to underscore the extraordinary musical cadences deliberately evoked in one of the major climactic statements of the poem."
99 *zephyr*: the west wind.
101 *Lawes*: Henry Lawes (1596–1662), English composer noted for his masques and airs for voice, generally upper-class music. Jenkyns: John Jenkins (1592–1678), English composer and musician to Charles I and II.
102 *Dolmetsch*: Arnold Dolmetsch (1858–1940), French musician and instrument maker; Dolmetsch Foundation (founded 1928) supports revivals of older music.
113 *Waller*: Edmund Waller (1606–1687), English poet; John Dowland (1563–1626), English composer.
115 *susteyne*: "your two eyes will slay me suddenly / I may the beauty of them not sustain," from "Mercilous Beauty," a love poem attributed to Geoffrey Chaucer (1340?–1400).
117 *mormorio*: (Italian) "And listening to the gentle murmur."
119 *hypostasis*: divine substance; here, Aphrodite.

120                but what the blindfold hides
          or at carneval
                              nor any pair showed anger
                Saw but the eyes and stance between the eyes,
          colour, diastasis,°
125                careless or unaware it had not the
                whole tent's room
          nor was place for the full Εἰδὼς°
          interpass, penetrate
                     casting but shade beyond the other lights
130                  sky's clear
                     night's sea
                     green of the mountain pool
                     shone from the unmasked eyes in half-mask's space.
          What thou lovest well remains,
                                        the rest is dross
135       What thou lov'st well shall not be reft from thee
          What thou lov'st well is thy true heritage
          Whose world, or mine or theirs
                              or is it of none?
          First came the seen, then thus the palpable
140            Elysium,° though it were in the halls of hell,
          What thou lovest well is thy true heritage
          What thou lov'st well shall not be reft from thee


          The ant's a centaur in his dragon world.
          Pull down thy vanity,° it is not man
145       Made courage, or made order, or made grace,
               Pull down thy vanity, I say pull down.
          Learn of the green world° what can be thy place
          In scaled invention or true artistry,
          Pull down thy vanity,
150                         Paquin° pull down!
          The green casque° has outdone your elegance.


          "Master thyself, then others shall thee beare"°
               Pull down thy vanity
          Thou art a beaten dog beneath the hail,
155       A swollen magpie in a fitful sun,
          Half black half white
          Nor knowst'ou wing from tail
          Pull down thy vanity
                         How mean thy hates

---

124 *diastasis*: interval, separation.
127 *Eidos*: (Greek) "knowing."
140 *Elysium*: according to Greek myth, the home of the virtuous after death, Paradise.
144 *vanity*: Cf. Ecclesiastes I: "Saith the preacher, vanity of vanity, all is vanity."
147 *green world*: nature.
150 *Paquin*: a famous Parisian dressmaker.
151 *green casque*: the green forms (as in helmet-like shells) of insects, hence natural beauty, surpass Paquin's creations.
152 *beare*: a paraphrase of Chaucer's poem "Truth: Ballade of Good Counsel," which Pound found in Speare's *Pocket Book.*

160     Fostered in falsity,
                Pull down thy vanity,
        Rathe° to destroy, niggard in charity,
        Pull down thy vanity,
                I say pull down.

165     But to have done instead of not doing
                this is not vanity
        To have, with decency, knocked
        That a Blunt° should open
                To have gathered from the air a live tradition
170     or from a fine old eye the unconquered flame
        This is not vanity.
                Here error is all in the not done,
        all in the diffidence that faltered . . .

                                                    *1948*


## CXVI

        Came Neptunus°
                his mind leaping
                        like dolphins,
        These concepts the human mind has attained.
5       To make Cosmos—
        To achieve the possible—
        Muss.,° wrecked for an error,
        But the record
                the palimpsest—

---

162 *Rathe*: (Middle English) "quick."
168 *Blunt*: Wilfred Scawen Blunt (1840–1922), an English poet and politician imprisoned for criticizing British imperialism and championing the cause of Irish home rule; he was much admired by Pound, who helped organize a dinner honoring him in 1914.
1 *Neptunus*: Neptune, according to Roman myth, the sea god; in Greek myth, Poseidon, whose son (Cyclops) Odysseus had blinded. Neptune appeared at the end of the first Canto to remind us that the sea god would delay Odysseus' return home. "Odysseus," the passage reads there, "Shalt return through spiteful Neptune, over dark seas." Roughly midway through the Cantos, in Canto XLVII, Pound retells the story of Odysseus' stay on Circe's island and again invokes Neptune's role in his journey. Now Neptune appears again at the end of the *Cantos* with perhaps a more personal inflection. The gods, it seems, have put many barriers in the way of Pound's own journey, and many obstacles have blocked the completion of the poem and the full realization of its original intention. Nor will Pound return home to the United States again. It is worth recalling that Gemisthus Pleton (c. 1355–1450), the Neoplatonist philosopher whose ashes Malatesta interred in the outside wall of the Tempio, made Neptune the greatest of the gods. Thus he is at once a blocking figure and the source of the poet's power.
7 *Muss*: Pound's fond nickname for Benito Mussolini (1883–1945), fascist dictator of Italy from 1922–1945 and ally of Adolf Hitler in World War II. Pound reasserts his admiration for Mussolini at the end and casts him as a leader who meant well and had admirable dreams, but failed partly out of his own mistakes and partly through the aggressions of others. From Pound's astonishing perspective, now sentimentalizing his own fascism decades later, "Muss" offered us "a little light / in great darkness."

10 a little light
                in great darkness—
      cuniculi°—
      An old "crank" dead in Virginia.
      Unprepared young burdened with records,
15    The vision of the Madonna°
                        above the cigar butts
                                  and over the portal.
      "Have made a mass of laws"
                            (mucchio di leggi)°
20    Litterae nihil sanantes°
                        Justinian's,°
      a tangle of works unfinished.
      I have brought the great ball of crystal;
                  who can lift it?
25    Can you enter the great acorn of light?°
                  But the beauty is not the madness
      Tho' my errors and wrecks lie about me.
      And I am not a demigod,
      I cannot make it cohere.
30    If love be not in the house there is nothing.
      The voice of famine unheard.
      How came beauty against this blackness,
      Twice beauty under the elms—
                  To be saved by squirrels and bluejays?
35                    "plus j'aime le chien"°

---

12 *cuniculi*: (Italian) "canals," or "underground passages." In Canto CI Pound cites the work of an Italian anthropologist who discovered canals near Rome that constituted an ideal irrigation system.

15 *Madonna*: in Canto CI Pound mentions the basilica of Torcello in the Venetian lagoon with a mosaic Madonna over the entrance.

19 *mucchio di leggi*: (Italian) "a mass of laws."

20 *Litterae* . . . : (Latin) "literature which heals nothing," from a June 28, 1812, letter from John Adams to Thomas Jefferson.

21 *Justinian's*: Justinian I, Flavius Petrus Sabbatius Justinianus (c. 482–565), emperor of the East Roman Empire from 527. His reign, through the generals he appointed, effectively restored the empire to its ancient limits. His general, Belisarius, regained the Vandal Kingdom of Africa (a success that for Pound foreshadows Mussolini's conquest of Ethiopia) and helped restore imperial authority in Rome. The fortifications he built anticipate Malatesta's fortress at Rimini. Meanwhile, Justinian's cultural contributions include the codification of Roman law in a series of volumes that have influenced the law of European countries to the present day. The mix of military and cultural work makes him another of Pound's heroes.

25 *crystal . . . acorn of light*: the image recalls neoplatonic philosophy; the "great acorn of light bulging outward" in Canto CVI is the primal, unseen light from which everything in the universe radiates. In Canto CVI it takes form in the flowers of paradise.

35 *"plus . . . chien"*: (French) "the more I love dogs," from Mme. Roland: "the more I know men, the more I love dogs."

Ariadne.°
    Disney° against the metaphysicals,
and Laforgue° more than they thought in him,
Spire° thanked me in proposito°
40     And I have learned more from Jules
                   (Jules Laforgue) since then
deeps in him,
        and Linnaeus.°
             chi crescerá i nostri°—
45     but about that terzo°
        third heaven,
           that Venere,°
again is all "paradiso"
     a nice quiet paradise
50             over the shambles,
and some climbing
         before the take-off,
to "see again,"
the verb is "see," not "walk on"
55     i.e. it coheres all right
          even if my notes° do not cohere.
Many errors,
        a little rightness,
to excuse his hell
60           and my paradiso.
And as to why they go wrong,
        thinking of rightness
And as to who will copy this palimpsest?
     al poco giorno
65          ed al gran cerchio d'ombra°
But to affirm the gold thread in the pattern
          (Torcello)°

---

36 *Ariadne*: in classical mythology, the daughter of King Minos who fell in love with The-
seus and helped him kill the Minotaur and escape from the labyrinth by giving him a ball
of string with which to mark his path. Theseus then betrayed her by abandoning her,
though the god Dionysus fell in love with her, married her, and took her off to Olympus.
*The Cantos* are of course rife with claims of betrayal, but here Ariadne also alludes to an
ideal at the center of the labyrinth of history.
37 *Disney*: Walt Disney (1901–1966), American filmmaker and entrepreneur whose cartoons
Pound admired.
38 *Laforgue*: Jules Laforgue (1860–1887), French symbolist poet.
39 *Spire*: Andre Spire (1868–1966), a French poet.
39 *in proposito*: (Italian) "for the intention."
43 *Linnaeus*: Karl von Linné (1707–1778), Swedish naturalist and physician, the founder
of modern scientific nomenclature for plants and animals, who went on to write more
philosophically about the diversity of life.
44 *chi crescerà*: (Italian) "Who will increase," from Dante, *Paradiso*, V, 105: "*Ecco chi
crescerà li nostri amori*," "Behold the man who will increase our loves."
45 *terzo*: (Italian) "third."
47 *Venere*: (Italian) "Venus," Roman goddess of love.
56 *my notes*: The *Cantos*.
65 *al poco . . . d'ombra*: (Italian) "In the small hours with the darkness describing a huge
circle," from Dante, *Rime* I, also quoted in Canto V.
67 *Torcello*: a city now sunk in the Venetian lagoon; a seventh century cathedral and two
palaces are preserved there.

al Vicolo d'oro°
      (Tigullio).°
70   To confess wrong without losing rightness:
Charity I have had sometimes,
      I cannot make it flow thru.
A little light, like a rushlight
      to lead back to splendour.

          *1968*

# Notes for CXVII et seq.°

For the blue flash and the moments
      benedetta°
the young for the old
      that is tragedy
5   And for one beautiful day there was peace.
     Brancusi's bird°
         in the hollow of pine trunks
or when the snow was like sea foam
     Twilit sky leaded with elm boughs.
10  Under the Rupe Tarpeia°
      weep out your jealousies—
To make a church
      or an altar to Zagreus° Ζαγρεύς
Son of Semele° Σεμέλη
15  Without jealousy
      like the double arch of a window
Or some great colonnade.

M'amour, m'amour°
      what do I love and
20       where are you?
That I lost my center
      fighting the world.

---

68 *al . . . d'oro*: street in Rapallo where a cross of blue sky is visible at the intersection.
69 *Tigullio*: the name of the gulf below Rapallo.
**poem title:** These notes were added by Pound's publisher long after the author's death; Pound had assumed *The Cantos* would end with CXVI.
2 *benedetta*: (Italian) "blessed."
6 *Brancusi's bird*: a famous sculpture ("Bird in Space," 1925) by the Romanian modernist sculptor Constantin Brancusi (1876–1957). His aim was simplification, to get to the essence of the thing. His "Sleeping Muse" (1910) was the first of a number of egg-shaped, highly polished carvings. A natural form in a tree on the grounds at St. Elizabeth's hospital reminded Pound of "Bird in Space."
10 *Rupe Tarpeia*: the Tarpeian Rock in ancient Rome was the place on the Capitoline Hill where criminals were hurled to their deaths.
13 *Zagreus*: alternative name for the god Dionysus, associated for Pound with religious ecstasy, fertility, and seasonal renewal.
14 *Semele*: Dionysus's mother, who was consumed by Jupiter's radiance when he appeared before her.
18 *M'amour . . .* : (French) "my love, my love."

          The dreams clash°
                    and are shattered—
25        and that I tried to make a paradiso
                              terrestre.°

          I have tried to write Paradise°
          Do not move
              Let the wind speak°
30                    that is paradise.


          Let the Gods forgive what I
                    have made°
          Let those I love try to forgive
                    what I have made.


35        La faillite° de François Bernouard°, Paris
          or a field of larks at Allègre,°
                    "es laissa cader"°
          so high toward the sun and then falling,
                    "de joi sas alas"°
40        to set here the roads of France.


          Two mice and a moth my guides—
          To have heard the farfalla° gasping
                    as toward a bridge over worlds.

---

23 *The dreams clash*: Daniele Varè was ambassador from Italy to the United States until Mussolini replaced him. Varè's memoir *The Two Imposters* details his readings of Mussolini's successes and failures, treating the absolutes of "triumph" or "disaster" equally as the "imposters" of the title; among his final chapters are "Harvesting of a Dream" and "The Dream Shattered."

26 *paradiso / terrestre*: an earthly paradise. Pound believed fascism would create an earthly paradise by centralizing power in the state, eliminating usury, and thus creating debt-free money. Even after the revelation of the holocaust he is able to sustain this fantasy. We can take the first-person voice here not only as Pound's own but also as that of the failed political heroes of *The Cantos*, from Malatesta to Mussolini.

27 *to write Paradise*: the stanza opens by admitting the failure of the modern idea that art can save us, while linking the literary project of *The Cantos* with the cultural and political aims of the historic soldier/patrons Pound idealizes. The allusion is broader, then, than the obvious reference to Dante's *Paradiso*.

29 *the wind speak*: once again Pound briefly allows that nature itself is paradise.

32 *forgive / what I have made*: whether or not this moment of contrition is convincing is open to debate.

35 *La faillite*: (French) "bankruptcy."

35 *Francois Bernouard*: a Paris publisher whom Pound knew in the 1920s; his firm declared bankruptcy in 1929.

36 *Allègre*: town in southern France associated with the troubador Bernart de Ventadorn (c. 1140-c. 1190). He wrote poems sung to music on behalf of his noble patrons, among them Eleanor of Aquitaine, who had him knighted in England; he ended his days in a monastery.

37 *es laissa cader*: (Provencal) "and let himself fall."

39 *de joi sas alas*: (Provencal) "[I see the lark moving] his wings with joy," from the first stanza of a Ventadorn song.

42 *farfalla*: (Italian) "butterfly."

That the kings meet in their island,
45                    where no food is after flight from the pole.
Milkweed° the sustenance
                    as to enter arcanum.°

To be men not destroyers.

                                                        1969

---

46 *Milkweed*: poisonous plant that provides a home for the Monarch butterfly; cited in
Canto CVI as "the king-wings in migration."
47 *arcanum*: the final mystery of life, unknowable.

# H.D. *(Hilda Doolittle) (1886–1961)*

H.D. was born and spent her early years in Bethlehem, Pennsylvania. Her father was a professor of astronomy and mathematics at Lehigh University. Her mother belonged to the Moravian Brotherhood, a Protestant sect that argued for a direct, sensuous perception of God, a belief that finds parallel expression in H.D.'s early imagist poetry. The family moved to Philadelphia in 1895 when the father became director of the University of Pennsylvania's observatory. Hilda enrolled at Bryn Mawr College, but found herself deeply conflicted. She had met and become engaged to the poet Ezra Pound but was simultaneously attracted to a girlfriend, Frances Gregg. Soon the women were on a boat to Europe, where Hilda became involved with Pound again; though the relationship faltered, Pound did come up with the name "H.D.," which she would continue to use. Although she visited the United States, her home thereafter would be abroad.

Doolittle met and married poet-translator Richard Aldington, published her first book of poetry, *Sea Garden* (1916), and soon the couple met and became intimately involved with D.H. and Frieda Lawrence. In the midst of the wartime chaos, H.D. also met the wealthy writer Winifred Ellerman ("Bryher"), who had committed the entirety of *Sea Garden* to memory; they would be lifelong friends.

From time to time, H.D. was beset by anxiety, and she even travelled to Vienna to be analyzed by Freud in the 1930s, but through it all she remained productive, writing poetry and fiction and doing translation from the Greek. During World War II she would write a major long poem, *Trilogy* (1944–1946), and follow it with another, *Helen in Egypt* (1961), but she has remained best known for the riveting power of the poems that simultaneously defined the imagist movement and exceeded what most other writers could do under its banner. H.D. calls up forces out of nature, intensifies them, and enlists them in vatic psychological demands. At moments in these poems, a transgressive otherness breaks through subjective identity. Myth and nature are placed in dynamic, transformative relationships with a poem's speaker. No readers who open themselves to her work can ever think of imagism as merely pictorial.

# Oread°

Whirl up, sea—
whirl your pointed pines,
splash your great pines
on our rocks,
5    hurl your green over us,
cover us with your pools of fir.

*1914*

# Mid-day

The light beats upon me.
I am startled—
a split leaf crackles on the paved floor—
I am anguished—defeated.

5    A slight wind shakes the seed-pods—
my thoughts are spent
as the black seeds.
My thoughts tear me,
I dread their fever.
10    I am scattered in its whirl.
I am scattered like
the hot shrivelled seeds.

The shrivelled seeds
are split on the path—
15    the grass bends with dust,
the grape slips
under its crackled leaf:
yet far beyond the spent seed-pods,
and the blackened stalks of mint,
20    the poplar is bright on the hill,
the poplar spreads out,
deep-rooted among trees.

O poplar, you are great
among the hill-stones,
25    while I perish on the path
among the crevices of the rocks.

*1916*

---

**poem title:** in Greek mythology, Oreads were nymphs who lived in the mountains. Like other nymphs, they were spirits personifying their particular setting.

## Sea Rose

Rose, harsh rose,
marred and with stint of petals,
meagre flower, thin,
sparse of leaf,

5    more precious
than a wet rose
single on a stem—
you are caught in the drift.

    Stunted, with small leaf,
10    you are flung on the sand,
you are lifted
in the crisp sand
that drives in the wind.

    Can the spice-rose
15    drip such acrid fragrance
hardened in a leaf?

*1916*

## Garden

### I

You are clear
O rose, cut in rock,
hard as the descent of hail.

    I could scrape the colour
5    from the petals
like spilt dye from a rock.

    If I could break you
I could break a tree.

    If I could stir
10    I could break a tree—
I could break you.

### II

O wind, rend open the heat,
cut apart the heat,
rend it to tatters.

15      Fruit cannot drop
        through this thick air—
        fruit cannot fall into heat
        that presses up and blunts
        the points of pears
20      and rounds the grapes.

        Cut the heat—
        plough through it,
        turning it on either side
        of your path.

                                                    *1916*

# The Helmsman

O be swift—
we have always known you wanted us.

We fled inland with our flocks,
we pastured them in hollows,
5       cut off from the wind
and the salt track of the marsh.

We worshipped inland—
we stepped past wood-flowers,
we forgot your tang,
10      we brushed wood-grass.

We wandered from pine-hills
through oak and scrub-oak tangles,
we broke hyssop and bramble,
we caught flower and new bramble-fruit
15      in our hair: we laughed
as each branch whipped back,
we tore our feet in half buried rocks
and knotted roots and acorn-cups.

We forgot—we worshipped,
20      we parted green from green,
we sought further thickets,
we dipped our ankles
through leaf-mould and earth,
and wood and wood-bank enchanted us—

25      and the feel of the clefts in the bark,
and the slope between tree and tree—
and a slender path strung field to field
and wood to wood
and hill to hill
30      and the forest after it.

We forgot—for a moment
tree-resin, tree-bark,
sweat of a torn branch
were sweet to the taste.

35      We were enchanted with the fields,
the tufts of coarse grass
in the shorter grass—
we loved all this.

But now, our boat climbs—hesitates—drops—
40      climbs—hesitates—crawls back—
climbs—hesitates—
O be swift—
we have always known you wanted us.

*1916*

# Eurydice°

## I

So you have swept me back,
I who could have walked with the live souls
above the earth,
I who could have slept among the live flowers
5      at last;

so for your arrogance
and your ruthlessness
I am swept back
where dead lichens drip
10      dead cinders upon moss of ash;

so for your arrogance
I am broken at last,
I who had lived unconscious,
who was almost forgot;

15      if you had let me wait
I had grown from listlessness
into peace,
if you had let me rest with the dead,
I had forgot you
20      and the past.

---

**poem title:** in Greek myth, Eurydice, wife of the singer and poet Orpheus, was bitten by a snake and died. The grief-stricken Orpheus plunged into Hades to bring her back. The music of his voice and lyre moved the gods of the underworld, and they granted his wish, but only on condition that he not look back at her until they reached the sunlight. In a moment of doubt, he looked back, and she was taken from him again, this time forever.

## II

Here only flame upon flame
and black among the red sparks,
streaks of black and light
grown colourless;

25          why did you turn back,
that hell should be reinhabited
of myself thus
swept into nothingness?

why did you turn?
30          why did you glance back?
why did you hesitate for that moment?
why did you bend your face
caught with the flame of the upper earth,
above my face?

35          what was it that crossed my face
with the light from yours
and your glance?
what was it you saw in my face?
the light of your own face,
40          the fire of your own presence?

What had my face to offer
but reflex of the earth,
hyacinth colour
caught from the raw fissure in the rock
45          where the light struck,
and the colour of azure crocuses
and the bright surface of gold crocuses
and of the wind-flower,
swift in its veins as lightning
50          and as white.

## III

Saffron from the fringe of the earth,
wild saffron that has bent
over the sharp edge of earth,
all the flowers that cut through the earth,
55          all, all the flowers are lost;

everything is lost,
everything is crossed with black,
black upon black
and worse than black,
60          this colourless light.

### IV

Fringe upon fringe
of blue crocuses,
crocuses, walled against blue of themselves,
blue of that upper earth,
65  blue of the depth upon depth of flowers,
lost;

flowers,
if I could have taken once my breath of them,
enough of them,
70  more than earth,
even than of the upper earth,
had passed with me
beneath the earth;

if I could have caught up from the earth,
75  the whole of the flowers of the earth,
if once I could have breathed into myself
the very golden crocuses
and the red,
and the very golden hearts of the first saffron,
80  the whole of the golden mass,
the whole of the great fragrance,
I could have dared the loss.

### V

So for your arrogance
and your ruthlessness
85  I have lost the earth
and the flowers of the earth,
and the live souls above the earth,
and you who passed across the light
and reached
90  ruthless;

you who have your own light,
who are to yourself a presence,
who need no presence;

yet for all your arrogance
95  and your glance,
I tell you this:

such loss is no loss,
such terror, such coils and strands and pitfalls
of blackness,
100  such terror
is no loss;

hell is no worse than your earth
above the earth,
hell is no worse,
105     no, nor your flowers
nor your veins of light
nor your presence,
a loss;

my hell is no worse than yours
110     though you pass among the flowers and speak
with the spirits above earth.

VI

Against the black
I have more fervour
than you in all the splendour of that place,
115     against the blackness
and the stark grey
I have more light;

and the flowers,
if I should tell you,
120     you would turn from your own fit paths
toward hell,
turn again and glance back

and I would sink into a place
even more terrible than this.

VII

125     At least I have the flowers of myself,
and my thoughts, no god
can take that;
I have the fervour of myself for a presence
and my own spirit for light;

130     and my spirit with its loss
knows this;
though small against the black,
small against the formless rocks,
hell must break before I am lost;

135     before I am lost,
hell must open like a red rose
for the dead to pass.

*1917*

# Helen°

All Greece hates
the still eyes in the white face,
the lustre as of olives
where she stands,
5     and the white hands.

All Greece reviles
the wan face when she smiles,
hating it deeper still
when it grows wan and white,
10    remembering past enchantments
and past ills.

Greece sees unmoved,
God's daughter, born of love,
the beauty of cool feet
15    and slenderest knees,
could love indeed the maid,
only if she were laid,
white ash amid funereal cypresses.

*1924*

from

# The Walls Do Not Fall°

To Bryher

*for Karnak* 1923
*from London* 1942

[1]

An incident here and there,
and rails gone (for guns)
from your (and my) old town square:

mist and mist-grey, no colour,
5     still the Luxor° bee, chick and hare
pursue unalterable purpose

---

**poem title:** *Helen:* Helen of Troy, the beautiful wife of King Menelaus of Greece. According to Greek myth, she was the daughter of the supreme God, Zeus, and Leda, a mortal woman. Zeus appeared to Leda in the guise of a swan. Helen's abduction by the Trojan prince Paris led to the Trojan war, which Greece won.
**poem title:** The first of three book-length poems comprising H.D.'s war trilogy. The other two are *Tribute to the Angels* and *The Flowering of the Rod.* Her comments in a letter are pertinent: "The parallel between ancient Egypt and 'ancient' London is obvious . . . . the 'fallen roof leaves the sealed room open to the air' is of course true of our own house of life—outer violence touching the deepest hidden subconscious terrors, etc. and we see so much of our past 'on show,' as it were 'another sliced wall where poor utensils show like rare objects in a museum.'"
5 *Luxor:* Egyptian town on the river Nile, in the vicinity of the ruins of Thebes. Images of a bee, a chick, and a hare are included on the Temple of Karnak at Thebes.

in green, rose-red, lapis;
they continue to prophesy
from the stone papyrus:

10    there, as here, ruin opens
the tomb, the temple; enter,
there as here, there are no doors:

the shrine lies open to the sky,
the rain falls, here, there
15    sand drifts; eternity endures:

ruin everywhere, yet as the fallen roof
leaves the sealed room
open to the air,

so, through our desolation,
20    thoughts stir, inspiration stalks us
through gloom:

unaware, Spirit announces the Presence;
shivering overtakes us,
as of old, Samuel:°

25    trembling at a known street-corner,
we know not nor are known;
the Pythian° pronounces—we pass on

to another cellar, to another sliced wall
where poor utensils show
30    like rare objects in a museum;

Pompeii° has nothing to teach us,
we know crack of volcanic fissure,
slow flow of terrible lava,

pressure on heart, lungs, the brain
35    about to burst its brittle case
(what the skull can endure!):

over us, Apocryphal° fire,
under us, the earth sway, dip of a floor,
slope of a pavement

---

24 *Samuel:* Cf. I Samuel, which reports Saul trembling at the sight of the Philistine army
and where the prophet Samuel is distressed at being raised from the dead.
27 *Pythian:* of or relating to Delphi, the temple of Apollo at Delphi, or its oracle.
31 *Pompeii:* the ancient Roman city on the bay of Naples, most famous for being buried
by the volcanic eruption of Mount Vesuvius in A.D. 79.
37 *Apocryphal:* the *Apocrypha* encompass various early Christian writings proposed as ad-
ditions to the New Testament but rejected as inauthentic; some suggest H.D. may have
meant "apocalyptic," as in the conflagration promised by the New Testament Apocalypse.

40  where men roll, drunk
with a new bewilderment,
sorcery, bedevilment:

the bone-frame was made for
no such shock knit within terror,
45  yet the skeleton stood up to it:

the flesh? it was melted away,
the heart burnt out, dead ember,
tendons, muscles shattered, outer husk dismembered,

yet the frame held:
50  we passed the flame: we wonder
what saved us? what for?

[6]

In me (the worm) clearly
is no righteousness, but this—

persistence; I escaped spider-snare,
55  bird-claw, scavenger bird-beak,

clung to grass-blade,
the back of a leaf

when storm-wind
tore it from its stem;

60  I escaped, I explored
rose-thorn forest,

was rain-swept
down the valley of a leaf;

was deposited on grass,
65  where mast by jewelled mast

bore separate ravellings
of encrusted gem-stuff

of the mist
from each banner-staff:

70  unintimidated by multiplicity
of magnified beauty,

such as your gorgon-great
dull eye can not focus

nor compass, I profit
75  by every calamity;

I eat my way out of it;
gorged on vine-leaf and mulberry,

parasite, I find nourishment:
when you cry in disgust,

80      a worm on the leaf,
a worm in the dust,

a worm on the ear-of-wheat,
I am yet unrepentant,

for I know how the Lord God
85      is about to manifest, when I,

the industrious worm,
spin my own shroud.

*1944*

# Robinson Jeffers (1887–1962)

Born in Pittsburgh, Pennsylvania, Jeffers' father was a minister and a professor of biblical literature. The family moved to northern California in 1903, before the area was fully settled. Jeffers himself was educated at Occidental College in Los Angeles. His initial interests were medicine and forestry, which he studied, respectively, at the University of Southern California and at the University of Washington. In 1914, he went to Carmel, California, where he built with his own hands a stone tower near his house overlooking the Pacific Ocean, and where he devoted himself to writing poetry. Many of the landscapes that figure in his work are from the area in which he lived. Jeffers developed a philosophy he called "inhumanism," in which he urged us to "uncenter the human mind from itself," to turn away from technology and incapacitating social regulation and look toward nature as a proper model of consciousness. Sometimes didactic, he is also capable of very effective exhortation, and is often capable of handling large themes with unusual dexterity. In nature he found a way of combining a fierce will with stoical endurance, twin values symbolized by the hawk and the rock; he also found in nature an indifference to human struggle that seemed to him the only spiritually sound and rational response to a world obsessed, alternatively, with mass murder and commodification. Although he is justly famous for his lyrics about nature, which use a Whitmanesque line to celebrate nature and decry its destruction by civilization, he also wrote many poems about national and international politics. "Fantasy," for example, is one of a group of long-suppressed poems intended for *The Double Axe* (1948); his publisher insisted on removing them from the book, and they were only published years later. He also wrote a number of long narrative poems, which were popular in the late 1920s and early 1930s, as well as several verse plays adapting Greek myths.

## Shine, Perishing Republic

While this America settles in the mould of its vulgarity, heavily
    thickening to empire,
And protest, only a bubble in the molten mass, pops and sighs out,
    and the mass hardens,

I sadly smiling remember that the flower fades to make fruit, the
    fruit rots to make earth.
Out of the mother; and through the spring exultances, ripeness and
    decadence; and home to the mother.

5      You making haste haste on decay: not blameworthy; life is good,
           be it stubbornly long or suddenly
       A mortal splendor: meteors are not needed less than mountains:
           shine, perishing republic.

       But for my children, I would have them keep their distance from
           the thickening center; corruption
       Never has been compulsory, when the cities lie at the monster's
           feet there are left the mountains.

       And boys, be in nothing so moderate as in love of man, a clever
           servant, insufferable master.
10     There is the trap that catches noblest spirits, that caught—they
           say—God, when he walked on earth.

                                                                    *1925*

# Hurt Hawks

## I

       The broken pillar of the wing jags from the clotted shoulder,
       The wing trails like a banner in defeat,
       No more to use the sky forever but live with famine
       And pain a few days: cat nor coyote
5      Will shorten the week of waiting for death, there is game without
           talons.
       He stands under the oak-bush and waits
       The lame feet of salvation; at night he remembers freedom
       And flies in a dream, the dawns ruin it.
       He is strong and pain is worse to the strong, incapacity is worse.
10     The curs of the day come and torment him
       At distance, no one but death the redeemer will humble that head,
       The intrepid readiness, the terrible eyes.
       The wild God of the world is sometimes merciful to those
       That ask mercy, not often to the arrogant.
15     You do not know him, you communal people, or you have forgotten
           him;
       Intemperate and savage, the hawk remembers him;
       Beautiful and wild, the hawks, and men that are dying, remember
           him.

## II

       I'd sooner, except the penalties, kill a man than a hawk; but the
           great redtail
       Had nothing left but unable misery
20     From the bone too shattered for mending, the wing that trailed un-
           der his talons when he moved.
       We had fed him six weeks, I gave him freedom,
       He wandered over the foreland hill and returned in the evening,
           asking for death,
       Not like a beggar, still eyed with the old

Implacable arrogance. I gave him the lead gift in the twilight. What
    fell was relaxed,
25    Owl-downy, soft feminine feathers; but what
Soared: the fierce rush: the night-herons by the flooded river cried
    fear at its rising
Before it was quite unsheathed from reality.

*1928*

## November Surf

Some lucky day each November great waves awake and are drawn
Like smoking mountains bright from the west
And come and cover the cliff with white violent cleanness: then
    suddenly
The old granite forgets half a year's filth:
5    The orange-peel, eggshells, papers, pieces of clothing, the clots
Of dung in corners of the rock, and used
Sheaths that make light love safe in the evenings: all the droppings
    of the summer
Idlers washed off in a winter ecstasy:
I think this cumbered continent envies its cliff then. . . . But all
    seasons
10    The earth, in her childlike prophetic sleep,
Keeps dreaming of the bath of a storm that prepares up the long
    coast
Of the future to scour more than her sea-lines:
The cities gone down, the people fewer and the hawks more nu-
    merous,
The rivers mouth to source pure; when the two-footed
15    Mammal, being someways one of the nobler animals, regains
The dignity of room, the value of rareness.

*1929*

## The Purse-Seine°

Our sardine fishermen work at night in the dark of the moon; day-
    light or moonlight
They could not tell where to spread the net, unable to see the
    phosphorescence of the shoals of fish.
They work northward from Monterey, coasting Santa Cruz; off
    New Year's Point or off Pigeon Point°
The look-out man will see some lakes of milk-color light on the
    sea's night-purple; he points, and the helmsman
5    Turns the dark prow, the motorboat circles the gleaming shoal and
    drifts out her seine-net. They close the circle
And purse the bottom of the net, then with great labor haul it in.

---

**poem title:** A purse-seine is a fishing net shaped like a bag.
3 *New Year's Point, Pigeon Point:* both in the Monterey Bay area of California.

                                          I cannot tell you
How beautiful the scene is, and a little terrible, then, when the
    crowded fish
Know they are caught, and wildly beat from one wall to the other
    of their closing destiny the phosphorescent
Water to a pool of flame, each beautiful slender body sheeted with
    flame, like a live rocket

10  A comet's tail wake of clear yellow flame; while outside the narrow-
    ing
Floats and cordage of the net great sea-lions come up to watch,
    sighing in the dark; the vast walls of night
Stand erect to the stars.

                    Lately I was looking from a night mountain-top
On a wide city, the colored splendor, galaxies of light: how could I
    help but recall the seine-net
Gathering the luminous fish? I cannot tell you how beautiful the
    city appeared, and a little terrible.

15  I thought, We have geared the machines and locked all together
    into interdependence; we have built the great cities; now
There is no escape. We have gathered vast populations incapable of
    free survival, insulated
From the strong earth, each person in himself helpless, on all de-
    pendent. The circle is closed, and the net
Is being hauled in. They hardly feel the cords drawing, yet they
    shine already. The inevitable mass-disasters
Will not come in our time nor in our children's, but we and our
    children

20  Must watch the net draw narrower, government take all powers—or
    revolution, and the new government
Take more than all, add to kept bodies kept souls—or anarchy, the
    mass-disasters.

                    These things are Progress;
Do you marvel our verse is troubled or frowning, while it keeps its
    reason? Or it lets go, lets the mood flow
In the manner of the recent young men into mere hysteria, splin-
    tered gleams, crackled laughter. But they are quite wrong.
There is no reason for amazement: surely one always knew that
    cultures decay, and life's end is death.

                                                      *1937*

## Fantasy

        Finally in white innocence
        The fighter planes like swallows dance,
        The bombers above ruined towns
        Will drop wreaths of roses down,
5       Doves will nest in the guns' throats
        And the people dance in the streets,
        Whistles will bawl and bells will clang,
        On that great day the boys will hang

Hitler and Roosevelt in one tree,
10      Painlessly, in effigy,
To take their rank in history;
Roosevelt, Hitler and Guy Fawkes
Hanged above the garden walks,
While the happy children cheer,
15      Without hate, without fear,
And new men plot a new war.

*1941*

## Cassandra°

The mad girl with the staring eyes and long white fingers
Hooked in the stones of the wall,
The storm-wrack hair and the screeching mouth: does it matter,
    Cassandra,
Whether the people believe
5    Your bitter fountain? Truly men hate the truth; they'd liefer
Meet a tiger on the road.
Therefore the poets honey their truth with lying; but religion-
Venders and political men
Pour from the barrel, new lies on the old, and are praised for
    kindly
10    Wisdom. Poor bitch, be wise.
No: you'll still mumble in a corner a crust of truth, to men
And gods disgusting.—You and I, Cassandra.

*1948*

## Vulture

I had walked since dawn and lay down to rest on a bare hillside
Above the ocean. I saw through half-shut eyelids a vulture
    wheeling high up in heaven,
And presently it passed again, but lower and nearer, its orbit
    narrowing, I understood then
That I was under inspection. I lay death-still and heard the
    flight-feathers
5    Whistle above me and make their circle and come nearer.
I could see the naked red head between the great wings
Bear downward staring. I said, "My dear bird, we are wasting time
    here.
These old bones will still work; they are not for you."
But how beautiful he looked, gliding down
10    On those great sails; how beautiful he looked, veering away in the
    sea-light over the precipice. I tell you solemnly

---

**poem title:** in Greek mythology, Cassandra, who was daughter to the king and queen of
Troy, had the gift of prophecy but no power to convince her listeners that her prophecies
were true. Thus she warned her people not to take the Trojan horse into their city, but
they ignored her. She went into a trance to deliver her prophecies.

That I was sorry to have disappointed him. To be eaten by that
  beak and become part of him, to share those wings and those
  eyes—
What a sublime end of one's body, what an enskyment; what a life
  after death.

*1954*

## Birds and Fishes

Every October millions of little fish come along the shore,
Coasting this granite edge of the continent
On their lawful occasions: but what a festival for the seafowl.
What a witches' sabbath of wings

5    Hides the dark water. The heavy pelicans shout "Haw!" like Job's
  friend's warhorse
And dive from the high air, the cormorants
Slip their long black bodies under the water and hunt like wolves
Through the green half-light. Screaming, the gulls watch,
Wild with envy and malice, cursing and snatching. What hysterical
  greed!

10   What a filling of pouches! the mob
Hysteria is nearly human—these decent birds!—as if they were
  finding
Gold in the street. It is better than gold,
It can be eaten: and which one in all this fury of wildfowl pities
  the fish?
No one certainly. Justice and mercy

15   Are human dreams, they do not concern the birds nor the fish nor
  eternal God.
However—look again before you go.
The wings and the wild hungers, the wave-worn skerries, the bright
  quick minnows
Living in terror to die in torment—
Man's fate and theirs—and the island rocks and immense ocean
  beyond, and Lobos

20   Darkening above the bay: they are beautiful?
That is their quality: not mercy, not mind, not goodness, but the
  beauty of God.

*1963*

# Marianne Moore (1887–1972)

Born in Kirkwood, Missouri, and raised in Carlisle, Pennsylvania, Moore was educated at Bryn Mawr College and Carlisle Commercial College. She shared a house with her mother all her life, much of it working at a series of jobs in the New York area, but always focusing on writing. Notably, her use of quotation in her poems is as elaborate as that of T.S. Eliot, but to quite different purposes. If Eliot aimed for magisterial allusiveness, Moore aimed for something more complex and subversive, to model the cultural constitution of knowledge and understanding. Her poems braided of multiple sources are, at their most ambitious, social and philosophical investigations of great subtlety. "Marriage" and "An Octopus" are the most important poems of this kind, so we include them both. She also had continuing political and historical interests, as two poems here about Ireland—"Sojourn in the Whale" and "Spenser's Ireland"—make clear.

On one level, Moore's "Marriage" is a strikingly even-handed demolition of the illusion that either party to a marriage can so divest himself or herself of self-absorption and self-interest as to make a union possible. "He loves himself so much," she writes, "he can permit himself / no rival in that love." But the poem is much more than an analysis of the pitfalls in gender relations. It actually moves centripetally and centrifugally at the same time, treating marriage not only as a site on which individuals and the culture as a whole act out their contradictory investments in independence and community but also as a figural resource that informs all compromised institutions in the culture. Thus the poem is at once about the marriage two people make and about the marriage the states made to form one country—"Liberty and union / now and forever." Both require "public promises / of one's intention / to fulfil a private obligation" and both "can never be more / than an interesting impossibility." Marriage is an institution constructed by contractualized idealization and a model for comparably problematic institutions of other sorts. Marriage in the poem is effectively thus both victim and purveyor of illusions within the culture.

# Poetry°

    I, too, dislike it: there are things that are important beyond all this
            fiddle.
     Reading it, however, with a perfect contempt for it, one
            discovers in
5      it after all, a place for the genuine.
          Hands that can grasp, eyes
            that can dilate, hair that can rise
               if it must, these things are important not because a

    high-sounding interpretation can be put upon them but because
10         they are
      useful. When they become so derivative as to become
            unintelligible,
     the same thing may be said for all of us, that we do not
            admire what
15      we cannot understand: the bat
              holding on upside down or in quest of something to

    eat, elephants pushing, a wild horse taking a roll, a tireless wolf
            under
     a tree, the immovable critic twitching his skin like a horse
20           that feels a flea, the base-
          ball fan, the statistician—
           nor is it valid
              to discriminate against 'business documents and

    school-books;° all these phenomena are important. One must
25         make a distinction
      however: when dragged into prominence by half poets,
            the result is not poetry,
     nor till the poets among us can be
            'literalists of
30      the imagination'°—above
            insolence and triviality and can present

---

**poem title:** A revised version of this poem, consisting largely of the first three lines, was published in *The Complete Poems* (1967), but Moore included the original 1921 version in her notes.

24 *school-books*: Moore's note—"*Diary of Tolstoy*, p. 84: 'Where the boundary between prose and poetry lies, I shall never be able to understand. The question is raised in manuals of style, yet the answer to it lies beyond me. Poetry is verse; prose is not verse. Or else poetry is everything with the exception of business documents and school books.' " Count Lev Nikolayevich (Nicholas) Tolstoy (1828–1910), major Russian novelist, dramatist, and social philosopher.

30 *literalists of the imagination*: Moore's note—"Yeats, *Ideas of Good and Evil* (A.H. Bullen 1930), p. 182: 'The limitation of his [Blake's] view was from the very intensity of his vision; he was a too literal realist of imagination, as others are of nature; and because he believed that the figures seen by the mind's eye, when exalted by inspiration, were "eternal existences," he hated every grace of style that might obscure their lineaments.' " From Yeats's essay "William Blake and His Illustrations."

for inspection, 'imaginary gardens with real toads in them,'
    shall we have
it. In the meantime, if you demand on the one hand,
35    the raw material of poetry in
        all its rawness and
    that which is on the other hand
        genuine, you are interested in poetry.

*1921*

## An Egyptian Pulled Glass Bottle in the Shape of a Fish

Here we have thirst
and patience, from the first,
    and art, as in a wave held up for us to see
    in its essential perpendicularity;

5    not brittle but
intense—the spectrum, that
    spectacular and nimble animal the fish,
    whose scales turn aside the sun's sword by their polish.

*1921*

## The Fish

wade
through black jade.
    Of the crow-blue mussel-shells, one keeps
    adjusting the ash-heaps;
5        opening and shutting itself like

an
injured fan.
    The barnacles which encrust the side
    of the wave, cannot hide
10        there for the submerged shafts of the

sun,
split like spun
    glass, move themselves with spotlight swiftness
    into the crevices—
15        in and out, illuminating

the
turquoise sea
    of bodies. The water drives a wedge
    of iron through the iron edge
20        of the cliff; whereupon the stars,°

---

20 *stars*: starfish.

pink
rice-grains, ink-
    bespattered jelly-fish, crabs like green
    lilies, and submarine
25         toadstools, slide each on the other.

    All
    external
    marks of abuse are present on this
    defiant edifice—
30         all the physical features of

ac-
cident—lack
    of cornice, dynamite grooves, burns, and
    hatchet strokes, these things stand
35         out on it; the chasm-side is

dead.
Repeated
    evidence has proved that it can live
    on what can not revive
        its youth. The sea grows old in it.

*1921*

## Sojourn in the Whale°

Trying to open locked doors with a sword, threading
    the points of needles, planting shade trees
    upside down; swallowed by the opaqueness of one whom the
                          seas
love better than they love you, Ireland—°

5    you have lived and lived on every kind of shortage.
    You have been compelled by hags to spin
    gold thread° from straw and have heard men say:
    "There is a feminine temperament in direct contrast to ours,

    which makes her do these things. Circumscribed by a
10     heritage of blindness and native
    incompetence, she will become wise and will be forced to give in.
    Compelled by experience, she will turn back;

---

**poem title:** refers to the Old Testament story of Jonah and the Whale. Jonah was swallowed by a whale in punishment for disobeying God, but his pleas for help won forgiveness and he was cast up again (Jonah 1–2).

4 *Ireland*: Ireland's sojourn in the whale was its long domination by England with its greater power and its historical domination of the seas. If Ireland was swallowed or devoured by England, it was also from time to time starved by the dominant country, as when the English declined to provide sufficient relief during the potato famine of the 1840s.

7 *gold thread*: in one of the folk stories published by the brothers Grimm, "Rumplestiltskin," a young girl must spin gold thread from common straw.

water seeks its own level":
    and you have smiled. "Water in motion is far
15        from level."° You have seen it, when obstacles happened to bar
the path, rise automatically.

                              *1921*

## A Grave

Man looking into the sea,
taking the view from those who have as much right to it as
                     you have to it yourself,
it is human nature to stand in the middle of a thing,
5   but you cannot stand in the middle of this;
the sea has nothing to give but a well excavated grave.
The firs stand in a procession, each with an emerald turkey-
                    foot at the top,
reserved as their contours, saying nothing;
10  repression, however, is not the most obvious characteristic of
                        the sea;
the sea is a collector, quick to return a rapacious look.
There are others besides you who have worn that look—
whose expression is no longer a protest; the fish no longer
15                    investigate them
for their bones have not lasted:
men lower nets, unconscious of the fact that they are
                  desecrating a grave,
and row quickly away—the blades of the oars
20  moving together like the feet of water-spiders as if there were
                no such thing as death.
The wrinkles progress among themselves in a phalanx°—
            beautiful under networks of foam,
and fade breathlessly while the sea rustles in and out of the
25                    seaweed;
the birds swim through the air at top speed, emitting cat-calls
              as heretofore—
the tortoise-shell scourges about the feet of the cliffs, in motion
            beneath them;
30  and the ocean, under the pulsation of lighthouses and noise of
            bell-buoys,
advances as usual, looking as if it were not that ocean in which
          dropped things are bound to sink—
in which if they turn and twist, it is neither with volition nor
             consciousness.

                              *1924*

---

15 "*. . . far from level*": Moore's note—"*Literary Digest.*"
22 *phalanx*: an ancient military formation consisting of closely spaced infantrymen.

# Silence

My father used to say,
"Superior people never make long visits,
have to be shown Longfellow's grave
or the glass flowers at Harvard.°
5  Self-reliant like the cat—
that takes its prey to privacy,
the mouse's limp tail hanging like a shoelace from its mouth—
they sometimes enjoy solitude,
and can be robbed of speech
10  by speech which has delighted them.
The deepest feeling always shows itself in silence;
not in silence, but restraint."
Nor was he insincere in saying, "Make my house your inn."°
Inns are not residences.

*1924*

# Peter°

Strong and slippery,
built for the midnight grass-party
confronted by four cats, he sleeps his time away—
the detached first claw on the foreleg corresponding
5  to the thumb, retracted to its tip; the small tuft of fronds
or katydid-legs above each eye numbering all units
in each group; the shadbones° regularly set about the mouth
to droop or rise in unison like porcupine-quills.
He lets himself be flattened out by gravity,
10  as seaweed is tamed and weakened by the sun,
compelled when extended, to lie stationary.
Sleep is the result of his delusion that one must
do as well as one can for oneself,
sleep—epitome of what is to him the end of life.
15  Demonstrate on him how the lady placed a forked stick
on the innocuous neck-sides of the dangerous southern snake.
One need not try to stir him up; his prune-shaped head
and alligator-eyes are not party to the joke.
Lifted and handled, he may be dangled like an eel
20  or set up on the forearm like a mouse;
his eyes bisected by pupils of a pin's width,
are flickeringly exhibited, then covered up.

---

4 *Harvard*: Moore's note—"My father used to say, 'Superior people never make long visits. When I am visiting, I like to go about by myself. I never had to be shown Longfellow's grave or the glass flowers at Harvard.' Miss A.M. Homans." The renowned poet Henry Wadsworth Longfellow (1807–1822) was buried in Cambridge, Massachusetts, the site of Harvard University's Peabody Museum, famous for its display of glass flowers.

13 *inn*: Moore's note—"Edmund Burke, in *Burke's Life* by Sir James Prior (1872): 'Throw yourself into a coach,' said he. 'Come down and make my house your inn.' "

**poem title:** Moore's note—"cat owned by Miss Magdalen Hueber and Miss Maria Weniger."

7 *shadbones*: the long, very fine bones of the shad fish.

May be? I should have said might have been;
when he has been got the better of in a dream—
25    as in a fight with nature or with cats, we all know it.
Profound sleep is not with him a fixed illusion.
Springing about with froglike accuracy, with jerky cries
when taken in hand, he is himself again;
to sit caged by the rungs of a domestic chair
30    would be unprofitable—human. What is the good of hypocrisy?
It is permissible to choose one's employment,
to abandon the nail, or roly-poly,
when it shows signs of being no longer a pleasure,
to score the nearby magazine with a double line of strokes.
35    He can talk but insolently says nothing. What of it?
When one is frank, one's very presence is a compliment.
It is clear that he can see the virtue of naturalness,
that he does not regard the published fact as a surrender.
As for the disposition invariably to affront,
40    an animal with claws should have an opportunity to use them.
The eel-like extension of trunk into tail is not an accident.
To leap, to lengthen out, divide the air, to purloin, to pursue.
To tell the hen: fly over the fence, go in the wrong way
in your perturbation—this is life;
to do less would be nothing but dishonesty.

                                                                1924


## Marriage°

This institution,
perhaps one should say enterprise
out of respect for which
one says one need not change one's mind
5    about a thing one has believed in,
requiring public promises
of one's intention
to fulfil a private obligation:
I wonder what Adam and Eve
10    think of it by this time,
this fire-gilt steel
alive with goldenness;
how bright it shows—
"of circular traditions and impostures,
15    committing many spoils,"°
requiring all one's criminal ingenuity
to avoid!
Psychology which explains everything
explains nothing,

---

**poem title:** In her notes to the poem, Moore rather modestly prefaces a list of sources
by calling them "statements that took my fancy which I tried to arrange plausibly." Of
course the nature of that "plausibility," which is here philosophically very complex, is ex-
actly what is at stake in "Marriage," one of her most ambitious poems.
15 *"of circular traditions . . . spoils"*: Moore's note—"Francis Bacon." Bacon (1561–1626),
British philosopher and scientist.

<pre>
20        and we are still in doubt.
          Eve: beautiful woman—
          I have seen her
          when she was so handsome
          she gave me a start,
25        able to write simultaneously°
          in three languages—
          English, German and French—
          and talk in the meantime;
          equally positive in demanding a commotion
30        and in stipulating quiet:
          "I should like to be alone";
          to which the visitor replies,
          "I should like to be alone;
          why not be alone together?"
35        Below the incandescent stars
          below the incandescent fruit,
          the strange experience of beauty;
          its existence is too much;
          it tears one to pieces
40        and each fresh wave of consciousness
          is poison.
          "See her, see her in this common world,"°
          the central flaw
          in that first crystal-fine experiment,
45        this amalgamation which can never be more
          than an interesting impossibility,
          describing it
          as "that strange paradise
          unlike flesh, stones,
50        gold or stately buildings,
          the choicest piece of my life:
          the heart rising
          in its estate of peace
          as a boat rises
55        with the rising of the water";°
          constrained in speaking of the serpent—
          shed snakeskin in the history of politeness
          not to be returned to again—
          that invaluable accident
</pre>

---

25 *write simultaneously*: Moore's note—" 'Miss A_____ will write simultaneously in three languages, English, German, and French, talking in the meantime. [She] takes advantage of her abilities in everyday life, writing her letters simultaneously with both hands; namely, the first, third, and fifth words with her left and the second, fourth, and sixth with her right hand. While generally writing outward, she is able as well to write inward with both hands.' 'Multiple Consciousness or Reflex Action of Unaccustomed Range.' *Scientific American,* January 1922."

42 *"see . . . world"*: Moore's note—"George Shock."

55 *". . . of the water"*: Moore's note—"Richard Baxter, *The Saints' Everlasting Rest*" (1650). Baxter (1615–1691), British preacher, theologian, and controversial figure.

60        exonerating Adam.
          And he has beauty also;
          it's distressing—the O thou
          to whom from whom,
          without whom nothing—Adam;
65        "something feline,°
          something colubrine"—how true!
          a crouching mythological monster
          in that Persian miniature° of emerald mines,
          raw silk—ivory white, snow white,
70        oyster white and six others—
          that paddock full of leopards and giraffes—
          long lemon-yellow bodies
          sown with trapezoids of blue.
          Alive with words,
75        vibrating like a cymbal
          touched before it has been struck,
          he has prophesied correctly—
          the industrious waterfall,
          "the speedy stream
80        which violently bears all before it,
          at one time silent as the air
          and now as powerful as the wind."
          "Treading chasms
          on the uncertain footing of a spear,"°
85        forgetting that there is in woman
          a quality of mind
          which as an instinctive manifestation
          is unsafe,
          he goes on speaking
90        in a formal customary strain,
          of "past states, the present state,
          seals, promises,
          the evil one suffered,
          the good one enjoys,
95        hell, heaven,
          everything convenient
          to promote one's joy."°
          In him a state of mind
          perceives what it was not
100      intended that he should;
          "he experiences a solemn joy

---

65 *feline*: Moore's note—"'We were puzzled and we were fascinated, as if by something feline, by something colubrine.' Philip Littell, reviewing Santayana's *Poems* in *The New Republic*, March 21, 1923." George Santayana (1863–1952), American philosopher, poet, and man of letters; the 1923 volume was a collected poems. Colubrine: snakelike.
68 *Persian miniature*: small, often intricately detailed paintings.
84 "*. . . spear*": Moore's note—"Hazlitt: 'Essay on Burke's Style.'" William Hazlitt (1778–1830), British essayist and critic.
97 "*. . . joy*": Moore's note—"Richard Baxter."

in seeing that he has become an idol."°
Plagued by the nightingale
in the new leaves,
105  with its silence—
not its silence but its silences,
he says of it:
"It clothes me with a shirt of fire."°
"He dares not clap his hands
110  to make it go on
lest it should fly off;
if he does nothing, it will sleep;
if he cries out, it will not understand."°
Unnerved by the nightingale
115  and dazzled by the apple,
impelled by "the illusion of a fire
effectual to extinguish fire,"°
compared with which
the shining of the earth
120  is but deformity—a fire
"as high as deep
as bright as broad
as long as life itself,"°
he stumbles over marriage,
125  "a very trivial object indeed"°
to have destroyed the attitude
in which he stood—
the ease of the philosopher
unfathered by a woman.
130  Unhelpful Hymen!°
a kind of overgrown cupid
reduced to insignificance
by the mechanical advertising
parading as involuntary comment,
135  by that experiment of Adam's
with ways out but no way in—
the ritual of marriage,

---

102 ". . . *idol*": Moore's note—"*A Travers Champs*, by Anatole France in *Filles et Garçons*
(Hachette): *'Le petit Jean comprend qu'el est beau et cette idée le pénétre d'un respect pro-
fond de lui-même. . . . Il goûte une joie pieuse à se sentir devenu une idole.'* " (French)
"Across the Fields," in *Girls and Boys*: "Little John understands that he is handsome and
this idea fills his being with a profound respect for himself. He joys in feeling that he has
become an idol." Anatole France, pseudonym of Anatole-François Thibault (1844–1924),
French poet and man of letters.
108 ". . . *shirt of fire*": Moore's note—"Hagop Boghossian in a poem, 'The Nightingale.' "
Boghossian was an Armenian poet.
113 ". . . *understand*": Moore's note—"Edward Thomas, *Feminine Influence on the Poets*
(Martin Secker, 1910)." Thomas (1878–1917), British poet and prose writer who died in
World War I.
117 ". . . *extinguish fire*": Moore's note—"Richard Baxter."
123 ". . . *itself*": Moore's note—"Richard Baxter."
125 ". . . *indeed*": Moore's note—"Godwin." William Godwin (1756–1836), British philoso-
pher and novelist, "Marriage is a law, and the very worst of all laws . . . a very trivial ob-
ject indeed."
130 *Hymen*: Greek god of marriage; cupid: child gods of love, often winged.

augmenting all its lavishness;
its fiddle-head ferns,
140     lotus flowers, opuntias,° white dromedaries,
its hippopotamus—
nose and mouth combined
in one magnificent hopper—
its snake and the potent apple.°
145     He tells us
that "for love that will
gaze an eagle blind,
that is with Hercules°
climbing the trees
150     in the garden of the Hesperides,
from forty-five to seventy
is the best age,"°
commending it
as a fine art, as an experiment,
155     a duty or as merely recreation.
One must not call him ruffian
nor friction a calamity—
the fight to be affectionate:
"no truth can be fully known
160     until it has been tried
by the tooth of disputation."°
The blue panther with black eyes,
the basalt panther with blue eyes,
entirely graceful—
165     one must give them the path—
the black obsidian Diana°
who "darkeneth her countenance
as a bear doth,"°
the spiked hand
170     that has an affection for one
and proves it to the bone,
impatient to assure you
that impatience is the mark of independence,
not of bondage.

---

140 *opuntias*: prickly pear cactuses, often with yellow flowers and edible fruit.

144 *potent apple*: convinced by the snake's arguments, Eve ate the forbidden apple of the tree of knowledge (of good and evil) in the Garden of Eden; as punishment, Adam and Eve were banished.

148 *Hercules*: A Latinized version of the Greek Heracles, the best-known and most popular hero in classical mythology. His many exploits include the famous twelve labors, numbered among them the charge to bring back the golden apples from the Garden of the Hesperides.

152 ". . . *age*": Moore's note—"Anthony Trollope, *Barchester Towers*." Trollope (1815–1882), one of the major novelists of the Victorian period.

161 ". . . *disputation*": Moore's note—"Robert of Sorbonne."

166 *Diana*: A roman goddess, always a virgin and eternally young; she was goddess of chastity and of the hunt; often vengeful herself, the ceremonies honoring her were sometimes violent and sacrificial; she joined with Hercules (above) to kill a giant. The "black obsidian Diana" is a statue of her.

168 ". . . *doth*": Moore's note—"Ecclesiasticus."

175  "Married people often look that way"—°
    "seldom and cold, up and down,
    mixed and malarial
    with a good day and a bad."°
    We Occidentals are so unemotional,
180  self lost, the irony preserved
    in "the Ahasuerus *tête-à-tête* banquet"°
    with its small orchids like snakes' tongues,
    with its "good monster, lead the way,"°
    with little laughter
185  and munificence of humor
    in that quixotic atmosphere of frankness
    in which "four o'clock does not exist,
    but at five o'clock
    the ladies in their imperious humility
190  are ready to receive you";°
    in which experience attests
    that men have power
    and sometimes one is made to feel it.
    He says, "What monarch would not blush
195  to have a wife
    with hair like a shaving-brush?"°
    The fact of woman
    is "not the sound of the flute
    but very poison."°
200  She says, "Men are monopolists
    of 'stars, garters, buttons
    and other shining baubles'—
    unfit to be the guardians
    of another person's happiness."°
205  He says, "These mummies
    must be handled carefully—
    'the crumbs from a lion's meal,
    a couple of shins and the bit of an ear';°

---

175 ". . . *that way*": Moore's note—"C. Bertram Hartman."

178 ". . . *bad*": Moore's note—"Richard Baxter."

181 *"Ahasuerus tête-à-tête banquet"*: Moore's note—"George Adam Smith, *Expositor's Bible.*" The intimate banquet where Queen Esther persuaded the Israelite King Ahasuerus that his counselor Haman had betrayed him.

183 ". . . *the way*": Moore's note—*"The Tempest."*

190 ". . . *receive you*": Moore's note—"Comtesse de Noailles, 'Le Thé,' *Femina*, December 1921. *'Dans leur impérieuse humilité elles jouent instinctivement leur rôles sur le globe.'* " (French) "In their imperious humility women instinctively play their roles on the planet."

196 ". . . *shaving-brush*": Moore's note—"From 'The Rape of the Lock,' a parody by Mary Frances Nearing, with suggestions by M. Moore."

199 ". . . *poison*": Moore's note—"A. Mitram Rihbany, *The Syrian Christ* (Houghton Mifflin, 1916). Silence of Women—'to an Oriental, this is as poetry set to music.' "

204 ". . . *happiness*": Moore's note—"Miss M. Carey Thomas, Founder's address, Mount Holyoke, 1921: 'Men, practically, reserve for themselves stately funerals, splendid monuments, memorial statues, membership in academies, medals, titles, honorary degrees, stars, garters, ribbons, buttons and other shining baubles, so valueless in themselves and yet so infinitely desirable because they are symbols of recognition by their fellow-craftsmen of difficult work well done.' "

208 ". . . *ear*": Moore's note—"Amos iii, 12, translation by George Adam Smith, *Expositor's Bible.*"

turn to the letter M
210    and you will find
that 'a wife is a coffin,'°
that severe object
with the pleasing geometry
stipulating space not people,
215    refusing to be buried
and uniquely disappointing,
revengefully wrought in the attitude
of an adoring child
to a distinguished parent."
220    She says, "This butterfly,
this waterfly, this nomad
that has 'proposed
to settle on my hand for life'—°
What can one do with it?
225    There must have been more time
in Shakespeare's day
to sit and watch a play.
You know so many artists who are fools."
He says, "You know so many fools
230    who are not artists."
The fact forgot
that "some have merely rights
while some have obligations,"°
he loves himself so much,
235    he can permit himself
no rival in that love.
She loves herself so much,
she cannot see herself enough—
a statuette of ivory on ivory,
240    the logical last touch
to an expansive splendor
earned as wages for work done:
one is not rich but poor
when one can always seem so right.
245    What can one do for them—
these savages
condemned to disaffect
all those who are not visionaries
alert to undertake the silly task
250    of making people noble?
This model of petrine° fidelity
who "leaves her peaceful husband

---

211 *"A wife is a coffin"*: Moore's note—"Ezra Pound."
223 *"for life"*: Moore's note—"Charles Reade, *Christie Johnston*." Reade (1814–1884), British dramatist and novelist.
233 *". . .obligations"*: Moore's note—" 'Asiatics have rights; Europeans have obligations.' Edmund Burke." Burke (1729–1797), Irish political writer and orator.
251 *". . . petrine"*: having the characteristics of the Apostle Peter, who denied Christ three times.

only because she has seen enough of him"—°
that orator reminding you,
255　"I am yours to command."
"Everything to do with love is mystery;
it is more than a day's work
to investigate this science."°
One sees that it is rare—
260　that striking grasp of opposites
opposed each to the other, not to unity,
which in cycloid inclusiveness
has dwarfed the demonstration
of Columbus with the egg°—
265　a triumph of simplicity—
that charitive Euroclydon°
of frightening disinterestedness
which the world hates,
admitting:

270　　"I am such a cow,
if I had a sorrow
I should feel it a long time;
I am not one of those
who have a great sorrow
275　in the morning
and a great joy at noon";

which says: "I have encountered it
among those unpretentious
protégés of wisdom,
280　where seeming to parade
as the debater and the Roman,
the statesmanship
of an archaic Daniel Webster°
persists to their simplicity of temper
285　as the essence of the matter:

　　'Liberty and union
　　now and forever';°

the Book on the writing-table;
the hand in the breast-pocket."

　　　　　　　　　　　　　*1924*

---

253 "*. . . enough of him*": Moore's note—"Simone Puget, advertisement entitled 'Change of Fashion,' *English Review*, June 1914: 'Thus proceed pretty dolls when they leave their old home to renovate their frame, and dear others who may abandon their peaceful husband only because they have seen enough of him.' "
258 "*. . . this science*": Moore's note—"F.C. Tilney, *Fables of La Fontaine*, 'Love and Folly,' Book XII, No. 14."
264 *egg*: there is a story that Columbus bragged he could make an egg stand on end; when the challenge was taken, he flattened one end and proved his point with the altered egg.
266 *Euroclydon*: a north wind (Acts 27.14).
283 "*Daniel Webster*": (1782–1852), American lawyer and politican, known as one of the great American orators of all time.
287 "*Liberty . . . forever*": Moore's note—"Daniel Webster (statue with inscription, Central Park, New York City)."

# An Octopus°

of ice. Deceptively reserved and flat,
it lies "in grandeur and in mass"
beneath a sea of shifting snow-dunes;
dots of cyclamen-red and maroon on its clearly defined

5                                                          pseudo-podia
made of glass° that will bend—a much needed invention—
comprising twenty-eight ice-fields from fifty to five hundred
                                                              feet thick,
of unimagined delicacy.

10      "Picking periwinkles from the cracks"°
or killing prey with the concentric crushing rigor of the python,
it hovers forward "spider fashion°
on its arms" misleadingly like lace;
its "ghostly° pallor changing

15      to the green metallic tinge of an anemone-starred pool."
The fir-trees, in "the magnitude of their root systems,"°
rise aloof from these maneuvers "creepy to behold,"°
austere specimens of our American royal families,
"each like the shadow° of the one beside it.

20      The rock seems frail compared with their dark energy of life,"
its vermilion and onyx and manganese-blue° interior expensiveness
left at the mercy of the weather;
"stained transversely by iron where the water drips down,"
recognized by its plants and its animals.

25      Completing a circle,
you have been deceived into thinking that you have progressed,

---

**poem title:** Based on a photograph of an octopus-shaped cap of ice and snow atop Mount Rainier in the state of Washington; the octopus's "tentacles" are formed by snow packed in gulleys or crevices, but Moore's many poems about animals and a deliberate rhetorical ambiguity in the poem put the other octopus, the sea creature, in play as well. Moore's note—"Quoted lines of which the source is not given are from the Department of the Interior Rules and Regulations, *The National Parks Portfolio* (1922)."

6 *glass:* Moore's note—"Sir William Bell, of the British Institute of Patentees has made a list of inventions which he says the world needs: glass that will bend; a smooth road surface that will not be slippery in wet weather; a furnace that will conserve ninety-five per cent of its heat; a process to make flannel unshrinkable; a noiseless aeroplane; a motor engine of one pound weight per horsepower; methods to reduce friction; a process to extract phosphorus from vulcanized india-rubber, so that it can be boiled up and used again; practical ways of utilizing the tides."

10 *"Picking periwinkles":* Moore's note—"M.C. Carey, *London Graphic,* August 25, 1923." A "periwinkle" is an edible snail living in a shell, appropriate food for a marine octopus, but it is also a cultivated herb.

12 *"Spider fashion":* Moore's note—"W.P. Pycraft, *Illustrated London News,* June 28, 1924."

14 *ghostly:* Moore's note—" 'Ghostly pallor, Creeping slowly . . .' Francis Ward, *Illustrated London News,* August 11, 1923."

16 *"Magnitude of their root systems":* Moore's note—"John Muir." Muir (1838–1914), American naturalist, author of numerous books.

17 *"creepy to behold":* Moore's note—"W.P. Pycraft, *Illustrated London News,* June 28, 1924."

19 *"Each like the shadow . . . .":* Moore's note—"Ruskin." John Ruskin (1819–1900), British art and social critic.

21 *blue:* Moore's note—"Lines 46, 53–54, 180, 184, 185: 'blue stone forests,' 'bristling, puny, swearing men,' 'tear the snow,' 'flat on the ground,' 'bent in a half circle.' Clifton Johnson, *What to See in America* (Macmillan, 1919)."

under the polite needles of the larches
"hung to filter, not to intercept the sunlight"—
met by tightly wattled spruce-twigs
30    "conformed to an edge like clipped cypress
as if no branch could penetrate the cold beyond its company";°
and dumps of gold and silver ore enclosing The Goat's Mirror—
that lady-fingerlike depression in the shape of the left human
                                                              foot,
35    which prejudices you in favor of itself
before you have had time to see the others;
its indigo, pea-green, blue-green, and turquoise,
from a hundred to two hundred feet deep,
"merging in irregular patches in the middle lake
40    where, like gusts of a storm
obliterating the shadows of the fir-trees, the wind makes lanes
                                                              of ripples."
What spot could have merits of equal importance
for bears, elk, deer, wolves, goats, and ducks?
45    Pre-empted by their ancestors,
this is the property of the exacting porcupine,
and of the rat "slipping along to its burrow in the swamp
or pausing on high ground to smell the heather";
of "thoughtful beavers
50    making drains which seem the work of careful men with shovels,"
and of the bears inspecting unexpectedly
ant-hills and berry-bushes.
Composed of calcium gems and alabaster pillars,
topaz, tourmaline crystals and amethyst quartz,
55    their den is somewhere else, concealed in the confusion
of "blue forests thrown together with marble and jasper and agate
as if whole quarries had been dynamited."
And farther up, in stag-at-bay position
as a scintillating fragment of these terrible stalagmites,
60    stands the goat,
its eye fixed on the waterfall which never seems to fall—
an endless skein swayed by the wind,
immune to force of gravity in the perspective of the peaks.
A special antelope
65    acclimated to "grottoes from which issue penetrating draughts
which make you wonder why you came,"
it stands its ground
on cliffs the color of the clouds, of petrified white vapor—
black feet, eyes, nose, and horns, engraved on dazzling ice-fields,
70    the ermine body on the crystal peak;
the sun kindling its shoulders to maximum heat like acetylene,
                                                              dyeing them white—

---

30–31 *conformed*: Moore's note—"Lines 29, 62, 80, 112, 116, 195: 'Conformed to an edge,'
'grottoes,' 'two pairs of trousers,' My old packer, Bill Peyto . . . would give one or two ner-
vous yanks at the fringe and tear off the longer pieces, so that his outer trousers disap-
peared day by day from below upwards . . . (He usually wears two pairs of trousers). 'Glass
eyes,' 'businessmen,' 'with a sound like the crack of a rifle,' W.D. Wilcox, *The Rockies of
Canada* (Putnam, 1903)."

upon this antique pedestal,
"a mountain with those graceful lines which prove it a volcano,"
75   its top a complete cone like Fujiyama's
till an explosion blew it off.
Distinguished by a beauty
of which "the visitor dare never fully speak at home
for fear of being stoned as an impostor,"
80   Big Snow Mountain is the home of a diversity of creatures:
those who "have lived in hotels
but who now live in camps—who prefer to";
the mountain guide evolving from the trapper,
"in two pairs of trousers, the outer one older,
85   wearing slowly away from the feet to the knees";
"the nine-striped chipmunk
running with unmammal-like agility along a log";
the water ouzel°
with "its passion for rapids and high-pressured falls,"
90   building under the arch of some tiny Niagara;
the white-tailed ptarmigan° "in winter solid white,
feeding on heather-bells and alpine buckwheat";
and the eleven eagles of the west,
"fond of the spring fragrance and the winter colors,"
95   used to the unegoistic action of the glaciers
and "several hours of frost every midsummer night."
"They make a nice appearance, don't they,"°
happy seeing nothing?
Perched on treacherous lava and pumice—
100   those unadjusted chimney-pots and cleavers
which stipulate "names and addresses of persons to notify
in case of disaster"—
they hear the roar of ice and supervise the water
winding slowly through the cliffs,
105   the road "climbing like the thread
which forms the groove around a snail-shell,
doubling back and forth until where snow begins, it ends."
No "deliberate wide-eyed wistfulness" is here
among the boulders sunk in ripples and white water
110   where "when you hear the best wild music of the forest
it is sure to be a marmot,"
the victim on some slight observatory,
of "a struggle between curiosity and caution,"
inquiring what has scared it:
115   a stone from the moraine descending in leaps,
another marmot, or the spotted ponies with glass eyes,
brought up on frosty grass and flowers
and rapid draughts of ice-water.
Instructed none knows how, to climb the mountain,

---

88 *water ouzel*: a bird (related to a thrush) that dives into swift mountain streams and walks on the bottom in search of food; now known as the American dipper.
91 *ptarmigan*: a plump-bodied species of bird with fully feathered feet, a form of grouse.
97 *"They make a nice appearance, don't they?"*: Moore's note—"Overheard at the circus."

120    by business men who require for recreation
       three hundred and sixty-five holidays in the year,
       these conspicuously spotted little horses are peculiar;
       hard to discern among the birch-trees, ferns, and lily-pads,
       avalanche lilies, Indian paint-brushes,
125    bear's ears° and kittentails,
       and miniature cavalcades of chlorophylless fungi
       magnified in profile on the moss-beds like moonstones in the water;
       the cavalcade of calico competing
       with the original American menagerie° of styles
130    among the white flowers of the rhododendron surmounting
                                                              rigid leaves
       upon which moisture works its alchemy,
       transmuting verdure into onyx.

       "Like happy souls in Hell," enjoying mental difficulties,
135                                                           the Greeks
       amused themselves with delicate behavior
       because it was "so noble° and so fair";
       not practised in adapting their intelligence
       to eagle-traps and snow-shoes,
140    to alpenstocks° and other toys contrived by those
       "alive to the advantage of invigorating pleasures."
       Bows, arrows, oars, and paddles, for which trees provide the
                                                              wood,
       in new countries more eloquent than elsewhere—
145    augmenting the assertion that, essentially humane,
       "the forest affords wood for dwellings and by its beauty
       stimulates the moral vigor of its citizens."
       The Greeks° liked smoothness, distrusting what was back
       of what could not be clearly seen,
150    resolving with benevolent conclusiveness,
       "complexities° which still will be complexities
       as long as the world lasts";
       ascribing what we clumsily call happiness,
       to "an accident or a quality,
155    a spiritual substance or the soul itself,
       an act, a disposition, or a habit,
       or a habit infused, to which the soul has been persuaded,

---

125 *bear's ears*: a yellow-flowered primrose native to the Alps; the surrounding lines include
references to a number of high woodland or mountain flowers.
129 *menagerie*: Moore's note—"Menagerie of styles. W.M., 'The Mystery of an Adjective
and of Evening Clothes,' *London Graphic*, June 21, 1924."
137 *noble*: Moore's note—" '*Rashness is rendered innocuous*,' 'So noble and so fair,' Cardi-
nal Newman, Historical Sketches." Cardinal John Henry Newman (1801–1890), British the-
ologian, Christian apologist, and writer on diverse social topics.
140 *alpenstocks*: long iron-pointed staffs used in mountain climbing.
148 *Greeks*: Moore's note—" 'The Greeks were emotionally sensitive.' W. D. Hyde, *The
Five Great Philosophies* (Macmillan, 1911)."
151 *complexities*: Moore's note—"Lines 145–146, 148–152. '*Complexities. . . ,*' '*an accident
. . . ,*' Richard Baxter, *The Saints' Everlasting Rest*." Baxter (1615–1691), British preacher,
theologian, and controversial figure.

or something distinct from a habit, a power"—
such power as Adam had and we are still devoid of.
160   "Emotionally sensitive, their hearts were hard";
their wisdom was remote
from that of these odd oracles of cool official sarcasm,
upon this game preserve
where "guns, nets, seines, traps and explosives,
165   hired vehicles, gambling and intoxicants are prohibited;
disobedient persons being summarily removed
and not allowed to return without permission in writing."
It is self-evident
that it is frightful to have everything afraid of one;
170   that one must do as one is told
and eat rice, prunes, dates, raisins, hardtack, and tomatoes
if one would "conquer the main peak of Mount Tacoma,
this fossil flower concise without a shiver,
intact when it is cut,
175   damned for its sacrosanct remoteness—
like Henry James° "damned by the public for decorum";
not decorum, but restraint;
it is the love of doing hard things
that rebuffed and wore them out—a public out of sympathy
180                                with neatness.
Neatness of finish! Neatness of finish!
Relentless accuracy is the nature of this octopus
with its capacity for fact.
"Creeping slowly as with meditated stealth,
185   its arms seeming to approach from all directions,"
it receives one under winds that "tear the snow to bits
and hurl it like a sandblast
shearing off twigs and loose bark from the trees."
Is "tree" the word for these things
190   "flat on the ground like vines"?
some "bent in a half circle with branches on one side
suggesting dust-brushes, not trees;
some finding strength in union, forming little stunted groves
their flattened mats of branches shrunk in trying to escape"
195   from the hard mountain "planed by ice and polished by the
                                    wind"—
the white volcano with no weather side;
the lightning flashing at its base,
rain falling in the valleys, and snow falling on the peak—
200   the glassy octopus symmetrically pointed,
its claw cut by the avalanche
"with a sound like the crack of a rifle,
in a curtain of powdered snow launched like a waterfall."

1924

---

176 *Henry James:* (1843–1916), American novelist.

# No Swan So Fine

"No water so still as the
         dead fountains of Versailles."° No swan,°
with swart blind look askance
and gondoliering legs, so fine
5            as the chintz china one with fawn-
brown eyes and toothed gold
collar on to show whose bird it was.

Lodged in the Louis Fifteenth
         candelabrum-tree of cockscomb-
10    tinted buttons, dahlias,
sea-urchins, and everlastings,
         it perches on the branching foam
of polished sculptured
flowers—at ease and tall. The king is dead.

*1932, 1951*


# The Pangolin°

Another armored animal—scale
         lapping scale with spruce-cone regularity until they
form the uninterrupted central
         tail-row! This near artichoke with head and legs and
5                                         grit-equipped gizzard,
         the night miniature artist engineer is,
         yes, Leonardo da Vinci's° replica—
              impressive animal and toiler of whom we seldom hear.
Armor seems extra. But for him,
10            the closing ear-ridge°
              or bare ear lacking even this small
              eminence and similarly safe

contracting nose and eye apertures
         impenetrably closable, are not;—a true ant-eater,
15    not cockroach-eater, who endures
         exhausting solitary trips through unfamiliar ground at night,
         returning before sunrise; stepping° in the moonlight,

---

2 *Versailles*: a palace fourteen miles southwest of Paris. Louis XV held court there in the
eighteenth century.
2 *swan*: Moore's note—"A pair of Louis XV candelabra with Dresden figures of swans be-
longing to Lord Balfour. 'There is no water so still as in the dead fountains of Versailles.'
Percy Phillip, *New York Times Magazine*, May 10, 1931."
**poem title:** The pangolin is an anteater.
7 *Leonardo da Vinci*: (1452–1519) Italian Renaissance painter, engineer, musician, scien-
tist; the most versatile genius of the period.
10 *ear-ridge*: Moore's note—"'The closing ear-ridge' and certain other detail, from 'Pan-
golins,' by Robert T. Hatt, *Natural History*, December 1935."
17 *stepping*: Moore's note—"'Stepping . . . peculiarly.' See Lydekker's *Royal Natural His-
tory*." Richard Lydekker (1849–1915) was a British naturalist.

on the moonlight peculiarly, that the outside
    edges of his hands may bear the weight and save the
20                                            claws
for digging. Serpentined about
    the tree, he draws
        away from danger unpugnaciously,
           with no sound but a harmless hiss; keeping

25     the fragile grace of the Thomas-
        of-Leighton Buzzard Westminster Abbey wrought-iron
                                  vine,° or
rolls himself into a ball that has
    power to defy all effort to unroll it; strongly intailed, neat
30     head for core, on neck not breaking off, with curled-in feet.
        Nevertheless he has sting-proof scales; and nest
          of rocks closed with earth from inside, which he can
                             thus darken.
    Sun and moon and day and night and man and beast
35         each with a splendor
           which man in all his vileness cannot
           set aside; each with an excellence!

"Fearful yet to be feared," the armored
    ant-eater met by the driver-ant does not turn back, but
40 engulfs what he can, the flattened sword-
    edged leafpoints on the tail and artichoke set leg- and
                              body-plates
quivering violently when it retaliates
    and swarms on him. Compact like the furled fringed frill
45     on the hat-brim of Gargallo's° hollow iron head of a
matador, he will drop and will
    then walk away
        unhurt, although if unintruded on,
        he cautiously works down the tree, helped

50 by his tail. The giant-pangolin-
    tail, graceful tool, as prop or hand or broom or ax, tipped like
an elephant's trunk with special skin,
    is not lost on this ant- and stone-swallowing uninjurable
    artichoke which simpletons thought a living fable
55     whom the stones had nourished, whereas ants had done
        so. Pangolins are not aggressive animals; between
        dusk and day they have the not unchain-like machine-like
        form and frictionless creep of a thing
60         made graceful by adversities, con-

versities. To explain grace requires
    a curious hand. If that which is at all were not forever,
why would those who graced the spires

---

27 *Buzzard's vine*: Moore's note—"a fragment of ironwork in Westminster Abbey."
45 *Gargallo*: Pablo Gargallo (1881–1934) was a Spanish artist.

with animals and gathered there to rest, on cold luxurious
65      low stone seats—a monk and monk and monk—between the
                                                        thus
            ingenious roof-supports, have slaved to confuse
                grace with a kindly manner, time in which to pay a
                                                        debt,
70          the cure for sins, a graceful use
                of what are yet
                    approved stone mullions° branching out across
                    the perpendiculars? A sailboat°

        was the first machine. Pangolins, made
75          for moving quietly also, are models of exactness,
        on four legs; on hind feet plantigrade,
            with certain postures of a man. Beneath sun and moon,
                                                    man slaving
            to make his life more sweet, leaves half the flowers worth
80                                                  having,
                needing to choose wisely how to use his strength;
                    a paper-maker like the wasp; a tractor of foodstuffs,
                like the ant; spidering a length
                of web from bluffs
85                  above a stream; in fighting, mechanicked
                    like the pangolin; capsizing in

        disheartenment. Bedizened or stark
    •           naked, man, the self, the being we call human, writing-
            master to this world, griffons° a dark
90          "Like does not like like that is obnoxious"; and writes error
                                                    with four
            r's. Among animals, *one* has a sense of humor.
                Humor saves a few steps, it saves years. Unignorant,
                    modest and unemotional, and all emotion,
95              he has everlasting vigor,
                    power to grow,
                        though there are few creatures who can make one
                        breathe faster and make one erecter.

        Not afraid of anything is he,
100         and then goes cowering forth, tread paced to meet an obstacle
        at every step. Consistent with the
            formula—warm blood, no gills, two pairs of hands and a few
                                                    hairs—that
            is a mammal; there he sits in his own habitat,
105             serge-clad, strong-shod. The prey of fear, he, always
                    curtailed, extinguished, thwarted by the dusk, work
                                                    partly done,

---

72 *mullions*: vertical strips dividing window panes.
73 *sailboat*: Moore's note—"*A sailboat was the first machine.* See F.L. Morse, *Power: Its Application from the 17th Dynasty to the 20th Century.*"
89 *griffons*: fabulous beasts with the head and wings of an eagle and the body of a lion, here adapted as a verb.

says to the alternating blaze,
   "Again the sun!
110     anew each day; and new and new and new,
   that comes into and steadies my soul."

*1936*

## Bird-Witted°

With innocent wide penguin eyes, three
   large fledgling mocking-birds below
the pussy-willow tree,
   stand in a row,
5   wings touching, feebly solemn,
till they see
     their no longer larger
     mother bringing
something which will partially
10  feed one of them.

Toward the high-keyed intermittent squeak
   of broken carriage-springs, made by
the three similar, meek-
   coated bird's-eye
15  freckled forms she comes; and when
from the beak
     of one, the still living
     beetle has dropped
out, she picks it up and puts
20  it in again.

Standing in the shade till they have dressed
   their thickly-filamented, pale
pussy-willow-surfaced
   coats, they spread tail
25  and wings, showing one by one,
the modest
     white stripe lengthwise on the
     tail and crosswise
underneath the wing, and the
30  accordion

is closed again. What delightful note
   with rapid unexpected flute-
sounds leaping from the throat
   of the astute
35  grown bird, comes back to one from
the remote
     unenergetic sun-
     lit air before
the brood was here? How harsh
40  the bird's voice has become.

---

**poem title:** Moore's note—"Sir Francis Bacon: 'If a boy be bird-witted.'"

A piebald cat observing them,
    is slowly creeping toward the trim
trio on the tree-stem.
    Unused to him
45    the three make room—uneasy
new problem.
        A dangling foot that missed
        its grasp, is raised
and finds the twig on which it
50    planned to perch. The

parent darting down, nerved by what chills
    the blood, and by hope rewarded—
of toil—since nothing fills
    squeaking unfed
55    mouths, wages deadly combat,
and half kills
        with bayonet beak and
        cruel wings, the
intellectual cautious-
ly creeping cat.

*1936, 1941*

## The Paper Nautilus°

    For authorities whose hopes
are shaped by mercenaries?
    Writers entrapped by
    teatime fame and by
5    commuters' comforts? Not for these
    the paper nautilus
    constructs her thin glass shell.

    Giving her perishable
souvenir of hope, a dull
10    white outside and smooth-
    edged inner surface
glossy as the sea, the watchful
    maker of it guards it
    day and night; she scarcely

---

**poem title:** Paper Nautilus, a mollusk with a delicate spiral, chambered shell; the outer layer resembles porcelain, the inner layer pearl; it gets its name (Nautilus, meaning "sailor") from its practice of carrying the gas-filled shell on the surface of the water, where it resembles a sail.

15              eats until the eggs are hatched.
            Buried eight-fold in her eight
                arms, for she is in
                a sense a devil-
            fish, her glass ram'shorn-cradled freight
20                is hid but is not crushed;
                as Hercules,° bitten

                by a crab loyal to the hydra,
            was hindered to succeed,
                the intensively
25          watched eggs coming from
            the shell free it when they are freed,—
                leaving its wasp-nest flaws
                of white on white, and close-

                laid Ionic° chiton-folds
30          like the lines in the mane of
                a Parthenon° horse,
                round which the arms had
            wound themselves as if they knew love
                is the only fortress
                strong enough to trust to.

                                        *1941, 1967*

## Spenser's Ireland°

            has not altered;—
                a place as kind as it is green,
                the greenest place I've never seen.
            Every name is a tune.°
5           Denunciations do not affect
                    the culprit; nor blows, but it
            is torture to him to not be spoken to.
            They're natural,—
                    the coat, like Venus'

---

21 *Hercules*: a Latinized version of the Greek Heracles, the best-known and most popular hero in classical mythology. His many exploits include the famous twelve labors, numbered among them the charge to kill the Hydra, a monstrous snake with multiple heads.
29 *Ionic*: a Greek style of architecture distinguished by the spiral volutes at the top of the Ionic column; the style is lighter and more graceful than Doric.
31 *Parthenon*: the principal building of the Athenian Acropolis in ancient Greece; its marble sculptures include processions of horses.
**poem title:** The English poet Edmund Spenser (1552–1599) went to Ireland in 1580 as secretary to Lord Grey de Wilton, who was going there to be Lord Deputy. When Grey was recalled, Spenser remained, becoming a landowner and later writing *A Veue of the Present State of Ireland* (1633). He returned to England in 1598 after his Irish castle was burned in an insurrection.
4 *a tune*: Moore's note—"Lines 5, 7–8, 51, 63–64: '*Every name is a tune*,' '*It is torture*,' '*ancient jewelry*,' '*Your trouble is their trouble*.' See 'Ireland: The Rock Whence I Was Hewn,' by Don Byrne, *National Geographic Magazine*, March 1927."

10    mantle° lined with stars,
        buttoned close at the neck,—the sleeves° new from disuse.

        If in Ireland
            they play the harp backward at need,
            and gather at midday the seed
15    of the fern, eluding
            their "giants all covered with iron," might
                    there be fern seed for unlearn-
        ing obduracy and for reinstating
        the enchantment?
20            Hindered characters
        seldom have mothers
        in Irish stories, but they all have grandmothers.

        It was Irish;
            a match not a marriage was made
25        when my great great grandmother'd said
        with native genius for
        disunion, "Although your suitor be
                    perfection, one objection
        is enough; he is not
30    Irish." Outwitting
                    the fairies, befriending the furies,
        whoever again
        and again says, "I'll never give in," never sees

        that you're not free
35        until you've been made captive by
            supreme belief,—credulity
        you say? When large dainty
        fingers tremblingly divide the wings
            of the fly° for mid-July
40    with a needle and wrap it with peacock-tail,
        or tie wool and
                    buzzard's wing, their pride,
        like the enchanter's
        is in care, not madness. Concurring hands divide

---

10 *Venus' mantle*: Moore's note—"Footnote, *Castle Rackrent*: 'The cloak, or mantle, as de-
scribed by Thady is of high antiquity. See Spenser's *View of the State of Ireland.*'"
11 *sleeves*: Moore's note—"In Maria Edgeworth's *Castle Rackrent*, as edited by Professor
Morley, Thady Quirk says, 'I wear a long greatcoat. . . ; it holds on by a single button
round my neck, cloak fashion.'" Edgeworth (1767–1849) was a British novelist; *Castle Rack-
rent* (1800) was a novel about Irish life, notable for chronicling the life of a family over
time but perhaps limited by the perspective of a rational, improving Anglo-Irish observer.
39 *fly*: Moore's note—"'The sad-yellow fly, made with the buzzard's wing' and 'the shell-
fly, for the middle of July,' Maria Edgeworth, *The Absentee.*" This novel (1812) continues
her narrative of Irish life.

45      flax° for damask
            that when bleached by Irish weather
            has the silvered chamois-leather
        water-tightness of a
        skin. Twisted torcs and gold new-moon-shaped
50              lunulae° aren't jewelry
        like the purple-coral fuschia-tree's.° Eire°—
        the guillemot°
                so neat and the hen
        of the heath and the
55      linnet spinet-sweet—bespeak relentlessness? Then

        they are to me
            like enchanted Earl Gerald° who
            changed himself into a stag, to
        a great green-eyed cat of
60      the mountain. Discommodity° makes
                them invisible; they've dis-
        appeared. The Irish say your trouble is their
        trouble and your
                joy their joy? I wish
65      I could believe it;
        I am troubled, I'm dissatisfied, I'm Irish.

                                                    *1941*

---

45 *flax*: a fine, light-colored textile fiber derived from the flax plant; damask: a fine linen.
50 *lunulae*: crescent-shaped ornaments.
51 *fuschia*: a tropical tree or bush widely cultivated for its dramatic, drooping flowers.
51 *Eire*: Ireland (from the Gaelic).
52 *guillemot, linnet*: Moore's note—" 'The guillemot.' 'The linnet.' Denis O'Sullivan, *Happy Memories of Glengarry*." A guillemot is a web-footed sea-diving bird; a linnet is a small Old World finch.
57 *Earl Gerald*: Moore's note—"From a lecture by Padraic Colum." Colum (1881–1972) was an Irish poet who was active in the Irish Renaissance before coming to the United States. In 1916, he founded the *Irish Review* with Thomas MacDonagh, later that year one of the leaders of the Easter Rebellion. Earl Gerald, or Gerald of Barry (c. 1147–1223) was a British chronicler whose *Topographia hiberniae* describes his 1185 expedition to Ireland in Prince John's company; his *Expugnatio hiberniae* celebrates Henry II's conquest of Ireland.
60 *Discommodity*: an inconvenience of no utility.

# T. S. Eliot (1888–1965)

When *The Waste Land* appeared on both sides of the Atlantic in 1922, it was not the first work to adapt techniques of visual collage to a literary text. Indeed, Agnes Ernst Meyer's and Marius De Zayas's 1915 "Mental Reactions" made much more radical and disruptive use of the space of the page than Eliot's poem did, and it even used graphic forms to make explicit the connection with artistic movements like cubism. But "Mental Reactions" was a one-shot experiment in a very small circulation journal. Moreover, though aimed at once for a pop-cultural celebration and parody of female stereotypes, it could hardly claim the cultural ambitions *The Waste Land* appeared to embody. Eliot's poem was published in the aftermath of World War I, and it evoked for many readers the ruined landscape left to them after the historically unique devastation of trench warfare and mass slaughter. Its fragments mirrored a shattered world, and its allusions, however erudite, recalled a civilized culture many felt they had lost. Even its tendency to taunt readers with failed possibilities of spiritual rebirth, along with its glimpses of a religious route to joining the pieces of a dismembered god and a broken society, struck a chord. Eliot was one of many major modernist writers to yearn for a mythic synthesis, which remained out of reach.

Years later, with hindsight, the benediction at the poem's end could seem to foreshadow the more explicit religiosity of "Burnt Norton" and the *Four Quartets*. But that was not apparent in 1922, nor were Eliot's monarchist political conservatism and his reactionary social and racial prejudices yet in evidence. So readers and writers from all points of the political spectrum found inspiration in Eliot's technical innovations. In a surprisingly short period of time, *The Waste Land* became the preeminent poem of modernism, the unquestioned symbol of what was actually a much more diverse movement. Eventually, as its shadow came to hide other kinds of modernism—from more decisively vernacular language to poems strongly identified with race or revolution—*The Waste Land* gathered a set of compensatory ambitions and resentments. Of course it was hardly Eliot's aim to make adulation of *The Waste Land* into a justification for ignoring the Harlem Renaissance, a movement barely under way when the poem was written, but conservative literary scholars turned the poem into a weapon with that sort of cultural power.

Meanwhile, the poem itself remains available to be reread. Its mix of multiple voices, its fusion of personal anguish with historical experience, its fragments of narrativity, its riveting imagery and layered allusiveness, all these remain hallmarks of the literary response to modernity. *The Waste Land* is among a tiny handful of poems that define Eliot's career, something that cannot be said of Robert Frost, Langston Hughes, Wallace Stevens, or William Carlos Williams, all of whom wrote large numbers of short poems from which people will choose different favorites. Eliot, on the other hand, has a career that runs more definitively from "The Love Song of J. Alfred Prufrock" through *The Waste Land* to *Four Quartets*.

Eliot grew up in St. Louis. He was educated first at Harvard University and then at Oxford University, with a break at the Sorbonne in Paris between his undergraduate and graduate degrees in Boston. He moved to England and began a strained marriage with Vivian Haigh-Wood in 1915. He supported himself by working at Lloyd's Bank in London from 1917–1925, then joined a publishing firm. In 1927, he became a British citizen and joined the Anglican Church, the latter decision shaping both "Journey of the Magi" and the later *Four Quartets*. He was drawn to European fascism in the 1930s, but, unlike Pound, remained uninvolved in politics. His literary criticism, both on individual poets and on general principles of analysis, heavily influenced the American "New Critical" movement from the 1930s through the 1960s. His more general social criticism was more idiosyncratic; its Christian cultural commitments earned him an audience, but its occasional anti-Semitism and severe conservatism isolated him from many readers. He had notable success with his verse plays, among them *Murder in the Cathedral* (1935) and *The Cocktail Party* (1949).

# The Love Song
# of J. Alfred Prufrock

*S'io credesse che mia risposta fosse*
*A persona che mai tornasse al mondo,*
*Questa fiamma staria senza piu scosse.*
*Ma perciocche giammai di questo fondo*
*Non torno vivo alcun, s'i'odo il vero,*
*Senza tema d'infamia ti rispondo.*°

Let us go then, you and I,
When the evening is spread out against the sky
Like a patient etherised° upon a table;
Let us go, through certain half-deserted streets,
5　　The muttering retreats
Of restless nights in one-night cheap hotels
And sawdust restaurants with oyster-shells:
Streets that follow like a tedious argument
Of insidious intent
10　　To lead you to an overwhelming question. . .
Oh, do not ask, "What is it?"
Let us go and make our visit.

---

**epigraph:** "If I thought my reply were to no one who could return to the world, this flame would stop flickering. But since no one returns alive from this pit, if what I hear is true, I answer you without fear of dishonor" (Italian), from *Inferno* (CCVII. 61–66), by Dante Alighieri (1265–1321). Spoken to the character Dante by Guido da Montefeltro, who, while wrapped in flame as punishment, confesses to the sin of fraudulent counseling.
3 *etherised*: anesthetized with ether.

In the room the women come and go
Talking of Michelangelo.°

15    The yellow fog that rubs its back upon the window-panes,
The yellow smoke that rubs its muzzle on the window-panes
Licked its tongue into the corners of the evening,
Lingered upon the pools that stand in drains,
Let fall upon its back the soot that falls from chimneys,
20    Slipped by the terrace, made a sudden leap,
And seeing that it was a soft October night,
Curled once about the house, and fell asleep.

And indeed there will be time°
For the yellow smoke that slides along the street,
25    Rubbing its back upon the window-panes;
There will be time, there will be time
To prepare a face to meet the faces that you meet;
There will be time to murder and create,
And time for all the works and days° of hands
30    That lift and drop a question on your plate;
Time for you and time for me,
And time yet for a hundred indecisions,
And for a hundred visions and revisions,
Before the taking of a toast and tea.

35    In the room the women come and go
Talking of Michelangelo.

And indeed there will be time
To wonder, "Do I dare?" and, "Do I dare?"
Time to turn back and descend the stair,
40    With a bald spot in the middle of my hair—
[They will say: "How his hair is growing thin!"]
My morning coat, my collar mounting firmly to the chin,
My necktie rich and modest, but asserted by a simple pin—
[They will say: "But how his arms and legs are thin!"]
45    Do I dare
Disturb the universe?
In a minute there is time°
For decisions and revisions which a minute will reverse.

---

14 *Michelangelo*: Michelangelo di Lodovoco Buonarroti Simoni (1475–1564), Italian artist whose sculpture includes the most famous statue of the Biblical "David" and whose paintings include the entire ceiling of the Sistine Chapel in Rome.
23 *there will be time*: Cf. "To His Coy Mistress," by the British poet Andrew Marvell (1621–1628), whose opening line is "Had we but world enough, and time."
29 *Works and Days*: an agricultural poem by the Greek poet Hesiod (eighth century B.C.).
47 *there is time*: all of Eliot's questions and assertions in stanzas 4 and 6 are antiheroic echoes of the magisterial litany of the prophet in Ecclesiastes 3.1–8: "to every thing there is a season, and a time to every purpose under heaven: A time to be born, and a time to die; a time to plant, and a time to pluck up that which is planted . . . ."

For I have known them all already, known them all:—
50    Have known the evenings, mornings, afternoons,
I have measured out my life with coffee spoons;
I know the voices dying with a dying fall°
Beneath the music from a farther room.
        So how should I presume?

55        And I have known the eyes already, known them all—
The eyes that fix you in a formulated phrase,
And when I am formulated, sprawling on a pin,
When I am pinned and wriggling on the wall,
Then how should I begin
60    To spit out all the butt-ends of my days and ways?
        And how should I presume?

        And I have known the arms already, known them all—
Arms that are braceleted° and white and bare
[But in the lamplight, downed with light brown hair!]
65    Is it perfume from a dress
That makes me so digress?
Arms that lie along a table, or wrap about a shawl.
        And should I then presume?
        And how should I begin?

                •  •  •  •  •

70    Shall I say, I have gone at dusk through narrow streets
And watched the smoke that rises from the pipes
Of lonely men in shirt-sleeves, leaning out of windows? . . .

        I should have been a pair of ragged claws
Scuttling across the floors of silent seas.

                •  •  •  •  •

75    And the afternoon, the evening, sleeps so peacefully!
Smoothed by long fingers,
Asleep . . . tired . . . or it malingers,
Stretched on the floor, here beside you and me.
Should I, after tea and cakes and ices,
80    Have the strength to force the moment to its crisis?
But though I have wept and fasted, wept° and prayed,
Though I have seen my head [grown slightly bald] brought in upon
        a platter,°
I am no prophet—and here's no great matter;
85    I have seen the moment of my greatness flicker,
And I have seen the eternal Footman hold my coat, and snicker,
And in short, I was afraid.

---

52 *dying fall:* Cf. "If music be the food of love, play on . . . That strain again! It had a dying fall," Shakespeare, *Twelfth Night* (1.1.1–4).
63 *braceleted:* Cf. "A bracelet of bright hair about the bone" from John Donne's (1572–1631) "The Relique," a line Eliot admired.
81 *fasted, wept:* Cf. 2 Samuel 1.12: "they mourned, and wept and fasted."
83 *upon a platter:* in Matthew 14:3–11, when Salome, Herodias's daughter, pleased Herod with her dancing, he promised her anything she requested. She asked for and received the head of the prophet John the Baptist, who had rejected her love, on a platter.

And would it have been worth it, after all,
After the cups, the marmalade, the tea,
90    Among the porcelain, among some talk of you and me,
Would it have been worth while,
To have bitten off the matter with a smile,
To have squeezed the universe into a ball°
To roll it toward some overwhelming question,
95    To say: "I am Lazarus,° come from the dead,
Come back to tell you all, I shall tell you all"°—
If one, settling a pillow by her head,
    Should say: "That is not what I meant at all.
    That is not it, at all."

100      And would it have been worth it, after all,
Would it have been worth while,
After the sunsets and the dooryards and the sprinkled streets,
After the novels, after the teacups, after the skirts that trail along
    the floor—
105    And this, and so much more?—
It is impossible to say just what I mean!
But as if a magic lantern threw the nerves in patterns on a screen:
Would it have been worth while
If one, settling a pillow or throwing off a shawl,
110    And turning toward the window, should say:
    "That is not it at all,
    That is not what I meant, at all."

           •    •    •    •    •

No! I am not Prince Hamlet, nor was meant to be;
Am an attendant lord, one that will do
115    To swell a progress,° start a scene or two,
Advise the prince; no doubt, an easy tool,
Deferential, glad to be of use,
Politic, cautious, and meticulous;
Full of high sentence, but a bit obtuse;°
120    At times, indeed, almost ridiculous—
Almost, at times, the Fool.

      I grow old . . . I grow old . . .
I shall wear the bottoms of my trousers° rolled.

---

93 *into a ball*: Cf.: "Let us roll all our strength and all / Our sweetness up into one ball / And tear our pleasures with rough strife / Through the iron gates of life," from Marvell, "To His Coy Mistress."
95 *Lazarus*: In John 11:1–44 Jesus raised Lazarus from the dead.
96 *tell you all*: Cf. Christ's promise about the Holy Ghost in John 14.26: "he shall teach you all things."
115 *progress*: a royal procession; in Elizabethan theater the fool was often a member.
119 *full of high sentence, but a bit obtuse*: modernizes "ful of hy sentence" from the General Prologue (l. 306) of Geoffrey Chaucer's (1343?–1400) *The Canterbury Tales*; following the reference to Shakespeare's *Hamlet*, we may also take this passage to evoke the character Polonius in the same play; sentence: judgment or opinion.
123 *trousers rolled*: trousers with cuffs were just coming into fashion.

Shall I part my hair behind?° Do I dare to eat a peach?
125    I shall wear white flannel trousers, and walk upon the beach.
I have heard the mermaids° singing, each to each.

I do not think that they will sing to me.

I have seen them riding seaward on the waves
Combing the white hair of the waves blown back
130    When the wind blows the water white and black.

We have lingered in the chambers of the sea
By sea-girls wreathed with seaweed red and brown
Till human voices wake us, and we drown.

*1915*

# Gerontion°

*Thou hast nor youth nor age*
*But as it were an after dinner sleep*
*Dreaming of both.°*

Here I am, an old man in a dry month,
Being read to by a boy, waiting for rain.°
I was neither at the hot gates°
Nor fought in the warm rain°
5    Nor knee deep in the salt marsh, heaving a cutlass,
Bitten by flies, fought.
My house is a decayed house,
And the jew° squats on the window sill, the owner,

---

124 *hair behind*: B.C. Southam comments, "in his autobiographical essay *Ushant* (1952) Eliot's Harvard contemporary Conrad Aiken [1889–1973] tells us what a sensation was caused when one of their fellow students returned from Paris 'in exotic Left Bank clothing, and with his hair parted behind.' Clearly, at the time, such a hair-style was regarded as daringly bohemian."
125 *mermaids*: Cf. "Teach me to heare Mermaids singing," from "Song" by John Donne. The mermaids were legendary sea creatures having the head and body of a woman and the tail of a fish; to the extent there is not just wistfulness, but also anxiety, in Prufrock's account, we may also recognize a reference to the Sirens of Greek mythology—sea demons, half woman and half bird, whose music drew sailors to their death.
**poem title:** Gerontion, from a Greek term for "an old man." Eliot had once intended this poem to serve as a prologue to *The Waste Land*, but Ezra Pound persuaded him to publish it separately.
**epigraph:** From Shakespeare's *Measure for Measure* (3.1.32–34), where the duke of Vienna describes death to Claudio, who is about to be executed.
2 *rain*: the first two lines adapt a passage from A.C. Benson, *Edward FitzGerald* (1905): "Here he sits, in a dry month, old and blind, being read to by a country boy, longing for rain."
3 *hot gates*: alludes to Thermopylae (Greek for "hot gates"), site of a mountain pass where the Spartans stood against the Persian forces in 480 B.C. The battles of Waterloo (1815) and Cannae (216 B.C.) may be invoked in the following images.
4 *warm rain*: probably a reference to the 1815 battle of Waterloo, where Napoleon was defeated by the Duke of Wellington.
8 *jew*: Eliot's anti-Semitism is not in doubt; it surfaced repeatedly in his work, early on and with singular vulgarity in such poems as "Sweeney among the Nightingales" (1918) and in lines Pound edited out of *The Waste Land*, and later in Eliot's essays. Here the Jew for Eliot symbolizes urban decay and a lack of deep and genuine cultural roots.

Spawned in some estaminet° of Antwerp,°
10  Blistered in Brussels, patched and peeled° in London.
The goat coughs at night in the field overhead;°
Rocks, moss, stonecrop,° iron, merds.°
The woman keeps the kitchen, makes tea,
Sneezes at evening, poking the peevish gutter.°
15                              I an old man,
A dull head among windy spaces.

Signs are taken for wonders. "We would see a sign!"°
The word within a word, unable to speak a word,
Swaddled with darkness. In the juvescence° of the year
20  Came Christ the tiger°

In depraved May,° dogwood and chestnut, flowering judas,°
To be eaten, to be divided, to be drunk°
Among whispers; by Mr. Silvero
With caressing hands, at Limoges°
25  Who walked all night in the next room;

By Hakagawa, bowing among the Titians;°
By Madame de Tornquist, in the dark room
Shifting the candles; Fräulein von Kulp
Who turned in the hall, one hand on the door.
30          Vacant shuttles
Weave the wind. I have no ghosts,
An old man in a draughty house
Under a windy knob.°

---

9 *estaminet:* (French) "tavern" or "cafe," a term brought back to England by soldiers returning from World War I.
9 *Antwerp:* a city in northern Belgium; reinforces anti-Semitic stereotypes, since it has been a stock market and a center of the diamond industry for centuries.
10 *blistered . . . peeled:* symptoms of, or cures for, venereal disease.
11 *field overhead:* the field on the hill overshadowing the house.
12 *stonecrop:* varieties of sedum, plants with flowers and fleshy leaves.
12 *merds:* (French) "excrement."
14 *peevish gutter:* sputtering fire.
17 *sign:* "Signs and wonders" are anticipated to prove Christ's divinity in John 4.48 and in Matthew 12.38 ("Master, we would see a sign from thee.") Eliot borrows from biblical commentary by Lancelot Andrews (1555–1626) in his *Works* I: "Signs are taken for wonders. 'Master we would fain see a sign,' that is a miracle."
19 *juvescence:* condensed from "juvenescence," or "youth"; hence the springtime of the year.
20 *Christ the tiger:* Gerontion's monologue images Christ as a powerful animal, rather than as a caring figure; the line refers to Christ's resurrection.
21 *depraved May:* echoes *The Education of Henry Adams* (1918) by Henry Adams (1838–1915): "the passionate depravity that marked the Maryland May."
21 *flowering Judas:* a tree so named because of the belief that Judas Iscariot hanged himself from one after betraying Jesus.
22 *eaten, divided, drunk:* alludes to the breaking and eating of the bread of Christ and the drinking of wine in the Christian communion.
24 *Limoges:* the French town renowned for its porcelain.
26 *Titians:* works by Titian (c. 1488–1576), the greatest of Venetian painters.
33 *knob:* hill.

After such knowledge, what forgiveness? Think now
35  History has many cunning passages, contrived corridors°
And issues, deceives with whispering ambitions,
Guides us by vanities. Think now
She gives when our attention is distracted
And what she gives, gives with such supple confusions
40  That the giving famishes the craving. Gives too late
What's not believed in, or if still believed,
In memory only, reconsidered passion. Gives too soon
Into weak hands, what's thought can be dispensed with
Till the refusal propagates a fear. Think
45  Neither fear nor courage saves us. Unnatural vices
Are fathered by our heroism. Virtues
Are forced upon us by our impudent crimes.
These tears are shaken from the wrath-bearing tree.°

The tiger springs° in the new year. Us he devours. Think at last
50  We have not reached conclusion, when I
Stiffen in a rented house. Think at last
I have not made this show purposelessly
And it is not by any concitation°
Of the backward devils.
55  I would meet you upon this honestly.
I that was near your heart was removed therefrom
To lose beauty in terror, terror in inquisition.
I have lost my passion: why should I need to keep it
Since what is kept must be adulterated?
60  I have lost my sight, smell, hearing, taste and touch:
How should I use them for your closer contact?

These with a thousand small deliberations
Protract the profit of their chilled delirium,
Excite the membrane, when the sense has cooled,
65  With pungent sauces, multiply variety
In a wilderness of mirrors. What will the spider do,
Suspend its operations, will the weevil
Delay? De Bailhache, Fresca, Mrs. Cammel, whirled
Beyond the circuit of the shuddering Bear°
70  In fractured atoms. Gull against the wind, in the windy straits
Of Belle Isle,° or running on the Horn,°

---

35 *contrived corridors*: B.C. Southam suggests "Eliot may have had a specific 'contrived corridor' in mind—the so-called Polish Corridor. This was a strip of land taken from Germany under the terms of the Treaty of Versailles (signed June 1919) and awarded to Poland. It was the most resented of the Treaty settlements."

48 *wrath-bearing tree*: not only the forbidden Tree of Knowledge in the Garden of Eden and the flowering Judas mentioned in line 21 but also every hanging tree in human history.

49 *tiger springs*: Christ the Tiger (of line 20) devours us with the knowledge he brings.

53 *concitation*: stirring up.

69 *Bear*: the Great Bear, a constellation of stars in the northern sky.

71 *Belle Isle*: straits between Labrador and Newfoundland on Canada's eastern seaboard.

71 *Horn*: Cape Horn, the southernmost point of land in South America, with notoriously dangerous waters.

White feathers in the snow, the Gulf° claims,
And an old man driven by the Trades°
To a sleepy corner.

75                      Tenants of the house,
Thoughts of a dry brain in a dry season.

*1920*

## The Waste Land°

*"Nam Sibyllam quidem Cumis ego ipse oculis meis vidi*
*in ampulla pendere, et cum illi pueri dicerent: Σιβυλλα*
*τι θέλεις; respondebat illa: ἀποθανεῖν θέλω."*°
For Ezra Pound
*il miglior fabbro.*°

---

72 *Gulf:* Gulf Stream, the warm ocean current flowing northward off eastern North America in the Atlantic.

73 *Trades:* the Trade winds.

**poem title:** Eliot's note reads—"Not only the title, but the plan and a good deal of the incidental symbolism of the poem was suggested by Miss Jessie L. Weston's book on the Grail legend: *From Ritual to Romance* (Cambridge). Indeed, so deeply am I indebted, Miss Weston's book will elucidate the difficulties of the poem much better than my notes can do; and I recommend it (apart from the great interest of the book itself) to any who think such elucidation of the poem worth the trouble. To another work of anthropology I am indebted in general, one which has influenced our generation profoundly; I mean *The Golden Bough*; I have used especially the two volumes *Adonis, Attis, Osiris.* Anyone who is acquainted with these works will immediately recognize in the poem certain references to vegetation ceremonies." Eliot was rather dismissive of his notes years later in *The Frontiers of Criticism* (1956): "When it came to print *The Waste Land* as a little book—for the poem on its first appearance in *The Dial* and *The Criterion* had no notes whatever—it was discovered that the poem was inconveniently short, so I set to work to expand the notes, in order to provide a few more pages of printed matter." Some have concluded the notes parody scholarly annotation, but they do clearly identify some of Eliot's narrative aims and sources, and their quotations serve as supplements to the original poem.

In Arthurian legends, a Fisher King is dead or wounded and his country has become a bleak, infertile wasteland; the land can only bloom again if the king is restored to life. For that, a knight must win through to the Perilous Chapel and learn the secrets of the Holy Grail (the cup used by Christ at the Last Supper and which was filled with the blood from the wound in his side at his crucifixion). According to Weston's *From Ritual to Romance*, the Arthurian legends themselves are preceded and paralleled by still earlier fertility myths, such as those described in Frazer's *Golden Bough.* For some cultures, myths of a leader's dismemberment and rebirth underwrite the human relationship with the cycle of the seasons.

A number of cultural theorists of Eliot's day believed that most religions of the world draw on these myths as resources and incorporate versions of them into their central stories. Certainly the story of Christ's death and resurrection, with its promise to redeem a fallen world, follows the pattern. Eliot found these myths suggestive in the shattered postwar world of modernity and in the midst of what seemed the emotional ruins of his personal life. These myths do not unify the five sections of *The Waste Land*, with its allusive fragments and multiple voices, into a single narrative, but they do haunt the poem, as perhaps they haunt modernity itself.

**epigraph:** "For I myself with my own eyes saw the Sibyl of Cumae hanging in a bottle, and when the boys asked her: 'Sibyl, what do you want?' she responded, 'I want to die,'" from *Satyricon* (Ch. 48), by the Roman satirist Petronius (?-A.D. 66). According to Roman myth, the sun god Apollo granted the Sibyl (a prophetess) immortality, but, having forgotten to ask for eternal youth, she was doomed to increasing decrepitude.

**dedication:** *il miglior fabbro:* (Italian) "the best maker" (better craftsman), from *Purgatorio* (XXVI. 117) by Dante Alighieri (1265–1321). Dante praises the Italian poet Guido Guinizelli (1240?–1274), who responds that the Provencal poet Arnaut Daniel (12th century B.C.) is the best maker of poetry. Pound edited *The Waste Land* prior to its publication.

## I. The Burial of the Dead°

April° is the cruellest month, breeding
Lilacs out of the dead land, mixing
Memory and desire, stirring
Dull roots with spring rain.
5      Winter kept us warm, covering
Earth in forgetful snow, feeding
A little life° with dried tubers.
Summer surprised us, coming over the Starnbergersee°
With a shower of rain; we stopped in the colonnade,
10     And went on in sunlight, into the Hofgarten,°
And drank coffee, and talked for an hour.
Bin gar keine Russin, stamm' aus Litauen, echt deutsch.°
And when we were children, staying at the archduke's,
My cousin's, he took me out on a sled,
15     And I was frightened. He said, Marie,
Marie, hold on tight. And down we went.
In the mountains, there you feel free.
I read, much of the night, and go south in the winter.

What are the roots that clutch, what branches grow
20     Out of this stony rubbish? Son of man,°
You cannot say, or guess, for you know only
A heap of broken images,° where the sun beats,
And the dead tree gives no shelter, the cricket° no relief,
And the dry stone no sound of water. Only
25     There is shadow under this red rock,°
(Come in under the shadow of this red rock),
And I will show you something different from either
Your shadow at morning striding behind you
Or your shadow at evening rising to meet you;
30     I will show you fear in a handful of dust.°

---

**Part I:** *Burial of the Dead:* from the title of the burial service in the Anglican *Book of Common Prayer.*

1 *April:* with this bleak view of April, Eliot simultaneously recalls and reverses the affirmative account in the opening to the General Prologue to *The Canterbury Tales* by Chaucer (1343?–1400).

7 *feeding / A little life:* Cf. "Our Mother feedeth thus our little life / That we in turn may feed her with our death," from "To Our Ladies of Death" by James Thomson (1834–1882).

8 *Starnbergersee:* a lake south of Munich, Germany. Lines 8–16 echo parts of *My Past* (1913) by Countess Marie Larisch.

10 *Hofgarten:* public garden with cafes in Munich.

12 *Bin . . . deutsch:* (German) "I am not at all Russian. I come from Lithuania, a real German."

20 *Son of Man:* Eliot's note—"Cf. Ezekiel II, i." There God tells the "Son of man," the prophet Ezekiel, "Stand upon they feet, and I will speak unto thee."

22 *broken images:* Cf. Ezekiel 6.6, "your images shall be broken," part of God's punishment for worshiping idols.

23 *cricket:* Eliot's note—"Cf. Ecclesiastes XII, v." There old age is said to be a time when "the grasshopper shall be a burden, and desire shall fail."

25 *rock:* Isaiah 32:1–2 predicts that the Messiah's arrival will be "as rivers of water in a dry place, as the shadow of a great rock in a weary land."

30 *handful of dust:* the phrase comes from John Donne's *Devotions Upon Emergent Occasions:* "what's become of man's great extent and proportion, when himself shrinks himself, and consumes himself to a handful of dust" (Meditation IV). *Fear* in a handful of dust adds anxiety about death to the image.

*Frisch weht der Wind*
*Der Heimat zu*
*Mein Irisch Kind,*
*Wo weilest du?*°

35 "You gave me hyacinths first a year ago;
"They called me the hyacinth girl."°
—Yet when we came back, late, from the Hyacinth garden,
Your arms full, and your hair wet, I could not
Speak, and my eyes failed, I was neither
40 Living nor dead, and I knew nothing,
Looking into the heart of light, the silence.
*Oed' und leer das Meer.*°

Madame Sosostris,° famous clairvoyante,
Had a bad cold, nevertheless
45 Is known to be the wisest woman in Europe,
With a wicked pack of cards.° Here, said she,
Is your card, the drowned Phoenician Sailor,°
(Those are pearls that were his eyes.° Look!)
Here is Belladonna,° the Lady of the Rocks,
50 The lady of situations.
Here is the man with three staves, and here the Wheel,°
And here is the one-eyed merchant, and this card,
Which is blank, is something he carries on his back,
Which I am forbidden to see. I do not find
55 The Hanged Man. Fear death by water.
I see crowds of people, walking round in a ring.
Thank you. If you see dear Mrs. Equitone,
Tell her I bring the horoscope myself:
One must be so careful these days.

---

31–34 *Frisch . . . du:* (German) "Fresh blows the wind / to the homeland / my Irish child / where are you waiting?" Eliot's note—"*Tristan and Isolde,* I, verses 5–8," an opera by Richard Wagner (1813–1883). Said to the dying Tristan as he awaits Isolde's arrival.
36 *hyacinth girl:* according to Greek myth, Hyacinthus was a youth accidentally killed by Apollo, who resurrected the boy as a flower, the hyacinth, which came to symbolize rebirth.
42 *Oed . . . Meer:* (German) "Empty and barren is the sea."
43 *Sosostris:* in *Chrome Yellow* (1921) by Aldous Huxley (1894–1963) Sosostris, the Sorceress of Ectabana, is a fake fortune-teller. The name is adapted from Sesotris, an Egyptian king.
46 *pack of cards:* Eliot's note—"I am not familiar with the exact constitution of the Tarot pack of cards, from which I have obviously departed to suit my own convenience. The Hanged Man, a member of the traditional pack, fits my purpose in two ways: because he is associated in my mind with the Hanged God of Frazer, and because I associate him with the hooded figure in the passage of the disciples to Emmaus in Part V. The Phoenician Sailor and the Merchant appear later; also the 'crowds of people,' and Death by Water is executed in Part IV. The Man with Three Staves (an authentic member of the Tarot pack) I associate, quite arbitrarily, with the Fisher King himself."
47 *Phoenician Sailor:* not actually a card in the Tarot pack. The Phoenicians were sea-going merchants who disseminated Egyptian fertility cults across the Mediterranean.
48 *his eyes:* in Shakespeare's *The Tempest* (1.2.397–402) Ariel sings to Ferdinand, who fears that his father has drowned, "Full fathom five thy father lies, /Of his bones are coral made; / Those are pearls that were his eyes; / Nothing of him that doth fade, /But doth suffer a sea-change / Into something rich and strange."
49 *Belladonna:* (Italian) "beautiful lady," the Virgin Mary of the painting *Madonna of the Rocks* by Leonardo da Vinci; also the poisonous plant nightshade and a cosmetic.
51 *Wheel:* the Wheel of Fortune appears on one of the Tarot cards.

60          Unreal City,°
        Under the brown fog of a winter dawn,
        A crowd flowed over London Bridge,° so many,
        I had not thought death had undone so many.°
        Sighs, short and infrequent, were exhaled,°
65      And each man fixed his eyes before his feet.
        Flowed up the hill and down King William Street,
        To where Saint Mary Woolnoth° kept the hours
        With a dead sound on the final stroke of nine.°
        There I saw one I knew, and stopped him, crying: "Stetson!°
70      "You who were with me in the ships at Mylae!
        "That corpse you planted last year in your garden,°
        "Has it begun to sprout? Will it bloom this year?
        "Or has the sudden frost disturbed its bed?
        "Oh keep the Dog far hence, that's friend to men,°
75      "Or with his nails he'll dig it up again!
        "You! hypocrite lecteur!—mon semblable,—mon frère!"°

---

60 *Unreal city:* Eliot's note—"Cf. Baudelaire: 'Fourmillante cité, cité pleine de rêves, / Où le spectre en plein jour raccroche le passant." (French) "Swarming city, city full of dreams, / Where the specter in broad daylight accosts the passerby," from *The Flowers of Evil* (1857) by the French symbolist Charles Baudelaire (1821–1867).

62 *London Bridge:* a bridge across the Thames River.

63 *so many:* Eliot's note—"Cf. *Inferno*, III, 55–57: 'si lunga tratta / di gente, ch'io non avrei mai creduto / che morte tanta n'avesse disfatta'" (Italian) "such a long train / of people, I should not have believed / that death had undone so many." Entering the Inferno, Dante sees hordes of people who made no choices in life and therefore have been rejected by both Heaven and Hell. Eliot's passage also evokes the aftermath of World War I, with massive loss of life in battle and the shell-shocked returning wounded.

64 *exhaled:* Eliot's note—"Cf. *Inferno*, IV, 25–27: 'Quivi, secondo che per ascoltare, / non avea pianto, ma' che di sospiri, / che l'aura eterna facevan tremare'" (Italian) "Here, to judge by hearing, there was no weeping but sighs / that made the eternal air tremble." Dante is in the first circle of the Inferno, Limbo, where the virtuous non-Christians suffer only from the fact that they can never see God.

67 *Saint Mary Woolnoth:* a London church on King William Street.

68 *stroke of nine:* Eliot's note—"A phenomenon which I have often noticed." In his own annotations, Sam Baskett writes, "Indeed he had, for it was partly the route Eliot took for many years to his desk at Lloyd's. If he passed under the clock of the 'Bankers Church' at nine, he would have been on time at the office, a few steps down the street. The church is also possibly an allusion to the Chapel Perilous in the Grail Legend. See also lines 388–389."

69 *Stetson:* possibly the hat manufacturer; Mylae: site of a Roman naval victory against Carthage (260 B.C.).

71 *garden:* in ancient fertility rites images of the gods were buried in fields devoted to agriculture.

74 *friend to man:* Eliot's note—"Cf. the Dirge in Webster's *White Devil*." John Webster's *The White Devil* ends, "But keep the wolf far hence, that's foe to men; / For with his nails he'll dig them up again," as one of the characters worries that her murdered relatives will be disinterred. Eliot's adaptation of the lines changes the wolf to a dog, now a friend rather than a foe. Lines 71–74 amount to a fallen, secularized parody of the resurrection of the fertility god.

76 *mon frère:* Eliot's note—"V. Baudelaire, Preface to *Fleurs du Mal*." Baudelaire's prefatory poem ends "You! Hypocritical reader!—my counterpart,—my brother!"

## II. A Game of Chess°

The Chair she sat in, like a burnished throne,°
Glowed on the marble, where the glass
Held up by standards wrought with fruited vines

80     From which a golden Cupidon° peeped out
(Another hid his eyes behind his wing)
Doubled the flames of sevenbranched candelabra
Reflecting light upon the table as
The glitter of her jewels rose to meet it,

85     From satin cases poured in rich profusion;
In vials of ivory and coloured glass
Unstoppered, lurked her strange synthetic perfumes,
Unguent, powdered, or liquid—troubled, confused
And drowned the sense in odours; stirred by the air

90     That freshened from the window, these ascended
In fattening the prolonged candle-flames,
Flung their smoke into the laquearia,°
Stirring the pattern on the coffered° ceiling.
Huge sea-wood fed with copper

95     Burned green and orange, framed by the coloured stone,
In which sad light a carvèd dolphin swam.
Above the antique mantel was displayed
As though a window gave upon the sylvan scene°
The change of Philomel,° by the barbarous king

100     So rudely forced; yet there the nightingale°
Filled all the desert with inviolable voice
And still she cried, and still the world pursues,
"Jug Jug"° to dirty ears.

---

**Part II:** *A Game of Chess:* probably refers to one of two plays by Thomas Middleton (1570?–1627), *A Game of Chess* (1624), a political satire, or *Women Beware Women* (1657), in which a woman is seduced while her mother-in-law plays chess nearby. Playing chess is a metaphor for the seduction.

77 *throne:* Eliot's note—"Cf. *Antony and Cleopatra*, II, ii, l. 190." In this Shakespeare play, Enobarbus, attempting to describe Cleopatra to Roman friends, begins his famous speech, "The barge she sat in, like a burnish'd throne, / Burned on the water."

80 *Cupidon:* a statue of the Roman god of love, Cupid.

92 *laquearia:* Eliot's note—"V. *Aeneid*, I, 726: dependent lychni laquearibus aureis incensi, et noctem flammis funalia vincunt," (Latin), "from the golden paneled ceiling hang lamps, and the torches conquer the night with their flames," a description of the banquet hall where Aeneas is welcomed to Carthage by Queen Dido, who later kills herself after Aeneas abandons her to found Rome.

93 *coffered:* decorated with sunken panels.

98 *sylvan scene:* Eliot's note—"V. Milton, *Paradise Lost*, IV, 140." In this epic by John Milton (1608–1674), which is Eliot's source for the phrase, but not for the events described here in *The Waste Land*, Satan comes to Eden for the first time and sees "A Sylvan Scene, and as the ranks ascend / Shade above shade, a woody Theatre / Of stateliest view?" (140–142).

99 *Philomel:* Eliot's note—"V. Ovid, *Metamorphosis*, VI, Philomela." In this narrative poem by the Roman Ovid (43 B.C.-A.D. 17?), Philomela is raped by King Tereus of Thrace, her brother-in-law, who cuts out her tongue to silence her; the gods transform her into a nightingale. Note the contrast from the Edenic sylvan scene anticipated by the previous line.

100 *nightingale:* Eliot's note—"Cf. Part III, l. 204" (of *The Waste Land*).

103 *Jug Jug:* a standard Elizabethan representation of the nightingale's song and a slang reference to sexual intercourse.

And other withered stumps of time
105    Were told upon the walls; staring forms
Leaned out, leaning, hushing the room enclosed.
Footsteps shuffled on the stair.
Under the firelight, under the brush, her hair
Spread out in fiery points
110    Glowed into words, then would be savagely still.


      "My nerves° are bad to-night. Yes, bad. Stay with me.
"Speak to me. Why do you never speak. Speak.
      "What are you thinking of? What thinking? What?
"I never know what you are thinking. Think."


115        I think we are in rats' alley°
Where the dead men lost their bones.


      "What is that noise?"
                              The wind under the door.°
"What is that noise now? What is the wind doing?"
120                            Nothing again nothing.
                                          "Do
"You know nothing? Do you see nothing? Do you remember
"Nothing?"


      I remember
125    Those are pearls that were his eyes.°
"Are you alive, or not? Is there nothing in your head?"°
                                                    But

O O O O that Shakespeherian Rag—°
It's so elegant
130    So intelligent
"What shall I do now? What shall I do?"
"I shall rush out as I am, and walk the street
"With my hair down, so. What shall we do to-morrow?
"What shall we ever do?"
135                        The hot water at ten.
And if it rains, a closed car at four.
And we shall play a game of chess,
Pressing lidless eyes and waiting for a knock upon the door.°

---

111 *nerves:* many now argue that portions of Part II of *The Waste Land*, such as lines 111–114, are informed by Eliot's disintegrating marriage to his first wife, Vivian Haigh-Wood.
115 *rat's alley:* Eliot's note—"Cf. Part III, l. 195" (of *The Waste Land*).
118 *door:* Eliot's note—"Cf. Webster: 'Is the wind in that door still?'" In Webster's *The Devil's Law Case* (1619?) (3.2), a doctor makes this comment when an attack fails to kill the victim, who is still breathing.
125 *eyes:* a line from Ariel's song in Shakespeare's *The Tempest*; see the note to line 48.
126 *your head:* Eliot's note—"Cf. Part I, l. 37, 48" (of *The Waste Land*).
127 *Rag:* "The Shakespearian Rag" (1912), lyrics by Gene Buck and Herman Ruby, music by Dave Stamper, contains the chorus: "That Shakespearian rag, / Most intelligent, very elegant . . . " Rag is short for ragtime, a style of jazz dance music.
138 *door:* Eliot's note—"Cf. the game of chess in Middleton's *Women Beware Women*."

When Lil's husband got demobbed,° I said—
140    I didn't mince my words, I said to her myself,
HURRY UP PLEASE ITS TIME°
Now Albert's coming back, make yourself a bit smart.
He'll want to know what you done with that money he gave you
To get yourself some teeth. He did, I was there.
145    You have them all out, Lil, and get a nice set,
He said, I swear, I can't bear to look at you.
And no more can't I, I said, and think of poor Albert,
He's been in the army four years, he wants a good time,
And if you don't give it him, there's others will, I said.
150    Oh is there, she said. Something o' that, I said.
Then I'll know who to thank, she said, and give me a straight look.
HURRY UP PLEASE ITS TIME
If you don't like it you can get on with it, I said.
Others can pick and choose if you can't.
155    But if Albert makes off, it won't be for lack of telling.
You ought to be ashamed, I said, to look so antique.
(And her only thirty-one.)
I can't help it, she said, pulling a long face,
It's them pills I took, to bring it off, she said.
160    (She's had five already, and nearly died of young George.)
The chemist° said it would be all right, but I've never been the
        same.
You are a proper fool, I said.
Well, if Albert won't leave you alone, there it is, I said,
What you get married for if you don't want children?
165    HURRY UP PLEASE ITS TIME
Well, that Sunday Albert was home, they had a hot gammon,°
And they asked me in to dinner, to get the beauty of it hot—
HURRY UP PLEASE ITS TIME
HURRY UP PLEASE ITS TIME
170    Goonight Bill. Goonight Lou. Goonight May. Goonight.
Ta ta. Goonight. Goonight.
Good night, ladies,° good night, sweet ladies, good night, good
        night.

---

139 *demobbed*: slang for "demobilized from the army," a change made by Pound.
141 *Hurry . . . Its Time*: a typical announcement of closing time in a London pub.
161 *chemist*: pharmacist.
166 *gammon*: ham or bacon, also, with "hot gammon," suggesting the human thigh.
172 *Good night, ladies*: quotes both Ophelia's speech before drowning herself in Shake-
speare's *Hamlet* (4.5.74–75) and the popular song "Good night ladies, we're going to leave
you now."

### III. The Fire Sermon°

The river's tent is broken: the last fingers of leaf
Clutch and sink into the wet bank. The wind
175    Crosses the brown land, unheard. The nymphs are departed.
Sweet Thames, run softly, till I end my song.°
The river bears no empty bottles, sandwich papers,
Silk handkerchiefs, cardboard boxes, cigarette ends
Or other testimony of summer nights. The nymphs are departed.
180    And their friends, the loitering heirs of city directors;°
Departed, have left no addresses.
By the waters of Leman I sat down and wept°. . .
Sweet Thames, run softly till I end my song,
Sweet Thames, run softly, for I speak not loud or long.
185    But at my back° in a cold blast I hear
The rattle of the bones, and chuckle spread from ear to ear.
A rat crept softly through the vegetation
Dragging its slimy belly on the bank
While I was fishing in the dull canal
190    On a winter evening round behind the gashouse
Musing upon the king my brother's wreck
And on the king my father's death° before him.
White bodies naked on the low damp ground
And bones cast in a little low dry garret,
195    Rattled by the rat's foot only, year to year.

---

**Part III:** *The Fire Sermon:* Buddha's fire sermon, referred to in Eliot's note to line 308. In the *Fire Sermon,* Buddha warns us against the fires of lust, envy, and anger and tells us everything is aflame: "forms are on fire . . . impressions received by the eye are on fire; and whatever sensation, pleasant, unpleasant, or indifferent, originates in dependence on impressions received by the eye, that also is on fire. And with what are these on fire? With the fire of passion, say I, with the fire of hatred, with the fire of infatuation." Sam Baskett writes, "The title of this section is especially evocative. It serves as a kind of rubric for the various scenes of lust, past and present, which follow, and it anticipates the express references to Buddha's *Fire Sermon* and St. Augustine's *Confessions* . . . . Given the accurate London geography of the poem and the fact that *The Waste Land* began as, and to some extent remains, a poem about London in the Dryden vein, it is worth noting that overlooking the scenes mentioned, especially in lines 262–268, is the imposing Monument to the Great Fire of London of 1666."
176 *song:* Eliot's note—"V. Spenser, *Prothalamion,*" the refrain to the 1596 marriage song by Edmund Spenser (1552?–1599), set on the Thames River near London.
180 *directors:* business directors in London's financial sector, the city.
182 *wept:* after "By the rivers of Babylon, there we sat down, yea, we wept, when we remembered Zion," from Psalm 137.1, in which the Jews mourn for their lost homeland. Leman is the French name for Lake Geneva, Switzerland, the site of the sanatorium where Eliot wrote much of *The Waste Land* while recovering from a nervous breakdown. "Leman" is an archaic term for mistress; hence the "waters of Leman" are also erotic longings.
185 *at my back:* after "But at my back I always hear / Time's wingéd chariot hurrying near," from the poem "To His Coy Mistress (21–22), by Andrew Marvell (1621–1678). The speaker, in his attempt to seduce his lady, reminds her of the inevitable passing of time.
192 *father's death:* Eliot's note—"Cf. *The Tempest,* I, ii." Ferdinand, son of the king of Naples, says, "Sitting on a bank, / Weeping again the King my father's wreck, / This music crept by me on the waters."

But at my back from time to time° I hear
The sound of horns and motors, which shall bring°
Sweeney to Mrs. Porter in the spring.
O the moon shone bright on Mrs. Porter°
200    And on her daughter
They wash their feet in soda water
*Et O ces voix d'enfants, chantant dans la coupole!°*

    Twit twit twit
Jug jug jug jug jug jug
205    So rudely forc'd.
Tereu°

    Unreal City
Under the brown fog of a winter noon
Mr. Eugenides, the Smyrna° merchant
210    Unshaven, with a pocket full of currants°
C.i.f. London: documents at sight,
Asked me in demotic° French
To luncheon at the Cannon Street Hotel°
Followed by a weekend at the Metropole.

215        At the violet hour, when the eyes and back
Turn upward from the desk, when the human engine waits
Like a taxi throbbing waiting,

---

196 *time to time:* Eliot's note—"Cf. Marvell, *To His Coy Mistress.*"
197 *shall bring:* Eliot's note—"Cf. Day, *Parliament of Bees:* 'When of the sudden, listen-
ing, you shall hear, / A noise of horns and hunting, which shall bring / Actaeon to Diana
in the spring, / Where all shall see her naked skin.'" According to classical myth, Actaeon,
as punishment for seeing Diana (Roman goddess of the hunt) bathing naked, was turned
into a stag and killed by his own hounds. *Parliament of Bees* is a satirical play by British
poet John Day (1574–1640?).
199 *Mrs. Porter:* Eliot's note—"I do not know the origin of the ballad from which these
lines are taken; it was reported to me from Sydney, Australia." In the song, a bawdy fa-
vorite of British troops during World War I and a parody of the popular ballad "Little Red-
wing," Mrs. Porter and her daughter are prostitutes. Eliot uses the character Sweeney
throughout his poetry as a vulgar person.
202 *Et . . . coupole:* (French) "And oh those voices of children, singing in the cupola!"
Eliot's note—"V. Verlaine, *Parsifal,*" the concluding line of a sonnet by the French sym-
bolist poet Paul Verlaine (1844–1896). In Wagner's opera *Parsifal* (1882), before the knight
Parsifal can approach the Holy Grail, his feet must be washed. Children sing at the cer-
emony.
206 *Tereu:* short for Tereus, who raped Philomel; also, another conventional Elizabethan
way of representing the nightingale's song; finally, a slang pronunciation of "true."
209 *Smyrna:* port in Turkey.
210 *currants:* Eliot's note—"The currants were quoted at a price 'carriage and insurance
free to London'; and the Bill of Lading, etc., were to be handed to the buyer upon pay-
ment of the sight draft."
212 *demotic:* popular, vernacular.
213 *Cannon St. Hotel:* a London hotel next to a station, typically full of travelers from Eu-
rope; the Metropole is a luxury hotel in Brighton, England, known as a sexual rendezvous.

I Tiresias,° though blind, throbbing between two lives,
Old man with wrinkled female breasts, can see
220      At the violet hour, the evening hour that strives
Homeward, and brings the sailor home from sea,°
The typist home at teatime, clears her breakfast, lights
Her stove, and lays out food in tins.
Out of the window perilously spread
225      Her drying combinations° touched by the sun's last rays,
On the divan are piled (at night her bed)
Stockings, slippers, camisoles, and stays.
I Tiresias, old man with wrinkled dugs
Perceived the scene, and foretold the rest—
230      I too awaited the expected guest.
He, the young man carbuncular,° arrives,
A small house agent's clerk, with one bold stare,
One of the low on whom assurance sits
As a silk hat on a Bradford° millionaire.
235      The time is now propitious, as he guesses,
The meal is ended, she is bored and tired,
Endeavours to engage her in caresses
Which still are unreproved, if undesired.
Flushed and decided, he assaults at once;
240      Exploring hands encounter no defence;
His vanity requires no response,
And makes a welcome of indifference.
(And I Tiresias have foresuffered all
Enacted on this same divan or bed;
245      I who have sat by Thebes below the wall°

---

218 *Tiresias:* Eliot's note—"Tiresias, although a mere spectator and not indeed a 'charac-
ter,' is yet the most important personage in the poem, uniting all the rest. Just as the one-
eyed merchant, seller of currants, melts into the Phoenician Sailor, and the latter is not
wholly distinct from Ferdinand Prince of Naples, so all the women are one woman, and
the two sexes meet in Tiresias. What Tiresias *sees,* in fact, is the substance of the poem.
The whole passage from Ovid is of great anthropological interest." Eliot then quotes from
Ovid's *Metamorphoses* (III. 320–338) the story of Tiresias, who upon seeing two snakes mat-
ing, strikes them and is turned into a woman. Seven years later he comes upon them again,
strikes them, and is turned back into a man. Because he has been both man and woman,
Tiresias is called upon to settle a quarrel between Jove and Juno (the supreme Roman god
and goddess) concerning whether men or women have more pleasure in love. Tiresias's
answer, that women have more pleasure, angered Juno, who struck him blind. To com-
pensate for the loss of sight, Jove granted Tiresias the gift of prophecy. Eliot's comments
have a good deal to teach us about the status of personae in the poem and about the im-
portance of sexuality, but it would be unwise to take his comments about Tiresias's cen-
trality literally.
221 *home from the sea:* Eliot's note—"This may not appear as exact as Sappho's lines, but
I had in mind the 'longshore' or 'dory' fisherman, who returns at nightfall." Sappho (early
sixth century B.C.) was a Greek lyric poet; another source is "Requiem" by Robert Louis
Stevenson (1850–1894): "Home is the sailor, home from the sea . . . ."
225 *combinations:* underwear.
231 *carbuncular:* pimpled.
234 *Bradford:* an English Midlands industrial town where fortunes were made during World
War I.
245 *wall:* below the wall of Thebes stretched the marketplace where Tiresias prophesied.

And walked among the lowest of the dead.)
Bestows one final patronising kiss,
And gropes his way, finding the stairs unlit . . .

She turns and looks a moment in the glass,
250      Hardly aware of her departed lover;
Her brain allows one half-formed thought to pass:
"Well now that's done: and I'm glad it's over."
When lovely woman stoops to folly° and
Paces about her room again, alone,
255      She smoothes her hair with automatic hand,
And puts a record on the gramophone.

"This music crept by me upon the waters"°
And along the Strand,° up Queen Victoria Street.
O City city, I can sometimes hear
260      Beside a public bar in Lower Thames Street,
The pleasant whining of a mandoline
And a clatter and a chatter from within
Where fishmen lounge at noon: where the walls
Of Magnus Martyr° hold
265      Inexplicable splendour of Ionian white and gold.

The river sweats°
Oil and tar
The barges drift
With the turning tide
270      Red sails
Wide
To leeward, swing on the heavy spar.
The barges wash
Drifting logs

---

253 *folly:* Eliot's note—"V. Goldsmith, the song in *The Vicar of Wakefield*," a 1766 novel
by Oliver Goldsmith (1728–1774), in which Olivia, having been seduced, sings, "When lovely
woman stoops to folly / And finds too late that men betray, / What charm can soothe her
melancholy, / What art can wash her guilt away? / The only art her guilt to cover, /To hide
her shame from every eye, / To give repentance to her lover / And wring his bosom—is to
die."
257 *waters:* the line is a direct quotation from *The Tempest* (1.2.391).
258 *Strand:* London street; Queen Victoria Street: London street near the Thames River.
264 *Magnus Martyr:* Eliot's note—"The interior of St. Magnus Martyr is to my mind one
of the finest among Wren's interiors. See *The Proposed Demolition of Nineteen City
Churches* (P.S. King & Son, Ltd.)." Magnus Martyr, a church designed by the English ar-
chitect Sir Christopher Wren (1632–1723), is in London, as are the other sites mentioned.
Near a fish market and a bar frequented by fishmen from the market, it was known as the
"fisherman's church."
266 *river sweats:* Eliot's note—"The Song of the (three) Thames-daughters begins here.
From line 292 to 306 inclusive they speak in turn. V. *Gotterdamerung*, III, i: the Rhine-
daughters." Lines 277–278 and 290–291 are the refrain of the Rhine maidens, who sing of
the deterioration of the Rhine River in Wagner's 1874 opera *Twilight of the Gods;* Eliot
adapts the song to the Thames River, borrowing some details from the description of the
river at the opening of *Heart of Darkness* (1899) by Joseph Conrad (1857–1924). The cry
"wei-a-la" is taken directly from Wagner.

275          Down Greenwich reach°
             Past the Isle of Dogs.°
                          Weialala leia
                          Wallala leialala

             Elizabeth and Leicester°
280          Beating oars
             The stern was formed
             A gilded shell
             Red and gold
             The brisk swell
285          Rippled both shores
             Southwest wind
             Carried down stream
             The peal of bells
             White towers°
290                          Weialala leia
                             Wallala leialala

             "Trams and dusty trees.
             Highbury bore me. Richmond and Kew°
             Undid me. By Richmond I raised my knees
295          Supine on the floor of a narrow canoe."

             "My feet are at Moorgate,° and my heart
             Under my feet. After the event
             He wept. He promised 'a new start.'
             I made no comment. What should I resent?"

---

275 *Greenwich reach:* south bank of the River Thames at Greenwich, downstream from London's center.

276 *Isle of Dogs:* peninsula in the Thames River, across from the borough of Greenwich, where Elizabeth I (1533–1603), queen of England from 1558 to 1603, was born.

279 *Leicester:* Eliot's note—"V. Froude, *Elizabeth,* Vol. I, ch. iv, letter of De Quadra to Philip of Spain: 'In the afternoon we were in a barge, watching the games on the river. (The queen) was alone with Lord Robert and myself on the poop, when they began to talk nonsense, and went so far that Lord Robert at last said, as I was on the spot there was no reason why they should not be married if the queen pleased.'" The British historian James Anthony Froude (1818–1894) wrote of the love affair between Elizabeth I and the Earl of Leicester, Robert Dudley (1532?–1588). Bishop De Quadra was the Spanish ambassador to England; the poop is a raised deck at a ship's stern.

289 *White towers:* perhaps the additional white stone towers of the Tower of London.

293 *Kew:* Eliot's note—"Cf. *Purgatorio,* V, 133: 'Ricorditi di me, che son la Pia; / Siena mi fe', disfecemi Maremma'" (Italian) "Remember me, who am Pia; Siena made me, Maremma unmade me." In the Antepurgatory Dante meets Pia, one of those who died without last rites, probably because her jealous husband had her killed because of suspicion of adultery. She was born in Siena and died in Maremma. Highbury is a London suburb; Richmond, a borough of London; Kew a London district noted for its botanical garden.

296 *Moorgate:* a London slum.

300    "On Margate Sands.°
       I can connect
       Nothing with nothing.
       The broken fingernails of dirty hands.
       My people humble people who expect
305    Nothing."
                    la la

       To Carthage° then I came

       Burning burning burning burning°
       O Lord Thou pluckest me out°
310    O Lord Thou pluckest

       burning

## IV. DEATH BY WATER°

Phlebas the Phoenician, a fortnight dead,
Forgot the cry of gulls, and the deep sea swell
And the profit and loss.
315                    A current under sea
Picked his bones° in whispers. As he rose and fell
He passed the stages of his age and youth
Entering the whirlpool.
                    Gentile or Jew
320    O you who turn the wheel and look to windward,
Consider Phlebas, who was once handsome and tall as you.

---

300 *Margate Sands:* a beach resort on the Thames, where the river opens into the Channel; emotionally stressed, Eliot spent a short time there and began work on *The Waste Land* before moving on to the sanatorium at Lake Geneva.

307 *Carthage:* Eliot's note—"V. St. Augustine's *Confessions:* 'to Carthage then I came, where a cauldron of unholy loves sang all about mine ears.'" Augustine is describing the errors of his youth.

308 *burning:* Eliot's note—"The complete text of the Buddha's Fire Sermon (which corresponds in importance to the Sermon on the Mount) from which these words are taken, will be found translated in the late Henry Clarke Warren's *Buddhism in Translation* (Harvard Oriental Series). Mr. Warren was one of the great pioneers of Buddhist studies in the Occident."

309 *pluckest me out:* Eliot's note—"From St. Augustine's *Confessions* again. The collocation of these two representatives of Eastern and Western asceticism, as the culmination of this part of the poem, is not an accident." Augustine's passage echoes Zechariah 3.2, where God calls the priest Joshua "a brand plucked out of the fire" when he converts from being a non-believer into being a follower of the Messiah.

**Part IV:** *Death By Water:* This short section, which Pound condensed considerably, was originally written in French as the conclusion to Eliot's poem "Dans le Restaurant" (1920) or "In the Restaurant."

315 *sea/picked his bones:* Cf. the passages quoted earlier from Ariel's song in *The Tempest.*

### V. What the Thunder Said°

After the torchlight red on sweaty faces
After the frosty silence in the gardens
After the agony in stony places
325    The shouting and the crying
Prison and palace and reverberation
Of thunder of spring over distant mountains
He who was living is now dead
We who were living are now dying
330    With a little patience

     Here is no water but only rock
Rock and no water and the sandy road
The road winding above among the mountains
Which are mountains of rock without water
335    If there were water we should stop and drink
Amongst the rock one cannot stop or think
Sweat is dry and feet are in the sand
If there were only water amongst the rock
Dead mountain mouth of carious° teeth that cannot spit
340    Here one can neither stand nor lie nor sit
There is not even silence in the mountains
But dry sterile thunder without rain
There is not even solitude in the mountains
But red sullen faces sneer and snarl
345    From doors of mudcracked houses
                      If there were water
     And no rock
     If there were rock
     And also water
350    And water
     A spring
     A pool among the rock
     If there were the sound of water only
     Not the cicada°
355    And dry grass singing
     But sound of water over a rock
     Where the hermit-thrush sings in the pine trees

---

**Part V:** *What the Thunder Said:* Eliot's note—"In the first part of Part V three themes are employed: the journey to Emmaus, the approach to the Chapel Perilous (see Miss Weston's book) and the present decay of eastern Europe." On the journey of Christ's disciples to Emmaus, which takes place after Christ's crucifixion and resurrection, see Luke 24.13–34. Jesus walks beside two of his disciples and engages them in conversation, but they first take him for a stranger. The first stanza deals with the events from Jesus' betrayal to his crucifixion. In the *Upanishads,* Vedic holy books, thunder is the language of god.

339 *carious:* decaying.

354 *cicada:* an insect with a stout body, blunt head, and wide transparent wings, that lives as a grub underground for most of its life and sings loudly when it surfaces; also known as locusts in some areas. Cf. the cricket of line 23.

Drip drop drip drop drop drop drop°
But there is no water

360    Who is the third who walks always beside you?°
When I count, there are only you and I together
But when I look ahead up the white road
There is always another one walking beside you
Gliding wrapt in a brown mantle, hooded
365    I do not know whether a man or a woman
—But who is that on the other side of you?

What is that sound high in the air°
Murmur of maternal lamentation
Who are those hooded hordes swarming
370    Over endless plains, stumbling in cracked earth
Ringed by the flat horizon only
What is the city over the mountains
Cracks and reforms and bursts in the violet air
Falling towers
375    Jerusalem Athens Alexandria
Vienna London
Unreal

A woman drew her long black hair out tight
And fiddled whisper music on those strings
380    And bats with baby faces in the violet light
Whistled, and beat their wings
And crawled head downward down a blackened wall
And upside down in air were towers
Tolling reminiscent bells, that kept the hours
385    And voices singing out of empty cisterns and exhausted wells.

---

358 *drop drop:* Eliot's note—"This is *Turdus aonalaschkae pallasii*, the hermit-thrush which I have heard in Quebec Province. Chapman says (*Handbook of Birds of Eastern North America*) 'it is most at home in secluded woodland and thickety retreats . . . Its notes are not remarkable for variety of volume, but in purity and sweetness of tone and exquisite modulation they are unequalled.' Its 'water-dripping song' is justly celebrated."

360 *beside you:* Eliot's note—"The following lines were stimulated by the account of one of the Antarctic expeditions (I forget which, but I think one of Shackleton's): it was related that the party of explorers, at the extremity of their strength, had the constant delusion that there was *one more member* than could actually be counted." Sir Henry Shackleton (1874–1922) was a British explorer who made three expeditions to Antarctica. Eliot is connecting the Antarctic experience with Jesus's unrecognized appearance before his two disciples on the way to Emmaus. As so often in *The Waste Land,* a modern event is a secularized, fallen version of an earlier archetype.

367 *in the air:* Eliot's note—"Cf. Hermann Hesse, *Blick ins Chaos*" (German) "A Glimpse Into Chaos" (1922) by novelist Hesse (1877–1962). Eliot then quotes a passage from the book, translated as, "Already half of Europe, already at least half of Eastern Europe, is on the way to chaos, going drunk in holy madness along the edge of the abyss and sings, sings drunkenly and hymnlike as Dimitri Karamazov sang. The bourgeois laughs, shocked at these songs; the saint and the prophet hear them with tears." The passage from Hesse refers to the Russian Revolution in 1917; Karamazov is a character in *The Brothers Karamazov* (1880) by Feodor Dostoevski (1821–1881).

In this decayed hole among the mountains
In the faint moonlight, the grass is singing
Over the tumbled graves, about the chapel°
There is the empty chapel, only the wind's home.
390    It has no windows, and the door swings,
Dry bones can harm no one.
Only a cock stood on the rooftree
Co co rico co co rico°
In a flash of lightning. Then a damp gust
395    Bringing rain

Ganga° was sunken, and the limp leaves
Waited for rain, while the black clouds
Gathered far distant, over Himavant.°
The jungle crouched, humped in silence.
400    Then spoke the thunder
D A
*Datta:°* what have we given?
My friend, blood shaking my heart
The awful daring of a moment's surrender
405    Which an age of prudence can never retract
By this, and this only, we have existed
Which is not to be found in our obituaries
Or in memories draped by the beneficent spider°
Or under seals broken by the lean solicitor
410    In our empty rooms
D A
*Dayadhvam:* I have heard the key°

---

388 *chapel:* we may recall the Chapel Perilous of the Arthurian Grail legend, where a knight must go in search of the Holy Grail.

393 *co rico:* according to folklore, a cock's crowing indicates that a ghost has departed. Cf. Shakespeare's *Hamlet* 1.1.157–59 and Matthew 26.34, 74, where a cock crows after Peter denies Christ three times.

396 *Ganga:* the Ganges River in India, sacred to Hindus, a site for symbolic purification.

398 *Himavant:* a Himalayan mountain.

402 *Datta:* Eliot's note—" 'Datta, dayadhvam, damyata' (Give, sympathize, control). The fable of the meaning of the Thunder is found in the *Brihadaranyaka—Upanishad,* 5, 1. A translation is found in Deussen's *Sechzig Upanishads des Veda,* p. 489." According to Hindu theology, "DA" is the command of the god Prajapati. *Da* is interpreted differently by gods, men, and demons—as "control ourselves," "give alms," and "have compassion." Prajapati informs them that when the god's voice, thunder, repeats the word *Da* it means *all three* things; thus humans should practice alms-giving, sympathy, and self-control. Paul Deussen (1845–1919) was a German philosopher and Sanskrit scholar who wrote *Sixty Vedic Upanishads.*

408 *spider:* Eliot's note—"Cf. Webster, *The White Devil,* V, vi: ' . . . they'll remarry / Ere the worm pierce your winding-sheet, ere the spider / Make a thin curtain for your epitaphs.'"

412 *key:* Eliot's note—"Cf. *Inferno,* XXXIII, 46: 'ed io sentii chiavar l'uscio di sotto / all'orribile torre.' [Italian, "And I heard them below locking the door / of the horrible tower."] Also F.H. Bradley, *Appearance and Reality,* p. 346. 'My external sensations are no less private to myself than are my thoughts or my feelings. In either case my experience falls within my own circle, a circle closed on the outside; and, with all its elements alike, every sphere is opaque to the others which surround it. . . . In brief, regarded as an existence which appears in a soul, the whole world for each is peculiar and private to that soul.'" The passage from the *Inferno* is spoken by Count Ugolino, whom Dante meets in Circle 9 of Hell, among those who were traitors to their countries. Ugolino was locked in a tower with his sons and grandsons and left to starve. F.H. Bradley (1846–1924) was an idealist English philosopher who was the subject of Eliot's dissertation.

Turn in the door once and turn once only
We think of the key, each in his prison
415    Thinking of the key, each confirms a prison
Only at nightfall, aethereal rumours
Revive for a moment a broken Coriolanus°
DA
*Damyata*: The boat responded
420    Gaily, to the hand expert with sail and oar
The sea was calm, your heart would have responded
Gaily, when invited, beating obedient
To controlling hands

                    I sat upon the shore
425    Fishing,° with the arid plain behind me
Shall I at least set my lands in order?°
London Bridge is falling down falling down falling down°
*Poi s'ascose nel foco che gli affina*°
*Quando fiam uti chelidon*—O swallow swallow°
430    *Le Prince d'Aquitaine à la tour abolie*°
These fragments I have shored against my ruins
Why then Ile fit you. Hieronymo's mad againe.°
Datta. Dayadhvam. Damyata.
       Shantih     shantih     shantih°

                                   1922

---

417 *Coriolanus*: Gaius Marcius Coriolanus (fifth century B.C.), a Roman hero who became the excessively proud protagonist of Shakespeare's play *Coriolanus* (1608), a figure ruined by his inability to sympathize with Rome's common people.

425 *Fishing*: Eliot's note—"V. Weston: *From Ritual to Romance*; chapter on the Fisher King." The Fisher King symbolizes resurrection.

426 *in order*: "Thus saith the Lord, Set thine house in order; for thou shalt die, and not live," from Isaiah 38.1.

427 *London bridge is falling down*: the refrain of a nursery rhyme.

428 *Poi . . . affina*: Eliot's note—"V. *Purgatorio*, XXVI, 148. 'Ara vos prec per aquella valor / que vos guida al som de l'escalina, / sovegna vos a temps de ma dolor. / Poi s'ascose nel foco che gli affina.'" "I pray you now in the name of that virtue / that guides you to the top of the stair [paradise], / remember in good time my suffering." On Ledge 7 of Purgatory, among the Lustful, Dante meets the poet Arnaut Daniel: Daniel speaks in Provencal; Dante, in Italian.

429 *swallow*: (Latin) 'When shall I be like the swallow?" Eliot's note—"V. *Pervigilium Veneris*. Cf. Philomela in Parts II and III." In the version of the myth in the anonymous poem "The Vigil of Venus," Philomela is turned into a swallow. "O Swallow, Swallow" is a phrase from English poet Alfred Lord Tennyson's (1809–1892) narrative poem "The Princess" (1847).

430 *Le Prince . . .*: (French) "The Prince of Aquitaine at the ruined tower." Eliot's note— "V. Gerard de Nerval, Sonnet *El Desdichado* [The Disinherited One]." It is the prince who has been disinherited in this sonnet from *Les Chimères* (1854), or *The Chimeras* (French), by the poet de Nerval (1808–1855).

432 *againe*: Eliot's note—"V. Kyd's *Spanish Tragedy*." "Why then Ile fit [supply] you" (with a play) refers to Hieronymo's plan to gain revenge while performing a play that has been requested by those he seeks to kill, from a 1594 drama by the English dramatist Thomas Kyd (1557?–1595?). "Hieronymo's mad againe" refers to the play's subtitle. Hieronymo bites out his tongue at the end of the play.

434 *Shantih*: Eliot's note—"Repeated as here, a formal ending to an Upanishad. 'The Peace which passeth understanding' is our equivalent to this word."

# The Hollow Men

*Mistah Kurtz—he dead.*°
A penny for the Old Guy

## I

We are the hollow men°
We are the stuffed men
Leaning together
Headpiece filled with straw. Alas!
5      Our dried voices, when
We whisper together
Are quiet and meaningless
As wind in dry grass
Or rats' feet over broken glass
10    In our dry cellar

    Shape without form, shade without colour,
Paralysed force, gesture without motion;

    Those who have crossed
With direct eyes, to death's other Kingdom
15    Remember us—if at all—not as lost
Violent souls, but only
As the hollow men
The stuffed men.

## II

Eyes I dare not meet in dreams
20    In death's dream kingdom
These do not appear:
There, the eyes are
Sunlight on a broken column
There, is a tree swinging
25    And voices are
In the wind's singing
More distant and more solemn
Than a fading star.

---

**epigraph & dedication:** "Mistah Kurtz—he dead" is a quotation from *Heart of Darkness* (1902) by Joseph Conrad (1857–1924); the line is spoken by a servant reporting Kurtz's death. In Conrad's novella, Kurtz, a trading company official up river in the African Congo, gradually went mad and became a demonic figure. "A penny for the Old Guy" is the phrase British children use on Guy Fawkes Day (November 5) to beg pennies for fireworks. Fawkes led a group conspiring to blow up the British House of Commons in 1605; captured before they could complete the plan, Fawkes was executed on 5 November. The Guy itself is a straw, rag, and paper filled effigy that is burned on Guy Fawkes Day.
1 *hollow men:* the phrase is from Shakespeare's *Julius Caesar* 4.2; Brutus remarks that his ally Cassius seems to be turning away from him: "hollow men . . . make gallant show and . . . like deceitful jades, / Sink in the trial." Kurtz in *Heart of Darkness* is described as a "hollow sham."

Let me be no nearer
30      In death's dream kingdom
Let me also wear
Such deliberate disguises
Rat's coat, crowskin, crossed staves
In a field°
35      Behaving as the wind behaves
No nearer—

Not that final meeting
In the twilight kingdom

### III

This is the dead land
40      This is cactus land
Here the stone images°
Are raised, here they receive
The supplication of a dead man's hand
Under the twinkle of a fading star.

45      Is it like this
In death's other kingdom
Waking alone
At the hour when we are
Trembling with tenderness
50      Lips that would kiss
Form prayers to broken stone.

### IV

The eyes are not here
There are no eyes here
In this valley of dying stars
55      In this hollow valley
This broken jaw of our lost kingdoms

In this last of meeting places
We grope together
And avoid speech
60      Gathered on this beach of the tumid river

Sightless, unless
The eyes reappear
As the perpetual star
Multifoliate rose°

---

33–34 *Rat's coat . . . staves /In a field:* scarecrows, and the country practice of hanging bodies of animals who eat crops in a field to scare off others.
41 *stone images:* as with idolatrous worship.
64 *multifoliate rose:* From *Paradiso* 28.30, the third volume of Dante Alighieri's (1265–1321) *Divine Comedy.* The multifoliate rose is the figure created by the souls of the saved encircling God.

65      Of death's twilight kingdom
        The hope only
        Of empty men.

                              V


        *Here we go round the prickly pear*°
        *Prickly pear prickly pear*
70      *Here we go round the prickly pear*
        *At five o'clock in the morning.*


            Between the idea
        And the reality
        Between the motion
75      And the act
        Falls the Shadow
                              *For Thine is the Kingdom*°


            Between the conception
        And the creation
80      Between the emotion
        And the response
        Falls the Shadow
                                      *Life is very long*°


            Between the desire
85      And the spasm
        Between the potency
        And the existence
        Between the essence
        And the descent
90      Falls the Shadow
                              *For Thine is the Kingdom*


            For Thine is
        Life is
        For Thine is the


95          *This is the way*° *the world ends*
        *This is the way the world ends*
        *This is the way the world ends*
        *Not with a bang but a whimper.*

                                              *1925*


---

68 *prickly pear:* Eliot uses a prickly pear as the central object in the traditional children's
verse "Here we go round the mulberry bush."
77 *For Thine is the Kingdom:* from the Lord's Prayer.
83 *Life is very long:* from Joseph Conrad's *An Outcast of the Islands* (1896).
95 *This is the way:* the phrase is the first half of a line from the same children's song
adapted above, "This is the way we clap our hands."

# Journey of the Magi°

'A cold coming we had of it,
Just the worst time of the year
For a journey, and such a long journey:
The ways deep and the weather sharp,
5    The very dead of winter.'°
And the camels galled,° sore-footed, refractory,
Lying down in the melting snow.
There were times we regretted
The summer palaces on slopes, the terraces,
10   And the silken girls bringing sherbet.
Then the camel men cursing and grumbling
And running away, and wanting their liquor and women,
And the night-fires going out, and the lack of shelters,
And the cities hostile and the towns unfriendly
15   And the villages dirty and charging high prices:
A hard time we had of it.
At the end we preferred to travel all night,
Sleeping in snatches,
With the voices singing in our ears, saying
20   That this was all folly.

Then at dawn we came down to a temperate valley,
Wet, below the snow line, smelling of vegetation;
With a running stream and a water-mill beating the darkness,
And three trees° on the low sky,
25   And an old white horse° galloped away in the meadow.
Then we came to a tavern with vine-leaves over the lintel,°
Six hands at an open door dicing for pieces of silver,°

---

**poem title:** One of Eliot's "Ariel" poems, unified by themes of death and rebirth. The speaker is one of the three Magi, or wise men, who journeyed to Bethlehem, bearing gifts for the newborn child Jesus (see Matthew 2.1–13).

5 *winter:* lines 1 to 5 are adapted from the 1622 Christmas sermon by Lancelot Andrewes (1555–1626)—"Last we consider the *time* of their coming, the season of the yeare. It was no *summer Progresse.* A cold coming they had of it, at this time of yeare; just, the worst time of the yeare, to take a journey, and especially a long journey, in. The wause deep, the weather sharp, the daies short, the sunn farthest off, *in solstiio brumali,* the very dead of *Winter.*"

6 *galled:* rubbed sore by their harness.

24 *three trees:* suggesting the crucifixion: according to Matthew 27.38, there were three crosses (two thieves were also crucified) and "darkness over the land."

25 *horse:* "Behold a white horse; and he that sat upon him was Faithful and True," from Revelation 19.11.

26 *lintel:* symbolizing homage to pagan gods of fertility, in contrast, for example, to the sacrificial blood with which the ancient Israelites marked their side posts and lintels (the crosspieces at the top of door frames) during the last of the plagues in Egypt: "when I [the Lord] see the blood, I will pass over you, and the plague shall not be upon you to destroy you, when I smite the land of Egypt," from Exodus 12.13.

27 *silver:* symbolizing Judas's betrayal of Jesus for 30 pieces of silver (see Matthew 26:14–16) and the soldiers' casting lots for his clothing (see Psalms 22.18).

And feet kicking the empty wine-skins.°
But there was no information, and so we continued
30        And arrived at evening, not a moment too soon
Finding the place; it was (you may say) satisfactory.

All this was a long time ago,° I remember,
And I would do it again, but set down
This set down
35        This: were we led all that way for
Birth or Death? There was a Birth, certainly,
We had evidence and no doubt. I had seen birth and death,
But had thought they were different; this Birth was
Hard and bitter agony for us, like Death, our death.
40        We returned to our places, these Kingdoms,
But no longer at ease here, in the old dispensation,°
With an alien people clutching their gods.
I should be glad of another death.

*1935*

from

# *Four Quartets*

## Burnt Norton°

τοῦ λόγου δ'ἐόντος ξυνοῦ ζώουσιν οι πολλοι
ὡς ιδιαν ἐχοντες φρόνησιν.
I. *p. 77. Fr. 2.*
ὁδὸς ἄνω κάτω μία καὶ ὠυτή.
I. *p. 89. Fr. 60.*
DIELS: *DIE FRAGMENTE DER VORSOKRATIKER* (HERAKLEITOS).°

I

Time present and time past
Are both perhaps present in time future,

---

28 *wine-skins:* "And no man putteth new wine into old bottles; else the new wine doth
burst the bottles," from Mark 2.22. The Magi are unable to interpret any of these symbols
because Jesus's life has not yet given them symbolic meaning.
32 *a long time ago:* the magus is recounting his tale for a listener who is to "set down /
This." William Butler Yeats's (1865–1939) prose piece "The Adoration of the Magi," in-
volving a comparable recounting, was reprinted in his *Mythologies* (1925) and may have
been Eliot's inspiration.
41 *the old dispensation:* the world and its belief system prior to Christianity.
**poem title:** Burnt Norton is the name of a manor house in Gloucestershire County in
southwest central England. The description of time in the opening lines adapts and elab-
orates on a passage in Ecclesiastes 3.15: "That which hath been is now; and that which is
to be hath already been." The poem is the first of Eliot's poem sequence *Four Quartets*:
"Burnt Norton" (1936), "East Coker" (1940), "The Dry Salvages" (1941), and "Little Gid-
ding" (1942), all titles referring to place names associated with Eliot's experience, thereby
suggesting that the local is the site of the transcendent and eternal. They were collected
as *Four Quartets* in 1943. One of the central motifs of "Burnt Norton" comes from the
Spanish mystic St. John of the Cross (1542–1591) who believed that the soul's meditative
movement toward God must pass through a "dark night of the soul."
**epigraph:** (Greek), from Heraclitus (540?–475 B.C.), "Though the word is common to all,
most people live as if each has an understanding uniquely his own"; "The way up and the
way down are the same."

And time future contained in time past.
If all time is eternally present
5    All time is unredeemable.
What might have been is an abstraction
Remaining a perpetual possibility
Only in a world of speculation.
What might have been and what has been
10   Point to one end, which is always present.
Footfalls echo in the memory
Down the passage which we did not take
Towards the door we never opened
Into the rose-garden.° My words echo
15   Thus, in your mind.
                But to what purpose
Disturbing the dust on a bowl of rose-leaves
I do not know.
            Other echoes
20   Inhabit the garden. Shall we follow?
Quick, said the bird, find them, find them,
Round the corner. Through the first gate,
Into our first world, shall we follow
The deception of the thrush? Into our first world.
25   There they were, dignified, invisible,
Moving without pressure, over the dead leaves,
In the autumn heat, through the vibrant air,
And the bird called, in response to
The unheard music hidden in the shrubbery,
30   And the unseen eyebeam crossed, for the roses
Had the look of flowers that are looked at.
There they were as our guests, accepted and accepting.
So we moved, and they, in a formal pattern,
Along the empty alley, into the box circle,°
35   To look down into the drained pool.
Dry the pool, dry concrete, brown edged,
And the pool was filled with water out of sunlight,
And the lotos rose,° quietly, quietly,
The surface glittered out of heart of light,°

---

14 *rose-garden:* the rose is an immensely complex and dual symbol, representing at once heavenly perfection and earthly passion, virginity and fertility, eternity and temporality, and finally both life and death. Here the rose-garden recalls the Garden of Eden as well as personal experience and missed opportunities for either passion or transcendence.

34 *box circle:* a circle formed of the evergreen shrub known as box or boxwood, a species widely used to construct hedges.

38 *lotus rose:* an aquatic plant whose blossoms float on the surface like a water lily, its symbolism is especially powerful. In Asia it is known as the "Flower of Light," symbolizing both a divine birth and the cosmos rising from the waters of pre-cosmic chaos. A symbol of perfect beauty, it is also the universal ground of existence. Sitting on the water in repose, it is a figure for enlightenment attained in meditation. Its temporal symbolism combines past, present, and future much in the manner of the poem's opening lines. In Taoism it is the Golden Flower of spiritual unfolding, the heart, and the cosmic wheel of manifestation. In Greek and Roman mythology, the lotus is linked with the goddess of love.

39 *heart of light:* continues the lotus symbolism and folds into it an allusion to Dante's *Paradiso* 12.28–29: "From out of the heart of one of the new lights there moved a voice."

40    And they were behind us, reflected in the pool.
      Then a cloud passed, and the pool was empty.
      Go, said the bird, for the leaves were full of children,
      Hidden excitedly, containing laughter.
      Go, go, go, said the bird: human kind
45    Cannot bear very much reality.
      Time past and time future
      What might have been and what has been
      Point to one end, which is always present.

## II

      Garlic and sapphires in the mud
50    Clot the bedded axle-tree.
      The trilling wire in the blood
      Sings below inveterate° scars
      And reconciles forgotten wars.
      The dance along the artery
55    The circulation of the lymph
      Are figured in the drift of stars
      Ascend to summer in the tree
      We move above the moving tree
      In light upon the figured leaf°
60    And hear upon the sodden floor
      Below, the boarhound and the boar
      Pursue their pattern as before
      But reconciled among the stars.

      At the still point of the turning world. Neither flesh nor fleshless;
65    Neither from nor towards; at the still point, there the dance is,
      But neither arrest nor movement. And do not call it fixity,
      Where past and future are gathered. Neither movement from nor
          towards,
      Neither ascent nor decline. Except for the point, the still point,
      There would be no dance, and there is only the dance.
70    I can only say, *there* we have been: but I cannot say where.
      And I cannot say, how long, for that is to place it in time.

      The inner freedom from the practical desire,
      The release from action and suffering, release from the inner
      And the outer compulsion, yet surrounded
75    By a grace of sense, a white light still and moving,
      *Erhebung*° without motion, concentration
      Without elimination, both a new world
      And the old made explicit, understood
      In the completion of its partial ecstasy,

---

52 *inveterate*: deep-rooted, persistent.
59 *figured leaf*: the British poet Alfred Lord Tennyson (1809–1892) characterizes death with similar language in *In Memoriam* (1850): "So that still garden of the souls / In many a figured leaf enrolls / The total world since life began."
76 *Erhebung*: (German) "exaltation."

80 The resolution of its partial horror.
  Yet the enchainment of past and future
  Woven in the weakness of the changing body,
  Protects mankind from heaven and damnation
  Which flesh cannot endure.
85         Time past and time future
  Allow but a little consciousness.
  To be conscious is not to be in time
  But only in time can the moment in the rose-garden,
  The moment in the arbour where the rain beat,
90 The moment in the draughty church at smokefall
  Be remembered; involved with past and future.
  Only through time time is conquered.

### III

  Here is a place of disaffection
  Time before and time after
95 In a dim light: neither daylight
  Investing form with lucid stillness
  Turning shadow into transient beauty
  With slow rotation suggesting permanence
  Nor darkness to purify the soul
100 Emptying the sensual with deprivation
  Cleansing affection from the temporal.
  Neither plenitude nor vacancy. Only a flicker
  Over the strained time-ridden faces
  Distracted from distraction by distraction
105 Filled with fancies and empty of meaning
  Tumid apathy with no concentration
  Men and bits of paper, whirled by the cold wind
  That blows before and after time,
  Wind in and out of unwholesome lungs
110 Time before and time after.
  Eructation of unhealthy souls
  Into the faded air, the torpid
  Driven on the wind that sweeps the gloomy hills of London,
  Hampstead and Clerkenwell, Campden and Putney,
115 Highgate, Primrose and Ludgate.° Not here
  Not here the darkness, in this twittering world.

   Descend lower, descend only
  Into the world of perpetual solitude,
  World not world, but that which is not world,
120 Internal darkness, deprivation
  And destitution of all property,
  Desiccation of the world of sense,
  Evacuation of the world of fancy,
  Inoperancy of the world of spirit;

---

114–115 *Hampstead . . . Ludgate:* London neighborhoods.

125     This is the one way, and the other
        Is the same, not in movement
        But abstention from movement; while the world moves
        In appetency,° on its metalled ways
        Of time past and time future.

                              IV

130     Time and the bell have buried the day,
        The black cloud carries the sun away.
        Will the sunflower turn to us, will the clematis°
        Stray down, bend to us; tendril and spray
        Clutch and cling?
135     Chill
        Fingers of yew be curled
        Down on us? After the kingfisher's° wing
        Has answered light to light, and is silent, the light is still
        At the still point of the turning world.

                              V

140     Words move, music moves
        Only in time; but that which is only living
        Can only die. Words, after speech, reach
        Into the silence. Only by the form, the pattern,
        Can words or music reach
145     The stillness, as a Chinese jar still
        Moves perpetually in its stillness.
        Not the stillness of the violin, while the note lasts,
        Not that only, but the co-existence,
        Or say that the end precedes the beginning,
150     And the end and the beginning were always there
        Before the beginning and after the end.
        And all is always now. Words strain,
        Crack and sometimes break, under the burden,
        Under the tension, slip, slide, perish,
155     Decay with imprecision, will not stay in place,
        Will not stay still. Shrieking voices
        Scolding, mocking, or merely chattering,
        Always assail them. The Word° in the desert
        Is most attacked by voices of temptation,
160     The crying shadow in the funeral dance,
        The loud lament of the disconsolate chimera.°

---

128 *appetency:* cravings, desires, affinities.
132 *clematis:* flowering vine.
137 *kingfisher:* a bird with a crested head and brilliant coloration that dives into water for fish.
158 *The Word:* Christ; desert: Cf. Christ's trial by temptation in the wilderness in Luke 4.1–4.
161 *chimera:* in Greek myth, a fire-breathing monster; also a term for hallucinations.

The detail of the pattern is movement,
As in the figure of the ten stairs.°
Desire itself is movement
165   Not in itself desirable;
Love is itself unmoving,
Only the cause and end of movement,
Timeless, and undesiring
Except in the aspect of time
170   Caught in the form of limitation
Between un-being and being.
Sudden in a shaft of sunlight
Even while the dust moves
There rises the hidden laughter
175   Of children in the foliage
Quick now, here, now, always—
Ridiculous the waste sad time
Stretching before and after.

*1936*

---

163 *ten stairs:* refers to St. John of the Cross's model for the soul's ascent to God, "The
Ten Degrees of the Mystical Ladder of Divine Love."

# John Crowe Ransom (1888–1974)

Born in Pulaski, Tennessee, Ransom was educated at Vanderbilt University and Christ Church College at Oxford University in England. After World War I service on the front in France, he joined Vanderbilt's faculty, where he helped lead the Agrarian Movement. It counted Allen Tate and Robert Penn Warren among its members, generally resisted racial integration, urged a renewal of religious belief in the context of a hierarchical society, and championed a southern agrarian economy as an antidote to northern industrialism. Later, at Kenyon College, he helped shape American New Criticism, with its preference for analysis of poems according to their internal character rather than their historical context. Elegant, ironic, carefully crafted, Ransom's own poems repeatedly attempt characterizations of fundamental differences between men and women. After 1927, most of his poetry writing consisted in repeatedly revising the poems he had already published, which he issued in new editions of his *Selected Poems* in 1945, 1963, and 1969. His ideas about gender are succinctly articulated in the titles to the first two sections of the *Selected Poems*: "The Innocent Doves" and "The Manliness of Men." Among his critical essays is a notoriously contemptuous piece on Edna St. Vincent Millay.

## Bells for John Whiteside's Daughter

There was such speed in her little body,
And such lightness in her footfall,
It is no wonder her brown study°
Astonishes us all.

5    Her wars were bruited in our high window.
We looked among orchard trees and beyond
Where she took arms against her shadow,
Or harried unto the pond

The lazy geese, like a snow cloud
10   Dripping their snow on the green grass,
Tricking and stopping, sleepy and proud,
Who cried in goose, Alas,

---

3 *brown study:* very still, as in a daydream or a reverie, or in deep thought.

For the tireless heart within the little
Lady with rod that made them rise
15    From their noon apple-dreams and scuttle
Goose-fashion under the skies!

But now go the bells, and we are ready,
In one house we are sternly stopped
To say we are vexed at her brown study,
Lying so primly propped.

*1924*

# Dead Boy

The little cousin is dead, by foul subtraction,
A green bough from Virginia's aged tree,
And none of the county kin like the transaction,
Nor some of the world of outer dark, like me.

5    A boy not beautiful, nor good, nor clever,
A black cloud full of storms too hot for keeping,
A sword beneath his mother's heart—yet never
Woman bewept her babe as this is weeping.

A pig with a pasty face, so I had said,
10   Squealing for cookies, kinned by poor pretense
With a noble house. But the little man quite dead,
I see the forbears' antique lineaments.

The elder men have strode by the box of death
To the wide flag porch, and muttering low send round
15   The bruit° of the day. O friendly waste of breath!
Their hearts are hurt with a deep dynastic wound.

He was pale and little, the foolish neighbors say;
The first-fruits, saith the Preacher, the Lord hath taken;
But this was the old tree's late branch wrenched away,
Grieving the sapless limbs, the shorn and shaken.

*1927*

---

15 *bruit:* rumors.

# Claude McKay (1889–1948)

Born Festus Claudius McKay to a Jamaican peasant family, McKay would write poems that inspired not only the Harlem Renaissance of the 1920s but also the Black Arts movement of the 1960s. As a young child he went to live with an older brother who was a schoolteacher. From him McKay received a background in both classical and British literature and philosophy, and before too long began to write poems in traditional forms. The sonnet tradition he imitated as a child he would dramatically transform as a young man in his 20s. McKay would take the romance and the consolations of the historical sonnet and replace them with a hand grenade of protest. Compressed and rhetorically proficient anger would now be among the sonnet's resources and its cultural aims; the form would never be quite the same again. Together with Millay, whose antiromantic sonnets turned the form about face, McKay reconceived the meaning of a centuries-long tradition.

But his first poems were actually rather different. A white British expatriate in Jamaica, Walter Jekyll, encouraged him to write dialect poems embodying Jamaican folklore. That he did in *Songs of Jamaica* (1912), and *Constab Ballads* (1912) drew on his brief stint as a policeman. That same year he emigrated to the United States to study farming, but soon abandoned that pursuit and headed for New York City. While working as a railroad dining car waiter he began to write radical poetry. "If We Must Die" appeared in the July 1919 issue of the leftwing magazine *Liberator*. McKay had been drawn to the radical union, the IWW, to several socialist groups, and to the *New Masses* radicals who were now issuing *Liberator*. For a time he was an active member of the New York left, even making a successful trip to the Soviet Union from 1922–1923.

His most influential book of poems, *Harlem Shadows*, appeared in 1922. A founding text of the Harlem Renaissance, many of its poems had inspired African American writers when they appeared in journals earlier. Even this small selection gives us a rich and multifaceted portrait of race in America, but the poems demand careful reading. "If We Must Die" should be read in the context of the race riots and the anticommunist red scare of 1919. "The White City" is not an attack on white people but rather a critique of race-based economic and political power.

The next decade of McKay's life was spent mostly in France, where he wrote two novels, *Home to Harlem* (1928) and *Banjo* (1929), struggled with illness, and finally returned to the United States in 1934. He would later write two autobiographical volumes and a nonfiction study, *Harlem: Negro Metropolis* (1940). Four years later he converted to Catholicism, associating himself with the progressive wing of Catholic activism. Although he became disenchanted with Soviet communism, he remained committed to international socialism. His final poems still carry the force of the work he had done decades earlier.

## The Harlem Dancer

Applauding youths laughed with young prostitutes
And watched her perfect, half-clothed body sway;
Her voice was like the sound of blended flutes
Blown by black players upon a picnic day.
5    She sang and danced on gracefully and calm,
The light gauze hanging loose about her form;
To me she seemed a proudly-swaying palm
Grown lovelier for passing through a storm.
Upon her swarthy neck black shiny curls
10   Luxuriant fell; and tossing coins in praise,
The wine-flushed, bold-eyed boys, and even the girls,
Devoured her shape with eager, passionate gaze;
But looking at her falsely-smiling face,
I knew her self was not in that strange place.

*1917*

## To the White Fiends

Think you I am not fiend and savage too?
Think you I could not arm me with a gun
And shoot down ten of you for every one
Of my black brothers murdered, burnt by you?
5    Be not deceived, for every deed you do
I could match—out-match: am I not Afric's son,
Black of that black land where black deeds are done?
But the Almighty from the darkness drew
My soul and said: Even thou shalt be a light
10   Awhile to burn on the benighted earth,
Thy dusky face I set among the white
For thee to prove thyself of higher worth;
Before the world is swallowed up in night,
To show thy little lamp: go forth, go forth!

*1919*

## If We Must Die°

If we must die, let it not be like hogs
Hunted and penned in an inglorious spot,
While round us bark the mad and hungry dogs,
Making their mock at our accursed lot.
5    If we must die, O let us nobly die,
So that our precious blood may not be shed

**poem title:** Written in response to race riots against Black Americans that took place in Chicago and other cities in the summer of 1919.

In vain; then even the monsters we defy
Shall be constrained to honor us though dead!
O kinsmen! we must meet the common foe!
10    Though far outnumbered let us show us brave,
And for their thousand blows deal one deathblow!
What though before us lies the open grave?
Like men we'll face the murderous, cowardly pack,
Pressed to the wall, dying, but fighting back!

*1919*


# The Lynching°

His Spirit in smoke ascended to high heaven.
His father, by the cruelest way of pain,
Had bidden him to his bosom once again;
The awful sin remained still unforgiven.
5    All night a bright and solitary star
(Perchance the one that ever guided him,
Yet gave him up at last to Fate's wild whim)
Hung pitifully o'er the swinging char.
Day dawned, and soon the mixed crowds came to view
10    The ghastly body swaying in the sun.
The women thronged to look, but never a one
Showed sorrow in her eyes of steely blue.

And little lads, lynchers that were to be,
Danced round the dreadful thing in fiendish glee.

*1920*


# The Tropics in New York

Bananas ripe and green, and ginger-root,
    Cocoa in pods and alligator pears,
And tangerines and mangoes and grape fruit,
    Fit for the highest prize at parish fairs,

5    Set in the window, bringing memories
    Of fruit-trees laden by low-singing rills,
And dewy dawns, and mystical blue skies
    In benediction over nun-like hills.

---

**poem title:** As an event when a mob murders someone accused of a crime, lynching has a long history in America. But only black men as a group have had to live under its shadow, to live in fear of being taken from their homes without reason and be beaten, dismembered, set afire, and hung. Far from treating it as a secret crime, lynching advocates defended the practice in print. In the period between the end of Reconstruction in the American South (1877) and the time McKay wrote his poem, thousands of African American men and women had been lynched. White families brought children to watch these sadistic rituals; newspapers sometimes announced the site in advance; and railroad companies made a profit selling excursion tickets. In 1915, the Ku Klux Klan, a racist organization that practiced lynching, was revived and grew to several million members by the early 1920s.

My eyes grew dim, and I could no more gaze;
10　　A wave of longing through my body swept,
And, hungry for the old, familiar ways,
　　I turned aside and bowed my head and wept.

1920

# The White City

I will not toy with it nor bend an inch.°
Deep in the secret chambers of my heart
I muse my life-long hate, and without flinch
I bear it nobly as I live my part.
5　My being would be a skeleton, a shell,
If this dark Passion that fills my every mood,
And makes my heaven in the white world's hell,°
Did not forever feed me vital blood.
I see the mighty city through a mist—
10　The strident trains that speed the goaded mass,
The poles and spires and towers° vapor-kissed,
The fortressed port through which the great ships
　　　pass,
The tides, the wharves, the dens I contemplate,
Are sweet like wanton loves because I hate.

1921

# America

Although she feeds me bread of bitterness,
And sinks into my throat her tiger's tooth,
Stealing my breath of life, I will confess
I love this cultured hell that tests my youth!
5　Her vigor flows like tides into my blood,
Giving me strength erect against her hate.
Her bigness sweeps my being like a flood.
Yet as a rebel fronts a king in state,
I stand within her walls with not a shred
10　Of terror, malice, not a word of jeer.
Darkly I gaze into the days ahead,
And see her might and granite wonders there,
Beneath the touch of Time's unerring hand,
Like priceless treasures sinking in the sand.

1921

---

1 *inch:* Cf. "I'll not budge an inch," in William Shakespeare's *The Taming of the Shrew.*
7 *hell:* McKay is alluding to lines 254–255 in Book I of John Milton's *Paradise Lost:* "The mind is its own place, and in itself / Can make a Heav'n of Hell, a Hell of Heav'n." Milton's narrator is commenting on Satan.
11 *towers:* McKay is alluding to (and reversing) the tone of William Wordsworth's "Composed Upon Westminster Bridge, Sept. 3, 1802": "This City now doth, like a garment, wear / The beauty of the morning; silent, bare, / Ships, towers, domes, theatres, and temples lie . . . All bright and glittering in the smokeless air."

## Outcast

For the dim regions whence my fathers came
My spirit, bondaged by the body, longs.
Words felt, but never heard, my lips would frame;
My soul would sing forgotten jungle songs.
5     I would go back to darkness and to peace,
But the great western world holds me in fee,
And I may never hope for full release
While to its alien gods I bend my knee.
Something in me is lost, forever lost,
10    Some vital thing has gone out of my heart,
And I must walk the way of life a ghost
Among the sons of earth, a thing apart.

For I was born, far from my native clime,
Under the white man's menace, out of time.

*1922*

## Mulatto

Because I am the white man's son—his own,
Bearing his bastard birth-mark on my face,
I will dispute his title to his throne,
Forever fight him for my rightful place.
5     There is a searing hate within my soul,
A hate that only kin can feel for kin,
A hate that makes me vigorous and whole,
And spurs me on increasingly to win.
Because I am my cruel father's child,
10    My love of justice stirs me up to hate,
A warring Ishmaelite, unreconciled,
When falls the hour I shall not hesitate
Into my father's heart to plunge the knife
To gain the utmost freedom that is life.

*1925*

## The Negro's Tragedy

It is the Negro's tragedy I feel
Which binds me like a heavy iron chain,
It is the Negro's wounds I want to heal
Because I know the keenness of his pain.
5     Only a thorn-crowned Negro and no white
Can penetrate into the Negro's ken,
Or feel the thickness of the shroud of night
Which hides and buries him from other men.

So what I write is urged out of my blood.
10  There is no white man who could write my book,
Though many think their story should be told
Of what the Negro people ought to brook.
Our statesmen roam the world to set things right.
This Negro laughs and prays to God for Light!

*1945*

## Look Within

Lord, let me not be silent while we fight
  In Europe Germans, Asia Japanese
For setting up a Fascist way of might
  While fifteen million Negroes on their knees
5  Pray for salvation from the Fascist yoke
  Of these United States. Remove the beam
(Nearly two thousand years since Jesus spoke)
  From your own eyes before the mote you deem
It proper from your neighbor's to extract!
10  We bathe our lies in vapors of sweet myrrh,
And close our eyes not to perceive the fact!
  But Jesus said: You whited sepulchre,
Pretending to be uncorrupt of sin,
  While worm-infested, rotten through within!

*1945*

## Tiger

The white man is a tiger at my throat,
Drinking my blood as my life ebbs away,
And muttering that his terrible striped coat
Is Freedom's and portends the Light of Day.
5  Oh white man, you may suck up all my blood
And throw my carcass into potter's field,
But never will I say with you that mud
Is bread for Negroes! Never will I yield.

Europe and Africa and Asia wait
10  The touted New Deal of the New World's hand!
New systems will be built on race and hate,
The Eagle and the Dollar will command.
Oh Lord! My body, and my heart too, break—
The tiger in his strength his thirst must slake!

*1946*

# Edna St. Vincent Millay (1892–1950)

Born in Rockville, Maine, Millay was educated at Vassar. In 1917, she moved to New York's Greenwich Village and joined the revolutionary mix of politics, modernism, and sexual experimentation that typified the community. Her poem "First Fig" is usually taken as the signature poem of an ecstatically romantic mode of writing, but it is offered here as an emblem of the more risky mix of commitments that shaped her life. She was in fact consistently involved in political causes through World War II and regularly wrote poems about them, as "Justice Denied in Massachusetts," "Say That We Saw Spain Die," and "I Forgot for a Moment" will demonstrate. But her most important legacy is no doubt the witty, antiromantic sonnets she wrote in significant number. Their rhetorical dexterity and confidence reflect an adaptation of Elizabethan sonnet style, while the gender instability and reversal of conventional gendered roles embody both her feminism and the rethinking of sexual identity that preoccupied modernist writers and the general public. These poems merit a major place in the history of the modern sonnet.

## First Fig

My candle burns at both ends;
　It will not last the night;
But ah, my foes, and oh, my friends—
　It gives a lovely light!

*1920*

## I, Being Born a Woman and Distressed

I, being born a woman and distressed
By all the needs and notions of my kind,
Am urged by your propinquity to find
Your person fair, and feel a certain zest
5　To bear your body's weight upon my breast:
So subtly is the fume of life designed,
To clarify the pulse and cloud the mind,
And leave me once again undone, possessed.
Think not for this, however, the poor treason
10　Of my stout blood against my staggering brain,
I shall remember you with love, or season
My scorn with pity,—let me make it plain:
I find this frenzy insufficient reason
For conversation when we meet again.

*1923*

## Love is not blind.

Love is not blind. I see with single eye
Your ugliness and other women's grace.
I know the imperfection of your face,—
The eyes too wide apart, the brow too high
5    For beauty. Learned from earliest youth am I
In loveliness, and cannot so erase
Its letters from my mind, that I may trace
You faultless, I must love until I die.
More subtle is the sovereignty of love:
10   So am I caught that when I say, "Not fair,"
'Tis but as if I said, "Not here—not there—
Not risen—not writing letters." Well I know
What is this beauty men are babbling of;
I wonder only why they prize it so.

*1923*

## Oh, oh, you will be sorry for that word!

Oh, oh, you will be sorry for that word!
Give back my book and take my kiss instead.
Was it my enemy or my friend I heard,
"What a big book for such a little head!"
5    Come, I will show you now my newest hat,
And you may watch me purse my mouth and prink!°
Oh, I shall love you still, and all of that.
I never again shall tell you what I think.
I shall be sweet and crafty, soft and sly;
10   You will not catch me reading any more:
I shall be called a wife to pattern by;
And some day when you knock and push the door,
Some sane day, not too bright and not too stormy,
I shall be gone, and you may whistle for me.

*1923*

## Sonnets from an Ungrafted Tree°

### I

So she came back into his house again
And watched beside his bed until he died,
Loving him not at all. The winter rain
Splashed in the painted butter-tub outside,
5    Where once her red geraniums had stood,
Where still their rotted stalks were to be seen;
The thin log snapped; and she went out for wood,

---

6 *prink*: primp.
**poem title:** Ungrafted tree, a tree which has its own natural roots; it has not been grown
from a branch grafted to another root stock, so it is not dependent on another set of roots
for its sustenance; also, therefore, a tree to which no branch has been grafted.

Bareheaded, running the few steps between
The house and shed; there, from the sodden eaves
10     Blown back and forth on ragged ends of twine,
Saw the dejected creeping-jinny vine,
  (And one, big-aproned, blithe, with stiff blue sleeves
Rolled to the shoulder that warm day in spring,
Who planted seeds, musing ahead to their far
    blossoming).

## II

15     The last white sawdust on the floor was grown
Gray as the first, so long had he been ill;
The axe was nodding in the block; fresh-blown
And foreign came the rain across the sill,
But on the roof so steadily it drummed
20     She could not think a time it might not be—
In hazy summer, when the hot air hummed
With mowing, and locusts rising raspingly,
When that small bird with iridescent wings
And long incredible sudden silver tongue
25     Had just flashed (and yet maybe not!) among
The dwarf nasturtiums—when no sagging springs
Of shower were in the whole bright sky, somehow
Upon this roof the rain would drum as it was drumming now.

## III

She filled her arms with wood, and set her chin
30     Forward, to hold the highest stick in place,
No less afraid than she had always been
Of spiders up her arms and on her face,
But too impatient for a careful search
Or a less heavy loading, from the heap
35     Selecting hastily small sticks of birch,
For their curled bark, that instantly will leap
Into a blaze, nor thinking to return
Some day, distracted, as of old, to find
Smooth, heavy, round, green logs with a wet, gray rind
40     Only, and knotty chunks that will not burn,
(That day when dust is on the wood-box floor,
And some old catalogue, and a brown, shriveled apple core).

## IV

The white bark writhed and sputtered like a fish
Upon the coals, exuding odorous smoke.
45     She knelt and blew, in a surging desolate wish
For comfort; and the sleeping ashes woke
And scattered to the hearth, but no thin fire
Broke suddenly, the wood was wet with rain.
Then, softly stepping forth from her desire,
50     (Being mindful of like passion hurled in vain

Upon a similar task, in other days)
She thrust her breath against the stubborn coal,
Bringing to bear upon its hilt the whole
Of her still body ... there sprang a little blaze ...
55 A pack of hounds, the flame swept up the flue!—
And the blue night stood flattened against the window,
    staring through.

### V

A wagon stopped before the house; she heard
The heavy oilskins of the grocer's man
Slapping against his legs. Of a sudden whirred
60 Her heart like a frightened partridge, and she ran
And slid the bolt, leaving his entrance free;
Then in the cellar way till he was gone
Hid, breathless, praying that he might not see
The chair sway she had laid her hand upon
65 In passing. Sour and damp from that dark vault
Arose to her the well-remembered chill;
She saw the narrow wooden stairway still
Plunging into the earth, and the thin salt
Crusting the crocks; until she knew him far,
70 So stood, with listening eyes upon the empty doughnut jar.

### VI

Then cautiously she pushed the cellar door
And stepped into the kitchen—saw the track
Of muddy rubber boots across the floor,
The many paper parcels in a stack
75 Upon the dresser; with accustomed care
Removed the twine and put the wrappings by,
Folded, and the bags flat, that with an air
Of ease had been whipped open skillfully,
To the gape of children. Treacherously dear
80 And simple was the dull, familiar task.
And so it was she came at length to ask:
How came the soda there? The sugar here?
Then the dream broke. Silent, she brought the mop,
And forced the trade-slip° on the nail that held his razor strop.

### VII

85 One way there was of muting in the mind
A little while the ever-clamorous care;
And there was rapture, of a decent kind,
In making mean and ugly objects fair:
Soft-sooted kettle-bottoms, that had been
90 Time after time set in above the fire,

---

84 *trade-slip*: receipt.

Faucets, and candlesticks, corroded green,
To mine again from quarry; to attire
The shelves in paper petticoats, and tack
New oilcloth in the ringed-and-rotten's place,
95      Polish the stove till you could see your face,
And after nightfall rear an aching back
In a changed kitchen, bright as a new pin,
An advertisement, far too fine to cook a supper in.

## VIII

She let them leave their jellies at the door
100     And go away, reluctant, down the walk.
She heard them talking as they passed before
The blind, but could not quite make out their talk
For noise in the room—the sudden heavy fall
And roll of a charred log, and the roused shower
105     Of snapping sparks; then sharply from the wall
The unforgivable crowing of the hour.
One instant set ajar, her quiet ear
Was stormed and forced by the full rout of day:
The rasp of a saw, the fussy cluck and bray
110     Of hens, the wheeze of a pump, she needs must hear;
She inescapably must endure to feel
Across her teeth the grinding of a backing wagon wheel.

## IX

Not over-kind nor over-quick in study
Nor skilled in sports nor beautiful was he,
115     Who had come into her life when anybody
Would have been welcome, so in need was she.
They had become acquainted in this way:
He flashed a mirror in her eyes at school;
By which he was distinguished; from that day
120     They went about together, as a rule.
She told, in secret and with whispering,
How he had flashed a mirror in her eyes;
And as she told, it struck her with surprise
That this was not so wonderful a thing.
125     But what's the odds?—It's pretty nice to know
You've got a friend to keep you company everywhere you go.

## X

She had forgotten how the August night
Was level as a lake beneath the moon,
In which she swam a little, losing sight
130     Of shore; and how the boy, who was at noon
Simple enough, not different from the rest,
Wore now a pleasant mystery as he went,
Which seemed to her an honest enough test
Whether she loved him, and she was content.

135 So loud, so loud the million crickets' choir . . .
So sweet the night, so long-drawn-out and late . . .
And if the man were not her spirit's mate,
Why was her body sluggish with desire?
Stark on the open field the moonlight fell,
140 But the oak tree's shadow was deep and black and secret as a well.

### XI

It came into her mind, seeing how the snow
Was gone, and the brown grass exposed again,
And clothes-pins, and an apron—long ago,
In some white storm that sifted through the pane
145 And sent her forth reluctantly at last
To gather in, before the line gave way,
Garments, board-stiff, that galloped on the blast
Clashing like angel armies in a fray,
An apron long ago in such a night
150 Blown down and buried in the deepening drift,
To lie till April thawed it back to sight,
Forgotten, quaint and novel as a gift—
It struck her, as she pulled and pried and tore,
That here was spring, and the whole year to be lived through once
more.

### XII

155 Tenderly, in those times, as though she fed
An ailing child—with sturdy propping up
Of its small, feverish body in the bed,
And steadying of its hands about the cup—
She gave her husband of her body's strength,
160 Thinking of men, what helpless things they were,
Until he turned and fell asleep at length,
And stealthily stirred the night and spoke to her.
Familiar, at such moments, like a friend,
Whistled far off the long, mysterious train,
165 And she could see in her mind's vision plain
The magic World, where cities stood on end . . .
Remote from where she lay—and yet—between,
Save for something asleep beside her, only the window screen.

### XIII

From the wan dream that was her waking day,
170 Wherein she journeyed, borne along the ground
Without her own volition in some way,
Or fleeing, motionless, with feet fast bound,
Or running silent through a silent house
Sharply remembered from an earlier dream,
175 Upstairs, down other stairs, fearful to rouse,
Regarding him, the wide and empty scream
Of a strange sleeper on a malignant bed,

And all the time not certain if it were
Herself so doing or some one like to her,
180    From this wan dream that was her daily bread,
Sometimes, at night, incredulous, she would wake—
A child, blowing bubbles that the chairs and carpet did not break!

### XIV

She had a horror he would die at night.
And sometimes when the light began to fade
185    She could not keep from noticing how white
The birches looked—and then she would be afraid,
Even with a lamp, to go about the house
And lock the windows; and as night wore on
Toward morning, if a dog howled, or a mouse
190    Squeaked in the floor, long after it was gone
Her flesh would sit awry on her. By day
She would forget somewhat, and it would seem
A silly thing to go with just this dream
And get a neighbor to come at night and stay.
195    But it would strike her sometimes, making the tea:
*She had kept that kettle boiling all night long, for company.*

### XV

There was upon the sill a pencil mark,
Vital with shadow when the sun stood still
At noon, but now, because the day was dark,
200    It was a pencil mark upon the sill.
And the mute clock, maintaining ever the same
Dead moment, blank and vacant of itself,
Was a pink shepherdess, a picture frame,
A shell marked Souvenir, there on the shelf.
205    Whence it occurred to her that he might be,
The mainspring being broken in his mind,
A clock himself, if one were so inclined,
That stood at twenty minutes after three—
The reason being for this, it might be said,
210    That things in death were neither clocks nor people, but only dead.

### XVI

The doctor asked her what she wanted done
With him, that could not lie there many days.
And she was shocked to see how life goes on
Even after death, in irritating ways;
215    And mused how if he had not died at all
'Twould have been easier—then there need not be
The stiff disorder of a funeral
Everywhere, and the hideous industry,
And crowds of people calling her by name
220    And questioning her, she'd never seen before,
But only watching by his bed once more

And sitting silent if a knocking came . . .
She said, at length, feeling the doctor's eyes,
"I don't know what you do exactly when a person dies."

### XVII

225 Gazing upon him now, severe and dead,
It seemed a curious thing that she had lain
Beside him many a night in that cold bed,
And that had been which would not be again.
From his desirous body the great heat
230 Was gone at last, it seemed, and the taut nerves
Loosened forever. Formally the sheet
Set forth for her today those heavy curves
And lengths familiar as the bedroom door.
She was as one who enters, sly, and proud,
235 To where her husband speaks before a crowd,
And sees a man she never saw before—
The man who eats his victuals at her side,
Small, and absurd, and hers: for once, not hers, unclassified.

      finis

                1923

## Well, I Have Lost You

Well, I have lost you; and I lost you fairly;
In my own way, and with my full consent.
Say what you will, kings in a tumbrel rarely
Went to their deaths more proud than this one went.
5 Some nights of apprehension and hot weeping
I will confess; but that's permitted me;
Day dried my eyes; I was not one for keeping
Rubbed in a cage a wing that would be free.
If I had loved you less or played you slyly
10 I might have held you for a summer more,
But at the cost of words I value highly,
And no such summer as the one before.
Should I outlive this anguish—and men do—
I shall have only good to say of you.

                1931

## Love Is Not All

Love is not all; it is not meat nor drink
Nor slumber nor a roof against the rain;
Nor yet a floating spar to men that sink
And rise and sink and rise and sink again;
5 Love can not fill the thickened lung with breath,
Nor clean the blood, nor set the fractured bone;
Yet many a man is making friends with death
Even as I speak, for lack of love alone.

It well may be that in a difficult hour,
10    Pinned down by pain and moaning for release,
Or nagged by want past resolution's power,
I might be driven to sell your love for peace,
Or trade the memory of this night for food.
It well may be. I do not think I would.

*1931*

## Justice Denied in Massachusetts°

Let us abandon then our gardens and go home
And sit in the sitting-room.
Shall the larkspur blossom or the corn grow under this cloud?
Sour to the fruitful seed
5    Is the cold earth under this cloud,
Fostering quack and weed, we have marched upon but cannot
    conquer;
We have bent the blades of our hoes against the stalks of them.

Let us go home, and sit in the sitting-room.
Not in our day
10    Shall the cloud go over and the sun rise as before,
Beneficent upon us
Out of the glittering bay,
And the warm winds be blown inward from the sea
Moving the blades of corn
15    With a peaceful sound.
Forlorn, forlorn,
Stands the blue hay-rack by the empty mow.
And the petals drop to the ground,
Leaving the tree unfruited.
20    The sun that warmed our stooping backs and withered the weed
    uprooted—
We shall not feel it again.
We shall die in darkness, and be buried in the rain.

What from the splendid dead
We have inherited—
25    Furrows sweet to the grain, and the weed subdued—
See now the slug and the mildew plunder.
Evil does overwhelm

---

**poem title:** Refers to what was the most notorious political trial in twentieth-century U.S. history, the trial of Nicola Sacco and Bartolomeo Vanzetti. They were two immigrant Italian anarchists, charged with robbery and murder in Massachusetts in 1920. Through the trial the themes of patriotism and radicalism were highlighted. International publicity convinced many that they had been selected for prosecution to suppress the anarchist movement. They were convicted in 1921. Evidence supporting motions for a new trial included a confession from a convicted bank robber, but the motion was denied. Widespread protests included the arrest of several writers, among them Millay. Sacco and Vanzetti were executed on August 23, 1927. The case led many to lose faith in the American justice system, to believe that class and politics trumped guilt or innocence.

The larkspur and the corn;
We have seen them go under.

30    Let us sit here, sit still,
Here in the sitting-room until we die;
At the step of Death on the walk, rise and go;
Leaving to our children's children this beautiful doorway,
And this elm,
35    And a blighted earth to till
With a broken hoe.

1927

## Say that We Saw Spain Die°

Say that we saw Spain die. O splendid bull, how well you fought!
Lost from the first.
                                            . . . the tossed, the replaced, the
watchful *torero*° with gesture elegant and spry,
5    Before the dark, the tiring but the unglazed eye deploying the
bright cape,
Which hid for once not air, but the enemy indeed, the authentic
shape,
A thousand of him, interminably into the ring released . . .
the turning beast at length between converging colours
caught.

Save for the weapons of its skull, a bull
10    Unarmed, considering, weighing, charging
Almost a world, itself without ally.

Say that we saw the shoulders more than the mind confused, so
profusely
Bleeding from so many more than the accustomed barbs, the
game gone vulgar, the rules abused.
Say that we saw Spain die from loss of blood, a rustic reason, in
a reinforced

---

**poem title:** Refers to the 1936–1939 Spanish Civil War, to the defeat of the Spanish Republic by General Francisco Franco (1892–1975), and to the combined forces of European fascism. The Spanish Civil War began in July 1936 when an alliance of reactionary military officers, wealthy industrialists, and conservative clergy staged a revolt against the democratically elected, progressive government. The Spanish people crushed the revolt in the major cities of Barcelona and Madrid, but rapid assistance from Germany's Adolf Hitler and Italy's Benito Mussolini made it possible to sustain the revolt. It also helped turn the war into the great international cause of the 1930s, since the support of the German and Italian dictators made it clear this was a decisive phase of the mounting worldwide conflict between democracy and fascism. While the Western democracies stood by and let Spain die, some 40,000 volunteers from 53 countries joined the communist-organized International Brigades and came to Spain's aid, but it was not enough to counterbalance German and Italian arms.
4 *torero*: (Spanish) "matador."

15        And proud punctilious land, no *espada*°—
          A hundred men unhorsed,
          A hundred horses gored, and the afternoon aging, and the crowd
            growing restless (all, all so much later than planned),
          And the big head heavy, sliding forward in the sand, and the
            tongue dry with sand,—no *espada*
          Toward that hot neck, for the delicate and final thrust, having
            dared trust forth his hand.

                                                                    *1938*


# I Forgot for a Moment

### *July 1940*

          I forgot for a moment France; I forgot England; I forgot my care:
          I lived for a moment in a world where I was free to be
          With the things and people that I love, and I was happy there.
          I forgot for a moment Holland, I forgot my heavy care.

5         I lived for a moment in a world so lovely, so inept
          At twisted words and crookèd deeds, it was as if I slept and dreamt.

          It seemed that all was well with Holland—not a tank had crushed
          The tulips there.
          Mile after mile the level lowlands blossomed—yellow square,
            white square,
10        Scarlet strip and mauve strip bright beneath the brightly clouded
            sky, the round clouds and the gentle air.

          Along the straight canals between striped fields of tulips in the
            morning sailed
          Broad ships, their hulls by tulip-beds concealed, only the sails showing.

          It seemed that all was well with England—the harsh foreign voice
            hysterically vowing,
          Once more, to keep its word, at length was disbelieved, and hushed.

15        It seemed that all was well with France, with her straight roads
          Lined with slender poplars, and the peasants on the skyline ploughing.

                                                                    *1940*

---

15 *espada*: (Spanish) "swordsman."

# Archibald MacLeish (1892–1982)

Born and raised in Illinois, MacLeish was educated at Yale University and Harvard Law School. He lived in Paris in the early 1920s, after frontline service in World War I. On the editorial board of *Fortune* magazine in the 1930s, MacLeish served as both Librarian of Congress and Assistant Secretary of State in the Roosevelt administration. Despite the self-sufficiency of poetic form he argues for in "Ars Poetica," he often addressed political topics in poems or radio plays. Thus he spoke out in support of the Spanish Republic, but, unlike many other Americans, never paid a price for doing so.

## Ars Poetica°

A poem should be palpable and mute
As a globed fruit,

Dumb
As old medallions to the thumb,

5    Silent as the sleeve-worn stone
Of casement ledges where the moss has grown—

A poem should be wordless
As the flight of birds.

•

A poem should be motionless in time
10   As the moon climbs,

Leaving, as the moon releases
Twig by twig the night-entangled trees,

Leaving, as the moon behind the winter leaves,
Memory by memory the mind—

15   A poem should be motionless in time
As the moon climbs.

---

**poem title:** (Latin): "The Art of Poetry," title of a treatise on poetics by the Roman poet Horace (65–8 B.C.).

•

A poem should be equal to:
Not true.

For all the history of grief
20    An empty doorway and a maple leaf.

For love
The leaning grasses and two lights above the sea—

A poem should not mean
But be.

1926

## The End of the World

Quite unexpectedly as Vasserot
The armless ambidextrian was lighting
A match between his great and second toe
And Ralph the lion was engaged in biting
5    The neck of Madame Sossman while the drum
Pointed, and Teeny was about to cough
In waltz-time swinging Jocko by the thumb—
Quite unexpectedly the top blew off:

And there, there overhead, there, there, hung over
10    Those thousands of white faces, those dazed eyes,
There in the starless dark the poise, the hover,
There with vast wings across the canceled skies,
There in the sudden blackness the black pall
Of nothing, nothing, nothing—nothing at all.

1926

# Dorothy Parker (1893–1967)

Born Dorothy Rothschild and raised in New York City, Parker worked early on for a number of magazines, including *Vogue* and *Vanity Fair*. She developed a reputation for cutting wit and a devastating ability to craft the perfect phrase—a reputation enhanced when Franklin Pierce Adams began quoting her conversation in his *New York Tribune* column "The Conning Tower"—and was for many the very model of the emancipated woman. At *The New Yorker* she wrote a regular column, "Constant Reader," published poems and stories, and was a highly visible figure on the New York literary scene. During the 1930s, she moved to Hollywood and wrote screenplays, helped to found the Screen Writers Guild, and continued the leftist political work she had begun in the 1920s, when she supported Sacco and Vanzetti, two Italian immigrants falsely accused of murder. She was an open communist, though by self-declaration rather than party membership, traveling to Spain in support of the Spanish Republic, taking a strong stand against fascism, and supporting civil rights. For all this she was blacklisted by the end of the 1940s and spent some years in isolation. Implicated in her wit is often a rather bleak view of both human relations and modern life.

## Unfortunate Coincidence

By the time you swear you're his,
   Shivering and sighing,
And he vows his passion is
   Infinite, undying—
5   Lady, make a note of this:
   One of you is lying.

*1926*

## Résumé

Razors pain you;
Rivers are damp;
Acids stain you;
And drugs cause cramp.
5   Guns aren't lawful;
Nooses give;
Gas smells awful;
You might as well live.

*1926*

# One Perfect Rose

A single flow'r he sent me, since we met.
    All tenderly his messenger he chose;
Deep-hearted, pure, with scented dew still wet—
    One perfect rose.

5      I knew the language of the floweret;
    "My fragile leaves," it said, "his heart enclose."
Love long has taken for his amulet
    One perfect rose.

Why is it no one ever sent me yet
10      One perfect limousine, do you suppose?
Ah no, it's always just my luck to get
    One perfect rose.

*1926*

# Genevieve Taggard (1894–1948)

Taggard was born in Waitsburg, Washington, where both her parents taught school and where her father was the school principal. Her parents were also active members of the Disciples of Christ, and, when Taggard was only two, they became missionaries and headed to Honolulu, Hawaii, to found and teach in a school there.

The family left Hawaii in 1914, at which point Taggard enrolled at the University of California at Berkeley, meanwhile joining the socialist political and literary community in the San Francisco Bay area. She graduated in 1919, having edited a Berkeley literary magazine and deepened her commitment to the radical left. The following year she was in New York. It was a decade when the socialist and communist left was in intense conflict and when revolutionary sentiment was entangled with artistic experimentation. Taggard edited *The Measure: A Magazine of Verse*, married the writer Robert Wolf, and participated in radical causes. In 1925, she edited *May Days*, a collection of poetry from the radical journals *The Masses* and *The Liberator*. By the end of the decade she had begun teaching college and eventually taught at Mount Holyoke, Bennington, and Sarah Lawrence. A Guggenheim year in Europe let her see Majorca, a memory that would be important when the Spanish Civil War broke out a few years later.

In 1934, Taggard was divorced and married Kenneth Durant, who headed the American office of Tass, the Soviet News Agency. This placed her at the center of left politics in the "red decade" of the 1930s. Tass would employ several Spanish Civil War vets, including poet Edwin Rolfe, in the 1940s, and Taggard came to know them well. The news agency meanwhile was charged with both disseminating and gathering information, a role that became critical when Hitler overran much of Europe. Taggard's politics would be most evident in the growing political eloquence of her poetry, notably in *Calling Western Union* (1936) and *Long View* (1942).

Like many women on the left, she combined radical politics with strong insight into women's issues. Her poetry thus took up the politics of gender, registered the human costs of the Great Depression with special eloquence, and addressed civil rights issues with great passion. Yet she also wrote *The Life and Mind of Emily Dickinson* (1930) and edited *Circumference* (1929), a collection of metaphysical verse. She died of the physical effects of hypertension.

## Everyday Alchemy

Men go to women mutely for their peace;
And they, who lack it most, create it when
They make, because they must, loving their men,
A solace for sad bosom-bended heads. There
5    Is all the meagre peace men get—no otherwhere;
No mountain space, no tree with placid leaves,
Or heavy gloom beneath a young girl's hair,
No sound of valley bell on autumn air
Or room made home with doves along the eaves,
10   Ever holds peace, like this, poured by poor women
Out of their heart's poverty, for worn men.

*1919*

## With Child

Now I am slow and placid, fond of sun,
Like a sleek beast, or a worn one,
No slim and languid girl—not glad
With the windy trip I once had,
5    But velvet-footed, musing of my own,
Torpid, mellow, stupid as a stone.

You cleft me with your beauty's pulse, and now
Your pulse has taken body. Care not how
The old grace goes, how heavy I am grown,
10   Big with this loneliness, how you alone
Ponder our love. Touch my feet and feel
How earth tingles, teeming at my heel!
Earth's urge, not mine,—my little death, not hers;
And the pure beauty yearns and stirs.

15   It does not heed our ecstasies, it turns
With secrets of its own, its own concerns,
Toward a windy world of its own, toward stark
And solitary places. In the dark
Defiant even now, it tugs and moans
To be untangled from these mother's bones.

*1921*

## Up State—Depression Summer

One of many patient farms under a cloud—
Clap-boarded house on up-land, Yankee as cider;
Mortgage the cloud, with another, second mortgage;
One old cloud with another one, drawn closer,
5    Size of a silver dollar, pouring trouble;
Bad luck everyway, short rations, and the old horse spavined.
Two cents a quart for milk and the feed sky-high.

June was sinister sweet. Can you eat wild flowers?
The world outside gilt-green, inside bone-bare.
10  No sugar, coffee . . . So the evil had them . . .
Evil, devil, pain in the belly hit them.
Taxes, words with the grocer, rage. . . .
                                    The trouble veered
And found a body small, for spring infection,
15  White as the May, slim shoulders and naked ear
Open for poison.
                        Behind June-morning eyes
The torpor spread.
                        Suddenly the kid was sick.

20  Emma found her in the yellow spare-room
That opened north, asleep across her doll
Face on the floor in stupor with thick breath.
And in her bed she hardly ever groaned.
Shut her eyes, stretched arms up, and went down
25  Deeper in stupor.
                        And days and weeks went by.
At first no telephone could get the doctor.
                                        Emma sat
Rubbing Nan's chest with goose grease, whipping egg
30  To make her vomit phlegm. Tom stormed and peeped
        at the child.
Banging the kitchen pots with no relief.
                                "Why haven't we
Medicine here, Emma," ranted Tom,
Knocking the bottles off the window-sill.
35  "Thermometer. Damn. This is like you.
You let the time go by till the kid gets sick
Before you even think to look or get one.
Go get some sleep. We both don't need to watch.
Go on, I tell you."
40                          Emma left the door
Open. Tom closed it. It was the closing door
That felt like death. Emma stared and stood.
And emerald lightning went on out of doors
Too vaguely flashed to rain and cut the web
45  Of woven heat that clustered in the trees.

And it was weeks along and still she lay.
The doctor came and went and wanted medicine
No one could buy. And weeks went on.
Hot spell came on; and rank weeds wilted. Haze.
50  Night's indifferent noise
Went slowly on. Day was the easier night-mare.

One day no one came out to feed the cows.
The house was like a rock stuck in the earth.
Tom's half-gone Ford
55  Stopped in the barn-yard middle. There the hens
Fluffed dust and slept beneath it. Desolation

Sat busy in the yard somewhere. The cows stamped on
Inside the barn with caking heavy udders.
The wind-mill pined and swung a point or two.
60     And Fanny, the cow, bore her calf and licked it clean.
No one molested. Nothing came
Out of the house till evening.
                                    Then poor Tom
Blundered about the porch and milked a little
65     And pumped some water and went in, afraid.
And the kid died as slowly as she could.
Then Emma was sick and would lie and look at nothing,
Or look at the elms and maples in the sky.
Or she spent a useless day with silent toil,
70     While the heat broke slowly. Cooking with no sense;
War on all living dirt; anger and fret
At all inanimate things that balked her hands.
Because the fire smoked she cried in a rage.

Tom found his cows, his second haying, found
75     The solid substance that he walked upon.
The roughness of his tools, the excellent
Hard silence of his clumsy cultivator.
And milking had its comfort, morning and evening.

In the gloom he came into the kitchen, bumping in,
80     To warn her not to let herself go on
While he was there to eat.
                                    Not possible now
To even roughly kiss her.
                                    They slept apart
85     Like grieving beasts that fall to sleep and lie
Their sour blood, their agony in them.

They sold the calf. That fall the bank took over.

                                                        *1936*


## Mill Town

(Dedicated to Paul de Kruif).

> *. . . the child died, the investigator said, for lack of*
> *proper food. After the funeral the mother went back to*
> *the mill. She is expecting another child . . .*

                              . . . then fold up without pause
The colored ginghams and the underclothes.
                              And from the stale
Depth of the dresser, smelling of medicine, take
5     The first year's garments. And by this act prepare
Your store of pain, your weariness, dull love,
To bear another child with doubled fists
And sucking face.

Clearly it is best, mill-mother,
10    Not to rebel or ask clear silly questions,
Saying womb is sick of its work with death,
Your body drugged with work and the repeated bitter
Gall of your morning vomit. Never try
Asking if we should blame you. Live in fear. And put
Soap on the yellowed blankets. Rub them pure.

*1936*

## Ode in Time of Crisis°

Now in the fright of change when bombed towns vanish
In fountains of debris
We say to the stranger coming across the sea
Not here, not here, go elsewhere!
5      Here we keep
Bars up. Wall out the danger, tightly seal
The ports, the intake from the alien world we fear.

It is a time of many errors now.
And this the error of children when they feel
10    But cannot say their terror. To shut off the stream
In which we moved and still move, if we move.
*The alien is the nation,* nothing more or less.
How set ourselves at variance to prove
The alien is not the nation. And so end the dream.
15    Forbid our deep resource from whence we came,
And the very seed of greatness.

This is to do
Something like suicide; to choose
Sterility—forget the secret of our past
20    Which like a magnet drew
A wealth of men and women hopeward. And now to lose
In ignorant blindness what we might hold fast.
The fright of change, not readiness. Instead
Inside our wall we will today pursue
25    The man we call the alien, take his print,
Give him a taste of the thing from which he fled,
Suspicion him. And again we fail.
How shall we release his virtue, his good-will
If by such pressure we hold his life in jail?
30    The alien is the nation. Nothing else.
And so we fail and so we jail ourselves.
Landlocked, the stagnant stream.
So ends the dream.

---

**poem title:** Alludes to several crises of national identity during World War II, from America's refusal to accept refugees from Nazi Germany to our decision to imprison American citizens of Japanese descent for the duration of the war.

O country-men, are we working to undo
35  Our lusty strength, our once proud victory?
Yes, if by this fright we break our strength in two.
If we make of every man we jail the enemy.
If we make ourselves the jailer locked in jail.
Our laboring wills, our brave, too brave to fail
40  Remember this nation by millions believed to be
Great and of mighty forces born; and resolve to be free,
To continue and renew.

1940

# To the Negro People

### I. SPIRITUALS

My way's cloudy, I cry out,
Cloudy, Lord.
Who found this way to speak?
Where is this poet's grave?
5   South is his burying ground. River Mississippi wide
Washes his dust along.
The Gulf dances level
Sapphire blue near his elbow, where his bones
Sleep in the dust of song, where we lift up our voices
10  Crying with the dark man when we cry
My way's cloudy.

### II. CITY OF THE BLUES

St. Louis, Mo.;
river side, piles rotted with river,
Y'hoo, Y'hoo, river whistle tuned harsh.
15  Get me back to St. Louis.
Burdocks, castor oil plants; ground pecked over by chickens, smeared
With droppings and moulted feathers. Fence, coop, mash-pans, wire
And a tub of white-wash. Faded rag rug and flat bottle.
(This nook and nobody here but the half-grown hens.)
20  Tug going by, puffpuff, small wave tapered. St. Louis dock
Stacked high, six blocks way, belted with wharves,
Coal smoke, winches, shovels,—crash of freight,
Pillars of white puffed upward, stiff white from the trains.
Bank all slums and slime, frame houses. Dark, wet, cold.
25  (So sweet, so cold, so fair.)
Castor oil plants and acanthus.
(When they kill, they kill
Here, and dump the body here.) The river, pale clay
Deep down stream. Y'hoo, Y'hoo yell the trains,
30  And the boats yell, too.
But the silence, the silence
Blows clean through your bones.

In the chicken yard, listlessly, beside the piles, waiting for nothing
The Negro boy, head bent, beating out his tattoo
35    Nimble and complex, on the fence . . .
Get ready to blow, trumpets, trumpets, trumpets,
O Gabriel,° O Willie Smith°
                              Take it away.

### III. Proud Day

*(Marian Anderson° on the steps of the Lincoln Memorial)*

Our sister sang on the Lincoln steps. Proud day.
40    We came to hear our sister sing. Proud day.
Voice out of depths, poise with memory,
What goodness, what splendor lay long under foot!
Our sister with a lasso of sorrow and triumph
Caught America, made it listen. Proud day.

45    The peaceful Lincoln sat so still. Proud day.
Waiting the Republic to be born again. Proud day.
Never, never forget how the dark people rewarded us
Giving out of their want and their little freedom
This blazing star. This blazing star.
50    Something spoke in my patriot heart. Proud day.

### IV. Chant for the Great Negro Poet of America Not Yet Born

He comes soon now, this spanning poet, the wide
Man, the dark, conscious of the apex, the place of his people.
He is sure to come,—up from the sorrowing side,
Born, awake, with the urgent rising of his people.

55    He will be our poet when he comes, he will wear
Scars. And a dazzling joy will give him the mark of his people.
We will hear his voice; in our nearness share
The struggle he joins, with the powerful mass of his people.

----

37 *Gabriel*: an angel named in both the Old and New Testaments; he is to blow the trum-
pet on Judgment Day.
37 *Willie Smith*: (1897–1973), legendary American jazz pianist.
*Marian Anderson*: (1902–1993), American singer renowned for her performance of spiritu-
als. She also devoted herself to the struggle for civil rights. "Proud Day" commemorates a
1939 concert that Marian Anderson presented on the steps of the Lincoln Memorial in
Washington, D.C., after her request to present an Easter Sunday concert at Constitution
Hall, the largest Washington auditorium, was turned town by the Hall's manager and by
its owners, the Daughters of the American Revolution. The D.A.R. maintained a "white
artists only" policy for Constitution Hall, and Marian Anderson was black; thus neither
that date nor any other was acceptable to them. In protest against the D.A.R.'s action,
Eleanor Roosevelt, then First Lady, resigned from the organization and helped arrange the
alternative concert at the memorial. It should be noted that Washington was a rigidly seg-
regated city during the 1930s.

His ancestors are splendid; they are ours also; but he is heir.
60      The Hebrew poets, so long the fellows of his people
Those who Englished them, anonymous, and also their
Kin—Blake, Whitman, and the honest preachers of his people.

He comes to us with the authority of those who cried
In darkness. He, to be the poet of all rising people.
65      A fervent kiss from all of us who have died
Going down, singing, for him, rising up in majesty, singing
with the universal
singing of his people.

*1939–1941*


## To the Veterans of the Abraham Lincoln Brigade°

Say of them
They knew no Spanish
At first, and nothing of the arts of war
At first,
how to shoot, how to attack, how to retreat
5       How to kill, how to meet killing
At first.
Say they kept the air blue
Grousing and griping,
Arid words and harsh faces. Say
10      They were young;
The haggard in a trench, the dead on the olive slope
All young. And the thin, the ill and the shattered,
Sightless, in hospitals, all young.

Say of them they were young, there was much they did not know,
15      They were human. Say it all; it is true. Now say
When the eminent, the great, the easy, the old,
And the men on the make
Were busy bickering and selling,
Betraying, conniving, transacting, splitting hairs,
20      Writing bad articles, signing bad papers,
Passing bad bills,
Bribing, blackmailing,
Whimpering, meaching, garroting,—they
Knew and acted
understood and died.

25      Or if they did not die came home to peace
That is not peace.
Say of them
They are no longer young, they never learned
The arts, the stealth of peace, this peace, the tricks of fear;
And what they knew, they know.
And what they dared, they dare.

*1941*

---

**poem title:** Refers to Americans who volunteered to help defend the democratically elected Spanish Republic from its own military and from fascist troops supplied by Hitler and Mussolini. Only two-thirds of the 2,800 American volunteers survived. The poem was written after these veterans of the 1936–1939 Spanish Civil War had their loyalty questioned by the House UnAmerican Activities Committee. For general background on the war see the note to Millay's "Say That We Saw Spain Die" (p. 329).

# E. E. Cummings (1894-1962)

E. (Edward) E. (Estlin) Cummings was born in Cambridge, Massachusetts, and educated at Harvard. When he began publishing in the 1920s, he lived in both New York and Paris, but he eventually spent most of his time in New York. From the outset there were powerfully contradictory impulses in his work. A strong component of sentimentality persisted throughout his career, but it is counterpointed either with blunt sexuality or with defamiliarizing typographic dislocation. "In Just-/ spring," he opens one poem, "when the world is puddle-wonderful," and children "come dancing / from hop-scotch and jump-rope," the "queer / old balloonman whistles"; that sounds innocent enough, despite the allusion to the Pied Piper, until he tells us at the end that the balloonman is "goat-footed," a lascivious satyr. So it was throughout his career. He was sardonic about organized religion, but maintained an almost transcendentalizing faith in human beings. He championed individuals against the power of the state, as with "i sing of Olaf glad and big," and as a result was drawn to the radical left early on, even translating Louis Aragon's poem "Red Front" from the French, but a visit to the Soviet Union turned him against communism. By temperament, he was, in some ways, more of an anarchist.

Cummings' father was a Congregationalist minister who taught at Harvard. Cummings himself began writing poetry while he was a student there, but his first major literary success came with the publication of his prose memoir *The Enormous Room* (1922), an account of his imprisonment in France after he served as an ambulance driver in World War I; the French censors had become offended by Cummings' remarks in his letters home. A certain irreverence was by then fundamental to his character; it would be apparent again in *Eimi* (1933), his experimental diary recounting his Soviet experience.

Interested in painting and himself a visual artist, Cummings throughout his career paid a great deal of attention to the visual appearance of the poem on the page. In some poems the eye must reassemble the broken pieces of the text before language can give us any representational access to the world. The influence of cubism and expressionism on his work is obvious, but he went farther than most poets in adapting visual technique at the level of individual words and passages—coining words or dividing and combining them unconventionally, punning, using disruptive hyphenation and line breaks, adopting idiosyncratic punctuation, mixing established stanzaic forms and free verse. Some of these experiments carried over into a play, *him* (1927) and a ballet, *Tom* (1935).

## Thy fingers make early flowers of

Thy fingers make early flowers of
all things.
thy hair mostly the hours love:
a smoothness which
5      sings, saying
(though love be a day)
do not fear, we will go amaying.

thy whitest feet crisply are straying.
Always
10     thy moist eyes are at kisses playing,
whose strangeness much
says; singing
(though love be a day)
for which girl art thou flowers bringing?

15     To be thy lips is a sweet thing
and small.
Death, Thee i call rich beyond wishing
if this thou catch,
else missing.
20     (though love be a day
and life be nothing, it shall not stop kissing).

*1923*

## in Just-

in Just-
spring      when the world is mud-
luscious the little
lame balloonman

5     whistles    far    and wee

and eddieandbill come
running from marbles and
piracies and it's
spring

10     when the world is puddle-wonderful

the queer
old balloonman whistles
far   and   wee
and bettyandisbel come dancing

15     from hop-scotch and jump-rope and

it's
spring
and
    the

20                      goat-footed

balloonMan    whistles
far
and
wee

## O sweet spontaneous

O sweet spontaneous
earth how often have
the
doting

5               fingers of
prurient philosophers pinched
and
poked

thee
10      , has the naughty thumb
of science prodded
thy

        beauty      . how
often have religions taken
15      thee upon their scraggy knees
squeezing and

buffeting thee that thou mightest conceive
gods
            (but
20      true

to the incomparable
couch of death thy
rhythmic
lover

25               thou answerest

them only with

            spring)

## Buffalo Bill 's°

Buffalo Bill 's
defunct
  who used to
  ride a watersmooth-silver
5         stallion
and break onetwothreefourfive pigeonsjustlikethat
             Jesus

  he was a handsome man
        and what i want to know is
10  how do you like your blueeyed boy
Mister Death

           *1920*

## Poem, or Beauty Hurts Mr. Vinal

take it from me kiddo
believe me
my country, 'tis of

you, land of the Cluett
5  Shirt Boston Garter and Spearmint
Girl With The Wrigley Eyes (of you
land of the Arrow Ide
and Earl &
Wilson
10  Collars) of you i
sing:land of Abraham Lincoln and Lydia E. Pinkham,°
land above all of Just Add Hot Water And Serve—
from every B. V. D.°

let freedom ring

15  amen. i do however protest, anent the un
-spontaneous and otherwise scented merde° which
greets one (Everywhere Why) as divine poesy per
that and this radically defunct periodical. i would
suggest that certain ideas gestures
20  rhymes, like Gillette Razor Blades
having been used and reused
to the mystical moment of dullness emphatically are
Not To Be Resharpened. (Case in point

---

**poem title:** William F. Cody (1846-1917) was known as "Buffalo Bill" after shooting al-
most five thousand buffalo in eight months to fulfill a contract to supply meat for work-
ers on the Kansas Pacific Railroad. He was a scout during the Sioux wars, but from 1883
on he was a showman, touring with his Wild West Show.
11 *Lydia Pinkham*: brand name for a nineteenth-century patent medicine.
13 *B.V.D.*: brand of men's underwear.
16 *merde*: (French) "excrement."

if we are to believe these gently O sweetly
25  melancholy trillers amid the thrillers
these crepuscular violinists among my and your
skyscrapers— Helen & Cleopatra° were Just Too Lovely,
The Snail's On The Thorn enter Morn and God's
In His andsoforth°

30  do you get me?) according
to such supposedly indigenous
throstles° Art is O World O Life
a formula: example, Turn Your Shirttails Into
Drawers and If It Isn't An Eastman It Isn't A
35  Kodak therefore my friends let
us now sing each and all fortissimo A-
mer
i

ca,I
40  love,
You.   And there're a
hun-dred-mil-lion-oth-ers, like
all of you successfully if
delicately gelded (or spaded)°
45  gentlemen (and ladies—pretty

littleliverpill-
hearted-Nujolneeding°-There's-A-Reason
americans (who tensetendoned and with
upward vacant eyes, painfully
50  perpetually crouched, quivering, upon the
sternly allotted sandpile
—how silently
emit a tiny violetflavoured nuisance:Odor?

ono.°
comes out like a ribbon lies flat on the brush

                                                    *1922*

---

27 *Cleopatra*: (69–30 B.C.), Egyptian queen who was Caesar's mistress; Helen, Greek beauty
whose abduction started the Trojan war in Homer's *Iliad*.
29 *Snail's . . . andsoforth*: parodies a song from *Pippa Passes* by Robert Browning (1812–
1889): "Morning's at seven,/The hillside's dewpearled;/The lark's on the wing;/The snail's
on the thorn;/God's in his heaven—/All's right with the world."
32 *throstles*: thrushes.
44 *spaded*: spayed.
47 *Nujolneeding*: this and the previous line burlesque two laxatives—Carters' Little Liver
Pills and Nujol.
54 *Odor?//ono*: the name of a deodorant, Odorono, bridges the stanza break.

## "next to of course god america i

"next to of course god america i
love you land of the pilgrims' and so forth oh
say can you see by the dawn's early my
country 'tis of centuries come and go
5   and are no more what of it we should worry
in every language even deafanddumb
thy sons acclaim your glorious name by gorry
by jingo by gee by gosh by gum
why talk of beauty what could be more beaut-
10  iful than these heroic happy dead
who rushed like lions to the roaring slaughter
they did not stop to think they died instead
then shall the voice of liberty be mute?"

He spoke.    And drank rapidly a glass of water

*1926*

## my sweet old etcetera

my sweet old etcetera
aunt lucy during the recent

war could and what
is more did tell you just
5   what everybody was fighting

for,
my sister

isabel created hundreds
(and
10  hundreds) of socks not to
mention shirts fleaproof earwarmers

etcetera wristers etcetera, my

mother hoped that

i would die etcetera
15  bravely of course my father used
to become hoarse talking about how it was
a privilege and if only he
could meanwhile my

self etcetera lay quietly
20  in the deep mud et

cetera
(dreaming,
et
        cetera,of
25  Your smile
eyes knees and of your Etcetera)

*1926*

## i sing of Olaf glad and big

i sing of Olaf glad and big
whose warmest heart recoiled at war:
a conscientious object-or°

     his wellbelovéd colonel(trig°
5     westpointer most succinctly bred)
took erring Olaf soon in hand;
but—though an host of overjoyed
noncoms°(first knocking on the head
him)do through icy waters roll
10    that helplessness which others stroke
with brushes recently employed
anent° this muddy toiletbowl,
while kindred intellects evoke
allegiance per blunt instruments—
15    Olaf(being to all intents
a corpse and wanting any rag
upon what God unto him gave)
responds, without getting annoyed
"I will not kiss your fucking flag"

20    straightway the silver bird looked grave
(departing hurriedly to shave)

but—though all kinds of officers
(a yearning nation's blueeyed pride)
their passive prey did kick and curse
25    until for wear their clarion
voices and boots were much the worse,
and egged the firstclassprivates on
his rectum wickedly to tease
by means of skilfully applied
30    bayonets roasted hot with heat
Olaf(upon what were once knees)
does almost ceaselessly repeat
"there is some shit I will not eat"

our president,being of which
35    assertions duly notified
threw the yellowsonofabitch
into a dungeon,where he died

Christ(of His mercy infinite)
i pray to see;and Olaf,too

---

3 *conscientious object-or*: a person who refuses to participate in war for moral or religious reasons; the U.S. military has always been reluctant or unwilling to credit such beliefs unless they are among the tenets of an established religion.
4 *trig*: smart, trim, neat in appearance.
8 *noncoms*: noncommissioned officers.
12 *anent*: regarding, concerning.

40 preponderatingly because
unless statistics lie he was
more brave than me:more blond than you.

1931

## Space being(don't forget to remember)Curved

Space being(don't forget to remember)Curved
(and that reminds me who said o yes Frost
Something there is which isn't fond of walls)°

an electromagnetic(now I've lost
5 the)Einstein expanded Newton's° law preserved
conTinuum(but we read that beFore)

of Course life being just a Reflex you
know since Everything is Relative or

to sum it All Up god being Dead(not to

10 mention inTerred)
LONG LIVE that Upwardlooking
Serene Illustrious and Beatific
Lord of Creation,MAN:
at a least crooking
15 of Whose compassionate digit,earth's most terrific

quadruped swoons into billiardBalls!

1931

## r-p-o-p-h-e-s-s-a-g-r

r-p-o-p-h-e-s-s-a-g-r
who
a)s w(e loo)k
upnowgath
5 PPEGORHRASS
eringint(o-
aThe):l
eA
!p:
10 S                                          a
(r
rIvInG              .gRrEaPsPhOs)
to
rea(be)rran(com)gi(e)ngly
,grasshopper;

1935

---

3 *walls*: a reworking of the first line of Robert Frost's poem "Mending Wall."
5 *Newton*: Albert Einstein (1879-1955), mathematical physicist whose theoretical work re-
vised our understanding of the universe; Sir Isaac Newton (1642–1727), English physicist
and mathematician.

## anyone lived in a pretty how town

anyone lived in a pretty how town
(with up so floating many bells down)
spring summer autumn winter
he sang his didn't he danced his did.

5 Women and men(both little and small)
cared for anyone not at all
they sowed their isn't they reaped their same
sun moon stars rain

children guessed(but only a few
10 and down they forgot as up they grew
autumn winter spring summer)
that noone loved him more by more

when by now and tree by leaf
she laughed his joy she cried his grief
15 bird by snow and stir by still
anyone's any was all to her

someones married their everyones
laughed their cryings and did their dance
(sleep wake hope and then)they
20 said their nevers they slept their dream

stars rain sun moon
(and only the snow can begin to explain
how children are apt to forget to remember
with up so floating many bells down)

25 one day anyone died i guess
(and noone stooped to kiss his face)
busy folk buried them side by side
little by little and was by was

all by all and deep by deep
30 and more by more they dream their sleep
noone and anyone earth by april
wish by spirit and if by yes.

Women and men(both dong and ding)
summer autumn winter spring
35 reaped their sowing and went their came
sun moon stars rain

1940

# Jean Toomer (1894–1967)

Born Nathan Pinchback Toomer in Washington, D.C., Toomer from the age of five was raised by his mother, until her death in 1909, and her father, P.B.S. Pinchback, lieutenant governor of Louisiana during Reconstruction, when blacks had political power in the South. By 1919, he had enrolled and left several schools, including the Universities of Wisconsin and Chicago, New York University, and the American College of Physical Training. When he returned to Washington, he had completed one of the prose pieces for *Cane* (1923), his greatest work and one of the most important experimental mixed form texts of American modernism. He changed his name to Jean Toomer in 1921 and took a summer job as acting principal at the Sparta Agricultural and Industrial Institute in Georgia. This first trip to the south galvanized him and generated the rest of the poems, prose poems, stories, and the drama that comprise *Cane*, from which these selections are taken. *Cane* was a major contribution to African American literature, but Toomer's own racial self-image was conflicted— a conflict, of course, that is only possible in a culture that insists one *have* a racial identity. His mother's parents had lived in both white and black neighborhoods in racially segregated Washington. Toomer referred to himself simply as an American. In 1936, he wrote a long poem, "Blue Meridian," describing the fusion of white, black, and Indian races into a new people, the blue men. By then he had become deeply committed to the philosophy of the Armenian spiritualist Gurdjieff.

## from

## *Cane*

### Reapers

Black reapers with the sound of steel on stones
Are sharpening scythes. I see them place the hones°
In their hip-pockets as a thing that's done,
And start their silent swinging, one by one.
Black horses drive a mower through the weeds.
And there, a field rat, startled, squealing bleeds.
His belly close to ground. I see the blade,
Blood-stained, continue cutting weeds and shade.

5

*1923*

---

2 *hones*: stones for sharpening blades.

# November Cotton Flower

Boll-weevil's coming, and the winter's cold,
Made cotton-stalks look rusty, season's old,
And cotton, scarce as any southern snow,
Was vanishing; the branch, so pinched and slow,
5    Failed in its function as the autumn rake;
Drouth fighting soil had caused the soil to take
All water from the streams; dead birds were found
In wells a hundred feet below the ground—
Such was the season when the flower bloomed.
10   Old folks were startled, and it soon assumed
Significance. Superstition saw
Something it had never seen before:
Brown eyes that loved without a trace of fear,
Beauty so sudden for that time of year.

*1923*

# Portrait in Georgia

Hair—braided chestnut,
coiled like a lyncher's rope,
Eyes—fagots,°
Lips—old scars, or the first red blisters,
5    Breath—the last sweet scent of cane,
And her slim body, white as the ash
    of black flesh after flame.

*1923*

# Her Lips Are Copper Wire

whisper of yellow globes
gleaming on lamp-posts that sway
like bootleg licker drinkers in the fog

and let your breath be moist against me
5    like bright beads on yellow globes

telephone the power-house
that the main wires are insulate

(her words play softly up and down
dewy corridors of billboards)

10   then with your tongue remove the tape
and press your lips to mine
till they are incandescent

*1921*

---

3 *fagots*: sticks or twigs bundled together.

# Charles Reznikoff (1894–1976)

Born in the Brooklyn Jewish community of the 1890s, Reznikoff earned a law degree but did not practice for long. He did work at a legal publishing firm in the 1930s, which proved a major inspiration in his writing. He began his career as a poet, however, as an imagist. His one-line poem "Aphrodite Vrania" (1921), its title fusing the Greek goddess of love with the muse of astronomy, reads simply "The ceaseless weaving of the uneven water." A decade later he was still writing in this mode. "About an excavation," another short poem announces, "a flock of bright red lanterns/has settled." As that untitled poem suggests, he regularly depicted New York settings in his short poems. But he also wrote imagist poems evoking the lives of poor immigrants and sometimes shaded imagism toward social commentary, as in an untitled 1918 eulogy to the sculptor Gaudier-Brezeska, killed in World War I:

> How shall we mourn you who are killed and wasted, sure that you would not die with your work unended, as if the iron scythe in the grass stops for a flower?

Many of these early poems appeared in hand-set books that Reznikoff published himself. Meanwhile, his focus began to shift. At a publishing firm he was summarizing court records of legal cases for publication in reference books. They provided a unique, often violent, history of American social life. While these court cases had all the persuasive, if sometimes surreal, idiosyncrasy of individual lived experience, their cumulative effect created a broad panorama of American life. He also found the spare prose of the court narratives powerful. Reznikoff refined and compressed some of the stories from court records for a 1934 prose collection, *Testimony*, and he began reworking the material into poems. The eventual result was a two-volume poem sequence, *Testimony: The United States (1885–1890): Recitative* (1965) and *Testimony: The United States (1891–1900): Recitative* (1968). Two further volumes covering the years up to 1915 were found among Reznikoff's papers after his death, and a new two-volume edition comprising all four sections was issued in 1978 and 1979. Portraits of African Americans and accounts of race relations are among his recurrent themes; I have compiled this selection from *Testimony* by gathering some of those sections together. Reznikoff divided the books into broad geographical units—"The North," "The South," and "The West"—and then gave section titles to sequences within them, such as "Social Life," "Domestic Difficulties," "Machine Age," "Neighbors," "Whites and Blacks," "Negroes," "Railroads," and "Property," often repeating these titles within a new geographical division. His 1975 book *Holocaust* used similar compositional techniques to create harrowing poems out of court testimony during the trials of Nazi war criminals. His sources, as he notes, are *Trials of the Criminals before the Nurem-*

berg *Military Tribunal* from 1945–1946 and the records of the 1961 Adolf Eich-
mann trial in Jerusalem. *Holocaust* consists of twelve numbered poems, "De-
portation," "Invasion," "Research," "Ghettos," "Massacres," "Gas Chambers
and Gas Trucks," "Work Camps," "Children," "Entertainment," "Mass Graves,"
"Marches," and "Escapes." In a way, *Testimony* and *Holocaust* are unified by
Reznikoff's sense that the Jewish poet should be a moral witness. Reznikoff
supported himself doing free-lance research, writing, and translation.

from

# Testimony: The United States (1885–1915): Recitative°

## Negroes

I

Alice's father was a white man,
of large estate,
and her mother a colored woman.
But her father and his wife treated Alice as his daughter—
5   in fact, as if she were *their* daughter;
although this, as a judge of the local court was to say,
was "revolting to the moral sense
and offensive against public policy."

She was sent to a boarding school in Washington,
10   and was now trying to establish herself
as a music teacher in that city.
After his wife's death, Alice's father wrote to her:
"Don't think that I will ever forget you:
I have promised this to my dear dead wife."

15   Alice's father had another daughter—
his child and his wife's.
When he made his will, he gave all of his large estate
to this daughter and her children;
but he had given Alice a deed to property in town that was worth
   about ten thousand dollars.
20   Only her father and his lawyer, and Alice and her friends,
knew of this;
and she was advised by her friends to place the deed on record
to protect the gift—
and she did.
25   By this time her father was old and feeble.
He was living with his white daughter
and spent most of his time just sitting on the porch.

As soon as Alice's half sister and her husband
learned of the gift to Alice,
30   they were furious—
although it was only a small part of her father's property.
They sent for his lawyer. When he came,

---

**volume title:** All that follows is based on law reports of the several states. The names of
all persons are fictitious and those of villages and towns have been changed. C.R.

the old man was sitting on the porch.
His daughter, holding a copy of the deed to Alice,
35    exclaimed: "See what Father has done!
I don't believe he knew what he was doing.
What can be done now?"

Her father finally said:
"I believe I can get Alice to reconvey the property.
40    1 don't think she will refuse."
And he and the lawyer arranged to take an early train the very next
     day
to where his colored daughter happened to be staying
on a visit to a friend.

They had breakfast with Alice and her friend
45    and then sat on the porch together
talking about everything but the deed;
most of the conversation was about Alice's life in Washington.
The old man could not bring himself to talk
about his errand.
50    Finally, he and his lawyer went for a walk together
while the young women—Alice and her friend—washed up the
     breakfast dishes.

On their return, the lawyer said:
"It will be best for you
to give the property back to your father."
55    And her father said: "You will not lose anything by it." Tears were
     in his eyes.
The lawyer added: "His family is much disturbed
about his giving you this property,
and his son-in-law says
he would rather see him burn down all the houses on it
60    than convey it to you.
As it is, it would only be the land there,
and would do you no good
because the people near there have said
no colored person should live there."

65    Her father said: "I thought that,
as I have done a great deal for you,
you would reconvey it to me."
"Do you want me to reconvey it
without any equivalent?"
70    "I have no equivalent to give you."
At this he went into the yard
and began walking backward and forward.
The lawyer on the porch said: "Has he not been very kind to you
and given you a great deal?
75    I think that under all the circumstances
you ought to grant his request.
You will not suffer by it."
"Has my father written his will?"

"Yes, I prepared a will for him which was signed."
80 But he did not tell her
that in the will there was nothing for her;
nor did she ask him.

She kept looking at her father
as the feeble old man
85 walked backward and forward in the yard,
weeping.
And Alice said: "I can't think of causing him distress
in his old age:
he has been too kind to me.
90 I will let him have the property."
At that, the lawyer took the deed that he had prepared the night
        before
out of his pocket. "I have a deed right here and will go for a notary,"
and hurried off.

When the deed was signed, witnessed, and in the lawyer's pocket
        again,
95 he turned to Alice and said: "You have acted nobly."

2

Wisdom and his wife and three or four other Negroes
with tickets as passengers
got on the train for Vicksburg.
The conductor met them on the platform of the car shouting:
100 "God damn you niggers! Get back and around!"
Wisdom explained that all they wanted to do
was to get through
to the car for colored people.
By way of answer the conductor pushed him to the ground,
105 knocking his hat off,
and as soon as all the Negroes were off the car
signaled the engineer to go ahead,
and the train left them standing at the station.

3

The Negro was living at a dugout on his own land
110 when a notice was posted in his neighborhood:
it had a rude drawing of a man hanging from a tree and a coffin
and read: "We don't allow a nigger on Hog Creek.
We give you warning in time;
so if you don't want to look up a tree
115 you had better leave. The White Caps."

Franklin and three or four others
were riding up to the Negro's dugout,
and Franklin was saying to the man riding beside him:

"I don't want to have anything to do with it;
120   I don't want to have any trouble with the Negroes.
All right, go ahead and buy the place
but I'll have nothing to do with it now,
and after you have made the trade
I'll come in."
125   But the Negro shot at them
and killed Franklin and another in the party.

4

The body was found in a swamp at the edge of town
forty or fifty yards from the wagon road
at the side of the swamp:
130   a leg was sticking out of the mud.
The dead body was that of a Negro—
girl or woman by the clothes:
the dress made out of homespun
and the buttons white
135   (homespun goods and white buttons
were common among the Negroes there).
One of the men got a pitchfork
put them in a box
and brought the box to the courthouse.
140   Hill had a daughter of fourteen or fifteen,
missing ever since July;
and some of the coroner's jury went to his house about sundown
and told him about the clothing
and asked him to go down to the courthouse
145   and see if he could identify the body.
He seemed unwilling to go
and had to be asked two or three times;
and when he did go
said there was nothing to prove to him
150   that it was his daughter;
and his wife, the girl's stepmother, agreed.

A large black oilcloth, about seven feet long and five wide,
had been found in the swamp, too,
about twenty-five or thirty yards from the body:
155   in size and color it looked like the one Hill had used to cover his
         wagon
(he would carry passengers in his wagon
out to mills and stills).

Among those who testified at the trial of Hill for murder
was a Negro woman who lived near the swamp
160   and on a night, about the beginning of August,
heard a girl screaming in the swamp;
and a Negro who had been in jail
for having a "fuss" with a preacher.
When the Negro was coming out on bail,

165    Hill who was then in jail said to him—
        so the witness said—
        "We colored people ought to stand by each other.
        If you will," said Hill, "I will see that you don't regret it."
        Then he said, "Go up to Georgia
170    and write a letter to me as my daughter,
        and sign my daughter's name to the letter:
        it will do me a lot of good in my case."
        And another witness said: "I am a fortuneteller
        and I tells a little something in the cards.
175    I was at Hill's restaurant"
        (in which his daughter had worked as a waitress)
        "and he said to me: 'Come into my room:
        I want you to do a little something for me.'
        I told him: 'You see that card? You are in trouble.
180    Tell me your trouble.'
        And Hill said: 'I killed my daughter.
        I got to fooling with her
        and bigged her.
        I told her not to tell anyone,
185    and when the time came I would send her off,
        but she told it around to white and black.
        My son held her hands
        and I cut her throat with my razor.'"

## 5

        Benton bought two tickets for seats in the orchestra of a theater in
            Kansas City
190    and he and his companion, a colored woman, went to the orchestra
            floor,
        where he gave the stubs to an usher,
        and the three started towards the seats.
        On the way, the usher was met by another usher
        and the two talked in whispers—
195    Benton overheard the word "nigger"—
        and, then one of the ushers told him he could not have the seats
            called for by the tickets:
        there had been a mistake.

        The usher was going to seat Benton and his companion in the balcony
        but Benton refused to follow him,
200    and went to the box-office instead
        where he showed the stubs to the man who had sold him the tickets
        and asked why he could not have the seats.
        The man said angrily, "Of course, you can!"
        and then looked at Benton again
205    and must have discovered, to use Benton's words,
        "that drop of African blood" in him
        and said: "It is a mistake. Those seats are occupied."
        He offered to give him seats in the balcony instead
        but Benton refused them
210    and with his companion left the theater.

The court held that Benton had no right to sit in the orchestra:
why, white persons at a place of amusement
especially for the colored
might very well be required to occupy separate seats!

6

215    It had been drizzling all afternoon
       but by eight o'clock it was clear:
       the streets, however, were still wet and muddy.
       At the entrance to the driveway
       leading to a stable in back of a house
220    was a swinging electric light,
       and there was another electric light in the street—
       strong and brilliant.
       Baldwin, a live-stock commission merchant—
       somewhat too fat—was on his way home.
225    He had two hundred dollars or so with him,
       and in his vest-pocket
       a gold watch with the likeness of his little dead son.

       Three Negro women were also going home
       along the street:
230    two of them servants who lived with the families for whom they
            worked,
       and now returning from church together,
       and Flo walking home alone.
       The women saw three men come up to Baldwin,
       heard something or other said,
235    and then saw the four of them tussling:
       the three men getting Baldwin against the hitching-post near the
            entrance to the driveway,
       hitting and kicking him, jerking him around,
       and one of them grabbing him by the throat and choking him
       until Baldwin was gurgling; and then they pulled him into the
            driveway
240    and he fell to the pavement.

       The tallest of the three got on Baldwin with his knees
       and was going through Baldwin's pockets;
       and one of the other two went to the sidewalk and, looking around,
       saw the colored women watching: "Get away from here!
245    What do you damned nigger bitches want, raising an excitement?
       It's only a friend of ours,
       and we are trying to get him away from the collars."
       "It's no such thing," said Flo,
       "that man there knocked him down!"
250    The second man rushed his hand into Baldwin's vest-pocket,
       pulled out the watch and said, "Come on, let's go!
       The collars will have us in a minute.
       Let's go!"
       The last to leave was the man who had been kneeling on Baldwin

255 and before he left gave him a farewell kick in the belly:
to one of the women it sounded like the slosh of water
in a slop-barrel on a wagon going down the street.
And the three men ran around a cable-car that was coming down.

Flo ran up to a man walking along the street calmly
260 and cried, "Those three men were beating this man to death!"
Baldwin tried to get up
but he was so weak he could hardly get his hand up.
"Oh," the man heard him say,
"they have my watch with my dead boy's picture in it."

7

265 The Negro went to his hogpen on a Sunday
bringing the hogs slops;
and just below the hogpen were two white men.
After the Negro had fed the hogs and started towards his house,
one of the men called to him:
270 he wanted a match.
The Negro told him he was in a hurry to get back home
to dress
and go to preaching,
but the man who had called him said,
275 "Come here, you!"
And the Negro answered, "I'll come."
The white man said, "You are too damned slow.
Why can't you come when I call you?"
The Negro answered, "I did."
280 At that the white man snatched the Negro's hat off
and said, "Take your hat off!
Like a damned nigger ought to when I talk to him,"
and taking a knife out of a coat pocket
put the blade against the Negro's throat,
285 and then tapped him on the head with the handle of the knife
and told him he could go home.

8

Four or five young Negroes working about the town
were arrested
and charged with breaking into stores and robbing them:
290 of meat, a sack of flour, some lard, and a pair of pants.
A day or two after they were arrested,
a constable, the jailer, and the sheriff of the county
took them out of jail about dusk.

A handkerchief was tied over the face of one of the young Negroes
295 and he was tied, hand and foot,
his pants pulled down
and he was whipped,
and then thrown into a pile of brush

and the brush set afire near where he was lying.
300     As for another, he was taken to the courtroom—
dark now except for the light of a candle
held by the jailer—
and a slick rope, perhaps to leave no mark,
put about the young Negro's neck
305     and he was pulled up until he was hanging
and was asked, "Where are those things?"
"I don't know," he said when they had lowered him.
He had almost lost his breath
and had to blow for it "mighty hard."
310     They had seen that the knot placed behind his neck was not
            hurting him
and turned it around until it was at his throat
and told him they would hang him until his tongue stuck out
unless he told them where the stolen goods were.
"You know where they are!" and he said again, "I don't."
315     and they pulled him up again.

9

The white man washing dishes at night in the restaurant
had only one leg and a crutch.
A Negro—in the habit of eating there—
was sitting at the table in the kitchen
320     at which Negroes had to eat.
The dishwasher had a fit of coughing
and the Negro, to be friendly, said,
"What in the hell is the matter with you?"
The dishwasher answered, "I am not bothering you.
325     Leave me alone!"
"By God," the Negro said, taking him literally,
"I don't have to go out until I am ready."
And, thinking that most of the help in the restaurant were friendly
and that he himself was not a man to be trifled with,
330     added, "You don't know me."
"Yes, I do," said the dishwasher. "You are a nigger."
The Negro stood up
and the dishwasher, leaning on the table,
shoved the crutch at him to ward him off;
335     but the Negro took a pistol from his pocket, held it in both hands,
and pointing it at the dishwasher
shot him in the belly.

10

A woman, just over thirty and well overweight,
was about to get off the streetcar
340     with her valise, a basket in which was cake and a bottle of syrup,
            and with a bundle of sugar cane.
The car stopped
and she went out on the platform.
When she put her foot on the step below the platform,

leaving the valise on the platform until she was on the ground,
345    the conductor, inside the car,
gave the signal to start,
and the car started.

She shifted the basket from her right hand to her arm at once
and her right hand free
350    held on to the bar on the side of the car to help passengers on or off
but was thrown from the car
and swung around it.
She held on to the bar
to be dragged a hundred feet and more
355    before the car stopped.

The conductor came out on the platform.
"If I had been a white lady," she said,
"you would have given me time to get off
before you rang the bell."
360    And the conductor replied,
"Go on, nigger;
you had time enough."

II

A young black, sixteen years of age,
earned a dollar and a half a day,
365    and gave almost all of it to his father
but kept the rest
to spend on himself:
buy tobacco, for example,
with which to make his cigarettes.

370    The train would stop for a while at the flag station
and he went into the car for colored people
where the "news butch" kept the newspapers, candy, tobacco, and
    whatever else was sold on the train
and the young black bought what he wanted,
and stood there talking to the "news butch" until the train was
    about to start
375    and then was walking to the platform of the car to get off.

Just then the conductor and the porter,
about to enter the car for white passengers,
saw him
and hurried up to him—
380    the train was now running pretty fast—
shoved him out of the door
and both threw him off the train.
"That damned nigger don't mind hitting the cross-ties," said the
    conductor,
as he and the porter turned back,
385    and the porter laughed.

The young black's body lay near the tracks,
his head one or two feet from the end of the railroad's cross-ties,
and his feet towards the ditch:
the head badly bruised on the side of the forehead
390      and the skull broken.

One of the passengers in the car for whites
saw what had happened,
but was advised by his friends
that the less he had to say about the matter the better.

*1965–1969*

## from

# *Holocaust°*

## Massacres°

I

The first day the Germans came into the city
where the young woman lived
they took Jewish men and ordered them to gather the dirt on the
   streets
with their hands.
5      Then the Jews had to undress
and behind each Jew was a German soldier with a fixed bayonet
who ordered him to run;
if the Jew stopped,
he would be stabbed in the back with the bayonet.
10     Almost all the Jews came home bleeding—
among them her father.
Later, after the German garrison had left the market place,
large trucks were suddenly there,
and about a dozen soldiers jumped off each truck—
15     in green uniforms with steel helmets:
these were S.S. men.
They went from house to house
and took Jewish men—young and old—
and brought them to the market place;
20     here the Jews had to hold their hands on the back of their necks.
About thirty Jews were taken that day;
among them the young woman's father.

---

**volume title:** All that follows is based on a United States government publication, *Trials of the Criminals before the Nuremberg Military Tribunal* and the records of the Eichmann trial in Jerusalem. C.R.

**poem title:** By 1941, the policy of the Nazis was changed to extermination of the Jews, not only in Germany but in all countries the Nazis annexed, invaded or dominated. It has been estimated that six million Jews lost their lives: about four and a half million in Poland and in the invaded parts of Russia. C.R.

They were then put on one of the trucks and carried off.°
The young woman ran after the truck
25 until she reached a woods in the neighborhood.
There she found all the Jews who had been taken—
dead.

They had been shot
and were stretched out on the ground
30 in a pattern:
Jews and Poles
in groups of five
but Jews and Poles in separate groups.
She kissed her father:
35 he was ice-cold
although it was only an hour after he had been taken.

2

Her father had a shop for selling leather
and was one of the notables in a Polish Jewish community
when the Germans entered.
40 They put their horses into the synagogue and turned it into a stable.
On a Saturday afternoon, peasants from neighboring villages
came to tell the Jews of the town
that the Germans were killing Jews: they should run away and hide.
But the rabbi and other elders of the town
45 thought running away useless;
besides, they thought the Germans might take a few of the young
    men to work for them
but that no one would be killed.

The next day, before sunrise, a Jew from a neighboring village
ran into the town shouting:
50 "Jews, run for your lives!
The Germans are out to kill us,"
and the townspeople saw the Germans coming in.
The young woman's grandfather said, "Run and hide, children,
    but I will stay:
they will do no harm to me."
55 those who could hid in a neighboring forest.
During the day they heard shooting—
single shots and cries;
but towards evening they thought the Germans would be leaving
    the town
and, sure enough, peasants from the neighborhood met them
60 and said: "You can go back now.
The Germans killed everybody left behind."

---

23 *off*: There was a standing order of the Germans that executions were not to be in a pub-
lic place and for this a wooded area was usual. C.R.

When the Jews came back,
they found that the Germans had rounded up about one hundred
    and fifty Jews,
including the rabbi and other notables.

65    They told the rabbi to take his prayer shawl along—
the other Jews had been gathered in the center of the town—
and he was told to put on his prayer shawl
and sing and dance. He would not

and was beaten up. And so were the other Jews.
70    Then they were driven to the cemetery.
Here a shallow grave had been dug for them.
They were told to lie down in fours
and were shot. But her father remained behind in the town—alive:
he had said he was cutting the leather in his shop for shoes
75    and was registered as a shoemaker.

Later, the Germans went into the town to take whatever they could
    find;
the place was swarming with Germans—four or five to every Jew.
Many were put upon a large truck;
those who could not climb on themselves
80    were thrown on; and those for whom there was no room on the
    truck
were ordered to run after it.
All the Jews were counted and the Germans searched for every
    missing person on their list.
The young woman was among those who ran,
her little daughter in her arms.
85    There were those, too, who had two or three children
and held them in their arms as they ran after the truck.
Those who fell were shot—right where they fell.

When the young woman reached the truck,
all who had been on it were down and undressed and lined up;
90    the rest of her family among them.
There was a small hill there and at the foot of the hill a dugout.
The Jews were ordered to stand on top of the hill
and four S.S. men shot them—killed each separately.
When she reached the top of the hill and looked down
95    she saw three or four rows of the dead already on the ground.
Some of the young people tried to run
but were caught at once
and shot right there.
Children were taking leave of their parents;
100    but her little daughter said to her,
"Mother, why are we waiting? Let us run!"

Her father did not want to take off all of his clothes
and stood in his underwear.
His children begged him to take it off
105    but he would not and was beaten.
Then the Germans tore off his underwear
and he was shot.

They shot her mother, too,
and her father's mother—
110    she was eighty years old
and held two children in her arms;
and they shot her father's sister;
she also had babies in her arms
and was shot on the spot.
115    Her younger sister went up to one of the Germans—
with another girl, one of her sister's friends—
and they asked to be spared,
standing there naked before him.
The German looked into their eyes
120    and shot them both—her sister and the young friend;
they fell
embracing each other.

The German who had shot her younger sister
turned to her
125    and asked, "Whom shall I shoot first?"
She was holding her daughter in her arms and did not answer.
She felt him take the child from her;
the child cried out and was shot.
Then he aimed at her: took hold of her hair
130    and turned her head around.
She remained standing and heard a shot
but kept on standing. He turned her head around again
and shot her;
and she fell into the dugout
135    among the bodies.

Suddenly she felt that she was choking;
bodies had fallen all over her.
She tried to find air to breathe
and began climbing towards the top of the dugout,
140    and felt people pulling at her
and biting at her legs.
At last she came to the top.
Bodies were lying everywhere
but not all of them dead:
145    dying, but not dead;
and children were crying, "Mamma! Papa!"
She tried to stand up but could not.

The Germans were gone.
She was naked,
150    covered with blood and dirty with the excrement of those in the
       dugout,
and found that she had been shot in the back of the head.
Blood was spurting from the dugout
in many places;
and she heard the cries and screams of those in it still alive.
150    She began to search among the dead for her little girl
and kept calling her name;
trying to join the dead,

and crying out to her dead mother and father,
"Why didn't they kill me, too?"

160     She was there all night.
Suddenly she saw Germans on horseback
and sat down in a field
and heard them order all the corpses heaped together;
and the bodies—many who had been shot but were still alive—
165     were heaped together with shovels.

Children were running about.
The Germans caught the children
and shot them, too;
but did not come near her. And left again
170     and with them the peasants from around the place—
who had to help—
and the machine-guns and trucks were taken away.

She remained in the field, stretched out.
Shepherds began driving their flocks into the field;
175     and threw stones at her,
thinking her dead or mad.
Afterwards, a passing farmer saw her,
fed her
and helped her join Jews in the forest nearby.

### 3

180     Jewish women were lined up by German troops in charge of the
        territory,
told to undress,
and they stood in their undergarments.
An officer, looking at the row of women—
stopped to look at a young woman—
185     tall, with long braided hair, and wonderful eyes.
He kept looking at her, then smiled and said,
"Take a step forward."
Dazed—as they all were—she did not move
and he said again: "Take a step forward!
190     Don't you want to live?"
She took that step
and then he said: "What a pity
to bury such beauty in the earth.
Go!
195     But don't look backwards.
There is the street to the boulevard.
Follow that."
She hesitated
and then began to walk as told.
200     The other women looked at her—
some no doubt with envy—
as she walked slowly, step by step.
And the officer took out his revolver
and shot her in the back.

4

205 The soldier doing the shooting was sitting at the narrow end of
　　 the pit,
　　 his feet dangling into it;
　　 smoking a cigarette,
　　 the machine-gun on his knees.

　　 As each truck came, those who had been on it—
210 Jewish men, women, and children of all ages—
　　 had to undress
　　 and put their clothing at fixed places,
　　 sorted in great piles—
　　 shoes, outer clothing, and underwear.

215 The S.S. man at the pit,
　　 shouted to his comrade
　　 and he counted off twenty, now completely naked,
　　 and told them to go down the steps cut in the clay wall of the pit:
　　 here they were to climb over the heads of the dead
220 to where the soldier pointed.
　　 As they went towards the pit,
　　 a slender young woman with black hair,
　　 passing a German civilian who was watching,
　　 pointed to herself and said,
225 "I am twenty-three."
　　 An old woman with white hair
　　 was holding a child about a year old
　　 in her arms,
　　 singing to it and tickling it,
230 and the child was cooing with delight;
　　 and a father was holding the hand of his little son—
　　 —the child about to burst into tears—
　　 speaking to the child softly,
　　 stroking his head
235 and pointing to the sky.

　　 Bodies were soon heaped in the large pit,
　　 lying on top of each other,
　　 heads still to be seen and blood running over their shoulders;
　　 but some were still moving,
240 lifting arms and turning heads.°

---

240 *heads:* There were different techniques: some commanders lined up those to be shot
and had them standing or kneeling on the edge of a pit, facing it; while others had those
to be shot standing with their backs to the pit; and still others had them go into the pit
while still alive and these were shot in the neck while standing or kneeling. This was the
most efficient, for of those shot above the pit all did not fall into it and then the soldiers
had the trouble of pushing them in; but if they were shot in the pit the next group to be
shot could come at once and fall on the bleeding corpses. But whatever the method of ex-
ecution it was, to quote an official report, "always honorable and done in a humane and
military manner." C.R.

5

They gathered some twenty *Hasidic* Jews from their homes,
in the robes these wear,
wearing their prayer shawls, too,
and holding prayer books in their hands.
245   They were led up a hill.
Here they were told to chant their prayers
and raise their hands for help to God
and, as they did so,
the officers poured kerosene under them
and set it on fire.

*1975*

# Herman Spector (1895–1959)

A lifelong resident of New York, Spector was a regular contributor to *New Masses* for several years, a key figure in the founding of the short-lived radical poetry journal *Dynamo*, and a contributor to many of the proletarian literature collections of the 1930s. Toward the end of the 1930s he worked for a year on the WPA Writers' Project. Thereafter he withdrew from his literary and political contacts, worked as a welder during the war, and finally survived in a series of marginal odd jobs before becoming a cab driver until his death. *Bastard in a Ragged Suit* (1977), which draws its title from a self-description in a 1929 poem, "Outcast," gathers together both his published poetry and prose and selections from the writing and drawing he continued to work on but never submitted for publication in the last years of his life.

## Wiseguy Type

The smart little gent with the shoebutton eyes
    and the folded nose, twice-over, so;
    with the diffident smile, and the spectacles
    like a hornèd owl, so wise, so wise,

5      Is a sharpshooter born in a cabaret to a rattle
    of drums and a spastic shudder;
    By a pinkish floozie with powdered thighs,
    and a monocled punk in a cutaway,
And a tinhorn song, and a clicking jig,
10      and a swift, pat fade
      and a getaway . . .

Is a wise, wise baby who won't take sides,
    playing the middle against the ends;
    shuffles the cards with a crack and a flutter,
15      looks sharp in the dark for omens and friends,
Concedes with a mutter, You may be right.
    It may be true but I can't decide,
    If the cards are stacked then what does it matter?
    If death is the answer, what's the use?
20    I'm a lonesome wolf in a cold, hard winter, he says
And the rest is up to Youse.

                              *1936*

# V. J. Jerome (1896–1965)

Born Isaac Jerome Romaine in a Polish ghetto, Victor Jeremy Jerome subsequently moved to London and from there came to New York. He joined the Communist party in 1927, and in 1937 he became chairman of the U.S. Communist Party's Cultural Commission and also began editing *The Communist*, which later became *Political Affairs*, the party's chief political journal. Arrested under the highly controversial Smith Act in 1951, he was convicted—on the inappropriate basis of his critical writings—of conspiracy to advocate the violent overthrow of the U.S. government, and he served three years in prison. "A Negro Mother to Her Child" was first published in *The Daily Worker* (November 15, 1930). An illustrated version appeared in *The Rebel Poet* in 1932, and the poem was set to music shortly thereafter. Jerome's interest in race in America would continue throughout his life, as exemplified by his poems "To a Black Man" (1932) and "Caliban Speaks" (1953), the latter inspired by the death of the black actor Canada Lee, as well as his pamphlet *The Negro in Hollywood* (1950). *A Lantern for Jeremy* (1952) is a fictionalized account of his childhood in Poland.

## A Negro Mother to Her Child

Quit yo' wailin' honey bo'
'Taint no use to cry
Rubber nipple, mammy's breast
Both am gone bone dry.

5      Daddy is a bolshevik
Locked up in de pen
Didn' rob nor didn' steal
Led de workin' men.

What's de use mah tellin' you
10     Silly li'l lamb
Gon'ter git it straight some day
When you is a man.

Wisht ah had a sea o' milk
Mek you strong an' soun'
15     Daddy's waitin' till you come
Brek dat prison down.

*1930*

# John Wheelwright (1897–1940)

Wheelright was born to a Boston Brahmin family; his father was an architect who designed a number of the city's well-known buildings. After his father's suicide in 1912, Wheelwright underwent a religious conversion, abandoning his family's historic Unitarianism and becoming an Anglican. At Harvard from 1916–1920, however, he became uneasy with his new commitment and joined the circle of Aesthetes, among them E.E. Cummings and Malcolm Cowley. Attracted to socialism, he remained at once emotionally connected to Christian myth and reluctant to embrace the uneducated masses. Many of his early poems register these conflicting impulses, though with the advent of the Great Depression he became increasingly committed to Marxism, aligning himself with its Trotskyite wing. Wheelwright died prematurely when he was struck down by a car in Boston in September 1940.

## Plantation Drouth

For Benjamin Rufus Kittredge, Jr.

It has not rained.
The fields lie powdered
under smoke and clouds.
The swamps are peopled
5  with smouldering cedar
reflected on black, hoarded water.
The furrow in the field
behind the negro's heels
smokes, as though the plowshare stirred
10  embers in the earth.
As the furrow lengthens,
the rising powder fades to sky-dust
below the powdered sky.
This spongy land is parched
15  and draws the salt sea to it,
up all its earthy rivers.
It drinks brine, like a thirsty goat.
The river reeds are withered.
It is April in the meadows
20  but, in the empty rice fields
it is Winter.
The roots of the cedars drink

slow fire under the sod.
A flame seeps up the core,—
25     a tall tree falls.
From the bark, the white smoke bleeds.
Midway between midnight and daybreak
the sky egg cracks across.
Goats move in sleep
30     Night then speaks with one dry boom.
The goats veer in their steps and stir
fire-flies from live oak trees
with their small lightnings.
One horned beast trots from the herd
35     more in disdain than fright
into the open, a little distance foraging.
The old devil knows
despite that bright, slow, loud antiphon
it will not rain.

*1933*

# Joseph Freeman (1897–1965)

Born in Ukraine, Freeman came to the United States in 1904. A socialist from age seventeen, he was one of the more visible figures of the left in the 1920s and 1930s as an editor of the *Liberator* and cofounder of *New Masses*. His poetry regularly appeared in journals, but it was never collected in a book. He worked for the Soviet news agency TASS from 1925–1931 but later broke with the party. His most famous work is his political autobiography *An American Testament* (1936). Twelve of his poems are reprinted in the anthology *Social Poetry of the 1930s* (1978).

## Our Age Has Caesars

Our age has Caesars, though they wear silk hats
And govern vaster continents than Rome;
The bishops tend their bellies and wear spats
And lie like ancient oracles; at home
5    Circe, bored with triumphs on the stage,
Sets the table and pours out the wine,
Varies her smiling makeup to engage,
Bewitch and rob her smug enamoured swine.
If we have prophets calling for revolts
10    Who shake the skies until the old worlds crack,
For every hero there are twenty dolts
And Tartuffe's° skulk behind Ilyich's° back;
And Madame Pompadour° and you, my dear,
Differ only in name and class and year.

1926

---

12 *Tartuffe*: title character in *Tartuffe* (1664) by French dramatist Molière (1622–1673). Tartuffe is a religious hypocrite, rogue, and imposter.
12 *Ilyich*: title character in *The Death of Ivan Ilyich* (1884) by the Russian writer Leo Tolstoy (1828–1910). A genial lawyer who hides from reality, Ilyich only faces reality as he nears death.
13 *Pompadour*: Madame de Pompadour (1721–1764), mistress of Louis XV of France, who had effective control of public affairs and swayed state policy for twenty years.

# Lucia Trent (1897–1977)

Trent's third book of poems, *Children of Fire and Shadow* (1929), a collection whose often witty radicalism anticipates some of the poetry of the next decade, is her most notable. A graduate of Smith College, she is also known for a number of editing projects, including the magazine *Contemporary Verse* and some ten books, on many of which she collaborated with her husband Ralph Cheyney. The most historically important of these may be *America Arraigned* (1928), a collection of poems about the Sacco and Vanzetti case. After Cheyney died, Trent remarried; for the last thirty years of her life she was known as Mrs. Ernest Glass. Living in Austin, Texas, she was bedridden for the last decade of her life after a stroke.

## Breed, Women, Breed

Breed, little mothers,
With tired backs and tired hands,
Breed for the owners of mills and the owners of mines,
Breed a race of danger-haunted men,
5    A race of toiling, sweating, miserable men,
Breed, little mothers,
Breed for the owners of mills and the owners of mines,
Breed, breed, breed!

Breed, little mothers,
10   With the sunken eyes and the sagging cheeks,
Breed for the bankers, the crafty and terrible masters of men,
Breed a race of machines,
A race of aenemic, round-shouldered, subway-herded machines!

Breed, little mothers,
15   With a faith patient and stupid as cattle,
Breed for the war lords,
Offer your woman flesh for incredible torment,
Wrack your frail bodies with the pangs of birth
For the war lords who slaughter your sons!

20      Breed, little mothers,
        Breed for the owners of mills and the owners of mines,
        Breed for the bankers, the crafty and terrible masters of men,
        Breed for the war lords, the devouring war lords,
        Breed, women, breed!

*1929*

# Black Men

Swift gusts of hollow night wind clatter by,
Tonight the earth is leper-pale and still;
The moon lies like a tombstone in the sky.
Three black men sway upon a lonely hill.

5     The pain has withered from each tortured face.
Soon earth will hide them with a mother's care.
But never God's great mercy can erase
A bitter scorn for those who hung them there.

*1929*

# Parade the Narrow Turrets

Thumb over your well-worn classics with clammy and accurate
    eyes,
Teach Freshmen to scan Homer and Horace and look wise.
Dress in your new Tuxedo as gauchely as you please.
And at official dinners kowtow to fat trustees.
5     Wince at the Evening Graphic, whose bold pink pages shriek,
Frown on the drooping shopgirl, rouging her lip and cheek.
Lecture to gray-haired ladies on ruins of ancient Rome,
And preach across a tea-cup on the sanctity of home.
What do you care if miner's brats shudder and starve and die.
10    What do you care if blacks are lynched° beneath a withering sky?
What do you care if two men° burn to death in a great steel chair
While the world shouts their innocence and honest men despair?
Go live in your Ivory Tower. Build it as high as you can,
And parade the narrow turrets as a cultivated man!

*1929*

---

10 *lynched:* see the notes to Claude McKay's "The Lynching" (p. 316).
11 *two men:* Sacco and Vanzetti, also the subject of Trent and Cheyney's important poetry
anthology *America Arraigned* (1928). See the notes to Millay's "Justice Denied in Massa-
chusetts" (p. 328).

# Louise Bogan (1897–1970)

Bogan was born in Livermore Falls, Maine. Her parents, of Irish descent, traveled across New England in search of work, and endured a tempestuous marriage. One of Bogan's brothers was killed in the First World War, while another died of alcoholism in his early 30s. Bogan attended Boston University for a year. After a brief, failed marriage, she settled in New York's Greenwich Village, became part of its vital literary life, and began publishing her intense but highly formal poetry in little magazines. In 1925, she married wealthy poet and editor Raymond Holden, but he lost his money in the stock market crash. After he became managing editor of *The New Yorker,* Bogan became poetry editor for the magazine, a post she held from 1931–1969. In addition to choosing poems for publication, she wrote two omnibus poetry reviews each year. Given the magazine's high rate of pay for poetry and its prestige, this position was a visible and influential one; Bogan was thus better known to some as a critic than as a poet.

She rejected any active involvement in the series of social and political concerns that moved so many of her contemporaries, but she was nonetheless acutely aware of gender issues. "I am a woman, and 'fundamental brainwork,' the building of logical structures, the abstractions, the condensations, the comparisons, the reasonings, *are not expected of me,*" she wrote in a 1930s journal. This is the same poet who in 1923 also spoke in the harsh persona of Medusa and who six years later stood with Cassandra, declaring herself "the shrieking heaven lifted over men, / Not the dumb earth, wherein they set their graves." Yet "Women" seems to elaborate generic metaphors of female passivity and male vitality. Indeed Bogan's bid to disentangle resistance from within prevailing commonplaces has often been misunderstood. The poem's subject is more properly understood not as "women" themselves but rather as masculinist discourses about women, the declarations about women that our culture habitually makes. "Women" mounts its feminist claims as counter-assertions, written against the grain of (and at work within) every patriarchal cliché about femininity. Thus "They do not see cattle cropping red winter grass," the line that opens the second stanza, exhibits exactly the precise visually observed detail that the line asserts women cannot see. The reader of either gender is provoked to visualize what the lines describe. The poem in most of its figures thereby undoes all its apparent propositions and assertions.

In her last decades, Bogan began to teach more regularly. She also did translations and published critical books. Her disciplined methods of composition and her exacting standards limited her output to 105 poems, but they are notable both for their craft and their fervor.

# Medusa°

I had come to the house, in a cave of trees,
Facing a sheer sky.
Everything moved,—a bell hung ready to strike,
Sun and reflection wheeled by.

5    When the bare eyes were before me
And the hissing hair,
Held up at a window, seen through a door.
The stiff bald eyes, the serpents on the forehead
Formed in the air.

10    This is a dead scene forever now.
Nothing will ever stir.
The end will never brighten it more than this,
Nor the rain blur.

The water will always fall, and will not fall,
15    And the tipped bell make no sound.
The grass will always be growing for hay
Deep on the ground.

And I shall stand here like a shadow
Under the great balanced day,
20    My eyes on the yellow dust, that was lifting in the wind,
And does not drift away.

*1923*

# The Crows

The woman who has grown old
And knows desire must die,
Yet turns to love again,
Hears the crows' cry.

5    She is a stem long hardened,
A weed that no scythe mows.
The heart's laughter will be to her
The crying of the crows,

Who slide in the air with the same voice
10    Over what yields not, and what yields,
Alike in spring, and when there is only bitter
Winter-burning in the fields.

*1923*

---

**poem title:** in Greek myth, Medusa was one of three sisters known as the Gorgons. Her head was entwined with snakes and her gaze so penetrating that anyone who looked in her flashing eyes was turned to stone. She was mortal, however, and was killed, while she slept, by Perseus, who avoided looking at her. Her severed head retained the power to turn people to stone.

# Women

Women have no wilderness in them,
They are provident instead,
Content in the tight hot cell of their hearts
To eat dusty bread.

5    They do not see cattle cropping red winter grass,
They do not hear
Snow water going down under culverts
Shallow and clear.

They wait, when they should turn to journeys,
10   They stiffen, when they should bend.
They use against themselves that benevolence
To which no man is friend.

They cannot think of so many crops to a field
Or of clean wood cleft by an axe.
15   Their love is an eager meaninglessness
Too tense, or too lax.

They hear in every whisper that speaks to them
A shout and a cry.
As like as not, when they take life over their door-sills
They should let it go by.

1923

# Cassandra°

To me, one silly task is like another.
I bare the shambling tricks of lust and pride.
This flesh will never give a child its mother,—
Song, like a wing, tears through my breast, my side,
5   And madness chooses out my voice again,
Again. I am the chosen no hand saves:
The shrieking heaven lifted over men,
Not the dumb earth, wherein they set their graves.

1929

# The Dragonfly

You are made of almost nothing
But of enough
To be great eyes
And diaphanous double vans;

---

**poem title:** In Greek mythology, Cassandra, who was daughter to the king and queen of Troy, had the gift of prophecy but no power to convince her listeners that her prophecies were true. Thus she warned her people not to take the Trojan horse into their city, but they ignored her. She went into a trance to deliver her prophecies.

5      To be ceaseless movement,
       Unending hunger
       Grappling love.

       Link between water and air,
       Earth repels you.
10     Light touches you only to shift into iridescence
       Upon your body and wings.

       Twice-born, predator,
       You split into the heat.
       Swift beyond calculation or capture
15     You dart into the shadow
       Which consumes you.

       You rocket into the day.
       But at last, when the wind flattens the grasses,
       For you, the design and purpose stop.

20     And you fall
       With the other husks of summer.

                                            *1963*

# Harry Crosby (1898–1929)

There is no other poet in our history quite like Crosby. He is above all else a poet of one unforgiving obsession: the image of the sun and every variation he can ring on it in poems of ecstatic incantation. Poems like "Pharmacie du Soleil" should be read aloud, preferably by a score of people speaking either in unison or in counterpoint. Born Henry Sturgis Crosby into an upper-class Boston family, his education at privileged Boston schools gives little hint of the iconoclastic Paris expatriate of the 1920s. But World War I changed him. He enlisted in the Ambulance Corps, went through the slaughter at Verdun, watched his own ambulance blown to bits while he was barely thirty feet away, and commemorated the moment as his "death day" every year thereafter. He won the Croix de Guerre medal at the end, but returned home radically alienated. At Harvard he fell in love in 1920 with Mary Phelps Jacob Peabody, a married woman who later changed her name to Caresse. Hoping to end the relationship, Crosby's mother arranged a job for him at uncle J.P. Morgan's Paris bank, but Caresse followed him and they were married on a return visit to New York in 1922. Back in France their wild parties, gambling, drinking, opium experiments, and blatantly open marriage gained them considerable notoriety among the expatriate community. Increasingly committed to writing poetry, Crosby and Caresse also cofounded Black Sun Press. They would publish Pound, Lawrence, Joyce, Crane, and such books as Crosby's own *Chariot of the Sun*. In Crosby's poetry he sought to transform the modern wasteland by the power of unconscious revelation, exploiting surrealism, incantation, declamation, and automatic writing. But he also began to craft his own ultimate nihilist performance. On a trip to New York, still married to Caresse, he successfully staged a joint murder and suicide with his willing mistress Josephine Rotch, the Mad Queen of his poetic mythology. He shot her first and then took his own life.

## Photoheliograph (For Lady A.)

```
        black black black black black
        black black black black black
        black black black black black
        black black black black black
5       black black S U N black black
        black black black black black
        black black black black black
        black black black black black
        black black black black black
10      black black black black black
```

1928

## Pharmacie du Soleil

**calcium iron hydrogen sodium nickel
magnesium cobalt silicon aluminium
titanium chromium strontium manganese
vanadium barium carbon scandium yttrium
zirconium molybdenum lanthanum niobium
palladium neodymium copper zinc cadmium
cerium glucinum germanium rhodium silver
tin lead erbium potassium iridium
tantalum osmium thorium platinum tungsten
ruthenium uranium**

5

10

*1928*

## Tattoo

I am the criminal whose chest is tattooed with a poinard above which are graven the words "mort aux bourgeois." Let us each tattoo this on our hearts.

I am the soldier with a red mark on my nakedness—when in a frenzy of love the mark expands to spell Mad Queen. Let us each tattoo our Mad Queen on our heart.

I am the prophet from the land of the Sun whose back is tattooed in the design of a rising sun. Let us each tattoo a rising sun on our heart.

*1928*

## *from* Short Introduction to the Word

1)

Take the word Sun which burns permanently in my brain. It has accuracy and alacrity. It is monomaniac in its intensity. It is a continual flash of insight. It is the marriage of Invulnerability with Yes, of the Red Wolf with the Gold Bumblebee, of Madness with Ra.

2)

Birdileaves, Goldabbits, Fingertoes, Auroramor, Barbarifire, Parabolaw, Peaglecock, Lovegown, Nombrilomane.

3)

I understand certain words to be single and by themselves and deriving from no other words as for instance the word I.

4)

I believe that certain physical changes in the brain result in a given word—this word having the distinguished characteristic of unreality being born neither as a result of connotation nor of conscious endeavor: Starlash.

5)

There is the automatic word as for instance with me the word Sorceress; when the word goes on even while my attention is focused on entirely different subjects just as in swimming my arms and legs go on automatically even when my attention is focused on subjects entirely different from swimming such as witchcraft for instance or the Sorceress.

*1928*

# Hart Crane (1899–1932)

Born in a small Ohio town, Crane grew up in Cleveland. He went to New York after leaving high school, but ended up returning to Cleveland until 1923, along the way accumulating work experience in advertising agencies, a newspaper, and in his father's businesses. He faced continual difficulty and much stress supporting himself and had to rely on relatives and a benefactor. The first six poems here come from this first phase of his career, among them the early imagist poem "October–November" and the remarkable "Episode of Hands," one of the most beautiful of explicitly homosexual poems from the modernist period.

The sheer ambition of his book-length project, *The Bridge*, frustrated Crane's attempts to begin it from 1923 to 1926. A change of location from New York City to a summer cottage on the Isles of Pines off the Cuban coast resulted in an outburst of new writing, and all but four of the poem's fifteen sections were substantially complete when an October 1926 hurricane devastated the island. This selection aims to make it possible to see the structure, style, main themes, and cultural ambitions of the poem. The poem sequence takes its title and the focus of its opening and closing poems, "Proem" and "Atlantis" from a much-celebrated piece of New York architecture and engineering, the Brooklyn Bridge. Widely considered both an aesthetic triumph and a highly successful technical project, Crane reasonably takes it as a symbol of American ambition and spirit combined. By reaching back into American history to Columbus's return voyage from the New World ("Ave Maria"), traveling through the Mississippi River region by train in the present day ("The River"), and then imaginatively flying by plane over the east coast of the United States ("Cape Hatteras"), Crane attempts to articulate a unifying vision of America.

Yet if the bridge is a transcendent and ecstatic symbol, the airplane in "Cape Hatteras" is sometimes a demonic one, given over to war rather than cultural poetry. The conflict is resolved, if at all, in the controversial bravado performance of "Atlantis," the final poem, which is one of the most rhetorically flamboyant texts among American long poems. Like Rukeyser's "The Book of the Dead" a few years later, *The Bridge* chooses commercial enterprises and construction projects as images of both greed and transcendence. Like her poem, too, it creates a unifying myth out of the most resistant materials. Reacting to Eliot's *The Waste Land*, both poets wrote long poem sequences that were American rather than international. Crane also wished to substitute cultural optimism for Eliot's bleak pessimism and to imagine that collaborative human work could offer some hope for the future. At the end, Crane saw little hope for his own; only thirty-three years old, he jumped overboard from a boat returning from Mexico and drowned.

## October–November

Indian-summer-sun
With crimson feathers whips away the mists;
Dives through the filter of trellises
And gilds the silver on the blotched arbor-seats.

5    Now gold and purple scintillate
On trees that seem dancing
In delirium;
Then the moon
In a mad orange flare
10  Floods the grape-hung night.

                              *1916*

## Black Tambourine°

The interests of a black man in a cellar
Mark tardy judgment on the world's closed door.
Gnats toss in the shadow of a bottle,
And a roach spans a crevice in the floor.

5    Aesop,° driven to pondering, found
Heaven with the tortoise and the hare;
Fox brush and sow ear top his grave
And mingling incantations on the air.

The black man, forlorn in the cellar,
10  Wanders in some mid-kingdom, dark, that lies,
Between his tambourine, stuck on the wall,
And, in Africa, a carcass quick with flies.

                              *1921*

---

**poem title:** In 1921, Crane worked in the storeroom of his father's Cleveland, Ohio confectionary, in company with a black porter, and the experience inspired "Black Tambourine." As he wrote in a letter to Gorham Munson, "the word 'mid-kingdom' is perhaps the key word to what ideas there are in it. The poem is a description and bundle of insinuations, suggestions bearing out the Negro's place somewhere between man and beast. That is why Aesop is brought in, etc.—the popular conception of Negro romance, the tambourine on the wall. The value of the poem is only, to me, in what a painter would call its 'tactile' quality,—an entirely aesthetic feature. A propagandist for either side of the Negro question could find anything he wanted to in it. My one declaration in it is that I find the Negro (in the popular, mind) sentimentally or brutally 'placed' in this midkingdom."
5 Aesop: traditional name of a Greek slave who was a writer of fables (sixth century BC). The fables use animals to make moral points.

## Chaplinesque°

We make our meek adjustments,
Contented with such random consolations
As the wind deposits
In slithered and too ample pockets.

5    For we can still love the world, who find
A famished kitten on the step, and know
Recesses for it from the fury of the street,
Or warm torn elbow coverts.

We will sidestep, and to the final smirk
10    Dally the doom of that inevitable thumb°
That slowly chafes its puckered index toward us,
Facing the dull squint with what innocence
And what surprise!

And yet these fine collapses are not lies
15    More than the pirouettes of any pliant cane;
Our obsequies° are, in a way, no enterprise.
We can evade you, and all else but the heart:°
What blame to us if the heart live on.

The game enforces smirks; but we have seen
20    The moon in lonely alleys make
A grail of laughter of an empty ash can,
And through all sound of gaiety and quest
Have heard a kitten in the wilderness.

1921

---

**poem title:** Crane admired the ability of comedian and film maker Charles Chaplin
(1889–1977) to make sentimentality "transcend itself into a new kind of tragedy, eccentric,
homely and yet brilliant." Inspired by Chaplin's film *The Kid* (1921), Crane explained to a
friend "Poetry, the human feelings, 'the kitten,' is so crowded out of the humdrum, rush-
ing, mechanical scramble of today that the man who would preserve them must duck and
camouflage for dear life to keep them or keep himself from annihilation. I have since
learned that I am by no means alone in seeing these things in the buffooneries of the
tragedian, Chaplin. . . . I have tried to express these 'social sympathies' in words corre-
sponding somewhat to the antics of the actor." To Gorham Munson, he wrote, "Chaplin
may be a sentimentalist, after all, but he carries the theme with such power and univer-
sal portent that sentimentality is made to transcend itself into a new kind of tragedy, ec-
centric, homely, and yet brilliant. . . . I feel that I have captured the arrested climaxes and
evasive victories of his gestures in words."
10 *thumb*: of a policeman.
16 *obsequies*: typically, funeral rites; but it also echoes "obsequious" and recalls Chaplin's
Little Tramp pretending to grovel and fawn before police and other figures of authority.
17 *heart*: Crane suggested this was a pun on his first name.

## Episode of Hands°

The unexpected interest made him flush.
Suddenly he seemed to forget the pain,—
Consented,—and held out
One finger from the others.

5     The gash was bleeding, and a shaft of sun
That glittered in and out among the wheels,
Fell lightly, warmly, down into the wound.

And as the fingers of the factory owner's son,
That knew a grip for books and tennis
10    As well as one for iron and leather,—
As his taut, spare fingers wound the gauze
Around the thick bed of the wound,
His own hands seemed to him
Like wings of butterflies
15    Flickering in sunlight over summer fields.

The knots and notches,—many in the wide
Deep hand that lay in his,—seemed beautiful.
They were like the marks of wild ponies' play,—
Bunches of new green breaking a hard turf.

20    And factory sounds and factory thoughts
Were banished from him by that larger, quieter hand
That lay in his with the sun upon it.
And as the bandage knot was tightened
The two men smiled into each other's eyes.

*1920*

## Porphyro in Akron°

### I

Greeting the dawn,
A shift of rubber workers presses down
South Main.
With the stubbornness of muddy water

---

**poem title:** Written in April 1920, after Crane had spent several months working in the warehouse of his father, a successful candy manufacturer, as a stock boy and handyman; though the boss's son, he did not begin at the top—thus allowing him a perspective on both figures in the poem.
**poem title:** Porphyro is the hero of John Keats' (1795–1821) poem "The Eve of Saint Agnes" (1820). Akron, a city in northeast Ohio located at the highest point on the Erie Canal between the Great Lakes and the Ohio River, was once known as "the rubber capital of the world"; its rubber factories expanded dramatically to supply tires for the growing automobile industry.

5        It dwindles at each cross-line
         Until you feel the weight of many cars
         North-bound, and East and West,
         Absorbing and conveying weariness,—
         Rumbling over the hills.

10       Akron, "high place",—
         A bunch of smoke-ridden hills
         Among rolling Ohio hills.

         The dark-skinned Greeks grin at each other
         In the streets and alleys.
15       The Greek grins and fights with the Swede,—
         And the Fjords and the Aegean are remembered.

         The plough, the sword,
         The trowel,—and the monkey wrench!
         O City, your axles need not the oil of song.
20       I will whisper words to myself
         And put them in my pockets.
         I will go and pitch quoits with old men
         In the dust of a road.

## II

         And some of them "will be Americans",
25       Using the latest ice-box and buying Fords;
         And others,—

                  I remember one Sunday noon,
         Harry and I, "the gentlemen",—seated around
         A table of raisin-jack and wine, our host
30       Setting down a glass and saying,—

                  "One month,—I go back rich.
         I ride black horse. . . . Have many sheep."
         And his wife, like a mountain, coming in
         With four tiny black-eyed girls around her
35       Twinkling like little Christmas trees.

         And some Sunday fiddlers,
         Roumanian business men,
         Played ragtime and dances before the door,
         And we overpayed them because we felt like it.

## III

40       Pull down the hotel counterpane
         And hitch yourself up to your book.

"Full on this casement shone the wintry moon,
And threw warm gules on Madeleine's fair breast,
As down she knelt for heaven's grace and boon . . ."°

45　　"Connais tu le pays . . .?"°

Your mother sang that in a stuffy parlour
One summer day in a little town
Where you had started to grow.
And you were outside as soon as you
50　　Could get away from the company
To find the only rose on the bush
In the front yard.......

But look up, Porphyro,—your toes
Are ridiculously tapping
55　　The spindles at the foot of the bed.

The stars are drowned in a slow rain,
And a hash of noises is slung up from the street.
You ought, really, to try to sleep,
60　　Even though, in this town, poetry's a
Bedroom occupation.

*1921*

## Voyages°

### I

Above the fresh ruffles of the surf
Bright striped urchins flay each other with sand.
They have contrived a conquest for shell shucks,
And their fingers crumble fragments of baked weed
5　　Gaily digging and scattering.

And in answer to their treble interjections
The sun beats lightning on the waves,
The waves fold thunder on the sand;
And could they hear me I would tell them:

10　　O brilliant kids, frisk with your dog,
Fondle your shells and sticks, bleached
By time and the elements; but there is a line
You must not cross nor ever trust beyond it
Spry cordage of your bodies to caresses
15　　Too lichen-faithful from too wide a breast.
The bottom of the sea is cruel.

*1923*

---

42–44 *"Full on this casement. . ."*: the first three lines of section XXV of Keats's "The Eve of St. Agnes."
45 *"Connais tu le pays. . ."*: (French) "Do you know the country . . . ?" from a French lullaby sung to Crane by his mother when he was a child: "One summer day in a little town/Where you had started to grow."
**poem title:** The first of a six-poem sequence, growing out of a passionate relationship with Emil Opffer, a seaman.

from

# The Bridge°

*From going to and fro in the earth,*
*and from walking up and down in it.*
THE BOOK OF JOB

Proem:
to
Brooklyn Bridge°

*How many dawns, chill from his rippling rest*
*The seagull's wings shall dip and pivot him,*
*Shedding white rings of tumult, building high*
*Over the chained bay waters Liberty—*

5      *Then, with inviolate curve, forsake our eyes*
*As apparitional as sails that cross*
*Some page of figures to be filed away;*
*—Till elevators drop us from our day . . .*

*I think of cinemas, panoramic sleights*
10     *With multitudes bent toward some flashing scene*
*Never disclosed, but hastened to again,*
*Foretold to other eyes on the same screen;*

*And Thee,° across the harbor, silver-paced*
*As though the sun took step of thee, yet left*
15     *Some motion ever unspent in thy stride,—*
*Implicitly thy freedom staying thee!*

---

**volume title:** Crane began writing *The Bridge* in 1923, published several of the poems from 1927–1928, and gathered the fifteen poems into an eight-part sequence for publication in 1930. After the proem (below) the sections are "Ave Maria," "Powhatan's Daughter," "Cutty Sark," "Cape Hatteras," "Three Songs," "Quaker Hill," "The Tunnel," and "Atlantis." In a 1926 letter to Waldo Frank he said that a bridge is "an act of faith besides being a communication." In a 1923 letter he wrote, "Very roughly, it concerns a mystical synthesis of 'America.' History and fact, location, etc., all have to be transfigured into abstract form that would almost function independently of its subject matter. The initial impulses of 'our people' will have to be gathered up toward the climax of the bridge, symbol of our constructive future, in which is included also our scientific hopes and achievements. . . . if I do succeed, such a waving of banners, such ascent of towers, such dancing, etc., will never before have been put down on paper! The form will be symphonic."
**poem title:** *Brooklyn Bridge:* a suspension bridge designed by John A. Roebling (1806–1869) and built from 1869 to 1883; it spans the East River from Brooklyn to Manhattan. It is the subject of many paintings and photographs.
13 *Thee:* Brooklyn Bridge.

*Out of some subway scuttle, cell or loft*
*A bedlamite° speeds to thy parapets,*
*Tilting there momently, shrill shirt ballooning,*
20     *A jest falls from the speechless caravan.*

*Down Wall,° from girder into street noon leaks,*
*A rip-tooth of the sky's acetylene;*
*All afternoon the cloud-flown derricks turn . . .*
*Thy cables breathe the North Atlantic still.*

25     *And obscure as that heaven of the Jews,°*
*Thy guerdon° . . . Accolade thou dost bestow*
*Of anonymity time cannot raise:*
*Vibrant reprieve and pardon thou dost show.*

*O harp and altar, of the fury fused,*
30     *(How could mere toil align thy choiring strings!)°*
*Terrific threshold of the prophet's pledge,*
*Prayer of pariah, and the lover's cry,—*

*Again the traffic lights that skim thy swift*
*Unfractioned idiom, immaculate sigh of stars,*
35     *Beading thy path—condense eternity:*
*And we have seen night lifted in thine arms.*

*Under thy shadow by the piers I waited;*
*Only in darkness is thy shadow clear.*
*The City's fiery parcels all undone,*
40     *Already snow submerges an iron year . . .*

*O Sleepless as the river under thee,*
*Vaulting the sea, the prairies' dreaming sod,*
*Unto us lowliest sometime sweep, descend*
*And of the curveship° lend a myth to God.*

1927

---

18 *bedlamite*: an insane person; after Bedlam, an insane asylum in London.
21 *Wall*: Wall Street, New York City's major financial district, site of the stock market, is
less than half a mile from the bridge's Manhattan side.
25 *the heaven of the Jews*: unlike Judaism, Christianity has developed elaborate theories
about and descriptions of heaven.
26 *guerdon*: reward.
30 *choiring strings*: the bridge's cables were spun on site from strands of steel wire.
44 *curveship*: Crane's coinage.

# Ave Maria°

*Venient annis, saecula seris,*
*Quibus Oceanus vincula rerum*
*Laxet et ingens pateat tellus*
*Tethysque novos detegat orbes*
*Nec sit terris ultima Tbule.*
              —SENECA°

Be with me, Luis de San Angel,° now—
Witness before the tides can wrest away                    *Columbus,*
The word I bring, O you who reined my suit                 *alone, gazing*
Into the Queen's great heart that doubtful day;            *toward Spain,*
5   For I have seen now what no perjured breath             *invokes the*
Of clown nor sage can riddle or gainsay;—                  *presence of*
To you, too, Juan Perez,° whose counsel fear               *two faithful*
And greed adjourned,—I bring you back Cathay!              *partisans of*
                                                           *his quest . . .*

Here waves climb into dusk on gleaming mail;
10  Invisible valves of the sea,—locks, tendons
Crested and creeping, troughing corridors
That fall back yawning to another plunge.
Slowly the sun's red caravel drops light
Once more behind us. . . . It is morning there—
15  O where our Indian emperies lie revealed,
Yet lost, all, let this keel one instant yield!

I thought of Genoa;° and this truth, now proved,
That made me exile in her streets, stood me
More absolute than ever—biding the moon
20  Till dawn should clear that dim frontier, first seen
—The Chan's° great continent. . . . Then faith, not fear
Nigh surged me witless. . . . Hearing the surf near—
I, wonder-breathing, kept the watch,—saw
The first palm chevron the first lighted hill.

---

**poem title:** (Spanish) "Hail Mary," traditional Roman Catholic reference to the Virgin Mary.

epigraph: *Seneca:* (4 B.C.–65 A.D.), Roman statesman and playwright. The epigraph is from his tragedy *Medea:* "There will come a time when the ocean will loosen the bonds of things, and the entire surface of the earth will be visible. Tethys will find new worlds, and Thule will no longer mark the farthest reaches of the world." Columbus's son claimed his father fulfilled this prophecy when he discovered the New World. Crane makes use of Columbus's journal of his first voyage to the New World, excerpted and retold in William Carlos Williams's *In the American Grain* (1925), but the issue in "Ave Maria" centers not on discovery (as in Williams) but on homecoming; the poem opens in Columbus's voice, with Columbus at mid-sea on the return voyage to Europe, anxious as to whether he will be able to deliver knowledge of a new world.

1 *Luis de San Angel:* one of Columbus's supporters at the Spanish Court, a Church tax collector.

7 *Juan Perez:* one of Columbus's supporters, a Franciscan who was confessor to Queen Isabella of Spain.

17 *Genoa:* birthplace of Columbus, a city in Italy.

21 *Chan:* Genghis Khan (1162–1227), Mongol conqueror whose empire reached from the Black Sea to the Pacific.

25      And lowered. And they came out to us crying,
        "The Great White Birds!" (O Madre Maria,° still
        One ship of these thou grantest safe returning;
        Assure us through thy mantle's ageless blue!)
        And record of more, floating in a casque,°
30      Was tumbled from us under bare poles scudding;
        And later hurricanes may claim more pawn. . . .
        For here between two worlds, another, harsh,

        This third, of water, tests the word; lo, here
        Bewilderment and mutiny heap whelming
35      Laughter, and shadow cuts sleep from the heart
        Almost as though the Moor's flung scimitar
        Found more than flesh to fathom in its fall.
        Yet under tempest-lash and surfeitings
        Some inmost sob, half-heard, dissuades the abyss,
40      Merges the wind in measure to the waves,

        Series on series, infinite,—till eyes
        Starved wide on blackened tides, accrete—enclose
        This turning rondure° whole, this crescent ring
        Sun-cusped and zoned with modulated fire
45      Like pearls that whisper through the Doge's° hands
        —Yet no delirium of jewels! O Fernando,°
        Take of that eastern shore, this western sea,
        Yet yield thy God's, thy Virgin's charity!

        —Rush down the plenitude, and you shall see
50      Isaiah° counting famine on this lee!

                        • • •

        An herb, a stray branch among salty teeth,
        The jellied weeds that drag the shore,—perhaps
        Tomorrow's moon will grant us Saltes Bar—
        Palos° again,—a land cleared of long war.
55      Some Angelus° environs the cordage° tree;
        Dark waters onward shake the dark prow free.

                        • • •

---

26 *O Madre Maria:* (Spanish) "Oh Mother Mary."
29 *casque:* helmet; R.W.B. Lewis suggests this is an attempted pun "which would fuse the
Admiral's helmet (as a symbol of authority) and the little barrel in which he dispatched
his all-important record [of his voyage]."
43 *turning rondure:* Cf. Whitman's call to the world ("O vast Rondure, swimming in space")
in "Passage to India," a poem that mentions Columbus enthusiastically.
45 *Doge:* chief magistrate in the former republics of Venice and Genoa.
46 *Fernando:* Ferdinand V (1452–1516) Spanish king who aided Columbus in his voyages
but turned against him after 1499.
50 *Isaiah:* in the Old Testament the prophet Isaiah warned against valuing wealth above
the spirit; the line echoes the punishment Isaiah prophesied.
54 *Palos:* the Spanish port that was Columbus's destination on his 1493 return voyage.
55 *Angelus Dominus:* Roman Catholic devotional song.
55 *cordage:* ship's rigging.

O Thou who sleepest on Thyself, apart
Like ocean athwart lanes of death and birth,
And all the eddying breath between dost search
60    Cruelly with love thy parable of man,—
Inquisitor! incognizable Word
Of Eden and the enchained Sepulchre,
Into thy steep savannahs, burning blue,
Utter to loneliness the sail is true.

65    Who grindest oar, and arguing the mast
Subscribest holocaust of ships, O Thou
Within whose primal scan consummately
The glistening seignories of Ganges swim;—
Who sendest greeting by the corposant,°
70    And Teneriffe's garnet°—flamed it in a cloud,
Urging through night our passage to the Chan;—
Te Deum laudamus,° for thy teeming span!

Of all that amplitude that time explores,
A needle in the sight, suspended north,—
75    Yielding by inference and discard, faith
And true appointment from the hidden shoal:
This disposition that thy night relates
From Moon to Saturn in one sapphire wheel:
The orbic wake of thy once whirling feet,
80    Elohim,° still I hear thy sounding heel!

White toil of heaven's cordons, mustering
In holy rings all sails charged to the far
Hushed gleaming fields and pendant seething wheat
Of knowledge,—round thy brows unhooded now
85    —The kindled Crown! acceded of the poles
And biassed by full sails, meridians reel
Thy purpose—still one shore beyond desire!
The sea's green crying towers a-sway, Beyond

And kingdoms
90                    naked in the
                              trembling heart—
            Te Deum laudamus
                        O Thou Hand of Fire

                                                        *1927*

---

69 *corposant*: Saint Elmo's fire, named after the patron saint of sailors—an eerie light, actually an electrical discharge, appearing on a ship's mast during a storm; Columbus reported seeing it in his journal.

70 *Teneriffe's garnet*: light from the Teneriffe Island volcano; Teneriffe is one of the Canary Islands of Spain in the Atlantic Ocean.

72 *Te Deum Laudamus*: from an ancient Latin hymn, "We praise thee, Lord," the Roman Catholic daily morning prayer.

80 *Elohim*: Hebrew name for God.

# The River°

Stick your patent name on a signboard
brother—all over—going west—young man      *. . . and past*
Tintex—Japalac—Certain-teed° Overalls ads      *the din and*
and lands sakes! under the new playbill ripped      *slogans of*
5    in the guaranteed corner—see Bert Williams° what?      *the year—*
Minstrels when you steal a chicken just
save me the wing for if it isn't
Erie° it ain't for miles around a
Mazda°—and the telegraphic night coming on Thomas

10    a Ediford°—and whistling down the tracks
a headlight rushing with the sound—can you
imagine—while an EXpress makes time like
SCIENCE—COMMERCE and the HOLYGHOST
15    RADIO ROARS IN EVERY HOME WE HAVE THE NORTHPOLE
WALLSTREET AND VIRGINBIRTH WITHOUT STONES OR
WIRES OR EVEN RUNning brooks° connecting ears
and no more sermons windows flashing roar
breathtaking—as you like it. . . eh?

So the 20th Century—so
20    whizzed the Limited°—roared by and left
three men, still hungry on the tracks, ploddingly
watching the tail lights wizen° and converge, slip-
ping gimleted and neatly out of sight.°

• • • • • •

---

**poem title:** The Mississippi River; "The River" is the third (of five) poems that make up "Powhatan's Daughter," the second section of *The Bridge*.

3 *Tintex—Japalac—Certain-teed*: brand names of a dye, a varnish, and overalls.

5 *Egbert Williams*: (1876–1922), a popular African American minstrel show performer.

8 *Erie*: town in northeast Pennsylvania; also, the Erie Railroad, whose New York-Chicago tracks Crane would have sometimes taken to his Cleveland home town.

9 *Mazda*: the electric light bulb, called by the trade name "Mazda" lamp.

10 *Thomas a Ediford*: combines references to Thomas A. Edison (1847–1931), who invented the incandescent lamp, to the automobile manufacturer Henry Ford (1863–1947), and to Saint Thomas à Beckett (1118?–1170), the archbishop of Canterbury, murdered after opposing King Henry II of England.

17 *brooks*: cf. "Books in the running brooks/Sermons in stones" (2.1.16–17), from Shakespeare's *As You Like It*.

20 *the Limited*: the Twentieth-Century Limited, an express train of the time.

22 *wizen*: wither, shrivel.

23 *sight*: (Crane's note), "The extravagance of the first twenty-three lines of this section is an intentional burlesque on the cultural confusion of the present—a great conglomeration of noises analogous to the strident impression of a fast express rushing by. The rhythm is jazz."

The last bear, shot drinking in the Dakotas
25    Loped under wires that span the mountain stream.
Keen instruments,° strung to a vast precision
Bind town to town and dream to ticking dream.        *to those*
But some men take their liquor slow—and count       *whose*
—Though they'll confess no rosary nor clue—         *addresses*
30    The river's minute by the far brook's year.          *are never near*
Under a world of whistles, wires and steam
Caboose-like they go ruminating through
Ohio, Indiana—blind baggage°—
To Cheyenne° tagging. . . Maybe Kalamazoo.

35    Time's rendings, time's blendings they construe
As final reckonings of fire and snow;
Strange bird-wit, like the elemental gist
Of unwalled winds they offer, singing low
*My Old Kentucky Home* and *Casey Jones,*
40    *Some Sunny Day.* I heard a road-gang chanting so.
And afterwards, who had a colt's eyes— one said,
"Jesus! Oh I remember watermelon days!" And sped
High in a cloud of merriment, recalled
"—And when my Aunt Sally Simpson smiled," he drawled—
"It was almost Louisiana, long ago."
"There's no place like Booneville° though, Buddy,"
One said, excising a last burr from his vest,
"—For early trouting." Then peering in the can,
"—But I kept on the tracks." Possessed, resigned,
50    He trod the fire down pensively and grinned,
Spreading dry shingles of a beard. . . .

Behind
My father's cannery works I used to see
Rail-squatters ranged in nomad raillery,
55    The ancient men—wifeless or runaway
Hobo-trekkers that forever search
An empire wilderness of freight and rails.
Each seemed a child, like me, on a loose perch,
Holding to childhood like some termless play.
60    John, Jake or Charley, hopping the slow freight
—Memphis to Tallahassee—riding the rods,°
Blind fists of nothing, humpty-dumpty clods.

---

26 *instruments:* telephone and telegraph.
33 *blind baggage:* hoboes lucky enough to ride blind baggage stood or crouched between
the coal tender of the engine and the first car in the train, usually a baggage or mail car
with its door locked. (I owe my knowledge of railroad jargon to Ed Brunner.)
34 *Cheyenne:* town in Wyoming; Kalamazoo: town in Michigan.
47 *Booneville:* town in Arkansas settled by Daniel Boone (1734–1820), American frontiers-
man and explorer.
61 *riding the rods:* hoboes sprawled their bodies across the brake rods that ran parallel to
the floors beneath freight cars.

Yet they touch something like a key° perhaps.
From pole to pole across the hills, the states
65 —They know a body under the wide rain; *but who have*
Youngsters with eyes like fjords, old reprobates *touched her,*
With racetrack jargon,—dotting immensity *knowing her*
They lurk across her, knowing her yonder breast *without name*
Snow-silvered, sumac-stained or smoky blue—
70 Is past the valley-sleepers,° south or west.
—As I have trod the rumorous midnights, too,

And past the circuit of the lamp's thin flame
(O Nights that brought me to her body bare!)
Have dreamed beyond the print that bound her name.
75 Trains sounding the long blizzards out—I heard
Wail into distances I knew were hers.
Papooses crying on the wind's long mane
Screamed redskin dynasties that fled the brain,
—Dead echoes!° But I knew her body there,
80 Time like a serpent down her shoulder, dark,
And space, an eaglet's° wing, laid on her hair.

Under the Ozarks, domed by Iron Mountain,°
The old gods of the rain lie wrapped in pools
Where eyeless fish curvet a sunken fountain *nor the*
85 And re-descend with corn from querulous crows. *myths of her*
Such pilferings make up their timeless eatage, *fathers. . .*
Propitiate them for their timber torn
By iron, iron—always the iron dealt cleavage!
They doze now, below axe and powder horn.

90 And Pullman° breakfasters glide glistening steel
From tunnel into field—iron strides the dew—
Straddles the hill, a dance of wheel on wheel.
You have a half-hour's wait at Siskiyou,°
Or stay the night and take the next train through.
95 Southward, near Cairo° passing, you can see

---

63 *key*: a pun, both the larger sense of a key as an "explanation"; also, messages and train orders were tapped out on a telegraph key.
70 *valley-sleepers*: a pun, the sleeping people a train passes in valleys at night; also, the wooden ties supporting rails were known as sleepers.
79 *Dead echoes*: acknowledging the Indian, railroads named engines (the New York Central System's "Mohawk" class 4–8–2) and built advertising slogans (the Milwaukee Road "Hiawathas" and the Sante Fe "Chief") to move across a landscape similarly strewn with traces of the Indian: Ohio, Wisconsin, Chicago, and so forth.
80–81 *Time/serpent and space/eaglet's wing*: serpent and eagle represented time and space in Aztec Indian mythology.
82 *Iron Mountain*: in southeastern Missouri; also, the St. Louis & Iron Mountain Railway.
90 *Pullman*: a railroad passenger car with convertible berths for sleeping, named after its inventor, G.P. Pullman (1831–1897).
93 *Siskiyou*: in northern California.
95 *Cairo*: city in southern Illinois, where the Ohio River merges with the Mississippi.

The Ohio merging,—borne down Tennessee;
And if it's summer and the sun's in dusk
Maybe the breeze will lift the River's musk
—As though the waters breathed that you might know
100  *Memphis Johnny, Steamboat Bill, Missouri Joe.*°
Oh, lean from the window, if the train slows down,
As though you touched hands with some ancient clown,
—A little while gaze absently below
And hum *Deep River*° with them while they go.

105  Yes, turn again and sniff once more—look see,
O Sheriff, Brakeman and Authority—
Hitch up your pants and crunch another quid,°
For you, too, feed the River timelessly.
And few evade full measure of their fate;
110  Always they smile out eerily what they seem.
I could believe he joked at heaven's gate—
Dan Midland°—jolted from the cold brake-beam.°

Down, down—born pioneers in time's despite,
Grimed tributaries to an ancient flow—
115  They win no frontier by their wayward plight,
But drift in stillness, as from Jordan's brow.°

You will not hear it as the sea; even stone
Is not more hushed by gravity. . . But slow,
As loth to take more tribute—sliding prone
120  Like one whose eyes were buried long ago

The River, spreading, flows—and spends your dream.
What are you, lost within this tideless spell?
You are your father's father, and the stream—
A liquid theme that floating niggers swell.

125  Damp tonnage and alluvial° march of days—
Nights turbid, vascular with silted shale
And roots surrendered down of moraine° clays:
The Mississippi drinks the farthest dale.

O quarrying passion, undertowed sunlight!
130  The basalt surface drags a jungle grace
Ochreous° and lynx-barred in lengthening might;
Patient! and you shall reach the biding place!

---

100 *Memphis Johnny, Steamboat Bill, Missouri Joe:* folk songs from the Mississippi River region.
104 *Deep River:* Mississippi River folk song.
107 *quid:* a wad of chewing tobacco.
112 *Dan Midland:* folklore hobo who died falling off a train.
112 *brake-beam:* part of a railroad car on which hobos often ride.
116 *Jordan's brow:* bank of the Jordan River in Palestine, symbolic of the boundary between Heaven and Earth, mentioned frequently in the Bible and in African American gospel music.
125 *alluvial:* depositional, sedimentary.
127 *moraine:* material deposited by a glacier.
131 *Ochreous:* an earthy clay containing iron ore, yellow or reddish brown in color.

Over De Soto's° bones the freighted floors
Throb past the City storied of three thrones.°
135    Down two more turns the Mississippi pours
(Anon tall ironsides° up from salt lagoons)

And flows within itself, heaps itself free.
All fades but one thin skyline 'round. . . Ahead
No embrace opens but the stinging sea;
140    The River lifts itself from its long bed,

Poised wholly on its dream, a mustard glow
Tortured with history, its one will—flow!
—The Passion° spreads in wide tongues, choked and slow,
Meeting the Gulf, hosannas silently below.

*1928*

## Cape Hatteras°

*The seas all crossed,*
*weathered the capes, the voyage done. . .*
      —WALT WHITMAN°

Imponderable the dinosaur
        sinks slow,
            the mammoth saurian
                ghoul, the eastern
5                        Cape . . .
While rises in the west the coastwise range,
            slowly the hushed land—
Combustion at the astral core—the dorsal change
Of energy—convulsive shift of sand . . .
10    But we, who round the capes, the promontories
Where strange tongues vary messages of surf
Below grey citadels, repeating to the stars
The ancient names—return home to our own
Hearths, there to eat an apple and recall
15    The songs that gypsies dealt us at Marseille°
Or how the priests walked—slowly through Bombay—°
Or to read you, Walt—knowing us in thrall

---

133 *De Soto*: Spanish explorer Hernando de Soto (1500–1542), buried in the Mississippi River by his men so that hostile Indians would not realize he was dead. Williams tells the story in *In the American Grain*.
134 *three thrones*: New Orleans, controlled at different times by the Spanish, French, and British.
136 *ironsides*: warships, not necessarily ironclad.
143 *the Passion*: Christ's agony and suffering during his crucifixion.
**poem title:** Cape Hatteras: peninsula at the southern end of Hatteras Island, off the eastern coast of North Carolina; site of Kitty Hawk, where the Wright brothers first flew their airplane. The flight at Kitty Hawk, and the subsequent development of aircraft, are, along with Walt Whitman, major points of reference in the poem.
epigraph: *Whitman*: the epigraph is from Whitman's "Passage to India."
15 *Marseille*: French city.
16 *Bombay*: city in India.

To that deep wonderment, our native clay
Whose depth of red, eternal flesh of Pocahontas°—
20 Those continental folded aeons, surcharged
With sweetness below derricks, chimneys, tunnels—
Is veined by all that time has really pledged us. . .
And from above, thin squeaks of radio static,
The captured fume of space foams in our ears—
25 What whisperings of far watches on the main
Relapsing into silence, while time clears
Our lenses, lifts a focus, resurrects
A periscope to glimpse what joys or pain
Our eyes can share or answer—then deflects
30 Us, shunting to a labyrinth submersed
Where each sees only his dim past reversed . . .

But that star-glistered salver of infinity,
The circle, blind crucible of endless space,
Is sluiced by motion,—subjugated never.
35 Adam and Adam's answer in the forest
Left Hesperus° mirrored in the lucid pool.
Now the eagle dominates our days, is jurist
Of the ambiguous cloud. We know the strident rule
Of wings imperious . . . Space, instantaneous,
40 Flickers a moment, consumes us in its smile:
A flash over the horizon—shifting gears—
And we have laughter, or more sudden tears.
Dream cancels dream in this new realm of fact
From which we wake into the dream of act;
45 Seeing himself an atom in a shroud—
Man hears himself an engine in a cloud!

"—Recorders ages hence"°—ah, syllables of faith!
Walt, tell me, Walt Whitman, if infinity
Be still the same as when you walked the beach
50 Near Paumanok°—your lone patrol—and heard the wraith
Through surf, its bird note° there a long time falling . . .
For you, the panoramas and this breed of towers,
Of you—the theme that's statured in the cliff,
O Saunterer on free ways still ahead!
55 Not this our empire yet, but labyrinth
Wherein your eyes, like the Great Navigator's° without ship,
Gleam from the great stones of each prison crypt

---

19 *Pocahontas*: an Indian princess who reportedly saved the life of Captain John Smith, leader of a group of American colonists. She married an Englishman, John Rolfe (1585–1622).
36 *Hesperus*: the planet Venus in its appearance as the evening star.
47 *"Recorders ages hence"*: a poem by Whitman.
50 *Paumanok*: the Native American name for Long Island, near New York City; Whitman used the name in his poem "Out of the Cradle Endlessly Rocking."
51 *bird note*: a reference to "Out of the Cradle Endlessly Rocking."
56 *Great Navigator*: Columbus.

Of canyoned traffic . . . Confronting the Exchange,
Surviving in a world of stocks,—they also range
60  Across the hills where second timber strays
Back over Connecticut farms, abandoned pastures,—
Sea eyes and tidal, undenying, bright with myth!

The nasal whine of power whips a new universe . . .
Where spouting pillars spoor the evening sky,
65  Under the looming stacks of the gigantic power house
Stars prick the eyes with sharp ammoniac proverbs,
New verities, new inklings in the velvet hummed
Of dynamos, where hearing's leash is strummed . . .
Power's script,—wound, bobbin-bound, refined—
70  Is stropped to the slap of belts on booming spools, spurred
Into the bulging bouillon, harnessed jelly of the stars.
Towards what? The forked crash of split thunder parts
Our hearing momentwise; but fast in whirling armatures,
As bright as frogs' eyes, giggling in the girth
75  Of steely gizzards—axle-bound, confined
In coiled precision, bunched in mutual glee
The bearings glint,—O murmurless and shined
In oilrinsed circles of blind ecstasy!

Stars scribble on our eyes the frosty sagas,
80  The gleaming cantos of unvanquished space . . .
O sinewy silver biplane, nudging the wind's withers!
There, from Kill Devils Hill at Kitty Hawk
Two brothers in their twinship left the dune;
Warping the gale, the Wright windwrestlers veered
85  Capeward, then blading the wind's flank, banked and spun
What ciphers risen from prophetic script,
What marathons new-set between the stars!
The soul, by naphtha fledged into new reaches
Already knows the closer clasp of Mars,—
90  New latitudes, unknotting, soon give place
To what fierce schedules, rife of doom apace!

Behold the dragon's covey—amphibian, ubiquitous
To hedge the seaboard, wrap the headland, ride
The blue's cloud-templed districts unto ether . . .
95  While Iliads glimmer° through eyes raised in pride
Hell's belt springs wider into heaven's plumed side.
O bright circumferences, heights employed to fly
War's fiery kennel masked in downy offings,—
This tournament of space, the threshed and chiselled height,
100  Is baited by marauding circles, bludgeon flail
Of rancorous grenades whose screaming petals carve us
Wounds that we wrap with theorems sharp as hail!

---

95 *Iliads glimmer:* in the eyes of those who believe the triumph of technology compares
to the deeds Homer chronicled.

Wheeled swiftly, wings emerge from larval-silver hangars.
Taut motors surge, space-gnawing, into flight;

105     Through sparkling visibility, outspread, unsleeping,
Wings clip the last peripheries of light . . .
Tellurian° wind-sleuths on dawn patrol,
Each plane a hurtling javelin of winged ordnance,
Bristle the heights above a screeching gale to hover;

110     Surely no eye that Sunward Escadrille° can cover!
There, meaningful, fledged as the Pleiades°
With razor sheen they zoom each rapid helix!
Up-chartered choristers of their own speeding
They, cavalcade on escapade, shear Cumulus—

115     Lay siege and hurdle Cirrus° down the skies!
While Cetus-like,° O thou Dirigible, enormous Lounger
Of pendulous auroral beaches,—satellited wide
By convoy planes, moonferrets that rejoin thee
On fleeing balconies as thou dost glide,

120     —Hast splintered space!

                   Low, shadowed of the Cape,
Regard the moving turrets! From grey decks
See scouting griffons° rise through gaseous crepe
Hung low . . . until a conch of thunder answers

125     Cloud-belfries, banging, while searchlights, like fencers,
Slit the sky's pancreas of foaming anthracite
Toward thee, O Corsair of the typhoon,—pilot, hear!
Thine eyes bicarbonated white by speed, O Skygak,° see
How from thy path above the levin's lance

130     Thou sowest doom thou hast nor time nor chance
To reckon—as thy stilly eyes partake
What alcohol of space . . ! Remember, Falcon-Ace,
Thou hast there in thy wrist a Sanskrit° charge
To conjugate infinity's dim marge°—

135     Anew. . !

            But first, here at this height receive
The benediction of the shell's deep, sure reprieve!
Lead-perforated fuselage, escutcheoned wings
Lift agonized quittance, tilting from the invisible brink

140     Now eagle-bright, now
                  quarry-hid, twist-
                         -ing, sink with

---

107 *Tellurian*: earthly.
110 *Escadrille*: (French) "squadron of airplanes."
111 *Pleiades*: a star cluster in the constellation Taurus.
115 *Cumulus and Cirrus*: cloud formations.
116 *Cetus*: whale, name of a constellation.
123 *griffons*: fabulous beasts with the head and wings of an eagle and the body of a lion; also a breed of dogs. Here, scouting aircraft.
128 *Skygak*: stunt pilot.
133 *Sanskrit*: an ancient language of India.
134 *marge*: margin.

Enormous repercussive list-
                                        -ings down
145 Giddily spiralled
                        gauntlets, upturned, unlooping
In guerrilla sleights, trapped in combustion gyr-
Ing, dance the curdled depth
                                down whizzing
150 Zodiacs,° dashed
                        (now nearing fast the Cape!)
                                down gravitation's
                                        vortex into crashed
.... dispersion ... into mashed and shapeless debris. ...
155 By Hatteras bunched the beached heap of high bravery!

· · · · · · ·

The stars have grooved our eyes with old persuasions
Of love and hatred, birth,—surcease of nations ...
But who has held the heights more sure than thou,
O Walt!—Ascensions of thee hover in me now
160 As thou at junctions elegiac, there, of speed
With vast eternity, dost wield the rebound seed!
The competent loam, the probable grass,—travail
Of tides awash the pedestal of Everest, fail
Not less than thou in pure impulse inbred
165 To answer deepest soundings! O, upward from the dead
Thou bringest tally, and a pact, new bound
Of living brotherhood!

                        Thou, there beyond—
Glacial sierras and the flight of ravens,
170 Hermetically past condor zones, through zenith havens
Past where the albatross has offered up
His last wing-pulse, and downcast as a cup
That's drained, is shivered back to earth—thy wand
Has beat a song, O Walt,—there and beyond!
175 And this, thine other hand, upon my heart
Is plummet ushered of those tears that start
What memories of vigils, bloody, by that Cape,—
Ghoul-mound of man's perversity at balk
And fraternal massacre! Thou, pallid there as chalk
180 Hast kept of wounds, O Mourner,° all that sum
That then from Appomattox° stretched to Somme!°

---

150 *Zodiacs:* arcs or circuits modeled on the paths of the planets.
180 *O Mourner:* alludes in part to Whitman's Civil War elegies.
181 *Appomattox:* Virginia town where the Confederacy surrendered to the Union in the American Civil War in 1865.
181 *Somme:* French river and surrounding area that was the site of costly, disastrous battles in World War I.

Cowslip° and shad-blow, flaked like tethered foam
Around bared teeth of stallions, bloomed that spring
When first I read thy lines, rife as the loam
185     Of prairies, yet like breakers cliffward leaping!
O, early following thee, I searched the hill
Blue-writ and odor-firm with violets, 'til
With June the mountain laurel broke through green
And filled the forest with what clustrous sheen!
190     Potomac lilies,—then the Pontiac rose,
And Klondike edelweiss of occult snows!
White banks of moonlight came descending valleys—
How speechful on oak-vizored palisades,
As vibrantly I following down Sequoia alleys
195     Heard thunder's eloquence through green arcades
Set trumpets breathing in each clump and grass tuft—'til
Gold autumn, captured, crowned the trembling hill!

*Panis Angelicus!* Eyes tranquil with the blaze
Of love's own diametric gaze, of love's amaze!
200     Not greatest, thou,—not first, nor last,—but near
And onward yielding past my utmost year.
Familiar, thou, as mendicants in public places;
Evasive—too—as dayspring's spreading arc to trace is:—
Our Meistersinger, thou set breath in steel;
205     And it was thou who on the boldest heel
Stood up and flung the span on even wing
Of that great Bridge, our Myth, whereof I sing!

Years of the Modern! Propulsions toward what capes?
But thou, *Panis Angelicus,* hast thou not seen
210     And passed that Barrier that none escapes—
But knows it leastwise as death-strife?—O, something green,
Beyond all sesames of science was thy choice
Wherewith to bind us throbbing with one voice,
New integers of Roman, Viking, Celt—
215     Thou, Vedic Caesar, to the greensward knelt!

And now, as launched in abysmal cupolas of space,
Toward endless terminals, Easters of speeding light—
Vast engines outward veering with seraphic grace
On clarion cylinders pass out of sight
220     To course that span of consciousness thou'st named
The Open Road—thy vision is reclaimed!
What heritage thou'st signalled to our hands!
And see! the rainbow's arch—how shimmeringly stands
Above the Cape's ghoul-mound, O joyous seer!
225     Recorders ages hence, yes, they shall hear
In their own veins uncancelled thy sure tread
And read thee by the aureole 'round thy head
Of pasture-shine, *Panis Angelicus!*
                                    yes, Walt,

---

182 *cowslip*: a primrose with fragrant yellow flowers; shad-blow: a shrub or tree with white
flowers and purplish fruit, also called shadbush or Juneberry.

230    Afoot again, and onward without halt,—
       Not soon, nor suddenly,—no, never to let go
              My hand
                     in yours,
                            Walt Whitman—
235                                 so—

                                                      *1930*

# Atlantis°

*Music is then the knowledge of that which
relates to love in harmony and system.*
                  —PLATO°

Through the bound cable strands, the arching path
Upward, veering with light, the flight of strings,—
Taut miles of shuttling moonlight syncopate
The whispered rush, telepathy of wires.
5      Up the index of night, granite and steel—
Transparent meshes—fleckless the gleaming staves—
Sibylline° voices flicker, waveringly stream
As though a god were issue of the strings. . . .

And through that cordage, threading with its call
10     One arc synoptic of all tides below—
Their labyrinthine mouths of history
Pouring reply as though all ships at sea
Complighted in one vibrant breath made cry,—
"Make thy love sure—to weave whose song we ply!"
15     —From black embankments, moveless soundings hailed,
So seven oceans answer from their dream.

And on, obliquely up bright carrier bars
New octaves trestle the twin monoliths
Beyond whose frosted capes the moon bequeaths
20     Two worlds of sleep (O arching strands of song!)—
Onward and up the crystal-flooded aisle
White tempest nets file upward, upward ring
With silver terraces the humming spars,
The loft of vision, palladium° helm of stars.

---

**poem title:** Atlantis was a mythical island in the Atlantic Ocean. Plato tells its story in the *Timaeus* and the *Critias*. In some versions of the story, Atlantis is overwhelmed by a flood sent in punishment for its inhabitants' sins. Some believed the island might rise up from the ocean floor again. "Atlantis" is the final section of *The Bridge*.
epigraph: *Plato:* the epigraph is from Plato's *Republic*.
7 *Sibylline:* oracular, ambiguous, and prophetic, like the ancient Sibyl's prophecies.
24 *palladium:* a natural metal, resembling platinum, that does not tarnish; also, a safeguard.

25    Sheerly the eyes, like seagulls stung with rime—
       Slit and propelled by glistening fins of light—
       Pick biting way up towering looms that press
       Sidelong with flight of blade on tendon blade
       —Tomorrows into yesteryear—and link
30    What cipher-script of time no traveller reads
       But who, through smoking pyres of love and death,
       Searches the timeless laugh of mythic spears.

       Like hails, farewells—up planet-sequined heights
       Some trillion whispering hammers glimmer Tyre:°
35    Serenely, sharply up the long anvil cry
       Of inchling aeons silence rivets Troy.°
       And you, aloft there—Jason!° hesting Shout!
       Still wrapping harness to the swarming air!
       Silvery the rushing wake, surpassing call,
40    Beams yelling Aeolus!° splintered in the straits!

       From gulfs unfolding, terrible of drums,
       Tall Vision-of-the-Voyage, tensely spare—
       Bridge, lifting night to cycloramic crest
       Of deepest day—O Choir, translating time
45    Into what multitudinous Verb the suns
       And synergy of waters ever fuse, recast
       In myriad syllables,—Psalm of Cathay!°
       O Love, thy white, pervasive Paradigm . . . !

       We left the haven hanging in the night—
50    Sheened harbor lanterns backward fled the keel.
       Pacific here at time's end, bearing corn,—
       Eyes stammer through the pangs of dust and steel.
       And still the circular, indubitable frieze
       Of heaven's meditation, yoking wave
55    To kneeling wave, one song devoutly binds—
       The vernal strophe chimes from deathless strings!

       O Thou steeled Cognizance° whose leap commits
       The agile precincts of the lark's return;
       Within whose lariat sweep encinctured sing
60    In single chrysalis the many twain,—
       Of stars Thou art the stitch and stallion glow
       And like an organ, Thou, with sound of doom—
       Sight, sound and flesh Thou leadest from time's realm
       As love strikes clear direction for the helm.

---

34 *Tyre*: an ancient Phoenician port city on the eastern Mediterranean Sea.
36 *Troy*: an ancient city that was also the legendary site of the Trojan war, in which it was captured and destroyed by the Greeks.
37 *Jason*: in Greek mythology, he led the Argonauts in the quest for the Golden Fleece, a magical ram's skin guarded by a dragon.
40 *Aeolus*: the Lord of the winds who appears in Homer's *Odyssey*.
47 *Cathay*: a medieval name for China.
57 *Cognizance*: perception, awareness.

65  Swift peal of secular light, intrinsic Myth
    Whose fell unshadow is death's utter wound,—
    O River-throated—iridescently upborne
    Through the bright drench and fabric of our veins;
    With white escarpments swinging into light,
70  Sustained in tears the cities are endowed
    And justified conclamant° with ripe fields
    Revolving through their harvests in sweet torment.

    Forever Deity's glittering Pledge, O Thou
    Whose canticle fresh chemistry assigns
75  To wrapt inception and beatitude,—
    Always through blinding cables, to our joy,
    Of thy white seizure springs the prophecy:
    Always through spiring cordage, pyramids
    Of silver sequel, Deity's young name
80  Kinetic of white choiring wings ... ascends.

    Migrations that must needs void memory,
    Inventions that cobblestone the heart,—
    Unspeakable Thou Bridge to Thee, O Love.
    Thy pardon for this history, whitest Flower,
85  O Answerer of all,—Anemone,°—
    Now while thy petals spend the suns about us, hold—
    (O Thou whose radiance doth inherit me)
    Atlantis,—hold thy floating singer late!

    So to thine Everpresence, beyond time,
90  Like spears ensanguined of one tolling star
    That bleeds infinity—the orphic° strings,
    Sidereal phalanxes, leap and converge:
    —One Song, one Bridge of Fire! Is it Cathay,
    Now pity steeps the grass and rainbows ring
95  The serpent with the eagle° in the leaves ... ?
    Whispers antiphonal in azure swing.

                                        *1930*


## The Mango Tree

    Let them return, saying you blush again for the great
    Great-grandmother. It's all like Christmas.
    When you sprouted Paradise a discard of chewing-gum
    took place. Up jug to musical, hanging jug just gay spiders

---

71 *conclamant*: derived from "conclamation," an outcry or shout by many voices together.
85 *Anemone*: a flowering plant; in Greek mythology, a white anemone sprouted from Aphrodite's tears when her lover Adonis was killed by a boar.
91 *orphic*: mystical, spell-binding, prophetic; from Orpheus, the Greek mythological figure whose voice and lyre moved the gods of the underworld.
95 *serpent with the eagle*: again, time and space in Aztec mythology; in the last line of "The Dance," the poem that follows "The River," the serpent and the eagle are a symbol of unity and Indian accessibility to eternal cycles.

5      yoked you first,—silking of shadows good underdrawers for
owls.

    First-plucked before and since the Flood, old hypno-
tisms wrench the golden boughs. Leaves spatter dawn from
emerald cloud-sprockets. Fat final prophets with lean ban-

10    dits crouch: and dusk is close

                        under your noon,
                        you Sun-heap, whose
ripe apple-lanterns gush history, recondite lightnings, irised.
                  O mister Señor
                  missus Miss
                  Mademoiselle
                  with baskets
                          Maggy, come on

                                      *1929*

# Allen Tate (1899–1979)

Tate was born John Orley Allen Tate in Winchester, Kentucky, and educated at Vanderbilt University. His roommate was Robert Penn Warren. After active participation in the Agrarian movement, which advocated traditional Southern values and a nonindustrial agricultural economy, Tate went on to write a number of elegiac poems regretting the loss of heroic ideals in the contemporary world. He was also active in introducing modernist verse to readers more accustomed to Victorian style; Vanderbilt's *The Fugitive*, a poetry-only bi-monthly magazine took on that project from 1921 to 1925, with Tate writing under the name "Henry Feathertop" in its early issues. Tate also wanted literature to be uncompromisingly serious, capable of taking on large philosophical issues, with its sobriety only broken with touches of the driest irony.

Much of his program is evident in "Ode to the Confederate Dead," its first version completed when Tate was only 29. Tate sought to evoke a certain emptiness, a lack of direction, that he associated with modernism's technological advances and with the social disruption caused by shifts in authority. He was sympathetic to T.S. Eliot's tone, but felt poetry retained vestiges of moral authority if the poet could but evoke them. The "Ode" dramatizes this fundamental conflict, so that from passage to passage we are never quite sure whether past greatness will be fully submerged or will re-emerge to press back upon the present moment.

## Ode to the Confederate Dead

Row after row with strict impunity
The headstones yield their names to the element,
The wind whirrs without recollection;
In the riven troughs the splayed leaves
5    Pile up, of nature the casual sacrament
To the seasonal eternity of death;
Then driven by the fierce scrutiny
Of heaven to their election in the vast breath,
They sough the rumour of mortality.

10    Autumn is desolation in the plot
Of a thousand acres where these memories grow
From the inexhaustible bodies that are not
Dead, but feed the grass row after rich row.
Think of the autumns that have come and gone!—
15    Ambitious November with the humors of the year,

With a particular zeal for every slab,
Staining the uncomfortable angels that rot
On the slabs, a wing chipped here, an arm there:
The brute curiosity of an angel's stare
20     Turns you, like them, to stone,
Transforms the heaving air
Till plunged to a heavier world below
You shift your sea-space blindly
Heaving, turning like the blind crab.

25          Dazed by the wind, only the wind
The leaves flying, plunge

You know who have waited by the wall
The twilight certainty of an animal,
Those midnight restitutions of the blood
30     You know—the immitigable pines, the smoky frieze
Of the sky, the sudden call: you know the rage,
The cold pool left by the mounting flood,
Of muted Zeno and Parmenides.°
You who have waited for the angry resolution
35     Of those desires that should be yours tomorrow,
You know the unimportant shrift of death
And praise the vision
And praise the arrogant circumstance
Of those who fall
40     Rank upon rank, hurried beyond decision—
Here by the sagging gate, stopped by the wall.

Seeing, seeing only the leaves
Flying, plunge and expire

Turn your eyes to the immoderate past,
45     Turn to the inscrutable infantry rising
Demons out of the earth—they will not last.
Stonewall, Stonewall,° and the sunken fields of hemp,
Shiloh, Antietam, Malvern Hill, Bull Run.°
Lost in that orient of the thick-and-fast
50     You will curse the setting sun.

---

33 *Parmenides*: (c.515–c.444 BC), the most influential of the Presocratic philosophers and
the first philosopher to insist on distinguishing between appearance and reality. Zeno of
Elea (c.490–c.420 BC) was a disciple of Parmenides who became famous for articulating
a series of paradoxes. Both believed the real universe was stable and unchanging; it is an
illusory world that is changing and unknowable.
47 *Stonewall*: Thomas Jonathan "Stonewall" Jackson (1824–1863) was a popular and suc-
cessful Confederate general in the American Civil War. He was accidentally killed by his
own troops at Chancellorsville.
48 *Shiloh . . . Bull Run*: early battles in the American Civil War (1861–1865). Shiloh (April
1862) was a Confederate defeat. Antietam (September 1862), the bloodiest battle of the
war, was inconclusive but a strategic setback for the South, as was Malvern Hill (July
1862). But both battles of Bull Run (1861 and 1862) were notable Confederate victories.

    Cursing only the leaves crying
    Like an old man in a storm

  You hear the shout, the crazy hemlocks point
  With troubled fingers to the silence which
55    Smothers you, a mummy, in time.

                    The hound bitch
  Toothless and dying, in a musty cellar
  Hears the wind only.

             Now that the salt of their blood
  Stiffens the saltier oblivion of the sea,
60    Seals the malignant purity of the flood,
  What shall we who count our days and bow
  Our heads with a commemorial woe
  In the ribboned coats of grim felicity,
  What shall we say of the bones, unclean,
65    Whose verdurous anonymity will grow?
  The ragged arms, the ragged heads and eyes
  Lost in these acres of the insane green?
  The gray lean spiders come, they come and go;
  In a tangle of willows without light
70    The singular screech-owl's tight
  Invisible lyric seeds the mind
  With the furious murmur of their chivalry.

    We shall say only the leaves
    Flying, plunge and expire

75    We shall say only the leaves whispering
  In the improbable mist of nightfall
  That flies on multiple wing;
  Night is the beginning and the end
  And in between the ends of distraction
80    Waits mute speculation, the patient curse
  That stones the eyes, or like the jaguar leaps
  For his own image in a jungle pool, his victim.
  What shall we say who have knowledge
  Carried to the heart? Shall we take the act
85    To the grave? Shall we, more hopeful, set up the grave
  In the house? The ravenous grave?

                     Leave now
  The shut gate and the decomposing wall:
  The gentle serpent, green in the mulberry bush,
90    Riots with his tongue through the hush—
  Sentinel of the grave who counts us all!

                             *1927/1937*

# Melvin B. Tolson (1900?–1966)

Tolson was born in Moberly, Missouri, the son of a Methodist Episcopalian minister. The family moved occasionally, as the father was assigned to new congregations. Tolson wrote poems as a child, and at the age of 14, he published one in an Iowa newspaper about the sinking of the *Titanic*, but it was not until after graduating from Lincoln University and teaching at Wiley College in Texas for most of the 1920s that he became a serious poet. While at Columbia University in 1931–1932 earning a graduate degree, he began to write poems that he published in some of the notable journals of the period. "Dark Symphony" won a prize in 1939.

Tolson's greatest achievement, however, may be *The Libretto for the Republic of Liberia* (1953), a late and still neglected triumph of literary modernism, written when Tolson was teaching at Langston University in Oklahoma. In 1947, Tolson had been named poet laureate of Liberia, a nation on the West African coast, by its president William S.V. Tubman, the son of Harriet Tubman of Underground Railroad fame. Liberia had been founded in 1822 as part of a long-running and controversial debate about whether to establish an African homeland for former slaves. By the time Tolson came to write his poem, however, the question he faced was rather different. What symbolic and cultural meaning did Liberia's founding now have for blacks here and across the world? In seeking an answer, reflecting on the history of slavery and writing while the memory of World War II and of the evil of European fascism was still fresh, Tolson came to major conclusions about the shape of Western civilization.

The dense, allusive poem was the result. It was originally published with jacket commentary designed to provide readers with necessary background and to gloss some of the abbreviated references in the poem:

> For the Liberian Centennial and International Exposition, two Afro-American artists received commissions: Duke Ellington, as composer, and M. B. Tolson, as poet laureate. Mr. Ellington's *Liberian Suite* had a successful premier in New York. . . . This odyssey [Tolson's *Libretto*] is rooted in the Liberian mentality as fact and symbol. Two hundred years after the *Mayflower* anchored off Plymouth Rock ["the unhinged gate" of Tolson's *Rendezvous with America* (1944)], the black Pilgrim Fathers sailed aboard the *Elizabeth* from America to West Africa in search of freedom. The idea had its inception three years before the Declaration of Independence, when Dr. Samuel Hopkins and Ezra Stiles, president of Yale College, suggested the colonization of freed persons of color.
>
> In January 1817, the American Colonization Society was organized with U.S. Supreme Court Justice Bushrod Washington, a nephew of George Washington, as president; Robert Finley, a former president of

the University of Georgia, and Francis Scott Key, author of "The Star-Spangled Banner," as vice-presidents; and Elijah Caldwell, clerk of the United States Supreme Court, as secretary.

Later, driven to Providence Island by hostile natives, the emigrants were saved by the courage and sagacity of Elijah Johnson, a black veteran of America's War of 1812; John Mill, a mulatto English trader along the West African Coast; and Jehudi Ashmun, a white agent of the Colonization Society.

On February 20, 1824, in the Supreme Court chamber of the Capitol Building at Washington, General Robert Harper of Maryland said to the Society: "I have thought of a name that is different, short, familiar and expresses the true object and nature of the establishment. I propose to call the colony *Liberia*." The principal city was named *Monrovia* in President Monroe's honor; and on July 28, 1847, a convention issued a document declaring the Commonwealth a free and independent nation, designated the *Republic of Liberia*. Joseph Jenkins Robert, a Negro born in Virginia, became the Republic's first president.

At the suggestion of poet Karl Shapiro, Tolson also provided a detailed set of notes to accompany the poem, but in the tradition of Spenser's *Shepheardes Calendar* (1579) and Eliot's *The Waste Land* (1922), the notes leave many references unidentified and constitute in part additions to the poem or directions for further study that raise further problems of interpretation. Since Tolson wrote sections of the *Libretto* in the form of parallel phrases, it is possible to miss some allusions and still recognize the poem's overall structure and argument. But the poem is full of intricately worded and very specific cultural and political judgments, many of which are at once strongly felt and wittily inventive. Without knowing Tolson's literary and historical sources, much of this is simply unavailable to the reader. We present here, for the first time, a fully annotated edition of the *Libretto* prepared by Edward Brunner.

## Dark Symphony

### I

*Allegro Moderato*°

Black Crispus Attucks° taught
        Us how to die
Before white Patrick Henry's° bugle breath
Uttered the vertical
5                Transmitting cry:
"Yea, give me liberty or give me death."

---

*Allegro Moderato*: (Italian, "moderately lively tempo"): a direction for musical performance; one direction precedes each of the poem's six sections.

1 *Attucks*: Crispus Attucks, escaped slave and American patriot, was one of five people killed by the British at the March 5, 1770, Boston Massacre, at an informal demonstration that partly led up to America's Revolutionary War. Ironically, then, one of the first killed in the struggle for independence was a man whose personal rights were not secure and would not be secured by independence. A statue honoring Attucks by Augustus Saint-Gaudens (1848–1907) was unveiled on Boston Commons in 1888.

3 *Patrick Henry*: (1736–1799), American patriot noted for his dramatic oratory in support of the Revolutionary War, including the 1775 declaration quoted three lines below; governor of Virginia.

Waifs of the auction block,
                    Men black and strong
The juggernauts of despotism withstood,
10          Loin-girt with faith that worms
                    Equate the wrong
And dust is purged to create brotherhood.

No Banquo's° ghost can rise
                    Against us now,
15          Aver we hobnailed Man beneath the brute,
Squeezed down the thorns of greed
                    On Labor's brow,
Garroted lands and carted off the loot.°

II

*Lento Grave°*

The centuries-old pathos in our voices
20          Saddens the great white world,
And the wizardry of our dusky rhythms
Conjures up shadow-shapes of ante-bellum years:

Black slaves singing *One More River to Cross*
In the torture tombs of slave-ships,
25          Black slaves singing *Steal Away to Jesus*
In jungle swamps,
Black slaves singing *The Crucifixion*
In slave-pens at midnight,
Black slaves singing *Swing Low, Sweet Chariot*
30          In cabins of death,
Black slaves singing *Go Down, Moses*
In the canebrakes of the Southern Pharaohs.

III

*Andante Sostenuto°*

They tell us to forget
The Golgotha° we tread . . .
35          We who are scourged with hate,
A price upon our head.
They who have shackled us
Require of us a song,
They who have wasted us
40          Bid us condone the wrong.

---

13 *Banquo*: a murdered lord in Shakespeare's *Macbeth*; his ghost haunts the title character.
18 *loot*: the last lines of the first section refer to the exploitation of American labor, which fueled the labor movement, and to American imperialist projects abroad, such as the conquest of the Philippines.
Lento Grave: From the Italian, "slow and solemn tempo."
Andante Sostenuto: From the Italian, "moderately slow and sustained tempo."
34 *Golgotha*: "Place of a Skull" (Hebrew): Calvary, the site of Jesus' crucifixion.

They tell us to forget
Democracy is spurned.
They tell us to forget
The Bill of Rights° is burned.
45     Three hundred years we slaved,
We slave and suffer yet:
Though flesh and bone rebel,
They tell us to forget!

Oh, how can we forget
50     Our human rights denied?
Oh, how can we forget
Our manhood crucified?
When Justice is profaned
And plea with curse is met,
55     When Freedom's gates are barred,
Oh, how can we forget?

**IV**

*Tempo Primo°*

The New Negro° strides upon the continent
In seven-league boots . . .
The New Negro
60     Who sprang from the vigor-stout loins
Of Nat Turner, gallows-martyr for Freedom,
Of Joseph Cinquez,° Black Moses of the Amistad Mutiny,
Of Frederick Douglass, oracle of the Catholic Man,
Of Sojourner Truth, eye and ear of Lincoln's legions,
65     Of Harriet Tubman, Saint Bernard° of the Underground Railroad.

---

44 *Bill of Rights*: the first ten amendments to the U.S. Constitution, adopted in 1791 and guaranteeing freedom of speech, freedom of religion, the press, and assembly, as well as legal procedure; designed to protect the individual against the power of the state.
Tempo Primo: From the Italian, "In the tempo of the first movement."
57 *New Negro*: since the 1890s, a term designed to signal a generation's determination to secure its rights and challenge stereotypes; linked with a new assertiveness and cultural pride in the 1920s during the Harlem Renaissance.
61–65 *Turner/Cinquez/Douglass/Truth/Tubman*: Nat Turner (1800–1831) led an 1831 slave revolt in Virginia; Joseph Cinquez led an 1839 mutiny aboard the slave ship *Amistad* (see Robert Hayden's poem "Middle Passage"); Frederick Douglass (1817–1895), African American writer and abolitionist, whose autobiography was one of the most influential books of its era; Sojourner Truth (c. 1797–1883), itinerant African American preacher, abolitionist, and feminist; Harriet Tubman: (1820?–1913), an escaped slave who helped others escape to the North through the Underground Railroad.
65 *Saint Bernard*: a double reference; a Saint Bernard is a species of dog, known for rescuing snowbound travelers in the far North; Tolson is thus first of all, in a familiarizing gesture typical of his approach to famous people, saying that Tubman was like the guide dog of the Underground Railroad, selflessly venturing out to help others; but Saint Bernard of Clairvaux (1090–1153) was also a monastic reformer who rallied support for the Second Crusade, a reference that provides a compensatory elevation.

The New Negro
Breaks the icons of his detractors,
Wipes out the conspiracy of silence,
Speaks to *his* America:
70          "My history-moulding ancestors
Planted the first crops of wheat on these shores,
Built ships to conquer the seven seas,
Erected the Cotton Empire,
Flung railroads across a hemisphere,
75          Disemboweled the earth's iron and coal,
Tunneled the mountains and bridged rivers,
Harvested the grain and hewed forests,
Sentineled the Thirteen Colonies,
Unfurled Old Glory at the North Pole,°
80          Fought a hundred battles for the Republic."

The New Negro:
His giant hands fling murals upon high chambers,
His drama teaches a world to laugh and weep,
His music leads continents captive,
85          His voice thunders the Brotherhood of Labor,
His science creates seven wonders,
His Republic of Letters challenges the Negro-baiters.

The New Negro,
Hard-muscled, Fascist-hating,° Democracy-ensouled,
90          Strides in seven-league boots
Along the Highway of Today
Toward the Promised Land of Tomorrow!

V

*Larghetto°*

None in the Land can say
To us black men Today:
95          You send the tractors on their bloody path,
And create Okies° for The *Grapes of Wrath.°*
You breed the slum that breeds a *Native Son*
To damn the good earth Pilgrim Fathers won.

---

79 *North Pole*: Matthew Henson (1866–1955), African American co-discoverer, with Robert Peary, of the North Pole; Old Glory: the American flag.
89 *Fascist-hating*: the nationalistic and authoritarian fascist movement was founded by Benito Mussolini in Italy in 1921, but it reached the peak of its influence in the Spanish Civil War and in Germany from 1930–1945. It involves the overthrow of all democratic institutions, suppression of trade unions and political dissent, a belligerent foreign policy, theories of national and racial superiority, and subservience to a dictatorial leader.
Larghetto: From the Italian, "somewhat slow tempo."
96 *Okies*: migrant farm workers, especially from ruined farms in the Oklahoma Dust Bowl during the 1930s Great Depression.
96 *The Grapes of Wrath*: John Steinbeck's (1902–1968) novel (1939) about an Oklahoma family's search for work in 1930s California; *Native Son*: Richard Wright's (1908–1960) novel (1940) about Bigger Thomas's struggle for life in a Chicago ghetto.

None in the Land can say
100      To us black men Today:
You dupe the poor with rags-to-riches tales,
And leave the workers empty dinner pails.
You stuff the ballot box, and honest men
Are muzzled by your demagogic din.

105      None in the Land can say
To us black men Today:
You smash stock markets with your coined blitzkriegs,°
And make a hundred million guinea pigs.
You counterfeit our Christianity,
110      And bring contempt upon Democracy.

None in the Land can say
To us black men Today:
You prowl when citizens are fast asleep,
And hatch Fifth Column° plots to blast the deep
115      Foundations of the State and leave the Land
A vast Sahara with a Fascist brand.

### VI

*Tempo di Marcia°*

Out of abysses of Illiteracy,
Through labyrinths of Lies,
Across waste lands of Disease . . .
120      We advance!

Out of dead-ends of Poverty,
Through wildernesses of Superstition,
Across barricades of Jim Crowism° . . .
We advance!

125      With the Peoples of the World° . . .
We advance!

*1944*

---

107 *blitzkreigs:* (German, "lightning wars"), Nazi World War II strategy of massive sudden
military campaigns.
114 *Fifth Column:* the term originated in 1936 during the Spanish Civil War, when fascist
general Francisco Franco (1892–1975) was leading four columns of troops toward the be-
sieged Spanish capital, Madrid. He bragged (falsely, as it happened) that a fifth column
of supporters within the city would rise up to support him. Now broadly applied to trai-
tors in sympathy with a national enemy.
Tempo di Marcia: From the Italian, "In March Tempo."
124 *Jim Crowism:* the term "Jim Crow" refers to legal efforts to segregate African Ameri-
cans from whites and restrict their social and economic opportunities. It dates back to the
1830s, but became a major practice in the American South after Reconstruction ended in
1877; further encouraged when the U.S. Supreme Court ruled in *Plessy v. Ferguson* (1896)
that "separate but equal" segregation was legal.
125 *Peoples of the World:* rhetoric of the antifascist popular front of the 1930s, now broadly
associated with international working class solidarity.

# Libretto for the Republic of Liberia

DO°

*Liberia?*
No micro-footnote in a bunioned book
Homed by a pedant
With a gelded look:°
5                    You are
The ladder of survival dawn men saw
In the quicksilver sparrow that slips
The eagle's claw!°


*Liberia?*
10          No side-show barker's bio-accident,°
No corpse of a soul's errand°
To the Dark Continent:°
You are
The lightning rod of Europe, Canaan's key,°

---

**poem title:** *Libretto*: (literally, "small book") The words of an opera or other work to be performed by singing; also, the book that contains those words. *Republic*: a nation where voting processes determine power. Liberia on the northwest African coast has been a republic since 1847. Note: Significant help in translating passages and identifying references came from Jay Bochner, Clinton Brand, Catalina Brand-Missas, Robert Howard, Cary Nelson, Arkady Plotnitsky, Mrinalini Sinha and Clarisse Zimra, and the work of previous scholars: Jon Stanton Woodson, Robert Farnsworth, Joy Flasch, Mariann Russell and Michael Bérubé.

*Do*: The first note in the 7-note sequence of the familiar (and so-called Western) diatonic scale. The opening poem is a set of contrasts resembling a call-and-response pattern in which we learn first what Liberia is not (in the second to fourth lines of each stanza) then learn what it is (in the sixth through eighth lines). This principle of apposition, in which Tolson makes a point then restates it from another angle, will continue as a helpful guide through esoteric passages.

3 *Gelded look*: Jon Stanton Woodson suggests Tolson's opening is a sharp rebuttal to "Heritage" (1925) by Countee Cullen (1903–1946): *"What is Africa to me?"* (line 10) and "Africa? A book one thumbs / Listlessly, till slumber comes" (lines 31–32).

8 *eagle's claw*: (Tolson's Note) "Cf. [John] Dryden [(1631–1700)], *All for Love*, II, i. ' . . . upon my eagle's wings / I bore this wren, till I was tired of soaring / and now he mounts above me.'" This passage from Dryden's rewrite of Shakespeare's *Antony and Cleopatra*, refers to a fable found in the Brothers Grimm. The birds agree to a contest: whoever can fly highest will be king. The eagle's strength raises him above all others, but just as victory seems assured, a shrewd wren who had been clinging to the eagle's feathers darts out and, fresh and rested, reaches heaven and claims victory—intellect triumphing over brute strength. The eagle is sometimes considered an emblem of America.

10 *bio-accident*: a carnival side-show specialized in peculiar aberrations that represented evolutionary errors.

11 *soul's errand*: (Tolson's Note) "Cf. [Sir Walter] Raleigh [(1552?–1618)], 'The Soul's Errand.'" Raleigh defines the soul's errand as "thankless" in "The Lie": "Go, soul, the body's guest, / Upon a thankless arrant [i.e., errand]" (lines 1–2).

12 *Dark Continent*: Africa, as named by non-Africans.

14 *lightning-rod . . . Canaan's key*: A complicated figure in which "Canaan" is at once the Promised Land of the Israelites which will "unlock" Europe, at the same time as it recalls the innovative experiment of Benjamin Franklin (1706–1790) with a kite and electricity. "Canaan" is also the son of Ham, Noah's second son, and traditionally the ancestor of Africans.

15      The rope across the abyss,°
        *Mehr licht°* for the Africa-To-Be!


                    *Liberia?*
        No haply° black man's X°
        Fixed to a Magna Charta° without a magic-square°
20      By Helon's leprous hand,° to haunt and vex:
                    You are
        The Orient of Colors everywhere,
        The oasis of Tahoua,° the salt bar of Harrar,°
        To trekkers in saharas, in sierras,° with Despair!


25                  *Liberia?*
        No oil-boiled Barabas,°
        No Darwin's bulldog° for ermined flesh,°

---

15 *rope across the abyss.* (Tolson's Note) "V. [Friedrich] Neitzsche [(1844–1900)], *Thus Spake Zarathustra.*" Nietzsche's prophet lectured: "Man is a rope, fastened between animal and Superman—a rope over an abyss. . . . What is great in man is that he is a bridge and not a goal" ("Zarathustra's Prologue," section 4, trans. R. J. Hollingdale).

16 *Mehr licht:* (German) "More light." The death-bed words of Johann Wolfgang von Goethe (1749–1832).

18 *No haply black man:* (Tolson's Note) "Cf. Shakespeare, *Othello*, III, iii: 'Haply, for I am black . . . '" [ll. 262–263]. The speech occurs after Iago has infected Othello with doubts about Desdemona's love for him, and Othello continues: "Haply for [i.e., perhaps because] I am black / And have not those soft parts of conversation / That chamberers [i.e., courtiers, or perhaps seducers] have . . . " The "haply black man" is the one who accepts as binding the judgment of others based on skin color.

18 *X:* Mark made in place of a signature by those not taught to write.

19 *Magna Charta:* originally the "great charter" of English liberties, forced from King John by English barons in 1215; now, any set of laws guaranteeing rights.

19 *Magic-Square:* (Tolson's note) "A symbol of equality. The diagram consists of a number of small squares each containing a number. The numbers are so arranged that the sum of those in each of the various rows is the same. Cf. [James] Thomson [(1834–1832)], *The City of Dreadful Night*, XXI, 1061." As his poem's climax, Thomson pictures a gigantic statue modeled on an Albrecht Dürer (1471–1528) engraving entitled "Melancholia"; she is surrounded by numerous symbols like the magic-square, but these remain mere images, never actualized. The statue represents "The sense that every struggle brings defeat / Because Fate holds no prize to crown success; / That all the oracles are dumb or cheat / Because they have no secret to express" (ll. 1103–1106).

20 *leprous hand:* (Tolson's Note) "Cf. [Nathaniel Parker] Willis [(1806–1867)], 'The Leper.'" Willis' 156-line narrative poem from 1844 portrays a handsome nobleman (Helon) stricken by leprosy and driven to suicide until healed by Christ.

23 *Tahoua:* town in southwest Nigeria.

23 *Harrar:* Province of eastern Ethiopia, also spelled "Harar" and "Harer." After abandoning the writing of poetry at 19, the visionary poet Arthur Rimbaud (1854–1891) moved to this region. He also figures in notes to lines 403, 422, 554, and 726.

24 *sierras:* range of hills with saw-like ridges; as opposite from "saharas" as an oasis from a salt bar.

26 *Barabas:* the over-reaching Machievellian villain in *The Jew of Malta* (1589) by Christopher Marlowe (1564–1593).

27 *Darwin's bulldog:* Charles Darwin (1800–1882), naturalist and author of *The Origin of Species* (1844).

27 *ermined flesh:* the fur of the ermine, a small weasel, is prized for ornamental purposes.

No braggart Lamech,° no bema's Ananias:°
You are
30      *Libertas*° flayed and naked by the road
To Jericho,° for a people's five score years°
Of bones for manna,° for balm an alien goad!°

*Liberia?*
No pimple on the chin of Africa,
35      No brass-lipped cicerone° of Big Top° democracy,
No lamb to tame a lion with a baa:°
You are
Black Lazarus° risen from the White Man's grave,°
Without a road to Downing Street,°
40      Without a hemidemisemiquaver° in an Oxford stave!°

---

28 *No braggart Lamech*: Last of Cain's descendants, Lamech chose not to put his trust in God but in the weapons invented by his sons that were designed to enhance his powers (see Genesis 4:18–24).

28 *Ananias*: probably the high priest who, from his "bema" or rostrum from which orators spoke, illegally ordered St. Paul to be struck when brought before him as a prisoner (see Acts 24).

30 *Libertas*: Liberty (Latin). (Tolson's Note) "The motto of Liberia: 'The love of liberty brought us here.'"

31 *Jericho*: A city in the Jordan Valley near the Dead Sea, taken from the Canaanites by Moses' successor, Joshua.

31 *five score years*: one hundred years, the century that has elapsed since the founding of Liberia in 1847.

32 *manna*: food that miraculously appears and sustains the Israelites as they search for the promised land.

32 *balm . . . goad*: (Tolson's Note) "Cf. [Thomas] Carlyle [(1795–1881)]: 'God has put into every white man's hand a whip to flog a black man.'" It is unusual for Carlyle to employ a term as neutral as "black man"; in essays such as "Shooting Niagara" and "The Nigger Question" he prefers more racist epithets, including "Quashee" (a derivation from the German *Quassi* [South American Negro]).

35 *cicerone*: a guide.

35 *Big Top*: main tent in a circus; also, slang for maximum security prison.

36 *No lamb . . . baa*: "The wolf also shall dwell with the lamb, and the leopard shall lie down with the kid; and the calf and the young lion and the fatling together; and a little child shall lead them" (Isaiah 11:6).

38 *Lazarus*: Raised from the dead by Christ (John 11:43–44).

38 *White man's grave*: (Tolson's Note) "Cf. The tavern scenes in [Thomas] Boulton's comic opera, 'The Sailor's Farewell [or, the Guinea Outfit].'" A subplot in this 1678 play centers on deceptions of Captain Sharp as he coaxes inexperienced laborers to join his crew and sail to West Africa: "In Guinea you have everything you could wish for. If you want money, Guinea's the place of its residence, for where do we get gold at but the Gold Coast. . . . Work? what? In Guinea! No, no, nothing to do there but lay your head on the knee of a delicate soft wench while she plays with your hair" (III, i). (In a later scene set in prison, two experienced sailors agree they are better off where they are than in Guinea.) Boulton shows that the captain's contempt for Africa and Africans is matched only by his disdain for those he hires.

39 *Downing Street*: shorthand for British government offices, all located at this address.

40 *hemidemisemiquaver*: a highly precise musical notation, a subtle vibration half the length of a demisemiquaver.

40 *stave*: musical staff (the five horizontal lines in a musical manuscript upon which notes are displayed to be performed).

Liberia?
No Cobra Pirate° of the Question Mark,°
No caricature° with a mimic flag
And golden joys° to fat the shark:
45                                 You are
American genius uncrowned° in Europe's charnel-house.°
Leave fleshpots° for the dogs and apes; for Man
The books whose head is golden° espouse!

---

42 *Cobra Pirate*: (Tolson's note) "V. [George] Hardy, *Les Grande Etapes de l'Histoire du Maroc* [(1921) *Major Stages in Moroccan History*], 50–54." Hardy portrays the Spanish moors as " 'corsairs' who descended unexpectedly upon the coasts or islands of the Mediterranean and they captured and sold as slaves the sailors and the passengers." The passage is cited in Chapter X of W.E.B. DuBois (1868–1963), *The World and Africa* (1946), a text Tolson credits in his footnote to line 80 and draws from in footnotes to lines 560, 566 and 576.

42 *The Question Mark*: (Tolson's note) "The shape of the map of Africa dramatizes two schools of thought among native African scholars. To the Christian educator, Dr. James E. Kwegyir Aggrey, it is a moral interrogation point that challenges the white world. According to Dr. Nnamdi Azikiwe, the leader of the nationalist movement on the West Coast, foreigners consider it 'a hambone designed by destiny for the carving-knife of European imperialism.' I have found very fruitful the suggestions and criticisms of Professor Diana Pierson, the Liberian, and Dr. Akiki Nyabongo, the Ugandian. I now know that the Question Mark is rough water between Scylla and Charybdis" [the rock and the whirlpool, respectively, between which smooth navigation is impossible: to avoid one is to be drawn toward the other]. Tolson describes Africa as the "Bloody Question Mark of Centuries" in his Nov. 21, 1942 newspaper column for the weekly Washington (D.C.) *Tribune*: "Every world conqueror has tried to conquer Africa. But in time Africa has swallowed them all. . . . And now the armies of Hitler and Mussolini are being swallowed in the African sands. Yes, Black Boy, Africa will swallow many a white army after we are dead and gone." The "question mark" figure reappears in lines 635–637.

43 *No caricature*: (Tolson's Note) "Cf. [Otto von] Bismarck [(1815–1898)]: 'They [Negroes] appear to me to be a caricature of the white man.'"

44 *golden joys*: (Tolson's Note) "Cf. Shakespeare, *Henry IV* [Part II], V, iii: 'A foutra for the world and worldings base! / I speak of Africa and golden joys'" (lines 100–101). With an obscene gesture to gloss "foutra," the character of Pistol speaks these lines that record an Elizabethan knowledge of Africa as a source of gold.

46 *American genius uncrowned*: (Tolson's Note) "Cf. [Ralph Waldo] Emerson [(1803–1882)]: 'While European genius is symbolized by some majestic Corinne crowned in the capitol at Rome, American genius finds its true type in the poor negro soldier lying in the trenches by the Potomac with his spelling book in one hand and his musket in the other.'" After a visit to Rome, Germaine de Staël (1766–1817) wrote *Corinne* (1807), a novel whose heroine pined away slowly once she learned of her lover's falsity. Among the sharp contrasts in Emerson's example, the European character is fictional while the American is actual.

46 *Europe's charnel house*: (Tolson's note) "V. [Rene] Maran, *Batouala* [: *A True Black Novel* (1922)], 9: 'Civilization, civilization, pride of the Europeans and charnel-house of innocents, Rabindranath Tagore, the Hindu poet, once, at Tokyo, told what you are! You have built your kingdom on corpses!'" Tolson quotes from the Preface of the 1923 translation by Adele Szold Seltzer.

47 *fleshpots*: worldly luxuries.

48 *The books whose head is golden*: (Tolson's Note) "Cf. [Dante Gabriel] Rossetti [(1828–1882)], 'Mary's Girlhood.'" Rossetti inscribed a sonnet on the frame of his first oil painting, "Mary's Girlhood," a portrait of the youthful Mary. The poem explains the symbolic meaning of objects in the picture. In these lines, St. Paul's approval of learning is quoted: "The books—whose head / Is golden Charity, as Paul hath said— / Those virtues are where the soul is rich" (ll. 10–12).

*Liberia?*
50   No waste land yet, nor yet a destooled elite,°
     No merry-andrew,° an Ed-dehebi° at heart,
     With St. Paul's root° and Breughel's cheat:°
               You are
     The iron nerve° of lame and halt and blind,
55               Liberia and not Liberia,°
     A moment of the conscience of mankind!°

---

50 *destooled*: (Tolson's Note) "On the Gold Coast the 'Stool' is the symbol of the soul of the nation, its Magna Charta. In 1900, Sir Frederick Hodgson, Governor of the Gold Coast, demanded that the Ashantis surrender their 'Stool.' They immediately declared war. 'Destooling' is a veto exercised by the sovereign people over unpopular rulers." The Ashanti, renown for their goldwork, had constructed a gold-covered stool which represented their confederacy that dated from the fifteenth century. Wars with the British from 1896 to 1901 resulted in the exile of their ruler and the breakup of the confederacy which was restored, with limited powers, in 1935. Edwin P. Smith opened *The Golden Stool* (1927), a study of African colonialism, with this anecdote as an example of the typically acute cultural conflict caused by outside settlers.

51 *merry-andrew*: clown.

51 *Ed-dehebi*: (Tolson's Note) "'The Master of Gold.' He was the conqueror of Songhai, with its fabulous gold mines." The Songhai civilization is described in "Re." Envying the salt and gold reserves in the Songhai empire, Sultan Ahmed Ed-Dehebi of Morocco in 1590 dispatched Spanish and Portuguese mercenaries armed with muskets who began an occupation of the region that led to the downfall of the empire.

52 *St. Paul's root*: Paul, originally Saul of Tarsus (?–67), early convert to Christianity whose letters to many churches he founded appear in the New Testament.

52 *Breughel's cheat*: Pieter Breughel the Elder (1520?–1569) painted scenes from the Bible, peasant life and fantastic scenes. Sons Pieter and Jan were also painters.

54 *Iron nerve*: (Tolson's Note) "Cf. [Alfred, Lord] Tennyson [(1809–1892)], 'Ode on the Death of the Duke of Wellington.'" The pertinent lines are addressed to the deceased Wellington: "O good gray head which all men knew, / O voice from which these omens all men drew, / O iron nerve to true occasion true" (section IV, lines 17–19).

55 *Liberia*: Jon Stanton Woodson suggests Tolson is playing on the "liberty" in the name of Liberia, calling it a nation whose slave heritage makes it both free yet not free.

56 *conscience of mankind*: (Tolson's Note) "V. the address of Anatole France [(1844–1924)] at the bier of Emile Zola [(1840–1902)]." France praised Zola's courage for his part in exposing the high-level cover-up that had unjustly condemned staff officer Louis Dreyfus (1859–1935) for treason. "Envy [Zola] his destiny and his heart, which made his lot that of the greatest," France said. "He was a moment in the conscience of man!"

RE°

The Good Gray Bard° in Timbuktu° chanted:
"*Brow tron lo—eta ne a new won oh gike!*"°

Before Liberia was, Songhai was: before
60    America set the raw foundling° on Africa's
Doorstep, before the Genoese° diced west,
Burnt warriors and watermen of Songhai
Tore into *bizarreries*° the uniforms of Portugal
And sewed an imperial quilt of tribes.

---

*Re*: second note in the diatonic scale. The poem depicts the Songhai civilization in north-
west Africa on the Niger River at the height of its fame (circa 1300–1500), detailing its
wealth, its devotion to learning (at a time when Europe was in the Dark Ages), and its
eventual destruction by Moroccans with Spanish and Portuguese mercenaries in 1591.
57 *Good Gray Bard*: American poet Walt Whitman (1819–1892) was described by his friend
William O'Connor as *The Good Gray Poet* (1866). Also see note to line 54.
57 *Timbuktu*: (Tolson's Note) "Cf. *A Memoir of Tennyson*, Vol I, 46, the letter of Arthur
Hallam to William Gladstone on the Timbuktu prize poem: 'I consider Tennyson as promis-
ing fair to be the greatest poet of our generation, perhaps of our century.'" [A 19-year-old
Alfred Tennyson won the Chancellor's Gold Medal in 1828 for verse on a preordained topic:
Timbuctoo. His 248-line descriptive poem "Timbuctoo" ended with a memory of a lost city
of "brilliant towers" giving way to a vision of "huts, / Black specks amid a waste of dreary
sand, / Low-built, mud-walled, Barbarian settlements. / How changed from this fair city!"]
"V. [Maurice] Delafosse, *Les Noirs d'Afrique* [(French) trans. as *The Negroes of Africa* (1928)
by F. Fligelman]. The Schomburg Collection, in Harlem, contains many rare items on the
civilization at Timbuktu. [Timbuktu (also Tombouctou) on the Niger River had been the
center of Songhai, largest of the ancient native empires of West Africa. The western edge
of present-day Liberia would have been on the fringe of the gold-producing area of the
empire. Founded circa 700, its rulers were converted to the Islamic religion around 1000.
Under Askia Mohammed the Great (1493–1528) the empire reached its pinnacle, with a
University at Sankoré that taught law, literature, geography, and surgery. When the em-
pire was shattered by an invading army in from Morocco in 1591, its downfall resulted in
a massive expansion of the trade in slaves which had previously been limited to local needs.]
Dr. Lorenzo Turner's *Africanisms in the Gullah Dialects* [(1949)], by tracing West Coast
derivatives to their Arabic and Moslem and Portuguese cultural roots, has revealed the
catholicity and sophistication of African antiquity and exploded the theory of the Old Eng-
lish origin of the Gullah dialects." The Gullahs were African Americans living on the coast
of Georgia and South Carolina. Turner assembled a lexicon of words from Gullah, then
matched them with equivalents from West African languages, defining Gullah not as a de-
terioration of English but as an extension of African.
58"*Brow . . . gike*": (Tolson's Note) "I am informed that variations of this *eironeia* or mock-
ery may be found in scores of African languages. It means here: 'The world is too large—
that's why we do not hear everything.' Cf. Pliny [(62?–114?)], *Historia Naturalis* [*Natural
History*], II: 'There is always something new from Africa.' Also [Jonathan] Swift
[(1667–1745)]: 'So geographers in Afric maps, / With savage pictures fill the gaps . . .'"
(lines 177–178, from "On Poetry: A Rhapsody" [1733]). As his footnotes especially reveal,
Tolson sees there are still gaps in our comprehension of world history, not only with re-
gard to Africa but also on other topics to which he returns: uprisings by the underclass,
their suppression, and a perennial desire for political freedom.
60 *raw foundling*: the new republic of Liberia.
61 *Genoese*: Christopher Columbus (1446?–1506).
63 *bizarreries*: (French) whimsical, odd, fragmentary.

65      In Milan and Mecca, in Balkh and Bombay,°
        Sea lawyers in the eyeservice° of sea kings
        Mixed liquors with hyperboles to cure deafness.
        Europe bartered Africa crucifixes for red ivory,
        Gewgaws for black pearls,° *pierres d'aigris*° for green gold:
70      Soon the rivers and roads became clog almanacs!

        The Good Gray Bard in Timbuktu chanted:
        *"Wanawake wanazaa ovyo! Kazi yenu wazungu!"*°

        Black Askia's fetish° was his people's health:
        The world his world, he gave the Bengal light°
75      Of Books the Inn of Court° in Songhai. *Beba mzigo!*°
        The law of empathy set the market price,
        Scaled the word and deed: the gravel-blind saw
        Deserts give up the ghost° to green pastures!

        Solomon in all his glory had no Oxford,°
80      Alfred the Great° no University of Sankoré:°

---

65 *Milan . . .* Bombay: Major trading centers in medieval times, located in Italy, Saudi Arabia, Afghanistan, and India. Mecca and Balkh were centers of Islamic religion, one the birthplace of Mohammed, the other home of the statesmen known as the Barmecides.

66 *eyeservice*: services so important they were performed exclusively under the watch of one's director.

69 *black pearls*: (Tolson's Note) "V. Shakespeare, *Two Gentlemen of Verona*, V, ii. [Jesting with Thurio and Julia, Proteus says: "The old saying is, / Black men are pearls in beauteous ladies' eyes" (lines 11–12).] "Also, *Othello*, I, i: 'Well prais'd! How if she be black and witty?'" [The line is spoken by Desdemona in an interchange with Iago (line 129).] "Mr. J.A. Rogers treats the subject and time and place adequately in *Sex and Race*." Rogers's 1942 study is subtitled "A History of White, Negro and Indian Miscegenation in the Two Americas" and cited in DuBois, *The World and Africa* (1946).

69 *Pierre d'aigris*: (French) "bitter stones."

72 *Wanawake wanazaa ovyo*: (Tolson's Note) "The women keep having children, right and left." *Kazi yenu wazungu*: "It's the work of you white men."

73 *Black Askia's fetish*: The Askia dynasty that ruled Songhai from the early 1500s onward were natives of the region, unlike the Sonni dynasty (Arabic), that had previously controlled the empire. Fetish: The name Europeans give to objects (usually small representative sculptures) whose presence among primitive peoples is regarded as a sign of belief in magic and other pre-scientific patterns of thought. Tolson uses the term to highlight the sophistication of the Songhai administrative infrastructure.

74 *Bengal light*: A vividly-colored light used as a signal. The Bengal region (portions of India and Pakistan) was conquered in 1200 by Moslems. Tolson's phrase suggests not only Moslem investment in learning but also the far reaches of its civilization.

75 *Inn of Court*: The British legal association that admits persons to practice as lawyers.

75 *Beba mzigo*: (Tolson's note) "'Lift the loads.' This repetend [in musical terms, a refrain] is tacked on *ex tempore* [extemporaneously] to ballads growing out of a diversity of physical and spiritual experiences."

78 *give up the ghost*: surrender.

79 *Solomon . . . Oxford*: (c. 972–c. 932 B.C.), king of the ancient Hebrews, renown for his wisdom. Oxford: traditional site of learning in England.

80 *Alfred the Great*: (849–899), king of Wessex in England.

80 *Sankoré*: (Tolson's note) "V. DuBois, *The World and Africa* [(1946)], a book to which I am deeply indebted for facts." DuBois quotes from Leo Africanus's fifteenth century eyewitness description of Songhai from *History and Description of Africa*, Volume III (the 1896 edition): "And hither are brought diuers manuscripts or written bookes out of Berberie, which are sold for more money than any other merchandise."

Footloose professors,° chimney sweeps of the skull,
From Europe and Asia; youths, souls in one skin,°
Under white scholars like El-Akit, under
Black humanists like Bagayogo.° *Karibu wee!*°

85      The Good Gray Bard in Timbuktu chanted:
"Europe is an empty python in hiding grass!"°

*Lia! Lia!*° The river Wagadu, the river Bagana,°
Became dusty metaphors where white ants ate canoes,
And the locust Portuguese raped the maiden crops,
90      And the sirocco° Spaniard razed the city-states,
And the leopard Saracen° bolted his scimitar° into
The jugular vein of Timbuktu. *Dieu seul est grand!*°

---

81 *Footloose professors*: (Tolson's note) "The nomadic pedagogues gathered at Timbuktu are not to be confused with the *vagantes* of the *Carmina Burana.*" By differentiating the Sankoré faculty from the *vagantes* or unemployed "wandering scholars" of the twelfth century who were the English version of the French troubadours and German minnesingers, and who rambled from one European university to another, composing burlesque versions of medieval hymns in a bastard Latin (collected as the *Carmina Burana* in 1907), Tolson again underscores the difference between a primitive England in the Middle Ages and the sophistication of the Songhai empire.

82 *souls in one skin*: (Tolson's note) "V. Firdousi, *The Dream of Dukiki*, I, A." The 56,000-line *Shāhnāma* (*The Book of Kings*), national epic of Iran written in the early eleventh century and recording 3,600 years of history, was begun by Daqiqi (?–980) and completed by Firdausi or Ferdowsi, the pen name of Abu'l Qâsim Mansûr (934?–1020). Tolson's note records cooperation between poets and stresses the duration and sophistication of Islamic culture.

83–84 *El-Akit, Bagayogo*: Delafosse in *Negroes of Africa* identifies El-Akit as white, Bagayogo as black. Both were educated in sixteenth century Timbuktu.

84 *Karibu wee*: (Tolson's note) "Among primitives hospitality is a thing poetic—and apostalic. *Jogoo linawika: Karibu wee*: 'The rooster crows: Welcome!' *Mbuzi wanalia: Karibu wee*. 'The goats bleat: welcome.'"

86 *empty python*: The python of European civilization in the late 1500s is "empty"—lacking a cultural tradition with institutions of learning but also hungry for conquest and pillage. In a later poem "Fa," Tolson equates nations at peace with wild animals who have been well-fed.

87 *Lia!*: (Tolson's note) "The word mean 'weep' and seems to follow the patterns of 'ototoi' in the Aeschylean chorus." The Greek dramatist Aeschylus (525–456 B.C.) highlighted the role of the chorus. "Otototoi" is an untranslatable exclamation of woe, pain or grief.

87 *Wagadu . . . Bagana*: "Wagadu" in the Sarakolle language and "Bagana" in the Mandingo language both signify a "country of herds, region of cattle raising."

90 *sirocco*: a hot and oppressive wind blowing from the Mediterranean into southern Europe.

91 *Saracen*: Used in the Middle Ages to designate Arabs (and by extension) Moslems.

91 *Scimitar*: a sword with a short curved blade.

92 *Dieu seul est grand!*: (French) "Only God is great!" (Tolson's note) "These first words of Massilon's exordium, delivered at the magnificent funeral of Louis XIV, brought the congregation to its feet in the cathedral. [Jean-Baptiste Massilon (1663–1742), Bishop of Clermont, was celebrated as a religious orator at the French courts of Louis XIV and Louis XV. The cry acknowledges how little control humans finally have over their fate.] For an account of the destruction of Timbuktu, see the *Tarikh el-Fettach*. [This sixteenth century manuscript by Mahmoud Kâti or Kòti, a member of the Songhai court, chronicles the Askia dynasty up to its conquest in the 1590s. Delafosse co-translated it into French in 1914.] The *askia* Issahak, in a vain attempt to stop the Spanish renegades at Tondibi, used cows as Darius had used elephants against the Macedonian phalanx." Issahak interposed cattle between his troops and the enemy, but the creatures were frightened by the novel sound of muskets firing and stampeded the Songhai warriors. Just as the defeat of Darius III (d. 330 B.C.) by Alexander the Great (356–323 B.C.) marked the close of the Persian empire, so Issahak's rout signaled the end of another major empire. *Askia* is the name of a family which, when it becomes a dynasty, then functions as a title conferring nobility.

And now the hyenas whine among the barren bones
Of the seventeen sun sultans of Songhai,°
95      And hooded cobras, hoodless mambas,° hiss
In the gold caverns of Falémé and Bambuk,°
And puff adders, hook scorpions, whisper
In the weedy corridors of Sankoré. *Lia! Lia!*

The Good Gray Bard chants no longer in Timbuktu:
100     "The maggots fat on yeas and nays of nut empires!"°

MI°

Before the bells of Yankee capital
Tolled for the feudal glory of the South°
And Frederick Douglass's Vesuvian mouth
Erupted amens crushing Copperheads,°

Old Robert Finley,° Jehovah's Damasias,
Swooped into Pennsylvania Avenue

---

94 *seventeen sun sultans of Songhai*: possibly a play on the names of the rulers of the Sonni dynasty (of whom DuBois, however, records eighteen).

95 *mambas*: a poisonous snake related to the cobra.

96 *The gold caverns of Falémé and Bambuk*: Gold holdings were a source of the Songhai empire's wealth. These two were located south of the Senegal River in present-day Senegal and Guinea, directly north of Liberia.

100 *Nut empires*: (Tolson's note): "Cf. Sagittarius [pseudonym under which editors published a weekly satirical verse], *New Statesman and Nation*, [XXV: 895], May 1, 1948, the poem entitled 'Pea-nuts': 'The sun of Empire will not set while Empire nuts abound [line 1].'" Playing on "nuts" as a term of derision, the poem ridicules a postwar economic scheme by England to import groundnuts from its colonies. The poem was noted in the "Introduction" to *Africa: Britain's Third Empire* (1949) by George Padmore (whose transcription error in the title Tolson repeats) who remarks: "Parliament, the press and radio—politicians, journalists and broadcasters—vie with one another in assuring the British people that what they have lost in Asia they will recover in Africa." In Chapter 8, Padmore points out that the success of the groundnuts plan hinges on a low wage scale for local labor and on seizing lands currently used for grazing livestock.

Mi: Third note of the diatonic scale. Tolson relates the personages and events in America leading up to the decision to finance the relocating of some African Americans to Africa. The emphasis throughout falls on political maneuvering, statesmanship, and foreign affairs, and the narrative leaps, at the end, from the early nineteenth-century to the recent events of World War II. The story of establishing Liberia on the West African coast will be continued in "Sol."

101–102 *Before the bells . . . of the South*: Tolson places the time frame of the poem as prior to the Civil War. By summarizing that war as a clash between the progressive economics of a Northern industrial economy and the regressive feudalism of a Southern agricultural economy, he also removes the issue of slave-holding from the equation.

103–104 *Frederick . . . mouth*: Douglass (c. 1817–1895), the well-known African American Abolitionist and author of *Narrative of the Life of Frederick Douglass* (1845). Vesuvian mouth: "Vesuvius" is the active volcano in the Bay of Naples in Italy whose eruption in 79 A.D. buried Pompeii. Copperheads: a term of reproach for Northerners sympathetic to the Southern causes; opposite to the Abolitionists.

105 *Robert Finley*: (1772–1817), Presbyterian clergyman, author of *Thoughts on the Colonization of Free Blacks* (1816), an organizer and Vice-President of the American Colonization Society, the alliance that sponsored the founding of what would become Liberia.

To pinion Henry Clay, the shuttlecock,°
And Bushrod Washington,° whose family name

Dwarfed signatures of blood:° his magnet Yea
Drew Lawyer Key, the hymnist primed to match
A frigate's guns,° and Bishop Meade,° God's purse,
And Doctor Torrey,° the People's clock: they eagled

The gospel for the wren Republic in
Supreme Court chambers. That decision's cash
And credit bought a balm for conscience,° verved
Black Pilgrim Fathers to Cape Mesurado,°

Where sun and fever, brute and vulture, spelled
The idioms of their faith in whited bones.
No linguist of the Braille of prophecy ventured:
*The rubber from Liberia shall arm*

*Free peoples and her airport hinterlands*
*Let loose the winging grapes of wrath° upon*

107 *Henry Clay, the shuttlecock*: Clay (1777–1852), Congressman and Secretary of State during John Adams' Presidency, was regarded as author of the "Missouri Compromise" of 1821 which, at a time when states were clamoring to enter the republic, established the custom of retaining a balance among the number of slave states and number of free states admitted.
108 *Bushrod Washington*: (1762–1829), son of George Washington's brother, Associate Justice of the Supreme Court, and President of the American Colonization Society.
109 *Dwarfed . . . blood*: Bushrod Washington inherited Mount Vernon, and was attacked in 1821 for having sold and transported 54 of its slaves to Louisiana, separating many from close family.
110–111 *Key . . . guns*: Francis Scott Key (1779–1843), poet, attorney, lyricist of the "Star Spangled Banner," written when he spotted the American flag flying over Fort McHenry after the British withdrawal from the burning of Washington, D.C. in 1814.
111 *Bishop Meade*: William Meade (1789–1862), Bishop of the Protestant Episcopal Church in Virginia, welcomed African American participation in church matters; freed his own slaves; offered early support to found Liberia.
112 *Doctor Torrey*: Possibly Charles Turner Torrey (1813–1846), editor and Abolitionist who died in jail after being sentenced to six years at hard labor in 1844 for aiding in the escape of slaves across the Virginia-Maryland border.
115 *balm for conscience*: After slavery was formally defined as piracy by the U.S. Congress in 1818, a supplementary act of 1819 provided that Africans captured from slave dealers should be returned "beyond the limits of the United States" to an area to be designated on the coast of Africa. $100,000 was appropriated for the program, later increased by smaller grants of $4,000 each.
116 *Cape Mesurado*: Isthmus on which is located Monrovia, capital of Liberia.
122 *winging . . . wrath*: (Tolson's note) "The airfields of Liberia sent 17,000 bombers a month against [Erwin] Rommel's *Afrika Korps*." *Grapes of Wrath*: The title of the 1939 protest novel by John Steinbeck (1902–1968), taken from the "Battle Hymn of the Republic" (1862) by Julia Ward Howe (1819–1910). Rommel (1891–1944) commanded the German forces in Egypt, Libya, and Tripoli. The information comes from Charles Morrow Wilson, *Liberia* (1947): "Liberia supplied several of the war's most important air bases. . . . Long-range bombers of the U.S. Army Air Forces and the Navy Air Command and of the Royal Air Force (as many as 17,000 per month) received shelter, bombs, fuel, miscellaneous supplies, and combat personnel at the great air bases in Liberia and from them proceeded to batter, harass, and paralyze Nazi supply lines and bases in North Africa, and the Mediterranean, to help break the back of Rommel's Afrika Corps, and in time to spearhead the Mediterranean offensive."

The Desert Fox's cocained nietzscheans°
A goosestep from the Gateway of the East!°

FA°

125      A fabulous mosaic log,
            the Bola boa° lies
            gorged to the hinges of his jaws,
            eyeless, yet with eyes . . .

            *in the interlude of peace*

130      The beaked and pouched assassin sags
            on to his corsair° rock,
            and from his talons swim the blood-
            red feathers of a cock . . .

            *in the interlude of peace.*

135      The tawny typhoon° striped with black
            torpors° in grasses tan:
            a doomsday cross, his paws uprear
            the leveled skull of a man . . .

            *in the interlude of peace*

SOL°

140      White Pilgrims, turn your trumpets west!
            Black Pilgrims, *shule, agrah,*° nor tread
            The Skull° of another's stairs!°

---

123 *The Desert Fox*: Rommel. *Cocained nietzscheans*: from Nietzsche's *Thus Spake Zarathus-
tra* (1886), Nazi intellectuals seized upon the concept of Nietzsche's Superman, distorting
it to justify the existence of a Master Race. In a Sept. 7, 1940, newspaper column for the
weekly Washington (D.C.) *Tribune*, Tolson called Nietzsche "that hateful German" and a
"brutal old philosopher" who "looked upon life as a struggle in which the fittest and slick-
est survived."
124 *Gateway of the East*: Africa as a potential corridor and supply-line for eastward conquests.
*Fa*: Fourth note in the diatonic scale. These three creatures are all satiated, so they are
temporarily not dangerous, but the refrain, *"in the interlude of peace,"* sounds disturbingly
hollow. Jon Stanton Woodson suggests that the sequence is brief and restrained because
peace is short-lived and temporary, a result of these animals having just dined.
126 *Boa*: a snake that kills by squeezing its prey.
131 *Corsair*: pirate.
135 *Typhoon*: The description resembles a tiger.
136 *torpors*: the verb in the sentence: "lazes" or "lounges."
*Sol*: Fifth note in the diatonic scale. Events at the opening and close are drawn from Wil-
son's *Liberia* (1947) and describe the first year of Liberia's founding. The history will con-
tinue in the next poem.
141 *Shule, agrah*: (Tolson's note) "'Move, my heart.' Cf. [Cecil James] Sharp, 'Shule, Shule,
Shule Agah.' It is a refrain from old Gaelic ballads." Sharp (1859–1924) collected English
and American folk songs.
142 *Skull*: (Tolson's note) "'gulgoleth,' a place of torment and martyrdom." [Golgotha is "skull"
in Hebrew, and also the name of the site outside Jerusalem where Jesus was crucified.]
142 *Another's stairs*: (Tolson's note) "Cf. [Dante Gabriel] Rossetti, 'Dante at Verona,' the epi-
graph from [Dante Alighieri (1265–1321)] *Paradiso* [(*Paradise*)], XVII: 'Yea, thou shalt learn how
salt his food who fares / Upon another's bread—how steep his path / Who treadeth up and
down another's stairs.'" Dante, exiled from Florence, refers to the pain of losing a homeland.

This is the horned American
Dilemma:° yet, this too, O Christ,
145    This too, O Christ, will pass!

The brig *Elizabeth*° flaunts her stern
At auction blocks° with the eyes of Cain°
And down-the-river° sjamboks.°

This is the Middle Passage:° here
150    Gehenna° hatchways vomit up
The debits of pounds of flesh.

This is the Middle Passage: here
The sharks wax fattest and the stench
Goads God to hold His nose!

---

143–144 *Dilemma*: (Tolson's note) "V. [Gunnar] Myrdal, *An American Dilemma* Cf. Aptheker, *The Negro People in America.* Also Cox, *Caste, Class and Race.*" Swedish sociologist Gunnar Myrdal's 1944 study was subtitled "The Negro Problem and Modern Democracy." As Woodson notes, Myrdal concluded that blacks were a type of "exaggerated American" who exhibit "pathological values." Tolson's invocation of two other scholars, then, stands as a corrective to Myrdal. Herbert Aptheker's 1946 volume was a critique of Myrdal from a Marxist perspective. Oliver Cromwell Cox, author of *Caste, Class and Race* (1948), was a Marxist sociologist and a former faculty colleague at Wiley College.

146 *Elizabeth*: In February 1820, the *Elizabeth,* with 86 freed slaves aboard and convoyed by a sloop-of-war of the U.S. Navy, was chartered by Congress to sail from Philadelphia to a location on the West African coast with authority and funds granted by President James Monroe to purchase Sherbo Island, a promontory off the present coast of Liberia, from native chiefs for colonization.

147 *Auction blocks*: (Tolson's note): "Cf. [John] Rolfe, *Diary, 1619:* 'About the last of August came a Dutch man of warre that sold us twenty negras.' Also [Marshall] Field, *Freedom Is More Than a Word* [(1948)]: 'And the Negroes have been in this country longer, on the average, than their white neighbors; they find they first came to this country on a ship called the 'Jesus' one year before the "'Mayflower. . . .'"'" Tolson marshals the evidence for Africans on American soil even before English Puritans, beginning with Rolfe, the celebrated Virginian who wed Pocahontas.

147 *With the eyes of Cain*: (Tolson's note) "Cf. Watson, *The World in Armor.*"

148 *down-the-river*: (Tolson's note) "Cf. John Davis, *Travels* [*in the United States of America: 1798 to 1802*], the chapter on a slave hanging alive on a gibbet in South Carolina: ' . . . the negro lolled out his tongue, his eyes starting from their sockets, and for three long days his only cry was Water! Water! Water!'" In Chapter X. Davis narrates this punishment of a Virginia slave who killed his master's son after finding the son "overficious with his wife" Davis records his disgust at South Carolina slavery in chapters II and III: "No casuistry can justify keeping a slave. . . . The supposed property of the master in the slave is an usurpation and not a right; because no one from being a person can become a thing" (III, 104–105).

148 *Sjamboks*: (Tolson's note) "Cf. [George] Padmore, *Africa* [(1949), p. 27]: 'The Africans are housed like cattle in a compound . . . they are guarded by foremen armed with the sjambok, a hide whip—the symbol of South African civilization.'" The description is of workers in the Transvaal gold mines.

149 *Middle Passage*: The route for shipping slaves across the Atlantic, usually to the West Indies from West Africa.

150 *Gehenna*: a place of torment; hell.

155        Elijah Johnson,° his *Tygers heart*°
           In the whale's belly, flenses° midnight:
           "How Long? How long? How long?"

           A dark age later the answer dawns
           When whitecap pythons thrash upon
160        The molar teeth of reefs

           And hallelujahs quake the brig
           From keel to crow's-nest and tomtoms gibber
           In cosmic *deepi-talki.*°

           Elijah feels the Forty Nights'
165        Octopus reach up to drag his mind
           Into man's genesis.

           He hears the skulls plowed under° cry:
           "*Griots,*° the quick owe the quick and dead.
           A man owes man to man!"

---

155 *Elijah Johnson*: (1780?–1849), African American, sailed on the founding voyage to Liberia, and resisted suggestions by other leaders to return to Sierra Leone after hostile natives discouraged settling on the West African coast. He homesteaded Monrovia, the capital city, and led settlers in battle against local tribes.

155 *Tygers heart*: (Tolson's note) "Greene's allusion to 'the onely Shake-scene.'" The Elizabethan playwright Robert Greene (1560?–1592) also called his rival "an upstart crow" in this outburst from 1592. Also see note to line 573.

156 *flenses*: (a technical term) to slice the blubber of a whale.

163 *deepi-talki*: (Tolson's note): "Cf. [probably, William J.] LaVarre: 'My black companions had two languages: *deepitalki*, a secret language no white man understands; and *talki-talki*, a concoction of many languages and idioms which I understood.'" Also see note to line 496.

167 *skulls plowed under*: (Tolson's note) "Cf. Sharp, *The Last Aboriginal.*"

168 *Griots*: (Tolson's Note): "'living encyclopedias.' [The translation is from Delafosse, chapter XV.] Giryama, Bantu, Amharic, Swahili, Yoruba, Vai, Thonga, Zulu, Jaba, Sudanese—these tribal scholars speak, with no basic change in idea and image, from line 173 to 214. The Africans have their *avant garde* in oral literature. Sometimes one of these bards becomes esoteric and sneers in a council of chiefs a line like this: 'The snake walks on its belly.' And thus elder statesmen are often puzzled by more than the seven ambiguities. [William Empson's *Seven Types of Ambiguity* (1930) fixed on the ability of poets to produce multiple meanings in single passages. As presented in Selwyn Gurney Champion's *Racial Proverbs: A Study of the World's Proverbs Arranged Linguistically* (1938), Thonga proverb no. 153 is "The snake walks on its belly" which he also translates as "the snake walks on its bowels." Champion glosses this to mean: "A man cannot work without tools or without money." Tolson's comment suggests that elder statesmen of any group are blind either to the needs of the working class or to obvious solutions to economic problems.] Delafosse feared that the mass production techniques introduce by missionaries and traders would contaminate art for art's sake in Africa." Delafosse's concern centered on "native" artifacts: "Even in Africa missionaries are developing these artistic industries among the natives. . . . Perhaps it is to be feared that the stimulus of an easier profit may push the Negro artisans to subordinate their own inspiration to the taste of the European buyer and to sacrifice their art to the temptation of mass production" (*Negroes of Africa*, 261).

170      "*Seule de tous les continents,*" the parrots
         chatter, "*l'Afrique n'a pas d'histoire!*"°
         *Mon petit doigt me l'a dit:*°

         "Africa is a rubber ball;
         the harder you dash it to the ground,
175      the higher it will rise.°

         "A lie betrays its mother tongue.
         The Eye said, 'Ear, the Belly is
         the foremost of the gods.'°

         "Fear makes a gnarl° a cobra's head.
180      One finger cannot kill a louse.
         The seed waits for the lily.

         "No fence's legs are long enough.
         The lackey licks the guinea's boot
         till holes wear in the tongue.

185      "A camel on its knees solicits
         the ass's load. Potbellies cook
         no meals for empty maws.

         "When skins are dry the flies go home.
         Repentance is a peacock's tail.
190      The cock is yolk and feed.

         "Three steps put man one step ahead.
         The rich man's weights are not the poor
         man's scales.° To each his coole.°

---

170–171 *Seule . . . d'histoire!*: (French) "Of all the continents, Africa alone has no history!" (Tolson's note): "These words of [Eugène] Guernier are no longer *ex cathedra* [accepted without question because of their speaker's prestige]: the scope of a native culture is vertical—not horizontal." Guernier is described as one of the parrots who speaks unthinkingly by imitating others. Author of several books on Africa, he was Professor at *l'Institut d'Etudes Politiques* (the Institute for Political Studies) at the University of Paris. Tolson may be suggesting that native culture is "vertical" in that it repeats and preserves wisdom from numerous generations without an emphasis on time changing, unlike a "horizontal" culture that values progress and conceives a timeline in which the future must be better than the past.

172 *Mon . . . dit*: (French) "My little finger has said to me!" Tolson replies (in French, for Guernier's benefit).

173–175 *African race . . . rise*: In several instances, the wordings of the proverbs Tolson uses closely resemble transcriptions in Champion, *Racial Proverbs* (1938). (One proverb from Champion formed the basis for Tolson's note to line 168.) Under "Bantu" the first proverb is: "The African race is an india-rubber ball; the harder you dash it to the ground, the higher it will rise." Tolson's version replaces the racialized "india-rubber" with simply "rubber."

177–178 *The Eye . . . gods*: The version in Champion's *Racial Proverbs* is simply: "The belly is foremost of the gods" (Yoruba proverb no. 7).

179 *gnarl*: a knot on the outside of a tree.

192–193 *The rich man's . . . scales*: The version in Champion's *Racial Proverbs*: "A chief's weights are not the same as a poor man's weights" (Oji [Ashanti] proverb no. 6).

193 *coole*: possibly an obsolete spelling of "cowle": a grant, particularly one that gives protection.

<br>

"A stinkbug° should not peddle perfume.
195        The tide that ebbs will flow again.
A louse that bites is in

"the inner shirt. An open door
sees both inside and out. The saw
that severs the topmost limb

200        "comes from the ground. God saves the black
man's soul but not his buttocks from
the white man's lash. The mouse

"as artist paints a mouse that chases
a cat. The diplomat's lie is fat
205        at home and lean abroad.

"It is the grass that suffers when
two elephants fight.° The white man solves
between white sheets his black

"problem. Where would the rich cream be
210        without skim milk? The eye can cross
the river in a flood.

"Law is a rotten tree; black man, rest
thy weight elsewhere, or like the goat
outrun the white man's stink!"

215        Elijah broods:° "The fevers hoed
Us under at Sherbro.° Leopard saints
Puked us from Bushrod Beach.°

"To Providence Island, where John Mill,°
The mulatto trader, fended off
220        The odds that bait the hook.

194 *A stinkbug*: (Tolson's note) "Cf. [Rudyard] Kipling [(1865–1936)], 'The White Man's Burden.'" Kipling's 1898 poem addresses America and insists that it assume responsibility for the natives of Cuba and the Philippine Islands after having released the islands from Spanish domination in the War against Spain in 1898.
205–206 *It is . . . fight*: The version in Champion's *Racial Proverbs*: "When two elephants struggle it is the grass that suffers" (Swahili proverb no. 57).
215 *broods*: Tolson returns us to the founding of Liberia.
216 *Sherbro*: Sherbro Island (now a promontory on the Liberian coast) had been previously chosen as the destination of the new colonizers, but Kru tribesmen refused to let it be "purchased"; 29 of the 86 colonizers died while struggling with the Kru.
217 *Bushrod Beach*: named for Bushrod Washington.
218 *Providence Island*: The British settlement near Freetown in Sierra Leone to which the colonizers retreated in 1820 after the collapse of their negotiations with the Kru.
218 *John Mill*: identified in the endjacket to *Libretto* (the hardcover edition by Twayne publishers) as "a mulatto English trader along the West African coast."

"The foxes have holes, the birds have nests,
And I have found a place to lay
My head, Lord of Farewells!"°

And every ark awaits its raven,
225    Its vesper dove with an olive-leaf,
Its rainbow over Ararat.°

### LA°

Glaciers had shouldered down
The cis-Saharan° snows,
Shoved antelope and lion
230    Past *Uaz-Oîriet*° floes.

Leopard, elephant, ape,
Rhinoceros and giraffe
Jostled in odysseys
To Africa: siamang° laugh

235    And curse impaled the frost
As Northmen brandished paws
And shambled Europe-ward,
Gnashing Cerberean° jaws.

---

222–223 *lay / my head*: (Tolson's note): "Cf. Matthew VIII, xx." "And Jesus saith unto him, 'The foxes have holes, and the birds of the air have nests; but the Son of Man hath not where to lay his head' " (Matthew 8:20).

224–226 *Ark . . . Ararat*: "And the ark [of Noah] rested . . . upon the mountains of Ararat" (Genesis: 8:4). After the flood waters had receded, Noah sent first a raven then a dove to determine whether there was any dry land. The dove returned with an olive-leaf (Genesis 8:8–12). (Tolson's note) "V. *New York Times*, 'Journey to Ararat,' April 17, 1949 [section B, p. 2. The article records an incident from the Cold War that shows the fragile nature of postwar peace. An Anglo-American archeological expedition to Mt. Ararat in Turkey to look for remains of the Ark was labeled by Russians as a "spying mission." Mount Ararat overlooked the Russian-Iranian border.] Cf. Maill's translation of a poem by an officer in the hospital at Erivan [Armenia]: 'Here is Mount Ararat. It has a brooding look . . . / One would think it was waiting to be set free.' "

*La*: Sixth note in the diatonic scale. After establishing a vast timeline that begins with the Ice Age, Tolson continues the history of Liberia's founding, beginning with a second wave of colonizers led by the white minister Jehudi Ashman.

228 *Cis-Saharan*: the prefix "cis-" designates that the speaker is on a particular side of the geographical place named.

230 *Uaz-Oîret*: (Tolson's note) "'The Very Green,' the ancient Egyptian name for the Mediterranean." From G. Gaston Maspero, *The Dawn of Civilization* (1901), Chapter I. See Tolson's note to line 692.

234 *siamang*: the black-haired gibbon ape of Sumatra.

238 *Cerberean jaws*: Cerberus was the multi-headed dog that guarded the entrance to Hades.

After *netami lennowak,*°
240          A white man spined with dreams°
Came to cudgel parrot scholars
And slay philistine schemes.

"The lion's teeth, the eagle's
Talons, shall break!" declared
245          Prophet Jehudi Ashmun,°
Christening the bones that dared.

When the black bat's ultima smote
His mate in the yoke, he felt
The seven swords'° *pis aller*°
250          Twist in his heart at the hilt.

He said: "My Negro kinsmen,
America is my mother,
Liberia is my wife,
And Africa my brother."

---

239 *netami lennowak*: (Tolson's note) "'the first men.'"

240 *spined with dreams*: (Tolson's note) "Cf. Virgil [(70–19 B.C.)], *Aeneid* Book IV, line 625: '*Excoriare aliquis!*'" The complete phrase is "*exoriare, aliquis . . . ultor!*" ("Arise, some avenger!), one of a series of curses that Dido, the beautiful Queen of Carthage (a city on the African coast), levels against Aeneas of Rome and "his progeny and all his race to come." (Not knowing by name her future avenger, he can only be "some" avenger.) Robert Howard points out that Virgil's audience would have understood Dido's curse to have been amply fulfilled by the three Punic wars with Carthage and the rise of Hannibal (247–183 B.C.), the general from Carthage who invaded Rome. Tolson's convoluted reference, with its narrative of betrayal and rage, perhaps complicates the kind of "dreams" a white man can be "spined with."

245 *Prophet Jehudi Ashmun*: (Tolson's note): "Lincoln University, the oldest Negro institution of its kind in the world, was founded as Ashmun Institute. The memory of the white pilgrim survives in old Ashmun Hall and in the Greek and Latin inscriptions cut in stones sacred to Lincoln men. The annual Lincoln-Liberian dinner is traditional, and two of the graduates have been ministers to Liberia." Ashmun (1794–1828), Congregational minister and journalist, sailed on the second expedition to Liberia in 1822, where he found the first wave of settlers decimated by fever and threatened by hostile tribes. His wife, who had accompanied him, died of malaria. Rallying the colonists, he repulsed attacks by natives with two cannons on loan from the U.S. Navy. Disease forced him home to America, where he died in 1828 at age 35.

249 *seven swords*: (Tolson's note): "V. [Guillaume] Appollinaire ([1880–1918]), '*La Chanson du Mal-Aimé*' ["Song of the Poorly-Loved," from *Alcools* (*Alcohols*, 1913)], the fifth and sixth sections." The seventh of the "seven swords of melancholy" that are wedged in the heart of those who have been treated poorly by love represents "a woman, a dead rose." The swords each sing in section 4, "The Seven Swords," and are introduced at the end of section 3, "Reply of the Zaporagian Cossacks to the Sultan of Constantinople." The poem is a blend of lyrical mourning for a lost love with outright anger at her betrayal (she left him). In French, the names of each sword sound slightly obscene, and the poem veers in and out of absurd lines. At one point, Appollinaire laments: "And oh my heart is as heavy / as the butt of a dame from Damascus" (lines 196–197).

249 *Pis aller*: (French) both "the worst possible choice" but also the only choice in a limited situation in which no other real option exists.

### TI°

255         O Calendar of the Century,
             red-letter° the Republic's birth!
             O Hallelujah,
             oh, let no *Miserere*°
             venom the spinal cord of Afric earth!
260                    *Selah!*°


             "*Ecce homo!*"°
             the blind men cowled in azure° rant
             before the Capitol,
             between the Whale and Elephant,°
265         where no longer stands Diogenes' hearse°
             readied for the ebony mendicant,°
             nor weeping widow Europe with her hands
             making the multitudinous seas incarnadine°
             or earth's *massebôth*° worse:

---

*Ti*: is the seventh note of the diatonic scale. The poem ranges widely across numerous historical, cultural, and political narratives, drawn from every corner of the globe, to suggest that while civilizations come and go, the conflicts between the few and the many, the elite and the masses, pervade human history. Tolson's controversial assertion is that no one ethnic group has a particular claim on being oppressed or on oppressing others.

256 *red-letter day*: special occasion.

258 *Miserere* [*Psalm* 51]: (Tolson's Note) "Cf. [John Henry] Newman [(1801–1890)], '*The Definition of a Gentleman*': '. . . we attended the Tenebrae, at the Sistine, for the sake of the Miserere.'" Possibly, at the Sistine chapel in Rome, Newman and company went to the evening service in order to appreciate the singing of the 51st Psalm, "Have Mercy on us, O God." Tolson presents the well-educated British sampling the finest moments of a religious culture for their aesthetic gratification rather than for their moral authority.

260 *Selah*: A Hebrew word sometimes marking the close of a Psalm. Its precise meaning is uncertain; it may signify a pause like a brief rest in musical notation.

261"*Ecce homo!*": "Behold the man!" Pilate's words as he presented Jesus Christ to the people (John 19:1–5).

262 *Cowled in azure*: (Tolson's note) "the cloak of deceit and false humility. Cf. Hafiz, *The Divan* (*Odes*), V. translated by Bicknell." The blue-colored cowl in the fifth ode signifies the elemental body, that which prevents the soul from a union with God. By referring to one of the several hundred odes in the *Divan* of the Persian poet Hafiz (d. 1388/1391?), all of which have been interpreted for their religious meaning, Tolson reminds us of alternatives to the Christian Bible, though these figures placed "before the Capitol" (line 263) seem closer to lobbyists and elected officials.

264 *Whale and elephant*: (Tolson's note) "The symbols [(Thomas)] Jefferson [(1743–1826)] used to designate Great Britain with her navy under [Horatio] Nelson [(1758–1805)] and France with her army under Napoleon [(1769–1821)]. V. [Robert Earle] Anderson, *Liberia* [: *America's African Friend* (1952)], X."

265 *Diogenes*: possibly the Greek philosopher (412?–323 B.C.) who had withdrawn from worldly wealth and whose "hearse" would not have amounted to much.

266 *mendicant*: beggar.

268 *making . . . incarnadine*: The murderer Macbeth believes that if he tried to wash the blood from his guilty hand in the ocean, it would turn the "multitudinous seas incarnadine" (i.e., flesh- or pink-colored) (*Macbeth*, II, ii, line 61).

269 *Massebôth*: (Tolson's note) "'sacred pillars.' [Numerous early cultures, including the Egyptian, conceived of the sky as being held up by pillars.] Cf. Genesis 28:18. [" . . . this is none other but the house of God, and this is the gate of heaven. And Jacob rose up early in the morning and took the stone that he had put for his pillows, and set it up for a pillar, and poured oil upon the top of it" (Genesis 28:17–18)]. Also the J Author." The "J Author" (ninth century B.C.) was presumed to have written an early history of the world that was the basis for the book of Genesis.

270  O Great White World, thou boy of tears,° omega hounds
     lap up the alpha laugh° and *du-haut-en-bas*° curse.
                    *Selah!*


               O Africa, Mother of Science
               . . . *lachen mit yastchekes* . . . °
275                   What dread hand,°
          to make tripartite one august event,°
               sundered Gondwanaland?°
          What dread grasp crushed your biceps and
                    back upon the rack
280                 chaos of chance and change
               fouled in Malebolgean° isolation?
          What dread *elboga*° shoved your soul
               into the *tribulum*° of retardation?
     melamin or melanin° dies to the world and dies:
285            Rome casketed herself in Homeric hymns.°
               Man's culture in barb and Arab lies:°
               The Jordan flows into the Tiber,°

---

270 *Thou boy of tears*: (Tolson's note) "Cf. Shakespeare, *Coriolanus*, V, v." When Cori-
olanus calls on Mars as the god of war, his enemy Aufidius jeers: "Name not the god, thou
boy of tears" (5, vi, line 101). What Coriolanus violently objects to, in the lines that follow,
is being addressed as "boy."
270–271 *omega . . . alpha*: "alpha" and "omega" as first and last letters of the Greek al-
phabet came to signify the beginning and the end.
271 *du-haut-en-bas*: (French) "downwards; from top to bottom."
274 *Lachen mit yastchekes*: (Tolson's note) [(Yiddish)] " 'laughing with needles being stuck
in you': ghetto laughter."
275 *what dread hand*: (Tolson's note) "Cf. [William] Blake [(1757–1827)], 'The Tyger.'"
"Tyger! Tyger! Burning bright / In the forest of the night, / What immortal hand or eye /
Could frame thy fearful symmetry?" (lines 1–4).
276 *august event*: (Tolson's note) "Cf. [Thomas] Hardy [(1840–1928)], 'The Convergence of
the Twain.'" Hardy's poem is subtitled "Lines on the loss of the 'Titanic'" and it envisions
the converging of the ship and "A Shape of Ice": "No mortal eye could see / The intimate
welding of their later history, / Or sign that they were bent / By paths coincident / On be-
ing anon the twin halves of one august event" (stanzas IX–X).
277 *Gondwanaland*: Name of the landmass formed when India, Africa, and South Amer-
ica were one unit.
281 *Malebolgean*: *Malebolge*: (Italian) "evil pockets." This was the nickname, as Dante
learned in Canto XVIII of the *Inferno*, of the ten stony ravines that rigidly separated the
violent sinners in lower hell.
282 *elboga*: (Anglo-Saxon) "elbow."
283 *tribulum*: (Latin) "threshing-sledge."
284 *melamin or melanin*: the pigments that determine skin color.
285 *Homeric hymns*: The writings of early Greek poets, ascribed to Homer, deeply admired
by a later Roman culture.
286 *barb and Arab*: (Tolson's note) "V. [W. P.] Pycraft, *Animals of the World*, 1941–1942.
*A fortiori* [i.e., necessarily] the American trotter is 'a combination of barb and Arab on En-
glish stock.'" The animals are horses.
287 *Jordan . . . Tiber*: (Tolson's note). "V. [Arthur] Christy, [ed.,] *The Asian Legacy and
American Life* [(1945)]. This book contains vital facts on oriental influences in the New
Poetry. What I owe the late professor Arthur E. Christy, a favorite teacher, is not limited
to the concept of 'the shuttle ceaselessly weaving the warp and weft of the world's cul-
tural fabric.'" Tolson quotes from Christy's Foreword in which Christy objects to "Spen-
glerian prophets of doom for the West" who "have thought too exclusively of domination
or decline."

the Yangtze into the Thames,
the Ganges into the Mississippi, the Niger
290                        into the Seine.°
Judge of the Nations, spare us: yet,
fool latins, alumni of one school,
on Clochan-na-n'all,° say *Phew*°
. . . *Lest we forget! Lest we forget!* . . . °
295        to dusky peers° of Roman, Greek, and Jew.
*Selah!*

Elders of Agâ's House,° keening
at the Eagles' feast, cringing
before the Red Slayer, shrinking
300        from the blood on Hubris' pall—
carked by cracks of myriad curbs,°

288–290 *Yangtze . . . Seine:* Tolson borrowed this from Christy's foreword (see note to line 287): "The legacies of Israel and Rome in Occidental civilization have been described as the Jordan flowing into the Tiber. In more recent times the Yangtze has flowed into the Thames and the Ganges into the Mississippi" (p. viii). Tolson also echoes the opening lines of Paul Verlaine (1844–1896)'s "Parisian Nocturne" (1866), a text he acknowledges in the footnote to line 405.

292 *Clochan-na-n'all:* (Tolson's note) 'the blind man's stepping stones.' Cf. [Samuel] Ferguson [(1810–1866)], 'The Welshmen of Tirawley.'" This low-water crossing in the Duvowen River in west Ireland was named thus after the males of the Lynott clan who had been blinded by members of a rival clan (the Barretts) and then forced to walk over "the slippery stepping-stones." The intricate revenge of the Lynotts, enacted over several decades and involving a third clan, resulted in the Barrett's loss of their freedom and virtual enslavement, as described in Ferguson's narrative poem in his *Lays of the Western Gael* (1886).

293 *Phew:* expression of relief.

294 *Lest we forget!:* The refrain from Kipling's "Processional" (1897), a hymn-like poem that was performed when representatives from all British colonies gathered in celebration of Queen Elizabeth's diamond jubilee. It asserts that British colonial rule is an extension of the hand of God ("God of our fathers . . . / Beneath whose awful Hand we hold / Dominion over palm and wine" [lines 1, 3–4]) but also claims that punishments will result if that power is used injudiciously. DuBois cited from the poem, describing it as an "epitaph" to the concept of the "White Man's Burden" in *The World and Africa* (1946), Chapter I.

295 *dusky peers:* Not just that Africans should be accorded equality with "Roman, Greek and Jew" but that African civilizations are fully equivalent to other great civilizations of the past and contributed significantly to ancient knowledge. We are all "alumni of one school" (line 293).

297 *Elders . . . House:* (Tolson's note) "V. [Aeschylus,] *Agamemnon.*" Possibly a reference to the House of Argos, of which Agamemnon was a descendant—a clan whose violence matches the events listed in lines 297–299.

301 *cracks . . . curbs:* (Tolson's note) "Cf. Shakespeare, *Coriolanus*, I, I, 67–76. See also Mr. Traversi's essay on this phase of the play." In the play, Menius is explaining to an angry crowed that it is futile for them to protest the Roman state because the state is indifferent to the masses: "you may as well / Strike at the heaven with your staves as lift them / Against the Roman state, whose course will on / The way it takes, cracking ten thousand curbs [i.e. restraints] / Of more strong link asunder than can ever / Appear in your impediment" (I, 1, lines 69–73). Derek Traversi's essay, in *Scrutiny* 6:1 (1937), cites and praises these lines for conveying the "sense of a social order hardened into insensitivity on the one hand and unworthiness on the other, the patricians and the people utterly out of contact with one another."

                    hitherto, against the Wailing Wall
                      of Ch'in,° the blind men cried:
                           All cultures crawl
305                           walk hard
                                fall,
                               flout
                        under classes under
                                Lout,
310              enmesh in ethos, in masôreth,° the poet's flesh,
              intone the Mass of the class as the requiem of the mass,
                   serve idola mentis° till the crack of will,
                   castle divorcee Art° in a blue-blood moat,
                         read the flesh of grass°
315                        into bulls and bears,°
                         let Brahmin° pens kill
                          Everyman the Goat,
                write Culture's epitaph in Notes upstairs.°
                         O Cordon Sanitaire,°
320              thy brain's tapeworm, extract, thy eyeball's mote!°
                               Selah!

---

303 *Ch'in*: (Tolson's note) "I came across these words somewhere: 'The Ch'in emperor built the Great Wall to keep out Mongolian enemies from the north and burned the books of China to destroy intellectual enemies from within.'" The Ch'in dynasty only ruled from 221 to 207 B.C. but during that time immense public works projects were undertaken, including roads, canals, and the Great Wall. The ruthless centralizing policy of its first emperor, Shih Huang-ti (259–210 B.C.) provoked such a reaction that after his death the empire collapsed.

310 *Masôreth*: (Tolson's note) "Cf. Akiba: '*Masôreth* is a fence for the sayings of the fathers.'" "Sayings" are not identical to the folk wisdom of the *Griots* because they are associated with "fathers" (whose "fence" is a form of control) while the *griots* are bards who speak for the whole of the people, including the underclass.

312 *Idola mentis*: (Tolson's note) [(Latin) "Idols of the Mind"]. "V. [Francis] Bacon [(1561–1626)], *Novum Organum*", [sections 23–46]. *Idola* can mean "image," "phantom," and "appearance." Bacon's phrase refers to the preconceived notions—the superstitions, beliefs, convictions—which, because they are part of our cultural background "so beset men's minds that they become difficult of access" and "even when access is obtained, will again meet and trouble us" (section 38).

313 *Divorcee art*: (Tolson's note) "Cf. [Rene de] Gourmont [(1858–1915)]: '*Car je crois que l'art est par essence, absolument inintelligible du peuple.*'" (French) "For I believe that art is, by its very essence, absolutely incomprehensible to the masses."

314 *flesh of grass*: "What shall I cry? All flesh is grass, and all the goodliness thereof is as the flower of the field" (Isaiah 40:6).

315 *bulls and bears*: Shorthand for the Wall Street stock exchange with buyers who are either confident ("bulls") or withdrawing ("bears," ready for hibernation). In Tolson's construction, they also devour the goodliness of flesh/grass.

316 *Brahmin*: a person from a long-established upper-class family.

318 *Notes upstairs*: footnotes designed to mystify rather than inform.

319 *Cordon Sanitaire*: originally, military posts on the borders of a disease-infected area that prevent a disease from spreading; in geopolitical terms, a ring of countries that serve to isolate another country and diminish its influence.

320 *mote*: "And why beholdest thou the mote that is in thy brother's eye, but considerest not the beam that is in thine own eye?" asks Christ in Matthew 7:3 and Luke 6:41.

Between pavilions
small and great
sentineled from capital to stylobate°
325      by crossbow, harquebus,° cannon, or Pegasus' bomb°
. . . *and none went in and none went out* . . . °
hitherto the State,°
in spite of Sicilian Vespers,° stout
from slave, feudal, bourgeois, or soviet grout,°
330      has hung its curtain°—scrim, foulard, pongee,
silk, lace, or iron°—helled in by Sancho's fears°
of the bitter hug of the Great Fear,° Not-To-Be—

---

324 *stylobate*: an architectural term for the pedestal upon which a series of columns stand.
325 *harquebus*: an early gun.
325 *Pegasus' bomb*: (Tolson's note) "Cf. [Austin] Dobson [(1840–1921)], 'On the Future of Poetry.'" Dobson's 1913 poem wonders: "Will Pegasus return again / in guise of modern aeroplane, / Descending from a cloudless blue / To drop on us a bomb or two?" (lines 9–12).
326 *none . . . out*: (Tolson's Note) "V. Joshua VI, i. 'Now Jericho was straitly shut up because of the children of Israel: none went out, and none came in'" (Joshua 6:1). Priests blowing on rams's horns and the people shouting in unison would soon shatter Jericho's walls.
327 *the State*: (Tolson's note) "Cf. [Heinrich von] Treitschke [(1834–1896)]: 'The State is Power. Of so unusual a type is its power that it has no power to limit its power. Hence no treaty, when it becomes inconvenient, can be binding; hence the very notion of arbitration is absurd; hence war is a part of the Divine order.' Contrast this idea with [Abraham] Lincoln [(1809–1865)]'s premise that the people can establish either a republic of wolves or a democracy of lambs, as instanced in the poem 'The Dictionary of the Wolf.' Cf. [probably, Otto von] Bismarck: 'The clause *rebus sic stantis* ["as things stand"] is understood in every contract.'"
328 *Sicilian Vespers*: The frailty of the state has been rarely dramatized so vividly as in the spontaneous uprising by Sicilian peasantry during an Easter vespers (evening) service in 1282 known as "Sicilian Vespers." It flared into a massacre of virtually all the French who had settled in as colonizers of Sicily. This indigenous revolt rapidly spread across the island, and eventually shifted the Mediterranean balance of power, fatally weakening the medieval papal monarchy.
329 *Soviet*: a council of delegates. *Grout*: (1) a rough or coarse meal; (2) mortar used for gaps in stone- and brick-work.
330 *Curtain*: (Tolson's note) "Cf. [George] Crile, *A Mechanistic View of War and Peace* (1915): 'France [is] a nation of forty million with a deep-rooted grievance and an iron curtain at its frontier.'" Crile's 1915 study of World War I is a disturbing photographic documentary of that war's inhumanity and a remarkably early attempt to intervene in the ongoing war. He was a surgeon from the Western Reserve University unit attached to the American Ambulance service at Neuilly-sur-Sein in France. "Iron curtain" was a term popularized by Winston Churchill after World Word II to describe the secrecy and censorship that Soviet Russia formed around itself.
329–330 "*Scrim . . . iron*": all materials from which curtains are made.
331 *Sancho's fears*: (Tolson's note) "V. [Miguel de] Cervantes [(1547–1616)], *Don Quixote de la Mancha, Part II*, translated by Peter Motteux, the episode of the letter: 'To Don Sancho Pança, Governor of the island of Barataria, to be delivered into his own hands or those of his secretary.'" Quixote had expected Sancho Pança to fail in his role as governor, he admits in this letter (in Chapter 51), but he has heard nothing but praise for his wise and practical actions.
332 *The Great Fear*: (Tolson's note) "V. [Louis] Madelin, *The French Revolution*, [(1926), p.] 69." "Ever since the beginning of April, Paris and its immediate neighborhood had been living in a state of terror, all the more poignant because it was undefined. . . . The whole country was in the grip of a sort of national hysteria, which historians will never be able to explain" (Part I, Chapter 2).

*oscuro Luzbel*,°<br>
with no bowels of mercy,°<br>
335         in the starlight°<br>
*de las canteras sin auroras*.°<br>
Behind the curtain, aeon after aeon,<br>
he who doubts the white book's° colophon°<br>
is Truth's, if not Laodicean,° wears<br>
340        the black flower° T of doomed Laocoön.°<br>
Before hammer and sickle or swastika,° two<br>
worlds existed: the Many, the Few.<br>
They sat at Delos', at Vienna's, at Yalta's,° ado:<br>
Macbeth, without three rings,° as host<br>
345        to Banquo's ghost.°<br>
*Selah!*

---

333 *oscuro Luzbel*: (Spanish) "Dark Lucifer." (Tolson's note) "[Rafael] Alberti [(b. 1902)], *Sobre los Angeles*" [*Concerning Angels* (1928)]. Tolson reprints parts of lines 12–13 from one of the poems in the collection, "*Los Dos Angeles*" ("The Two Angels") which he returns to cite in line 336. Lucifer is the "Son of Light," the fallen angel who revolted against heaven and thus became Devil.

334 *mercy*: (Tolson's note) "Cf. The aphorism: '*La politique n'a pas d'entrailles*.'" "Politics has no bowels of mercy."

335 *Starlight*: (Tolson's note) "Cf. [George] Meredith: [(1828–1909)], 'Lucifer in the Starlight.'" In this 1883 sonnet, Lucifer soars around the world only to discover his limits when he looks to the stars and recognizes they are a barrier to his ambitions.

336 *De las canteras sin auroras*: (Spanish) "of the quarry without dawn." This follows a phrase from the Alberti poem in line 333. The entire stanza reads: "You are burning me alive. / Fly away from me now, dark / Lucifer of the quarry without dawn, / of the wells with no water, / of the abyss with no sleep, / now coal of the soul, / sun, moon" (lines 11–17).

338 *white book*: the white book (so called for its white binder) originated as a government's official position on political affairs, but in totalitarian governments, it often became a list of approvals and prohibitions.

338 *colophon*: publisher's imprint—for a white book, the State.

339 *Laodicean*: The early Christians of Laodicea lacked intensity of religious feeling.

340 *black flower T*: (Tolson's note) "Cf. [Nathaniel] Hawthorne [(1804–1864)], *The Scarlet Letter*: 'The black flower of civilized society, a prison [(Chapter 1)].'" Hawthorne's heroine wore a scarlet "A" for adultery; Tolson's "T" represents truth. Tolson's complex metaphor inverts conventional color symbolism: the "white book" may carry lies and the "black flower" of prison in a totalitarian nation may be an honorable place to reside.

340 *Laocoön*: Because he had warned the Trojans against the wooden horse, Laocoön and two sons were destroyed by sea serpents. A famous sculpture shows all three elaborately entangled in the serpent's coils. Tolson suggests that those who question state-sponsored "truth" will meet this fate.

341 *hammer and sickle or swastika*: patriotic symbols of Soviet Russia and Nazi Germany.

343 *Delos, Vienna, Yalta*: locations where governments negotiated peace treaties.

344 *three rings*: (Tolson's note) "V. [Giovanni] Boccaccio [(1313–1375)], 'The Three Rings.' Cf. [Gotthold E.] Lessing [(1729–1781)], *Nathan the Wise*." In Boccaccio's *Decameron*, the third story told by travelers on the first day is about a father who wishes to distribute his property equally among all three sons. He has two copies made of the ring that he will pass on after his death to designate his sole heir. The copies are so true to the original that no one can determine which is real and the sons thus learn they must equally share their heritage. In Lessing's play, Nathan shrewdly tells Boccaccio's story when he is asked: "which of all religions is the true one?" No one can tell whether Judaism, Mohammedism, or Christianity is the genuine article.

344–345 *host / to Banquo's ghost*: In *Macbeth* III, iv, the ghost of Banquo, whose slaying had been commissioned by Macbeth, appears to Macbeth alone, sitting in Macbeth's place, at a large state banquet. Lacking direction from the parable of the three rings, Macbeth murdered to inherit his throne.

Like some gray ghoul from Alcatraz,°
old Profit, the bald rake *paseq*,° wipes the bar,
polishes the goblet vanity,
350        leers at the tigress Avarice
as
she harlots roués° from afar:
swallowtails° unsaved by loincloths,
famed enterprises° prophesying war,
355     hearts of rags (*Hanorish tharah sharinas*°) souls of chalk,°
laureates with sugary grace° in zinc buckets of verse,°

---

347 *Alcatraz*: Maximum security prison on an island in San Francisco Bay.

348 *Paseq*: (Tolson's note) "divider. This is a vertical line that occurs about 480 times in our Hebrew Bible. Although first mentioned in the *Midrash Rabba* in the eleventh century, it is still the most mysterious sign in literature." (Also see Tolson's note to line 367.) Though "Peseq" and "Paseq" in Hebrew mean "separator" or "separated," the sign itself (a vertical bar that resembles this mark: | ) was not intended to cause separation when it appears in a text. This "note-line" appears between words, never letters, and scholars conjecture that scribes placed this simple mark to call attention to a noteworthy or questionable passage as an assurance that this text, though unusual, was exactly the same as a previous manuscript. It functions most often like our own "[sic]." A simple example occurs in Isaiah 6:3 where the words "holy, holy, holy!" are separated by | to indicate this repetition is not an error of transcription. A *Midrash* (Hebrew for "explanation") is a commentary on the Hebrew Bible, and the *Midrash Rabbah* was one of the earliest, circa 1200 A.D. In his passage, Tolson uses "Paseq" to suggest that the desire for "Profit" has been the divisive factor in many societies.

352 *roués*: a dissipated man, a rake.

352 *from afar*: (Tolson's note) "Cf. [C. P.] Cavafy [(1863–1933)], 'Waiting for the Barbarians.'" In Cavafy's poem, senators put on "amethyst-studded bracelets" and "rings with glittering emeralds," dressing this way, they say, to please the simple barbarians. Civilizations define themselves by identifying those they see as "barbarians" but they also use them as an excuse to take on "outlawed" attributes.

353 *swallowtails*: man's full-dress coat, with a back that tapers into two long tails.

354 *Famed enterprises*: (Tolson's note) "V. Erasmus [(1466?–1536)], *The Praise of Folly*, 'Soldiers and Philosophers,' *in toto*, the revised translation by John Wilson."

355 *Hearts of rags . . . souls of chalk*: (Tolson's note) "[(Walt)] Whitman's epithets for the 'floating mass' that vote early and often for bread and circuses."

355 *Hanorish tharah sharinas*: (Tolson's note) "'Man is a being of varied, manifold and inconstant nature.' Vide [Giovanni Pico] della Mirandola [(1463–1494)], *Oration on the Dignity of Man*. Cf. [Euclydes da] Cunha [(1866–1909)]: 'The fantasy of universal suffrage [is] the Hercules' club of our dignity.'" The quote is from Chapter II, Section V, "Depredations" in the Samuel Putnam translation of Cunha's 1902 history *Os Sertões* ("The Backlands") entitled *Rebellion in the Backlands* (1944). Hercules' club was a large one. Tolson will now cite from Cunha's history with increasing frequency. A civil engineer, Cunha wrote history on a grand scale, composing an exhaustive study of the geography, ethnic groups, and social structures of the south of Brazil in order to explain why the state would perceive as a threat the peaceful settlement of a large mass of poor people who were the religious followers of a self-declared prophet. After several battles, the Brazilian military succeeded in massacring the group, including women and children. Cunha's widely praised study has been described as the national epic of Brazil. See Tolson's notes to lines 491 and 533.

356 *Sugary grace*: (Tolson's note) "Cf. Martial [(40–102?)], 'To a Rival Poet.'" "Your verses are full of sugary grace, / As spotless and pure as a well-powdered face" (Book VII, poem 25, lines 1–2 in the J. A. Pott and F. A. Wright translation that Tolson used).

356 *Zinc . . . verse*: (Tolson's note) "V. [Boris] Pasternak [(1890–1960)], 'Definition of Poetry.'" From the last stanza of "Poetry" (1922) in the Eugene M. Kayden translation: "When undoubted truths, O Poetry, / Are held like buckets at the tap, / The hoarded stream will spout—for me / In my open copybook to tap."

myths rattled by the blueprint's talk,
ists° potted and pitted by a feast,
Red Ruin's° skeleton horsemen,° four abreast
360 . . . galloping . . .
Marx, the exalter, would not know his East
. . . galloping . . .
nor Christ, the Leveler,° His West.
*Selah!*


365               O Age of Tartuffe°
*. . . a lighthouse with no light atop . . .*
O Age, pesiq,° O Age,
kinks internal and global stinks

---

358 *ists*: "ist" is a suffix that means "one who believes in" or "practices."

359 *Red Ruin*: (Tolson's note) "Cf. [Alfred, Lord] Tennyson, *Idylls of the King* [(1885)]: 'Red ruin, and the breaking of laws.'" King Arthur chastises the Queen for her unfaithfulness: "Well is it that no child is born of thee. / The children born of thee are sword and fire, / Red ruin, and the breaking up of laws" (from "Guinevere," lines 422–424).

359 *skeleton horsemen*: (Tolson's note) "V. Revelations VI. [This passage from the Book of Revelations introduces the four horsemen of the Apocalypse who appear at the end of the world.] Cf. [Pierre Jean] Jouve [(b. 1887)], '*La Resurrection des Morts*' ["The Resurrection of the Dead"]. See the White Horse, the Red Horse, the Black Horse and the fourth horse, the worst: '*Tu es jaune et ta forme coule à ta charpente / Sur le tonneau ajouré de tes côtes / Les lambeaux certis tombent plus transparents / La queue est chauve et le bassin a des béquilles / Pour le stérile va-et-vient de la violence . . .*'" Jouve's distorted description of the fourth horse eludes smooth translation: "You are pale-yellow and your form is stretched tightly on your frame / On the barrel [of your torso] light shows up your slatted sides / The tightly inserted shreds fell more transparent / The tail is bald and the pelvis leans on crutches / For the pale to-and-fro of violence." The book-length poem *Kyrie* (1946) which includes "*Les Quatres Cavaliers*" (French: "The Four Horsemen") was written during World War II and translates the prophecies from the Book of Revelation into a current history in which Hitler is the anti-Christ.

363 *The Leveler*: (Tolson's note) "V. Acts 3:32–36." "And the multitude that believed were of one heart and of one soul: neither said any of them that ought of the things which he possessed was his own; but they had all things common (Acts 3:32) . . . a distribution was made unto every man according to his need" (Acts 3:35).

365 *Tartuffe*: In the 1664 play of the same name by Moliere [1622–1673], he is the very type of the pious hypocrite.

367 *Pesiq*: (Tolson's note) [(Hebrew)] "'divided.' V. Fuchs, *Pesiq ein Glossenzeichen* [(German) *Pesiq as Comment-Sign*]. It seems to me that this linguistic symbol gives us a concrete example of the teleological—perhaps the only one. By an accident of *a priori* probability, the sign in itself indicates both cause and effect, and the index of the relationship is served synchronously by either *paseq* or *pasiq*. Of course the protagonist of the poem uses them for his own purpose on another level." Like "paseq" itself as Tolson discussed it in his earlier note to line 348, these remarks are "the most mysterious" of all the footnotes. Tolson may be suggesting that the note-sign as "paseq" (which he translates as "divider") when placed in a text at once brings about the condition of "pesiq" (which he translates as "divided"), as if the marking that was intended to be unobtrusive now actively intrudes. The final sentence implies that Tolson reserves for the poem a limited use of "pesiq" as "divided" or "separated" perhaps to indicate the numerous separations in modern culture—as in class and race.

fog the bitter black estates° of Buzzard° and Og.°
370     A Dog, I'd rather be, o sage, a Monkey or a Hog.°
O Peoples of the Brinks,°
come with the hawk's resolve,
the skeptic's optic nerve, the prophet's *tele*° verve
and Oedipus' guess, to solve
375     the riddle of
the Red Enigma and the White Sphinx.°
*Selah!*


O East . . . *el grito de Dolores*° . . . O West,
pacts, disemboweled, crawl off to die;
380     white books,° *fiers instants promis à la faux,*°
in sick bay choke on mulligan° truth and lie;

---

369 *Bitter black estates*: (Tolson's note) "Cf. [Francesco] Petrarch [(1304–1374)], 'The Spring
Returns, but Not To Him Returns' [*Zefira torna*," sonnet 310] translated by [Joseph] Aus-
lander". In Auslander's melodramatic rendering, all of the beauties of spring—"these mead-
ows, blossoms, birds / these lovely gentle girls" are, because Laura is gone, just "words,
empty words, / As bitter as the black estates of death!" (lines 12–14).
369 *Buzzard*: (Tolson's note) "V. [John] Dryden, 'The Hind and the Panther.'" The poem
is an allegory of political power in which certain animals represent various factions. Lines
1120–1280 describe the unattractive buzzard.
369 *Og*: (Tolson's note) "V. Tate, 'The Second Part of Absalom and Achitophel,' the pas-
sage inserted by Dryden." Dryden's 1682 sequel continues his attack on fellow poet Thomas
Shadwell (1642?–1692) here designated as "Og" and previously targeted in *MacFlecknoe*:
"With all his bulk there's nothing lost in Og, / For ev'ry inch that is not fool is rogue: / A
monstrous mass of foul corrupted matter, / As all the devils had spewed to make the bat-
ter."
370 *a Hog*: (Tolson's note) "V. [John Wilmot, Earl of] Rochester [(1647–1680)], 'Satyr against
Mankind.' [Lines 1–7: "Were I . . . A spirit free to choose . . . What case of flesh and blood
I pleased to wear, / I'd be a dog, a monkey, or a bear, / Or anything but that vain animal
/ Who is so proud of being rational."] Cf. [Jean] Cocteau [(1889–1963)], *Le Cap de Bonne
Espérance*: '*J'ai mal d'être homme.*' "I am sick of being a man," from "Attempt to Escape,"
the second poem in Cocteau's first collection, *Cape of Good Hope* (1916), an exploration
of the destructive role of the airplane in modern warfare.
371 *Brinks*: Robert Farnsworth suggests this refers both to the Brink's Armored Car Ser-
vice, which delivers money safely to banks, and the cold war foreign policy of "brinks-
manship" in which America and Russia were always testing each other's resolve.
373 *tele*: perhaps from the Greek *telos*, "an end."
376 *Red Enigma and White Sphinx*: Possibly an allusion to the Cold War stalemate be-
tween Soviet communism and capitalist democracy. But Tolson used these same terms
broadly in *Harlem Gallery* (1965): "the poet's mind kept shuttling between / the sphinx of
yesterday and the enigma of today."
378 *el grito de Dolores*: (Spanish) literally, "the cry of Dolores (Death)." (Tolson's note)
"The watchword of [Miguel] Hidalgo [y Costilla (1753–1811)], 'Captain General of Amer-
ica.'" In 1810, Mexican Priest Miguel Hidalgo's "Cry of Dolores" announced an anti-Span-
ish revolutionary movement that proclaimed the emancipation of slaves, return of land to
native Indians, and numerous social reforms. Though initially successful in battle, his army
was eventually routed. While heading north to seek refuge in the United States he was
betrayed, captured by Royalist forces, tortured, and executed.
380 *white books*: see note to line 338.
380 *fiers . . . faux*: (Tolson's note) "Cf. [Vincent] Muselli [(d. 1956)], '*Ballade de Contra-
diction*': '*Fiers instants promis à la faux, / Éclairs sombrés au noir domaine.*'" (French):
"Proud moments, already claimed by the scythe [of death], / Lightning-streaks tumbling
down the black domain" (lines 21–22) of the sixth *ballade* in *Sept Ballades de Contradic-
tion* (1941) (*Seven Ballads of Contradiction*).
381 *mulligan truth*: A mulligan stew was a random mix of ingredients.

the knife of Rousseau° hacks the anatomy
of the fowl necessity;
dead eyes accuse red Desfourneau,°
385        whose sit-down strike° gives High-Heels vertigo;°
the wind blows through the keyhole°
and the fettered pull down the shades;
while il *santo* and *pero*° hone phillipics,°
*Realpolitik*° explodes the hand grenades
390                    *faits accomplis*°
in the peace of parades;
caught in the blizzard *divide et impera,*°
the little gray cattle° cower
before the Siamese wolves,
395                    pomp and power;°
Esperanto° trips the heels of Greek;
in brain-sick lands° the pearls too rich for swine

---

382 *Rousseau*: Jean-Jacques Rousseau (1712–1778), French philosopher who insisted that humans were inherently good but became corrupted by civilization.

384 *Desfourneau*: (Tolson's note) "Cf. [Albert] Camus [(1913–1960)], 'The Artist as Witness of Freedom' [*Commentary* 8: 12 (December 1949), 534–538; a translation by Bernard Frechtman of "*Le Témoin de la Liberté*" 1948.] M. Desfourneau's '. . . demands were clear. He naturally wanted a bonus for each execution, which is customary in any enterprise. But, more important, he vigorously demanded that he be given . . . an administrative status. Thus came to an end, beneath the weight of history, one of the last of our liberal professions . . . Almost everywhere else in the world, executioners have already been installed in ministerial chairs. They have merely substituted the rubber stamp for the axe'" (535). Defourneau was official executioner for Paris. His demands for improved status and better working conditions occurred during the general strike of November 1947 (see line 385).

385 *sit-down strike*: employees halt work and refuse to leave the workplace until an agreement is reached.

385 *Vertigo*: dizziness.

386 *wind . . . keyhole*: (Tolson's note) "Cf. Nietzsche, *Thus Spoke Zarathustra.*" From "Of Involuntary Bliss" (Book III): "The wind blew through the keyhole and said 'Come!' The door sprang cunningly open and said 'Go!' . . . In symbols everything called to me: 'It is time!' But I—did not hear" (R. J. Hollingdale translation).

388 *santo . . . pero*: (Tolson's note) "*Il Santo* ["the Holy"] and *Pero* ["However"]: respectively, the nicknames of Neitzsche and [Leon] Trotsky [(1877–1940)]—the first innocently ironical, the second ironically innocent." Trotsky was one of the revolutionary founders of Soviet Russia.

388 *Phillipics*: a speech dominated by harsh invective.

389 *Realpolitik*: (German) "power politics."

390 *faits accomplis*: (French) acts or situations irreversibly concluded.

392 *divide et impera*: (Latin) "divide and conquer."

393 *cattle*: (Tolson's note) "Cf. The remark of Nicholas I [Czar of Russia, 1825–1855]: 'We have plenty of little gray cattle.'" The Czar had in mind the Russian peasant.

394–395 *Siamese wolves . . . pomp and power*: Like permanently linked Siamese twins, "pomp and power" cannot be separated.

396 *Esperanto*: an artificial language for international use, based on words common to the main European languages.

397 *brain-sick lands*: (Tolson's note) "Cf. [George] Meredith, 'On the Danger of War.'" From a poem published in 1885 and addressing the border dispute between Afghanistan and Russia (over which England threatened war), lines 2–4 define a land as "brain-sick / When nations gain the pitch where rhetoric / Seems reason."

the claws of the anonymous seek;°
the case Caesarean,° Lethean° brew
400    nor instruments obstetrical° at hand,
the midwife° of the old disenwombs the new.
*Selah!*

The *Höhere°* of Gaea's° children
is beyond the *dérèglement de tous les sens,°* is beyond
405    gold fished from cesspools° the *galerie des rois,°*
the seeking of cows,° *apartheid,°* Sisyphus' despond,°
the Ilande intire of itselfe° with *die Schweine°* in mud,
the potter's wheel° that stocks the potter's field,°
Kchesinskaja's balcony° with epitaphs in blood,

---

398 *claws . . . anonymous:* (Tolson's note) "In the fables of Antisthenes, when the hares demanded equality for all, the lions said: 'Where are your claws?' Cf. Martial, *Epigram* XII, 92: '*Die mihi, si fias tu leo, qualis eris?*'" "What sort of a lion will you be / If you become a lion?" (lines 7–8 in the J. A. Potts and F. A. Wright translation cited elsewhere by Tolson).

399 *Caesarean:* surgical delivery of a baby.

399 *Lethean:* Lethean waters induce forgetfulness.

400 *instruments obstetrical:* technical devices like forceps to aid in childbirth.

401 *midwife:* woman who assists in childbirth.

403 *Höhere:* (Tolson's note) ["the heights"]: "Cf. [Gaius] Petronious [(?–66 A.D.)]: '*Proecipitandus est liber spiritus.*'" "The free spirit must be brought down." Gaea: the planet earth. In the next four stanzas, Tolson affirms the greatness of humankind by listing all the evils, the limitations, and the misconceptions that such greatness should be beyond.

404 *dérèglement . . . sens:* Rimbaud the visionary-in-training wrote to his old teacher: "The point is, to arrive at the unknown by the disordering of *all the senses*" (his italics, 13 May 1871 letter). As a rallying-cry for experimental modernism and surrealism, the concept has been sometimes invoked with the effect of detaching art from social engagement.

405 *gold . . . cesspools:* (Tolson's note) "In the Gilded Era [the era of rapid growth in America from 1865 to 1900], cynics said of Babcock [possibly James F. Babcock (1844–1897), chemist and inventor]: 'He fished for gold in every stinking cesspool.'"

405 *galeries de rois:* (Tolson's note) "Cf. [Paul] Verlaine, '*Nocturnal Parisien*' ["Parisian Nocturne"], the reference to the twenty-eight statues of French Kings." Verlaine's 1866 description of the River Seine in Paris at night is a portrait that mixes disgust with affection.

406 *The seeking of cows:* (Tolson's note) "This is the literal meaning of the word 'battle' among the ancient Aryans who ravaged the Indo-Gangetic plains. The backwardness of their culture is attested by their failure to fumigate and euphemize their war aims."

406 *apartheid:* (Tolson's note) "The South African system of multi-layered segregation." "Apartheid" means "apartness" in the Afrikaaner language. See Tolson's notes to lines 348 and 367 on "paseq."

406 *Sisyphus:* in Greek myth, a man condemned to roll uphill a marble block which reached the top always to roll down again.

407 *the Ilande intire of itselfe:* words from Meditation XVII in *Devotions upon Emergent Occasions* (1624) by John Donne (1573–1631) were made famous by the epigraph to *For Whom the Bell Tolls* (1940) by Ernest Hemingway (1898–1961): "No man is an *Iland*, intire of itself; every man is a peece of the *Continent*, a part of the *maine.*"

407 *die Schweine:* (German) "the pigs."

408 *potter's wheel:* instrument used for forming vases out of clay.

408 *potter's field:* a field set aside for burial of criminals, poor people, and the unknown dead, named for a Jerusalem site once owned by a potter.

409 *Kchesinskaja's balcony:* Mathilde Kchesinskaya (sometimes spelled Kzeczinska) (1872–1971), as Prima Ballerina of the Kirov ballet and mistress of Czar Nicholas II (1868–1918), enjoyed her own palace just across from the Czar's Winter Palace. One of the first places to be stormed when the Bolshevik revolutionaries wrested power from the Czar in the October Revolution of 1917, her palace became Bolshevik headquarters and Vladimir Lenin (1870–1924) first delivered speeches to people in large numbers from its balcony.

410          deeds hostile all,° O Caton,° to hostile eyes,
             the breaking of foreheads against the walls,°
             gazing at navels, thinking with thighs

                                    •

             The *Höhere* of God's stepchildren
             is beyond the sabotaged world,° is beyond
415              *das Diktat der Menschenverachtung,*°
             *la muerte sobre el esqueleto de la nada,*°
             the pelican's breast rent red to feed the young,°

---

410 *deeds hostile to all*: (Tolson's note) "These words are from the Chorus to *Ajax* by Sopho-
cles, which Mr. [James] Forrestal [(1892–1949)] apparently read just before his death." De-
pression leading to suicide or thoughts of suicide is common to this and the following ref-
erences. Forrestal participated in the war effort as Secretary of the Navy for Roosevelt and
Secretary of Defense for Truman, and his last diary entry before he jumped from his six-
teenth-story hotel room was a 17-line excerpt from the Chorus in *Ajax*, ending with the
thoughts of a mother struggling to accept the loss of her son: "Woe to her desolate heart
and temples gray, / When she shall hear / Her loved one's story whispered in her heart /
'Woe, woe!' will be the cry— / No quiet murmur like the tremulous wail / Of the lone bird,
the querulous nightingale—."
410 *O Caton*: (Tolson's note) "Cato the Younger committed suicide in 46 B.C. He had
spent the previous night reading Plato's *Phaedo*. [After death, the soul enters a new life
in which one's earthly conduct is judged, Plato (427?–327 B.C.) argues in *Phaedo*. Cato
the Younger (95–46 B.C.), member of a prestigious Roman family, had served as a mili-
tary tribune in Macedonia.] Cf. [Alphonse Marie Louis de] Lamartine [(1790–1869)]: '*Le
Désespoir*'" (French): "Despair" (1818), a 126-line poem from *Poetic Meditations* (1820) in
which Lamartine alludes to Cato's suicide in lines 104–105.
411 *the walls*: (Tolson's note) "'economic doctrines.' The figure is Blok's." Most likely
Alexander Blok, Russian poet (1880–1921).
414 *sabotaged world*: (Tolson's note) "Cf. [Andre] Salmon [(b. 1881)], '*Age de l'Humanité*.'"
"Age of Humanity," Salmon's two-page prose memoir recalls a 1919 Paris march by a mas-
sive group of citizens and military veterans from all social classes who converged on the
home of the assassinated Socialist Jean Jaurès (1859–1914) to participate in and witness a
ceremonial discarding of military honors and decorations by veterans. Salmon drily notes
that the medals had all to be retrieved for them to be distributed again a few decades later.
415 *Diktat der Menschenverachtung*: (German) "Dictates of the Men of Contempt." (Tol-
son's note) "V. [Alexander] Mitscherlich and [Andre] Mielke, *Doctors of Infamy*, translated
by Norden. Cf. [Hugo] Grotius [(1583–1645)], *De Jure Belli et Pacis* [On the Rules of War
and Peace], 'Prolegomena,' XVIII: '. . . a people which violates the Laws of Nature and
Nations, beats down the bulwark of its own tranquility for future time.'" In this context,
the "people" here referred to seem to be the German nation.
416 *la muerte . . . la nada*: (Spanish) "the death on the skeleton of nothingness": the final
words in Rafael Alberti's "*Castigos*" ("Punishments") from *Sobre Los Angeles* ["Concerning
Angels," (1928)]), a poem whose overwhelming bleakness (a typical passage: "There are
nights in which hours become stone in space, / in which one's veins do not flow") culmi-
nates in this image of utter collapse.
417 *pelican's . . . young*: (Tolson's note) "Cf. [Pierre de] Ronsard [(1524–1585)], *Le Bocage*
[*The Royal Woods*, (1587)]. Also [Alfred de] Musset [(1810–1857)], '*La Nuit de mai*'" ["May
Night" from *New Poems* (1852)]. Both de Musset in "May Night" and Ronsard in "Dia-
logue between the Dislodged Muses" place the poet in dialogue with hard-working muses.
In the case of de Musset, the muse compares herself to the self-sacrificing pelican whom
naturalists once believed tore its breast to feed its young.

summer's third-class ticket,° the *Revue des morts,*°
the skulls trepanned° to hold ideas plucked from dung,
420       Dives' crumbs° in the church of the unchurched,
absurd life shaking its ass's ears° among
the colors of vowels° and Harrar blacks°
with Nessus shirts° from Europe on their backs

•

---

418 *summer's third-class ticket*: Third-class accommodations would be especially uncomfortable in summer, crowded with vacationers.

418 *Revue des morts*: (French) "review of the dead." (Tolson's note) "V. [Theophile] Gautier [(1811–1872)] '*Vieux de la vieille*' [(French) "Veterans of the Old Guard"), the reference to Raffet's *nocturne* showing Napoleon's spirit reviewing spectral troops." In the poem (from *Enamels and Cameos*, 1852), the poet strolling in the evening thinks he sees five ghosts like those in "The lithograph . . . / Wherein one ray shines down upon / The dead, that Raffet deifies, / That pass and shout 'Napoleon'!" (lines 33–36, Agnes Lee translation). They turn out to be real persons so aged and worn they resembles ghosts. Denis Raffet (1804–1860) was an illustrator and lithographer.

419 *skulls trepanned*: (Tolson's note) "Plekhanov had Alexander II in mind when he used the trepan figure." The "reforms" of Czar Alexander II (1818–1881) further burdened Russian peasantry. Georgi Plekhanov (1857–1918) was a political philosopher who influenced Lenin but opposed the 1918 revolution. "This Neanderthal skull," Plekhanov said, referring to Alexander's, "has to be trepanned with a bomb to press into it any idea of the political demands of modern Russia." The quote is from Chapter 12 of Jan Kucharzewski's *Origins of Modern Russia* (1948), a text Tolson draws upon for notes on lines 504, 511 and 551.

420 *Dives' crumbs*: Dives was the wealthy man who was "clothed in purple and fine linen and fared sumptuously every day" (Luke 16:19). Lazarus, poor and ill, desired the crumbs that fell from his table.

421 *absurd . . . ears:* (Tolson's note) "V. [Blaise] Cendrars [(1887–1961)], '*Éloge de la vie dangereuse*'" (French) "In Praise of the Dangerous Life" (1922). The entire sentence reads: "So there is no truth, only absurd life waggling its donkey's ears."

422 *colors of vowels*: Rimbaud's "*Voyelles*" ("Vowels") assigns each vowel a color.

422 *Harrar blacks*: (Tolson's note) "Rimbaud, in a town near the Red Sea, looked toward Khartoum and wrote: "*Leur Gordon est un idiot, leur Wolseley un âne, et toutés leurs enterprises une suite insensées d'absurdités et de déprédations.*' [(French) "Your Gordon is an idiot, your Wolseley an ass, and all their projects a conglomeration of inanities and misappropriations." British General Charles George Gordon (1833–1885, also known as "Chinese Gordon") was caught in the 1884 siege of Khartoum and died there two days' before the tardy arrival of Garnet Wolseley (1833–1913) with reinforcements. Ex-poet Rimbaud, as an arms-dealer in Harar who had journeyed into Abyssinia and worked with slave dealers, was appraising British foreign policy failures from a local vantage.] But fifty years later, when the Black Shirts [of Mussolini] entered Harrar, the ex-poet who plotted with Menelik against Italy was not there to hear Vittorio Mussolini's poetic account: 'I still remember the effect produced on a small group of Galla tribesmen massed around a man in black clothes. I dropped an aerial bomb right in the center, and the group opened up like a flowering rose. It was most entertaining.'" Mussolini encouraged both his sons, Vittorio and Bruno, to participate as fliers in the air-bombing of Adowa—notable as the place where the Italian army, in an 1896 attempt by Italy to conquer Ethiopia, had been soundly defeated by King Menelek, vassal of the Ethiopian emperor John. Menelek fought his battles using arms smuggled to him by Rimbaud who had hoped to make his fortune in the deal but barely covered his expenses.

423 *Nessus shirts . . . backs*: Nessus, a centaur, attempted to rape Hercules' wife, Delanira, and Hercules shot him in the heart. Before dying, Nessus urged Delanira to soak a shirt with his blood to use as a love charm that would bind her to Hercules. But his blood had been poisoned by Hercules' arrow and when Delanira, fearful of a rival's charms, urged Hercules to wear the shirt, he was poisoned by it.

The *Höhere* of X's children
425 is beyond Heralds' College,° the *filets d' Arachné*,° is beyond
maggot democracy, the *Mal éternel*,° the Bells of Ys,
the doddering old brigades with aorist° medicines of poetry,
the *Orizaba* with its Bridge of Sighs,°
the *oasis d'horreur dans un déserte d'ennui*,°
430 the girasol° rocks of Secunderabad,°
Yofan's studio° and *Shkola Nenavisti*,°
the *otototoi*°—in Crimson Tapestries—of the *hoi polloi*,°
Euboean defeats°
in the Sausage Makers' bout
435 the fool himself finds out
and in the cosmos of his chaos
repeats.
*Selah!*

---

425 *Heralds' College*: English institution organized to trace and preserve the genealogies of fine families.

425 *filets d'Arachné* [(French) "webs of Arachne"]: (Tolson's note) "Cf. [Andre] Chenier [(1762–1794)]: '*Qui? Moi? De Phébus to dicter les leçons?*'" "Who? Me? Give You the Lessons that Only Apollo Can Teach?" (XVIII in his *Elegies*) was a letter-poem to his friend the Marquis de Brazais. Arachne's skill as a weaver led to the events in which she was transformed into a spider, whose skills served not to free but entangle her.

426 *Mal éternel*: (Tolson's note) [(French) "eternal evil"]. "Cf. [Charles Marie Leconte de] Lisle [(1818–1894)], '*Dies Irae*.'" (Latin: "Days of Wrath"—opening words of the Mass for the dead.): "*Oui! Le mal éternel est dans sa plénetude! / L'air du siècle est mauvais aux esprits ulcérés*" (lines 93–94). (French) "Yes, eternal evil has attained its fullness! / The air of the century is foul with its festering spirit."

427 *aorist*: a verb tense of action that does not indicate whether it is completed, repeated, or continued.

428 *The Orizaba . . . sighs*: Jon Stanton Woodson notes that the *Orizaba* was the ship from which Hart Crane (1899–1932), author of the American epic *The Bridge* (1930), jumped to commit suicide. Woodson points out that DuBois in *The World and Africa* mentions that the *Orizaba* had carried him to France in December 1918 where he hoped to convince the Peace Conference at Versailles, then establishing terms for ending World War I, to call a Pan-African congress.

429 *oasis . . . d'ennui*: (French) "oasis of horror in a desert of tedium." (Tolson's note) "Cf. [Charles] Baudelaire [(1821–1867)], '*Le voyage*'" ["The Voyage," poem VII, line 4].

430 *girasol*: (also girosol) an opal with a reddish gleam; fire opal.

430 *rocks of Secunderabad*: (Tolson's note) "Cf. [Victor] Robinson, the Preface to *The Story of Medicine*" [(1931)]. The preface is a dedication to Sir Ronald Ross (1857–1932), whose field research identified the mosquito as the origin of malaria, and who now lives in poverty: "Had he devoted himself to ledgers instead of laboratory notebooks, had he camped on fashionable Harley Street [in London, where physicians practice] instead of the sun-scorched rocks of Secunderabad, he might be enjoying a comfortable income today." Secunderabad was at one time one of the largest British military installations in India.

431 *Yofan's studio*: (Tolson's note) "Napoleon's old residence by the Kremlin wall." Napoleon's army was broken by its effort to conquer Russia just as Hitler's was.

431 *Shkola Nenavisti*: (Tolson's note) [(Russian) "School of Hate"]: "a Berlin film on a Dublin subject in a Moscow theater."

432 *otototoi*: (Tolson's note) "Cf. Gilbert Murray's Notes to *Aeschylus*." In ancient Greek, "otototoi" was an outburst that voiced grief, a wailing noise as untranslatable as "oh me oh my." Tolson also uses the phrase in line 87.

432 *hoi polloi*: (Greek) "the people, the masses."

433 *Euboean defeats*: (Tolson's note) "Cf. Ovid [(43 B.C.–17 A.D.), *Tristia*, quoted by [Michel de] Montaigne [(1533–1592)] in 'Of Three Commerces' [essay XXXIV]: 'Whoever of the Grecian fleet has escaped the Capharean rocks ever takes care to steer clear from those of the Euobean sea'" [(I, 1, line 83)]. One who suffers a "Euoebean defeat" has presumably not heard or learned from Ovid's advice.

The *Höhere* of one's pores En Masse°

440          . . . Christians, Jews, *ta ethne*° . . .

makes as apishly

brazen as the brag and brabble of brass

the flea's fiddling

on the popinjay,°

445          the pollack's° pout

in the net's hurray,

the jerboa's feat°

in the fawn and the flout

of

450          Quai d'Orsay,°

White House,

Kremlin,

Downing Street.

Again black Aethiop° reaches at the sun, O Greek

455          Things-as-they-are-for-us, *nullius in verba*,°

speak!

O East, O West,

on tenotomy° bent,

Chang's tissue is

460          Eng's ligament!°

*Selah!*

---

439 *En Masse*: in one large group; all together. (Tolson's note) "Cf. [Alphone Marie de] Lamartine [(1790–1869)]: *'Il faut . . . Avec l'humanité t'unir par chaque pore'* ["It is essential to unite yourself with humanity through each pore."] Cf. [Victor] Hugo [(1802–1885)], the Preface to *Les Contemplations* ["Contemplations," 1856]: 'When I speak to you of myself, I am speaking to you of you.' ["*Quand je vous parle de moi, je vous parle de vous*"]. And again, [Jules] Romains [(1885–1972)]: 'Il faut bien qu'un jour on soit l'humanité!'" ["We will have to become humanity eventually!"].

440 *ta ethne*: (Greek) "the people; the race."

444 *popinjay*: "parrot"; applied to persons who mechanically repeat phrases.

445 *pollack*: a salt-water food fish.

447 *jerboa's feet*: small African rodent, remarkable for its jumping skills.

450 *Quai d'Orsay*: Paris street, site of French Ministry of Foreign Affairs. This and three following locations designate governments victorious after World War II: France, America, Russia, Great Britain.

454 *Black Aethiop*: (Tolson's note) "Cf. Shakespeare, *Pericles*, II, ii [lines 18–21]: 'A knight of Sparta, my renowned father, / And the device he bears upon his shield / Is a black Aethiop, reaching at the sun, / The word, *Lux tua vita mihi*'" [(Latin) "Thy light is life to me."] The words are spoken by Thaisa, one of a number of successful warriors who are strutting about, comparing shields and family mottoes. His shield proudly indicates mobility upward from slavery.

455 *nullius in verba*: (Tolson's note) [(Latin) perhaps "into the words of nobody"]. "Cf. [Henry G.] Lyons, *The Royal Society*" [(1944)].

458 *tenotomy*: cutting or division of a tendon.

460 *ligament*: tissue connecting one bone to another. Chang and Eng (1811–1874) were Siamese twins, whose names are said to mean left and right. They were the first such twins on record.

Between Yesterday's wars
now hot now cold
the grief-in-grain° of Man

465

dripping dripping dripping
from the Cross of Iron°
dripping
drew jet vampires
of the Skull;

470

Between Yesterday's wills of Tanaka,° between
golden goblet and truckling trull°
and the ires
of rivers red with the reflexes of fires,
the ferris wheel°

475

of race, of caste, of class°
dumped and alped° cadavers till the ground
fogged the Pleiades° with Gila° rot: Today the mass,
the Beast with a Maginot Line° in its Brain,
the staircase Avengers of base alloy,°

---

464 *grief-in-grain*: (Tolson's note) "The 'grain' I have in mind in this figure consists of the dried female bodies of a scale insect found on cacti in Mexico and Central America. The dye is red and unfading. Cf. [W. E.] Henley [(1849–1903)], 'To James McNeill Whistler,' *in toto*." In poem XII of *Rhymes and Rhythms* (1862), subtitled "to James McNeill Whistler," the poet hears "a broken tune . . . So melancholy a soliloquy / It sounds as it might tell / The secret of the unending grief-in-grain, / The terror of Time and Change and Death / That wastes this floating, transitory world" (lines 11–15).

466 *Cross of Iron*: Possibly *das eiserne kreus*, a German and Austrian decoration for distinguished wartime service.

470 *wills of Tanaka*: Baron Glichi Tanaka (1863–1929), Japanese General usually considered author of a 1927 plan for future foreign conquest.

471 *truckling trull*: servile harlot.

474 *the ferris wheel*: As Robert Farnsworth has noted, Tolson's Oct. 19, 1940, newspaper column in the weekly Washington (D.C.) *Tribune* on "The Merry-Go-Round and the Ferris Wheel of History" first developed the contrast between a history in which nations rise and fall as one ruling class battles another and a history in which democracy fosters equality. "As long as there are upper classes and superior races, there will be wars and revolutions. The class or race that is up today will be wars and revolutions. . . . On the merry-go-round all the seats are on the same level. Nobody goes up; therefore, nobody comes down." A variant of this stanza once stood as the conclusion in an earlier version of the poem. Farnsworth's study reprints part of a letter by Tolson to his book editor in which *Libretto* was to conclude with "the theme a world at peace. I use the Ferris Wheel of Tyranny and the Merry-go-round of democracy as my symbols, one for the past, the other for the future." In that version, the trans-Africa voyages in the last half of what is now section eight constituted section seven. Also see Tolson's extensive note to line 621.

475 *race, caste, class*: a deliberate echo of the title of the book by Tolson's Wiley College colleague, the Marxist sociologist Oliver Cromwell Cox: *Caste, Class, and Race* (1948).

476 *alped*: (Tolson's coinage) "piled as high as the alps."

477 *Pleiades*: cluster of distant stars.

477 *Gila*: a venomous lizard found in the desert.

478 *Maginot Line*: A system of fortified outposts, traps, and barriers on France's eastern frontier that were designed to repel invaders.

479 *staircase . . . alloy*: (Tolson's note): "Cf. [C.P.] Cavafy, 'The Footsteps.'" The "iron footsteps that shake the staircase" in Cavafy's poem approach a sleeping Nero, emperor of Rome, and belong to the Furies (or Eumenides, the so-called "Kindly Ones" who the Greeks believed avenge certain crimes) who will punish him for matricide.

480        the *vile canaille°—Gorii!*—the *Bastard-rasse,°*
the *uomo qualyque,°* the *hoi barbaroi,°*
the *raya°* in the *Oeil de Boeuf,°*
the *vschelovek,°* the *descamisados,°* the *hoi polloi,°*
the Raw from the Coliseum of the Cooked,°
485        Il Duce's Whore,° Vardaman's Hound°—
unparadised nobodies° with maps of Nowhere
ride the merry-go-round!
*Selah!*

---

480 *vile canaille*: (French) "low riff-raff."

480 *Gorii*: (Tolson's note) "The voyage of the Carthaginian general Hanno carried him as far as what is now Liberia. The aborigines he saw were called *Gorii*, which later Greek and Latin scholars turned into 'gorilla.' However, to Hanno's interpreter and in the Wolof language today, the expression means 'These too are men.'" Tolson's authority is Delafosse, *The Negroes of Africa* (1928), Chapter 1.

480 *Bastard-rasse*: "Bastard Race" (German).

481 *Uomo qualyque*: possibly *uomo qualunque*, (Italian) "the man in the street." *Hoi barbaroi*: (Greek) "the barbarians."

482 *raya*: (Tolson's note) "In the Turkish conquest of the Southern Slavs, the maltreated people became *raya* or cattle. Conquest salves its conscience with contempt. Among the *raya* for five hundred years, the ballads of the wandering *guslars* kept freedom alive."

482 *Oeil de Boeuf*: (Tolson's note) [literally "bull's eye"; a small circular window] "a waiting room at Versailles. Cf. [Austin] Dobson, 'On a Fan that Belonged to the Marquise de Pompadour.'" Dobson's 1878 poem imagines the fan skillfully being deployed as an erotic extension of its owner. As this erotic symbol fluttered, "Thronging the *Oeil de Boeuf* through" (line 10), it could influence history's course by scrambling great men's brains— a sharp contrast to the artistry of the wandering balladeers in the previous note whose songs kept the concept of freedom alive for five hundred years.

483 *vschelovek*: (Tolson's note) [(Russian)] "'universal man.' In spite of its global image, this concept has a taint of *blut und boden* [the "blood and soil" associated with Nazi Germany]. Ever since [Feodor] Dostoevski [(1821–1881)], in a eulogy on [Alexander] Pushkin [(1799–1837)], identified the latter's genius with *vschelovek*, the term has created pros and cons. Cf. The Latin: 'Paul is a Roman and not a Roman.'"

483 *descamisados*: (Tolson's note) "the shirtless ones."

483 *the hoi polloi*: (ancient Greek) "the masses."

484 *Raw . . . Cooked*: (Tolson's note) "The line was suggested by the history of the *Crudes* and *Asados* of Uruguay." Uruguayan cultures revealed their level of sophistication by how they prepared their food, cooked or raw. The Coliseum: large building for public events.

485 *Il Duce's Whore*: (Tolson's note) "V. *Ciano Diaries*, 1939–43, ed. by [Hugh] Gibson. This is one of the 'many instances of the vast contempt in which Il Duce held his people.'" Il Duce was Benito Mussolini (1883–1945), and Galeazzo Ciano a high-level official opposed to many aspects of World War II—but not opposed enough to protest them. (Ciano, then, may be Il Duce's whore.)

485 *Vardaman's hound*: Possibly a reference to J. K. Vardaman (1861–1930), a Mississippi Governor, U.S. Senator and racist demagogue who was responsible for numerous Jim Crow laws and who built the infamous Parchman prison.

486 *unparadised nobodies*: (Tolson's note) "Cf. [John] Milton [(1608–1674)], the outline of *Adam Unparadised*." The four drafts (written around 1640) grow from an initial list of the names of sixteen players to a full-scale 300-word treatment of the story of the fall of mankind.

DO°

490
<blockquote>
a <i>pelageya</i>° in <i>as seccas</i>° the old she-fox today°<br>
eyes dead letters mouth a hole in a privy°<br>
taschunt° a corpse's in a mud-walled troy of jagunços°<br>
(<i>naze naze desu ka</i>° servant de dakar°) (<i>el grito de yara</i>°)
</blockquote>

---

Do: Although "Do" is identical to the title of the opening, this eighth section is (in the example of the musical scale), also the note that sounds one whole octave above the first. Its opening stanzas depend heavily on the footnote as an informative (and subversive) device. The poem opens in sheer cacophony, its collage of voices representing the confusion of the postwar moment. Tolson maintains a tightrope-walk between both positive and negative, between the discourse of James Joyce's *Finnegans Wake* (1939) with its mythic narratives that overlap fragments of different languages, which glimpse an underlying universality, and the discourse of a literature of automatic writing and surrealism with its sense of unbridled chaos and undirected "release." This semantic thicket is compounded by Tolson's footnotes, which become so allusive and fragmentary as to evade all but the specialist. (Many resist complete explanation.) The opening eleven six-line stanzas enact a crisis that can be linked with the collapse of Europe and the subsequent questioning of Western values. But Tolson then posits a counter vision (after a one-stanza transition that returns to the centered-line form of "Ti") by launching into a finale that takes us upon journeys projected into an Africa of the future that has resolved the chaos of the contemporary and is now equal if not superior to any civilization.

489 *pelagaya*: (Tolson's note) "the wench of the draft constitution. V. [Nikolai] Gogol's [(1809–1852)] *Dead Souls*." Pelagaya was the mud-soaked and illiterate 11-year-old servant girl whom a rural family loaned to Gogol's hero Tchitchikov to guide him back to the main road, which she did quite successfully.

489 *as seccas*: (Tolson's note) [Portuguese] "the devastating periodic droughts of Brazil."

489 *old she-fox today*: Most likely, the globe and all its nations, cunning and cautious as a fox because of the recent world war.

490 *privy*: outhouse.

491 *taschunt*: (Tolson's note) "Cf. [Leo] Frobenius [(1873–1938)], *African Genesis* [(1937)], 47 (Faber & Faber Ltd.): 'He felt that he had a *thabuscht*.'" From "Kabyl Legends of Creation": "The man saw the woman lying strange and naked before him. He saw that she had a taschunt. He felt that he had a thabuscht. He looked at the taschunt and asked: 'What is that for?' The woman said: 'That is good.' The man lay upon the woman." But with *taschunt* a corpse the elemental vitality of this legend has receded, as in the previous line where usual emblems of life, eyes and mouth, are horrifyingly debased.

491 *A mudwalled troy of jaguncos*: (Tolson's note) [(Brazil) "ruffian"]: "the home of Maciel's fanatics." One of the continuing references to Cunha's *Os Sertões* (see notes to lines 355 and 534). Antonio Conselheiro Maciel (d. 1897) was the Brazilian mystic whose religious convictions attracted followers among the poor in enormous numbers. Troy: ancient Greek town placed under siege in the Trojan War.

492 *naze naze desu ka*: (Tolson's note) ["Why, Why is it?"]. "V. [Norman] Mailer [(b. 1923)], *The Naked and the Dead* [(1948)], the diary of Major Ishimira, 247." When we read Ishimira's diary, he is a dead man: "He had fallen, shrieking no doubt, a unit in an anonymous exalted mass."

492 *servant of dakar*: (Tolson's note) "Also [Guillaume] Apollinaire, '*Les Soupirs du Servant de Dakar*.'" (French): "The Sighs of the Gunner from Dakar" from *Caligrammes: Poems of Peace and War* (1916). The poem ends with the speaker also asking "why?" "Why is it better to be white than black / Why not dance and give speeches / eat and then sleep" (lines 56–58).

492 *el grito de yara*: (Tolson's note) "the watchword at Manzanillo, October 10, 1868." The Ten Years War (1868–1878) in which Cuba first attempted to break from Spanish rule was launched by Carlos Manuel de Cespedes (1819–1874) who proclaimed a revolution at Yara and issued *el grito de Yara* ("the protest from Yara"), a declaration of Cuban independence, published on October 10, 1868 in Manzanillo.

cackles among the garbage cans of mummy truths°
o frontier saints° bring out your dead°

495  the aria° of the old *sookin sin*° breaks my shoulders°
*lasciatemi morire*° o africa (*maneno matupu*°)
the fat of fame didn't outlast a night in hog's wash°
nor geneva's church nor the savage's ten pounds°

---

493 *Mummy truths*: disturbing wisdom. W. B. Yeats (1865–1939), "All Souls' Night" (from *The Tower* [1928]): "I have mummy truths to tell / Whereat the living mock, / Though not for sober ear, / For maybe all that hear / Should laugh and weep an hour upon the clock" (lines 95–99).

494 *frontier saints*: (Tolson's note) "Cf. Francia: '. . . now I know that bullets are the best saints you can face on the frontiers.'"

494 *bring out your dead*: (Tolson's note) "the cry of the bellman walking by night in front of the dead cart. V. [Daniel] Defoe [(1659–1731)], *Journal of the Plague Year*" [(1722)]. During the plague, a nightly cart made rounds to collect corpses, its arrival signaled by the bellman.

495 *aria*: (Tolson's note) "Cf. [possibly, Emil] Ludwig: 'Dictatorship is always an aria, never an opera.'"

495 *sookin sin*: (Tolson's note) [(Russian) "Son-of-a-bitch"]: "V. [Harry] Duhanty, *One Life, One Kopeck*, [(1937)], 3." The kopeck is a very small unit of Russian money. Duhanty explains his title rephrases a Russian saying, *Dzizn Kopeika*, "Life is a little kopeck" (that is, not worth much).

495 *breaks my shoulders*: (Tolson's note) "Cf. Baudelaire: '*Pour ne pas sentir l'horrible fardeau du temps qui brise vos épaules et vous penches vers terre, il faut vous enivrer sans trêve.*'" (French) "In order not to feel the horrible burden of time breaking your shoulders and pushing you to the ground, you must get intoxicated unceasingly" (XXXIII from *Spleen de Paris: Petits Poèmes en Prose* [*Ill Temper of Paris: Brief Prose Poems*]).

496 *lasciatemi morire*: (Tolson's note) [(Italian) "Oh let me die"]. "V. [Claudio] Monteverdi [(1567–1643)], *Lament of Arianna* [(1608)]. The libretto is by Ottavio Rinuccini. "Arianna" is Ariadne, the wife whom Theseus deserted, and she is lamenting his absence: "Oh let me die! / Whom would you have comfort me / In this sad plight, / In this bitter anguish?"] Cf. [Felix] Mendelssohn [(1809–1847)], Aria from *Elijah*: '[It is enough] O Lord, [now] take away my life, for I am not better than my fathers.' [The lines begin an aria, and they borrow words from Job 7:16.] See also Maecenas [(70?–8 B.C.]: '*Debilem, facito manu, / Debilem pede, coxâ; / Lubricos quate dentes: / Vita dum superest, bene est . . .*'": (Latin) "Make him disabled in his hand, / Disabled in his foot and hip; / Break his slippery teeth: / While life survives, he is well . . ."

496 *maneno matupu*: (Tolson's note) "'empty words.' Epithet used in *deepi-talki*—not *talki-talki*." The implication is that natives could not openly criticize those who had hired them. Also see Tolson's note to line 163.

497 *hog's wash*: (Tolson's note) "a London newspaper edited by Daniel Isaac Eaton during the 'Anti-Jacobin Terror.' Its name was an ironical allusion to [Edmund] Burke [(1729–1797)]'s epithet, 'the swinish multitudes.'" England was nervous that the French revolutionary fervor of the Jacobins would spread beyond France. Eaton's title is an example of embracing a negative epithet as deliberate oppositional discourse.

498 *savage's ten pounds*: (Tolson's note) "Cf. [(Francois M.A.] Voltaire [(1694–1778)], *Irene*, the preliminary letter: 'Shakespeare is a savage with sparks of genius in a dreadful darkness of night' ["Introduction to *Irene*: Letter to the French Academy"]. See Shakespeare's will and epitaph." The £10 Shakespeare left in his will to the "poor of Stratford" was considered a generous amount for a man of his means.

for stratford's° poor (bles be ye man for jesvs sake)°
500    here one singeth° *per me si va nella città dolente*°

below the triumvirate flag° & tongue & mammon
while *blut und boden*° play the anthemn *iron masters gold*°
ruble shilling franc yen lira baht and dime°
brass-knuckled (*la légalité nous tue*)° and iron-toed
505    wage armageddon in the temple of *dieu et l'état*°
o earl of queensberry° o last christian on the cross

---

499 *Stratford*: Shakespeare's home and place of death.

499(*Bles be ye man for jesvs sake*): Shakespeare's epitaph reads: "Good friend, for Jesvs' sake forbear / To dig the dust enclosed heare: / Blese be ye man that spares the stones, / And curst be he that moves my bones."

500 *here one singeth*: (Tolson's note) "Cf. *Aucassin and Nicolette*, translated by Andrew Lang, the warning *aubade*, or 'dawn song,' of the sentinel on the tower above the trysting place." The medieval tale is a mixture of narrative and rhymed lyrics like an aria in opera. Each lyric is introduced by a stock phrase, which Lang renders as "Here one singeth."

500 *Per me si va nella città dolente*: (Italian) "Through me one goes into the city of suffering." The first of the phrases inscribed above the Gate of Hell in Dante's *Inferno*, III, line 1.

501 *triumvirate flag*: possibly the tricolor or three-colored flag of the French revolution, here signifying political strife.

502 *blut und boden*: (German) "blood and soil."

502 *iron . . . gold*: (Tolson's note) "When Croesus showed Solon his gold, the sage said, 'Sir, if any other come that hath better iron than you, he will be master of all this gold.'" Solon's brutal remark states that those with superior technical and military skills will simply take the gold.

503 *ruble . . . dime*: monetary units in different countries.

504 *la légalitè nous tue*: (Tolson's note) [(French) "Legality is killing us"]. "[Michael] Muraviev, the Hangman, when he was governor general of Poland, wrung this cry from the people." Muraviev was appointed by Czar Alexander II (1818–1881) to oversee Lithuania (part of Poland occupied by Russia). His brutal disregard for lawful procedures led to the general insurrection known as the January Insurrection (1863) and prompted the *St. Petersburg (Russia) Journal* to cite this French aphorism. Also see notes to lines 419, 511, and 551.

505 *dieu et l'état*: (French) "god and the state."

506 *earl of queensberry*: Sir John Douglas (1844–1900) brought fair play into the physical violence of boxing by formulating the Marquis of Queensberry rules in 1867. Tolson's bitter stanza proposes that anyone interested in promoting civility and fairness is as obsolete as the "last Christian on the cross," for modern history is dominated by nations willing to arm themselves and use their might to seize wealth. The issues are not "god and the state" (religion and civil order) but "iron and gold"—technical advancement and economic domination.

*vexilla regis prodeunt inferni*° what is man f.r.a.t.° *tò tí*°
(a professor° of metaphysicotheologicocosmonigology°
a tooth puller° a pataphysicist° in a cloaca of error°
510      a belly's wolf° a skull's tabernacle° a #13 with stars°
a muses' darling a busie bee *de sac et de corde*°
a neighbor's bed-shaker a walking hospital on the walk)°

---

507 *vexilla regis prodeunt inferni*: (Tolson's note) [(Italian) "The banners of the king advance into hell"]. "Cf. Dante, *Inferno*, Canto XXXIV" [line 1].

507 *f. r. a. i.*: "fellow of the royal archeological institute." Tolson ironically suggests that only duly certified professionals are now qualified to answer the question "what is man?"

507 *tò tí*: (Tolson's note) [(Greek)] " 'What is it?' This was the old gadfly's everlasting question." Plato described Socrates as the gadfly sent to sting the state. The stanza opens with Plato's question, then offers examples of mankind in which good and bad are mixed, and ends by returning to the Platonic dialogues, describing the human as a figure of destruction (a "walking hospital") capable of the highest aspirations (on "the walk" in Athens with Socrates). Jon Stanton Woodson notes that Tolson pursues the very question that T. S. Eliot's Prufrock defers: "O do not ask, 'What is it?' / Let us go and make our visit" ("The Love Song of J. Alfred Prufrock," lines 11–12).

508 *professor*: (Tolson's note) "Cf. [Nicolas] Boileau [(1636–1711)], *Satires* IV, 5–10." "A pedant, proud of Greek and stuffed with hollow science, / Inflate belike with pride and arrogant defiance, / Who knows a thousand authors, word by word, alas! / And all by rote, himself may be a solemn ass. / He deems what's not in books to be of no account, / Thinks only Aristotle sense and reason's fount" (lines 5–10 in the Hayward Porter translation).

508 *metaphysicotheologicocosmonigology*: The subject taught by the outrageous Professor Pangloss in Voltaire's *Candide* (Chapter I).

509 *tooth puller*: (Tolson's note) " '*Tiradentes*,' the nickname of the first martyr of Brazilian independence." Jose Joaquim da Silva Xavier (1748–1792) was inspired by the American Revolution to lead a movement for revolutionary democracy in Brazil, for which he was imprisoned and executed by Portuguese rulers.

509 *pataphysicist*: (Tolson's note) "Cf. [Alfred] Jarry [(1873–1907)], '*Gestes et Opinions du Dr. Pataphysicien.*'" *Exploits and Opinions of Dr. Faustroll, Pataphysician* (1911). Jarry sets out to outrage his educated audience by inventing Pataphysics as a "science of imaginary solutions."

509 *a cloaca of error*: (Tolson's note) "See [Blaise] Pascal [(1623–1662)]'s doctrine of the Thinking Reed." "Man is but a reed, the most feeble thing in nature; but he is a thinking reed. . . . If the universe were to crush him, man would still be more noble than that which killed him, because he knows that he has ideas and the advantage which the universe has over him; the universe knows nothing of this" (*Pensées*, 347.)

510 *a belly's wolf*: (Tolson's note) "Cf. [Francis] Beaumont [(1584–1616)] and [John] Fletcher [(1579–1625)], *Woman Pleased*." In this 1647 play, Lopez's servant Penuria is complaining of hunger in I, ii. Asked by his master what he is doing he explains he is "Hunting, sir, for a second course of flies here. / They are rare new salads." His miserly master responds: "This ravening fellow has a wolf in's belly: / Untempered knave, will nothing quench thy appetite? / I saw him eat two apples, which is monstrous" (lines 81–83).

510 *skull's tabernacle*: (Tolson's note) "Also Malley: 'Religion is a process of turning your skull into a tabernacle, not of going up to Jerusalem once a year.'"

510 *#13 with stars*: (Tolson's note) "James Wilkinson [1757–1825], American general and secret Spanish agent, who sought to establish an empire in the Southwest under his own sword and sceptre." In the 1790s, when Spain controlled the flow of goods on the Mississippi River, Wilkinson (who began his military career in the Revolutionary War when there were thirteen stars on the flag) was paid by Spain to encourage Kentucky to secede from the union.

511 *sac . . . corde*: (Tolson's note) "[Alexey] Orlov in a letter to [Alexander] Golovnin branded [Michael] Muraviev as '*un homme de sac et de corde*'" (French): "utter scoundrel." Orlov was then Chief of the Russian Secret Police, and Golovnin was Minister of Education. See Tolson's notes to lines 419, 504, and 551.

512 *the walk*: (Tolson's note) "the *Peripatos* [(Greek): "walkway"] of the Lyceum." The covered walkways in the public space of the Lyceum in Athens were where Aristotle discussed issues with his followers, the "peripatetic" school of philosophers.

lincoln° walks the midnight epoch of the ant-hill°
and barbaric yawps° shatter the shoulder-knots° of white peace
515 *jai hind*° (dawn comes up like thunder °*pakistan zindabad*°
britannia rules the waves° *my pokazhem meeru*°
the world is my parish° *muhammad rasulu 'llah*°
*hara ga hette iru*° oh yeah *higashi no kazeame*°

naïfs pray for a guido's scale° of good and evil to match
520 worldmusic's sol-fa syllables° (*o do de do de do de*)°
worldmathematics' arabic and roman figures°
worldscience's greek and latin symbols°
the letter killeth° five hundred global tongues
before esperanto garrotes voläpuk° *vanitas vanitatum*°

---

513 *lincoln*: Abraham Lincoln (1809–1865), U.S. President during the Civil War whose Emancipation Proclamation stipulated an end to slavery in America.

513 *epoch of the ant-hill*: (Tolson's note) "Cf. [Henri Frédéric] Amiel [(1821–1881)], *Journal* [(1882)]: 'The age of great men is going.'"

514 *barbaric yawps*: Walt Whitman, *Song of Myself*: "I sound my barbaric yawp over the roof of the world" (poem 52, line 1323).

514 *shoulder-knots*: (Tolson's note) "Cf. [Jonathan] Swift, 'A Tale of a Tub.'" "Shoulder-knots were a 1670 fad: knots of ribbon or lace, and occasionally jewels, worn in the hair at the point where it touched the shoulder: "Strait, all the World was *Shoulder-knots*; no approaching the Ladies *Ruelles* [bedsides] without the *Quota* of *Shoulder-knots: That Fellow*, cries one, *has no Soul; where is his Shoulder-knot?*" (Chapter II).

515 *jai hind*: (Urdu) "Victory to India." A patriotic slogan.

515 *dawn comes up like thunder*: (Tolson's note) "Cf. [Rudyard] Kipling, 'Mandalay.'" Kipling's lower-class speaker, an ex-soldier back in England, longs nostalgically for a landscape of sensual freedom ("Where there aren't no Ten Commandments, an' a man can raise a thirst") and specifically for the pleasures of "Supi-yaw-lat," a Burmese native woman with whom he had an alliance.

515 *pakistan zindabad*: (Urdu) "Long live Pakistan." Pakistan and India, long-time rivals, are represented with slogans identical in their competitiveness.

516 *brittania rules the waves*: From lines credited to James Thomson (1700–1748) and set to music in *Alfred: A Masque* (1740) to become a patriotic tune: "Rule Britannia, rule the waves, / Britons never will be slaves."

516 *my pokazhem meeru*: (Tolson's note) "'[(Russian)] We'll show the world.'"

517 *the world is my parish*: (Tolson's note) "[John] Wesley's announcement of his mission." Wesley (1703–1791), developed the Methodist Church out of the study of the scriptures practiced at Oxford University.

517 *muhammed rasulu 'llah*: (Arabic) "Mohammed the messenger of God."

518 *hara ga hette iru*: (Tolson's note) "'[(Japanese)] The belly has shrunken.'"

518 *higashi no kazeame*: (Tolson's note) "the code words all Japanese embassies had received by mid-November, 1941. This phrase—'East wind rain'—was to be repeated in a short-wave news broadcast in case of a rupture in Japanese-American relations."

519 *guido's scale*: Guido Arezzo (995?–1050?), Benedictine monk and music reformer, who conceived additional notations for the musical staff and reconceived the basis for harmony in the musical scale.

520 *worldmusic's sol-fa syllables*: "sol" and "fa" are the fifth and fourth tones above the "do." Arezzo's reforms (see line 518), by helping standardize musical notation and pitch, made it possible for singers to perform in a group. Tolson suggests his reforms allowed music to be a possible universal form of communication.

520 *o do de do de do de*: (Tolson's note) "V. Shakespeare, *King Lear*, III, iv." Edgar, in disguise as a madman, meets Lear and the Fool on the heath and pretends to babble.

521 *arabic and roman figures*: numerals in mathematics have Arabic and Roman origins.

522 *greek and latin symbols*: in chemistry, for example, Greek and Latin letters were a shorthand for certain elements.

523 *The letter killeth*: ". . . for the letter killeth, but the spirit giveth life" (2 Corinthians, 3:5–6). Tolson uses the quote flippantly, however: the "five hundred global tongues" present insurmountable obstacles to a universal language of global understanding.

524 *esperanto . . . voläpuk*: Esperanto and Volapuk were different artificial languages for international use, one invented in 1877, the other in 1879. Garrotes: strangles.

524 *Vanitas vanitatum*: (Latin) "vanity of vanities."

525 o majesty-dwarf'd° brothers *en un solo espasmo sexual°*
ye have mock'd the golden rules of eleven sons of god
smitten to rubble *ein feste burg°* for a few acres of snow°
buried the open sesame° *satya bol gat hai°* among dry bones
wasted the balm *assalamu aleykum°* on lice and maggots
530 snarled the long spoon for the scaly horror°

pin-pricks° precede blitzkriegs° *mala' oun el yom yomek°*
idiots carol happy dashes° in st. innocent's° little acre

---

525 *majesty-dwarf'd*: (Tolson's note) "V. [John Henry] Newman, 'The Dream of Gerontius.'"
"O man, strange composite of heaven and earth! / Majesty dwarf'd to baseness!" (section
2, second Angel's speech, lines 25–26).
525 *en un . . . sexual*: (Spanish) "in only one sexual spasm." (Tolson's note) "Cf. [José Asun-
cion] Silva [(1865–1896)]: *'Juan Ianas, el mozo de esquina, / Es absolutamente igual / Al Em-
perador de la China; / Los dos son un mismo animal.'"* (Spanish) "Juan Lanas, a manual
laborer, / is absolutely equal / To the Chinese Emperor: / They are the same animal" (from
"*Egalite*," ["Equality"], lines 1–4). Silva proposes all humans are equal in that all experi-
ence sexual desire. The passage quoted in line 525 appears in this context: "And if to Juan
a Juana / Gives herself in a brutal mode / And the human beast palpitates / In only one
sexual spasm. / Juan Lanas, the laborer, / Is absolutely equal / To the Chinese emperor: /
They are both the same animal" (lines 21–25).
527 *ein feste burg*: (German) "a mighty fortress." (Tolson's note) "V. [Martin] Luther
[(1483–1546)]: *'Ein feste Burge ist unser Gott / Ein gute Wehr and Waffen.'"* The opening
lines of Luther's famous hymn, based on Psalm 46 (which begins "God is our refuge and
strength, a very present help in trouble"), often called the national hymn of Protestant Ger-
many. Existing in over a dozen translations, it has become most familiar in its 1872 version:
"A mighty fortress is our God, / A trusty shield and weapon." The well-known German hymn
stresses the connection between religious values and military might (unlike Psalm 46).
527 *acres of snow*: (Tolson's note) "Voltaire looked upon the Seven Years' War as the dev-
astation of Europe to settle whether England or France should win 'a few acres of snow'
in Canada." One outcome of this 1756–1763 war was that the French lost Canada to the
British; another was the ascendancy of Prussia as a major power.
528 *open sesame*: a door opened when these words were spoken.
528 *satya bol gat hai*: (Tolson's note) "'In truth lies salvation.'"
529 *Assalamu aleykum*: (Tolson's note) "Peace to you."
530 *Long . . . horror*: "He who sups with the devil must have a long spoon" (old saying).
531 *Pin-pricks*: (Tolson's note) "Cf. Napoleon's words to Czar Alexander I at Tilsit, June
22, 1807: 'If they want peace, nations should avoid the pin-pricks that precede cannon-
shots.'" The Russian-French alliance signed at Tilsit arranged for vast amounts of Pruss-
ian territory to be transferred to France. The treaty collapsed in 1812.
531 *blitzkrieg*: (German) "lightning-strike." The strategy of surprise the German military
employed under Hitler.
531 *mala' oun el yom yomek*: (Tolson's note) "It is said that Taha Shanin, the Dongolawi,
as he plunged his spear into General Gordon, cried: 'O cursèd one, your time has come!'"
Gordon was defending Khartoum, and his attackers had been instructed to take him alive.
Also see note to line 422.
532 *happy dashes*: (Tolson's note) "The hag Today in the poem says the idiots have a word
for it. In China it means 'Kong Hi Sing Yen'; in Africa 'Happy Dashes'; in America, 'Merry
Christmas.' ["Dashes" means "gifts," according to Wilson, *Liberia*, who associates the
phrase with Christmas greetings in his Chapter 4.] Cf. F.P.A. [Franklin P. Adams
(1881–1960), American humorist and columnist], 'For the Other 364 Days': 'Christmas is
over and Business is Business.'"
532 *st. innocent's* (Tolson's note) "Cf. [Thomas] Browne [(1605–1682)], *Hydriotaphia or Urn
Burial* [: "'Tis all one to lie in St. Innocent's churchyard as in the sands of Egypt" (final
sentence).] Also Job XIV, vii." "For there is hope of a tree, if it be cut down, that it will
sprout again, and that the tender branch thereof will not cease" (Job 14:7).

of rags and bones° without brasses black and red°
booby mouths looted of the irritating parenthesis°
535          patrol skulls unhonored by a cromwell's pike°
snaggleteeth° glutted *in sudori vultus alieni*°

o sweet chariot° these aesop's flies without mirth
these *oh-mono*° without music in greed's akeldama°
are one with the great auk° of the north star
540          mouldy rolls of noah's ark and wall street
nuclei fed to demogorgon's mill°
alms for oblivion raindrops minus h₂o

o's without figures on ice the sun licks
pebbles let fall in the race of a night sea
545          jockeyed by beaufort no. 12°

---

532–533 *little acre / of rags and bones*: the burial plot. But Tolson's phrase echoes the title
of Erskine Caldwell's scandalous best-seller *God's Little Acre* (1933).

533 *brasses black and red*: (Tolson's note) "Cf. [Sir Henry] Newbolt [(1862–1938)], 'He Fell
Among Thieves.' Also his 'Clifton Chapel,' the inscription which gives an epitome of two
or three brasses in the Chapel: "*Qui procul hinc,*" the legend's writ— / The frontier-grave
is far away— / "*Qui ante diem periit:* / *Sed miles, sed pro patria.*"'" Newbolt romanticized
exploits of noble Englishmen in far-off lands. Outnumbered 5-to-1 and captured by thieves,
the protagonist in the first poem summons a vision of rural England before he is executed:
"He saw the little gray church across the park, / The mounds that hide the loved and hon-
ored dead; / The Norman arch, the chancel softly dark, / The brasses dark and red" (lines
21–24). "Clifton Chapel" records the Latin inscriptions on those brasses: "He who is far
from here" and "who perished before his time, / Who perished a soldier, for his father
land." Both poems, collected in *The Island Race* (1898), suggest how easily the evils of
colonialism shelter behind patriotism.

534 *irritating parenthesis*: (Tolson's note) "[Euclydes da] Cunha's figure for the problem of
miscegenation. Cf. Cunha, *Os Sertões*, II, ii, 108–110." "Irritating Parenthesis" is the lead-
in title for a section in which Cunha displays his knowledge of the racist theories of bio-
logical determinism that were widely accepted in 1898. He classified the mixed-race "mes-
tizo" as a "degenerate type, lacking the physical energy of his savage ancestors." Also see
notes to lines 355 and 491.

535 *cromwell's pike*: Oliver Cromwell (1599–1685), Puritan leader in seventeenth century
England, who demanded the king's execution. Pike: long iron pole for displaying the skulls
of the beheaded.

536 *snaggleteeth*: broken or crooked teeth.

536 *in sudori vultus alieni*: (Latin) "in the sweat of a strange face."

537 *o sweet chariot*: (Tolson's note) "I have in mind the Negro spiritual." "Swing low, sweet
chariot, / Comin' for to carry me home."

538 *oh-mono*: (Tolson's note) "high muck-a-mucks."

538 *greed's akeldama*: (Tolson's note) [(Greek) "Acheldama": the place where Judas Iscar-
iot committed suicide.]. "V. The Acts I, xv-xxi." These passages translate "Aceldama" [sic]
as "field of blood" (Acts 1:19).

539 *great auk*: extinct since 1844, the great auk was a penguin-like diving bird of the North-
ern seas.

541 *demogorgon's mill*: (Tolson's note) "Cf. [Percy Bysse] Shelley [(1792–1822)], *Prometheus
Unbound*" (1820). In Shelley's allegorical poem, Demogorgon was the primal power of the
world.

545 *beaufort no.* 12: 12 is the highest point on the Beaufort scale for wind velocities and
registers hurricane-strength speeds of 75 miles per hour and over.

iotas of the *yod*° of god in a rolls royce°
   the seven trumpets° of today's baby boys° summon peace
   and the walls come tumblin' down° (christ sleeps)°

   and no mourners go crying *dam-bid-dam*°
550   about the ex-streets of scarlet letters
      only the souls of hyenas whining *teneo te africa*°
      only the blind men gibbering *mboagan*° in greek

---

546 *yod*: in occult lore, the active or "male" principle that vitally interacts with the passive "female" principle.

546 *god in a rolls royce*: (Tolson's note) "Father Divine. Some years ago in a jeremiad issued from one of his 'heavens' he announced that he had reduced the Mayor of New York City 'to a little tittle of a jot' during the Harlem riot." Father Divine (1883?–1965) was a mysterious, highly successful African American Messiah figure whose "Peace Mission" worked across racial boundaries to form business ventures in ghetto areas. The March 1935 Harlem riot pitted New York City blacks against whites.

547 *the seven trumpets*: (Tolson's note) "Cf. Joshua VI, viii." "And it came to pass, when Joshua had spoken unto the people, that the seven priests bearing the seven trumpets of rams' horns passed on before the Lord and blew with the trumpets: and the ark of the covenant of the Lord followed them" (Joshua 6:8). Also see note to line 326.

547 *today's baby boys*: (Tolson's note) "The code word for the A-bombs. The day after it was proved at Alamagordo, New Mexico, that the weapon worked, the late Henry L. Stimson [(1867–1950)], then Secretary of War, received the message: 'Baby boy born today mother and child doing well.'"

548 *And the walls came tumblin' down*: a phrase from an African American spiritual that describes the fall of Jericho after the trumpets and shouts in the Book of Joshua.

548 *(christ sleeps)*: (Tolson's note) "In the days of the Norman King Stephen (1135–1154) men cried out that 'Christ and His saints slept.'"

549 *dam-bid-dam*: (Tolson's note) "'blood for blood.' This was the way the Saadists phrased the idea of talion at the Abbasiya mausoleum of Nokrashy Pasha. ["Talion" is a form of punishment that resembles the crime. Tolson may have in mind a passage from the Persian author Saadi or Sadi (1200?–1291), who wrote didactic tales interspersed with short verses that delivered a moral.] Cf. Leviticus XXIV, xvii-xxi." "And he that killeth any man shall surely be put to death. And he that killeth a beast shall make it good; beast for beast. And if a man cause a blemish in his neighbor; as he hath done, so shall it be done to him; Breach for breach, eye for eye, tooth for tooth: as he hath caused a blemish to a man so shall it be done to him again. And he that killeth a beast, he shall restore it; and he that killeth a man, he shall be put to death."

551 *souls of hyenas*: (Tolson's note) "Another reference to the bloody Muraviev, 'this loathsome figure with a bulldog's face and a hyena's soul.'" The phrase is from [Jan] Kucharzewski, *The Origins of Modern Russia* (1948), Chapter 10. See Tolson's notes to lines 419, 504, and 511.

551 *teneo te africa*: (Tolson's note) "The words uttered by Caesar when he stumbled and fell on touching the shore of Africa. Cf. Suetonious [(2nd c.)], *Lives of the Caesars*." "He had also slipped and fallen as he disembarked on the coast of Africa but turned an unfavorable omen into a favorable one by clasping the ground and shouting: 'Africa, I have tight hold of you!'" (paragraph 59, "Julius Caesar").

552 *mboagan*: (Tolson's note) "death."

against sodom's pillars of salt
below the mountain of rodinsmashedstatues° *aleppe*°

• • • • • • •

555        Tomorrow . . . O . . . Tomorrow,°
Where is the glory of the *mestizo*° Pharaoh?
The Mahdi's° tomb of the foul deed?
Black Clitus of the fatal verse° and Hamlet's arras?°
The cesspool of the reef of gold?°

---

554 *rodinsmashedstatues*: (Tolson's note) "The twisted version of the hag Today keeps her from seeing that only the hands of the statues have been chopped off; and thus she misses the apocalypse in the Rodin image, the magnetic needle of whose compass points toward the Africa-To-Be (*Höhere* ["the heights," see note to line 403] and *Khopirû* ["To Be," see note to line 610], set as the goal, by the protagonist, in the first section. For an elucidation of this Janus-faced image, see Lajos Egri, *The Art of Dramatic Writing* [(1946)], pp. 30–31." In Egri's telling, Auguste Rodin (1840–1917) smashed and removed the hands from a sculpture because the quality of their craftsmanship distracted from the composition. "No part is more important than the whole" is Rodin's advice. Tolson may be suggesting that though the high culture of Europe has been destroyed by World War II the void left only implies a future role for nations outside Europe. Although the two faces of Janus, Roman God of beginnings, face in opposite directions and can represent pure opposition, here "Janus-faced" seems to mean "looking all ways."

554 *alleppe*: "Cf. Dante, *Inferno*, Canto VII: '*Pape Satan! Pape, aleppe!*'" (line 1). Gibberish barked out by Plutus, god of wealth and guardian of the fourth circle of Hell, who collapses at once upon a word from Dante's guide Virgil.

555 *Tomorrow*: (Tolson's note) "V. [William] Blake, 'The Bard' [perhaps the "Introduction" to *Songs of Experience* (1794): "Hear the voice of the Bard! / Who Present, Past, & Future sees!" (lines 1–2).] Cf. [Arthur] Rimbaud: '*Je vais dévoiler tous les mystères . . . mort, naissance, avenir, passé, cosmogonie, neant.*' [(French) "I shall now unveil all the mysteries . . . death, birth, future, past, cosmos, nothingness" from "Night in Hell" in *A Season of Hell* (1874).] Also [Johann Wolfgang von] Goethe, *Faust* [Part Two, line] 7433: 'Enough, the poet is not bound by time'" (Act 2, in the George Madison Priest translation). The theme of poet as visionary signals a transition toward Tolson's portrayal of a future in which Africa is included as a continent with a thriving economy and a positive civilization. But first, he pauses in this stanza between lost or forgotten historical moments—some positive, some negative, some undetermined—whose ultimate significance will depend upon the course the future takes.

556 *mestizo*: mixed-race.

557 *Mahdi*: The Moslem prophet whose appearance will indicate the end of the world. The title has been assumed several times by various leaders, including Mohammed Ahmed in 1883 in the war in the Egyptian Sudan in which Khartoum fell and Gordon was killed.

558 *the fatal verse*: (Tolson's note) "Alexander the Great made Black Clitus, 'his best beloved,' King of Bactria and commander of his celebrated cavalry, which synchronized with the Macedonian phalanx to deliver a battle's one-two punch. Dropsica, Clitus' mother, was Alexander's nurse. During the Persian campaign a furious argument broke out at the king's supper table. He snatched a spear from a soldier and ran it through Clitus as he came from behind a curtain shouting a verse from Euripedes' *Andromache*: 'In Greece, alas, how ill things ordered are!' V. Plutarch [(46?–120?], *Lives*, 'Alexander'" [sections L-LI].

558 *arras*: (Tolson's note) "Cf. Shakespeare, *Hamlet*, III, iv." Hamlet kills the eavesdropper behind an arras, an eavesdropper whom he had thought to be his stepfather, the king, but was in fact the counselor, Polonius.

559 *cesspool of the reef of gold*: (Tolson's note) "The epithet African intellectuals give to Johannesburg." In the South African capital, black and white were separated by rigid laws.

560          *Der Schwarze Teufel*, Napoleon's savior?°
          The Black Virgin° of Creation's Hell Hole?°
          Tomorrow . . . O . . . Tomorrow,
          Where is Jugurtha° the dark Iago?
          The witches' Sabbath of sleeping sickness?°
565          The *Nye ke mi*° eyeless in the River of Blood?°
          The Tagus° that imitates the Congo?°
          The *Mein Kampf*° of *kitab al sudan wa'lbidan*?°

---

560 *Die Schwarze Teufel*: (German) "The black devil." (Tolson's note) "V. the German army's nickname for General [Alexandre] Dumas, who rescued Napoleon from the Mamelukes [the elite Egyptian calvary forces that harassed the French in their 1798 African campaign] by riding a stallion into a mosque in Cairo. The general's astounding feats kept him from getting a marshal's baton. He never recovered from the blow."

561 *Black Virgin*: (Tolson's note) "Cf. Xenophanes [(6th c. B.C.): 'Men have always made their gods in their own image—the Greeks like Greeks, the Ethiopians like Ethiopians.' [Tolson's version removes physical features from a couplet that is usually translated more literally: "Ethiopians say that their gods are snub-nosed and black, / Thracians that theirs have light blue eyes and red hair" (Fragment 16).] Again Professor [Arthur] Christy's figure of 'the world's cultural fabric' is evidenced in the statues of the Black Virgin Mary and Negro saints which were common in Germany and Latin Europe, as well as northern Africa, during the Middle Ages. The stained glass of the Cathedral at Chartres has portraits in ebony." This information Tolson also developed from a passage in Chapter X of DuBois, *The World and Africa* (1946). See note to line 577. For more on Christy, see Tolson's note to line 287.

561 *Creation's Hell Hole*: (Tolson's note) "the name the Italians gave the Danakil desert." *Hell-Hole of Creation: The Exploration of Abyssinian Danakil* by L. M. Nesbitt was published in 1935. Another reference to the difficulties of the Italians as would-be African conquerors.

563 *Jugurtha*: African prince (d. 104 B.C.) from Carthage who waged war against Rome from 111–106 B.C., but was defeated and displayed as a captive in Rome, where he died.

564 *sleeping sickness*: an infectious disease of tropical Africa, transmitted by the tse-tse fly.

565 *The Nye ke mi*: "doctor" in the Mano dialect, but a literal reading would be "the one who channels the power of the essence of things." Wilson discusses the phrase in *Liberia* (1947), Chapter Ten, where he cites a local doctor explaining, "Nye is that which has more power than a casual examination might reveal. *Nye* is any substance or fetish used in making medicine or controlling illness . . . Certain rare and precious medicines are thought to have sight and speech, even the ability to assume human form and move about."

565 *River of Blood*: Rivers of Blood are all too common in history, but Tolson may have had in mind the decisive 1838 Battle of Blood River in which the slaughter of spear-carrying Zulu warriors by Dutch soldiers with rifles began to weaken the massive Zulu African empire.

566 *Tagus*: The longest river in the Iberian peninsula, it flows through Spain and Portugal, entering the Atlantic at Lisbon. (Tolson's note) "Cf. [Vianna] Moog, *Um Rio imita o Rheno* [(Portuguese) "Rio Imitates the Rhine"]. Moog created his symbol to suggest the heavy German settlement on Rio Grande do Sul [southernmost state of Brazil]. The line indicates a historic parallel when 10,000 Negroes gathered in Lisbon and threatened to outnumber the whites." Possibly a reference to the forced removal of the Moors from Lisbon in 1147 by Alfonso I, the beginning of the end of African influence in Portugal.

567 *Mein Kampf*: (German) "My Struggle." The book in which Adolf Hitler (1889–1945) flaunted his anti-Semitism and explained his ambitions for world conquest.

567 *kitab al sudan wa 'lbidan*: (Tolson's note) "'the superiority of the black race over the white.' Before the swastika gave Nordicism the Stuka, an Arab scholar Al-Jahiz issued his racist theory in reverse: another instance of similarity in dissimilarity." DuBois in Chapter X of *The World and Africa* mentioned "Al-Jahiz, a writer, whom [British historian] Christopher Dawson called the greatest Arab scholar and stylist of the nineteenth century." His book was entitled *The Superiority of the Black Race over the White*. Swastika: symbol of the Nazis. Nordicism: "scientific" theorists of racism in the early twentieth century divided Europeans into three classes: the Nordic or highest, the Alpine or next highest, and the Mediterranean, the lowest. Stuka: a German dive-bombing airplane of World War II.

The black albatross about the white man's neck?°
O Tomorrow,
570        Where is the graven image *pehleh*° of *Nash Barin*?°
Their white age of their finest black hour?
The forged minute book of ebony Hirsch?°
The chattel whose Rock° vies with the Rime of the upstart Crow?°
*Ppt. knows.*°

• • • • • • •

575        The Futurafrique, the *chef d'oeuvre*° of Liberian
Motors  slips  through  the  traffic

568 *albatross . . . neck*: In Samuel Taylor Coleridge (1772–1834)'s "Rime of the Ancient
Mariner" (1798), the mariner has "inhospitably killed" the albatross, a "pious bird of good
omen," and his shipmates attempt to place guilt entirely on the mariner by hanging the
dead bird around his neck.

570 *pehleh*: (Tolson's note) [(Russian)] "money."

570 *Nash Barin*: (Tolson's note) "before the October Revolution, this expression meant
'Our Master' or God. I don't know its present meaning. [The October Revolution of 1918
overthrew the Russian aristocracy.] Cf. I Timothy VI, v. ["Perverse disputings of men of
corrupt minds, and destitute of the truth, supposing that gain is godliness: from such with-
draw thyself" (I Timothy 6:5).] Also, [John] Milton, *Paradise Lost* [line] 678." "*Mammon*
led them on, / *Mammon*, the least erected Spirit that fell / From Heav'n, for ev'n in Heav'n
his looks and thoughts / Were always downward bent, admiring more / The riches of
Heav'n's pavement, trodd'n Gold, / Than aught divine or holy else enjoy'd / In vision be-
atific" (Book I, lines 678–684).

572 *ebony Hirsch*: Possibly Moritz (or Maurice) de Hirsch (1831–1896), philanthropist who
founded and financed the Jewish Colonization Association to promote the emigration of
Jews from Europe and Asia. He was especially active in transferring Russian Jews to Ar-
gentina. Russia rejected his offer of a $10 million subsidy to upgrade educational condi-
tions for Jews. Tolson will apply the epithet "ebony" to those whose actions have been
friendly toward Africans.

573 *The chattel*: (Tolson's note) "'Tariq.' Rock: Gibraltar was named for this black general
and ex-slave." Moslem rule in Spain began in 711 after the invasion of Tarik ibn Zayad.
The outcropping in the Mediterranean Sea was named *Djebel Tarik* (or "mountain of
Tarik"), corrupted to "Gibraltar." DuBois in *The World and Africa* (1946) notes this, citing
from W. A. Rogers in *Sex and Race* (1942). Rogers is cited in a note to line 69.

573 *the Rime of the upstart Crow*: (Tolson's note) "Cf. Shakespeare, Sonnet LV: 'Not mar-
ble, nor the gilded monuments / Of Princes, shall outlive this powerful rime.'" Robert
Greene called Shakespeare "an upstart crow." See note to line 155.

574 *Ppt. knows*: (Tolson's note) "V. [Jonathan] Swift, *Journal to Stella*, March 15, 1712."
"Ppt" was shorthand in Swift's journal for Esther Johnson (the "Stella" of his poems) with
whom he had a life-long attachment. The initials stood for "poor pretty thing" or "poppet"
(a term of endearment reserved for a child). The 15 March 1712 entry surrounds with un-
certainty a possible meeting of Parliament that neither Queen nor Ministers can be as-
sured will occur: "for it depends on winds and weather, and circumstances of negotiation.
However, we go on as if it was certainly to meet; and I am to be at Lord Treasurer's to-
morrow, upon that supposition, to settle some things relating that way. Ppt. may under-
stand me." For Robert Farnsworth, the line records "the need to act with faith in the midst
of uncertainty. . . . 'Ppt. knows' asserts that the truth, though guarded, is known; thus it
expresses a quietly wistful assurance of the future." Jon Stanton Woodson sees Tolson as
acutely sensitive to worldwide nuclear destruction—indeed, Tolson's finale of a triumphant
Africa, Woodson sees as emerging from such a future disaster—and for him Swift's jour-
nal entry echoes a Cold War scenario in which the good but helpless citizen must pretend
that the future is a certainty. Finally, Tolson's use of so diminished a phrase ("ppt.") at so
crucial a moment in his work also suggests he wants attention drawn to figures only ac-
corded space in history along the sidelines, reduced to shorthand entries in journals. Their
silencing is unjust, and their perspective is valuable for its special sensitivity.

575 *The Futurafrique*: name of an automobile, the *chef d'oeuvre* ("masterpiece") of Liber-
ian Motors, first of four modes of transportation that will transport us across a series of
landscapes set in an African future.

swirl of axial Parsifal-Feirefiz°
Square, slithers past the golden
statues of the half-brothers as
580       brothers, with *cest prace*° . . .
The Futurafrique, the accent on youth and speed
and beauty, escalades the Mount
Sinai° of Tubman University,° the
vistas of which bloom with co-
585       eds from seven times seven lands . . .
The Futurafrique, windows periscopic, idles past
the entrance to the 70A subway
station,° volplanes into the aria
of Swynnerton Avenue,° zooms
590       by the Zorzor Monument,° zigzags
between the factory hierarchies,
rockets upcountry and backcoun-
try, arcs the ad-libbing soapy
blue harbor crossroads of Wal-
595       dorf Astorias° at anchor, atom-
fueled and burnished in ports
of the six seagirt worlds . . .
The Futurafrique strokes the thigh of Mount Bar-
clay° and skis toward the Good-

---

577 *Parsifal-Feirefiz*: (Tolson's note) "Cf. [Wolfram von] Eschenbach [(1170?–1220?)], *Parzi-val*. Also [W.E.B.] DuBois, *The World and Africa* [chapter] X." DuBois summarizes the plot of *Parzival*, a story of the search for the Holy Grail. Early on, Parzival falls into bat-tle with Feirefiz, a *bunte sohn* or "colored man" who spares Parzival's life after his sword breaks and who is revealed as Parzival's half-brother, offspring of his father's love of Queen Belakane (whose people were described as "even blacker than the night"). DuBois con-cludes: "This story of the crossing of the paths of Parsifal and Fierefiz is more than a side issue to the main story of the Holy Grail. It points toward the bridging of the gaps be-tween creeds and races and is of great significance in revealing the thought of enlightened and civilized society in Europe in the thirteenth century."

580 *cest prace*: (Tolson's note) "all honor to labor."

583 *Mount Sinai*: traditionally, the mountain on which Moses received the Ten Com-mandments.

583 *Tubman University*: William Tubman, born in 1895 and President of Liberia when Tol-son was writing, was a reformer who extended voting rights to women and tribesmen.

587 *70A subway*: (Tolson's note) "V. [Charles Morrow] Wilson, *Liberia* [(1947)], for many of these references." Since the journeys embarked upon here take place in the future, sev-eral place names and references that Tolson cites are imaginary projections that nonethe-less record actual moments of distinction from the country's past. When Tolson wrote, there was no subway in Monrovia, a town of 40,000. "70A" was the number assigned to the experimental drug phenylarsenoxide, discovered in the 1940s to be effective against sleeping sickness.

589 *Swynnerton Avenue*: Charles Swynnerton, British naturalist, traced the origin of sleep-ing sickness to the tse-tse fly.

590 *Zorzor Monument*: (Tolson's note) "The Zorzor twins were miracle workers in iron, see line 273." Line 273 reads: "O Africa, Mother of Science." The twins appear in Wilson's *Liberia* as "two crippled smiths, both victims of infantile paralysis. They . . . crawl about with the help of hand grips. . . . For bellows they use tubes made of hide set into low clay walls, and for anvils, blocks of granite" (Chapter 3).

595 *Waldorf Astorias*: luxury hotels.

599 *Mt. Barclay*: Actual mountain named after two Presidents of Liberia, Arthur (1904–1912) and Edwin (1930–1944).

600            lowe Straightaway, whose colo-
               ratura sunset is the alpenglow
               of cultures in the Shovelhead Era
               of the Common Man . . .
       The Futurafrique glitters past bronze Chomolungma, odic
605            memorial to Matilda Newport—°
               on and on and on, outracing the
               supercoach of the Momolu Bu-
               kere Black-Hound winging along
               the seven-lane Equatorial High-
610            way toward Khopirû° . . .
       The Futurafrique, flight-furbished ebony astride
               velvet-paved miles, vies with the
               sunflower   magnificence   of   the
               Oriens, challenges the snow-lily
615            diadem of the Europa° . . .
       The Futurafrique, with but a scintilla of its Niagara
               power,   slices   Laubach   Park,°
               eclipses the Silver Age Gibbet
               of Shikata-gai-nai,° beyond the

---

605 *Matilda Newport*: heroine of the earliest days of Liberia, she went beyond the stock-
ade's protective walls to fire a cannon with a coal from her pipe when tribesmen had placed
the new colonists under siege in 1822.
610 *Khopirû*: (Tolson's note) " 'To Be.' The concept embraces the Eternity of Thence; which,
free from blind necessity, contains the good life."
614–615 *Oriens and Europa*: These variants on "Orient" and "Europe" also sound like brand-
names or rival car models.
617 *Laubach Park*: American Missionary Frank Laubach (1884–1970) devised a simple way
to teach reading and writing which he applied in Asia, India, and Latin America, and which
he described in *Teaching the World to Read* (1948).
619 *Shikata-gai-nai*: (Tolson's note) " 'It cannot be helped.' This is the stoicism with which
Japanese villagers meet the earth convulsions of sacred Fujiyama [a volcano in Japan]. In
other lands it is fate, kismet, predestination, artistries of Circumstance, economic deter-
minism, necessitarianism—from Aeschylus' Nemesis to [Andre] Chenier's *filets d'Arachné*
[(French) "webs of the spider"]. Sometimes it takes the form of the sophistry, *human na-
ture does not change*. As a hidden premise it blocks the kinetic; it confuses the feral with
the societal and leads to *petitio principii* [(Latin) "little principles" or petty bureaucracy].
History, then, remains a Heraclitean continuum of a world flaring up and dying down as
'it always was, is, and shall be.' [The pre-Socratic Greek philosopher Heraclitus (sixth-fifth
c. B.C.) believed there was no reality except endless change, and that all things were de-
fined by the opposites they carried within them. T. S. Eliot cited him in the epigraph to
*Four Quartets* (1944).] Some moderns have turned this ancient seesaw figure of a crude
dialectics into a *locomotive of history*. In the poem, however, the flux of men and things
is set forth in symbols whose motions are vertical-circular, horizontal-circular, and recti-
linear [straight line]. In spite of the diversity of phenomena, the underlying unity of the
past is represented by the ferris wheel; the present by the merry-go-round; and the future
by the automobile, the train, the ship, and the airplane. I placed the ship image in the
middle of the images of swifter vehicles to indicate the contradiction in the essence of
things, the struggle of opposites, which mankind will face even in *Khopirû* and *Hōhere*.
By the Law of Relativity, history will always have its silver age as well as its golden, and
each age will contain some of the other's metal. Because of these upward and onward lags
and leaps, it is not an accident that Liberia reaches her destination, the Parliament of
African Peoples, after the aerial symbol. Cf. [George] Meredith, 'The World's Advance,'
the figure of the reeling spiral." Meredith's sonnet begins with the figure of a drunken
man, weaving to and fro but pressing onward: "our world's advance presents / That figure
on a flat; the way of worms. / Cherish the promise of its good intents. . . . " (lines 10–12).

620 *ars* of Phidias;° on and on, herds
  only blears of rotor masts roulet-
  ting, estates only rococo decks
  and sails swirling, the Futur-
  afrique, the Oriens, the Auster,
625 the Americus, the Europa,° rend
  space, gut time, arrowing past
  tiering Nidaba,° glissading side
  by side, into the cosmopolis of
  Höhere—the bygone habitat of
630 mumbo jumbo and blue tongue,
  of sasswood-bark jury° and tsetse
  fly, aeons and aeons before the
  Unhappie Wight of the Ques-
  tion Mark° crossed the Al Sirat!°

635 The United Nations Limited volts over the unten-
  anted, untitled grave of Black
  Simoom, the red Chaka of *ruse
  de guerre,*° the Cheops° of pyra-
  mids with the skulls of Pygmy
640 and Britisher, Boer and Arab . . .
 The United Nations Limited careers across Seretse
  Khama's Bechuanaland,° yester-
  day and yesterday and yester-
  day after the body of Living-
645 stone° knelled its trek in dry salt

---

620 *ars* [*art*] *of Phidias*: (Tolson's note) "Cf. [Auguste] Rodin: 'Beyond Phidias sculpture will never advance.' Also Shakespeare, *Troilus and Cressida*: 'The baby figure of the giant mass / Of things to come'" (Act 1 scene 3, lines 345–346). In the passage Nestor says small details can predict larger and more significant events.

624–625 *Auster, Americus*: Australia, America; See note to line 615.

627 *Nidaba*: (Tolson's note) "Cf. Dr. Samuel Noah Kramer's translation of a Sumerian tablet in the Museum of the Ancient Orient: 'You have called Nidaba the Queen of the places of learning.'" Nidaba was the Sumerian goddess of writing, learning, and accounting. Kramer was the author of *History Begins at Sumer* (1953), popular scholarship that identifies the non-Semitic people of the Sumerian civilization 3000 B.C. with several "firsts."

632 *sasswood-bark jury*: Tribal courts permit "trial by sasswood": "the accused drinks six cupfuls of a heavy tea brewed from the bark of the sasswood or *gli* tree. . . . According to folk belief, if the accused is innocent he will vomit up the fluid which has considerable emetic quality. If guilty he is unable to vomit, becomes ill, and frequently dies of the dosage, which presently acts as a violent cathartic" (Wilson, *Liberia*, Chapter Ten).

634 *Wight*: (Middle English): creature, living being. *Question Mark*: Africa's shape on a map. See note to line 42.

634 *Al Sirat*: probably shorthand for *al-Sirat al-Mustaqim*: (Arabic) "straight path, right path." Figuratively, the Islamic faith, and more generally, "that which pleases God."

635 *The United Nations Limited*: an express train.

636–638 *Black . . . ruse de guerre*: (French: "tricks of war"). Chaka or more commonly, Shaka (1787–1828), Zulu chief and tactician, expanded the territory over which he ruled to 200,000 square miles until assassinated by one of his brothers. *Simoon (or simoom)*: hot and sandy blowing winds that could prove fatal to travelers in Arabia and Syria.

638 *Cheops*: king of ancient Egypt who built the largest pyramid at Gizeh.

642 *Bechuanaland*: Currently Botswana.

644 *Livingstone*: David Livingstone (1813–1873), Scottish missionary and explorer who named "Victoria Falls" and witnessed Lake Bangeula. His body was transported from Africa for burial in Westminster Abbey.

from Lake Bangeula to the sab-
bath of Westminster Abbey . . .
The United Nations Limited horseshoe-curves° Stan-
ley Falls,° sheens the surrealistic
650 harlotry of the mirage-veiled
Sahara, quakes the dinosaurian
teeth bolted in the jaws of Ti-
besti,° zoom-zooms through the
Ptolemaic Subterane like a silver
655 sirocco . . .
The United Nations Limited, stream-phrased and air-
chamoised and spong-cush-
ioned, telescopes the polyge-
netic metropolises polychro-
660 matic between Casablanco and
Mafeking, Freetown and Addis
Ababa!°

The Bula Matadi,° diesel-engined, fourfold-decked,
swan-sleek, glides like an ice-
665 ballet skater out of the Bight of
Benin,° the lily lyricism of whose
ivory and gold figurines larked
space oneness on the shelf ice
of avant-garde Art . . .
670 The Bula Matadi swivels past isled Ribat,° where, in
a leaden age's iliads,° the Black
Messiah and his Black Puritans,
exsected° by Sodoms and Go-
morrahs, daunted doxy° doubts
675 with skeletons of dharna° . . .
The Bula Matadi skirrs up the Niger,° with her Khufu°
cargo from Tel Aviv and Hiro-

---

648 *horseshoe-curves*: a verb. The U.N. Limited navigates a turn similar to the Horseshoe Curve near Altoona, Pennsylvania, on the westward lines of the Pennsylvania Railroad.
649 *Stanley Falls*: Named for Sir Henry Stanley (1841–1904), journalist and adventurer, these are cascades that feed into the Congo River.
653 *Tibesti*: a mountain range in north-central Africa.
660–662 *Casablanco . . . Addis Ababa*: widely-separated centers of civilization on the African continent.
663 *Bula Matadi*: a sailing vessel, named after the Atlantic Ocean port at the entrance to the Congo River.
666 *bight of Benin*: City in southwest Nigeria, whose ivory carvings and sculpture were much prized by collectors and originators of modern art.
670 *Ribat*: Arabic for a particular kind of settlement, usually one located near a saint's grave and with a small mosque.
671 *leaden age's iliads*: tales of warfare like the *Iliad* of Homer, but from an age more recent that the "golden age" of Greece.
673 *exsected*: cut out.
674 *doxy*: a doctrine or creed, especially in religion; also, a loose woman.
675 *dharna*: The method of attaining justice in India by sitting at the door of one's debtor and fasting until justice is served.
676 *Niger*: River in West Africa.
677 *Khufu cargo*: Cheops was also called Khufu. (See note to line 641.) Khufu cargo may be wealth like that with which the pharoahs were surrounded in the pyramids.

shima, Peiping and San Salva-
dor, Monrovia and Picayune!°

680    *Le Premier des Noirs*,° of Pan-African Airways, whirs
        beyond the copper cordilleran°
        climaxes of glass skyscrapers on
        pavonine° Cape Mesurado° . . .
    *Le Premier des Noirs* meteors beyond the Great White
685         Way of Kpandemai, aglitter
        with the ebony *beau monde*° . . .
    *Le Premier des Noirs* waltzes across Lake Chad,° curv-
        ets above the Fifth Cataract,
        wantons with the friar stars of
690         the Marra Mountains, eagles its
        steeple-nosed prow toward the
        Very Black° and the iron cur-
        tainless Kremlin!°

    The Parliament of African Peoples plants the winged
695         *lex scripta*° of its New Order on
        Roberts Avenue, in Bunker Hill,
        Liberia . . .
    The Parliament of African Peoples pinnacles *Novus*
        *Homo*° in the Ashmun Interna-
700         tional House,° where, free and
        joyful again,° all mankind unites,
        without heralds of earth and
        water° . . .

---

679 *Picayune*: a small town in southern Mississippi, included in this list somewhat outra-
geously.
680 *Le Premier des Noirs*: (French) "First of the Blacks." (Tolson's note) "When Napoleon
became First Consul, Toussaint l'Ouverture addressed him in this manner. 'From the First
of the Blacks to the First of the Whites.'" L'Ouverture (1743–1803) wrenched control of
Haiti from the British, the Spanish, and the French, and governed the island successfully
until captured and sent to France to die in a dungeon.
681 *cordilleran*: the principal mountain range of a location.
683 *pavonine*: iridescent, like the peacock's tail.
683 *Cape Mesurado*: isthmus of the Liberian capital, Monrovia.
686 *beau monde*: (French) "high society."
687 *Lake Chad*: in northwest central Africa, at the junction of Nigeria and Chad.
692 *the Very Black*: (Tolson's note) "'Qim-Oîrit,' or the Red Sea. V. [G. Gaston] Maspero,
*The Dawn of Civilization* [(1901), Chapter] I."
693 *iron curtainless Kremlin*: Russia without restrictions on its people. See Tolson's note
to line 330.
695 *lex scripta*: (Latin) "written law."
699 *Novus Homo*: (Latin) "new man."
700 *Ashmun International House*: See note to line 245.
701 *free and joyful*: (Tolson's note) "Cf. [Ludwig van] Beethoven [(1770–1827)], *Ninth Sym-
phony*, 'Finale.'" This chorale ending features the "Ode to Joy" of Johann von Schiller
(1759–1805).
703 *heralds of earth and water*: (Tolson's note) "ancient symbols of submission." These
"symbols of submission" were emphasized in Tolson's footnote to line 117 of "E. & O. E.,"
as published in *Poetry* (September 1951): "The symbol of submission among the Indo-Aryans
was earth and water. Some African tribes still use this symbol."

The Parliament of African Peoples churns with magic
705                potions, monsoon spirits, zonal
                   oscillations, kinetic credenda,
                   apocalyptic projects—shudder-
                   ing at its own depth,° shudder-
                   ing as if Shakespeare terrified
710                Shakespeare . . .
The Parliament of African Peoples, chains riven in
                   an age luminous with alpha ray
                   ideas, rives the cycle of years
                   lean and fat, poises the scales
715                of Head and Hand, gives Sci-
                   ence dominion over Why and
                   Art over How, bids Man cross
                   the bridge of Bifrost° and drink
                   draughts of rases° from verved
720                and loined apes of God° with
                   leaves of grass and great audi-
                   ences° . . .
The Parliament of African Peoples, After the Deluge,°
                   wipes out the zymotic zombi°
725                cult of God's wounds, exscinds
                   the fetid fetish Zu'lkadah,° bans
                   the genocidal *Siyáfa,°* enroots
                   the Kiowa anthem° *Geh Tai*
                   *Gea°* . . .
730        The Parliament of African Peoples pedestals a new
                   golden calendar of Höhere and
                   quickens the death-in-life of the

---

708 *its own depth*: (Tolson's note) "In this phrase [Victor] Hugo was describing Hugo." Possibly from the 1856 Preface cited earlier in line 439, where Hugo invites readers to meditate on his poetry and "recover their appropriate image in that deep and mournful water, which was amassed slowly, as from the depth of a soul."

718 *bridge of Bifrost*: in Norse mythology, the rainbow bridge that leads to Valhalla, hall of the Gods.

719 *draughts of rases*: perhaps drinks raised in a toast to erasing the past.

720 *apes of God*: for Tolson the phrase defines human beings.

722 *leaves of grass and great audiences*: *Leaves of Grass* author Whitman stated that "To have great poets there must be great audiences too"—adopted as the motto of *Poetry* magazine.

723 *After the Deluge*: After the Flood. Jon Stanton Woodson notes the phrase may allude to the title of the opening prose poem in Arthur Rimbaud's *Illuminations*, "Après le Déluge."

724 *zymotic*: caused by fermentation. *Zombi*: a corpse in a state of trancelike animation.

726 *Zu'lkadah*: (Also dhu-l-kada). The time in the Islamic calendar that occurs before the time in which the pilgrimage to Mecca is taken; thus, for some, an emotional low point.

727 *Siyáfa*: (Tolson's note) "'We Die.'"

728 *anthem*: Tolson's phrasing recalls the closing line of Whitman's "Prayer of Columbus": "anthems in new tongues I hear saluting me."

729 *Geh Tai Gea*: (Tolson's note) [(Kiowa?)] "'All is Well.'"

           unparadised° with the olive al-
           penstocks° of the Violent Men° . . .

735    The Parliament of African Peoples decrees the Zu'l-
           hijyah° of Everyman and eter-
           nizes *Afrika sikelél' iAfrika°* . . .

       The Parliament of African Peoples hormones the Iscariot-
           cuckolded Four Freedoms,° up-
740           holsters warehoused *unto each*
           *according as any one has need,*
           keystones italics ushered in by
           epee° Pros and Cons Incorrup-
           tible, banishes cicerones° of the
745           witch hunt under the aegis of
           Flag and Cross,° while the tiered
           galleries and television conti-
           nents hosanna the Black Jews
           from the cis-Danakil Desert,
750           the Ashantis from the Great
           Sierra Nile, the Hottentots from
           Bushland, the Mpongwes from
           the Cameroon Peoples' Repub-
           lic, the Pygmies from the United
755           States of Outer Ubangi° . . .

       The Parliament of African Peoples signets° forever
           the *Recessional of Europe°* and

---

732–733 *quickens . . . unparadised:* restores life to those groups who had been in a suspended state because they did not conform to a ready formula for achievement.

734 *alpenstocks:* iron-tipped staff for mountain climbing.

734 *the Violent Men:* (Tolson's note) "the stigmatized advocates of the Declaration of Independence in the First and Second Continental Congress. V. [Cornelia] Meigs, *The Violent Men.*" Meigs's scholarship is subtitled *A Study of Human Relations in the First American Congress* (1949): "To stand as a small minority against the natural timidity, against the distrust of change, against the clinging to security which dominated the minds of the majority; to feel the new pressure of liberty and freedom as it crowded an age of selfish conservatism; to be forward-looking in a time of confusion and hopeful in the face of every temptation to despair—that is what it was, in the years 1774, 1775, and 1776, to be a 'violent' man" (end of Chapter III).

736 *Zu'lhijyah:* (also Dhu-l-Hijja). The month in the Islamic calendar when the all-important pilgrimage to Mecca occurs, an event uniting believers who are otherwise geographically scattered.

737 *Afrika sikelél iAfrika:* (Tolson's note) "'Africa save Africa.'"

739 *Four Freedoms:* Franklin D. Roosevelt's 1941 assertion that the world should enjoy freedom of speech and expression, freedom of worship, freedom from want, and freedom from fear.

743 *epee:* a thin, pointed sword used in fencing.

744 *cicerones:* guides.

745–746 *witch hunt . . . Flag and Cross:* In the 1950s, conservative factions in the state conducted trials known as witch hunts to brand liberal thinkers as dangerous radicals opposed to the nation and Christianity ("Flag and Cross").

748–754 *Black Jews, Ashantis, Hottentots, Mpongwes, Pygmies:* diverse groups from various places in the African continent.

756 *signets:* the signet ring marked an official government seal.

757 *Recessional of Europe:* a recessional was a hymn sung to indicate the formal close of a church service.

trumpets the abolition of itself:
and no nation uses *Felis leo* or
760  *Aquila heliaca*° as the emblem of
*blut und boden*,° and the hyenas
whine no more among the bar-
ren bones of the seventeen sun-
set sultans of Songhai; and the
765  deserts that gave up the ghost
to green pastures° chant in the
ears and teeth of the Dog, in
the Rosh Hashana° of the Afric
calends: "*Honi soit qui mal y*
770  *pense!*"°

1953

---

759–760 *Felis leo*: (Latin) a lion. *Aquila heliaca*: (Latin) a type of eagle. Both emblems stress strength and power. With the reference to the eagle, Tolson echoes the opening lines of the poem and the contrast with the "quicksilver sparrow."

761 *Blut und boten*: (German) "Blood and soil." See notes to line 483 and 502.

766 *pastures*: Tolson here recasts phrases used in "Re" when mourning the lost civilization of Songhai, in lines 93–94 ("And now the hyenas whine among the barren bones / Of the seventeen sun sultans of Songhai") and 77–78 ("the gravel-blind saw / Deserts give up the ghost to green pastures!").

768 *Rosh Hashana*: Name of the Jewish New Year, whose first day is traditionally a Judgment Day, when the Lord reviews everyone on earth and determines whether to enter their names into the Book of Life or the Book of Death.

769–770 *Honi soit aui mal y pense*: (French) "Shamed be he who thinks evil of it," motto of the Order of the Garter and reportedly spoken by Edward III (1312–1377), wearing without shame the garter of the Countess of Salisbury. In concluding, these words deny outright either/or judgments and initiate a self-reflective process of understanding and acceptance.

# Yvor Winters (1900–1968)

Arthur Yvor Winters was born in Chicago. He first published as an imagist poet, and his work was much admired in the 1920s. *The Magpie's Shadow* (1922) is composed entirely of one-line poems, six syllables to the line. But even as a young poet he thought about critical matters. His 1924 essay "The Testament of a Stone," about the poetic image, was important enough for the editors of *Secession* to devote an entire issue to it. Hart Crane was a contemporary and a friend, but one whose excess Winters found disturbing. Winters felt William Carlos Williams's free verse was erratic. Poetry, he believed, should aspire to an almost epigrammatic clarity. Some of the seriousness and intensity Winters brought to the act of critical judgment is evident in "Sir Gawaine and the Green Knight," a poem that teases out and complicates some of the moral implications of the medieval romance of the same name. At Stanford, Winters was mentor to a number of young poets, including Philip Levine and Robert Hass.

## Sir Gawaine and the Green Knight°

Reptilian green the wrinkled throat,
Green as a bough of yew the beard;
He bent his head, and so I smote;
Then for a thought my vision cleared.

5      The head dropped clean; he rose and walked;
He fixed his fingers in the hair;
The head was unabashed and talked;
I understood what I must dare.

---

**poem title:** The title of a fourteenth-century Arthurian romance, a long narrative poem describing how a Green Knight arrives at King Arthur's court and challenges any knight to behead him that night, provided that he give the beheader a similar blow a year later. Sir Gawaine takes the challenge and beheads the Green Knight, who picks up his head and tells Gawaine to meet him in one year. Later, Gawaine arrives at a castle where he is warmly entertained, not realizing that his host is the Green Knight. The lady of the castle tries to seduce Gawaine, who resists her but accepts a magic protective girdle that he conceals from his host. When the time for the beheading comes, Gawaine does not flinch, but the Green Knight gives him only a slight wound, and that because he concealed the girdle. The entire adventure is a plot to test the honor and courage of the knights.

His flesh, cut down, arose and grew.
10    He bade me wait the season's round,
And then, when he had strength anew,
To meet him on his native ground.

The year declined; and in his keep
I passed in joy a thriving yule;
15    And whether waking or in sleep,
I lived in riot like a fool.

He beat the woods to bring me meat.
His lady, like a forest vine,
Grew in my arms; the growth was sweet;
20    And yet what thoughtless force was mine!

By practice and conviction formed,
With ancient stubbornness ingrained,
Although her body clung and swarmed,
My own identity remained.

25    Her beauty, lithe, unholy, pure
Took shapes that I had never known;
And had I once been insecure,
Had grafted laurel in my bone.

And then, since I had kept the trust,
30    Had loved the lady, yet was true,
The knight withheld his giant thrust
And let me go with what I knew.

I left the green bark and the shade,
Where growth was rapid, thick, and still;
35    I found a road that men had made
And rested on a drying hill.

*1943*

# Sterling A. Brown (1901–1989)

Brown was born and raised in the strictly segregated Washington, D.C., of the first decades of the century. His family was middle class (his father was a professor of religion), and he was educated at Williams Collage and Harvard. At Harvard, he read the new American poetry of early modernism and was struck especially by the use of the vernacular in Frost, Sandburg, and others. To this he would add knowledge of black folk traditions sought out in the southern countryside during several college teaching jobs in the 1920s. The result was the stunning debut volume *Southern Road* (1932), which in many ways revolutionized African American poetry throughout the rest of the century.

The critical issue was Brown's use of black dialect in his poetry. Criticized by James Weldon Johnson and others because of its long association with plantation life and minstrel shows, black dialect was faulted for reinforcing stereotypes, substituting pathos for dignity, and even promoting belief in black ignorance. But Brown's poetry overturned all these assumptions. His revolutionary use of dialect went much further than crediting the vitality of independent folk traditions. Dialect in Brown becomes an extraordinarily compressed register for an ironic sense of cultural difference, for pride in an alternative knowledge amidst racial oppression. Dialect registers class and race awareness, along with a basic understanding of power relations in America, in a witty form that goes unnoticed by the ruling classes. It is a special form, at once a form of wit and wisdom.

Because Brown's first book of poems appeared at the outset of the Great Depression, it missed the widespread attention it might have attracted only a few years earlier. Brown returned to Harvard for graduate study and produced two ground-breaking critical studies of African American literature in the 1930s. His major anthology *The Negro Caravan* appeared in 1941, but his *Collected Poems* was not published until 1980.

## Scotty Has His Say

Whuh folks,° whuh folks; don' wuk muh brown too hahd!

'Cause Ise crazy 'bout muh woman,
An' ef yuh treats huh mean,

---

1 *Whuh folks*: Black vernacular pronunciation of "white folks."

I gonna sprinkle goofy dus'°

5          In yo' soup tureen.


Whuh folks, whuh folks; don' wuk muh brown too hahd!

Muh brown what's tendin' chillen in yo' big backyahd.


Oh, dat gal is young an' tender,

So jes' don' mistreat huh please,

10         Or I'll put a sprig of pisen ivy

In yo' B.V.D.'s.


I got me a Blackcat's wishbone,

Got some Blackcat's ankle dus',

An' yuh crackers better watch out

15         Ef I sees yo' carcass fus'—


Whuh folks, whuh folks; don' wuk muh brown too hahd!

Muh brown what's wringin' chicken necks in yo' backyahd.


'Cause muh brown an' me, we'se champeens

At de St. Luke's Hall;

20         An' yo' cookin' an' yo' washin'

Jes' ain't in it, not at all,


Wid de way we does de Chahlston,°

De Black Bottom° an' cake walkin',

Steppin' on de puppies' tail;

25         Whuh folks, ain' no need in talkin',—


You is got muh purty brownskin

In yo' kitchen an' yo' yahd,

Lemme tell yuh rebs one sho thing

Doncha wuk muh brown too hahd—


30         Whuh folks, whuh folks; don' wuk muh brown too hahd!

Who's practisin' de Chahlston in yo' big backyahd.

                                                    *1932*

---

4 *dus*: Scotty's threat to sprinkle "goofy dust" in the white owner's soup is the first of several proto-revolutionary threats based on folk or voodoo knowledge; it is followed by the threat to place poison ivy in the master's underpants and by Scotty's warning that he has a black cat's wishbone available as a weapon.

22 *Chahlston*: the Charleston was a popular dance that probably had African origins; it became popular through black musicals of the early 1920s. With its eccentric kicks and dynamic syncopations, it typifies the 1920s.

23 *Black Bottom*: a jazz dance that originated around the turn of the century and was popularized in vaudeville and minstrel shows; it became a craze in 1927, displacing the Charleston in popularity. Its name may refer to one of the dance's original movements, slapping the buttocks.

# Memphis Blues

### I

Nineveh, Tyre,
Babylon,°
Not much lef'
Of either one.
5    All dese cities
Ashes and rust,
De win' sing sperrichals
Through deir dus' . . .
Was another Memphis°
10    Mongst de olden days,
Done been destroyed
In many ways. . . .
Dis here Memphis°
It may go;
15    Floods may drown it;
Tornado blow;
Mississippi wash it
Down to sea—
Like de other Memphis in
20    History.

### II

Watcha gonna do when Memphis on fire,
    Memphis on fire, Mistah Preachin' Man?
Gonna pray to Jesus and nebber tire,
    Gonna pray to Jesus, loud as I can,
25        Gonna pray to my Jesus, oh, my Lawd!

Watcha gonna do when de tall flames roar,
    Tall flames roar, Mistah Lovin' Man?
Gonna love my brownskin better'n before—
    Gonna love my baby lak a do right man,
30        Gonna love my brown baby, oh, my Lawd!

Watcha gonna do when Memphis falls down,
    Memphis falls down, Mistah Music Man?
Gonna plunk on dat box as long as it soun',
    Gonna plunk dat box fo' to beat de ban',
35        Gonna tickle dem ivories, oh, my Lawd!

---

1–2 *Nineveh, Tyre, Babylon*: according to the Old Testament, three cities that were each
the object of divine wrath.
9 *Memphis*: a city on the Nile River, capital of Lower Egypt under the pharaohs.
13 *Memphis*: the American city on the Mississippi River in Tennessee.

Watcha gonna do in de hurricane,
  In de hurricane, Mistah Workin' Man?
Gonna put dem buildings up again,
  Gonna put em up dis time to stan',
40        Gonna push a wicked wheelbarrow, oh, my Lawd!

Watcha gonna do when Memphis near gone,
  Memphis near gone, Mistah Drinkin' Man?
Gonna grab a pint bottle of Mountain Corn,
  Gonna keep de stopper in my han',
45        Gonna get a mean jag° on, oh, my Lawd!

Watcha gonna do when de flood roll fas',
  Flood roll fas', Mistah Gamblin' Man?
Gonna pick up my dice fo' one las' pass—
  Gonna fade my way to de lucky lan',
50        Gonna throw my las' seven—oh, my Lawd!

III

Memphis go
By Flood or Flame;
Nigger won't worry
All de same—
55    Memphis go
Memphis come back,
Ain' no skin
Off de nigger's back.
All dese cities
60    Ashes, rust. . . .
De win' sing sperrichals
Through deir dus'.

1931

# Slim in Atlanta°

Down in Atlanta,
  De whitefolks got laws
For to keep all de niggers
  From laughin' outdoors.

5        Hope to Gawd I may die
  If I ain't speakin' truth
Make de niggers do deir laughin'
  In a telefoam booth.

---

45 *jag*: drinking binge.
**poem title:** from a series of five poems about the Slim Greer character.

Slim Greer hit de town
10      An' de rebs° got him told,—
"Dontcha laugh on de street,
    If you want to die old."

    Den dey showed him de booth,
      An' a hundred shines°
15    In front of it, waitin'
      In double lines.

Slim thought his sides
    Would bust in two,
Yelled, "Lookout, everybody,
20    I'm coming through!"

    Pulled de other man out,
      An' bust in de box,
    An' laughed four hours
      By de Georgia clocks.

25    Den he peeked through de door,
    An' what did he see?
*Three* hundred niggers there
    In misery.—

    Some holdin' deir sides,
30      Some holdin' deir jaws,
    To keep from breakin'
      De Georgia laws.

An' Slim gave a holler,
    An' started again;
35    An' from three hundred throats
    Come a moan of pain.

    An' everytime Slim
      Saw what was outside,
    Got to whoopin' again
40      Till he nearly died.

An' while de poor critters
    Was waitin' deir chance,
Slim laughed till dey sent
    Fo' de ambulance.

---

10 *rebs*: rebels, Southerners; originally applied to supporters of the Confederacy in the American Civil War.
14 *shines*: black people.

45
>De state paid de railroad
>    To take him away;
>Den, things was as usural
>    In Atlanta, Gee A.°

*1932*

## Slim in Hell°

I

>Slim Greer went to heaven;
>    St. Peter said, "Slim,
>You been a right good boy."
>    An' he winked at him.

5
>        "You been a travelin' rascal
>            In yo' day.
>        You kin roam once mo';
>            Den you comes to stay.

>"Put dese wings on yo' shoulders,
10
>        An' save yo' feet."
>Slim grin, and he speak up
>        "Thankye, Pete."

>        Den Peter say, "Go
>            To Hell an' see,
15
>        All dat is doing, and
>            Report to me.

>"Be sure to remember
>        How everything go."
>Slim say, "I be seein' yuh
20
>        On de late watch, bo."

>        Slim got to cavortin',
>            Swell as you choose,
>        Like Lindy in de "Spirit
>            Of St. Louis Blues!"°

---

48 *Gee A*: abbreviation for Georgia (Ga.).

**poem title:** Slim's journey to Hell draws on or alludes to numerous literary and folk traditions: the Greek myth of Orpheus and Eurydice, the Italian poet Dante Alighieri's (1265–1321) depiction of a journey into Hell in *The Divine Comedy*, the tall tale tradition, and folktales about "the colored man in heaven."

24 *Blues*: the second half of this stanza conflates Charles Lindberg's historic 1927 solo airplane flight across the Atlantic in the "Spirit of St. Louis" with W.C. Handy's 1914 "St. Louis Blues," an immensely influential composition that moved popular music from ragtime toward the blues. The passage performs this collation partly through Brown's reference to the Lindy Hop, a lively, athletic dance of black origin that had a surge in popularity when it was associated with Lindberg's feat. One of my students suggested we take Lindberg's flight as a symbolic counterpoint to the middle passage.

25  He flew an' he flew,
    Till at last he hit
A hangar wid de sign readin'
    DIS° IS IT.

    Den he parked his wings,
30      An' strolled aroun'
    Gettin' used to his feet
      On de solid ground.

## II

Big bloodhound came aroarin'
    Like Niagry Falls,
35  Sicked on by white devils
    In overhalls.

Now Slim warn't scared,
    Cross my heart, it's a fac',
An' de dog went on a bayin'
40    Some po' devil's track.

    Den Slim saw a mansion
      An' walked right in;
    De Devil looked up
      Wid a sickly grin.

45  "Suttinly didn't look
    Fo' you, Mr. Greer,
How it happen you comes
    To visit here?"

    Slim say—"Oh, jes' thought
50      I'd drap by a spell."
    "Feel at home, seh, an' here's
      De keys to Hell."

Den he took Slim around
    An' showed him people
55  Raisin' hell as high as
    De First Church Steeple.

    Lots of folks fightin'
      At de roulette wheel,
    Like old Rampart Street,
60      Or leastwise Beale.

---

28 *Dis*: a pun, not only black dialect but also Dante's name for the ninth circle of hell;
Brown thereby turns black dialect into a discourse of erudition.

Showed him bawdy houses
  An' cabarets,
Slim thought of New Orleans
  An' Memphis days.

65      Each devil was busy
          Wid a devilish broad,
        An' Slim cried, "Lawdy,
          Lawd, Lawd, Lawd."

Took him in a room
70        Where Slim see
De preacher wid a brownskin
  On each knee.

        Showed him giant stills,
          Going everywhere
75        Wid a passel of devils,
          Stretched dead drunk there.

Den he took him to de furnace
  Dat some devils was firing,
Hot as hell, an' Slim start
80        A mean presspirin';

        White devils wid pitchforks
          Threw black devils on,
        Slim thought he'd better
          Be gittin' along.

85    An' he say—"Dis makes
        Me think of home—
Vicksburg, Little Rock, Jackson,
  Waco, and Rome."

        Den de devil gave Slim
90        De big Ha-Ha;
        An' turned into a cracker,
          Wid a sheriff's star.

Slim ran fo' his wings,
  Lit out from de groun'
95    Hauled it back to St. Peter,
        Safety boun'.

**III**

St. Peter said, "Well,
  You got back quick.
How's de devil? An' what's
100       His latest trick?"

An' Slim say, "Peter,
    I really cain't tell,
De place was Dixie
    Dat I took for Hell."

105     Then Peter say, "You must
            Be crazy, I vow,
        Where'n hell dja think Hell *was*,
            Anyhow?

"Git on back to de yearth,
110     Cause I got de fear,
You'se a leetle too dumb,
    Fo' to stay up here . . ."

                                        1932

# Rent Day Blues

I says to my baby
"Baby, but de rent is due;
Can't noways figger
What we ever gonna do."

5   My baby says, "Honey,
Dontcha worry 'bout de rent.
Looky here, daddy,
At de money what de good Lord sent."

Says to my baby,
10  "Baby, I been all aroun';
Never knowed de good Lord
To send no greenbacks down."

Baby says, "Dontcha
Bother none about de Lord;
15  Thing what I'm figgerin'
Is how to get de next month's board."

Says to my baby,
"I'd best get me on a spell;
Get your rent from heaven,
20  Maybe get your food from hell."

Baby says, "One old
Miracle I never see
Dat a man lak you
Can ever get away from me."

25  I says, "Ain't no magician,
Baby, dat's a sho-Gawd fact;
But jest you watch me
Do de disappearin' act."

"Ef you do, you're better
30    Dan de devil or de Lord on high";
An' I stayed wid my baby
Fo' a devilish good reason why.

1932

## Old Lem

I talked to old Lem
and old Lem said:
        "They weigh the cotton
        They store the corn
5            We only good enough
            To work the rows;
        They run the commissary
        They keep the books
            We gotta be grateful
10           For being cheated;
        Whippersnapper clerks
        Call us out of our name
            We got to say mister
            To spindling boys
15       They make our figgers
        Turn somersets
        We buck in the middle
            Say, "Thankyuh, sah."
            They don't come by ones
20           They don't come by twos
            But they come by tens.

        "They got the judges
        They got the lawyers
        They got the jury-rolls
25       They got the law
            They don't come by ones
        They got the sheriffs
        They got the deputies
                    They don't come by twos
30       They got the shotguns
        They got the rope
            We git the justice
            In the end
                And they come by tens.

35       "Their fists stay closed
        Their eyes look straight
            Our hands stay open
            Our eyes must fall
                They don't come by ones
40       They got the manhood
        They got the courage
                They don't come by twos

We got to slink around
Hangtailed hounds.
45     They burn us when we dogs
They burn us whem we men
    They come by tens . . .

"I had a buddy
Six foot of man
50     Muscled up perfect
Game to the heart
        They don't come by ones
Outworked and outfought
Any man or two men
55         They don't come by twos
He spoke out of turn
At the commissary
They gave him a day
To git out the county
60     He didn't take it.
He said 'Come and get me.'
They came and got him
        And they came by tens.
He stayed in the county—
65     He lays there dead.

        They don't come by ones
        They don't come by twos
        But they come by tens."

                      *1939*

## Sharecroppers

When they rode up at first dark and called his name,
He came out like a man from his little shack.
He saw his landlord, and he saw the sheriff,
And some well-armed riff-raff in the pack.
5     When they fired questions about the meeting,
He stood like a man gone deaf and dumb,
But when the leaders left their saddles,
He knew then that his time had come.
In the light of the lanterns the long cuts fell,
10     And his wife's weak moans and the children's wails
Mixed with the sobs he could not hold.
But he wouldn't tell, he would not tell.
The Union was his friend, and he was Union,
And there was nothing a man could say.
15     So they trussed him up with stout ploughlines,
Hitched up a mule, dragged him far away
Into the dark woods that tell no tales,
Where he kept his secrets as well as they.

He would not give away the place,
20      Nor who they were, neither white nor black,
Nor tell what his brothers were about.
They lashed him, and they clubbed his head;
One time he parted his bloody lips
Out of great pain and greater pride,
25      One time, to laugh in his landlord's face;
Then his landlord shot him in the side.
He toppled, and the blood gushed out.
But he didn't mumble ever a word,
And cursing, they left him there for dead.
30      He lay waiting quiet, until he heard
The growls and the mutters dwindle away;
"Didn't tell a single thing," he said,
Then to the dark woods and the moon
He gave up one secret before he died:
35      "We gonna clean out dis brushwood° round here soon,
Plant de white-oak and de black-oak side by side."

1939

## Southern Cop

Let us forgive Ty Kendricks.
The place was Darktown. He was young.
His nerves were jittery. The day was hot.
The Negro ran out of the alley.
5       And so he shot.

Let us understand Ty Kendricks.
The Negro must have been dangerous,
Because he ran;
And here was a rookie with a chance
10      To prove himself a man.

Let us condone Ty Kendricks
If we cannot decorate.
When he found what the Negro was running for,
It was too late;
15      And all we can say for the Negro is
It was unfortunate.

Let us pity Ty Kendricks,
He has been through enough,
Standing there, his big gun smoking,
20      Rabbit-scared, alone,
Having to hear the wenches wail
And the dying Negro moan.

1936

---

35 *brushwood*: white racists.

## Choices

Don't want no yaller gal, dat's a color will not stay,
Don't want no yaller, yaller nevah known to stay,
Git caught in a storm, de yaller sho' will fade away.

Don't want no pretty pink, pink ain't de shade fo' me,
5    Don't want no pretty pink, pink it ain't de shade fo' me.
When you think you's got her, ain't nuffin' but yo' used to be.

Don't want no black gal, gums blue lak de sea,
Don't want no blue gums, blue jus' lak de deep blue sea,
Fraid that when I kiss her, bluine run all over me.

10    Don't want no brownskin, choklit to de bone,
Don't want no brownskin, choklit to de bone,
Choklit melts jes lak vanilla, and runs all out de cone.

Don't want no charcoal, soot's a mess what I despise,
Don't want no charcoal, soot's a mess what I despise,
15    Want to know whah my gals' at, anytime she shets her eyes.

Don't want no Geechie gal, talkin' lak a nachel zoo,
Don't want no Geechie, talkin' lak a nachel zoo,
Jabber lak a monkey, make a monkey outa you.

Don't care for de Ofays, got no dealins wif Miss Ann,°
20    Don't care for de Ofay, got no dealins wif Miss Ann,
Don't lak her brother Hemp, nor her cousin Mr. Cool Oil Can.

Don't want me no Injin, no Injin squaw of red,
Don't want me no Injin, no Injin squaw of red,
Ain't got much hair, want it left on top by frazzly head.

25    Don't want no blue woman, moanin' wid de lonesome blues,
Don't want no blue woman, moanin' wid de graveyard blues,
Got mo' blues myself now dan a man could evah use.

Gonna git me a green gal, if a green gal's to be found,
Git me a green gal, if a green gal is to be found,
30    But I spec' she ain't born yet, and her mama she in the ground.

*c. 1939*

---

19 *Miss Ann*: a white woman; her "brother Hemp" is a lynching rope. An "Ofay" is a term
for a white person in Black English. A "Geechie," in the previous stanza, is a Gullah-speak-
ing black person from the tide-water section of Georgia and South Carolina, or more
broadly, any poorly educated rural black speaking a hard-to-understand dialect. The poem
as as whole satirizes attitudes toward skin color *within* the black community.

# Laura (Riding) Jackson (1901–1991)

Born in New York City as Laura Reichenthal into a family whose father (a tailor by trade) was a committed socialist, she was encouraged to form strong opinions. She was attending Cornell University when she met and married historian Louis Gottschalk, accompanying him to academic posts in Illinois and Kentucky, and beginning to publish poetry in periodicals, including *The Fugitive*. A divorce returned her to New York City, where Hart Crane, her companion in several escapades, honored her outspoken confidence by dubbing her "Laura Riding-Roughshod." She joined British poet Robert Graves's extended family in England in 1925, coauthoring *A Survey of Modern Poetry* with him in 1927. That same year she legally adopted the surname Riding.

She was meanwhile developing an intense, paradoxical poetic style that made heavy demands on its readers. She had written about Gertrude Stein, and some of the poetry, like "Elegy in a Spider's Web," showed Stein's influence. Her assertions of independence echoed feminist sentiments. But, unlike Stein, wit and play were not among her more reliable strengths. Clashing assertions and compressed, telegraphic metaphors were her natural mode. The poetry imposed lessons of difficulty; anything less seemed hardly worth the effort.

A crisis came in 1929, when an Irish poet strongly drawn to her joined the Graves group. She leapt from a third-story window and broke her back, but survived. Moving to Mallorca with Graves, she wrote poems that often emphasized physical and mental suffering, while also completing several satiric works. Then she met Schuyler Jackson, a *Time* editor who had written intelligently of her 1938 *Collected Poems*. He divorced his wife, and they were married. With Jackson, she began to work on a dictionary project aimed at achieving an exceptional exactitude in definition. In 1941, she renounced writing poetry on grounds of linguistic principle, holding that "poetry obstructs general attainment to something better in our linguistic way-of-life than we have," that it distracts us by appealing to the senses rather than the intellect. She outlined her theories of language in *The Telling* (1972) and *Rational Meaning* (1974).

# Helen's Burning°

Her beauty, which we talk of,
Is but half her fate.
All does not come to light
Until the two halves meet
5  And we are silent
And she speaks,
Her whole fate saying,
She is, she is not, in one breath.

But we tell only half, fear to know all
10  Lest all should be to tell
And our mouths choke with flame
Of her consuming
And lose the gift of prophecy.

*1938*

# The Wind Suffers

The wind suffers of blowing,
The sea suffers of water,
And fire suffers of burning,
And I of a living name.

5  As stone suffers of stoniness,
As light of its shiningness,
As birds of their wingedness,
So I of my whoness.

And what the cure of all this?
10  What the not and not suffering?
What the better and later of this?
What the more me of me?

How for the pain-world to be
More world and no pain?
How for the old rain to fall
15  More wet and more dry?

How for the wilful blood to run
More salt-red and sweet-white?
And how for me in my actualness
20  To more shriek and more smile?

---

**poem title:** Helen of Troy, the beautiful wife of King Menelaus of Greece. According to Greek myth, she was the daughter of the supreme God, Zeus, and Leda, a mortal woman. Zeus appeared to Leda in the guise of a swan. Helen's abduction by the Trojan prince Paris led to the Trojan war, which Greece won.

By no other miracles,
By the same knowing poison,
By an improved anguish,
By my further dying.

1938

## Elegy in a Spider's Web

What to say when the spider
Say when the spider what
When the spider the spider what
The spider does what
5     Does does dies does it not
Not live and then not
Legs legs then none
When the spider does dies
Death spider death
10     Or not the spider or
What to say when
To say always
Death always
The dying of always
15     Or alive or dead
What to say when I
When I or the spider
No I and I what
Does what does dies
20     No when the spider dies
Death spider death
Death always I
Death before always
Death after always
25     Dead or alive
Now and always
What to say always
Now and always
What to say now
30     Now when the spider
What does the spider
The spider what dies
Dies when then when
Then always death always
35     The dying of always
Always now I
What to say when I
When I what
When I say
40     When the spider
When I always
Death always
When death what
Death I says say

45 Dead spider no matter
How thorough death
Dead or alive
No matter death
How thorough I
50 What to say when
When who when the spider
When life when space
The dying of oh pity
Poor how thorough dies
55 No matter reality
Death always
What to say
When who
Death always
60 When death when the spider
When I who I
What to say when
Now before after always
When then the spider what
65 Say what when now
Legs legs then none
When the spider
Death spider death
The genii who cannot cease to know
70 What to say when the spider
When I say
When I or the spider
Dead or alive the dying of
Who cannot cease to know
75 Who death who I
The spider who when
What to say when
Who cannot cease
Who cannot
80 Cannot cease
Cease
Cannot
The spider
Death
85 I
We
The genii
To know
What to say when the
90 Who cannot
When the spider what
Does what does dies
Death spider death
Who cannot
95 Death cease death
To know say what
Or not the spider

Of if I say
Or if I do not say
100  Who cannot cease to know
Who know the genii
Who say the I
Who they we cannot
Death cease death
105  To know say I
Oh pity poor pretty
How thorough life love
No matter space spider
How horrid reality
110  What to say when
What when
Who cannot
How cease
The knowing of always
115  Who these this space
Before after here
Life now my face
The face love the
The legs real when
120  What time death always
What to say then
What time the spider

*1938*

# Angel Island: Poems by Chinese Immigrants, 1910–1940

Over a period of thirty years, a series of Chinese immigrants passing through Angel Island in San Francisco Bay wrote poems about their lives on the walls of the wooden barracks in which they were detained. Some were being deported back to China; others were waiting to see if they fell within the few exempted classes established in the racist 1882 Chinese Exclusion Act and could thus gain entry to the United States. Although people from other countries were processed quickly, Chinese immigrants were typically detained for months, either waiting for medical examinations or undergoing highly detailed interrogations to test whether they really had relatives in the United States and were thus entitled to entrance under the law. Those who chose to appeal their cases could spend years essentially imprisoned on the island. The poems they wrote on the barracks walls in Chinese characters (here translated into English) talk about the voyage from China ("I ate wind and tasted waves for more than twenty days"), about the strain of incarceration ("The harsh laws pile layer upon layer; how can I dissipate my hatred?"), about the American officials they dealt with ("Even while they are tyrannical, they still claim to be humanitarian"), and about their fantasies of revenge ("I will not speak of love when I level the immigration station"). These poets were not only inscribing a record of their passage; they were also giving a cultural education to those who would follow them. Indeed, some of the poems comment on one another. Of the poems that survive—somewhat more than 130—about half are four lines long. Closed for decades, the wooden barracks was scheduled for demolition in 1970, when a park ranger noticed the inscriptions and asked a local scholar to examine them. As a result, the building was preserved, and those poems that were legible were translated by Him Mark Lai, Genny Lim, and Judy Yung, and published in 1980.

## Poems from Angel Island

As a traveller in wind and dust, half the time it was
    difficult.
In one month, I crossed to the end of the ocean.
I told myself that going by this way would be easy.
Who was to know that I would be imprisoned at
    Devil's Pass?

•

Instead of remaining a citizen of China, I
    willingly became an ox.
I intended to come to America to earn a
    living.
The Western styled buildings are lofty; but I
    have not the luck to live in them.
How was anyone to know that my dwelling
    place would be a prison?

•

I am distressed that we Chinese are detained
    in this wooden building.
It is actually racial barriers which cause
    difficulties on Yingtai Island.°
Even while they are tyrannical, they still
    claim to be humanitarian.
I should regret my taking the risks of coming
    in the first place.

•

America has power, but not justice.
In prison, we were victimized as if we were
    guilty.
Given no opportunity to explain, it was really
    brutal.
I bow my head in reflection but there is
    nothing I can do.

•

The low building with three beams merely
    shelters the body.
It is unbearable to relate the stories
    accumulated on the Island slopes.
Wait till the day I become successful and
    fulfill my wish!
I will not speak of love when I level the
    immigration station!

                    By One From Taishan°

•

The dragon out of water is humiliated by
    ants;
The fierce tiger who is caged is baited by a
    child.
As long as I am imprisoned, how can I dare
    strive for supremacy?
An advantageous position for revenge will
    surely come one day.

---

2 *Yingtai*: the poet is making an analogy to Yingtai Island in the Southern Lake west of
the Forbidden City in Peking; Emperor Guangxu (1875–1908) was imprisoned there by the
Empress Dowager Cixi in 1898 after a coup to halt his reform programs.
**poet:** *Taishan*: a mountain in Shandong province, in China, that has been considered sa-
cred for several thousand years.

The silvery red shirt is half covered with dust.°
A flickering lamp keeps this body company.
I am like pear blossoms which have already fallen;
Pity the bare branches during the late spring.

•

# Poem by One Named Xu, From Xiangshan,° Consoling Himself

Over a hundred poems are on the walls.
Looking at them, they are all pining at the
    delayed progress.
What can one sad person say to another?
Unfortunate travellers everywhere wish to
    commiserate.
5    Gain or lose, how is one to know what is
    predestined?
Rich or poor, who is to say it is not the will
    of heaven?
Why should one complain if he is detained
    and imprisoned here?
From ancient times, heroes often were the
    first ones to face adversity.

•

Leaving behind my writing brush and
    removing my sword, I came to America.
Who was to know two streams of tears would
    flow upon arriving here?
If there comes a day when I will have
    attained my ambition and become successful,
I will certainly behead the barbarians and
    spare not a single blade of grass.

*1910–1940*

---

1 *"covered with dust"*: a phrase conventionally used to describe fleeing in troubled times.
**poem title:** Xiangshan, town in eastern China, 120 miles south of Shanghai on the south shore of Xiangshan Bay, an inlet of the East China Sea.

# Kenneth Fearing (1902–1961)

Fearing was born in Oak Park, Illinois, now a Chicago neighborhood. His father was an attorney, though the family broke up a year after Fearing was born, and he moved in with an aunt. He was educated at the Universities of Illinois and Wisconsin, and moved to New York in 1924. There he supported himself with a series of brief jobs, usually working at most for a few months. He sold pants in a department store, worked for the WPA, for *Time* magazine, for the United Jewish Appeal, and for the Federation of Jewish Philanthropies. He also published pulp fiction: detective novels published under his own name and soft-core pornography published under the pseudonym Kirk Wolff. After 1933, when he was married, and until 1942, when the marriage disintegrated, his wife Rachel was the reliable breadwinner. Fearing himself was notoriously unkempt and a serious alcoholic.

Meanwhile, from the time he arrived in New York he published poetry steadily and wrote serious fiction, placing over forty poems in journals like *New Masses* before publishing his first book of poetry in 1929. With the advent of the Great Depression, he was drawn to the Communist left, though he remained an irreverent and iconoclastic fellow traveler. His revolutionary and anticapitalist 1935 *Poems* helped define a dynamic relation between proletarian poetry and experimental modernism. It included several exuberant, Whitmanesque social satires focused on the mass culture of consumer capitalism, and it successfully employed modernist techniques for political ends. The book was also devoted to the poor, but Fearing was simultaneously ruthless about all the idealizations that drive self-delusion in modern culture. His one great commercial success was his 1946 novel *The Big Clock*, which was made into a film by Paramount. In his 1956 *New and Selected Poems*, he attacked the anticommunist witch hunts in both prose and verse.

## Dear Beatrice Fairfax:°

*Is it true that Father Coughlin and Miss Aimee Semple*
*McPherson and Mr. H.L. Mencken and Peter Pan?°*

Foolproof baby with that memorized smile,
    burglarproof baby, fireproof baby with that rehearsed
        appeal,
    reconditioned, standardized, synchronized, amplified,
5        best-by-test baby with those push-the-button tears,

Your bigtime sweetheart worships you and you alone,
    your goodtime friend lives for you, only you,
    he loves you, trusts you, needs you, respects you, gives
        for you, fascinated, mad about you,
10    all wrapped up in you like the accountant in the trust,
    like the banker trusts the judge, like the judge
    respects protection, like the gunman needs his
    needle, like the trust must give and give—

He's with you all the way from the top of the bottle to the
15        final alibi,
    from the handshake to the hearse, from the hearse
    to the casket,
    to the handles on the casket, to the nails, to the hinges,
    to the satin, to the flowers, to the music, to the
20    prayer, to the graveyard, to the tomb,

But just the same, baby, and never forget,
    it takes a neat, smart, fast, good, sweet doublecross
    to doublecross the gentleman who doublecrossed the
    gentleman who doublecrossed
    your doublecrossing, doublecrossing, doublecross friend.

*1934*

## $2.50

But that dashing, dauntless, delphic, diehard, diabolic
    cracker likes his fiction turned with a certain elegance
    and wit; and that anti-anti-anti slum-congestion
    clublady prefers romance;

---

**poem title:** Fairfax, a widely read newspaper sob columnist.
**epigraph:** Charles Coughlin (1891–1979), Canadian-born American Catholic demagogic "radio priest" of the 1930s; on radio and at rallies, he spoke against Roosevelt, communism, Jews. and Wall Street. Aimee Semple McPherson (1890–1944), flamboyant American evangelist of the 1910s and 1920s who lost her following when a widely publicized 1926 "kidnapping" was revealed to be a tryst with a married lover. Henry Louis Mencken (1880–1956), American author, social critic, satirist, and philologist, editor of the *American Mercury*, the only person of these three Fearing admired. Peter Pan: the title character in the 1904 children's tale *Peter Pan* by James Barrie (1860–1937). This is a revised epigraph from a later edition.

5  search through the mothballs, comb the lavendar and
    lace,
  were her desires and struggles futile or did an innate
    fineness bring him at last to a prouder, richer peace
    in a world gone somehow mad?

10 We want one more compelling novel, Mr. Filbert Sopkins
    Jones,
  all about it, all about it,
  with signed testimonials to its stark, human, while-u-
    wait, iced-or-heated, taste-that-sunshine tenderness
15    and truth;
  one more comedy of manners, Sir Warwick Aldous
    Wells, involving three blond souls; tried in the
    crucible of war, Countess Olga out-of-limbo by
    Hearst through the steerage peerage,
20  glamorous, gripping, moving, try it, send for a 5 cent,
    10 cent sample, restores faith to the flophouse,
    workhouse, warehouse, whorehouse, bughouse life
    of man,
  just one more long poem that sings a more heroic age,
25    baby Edwin, 58,

But the faith is all gone,
  and all the courage is gone, used up, devoured on the
    first morning of a home relief menu,
  you'll have to borrow it from the picket killed last
30    Tuesday on the fancy knitgoods line;
  and the glamor, the ice for the cocktails, the shy appeal,
    the favors for the subdeb ball? O.K.,
  O.K.,
  but they smell of exports to the cannibals,
35  reek of something blown away from the muzzle of a
    twenty inch gun;

Lady, the demand is for a dream that lives and grows and
    does not fade when the midnight theater special
    pulls out on track 15;
40  cracker, the demand is for a dream that stands and
    quickens and does not crumble when a General
    Motors dividend is passed;
  lady, the demand is for a dream that lives and grows
    and does not die when the national guardsmen fix
45    those cold, bright bayonets;
  cracker, the demand is for a dream that stays, grows
    real, withstands the benign, afternoon vision of the
    clublady, survives the cracker's evening fantasy of
    honor, and profit, and grace.

1934

# Dirge

1-2-3 was the number he played but today the number came
 3-2-1;
  bought his Carbide° at 30 and it went to 29; had the
  favorite at Bowie° but the track was slow—

5 O, executive type, would you like to drive a floating power,
  knee-action, silk-upholstered six? Wed a Hollywood
  star? Shoot the course° in 58? Draw to the ace,
  king, jack?
  O, fellow with a will who won't take no, watch out for
10  three cigarettes on the same, single match; O,
  democratic voter born in August under Mars,
  beware of liquidated rails—

Denoument to denoument, he took a personal pride in the
  certain, certain way he lived his own, private life,
15 but nevertheless, they shut off his gas; nevertheless, the
  bank foreclosed; nevertheless, the landlord called;
  nevertheless, the radio broke,

And twelve o'clock arrived just once too often,
  just the same he wore one grey tweed suit, bought one
20  straw hat, drank one straight Scotch, walked one
  short step, took one long look, drew one deep
  breath,
  just one too many,

And wow he died as wow he lived,
25  going whop to the office and blooie home to sleep and
  biff got married and bam had children and oof got
  fired,
  zowie did he live and zowie did he die,

With who the hell are you at the corner of his casket, and
30  where the hell we going on the right-hand silver
  knob, and who the hell cares walking second from
  the end with an American Beauty° wreath from why
  the hell not,

Very much missed by the circulation staff of the New York
35  Evening Post; deeply, deeply mourned by the
  B.M.T.,°

---

2 *Carbide*: Union Carbide Corporation stock, purchased at $30 per share.
3 *Bowie*: a race track in Maryland.
7 *the course*: golf course.
32 *American beauty*: variety of rose.
36 *B.M.T.*: a subway line in New York City.

Wham, Mr. Roosevelt; pow, Sears Roebuck; awk, big
    dipper; bop, summer rain;
bong, Mr., bong, Mr., bong, Mr., bong.

*1934*

# Denouement

### 1

Sky, be blue, and more than blue; wind, be flesh and blood;
    flesh and blood, be deathless;
    walls, streets, be home;
    desire of millions, become more real than warmth and
5        breath and strength and bread;
    clock, point to the decisive hour and, hour without name
        when stacked and waiting murder fades, dissolves,
        stay forever as the world grows new;

Truth, be known, be kept forever, let the letters, letters,
10      souvenirs, documents, snapshots, bills be found at
        last, be torn away from a world of lies, be kept as
        final evidence, transformed forever into more than
        truth;
    change, change, rows and rows and rows of figures,
15      spindles, furrows, desks, change into paid-up rent
        and let the paid-up rent become South Sea music;
    magic film, unwind, unroll, unfold in silver on that
        million mile screen, take us all, bear us again to the
        perfect denouement,

20  Where everything lost, needed, each forgotten thing, all
        that never happens,
    gathers at last into a dynamite triumph, a rainbow
        peace, a thunderbolt kiss,
    for you, the invincible, and I, grown older, and he, the
25      shipping clerk, and she, an underweight blond
        journeying home in the last express.

### 2

But here is the body found lying face down in a burlap
        sack, strangled in the noose jerked shut by these
        trussed and twisted and frantic arms;
30      but here are the agents come to seize the bed;
    but here is the vase holding saved-up cigarstore
        coupons, and here is a way to save on cigars and
        to go without meat;
    but here is the voice that strikes around the world, "My
35      friends . . . my friends," issues from the radio and
        thunders "My friends" in newsreel close-ups, ex-
        plodes across headlines, "Both rich and poor, my

friends, must sacrifice," re-echoes, murmuring,
through hospitals, deathcells, "My friends . . . my
friends . . . my friends . . . my friends . . ."

And who, my friend, are you?
Are you the one who leaped to the blinds of the cannon-
ball express? Or are you the one who started life
again with three dependents and a pack of
45     cigarettes?

But how can these things be made finally clear in a post-
mortem room with the lips taped shut and the blue
eyes cold, wide, still, blind, fixed beyond the steady
glare of electric lights, through the white-washed
50     ceiling and the crossmounted roof, past the drifting
clouds?

Objection, over-ruled, exception, proceed:

Was yours the voice heard singing one night in a flyblown,
sootbeamed, lost and forgotten Santa Fe saloon?
55     Later bellowing in rage? And you boiled up a shirt
in a Newark furnished room? Then you found
another job, and pledged not to organize or go on
strike?

We offer this union book in evidence. We offer these rent
60     receipts in evidence. We offer in evidence this
vacation card marked, "This is the life. Regards
to all."

You, lodge member, protestant, crossborn male, the placenta
discolored, at birth, by syphilis, you, embryo four
65     inches deep in the seventh month,
among so many, many sparks struck and darkened at
conception,
which were you,
you, six feet tall on the day of death?

70 Then you were at no time the senator's son? Then you
were never the beef king's daughter, married in a
storm of perfume and music and laughter and rice?
And you are not now the clubman who waves and nods
and vanishes to Rio in a special plane?
75 But these are your lungs, scarred and consumed? These
are your bones, still marked by rickets? These are
your pliers? These are your fingers, O master
mechanic, and these are your cold, wide, still, blind
eyes?

80 The witness is lying, lying, an enemy, my friends, of Union
Gas and the home:

But how will you know us, wheeled from the icebox and
     stretched upon the table with the belly slit wide
     and the entrails removed, voiceless as the clippers
     bite through ligaments and flesh and nerves and
     bones,
     but how will you know us, attentive, strained, before
     the director's desk, or crowded in line in front of
     factory gates,
90     but how will you know us through ringed machinegun
     sights as we run and fall in gasmask, steel helmet,
     flame-tunic, uniform, bayonet, pack,
     but how will you know us, crumbled into ashes, lost in
     air and water and fire and stone,
95     how will you know us, now or any time, who will ever
     know that we have lived or died?

And this is the truth? So help you God, this is the truth?
     The truth in full, so help you God? So help you
     God?
100    But the pride that was made of iron and could not be
     broken, what has become of it, what has become
     of the faith that nothing could destroy, what has
     become of the deathless hope,
     you, whose ways were yours alone, you, the one like no
105    one else, what have you done with the hour you
     swore to remember, where is the hour, the day, the
     achievement that would never die?

Morphine. Veronal. Veronal. Morphine. Morphine.
     Morphine. Morphine.

3

110   Leaflets, scraps, dust, match-stubs strew the linoleum that
     leads upstairs to the union hall, the walls of the
     basement workers' club are dim and cracked and
     above the speaker's stand Vanzetti's face shows
     green, behind closed doors the committeeroom is
115    a fog of smoke,

Who are these people?

All day the committee fought like cats and dogs and
     twelve of Mr. Kelly's strongarm men patrolled the
     aisles that night, them blackjack guys get ten to
120    twenty bucks a throw, the funds were looted, sent
     to Chicago, at the meeting the section comrade
     talked like a fool, more scabs came through in trucks
     guarded by police,
     workers of the world, workers of the world, workers
125    of the world,

Who are these people and what do they want, can't they be
    decent, can't they at least be calm and polite,
    besides the time is not yet ripe, it might take years, like
    Mr. Kelly said, years,

130    Decades black with famine and red with war, centuries on
    fire, ripped wide,

Who are these people and what do they want, why do they
    walk back and forth with signs that say "Bread Not
    Bullets," what do they mean "They Shall Not Die"

135    as they sink in clouds of poison gas and fall beneath
    clubs, hooves, rifles, fall and do not arise, arise,
    unite,
    never again these faces, arms, eyes, lips,

Not unless we live, and live again,

140    return, everywhere alive in the issue that returns, clear
    as light that still descends from a star long cold,
    again alive and everywhere visible through and
    through the scene that comes again, as light on
    moving water breaks and returns, heard only in the

145    words, as millions of voices become one voice, seen
    only in millions of hands that move as one,

Look at them gathered, raised, look at their faces, clothes,
    who are these people, who are these people,
    what hand scrawled large in the empty prison cell "I

150    have just received my sentence of death. Red
    Front," whose voice screamed out in the silence
    "Arise"?

And all along the waterfront, there, where rats gnaw into
    the leading platforms, here, where the wind whips

155    at warehouse corners, look, there, here,
    everywhere huge across the walls and gates "Your
    party lives,"
    where there is no life, no breath, no sound, no touch,
    no warmth, no light but the lamp that shines on a
    trooper's drawn and ready bayonet.

*1935*

# Langston Hughes (1902–1967)

For several decades, Langston Hughes was simultaneously the foremost African American poet and the premier poet of the American left. Without understanding that double identity and dual cultural role, there is little chance of winning a full or fair appreciation of his life and work. Few American writers, moreover, have been at once so deeply loved and so viciously reviled. His poem "Let America Be America Again" became an anthem for a generation; memorized, read aloud, it symbolized at once their political aspirations and their historical memory. Yet at the same time, extreme right-wing groups picketed his readings and distributed hate literature about him.

All this came to a head during the McCarthy period of the 1950s. Hughes had at the very least been a fellow traveler of the American Communist Party (CP) since the late 1920s. That is hardly surprising. The American party had taken the cause of civil rights seriously almost from its inception; it was hard to find a leading black intellectual or artist who was not either a formal CP member or a close collaborator on a whole range of cultural issues. Hughes was active in the Young Communist League in the 1920s, and thereafter published in CP newspapers and through CP imprints repeatedly. In the 1950s, under pressure from the House UnAmerican Activities Committee, with poems like "Goodbye Christ" denounced in the U.S. Congress, Hughes offered a muted disclaimer for his radical politics and issued a *Selected Poems* (1959) that eliminated all his most radical poems and even some of his stronger poems about racial injustice. A true *Collected Poems* did not correct the picture until 1994, though Hughes put together the progressive collection, *The Panther and the Lash*, in an effort to right the balance in the year of his death.

What a full representation of Hughes' poetry would entail, however, is still open to debate. Some of his late revisions weakened the rhetorical force of his poems; we thus offer "Christ in Alabama" in its first published form. That poem also came with a powerful illustration by Hughes' long-time male companion, Zoe Ingram. "Come to the Waldorf-Astoria" appeared integrated with a fine illustration by socialist artist Walter Steinhilber. Both illustrated versions appear here in an appendix. Hughes was probably the most widely and successfully illustrated of modern American poets, but one would not know this from those of his books now in print.

Hughes was born in Joplin, Missouri, but grew up mainly in Lawrence, Kansas. Before enrolling at the historically black Lincoln University, he had worked at numerous menial jobs, but had also seen Africa, Mexico, and Paris. He would later make trips to the Soviet Union and to Spain during the Spanish Civil War. "Letter from Spain" was written in the midst of that war, and was handed to American poet Edwin Rolfe in Madrid for publication in the

International Brigades magazine *Volunteer for Liberty* in November 1937.
Hughes would also write several stage plays and musicals, along with numer-
ous newspaper columns, an autobiography, and several collections of short
stories featuring his character Simple. Jazz and the blues remained a strong
influence, from his first books to the masterful collage poem *Ask Your Mama*
(1962). Throughout his career, the typical Hughes poem communicated a rich
social and political vision through deceptively simple language; his apparently
straightforward rhetorical surfaces are intricately nuanced. He wrote some of
America's most telling indictments of racism, but also reached out to the poor
of all ethnic backgrounds. And he was one of the few male poets of his gen-
eration would could write persuasively both about women and within a female
persona.

## Negro

I am a Negro:
    Black as the night is black,
    Black like the depths of my Africa.

I've been a slave:
5    Caesar told me to keep his door-steps clean.
    I brushed the boots of Washington.

I've been a worker:
    Under my hand the pyramids arose.
    I made mortar for the Woolworth Building.

10    I've been a singer:
    All the way from Africa to Georgia
    I carried my sorrow songs.
    I made ragtime.

I've been a victim:
15    The Belgians cut off my hands in the Congo.
    They lynch me still in Mississippi.

I am a Negro:
    Black as the night is black,
    Black like the depths of my Africa.

*1922*

## The Negro Speaks of Rivers

I've known rivers:
I've known rivers ancient as the world and older than the
    flow of human blood in human veins.

My soul has grown deep like the rivers.

5      I bathed in the Euphrates° when dawns were young.
       I built my hut near the Congo° and it lulled me to sleep.
       I looked upon the Nile and raised the pyramids above it.
       I heard the singing of the Mississippi when Abe Lincoln
           went down to New Orleans,° and I've seen its muddy
10         bosom turn all golden in the sunset.

       I've known rivers:
       Ancient, dusky rivers.

       My soul has grown deep like the rivers.

                                                    *1921*


## The Weary Blues

       Droning a drowsy syncopated tune,
       Rocking back and forth to a mellow croon,
           I heard a Negro play.
       Down on Lenox Avenue° the other night
5      By the pale dull pallor of an old gas light
           He did a lazy sway. . . .
           He did a lazy sway. . . .
       To the tune o' those Weary Blues.
       With his ebony hands on each ivory key
10     He made that poor piano moan with melody.
           O Blues!
       Swaying to and fro on his rickety stool
       He played that sad raggy tune like a musical fool.
           Sweet Blues!
15     Coming from a black man's soul.
           O Blues!
       In a deep song voice with a melancholy tone
       I heard that Negro sing, that old piano moan—
           "Ain't got nobody in all this world,
20             Ain't got nobody but ma self.
               I's gwine to quit ma frownin'
               And put ma troubles on the shelf."

       Thump, thump, thump, went his foot on the floor.
       He played a few chords then he sang some more—
25             "I got the Weary Blues
               And I can't be satisfied.
               Got the Weary Blues

---

5 *Euphrates*: Euphrates River, the cradle of ancient Babylonian civilization, which flows
from eastern Turkey through Syria and Iraq into the Persian Gulf.
6 *Congo*: Congo River, which flows through west-central Africa into the Atlantic.
9 *New Orleans*: Lincoln's interest in ending slavery was reported to have sprung from a
visit he made to New Orleans, Louisiana, as a young man.
4 *Lenox Avenue*: major street in New York City's Harlem, since renamed Adam Clayton
Powell Boulevard.

And can't be satisfied—
I ain't happy no mo'
30         And I wish that I had died."
And far into the night he crooned that tune.
The stars went out and so did the moon.
The singer stopped playing and went to bed
While the Weary Blues echoed through his head.
He slept like a rock or a man that's dead.

            *1925*

# The Cat and the Saxophone (2 a.m.)

    EVERYBODY
    Half-pint,—
    Gin?
    No, make it
5     LOVES MY BABY°
    corn. You like
    liquor,
    don't you, honey?
    BUT MY BABY
10     Sure. Kiss me,
    DON'T LOVE NOBODY
    daddy.
    BUT ME.
    Say!
15     EVERYBODY
    Yes?
    WANTS MY BABY
    I'm your
    BUT MY BABY
20     sweetie, ain't I?
    DON'T WANT NOBODY
    Sure.
    BUT
    Then let's
25     ME,
    do it!
    SWEET ME.
    Charleston,
    mamma!
    !

            *1926*

---

5 *LOVES MY BABY*: Hughes incorporates lines from the 1924 popular song "Everybody Loves My Baby, but My Baby Don't Love Nobody but Me" by Jack Palmer and Spencer Williams.

## To the Dark Mercedes of "El Palacio de Amor"°

Mercedes is a jungle-lily in a death house.
Mercedes is a doomed star.
Mercedes is a charnel rose.
Go where gold
5    Will fall at the feet of your beauty,
Mercedes.
Go where they will pay you well
For your loveliness.

                                                    *1926*


## Mulatto

*I am your son, white man!*

Georgia dusk
And the turpentine woods.
One of the pillars of the temple fell.

5        *You are my son!*
         *Like hell!*

The moon over the turpentine woods.
The Southern night
Full of stars,
10   Great big yellow stars.
         What's a body but a toy?
             Juicy bodies
             Of nigger wenches
             Blue black
15           Against black fences.
         O, you little bastard boy,
         What's a body but a toy?
The scent of pine wood stings the soft night air.
         *What's the body of your mother?*
20   Silver moonlight everywhere.
         *What's the body of your mother?*
Sharp pine scent in the evening air.
             A nigger night,
             A nigger joy,
5            A little yellow
             Bastard boy.

         *Naw, you ain't my brother.*
         *Niggers ain't my brother.*
         *Not ever.*
30       *Niggers ain't my brother.*

---

**poem title:** "El Palacio de Amor" (Spanish, "The Palace of Love") a house of prostitution at Las Palmas in the Azores (islands 900 miles west of Portugal) where Hughes and his shipmates spent a night in 1923; Hughes was on his way to Africa.

The Southern night is full of stars,
Great big yellow stars.
     O, sweet as earth,
     Dusk dark bodies
35          Give sweet birth
To little yellow bastard boys.

     *Git on back there in the night,*
     *You ain't white.*

The bright stars scatter everywhere.
40  Pine wood scent in the evening air.
     A nigger night,
     A nigger joy.

     *I am your son, white man!*

     A little yellow
     Bastard boy.

                       *1927*

## Justice

That Justice is a blind goddess
Is a thing to which we black are wise.
Her bandage hides two festering sores
That once perhaps were eyes.

                       *1923*

## Fire

     Fire,
     Fire, Lord!
     Fire gonna burn ma soul!

     I ain't been good,
5     I ain't been clean—
     I been stinkin', low-down, mean.

     Fire,
     Fire, Lord!
     Fire gonna burn ma soul!

10    Tell me, brother,
     Do you believe
     If you wanta go to heaben
     Got to moan an' grieve?

     Fire,
15    Fire, Lord!
     Fire gonna burn ma soul!

I been stealin'.
5      Been tellin' lies,
     Had more women
20      Than Pharoah had wives.

Fire,
Fire, Lord!
Fire gonna burn ma soul!
I means Fire, Lord!
Fire gonna burn ma soul!

*1927*

## White Shadows°

I'm looking for a house
In the world
Where the white shadows
Will not fall.

5      *There is no such house,*
*Dark brothers,*
*No such house*
*At all.*

*1931*

## Christ in Alabama

Christ is a Nigger,
Beaten and black—
*O, bare your back.*

Mary is His Mother—
5      *Mammy of the South,*
*Silence your mouth.*

God's His Father—
*White Master above,*
*Grant us your love.*

10      Most holy bastard
Of the bleeding mouth:
*Nigger Christ*
*On the cross of the South.*

*1931*

---

**poem title:** retitled "House in the World" when reprinted in 1934.

# THREE SONGS ABOUT LYNCHING°

**SILHOUETTE**

(With Violins)

Southern gentle lady,
Do not swoon.
They've just hung a nigger

In the dark of the moon.
5    They've hung a black nigger
To a roadside tree
In the dark of the moon
For the world to see
How Dixie protects
10   Its white womanhood.

Southern gentle lady,
Be good! Be good!

*The first with satirically sentimental music.*

**FLIGHT**

(With Oboe and Drums)

Plant your toes in the cool swamp mud.
Step and leave no track.
15   Hurry, sweating runner!
The hounds are at your back.

No, I didn't touch her.
White flesh ain't for me.

Hurry, black boy, hurry!
20   Or they'll swing you to a tree.

*The second to a sylvan air with an under-current of fear and death.*

**LYNCHING SONG**

(With Trumpets)

Pull at the rope! O!
Pull it high!
Let the white folks live
And the nigger die.

25   Pull it, boys,
With a bloody cry
As the nigger spins
And the white folks die.

*The third to a blast of childish trumpets full of empty wonder— and life not dead at all.*

---

**poem title:** Hughes published these poems as a group in *Opportunity* in 1936. For general information about lynching see the notes to Claude McKay's "The Lynching" (p. 316).

30
*The white folks die?*
*What do you mean—*
*The white folks die?*

*The nigger's*
*Still body*
*Says*

NOT I.

*1930–1936*

# Come to the Waldorf-Astoria

### FINE LIVING . . . *a la carte??*

#### LISTEN HUNGRY ONES!

Look! See what Vanity Fair says about the new Waldorf-Astoria:
  "All the luxuries of private home . . ."
Now, won't that be charming when the last flop-house has turned
  you down this winter? Furthermore:
"It is far beyond anything hitherto attempted in the hotel
  world . . ." It cost twenty-eight million dollars. The famous Oscar
  Tschirky is in charge of banqueting. Alexandre Gastaud is chef.
  It will be a distinguished background for society.

5   So when you've got no place else to go, homeless and hungry ones,
  choose the Waldorf as a background for your rags—
(Or do you still consider the subway after midnight good enough?)

#### ROOMERS

Take a room at the new Waldorf, you down-and-outers—sleepers in
  charity flop-houses where God pulls a long face, and you have
  to pray to get a bed.
They serve swell board at the Waldorf Astoria.

10   Look at this menu, will you:
          GUMBO CREOLE
     CRABMEAT IN CASSOLETTE
     BOILED BRISKET OF BEEF
    SMALL ONIONS IN CREAM
     WATERCRESS SALAD
       PEACH MELBA
Have luncheon there this afternoon, all you jobless.
  Why not?
Dine with some of the men and women who got rich off of your la-
  bor, who clip coupons with clean white fingers because your
  hands dug coal, drilled stone, sewed garments, poured steel—to
  let other people draw dividends and live easy.

20   (Or haven't you had enough yet of the soup-lines and the bitter
  bread of charity?)
Walk through Peacock Alley tonight before dinner, and get warm,
  anyway. You've got nothing else to do.

### Evicted Families

All you families put out in the street: Apartments in the Towers are
only $10,000 a year. (Three rooms and two baths.) Move in
there until times get good, and you can do better. $10,000 and
$1.00 are about the same to you, aren't they?
Who cares about money with a wife and kids homeless, and no-
body in the family working? Wouldn't a duplex high above the
street be grand, with a view of the richest city in the world at
your nose?
"A lease, if you prefer; or an arrangement terminable at will."

### Negroes

25     O, Lawd, I done forgot Harlem!
      Say, you colored folks, hungry a long time in 135th Street—they
got swell music at the Waldorf-Astoria. It sure is a mighty
nice place to shake hips in, too. There's dancing after supper
in a big warm room. It's cold as hell on Lenox Avenue. All
you've had all day is a cup of coffee. Your pawnshop over-
coat's a ragged banner on your hungry frame. . . . You know,
down-town folks are just crazy about Paul Robeson.° Maybe
they'd like you, too, black mob from Harlem. Drop in at the
Waldorf this afternoon for tea. Stay to dinner. Give Park Av-
enue a lot of darkie color—free—for nothing! Ask the Junior
Leaguers to sing a spiritual for you. They probably know 'em
better than you do—and their lips won't be so chapped with
cold after they step out of their closed cars in the undercover
driveways.
      Hallelujah! under-cover driveways!
      Ma soul's a witness for de Waldorf-Astoria!
(A thousand nigger section-hands keep the road-beds smooth, so
investments in railroads pay ladies with diamond necklaces
staring at Sert° murals.)
30       Thank God A-Mighty!
(And a million niggers bend their backs on rubber plantations, for
rich behinds to ride on thick tires to the Theatre Guild tonight.)
      Ma soul's a witness!
(And here we stand, shivering in the cold, in Harlem.)
35       Glory be to God—
      De Waldorf-Astoria's open!

### Everybody

So get proud and rare back, everybody! The new Waldorf-Astoria's
open!
(Special siding for private cars from the railroad yards.)
You ain't been there yet?
(A thousand miles of carpet and a million bath rooms.)
40     What's the matter? You haven't seen the ads in the papers? Didn't
you get a card? Don't you know they specialize in American
cooking?

---

27 *Robeson:* (1898–1976) African American singer, actor, and spokesman for revolutionary
cultural and political change.
29 *Sert:* José Maria Sert (1876–1945), Spanish painter.

Ankle on down to 49th Street at Park Avenue. Get up off that sub-
way bench tonight with the evening POST for cover! Come on
out o' that flop-house! Stop shivering your guts out all day on
street corners under the L.
Jesus, ain't you tired yet?

**CHRISTMAS CARD**

Hail Mary, Mother of God!
The new Christ child of the Revolution's about to be born.
45      (Kick hard, red baby, in the bitter womb of the mob.)
Somebody, put an ad in Vanity Fair quick!
Call Oscar of the Waldorf—for Christ's sake!
It's almost Christmas, and that little girl—turned whore because
    her belly was too hungry to stand it any more—wants a nice
    clean bed for the Immaculate Conception.
Listen, Mary, Mother of God, wrap your new born babe in the red
    flag of Revolution:
50      The Waldorf-Astoria's the best manger we've got.
For reservations: Telephone
          Eldorado 5-3000.

                                      *1931*

# Goodbye Christ°

Listen, Christ,
You did alright in your day, I reckon—
But that day's gone now.
They ghosted you up a swell story, too,
5    Called it Bible—
But it's dead now,
The popes and the preachers've
Made too much money from it.
They've sold you to too many

10    Kings, generals, robbers, and killers—
Even to the Tzar and the Cossacks,
Even to Rockefeller's Church,
Even to THE SATURDAY EVENING POST.
You ain't no good no more.
15    They've pawned you
Till you've done wore out.

---

**poem title:** "Goodbye Christ" was written in the Soviet Union and first published in *The
Negro Worker*, probably without Hughes' permission, in 1932. That appearance was, how-
ever, a good deal less important than its subsequent redistribution in a prolonged racist
and anticommunist campaign against Hughes, which included its republication in the *Sat-
urday Evening Post* in 1940, its quotation in a J. Edgar Hoover speech in 1947 (read by one
of Hoover's deputies), and its being read into the U.S. Senate Record in 1948. It was also
reprinted on hate sheets several times in the early and late 1940s as part of national right-
wing smear campaigns against Hughes. Hughes repudiated the poem in the midst of the
postwar anticommunist crusades.

Goodbye,
Christ Jesus Lord God Jehova,
Beat it on away from here now.
20   Make way for a new guy with no religion at all—
A real guy named
Marx Communist Lenin Peasant Stalin Worker ME—

I said, ME!

Go ahead on now,
25   You're getting in the way of things, Lord.
And please take Saint Gandhi° with you when you go,
And Saint Pope Pius,°
And Saint Aimee McPherson,°
And big black Saint Becton°
30   Of the Consecrated Dime.
And step on the gas, Christ!
Move!

Don't be so slow about movin'!
The world is mine from now on—
35   And nobody's gonna sell ME
To a king, or a general,
Or a millionaire.

                                        *1932*

## Ballad of Roosevelt

The pot was empty,
The cupboard was bare.
I said, Papa,
What's the matter here?
5    I'm waitin' on Roosevelt, son,
Roosevelt, Roosevelt,
Waitin' on Roosevelt, son.

The rent was due
And the lights was out.
10   I said, Tell me, Mama,
What's it all about?
We're waitin' on Roosevelt, son,
Roosevelt, Roosevelt,
Just waitin' on Roosevelt.

---

26 *Gandhi*: Mohandas K. Gandhi (1869–1948) was the central figure of India's movement for independence; he urged nonviolent protest against British rule.

27 *Saint Pope Pius*: Pius XI headed the Roman Catholic Church from 1922–1939. He was an opponent of the left and of progressive causes throughout his reign.

28 *Aimee McPherson*: (1890–1944), American evangelist who founded a religious movement centered in Los Angeles—emphasizing spectacle, faith healing, and adult baptism—and was entangled in accusations of monetary and sexual improprieties.

29 *Becton*: George Wilson Becton was the leader of a Harlem religious sect that funded its activities through supposedly consecrated ten-cent donations. He was murdered in 1933.

15      Sister got sick
        And the doctor wouldn't come
        Cause we couldn't pay him
        The proper sum—
        A-waitin' on Roosevelt,
20      Roosevelt, Roosevelt,
        A-waitin' on Roosevelt.

        Then one day
        They put us out o' the house.
        Ma and Pa was
25      Meek as a mouse
        Still waitin' on Roosevelt,
        Roosevelt, Roosevelt.

        But when they felt those
        Cold winds blow
30      And didn't have no
        Place to go
        Pa said, I'm tired
        O' waitin' on Roosevelt,
        Roosevelt, Roosevelt.
35      Damn tired o' waitin' on Roosevelt.

        I can't git a job
        And I can't git no grub.
        Backbone and navel's
        Doin' the belly-rub—
40      A-waitin' on Roosevelt,
        Roosevelt, Roosevelt.

        And a lot o' other folks
        What's hungry and cold
        Done stopped believin'
45      What they been told
        By Roosevelt,
        Roosevelt, Roosevelt—

        Cause the pot's still empty,
        And the cupboard's still bare,
50      And you can't build a bungalow
        Out o' air—
        Mr. Roosevelt, listen!
        What's the matter here?

                                        1934


# Park Bench

        I live on a park bench.
        You, Park Avenue.
        Hell of a distance
        Between us two.

5 I beg a dime for dinner—
You got a butler and maid.
But I'm wakin' up!
Say, ain't you afraid

That I might, just maybe,
10 In a year or two,
Move on over
To Park Avenue?

1934

## Let America Be America Again

Let America be America again.
Let it be the dream it used to be.
Let it be the pioneer on the plain
Seeking a home where he himself is free.

5 (America never was America to me.)

Let America be the dream the dreamers dreamed—
Let it be that great strong land of love
Where never kings connive nor tyrants scheme
That any man be crushed by one above.

10 (It never was America to me.)

O, let my land be a land where Liberty
Is crowned with no false patriotic wreath,
But opportunity is real, and life is free,
Equality is in the air we breathe.

15 (There's never been equality for me,
Nor freedom in this "homeland of the free.")

*Say, who are you that mumbles in the dark?*
*And who are you that draws your veil across the stars?*

I am the poor white, fooled and pushed apart,
20 I am the Negro bearing slavery's scars.
I am the red man driven from the land,
I am the immigrant clutching the hope I seek—
And finding only the same old stupid plan
Of dog eat dog, of mighty crush the weak.

25 I am the young man, full of strength and hope,
Tangled in that ancient endless chain
Of profit, power, gain, of grab the land!
Of grab the gold! Of grab the ways of satisfying need!
Of work the men! Of take the pay!
30 Of owning everything for one's own greed!

I am the farmer, bondsman to the soil.
I am the worker sold to the machine.
I am the Negro, servant to you all.
I am the people, humble, hungry, mean—
35    Hungry yet today despite the dream.
Beaten yet today—O, Pioneers!
I am the man who never got ahead,
The poorest worker bartered through the years.

Yet I'm the one who dreamt our basic dream
40    In that Old World while still a serf of kings,
Who dreamt a dream so strong, so brave, so true,
That even yet its mighty daring sings
In every brick and stone, in every furrow turned
That's made America the land it has become.
45    O, I'm the man who sailed those early seas
In search of what I meant to be my home—
For I'm the one who left dark Ireland's shore,
And Poland's plain, and England's grassy lea,
And torn from Black Africa's strand I came
50    To build a "homeland of the free."

The free?

Who said the free? Not me?
Surely not me? The millions on relief today?
The millions shot down when we strike?
55    The millions who have nothing for our pay?
For all the dreams we've dreamed
And all the songs we've sung
And all the hopes we've held
And all the flags we've hung,
60    The millions who have nothing for our pay—
Except the dream that's almost dead today.

O, let America be America again—
The land that never has been yet—
And yet must be—the land where *every* man is free.
65    The land that's mine—the poor man's, Indian's, Negro's, ME—
Who made America,
Whose sweat and blood, whose faith and pain,
Whose hand at the foundry, whose plow in the rain,
Must bring back our mighty dream again.

70    Sure, call me any ugly name you choose—
The steel of freedom does not stain.
From those who live like leeches on the people's lives,
We must take back our land again,
America!

75    O, yes,
I say it plain,
America never was America to me,
And yet I swear this oath—
America will be!

80  Out of the rack and ruin of our gangster death,
    The rape and rot of graft, and stealth, and lies,
    We, the people, must redeem
    The land, the mines, the plants, the rivers.
    The mountains and the endless plain—
85  All, all the stretch of these great green states—
    And make America again!

                                                    *1936*


# Letter from Spain°

Addressed to Alabama

                        Lincoln Battalion,
                        International Brigades,
                        November Something, 1937.


Dear Brother at home:

We captured a wounded Moor today.
He was just as dark as me.
I said, Boy, what you been doin' here
Fightin' against the free?

He answered something in a language
10  I couldn't understand.
    But somebody told me he was sayin'
    They nabbed him in his land

And made him join the fascist army
And come across to Spain.
15  And he said he had a feelin'
    He'd never get back home again.

He said he had a feelin'
This whole thing wasn't right.
He said he didn't know
20  The folks he had to fight.

    And as he lay there dying
    In a village we had taken,
    I looked across to Africa
    And seed foundations shakin'.

25      Cause if a free Spain wins this war,
        The colonies, too, are free—
        Then something wonderful'll happen
        To them Moors as dark as me.

---

**poem title:** written while Hughes was in Spain visiting American volunteers. For general information on the Spanish Civil War see the notes to Millay's "Say That We Saw Spain Die" and Rolfe's "Elegia."

30     I said, I guess that's why old England
    And I reckon Italy, too,
    Is afraid to let a workers' Spain
    Be too good to me and you—

    Cause they got slaves in Africa—
    And they don't want 'em to be free.
35     Listen, Moorish prisoner, hell!
    Here, shake hands with me!

    I knelt down there beside him,
    And I took his hand—
    But the wounded Moor was dyin'
40     And he didn't understand.

              Salud,
              Johnny

                 *1937*

# The Bitter River

(Dedicated to the memory of Charlie Lang and Ernest
Green, each fourteen years old when lynched together
beneath the Shubuta Bridge over the Chicasawhay River
in Mississippi, October 12TH, 1942.)

    There is a bitter river
    Flowing through the South.
    Too long has the taste of its water
    Been in my mouth.
5     There is a bitter river
    Dark with filth and mud.
    Too long has its evil poison
    Poisoned my blood.

    I've drunk of the bitter river
10     And its gall coats the red of my tongue,
    Mixed with the blood of the lynched boys
    From its iron bridge hung,
    Mixed with the hopes that are drowned there
    In the snake-like hiss of its stream
15     Where I drank of the bitter river
    That strangled my dream:
    The book studied—but useless,
    Tool handled—but unused,
    Knowledge acquired but thrown away,
20     Ambition battered and bruised.
    Oh, water of the bitter river
    With your taste of blood and clay,
    You reflect no stars by night,
    No sun by day.

25 The bitter river reflects no stars—
It gives back only the glint of steel bars
And dark bitter faces behind steel bars:
The Scottsboro boys behind steel bars,
Lewis Jones behind steel bars,
30 The voteless share-cropper behind steel bars,
The labor leader behind steel bars,
The soldier thrown from a Jim Crow bus behind steel bars,
The 15¢ mugger behind steel bars,
The girl who sells her body behind steel bars,
35 And my grandfather's back with its ladder of scars,
Long ago, long ago—the whip and steel bars—
The bitter river reflects no stars.

"Wait, be patient," you say.
"Your folks will have a better day."
40 But the swirl of the bitter river
Takes your words away.
"Work, education, patience
Will bring a better day."
The swirl of the bitter river
45 Carries your "patience" away.
"Disrupter! Agitator!
Trouble maker!" you say.

The swirl of the bitter river
Sweeps your lies away.
50 I did not ask for this river
Nor the taste of its bitter brew.
I was given its water
As a gift from you.
Yours has been the power
55 To force my back to the wall
And make me drink of the bitter cup
Mixed with blood and gall.

You have lynched my comrades
Where the iron bridge crosses the stream,
60 Underpaid me for my labor,
And spit in the face of my dream.
You forced me to the bitter river
With the hiss of its snake-like song—
Now your words no longer have meaning—
65 I have drunk at the river too long:
Dreamer of dreams to be broken,
Builder of hopes to be smashed,
Loser from an empty pocket
Of my meagre cash,
70 Bitter bearer of burdens
And singer of weary song,
I've drunk at the bitter river
With its filth and its mud too long.

Tired now of the bitter river,
75    Tired now of the pat on the back,
Tired now of the steel bars
Because my face is black,
I'm tired of segregation,
Tired of filth and mud,
80    I've drunk of the bitter river
And it's turned to steel in my blood.

Oh, tragic bitter river
Where the lynched boys hung,
The gall of your bitter water
85    Coats my tongue.
The blood of your bitter water
For me gives back no stars.
I'm tired of the bitter river!
Tired of the bars!

                                             *1942*

# Ku Klux

They took me out
To some lonesome place.
They said, "Do you believe
In the great white race?"

5     I said, "Mister,
To tell you the truth,
I'd believe in anything
If you'd just turn me loose."

The white man said, "Boy,
10    Can it be
You're a-standin' there
A-sassin' me?"

They hit me in the head
And knocked me down.
15    And then they kicked me
On the ground.

A klansman said, "Nigger,
Look me in the face—
And tell me you believe in
The great white race."

                                             *1942*

## Shakespeare in Harlem

Hey ninny neigh!°
And a hey nonny noe!
Where, oh, where
Did my sweet mama go?

Hey ninny neigh
With a tra-la-la-la!
They say your sweet mama
Went home to her ma.

*1942*

## Madam and the Phone Bill

You say I O.K.ed
LONG DISTANCE?
O.K.ed it when?
My goodness, Central,
5    That was *then*!

I'm mad and disgusted
With that Negro now.
I don't pay no REVERSED
CHARGES nohow.

10    You say, I will pay it—
Else you'll take out my phone?
You better let
My phone alone.

I didn't ask him
15    To telephone me.
Roscoe knows darn well
LONG DISTANCE
Ain't free.

If I ever catch him,
20    Lawd, have pity!
Calling me up
From Kansas City

Just to say he loves me!
I knowed that was so.
25    Why didn't he tell me some'n
I don't know?

---

1 *Hey ninny neigh*: See Shakespeare's *The Two Noble Kinsmen* (3.04.21): "hey nonny, nonny, nonny."

For instance, what can
Them other girls do
That Alberta K. Johnson
30    Can't do—*and more, too?*

What's that, Central?
You say you don't care
Nothing about my
Private affair?

35    Well, even less about your
PHONE BILL does I care!

Un-humm-m! . . . Yes!
You say I gave my O.K.?
Well, that O.K. you may keep—

But I *sure* ain't gonna pay!

          *1949*

## Ballad of the Landlord

Landlord, landlord,
My roof has sprung a leak.
Don't you 'member I told you about it
Way last week?

5    Landlord, landlord,
These steps is broken down.
When you come up yourself
It's a wonder you don't fall down.

Ten Bucks you say I owe you?
10    Ten Bucks you say is due?
Well, that's Ten Bucks more'n I'll pay you
Till you fix this house up new.

What? You gonna get eviction orders?
You gonna cut off my heat?
15    You gonna take my furniture and
Throw it in the street?

Um-huh! You talking high and mighty.
Talk on—till you get through.
You ain't gonna be able to say a word
20    If I land my fist on you.

*Police! Police!*
*Come and get this man!*
*He's trying to ruin the government*
*And overturn the land!*

25    Copper's whistle!
    Patrol bell!
    Arrest.

    Precinct Station.
    Iron cell.
30    Headlines in press:

MAN THREATENS LANDLORD

TENANT HELD NO BAIL

JUDGE GIVES NEGRO 90 DAYS IN COUNTY JAIL.

*1940–1943*

# Harlem

What happens to a dream deferred?
5    Does it dry up
like a raisin in the sun?
Or fester like a sore—
5    And then run?
Does it stink like rotten meat?
Or crust and sugar over—
like a syrupy sweet?

Maybe it just sags
10    like a heavy load.

*Or does it explode?*

*1951*

# Late Corner

The street light
On its lonely arm
Becomes
An extension
5    Of the Cross—
The Cross itself
A lonely arm
Whose light is lost

*Oh, lonely world!*
10    *Oh, lonely light!*
*Oh, lonely Cross!*

*1957*

## Dinner Guest: Me

I know I am
The Negro Problem
Being wined and dined,
Answering the usual questions
5    That come to white mind
Which seeks demurely
To probe in polite way
The why and wherewithal
Of darkness U.S.A.—
10    Wondering how things got this way
In current democratic night,

Murmuring gently
Over *fraises du bois*,°
"I'm so ashamed of being white."

15    The lobster is delicious,
The wine divine,
And center of attention
At the damask table, mine.
To be a Problem on
20    Park Avenue at eight
Is not so bad.
Solutions to the Problem,
Of course, wait.

*1965*

## The Backlash Blues

Mister Backlash, Mister Backlash,
Just who do you think I am?
Tell me, Mister Backlash,
Who do you think I am?
5    You raise my taxes, freeze my wages,
Send my son to Vietnam.

You give me second-class houses,
Give me second-class schools,
Second-class houses
10    And second-class schools.
You must think us colored folks
Are second-class fools.

When I try to find a job
To earn a little cash,
15    Try to find myself a job
To earn a little cash,
All you got to offer
Is a white backlash.

---

13 *fraises du bois* (French) strawberries.

But the world is big,
20      The world is big and round,
        Great big world, Mister Backlash,
        Big and bright and round—
        And it's full of folks like me who are
        Black, Yellow, Beige, and Brown.

35      Mister Backlash, Mister Backlash,
        What do you think I got to lose?
        Tell me, Mister Backlash,
        What you think I got to lose?
        I'm gonna leave you, Mister Backlash,
30      Singing your mean old backlash blues.

            *You're the one,*
            *Yes, you're the one*
            *Will have the blues.*

                                                        *1967*

## Bombings in Dixie

        It's not enough to mourn
        And not enough to pray.
        Sackcloth and ashes, anyhow,
        Save for another day.

5       The Lord God Himself
        Would hardly desire
        That men be burned to death—
        *And bless the fire.*

                                                        *1967*

## Arna Bontemps (1902–1973)

Born in Alexandria, Louisiana, Bontemps grew up in California and was educated at Pacific Union College. His father was a bricklayer and his mother a teacher. After college he moved to Harlem to teach at the Seventh Day Adventist academy, arriving at the height of the Harlem Renaissance. His poetry began to win awards, but the Adventists reassigned him to Oakwood Junior College in Huntsville, Alabama, in 1931. Although he was in conflict with conservative school officials, the experience of the South helped inspire some of his best work. Bontemps left Alabama in 1934, first for California and then for Chicago, where he earned a library science degree from the University of Chicago, and where he published his second novel, *Black Thunder* (1936). Bontemps' poems combine a strong sense of black history with an almost meditative quality of witness.

### A Black Man Talks of Reaping

I have sown beside all waters in my day.
I planted deep within my heart the fear
That wind or fowl would take the grain away.
I planted safe against this stark, lean year.

5    I scattered seed enough to plant the land
In rows from Canada to Mexico.
But for my reaping only what the hand
Can hold at once is all that I can show

Yet what I sowed and what the orchard yields
10   My brother's sons are gathering stalk and root,
Small wonder then my children glean in fields
They have not sown, and feed on bitter fruit.

*1926*

### Southern Mansion

Poplars are standing there still as death
And ghosts of dead men
Meet their ladies walking
Two by two beneath the shade
And standing on the marble steps.

There is a sound of music echoing
Through the open door
And in the field there is
Another sound tinkling in the cotton:
Chains of bondmen dragging on the ground.

The years go back with an iron clank,
A hand is on the gate,
A dry leaf trembles on the wall.
Ghosts are walking.
They have broken roses down
And poplars stand there still as death.

*1931*

# Gwendolyn Bennett (1902–1981)

Born in Giddings, Texas, Bennett and her family moved to Nevada and Washington, D.C, before the marriage broke up and her father took her to Pennsylvania and then Brooklyn, New York. She studied fine arts at both Columbia University and Pratt Institute. While teaching art at Harvard University she won a scholarship to study in Paris for a year. She had published "Heritage" in 1923, and when she returned to Harlem in 1926 she continued doing both literary and graphic work for magazines like *Opportunity* and the *Crisis*. Her accomplished graphic art had both wit and style, and remains immensely appealing today. Her poetry, consistently elegant, celebrated a black difference with an effortless ease that set it apart from much of the more anguished protest poetry of the period. After her husband died, she had less time to write and worked in a government job until the anticommunist witch hunts saw her fired and blacklisted.

## To a Dark Girl

I love you for your brownness
And the rounded darkness of your breast.
I love you for the breaking sadness in your voice
And shadows where your wayward eye-lids rest.

5      Something of old forgotten queens
Lurks in the lithe abandon of your walk,
And something of the shackled slave
Sobs in the rhythm of your talk.

Oh, little brown girl, born for sorrow's mate,
10    Keep all you have of queenliness,
Forgetting that you once were slave,
And let your full lips laugh at Fate!

*1923*

## Heritage

I want to see the slim palm-trees,
Pulling at the clouds
With little pointed fingers. . . .

I want to see lithe Negro girls,
Etched dark against the sky
While sunset lingers.

I want to hear the silent sands,
Singing to the moon
Before the Sphinx-still face. . . .

I want to hear the chanting
Around a heathen fire
Of a strange black race.

I want to breathe the Lotus flow'r,
Sighing to the stars
With tendrils drinking at the Nile. . . .

I want to feel the surging
Of my sad people's soul
Hidden by a minstrel-smile.

*1923*

## Street Lamps in Early Spring

Night wears a garment
All velvet soft, all violet blue . . .
And over her face she draws a veil
As shimmering fine as floating dew . . .
And here and there
In the black of her hair
The subtle hands of Night
Move slowly with their gem-starred light.

*1926*

# Countee Cullen (1903–1946)

Cullen was probably born in Louisville, Kentucky, though Cullen himself
later liked to claim New York as his birthplace. In any case, he was at some
point informally adopted by the Reverend A. and Carolyn Belle Cullen; prior
to that he used the name Countee Porter. The Reverend was not only a min-
ister but also a black activist in Harlem. Cullen himself absorbed the activism,
but realized that his literary inclinations and homosexuality—see the simulta-
neously racial and sexual transgression of "Tableau"—would take him in dif-
ferent directions. He wrote much of his early poetry while a student at New
York University from 1921–1925 and at Harvard from 1925–1927, and it is no-
table not only for its sometimes unforgettable concision and its almost musi-
cal politics and racial commentary, but also for its ground-breaking use of
purportedly "white" traditional forms. Unlike Langston Hughes, he had little
interest in how jazz or the blues might be adapted by black poets; unlike Ster-
ling Brown, dialect was not to be the ground of his achievement.

A much celebrated 1928 marriage to W.E.B. Du Bois's daughter collapsed
almost immediately. Thereafter Cullen worked as an English and French
teacher at Frederick Douglass Junior High School, wrote a novel, translated
Euripides's play *Medea* from the Greek, and wrote two collections of children's
verse. See *My Soul's High Song: The Collected Writings of Countee Cullen*
(1991).

## Incident

(For Eric Walrond)

Once riding in old Baltimore,
   Heart-filled, head-filled with glee,
I saw a Baltimorean
   Keep looking straight at me.

5     Now I was eight and very small.
   And he was no whit bigger,
And so I smiled, but he poked out
   His tongue, and called me, "Nigger."

I saw the whole of Baltimore
10    From May until December;
Of all the things that happened there
   That's all that I remember.

*1925*

## For a Lady I Know

She even thinks that up in heaven
   Her class lies late and snores,
While poor black cherubs rise at seven
   To do celestial chores.

                                        1925

## Yet Do I Marvel

I doubt not God is good, well-meaning, kind,
And did He stoop to quibble could tell why
The little buried mole continues blind,
Why flesh that mirrors Him must some day die,
Make plain the reason tortured Tantalus°
Is baited by the fickle fruit, declare
If merely brute caprice dooms Sisyphus°
To struggle up a never-ending stair.
Inscrutable His ways are, and immune
To catechism° by a mind too strewn
With petty cares to slightly understand
What awful brain compels His awful hand.
Yet do I marvel at this curious thing:
To make a poet black, and bid him sing!

                                        1925

## Near White

Ambiguous of race they stand,
   By one disowned, scorned of another,
Not knowing where to stretch a hand,
   And cry, "My sister" or "My brother."

                                        1925

## Tableau

(For Donald Duff)

Locked arm in arm they cross the way,
   The black boy and the white,
The golden splendor of the day,
   The sable pride of night.

---

5 *Tantalus*: there is more than one version of the Tantalus story in Greek myth, but in all of them he is punished after death for one or another crime against the gods. In one story he is burdened with continual thirst and plunged into water up to his neck, water that withdraws whenever he reaches toward it; in another, a branch laden with fruit hangs eternally over his head, but springs away when he reaches for it.
7 *Sisyphus*: in Greek myth, Sisyphus, the least scrupulous of mortals, is punished in the underworld by being condemned to roll an enormous rock eternally up a hill. Each time the rock approached the summit, it rolled down and had to be pushed up again.
10 *catechism*: understanding.

5          From lowered blinds the dark folk stare,
                And here the fair folk talk,
            Indignant that these two should dare
                In unison to walk.

            Oblivious to look and word
10              They pass, and see no wonder
            That lightning brilliant as a sword
                Should blaze the path of thunder.

                                                                1925


## Heritage

(For Harold Jackman)

            What is Africa to me:
            Copper sun or scarlet sea,
            Jungle star or jungle track,
            Strong bronzed men, or regal black
5           Women from whose loins I sprang
            When the birds of Eden sang?
            *One three centuries removed*
            *From the scenes his fathers loved,*
            *Spicy grove, cinnamon tree,*
10          *What is Africa to me?*

            So I lie, who all day long
            Want no sound except the song
            Sung by wild barbaric birds
            Goading massive jungle herds,
15          Juggernauts of flesh that pass
            Trampling tall defiant grass
            Where young forest lovers lie,
            Plighting troth beneath the sky.
            So I lie, who always hear,
20          Though I cram against my ear
            Both my thumbs, and keep them there,
            Great drums throbbing through the air.
            So I lie, whose fount of pride,
            Dear distress, and joy allied,
25          Is my somber flesh and skin,
            With the dark blood dammed within
            Like great pulsing tides of wine
            That, I fear, must burst the fine
            Channels of the chafing net
30          Where they surge and foam and fret.

            Africa? A book one thumbs
            Listlessly, till slumber comes.
            Unremembered are her bats
            Circling through the night, her cats
35          Crouching in the river reeds,

Stalking gentle flesh that feeds
By the river brink; no more
Does the bugle-throated roar
Cry that monarch claws have leapt

40          From the scabbards where they slept.
Silver snakes that once a year
Doff the lovely coats you wear,
Seek no covert in your fear
Lest a mortal eye should see;

45          What's your nakedness to me?
Here no leprous flowers rear
Fierce corolas° in the air;
Here no bodies sleek and wet,
Dripping mingled rain and sweat,

50          Tread the savage measures of
Jungle boys and girls in love.
What is last year's snow to me,
Last year's anything? The tree
Budding yearly must forget

55          How its past arose or set—
Bough and blossom, flower, fruit,
Even what shy bird with mute
Wonder at her travail there,
Meekly labored in its hair.

60          *One three centuries removed*
*From the scenes his fathers loved,*
*Spice grove, cinnamon tree,*
*What is Africa to me?*

So I lie, who find no peace

65          Night or day, no slight release
From the unremittant beat
Made by cruel padded feet
Walking through my body's street.
Up and down they go, and back,

70          Treading out a jungle track.
So I lie, who never quite
Safely sleep from rain at night—
I can never rest at all
when the rain begins to fall;

75          Like a soul gone mad with pain
I must match its weird refrain;
Ever must I twist and squirm,
Writhing like a baited worm,
While its primal measures drip

80          Through my body, crying, "Strip!
Doff this new exuberance.
Come and dance the Lover's Dance!"
In an old remembered way
Rain works on me night and day.

---

47 *corollas:* petals.

85      Quaint, outlandish heathen gods
        Black men fashion out of rods,
        Clay, and brittle bits of stone,
        In a likeness like their own,
        My conversion came high-priced;
90      I belong to Jesus Christ,
        Preacher of humility;
        Heathen gods are naught to me.

        Father, Son, and Holy Ghost,
        So I make an idle boast;
95      Jesus of the twice-turned cheek,°
        Lamb of God, although I speak
        With my mouth thus, in my heart
        Do I play a double part.
        Ever at Thy glowing altar
100     Must my heart grow sick and falter,
        Wishing He I served were black,
        Thinking then it would not lack
        Precedent of pain to guide it,
        Let who would or might deride it;
105     Surely then this flesh would know
        Yours had borne a kindred woe.
        Lord, I fashion dark gods, too,
        Daring even to give You
        Dark despairing features where,
110     Crowned with dark rebellious hair,
        Patience wavers just so much as
        Mortal grief compels, while touches
        Quick and hot, of anger, rise
        To smitten cheek and weary eyes.
115     Lord, forgive me if my need
        Sometimes shapes a human creed.

        *All day long and all night through,*
        *One thing only must I do:*
        *Quench my pride and cool my blood,*
120     *Lest I perish in the flood.*

        *Lest a hidden ember set*
        *Timber that I thought was wet*
        *Burning like the dryest flax,*
        *Melting like the merest wax,*
125     *Lest the grave restore its dead.*
        *Not yet has my heart or head*
        *In the least way realized*
        *They and I are civilized.*

                                        1925

---

95 *cheek:* Jesus urges "that ye resist not evil: but whosoever shall smite thee on the right cheek, turn to him the other also" (Matthew 5:39).

# From the Dark Tower

(To Charles S. Johnson)

We shall not always plant while others reap
The golden increment of bursting fruit,
Not always countenance, abject and mute,
That lesser men should hold their brothers cheap;
5    Not everlastingly while others sleep
Shall we beguile their limbs with mellow flute,
Not always bend to some more subtle brute;
We were not made eternally to weep.

The night whose sable breast relieves the stark,
10   White stars is no less lovely being dark,
And there are buds that cannot bloom at all
In light, but crumple, piteous, and fall;
So in the dark we hide the heart that bleeds,
And wait, and tend our agonizing seeds.

*1927*

# Lorine Niedecker (1903–1970)

Niedecker lived most of her life on Black Hawk Island. It is on the Rock River near where it flows into Lake Koshkonong by the town of Fort Atkinson in Wisconsin. For her it is the place evoked in her poem "Paean to Place." But it is also a place from which we can all draw a lesson about the interconnectedness of natural process and human endeavor. Her father netted carp for a living; her mother helped, struggling with deafness that came on after her daughter's birth. There were the boats, the marshes, birds, and trees, and the uncertainties of a marginal economic existence, vulnerable to floods and market fluctuations. Niedecker attended Beliot College for a year, but returned to help her family, then worked as a library assistant at the end of the 1920s. She read Zukofsky's "Objectivist" issue of *Poetry* magazine in 1931 and began an extended correspondence with him. Her spare diction and intense focus on the spatial effects of the page resonated with elements of Zukofsky's aesthetic, though neither her evocation of a rural woman's experience nor her depictions of "Muskrats / gnawing / doors" raised many echoes with the metropolitan subjects the Objectivists typically treated. Late in her life she began to have some contact with other writers, but she mostly avoided the poetry establishment. Indeed, she often struggled to support herself, cleaning kitchens and scrubbing floors at Fort Atkinson Memorial Hospital from 1957 to 1963.

## Paean to Place

*And the place was water*

Fish
    fowl
       flood
          Water lily mud
5    My life

in the leaves and on water
My mother and I
           born
10    in swale and swamp and sworn
to water

My father
thru marsh fog
    sculled down
15          from high ground
saw her face

at the organ
bore the weight of lake water
  and the cold—
20  he seined for carp to be sold
that their daughter

might go high
on land
  to learn
25  Saw his wife turn
deaf

and away
She
  who knew boats
30    and ropes
no longer played


She helped him string out nets
for tarring
  And she could shoot
35    He was cool
to the man

who stole his minnows
by night and next day offered
  to sell them back
40    He brought in a sack
of dandelion greens

if no flood
No oranges—none at hand
  No marsh marigolds
45    where the water rose
He kept us afloat


I mourn her not hearing canvasbacks
their blast-off rise
  from the water
50    Not hearing sora
rail's sweet

spoon-tapped waterglass-
descending scale-
  tear-drop-tittle
55    Did she giggle
as a girl?


His skiff skimmed
the coiled celery now gone
  from these streams
60    due to carp
He knew duckweed

fall-migrates
toward Mud Lake bottom
   Knew what lay
65         under leaf decay
and on pickerelweeds

before summer hum
To be counted on:
   new leaves
70        new dead
leaves

He could not
—like water bugs—
   stride surface tension
75        He netted
loneliness

As to his bright new car
my mother—her house
   next his—averred:
80        A hummingbird
can't haul

Anchored here
in the rise and sink
   of life—
85        middle years' nights
he sat

beside his shoes
rocking his chair
   Roped not 'looped
90        in the loop
of her hair'

I grew in green
slide and slant
   of shore and shade
95        Child-time—wade
thru weeds

Maples to swing from
Pewee-glissando
   sublime
100        slime-
song
     . . .

Grew riding the river
Books
   at home-pier
105        Shelley could steer
as he read

I was the solitary plover
a pencil
        for a wing-bone
110   From the secret notes
I must tilt

upon the pressure
execute and adjust
        In us sea-air rhythm
115   'We live by the urgent wave
of the verse'

Seven-year molt
for the solitary bird
        and so young
120   Seven years the one
dress

for town once a week
One for home
        faded blue-striped
125   as she piped
her cry

Dancing grounds
my people had none
        woodcocks had—
130           backland-
air around

Solemnities
such as what flower
        to take
135           to grandfather's grave
unless

water lilies—
he who'd bowed his head
        to grass as he mowed
140           Iris now grows
on fill

for the two
and for him
        where they lie
145           How much less am I
in the dark than they?

Effort lay in us
before religions
        at pond bottom
150               All things move toward
the light

except those
that freely work down
    to oceans' black depths
155          In us an impulse tests
the unknown


River rising—flood
Now melt and leave home
    Return—broom wet
160          naturally wet
Under


soak-heavy rug
water bugs hatched—
    no snake in the house
165          Where were they?—
she


who knew how to clean up
after floods
    he who bailed boats, houses
170          Water endows us
with buckled floors


You with sea water running
in your veins sit down in water
    Expect the long-stemmed blue
175          speedwell to renew
itself


O my floating life
Do not save love
    for things
180          Throw *things*
to the flood


ruined
by the flood
    Leave the new unbought—
185          all one in the end—
water


I possessed
the high word:
    The boy my friend
190          played his violin
in the great hall


On this stream
my moonnight memory
    washed of hardships
195          maneuvers barges
thru the mouth

of the river
They fished in beauty
    It was not always so
200          In Fishes
red Mars

rising
rides the sloughs and sluices
    of my mind
205          with the persons
on the edge

                  *1970*

# Poet's work

Grandfather
    advised me:
        Learn a trade

5     I learned
        to sit at desk
           and condense

    No layoff
        from this
           condensery

                  *1968*

# Kay Boyle (1903–1993)

Born in St. Paul, Minnesota, Boyle studied architecture at Parson's School of Fine and Applied Arts in New York and elsewhere, took courses at Columbia, and studied violin at the Cincinnati Conservatory of Music. She lived mostly in France from 1923 to 1941, where she was well known among the American expatriate community. Back in the U.S., she was active in progressive movements for decades and was blacklisted during the McCarthy period. She published ten novels, half a dozen short novels and numerous short story collections, three children's books, along with essays and several volumes of poetry.

## A Communication to Nancy Cunard°

These are not words set down for the rejected
Nor for outcasts cast by the mind's pity
Beyond the aid of lip or hand or from the speech
Of fires lighted in the wilderness by lost men
5      Reaching in fright and passion to each other.
This is not for the abandoned to hear.

---

**poem title:** The poem is based on the famous Scottsboro case in which nine young black teenagers (Charlie Weems, Ozie Powell, Clarence Norris, Olen Montgomery, Willie Robertson, Haywood Patterson, Andy Wright, Roy Wright, and Eugene Williams) were accused and convicted of raping two white woman, Ruby Bates and Victoria Price, in 1931 in Alabama. The convictions, based on false testimony, produced death sentences and worldwide protests; despite their innocence, they spent years in prison.

Nancy Cunard (1896–1965) was a British poet and heiress who was prominent in avant-garde literary circles in the 1920s and 1930s. Her relationship with black musician Henry Crowder provoked prejudicial controversy, and that propelled her into activism. She joined the Scottsboro protests, wrote *Black Man and White Ladyship* (1931), and edited the massive and highly innovative anthology *Negro* (1934), which included "Scottsboro and Other Scottsboros," her own detailed documentary account of events leading up to the first Scottsboro trials in 1931–1932.

Boyle's working title for the poem had a subtitle, "Scottsboro, 1937," which is the title Cunard preferred, in part because it continued the ongoing documentary tradition about the case. "Scottsboro" was indeed far from a finished story at the time Boyle wrote the poem. The poem was first published in *The New Republic* on June 9, 1937, where it carried Boyle's note remarking that "much of the detail in this poem is due to Carleton Beales," whose coverage of the trials appeared in *The Nation* on February 5 and 12 in 1936. Beales' account is the source of the comments by the "Sheriff with the gold pin," words Beales actually attributes to a juror, and by the "Sunday-school teacher who addressed the jury" (Melvin Hutson, county solicitor). Boyle also quotes from a letter defendant Haywood Pat-

It begins in the dark on a boxcar floor, the groaning timber
Stretched from bolt to bolt above the freight-train wheels
That grind and cry aloud like hounds upon the trail, the breathing weaving
10 Unseen within the dark from mouth to nostril, nostril to speaking mouth.
This is the theme of it, stated by one girl in a boxcar saying:
"Christ, what they pay you don't keep body and soul together."
"Where was you working?" "Working in a mill town."
The other girl in the corner saying: "Working the men when we could get them."
15 "Christ, what they pay you," wove the sound of breathing, "don't keep shoes on your feet.
Don't feed you. That's why we're shoving on."

(This is not for Virginia Price or Ruby Bates, the white girls dressed like boys to go; not for Ozie Powell, six years in a cell playing the little harp he played tap-dancing on the boxcar boards; not for Olen Montgomery, the blind boy traveling towards Memphis that night, hopping a ride to find a doctor who could cure his eyes; not for Eugene Williams or Charlie Weems, not for Willie Robertson nor for Leroy and Andy Wright, thirteen years old the time in March they took him off the train in Paint Rock, Alabama; this is not for Clarence Norris or Haywood Patterson, sentenced three times to die.)

This is for the sheriff with a gold lodge pin
And for the jury venireman who said: "Now, mos' folk don't go on
And think things out. The Bible never speaks
20 Of sexual intercourses. It jus' says a man knows a woman.
So after Cain killed Abel he went off and knew a woman
In the land of Nod. But the Bible tells as how
There couldn't be no human folk there then.
Now, jus' put two and two together. Cain had offspring
25 In the land of Nod so he musta had him a female baboon
Or chimpanzee or somethin' like it.
And that's how the nigger race begun."

---

terson had written her. When *The New Republic* sent her a $25 fee for the poem, she directed that Patterson be paid $7 for his contribution.

The basic facts of the case are these: On March 25, 1931, some young black and white boys on an Alabama train got into a scuffle. When deputies arrived it was decided to teach the black teenagers a more definitive lesson, so two lower-class white women of casual morals on the train (but not part of the scuffle) were encouraged to invent a story of gang rape by the black teenagers, which they did. Alabama newspapers inflamed public opinion against the defendants, and they were convicted and sentenced to death in early April. The following year, Ruby Bates admitted there had not actually been any rape on the train, that the whole story was fabricated, a fact she testified to in Haywood Patterson's second trial in 1933. No matter, they were all convicted again. The U.S. Supreme Court twice threw out convictions from several of the trials, issuing a historic ruling against the practice of excluding blacks from juries. No matter. Alabama tried them again. Patterson was tried and convicted four times. He finally escaped from prison in 1948 and was arrested in Detroit, but Michigan's governor refused Alabama's extradition request in 1950. Patterson died two years later. Alabama pardoned defendant Clarence Norris in 1976.

This is for the Sunday-school teacher with the tobacco plug
Who addressed the jury, the juice splattering on the wall,
30    Pleading: "Whether in overalls or furs a woman is protected by the
            Alabama law
Against the vilest crime the human species knows. Now, even dogs
            choose their mates,
But these nine boys are lower than the birds of the air,
Lower than the fish in the sea, lower than the beasts of the fields.
There is a law reaching down from the mountaintops to the
            swamps and caves—
35    It's the wisdom of the ages, there to protect the sacred parts of the
            female species
Without them having to buckle around their middles
Six-shooters or some other method of defense."

        This is set down for the others: people who go and come,
        Open a door and pass through it, walk in the streets
40      With the shops lit, loitering, lingering, gazing.
        This is for two men riding, Deputy Sheriff Sandlin, Deputy
            Sheriff Blacock,
            With Ozie Powell, handcuffed. Twelve miles out of Cullman
            They shot him through the head.°

                        **THE TESTIMONY**

        *Haywood Patterson:*                            *Victoria Price*

        "So here goes an I shell try
45      Faitfully an I possibly can
        Reference to myself in                              "I
            particularly                                   cain't
        And concerning the other boys                    remember."
            personal pride
        And life time up to now.
        You must be patiene with me
            and remember
50      Most of my English is not of                         "I
            much interest                                  cain't
        And that I am continually                        remember."
        Stopping and searching for the
            word."

So here goes and I shall try faithfully as possible to tell you as I un-
derstand if not mistaken that Olen Montgomery, who was part blind
then, kept saying because of the dark there was inside the boxcar and
outside it: "It sure don't seem to me we're getting anywheres. It sure
don't seem like it to me." I and my three comrades whom were with
me, namely Roy Wright and his brother Andy and Eugene Williams,

---

43 *head*: the bullet was removed, but it had penetrated an inch into his brain; Powell sur-
vived, but he was never the same.

and about my character I have always been a good natural sort of boy, but as far as I am personally concerned about those pictures of me in the papers, why they are more or less undoubtedly not having the full likeness of me for I am a sight better-looking than those pictures make me out. Why all my life I spent in and around working for Jews° in their stores and so on and I have quite a few Jew friends whom can and always have gave me a good reputation as having regards for those whom have regards for me. The depression ran me away from home, I was off on my way to try my very best to find some work some else-where but misfortune befalled me without a moving cause. For it is events and misfortune which happens to people and how some must whom are less fortunate have their lives taken from them and how people die in chair for what they do not do.

### THE SPIRITUAL FOR NINE VOICES

I went last night to a turkey feast (Oh, God, don't fail your
    children now!)
55    My people were sitting there the way they'll sit in heaven
With their wings spread out and their hearts all singing
Their mouths full of food and the table set with glass
(Oh, God, don't fail your children now!)
There were poor men sitting with their fingers dripping honey
60    All the ugly sisters were fair. I saw my brother who never had a
    penny
With a silk shirt on and a pair of golden braces
And gems strewn through his hair.

(Were you looking, Father, when the sheriffs came in?
Was your face turned towards us when they had their say?)

65    There was baked sweet potato and fried corn pone
There was eating galore, there was plenty in the horn.
(Were you there when Victoria Price took the stand?
Did you see the state attorney with her drawers in his hand?
Did you hear him asking for me to burn?)

70    There were oysters cooked in amplitude
There was sauce in every mouth.
There was ham done slow in spice and clove
And chicken enough for the young and the old.
(Was it you stilled the water on horse-swapping day
75    When the mob came to the jail? Was it you come out in a long
    tail coat
Come dancing high with the word in your mouth?)

---

*Jews:* anti-Semitism became a major feature of publicity about the case after Samuel Lei-bowitz (1893–1978), a Jewish lawyer from New York, came on board to head the Scotts-boro defense in January of 1933. The defense was also relentlessly red-baited because it was organized by the Communist Party's legal affiliate, the International Labor Defense. Leibowitz, who was tireless in his efforts, was himself a democrat, not a radical.

I saw my sister who never had a cent
Come shaking and shuffling between the seats.
Her hair was straight and her nails were pointed
80     Her breasts were high and her legs double-jointed.

(Oh, God, don't fail your children now!)

### The Sentence

Hear how it goes, the wheels of it traveling fast on the rails
    The boxcars, the gondolas running drunk through the night.
85   Hear the long high wail as it flashes through stations unlit
    Past signals ungiven, running wild through a country
A time when sleepers rouse in their beds and listen
    And cannot sleep again.
Hear it passing in no direction, to no destination
90   Carrying people caught in the boxcars, trapped on the coupled
    chert cars°
(Hear the rattle of gravel as it rides whistling through the day and
    night.)
Not the old or the young on it, nor people with any difference in
    their color or shape,
Not girls or men, Negroes or white, but people with this in
    common:
People that no one had use for, had nothing to give to, no place to
    offer
95   But the cars of a freight train careening through Paint Rock,
    through Memphis,
    Through town after town without halting.
The loose hands hang down, and swing with the swing of the
    train in the darkness,
Holding nothing but poverty, syphilis white as a handful of dust,
    taking nothing as baggage
100  But the sound of the harp Ozie Powell is playing or the voice of
    Montgomery
Half-blind in oblivion saying: "It sure don't seem to me like we're
    getting anywheres.
It don't seem to me like we're getting anywheres at all."

    *1937*

---

90 *chert cars:* regional slang for open-top high-sided gondolas used for hauling gravel.

# Carl Rakosi (b. 1903)

Born in Berlin, the son of Hungarian nationals, Rakosi came to the United States in 1910. He was educated at the University of Wisconsin and the University of Minnesota. He changed his name legally to Callman Rawley but retained the name Rakosi for his literary work. First associated with the Objectivists, Rakosi wrote no poetry from 1939 to 1965, feeling, as he told an interviewer, that "in the wake of the Depression and World War II, his intensely individual lyricism was irrelevant and impossible to continue." His lyric impulses are often counterpointed with sudden shifts in diction, sound, and thematic focus, as he cuts back and forth across the page and back and forth from seriousness to playfulness. The aim in part is to catch the unstable relationship between consciousness and the physical world. For many years, Rakosi supported himself as a social worker in the Midwest. The experience no doubt contributed to projects like his "Americana" series that give his account of American beliefs and political currents.

## The Menage

Up stand
        six
yellow
        jonquils
5     in a
        glass/
the stems
         dark green,
paling
10         as they descend
into the water/
          seen through
a thicket
        of baby's breath, "a tall herb
15   bearing numerous small,
            fragrant white flowers."
I have seen
        snow-drops larger.
I bent my face down.
20           To my delight
they were convoluted
         like a rose.

They had no smell,
      their white
25  the grain of Biblical dust,
          which like the orchid itself
is as common as hayseed.
        Their stems were thin and woody
but as tightly compacted
30          as a tree trunk,
greenish rubbings showing in spots
          through the brown;
wiry, forked twigs so close,
        they made an impassable bush
35  which from a distance
       looked like mist.
I could barely escape
      from that wood of particulars.
the jonquils whose air within
40         was irradiated topaz,
silent as in an ear,
       the stems leaning lightly
against the glass,
       trisecting its inner circle
45  in the water,
       crossed like reverent hands
(ah, the imagination!
       Benedicite.
Enter monks.
50       Oops, sorry!
Trespassing
      on Japanese space.
Exit monks
     and all their lore
55  from grace).

I was moved by all this
        and murmured
to my eyes, "Oh, Master!"
        and became engrossed again
60  in that wood of particulars
        until I found myself
out of character, singing
  "Tell me why you've settled here."

  "Because my element is near."
65  and reflecting,
      "The eye of man cares. Yes!"

But a familiar voice
      broke into the wood,
a shade of mockery in it,
70       and in her smile
a fore-knowledge
      of something playful,

something forbidden,
                    something make-believe
75      something saucy,
                    something delicious
        about to pull me
                    off guard:
        "Do you want to be my Cupid-o?"

80      In fairness to her
                    it must be said
        that her freckles
                    are always friendly
        and that the anticipation
85                          of a prank
        makes them radiate
                    across her face
        the way dandelions
                    sprout in a field
90      after a summer shower.

        "What makes you so fresh,
                    my Wife of Bath?
        What makes you so silly,
                    o bright hen?"

95      "That's for you to find out,
                    old shoe, old shoe.
        That's for you to find out
                    if you can."

        "Oh yeah!"
                    (a mock chase and capture)
100     "Commit her
                    into jonquil's custody.
        She'll see a phallus
                    in the pistil.
105     Let her work it off there."

        But I was now myself
                    under this stringent force
        which ended,
                    as real pastorals in time must,
110     in bed, with the great
                    eye of man, rolling.

                                        *c. 1939*

# Aqua Laluah (1904–1950)

Aqua Laluah was the pen name of Gladys May Casely-Hayford, an American national born in Axim, Gold Coast (now Ghana), West Africa. Her father was a politician and lawyer, her mother a teacher. Casely-Hayford was educated in Sierra Leone and in Wales. In the 1920s, she danced with a jazz band in Germany; she also began publishing poems in journals like *Opportunity*, *Atlantic Monthly*, and *Philadelphia Tribune* under her pseudonym. Her one collection is *Take 'um so* (1948). She died of black water fever in 1950.

## The Serving Girl

The calabash wherein she served my food
Was smooth and polished as sandalwood;
Fish, as white as the foam of the sea,
Peppered, and golden fried for me.
5    She brought palm wine that carelessly slips
From the sleeping palm tree's honeyed lips.
But who can guess, or even surmise,
The countless things she served with her eyes?

*1927*

## Lullaby

Close your sleepy eyes, or the pale moonlight will steal you,
Else in the mystic silence, the moon will turn you white.
Then you won't see the sunshine, nor smell the open roses,
Nor love your Mammy anymore, whose skin is dark as night.
5    You will only love the shadows, and the foam upon the billows,
The shadow of the vulture's wings, the call of mystery,
The hooting of the night owl, and the howling of the jackal,
The sighing of the evil winds, the call of mystery.
Wherever moonlight stretches her arms across the heavens,
10   You will follow, always follow, till you become instead,
A shade in human draperies, with palm fronds for your pillow,
In place of Mammy's bibini, asleep on his wee bed.

*1929*

# Louis Zukofsky (1904–1978)

Born in New York of Russian immigrant parents and raised on Manhattan's Lower East Side, Zukofsky's childhood reading was done in Yiddish. He was educated at Columbia University. Earning money teaching English at the Polytechnic Institute of Brooklyn, among other jobs, he began writing and publishing early on. He defined a de facto movement, whose members he called "Objectivists," when he edited a special issue of *Poetry* magazine in 1931; Pound had convinced the editor Harriet Monroe to let Zukofsky do the issue. *An "Objectivists" Anthology* appeared the following year. The collections included Oppen, Pound, Rakosi, Rexroth, Reznikoff, Williams, and Zukofsky himself. All the contributors shared at least a partial interest in the material presence of the poem and in its linguisticality. Zukofsky himself added a strong belief in historically contextualized poetry and a highly developed musical sense. Read aloud, Zukofsky's poems sometimes show how he used sound effects to add additional layers of meaning to the text. In addition to *All: The Collected Shorter Poems*, Zukofsky's writing includes one of the major book-length poem sequences of American modernism, *"A"*, and a massive theoretical work, *Bottom: On Shakespeare*. He collaborated with his wife Celia on a translation of Catullus, and she wrote musical settings for some of his lyrics.

## To My Wash-stand

> To my wash-stand
> in which I wash
> my left hand
> and my right hand
>
> 5　　To my wash-stand
> whose base is Greek
> whose shaft
> is marble and is fluted
>
> To my wash-stand
> 10　whose wash-bowl
> is an oval
> in a square
>
> To my wash-stand
> whose square is marble
> 15　　and inscribes two
> smaller ovals to left and right for soap

Comes a song of
water from the right faucet and the left
my left and my
20    right hand mixing hot and cold

Comes a flow which
if I have called a song
is a song
entirely in my head

25                a song out of imagining
modillions described above
my head    a frieze
of stone completing what no longer

is my wash-stand
30    since its marble has completed
my getting up each morning
my washing before going to bed

my look into a mirror
to glimpse half an oval
35                as if its half
were half-oval in my head    and the

climates of many
inscriptions human heads shapes'
horses' elephants' (tusks) others'
40    scratched in marble tile

so my wash-stand
in one particular breaking of the
tile at which I have
looked and looked

45                has opposed to my head
the inscription of a head
whose coinage is the
coinage of the poor

observant in waiting
50    in their getting up mornings
and in their waiting
going to bed

carefully attentive
to what they have
55                and to what they do not
have

when a flow of water
doubled in narrow folds

<pre>
          occasions invertible counterpoints
60              over a head   and

              an age in a wash-stand
          and in their own heads
</pre>

*1931*

# Mantis

Mantis! praying mantis! since your wings' leaves
And your terrified eyes, pins, bright, black and poor
Beg—"Look, take it up" (thoughts torsion)! "save it!"
I who can't bear to look, cannot touch,—You—
5   You can—but no one sees you steadying lost
In the cars' drafts on the lit subway stone.

Praying mantis, what wind-up brought you, stone
On which you sometimes prop, prey among leaves
(Is it love's food your raised stomach prays?), lost
10  Here, stone holds only seats on which the poor
Ride, who rising from the news may trample you—
The shops' crowds a jam with no flies in it.

Even the newsboy who now sees knows it
No use, papers make money, makes stone, stone,
15  Banks, "it is harmless," he says moving on—You?
Where will he put *you*? There are no safe leaves
To put you back in here, here's news! too poor
Like all the separate poor to save the lost.

Don't light on my chest, mantis! do—you're lost,
20  Let the poor laugh at my fright, then see it:
My shame and theirs, you whom old Europe's poor
Call spectre, strawberry, by turns; a stone—
You point—they say—you lead lost children—leaves
Close in the paths men leave, saved, safe with you.

25  Killed by thorns (once men), who now will save you
Mantis? what male love bring a fly, be lost
Within your mouth, prophetess, harmless to leaves
And hands, faked flower,—the myth is: dead, bones, it
Was assembled, apes wing in wind: On stone,
30  Mantis, you will die, touch, beg, of the poor.

Android, loving beggar, dive to the poor
As your love would even without head to you,
Graze like machined wheels, green, from off this stone
And preying on each terrified chest, lost
35  Say, I am old as the globe, the moon, it
Is my old shoe, yours, be free as the leaves.

Fly, mantis, on the poor, arise like leaves
The armies of the poor, strength: stone on stone
And build the new world in your eyes, Save it!

*1934*

# A Song for the Year's End

### 1

Daughter of music
and her sweet son
so that none rule
the dew to his own hurt
5      with the year's last sigh
awake
the starry sky and bird.

### 2

I shall go back to my mother's grave after this war
Because there are those who'll still speak of loyalty
10      In the outskirts of Baltimore
Or wherever Jews are not the right sort of people,
And say to her one of the dead I speak to—
There are less Jews left in the world,
While they were killed
15      I did not see you in a dream to tell you,
And that I now have a wife and son.

Then I shall go and write of my country,
Have a job all my life
Seldom write with grace again, be part of the world,
20      See every man in forced labor,
Dawn only where suburbs are *restricted*
To people who take trains every morning,
Never the gentleness that can be,
The hope of the common man, the eyes that love leaves
25      Any shade, thought or thing that makes all man uncommon,

But always the depraved bark
Fight or work,
Dawn the red poster, the advertiser's cock crow,
Sunset a lack of wonder, the lone winged foot of Mercury in
    tie with a tire,
30      The fashion model
Her train stopped in the railroad cut
Looking up to a billboard of herself
As she goes home to her small son asleep,

So early and so late in the fortunes that followed
    me from my mother's grave
35      A lovely air follows her

And the dead President who is worth it:
'Dear death, like peace, I end not speaking,
The chitchat has died
And the last smile is unwilled
40     I am dead, I can't talk
To blossoms or spring in the world.'

### 3

     "Because he was crying
I like him most of all," says my son
"Because he was crying,"—the red fox
45     With three porcupine quills in his paw—
Who brings tears to the eyes,
     button nose against shambles,
Valentines all day, all night, tomorrow
The simplest the keyboard can play,
'Pony gay, on your way,' love's hair
50     With two gray, Papa Bear's Song
     new to renew,
'Who's been sitting in my chair?'

                                        1945–46

## Because Tarzan Triumphs

Because Tarzan triumphs
See Tarzan the He-man
Go to sleep with boy in jungle corral
And chimpanzee, the best man, delouse
5     By the bed, hear that movie goer's giggle!
Clean,
Tarzan gives up his bed
                    lush couch—
Thru with women: that girl
With her hair down in the world
10     Can take care of herself in his bed.

"Tarzan, boy's mother," he says slapping
The boy's rear, and
Reared by the jungle
He beats a man's breasts on his chest,
15     "He likes swimming," boy teases princess
"Swim with him!"

—Cupid, your thighs do play Cupid, boy,
She won't get far
If she wants thighs
20     Instead of high morals.
"She says you're an isolationist, Tarzan!"
Thwarted, the boy dawdles on the syllable *Tar:*
"A what! Boy?"
—Wait till he finds out!

25     You'll *have* to see how they do it
Tho evening prices go up quickly at noon.
"Nazi!" Tarzan says coyly
"Nazi," Tarzan says
And lures some celluloid to the lion's maw:
30     And all the earth's problems are solved.
You have seen
A rain of dried peas does not stick to a screen,
A non-stop reflector,
(Not the black sheet of a bed),
35     But an heroic
Which excretes and laughs.

*1940–48*

# Non Ti Fidar°

*in opera poetry must be the obedient daughter of music*
MOZART

The hand a shade of moonlight on the pillow
And that a shadowed white would seem above or below
Their heads ear to ear, hearing water
Not like the word, the flickflack of the eye opening on it
5     With what happiness
Where the word is the obedient daughter of music
And Don Giovanni's shapely seat and heart live in hell
Lovable as its fire
As all loves that breathe and kiss
10     Simply by life
Rocking to sleep and flame:
So frail is judgment
It must light up, an overseer
With some truckling in hell,
15     A song that lovers' heads
Ear to, and on ear foretell.

*1949*

---

**poem title:** *"Non ti fidar, o misera"* (Italian) "Never trust that evil man" is a quartet sung in Wolfgang Amadeus Mozart's (1756–1791) opera *Don Giovanni* (1787), Act I. Alvira, a previous conquest of Giovanni's, sings this warning to Anna, the most recent object of Giovanni's attentions. Giovanni then addresses Anna, hoping to undermine Alvira's credibility. Anna's betrothed, Ottavia, then pleads with her to heed Alvira's words.

# John Beecher (1904–1980)

Beecher was born in New York, the great-great-nephew of Abolitionists Harriet Beecher Stowe and Henry Ward Beecher; it was a heritage his life would honor. He grew up in Birmingham, Alabama, where his father was a U.S. Steel executive, but Beecher entered the industry at the bottom. From age 16, he worked twelve-hour shifts on the open hearth furnaces. Educated at Cornell, Alabama, Harvard, and North Carolina Universities, Beecher worked eight years during the New Deal era as a field administrator of social programs devoted to sharecroppers and migrant workers. He then took up a teaching career. But when he refused to sign California's unconstitutional "loyalty" oath in 1950, he was fired and blacklisted. He began ranching in the redwoods, and, along with his wife Barbara, founded a press to publish himself and other blacklisted writers. During the civil rights movement he became a Southern correspondent for *Ramparts* and the *San Francisco Chronicle*. In 1977, nearly 30 years after being fired, he was reappointed to the San Francisco State University faculty. See his *Collected Poems 1924–1974* (1974).

## Report to the Stockholders

### I

he fell off his crane
and his head hit the steel floor and broke like an egg
he lived a couple of hours with his brains bubbling out
and then he died
5    and the safety clerk made out a report saying
it was carelessness
and the craneman should have known better
from twenty years experience
than not to watch his step
10    and slip in some grease on top of his crane
and then the safety clerk told the superintendent
he'd ought to fix that guardrail

### II

out at the open hearth
they all went to see the picture
15    called Men of Steel

about a third-helper who
worked up to the top
and married the president's daughter
and they liked the picture
20      because it was different

### III

a ladle burned through
and he got a shoeful of steel
so they took up a collection through the mill
and some gave two bits
25      and some gave four
because there's no telling when

### IV

the stopper-maker
puts a sleeve brick on an iron rod
and then a dab of mortar
30      and then another sleeve brick
and another dab of mortar
and when he has put fourteen sleeve bricks on
and fourteen dabs of mortar
and fitted on the head
35      he picks up another rod
and makes another stopper

### V

a hot metal car ran over the Negro switchman's leg
and nobody expected to see him around here again
except maybe on the street with a tin cup
40      but the superintendent saw what an ad
the Negro would make with his peg leg
so he hung a sandwich on him
with safety slogans
and he told the Negro just to keep walking
45      all day up and down the plant
and be an example

### VI

he didn't understand why he was laid off
when he'd been doing his work
on the pouring tables OK
50      and when men with less age than he had
weren't laid off
and he wanted to know why
but the superintendent told him to get the hell out
so he swung on the superintendent's jaw
55      and the cops came and took him away

## VII

he's been working around here ever since there was
   a plant
he started off carrying tests when he was fourteen
and then he third-helped
and then he second-helped
60   and then he first-helped
and when he got to be sixty years old
and was almost blind from looking into furnaces
the bosses let him
carry tests again

## VIII

65   he shouldn't have loaded and wheeled
a thousand pounds of manganese
before the cut in his belly was healed
but he had to pay his hospital bill
and he had to eat
70   he thought he had to eat
but he found out
he was wrong

## IX

in the company quarters
you've got a steelplant in your backyard
75   very convenient
gongs bells whistles mudguns steamhammers and slag-
   pots blowing up
you get so you sleep through it
but when the plant shuts down
you can't sleep for the quiet

*1925*

## Beaufort Tides

Low tide.
The scavenging gulls
scour the reaches of mud.
No slavers ride
5   at anchor in the roads. Rotting hulls
are drawn up on the shore.

Full stood
the tide here
when through this colonnaded door
10   into the raw land passed bond and free,
the one in hope leading the other in fear,
chained each to each by destiny.

Not only tide
but time and blood
15    can turn, can ebb and flow.
Time ebbs, blood flows, the fear
shows in the master's eye while jubilee
bursts from the bondsman's throat.

Now
20    no shout
rings out.
Neither hopes. Both fear.
What future tide will free
these captives of their history?

1934

## Engagement at the Salt Fork

Like tumbleweeds before the wind we moved
across the continent's huge heedless face.
Fat sheriffs' radios kept hot with news
of our invasion. Squad-cars tailed the walk.
5    Blasts born on Yukon tundras knifed us through
and buffeted our sign: *Man Will End War
Or War Will End Man.* Handful that we were,
armed men patrolled us, secret agents sped
ahead to warn the elevator towns.
10    Christians heard now that if they harbored us
and let us spread our sleeping-bags on floors
of Sunday schools, religion would be lost.
Whoever opened up his door to us
was spotted by a telephoto lens,
15    proclaimed suspect, anathema to all
right-thinking patriots. As if we were
the ghosts of banished Cherokees come back,
the guilty Strip shook in its cowboy boots.
We camped one night beside the Salt Fork, near
20    a town through which they'd hustled us with guns
and imprecations lest ideas start
an epidemic there. Our campfire lit,
potatoes boiling and someone's guitar
strumming *Down by the Riverside,* people
25    began to drift in from the country round.
Skylarking students with a bugle, torches,
burlesquing us with signs: *Workers Arise!
You Have Nothing to Lose but Your Thirst! Drink Beer!*
Good kids they proved to be and soon knocked off
30    the clowning. Faces in the firelight grew
into hundreds, boys with their dates, big-hats
from nearby ranches, preachers whose wives had brought
us popcorn, apples. A dozen arguments
swirled into being as good-humoredly
35    they challenged us to win their minds with fact

and logic. Raw though the night, shirt-sleeved they stood
and battled with us till they came to see
the meaning of our walk. Some would have joined
had we sought that. One horse-breeder, Stetsoned
40    and powerful of frame, told of campaigns
he'd fought in Italy. Fondling his son,
a lad of eight, he blessed our walk for peace.
"Each war *we* fight, *they* promise is the last,"
he said, "and here they go ag'in. This boy
45    is one they ain't a-goin' to git, by God!"
Long after midnight it was when the last
of them went home. I could not sleep for pride
in these my people, still square-shooters, still
ready to tote fair with the other man.
50    I could not sleep for sadness too, to think
how these great hearts are gulled with lies.
God help the liars when my people wake!

1961

# Kenneth Rexroth (1905–1982)

Born in South Bend, Indiana, Rexroth moved to Chicago with his family at age twelve. Although he attended classes at Chicago's Art Institute and later at the Art Students League in New York, he was largely (and prodigiously) self-educated. He would learn several languages, translate poems from the Chinese, French, Spanish, and Japanese, and exhibit his own paintings in several cities. He also worked early on as a fruit picker, a forest patrolman, a factory hand, and an attendant at a mental institution. Later he was a columnist for the *San Francisco Examiner* and the *San Francisco Bay Guardian* and a teacher at several universities.

Rexroth's long career and interesting life are not easy to represent fully. He was a fellow traveler of the Communist Party, a key figure in the West Coast anarchist movement, a conscientious objector in World War II, and a long-time Buddhist. His early political poetry is notable for its capacity for intellectual reflection; his nature poetry virtually established the genre in California. He championed a number of younger poets, including the Beats, and helped found several West Coast cultural institutions. Rather than sample his varied career, we reprint here one of his neglected masterpieces, "The Love Poems of Marichiko." The sequence has been somewhat neglected because Rexroth pretended it was a translation; actually Marichiko is an invented persona. Rexroth is "translating" from her imaginary consciousness.

## The Love Poems of Marichiko°

### I

I sit at my desk.
What can I write to you?
Sick with love,
I long to see you in the flesh.
5    I can write only,
"I love you. I love you. I love you."
Love cuts through my heart
And tears my vitals.
Spasms of longing suffocate me
10   And will not stop.

---

**poem title:** Marichiko is an invented persona; the "translations" from her imaginary consciousness are all original poetry by Rexroth. Rexroth's own notes begin on p. 572.

## II

If I thought I could get away
And come to you,
Ten thousand miles would be like one mile.
But we are both in the same city
15 And I dare not see you,
And a mile is longer than a million miles.

## III

Oh the anguish of these secret meetings
In the depth of night,
I wait with the shoji open.
20 You come late, and I see your shadow
Move through the foliage
At the bottom of the garden.
We embrace—hidden from my family.
I weep into my hands.
25 My sleeves are already damp.
We make love, and suddenly
The fire watch loom up
With clappers and lantern.
How cruel they are
30 To appear at such a moment.
Upset by their apparition,
I babble nonsense
And can't stop talking
Words with no connection.

## IV

35 You ask me what I thought about
Before we were lovers.
The answer is easy.
Before I met you
I didn't have anything to think about.

## V

40 Autumn covers all the world
With Chinese old brocade.
The crickets cry, "We mend old clothes."
They are more thrifty than I am.

## VI

Just us.
45 In our little house
Far from everybody,
Far from the world,
Only the sound of water over stone.
And then I say to you,
50 "Listen. Hear the wind in the trees."

### VII

Making love with you
Is like drinking sea water.
The more I drink
The thirstier I become,
55          Until nothing can slake my thirst
But to drink the entire sea.

### VIII

A single ray in the dawn,
The bliss of our love
Is incomprehensible.
60          No sun shines there, no
Moon, no stars, no lightning flash,
Not even lamplight.
All things are incandescent
With love which lights up all the world.

### IX

65          You wake me,
Part my thighs, and kiss me.
I give you the dew
Of the first morning of the world.

### X

Frost covers the reeds of the marsh.
70          A fine haze blows through them,
Crackling the long leaves.
My full heart throbs with bliss.

### XI

Uguisu sing in the blossoming trees.
Frogs sing in the green rushes.
75          Everywhere the same call
Of being to being.
Somber clouds waver in the void.
Fishing boats waver in the tide.
Their sails carry them out.
80          But ropes, as of old, woven
With the hair of their women,
Pull them back
Over their reflections on the green depths,
To the ports of love.

### XII

85          Come to me, as you come
Softly to the rose bed of coals
Of my fireplace
Glowing through the night-bound forest.

### XIII

90
Lying in the meadow, open to you
Under the noon sun,
Hazy smoke half hides
My rose petals.

### XIV

On the bridges
And along the banks
95
Of Kamo River, the crowds
Watch the character "Great"
Burst into red fire on the mountain
And at last die out.
Your arm about me,
100
I burn with passion.
Suddenly I realize—
It is life I am burning with.
These hands burn,
Your arm about me burns,
105
And look at the others,
All about us in the crowd, thousands,
They are all burning—
Into embers and then into darkness.
I am happy.
110
Nothing of mine is burning.

### XV

Because I dream
Of you every night,
My lonely days
Are only dreams.

### XVI

115
Scorched with love, the cicada
Cries out. Silent as the firefly,
My flesh is consumed with love.

### XVII

Let us sleep together here tonight.
Tomorrow, who knows where we will sleep?
120
Maybe tomorrow we will lie in the fields,
Our heads on the rocks.

### XVIII

Fires
Burn in my heart.
No smoke rises.
125
No one knows.

## XIX

I pass the day tense, day-
Dreaming of you. I relax with joy
When in the twilight I hear
The evening bells ring from temple to temple.

## XX

130     Who is there? Me.
Me who? I am me. You are you.
You take my pronoun,
And we are us.

## XXI

The full moon of Spring
135     Rises from the Void,
And pushes aside the net
Of stars, a pure crystal ball
On pale velvet, set with gems.

## XXII

This Spring, Mercury
140     Is farthest from the sun and
Burns, a ray of light,
In the glow of dawn
Over the uncountable
Sands and waves of the
145     Illimitable ocean.

## XXIII

I wish I could be
Kannon of eleven heads
To kiss you, Kannon
Of the thousand arms,
150     To embrace you forever.

## XXIV

I scream as you bite
My nipples, and orgasm
Drains my body, as if I
Had been cut in two.

## XXV

155     Your tongue thrums and moves
Into me, and I become
Hollow and blaze with
Whirling light, like the inside
Of a vast expanding pearl.

## XXVI

160 It is the time when
The wild geese return. Between
The setting sun and
The rising moon, a line of
Brant write the character "heart."

## XXVII

165 As I came from the
Hot bath, you took me before
The horizontal mirror
Beside the low bed, while my
Breasts quivered in your hands, my
170 Buttocks shivered against you.

## XXVIII

Spring is early this year.
Laurel, plums, peaches,
Almonds, mimosa,
All bloom at once. Under the
175 Moon, night smells like your body.

## XXIX

Love me. At this moment we
Are the happiest
People in the world.

## XXX

Nothing in the world is worth
180 One sixteenth part of the love
Which sets free our hearts.
Just as the Morning Star in
The dark before dawn
Lights up the world with its ray,
185 So love shines in our hearts and
Fills us with glory.

## XXXI

Some day in six inches of
Ashes will be all
That's left of our passionate minds,
190 Of all the world created
By our love, its origin
And passing away.

### XXXII

I hold your head tight between
My thighs, and press against your
195 Mouth, and float away
Forever, in an orchid
Boat on the River of Heaven.

### XXXIII

I cannot forget
The perfumed dusk inside the
200 Tent of my black hair,
As we awoke to make love
After a long night of love.

### XXXIV

Every morning, I
Wake alone, dreaming my
205 Arm is your sweet flesh
Pressing my lips.

### XXXV

The uguisu sleeps in the bamboo grove,
One night a man traps her in a bamboo trap,
Now she sleeps in a bamboo cage.

### XXXVI

210 I am sad this morning.
The fog was so dense,
I could not see your shadow
As you passed my shoji.

### XXXVII

Is it just the wind
215 In the bamboo grass,
Or are you coming?
At the least sound
My heart skips a beat.
I try to suppress my torment
220 And get a little sleep,
But I only become more restless.

### XXXVIII

I waited all night.
By midnight I was on fire.
In the dawn, hoping
225 To find a dream of you,

I laid my weary head
On my folded arms,
But the songs of the waking
Birds tormented me.

### XXXIX

230    Because I can't stop,
Even for a moment's rest from
Thinking of you,
The obi° which wound around me twice,
Now goes around me three times.

### XL

235    As the wheel follows the hoof
Of the ox that pulls the cart,
My sorrow follows your footsteps,
As you leave me in the dawn.

### XLI

On the mountain,
240    Tiring to the feet,
Lost in the fog, the pheasant
Cries out, seeking her mate.

### XLII

How many lives ago
I first entered the torrent of love,
245    At last to discover
There is no further shore.
Yet I know I will enter again and again.

### XLIII

Two flowers in a letter.
The moon sinks into the far off hills.
250    Dew drenches the bamboo grass.
I wait.
Crickets sing all night in the pine tree.
At midnight the temple bells ring.
Wild geese cry overhead.
255    Nothing else.

### XLIV

The disorder of my hair
Is due to my lonely sleepless pillow.
My hollow eyes and gaunt cheeks
Are your fault.

---

233 *obi*: a broad sash with a bow in back.

### XLV

260 When in the Noh theater
We watched Shizuka Gozen
Trapped in the snow,
I enjoyed the tragedy,
For I thought,
265 Nothing like this
Will ever happen to me.

### XLVI

Emitting a flood of light,
Flooded with light within,
Our love was dimmed by
270 Forces which came from without.

### XLVII

How long, long ago.
By the bridge at Uji,
In our little boat,
We swept through clouds of fireflies.

### XLVIII

275 Now the fireflies of our youth
Are all gone,
Thanks to the efficient insecticides
Of our middle age.

### XLIX

Once again I hear
280 The first frogs sing in the pond.
I am overwhelmed by the past.

### L

In the park a crow awakes
And cries out under the full moon,
And I awake and sob
285 For the years that are gone.

### LI

Did you take me because you loved me?
Did you take me without love?
Or did you just take me
To experiment on my heart?

## LII

290 Once I shone afar like a
Snow-covered mountain.
Now I am lost like
An arrow shot in the dark.
He is gone and I must learn
295 To live alone and
Sleep alone like a hermit
Buried deep in the jungle.
I shall learn to go
Alone, like the unicorn.

## LIII

300 Without me you can only
Live at random like
A falling pachinko ball.
I am your wisdom.

## LIV

Did a cuckoo cry?
305 I look out, but there is only dawn and
The moon in its final night.
Did the moon cry out
Horobirete! Horobirete!
Perishing! Perishing!

## LV

310 The night is too long to the sleepless.
The road is too long to the footsore.
Life is too long to a woman
Made foolish by passion.
Why did I find a crooked guide
315 On the twisted paths of love?

## LVI

This flesh you have loved
Is fragile, unstable by nature
As a boat adrift.
The fires of the cormorant fishers
320 Flare in the night.
My heart flares with this agony.
Do you understand?
My life is going out.
Do you understand?
325 My life.
Vanishing like the stakes
That hold the nets against the current
In Uji River, the current and the mist
Are taking me.

## LVII

330      Night without end. Loneliness.
The wind has driven a maple leaf
Against the shoji. I wait, as in the old days,
In our secret place, under the full moon.
The last bell crickets sing.
335      I found your old love letters,
Full of poems you never published.
Did it matter? They were only for me.

## LVIII

Half in a dream
I become aware
340      That the voices of the crickets
Grow faint with the growing Autumn.
I mourn for this lonely
Year that is passing
And my own being
345      Grows fainter and fades away.

## LIX

I hate this shadow of a ghost
Under the full moon.
I run my fingers through my greying hair,
And wonder, have I grown so thin?

## LX

350      Chilled through, I wake up
With the first light. Outside my window
A red maple leaf floats silently down.
What am I to believe?
Indifference?
355      Malice?
I hate the sight of coming day
Since that morning when
Your insensitive gaze turned me to ice
Like the pale moon in the dawn.

*1974*

---

Rexroth's notes: Marichiko is the pen name of a contemporary young woman who lives near the temple of Marishi-ben in Kyoto.

Marishi-ben is an Indian, pre-Aryan, goddess of the dawn who is a bodhisattva in Buddhism and patron of geisha, prostitutes, women in childbirth, and lovers, and, in another aspect, once of samurai. Few temples or shrines to her or even statues exist in Japan, but her presence is indicated by statues, often in avenues like sphinxes, of wild boars, who also draw her chariot. She has three faces: the front of compassion; one side, a sow; the other a woman in ecstasy. She is a popular, though hidden, deity of tantric, Tachigawa Shingon. As the Ray of Light, the Shakti, or Prajna, the Power or Wisdom of Vairocana (the primordial Buddha, Dainichi Nyorai), she is seated on his lap in sexual bliss, Myōjō—the Morning Star.

Marichiko writes me, now that I am doing so many of her poems, in reference to the note on her in my *One Hundred More Poems from the Japanese,* "Although Marichi is the Shakti, or power, of the Indian god of the sun, she is the Prajna, or wisdom, of Dainichi Nyorai. Dainichi means Great Sun, but he is that only in a metaphorical sense, the Illuminator of the compound infinity of infinities of universes. The Buddhas and Bodhisattvas of Mahayana do not have Shaktis as consorts, for the simple reason that there is no such thing as power in Buddhism. Power is ignorance and grasping. With illumination, it turns into wisdom."

Notice, that like the English seventeenth-century poet Rochester, many of her poems turn religious verse into erotic, and she also turns traditional geisha songs into visionary poems. They therefore bear comparison with Persian Sufi poets, Hafidh, Attar, Sa'adi, and others, and with the Arab, Ibn el Arabi—with all of whom she is familiar in translation.

The series of poems, as should be obvious, form a sort of little novel and recall the famous *Diary of Izumi Shikibu* without the connecting prose. Notice that the sex of the lover is ambiguous.

Poem IV. Echoes Fujiwara no Atsutada, "Ai minto no."

Poem V. Narihira compares the leaf covered water of Tatsuta River to Chinese old brocade.

Poem VI. Echoes several "honeymoon houses," the modern one by Yosano Akiko.

Poem VII. Echoes a passage in the *Katha Upanishad.*

Poem VIII. Echoes a passage in the *Katha Upanishad.*

Poem XI. The uguisu, often translated "nightingale," is not a nightingale and does not sing at night. It is the Japanese bush warbler, *Horeites cantans cantans,* or *Cettia diphone.*

Poem XIV. Refers to the Festival, Daimonji Okuribi, sending of the dead back to heaven, when huge bonfires in the shape of characters are lit on the mountain sides around Kyoto. There is a paraphrase of Buddha's Fire Sermon and a paraphrase of Rilke's paraphrase of that.

Poem XVI. Based on a geisha song in many forms.

Poem XVII. Either the poem on Hitomaro's (Japan's greatest poet—b.?–d.739) death or his own poem on a friend's death.

Poem XX. This poem, though syntactically barely possible, would be inconceivable in classical Japanese.

Poem XXI. There is an implied reference to the doctrine of Void Only and then to the Avatamsaka Sutra (Kegongyo) as the Net of Indra.

Poem XXII. The ray of light of the Morning Star—Marishiten—Myogo.

Poem XXIII. Both forms of Kannon (Avalokitesvara) are common statues. Sanjusangendo, across from the Kyoto Art Museum, is a hall of over a thousand such, each very slightly different.

Poem XXVI. Brant, *Branta bernicia* is Japanese Koku-gan, are small, dark geese, who winter in the north of Honshu, the main island. Unlike many birds of the family, they do not fly in arrow formations, but in an irregular line.

Poem XXVII. The horizontal mirror is a narrow mirror, closed by sliding panels, alongside the bed in many Japanese inns (ryokan). Shunga erotic woodblock prints, representing them, are usually called "seen through the slats of a bamboo screen" by Westerners— Japanese until recent times had nothing resembling our venetian blinds.

Poem XXX. Echoes the Buddhist sutra Itivuttaka, III, 7.

Poem XXXI. Echoes the Buddhist sutra, Samyutta Nikaya, II, 3, 8.

Poem XXXII. "Orchid boat" is a metaphor for the female sexual organ.

Poem XXXIII. Echoes Yosano Akiko.

Poem XXXVI. Shoji—sliding doors or windows with "panes" of paper.

Poem XXXVIII. Ono no Komachi (834–880) is certainly Japan's greatest woman poet. Marichiko echoes her most famous poem—"Hito no awan/Tsuki no naki ni wa/Omoiokite/ Mune hashibiri ni/Kokoro yakeori."

Poem XL. Echoes the first lines of the Dhammapada, the ancient popular exposition of Theravada Buddhism.

Poem XLI. Echoes an anonymous poem usually attributed to Hitomaro.

Poem XLII. Echoes a Buddhist sutra.

Poem XLIV. There are a great many midaregami, "tangled hair" poems, from an exchange between Mikata and his wife in the *Manyoshu*—eighth century—to the first great book of Yosano Akiko, called *Midaregami,* the early twentieth-century woman poet and still the unequalled poet of modern verse in classical (tanka) form.

Poem XLV. Shizuka Gozen (twelfth century) was a white dress dancer of spectacular beauty who became the lover of Minamoto no Yoshitsune, the tragic hero of the epic of the war between the Taira and Minamoto, which brought to an end the great years of early Japanese civilization. He was the principal general of his brother Yoritomo, and broke the power of the Taira in a series of battles. After Yoritomo outlawed his brother, Shizuka was captured fleeing through the snowbound wilderness on Mt. Yoshino. When Yorimoto and his courtiers were worshipping at the Tsuruga-Oka Shrine at Kamakura, he commanded Shizuka to perform her most famous dance. She refused but was finally forced to dance. Shortly after, she gave birth to Yoshitsune's son, whom Yoritomo murdered. She then became a Buddhist nun and lived to an old age, long after Yoshitsune had been destroyed in his refuge in the far North. She is not a great poet but, with Yoshitsune, one of the tragic figures of Japanese history. Her dance occurs in several Noh plays.

Poem XLVI. Echoes a Buddhist sutra, but also refers to herself as Marichi—Ray of Light—and Dainichi (Vairocana)—The Transcendent Sun.

Poem XLVII–XLVIII. These two poems are factual—D.D.T. exterminated most of the fireflies of Japan, and the Hotaru Matsuri—Firefly Festivals—are no longer held, or even remembered by the younger generation.

Poem LII. Echoes a Buddhist sutra, the poems of Yokobue and her lover in the *Heike Monogatori,* and finally Buddha's Unicorn (often called "Rhinoceros") Sermon.

Poem LIII. Pachinko is a form of vertical pinball—and immense pachinko parlors, crowded with hypnotized players, litter Japan. It is a symbol of total immersion in the world of illusion, ignorance, suffering, and grasping. Wisdom is Prajna—the female consort of a Buddha in esoteric Shingon Buddhism, corresponding to the Shakti, power, the consort of a Hindu god. Note that Prajna is, in a sense, the contradictory of Shakti.

Poem LIV. The first cuckoo in the dawn poem probably dates back before the *Kokinshu,* the second Imperial Anthology. There are many geisha songs that essentially repeat it. But Marichiko says, "was it the moon itself that cried out?" a completely novel last line. The hototogisu does not say "cuckoo," but something like the five syllables of its name, or "horobirete," perishing. It is *Cuculus poliocephalus.*

Poem LV. Echoes a Buddhist sutra.

Poem LVII. The bell cricket is the Tsukutsuku boshi, *Cosmopsal tria colorata.*

As I finish these notes, I realize that, whereas Westerners, alienated from their own culture, embrace Zen Buddhism, most young Japanese consider it reactionary, the religion of the officer caste, the great rich, and foreign hippies. There is however a growing movement of appreciation of Theravada (Hinayana) Buddhism, hitherto hardly known except to scholars in Japan. Marichiko's poems are deeply influenced by Theravada suttas, Tachigawa Shingon, folksongs, Yosano Akiko, and the great women poets of Heian Japan—Ono no Komachi, Murasaki Shikibu, and Izumi Shikibu.

# Robert Penn Warren (1905–1989)

Born in Guthrie, Kentucky, Warren was educated at Vanderbilt University, the University of California at Berkeley, Yale University, and Oxford University. At Vanderbilt, he was associated with the literary group called the Fugitives, which evolved into the Agrarian movement. The Agrarians advocated traditional values and an agricultural economy as a way of opposing industrialization and its accompanying alienation. At the time, Warren also wrote in support of racial segregation, a position he later came to regret. At Louisiana State University he cofounded the *Southern Review* before moving on to teach at Minnesota and Yale. His poetry of the 1930s and 1940s showed the combined influence of key modernists like Eliot and of his fellow "Fugitive," Allen Tate, along with the seventeenth-century metaphysical poets. By the late 1930s, he was also devoting much of his time to writing fiction, and from 1944 until 1953 he published no poetry. Thereafter, while he remained strongly interested in narrative poetry and often mounted moral arguments in verse, he also adopted more open forms, more colloquial diction, and more historically engaged subjects.

## Bearded Oaks

The oaks, how subtle and marine,
Bearded, and all the layered light
Above them swims; and thus the scene,
Recessed, awaits the positive night.

5     So, waiting, we in the grass now lie
Beneath the languorous tread of light:
The grasses, kelp-like, satisfy
The nameless motions of the air.

     Upon the floor of light, and time,
10    Unmurmuring, of polyp made,
We rest; we are, as light withdraws,
Twin atolls on a shelf of shade.

     Ages to our construction went,
Dim architecture, hour by hour:
15    And violence, forgot now, lent
The present stillness all its power.

The storm of noon above us rolled,
Of light the fury, furious gold,
The long drag troubling us, the depth:
20    Dark is unrocking, unrippling, still.

Passion and slaughter, ruth,° decay
Descend, minutely whispering down,
Silted down swaying streams, to lay
Foundation for our voicelessness.

25    All our debate is voiceless here,
As all our rage, the rage of stone;
If hope is hopeless, then fearless is fear,
And history is thus undone.

Our feet once wrought the hollow street
30    With echo when the lamps were dead
At windows, once our headlight glare
Disturbed the doe that, leaping, fled.

I do not love you less that now
The caged heart makes iron stroke,
35    Or less that all that light once gave
The graduate dark should now revoke.

We live in time so little time
And we learn all so painfully,
That we may spare this hour's term
To practice for eternity.

*1942*

## Evening Hawk

From plane of light to plane, wings dipping through
Geometries and orchids that the sunset builds,
Out of the peak's black angularity of shadow, riding
The last tumultuous avalanche of
5    Light above pines and the guttural gorge,
The hawk comes.

            His wing
Scythes down another day, his motion
Is that of the honed steel-edge, we hear
10    The crashless fall of stalks of Time.

The head of each stalk is heavy with the gold of our error.

---

21 *ruth:* pity.

Look! Look! he is climbing the last light
Who knows neither Time nor error, and under
Whose eye, unforgiving, the world, unforgiven, swings
15    Into shadow.

          Long now,
The last thrush is still, the last bat
Now cruises in his sharp hieroglyphics. His wisdom
Is ancient, too, and immense. The star
20    Is steady, like Plato, over the mountain.

If there were no wind we might, we think, hear
The earth grind on its axis, or history
Drip in darkness like a leaking pipe in the cellar.

*1975*

# Heart of Autumn

Wind finds the northwest gap, fall comes.
Today, under gray cloud-scud and over gray
Wind-flicker of forest, in perfect formation, wild geese
Head for a land of warm water, the *boom,* the lead pellet.

5    Some crumple in air, fall. Some stagger, recover control,
Then take the last glide for a far glint of water. None
Knows what has happened. Now, today, watching
How tirelessly *V* upon *V* arrows the season's logic,

Do I know my own story? At least, they know
10    When the hour comes for the great wing-beat. Sky-strider,
Star-strider—they rise, and the imperial utterance,
Which cries out for distance, quivers in the wheeling sky.

That much they know, and in their nature know
The path of pathlessness, with all the joy
15    Of destiny fulfilling its own name.
I have known time and distance, but not why I am here.

Path of logic, path of folly, all
The same—and I stand, my face lifted now skyward,
Hearing the high beat, my arms outstretched in the tingling
20    Process of transformation, and soon tough legs,

With folded feet, trail in the sounding vacuum of passage,
And my heart is impacted with a fierce impulse
To unwordable utterance—
Toward sunset, at a great height.

*1978*

# Stanley Kunitz (b. 1905)

Born and raised in Worcester, Massachusetts, Kunitz was educated at Harvard. Declaring himself a pacifist, he served in the army during World War II cleaning latrines. Since then, he has taught poetry workshops at several colleges, coedited a number of biographical dictionaries, helped to establish the Provincetown Fine Arts Work Center, edited the Yale Series of Younger Poets (from 1974–1976), and refined an increasingly open, almost conversational poetic voice. A 1967 trip to the Soviet Union led to his translating several poets from the Russian.

## The Wellfleet Whale°

*A few summers ago, on Cape Cod, a whale foundered on the beach, a sixty-three-foot finback whale. When the tide went out, I approached him. He was lying there, in monstrous desolation, making the most terrifying noises—rumbling—groaning. I put my hands on his flanks and I could feel the life inside him. And while I was standing there, suddenly he opened his eye. It was a big, red, cold eye, and it was staring directly at me. A shudder of recognition passed between us. Then the eye closed forever. I've been thinking about whales ever since.*
—JOURNAL ENTRY

I

You have your language too,
    an eerie medley of clicks
      and hoots and trills,
location-notes and love calls,
5      whistles and grunts. Occasionally,
        it's like furniture being smashed,
or the creaking of a mossy door,
    sounds that all melt into a liquid
      song with endless variations,
10    as if to compensate
      for the vast loneliness of the sea.
      Sometimes a disembodied voice

---

**poem title:** Wellfleet is a town on the Massachusetts coast.

breaks in, as if from distant reefs,
    and it's as much as one can bear
15        to listen to its long mournful cry,
a sorrow without a name, both more
    and less human. It drags
        across the ear like a record
running down.

2

20  No wind. No waves. No clouds.
    Only the whisper of the tide,
        as it withdrew, stroking the shore,
a lazy drift of gulls overhead,
    and tiny points of light
25        bubbling in the channel.
It was the tag-end of summer.
    From the harbor's mouth
    you coasted into sight,
flashing news of your advent,
30        the crescent of your dorsal fin°
    clipping the diamonded surface.
We cheered at the sign of your greatness
    when the black barrel of your head
    erupted, ramming the water,
35  and you flowered for us
    in the jet of your spouting.

3

All afternoon you swam
    tirelessly round the bay,
    with such an easy motion,
40  the slightest downbeat of your tail,
    an almost imperceptible
    undulation of your flippers,
you seemed like something poured,
    not driven; you seemed
45        to marry grace with power.
And when you bounded into air,
    slapping your flukes,°
    we thrilled to look upon
pure energy incarnate
50    as nobility of form.
    You seemed to ask of us
not sympathy, or love,
    or understanding,
        but awe and wonder.

---

30 *dorsal:* back fin.
47 *flukes:* the two flattened portions of a whale's tail.

55      That night we watched you
            swimming in the moon.
        Your back was molten silver.
    We guessed your silent passage
        by the phosphorescence in your wake.
60          At dawn we found you stranded on the rocks.


                            4


    There came a boy and a man
        and yet other men running, and two
            schoolgirls in yellow halters
    and a housewife bedecked
65          with curlers, and whole families in beach
            buggies with assorted yelping dogs.
    The tide was almost out.
        We could walk around you,
            as you heaved deeper into the shoal,
70  crushed by your own weight,
        collapsing into yourself,
            your flippers and your flukes
    quivering, your blowhole
        spasmodically bubbling, roaring.
75          In the pit of your gaping mouth
    you bared your fringework of baleen,°
        a thicket of horned bristles.
            When the Curator of Mammals
    arrived from Boston
80          to take samples of your blood
            you were already oozing from below.
    Somebody had carved his initials
        in your flank. Hunters of souvenirs
            had peeled off strips of your skin,
85  a membrane thin as paper.
        You were blistered and cracked by the sun.
            The gulls had been pecking at you.
    The sound you made was a hoarse and fitful bleating.

    What drew us, like a magnet, to your dying?
90      You made a bond between us,
            the keepers of the nightfall watch,
    who gathered in a ring around you,
        boozing in the bonfire light.
            Toward dawn we shared with you
95  your hour of desolation,
        the huge lingering passion
            of your unearthly outcry,
    as you swung your blind head
        toward us and laboriously opened
100         a bloodshot, glistening eye,
    in which we swam with terror and recognition.

---

76 *baleen:* a horny sieve in the mouths of some whale species that strains and collects food.

5

Voyager, chief of the pelagic° world,
　　you brought with you the myth
　　　　of another country, dimly remembered,
105　　where flying reptiles
　　　　lumbered over the steaming marshes
　　　　　　and trumpeting thunder lizards
wallowed in the reeds.
　　　　While empires rose and fell on land,
110　　　　your nation breasted the open main,
rocked in the consoling rhythm
　　of the tides. Which ancestor first plunged
　　　　head-down through zones of colored twilight
to scour the bottom of the dark?
115　　　　You ranged the North Atlantic track
　　　　　　from Port-of-Spain to Baffin Bay,°
edging between the ice-floes
　　through the fat of summer,
　　　　lob-tailing, breaching, sounding,°
120　　grazing in the pastures of the sea
　　　　on krill-rich orange plankton,°
　　　　　　crackling with life.
You prowled down the continental shelf,
　　guided by the sun and stars
125　　　　and the taste of alluvial silt°
on your way southward
　　to the warm lagoons,
　　　　the tropic of desire,
where the lovers lie belly to belly
130　　in the rub and nuzzle of their sporting;
　　　　and you turned, like a god in exile,
out of your wide primeval element,
　　delivered to the mercy of time.
　　　　Master of the whale-roads,°
135　　let the white wings of the gulls
　　　　spread out their cover.
　　　　　　You have become like us,
disgraced and mortal.

　　　　　　　　　　　　　　　　　　1983

---

102 *pelagic*: of the open sea.
116 *Baffin Bay*: running north from the Trinidad town of Port-of-Spain to Greenland's Baffin Bay.
119 *sounding*: diving suddenly toward the ocean depths.
121 *plankton*: tiny organisms strained by whale baleen for food.
125 *alluvial silt*: debris deposited from running water.
134 *whale-road*: an Old English figure for the sea.

## The Snakes of September

All summer I heard them
rustling in the shrubbery,
outracing me from tier
to tier in my garden,
5    a whisper among the viburnums,
a signal flashed from the hedgerow,
a shadow pulsing
in the barberry thicket.
Now that the nights are chill
10   and the annuals spent,
I should have thought them gone,
in a torpor of blood
slipped to the nether world
before the sickle frost.
15   Not so. In the deceptive balm
of noon, as if defiant of the curse
that spoiled another garden,
these two appear on show
through a narrow slit
20   in the dense green brocade
of a north-country spruce,
dangling head-down, entwined
in a brazen love-knot.
I put out my hand and stroke
25   the fine, dry grit of their skins.
After all,
we are partners in this land,
co-signers of a covenant.
At my touch the wild
30   braid of creation
trembles.

*1985*

# Joseph Kalar (1906–1972)

Joseph Kalar worked in the lumber and papermill industries and then became active in union activities and the political efforts of the Farm Labor Party of Minnesota. From 1928–1930 he traveled across the country taking odd jobs and reporting to the radical journal *New Masses* on conditions everywhere he went. In addition to poetry, he published fiction and a particularly savage brand of cultural satire. Along with Sol Funaroff, Edwin Rolfe, and Herman Spector, he was one of the poets presented in the collection *We Gather Strength* (1933). "Papermill" is one of the notable examples of the proletarian poetry of the 1930s. A limited edition of his work, *Joseph Kalar, Poet of Protest* was issued by his family in 1985.

## Papermill

    Not to be believed, this blunt savage wind
    Blowing in chill empty rooms, this tornado
    Surging and bellying across the oily floor
    Pushing men out in streams before it;
5   Not to be believed, this dry fall
    Of unseen fog drying the oil
    And emptying the jiggling greasecups;
    Not to be believed, this unseen hand
    Weaving a filmy rust of spiderwebs
10  Over these turbines and grinding gears,
    These snarling chippers and pounding jordans;°
    These fingers placed to lips saying shshsh;
    Keep silent, keep silent, keep silent;
    Not to be believed hardly, this clammy silence
15  Where once feet stamped over the oily floor,
    Dinnerpails clattered, voices rose and fell
    In laughter, curses, and songs. Now the guts
    Of this mill have ceased their rumbling, now
    The fires are banked and red changes to black,
20  Steam is cold water, silence is rust, and quiet
    Spells hunger. Look at these men, now,
    Standing before the iron gates, mumbling,
    "Who could believe it? Who could believe it?"

*1931*

---

11 *jordans:* machines employed at a paper mill.

# Richard Wright (1908–1960)

Born on a farm near Natchez, Mississippi, Wright understood racism and its impact on black lives early on. After growing up in the South, he moved to Chicago where he became active in the Communist Party's John Reed Club. Though primarily known for his fiction and autobiographies, work that transformed the landscape of African American writing, Wright also wrote a group of revolutionary poems during the 1930s, of which "We of the Streets" is an example. Wright's poetry is gathered together as "Appendix B" to Michael Fabre, *The World of Richard Wright* (1985).

## We of the Streets

Streets are full of the scent of us—odors of onions drifting from
    doorways, effluvium of baby new-born downstairs, seeping
    smells of warm soap-suds—the streets as lush with the fer-
    ment of our living.
Our sea is water swirling in gutters; our lightning is the blue flame
    of an acetylene torch; billboards blossom with the colors of a
    billion flowers; we hear thunder when the "L" roars; our
    strip of sky is a dirty shirt.
We have grown used to nervous landscapes, chimney-broken hori-
    zons, and the sun dying between tenements; we have grown
    to love streets, the ways of streets; our bodies are hard like
    worn pavement.
Our emblems are street emblems: stringy curtains blowing in win-
    dows; sticky-fingered babies tumbling on door-steps; deep-
    cellared laughs meant for everybody; slow groans heard in
    area-ways.
5    Our sunshine is a common hope; our common summer and com-
    mon winter a common joy and a common sorrow; our frater-
    nity is shoulder-rubbing, crude with unspoken love; our pass-
    word the wry smile that speaks a common fate.
Our love is nurtured by the soft flares of gas-lights; our hate is an
    icy wind screaming around corners.
And there is something in the streets that made us feel immortality
    when we rushed along ten thousand strong, hearing our
    chant fill the world, wanting to do what none of us would do
    alone, aching to shout the forbidden word, knowing that we
    of the streets are deathless. . . .

*1937*

# Theodore Roethke (1908–1963)

Roethke was born and raised in Saginaw, Michigan, where his family managed greenhouses, which were the subject of several of his early lyrics. In these densely nurtured spaces, Roethke began to forge a kind of mystical animism that stayed with him throughout his career. From these contained, miniature natural worlds, embodying a whole range of human sexual and generative impulses, he would eventually reach outward to the large-scale visionary landscape poems of "North American Sequence," landscapes at once meticulously observed and psychologically suggestive. Along the way he composed major elegies and love poems and a series of sequences that each broke unique ground. "The Lost Son" is a sequence of self-discovery that combines psychoanalytic depth with surrealism and elements from nursery rhyme technique. "Meditations of an Old Woman" is an astonishing identification with a female persona. Throughout these poems despair contends with a will to transcendence.

Roethke was educated at the University of Michigan and Harvard, and for the last decade and a half of his life taught at the University of Washington. He was subject throughout his adult life to frequent mood swings, sometimes alternating between extravagant bravado and paralyzing self-doubt. He also went on numerous drinking binges and suffered a series of mental breakdowns that required hospitalization, but he also clearly learned from them things he used in his writing.

## Cuttings

Sticks-in-a-drowse droop over sugary loam,
Their intricate stem-fur dries;
But still the delicate slips keep coaxing up water;
The small cells bulge;

5    One nub of growth
Nudges a sand-crumb loose,
Pokes through a musty sheath
Its pale tendrilous horn.

1948

## Cuttings
### (*later*)

This urge, wrestle, resurrection of dry sticks,
Cut stems struggling to put down feet,
What saint strained so much,
Rose on such lopped limbs to a new life?

5      I can hear, underground, that sucking and sobbing,
In my veins, in my bones I feel it,—
The small waters seeping upward,
The tight grains parting at last.
When sprouts break out,
10      Slippery as fish,
I quail, lean to beginnings, sheath-wet.

                                        *1948*


## Frau Bauman, Frau Schmidt, and Frau Schwartze°

Gone the three ancient ladies
Who creaked on the greenhouse ladders,
Reaching up white strings
To wind, to wind
5      The sweet-pea tendrils,° the smilax,°
Nasturtiums, the climbing
Roses, to straighten
Carnations, red
Chrysanthemums; the stiff
10      Stems, jointed like corn,
They tied and tucked,—
These nurses of nobody else.
Quicker than birds, they dipped
Up and sifted the dirt;
15      They sprinkled and shook;
They stood astride pipes,
Their skirts billowing out wide into tents,
Their hands twinkling with wet;
Like witches they flew along rows
20      Keeping creation at ease;
With a tendril for needle
They sewed up the air with a stem;
They teased out the seed that the cold kept asleep,—
All the coils, loops, and whorls.
25      They trellised° the sun; they plotted for more than themselves.

---

**poem title:** Roethke's family was of German origin; the father was a florist in Saginaw, Michigan, and Roethke played in his father's greenhouses as a child. The women in the title were among the greenhouse employees.
5 *tendrils:* tiny, twisting, threadlike growth by which a vine anchors itself.
5 *smilax:* slender vine with glossy foliage.
25 *trellised the sun:* in effect, not only trained plants to grow on trellises in the sunlight but also trained the very sun to grow on a trellis.

I remember how they picked me up, a spindly kid,
Pinching and poking my thin ribs
Till I lay in their laps, laughing,
Weak as a whiffet;°
30    Now, when I'm alone and cold in my bed,
They still hover over me,
These ancient leathery crones,
With their bandannas stiffened with sweat,
And their thorn-bitten wrists,
And their snuff-laden breath blowing lightly over me in my first
    sleep.

*1948*

from

# The Lost Son

## 1. The Flight

At Woodlawn° I heard the dead cry:
I was lulled by the slamming of iron,
A slow drip over stones,
Toads brooding wells.°
5    All the leaves stuck out their tongues;
I shook the softening chalk of my bones,
Saying,
Snail, snail, glister° me forward,
Bird, soft-sigh me home,
10    Worm, be with me.
This is my hard time.

Fished in an old wound,
The soft pond of repose;
Nothing nibbled my line,
15    Not even the minnows came.

Sat in an empty house
Watching shadows crawl,
Scratching.
There was one fly.

20    Voice, come out of the silence.
Say something.
Appear in the form of a spider
Or a moth beating the curtain.

---

29 *whiffet:* perhaps a corruption of "whippet," a small racing dog, hence a little (and as
yet unimportant) person.
1 *Woodlawn:* a cemetery in the Bronx in New York City.
4 *Toads brooding wells:* not merely brooding *in* wells but also evoking the depth of wells
in their brooding.
8 *glister:* archaic variant of glisten; snails produce a mucus trail along which they glide.

Tell me:
25  Which is the way I take;
Out of what door do I go,
Where and to whom?

Dark hollows said, lee to the wind,
The moon said, back of an eel,
30  The salt said, look by the sea,
Your tears are not enough praise,
You will find no comfort here,
In the kingdom of bang and blab.°

Running lightly over spongy ground,
35  Past the pasture of flat stones,
The three elms,
The sheep strewn on a field,
Over a rickety bridge
Toward the quick-water, wrinkling and rippling.

40  Hunting along the river,
Down among the rubbish, the bug-riddled foliage,
By the muddy pond-edge, by the bog-holes,
By the shrunken lake, hunting, in the heat of summer.

The shape of a rat?
45          It's bigger than that.
It's less than a leg
And more than a nose,
Just under the water
It usually goes.

50  Is it soft like a mouse?
Can it wrinkle its nose?
Could it come in the house
On the tips of its toes?

Take the skin of a cat
55  And the back of an eel,
Then roll them in grease,—
That's the way it would feel.

It's sleek as an otter
With wide webby toes
60  Just under the water
It usually goes.

1948

---

33 *bang and blab:* noise and idle chatter.

## I Knew a Woman

I knew a woman, lovely in her bones,
When small birds sighed, she would sigh back at them;
Ah, when she moved, she moved more ways than one:
The shapes a bright container can contain!
5 Of her choice virtues only gods should speak,
Or English poets who grew up on Greek
(I'd have them sing in chorus, cheek to cheek).

How well her wishes went! She stroked my chin,
She taught me Turn, and Counter-turn, and Stand;°
10 She taught me Touch, that undulant white skin;
I nibbled meekly from her proffered hand;
She was the sickle; I, poor I, the rake,
Coming behind her for her pretty sake
(But what prodigious mowing we did make).

15 Love likes a gander, and adores a goose:
Her full lips pursed, the errant note to seize;
She played it quick, she played it light and loose;
My eyes, they dazzled at her flowing knees;
Her several parts could keep a pure repose,
20 Or one hip quiver with a mobile nose
(She moved in circles, and those circles moved).

Let seed be grass, and grass turn into hay:
I'm martyr to a motion not my own;
What's freedom for? To know eternity.
25 I swear she cast a shadow white as stone.
But who would count eternity in days?
These old bones live to learn her wanton ways:
(I measure time by how a body sways).

*1958*

# North American Sequence

## The Longing

### I

On things asleep, no balm:
A kingdom of stinks and sighs,
Fetor of cockroaches, dead fish, petroleum,
Worse than castoreum of mink or weasels,
5 Saliva dripping from warm microphones,

---

9 *Turn . . . Stand:* Strophe, antistrophe, and epode, or the three stanzas around which the odes of the Greek poet Pindar (522–422 B.C.) are organized. Usually elevated in tone, Pindaric odes have a complex metrical structure reflecting the dance movements they were written to accompany. The pattern of the strophe is repeated in the antistrophe but not in the concluding epode.

Agony of crucifixion on barstools.
    Less and less the illuminated lips,
    Hands active, eyes cherished;
    Happiness left to dogs and children—
10     (Matters only a saint mentions!)
Lust fatigues the soul.
How to transcend this sensual emptiness?
(Dreams drain the spirit if we dream too long.)
In a bleak time, when a week of rain is a year,
15   The slag-heaps fume at the edge of the raw cities:
The gulls wheel over their singular garbage;
The great trees no longer shimmer;
Not even the soot dances.

And the spirit fails to move forward,
20   But shrinks into a half-life, less than itself,
Falls back, a slug, a loose worm
Ready for any crevice,
An eyeless starer.

2

A wretch needs his wretchedness. Yes.
25   O pride, thou art a plume upon whose head?

How comprehensive that felicity! . . .
A body with the motion of a soul.
What dream's enough to breath in? A dark dream.
The rose exceeds, the rose exceeds us all.
30   Who'd think the moon could pare itself so thin?
A great flame rises from the sunless sea;
The light cries out, and I am there to hear—
I'd be beyond; I'd be beyond the moon,
Bare as a bud, and naked as a worm.

35   To this extent I'm a stalk.
    —How free; how all alone.
Out of these nothings
    —All beginnings come.

3

I would with the fish, the blackening salmon, and the mad
    lemmings,
40   The children dancing, the flowers widening.
Who sighs from far away?
I would unlearn the lingo of exasperation, all the distortions of
    malice and hatred;
I would believe my pain: and the eye quiet on the growing rose;
I would delight in my hands, the branch singing, altering the
    excessive bird;

45 I long for the imperishable quiet at the heart of form;
I would be a stream, winding between great striated rocks in late
summer;
A leaf, I would love the leaves, delighting in the redolent disorder
of this mortal life,
This ambush, this silence,
Where shadow can change into flame,
50 And the dark be forgotten.
I have left the body of the whale, but the mouth of the night is
still wide;
On the Bullhead, in the Dakotas, where the eagles eat well,
In the country of few lakes, in the tall buffalo grass at the base of
the clay buttes,
In the summer heat, I can smell the dead buffalo,
55 The stench of their damp fur drying in the sun,
The buffalo chips drying.

Old men should be explorers?°
I'll be an Indian.
Ogalala?
60 Iroquois.

## Meditation at Oyster River

I

Over the low, barnacled, elephant-colored rocks,
Come the first tide-ripples, moving, almost without sound, toward
me,
Running along the narrow furrows of the shore, the rows of dead
clam shells;
Then a runnel behind me, creeping closer,
5 Alive with tiny striped fish, and young crabs climbing in and out of
the water.

No sound from the bay. No violence.
Even the gulls quiet on the far rocks,
Silent, in the deepening light,
Their cat-mewing over,
10 Their child-whimpering.

At last one long undulant ripple,
Blue-black from where I am sitting,
Makes almost a wave over a barrier of small stones,
Slapping lightly against a sunken log.
15 I dabble my toes in the brackish foam sliding forward,
Then retire to a rock higher up on the cliff-slide.
The wind slackens, light as a moth fanning a stone:
A twilight wind, light as a child's breath
Turning not a leaf, not a ripple.
20 The dew revives on the beach-grass;

---

57 *explorers*: T.S. Eliot writes "Old men ought to be explorers" at the end of his poem "East
Coker."

The salt-soaked wood of a fire crackles;
A fish raven turns on its perch (a dead tree in the rivermouth),
Its wings catching a last glint of the reflected sunlight.

2

The self persists like a dying star,
25   In sleep, afraid. Death's face rises afresh,
Among the shy beasts, the deer at the salt-lick,
The doe with its sloped shoulders loping across the highway,
The young snake, poised in green leaves, waiting for its fly,
The hummingbird, whirring from quince-blossom to morning-
          glory—
30   With these I would be.
And with water: the waves coming forward, without cessation,
The waves, altered by sand-bars, beds of kelp, miscellaneous
          driftwood,
Topped by cross-winds, tugged at by sinuous undercurrents
The tide rustling in, sliding between the ridges of stone,
35   The tongues of water, creeping in, quietly.

3

In this hour,
In this first heaven of knowing,
the flesh takes on the pure poise of the spirit,
Acquires, for a time, the sandpiper's insouciance,
40   The hummingbird's surety, the kingfisher's cunning—
I shift on my rock, and I think:
Of the first trembling of a Michigan brook in April,
Over a lip of stone, the tiny rivulet;
And that wrist-thick cascade tumbling from a cleft rock,
45   Its spray holding a double rain-bow in early morning,
Small enough to be taken in, embraced, by two arms,—
Or the Tittebawasee, in the time between winter and spring,
When the ice melts along the edges in early afternoon.
And the midchannel begins cracking and heaving from the pressure
          beneath,
50   The ice piling high against the iron-bound spiles,
Gleaming, freezing hard again, creaking at midnight—
And I long for the blast of dynamite,
The sudden sucking roar as the culvert loosens its debris of
          branches and sticks,
Welter of tin cans, pails, old bird nests, a child's shoe riding a log,
55   As the piled ice breaks away from the battered spiles,
And the whole river begins to move forward, its bridges shaking.

4

Now, in this waning of light,
I rock with the motion of morning;
In the cradle of all that is,
60   I'm lulled into half-sleep

By the lapping of water,
Cries of the sandpiper.
Water's my will, and my way,
And the spirit runs, intermittently,
65  In and out of the small waves,
runs with the intrepid shorebirds—
How graceful the small before danger!

In the first of the moon,
All's a scattering,
70  A shining.

## Journey to the Interior

1

In the long journey out of the self,
There are many detours, washed-out interrupted raw places
Where the shale slides dangerously
And the back wheels hang almost over the edge
5  At the sudden veering, the moment of turning.
Better to hug close, wary of rubble and falling stones.
The arroyo cracking the road, the wind-bitten buttes, the canyons,
Creeks swollen in midsummer from the flash-flood roaring into the
        narrow valley.
Reeds beaten flat by wind and rain,
10  Grey from the long winter, burnt at the base in the late summer.
—Or the path narrowing,
Winding upward toward the stream with its sharp stones,
The upland of alder and birchtrees,
Through the swamp alive with quicksand,
15  The way blocked at last by a fallen fir-tree,
The thickets darkening,
The ravines ugly.

2

I remember how it was to drive in gravel,
Watching for dangerous down-hill places, where the wheels whined
        beyond eighty—
20  When you hit the deep pit at the bottom of the swale,
The trick was to throw the car sideways and charge over the hill,
        full of the throttle.
Grinding up and over the narrow road, spitting and roaring.
A chance? Perhaps. But the road was part of me, and its ditches,
And the dust lay thick on my eyelids,—Who ever wore goggles?—
25  Always a sharp turn to the left past a barn close to the roadside,
To a scurry of small dogs and a shriek of children,
The highway ribboning out in a straight thrust to the North,
To the sand dunes and fish flies, hanging, thicker than moths,
Dying brightly under the street lights sunk in coarse concrete,

30   The towns with their high pitted road-crowns and deep gutters,
     Their wooden stores of silvery pine and weather-beaten red
          courthouses,
     An old bridge below with a buckled iron railing, broken by some
          idiot plunger;
     Underneath, the sluggish water running between weeds, broken
          wheels, tires, stones.
     And all flows past—
35   The cemetery with two scrubby trees in the middle of the prairie,
     The dead snakes and muskrats, the turtles gasping in the rubble,
     The spikey purple bushes in the winding dry creek bed—
     the floating hawks, the jackrabbits, the grazing cattle—
     I am not moving but they are,
40   And the sun comes out of a blue cloud over the Tetons,
     While, farther away, the heat-lightning flashes.
     I rise and fall in the slow sea of a grassy plain,
     The wind veering the car slightly to the right,
     Whipping the line of white laundry, bending the cottonwoods
          apart,
45   The scraggly wind-break of a dusty ranch-house.
     I rise and fall, and time folds
     Into a long moment;
     And I hear the lichen speak,
     And the ivy advance with its white lizard feet—
50   On the shimmering road,
     On the dusty detour.


                              3


     I see the flower of all water, above and below me, the never
          receding,
     Moving, unmoving in a parched land, white in the moonlight:
     The soul at a still-stand,
55   At ease after rocking the flesh to sleep,
     Petals and reflections of petals mixed on the surface of a glassy
          pool,
     And the waves flattening out when the fishermen drag their nets
          over the stones.

     In the moment of time when the small drop forms, but does not
          fall,
     I have known the heart of the sun,—
60   In the dark and light of a dry place,
     In a flicker of fire brisked by a dusty wind.
     I have heard, in a drip of leaves,
     A slight song,
     After the midnight cries.

65   I rehearse myself for this:
     The stand at the stretch in the face of death,
     Delighting in surface change, the glitter of light on waves,
     And I roam elsewhere, my body thinking,
     turning toward the other side of light,

70    In a tower of wind, a tree idling in air,
Beyond my own echo,
Neither forward nor backward,
Unperplexed, in a place leading nowhere.

As a blind man, lifting a curtain, knows it is morning,
75    I know this change:
On one side of silence there is no smile;
But when I breathe with the birds,
The spirit of wrath becomes the spirit of blessing,
And the dead begin from their dark to sing in my sleep.

## The Long Waters

### I

Whether the bees have thoughts, we cannot say,
But the hind part of the worm wiggles the most,
Minnows can hear, and butterflies, yellow and blue,
Rejoice in the language of smells and dancing.
5    Therefore I reject the world of the dog
Though he hear a note higher than C
And the thrush stopped in the middle of his song.

And I acknowledge my foolishness with God,
My desire for the peaks, the black ravines, the rolling mists
10    Changing with every twist of wind,
The unsinging fields where no lungs breathe,
Where light is stone.
I return where fire has been,
To the charred edge of the sea
15    Where the yellowish prongs of grass poke through the blackened
        ash,
And the bunched logs peel in the afternoon sunlight,
Where the fresh and salt waters meet,
And the sea-winds move through the pine trees,
A country of bays and inlets, and small streams flowing seaward.

### 2

20    Mnetha, Mother of Har, protect me
From the worm's advance and retreat, from the butterfly's havoc,
From the slow sinking of the island peninsula, the coral
        efflorescence,
The dubious sea-change, the heaving sands, and my tentacled sea-
        cousins.

But what of her?—
25    Who magnifies the morning with her eyes,
That star winking beyond itself,
The cricket-voice deep in the midnight field,
The blue jay rasping from the stunted pine.

How slowly pleasure dies!—
30      The dry bloom splitting in the wrinkled vale,
The first snow of the year in the dark fir.
Feeling, I still delight in my last fall.

### 3

In time when the trout and young salmon leap for the low-flying
        insects,
And the ivy-branch, cast to the ground, puts down roots into the
        sawdust,
35      And the pine, whole with its roots, sinks into the estuary,
Where it leans, tilted east, a perch for the osprey,
And a fisherman dawdles over a wooden bridge,
These waves, in the sun, remind me of flowers:
The lily's piercing white,
40      The mottled tiger, best in the corner of a damp place,
The heliotrope, veined like a fish, the persistent morning-glory,
And the bronze of a dead burdock at the edge of a prairie lake,
Down by the muck shrinking to the alkaline center.

I have come here without courting silence,
45      Blessed by the lips of a low wind,
To a rich desolation of wind and water,
To a landlocked bay, where the salt water is freshened
By small streams running down under fallen fir trees.

### 4

In the vaporous grey of early morning,
50      Over the thin, feathery ripples breaking lightly against the irregular
        shoreline—
Feathers of the long swell, burnished, almost oily—
A single wave comes in like the neck of a great swan
Swimming slowly, its back ruffled by the light cross-winds,
To a tree lying flat, its crown half broken.

55      I remember a stone breaking the eddying current,
Neither white nor red, in the dead middle way,
Where impulse no longer dictates, nor the darkening shadow,
A vulnerable place,
Surrounded by sand, broken shells, the wreckage of water.

### 5

60      As light reflects from a lake, in late evening,
When bats fly, close to slightly tilting brownish water,
And the low ripples run over a pebbly shoreline,
As a fire, seemingly long dead, flares up from a downdraft of air in
        a chimney,
Or a breeze moves over the knees from a low hill,
65      So the sea wind wakes desire.
My body shimmers with a light flame.

I see in the advancing and retreating waters
The shape that came from my sleep, weeping:
The eternal one, the child, the swaying vine branch,
70    The numinous ring around the opening flower,
The friend that runs before me on the windy headlands,
Neither voice nor vision.

I, who came back from the depths laughing too loudly,
Become another thing;
75    My eyes extend beyond the farthest bloom of the waves;
I lose and find myself in the long water;
I am gathered together once more;
I embrace the world.

## The Far Field

### 1

I dream of journeys repeatedly:
Of flying like a bat deep into a narrowing tunnel,
Of driving alone, without luggage, out a long peninsula,
The road lined with snow-laden second growth,
5    A fine dry snow ticking the windshield,
Alternate snow and sleet, no on-coming traffic,
And no lights behind, in the blurred side-mirror,
The road changing from glazed tarface to a rubble of stone,
Ending at last in a hopeless sand-rut,
10    Where the car stalls,
Churning in a snowdrift
Until the headlights darken.

### 2

At the field's end, in the corner missed by the mower,
Where the turf drops off into a grass-hidden culvert,
15    Haunt of the cat-bird, nesting-place of the field-mouse,
Not too far away from the ever-changing flower-dump,
Among the tin cans, tires, rusted pipes, broken machinery,—
One learned of the eternal;
And in the shrunken face of a dead rat, eaten by rain and ground-
    beetles
20    (I found it lying among the rubble of an old coal bin)
And the tom-cat, caught near the pheasant-run,
Its entrails strewn over the half-grown flowers,
Blasted to death by the night watchman.

I suffered for birds, for young rabbits caught in the mower,
25    My grief was not excessive.
For to come upon warblers in early May
Was to forget time and death:
How they filled the oriole's elm, a twittering restless cloud, all one
    morning,

And I watched and watched till my eyes blurred from the bird
    shapes,—
30    Cape May, Blackburnian, Cerulean,—°
Moving, elusive as fish, fearless,
Hanging, bunched like young fruit, bending the end branches,
Still for a moment,
Then pitching away in half-flight,
35    Lighter than finches,
While the wrens bickered and sang in the half-green hedgerows,
And the flicker drummed from his dead tree in the chicken-yard.

—Or to lie naked in sand,
In the silted shallows of a slow river,
40    Fingering a shell,
Thinking:
Once I was something like this, mindless,
Or perhaps with another mind, less peculiar;
Or to sink down to the hips in a mossy quagmire;
45    Or, with skinny knees, to sit astride a wet log,
Believing:
I'll return again,
As a snake or a raucous bird,
Or, with luck, as a lion.

50    I learned not to fear infinity,
The far field, the windy cliffs of forever,
The dying of time in the white light of tomorrow,
The wheel turning away from itself,
The sprawl of the wave,
55    The on-coming water.

### 3

The river turns on itself,
The tree retreats into its own shadow.
I feel a weightless change, a moving forward
As of water quickening before a narrowing channel
60    When banks converge, and the wide river whitens;
Or when two rivers combine, the blue glacial torrent
And the yellowish-green from the mountainy upland,—
At first a swift rippling between rocks,
Then a long running over flat stones
65    Before descending to the alluvial plain,
To the clay banks, and the wild grapes hanging from the elmtrees.
The slightly trembling water
Dropping a fine yellow silt where the sun stays;
And the crabs bask near the edge,
70    The weedy edge, alive with small snakes and bloodsuckers,—
I have come to a still, but not a deep center,
A point outside the glittering current;
My eyes stare at the bottom of a river,

---

30 *Cerulean:* three species of warblers.

At the irregular stones, iridescent sandgrains,
75  My mind moves in more than one place,
In a country half-land, half-water.

I am renewed by death, thought of my death,
The dry scent of a dying garden in September,
The wind fanning the ash of a low fire.
80  What I love is near at hand,
Always, in earth and air.

4

The lost self changes,
Turning toward the sea,
A sea-shape turning around,—
85  An old man with his feet before the fire,
In robes of green, in garments of adieu.

A man faced with his own immensity
Wakes all the waves, all their loose wandering fire.
The murmur of the absolute, the why
90  Of being born fails on his naked ears.
His spirit moves like a monumental wind
That gentles on a sunny blue plateau.
He is the end of things, the final man.

All finite things reveal infinitude:
95  The mountain with its singular bright shade
Like the blue shine on freshly frozen snow,
The after-light upon ice-burdened pines;
Odor of basswood on a mountain-slope,
A scent beloved of bees;
100  Silence of water above a sunken tree:
The pure serene of memory in one man,—
A ripple widening from a single stone
Winding around the waters of the world.

# The Rose

1

There are those to whom place is unimportant,
But this place, where sea and fresh water meet,
Is important—
Where the hawks sway out into the wind,
5  Without a single wingbeat,
And the eagles sail low over the fir trees,
And the gulls cry against the crows
In the curved harbors;
And the tide rises up against the grass
10  Nibbled by sheep and rabbits.

A time for watching the tide,
For the heron's hieratic fishing,
For the sleepy cries of the towhee,
The morning birds gone, the twittering finches,
15      But still the flash of the kingfisher, the wingbeat of the scoter,
The sun a ball of fire coming down over the water,
The last geese crossing against the reflected afterlight,
The moon retreating into a vague cloud-shape
To the cries of the owl, the eerie whooper.
20      The old log subsides with the lessening waves,
And there is silence.

I sway outside myself
Into the darkening currents,
Into the small spillage of driftwood,
25      The waters swirling past the tiny headlands.
Was it here I wore a crown of birds for a moment
While on a far point of the rocks
The light heightened,
And below, in a mist out of nowhere,
30      The first rain gathered?

2

As when a ship sails with a light wind—
The waves less than the ripples made by rising fish,
The lacelike wrinkles of the wake widening, thinning out,
Sliding away from the traveler's eye,
35      The prow pitching easily up and down,
The whole ship rolling slightly sideways,
The stern high, dipping like a child's boat in a pond—
Our motion continues.

But this rose, this rose in the sea-wind,
40      Stays,
Stays in its true place,
Flowering out of the dark,
Widening at high noon, face upward,
A single wild rose, struggling out of the white embrace of the
        morning-glory,
45      Out of the briary hedge, the tangle of matted underbrush,
Beyond the clover, the ragged hay,
Beyond the sea pine, the oak, the wind-tipped madrona,
Moving with the waves, the undulating driftwood,
Where the slow creek winds down to the black sand of the shore
50      With its thick grassy scum and crabs scuttling back into their
        glistening craters.

And I think of roses, roses,
White and red, in the wide six-hundred-foot greenhouses,
And my father standing astride the cement benches,
Lifting me high over the four-foot stems, the Mrs. Russells, and his
        own elaborate hybrids,

55    And how those flowerheads seemed to flow toward me, to beckon
          me, only a child, out of myself.

      What need for heaven, then,
      With that man, and those roses?

                              3

      What do they tell us, sound and silence?
      I think of American sounds in this silence:
60    On the banks of the Tombstone, the wind-harps having their say,
      The thrush singing alone, that easy bird,
      The killdeer whistling away from me,
      The mimetic chortling of the catbird
      Down in the corner of the garden, among the raggedy lilacs,
65    The bobolink skirring from a broken fencepost,
      The bluebird, lover of holes in old wood, lilting its light song,
      And that thin cry, like a needle piercing the ear, the insistent
          cicada,
      And the ticking of snow around oil drums in the Dakotas,
      The thin whine of telephone wires in the wind of a Michigan
          winter,
70    The shriek of nails as old shingles are ripped from the top of a
          roof,
      The bulldozer backing away, the hiss of the sandblaster,
      And the deep chorus of horns coming up from the streets in early
          morning.
      I return to the twittering of swallows above water,
      And that sound, that single sound,
75    When the mind remembers all,
      And gently the light enters the sleeping soul,
      A sound so thin it could not woo a bird,

      Beautiful my desire, and the place of my desire.

      I think of the rock singing, and light making its own silence,
80    At the edge of a ripening meadow, in early summer,
      The moon lolling in the close elm, a shimmer of silver,
      Or that lonely time before the breaking of morning
      When the slow freight winds along the edge of the ravaged hillside,
      And the wind tries the shape of a tree,
85    While the moon lingers,
      And a drop of rain water hangs at the tip of a leaf
      Shifting in the wakening sunlight
      Like the eye of a new-caught fish.

                              4

      I live with the rocks, their weeds,
90    Their filmy fringes of green, their harsh
      Edges, their holes
      Cut by the sea-slime, far from the crash
      Of the long swell,

The oily, tar-laden walls
95      Of the toppling waves,
Where the salmon ease their way into the kelp beds,
And the sea rearranges itself among the small islands.

Near this rose, in this grove of sun-parched, wind-warped
          madronas,
Among the half-dead trees, I came upon the true ease of myself,
100     As if another man appeared out of the depths of my being,
And I stood outside myself,
Beyond becoming and perishing,
A something wholly other,
As if I swayed out on the wildest wave alive,
105     And yet was still.
And I rejoiced in being what I was:
In the lilac change, the white reptilian calm,
In the bird beyond the bough, the single one
With all the air to greet him as he flies,
110     The dolphin rising from the darkening waves;

And in this rose, this rose in the sea-wind,
Rooted in stone, keeping the whole of light,
Gathering to itself sound and silence—
Mine and the sea-wind's.

                                                          *1964*

# George Oppen (1908–1984)

Born in New York and raised in San Francisco, Oppen enrolled at Oregon State University but left after his future wife, also a student there, was expelled when they stayed out all night on a date. The couple went to France, where they founded a small press, publishing Louis Zukofsky's *An "Objectivists" Anthology* in 1932. In addition to Oppen and Zukofsky, the loose confederation of objectivists included Pound, Reznikoff, and Williams. All shared at least a partial interest in the material presence of the poem and in its linguisticality. Oppen returned to New York in 1933 and published his first book, *Discrete Series*, the following year. Then, in the midst of the country's political, social, and economic crisis, he stopped publishing poetry and devoted himself to the New York State Workers Alliance. In the following decade, he took up a variety of other projects for the Communist Party, meanwhile supporting himself as a factory worker in Detroit and a cabinetmaker in California. He served in the army in World War II and was wounded. Then in the 1950s, under the shadow of McCarthyism, Oppen, like so many other progressive artists, was hounded by the FBI and the inquisition. He left for Mexico, where he remained for eight years. On his return, he took up poetry again, publishing a series of books, the first appearing in 1962.

Oppen's poems can sometimes seem too cerebral, and they are certainly rhetorically restrained, with Oppen resisting elaborate metaphor, but they often display powerful feeling despite their constraint and frequent silences. They are also deeply invested in the problematics of language, with what can be said truthfully within a spare and heavily tested diction.

## Image of the Engine

I

Likely as not a ruined head gasket
Spitting at every power stroke, if not a crank shaft
Bearing knocking at the roots of the thing like a pile-driver:
A machine involved with itself, a concentrated
5     Hot lump of a machine
Geared in the loose mechanics of the world with the valves
     jumping
And the heavy frenzy of the pistons. When the thing stops,
Is stopped, with the last slow cough
In the manifold, the flywheel blundering
10   Against compression, stopping, finally

Stopped, compression leaking
From the idle cylinders will one imagine
Then because he can imagine
That squeezed from the cooling steel

15   There hovers in that moment, wraith-like and like a plume of
            steam, an aftermath,
A still and quiet angel of knowledge and of comprehension.

2

Endlessly, endlessly,
The definition of mortality

The image of the engine

20   That stops.
We cannot live on that.
I know that no one would live out
Thirty years, fifty years if the world were ending
With his life.

25   The machine stares out,
Stares out
With all its eyes

Thru the glass
With the ripple in it, past the sill

30   Which is dusty—If there is someone
In the garden!
Outside, and so beautiful.

3

What ends
Is that.

35            Even companionship
Ending.

'I want to ask if you remember
When we were happy! As tho all travels

Ended untold, all embarkations

40   Foundered.

4

On that water
Grey with morning
The gull will fold its wings
And sit. And with its two eyes

45   There as much as anything
Can watch a ship and all its hallways
And all companions sink.

5

*Also he has set the world*
*In their hearts.* From lumps, chunks,

50      We are locked out: like children, seeking love
At last among each other. With their first full strength
The young go search for it,

Native in the native air.
But even in the beautiful bony children
55      Who arise in the morning have left behind
them worn and squalid toys in the trash

Which is a grimy death of love. The lost
Glitter of the stores!
The streets of stores!
60      Crossed by the streets of stores
And every crevice of the city leaking
Rubble: concrete, conduit, pipe, a crumbling
Rubble of our roots

                 But they will find
65      In flood, storm, ultimate mishap:
Earth, water, the tremendous
Surface, the heart thundering
Absolute desire.

                                   *1962*

## In Alsace°

In Alsace, during the war, we found ourselves on the edge of the
Battle of the Bulge. The front was inactive, but we were spread so thin
that the situation was eerily precarious. We hardly knew where the next
squad was, and it was not in sight—a quiet and deserted hill in front
of us. We dug in near a farmhouse. Pierre Adam, tho he was a jour-
neyman mason, lived with his wife and his children in that farmhouse.

During the occupation the Germans had declared Alsace a part of
Greater Germany. Therefore they had drafted Alsatian men into the
German army. Many men, learning in their own way that they were to
be called, dug a hole. The word became a part of the language: *faire*
*une trou.* Some men were in those holes as long as two and three years.
It was necessary that someone should know where those holes were;

---

poem title: Alsace-Lorraine is an ancient region of eastern France bordering on Germany,
Luxembourg, and Switzerland. Germany gained control of the region after the Franco-
Prussian War (1870–1871), but France regained the territory after World War I. Seized
again by the Germans in World War II, it was liberated after the Allies landed in France
in 1944. The Battle of the Bulge lasted from December 16, 1944, to January 28, 1945.

in winter it was impossible for a man to come out of his hole without leaving footprints in the snow. While snow was actually falling, however, a friend could come to the hole with food and other help. Pierre, whom many people trusted, knew where some two dozen of those holes were.

The Germans became aware that men were going into hiding, and they began to make reprisals. If the man was young and unmarried, they killed his parents. If the man was married, they took his wife into Germany to the army brothels, it was said. They took the children into Germany, and it was not certain whether those children would remember where they came from. Pierre told me this story:

Men would come to Pierre and they would say: I am thinking of making a hole. Pierre would say: yes. They would say then: but if I do they will kill my parents; or: they will take my wife and my children. Then Pierre would say, he told me: *if* you dig a hole,   I will help you.

He knew, of course, what he was telling me. You must try to put yourself into those times. If one thought he knew anything, it was that a man should not join the Nazi army. Pierre himself learned, shortly before the Americans arrived, that he was about to be drafted. He and his wife discussed the children. They thought of tattooing the children's name and addresses on their chests so that perhaps they could be found after the war. But they thought that perhaps the tattooing would be cut out of the children . . . They did not, finally, have to make that decision, as it turned out. But what a conversation between a man and his wife—

There was an escape from that dilemma, as, in a way, there always is. Pierre told me of a man who, receiving the notification that he was to report to the German army, called a celebration and farewell at his home. Nothing was said at that party that was not jovial. They drank and sang. At the proper time, the host got his bicycle and waved goodbye. The house stood at the top of a hill and, still waving and calling farewells, he rode with great energy and as fast as he could down the hill, and, at the bottom, drove into a tree.

It must be hard to do. Probably easier in an automobile. There is, in an automobile, a considerable time during which you cannot change your mind. Riding a bicycle, since in those woods it is impossible that the tree should be a redwood, it must be necessary to continue aiming at the tree right up to the moment of impact. Undoubtedly difficult to do. And, of course, the children had no father. Thereafter.

*1968*

## Exodus

| Miracle of the children | the brilliant |
| Children      the word | |
| Liquid as woodlands | Children? |

When she was a child I read Exodus
5   To my daughter       'The children of Israel . . . '

Pillar of fire
Pillar of cloud

We stared at the end
Into each other's eyes        Where
10   She said hushed

Were the adults       We dreamed to each other
Miracle of the children
The brilliant children        Miracle

Of their brilliance        Miracle
of

1972

# Edwin Rolfe (1909-1954)

Born Solomon Fishman in New York, Rolfe grew up on Coney Island. He took the pen name Rolfe in high school and eventually adopted it as his only name. Both his parents were politically active, though they were committed to competing wings of the Communist Party. Rolfe began writing revolutionary poems while he was still in high school and was soon publishing them in the Party's newspaper, the *Daily Worker*. Along with Langston Hughes, he read his poems at the party's "Red Poets Night" in 1928, but the following year, disenchanted with rigid party functionaries and alienated by the infighting that helped destroy his parents' marriage, he quit the party and enrolled at the Experimental College at the University of Wisconsin. Two years later, in the midst of the Great Depression, it no longer seemed possible to opt out of revolutionary politics. Rolfe in any case had never abandoned his identification with working people or his theoretical devotion to international socialism. He returned to New York, rejoined the party, and became features editor of the *Daily Worker*. But the decisions to quit and rejoin, highly unconventional, would mark him as untrustworthy to some party bureaucrats thereafter. When the Spanish Civil War broke out, he recognized that fascism put the world at peril and saw the opportunity for a properly international political commitment. He joined the Abraham Lincoln Brigade in 1937. That summer he was in Madrid editing the English language magazine of the International Brigades; the following year he joined his comrades in the field for the Ebro campaign.

He had published his first book of poems in 1936; it was reviewed in the *New York Times Book Review*, accompanied by his photograph. It was the last mainstream attention he would receive until the *New York Review of Books* devoted a full page to his *Collected Poems* more than 50 years later. If his first book was focused on the Great Depression, his second, privately printed in 1951, was centered on Spain and pervaded by the haunting lyricism associated with the lost cause of the 1930s. By then Rolfe had been drafted for World War II service but was sent home when he became ill in training. He moved to Los Angeles in 1943, supporting his poetry writing by part-time work on the fringes of the motion picture industry. A breakthrough came in 1947, when Humphrey Bogart and Lauren Bacall were signed to star in a film based on one of his scripts, but within months the anticommunist House UnAmerican Activities Committee hearings arrived in Hollywood; Rolfe was blacklisted and his film abandoned by Warner Brothers. He then took up his last great subject, the nightmare of the long inquisition that culminated in McCarthyism, writing stronger poems on the topic than any other American. Some, like "Little Ballad for Americans—1954," or "Are You Now or Have You Ever Been," proved unpublishable at the time. After Rolfe died of a heart attack in 1954, poet Thomas McGrath assembled some of his poems for a posthumous volume, but a number of Rolfe's poems were not published until 1993.

## Asbestos°

Knowing (as John did) nothing of the way
men act when men are roused from lethargy,
and having nothing (as John had) to say
to those he saw were starving just as he

5    starved, John was like a workhorse. Day by day
he saw his sweat cement the granite tower
(the edifice his bone had built), to stay
listless as ever, older every hour.

John's deathbed is a curious affair:
10   the posts are made of bone, the spring of nerves,
the mattress bleeding flesh. Infinite air,
compressed from dizzy altitudes, now serves

his skullface as a pillow. Overhead
a vulture leers in solemn mockery,
15   knowing what John had never known: that dead
workers are dead before they cease to be.

*1928*

## Season of Death

This is the sixth winter:
this is the season of death
when lungs contract and the breath of homeless men
freezes on restaurant window panes—men seeking
5    the sight of rare food
before the head is lowered into the upturned collar
and the shoulders hunched and the shuffling feet
move away slowly, slowly disappear
into a darkened street.

10   This is the season when rents go up:
men die, and their dying is casual.
I walk along a street, returning
at midnight from my unit. Meet a man
leaning against an illumined wall
15   and ask him for a light.
                His open eyes
stay fixed on mine. And cold rain falling
trickles down his nose, his chin.
"Buddy," I begin . . . and look more closely—
20   and flee in horror from the corpse's grin.

---

**poem title:** The poem was titled "The 100 Percenter" when first published in the *Daily Worker* in 1928. It was retitled "Asbestos" for its 1933 reprinting in *We Gather Strength*.

The eyes pursue you even in sleep and
when you awake they stare at you from the ceiling;
you see the dead face peering from your shoes;
the eggs at Thompson's are the dead man's eyes.
25   Work dims them for eight hours, but then—
the machines silent—they appear again.

Along the docks, in the terminals, in the subway, on the street,
in restaurants—the eyes
are focused from the river
30   among the floating garbage
that other men fish for,
their hands around poles
almost in prayer—
wanting to live,
35   *wanting to live!* who also soon
will stand propped by death against a stone-cold wall.

                                                    *1935*


## First Love°

Again I am summoned to the eternal field
green with the blood still fresh at the roots of flowers,
green through the dust-rimmed memory of faces
that moved among the trees there for the last time
5    before the final shock, the glazed eye, the hasty mound.

But why are my thoughts in another country?
Why do I always return to the sunken road through corroded hills,
with the Moorish castle's shadow casting ruins over my shoulder
and the black-smocked girl approaching, her hands laden with
         grapes?

10   I am eager to enter it, eager to end it.
Perhaps this one will be the last one.
And men afterward will study our arms in museums
and nod their heads, and frown, and name the inadequate dates
and stumble with infant tongues over the strange place-names.

15   But my heart is forever captive of that other war
that taught me first the meaning of peace and of comradeship

and always I think of my friend who amid the apparition of bombs
saw on the lyric lake the single perfect swan.

                                                    *1943*

---

**poem title:** The poem was composed at Camp Wolters in Texas in 1943, while Rolfe was in training in the U.S. Army. He is reflecting on his 1937–1938 experience as a volunteer in the Spanish Civil War on the eve of returning to Europe to fight fascism yet again. Shortly after writing the poem Rolfe became ill and was discharged.

# Elegia°

Madrid   Madrid   Madrid   Madrid
I call your name endlessly, savor it like a lover.
Ten irretrievable years have exploded like bombs
since last I saw you, since last I slept
5      in your arms of tenderness and wounded granite.
Ten years since I touched your face in the sun,
ten years since the homeless Guadarrama winds°
moaned like shivering orphans through your veins
and I moaned with them.
                        When I think of you, Madrid,
10     locked in the bordello of the Universal Pimp,
the blood that rushes to my heart and head
blinds me, and I could strangle your blood-bespattered jailors,
choke them with these two hands which once embraced you.
When I think of your breathing body of vibrancy and sun,
15     silently I weep, in my own native land
which I love no less because I love you more.
Yet I know, in the heart of my heart, that until your liberation
rings through the world of free men near and far
I must wander like an alien everywhere.


20     Madrid, in these days of our planet's anguish,
forged by the men whose mock morality
begins and ends with the tape of the stock exchanges,
I too sometimes despair. I weep with your dead young poet.
Like him I curse our age and cite the endless wars,
25     the exiles, dangers, fears, our weariness
of blood, and blind survival, when so many
homes, wives, even memories, are lost.


Yes, I weep with Garcilaso.° I remember
your grave face and your subtle smile

---

**poem title:** (Spanish) "elegy." "Elegia" was written in Los Angeles in 1948, after the Hollywood blacklist was in place and the long postwar purge of the left had begun. Its sense of mourning for an antifascist alliance politics is thus relevant not only to Spain but also to the United States.

7 *Guadarrama winds:* Madrid is situated on a 2,120-foot high plateau, and it is encircled by the Guadarrama mountains to the north. The winds that sweep down off the Guadarrama mountains are a distinctive part of the city's climate.

28 "*Yes, I weep with Garcilaso*": Like Rolfe himself, and like some of the young men in the trenches in Madrid, Garcilaso de la Vega (1501–1536) was a soldier-poet. In an unpublished essay on poetics, Rolfe mentions that Garcilaso de la Vega's "First Elegy" is one of his favorite poems. His poetic output was small but highly polished, so that he became the undisputed classic poet of the Golden Age of Spanish literature. The recurrent theme in his poetry is love, and the melancholy and frustrated idealism with which it is treated no doubt owes something to his own unrequited love for Isabel Freire, a Portuguese lady-in-waiting to the Empress. Rolfe's own love for Madrid here is, of course, frustrated by Franco's domination of Spain. Although the balance of the stanza is addressed to Madrid, the reference to Garcilaso continues to permeate it. The sons and daughters of the city, when they fall in love, are also figuratively children of Garcilaso's romantic poems. Finally, it is worth noting that Garcilaso was mortally wounded when leading an assault on an unimportant but well-fortified position, a story with no lack of parallels to the battles of the Spanish Civil War.

30    and the heart-leaping beauty of your daughters and even
      the tattered elegance of your poorest sons.
      I remember the gaiety of your *milicianos*°—
      my comrades-in-arms. What other city
      in history ever raised a battalion of barbers
35    or reared its own young shirt-sleeved generals?
      And I recall them all. If I ever forget you,
      Madrid, Madrid, may my right hand lose its cunning.

      I speak to you, Madrid, as lover, husband, son.
      Accept this human trinity of passion.
40    I love you, therefore I am faithful to you
      and because to forget you would be to forget
      everything I love and value in the world.
      Who is not true to you is false to every man
      and he to whom your name means nothing never loved
45    and they who would use your flesh and blood again
      as a whore for their wars and their wise investments,
      may they be doubly damned! the double murderers
      of you and their professed but fictional honor,
      of everything untarnished in our time.

50    Wandering, bitter, in this bitter age,
      I dream of your broad avenues like brooks in summer
      with your loveliest children alive in them like trout.
      In my memory I walk the Calle de Velasquez°
      to the green Retiro and its green gardens.°
55    Sometimes when I pace the streets of my own city
      I am transported to the flowing Alcalá°
      and my footsteps quicken, I hasten to the spot
      where all your living streams meet the Gateway to the Sun.°
      Sometimes I brood in the shadowed Plaza Mayor°

---

32 *milicianos*: members of the largely untrained volunteer militias that rose up to defeat
the fascist rebels in cities like Madrid and Barcelona.

53 *Calle de Velasquez*: The Madrid Street where the International Brigades building was
located and where Rolfe edited the English language magazine of the brigades, *Volunteer
for Liberty*, from 1937 to the beginning of 1938.

54 *"the green Retiro and its green gardens"*: Spread out in the middle of Madrid, the *Re-
tiro* is one of Spain's most beautiful parks. It encompasses a lake and number of distinct
squares, open spaces, and formal gardens. Laid out in the seventeenth century, the park's
320 acres originally served as a royal retreat (*retiro*).

56 *Alcala*: A major highway that heads east from its origin in the *Puerta del Sol*. Rolfe of-
ten walked along the Alcala in the fall of 1937. In the 1930s, the portion of the Alcala in
the downtown area was the major cafe street in the city.

58 *Gateway to the Sun: Puerta del Sol*, the central plaza of Madrid.

59 *Plaza Mayor*: A beautifully proportioned, rectangular, seventeenth-century, cobbled, ar-
caded square. Some 130 yards long and 100 yards wide, it was planned by Felipe II and his
architect to serve as a public meeting place for the new capital; it was finished in 1619 dur-
ing the reign of Felipe III. A 1613 bronze statue of Felipe III on horseback is in the cen-
ter of the square. The Plaza Mayor has been a frequent site for public spectacles—from
processions of flagellants and penitents to bullfights—as well as the site of some of Spain's
major public ceremonies—such as the crowning of kings—and the site, finally, of some of
its more traumatic historical moments. Thus it was here that the Inquisition held its *au-
tos-da-fe* and executed its victims. Balconies on all four sides of the square provided van-
tage points for spectators. The *Plaza Mayor* is located off *Calle Mayor*, a few blocks from
*Puerta del Sol*. The streets of Old Madrid radiate from the *Plaza Mayor*.

60      with the ghosts of old Kings and Inquisitors
        agitating the balconies with their idiot stares
        (which Goya later knew) and under whose stone arches,
        those somber rooms beneath the colonnades,
        the old watchmaker dreams of tiny, intricate minutes,
65      the old woman sells pencils and gaudy amber combs,
        dreaming of the days when her own body was young,
        and the rheumatic peasant with fingers gnarled as grapevines
        eagerly displays his muscat raisins;
        and the intense boys of ten, with smouldering aged eyes,
70      kneel, and gravely, quixotically,
        polish the rawhide boots of the soldiers in for an hour
        from the mined trenches of the Casa de Campo,°
        from their posts, buzzing with death, within the skeleton
        of University City.°
75                          And the girls stroll by,
        the young ones, conscious of their womanhood,
        and I hear in my undying heart called Madrid
        the soldiers boldly calling to them: Oye, guapa, oye!

        I remember your bookshops, the windows always crowded
80      with new editions of the Gypsy Ballads,°
        with *Poetas en la España Leal*

---

72 *Casa de Campo:* A sprawling wooded park northwest of the city that was the scene of
major fighting during the attacks on Madrid. Its hills and scrub brush made rapid troop
movement difficult but provided excellent cover for the nationalist troops. In the summer
of 1936, when terror reigned in both Nationalist and Republican cities, the Casa de Campo
was the scene of frequent summary executions.

74 *University City:* The hillside campus of the University of Madrid, which was the scene
of dramatic fighting during the struggle for the city. Hoping to end the war quickly with
one decisive stroke, Franco ordered a major assault against the Spanish capital in the fall
of 1936. After being halted by the people's militias, Franco's troops were preparing addi-
tional attacks on the city when the International Brigades marched through Madrid on
November 8th to take up positions in their first major battles. On November 9th Interna-
tional Brigade troops spear-headed a counter-attack among the gum and ilex trees of the
*Casa de Campo.* In a series of bloody bayonet charges ending in hand-to-hand combat, the
Internationals helped retake portions of the park, though Nationalist troops remained en-
trenched there. A week later, the Internationals were engaged in hand-to-hand combat in
University City, much of which was reduced to rubble in the process. Buildings were sand-
bagged; doors and windows were barricaded. Machine guns swept all the open approaches.
At one point, the ground floor of one building was held by the Thaelmann battalion of the
Internationals and the other floors by Franco's Moors. On another day, one room in the
Hall of Philosophy changed hands four times. The battle for University City continued un-
til November 23; the fascist advance had been stopped, but University City remained di-
vided between the opposing armies for the rest of the war. The grounds were deeply en-
trenched, tunnels were dug under streets exposed to fire, and various buildings remained
in either Nationalist or Republican hands.

80 *Gypsy Ballads* (*Romancero Gitano*, 1928): A book of poems by Federico García Lorca
that Rolfe acquired in Albacete in 1937. Lorca was murdered by Nationalist partisans just
after the outbreak of the Spanish Civil War.

and *Romanceros de los Soldados en las Trincheras.*°
There was never enough food, but always poetry.
Ah the flood of song that gushed with your blood
85          into the world during your three years of glory!

And I think: it is a fine thing to be a man
only when man has dignity and manhood.
It is a fine thing to be proud and fearless
only when pride and courage have direction, meaning.
90          And in our world no prouder words were spoken
in those three agonized years that *I am from Madrid.*

Now ten years have passed with small explosions of hope,
yet you remain, Madrid, the conscience of our lives.
So long as you endure, in chains, in sorrow,
95          I am not free, no one of us is free.
Any man in the world who does not love Madrid
as he loves a woman, as he values his sex,
that man is less than a man and dangerous,
and so long as he directs the affairs of our world
100          I must be his undying enemy.

Madrid   Madrid   Madrid   Madrid
Waking and sleeping, your name sings in my heart
and your need fills all my thoughts and acts
(which are gentle but have also been intimate with rifles).
105          Forgive me, I cannot love you properly from afar—
no distant thing is every truly loved—
but this, in the wrathful impotence of distance,
I promise: Madrid, if I ever forget you,
may my right hand lose its human cunning,
110          may my arms and legs wither in their sockets,
may my body be drained of its juices and my brain
go soft and senseless as an imbecile's.
And if I die before I can return to you,
or you, in fullest freedom, are restored to us,
115          my sons will love you as their father did
Madrid   Madrid   Madrid

*1948*

---

82 *Poetas en La España Leal and Romanceros de los Soldados en las Trincheras:* Two of a
number of poetry anthologies issued in Spain by Loyalist supporters during the war. *Po-
etas en la España Leal,* containing forty-four poems, was published in July of 1937 to honor
the Second International Congress of Anti-fascist Writers which met in Spain that year.
It was compiled by the editors of the journal *Hora de España,* which had previously pub-
lished most of the poems in the book. Rolfe's entry in his diary for September 11, 1937,
notes that he purchased three copies of *Poetas en la España Leal* in Madrid that day.

## After Tu Fu (A.D. 713–770)

The innocents were condemned to death in the Hall of Justice.
In the Hall of Peace, the war was declared.
In the name of Mercy, the bomb was dropped on the two cities.
O my maimed brothers, beloved stricken brothers,
5    dig deep again in the great caves of the East:
again our wise men talk in the Hall of Peace.

*c. 1953*

## Now the Fog

Now the fog falls on the land.
Imagination's eyes go blind.
And the smoke, sole residue of written wisdom,
bears poet and prophet to their doom,
5    their grave, their wavering edgeless tomb.

Knaves masqued like sovereigns decree
what we shall say, listen to, see.
The habit of slavery, long discarded,
becomes our normal comfortable suit.
10   Soon we will savor the spoiled fruit
as taste-buds wither on nerveless tongues.
The belly will defeat the brain
in combat perfunctory and painless,
and the gutted brain not find it hard
15   to crawl inside the colorless Pale
of a stamped official registration card.

And this was the land that Ponce found
seeking his lost youth; the land
young mariners, following old stars, set free . . .

20   The fog falls, settles, seeps into the land
among the despairing, the despised, the blind;
and only rare and blest oases of courage
mark the blurred landscape, lest even the iron
rust—in all of us, agèd and young—
of the English tongue.

*1950*

## A Letter to the Denouncers

Dear sir: the summum bonum is
Solvency, which sufficiently defined most simply means
Spuds in sufficient quantities,
an untapped phone, and daily pork and beans.

5   Sir, as you start for work each morning, please
    check your clothes-closet for skeletons,
    your dreams for inconsistencies,
    the radio in your car for microphones.

    This too remember: old man, tired man, fool,
10  after their final sessions with their analysts,
    shape all their Methods to one glowing Goal—
    Safety. And so they draw up lists.

    And *what* lists! One, born of maliciousness,
    another of envy, a third of gratitude—
15  name first the friend who straightened out their mess,
    then him who found them work, and self-respect, and bread.

    Naturally they're honest; they've merely changed their views.
    They flinch before the paradox of Means and Ends.
    So, hating dubious Means, each casually betrays
20  his benefactors, boon-companions, friends.

    A crazy crowd applauds these eager choristers
    who sing as wingless birds have never sung before.
    But you, dear friendless friends, dear lonely sirs,
    recall whom *you've* befriended, and beware, beware.

                                                    *c. 1952*

## Are You Now or Have You Ever Been

    I admit it: there was a moment of pity
    a vulnerable second of sympathy
    my defenses were down
    and I signed the letter asking clemency
5   for the six Negroes the letter
    hereinafter known as Exhibit A

    I signed the letter yes
    the signature is indubitably mine
    and later this at another time
10  I wrote a small check yes small
    since my income is small
    perhaps ten dollars not more
    for the fund these people were collecting
    to keep the refugees alive
15  and then again in a moment of weakness
    I promised and kept my promise
    to join the demonstration at the city hall
    protesting the raising of rents
    no you needn't show me the photograph
20  I was there I admit I was there

    but please   believe me
    everything I did was done through weakness if you will
    but it's strange how weakness of this kind snowballs
    multiplies

25 before they approached me with that innocent petition
I was may it please the court exactly
like you like every other man
I lived my own life solely suffered
only my own sorrows and enjoyed my own triumphs
30 small ones I grant you
asked nothing from
gave nothing to
any man
except myself my wife my children
35 so there you have it
it is all true
Exhibits A and B and C
and the witnesses don't lie
I wanted to help those six men stay alive
40 I thought them innocent
I honestly believed the rents were too high
(no, I own no tenements)
and the anguish of the refugees starving far from home
moved me I admit more than it should have
45 perhaps because I still retain
a fleeting childhood picture of my great grandfather's face
he too was a refugee

            *c. 1952*

## A Poem to Delight My Friends
## Who Laugh at Science-Fiction

That was the year
the small birds in their frail and delicate battalions
committed suicide against the Empire State,
having, in some never-explained manner,
5 lost their aerial radar, or ignored it.

That was the year
men and women everywhere stopped dying natural deaths.
The aged, facing sleep, took poison;
the infant, facing life, died with the mother in childbirth;
10 and the whole wild remainder of the population,
despairing but deliberate, crashed in auto accidents
on roads as clear and uncluttered as ponds.

That was the year every ship on every ocean,
every lake, harbor, river, vanished without trace;
15 and even ships docked at quays
turned over like harpooned whales, or wounded Normandies.

Yes, and the civilian transcontinental planes
found, like the war-planes, the sky-lanes crowded
and, praising Icarus, plunged to earth in flames.
20 Many, mild stay-at-homes, slipped in bath tubs,
others, congenital indoors-men, descending stairs,

and some, irrepressible roisterers, playing musical chairs.
Tots fell from scooter cars and tricycles
and casual passersby were stabbed by falling icicles.

25    Ah, what carnage! It was reported
that even bicarb and aspirin turned fatal,
and seconal too, to those with mild headaches,
whose stomachs were slightly acid, or who found they could not
    sleep.
All lovers died in bed, as all seafarers on the deep.

30    Till finally the only people left alive
were the soldiers sullenly spread on battlefields

among the shell-pocked hills and the charred trees.
Thus, even the indispensable wars died of ennui.

But not the expendable conscripts: they remained as always.
35    However, since no transport was available anywhere,
and home, in any case, was dead, and bare,
the soldiers wandered eternally
in their dazed, early-Chirico landscapes,
like drunken stars in their shrinking orbits
40    round and round and round and round

and (since I too died in the world-wide suicide)
they may still, for all I know, be there.
Like forsaken chessmen abandoned by paralyzed players.
they may still be there,
may still be there.

                                        *1953*


# In Praise Of

To understand the strength of those dark forces
phalanxed against him would have spelled surrender:
the spiked fist, the assassin's knife, the horses'
eyeless hooves above as he fell under.
5    To understand the sum of all this terror
would *a priori* have meant defeat, disaster.
Born of cold panic, error would pile on error,
heart and mind fall apart like fragile plaster.

Therefore I honor him, this simple man
10    who never clearly saw the threatening shapes, yet fought
his complex enemies, the whole sadistic clan,
persistently, although unschooled. Untaught,
he taught us, who could talk so glibly, what
the world's true shape should be like, and what not.

                                        *1953*

## Little Ballad for Americans—1954°

Brother, brother, best avoid your workmate—
Words planted in affection can spout a field of hate.

Housewife, housewife, never trust your neighbor—
A chance remark may boomerang to five years at hard labor.

5    Student, student, keep mouth shut and brain spry—
Your best friend Dick Merriwell's employed by the F.B.I.

Lady, lady, make your phone calls frugal—
The chief of all Inquisitors has ruled the wire-tap legal.

Daughter, daughter, learn soon your heart to harden—
10    They've planted stoolies everywhere; why not in kindergarten?

Lovers, lovers, be careful when you're wed—
The wire-tap grows in living-room, in auto, and in bed.

Give full allegiance only to circuses and bread;
No person's really trustworthy until he's dead.

*1954*

---

**poem title:** Rolfe's title no doubt alludes ironically to Earl Robinson's famous 1939 patriotic cantata *Ballad for Americans*, which set to music John Latouche's 1935 poem of the same title. The reference to Robinson's *Ballad for Americans* underlines the difference between the idealized image of America and its reality during the inquisition. *Ballad for Americans* is an inclusive, Whitmanesque celebration of all the ethnic, religious, and racial groups that make up America; during the McCarthy period, the dominant culture was obsessed instead with casting people out as un-American.

# Charles Olson (1910-1970)

Born and raised in Worcester, Massachusetts, the son of a postal worker, Olson was educated at Wesleyan, Harvard, and Yale universities. As a child he spent summers on the Massachusetts coast at Gloucester, the city that would be the setting for his major poem sequence *The Maximus Poems*. Anticipating a scholarly career, he completed doctoral research for a project on Herman Melville. It was interrupted by work for the American Civil Liberties Union in New York and for the Office of War Information in Washington. After resigning the latter job in protest against censorship, he proceeded to write *Call Me Ishmael,* a powerful, visionary study of Melville and the American obsession with space. Then he had the opportunity to fill in at Black Mountain College in North Carolina, which would become his home until 1956. He ended up running the college, and wrote many of his key early poems there, along with his widely read manifestoes on poetics, "Projective Verse" and "Human Universe."

One of the major practitioners of open form poetry, Olson often sought to record the mental process of composition in his poetry. *The Maximus Poems* in particular tracks ongoing perceptions while drawing in both classical allusions and references to modern science and philosophy. Often disjunctive, the poems can be lyrical at some moments, decidedly didactic at others. Because the sequence is difficult to represent effectively in excerpts, we have chosen one poem from the sequence that works well on its own (Cole's Island), along with one of Olson's more appealing independent poems, as introductions to his work.

## Variations Done for Gerald Van De Wiele°

### 1. Le Bonheur°

dogwood flakes
what is green

the petals
from the apple
5    blow on the road

---

**poem title:** Van De Wiele was a student at Black Mountain College in the 1950s while Olson was director there.
1 *Le Bonheur:* (French, "happiness"), title of a poem by French poet Arthur Rimbaud (1854–1891), the last text of Rimbaud's experimental sequence *A Season in Hell* (1873). A number of echoes of Rimbaud's book are woven into Olson's poem.

mourning doves
mark the sway
of the afternoon, bees
dig the plum blossoms

10  the morning
stands up straight, the night
is blue from the full of the April moon

iris and lilac, birds
birds, yellow flowers
15  white flowers, the Diesel
does not let up dragging
the plow

         as the whippoorwill,
the night's tractor, grinds
20  his song

         and no other birds but us
are as busy (O saisons,° o chateaux!

Délires!°

         What soul
25  is without fault?

Nobody studies
happiness

Every time the cock crows
I salute him

30  I have no longer any excuse
for envy. My life

has been given its orders: the seasons
seize

the soul and the body, and make mock
35  of any dispersed effort. The hour of death

is the only trespass

## II. The Charge

dogwood flakes
the green

the petals from the apple-trees
40  fall for the feet to walk on

---

22 *O saisons:* "Oh seasons, oh castles!"; the first line of "Le Bonheur."
23 *Délires:* ("frenzies") the title of two sections of *A Season in Hell.*

the birds are so many they are
loud, in the afternoon

they distract, as so many bees do
suddenly all over the place

45      With spring one knows today to see
that in the morning each thing

is separate but by noon
they have melted into each other

and by night only crazy things
50      like the full moon and the whippoorwill

and us, are busy. We are busy
if we can get by that whiskered bird,

that nightjar,° and get across, the moon
is our conversation, she will say

55      what soul
isn't in default?

can you afford not to make
the magical study

which happiness is? do you hear
60      the cock when he crows? do you know the charge,

that you shall have no envy, that your life
has its orders, that the seasons

seize you too, that no body and soul are one
if they are not wrought

65      in this retort? that otherwise efforts
are efforts? And that the hour of your flight

will be the hour of your death?

### III. Spring

The dogwood
lights up the day.

70      The April moon
flakes the night.

Birds, suddenly,
are a multitude

---

53 *nightjar:* a European bird of the goatsucker family, named for its harsh call.

The flowers are ravined°
75     by bees, the fruit blossoms

are thrown to the ground, the wind
the rain forces everything. Noise—

even the night is drummed
by whippoorwills, and we get

80     as busy, we plow, we move,
we break out, we love. The secret

which got lost neither hides
nor reveals itself, it shows forth

tokens. And we rush
85     to catch up. The body

whips the soul. In its great desire
it demands the elixir

In the roar of spring,
transmutations. Envy

90     drags herself off. The fault of the body and the soul
—that they are not one—

the matutinal° cock clangs
and singleness: we salute you

season of no bungling

                             *1960*

# Cole's Island

I met Death—he was a sportsman—on Cole's
Island.° He was a property-owner. Or maybe
Cole's Island, was his. I don't know. The
point was I was there, walking, and—as it
5     often is, in the woods—a stranger, suddenly
showing up, makes the very thing you were do-
ing no longer the same. That is suddenly
what you thought, when you were alone, and
doing what you were doing, changes because someone else
10    shows up. He didn't bother me, or say anything. Which is
not surprising, a person might not, in the circumstances;
or at most a nod or something. Or they would. But they wouldn't,

---

74 *ravined:* emptied out.
92 *matutinal:* morning.
2 *Cole's Island:* Located in West Gloucester on the Essex River, Cole's Island is not a true
island but is attached to the mainland by marshes and a road.

or you wouldn't think to either, if it was Death. And
He certainly was, the moment I saw him. There wasn't any
         question

15 about that even though he may have looked like a sort of country
gentleman, going about his own land. Not quite. Not it being He.

A fowler, maybe—as though he was used to
hunting birds, and was out, this morning, keeping
his hand in, so to speak, moving around, noticing
20 what game were about. And how they seemed. And how the woods
were. As a matter of fact just before he had shown up,
so naturally, and as another person might walk
up on a scene of your own, I had noticed
a cock and hen pheasant cross easily the
25 road I was on and had tried, in fact,
to catch my son's attention quick enough for him
to see before they did walk off into the bayberry
or arbor vitae along the road.

                My impression is we did—
30 that is, Death and myself, regard each other. And
there wasn't anything more than that, only that he had appeared,
and we did recognize each other—or I did, him, and he seemed
to have no question
about my presence there, even though I was uncomfortable.
35     That is,
Cole's Island
is a queer isolated and gated place, and I was only there by will
to know more of the topography of it lying as it does out
over the Essex River. And as it now is, with no tenants that one
    can speak of,
40 it's more private than almost any place one might imagine.
And down in that part of it where I did meet him (about half way
    between the
two houses over the river and the carriage house
at the entrance) it was as quiet and as much a piece
of the earth as any place can be. But my difficulty,
45 when he did show up, was immediately at least that I was
an intruder, by being there at all
and yet, even if he seemed altogether
used to Cole's Island, and, like I say, as though he owned it,
even if I was sure he didn't, I noticed him, and he me, and he
50 went on without anything extraordinary at all.

Maybe he had gaiters on, or almost
a walking stick, in other words much more
habited than I,
who was in chinos actually and
55 only doing what I had set myself to do here
& in other places on Cape Ann.

    It was his eye perhaps which makes me
render him as Death? It isn't true, there wasn't anything

that different about his eye,
60          it was not one thing more than that he was Death instantly
that he came into sight. Or that I was aware there was a person
here as well as myself. And son.

We did exchange some glance. That is the fullest possible
account I can give, of the encounter.

*1964*

# Sol Funaroff (1911–1942)

Funaroff was born of Russian parents; his father died in Palestine after the family fled across Europe. While Funaroff's mother was working in a sweatshop in 1915, the tenement they lived in on New York's Lower East Side slums burned down. Neighbors carried Sol gasping from the building, but his lungs were weak thereafter. As a child, he and his brother sold candy and fruit to garment workers. Later he worked in a matzo factory and in an upholstery shop. During the depression, Funaroff got part-time work as a relief investigator, as a reporter for the *New York World* and other news services, and did some editorial work for the *New Republic* and *Scribner's*. The WPA Writer's Project gave him some steady work in the late 1930s. Meanwhile he wrote poetry and became an important organizer for the proletarian poetry movement in the 1930s. He founded Dynamo Press, which published *Dynamo* magazine and books by Fearing, Rolfe, and Funaroff himself. His two poetry collections are *The Spider and the Clock* (1938) and the posthumous *Exile from a Future Time* (1943), from which the poems below are taken. "Going Mah Own Road" is from his musical in black dialect, *Tough Scufflin'*. "The Bull in the Olive Field" was written in response to the Spanish Civil War; during its opening months, Spanish workers rose up to put down the military rebellion in major cities. Always ill, Funaroff died young. The title of his second book is taken from lines in the opening poem of his first collection: "I am that exile / from a future time," he writes, "from shores of freedom / I may never know."

## The Man at the Factory Gate

A VAN DE LUBBE POEM

A man is tortured in a cell in Germany.
He is an innocent man. He committed no crime.
There are men like that in the prisons of America.
Men like that walk the streets of America
5    Millions of men in the streets await death.

Do you know this man? He is the son of poor workers.
He was a dock worker in the port of Hamburg.
He was a soldier in the war. He committed no crime
And he is tortured in a cell in Germany.

10   They gouge his eyes. They tear at his genitals.
They beat him with steel rods.

They burn matches under the soles of his feet.
Sit down. Stand up. Confess. Who was it?
Who was it burned the Reichstag?
15 Who?

Do you remember the man at the factory gate in the early
morning?
Do you recall the leaflets he gave you and your comrades?
Do you recall the slogans:
"Strike Against Wage-cuts! Fight Against Hunger!
20 Fight Against War and Fascism! Our cause is your cause!"?
Do you remember this man?

A man in a top-hat hacked his head on a block in Berlin.
His head was stuck on a pike in the streets of Shanghai.
His limbs were found in a shark in the Bay of Havana.
25 His body was burned under a tree in Alabama.
For good-luck charms, the citizens kept his fingers.

Do you remember the man at the factory gate in the early
morning?
Do you recall?
He was a good shoemaker. He was a poor fish peddler.
30 He was an organizer in a labor union in San Francisco.
He committed no crime, he is an innocent man.
He is a Communist. He is a leader of an oppressed people.

They gouge his eyes.
They burn matches under the soles of his feet.
35 They beat him with steel rods.
Sit down.   Stand up.   Who was it?
Who burned the Reichstag?
Who played with fire and lit an unquenchable flame?

*c. 1939*

## The Bull in the Olive Field°

With the first banderillas of daybreak
the darkness lowered its head,
a drip of bloody snot in its nostrils,
and Madrid awoke,
5 toreador in overalls:

A storm of people poured like rain
upon the face of the streets,
thundering with firearms
across barricades:

---

**poem title:** Written in response to the Spanish Civil War. See the note to Millay's "Say
That We Saw Spain Die" (p. 325).

10        Against the darkness bearing
          dust winds from the desert,
          hot blasts in the mouths of cannon,
          drouth and carnage in the olive land:

          Death, in his black cassock,
15        bull with the black hide,
          hooded, gold cross at the neck,
          fat and in folds like velvet;

          his crotch full, a purse with coins,
          rutted with the cows,
20        the whores of the old world,
          rotted with the disease
          in the rotten lands,

          The fields sickened
          in the hate of dry winds:

25        the hate hot in the mouths of clerks,
          the gatherers of taxes under
          the smoking rifles of civil guards;

          the hate hot in the brand of latifundia,
          seal of state stamped in the arroyos,
30        hooves in the gullies and stone-choked soil;

          and unloosed the blessed bastards,
          the young bulls, aristocrats, all of them,
          raised in the sanctuaries of the dons,
          bred in the stables of
35        Salamanca, Rome, Berlin.

          The fields filled with bullfire
          and the hatred of beasts; their breaths
          scorching siroccos,
          hot winds burning hatred against US:

40        the layers of water,
          bidders for water rented for dry land,
          haulers of water in jars at the village well,
          blind mules turning the water mill,
          circling the centuries in ciphers of debt.

45        the hate in the dust of documents
          drifting in the hot winds
          in the buzzing mouths of officials
          breeding swarms of idlers
          like flies on our bread.

50        Breeding illness of their idleness:
          horrors on the path to the bullring,

beggars in the path of the bull:

trees sick with spore diseases,
tubercular, stunted,
55    the bark parched and peeling,
trunks gored and their wounds
swathed in bandages of lime;
Their limbs tortured, lifting up
bare branches of their poverty,
twisted in agony like christs in the grove.

*c. 1938*

## Goin Mah Own Road

Goin mah own road
Goin mah own road
Goin to wuhk foh mahse'f

Ah need some clo's
5    Ah need some shoes
Ah need a loaf of bread
Ah need a roof ovah mah head

Ah hired me out for a pair of shoes
Ah hired me out for a coat and suit
10    Make me a roof ovah mah head
Ah worked hard to make my bread

Ah wukked mah time and ovahtime
Ah wukked mah time and too much time
When ah quit wuk
15    Ah hadn't a dime.

Goin mah own road
Goin mah own road
Goin to wuk foh mahse'f

Ah tol' the boss you go to hell
20    Ah kicked his ass, you go to hell
Me an mah kind don need you.
Me an mah kind kin wuk foh ourselves.

Ah tol' the boss "Ah take what's mine"
You hired mah labor, Ah made what's mine
25    Me and my kin don need you
Ah'm going to wuk for mahse'f.

Ah'll make mah clothes
Ah'll make mah shoes
Ah'll make a loaf of bread,
30    Make me a roof ovah mah head

Walkin mah own road

Walkin mah own road
Goin to wuk foh mahse'f

Ah wukked mah time an overtime
35    Ah wukked mah time an too much time.
When Ah quit wuk Ah hadn't a dime.

    Aint gonna let them two time me no mo.
    Ah was small time, but Ah'm gonna be
        big time now.

40    Goin mah own road
Goin mah own road
Goin to wuk for mahse'f

Ah tol' the boss, Ah been a goddamn fool,
Ah tol' the boss, Ah been a goddamn fool,
45    Let him drive me like a mule.

Ah'm gonna hand that harness up on a shelf
Ah'm gonna hand that harness up on a shelf
Ah'm gonna wuk foh mahse'f.

Goin mah own road
50    Goin mah own road
Goin to work foh mahse'f.

                                        *c. 1939*

# Elizabeth Bishop (1911–1979)

Born in Worcester, Massachusetts, Bishop's childhood was structured around a sequence of tragedies. Her father died when she was less than one year old. Her mother endured a series of emotional breakdowns and was permanently institutionalized when Bishop was five years old; they never saw each other again. At that point, Elizabeth was living in Nova Scotia, but after a few years her grandparents returned with her to Worcester. Then she lived with an aunt, meanwhile suffering from asthma and other illnesses. After an education at Vassar, she lived in New York and Florida, but on a fellowship to Brazil she decided to stay there with Lota de Macedo Soares, a Brazilian architect. She remained for sixteen years, until his suicide in 1967. In 1970, she began a seven-year teaching career at Harvard.

If other poets of her generation were to exploit their pain, Bishop instead chose restraint in her early work. She practiced exacting description coupled with distinctly unsentimental introspection, but she also discovered a style of frank, but crafted, spontaneity. With her third book, *Questions of Travel* (1965), which focused on her Brazil experience, her technical skills and her unsentimental wit supported her in a journey into boldly unconventional social and cultural commentary of a sort no other American poet has attempted. If anything, the Brazil poems have become more surprising with a few decades distance. It would be hard to imagine anyone writing them now.

## The Fish

I caught a tremendous fish
and held him beside the boat
half out of water, with my hook
fast in a corner of his mouth.
5  He didn't fight.
He hadn't fought at all.
He hung a grunting weight,
battered and venerable
and homely. Here and there
10  his brown skin hung in strips
like ancient wallpaper,
and its pattern of darker brown
was like wallpaper:
shapes like full-blown roses
15  stained and lost through age.
He was speckled with barnacles,

fine rosettes° of lime,
and infested
with tiny white sea-lice,
20      and underneath two or three
rags of green weed hung down.
While his gills were breathing in
the terrible oxygen
—the frightening gills,
25      fresh and crisp with blood,
that can cut so badly—
I thought of the coarse white flesh
packed in like feathers,
the big bones and the little bones,
30      the dramatic reds and blacks
of his shiny entrails,
and the pink swim-bladder
like a big peony.
I looked into his eyes
35      which were far larger than mine
but shallower, and yellowed,
the irises backed and packed
with tarnished tinfoil
seen through the lenses
40      of old scratched isinglass.°
They shifted a little, but not
to return my stare.
—It was more like the tipping
of an object toward the light.
45      I admired his sullen face,
the mechanism of his jaw,
and then I saw
that from his lower lip
—if you could call it a lip—
50      grim, wet, and weaponlike,
hung five old pieces of fish-line,
or four and a wire leader°
with the swivel still attached,
with all their five big hooks
55      grown firmly in his mouth.
A green line, frayed at the end
where he broke it, two heavier lines,
and a fine black thread
still crimped from the strain and snap
60      when it broke and he got away.
Like medals with their ribbons
frayed and wavering,
a five-haired beard of wisdom
trailing from his aching jaw.

---

17 *rosettes:* roselike marking, like an ornamental badge.
40 *isinglass:* thin, transparent sheets of mica, a crystallized mineral, used for windows; in context, we are to remember that "isinglass" also refers to a very pure form of gelatin made from the air bladders of sturgeons or other fish.
52 *leader:* connects fish hook and fishline.

65      I stared and stared
        and victory filled up
        the little rented boat,
        from the pool of bilge
        where oil had spread a rainbow
70      around the rusted engine
        to the bailer rusted orange,
        the sun-cracked thwarts,
        the oarlocks on their strings,
        the gunnels°—until everything
75      was rainbow, rainbow, rainbow!
        And I let the fish go.

                                                    1946

## The Man-Moth°

            Here, above,
    cracks in the buildings are filled with battered moonlight.
    The whole shadow of Man is only as big as his hat.
    It lies at his feet like a circle for a doll to stand on,
5   and he makes an inverted pin, the point magnetized to the moon.
    He does not see the moon; he observes only her vast properties,
    feeling the queer light on his hands, neither warm nor cold,
    of a temperature impossible to record in thermometers.

            But when the Man-Moth
10  pays his rare, although occasional, visits to the surface,
    the moon looks rather different to him. He emerges
    from an opening under the edge of one of the sidewalks
    and nervously begins to scale the faces of the buildings.
    He thinks the moon is a small hole at the top of the sky,
15  proving the sky quite useless for protection.
    He trembles, but must investigate as high as he can climb.

            Up the façades,
    his shadow dragging like a photographer's cloth behind him,
    he climbs fearfully, thinking that this time he will manage
20  to push his small head through that round clean opening
    and be forced through, as from a tube, in black scrolls on the light.
    (Man, standing below him, has no such illusions.)
    But what the Man-Moth fears most he must do, although
    he fails, of course, and falls back scared but quite unhurt.

25          Then he returns
    to the pale subways of cement he calls his home. He flits,
    he flutters, and cannot get aboard the silent trains
    fast enough to suit him. The doors close swiftly.
    The Man-Moth always seats himself facing the wrong way

---

74 *gunnels:* "bailer," bucket used to bail water out of the boat; "thwarts," seats or benches
across a boat for rowers to sit on; "oarlocks," metal brackets that anchor the oars but al-
low them to swivel; "gunnels," the upper edges on the sides of a boat.
**poem title:** (Bishop's note), a newspaper misprint for "mammoth."

30    and the train starts at once at its full, terrible speed,
      without a shift in gears or a gradation of any sort.
      He cannot tell the rate at which he travels backwards.

                    Each night he must
      be carried through artificial tunnels and dream recurrent dreams.
35    Just as the ties recur beneath his train, these underlie
      his rushing brain. He does not dare look out the window,
      for the third rail, the unbroken draught of poison,
      runs there beside him. He regards it as a disease
      he has inherited the susceptibility to. He has to keep
40    his hands in his pockets, as others must wear mufflers.

                    If you catch him,
      hold up a flashlight to his eye. It's all dark pupil,
      an entire night itself, whose haired horizon tightens
      as he stares back, and closes up the eye. Then from the lids
45    one tear, his only possession, like the bee's sting, slips.
      Slyly he palms it, and if you're not paying attention
      he'll swallow it. However, if you watch, he'll hand it over,
      cool as from underground springs and pure enough to drink.

                                                        *1946*


## At the Fishhouses

      Although it is a cold evening,
      down by one of the fishhouses
      an old man sits netting,
      his net, in the gloaming almost invisible,
5     a dark purple-brown,
      and his shuttle worn and polished.
      The air smells so strong of codfish
      it makes one's nose run and one's eyes water.
      The five fishhouses have steeply peaked roofs
10    and narrow, cleated gangplanks slant up
      to storerooms in the gables
      for the wheelbarrows to be pushed up and down on.
      All is silver: the heavy surface of the sea,
      swelling slowly as if considering spilling over,
15    is opaque, but the silver of the benches,
      the lobster pots, and masts, scattered
      among the wild jagged rocks,
      is of an apparent translucence
      like the small old buildings with an emerald moss
20    growing on their shoreward walls.
      The big fish tubs are completely lined
      with layers of beautiful herring scales
      and the wheelbarrows are similarly plastered
      with creamy iridescent coats of mail,
25    with small iridescent flies crawling on them.
      Up on the little slope behind the houses,
      set in the sparse bright sprinkle of grass,

is an ancient wooden capstan,
cracked, with two long bleached handles
30   and some melancholy stains, like dried blood,
where the ironwork has rusted.
The old man accepts a Lucky Strike.
He was a friend of my grandfather.
We talk of the decline in the population
35   and of codfish and herring
while he waits for a herring boat to come in.
There are sequins on his vest and on his thumb.
He has scraped the scales, the principal beauty,
from unnumbered fish with that black old knife,
40   the blade of which is almost worn away.

Down at the water's edge, at the place
where they haul up the boats, up the long ramp
descending into the water, thin silver
tree trunks are laid horizontally
45   across the gray stones, down and down
at intervals of four or five feet.

Cold dark deep and absolutely clear,
element bearable to no mortal,
to fish and to seals . . . One seal particularly
50   I have seen here evening after evening.
He was curious about me. He was interested in music;
like me a believer in total immersion,
so I used to sing him Baptist hymns.
I also sang "A Mighty Fortress Is Our God."
55   He stood up in the water and regarded me
steadily, moving his head a little.
Then he would disappear, then suddenly emerge
almost in the same spot, with a sort of shrug
as if it were against his better judgment.
60   Cold dark deep and absolutely clear,
the clear gray icy water . . . Back, behind us,
the dignified tall firs begin.
Bluish, associating with their shadows,
a million Christmas trees stand
65   waiting for Christmas. The water seems suspended
above the rounded gray and blue-gray stones.
I have seen it over and over, the same sea, the same,
slightly, indifferently swinging above the stones,
icily free above the stones,
70   above the stones and then the world.
If you should dip your hand in,
your wrist would ache immediately,
your bones would begin to ache and your hand would burn
as if the water were a transmutation of fire
75   that feeds on stones and burns with a dark gray flame.
If you tasted it, it would first taste bitter,
then briny, then surely burn your tongue.
It is like what we imagine knowledge to be:
dark, salt, clear, moving, utterly free,

80    drawn from the cold hard mouth
      of the world, derived from the rocky breasts
      forever, flowing and drawn, and since
      our knowledge is historical, flowing, and flown.

                                                          *1955*


## Filling Station

       Oh, but it is dirty!
       —this little filling station,
       oil-soaked, oil-permeated
       to a disturbing, over-all
5      black translucency.
       Be careful with that match!

       Father wears a dirty,
       oil-soaked monkey suit
       that cuts him under the arms,
10     and several quick and saucy
       and greasy sons assist him
       (it's a family filling station),
       all quite thoroughly dirty.

       Do they live in the station?
15     It has a cement porch
       behind the pumps, and on it
       a set of crushed and grease-
       impregnated wickerwork;
       on the wicker sofa
20     a dirty dog, quite comfy.

       Some comic books provide
       the only note of color—
       of certain color. They lie
       upon a big dim doily
25     draping a taboret°
       (part of the set), beside
       a big hirsute begonia.

       Why the extraneous plant?
       Why the taboret?
30     Why, oh why, the doily?
       (Embroidered in daisy stitch
       with marguerites,° I think,
       and heavy with gray crochet.)

----

25 *taboret*: small, drum-shaped table or stand.
32 *marguerites*: small daisies.

Somebody embroidered the doily.
35      Somebody waters the plant,
or oils it, maybe. Somebody
arranges the rows of cans
so that they softly say:
Esso°—so—so—so
40      to high-strung automobiles.
Somebody loves us all.

1965

## Questions of Travel

There are too many waterfalls here; the crowded streams
hurry too rapidly down to the sea,
and the pressure of so many clouds on the mountaintops
makes them spill over the sides in soft slow-motion,
5       turning to waterfalls under our very eyes.
—For if those streaks, those mile-long, shiny, tearstains,
aren't waterfalls yet,
in a quick age or so, as ages go here,
they probably will be.
10      But if the streams and clouds keep travelling, travelling,
the mountains look like the hulls of capsized ships,
slime-hung and barnacled.

Think of the long trip home.
Should we have stayed at home and thought of here?
15      Where should we be today?
Is it right to be watching strangers in a play
in this strangest of theatres?
What childishness is it that while there's a breath of life
in our bodies, we are determined to rush
20      to see the sun the other way around?
The tiniest green hummingbird in the world?
To stare at some inexplicable old stonework,
inexplicable and impenetrable,
at any view,
25      instantly seen and always, always delightful?
Oh, must we dream our dreams
and have them, too?
And have we room
for one more folded sunset, still quite warm?

30      But surely it would have been a pity
not to have seen the trees along this road,
really exaggerated in their beauty,
not to have seen them gesturing
like noble pantomimists, robed in pink.
35      —Not to have had to stop for gas and heard

---

39 *Esso:* a brand of gasoline.

the sad, two-noted, wooden tune
of disparate wooden clogs
carelessly clacking over
a grease-stained filling-station floor.
40 (In another country the clogs would all be tested.
Each pair there would have identical pitch.)
—A pity not to have heard
the other, less primitive music of the fat brown bird
who sings above the broken gasoline pump
45 in a bamboo church of Jesuit baroque:
three towers, five silver crosses.
—Yes, a pity not to have pondered,
blurr'dly and inconclusively,
on what connection can exist for centuries
50 between the crudest wooden footwear
and, careful and finicky,
the whittled fantasies of wooden cages.
—Never to have studied history in
the weak calligraphy of songbirds' cages.
55 —And never to have had to listen to rain
so much like politicians' speeches:
two hours of unrelenting oratory
and then a sudden golden silence
in which the traveller takes a notebook, writes:

60 *"Is it lack of imagination that makes us come*
*to imagined places, not just stay at home?*
*Or could Pascal have been not entirely right*
*about just sitting quietly in one's room?*

*Continent, city, country, society:*
65 *the choice is never wide and never free.*
*And here, or there . . . No. Should we have stayed at home,*
*wherever that may be?"*

*1965*

# The Armadillo

(For Robert Lowell)

This is the time of year
when almost every night
the frail, illegal fire balloons appear.
Climbing the mountain height,

5 rising toward a saint
still honored in these parts,
the paper chambers flush and fill with light
that comes and goes, like hearts.

Once up against the sky it's hard
10      to tell them from the stars—
planets, that is—the tinted ones:
Venus going down, or Mars,

or the pale green one. With a wind,
they flare and falter, wobble and toss;
15      but if it's still they steer between
the kite sticks of the Southern Cross,°

receding, dwindling, solemnly
and steadily forsaking us,
or, in the downdraft from a peak,
20      suddenly turning dangerous.

Last night another big one fell.
It splattered like an egg of fire
against the cliff behind the house.
The flame ran down. We saw the pair

25      of owls who nest there flying up
and up, their whirling black-and-white
stained bright pink underneath, until
they shrieked up out of sight.

The ancient owls' nest must have burned.
30      Hastily, all alone,
a glistening armadillo left the scene,
rose-flecked, head down, tail down,

and then a baby rabbit jumped out,
*short*-eared, to our surprise.
35      So soft!—a handful of intangible ash
with fixed, ignited eyes.

*Too pretty, dreamlike mimicry!*
*O falling fire and piercing cry*
*and panic, and a weak mailed fist*
*clenched ignorant against the sky!*

                                        *1965*


## In the Waiting Room

In Worcester, Massachusetts,
I went with Aunt Consuelo
to keep her dentist's appointment
and sat and waited for her
5      in the dentist's waiting room.

---

16 *Southern Cross:* a constellation.

It was winter. It got dark
early. The waiting room
was full of grown-up people,
arctics and overcoats,
10     lamps and magazines.
My aunt was inside
what seemed like a long time
and while I waited I read
the *National Geographic*
15     (I could read) and carefully
studied the photographs:
the inside of a volcano,
black, and full of ashes;
then it was spilling over
20     in rivulets of fire.
Osa and Martin Johnson°
dressed in riding breeches,
laced boots, and pith helmets.
A dead man slung on a pole
25     —"Long Pig,"° the caption said.
Babies with pointed heads
wound round and round with string;
black, naked women with necks
wound round and round with wire
30     like the necks of light bulbs.
Their breasts were horrifying.
I read it right straight through.
I was too shy to stop.
And then I looked at the cover:
35     the yellow margins, the date.

Suddenly, from inside,
came an *oh!* of pain
—Aunt Consuelo's voice—
not very loud or long.
40     I wasn't at all surprised;
even then I knew she was
a foolish, timid woman.
I might have been embarrassed,
but wasn't. What took me
45     completely by surprise
was that it was *me*:
my voice, in my mouth.
Without thinking at all
I was my foolish aunt,
50     I—we—were falling, falling,
our eyes glued to the cover
of the *National Geographic*,
February, 1918.

---

21 *Johnson*: Osa Johnson (1894–1953) and her husband Martin Johnson (1884–1937) filmed
Africa's vanishing wildlife for the American Museum of Natural History.
25 *Long Pig*: the name Polynesian cannibals used for the body of a dead person.

I said to myself: three days
55 and you'll be seven years old.
I was saying it to stop
the sensation of falling off
the round, turning world
into cold, blue-black space.
60 But I felt: you are an *I*,
you are an *Elizabeth*,
you are one of *them*.
*Why* should you be one, too?
I scarcely dared to look
65 to see what it was I was.
I gave a sidelong glance
—I couldn't look any higher—
at shadowy gray knees,
trousers and skirts and boots
70 and different pairs of hands
lying under the lamps.
I knew that nothing stranger
had ever happened, that nothing
stranger could ever happen.
75 Why should I be my aunt,
or me, or anyone?
What similarities—
boots, hands, the family voice
I felt in my throat, or even
80 the *National Geographic*
and those awful hanging breasts—
held us all together
or made us all just one?
How—I didn't know any
85 word for it—how "unlikely" . . .
How had I come to be here,
like them, and overhear
a cry of pain that could have
got loud and worse but hadn't?

90 The waiting room was bright
and too hot. It was sliding
beneath a big black wave,
another, and another.

Then I was back in it.
95 The War° was on. Outside,
in Worcester, Massachusetts,
were night and slush and cold,
and it was still the fifth
of February, 1918.

*1976*

---

95 *the War:* World War I.

# Pink Dog

### [RIO DE JANEIRO]°

The sun is blazing and the sky is blue.
Umbrellas clothe the beach in every hue.
Naked, you trot across the avenue.

Oh, never have I seen a dog so bare!
5     Naked and pink, without a single hair . . .
Startled, the passersby draw back and stare.

Of course they're mortally afraid of rabies.
You are not mad; you have a case of scabies°
but look intelligent. Where are your babies?

10     (A nursing mother, by those hanging teats.)
In what slum have you hidden them, poor bitch,
while you go begging, living by your wits?

Didn't you know? It's been in all the papers,
to solve this problem, how they deal with beggars?
15     They take and throw them in the tidal rivers.

Yes, idiots, paralytics, parasites
go bobbing in the ebbing sewage, nights
out in the suburbs, where there are no lights.

If they do this to anyone who begs,
20     drugged, drunk, or sober, with or without legs,
what would they do to sick, four-leggèd dogs?

In the cafés and on the sidewalk corners
the joke is going round that all the beggars
who can afford them now wear life preservers.

25     In your condition you would not be able
even to float, much less to dog-paddle.
Now look, the practical, the sensible

solution is to wear a *fantasía.*°
Tonight you simply can't afford to be a-
30     n eyesore. But no one will ever see a

---

*Rio de Janeiro*: Port city in southeast Brazil.
8 *scabies*: an itchy skin condition caused by infestation with the itch-mite; in the tropics, sometimes accompanied by secondary infections.
28 *fantasía*: carnival costume (Bishop's note).

dog in *máscara* this time of year.
Ash Wednesday'll° come but Carnival is here.
What sambas° can you dance? What will you wear?

They say that Carnival's degenerating
35    —radios, Americans, or something,
have ruined it completely. They're just talking.

Carnival is always wonderful!
A depilated dog would not look well.
Dress up! Dress up and dance at Carnival!

1979

## Crusoe in England

A new volcano has erupted,
the papers say, and last week I was reading
where some ship saw an island being born:
at first a breath of steam, ten miles away;
5    and then a black fleck—basalt, probably—
rose in the mate's binoculars
and caught on the horizon like a fly.
They named it. But my poor old island's still
un-rediscovered, un-renamable.
10    None of the books has ever got it right.

Well, I had fifty-two
miserable, small volcanoes I could climb
with a few slithery strides—
volcanoes dead as ash heaps.
15    I used to sit on the edge of the highest one
and count the others standing up,
naked and leaden, with their heads blown off.
I'd think that if they were the size
I thought volcanoes should be, then I had
20    become a giant;
and if I had become a giant,
I couldn't bear to think what size
the goats and turtles were,
or the gulls, or the overlapping rollers
25    —a glittering hexagon of rollers
closing and closing in, but never quite,
glittering and glittering, though the sky
was mostly overcast.

---

32 *Ash Wednesday:* in the Christian calendar, the first day of Lent, the forty days leading
up to the date of Christ's crucifixion. Catholics mark the day by placing a cross of ash on
their foreheads, a token of penitence and mortality.
33 *sambas:* Brazilian dances.

My island seemed to be
30     a sort of cloud-dump. All the hemisphere's
left-over clouds arrived and hung
above the craters—their parched throats
were hot to touch.
Was that why it rained so much?
35     And why sometimes the whole place hissed?
The turtles lumbered by, high-domed,
hissing like teakettles.
(And I'd have given years, or taken a few,
for any sort of kettle, of course.)
40     The folds of lava, running out to sea,
would hiss. I'd turn. And then they'd prove
to be more turtles.
The beaches were all lava, variegated,
black, red, and white, and gray;
45     the marbled colors made a fine display.
And I had waterspouts. Oh,
half a dozen at a time, far out,
they'd come and go, advancing and retreating,
their heads in cloud, their feet in moving patches
50     of scuffed-up white.
Glass chimneys, flexible, attenuated,
sacerdotal beings of glass . . . I watched
the water spiral up in them like smoke.
Beautiful, yes, but not much company.

55     I often gave way to self-pity.
"Do I deserve this? I suppose I must.
I wouldn't be here otherwise. Was there
a moment when I actually chose this?
I don't remember, but there could have been."
60     What's wrong about self-pity, anyway?
With my legs dangling down familiarly
over a crater's edge, I told myself
"Pity should begin at home." So the more
pity I felt, the more I felt at home.

65     The sun set in the sea; the same odd sun
rose from the sea,
and there was one of it and one of me.
The island had one kind of everything:
one tree snail, a bright violet-blue
70     with a thin shell, crept over everything,
over the one variety of tree,
a sooty, scrub affair.
Snail shells lay under these in drifts
and, at a distance,
75     you'd swear that they were beds of irises.
There was one kind of berry, a dark red.
I tried it, one by one, and hours apart.
Sub-acid, and not bad, no ill effects;
and so I made home-brew. I'd drink

80    the awful, fizzy, stinging stuff
that went straight to my head
and play my home-made flute
(I think it had the weirdest scale on earth)
and, dizzy, whoop and dance among the goats.

85    Home-made, home-made! But aren't we all?
I felt a deep affection for
the smallest of my island industries.
No, not exactly, since the smallest was
a miserable philosophy.

90    Because I didn't know enough.
Why didn't I know enough of something?
Greek drama or astronomy? The books
I'd read were full of blanks;
the poems—well, I tried

95    reciting to my iris-beds,
"They flash upon that inward eye,
which is the bliss . . ." The bliss of what?
One of the first things that I did
when I got back was look it up.

100    The island smelled of goat and guano.
The goats were white, so were the gulls,
and both too tame, or else they thought
I was a goat, too, or a gull.
*Baa, baa, baa* and *shriek, shriek, shriek,*

105    *baa . . . shriek . . . baa . . .* I still can't shake
them from my ears; they're hurting now.
The questioning shrieks, the equivocal replies
over a ground of hissing rain
and hissing, ambulating turtles

110    got on my nerves.

When all the gulls flew up at once, they sounded
like a big tree in a strong wind, its leaves.
I'd shut my eyes and think about a tree,
an oak, say, with real shade, somewhere.

115    I'd heard of cattle getting island-sick.
I thought the goats were.
One billy-goat would stand on the volcano
I'd christened *Mont d'Espoir* or *Mount Despair*
(I'd time enough to play with names),

120    and bleat and bleat, and sniff the air.
I'd grab his beard and look at him.
His pupils, horizontal, narrowed up
and expressed nothing, or a little malice.
I got so tired of the very colors!

125    One day I dyed a baby goat bright red
with my red berries, just to see
something a little different.
And then his mother wouldn't recognize him.

Dreams were the worst. Of course I dreamed of food
130        and love, but they were pleasant rather
than otherwise. But then I'd dream of things
like slitting a baby's throat, mistaking it
for a baby goat. I'd have
nightmares of other islands
135        stretching away from mine, infinities
of islands, islands spawning islands,
like frogs' eggs turning into polliwogs
of islands, knowing that I had to live
on each and every one, eventually,
140        for ages, registering their flora,
their fauna, their geography.

Just when I thought I couldn't stand it
another minute longer, Friday came.
(Accounts of that have everything all wrong.)
145        Friday was nice.
Friday was nice, and we were friends.
If only he had been a woman!
I wanted to propagate my kind,
and so did he, I think, poor boy.
150        He'd pet the baby goats sometimes,
and race with them, or carry one around.
—Pretty to watch; he had a pretty body.

And then one day they came and took us off.

Now I live here, another island,
155        that doesn't seem like one, but who decides?
My blood was full of them; my brain
bred islands. But that archipelago
has petered out. I'm old.
I'm bored, too, drinking my real tea,
160        surrounded by uninteresting lumber.
The knife there on the shelf—
it reeked of meaning, like a crucifix.
It lived. How many years did I
beg it, implore it, not to break?
165        I knew each nick and scratch by heart,
the bluish blade, the broken tip,
the lines of wood-grain on the handle . . .
Now it won't look at me at all.
The living soul has dribbled away.
170        My eyes rest on it and pass on.

The local museum's asked me to
leave everything to them:
the flute, the knife, the shrivelled shoes,
my shedding goatskin trousers
175        (moths have got in the fur),
the parasol that took me such a time
remembering the way the ribs should go.

It still will work but, folded up,
looks like a plucked and skinny fowl.
180 How can anyone want such things?
—And Friday, my dear Friday, died of measles
seventeen years ago come March.

1976

# One Art

The art of losing isn't hard to master;
so many things seem filled with the intent
to be lost that their loss is no disaster.

Lose something every day. Accept the fluster
5 of lost door keys, the hour badly spent.
The art of losing isn't hard to master.

Then practice losing farther, losing faster:
places, and names, and where it was you meant
to travel. None of these will bring disaster.

10 I lost my mother's watch. And look! my last, or
next-to-last, of three loved houses went.
The art of losing isn't hard to master.

I lost two cities, lovely ones. And, vaster,
some realms I owned, two rivers, a continent.
15 I miss them, but it wasn't a disaster.

—Even losing you (the joking voice, a gesture
I love) I shan't have lied. It's evident
the art of losing's not too hard to master
though it may look like (*Write* it!) like disaster.

1976

# William Everson (1912–1994)

Born in Sacramento, California, Everson was the son of a Norwegian composer. He attended Fresno State College until leaving in 1935 to write poetry. Robinson Jeffers was one of his strongest literary influences at the time. He was a conscientious objector during World War II, working as a forester in Oregon for three years, and soon afterwards joined the San Francisco anarcho-pacifist group centered around poet Kenneth Rexroth. In 1949, Everson converted to Roman Catholicism, and the following year he joined the Catholic Worker Movement. In 1951, he entered the Dominican Order as a lay brother without vows and took the name Brother Antoninus, but he left the monastery and rejoined the secular world in 1969. Before his conversion Everson had written poems of erotic mysticism and pantheism, as well as poems against war. In the early 1950s, the period when "A Canticle to the Waterbirds" was written, he wrote poems of great religious passion, but the differences between the poems were not absolute. The "Canticle" is essentially a proof of the existence of God based on the evidence of nature's fecundity.

## A Canticle° to the Waterbirds

Clack your beaks you cormorants° and kittiwakes,
North on those rock-croppings finger-jutted into the rough Pacific
surge;
You migratory terns and pipers who leave but the temporal claw-
track written on sandbars there of your presence;

---

**poem title:** *canticle*: a song or chant, often a hymn with words taken from a biblical text. The poem is devoted to the waterbirds on a long stretch of Pacific coast from San Francisco/Oakland, California, north along Oregon and Washington to British Columbia, Canada. In a preface to the poem, Everson explains: "In the long summer dusks we used to walk to the Oakland estuary among the deserted factories and warehouses, and out along the silent piers. Where all day long an inferno of deafening racket enveloped the machines, now lay a most blessed peace. In these moments of solitude we thought of the men back at the hospice, broken, shabby, wine-sotted, hopeless. Out there on the estuary, over the water, the gulls lifted their wings in a gesture of pure felicity. Something hidden and conclusive broke bondage within me, something born of the nights and the weeks and the months. My mind shot north up the long coast of deliverance, encompassing all the areas of my ancient quest, that ineluctable instinct for the divine—the rivermouths and the sand-skirted beaches, sea-granite capes and bastions and basalt-founded cliffs—where despite all man's meanness a presence remains unspoiled, the sacred zone between earth and sea, and pure."
[1]*cormorants*: marine diving birds with webbed feet and slender hooked bills; kittiwakes: cliff-nesting gulls. These are among the many species of sea and fresh water birds, large and small, mentioned in the poem; we have identified only a few.

Grebes and pelicans; you comber-picking° scoters° and you shore-
   long gulls;
5    All you keepers of the coastline north of here to the Mendocino°
   beaches;
All you beyond upon the cliff-face thwarting the surf at Hecate
   Head;
Hovering the under-surge where the cold Columbia° grapples at
   the bar;
North yet to the Sound,° whose islands float like a sown flurry of
   chips upon the sea;
Break wide your harsh and salt-encrusted beaks unmade for song
10   And say a praise up to the Lord.

And you freshwater egrets° east in the flooded marshlands skirting
   the sea-level rivers, white one-legged watchers of shallows;
Broad-headed kingfishers minnow-hunting from willow stems on
   meandering valley sloughs;
You too, you herons, blue and supple-throated, stately, taking the
   air majestical in the sunflooded San Joaquin,°
Grading down on your belted wings from the upper lights of sun-
   set,
15    Mating over the willow clumps or where the flatwater rice fields
   shimmer;
You killdeer, high night-criers, far in the moon-suffusion sky;
Bitterns, sand-waders, all shore-walkers, all roost-keepers,
Populates of the 'dobe° cliffs of the Sacramento:
Open your water-dartling beaks,
20   And make a praise up to the Lord.

For you hold the heart of His mighty fastnesses,
And shape the life of His indeterminate realms.
You are everywhere on the lonesome shores of His wide creation.
You keep seclusion where no man may go, giving Him praise;
25    Nor may a woman come to lift like your cleaving flight her clear
   contralto° song
To honor the spindrift° gifts of His soft abundance.
You sanctify His hermitage° rocks where no holy priest may kneel

---

4 *comber-picking*: searching for food among long waves that have reached their peak or broken into foam.
4 *scoters*: ducks of northern coastal areas.
5 *Mendocino*: Northern California coastal county and city.
7 *cold Columbia*: the Columbia River rises in southeast British Columbia, Canada, and flows south and west toward the Pacific ocean along the Washington-Oregon border.
8 *the Sound*: probably Queen Charlotte Sound, running from Vancouver Island north to Hecate Strait and the Queen Charlotte Islands along the Pacific coast in British Columbia, Canada; a sound is a long, wide body of water, larger than a strait or channel, as in an ocean inlet.
11 *egret*: a species of heron, often white, displaying long, dramatic drooping plumes during the mating season.
13 *San Joaquin*: river in central California rising in the Sierra Nevada mountains and flowing northwest to form a large delta with the Sacramento River.
18 *'dobe*: adobe, a form of clay.
25 *contralto*: the lowest female voice, intermediate between soprano and tenor.
26 *spindrift*: windblown sea spray.
27 *hermitage*: monastery.

to adore, nor holy nun assist;
And where His true communion-keepers are not enabled to enter.

And well may you say His praises, birds, for your ways
30  Are verved with the secret skills of His inclinations,
And your habits plaited and rare with the subdued elaboration of
    His intricate craft;
Your days intent with the direct astuteness needful for His out-
    working,
And your nights alive with the dense repose of His infinite sleep.
You are His secretive charges and you serve His secretive ends,
35  In His clouded, mist-conditioned stations, in His murk,
Obscure in your matted nestings, immured in His limitless ranges.
He makes you penetrate through dark interstitial° joinings of His
    thicketed kingdoms,
And keep your concourse in the deeps of His shadowed world.

Your ways are wild but earnest, your manners grave,
40  Your customs carefully schooled to the note of His serious mien.
You hold the prime condition of His clean creating,
And the swift compliance with which you serve His minor means
Speaks of the constancy with which you hold Him.
For what is your high flight forever going home to your first begin-
    nings,
45  But such a testament to your devotion?
You hold His outstretched world beneath your wings, and mount
    upon His storms,
And keep your sheer wind-lidded sight upon the vast perspectives
    of His mazy latitudes.

But mostly it is your way you bear existence wholly within the con-
    text of His utter will and are untroubled.
Day upon day you do not reckon, nor scrutinize tomorrow, nor
    multiply the nightfalls with a rash concern,
50  But rather assume each instant as warrant sufficient of His final
    seal.
Wholly in Providence you spring, and when you die you look on
    death in clarity unflinched,
Go down, a clutch of feather ragged upon the brush;
Or drop on water where you briefly lived, found food,
And now yourselves made food for His deep current-keeping fish,
    and then are gone:
55  Is left but the pinion-feather° spinning a bit on the uproil°
Where lately the dorsal° cut clear air.

---

37 *interstitial*: narrow spaces created between multiple connections.
55 *pinion-feather*: one of a bird's primary wing feathers.
55 *uproil*: small section of turbulent water (or air) moving rapidly upward.
56 *dorsal*: main fin located on the back of fishes and marine mammals.

You leave a silence. And this for you suffices, who are not of the
    ceremonials of man,
And hence are not made sad to now forgo them.
Yours is of another order of being, and wholly it compels.
60    But may you, birds, utterly seized in God's supremacy,
Austerely living under His austere eye—
Yet may you teach a man a necessary thing to know,
Which has to do of the strict conformity that creaturehood entails,
And constitutes the prime commitment all things share.
65    For God has given you the imponderable grace to *be* His verifica-
    tion,
Outside the mulled incertitude of our forensic° choices;
That you, our lessers in the rich hegemony of Being,
May serve as testament to what a creature is,
And what creation owes.

70    Curlews, stilts and scissortails, beachcomber gulls,
Wave-haunters, shore-keepers, rockhead-holders, all cape-top vigi-
    lantes,
Now give God praise.
Send up the strict articulation of your throats,
And say His name.

*1950*

---

66 *forensic*: rhetorical, argumentative.

# Tillie Lerner Olsen (b. 1912)

Born in Nebraska of Russian parents who participated in the 1905 revolution and fled when it failed, Tillie Lerner (the name she published under before her marriage) had to leave school to work after the eleventh grade. She trimmed meat in a packing house, worked as a waitress and a domestic, and meanwhile joined the Young Communist League. Her father had become state secretary of the Nebraska Socialist Party. Lerner herself went to jail for trying to organize packing house workers. Meanwhile, when she was only nineteen, she began to write, starting the novel that would become *Yonnondio* years later. She moved to California in the early 1930s, publishing "I Want You Women Up North to Know" in the West coast John Reed Club magazine, *Partisan*, in 1934. She was harassed repeatedly by the FBI during the McCarthy period. Her story "Tell Me a Riddle" is her most famous work.

## I Want You Women Up North to Know

*(Based on a Letter by Felipe Ibarro in* New Masses, *Jan. 9th, 1934.)*

     i want you women up north to know
     how those dainty children's dresses you buy
        at macy's, wanamakers, gimbels, marshall fields,°
     are dyed in blood, are stitched in wasting flesh,
5      down in San Antonio,° "where sunshine spends the winter."°

     I want you women up north to see
     the obsequious smile, the salesladies trill
        "exquisite work, madame, exquisite pleats"
     vanish into a bloated face, ordering more dresses,
10     gouging the wages down,
     dissolve into maria, ambrosa, catalina,
        stitching these dresses from dawn to night,
        in blood, in wasting flesh.

     Catalina Rodriguez, 24,
15     body shrivelled to a child's at twelve,
     catalina rodriguez, last stages of consumption,
        works for three dollars a week from dawn to midnight.

---

3 *macy's . . . marshall fields*: four U.S. department stores.
5 *San Antonio*: Texas city.
5 *winter*: phrase from a San Antonio Chamber of Commerce brochure.

A fog of pain thickens over her skull, the parching heat
    breaks over her body.
20    and the bright red blood embroiders the floor of her room.
      White rain stitching the night, the bourgeois poet would say,
      white gulls of hands, darting, veering,
      white lightning, threading the clouds,
    this is the exquisite dance of her hands over the cloth,
25    and her cough, gay, quick, staccato,°
      like skeleton's bones clattering,
    is appropriate accompaniment for the esthetic dance
      of her fingers,
    and the tremolo, tremolo° when the hands tremble with pain.
30    Three dollars a week,
    two fifty-five,
    seventy cents a week,
    no wonder two thousands eight hundred ladies of joy
    are spending the winter with the sun after he goes down—
35    for five cents (who said this was a rich man's world?) you can
      get all the lovin you want
    "clap and syph aint much worse than sore fingers, blind eyes, and
    t.m."

Maria Vasquez, spinster,
40    for fifteen cents a dozen stitches garments for children she has
    never had,
Catalina Torres, mother of four,
    to keep the starved body starving, embroiders from dawn to
    night.
45    Mother of four, what does she think of,
    as the needle pocked fingers shift over the silk—
    of the stubble-coarse rags that stretch on her own brood,
    and jut with the bony ridge that marks hunger's landscape
    of fat little prairie-roll bodies that will bulge in the
50    silk she needles?
(Be not envious, Catalina Torres, look!
    on your own children's clothing, embroidery,
    more intricate than any a thousand hands could fashion,
    there where the cloth is ravelled, or darned,
55    designs, multitudinous, complex and handmade by Poverty
    herself.)

Ambrosa Espinoza trusts in god,
    "Todos es de dios, everything is from god,"
    through the dwindling night, the waxing day, she bolsters herself
60    up with it—
but the pennies to keep god incarnate, from ambrosa,
and the pennies to keep the priest in wine, from ambrosa,
ambrosa clothes god and priest with hand-made children's dresses.

---

25 *staccato*: series of short, abrupt, disjointed sounds or motions.
29 *tremolo*: from music, a rapid reiteration of a tone or rapid variation of pitch; here the music of pain.

Her brother lies on an iron cot, all day and watches,
65    on a mattress of rags he lies.
For twenty-five years he worked for the railroad, then they laid him off.
    (racked days, searching for work; rebuffs; suspicious eyes of
        policemen.)
    goodbye ambrosa, mebbe in dallas I find work; desperate swing
       for a freight,
70    surprised hands, clutching air, and the wheel goes over a
    leg,
the railroad cuts it off, as it cut off twenty-five years of his life.)
She says that he prays and dreams of another world, as he lies
    there, a heaven (which he does not know was brought to earth
75    in 1917 in Russia,° by workers like him).

Women up north, I want you to know
when you finger the exquisite hand made dresses
what it means, this working from dawn to midnight,
on what strange feet the feverish dawn must come
80    to maria, catalina, ambrosa,
how the malignant fingers twitching over the pallid faces jerk them
    to work,
and the sun and the fever mounts with the day—
    long plodding hours, the eyes burn like coals, heat jellies the
    flying fingers,
down comes the night like blindness.
85    long hours more with the dim eye of the lamp, the breaking
    back,
    weariness crawls in the flesh like worms, gigantic like earth's in
    winter.
And for Catalina Rodriguez comes the night sweat and the blood
    embroidering the darkness.
    for Catalina Torres the pinched faces of four huddled
90    children,
    the naked bodies of four bony children,
    the chant of their chorale of hunger.
And for twenty eight hundred ladies of joy the grotesque act gone
    over—
    the wink—the grimace—the "feeling like it baby?"
95    And for Maria Vasquez, spinster, emptiness, emptiness.
    flaming with dresses for children she can never fondle.
And for Ambrosa Espinoza—the skeleton body of her brother on
    his mattress
of rags, boring twin holes in the dark with his eyes to the image of
    christ
remembering a leg, and twenty-five years cut off from his life by
    the railroad.

100    Women up north, I want you to know,
I tell you this can't last forever.

I swear it won't.

1934

---

74 *Russia*: the 1917 Russian Revolution ushered in the era of communism.

# Muriel Rukeyser (1913–1980)

From the outset, Rukeyser was at once a political poet and a visionary. At times, as at points in "The Book of the Dead," those qualities were intensified, and in those moments she was simultaneously a revolutionary and a mystic. But to grasp the forces that drive her work—through a career that spanned five decades of American history—we have to come to terms with a visionary impulse rooted in time, embedded in a struggle with lived history. Consider as a case in point the rhapsodic images Rukeyser crafts to voice the mother's anguish at the death of her sons in "Absalom." To understand her work we must also embrace the larger, wiser notion of politics that underlies all her poetry. For she understood early on what so many of us could not: that politics encompasses all the ways that social life is hierarchically structured and made meaningful. Politics is not only the large-scale public life of nations. It is also the advantages and inequities and illusions that make daily life very different for different groups. Thus Rukeyser understood that race and gender are integral parts of our social and political life. Never officially a feminist, she nonetheless devoted herself, as she does in "Rite," to voicing women's distinctive experience throughout her career.

Although Rukeyser wrote numerous short, tightly controlled poems like "The Minotaur," it may well be that her most rich and suggestive accomplishments are her poem sequences. "The Book of the Dead" is one of the major poem sequences of American modernism. Based on Rukeyser's own research in West Virginia, it combines historical background, congressional testimony, and the voices of a number of victims in telling the story of a 1930s industrial scandal: a company building a tunnel for a dam decided to double its profit by rapidly mining silica at the same time (without any of the necessary precautions). A great many workers died of lung disease as a result. "The Book of the Dead" is thus also one of Rukeyser's many poems that reflect and contribute to her political activism.

Rukeyser was born and raised in New York City and educated at Vassar College and Columbia University. During the 1930s, Rukeyser regularly wrote for Communist Party publications like *New Masses*. She was in Spain to cover the antifascist Olympics in Barcelona when the Spanish Civil War broke out. She described that experience in the long poem "Mediterranean" and returned to the subject throughout her life. Years later, in 1975, she went to South Korea to protest the poet Kim Chi-Ha's imprisonment and anticipated execution; the poem sequence "The Gates" grew out of that trip. Rukeyser meditates on her poetics in *The Life of Poetry* (1949). She also published a novel, *The Orgy* (1966), as well as two biographies, *Willard Gibbs* (1942) and *The Traces of Thomas Harriot* (1971).

# The Book of the Dead°

## THE ROAD

These are roads to take when you think of your country
and interested bring down the maps again,
phoning the statistician, asking the dear friend,

reading the papers with morning inquiry.
5    Or when you sit at the wheel and your small light
chooses gas gauge and clock; and the headlights

indicate future of road, your wish pursuing
past the junction, the fork, the suburban station,
well-travelled six-lane highway planned for safety.

10   Past your tall central city's influence,
outside its body: traffic, penumbral crowds,
are centers removed and strong, fighting for good reason.

These roads will take you into your own country.
Select the mountains, follow rivers back,
15   travel the passes. Touch West Virginia where

the Midland Trail leaves the Virginia furnace,
iron Clifton Forge, Covington iron, goes down
into the wealthy valley, resorts, the chalk hotel.

Pillars and fairway; spa; White Sulphur Springs.
20   Airport. Gay blank rich faces wishing to add
history to ballrooms, tradition to the first tee.

---

**poem title:** *The Book of the Dead* is a twenty-poem sequence published in Rukeyser's second book (*U.S. 1*, 1938). The sequence explores the 1929–1932 outbreak of silicosis, a fatal lung disease, in the Hawk's Nest tunneling project in Gauley Bridge, West Virginia. Undertaken by the Rinehart and Dennis company as a tunnel to divert water from the New River to the New Kanawha power plant, the tunnel became a mining operation when workers discovered large deposits of pure silica, an element used in the electroprocessing of steel. Two thousand workers in the tunnel contracted silicosis after breathing silica dust in high concentrations. Investigated by a congressional subcommittee and widely covered in the national news media, the Hawk's Nest industrial disaster caught Rukeyser's attention in the mid-1930s. Intending to make a documentary film with her college classmate and lifelong friend, the photographer Nancy Naumberg, Rukeyser traveled to Gauley Bridge in 1936 and interviewed survivors and workers' families. Her impressions and interviews, along with the subcommittee's hearings testimony, provided the source material for Rukeyser's poetic treatment of Hawk's Nest, of workers' sufferings, and of corporate responsibility for the disaster. The sequence's genesis in thirties documentary culture is especially obvious in the monologue or portrait poems but, influenced by other modernist poets, especially Ezra Pound and T.S. Eliot, Rukeyser combined the earmarks of social documentary with the consolatory myth system of the Egyptian *Book of the Dead*, whose progression of spells to guide the dead into new life serves as a structuring device for her sequence. Rukeyser titles her book, *U.S. 1*, after the guidebook to U.S. Highway 1, published by the Works Progress Administration Writers' Project. She intended her collection of poems to expand on and explore the guidebook's presentation of the Atlantic Seaboard.

*Book of the Dead*—(first compiled c 1550 BCE) Egyptian collection of funerary spells and ritual practices supposed to ensure the dead a happy afterlife in "the blessed realm of Osiris," the Egyptian deity ritually killed, dispersed, and reborn every year.

The simple mountains, sheer, dark-graded with pine
in the sudden weather, wet outbreak of spring,
crosscut by snow, wind at the hill's shoulder.

25    The land is fierce here, steep, braced against snow,
rivers and spring. KING COAL HOTEL, Lookout,
and swinging the vicious bend, New River Gorge.

Now the photographer unpacks camera and case,
surveying the deep country, follows discovery
30    viewing on groundglass an inverted image.

John Marshall° named the rock (steep pines, a drop
he reckoned in 1812, called) Marshall's Pillar,
but later, Hawk's Nest. Here is your road, tying

you to its meanings: gorge, boulder, precipice.
35    Telescoped down, the hard and stone-green river
cutting fast and direct into the town.

### WEST VIRGINIA

They saw rivers flow west and hoped again.
Virginia speeding to another sea!
1671—Thomes Batts, Robert Fallam,
40    Thomas Wood, the Indian Perecute,
and an unnamed indentured English servant
followed the forest past blazed trees, pillars of God,
were the first whites emergent from the east.
They left a record to our heritage,
45    breaking of records. Hoped now for the sea,
*for all mountains have their descents about them,*
*waters, descending naturally, doe alwaies resort*
*unto the seas invironing those lands . . .*
*yea, at home amongst the mountaines in England.*

50    Coming where this road comes,
flat stones spilled water which the still pools fed.
Kanawha Falls, the rapids of the mind,
fast waters spilling west.

Found Indian fields, standing low cornstalks left,
55    learned three Mohetons planted them; found-land
farmland, the planted home, discovered!

War-born:
The battle at Point Pleasant, Cornstalk's tribes,
last stand, Fort Henry,° a revolution won;
60    the granite SITE OF THE precursor EXECUTION

---

31 *John Marshall:* (1755–1835), Virginia legislator, U.S. Supreme Court Chief Justice.
59 *Point Pleasant, Fort Henry:* military engagements in the American Revolution.

sabres, apostles OF JOHN BROWN° LEADER OF THE
War's brilliant cloudy RAID AT HARPERS FERRY.
Floods, heavy wind this spring, the beaten land
blown high by wind, fought wars, forming a state,

65       a surf, frontier defines two fighting halves,
two hundred battles in the four years: troops
here in Gauley Bridge, Union headquarters, lines
bring in the military telegraph.
Wires over the gash of gorge and height of pine.

70       But it was always the water
the power flying deep
green rivers cut the rock
rapids boiled down,
a scene of power.

75       Done by the dead.
Discovery learned it.
And the living?

Live country filling west,
knotted the glassy rivers;
80       like valleys, opening mines,
coming to life.

### STATEMENT: PHILIPPA ALLEN°

—You like the State of West Virginia very much, do you not?
—I do very much, in the summertime.
—How much time have you spent in West Virginia?
85       —During the summer of 1934, when I was doing social work
down there, I first heard of what we were pleased to call
the Gauley tunnel tragedy, which involved about 2,000
men.
—What was their salary?
—It started at 40¢ and dropped to 25¢ an hour.
—You have met these people personally?
—I have talked to people; yes.
90       According to estimates of contractors
2,000 men were
employed there
period, about 2 years
drilling, 3.75 miles of tunnel.

---

61 *John Brown:* (1800–1859), militant abolitionist who led an inflammatory raid on the U.S. Armory at Harper's Ferry, West Virginia, on October 17, 1859. After a battle with U.S. Army troops, Brown was captured and convicted of treason. He was executed on December 2, 1859, but was broadly seen in the north as a martyr for the abolitionist cause.
**section head:** *Philippa Allen:* a social worker from New York who traveled to West Virginia in 1934 to work with victims and families of Gauley Bridge and the surrounding area. Allen testified at length before the 1936 subcommittee of the U.S. House of Representatives' Labor Committee, which investigated the Hawk's Nest incident, and is credited by Rukeyser, in the "Note" at the back of *U.S. 1*, with making the poem possible.

95           To divert water (from New River)
            to a hydroelectric plant (at Gauley Junction).
       The rock through which they were boring was of a high
          silica content.
       In tunnel No. 1 it ran 97–99% pure silica.
       The contractors
100           knowing pure silica
          30 years' experience
          must have known danger for every man
   neglected to provide the workmen with any safety device. . . .
   —As a matter of fact, they originally intended to dig that
       tunnel a certain size?
105    —Yes.
   —And then enlarged the size of the tunnel, due to the fact
       that they discovered silica and wanted to get it out?
   —That is true for tunnel No. 1.
       The tunnel is part of a huge water-power project
          begun, latter part of 1929
110           direction: New Kanawha Power Co.
                   subsidiary of Union Carbide & Carbon Co.
       That company—licensed:
       to develop power for public sale.
       Ostensibly it was to do that; but
115           (in reality) it was formed to sell all the power to
           the Electro-Metallurgical Co.
          subsidiary of Union Carbide & Carbon Co.
           which by an act of the State legislature
           was allowed to buy up
120           New Kanawha Power Co. in 1933.
   —They were developing the power. What I am trying to
       get at, Miss Allen, is, did they use this silica from the
       tunnel; did they afterward sell it and use it in commerce?
   —They used it in the electro-processing of steel.
       $SiO_2$         $SiO_2°$
       The richest deposit.
125        Shipped on the C & O down to Alloy.
       It was so pure that
               $SiO_2$
       they used it without refining.
   —Where did you stay?
130    —I stayed at Cedar Grove. Some days I would have to hitch
       into Charleston, other days to Gauley Bridge.
   —You found the people of West Virginia very happy to pick
       you up on the highway, did you not?
   —Yes; they are delightfully obliging.
       (All were bewildered. Again at Vanetta they are asking,
         "What can be done about this?")
135        I feel that this investigation may help in some manner.

---

123 *$SiO_2$*: silica, or silicon oxide, a mineral used in the electroprocessing of steel; silica dust particles, inevitably raised when the mineral is mined, are tiny shards of glass which lacerate lung tissue when they are inhaled.

I do hope it may.
I am now making a very general statement as a beginning.
  There are many points that I should like to develop
  later, but I shall try to give you a general history of
  this condition first. . . .

### GAULEY BRIDGE

Camera at the crossing sees the city
a street of wooden walls and empty windows,
140    the doors shut handless in the empty street,
and the deserted Negro standing on the corner.

The little boy runs with his dog
up the street to the bridge over the river where
nine men are mending road for the government.
145    He blurs the camera-glass fixed on the street.

Railway tracks here and many panes of glass
tin under light, the grey shine of towns and forests:
in the commercial hotel (Switzerland of America)
the owner is keeping his books behind the public glass.

150    Postoffice window, a hive of private boxes,
the hand of the man who withdraws, the woman who reaches
    her hand
and the tall coughing man stamping an envelope.

The bus station and the great pale buses stopping for food;
April-glass-tinted, the yellow-aproned waitress;
155    coast-to-coast schedule on the plateglass window.

The man on the street and the camera eye:
he leaves the doctor's office, slammed door, doom,
any town looks like this one-street town.

Glass, wood, and naked eye: the movie-house
160    closed for the afternoon frames posters streaked with rain,
advertise "Racing Luck" and "Hitch-Hike Lady."

Whistling, the train comes from a long way away,
slow, and the Negro watches it grow in the grey air,
the hotel man makes a note behind his potted palm.

165    Eyes of the tourist house, red-and-white filling station,
the eyes of the Negro, looking down the track,
hotel-man and hotel, cafeteria, camera.

And in the beerplace on the other sidewalk
always one's harsh night eyes over the beerglass
170    follow the waitress and the yellow apron.

The road flows over the bridge,
Gamoca pointer at the underpass,
opposite, Alloy, after a block of town.

What do you want—a cliff over a city?
175    A foreland, sloped to sea and overgrown with roses?
These people live here.

### THE FACE OF THE DAM: VIVIAN JONES°

On the hour he shuts the door and walks out of town;
he knows the place up the gorge where he can see
his locomotive rusted on the siding,
180    he sits and sees the river at his knee.

There, where the men crawl, landscaping the grounds
at the power-plant, he saw the blasts explode
the mouth of the tunnel that opened wider
when precious in the rock the white glass showed.

185    The old plantation-house (burned to the mud)
is a hill-acre of ground. The Negro woman throws
gay arches of water out from the front door.
It runs down, wild as grass, falls and flows.

On the quarter he remembers how they enlarged
190    the tunnel and the crews, finding the silica,
how the men came riding freights, got jobs here
and went into the tunnel-mouth to stay.

Never to be used, he thinks, never to spread its power,
jinx on the rock, curse on the power-plant,
195    hundreds breathed value, filled their lungs full of glass
(O the gay wind the clouds the many men).

On the half-hour he's at Hawk's Nest over the dam,
snow springs up as he reaches the great wall-face,
immense and pouring power, the mist of snow,
200    the fallen mist, the slope of water, glass.

O the gay snow the white dropped water, down,
all day the water rushes down its river,
unused, has done its death-work in the country,
proud gorge and festive water.

205    On the last quarter he pulls his heavy collar up,
feels in his pocket the picture of his girl,
touches for luck—he used to as he drove
after he left his engine; stamps in the deep snow.

---

**section head:** *Vivian Jones*: an engineer on the Hawk's Nest project, one of the design-
ers of the tunnel and power plant.

And the snow clears and the dam stands in the gay weather,
210   O proud O white O water rolling down,
he turns and stamps this off his mind again
and on the hour walks again through town.

PRAISE OF THE COMMITTEE

*These are the lines on which a committee is formed.*
      Almost as soon as work was begun in the tunnel
215   men began to die among dry drills. No masks.
      Most of them were not from this valley.
      The freights brought many every day from States
      all up and down the Atlantic seaboard
      and as far inland as Kentucky, Ohio.
220   After the work the camps were closed or burned.
      The ambulance was going day and night,
      White's undertaking business thriving and
      his mother's cornfield put to a new use.
      "Many of the shareholders at this meeting
225   "were nervous about the division of the profits;
      "How much has the Company spent on lawsuits?
      "The man said $150,000. Special counsel:
      "I am familiar with the case. Not  :  one  :  cent.
      " 'Terms of the contract. Master liable.'
230   "No reply. Great corporation disowning men who made. . . ."
      After the lawsuits had been instituted. . . .
*The Committee is a true reflection of the will of the people.*
      Every man is ill. The women are not affected,
      This is not a contagious disease. A medical commission,
235   Dr. Hughes, Dr. Hayhurst examined the chest
      of Raymond Johnson, and Dr. Harless, a former
      company doctor. But he saw too many die,
      he has written his letter to Washington.
*The Committee meets regularly, wherever it can.*
240   Here are Mrs. Jones, three lost sons, husband sick,
      Mrs. Leek, cook for the bus cafeteria,
      the men: George Robinson, leader and voice,
      four other Negroes (three drills, one camp-boy)
      Blankenship, the thin friendly man, Peyton the engineer,
245   Juanita° absent, the one outsider member.
      Here in the noise, loud belts of the shoe-repair shop,
      meeting around the stove beneath the one bulb hanging.
      They come late in the day. Many come with them
      who pack the hall, wait in the thorough dark.
250   *This is a defense committee. Unfinished business:*
      Two rounds of lawsuits, 200 cases
      Now as to the crooked lawyers
      If the men had worn masks, their use would have involved
      time every hour to wash the sponge at mouth.

---

240–245 *Mrs. Jones, Blankenship, Peyton, Juanita, Robinson*: members of the Gauley Bridge
community's defense committee, which undertook lawsuits against Union Carbide and its
subsidiaries; each is the subject of a poem later in the sequence.

255      Tunnel, 3¹/₈ miles long. Much larger than
          the Holland Tunnel or Pittsburgh's Liberty Tubes.
          Total cost, say, $16,000,000.
       *This is the procedure of such a committee*:
          To consider the bill before the Senate.
260      To discuss relief.
             Active members may be cut off relief,
                16-mile walk to Fayetteville for cheque—
                WEST VIRGINIA RELIEF ADMINISTRATION, #22991,
                TO JOE HENIGAN, GAULEY BRIDGE, ONE AND 50/100,
265                 WINONA NATIONAL BANK. PAID FROM STATE FUNDS.
       Unless the Defense Committee acts;
       the *People's Press*, supporting this fight,
       signed editorials, sent in funds.
       Clothing for tunnel-workers.
270           Rumored, that in the post-office
          parcels are intercepted.
          Suspected: Conley. Sheriff, hotelman,
          head of the town ring—
          Company whispers. Spies,
275           The Racket.
       Resolved, resolved.
       George Robinson holds all their strength together:
       To fight the companies   to make somehow a future.
       "At any rate, it is inadvisable to keep a community of dying
280           persons intact."
       "Senator Holt.° Yes. This is the most barbarous example of
          industrial construction that ever happened in the world."
          Please proceed.
     "In a very general way° Hippocrates'° *Epidemics* speaks
285           of the metal digger who breathes with difficulty,
          having a pale and wan complexion.
          Pliny, the elder°. . . ."
     "Present work of the Bureau of Mines. . . ."

     The dam's pure crystal slants upon the river.
290           A dark and noisy room, frozen two feet from stove.
          The cough of habit. The sound of men in the hall
          waiting for word.

          These men breathe hard
          but the committee has a voice of steel.
295           One climbs the hill on canes.
          They have broken the hills and cracked the riches wide.

---

281 *Senator Holt*: Senator Rush Dew Holt of West Virginia, who testified before the Sub-committee.

284 *"In a very general way . . ."*: from the congressional testimony of John Finch, Director of the U.S. Bureau of Mines.

284 *Hippocrates*: (460–377 BCE) Greek physician, "father of medicine," and author of *Epidemics*, among the earliest extant treatises on clinical medicine.

287 *Pliny the elder*: (23–79 AD) Roman official, author of *Natural History*, among the most important works of classical Latin literature.

In this man's face
family leans out from two worlds of graves—
here is a room of eyes,
300        a single force looks out, reading out life.

Who stands over the river?
Whose feet go running in these rigid hills?
Who comes, warning the night,
shouting and young to waken our eyes?

305        Who runs through electric wires?
Who speaks down every road?
Their hands touched mastery; now they
demand an answer.

### MEARL BLANKENSHIP°

He stood against the stove
310        facing the fire—
Little warmth, no words,
loud machines.

Voted relief,
wished money mailed,
315        quietly under the crashing:

"I wake up choking, and my wife
"rolls me over on my left side;
"then I'm asleep in the dream I always see:
"the tunnel choked
320        "the dark wall coughing dust.
"I have written a letter.
"Send it to the city,
"maybe to a paper
"if it's all right."

325        Dear Sir, my name is Mearl Blankenship.
I have Worked for the rhinehart & Dennis Co
Many days & many nights
& it was so dusty you couldn't hardly see the lights.
I helped nip steel for the drills
330        & helped lay the track in the tunnel
& done lots of drilling near the mouth of the tunnell
& when the shots went off the boss said
If you are going to work Venture back
& the boss was Mr. Andrews
335        & now he is dead and gone
But I am still here
a lingering along

---

**section head:** *Blankenship*: a laborer on the Hawk's Nest tunnel project who contracted silicosis while working on the tunnel; he did not testify before the subcommittee, but Rukeyser and Naumberg met him when they traveled to Gauley Bridge.

He stood against the rock
facing the river
340 grey river grey face
the rock mottled behind him
like X-ray plate enlarged
diffuse and stony
his face against the stone.

345      J C Dunbar said that I was the very picture of health
when I went to Work at that tunnel.
I have lost eighteen lbs on that Rheinhart ground
and expecting to loose my life
& no settlement yet & I have sued the Co. twice
350 But when the lawyers got a settlement
they didn't want to talk to me
But I didn't know whether they were sleepy or not.
I am a Married Man and have a family.   God
knows if they can do anything for me
355 it will be appreciated
if you can do anything for me
let me know soon

### ABSALOM°

I first discovered what was killing these men.
I had three sons who worked with their father in the tunnel:
360 Cecil, aged 23, Owen, aged 21, Shirley, aged 17.
They used to work in a coal mine, not steady work
for the mines were not going much of the time.
A power Co. foreman learned that we made home brew,
he formed a habit of dropping in evenings to drink,
365 persuading the boys and my husband—
give up their jobs and take this other work.
It would pay them better.
Shirley was my youngest son; the boy.
He went into the tunnel.

370      *My heart      my mother      my heart      my mother*
*My heart      my coming into being.*

·   My husband is not able to work.
He has it, according to the doctor.
We have been having a very hard time making a living since
this trouble came to us.
375 I saw the dust in the bottom of the tub.
The boy worked there about eighteen months,
came home one evening with a shortness of breath.

---

**section head:** *Absalom*: the youngest son of King David who rebels against his father and,
after forcing David into a brief retreat across the Jordan, is defeated by David's army and
killed by Joab, David's faithful captain (II Samuel 13–19). In the voice of Mrs. Dora Jones,
this section draws on testimony scattered throughout the hearings, most of it not actually
given by Mrs. Jones, but given instead by Philippa Allen and Mrs. Jones' husband, Charles.

He said, "Mother, I cannot get my breath."
Shirley was sick about three months.
380    I would carry him from his bed to the table,
from his bed to the porch, in my arms.

*My heart is mine in the place of hearts,*
*They gave me back my heart, it lies in me.*

When they took sick, right at the start, I saw a doctor.
385    I tried to get Dr. Harless to X-ray the boys.
He was the only man I had any confidence in,
the company doctor in the Kopper's mine,
but he would not see Shirley.
He did not know where his money was coming from.
390    I promised him half if he'd work to get compensation,
but even then he would not do anything.
I went on the road and begged the X-ray money,
the Charleston hospital made the lung pictures,
he took the case after the pictures were made.
395    And two or three doctors said the same thing.
The youngest boy did not get to go down there with me,
he lay and said, "Mother, when I die,
"I want you to have them open me up and
"see if that dust killed me.
400    "Try to get compensation,
"You will not have any way of making your living
"when we are gone,
"and the rest are going too."

*I have gained mastery over my heart*
405    *I have gained mastery over my two hands*
*I have gained mastery over the waters*
*I have gained mastery over the river.*

The case of my son was the first of the line of lawsuits.
They sent the lawyers down and the doctors down;
410    they closed the electric sockets in the camps.
There was Shirley, and Cecil, Jeffrey and Oren,
Raymond Johnson, Clev and Oscar Anders,
Frank Lynch, Henry Palf, Mr. Pitch, a foreman;
a slim fellow who carried steel with my boys,
415    his name was Darnell, I believe. There were many others,
the towns of Glen Ferris, Alloy, where the white rock lies,
six miles away; Vanetta, Gauley Bridge,
Gamoca, Lockwood, the gullies,
the whole valley is witness.
420    I hitchhike eighteen miles, they make checks out.
They asked me how I keep the cow on $2.
I said one week, feed for the cow, one week, the children's flour.
The oldest son was twenty-three.
The next son was twenty-one.
425    The youngest son was eighteen.

They called it pneumonia at first.
They would pronounce it fever.
Shirley asked that we try to find out.
That's how they learned what the trouble was.

430     *I open out a way, they have covered my sky with crystal*
    *I come forth by day, I am born a second time,*
    *I force a way through, and I know the gate*
    *I shall journey over the earth among the living.*

    He shall not be diminished, never;
435     I shall give a mouth to my son.

### The Disease°

This is a lung disease. Silicate dust makes it.
The dust causing the growth of

This is the X-ray picture taken last April.
I would point out to you: these are the ribs;
440     this is the region of the breastbone;
this is the heart (a wide white shadow filled with blood).
In here of course is the swallowing tube, esophagus.
The windpipe. Spaces between the lungs.

        Between the ribs?

445     Between the ribs. These are the collar bones.
Now, this lung's mottled, beginning, in these areas.
You'd say a snowstorm had struck the fellow's lungs.
About alike, that side and this side, top and bottom.
The first stage in this period in this case.

450         Let us have the second.

Come to the window again. Here is the heart.
More numerous nodules, thicker, see, in the upper lobes.
You will notice the increase : here, streaked fibrous tissue—

        Indicating?

455     That indicates the progress in ten months' time.
And now, this year—short breathing, solid scars
even over the ribs, thick on both sides.
Blood vessels shut. Model conglomeration.

---

**section head:** *"The Disease"*: drawn from the Congressional testimony of Dr. Leonard Goldwater, chief of the occupational diseases clinic of the New York University College of Medicine.

                        What stage?

460      Third stage. Each time I place my pencil point:
         There and there and there, there, there.

             "It is growing worse every day. At night
             "I get up to catch my breath. If I remained
             "flat on my back I believe I would die."°
465      It gradually chokes off the air cells in the lungs?
         I am trying to say it the best I can.
         That is what happens, isn't it?
         A choking-off in the air cells?

         Yes.
470      There is difficulty in breathing.
         Yes.
             And a painful cough?
         Yes.

             Does silicosis cause death?

475      Yes, sir.

                    GEORGE ROBINSON: BLUES°

         Gauley Bridge is a good town for Negroes, they let us stand
             around, they let us stand
         around on the sidewalks if we're black or brown.
         Vanetta's over the trestle, and that's our town.

         The hill makes breathing slow, slow breathing after you row the river,
480      and the graveyard's on the hill, cold in the springtime blow,
         the graveyard's up on high, and the town is down below.

         Did you ever bury thirty-five men in a place in back of your house,
         thirty-five tunnel workers the doctors didn't attend,
         died in the tunnel camps, under rocks, everywhere, world
             without end.

485      When a man said I feel poorly, for any reason, any weakness or such,
         letting up when he couldn't keep going barely,
         the Cap and company come and run him off the job surely.

         I've put them
         DOWN from the tunnel camps
490      to the graveyard on the hill,
         tin-cans all about—it fixed them!—
         TUNNELITIS

---

462–464 *"It is growing worse . . ."*: from tunnel worker George Robinson's testimony at the
Subcommittee hearings; see next note.
**section head**: *George Robinson*: African American laborer on the Hawk's Nest project
whose actual name was George Robison; drawn from his lengthy congressional testimony.

hold themselves up
at the side of a tree,
495    I can go right now
to that cemetery.

When the blast went off the boss would call out, Come, let's go back,
when that heavy loaded blast went white, Come, let's go back,
telling us hurry, hurry, into the falling rocks and muck.

500    The water they would bring had dust in it, our drinking water,
the camps and their groves were colored with the dust,
we cleaned our clothes in the groves, but we always had the dust.
Looked like somebody sprinkled flour all over the parks and groves,
it stayed and the rain couldn't wash it away and it twinkled
505    that white dust really looked pretty down around our ankles.

As dark as I am, when I came out at morning after the tunnel at
    night,
with a white man, nobody could have told which man was white.
The dust had covered us both, and the dust was white.

### JUANITA TINSLEY°

Even after the letters, there is work,
510    sweaters, the food, the shoes
and afternoon's quick dark

draws on the windowpane
my face, the shadowed hair,
the scattered papers fade.

515    Slow letters! I shall be
always—the stranger said
"To live stronger and free."

I know in America there are songs,
forgetful ballads to be sung,
520    but at home I see this wrong.

When I see my family house,
the gay gorge, the picture-books,
they raise the face of General Wise

aged by enemies, like faces
525    the stranger showed me in the town.
I saw that plain, and saw my place.

The scene of hope's ahead; look, April,
and next month with a softer wind,
maybe they'll rest upon their land,

---

**section head:** *Juanita Tinsely:* member of the local defense committee, resident of Gauley
Bridge.

530          and then maybe the happy song, and love,
             a tall boy who was never in a tunnel.


                        THE DOCTORS°


             —Tell the jury your name.
             —Emory R. Hayhurst.
             —State your education, Doctor, if you will.
535          Don't be modest about it; just tell about it.


             High school Chicago 1899
             Univ. of Illinois 1903
             M.A. 1905, thesis on respiration
             P & S Chicago 1908
540          2 years' hospital training;
             at Rush on occupational disease
             director of clinic 2½ years.
             Ph.D. Chicago 1916
             Ohio Dept. of Health, 20 years as
545          consultant in occupational diseases.
             Hygienist, U.S. Public Health Service
             and Bureau of Mines
             and Bureau of Standards


             Danger begins at 25%
550          here was pure danger
             Dept. of Mines
             came in, was kept away.


             Miner's phthisis, fibroid phthisis,
             grinder's rot, potter's rot,
555          whatever it used to be called,
             these men did not need to die.


             —Is silicosis an occupational disease?
             —It is.
             —Did anyone show you the lungs of Cecil Jones?
560          —Yes, sir.
             —Who was that?
             —It was Dr. Harless.


"We talked to Dr. L. R. Harless, who had handled many of the cases,
more than any other doctor there. At first Dr. Harless did not like to
talk about the matter. He said he had been subjected to so much pub-
licity. It appeared that the doctor thought he had been involved in too

---

**section head:** *"The Doctors"*: compiled from the congressional testimony of Dr. Leonard
Goldwater, Dr. Emory Hayhurst, a member of the medical commission charged with de-
termining the extent of the Gauley Bridge silicosis problem, and of Gilbert Love, a jour-
nalist who had visited the area; from transcripts of testimony at two civil trials held in
West Virginia, read into the subcommittee's record; and from a telegram and letter sent
by Dr. L.R. Harless of West Virginia in lieu of testimony; this poem exemplifies Rukeyser's
practice of editing and juxtaposing fragments from the subcommittee hearings both to add
coherence by giving the impression of a single speaker and to construct the light in which
(or lens through which) readers see individual speakers.

many of the court cases; but finally he opened up and told us about
the matter."
—Did he impress you as one who thought this was a very serious thing
in that section of the country?
"Yes, he did. I would say that Dr. Harless has probably become very
self-conscious about this matter. I cannot say that he has retracted
what he told me, but possibly he had been thrust into the limelight so
much that he is more conservative now than when the matter was sim-
ply something of local interest."

Dear Sir: Due to illness of my wife and urgent professional duties, I
am unable to appear as per your telegram.
    Situation exaggerated. Here are facts:
    We examined. 13 dead. 139 had some lung damage.
    2 have died since, making 15 deaths.
    Press says 476 dead, 2,000 affected and doomed.
    I am at a loss to know where those figures were obtained.
    At this time, only a few cases here,
    and these only moderately affected.
    Last death occurred November, 1934.
It has been said that none of the men knew of the hazard connected
with the work. This is not correct. Shortly after the work began many
of these workers came to me complaining of chest conditions and I
warned many of them of the dust hazard and advised them that con-
tinued work under these conditions would result in serious lung dis-
ease. Disregarding this warning many of the men continued at this
work and later brought suit against their employer for damages.
While I am sure that many of these suits were based on meritorious
grounds, I am also convinced that many others took advantage of this
situation and made out of it nothing less than a racket. In this letter
I have endeavored to give you the facts which came under my obser-
vation. . . .
If I can supply further information. . . .
Mr. Marcantonio.° A man may be examined a year after he has worked
in a tunnel and not show a sign of silicosis, and yet the silicosis may
develop later; is not that true?
—Yes, it may develop as many as ten years after.
Mr. Marcantonio. Even basing the statement on the figures, the doc-
tor's claim that this is a racket is not justified?
—No; it would not seem to be justified.
Mr. Marcantonio. I should like to point out that Dr. Harless contra-
dicts his "exaggeration" when he volunteers the following:
"I warned many. . . ."
(Mr. Peyton. I do not know. Nobody knew the danger around there.)

Dr. Goldwater. First are the factors involving the individual.
        Under the heading B, external causes.
        Some of the factors which I have in mind—
        those are the facts upon the blackboard,
        the influencing and controlling factors.

---

*Mr. Marcantonio*: Vito Marcantonio, Congressman from New York and member of the
subcommittee.

Mr. Marcantonio. Those factors would bring about acute silicosis?
Dr. Goldwater. I hope you are not provoked when I say "might."
     Medicine has no hundred percent.
     We speak of possibilities, have opinions.
Mr. Griswold.° Doctors testify answering "yes" and "no." Don't they?
Dr. Goldwater. Not by the choice of the doctor.
Mr. Griswold. But that is usual, isn't it?
Dr. Goldwater. They do not like to do that.
     A man with a scientific point of view—
     unfortunately there are doctors without that—
     I do not mean to say all doctors are angels—
     but most doctors avoid dogmatic statements.
     avoid assiduously "always," "never."
Mr. Griswold. Best doctor I ever knew said "no" and "yes."
Dr. Goldwater. There are different opinions on that, too.
     We were talking about acute silicosis.

   The man in the white coat is the man on the hill,
   the man with the clean hands is the man with the drill,
   the man who answers "yes" lies still.

—Did you make an examination of those sets of lungs?
—I did.
—I wish you would tell the jury whether or not those lungs were
 silicotic.
—We object.
—Objection overruled.
—They were.

### THE CORNFIELD

   Error, disease, snow, sudden weather.
   For those given to contemplation : this house,
565  wading in snow, its cracks are sealed with clay,
   walls papered with print, newsprint repeating,
   in-focus grey across the room, and squared
   ads for a book : HEAVEN'S MY DESTINATION,
   HEAVEN'S MY . . . HEAVEN. . . . THORNTON WILDER.°
570  The long-faced man rises long-handed jams the door
   tight against snow, long-boned, he shivers.
   Contemplate.

      Swear by the corn,
   the found-land corn, those who like ritual. *He*
   rides in a good car. They say blind corpses rode
575  with him in front, knees broken into angles,
   head clamped ahead. Overalls. Affidavits.
   He signs all papers. His office : where he sits.

---

*Mr. Griswold*: Glenn Griswold, Congressman from Indiana and chair of the subcommittee.
569 *Thornton Wilder*: (1897–1975) popular American playwright and novelist, author of
*Heaven's My Destination* (1935), a satiric study of a Midwestern book salesman.

feet on the stove, loaded trestles through door,
satin-lined, silk-lined, unlined, cheap,
580    The papers in the drawer. On the desk, photograph
H. C. White, Funeral Services (new car and eldest son);
tells about Negroes who got wet at work,
shot craps, drank and took cold, pneumonia, died.
Shows the sworn papers. Swear by the corn.
585    Pneumonia, pneumonia, pleurisy, t.b.

For those given to voyages : these roads
discover gullies, invade, Where does it go now?
Now turn upstream twenty-five yards. Now road again.
Ask the man on the road. Saying, That cornfield?
590    Over the second hill, through the gate,
watch for the dogs. Buried, five at a time,
pine boxes, Rinehart & Dennis paid him $55
a head for burying these men in plain pine boxes.
His mother is suing him : misuse of land.

595    George Robinson : I knew a man
who died at four in the morning at the camp.
At seven his wife took clothes to dress her dead
husband, and at the undertaker's
they told her the husband was already buried.
600    —Tell me this, the men with whom you are acquainted,
the men who have this disease
have been told that sooner or later they are going to die?
—Yes, sir.
—How does that seem to affect the majority of the people?
605    —It don't work on anything but their wind.
—Do they seem to be living in fear
or do they wish to die?
—They are getting to breathe a little faster.

For those given to keeping their own garden:
610    Here is the cornfield, white and wired by thorns,
old cornstalks, snow, the planted home.
Stands bare against a line of farther field,
unmarked except for wood stakes, charred at tip,
few scratched and named (pencil or nail).
615    Washed-off. Under the mounds,
all the anonymous.
Abel America, calling from under the corn,
Earth, uncover my blood!
Did the undertaker know the man was married?
620    Uncover.
Do they seem to fear death?
Contemplate.
Does Mellon's° ghost walk, povertied at last,
walking in furrows of corn, still sowing,

---

623 *Mellon*: (William Andrew, 1855–1937) American industrialist and financier, Secretary
of the U.S. Treasury (1921–1932).

625    do apparitions come?
       Voyage.
       Think of your gardens. But here is corn to keep.
       Marked pointed sticks to name the crop beneath.
       Sowing is over, harvest is coming ripe.

630    —No, sir; they want to go on.
       They want to live as long as they can.


                    Arthur Peyton°

       Consumed. Eaten away. And love across the street.
       I had a letter in the mail this morning
       Dear Sir, . . . pleasure . . . enclosing herewith our check . . .
635    payable to you, for $21.59
                    being one-half of the residue which
                    we were able to collect in your behalf
                    in regard to the above case.
       In winding up the various suits,
640                 after collecting all we could,
                    we find this balance due you.
       With regards, we are
                    Very truly,


       After collecting
645                 the dust      the failure      the engineering corps
       O love      consumed      eaten away      the foreman laughed
       they wet the drills when the inspectors came
       the moon blows glassy over our native river.

       O love tell the committee that I know:
650    never repeat you mean to marry me.
       In mines, the fans are large (2,000 men unmasked)
       before his verdict the doctor asked me      How long
       I said, Dr. Harless, tell me how long?
       —Only never again tell me you'll marry me.
655    I watch how at the tables you all day
       follow a line of clouds      the dance of drills,

       and, love, the sky birds who crown the trees
       the white white hills standing upon Alloy
       —I charge negligence, all companies concerned—
660    two years O love two years he said he gave.

       The swirl of river at the tidy house
       the marble bank-face of the liquor store
       I saw the Negroes driven with pick handles
       on these other jobs I was not in tunnel work.

---

**section head:** *Arthur Peyton:* Peyton was an engineer at the Hawk's Nest tunnel project
who contracted silicosis from work in the tunnel; he testified before the subcommittee
about the inadequacy of tunnel ventilation equipment; drawn from his congressional tes-
timony.

665    Between us, love
                              the buses at the door
       the long glass street      two years, my death to yours
       my death upon your lips
       my face becoming glass
670    strong challenged time making me win immortal
       the love a mirror of our valley
       our street    our river    a deadly glass to hold.
       Now they are feeding me into a steel mill furnace
       O love the stream of glass a stream of living fire.

### ALLOY

675    This is the most audacious landscape. The gangster's
       stance with his gun smoking and out is not so
       vicious as this commercial field, its hill of glass.

       Sloping as gracefully as thighs, the foothills
       narrow to this, clouds over every town
670    finally indicate the stored destruction.

       Crystalline hill: a blinded field of white
       murdering snow, seamed by convergent tracks;
       the travelling cranes reach for the silica.

       And down the track, the overhead conveyor
675    slides on its cable to the feet of chimneys.
       Smoke rises, not white enough, not so barbaric.

       Here the severe flame speaks from the brick throat,
       electric furnaces produce this precious, this clean,
       annealing the crystals, fusing at last alloys.

680    Hottest for silicon, blast furnaces raise flames,
       spill fire, spill steel, quench the new shape to freeze,
       tempering it to perfected metal.

       Forced through this crucible, a million men.
       Above this pasture, the highway passes those
685    who curse the air, breathing their fear again.

       The roaring flowers of the chimney-stacks
       less poison, at their lips in fire, than this
       dust that is blown from off the field of glass;

       blows and will blow, rising over the mills,
690    crystallized and beyond the fierce corrosion
       disintegrated angel on these hills.

### POWER

       The quick sun brings, exciting mountains warm,
       gay on the landscapers and green designs,
       miracle, yielding the sex up under all the skin,

695 until the entire body watches the scene with love,
 sees perfect cliffs ranging until the river
 cuts sheer, mapped far below in delicate track,
 surprise of grace, the water running in the sun,
 magnificent flower on the mouth, surprise
700 as lovers who look too long on the desired face
 startle to find the remote flesh so warm.
 A day of heat shed on the gorge, a brilliant
 day when love sees the sun behind its man
 and the disguised marvel under familiar skin.

705 Steel-bright, light-pointed, the narrow-waisted towers
 lift their protective network, the straight, the accurate
 flex of distinction, economy of gift,
 gymnast, they poise their freight; god's generosity! give
 their voltage low enough for towns to handle.
710 The power-house stands skin-white at the transmitters' side
 over the rapids  the brilliance  the blind foam.

 This is the midway between water and flame,
 this is the road to take when you think of your country,
 between the dam and the furnace, terminal.
715 The clean park, fan of wires, landscapers,
 the stone approach. And seen beyond the door,
 the man with the flashlight in his metal hall.
 Here, the effective green, grey-toned and shining,
 tall immense chamber of cylinders. Green,
720 the rich paint catches light from three-story windows,
 arches of light vibrate erratic panels on
 sides of curved steel. Man pockets flashlight,
 useless, the brilliant floor casts tiled reflection up,
 bland walls return it, circles pass it round.
725 Wheels, control panels, dials, the vassal instruments.
 This is the engineer Jones, the blueprint man,
 loving the place he designed, visiting it alone.
 Another blood, no cousin to the town;
 rings his heels on stone, pride follows his eyes,
730 "This is the place."

 Four generators, smooth green, and squares of black,
 floored-over space for a fifth.
         The stairs. Descend.
 "They said I built the floor like the tiles of a bank,
735 I wanted the men who work here to be happy."
 Light laughing on steel, the gay, the tall sun
 given away; mottled; snow comes in clouds;
 the iron steps go down as roads go down.
 This is the second circle, world of inner shade,
740 hidden bulk of generators, governor shaft,
 round gap of turbine pit. Flashlight, tool-panels,
 heels beating on iron, cold of underground,
 stairs, wire flooring, the voice's hollow cry.
 This is the scroll, the volute case of night,

745     quick shadow and the empty galleries.

Go down; here at the outlets, butterfly valves
open from here, the tail-race, vault of steel,
the spiral staircase ending, last light in shaft.
"Gone," says the thin straight man.
750     "'Hail, holy light, offspring of Heav'n first-born,
'Or of th' Eternal Coeternal beam
'May I express thee unblamed?' "°
                              And still go down.

Now ladder-mouth; and the precipitous fear,
755     uncertain rungs down into after-night.
"This is the place. Away from this my life
I am indeed Adam unparadiz'd.
Some fools call this the Black Hole of Calcutta,
I don't know how they ever get to Congress."

760     Gulfs, spirals, that the drunken ladder swings,
its rungs give, pliant, beneath the leaping heart.
Leaps twice at midnight. But a naked bulb
makes glare, turns paler, burns to dark again.
Brilliance begins, stutters. And comes upon
765     after the tall abstract, the ill, the unmasked men,
the independent figure of the welder
masked for his work; acts with unbearable flame.
His face is a cage of steel, the hands are covered,
points dazzle hot, fly from his writing torch,
770     brighten the face and hands and marrying steel.
Says little, works   :   only   :   "A little down,
five men were killed in the widening of the tunnel."

Shell of bent metal; walking along an arc
the tube rounds up about your shoulders, black
775     circle, great circle, down infinite mountains rides,
echoes words, footsteps, testimonies.
"One said the air was thin, Fifth-Avenue clean."
The iron pillars mark a valve division,
four tunnels merging. Iron on iron resounds,
780     echoes along created gorges. "Sing,
test echoes, sing : Pilgrim," he cries,
singing *Once More, Dear Home,*
as all the light burns out.
Down the reverberate channels of the hills
785     the suns declare midnight, go down, cannot ascend,
no ladder back; see this, your eyes can ride through steel,
this is the river Death, diversion of power,
the root of the tower and the tunnel's core,
this is the end.

---

752 *Hail, holy light, offspring of Heav'n first-born . . .*": Milton, *Paradise Lost* (III, 1–3).

## The Dam

790  All power is saved, having no end. Rises
In the green season, in the sudden season
the white the budded
      and the lost.
Water celebrates, yielding continually
795  sheeted and fast in its overfall
slips down the rock, evades the pillars
building its colonnades, repairs
in stream and standing wave
retains its seaward green
800  broken by obstacle rock; falling, the water sheet
spouts, and the mind dances, excess of white.
White brilliant function of the land's disease.

Many-spanned, lighted, the crest leans under
concrete arches and the channelled hills,
805  turns in the gorge toward its release;
kinetic and controlled, the sluice
urging the hollow, the thunder,
the major climax
      energy
810  total and open watercourse
praising the spillway, fiery glaze,
crackle of light, cleanest velocity
flooding, the moulded force.

   *I open out a way over the water*
815     *I form a path between the Combatants:*
   *Grant that I sail down like a living bird,*
   *power over the fields and Pool of Fire.*
   *Phoenix,° I sail over the phoenix world.*

Diverted water, the fern and fuming white
820  ascend in mist of continuous diffusion.
Rivers are turning inside their mountains,
streams line the stone, rest at the overflow
lake and in lanes of pliant color lie.
Blessing of this innumerable silver,
825  printed in silver, images of stone
walk on a screen of falling water
in film-silver in continual change
recurring colored, plunging with the wave.

Constellations of light, abundance of many rivers.
830  The sheeted island-cities, the white surf filling west,
the hope, fast water spilled where still pools fed.
Great power flying deep: between the rock and the sunset,
the caretaker's house and the steep abutment,
hypnotic water fallen and the tunnels under

---

818 *Phoenix*: mythological bird which arises alive out of the ashes of its own immolation.

835      the moist and fragile galleries of stone,
            mile-long, under the wave. Whether snow fall,
            the quick light fall, years of white cities fall,
            flood that this valley built falls slipping down
            the green turn in the river's green.
840      Steep gorge, the wedge of crystal in the sky.

            How many feet of whirlpools?
            What is a year in terms of falling water?
            Cylinders; kilowatts; capacities.
            Continuity: $\Sigma \, Q = 0°$
845      Equations for falling water. The streaming motion.
            The balance-sheet of energy that flows
            passing along its infinite barrier.

            It breaks the hills, cracking the riches wide,
            runs through electric wires;
850      it comes, warning the night,
            running among these rigid hills,
            a single force to waken our eyes.

            They poured the concrete and the columns stood,
            laid bare the bedrock, set the cells of steel,
855      a dam for monument was what they hammered home.
            Blasted, and stocks went up;
            insured the base,
            and limousines
            wrote their own graphs upon
860      roadbed and lifeline.

        Their hands touched mastery:
        wait for defense, solid across the world.
        Mr. Griswold. "A corporation is a body without a soul."
        Mr. Dunn.° When they were caught at it they resorted to the
            methods employed by gunmen, ordinary machine gun racke-
            teers. They cowardly tried to buy out the people who had the
            information on them.
865      Mr. Marcantonio. I agree that a racket has been practised, but the
            most damnable racketeering that I have ever known is the
            paying of a fee to the very attorney who represented these
            victims. That is the most outrageous racket that has ever come
            within my knowledge.
        Miss Allen. Mr. Jesse J. Ricks, the president of the Union Carbide
            & Carbon Corporation, suggested that the stockholder had
            better take this question up in a private conference.
        The dam is safe. A scene of power.
        The dam is the father of the tunnel.
        This is the valley's work, the white, the shining.

---

844 $\Sigma \, Q = 0$: equation for the conversion of rushing or falling water's kinetic energy into electricity.
864 *Mr. Dunn*: Matthew Dunn, Congressman from Pennsylvania and member of the subcommittee.

870

| High | Low | Stock and Dividend in Dollars° | Open | High | Low | Last | Net Chge. | Closing Bid | Ask | Sales |
|---|---|---|---|---|---|---|---|---|---|---|
| 111 | 61¼ | Union Carbide (3.20) . . . . | 67¼ | 69½ | 67¼ | 69½ | +3 | 69¼ | 69½ | 3,400 |

The dam is used when the tunnel is used.
The men and the water are never idle,
have definitions.
This is a perfect fluid, having no age nor hours,
875    surviving scarless, unaltered, loving rest,
willing to run forever to find its peace
in equal seas in currents of still glass.
Effects of friction : to fight and pass again,
learning its power, conquering boundaries,
880    able to rise blind in revolts of tide,
broken and sacrificed to flow resumed.
Collecting eternally power. Spender of power,
torn, never can be killed, speeded in filaments,
million, its power can rest and rise forever,
885    wait and be flexible. Be born again.
Nothing is lost, even among the wars,
imperfect flow, confusion of force.
It will rise. These are the phases of its face.
It knows its seasons, the waiting, the sudden.
890    It changes. It does not die.

### THE DISEASE : AFTER-EFFECTS

This is the life of a Congressman.
Now he is standing on the floor of the House,
the galleries full; raises his voice; presents the bill.
Legislative, the fanfare, greeting its heroes with
895    ringing of telephone bells preceding entrances,
snapshots (Grenz rays, recording structure) newsreels.
This is silent, and he proposes:
                       embargo on munitions
to Germany and Italy
900    as states at war with Spain.°
He proposes
              Congress memorialize
the governor of California : free Tom Mooney,°

---

870 *stock quote*: an actual newspaper quote for Union Carbide stock, showing its gain in value over one day's trading.
900 *Spain*: During the 1936–1939 Spanish Civil War German and Italian troops fought to overthrow the elected government.
903 *Tom Mooney*: (1892–1942) labor activist, unjustly convicted in 1916 and served 23 years for purported involvement in a fire bomb attack on the Preparedness Day parade in San Francisco. Mooney's conviction was widely recognized as a government frame-up and became a cause celebre on the American Left (see note to Lola Ridge's "Stone Face").

A bill for a TVA° at Fort Peck Dam.
905   A bill to prevent industrial silicosis.

This is the gentleman from Montana.
—I'm a child, I'm leaning from a bedroom window,
clipping the rose that climbs upon the wall,
the tea roses, and the red roses,
910   one for a wound, another for disease,
remembrance for strikers. I was five, going on six,
my father on strike at the Anaconda mine;
they broke the Socialist mayor we had in Butte,
the sheriff (friendly), found their judge. Strike-broke.
915   Shot father. He died : wounds and his disease.
My father had silicosis.

Copper contains it, we find it in limestone,
sand quarries, sandstone, potteries, foundries,
granite, abrasives, blasting; many kinds of grinding,
920   plate, mining, and glass.

Widespread in trade, widespread in space!
Butte, Montana; Joplin, Missouri; the New York tunnels,
the Catskill Aqueduct.° In over thirty States.
A disease worse than consumption.

925   Only eleven States have laws.
There are today one million potential victims.
500,000 Americans have silicosis now.
These are the proportions of a war.

          Pictures rise, foreign parades, the living faces,
930          Asturian miners° with my father's face,
          wounded and fighting, the men at Gauley Bridge,
          my father's face enlarged; since now our house

          and all our meaning lies in this
          signature: power on a hill
935          centered in its committee and its armies
          sources of anger, the mine of emphasis.

          No plane can ever lift us high enough
          to see forgetful countries underneath,
          but always now the map and X-ray seem
940          resemblent pictures of one living breath
          one country marked by error
          and one air.

---

904 *TVA*: Tennessee Valley Authority, an agency of the Federal government created in
1933, charged with the development of the Tennessee River basin and surrounding area
(44,000 square miles, covering parts of seven states) to provide public works jobs and hy-
droelectric power for the region.
922–923 *Butte, Montana; Joplin, Missouri; the New York tunnels, the Catskill aqueduct*: lo-
cations of earlier silicosis outbreaks, mentioned in the congressional testimony of two Bu-
reau of Mines officials.
930 *miners*: Asturian miners in northwest Spain revolted against the government in 1934.

It sets up a gradual scar formation;
this increases, blocking all drainage from the lung,
945    eventually scars, blocking the blood supply,
and then they block the air passageways.
Shortness of breath,
pains around the chest,
he notices lack of vigor.

950    Bill blocked; investigation blocked.

These galleries produce their generations.
The Congressmen are restless, stare at the triple tier,
the flags, the ranks, the walnut foliage wall;
a row of empty seats, mask over a dead voice.
955    But over the country, a million look from work,
five hundred thousand stand.

### THE BILL°

The subcommittee submits:
Your committee held hearings, heard many witnesses; finds:

THAT the Hawk's Nest tunnel was constructed
960            Dennis and Rinehart, Charlottesville, Va., for
New Kanawha Power Co., subsidiary of
Union Carbide & Carbon Co.

THAT a tunnel was drilled
app. dist. 3.75 mis.
965            to divert water (from New River)
to hydroelectric plant (Gauley Junction).

THAT in most of the tunnel, drilled rock contained
90—even 99 percent pure silica.

This is a fact that was known.

970    THAT silica is dangerous to lungs of human beings.
When submitted to contact. Silicosis.

THAT the effects are well known.
Disease incurable.
Physical incapacity, cases fatal.

975    THAT the Bureau of Mines has warned for twenty years.

THAT prevention is: wet drilling, ventilation,
respirators, vacuum drills.
Disregard : utter. Dust : collected. Visibility : low.
Workmen left work, white with dust.

---

**section head:** *The Bill*: drawn from the subcommittee's report to the House of Repre-
sentatives Labor Committee, 5 February 1936.

980           Air system : inadequate.
          It was quite cloudy in there.
          When the drills were going, in all the smoke and dust,
          it seemed like a gang of airplanes going through that
            tunnel.
          Respirators, not furnished.
985           I have seen men with masks, but simply on their
            breasts.
          I have seen two wear them.
          Drills : dry drilling, for speed, for saving.
          A fellow could drill three holes dry for one hole wet.
          They went so fast they didn't square at the top.
990           Locomotives : gasoline. Suffering from monoxide gas.
          There have been men that fell in the tunnel. They had
            to be carried out.
       The driving of the tunnel.
          It was begun, continued, completed, with gravest
            disregard.
          And the employees? Their health, lives, future?
995        Results and infection.
          Many died. Many are not yet dead.
          Of negligence. Willful or inexcusable.
       Further findings:
          Prevalence : many States, mine, tunnel operations.
1000           A greatest menace.
       We suggest hearings be read.
          This is the dark. Lights strung up all the way.
          Depression; and, driven deeper in,
          by hunger, pistols, and despair,
1005           they took the tunnel.
       Of the contracting firm
          P. H. Faulconer, Pres.
          E. J. Perkins, Vice-Pres.
          have declined to appear.
1010           They have no knowledge of deaths from silicosis.
          However, their firm paid claims.
          I want to point out that under the statute $500 or $1000,
          but no more, may be recovered.

       We recommend.
          Bring them. Their books and records.
1015           Investigate. Require.
       Can do no more.
          These citizens from many States
          paying the price for electric power,
          To Be Vindicated.
1020
"If by their suffering and death they will have made a future life safer
for work beneath the earth, if they will have been able to establish a
new and greater regard for human life in industry, their suffering may
not have been in vain."
          Respectfully,
1025           Glenn Griswold
          Chairman, Subcommittee

Vito Marcantonio
W. P. Lambertson°
Matthew A. Dunn

1030     The subcommittee subcommits.
         Words on a monument.
         Capitoline thunder. It cannot be enough.
         The origin of storms is not in clouds,
         our lightning strikes when the earth rises,
1035     spillways free authentic power:
         dead John Brown's body walking from a tunnel
         to break the armored and concluded mind.

### THE BOOK OF THE DEAD

         These roads will take you into your own country.
         Seasons and maps coming where this road comes
1040     into a landscape mirrored in these men.

         Past all your influences, your home river,
         constellations of cities, mottoes of childhood,
         parents and easy cures, war, all evasion's wishes.

         What one word must never be said?
1045     Dead, and these men fight off our dying,
         cough in the theatres of the war.

         What two things shall never be seen?
         They : what we did. Enemy : what we mean.
         This is a nation's scene and halfway house.

1050     What three things can never be done?
         Forget.      Keep silent.      Stand alone.
         The hills of glass, the fatal brilliant plain.

         The facts of war forced into actual grace.
         Seasons and modern glory.      Told in the histories,
1055            how first ships came

         seeing on the Atlantic thirteen clouds
         lining the west horizon with their white
                 shining halations;

         they conquered, throwing off impossible Europe—
1060     could not be used to transform; created coast—
                 breathed-in America.

         See how they took the land, made after-life
         fresh out of exile, planted the pioneer
                 base and blockade,

---

1028 *W.P. Lambertson*: Congressman from Kansas and member of the subcommittee; the final member of the subcommittee, Jennings Randolph of West Virginia, submitted a separate concurring report from which Rukeyser drew some phrases in this poem.

1065     pushed forests down in an implacable walk
        west where new clouds lay at the desirable
                body of sunset;

        taking the seaboard. Replaced the isolation,
        dropped cities where they stood, drew a tidewater
1070               frontier of Europe,

        a moment, and another frontier held,
        this land was planted home-land that we know.
              Ridge of discovery,

        until we walk to windows, seeing America
1075         lie in a photograph of power, widened
              before our forehead,

        and still behind us falls another glory,
        London unshaken, the long French road to Spain,
              the old Mediterranean

1080     flashing new signals from the hero hills
        near Barcelona, monuments and powers,
              parent defenses.

        Before our face the broad and concrete west,
        green ripened field, frontier pushed back like river
1085               controlled and dammed;

        the flashing wheatfields, cities, lunar plains
        grey in Nevada, the sane fantastic country
              sharp in the south,

        liveoak, the hanging moss, a world of desert,
1090         the dead, the lava, and the extreme arisen
              fountains of life,

        the flourished land, peopled with watercourses
        to California and the colored sea;
              sums of frontiers

1095     and unmade boundaries of acts and poems,
        the brilliant scene between the seas, and standing,
              this fact and this disease.

———————

        Half-memories absorb us, and our ritual world
        carries its history in familiar eyes,
1100         planted in flesh it signifies its music

        in minds which turn to sleep and memory,
        in music knowing all the shimmering names,
        the spear, the castle, and the rose.

But planted in our flesh these valleys stand,
1105    everywhere we begin to know the illness,
are forced up, and our times confirm us all.

In the museum life, centuries of ambition
yielded at last a fertilizing image:
the Carthaginian stone meaning a tall woman

1110    carries in her two hands the book and cradled dove,
on her two thighs, wings folded from the waist
cross to her feet, a pointed human crown.

This valley is given to us like a glory.
To friends in the old world, and their lifting hands
1115    that call for intercession. Blow falling full in face.

All those whose childhood made learn skill to meet,
and art to see after the change of heart;
all the belligerents who know the world.

You standing over gorges, surveyors and planners,
1120    you workers and hope of countries, first among powers;
you who give peace and bodily repose,

opening landscapes by grace, giving the marvel lowlands
physical peace, flooding old battlefields
with general brilliance, who best love your lives;

1125    and you young, you who finishing the poem
wish new perfection and begin to make;
you men of fact, measure our times again.

--------------------

These are our strength, who strike against history.
These who corrupt cells owe their new styles of weakness
1130            to our diseases;

these carrying light for safety on their foreheads
descended deeper for richer faults of ore,
                drilling their death.

These touching radium and the luminous poison,
1135    carried their death on their lips and with their warning
                glow in their graves.

These weave and their eyes water and rust away,
these stand at wheels until their brains corrode,
                these farm and starve,

1140    all these men cry their doom across the world,
meeting avoidable death, fight against madness,
                find every war.

Are known as strikers, soldiers, pioneers,
fight on all new frontiers, are set in solid
1145           lines of defense.

Defense is sight; widen the lens and see
standing over the land myths of identity,
                new signals, processes:

Alloys begin : certain dominant metals.
1150     Deliberate combines add new qualities,
                sums of new uses.

Over the country, from islands of Maine fading,
Cape Sable fading south into the orange
                detail of sunset,

1155     new processes, new signals, new possession.
A name for all the conquests, prediction of victory
                deep in these powers.

Carry abroad the urgent need, the scene,
to photograph and to extend the voice,
1160            to speak this meaning.

Voices to speak to us directly. As we move.
As we enrich, growing in larger motion,
                this word, this power.

Down coasts of taken countries, mastery,
1165     discovery at one hand, and at the other
                frontiers and forests,

fanatic cruel legend at our back and
speeding ahead the red and open west,
                and this our region,

1170     desire, field, beginning. Name and road,
communication to these many men,
as epilogue, seeds of unending love.

                                                    *1938*

# The Minotaur°

Trapped, blinded, led; and in the end betrayed
Daily by new betrayals as he stays
Deep in his labyrinth, shaking and going mad.
Betrayed.  Betrayed.  Raving, the beaten head
5     Heavy with madness, he stands, half-dead and proud.
No one again will ever see his pride.
No one will find him by walking to him straight
But must be led circuitously about,
Calling to him and close and, losing the subtle thread,
10    Lose him again; while he waits, brutalized
By loneliness.   Later, afraid
Of his own suffering.   At last, savage and made
Ravenous, ready to prey upon the race
If it so much as learn the clews of blood
15    Into his pride his fear his glistening heart.
Now is the patient deserted in his fright
And love carrying salvage round the world
Lost in a crooked city; roundabout,
By the sea, the precipice, all the fantastic ways
20    Betrayal weaves its trap; loneliness knows the thread,
And the heart is lost, lost, trapped, blinded and led,
Deserted at the middle of the maze

*1944*

# (To be a Jew in the Twentieth Century)

To be a Jew in the twentieth century
Is to be offered a gift. If you refuse,
Wishing to be invisible, you choose
Death of the spirit, the stone insanity.
5    Accepting, take full life. Full agonies:
Your evening deep in labyrinthine blood
Of those who resist, fail, and resist; and God
Reduced to a hostage among hostages.

The gift is torment. Not alone the still
10    Torture, isolation; or torture of the flesh.
That may come also. But the accepting wish,
The whole and fertile spirit as guarantee
For every human freedom, suffering to be free,
Daring to live for the impossible.

*1944*

---

**poem title:** In Greek myth, the Minotaur was a monster with the head of a bull and the body of a man. Periodically, seven youths and seven maidens were fed to the creature, who was confined in a huge palace-prison constructed as a labyrinth. One year, Theseus joined the group, killed the Minotaur, and found his way out of the labyrinth with the aid of a thread given to him by Ariadne, the daughter of King Minos.

## Rite

My father groaned; my mother wept.
Among the mountains of the west
A deer lifted her golden throat.

They tore the pieces of the kill
5     While two dark sisters laughed and sang.—
The hidden lions blare until

The hunters charge and burn them all.
And in the black apartment halls
Of every city in the land

10   A father groans; a mother weeps;
A girl to puberty has come;
They shriek this, this is the crime

The gathering of the powers in.
At this first sign of her next life
15   America is stricken dumb.

The sharpening of your rocky knife!
The first blood of a woman shed!
The sacred word: Stand Up You Dead.

Mothers go weep; let fathers groan,
70   The flag of infinity is shown.
Now you will never be alone.

*1958*

## The Poem as Mask

### ORPHEUS°

When I wrote of the women in their dances and wildness, it
    was a mask,
on their mountain, gold-hunting, singing, in orgy,
it was a mask; when I wrote of the god,
fragmented, exiled from himself, his life, the love gone down
    with song,
5   it was myself, split open, unable to speak, in exile from myself.

There is no mountain, there is no god, there is memory
of my torn life, myself split open in sleep, the rescued child
beside me among the doctors, and a word
of rescue from the great eyes.

---

*Orpheus:* In Greek mythology, Orpheus, child of the sun-god Apollo, is the singer whose
music enraptures all creatures; he was dismembered by the Maenads, a tribe of wild women.

10        No more masks! No more mythologies!

Now, for the first time, the god lifts his hand,
the fragments join in me with their own music.

1968


## Poem

I lived in the first century of world wars.
Most mornings I would be more or less insane,
The newspapers would arrive with their careless stories,
The news would pour out of various devices
5    Interrupted by attempts to sell products to the unseen.
I would call my friends on other devices;
They would be more or less mad for similar reasons.
Slowly I would get to pen and paper,
Make my poems for others unseen and unborn.
10    In the day I would be reminded of those men and women
Brave, setting up signals across vast distances,
Considering a nameless way of living, of almost unimagined
        values.
As the lights darkened, as the lights of night brightened,
We would try to imagine them, try to find each other.
15    To construct peace, to make love, to reconcile
Waking with sleeping, ourselves with each other,
Ourselves with ourselves. We would try by any means
To reach the limits of ourselves, to reach beyond ourselves,
To let go the means, to wake.

I lived in the first century of these wars.

1968


## Poem White Page
## White Page Poem

Poem      white page      white page      poem
something is streaming out of a body in waves
something is beginning from the fingertips
they are starting to declare for my whole life
5    all the despair and the making music
something like wave after wave
that breaks on a beach
something like bringing the entire life
to this moment
10    the small waves bringing themselves to white paper
something like light stands up and is alive

1978

# Robert Hayden (1913–1980)

Hayden was born Asa Bundy Sheffey to a couple in financial and personal difficulty. When they separated, Hayden was taken in by a foster family and received a new name. The new family, unfortunately, was equally conflicted, and Hayden's childhood—spent in the Detroit ghetto called "Paradise Valley"—was frequently traumatic. Reading was a form of escape, but it also prepared him for a career. He enrolled at Detroit City College, but left in 1936 to research black history and culture, including Michigan's Underground Railroad, for the Federal Writers' Project. Then in the early 1940s, he studied with W.H. Auden at the University of Michigan. The other major development in his life occurred when he committed himself to the Bahai faith in the 1940s, eventually editing its journal *World Order* in the late 1960s and in the 1970s.

All this experience finds its way into his poetry, for he wrote about his Detroit neighborhood and about black history, as in "Middle Passage" and "Runagate, Runagate." Technically meticulous, Hayden adapted his style and voice to the subject matter, using montage, and mixing narrative and lyric passages in "Middle Passage," adopting imagist and symbolist techniques, varying line length considerably. Some of his poems are meditative, others strongly narrative. He also aimed for a universal audience, believing that African American history had vital lessons for all readers. And he refused to write exclusively about black subject matter, despite crafting a distinctive form of rhetorically intricate protest and deploying it for decades. Hayden taught for many years at Fisk University, returning at the end of his career to the University of Michigan.

## Middle Passage°

### I

*Jesús, Estrella, Esperanza, Mercy:*°
    Sails flashing to the wind like weapons,
    sharks following the moans the fever and the dying;
    horror the corposant° and compass rose.°

---

**poem title:** The "middle passage" was the name of the route slave ships took across the Atlantic Ocean from Africa to North or South America. Robert Hayden's note: Part III follows in the main the account of the *Amistad* mutiny given by Muriel Rukeyser in her biography of Willard Gibbs.
1 *Jesús, Estrella* (Spanish, *"star"*), *Esperanza* (Spanish, *"hope"*), *Mercy:* names of slave ships.
4 *corposant:* Saint Elmo's fire, named after the patron saint of sailors—an eerie light, actually an electrical discharge, appearing on a ship's mast during a storm.
4 *compass rose:* the printed guide to compass directions included on maps.

Anthology of Modern American Poetry

5      Middle Passage:
                voyage through death
                        to life upon these shores.

                "10 April 1800—
            Blacks rebellious. Crew uneasy. Our linguist says
10          their moaning is a prayer for death,
            ours and their own. Some try to starve themselves.
            Lost three this morning leaped with crazy laughter
            to the waiting sharks, sang as they went under."

        *Desire, Adventure, Tartar, Ann:*

15          Standing to America, bringing home
            black gold, black ivory, black seed.

                *Deep in the festering hold thy father lies,*
                *of his bones New England pews are made,*
                *those are altar lights that were his eyes.°*

20      Jesus   Saviour   Pilot   Me°
        Over   Life's   Tempestuous   Sea

        We pray that Thou wilt grant, O Lord,
        safe passage to our vessels bringing
        heathen souls unto Thy chastening.

25      Jesus   Saviour

                "8 bells. I cannot sleep, for I am sick
            with fear, but writing eases fear a little
            since still my eyes can see these words take shape
            upon the page & so I write, as one
30          would turn to exorcism. 4 days scudding,°
            but now the sea is calm again. Misfortune
            follows in our wake like sharks (our grinning
            tutelary° gods). Which one of us
            has killed an albatross?° A plague among
35          our blacks—Ophthalmia: blindness—& we
            have jettisoned the blind to no avail.
            It spreads, the terrifying sickness spreads.
            Its claws have scratched sight from the Capt.'s eyes

---

19 *eyes:* A devastating adaptation of Ariel's song in Shakespeare's *The Tempest.* In the play, it was to offer a certain consolation to Ferdinand about the father he feared had drowned: "Full fathom five thy father lies, / Of his bones are coral made; / Those are pearls that were his eyes; / Nothing of him that doth fade, / But doth suffer a sea-change / Into something rich and strange."

20 *Jesus Saviour Pilot Me* . . . : from a Protestant hymn.

30 *scudding:* running before a strong wind with little or no sail set.

33 *tutelary:* protector or guardian.

34 *albatross:* a large web-footed sea bird. They are considered to bring luck unless they are killed. In Samuel Taylor Coleridge's (1772–1834) poem "The Rime of the Ancient Mariner," a sailor who kills an albatross must wear it around his neck as a penance.

40    & there is blindness in the fo'c'sle°
      & we must sail 3 weeks before we come
      to port."

          *What port awaits us, Davy Jones'*
          *or home? I've heard of slavers drifting, drifting,*
          *playthings of wind and storm and chance, their crews*
45        *gone blind, the jungle hatred*
          *crawling up on deck.*

    Thou   Who   Walked   On   Galilee

      "Deponent° further sayeth *The Bella J*
      left the Guinea Coast
50    with cargo of five hundred blacks and odd
      for the barracoons° of Florida:

      "That there was hardly room 'tween-decks for half
      the sweltering cattle stowed spoon-fashion there;
      that some went mad of thirst and tore their flesh
55    and sucked the blood:

      "That Crew and Captain lusted with the comeliest
      of the savage girls kept naked in the cabins;
      that there was one they called The Guinea Rose
      and they cast lots and fought to lie with her:

60    "That when the Bo's'n piped all hands,° the flames
      spreading from starboard already were beyond
      control, the negroes howling and their chains
      entangled with the flames:

      "That the burning blacks could not be reached,
65    that the Crew abandoned ship,
      leaving their shrieking negresses behind,
      that the Captain perished drunken with the wenches:

      "Further Deponent sayeth not."

    Pilot   Oh   Pilot   Me

                            II

70    Aye, lad, and I have seen those factories,
      Gambia, Rio Pongo, Calabar;°
      have watched the artful mongos° baiting traps
      of war wherein the victor and the vanquished

---

39 *fo'c'sle*: forecastle, a superstructure at the bow of a merchant ship where the crew is
housed.
48 *Deponent*: person offering evidence.
51 *barracoons*: temporary confinement for slaves or convicts.
60 *Bo's'n piped all hands*: boatswain called the crew.
71 *Calabar*: a Nigerian city; Gambia: a country in west Africa; Rio Pongo: African river.
72 *mongos*: Bantu-speaking people native to the African country of Zaire.

Were caught as prizes for our barracoons.
75    Have seen the nigger kings whose vanity
and greed turned wild black hides of Fellatah,
Mandingo, Ibo, Kru° to gold for us.

And there was one—King Anthracite we named him—
fetish face beneath French parasols
80    of brass and orange velvet, impudent mouth
whose cups were carven skulls of enemies:

He'd honor us with drum and feast and conjo°
and palm-oil-glistening wenches deft in love,
and for tin crowns that shone with paste,
85    red calico and German-silver trinkets

Would have the drums talk war and send
his warriors to burn the sleeping villages
and kill the sick and old and lead the young
in coffles° to our factories.

90    Twenty years a trader, twenty years,
for there was wealth aplenty to be harvested
from those black fields, and I'd be trading still
but for the fevers melting down my bones.

### III

Shuttles in the rocking loom of history,
95    the dark ships move, the dark ships move,
their bright ironical names
like jests of kindness on a murderer's mouth;
plough through thrashing glister toward
fata morgana's° lucent melting shore,
100    weave toward New World littorals° that are
mirage and myth and actual shore.

Voyage through death,
                 voyage whose chartings are unlove.

A charnel stench, effluvium of living death
105    spreads outward from the hold,
where the living and the dead, the horribly dying,
lie interlocked, lie foul with blood and excrement.

---

77 *Fellatah, Mandingo, Ibo, Kru*: African tribes. The Mandingo are Mande-speaking agricultural people from Mali, Guinea, and Senegal; the Ibo are agricultural tribes from Nigeria; the Kru are fisherman from Liberia and the Ivory Coast.
82 *conjo*: dance.
89 *coffles*: slaves chained together in a line; the term also refers to the same practice applied to criminals or animals.
99 *fata morgana*: mirage.
100 *littorals*: shores or coastal regions.

*Deep in the festering hold thy father lies,*
*the corpse of mercy rots with him,*
110     *rats eat love's rotten gelid eyes.*

*But, oh, the living look at you*
*with human eyes whose suffering accuses you,*
*whose hatred reaches through the swill of dark*
*to strike you like a leper's claw.*

115     *You cannot stare that hatred down*
*or chain the fear that stalks the watches*
*and breathes on you its fetid scorching breath;*
*cannot kill the deep immortal human wish,*
*the timeless will.*

120     "But for the storm that flung up barriers
of wind and wave, *The Amistad*° señores,
would have reached the port of Príncipe in two,
three days at most; but for the storm we should
have been prepared for what befell.
125     Swift as the puma's leap it came. There was
that interval of moonless calm filled only
with the water's and the rigging's usual sounds,
then sudden movement, blows and snarling cries
and they had fallen on us with machete
130     and marlinspike. It was as though the very
air, the night itself were striking us.
Exhausted by the rigors of the storm,
we were no match for them. Our men went down
before the murderous Africans. Our loyal
135     Celestino ran from below with gun
and lantern and I saw, before the cane-
knife's wounding flash, Cinquez,
that surly brute who calls himself a prince,
directing, urging on the ghastly work.
140     He hacked the poor mulatto down, and then
he turned on me. The decks were slippery
when daylight finally came. It sickens me
to think of what I saw, of how these apes
threw overboard the butchered bodies of
145     our men, true Christians all, like so much jetsam.
Enough, enough. The rest is quickly told:
Cinquez was forced to spare the two of us
you see to steer the ship to Africa,
and we like phantoms doomed to rove the sea

---

121 *Amistad*: (Spanish, "Friendship"), A Spanish slave ship out of Havana that was the site
of a famous 1839 rebellion. Cinquez led the fifty-three slaves in revolt, in which the cap-
tain, the mate, and the captain's slave Celestino were killed. The *Amistad* was held when
it arrived at Long Island; the owners, who were spared during the mutiny, tried to have
the slaves sent to Cuba to be tried for murder. The case was decided in the U.S. Supreme
Court in 1841, with John Quincy Adams, former U.S. president, helping (successfully) to
defend the surviving slaves.

150 voyaged east by day and west by night,
  deceiving them, hoping for rescue,
  prisoners on our own vessel, till
  at length we drifted to the shores of this
  your land, America, where we were freed
155 from our unspeakable misery. Now we
  demand, good sirs, the extradition of
  Cinquez and his accomplices to La
  Havana. And it distresses us to know
  there are so many here who seem inclined
160 to justify the mutiny of these blacks.
  We find it paradoxical indeed
  that you whose wealth, whose tree of liberty
  are rooted in the labor of your slaves
  should suffer the august John Quincy Adams
165 to speak with so much passion of the right
  of chattel slaves to kill their lawful masters
  and with his Roman rhetoric weave a hero's
  garland for Cinquez. I tell you that
  we are determined to return to Cuba
170 with our slaves and there see justice done. Cinquez—
  or let us say 'the Prince'—Cinquez shall die."

The deep immortal human wish,
the timeless will:

Cinquez its deathless primaveral image,
175 life that transfigures many lives.

Voyage through death
                to life upon these shores.

                                    *1962*

## Runagate Runagate°

### I.

Runs falls rises stumbles on from darkness into darkness
and the darkness thicketed with shapes of terror
and the hunters pursuing and the hounds pursuing
and the night cold and the night long and the river
5 to cross and the jack-muh-lanterns° beckoning beckoning
and blackness ahead and when shall I reach that somewhere
morning and keep on going and never turn back and keep on going

        Runagate
                Runagate
10                      Runagate

---

**poem title:** *Runagate:* archaic for "runaway"; the poem is about America's Underground
Railroad, a pre-Civil War system set up by abolitionists to help slaves escape to the North.
5 *lanterns:* Jack-o'-lanterns, or will-o'-the-wisps, elusive lights seen over marshes at night.

Many thousands rise and go
many thousands crossing over

     O mythic North
    O star-shaped yonder Bible city°

15 Some go weeping and some rejoicing
  some in coffins and some in carriages
  some in silks and some in shackles

    Rise and go or fare you well

  No more auction block for me
20 no more driver's lash for me

    If you see my Pompey, 30 yrs of age,
    new breeches, plain stockings, negro shoes;
    if you see my Anna, likely young mulatto°
    branded E on the right cheek, R on the left,
25   catch them if you can and notify subscriber.
    Catch them if you can, but it won't be easy.
    They'll dart underground when you try to catch them,
    plunge into quicksand, whirlpools, mazes,
    turn into scorpions when you try to catch them.

30 And before I'll be a slave
  I'll be buried in my grave

    North star and bonanza gold
    I'm bound for the freedom, freedom-bound
    and oh Susyanna don't you cry for me°

35     Runagate

      Runagate

     **II.**

Rises from their anguish and their power,

    Harriet Tubman,°

    woman of earth, whipscarred,
40   a summoning, a shining

    Mean to be free

---

14 *Bible city*: Bethlehem, Pennsylvania, just north of the Mason-Dixon line, the line di-
viding slave from free states, in pre-Civil War days.
23 *mulatto*: a person of mixed race, child of both black and white parents.
34 *cry for me*: the first line of the song "Oh Susanna" (1848) by the composer of popular
music Stephen Collins Foster (1826–1864).
38 *Tubman*: (1820?–1913), an escaped slave who helped others escape to the North through
the Underground Railroad.

And this was the way of it, brethren brethren,
way we journeyed from Can't to Can.
Moon so bright and no place to hide,
45　　the cry up and the patterollers° riding,
hound dogs belling in bladed air.
And fear starts a-murbling, Never make it,
we'll never make it. *Hush that now,*
and she's turned upon us, levelled pistol
50　　glinting in the moonlight:
Dead folks can't jaybird-talk, she says;
you keep on going now or die, she says.

Wanted　　Harriet Tubman　　alias The General
alias Moses　　Stealer of Slaves

55　　In league with Garrison　Alcott　Emerson
Garrett　Douglass　Thoreau　John Brown°

Armed and known to be Dangerous

Wanted　　Reward　　Dead or Alive

Tell me, Ezekiel,° oh tell me do you see
60　　mailed Jehovah coming to deliver me?

Hoot-owl calling in the ghosted air,
five times calling to the hants° in the air.
Shadow of a face in the scary leaves,
shadow of a voice in the talking leaves:

65　　Come ride-a my train

*Oh that train, ghost-story train*
*through swamp and savanna movering movering,*
*over trestles of dew, through caves of the wish,*
*Midnight Special on a sabre track movering movering,*
70　　*first stop Mercy and the last Hallelujah.*

Come ride-a my train

Mean mean mean to be free.

1962

---

45 *patterollers:* patrollers.
56 *Brown:* abolitionists. The editor William Lloyd Garrison (1805–1879); the educator and reformer Amos Bronson Alcott (1799–1888); the essayist and poet Ralph Waldo Emerson (1803–1882); the Quaker leader Thomas Garrett (1789–1871); the African American journalist and statesman Frederick Douglass (1818?–1895); the writer and naturalist Henry David Thoreau (1817–1862); John Brown (1800–1859), the leader of a raid on the arsenal at Harper's Ferry, West Virginia, to start a slave uprising.
59 *Ezekiel:* sixth-century B.C. Hebrew prophet; Jehovah is the Judeo-Christian God.
62 *hants:* haunts, ghosts.

# A Letter from Phillis Wheatley°

## *London, 1773*

Dear Obour°
        Our crossing was without
event. I could not help, at times,
reflecting on that first—my Destined—
5    voyage long ago (I yet
have some remembrance of its Horrors)
and marvelling at God's Ways.
        Last evening, her Ladyship° presented me
to her illustrious Friends.
10    I scarce could tell them anything
of Africa, though much of Boston
and my hope of Heaven. I read
my latest Elegies to them.
"O Sable° Muse!" the Countess cried,
15    embracing me, when I had done.
I held back tears, as is my wont,
and there were tears in Dear
Nathaniel's° eyes.
        At supper—I dined apart
20    like captive Royalty—
the Countess and her Guests promised
signatures affirming me
True Poetess, albeit once a slave.
Indeed, they were most kind, and spoke,
25    moreover, of presenting me
at Court (I thought of Pocahontas)°—
an Honor, to be sure, but one,
I should, no doubt, as Patriot decline.
        My health is much improved;
30    I feel I may, if God so Wills,
entirely recover here.

---

**poem title:** Wheatley (c. 1753–1784) was brought to the United States as a slave from Gambia in West Africa. She was put up for auction on the Boston slave block in 1761 and sold to John and Susannah Wheatley. Despite being a slave, she mastered English well enough to begin writing letters and poems. A few were published and she came to the attention of people both in the U.S. and in England. It was the British attention that persuaded John Wheatley to set her free. By then, her book *Poems on Various Subjects, Religious, and Moral* had already appeared. Only the second woman (and the first African American) to publish a book in the colonies on any subject, Wheatley is considered a founding figure of the black literary tradition.
1 *Obour* (Tanner): a young, free black woman who was Wheatley's most regular correspondent.
8 *Ladyship:* Selina Hastings, philanthropist and Countess of Hastings, who helped Wheatley find a publisher for her book.
14 *Sable:* Cf. Wheatley's line "Some view our sable [black] race with scornful eye" in her delicately sardonic poem "On Being Brought from Africa to America."
18 *Nathaniel:* Wheatley's son, who accompanied Wheatley on her 1773 trip to London.
26 *Pocahontas:* an Indian princess who reportedly saved the life of Captain John Smith, leader of a group of American colonists. She married an Englishman, John Rolfe (1585–1622), who presented her to the British court in 1616.

Idyllic England! Alas, there is
no Eden without its Serpent. Under
the chiming Complaisance I hear him Hiss;
35      I see his flickering tongue
when foppish would-be Wits
murmur of the Yankee Pedlar°
and his Cannibal Mockingbird.
        Sister, forgive th'intrusion of
40      my Sombreness—Nocturnal Mood
I would not share with any save
your trusted Self. Let me disperse,
in closing, such unseemly Gloom
by mention of an Incident
45      you may, as I, consider Droll:
Today, a little Chimney Sweep,
his face and hands with soot quite Black,
staring hard at me, politely asked:
"Does you, M'lady, sweep chimneys too?"
50      I was amused, but dear Nathaniel
(ever Solicitous) was not.
      I pray the Blessings of our Lord
and Saviour Jesus Christ be yours
Abundantly. In his Name,

Phillis

1978

# Night, Death, Mississippi

I

A quavering cry. Screech-owl?
Or one of them?
The old man in his reek
and gauntness laughs—

5      One of them, I bet—
and turns out the kitchen lamp,
limping to the porch to listen
in the windowless night.

Be there with Boy and the rest
10      if I was well again.
Time was. Time was.
White robes like moonlight

In the sweetgum dark.°
Unbucked that one then
15      and him squealing bloody Jesus
as we cut it off.

---

37 *Yankee Pedlar and his Cannibal Mockingbird:* derogatory terms for John Wheatley and
poet Phillis Wheatley; as a "mockingbird," she is in effect only mimicking other poets.
13 *sweetgum dark:* the deep woods of the North American sweet gum tree.

Time was. A cry?
A cry all right.
He hawks and spits,
20      fevered as by groinfire.

Have us a bottle,
Boy and me—
he's earned him a bottle—
when he gets home.

## II

25      Then we beat them, he said,
beat them till our arms was tired
and the big old chains
messy and red.

*O Jesus burning on the lily cross*

30      Christ, it was better
than hunting bear
which don't know why
you want him dead.

*O night, rawhead and bloodybones night*

35      You kids fetch Paw
some water now so's he
can wash that blood
off him, she said.

*O night betrayed by darkness not its own*

1966

## Aunt Jemima of the Ocean Waves°

### I

Enacting someone's notion of themselves
(and me), The One And Only Aunt Jemima
and Kokimo The Dixie Dancing Fool
do a bally for the freak show.

---

**poem title:** Adapted from a minstrel show, Aunt Jemima has been the symbol for a popular pancake mix since 1899. As Nagueyalti Warren writes in the *Oxford Companion to African American Literature*, "Jemima, the offshoot of irascible mammy [a still earlier popular stereotype], was sweet, jolly, even-tempered, and polite. Jemima, Hebrew for 'dove,' was Job's youngest daughter, symbolizing innocence, gentleness, and peace. But the name belies its meaning. The caricature connotes not naiveté but stupidity, not peace but docility. Jemima was an obese, darkly pigmented, broad-bosomed, handkerchief-headed, gingham-dressed, elderly servant content in her subjugation. . . . By 1900, more than 200,000 Jemima dolls, 150,000 Jemima cookie jars, and numerous memorabilia in the form of blackfaced buttons and toothpick holders had been sold."

5       I watch a moment, then move on,
        pondering the logic that makes of them
        (and me) confederates
        of The Spider Girl, The Snake-skinned Man. . . .

        Poor devils have to live somehow.

10      I cross the boardwalk to the beach,
        lie in the sand and gaze beyond
        the clutter at the sea.

                        II

        Trouble you for a light?
        I turn as Aunt Jemima settles down
15      beside me, her blue-rinsed hair
        without the red bandanna now.

        I hold the lighter to her cigerette.
        Much obliged. Unmindful (perhaps)
        of my embarrassment, she looks
20      at me and smiles: You sure

        do favor a friend I used to have.
        Guess that's why I bothered you
        for a light, So much like him that I—
        She pauses, watching white horses rush

25      to the shore. Way them big old waves
        come slamming whopping in,
        sometimes it's like they mean to smash
        this no-good world to hell.

        Well, it could happen. A book I read—
30      Crossed that very ocean years ago.
        London, Paris, Rome,
        Constantinople too—I've seen them all.

        Back when they billed me everywhere
        as the Sepia High Stepper.
35      Crowned heads applauded me.
        Years before your time. Years and years.

        I wore me plenty diamonds then,
        and counts or dukes or whatever they were
        would fill my dressing room
40      with the costliest flowers. But of course

        there was this one you resemble so.
        Get me? The sweetest gentleman.
        Dead before his time. Killed in the war
        to save the world for another war.

45 High-stepping days for me
were over after that. Still I'm not one
to let grief idle me for long.
I went out with a mental act—

mind-reading—Mysteria From
50 The Mystic East—veils and beads
and telling suckers how to get
stolen rings and sweethearts back.

One night he was standing by my bed,
seen him plain as I see you,
55 and warned me without a single word:
Baby, quit playing with spiritual stuff.

So here I am, so here I am,
fake mammy to God's mistakes.
And that's the beauty part,
60 I mean, ain't that the beauty part.

She laughs, but I do not, knowing what
her laughter shields. And mocks.
I light another cigarette for her.
She smokes, not saying any more.

65 Scream of children in the surf,
adagios of sun and flashing foam,
the sexual glitter, oppressive fun. . . .
An antique etching comes to mind:

"The Sable Venus" naked on
70 a baroque Cellini shell—voluptuous
imago floating in the wake
of slave-ships on fantastic seas.

Jemima sighs, Reckon I'd best
be getting back. I help her up.
75 Don't you take no wooden nickels, hear?
Tin dimes neither. So long, pal.

        *1978*

# from *Elegies for Paradise Valley*

## I

My shared bedroom's window
opened on alley stench.
A junkie died in maggots there.
I saw his body shoved into a van.
5 I saw the hatred for our kind
glistening like tears
in the policemen's eyes.

        *1978*

# The Dogwood Trees

(for Robert Slagle)

Seeing dogwood trees in bloom,
I am reminded, Robin,
of our journey through the mountains
in an evil time.

5          Among rocks and rock-filled streams
white bracts of dogwood
clustered. Beyond, nearby, shrill slums
were burning,

the crooked crosses flared. We drove
10         with bitter knowledge
of the odds against comradeship we dared
and were at one.

*1978*

# O Daedalus, Fly Away Home°

(For Maia and Julie)

Drifting night in the Georgia pines,
coonskin drum and jubilee banjo.
　　　Pretty Malinda, dance with me.

Night is juba, night is conjo.°
5          　　　Pretty Malinda, dance with me.

Night is an African juju man
weaving a wish and a weariness together
　　　to make two wings.

　　　*O fly away home fly away*

10         Do you remember Africa?

　　　*O cleave the air fly away home*

My gran, he flew back to Africa,
just spread his arms and
　　　flew away home.

---

**poem title:** In Greek mythology, Daedalus and his son Icarus set out to free themselves
from the Minotaur's labyrinth. Daedalus made wings for his son out of wax and feathers,
but Icarus flew too near the sun, and the wax melted. Icarus perished when he fell into
the sea, but Daedalus escaped.
4 *juba, conjo:* dances.

15          Drifting night in the windy pines;
            night is a laughing, night is a longing.
                    Pretty Malinda, come to me.

            Night is a mourning juju man°
            weaving a wish and a weariness together
20                  to make two wings.

                *O fly away home fly away*

                                                                1962

---

18 *juju man*: one adept in the system of conjuring or magic known as "hoodoo," "mojo,"
"obeah," or "juju." A juju man is a practioner of folk medicine, a visionary, a spiritual guide,
a shape changer, and a practicer of black magic.

# Charles Henri Ford (b. 1913)

Born in Brookhaven, Massachusetts, Ford was first known as the editor of *Blues: A Magazine of Verse* (1929–1930), after which he lived in Paris for several years. He edited the beautiful surrealist magazine *View* in New York from 1940–1947 and lived in Italy from 1952–1957. He began publishing his own surrealist poetry in the 1930s, and began to exhibit his paintings worldwide in the 1950s. In the 1960s, he collaborated with Andy Warhol on film and multimedia projects. Ford has frequently lived in Greece and has spent some time in Tibet.

## Plaint

*Before A Mob of 10,000 At Owensboro, Ky.*

I, Rainey Betha, 22,
from the top-branch of race-hatred look at you.
My limbs are bound, though boundless the bright sun
like my bright blood which had to run
5     into the orchard that excluded me:
now I climb death's tree.

The pruning hooks of many mouths
cut the black-leaved boughs.
The robins of my eyes hover where
10    sixteen leaves fall that were a prayer:
sixteen mouths are open wide;
the minutes like black cherries
drop from my shady side.

*Oh, who is the forester must tend such a tree, Lord?*
*Do angels pick the cherry-blood of folk like me, Lord?*

1937

# Flag of Ecstasy

for Marcel Duchamp

Over the towers of autoerotic honey
Over the dungeons of homicidal drives

Over the pleasures of invading sleep
Over the sorrows of invading a woman

5      Over the voix céleste°
Over vomito° negro

Over the unendurable sensation of madness
Over the insatiable sense of sin

Over the spirit of uprisings
10     Over the bodies of tragediennes

Over tarantism:° "melancholy stupor and an
    uncontrollable desire to dance"
Over all

Over ambivalent virginity
15     Over unfathomable succubi°

Over the tormentors of Negresses
Over openhearted sans-culottes°

Over a stactometer° for the tears of France
Over unmanageable hermaphrodites

20     Over the rattlesnake sexlessness of art lovers
Over the shithouse enigmas of art haters

Over the sun's lascivious° serum
Over the sewage of the moon

---

5 *voix céleste*: (French) "heavenly voice," an organ stop producing a sound of stringlike quality.
6 *vomito negro*: (Italian) "black vomit." Cf. "vomitus niger" (Latin), "black vomit."
11 *tarantism*: a dancing mania of late medieval Europe, defined in the quoted phrase.
15 *succubi*: demons who take female form in order to have intercourse with men in their sleep; also, more broadly, prostitutes.
17 *sans-culottes*: (French) "without breeches," a term of reproach used by the aristocrats for the extreme republicans (wearers of pantaloons rather than knee breeches) in the French Revolution; in other words, a violent revolutionist.
18 *stactometer*: a device used to measure the number of drops in a given volume of liquid.
22 *lascivious*: wanton, lewd.

Over the saints of debauchery
25   Over criminals made of gold

Over the princes of delirium
Over the paupers of peace

Over signs foretelling the end of the world
Over signs foretelling the beginning of a world

30   Like one of those tender strips of flesh
On either side of the vertebral column

Marcel,° wave!

1944

---

32 *Marcel*: Duchamp (1887–1968), French painter and theorist, an avant-garde icon who
moved to New York in 1915 and became the center of a group of Dada artists. Note in the
poem the element of collage, the use of phrases that are almost the equivalent of found
objects, and the unstable dichotomies in the couplets.

# Weldon Kees (1914–1955)

Born in Beatrice, Nebraska, Kees graduated from the University of Nebraska. After an editorial job with the Federal Writers' Project in Lincoln, he moved to Denver to direct its bibliographic center. A few years later, he left for New York, where he earned a living for a while writing for *Time* magazine, until he moved to San Francisco in 1951. He also became a committed Trotskyite, the Marxist group cast out of the official communist party. Kees was not only a poet—one often cynical about American middle-class values—but also a painter, a pianist, and a jazz composer. In California, he also collaborated with psychiatrist Jurgen Ruesch on the book *Non-Verbal Communication*, which is illustrated with Kees' photographs. Little known as a poet during his own life, he disappeared in 1955 and is presumed to have committed suicide; his car was found abandoned on the approach to Golden Gate Bridge, but his body was never found. His fictional satire of scholarly life, *Fall Quarter*, was written in the 1930s but not published until 1990.

## Travels in North America

*(To Lorraine and Robert Wilbur)*

Here is San Luis Obispo. Here
Is Kansas City, and here is Rovere,
Kentucky. And here, a small black dot,
Unpronounceable but hard to forget,
5    Is where we stopped at the Seraphim Motel,
And well-fed moths flew out to greet us from the walls
On which a dado of petunias grew.
We threw a nickel in the wishing well,
But the moths remained, and the petunias too.

10    And here is Santa Barbara where
They had the heated swimming pool.
Warm in our room, we watched the bathers' breaths. My hair
Fell out in Santa Barbara, and the cold
Came blowing off the sea. An ancient gull
15    Dropped down to shiver gravely in the steady rain.
The sea-food dinner Duncan Hines° had praised

---

16 *Hines:* (1880–1959); he published the notes he accumulated from years of eating at American restaurants as a traveling salesman as *Adventures in Good Eating* (1936). The book launched him on a career as a publisher and sponsor of packaged food products.

Gave off a classic taste of tin. The weather was unseasonable.
There was a landmark, I remember, that was closed.

Here is the highway in and out of Cincinnati.
20    An inch or so of line along the river. Driving west
One Sunday in a smoky dawn, burnt orange along the land-
    scape's rim,
The radio gave forth five solid and remembered hours
Of gospel singers and New Orleans jazz,
With terse, well-phrased commercials for a funeral home.
25    They faded out—Cleves, Covington, North Bend
Made way for Evansville and Patti Page.° The roads end
At motels. The one that night had an Utrillo° in a velvet frame.

The stars near Santa Fe are blurred and old, discolored
By a milky haze; a ragged moon
30    Near Albuquerque shimmers the heat. Autumnal light
Falls softly on a file of candy skulls
And metal masks. Sand drifts at noon, at nine,
And now at midnight on a Navajo in levis reading
Sartre° in an Avon Pocket Book, against the window
35    Of a Rexall store. Here one descends
To shelvings of the pit. The valleys hollow out.

The land is terraced near Los Alamos°: scrub cedars,
Piñon pines and ruined pueblos, where a line
Of tall young men in uniform keep watch upon
40    The University of California's atom bomb.
The sky is soiled and charitable
Behind barbed wire and the peaks of mountains—
Sangre de Christo, Blood of Christ, this "fitting portent
For the Capital of the Atomic Age." We meant
45    To stop, but one can only see so much. A mist
Came over us outside Tryuonyi: caves, and a shattered cliff.

And possibly the towns one never sees are best,
Preserved, remote, and merely names and distances.
Cadiz, Kentucky, "noted for the quality of hams it ships,
50    The home of wealthy planters," Dalton, Georgia,
"Center of a thriving bedspread industry, where rainbow lines
Of counterpanes may be observed along the highway. Here
The man whose *Home, Sweet Home* is known to all,
The champion of the Cherokee, John Howard Payne,° was tried."
55    —Wetumka, Oklahoma; Kipling, Michigan;

---

26 *Page:* (b. 1927) American singer who recorded a number of hit records in the 1950s and
was often heard on the radio.
27 *Utrillo:* Maurice Utrillo (1883–1955), French painter.
34 *Sartre:* Jean-Paul Sartre (1905–1980), French existentialist philosopher, novelist, and
critic.
37 *Los Alamos:* New Mexico site where the atom bomb was constructed from 1943–1945.
54 *Payne:* (1791–1852), American actor, playwright, and composer (and frequent debtor)
who wrote the words to the song "Home, Sweet Home" for his operetta *Clari* (1823). He
once took on a campaign to help the Cherokee.

Glenrock, Wyoming; and Chehalis, Washington
Are momentarily the shifting centers of a dream,
Swept bare of formica and television aerials
And rows of cars that look a little more like fish each year.
60    —A dream that ends with towns that smell of rubber smouldering;
A brownish film sticks to the windshields
And the lungs; the skies are raining soot
And other specks that failed to fit into the paint
Or the salami. A cloud of grit sweeps over you and down the street.

65    And sometimes, shivering in St. Paul or baking in Atlanta,
The sudden sense that you have seen it all before:
The man who took your ticket at the Gem in Council Bluffs
Performed a similar function for you at the Shreveport Tivoli.
Joe's Lunch appears again, town after town, next door
70    To Larry's Shoe Repair, adjoining, inescapably, the Acme
          Doughnut Shop.
Main, First, and Market fuse together.
Bert and Lena run the laundromat. John Foster, D.D.S.,
Has offices above the City Bank.—At three or four,
On winter afternoons, when school is letting out
75    And rows of children pass you, near the firehouse,
This sense is keenest, piercing as the wind
That sweeps you toward the frosted door of your hotel
And past the portly hatted traveler with moist cigar
Who turns his paper as you brush against the rubber plant.
80    You have forgotten singularities. You have forgotten
Rooms that overlooked a park in Boston, brown walls hung

With congo masks and Mirós,° rain
Against a skylight, and the screaming girl
Who threw a cocktail shaker at a man in tweeds
85    Who quoted passages from Marlowe and 'Tis Pity She's a Whore.°
You have forgotten yellow lights of San Francisco coming on,
the bridges choked with cars, and islands in the fog.
Or have forgotten why you left or why you came to where you are,
Or by what roads and passages,
90    Or what it was, if anything, that you were hoping for.

Journeys are ways of marking out a distance,
Or dealing with the past, however ineffectually,
Or ways of searching for some new enclosure in this space
Between the oceans.—Now the smaller waves of afternoon retrace
95    This sand where breakers threw their cargoes up—
Old rafts and spongy two-by-fours and inner tubes,
The spines of sharks and broken codheads,
Tinned stuff with the labels gone, and yellow weeds
Like entrails; mattresses and stones, and, by a grapefruit crate,
100    A ragged map, imperfectly enclosed by seaworn oilskin.

---

82 *Mirós*: paintings by Spanish artist Joán Miró (1893–1983).
85 *'Tis Pity She's a Whore*: 1628 play by British dramatist John Ford (1586–1640); Christo-
pher Marlowe (1564–1593), British dramatist.

Two tiny scarlet crabs run out as I unfold it on the beach.
Here, sodden, fading, green ink blending into blue,
Is Brooklyn Heights, and I am walking toward the subway
In a January snow again, at night, ten years ago. Here is Milpitas,
105   California, filling stations and a Ford
Assembly plant. Here are the washboard roads
Of Wellfleet, on the Cape, and summer light and dust.
And here, now textured like a blotter, like the going years
And difficult to see, is where you are, and where I am,
And where the oceans cover us.

*1952*

# Randall Jarrell (1914–1965)

Born in Nashville, Tennessee, Jarrell was educated at Vanderbilt University, and taught at a number of colleges and universities, meanwhile acquiring a reputation as a devastatingly witty reviewer of other people's poetry. After enlisting in the Army air force in 1942, he was assigned to an aviation facility in Tucson, Arizona, where he became a celestial training navigator. It may well have been his very distance from the World War II front that made him an attentive listener to B-29 crews, other returning soldiers, and home front family members, and led him to retell their stories so effectively. Influenced by W. H. Auden early on, the war inspired him to use a less intricate, more conversational idiom. Both then and later in his career, he sometimes adopted a woman's persona to tell a gendered narrative. Overall, it is the body of poetry he wrote about World War II, some of the most successful written by any American, that constitutes his most distinctive and important contribution to his country's literature. A 1954 novel, *Pictures from an Institution*, uses Sarah Lawrence College as a model for its satire.

## The Death of the Ball Turret Gunner°

From my mother's sleep I fell into the State,
And I hunched in its belly till my wet fur froze.
Six miles from earth, loosed from its dream of life,
I woke to black flak° and the nightmare fighters.
When I died they washed me out of the turret with a hose.

*1945*

---

**poem title:** Jarrell's note, "A ball turret was a plexiglass sphere set into the belly of a B-17 or B-24 [bomber], and inhabited by two .50 caliber machine-guns and one man, a short, small man. When this gunner tracked with his machine-gun a fighter attacking his bomber from below, he revolved with the turret; hunched upside-down in his little sphere, he looked like the foetus in the womb. The fighters that attacked him were armed with cannon firing explosive shells. The hose was a steam hose."
4 *flak*: noise and fire of anti-aircraft guns.

# A Front°

Fog over the base: the beams ranging
From the five towers pull home from the night
The crews cold in fur, the bombers banging
Like lost trucks down the levels of the ice.
5     A glow drifts in like mist (how many tons of it?),
Bounces to a roll, turns suddenly to steel
And tires and turrets, huge in the trembling light.
The next is high, and pulls up with a wail,
Comes round again—no use. And no use for the rest
10    In drifting circles out along the range;
Holding no longer, changed to a kinder course,
The flights drone southward through the steady rain.
The base is closed. . . . But one voice keeps on calling,
The lowering pattern of the engines grows;
15    The roar gropes downward in its shaky orbit
For the lives the season quenches. Here below
They beg, order, are not heard; and hear the darker
Voice rising: *Can't you hear me? Over. Over*—
All the air quivers, and the east sky glows.

*1945*

# Losses

It was not dying: everybody died.
It was not dying: we had died before
In the routine crashes—and our fields
Called up the papers, wrote home to our folks,
5    And the rates rose, all because of us.
We died on the wrong page of the almanac,
Scattered on mountains fifty miles away;
Diving on haystacks, fighting with a friend,
We blazed up on the lines we never saw.
10    We died like aunts or pets or foreigners.
(When we left high school nothing else had died
For us to figure we had died like.)

In our new planes, with our new crews, we bombed
The ranges by the desert or the shore,
15    Fired at towed targets, waited for our scores—
And turned into replacements and woke up
One morning, over England, operational.
It wasn't different: but if we died
It was not an accident but a mistake
20    (But an easy one for anyone to make).
We read our mail and counted up our missions—
In bombers named for girls, we burned

---

**poem title:** Jarrell's note: "A front is closing in over a bomber base; the bombers, guided in by signals from the five towers of the radio range, are landing. Only one lands before the base is closed; the rest fly south to fields that are still open. One plane's radio has gone bad—it still transmits, but doesn't receive—and this plane crashes."

The cities we had learned about in school—
Till our lives wore out; our bodies lay among
The people we had killed and never seen.
When we lasted long enough they gave us medals;
When we died they said, "Our casualties were low."
They said, "Here are the maps"; we burned the cities.

It was not dying—no, not ever dying;
But the night I died I dreamed that I was dead,
And the cities said to me: "Why are you dying?
We are satisfied, if you are; but why did I die?"

1948

## Second Air Force

Far off, above the plain the summer dries,
The great loops of the hangars sway like hills.
Buses and weariness and loss, the nodding soldiers
Are wire, the bare frame building, and a pass
To what was hers; her head hides his square patch
And she thinks heavily: My son is grown.
She sees a world: sand roads, tar-paper barracks,
The bubbling asphalt of the runways, sage,
The dunes rising to the interminable ranges,
The dim flights moving over clouds like clouds.
The armorers in their patched faded green,
Sweat-stiffened, banded with brass cartridges,
Walk to the line; their Fortresses, all tail,
Stand wrong and flimsy on their skinny legs,
And the crews climb to them clumsily as bears.
The head withdraws into its hatch (a boy's),
The engines rise to their blind laboring roar,
And the green, made beasts run home to air.
Now in each aspect death is pure.
(At twilight they wink over men like stars
And hour by hour, through the night, some see
The great lights floating in—from Mars, from Mars.)
How emptily the watchers see them gone.

They go, there is silence; the woman and her son
Stand in the forest of the shadows, and the light
Washes them like water. In the long-sunken city
Of evening, the sunlight stills like sleep
The faint wonder of the drowned; in the evening,
In the last dreaming light, so fresh, so old,
The soldiers pass like beasts, unquestioning,
And the watcher for an instant understands
What there is then no need to understand;
But she wakes from her knowledge, and her stare,
A shadow now, moves emptily among
The shadows learning in their shadowy fields
The empty missions.
                    Remembering,
She hears the bomber calling, *Little Friend*!

40  To the fighter hanging in the hostile sky,
And sees the ragged flame eat, rib by rib,
Along the metal of the wing into her heart:
The lives stream out, blossom, and float steadily
To the flames of the earth, the flames
That burn like stars above the lands of men.

45  She saves from the twilight that takes everything
A squadron shipping, in its last parade—
Its dogs run by it, barking at the band—
A gunner walking to his barracks, half-asleep,
Starting at something, stumbling (above, invisible,
50  The crews in the steady winter of the sky
Tremble in their wired fur); and feels for them
The love of life for life. The hopeful cells
Heavy with someone else's death, cold carriers
Of someone else's victory, grope past their lives
55  Into her own bewilderment: The years meant *this*?

But for them the bombers answer everything.

                                                        *1945*

## Protocols

*(Birkenau°, Odessa;° the children speak alternately.)*

We went there on the train. *They had big barges that they towed,*
*We stood up, there were so many I was squashed.*
There was a smoke-stack, then they made me wash.
It was a factory, I think. *My mother held me up*
5  *And I could see the ship that made the smoke.*

When I was tired my mother carried me.
She said, "Don't be afraid." But I was only tired.
*Where we went there is no more Odessa.*
They had water in a pipe—like rain, but hot;
10  *The water there is deeper than the world*

*And I was tired and fell in in my sleep*
*And the water drank me. That is what I think.*
And I said to my mother, "Now I'm washed and dried,"
My mother hugged me, and it smelled like hay
*And that is how you die. And that is how you die.*

                                                        *1948*

---

**subtitle:** *Birkenau:* a village in southern Poland next to the Auschwitz-Birkenau concentration camp, the most notorious World War II Nazi death camp. *Odessa:* a city in the Ukraine in the former Soviet Union, located on Odessa Bay off the Black Sea; a major seaport and industrial center. After experiencing heavy damage and loss of life from bombardment and being largely cut off, the city was evacuated and abandoned by the Russians in 1941. The Nazis occupied Odessa from 1941–1944 at the height of World War II. The Germans also brought the "final solution," their plan for the murder of all the Jews of Europe, with them to the Ukraine, where they killed Jews whenever the opportunity arose.

# Japanese American Concentration Camp Haiku, 1942–1944

Shortly after the bombing of Pearl Harbor and the United States' entry into the Second World War, U.S. President Franklin Delano Roosevelt signed the now infamous Executive Order 9066, which authorized the forced roundup, relocation, and detention of Japanese Americans. The Executive Order would later be declared unconstitutional, but such legal niceties were ignored during the war. Its motivation was racist. No comparable abrogation of citizenship and due process was effected for German Americans. So more than 120,000 Japanese Americans, most of them American born, were suddenly taken from their homes and confined in concentration camps set up in the swampland of Arkansas or the deserts of Arizona, California, and New Mexico. Meanwhile, some Japanese Americans fought and died in the U.S. Army on behalf of the country that was imprisoning their families.

Among the imprisoned Japanese Americans were members of California Haiku-writing clubs that had adopted the free-verse Haiku first developed after 1915 and more widely popularized in the 1930s. These modernist haiku were not restricted to seasonal vocabularies or to the strict syllable structure of traditional haiku. When these amateur poets found themselves exiles in their own country, they turned to haiku to express their feelings, and some of the haiku were issued in camp newspapers. Many of the poems did not survive the war, but Violet Kazue de Cristoforo has translated over 300 of them from the Japanese in *May Sky—There is Always Tomorrow: An Anthology of Japanese American Concentration Camp Kaiko Haiku* (1997), from which the following selection is taken.

Of the eighteen poets represented here, few biographical details are known. Neiji Ozawa (1886–1967) was born in Nagano Prefecture in Japan. He came to the United States in 1907, studied pharmacology at Berkeley, and opened a drug store in Fresno, California, where he also organized a haiku club. Kyotaro Komuro (1885–1953) came to the United States on the same boat as Ozawa; before being taken from his home he had become president and publisher of the *Stockton Times* in California. Hekisamei Matsuda (1906–1970) was owner and manager of the Matsuda Book Shop in Fresno when war broke out; he was repatriated to Japan in 1945. Sadayo Taniguchi, born in Japan in 1905, was separated from her family during her five-year internment; she later died in Texas. Hankuro Wada was born in Stockton, California, but was also expatriated to Japan in 1945. Shokoshi Saga, the pen name of Hideo Ito, was born in Mie Prefecture, Japan. Before the war he was a Japanese language school teacher and a correspondent for a Japanese newspaper. He settled in San Francisco after the war and died there in 1988. Shizuku Uyemaruko, the pen name of Sachiko Uyemaruko (1898–1992), was born in Hiroshima and emigrated to the United States in 1917; she declined to share other details of her biography with de Cristoforo. Shiho Okamoto (1888–1967) wrote haiku for many decades. Senbinshi Takaoka was both a poet and an artist; he returned to Japan and died in Kyoto. Jyosha Yamada (1883–1969) was born in Japan and died in Stockton, California. Hangetsu Tsunekawa returned to Stockton, California, after being released. Ryokuin Matsui died soon after the war. About fifty of Hyakuissei's haiku survive, including some composed as a travel diary between Rohwer concentration camp in Arkansas and the Tule Lake camp in northern California in 1943. Little is known about Shonan Suzuki, Hyakuissei Okamoto, Tokuji Hirai, Suiko Matsushita, or Sei Sagara. In order to emphasize the narrative potential that is revealed when the poems are treated as a collective enterprise, we have removed the poets' names from the poems here, though they are listed in the book's contents. This sequence begins with arrest in summer and moves through the experience of internment.

> Being arrested—
> at home peony bud
> still firm
>
> Hand-cuffed and taken away
> 5  I see my husband
> even today
>
> Lingering summer heat—
> Japanese proceeding under guard
> on dusty white road
>
> 10  Passed guard tower
> without glancing up
> before summer daybreak
>
> In the shade of summer sun
> guard tapping rock
> 15  with club
>
> Withered grass on ground
> army tank creaking
> in the wind
>
> Young grass red and shriveled
> 20  wide sandy flat
> and gritty wind
>
> Dandelion has bloomed
> a moment of bitterness—
> of what consequence?
>
> 25  On certain days
> heart is full of hypocrisy
> flowers of *gobo*° are purple

---

27 *gobo*: Burdock.

Released seagull
after writing NIPPON in red on its belly
30   summer morning in highlands

Sprinkling water outside
barracks occupants
in full force and barefooted

Want to be with children
35   playing in water
of irrigation ditch

Even the croaking of frogs
comes from outside the barbed wire fence
this is our life

40   Sentry at main gate
face clearly exposed
in evening sun

Thin shadow of tule reed
blazing sunset
45   on barbed wire fence

Looking at summer moon
On Castle Rock
we are living in alien (enemy) land

Moon shadows on internment camp
50   I hear the cries of geese
again this year

Early moon has set
people unable to sleep
whispering

55   Rain shower from mountain
quietly soaking
barbed wire fence

Desert rain falling
spitting blood
then fall asleep

60   Frosty morning
handed a hatchet
today I became a woodcutter

Black clouds instantly shroud
autumn sky
65   hail storming against us today also

Winter wind
relentlessly blasting shed
goat bleating

70          Doll without a head
lying on desk top
one evening

Suddenly awakened
listening to bugle from guard house
75          moonlight

Jeep patrolling slowly
stove is glowing
at night

Grieving within
80          another victim°
oats on the ground

In the sage brush
two new earth mounds°
torrid wind blows

85          Oh shells—
the cliff, your bygone world
is slowly crumbling

---

80 *victim*: Soichi James Okamoto, a construction worker, was asking permission to pass
through the Tule Lake Camp gate when he was fatally shot, on May 24, 1944. The sentry
who fired the fatal bullet was later acquitted after being fined $1.00 for the "unauthorized
use of government property."
83 *mounds*: The mounds (graves) were for two critically ill internees who had just arrived
from a camp in Bismark, North Dakota, and were shot dead by sentries who later alleged
the two were "trying to escape from the camp."

# John Berryman (1914–1972)

Berryman was born John Smith in McAlester, Oklahoma. At age twelve, after his family had moved to Florida, Berryman's father shot himself to death outside his son's window. His surname comes from his mother's second marriage, which occurred after the family moved to New York. Berryman was educated at Columbia and Cambridge universities and himself became an influential teacher at Harvard, Princeton, and Minnesota. But he struggled with alcoholism and madness throughout his life. In the end, he leapt to his death from a bridge in Minneapolis.

Although he wrote short poems, a long poem and a 385-poem sequence, *Homage to Mistress Bradstreet* (1956) and *The Dream Songs* (1964–1968) are his major achievements. In the later work Berryman performs, exhibits, and burlesques his psychic struggles and his attitudes toward contemporary culture through a series of personae. Stylistically and rhetorically inventive, these poems are quite unlike anything else in modern poetry.

## from *The Dream Songs*°

### I

Huffy Henry hid     the day,
unappeasable Henry sulked.
I see his point,—a trying to put things over.
It was the thought that they thought
5     they could *do* it made Henry wicked & away.
But he should have come out and talked.

All the world like a woolen lover
once did seem on Henry's side.
Then came a departure.

---

**volume title:** Most of these poems were first published in 77 *Dream Songs* (1967) or in *His Toy, His Dream, His Rest* (1968) and then collected in *The Dream Songs* (1969). Throughout the "dream songs" appear Berryman's persona, Henry, and Henry's alter ego, Mister Bones (a name given to the character who rattled bones as a sound effect in minstrel shows). Berryman's note: "The poem, then, whatever its wide cast of characters, is essentially about an imaginary character (not the poet, not me) named Henry, a white American in early middle age sometimes in blackface, who has suffered an irreversible loss and talks about himself sometimes in the first person, sometimes in the third, sometimes even in the second; he has a friend, never named, who addresses him as Mr. Bones and variants thereof. Requiescant in pace" ["Rest in peace" (Latin)].

10      Thereafter nothing fell out as it might or ought.
        I don't see how Henry, pried
        open for all the world to see, survived.

        What he has now to say is a long
        wonder the world can bear & be.
15      Once in a sycamore I was glad
        all at the top, and I sang.
        Hard on the land wears the strong sea
        and empty grows every bed.

*1964*


## 4

        Filling her compact & delicious body
        with chicken páprika, she glanced at me
        twice.
        Fainting with interest, I hungered back
5       and only the fact of her husband & four other people
        kept me from springing on her

        or falling at her little feet and crying
        'You are the hottest one for years of night
        Henry's dazed eyes
10      have enjoyed, Brilliance.' I advanced upon
        (despairing) my spumoni.—Sir Bones: is stuffed,
        de world, wif feeding girls.

        —Black hair, complexion Latin, jewelled eyes
        downcast . . . The slob beside her   feasts . . . What wonders is
15      she sitting on, over there?
        The restaurant buzzes. She might as well be on Mars.
        Where did it all go wrong? There ought to be a law against Henry.
        —Mr. Bones: there is.

*1964*


## 5

        Henry sats in de bar & was odd,
        off in the glass from the glass,
        at odds wif de world & its god,
        his wife is a complete nothing,
5       St Stephen
        getting even.

        Henry sats in de plane & was gay.
        Careful Henry nothing said aloud
        but where a Virgin out of cloud
10      to her Mountain dropt in light,
        his thought made pockets & the plane buckt.
        'Parm me, lady.' 'Orright.'

Henry lay in de netting, wild,
while the brainfever bird did scales;
15　Mr Heartbreak,° the New Man,
come to farm a crazy land;
an image of the dead on the fingernail°
of a newborn child.

1964

## 14

Life, friends, is boring. We must not say so.
After all, the sky flashes, the great sea yearns,
we ourselves flash and yearn,
and moreover my mother told me as a boy
5　(repeatingly) 'Ever to confess you're bored
means you have no

Inner Resources.' I conclude now I have no
inner resources, because I am heavy bored.
Peoples bore me,
10　literature bores me, especially great literature,
Henry bores me, with his plights & gripes
as bad as achilles,°

who loves people and valiant art, which bores me.
And the tranquil hills, & gin, look like a drag
15　and somehow a dog
has taken itself & its tail considerably away
into mountains or sea or sky, leaving
behind: me, wag.

1964

## 22

### Of 1826

I am the little man who smokes & smokes.
I am the girl who does know better but.
I am the king of the pool.
I am so wise I had my mouth sewn shut.

---

15 *Heartbreak*: translates the last name of J. Hector St. John Crèvecoeur, whose *Letters from an American Farmer* (1782) introduces the notion of the American as the "New Man" in its third chapter.
17 *fingernail*: from Miguel de Cervantes, whose *The Colloquoy of the Dogs* (1613) notes that the witch of Kamacha could "cause the living or dead to appear in a mirror on the fingernail of a newborn child."
12 *achilles*: hero of *The Iliad*, by the Greek epic poet Homer (eighth century B.C.); because of injured pride after a slight from Agamemnon, Achilles sulked in his tent, refusing to fight the Trojans. Berryman commented that *The Dream Songs* borrows some of its structure from *The Illiad*.

5      I am a government official & a goddamned fool.
       I am a lady who takes jokes.

       I am the enemy of the mind.
       I am the auto salesman and lóve you.
       I am a teenage cancer, with a plan.
10     I am the blackt-out man.
       I am the woman powerful as a zoo.
       I am two eyes screwed to my set, whose blind—

       It is the Fourth of July.
       Collect: while the dying man,°
15     forgone by you creator, who forgives,
       is gasping 'Thomas Jefferson still lives'
       in vain, in vain, in vain.
       I am Henry Pussy-cat! My whiskers fly.

                                              *1964*


                          29

       There sat down, once, a thing on Henry's heart
       só heavy, if he had a hundred years
       & more, & weeping, sleepless, in all them time
       Henry could not make good.
5      Starts again always in Henry's ears
       the little cough somewhere, an odour, a chime.

       And there is another thing he has in mind
       like a grave Sienese face° a thousand years
       would fail to blur the still profiled reproach of. Ghastly,
10     with open eyes, he attends, blind.
       All the bells say: too late. This is not for tears;
       thinking.

       But never did Henry, as he thought he did,
       end anyone and hacks her body up
15     and hide the pieces, where they may be found.
       He knows: he went over everyone, & nobody's missing.
       Often he reckons, in the dawn, them up.
       Nobody is ever missing.

                                              *1964*


---

14 *dying man*: John Adams (1735–1826), second president of the United States, defeated
for reelection by Thomas Jefferson (1743–1826). They died on the same day, July 4, 1826,
with Jefferson dying first, but Adams did not know that when he gasped his last words.
8 *Sienese face*: like an austere face seen in the religious paintings by thirteenth- and four-
teenth-century Italian artists in Siena.

## 40

I'm scared a lonely. Never see my son,
easy be not to see anyone,
combers° out to sea
know they're goin somewhere but not me.
5    Got a little poison, got a little gun,
I'm scared a lonely.

I'm scared a only one thing, which is me,
from othering I don't take nothin, see,
for any hound dog's sake.
10    But this is where I livin, where I rake
my leaves and cop my promise,° this' where we
cry oursel's awake.

Wishin was dyin but I gotta make
it all this way to that bed on these feet
15    where peoples said to meet.
Maybe but even if I see my son
forever never, get back on the take,
free, black° & forty-one.

1964

## 45

He stared at ruin. Ruin stared straight back.
He thought they was old friends. He felt on the stair
where her papa found them bare
they became familiar. When the papers were lost
5    rich with pals' secrets, he thought he had the knack
of ruin. Their paths crossed

and once they crossed in jail; they crossed in bed;
and over an unsigned letter their eyes met,
and in an Asian city
10    directionless & lurchy at two & three,
or trembling to a telephone's fresh threat,
and when some wired his head

to reach a wrong opinion, 'Epileptic',°
But he noted now that: they were not old friends.
15    He did not know this one.
This one was a stranger, come to make amends

---

3 *combers*: long, breaking waves.
11 *cop my promise*: the phrase cuts two ways, suggesting at once *increasing* his promise or capacities and backing down on, or going back on, his word.
18 *free, black*: a play on "free, white, and twenty-one," a colloquialism for "legally independent."
13 *Epileptic*: Berryman was incorrectly diagnosed with epilepsy in 1939.

for all the imposters, and to make it stick.
Henry nodded, un-.

                                                        *1964*


## 46

I am, outside. Incredible panic rules.°
People are blowing and beating each other without mercy.
Drinks are boiling. Iced
drinks are boiling. The worse anyone feels, the worse
5      treated he is. Fools elect fools.
A harmless man at an intersection said, under his breath: "Christ!"

That word, so spoken, affected the vision
of, when they trod to work next day, shopkeepers
who went & were fitted for glasses.
10     Enjoyed they then an appearance of love & law.
Millenia whift & waft—one, one—er, er . . .
Their glasses were taken from them, & they saw.

Man has undertaken the top job of all,
*son fin.*° Good luck.
15     I myself walked at the funeral of tenderness.
Followed other deaths. Among the last,
Like the memory of a lovely fuck,
was: *Do, ut des.*°

                                                        *1964*


## 55

Peter's not friendly. He gives me sideways looks.
The architecture is far from reassuring.
I feel uneasy.
A pity,—the interview began so well:
5      I mentioned fiendish things, he waved them away
and sloshed out a martini

strangely needed. We spoke of indifferent matters—
God's health, the vague hell of the Congo,
John's energy,
10     anti-matter matter. I felt fine.
Then a change came backward. A chill fell.
Talk slackened,

---

1 *rules*: the first line alludes to a dream recorded by Wilhelm Stekel in *Sadism and Masochism* (1935).
14 *son fin*: (French) "his end."
18 *Do, ut des*: (German) "I give that thou shalt give," Wilhelm Stekel.

died, and he began to give me sideways looks.
'Christ,' I thought 'what now?' and would have askt for another
15 but didn't dare.
I feel my application    failing. It's growing dark,
some other sound is overcoming. His last words are:
'We betrayed me.'

1964

## 76

### *Henry's Confession*

Nothin very bad happen to me lately.
How you explain that?—I explain that, Mr Bones,
terms o' your bafflin odd sobriety.
Sober as man can get, no girls, no telephones,
5 what could happen bad to Mr Bones?
—*If* life is a handkerchief sandwich,

in a modesty of death I join my father
who dared so long agone leave me.
A bullet on a concrete stoop
10 close by a smothering southern sea
spreadeagled on an island, by my knee.
—You is from hunger, Mr Bones,

I offers you this handkerchief, now set
your left foot by my right foot,
15 shoulder to shoulder, all that jazz,
arm in arm, by the beautiful sea,°
hum a little, Mr Bones.
—I saw nobody coming, so I went instead.

1964

## 382

At Henry's bier let some thing fall out well:
enter there none who somewhat has to sell,
the music ancient & gradual,
the voices solemn but the grief subdued,
5 no hairy jokes but everybody's mood
subdued, subdued,

until the Dancer comes, in a short short dress
hair black & long & loose, dark dark glasses,
uptilted face,
10 pallor & strangeness, the music changes
to 'Give!' & 'Ow!' and how! the music changes,
she kicks a backward limb

---

16 *beautiful sea*: from a popular song of 1914.

on tiptoe, pirouettes, & she is free
to the knocking music, sails, dips, & suddenly
15      returns to the terrible gay
occasion hopeless & mad, she weaves, it's hell,
she flings to her head a leg, bobs, all is well,
she dances Henry away.

*1968*


## 384

The marker slants, flowerless, day's almost done,
I stand above my father's grave with rage,
often, often before
I've made this awful pilgrimage to one
5       who cannot visit me, who tore his page
out: I come back for more,

I spit upon this dreadful banker's grave
who shot his heart out in a Florida dawn
O ho alas alas
10      When will indifference come, I moan & rave
I'd like to scrabble till I got right down
away down under the grass

and ax the casket open ha to see
just how he's taking it, which he sought so hard
15      we'll tear apart
the mouldering grave clothes ha & then Henry
will heft the ax once more, his final card,
and fell it on the start.

*1968*

# William Stafford (1914–1993)

Born in rural Kansas, Stafford was a conscientious objector during World War II and was active in pacifist organizations. After earning degrees from the University of Kansas, he went on to study at the Writer's Workshop at the University of Iowa, where he also earned a Ph.D. He taught at Lewis and Clark College in Portland, Oregon, from 1956 to 1979, publishing his first book, *West of Your City*, in 1960. Stafford's writing process, as he explained it, was to rise early and work in the quiet before others awoke. One way to describe his poetry is to compare it with the pure quiet of the pre-dawn hours. Everything about his writing, from its careful parceling into stanzas to the clear steps that guide us from passage to passage, suggests there is a virtue to calm, thoughtful, understated observation. Many of his poems depict Midwestern towns and landscapes; others take up personal and family experiences, but he has also taken up public topics on occasion.

## Traveling Through the Dark

Traveling through the dark I found a deer
dead on the edge of the Wilson River road.
It is usually best to roll them into the canyon:
that road is narrow; to swerve might make more dead.

5  By glow of the tail-light I stumbled back of the car
and stood by the heap, a doe, a recent killing;
she had stiffened already, almost cold.
I dragged her off; she was large in the belly.

My fingers touching her side brought me the reason—
10  her side was warm; her fawn lay there waiting,
alive, still, never to be born.
Beside that mountain road I hesitated.

The car aimed ahead its lowered parking lights;
under the hood purred the steady engine.
15  I stood in the glare of the warm exhaust turning red;
around our group I could hear the wilderness listen.

I thought hard for us all—my only swerving—,
then pushed her over the edge into the river.

1960

## At the Bomb Testing Site

At noon in the desert a panting lizard
waited for history, its elbows tense,
watching the curve of a particular road
as if something might happen.

5      It was looking for something farther off
than people could see, an important scene
acted in stone for little selves
at the flute end of consequences.

There was just a continent without much on it
under a sky that never cared less.

*1966*


## The Indian Cave Jerry Ramsey Found°

Brown, brittle, wait-a-bit weeds
block the entrance. I untangle their
whole summer embrace. Inside—soot from
a cold fire, powder of bones,
5      a piece of ceremonial horn: cool
history comes off on my hands.
Outside, I stand in a canyon so
quiet its pool almost remembers its
old reflections. And then I breathe.

*1983*

---

**poem title:** Jarold Ramsey (b. 1937), American poet and critic who studies Native American literature.

# Dudley Randall (b. 1914)

Randall was born in Washington, D.C., but moved to Detroit in 1920. He worked in a foundry early on, then served in the military during World War II, an experience described in some of his poems. He earned degrees in English and library science and took several library positions during his career, but he is perhaps most famous as the 1965 founder of Detroit's Broadside Press. The press issued the first books of a considerable number of black writers, along with an extensive series of historic poetry broadsides. Randall himself worked both in traditional stanzaic forms and in blues styles, often writing poems of articulate protest. See his *A Litany of Friends: New and Selected Poems* (1983).

## Ballad of Birmingham°

(On the bombing of a church in Birmingham, Alabama, 1963)

"Mother dear, may I go downtown
Instead of out to play,
And march the streets of Birmingham
In a Freedom March today?"

5     "No, baby, no, you may not go,
For the dogs are fierce and wild,
And clubs and hoses, guns and jails
Aren't good for a little child."

"But, mother, I won't be alone.
10    Other children will go with me,
And march the streets of Birmingham
To make our country free."

"No, baby, no, you may not go,
For I fear those guns will fire.
15    But you may go to church instead
And sing in the children's choir."

---

**poem title:** the Rev. Martin Luther King, Jr. led nonviolent civil rights demonstrations in Birmingham, Alabama, two weeks after his famous August 23rd March on Washington, D.C.; the Birmingham demonstrators were confronted with attack dogs, tear gas, fire hoses, and cattle prods.

She has combed and brushed her night-dark hair,
And bathed rose petal sweet,
And drawn white gloves on her small brown hands,
20 And white shoes on her feet.

The mother smiled to know her child
Was in the sacred place,
But that smile was the last smile
To come upon her face.

25 For when she heard the explosion,
Her eyes grew wet and wild.
She raced through the streets of Birmingham
Calling for her child.

She clawed through bits of glass and brick,
30 Then lifted out a shoe.
"O, here's the shoe my baby wore,
But, baby, where are you?"

*1969*

# Joy Davidman (1915–1960)

Davidman's first publications appeared while she was still an undergraduate at Hunter College. *Poetry* began to publish her poems in 1936. Within a year or two, she had joined the Communist party. *Letter to a Comrade*, the only collection of her own poems, was published in the Yale Series of Younger Poets in 1938. She spent the latter half of 1939 in Hollywood as an assistant screen writer for M-G-M, an experience that led her to write a number of film reviews for *New Masses* in the early 1940s. She contributed new poems to her massive anthology *War Poems of the United Nations* (1943) and to *Seven Poets in Search of an Answer* (1944), from which "For the Nazis" is reprinted. She wrote two novels, and converted to Christianity after a religious experience in 1946. She divorced her first husband, the Spanish Civil War veteran William Gresham, and married the British writer C.S. Lewis in 1956; the 1993 feature film *Shadowlands* tells a version of her relationship with Lewis.

## This Woman

Now do not put a ribbon in your hair;
Abjure the spangled insult of design,
The filigree sterility, nor twine
A flower with your strength; go bare, go bare.

5     The elements foregathered at your birth
Gave your hard throat an armor for despair,
Burned you and bathed you, nourished you with air,
And carved your body like a tree of earth.

This is the symbol that I shape of you;
10    Branching from the broad column of your flesh
Into the obdurate and fibrous mesh
Stubborn to break apart and stiff to hew;
Lost at your core a living skeleton
Like sharp roots pointing downward from the sun.

*1938*

# For the Nazis

When you see red
it will be too late;
the night will be dead,
the sun will not wait;
5    say, can you see
what the sunrise will be?

When you command
the sea to stand still
at the safe edge of the sand,
10    do you think that it will?
say, do you know
where the high tide will go?

Call for your cannon,
call for your drum,
15    buzz with the airplane;
burst with the bomb;
you're up a tree now;
say, while you rave,
say, can you see now
the depth of your grave?

1944

# Margaret Walker (1915–1998)

Born in Birmingham, Alabama, to a middle-class black family that moved to New Orleans a decade later, Walker first enrolled at New Orleans University. Then she met poet Langston Hughes, who encouraged her writing and advised her to go north to complete her education, which she did at Northwestern University. It was in Chicago, in 1936, that she met novelist and poet Richard Wright, about whom she would publish a critical biography fifty-two years later. She became a teacher and a novelist, and continued publishing poetry after the dramatic success of the poems of *For My People* (1942).

## For My People

For my people everywhere singing their slave songs
    repeatedly: their dirges and their ditties and their blues
    and jubilees, praying their prayers nightly to an
    unknown god, bending their knees humbly to an
5    unseen power;

For my people lending their strength to the years, to the
    gone years and the now years and the maybe years,
    washing ironing cooking scrubbing sewing mending
    hoeing plowing digging planting pruning patching
10    dragging along never gaining never reaping never
    knowing and never understanding;

For my playmates in the clay and dust and sand of Alabama
    backyards playing baptizing and preaching and doctor
    and jail and soldier and school and mama and cooking
15    and playhouse and concert and store and hair and Miss
    Choomby and company;

For the cramped bewildered years we went to school to learn
    to know the reasons why and the answers to and the
    people who and the places where and the days when, in
20    memory of the bitter hours when we discovered we
    were black and poor and small and different and nobody
    cared and nobody wondered and nobody understood;

For the boys and girls who grew in spite of these things to
    be man and woman, to laugh and dance and sing and
25       play and drink their wine and religion and success, to
    marry their playmates and bear children and then die
    of consumption and anemia and lynching;

For my people thronging 47th Street in Chicago and Lenox
    Avenue in New York and Rampert Street in New
30       Orleans, lost disinherited dispossessed and happy
    people filling the cabarets and taverns and other
    people's pockets needing bread and shoes and milk and
    land and memory and something—something all our own;

For my people walking blindly spreading joy, losing time
35       being lazy, sleeping when hungry, shouting when
    burdened, drinking when hopeless, tied, and shackled
    and tangled among ourselves by the unseen creatures
    who tower over us omnisciently and laugh;

For my people blundering and groping and floundering in
40       the dark of churches and schools and clubs and
    societies, associations and councils and committees and
    conventions, distressed and disturbed and deceived and
    devoured by money-hungry glory-craving leeches,
    preyed on by facile force of state and fad and novelty, by
45       false prophet and holy believer;

For my people standing staring trying to fashion a better way
    from confusion, from hypocrisy and misunderstanding,
    trying to fashion a world that will hold all the people,
    all the faces, all the adams and eves and their countless
50       generations;

Let a new earth rise. Let another world be born. Let a
    bloody peace be written in the sky. Let a second
    generation full of courage issue forth; let a people
    loving freedom come to growth. Let a beauty full of
55       healing and a strength of final clenching be the pulsing
    in our spirits and our blood. Let the martial songs be
    written, let the dirges disappear. Let a race of men now
    rise and take control.

*1937*

# Ruth Stone (b. 1915)

Born in Roanoke, Virginia, Stone grew up in Indiana and Illinois, and was educated at the University of Illinois. Although she did not publish her first book until 1958, and withheld her next book until 1970, she has nevertheless had a long and distinguished career. It has also, however, been a career very much on the margins of the poetry establishment, about which "Some Things You'll Need to Know/Before You Join the Union" testifies with devastating wit. She has gone her own way, devoted more to writing her poetry than publishing it, courting few journals, living on a New England farm, while serving occasionally as poet-in-residence at various universities, including the State University of New York at Binghamton, and all the while honing an intensely lyrical voice with a sharp edge of awareness about the politics of gender in America.

## In an Iridescent Time

My mother, when young, scrubbed laundry in a tub,
She and her sisters on an old brick walk
Under the apple trees, sweet rub-a-dub.
The bees came round their heads, the wrens made talk.
5    Four young ladies each with a rainbow board
Honed their knuckles, wrung their wrists to red,
Tossed back their braids and wiped their aprons wet.
The Jersey calf beyond the back fence roared;
And all the soft day, swarms about their pet
10   Buzzed at his big brown eyes and bullish head.
Four times they rinsed, they said. Some things they starched,
Then shook them from the baskets two by two,
And pinned the fluttering intimacies of life
Between the lilac bushes and the yew:
Brown gingham, pink, and skirts of Alice blue.

*1959*

## I Have Three Daughters

I have three daughters
Like greengage plums.
They sat all day
Sucking their thumbs.

5      And more's the pity,
       They cried all day,
       Why doesn't our mother's brown hair
       Turn gray?

       I have three daughters
10     Like three cherries.
       They sat at the window
       The boys to please.
       And they couldn't wait
       For their mother to grow old.
15     Why doesn't our mother's brown hair
       Turn to snow?

       I have three daughters
       In the apple tree
       Singing Mama send Daddy
20     With three young lovers
       To take them away from me.

       I have three daughters
       Like greengage plums,
       Sitting all day
25     And sighing all day
       And sucking their thumbs;
       Singing, Mama won't you fetch and carry,
       And Daddy, won't you let us marry,
       Singing, sprinkle snow down on Mama's hair
       And lordy, give us our share.

                                                        *1970*

## Pokeberries

       I started out in the Virginia mountains
       with my grandma's pansy bed
       and my Aunt Maud's dandelion wine.
       We lived on greens and back-fat and biscuits.
5      My Aunt Maud scrubbed right through the linoleum.
       My daddy was a northerner who played drums
       and chewed tobacco and gambled.
       He married my mama on the rebound.
       Who would want an ignorant hill girl with red hair?
10     They took a Pullman up to Indianapolis
       and someone stole my daddy's wallet.
       My whole life has been stained with pokeberries.
       No man seemed right for me. I was awkward
       until I found a good wood-burning stove.
15     There is no use asking what it means.
       With my first piece of ready cash I bought my own
       place in Vermont; kerosene lamps, dirt road.
       I'm sticking here like a porcupine up a tree.
       Like the one our neighbor shot. Its bones and skin

20  hung there for three years in the orchard.
No amount of knowledge can shake my grandma out of me;
or my Aunt Maud; or my mama, who didn't just bite an apple
with her big white teeth. She split it in two.

*1987*

## American Milk

Then the butter we put on our white bread
was colored with butter yellow, a cancerous dye,
and all the fourth grades were taken by streetcar
to the Dunky Company to see milk processed; milk bottles
5   riding on narrow metal cogs through little doors that flapped.
The sour damp smell of milky-wet cement floors:
we looked through great glass windows at the milk.
Before we were herded back to the streetcar line,
we were each given a half pint of milk in tiny
10  milk bottles with straws to suck it up. In this way
we gradually learned about our country.

*1987*

## From the Arboretum

The bunya-bunya is a great louse that sucks.
From its center many limbs are fastened to the sky
which lies behind it placidly suffering.
At its bottom it wears the ruffles of a cancan girl.
5   Bird dung and nits drip with its resinous sweat.
Its forgotten threads underground are anaerobic
with the maximum strength of steel. For every stretch
upward it splits and bleeds—fingers grow out of fingers.
Rings of ants, bark beetles, sponge molds,
10  even cockroaches communicate in its armpits.
But it protests only with the voices of starlings,
their colony at its top in the forward brush.
To them it is only an old armchair, a brothel, the front porch.

*1987*

## Drought in the Lower Fields

Steers are dumb like angels,
moony-eyed, and soft-calling
like channel bells
to sound the abyss,
5   the drop-off in the fog
that crows circle
and gliding buzzards
yearn down into with their small
red heads bent
10  looking for dead souls to pick.

Steers nod their heads, yes,
browsing the scalded grass,
they eat around the scarce
blue stars of chicory.

*1987*


# Some Things You'll Need to Know
# Before You Join the Union

### I

At the poetry factory
body poems are writhing and bleeding.
An angry mob of women
is lined up at the back door
5    hoping for jobs.
Today at the poetry factory
they are driving needles through the poems.
Everyone's excited.
Mr. Po-Biz himself comes in from the front office.
10   He clenches his teeth.
"Anymore wildcat aborting out there," he hisses
"and you're all blacklisted."
The mob jeers.

### II

The antiwar and human rights poems
15   are processed in the white room.
Everyone in there wears sterile gauze.
These poems go for a lot.
No one wants to mess up.
There's expensive equipment involved,
20   The workers have to be heavy,
very heavy.
These poems are packaged in cement.
You frequently hear them drop with a dull thud.

### III

Poems are being shipped out
25   by freight car.
Headed up the ramp
they can't turn back.
They push each other along.
They will go to the packing houses.
30   The slaughter will be terrible,
an inevitable end of overproduction,
the poetry factory's GNP.
Their shelf life will be brief.

### IV

They're stuffing at the poetry factory today.
35  They're jamming in images
saturated with *as* and *like*.
Lines are being stuffed to their limits.
If a line by chance explodes,
there's a great cheer.
40  However, most of them don't explode.
Most of them lie down and groan.

### V

In the poetry factory
it's very hot.
The bellows are going,
45  the pressure is building up.
Young poems are being rolled out
ready to be cut.
Whistles are blowing.
Jive is rocking.
50  Barrels of thin words line the walls.
Fat words like links of sausages
hang on belts.
Floor walkers and straw bosses
take a coffee break.
55  Only the nervous apprentice
is anywhere near the machines
when a large poem
seems about to come off the assembly line.
"This is it," the apprentice shouts.
60  "Get my promotion ready!
APR, the quarterlies,
a chapbook, NEA,
a creative writing chair,
the poetry circuit, Yaddo!"
65  Inside the ambulance
as it drives away
he is still shouting,
"I'll grow a beard,
become an alcoholic,
consider suicide."

*1987*

# Thomas McGrath (1916–1990)

Born on a farm near Sheldon, North Dakota, the grandchild of Irish Catholic homesteaders, McGrath was educated at the University of North Dakota, Louisiana State University, New College, and Oxford University, the latter as a Rhodes Scholar. He was in the U.S. Air Force in the Aleutian Islands during World War II, isolated from combat in a unit full of radicals feared by the high command. He moved to Hollywood on his return and married Alice Greenfield (McGrath), a communist organizer in Los Angeles who is the real social worker behind the heroine of Luis Valdez's play (and later film) *Zoot Suit*. In 1953, at the height of the long postwar inquisition that culminated in the McCarthy Era, McGrath was teaching at Los Angeles State College when he was called before the House UnAmerican Activities Committee. Citing his constitutional guarantees of free speech and political association, guarantees the government swept aside, McGrath refused to answer the committee's questions about his own beliefs or to betray his friends. "Poets have been notorious non-cooperators where committees of this sort are concerned," he added, "I do not wish to bring dishonor upon my tribe." McGrath was fired from his teaching job and blacklisted as a result. A lifelong socialist and prairie populist, veteran of failed farms during the Great Depression, occasional welder and logger, McGrath then pieced together a living doing labor organizing, writing scripts for documentary films, and eventually, when the inquisition had run its course, by teaching. In 1975, he was investigated by a grand jury for possible third-degree murder in the shooting death of a Minnesota man; though the grand jury returned a no-charge verdict and he was not brought to trial, the incident hurt him deeply. Through it all he remained a revolutionary and an ironist, writing short poems notable not only for their rhetorical intricacy and political wit but also for their passionate commitment to justice and sanity. He would also write one of the great American book-length poem sequences, *Letter to an Imaginary Friend*, finally issued in its entirety posthumously in 1997.

## Deep South

*Baton Rouge, 1940*

These are savannas bluer than your dreams
Where other loves are fashioned to older music,
And the romantic in his light boat
Puts out among flamingos and water moccasins
5   Looking for the river that went by last year.

Even the angels wear confederate uniforms;
And when the magnolia blooms and the honeysuckle,
Golden lovers, brighter than the moon,
Read Catullus in the flaring light
10 Of the burning Negro in the open eye of midnight.

And the Traveller, moving in the hot swamps,
Where every human sympathy sends up the temperature,
Comes of a sudden on the hidden glacier,
Whose motives are blonder than Hitler's choir boys.

15 Here is the ambiguous tenderness of 'gators
Trumpeting their loves along a hundred miles
Of rivers writhing under trees like myths—
And human existence pursues the last,
The simple and desperate life of the senses.
20 Since love survives only as ironic legend—
Response to situations no longer present—
Men lacking dignity are seized by pride,
Which is the easy upper-class infection.

The masters are at home in this merciless climate
25 But deep in the caves of their minds some animal memory
Warns of the fate of the mammoth at the end of the ice-age;
As sleeping children a toy, they hug the last, fatal error,
But their eyes are awake and their dreams shake as with palsy.

    * * *

Over Birmingham where the blast furnace flowers
30 And beyond the piney woods in cotton country,
Continually puzzling the pale aristocrats,
The sun burns equally white man and black.

The labor which they do makes more and more
Their brotherhood condition for their whole existence;
35 They mint their own light, and their fusing fires
Will melt at last these centuries of ice.

This is a nightmare nimble in the Big House,
Where sleepers are wakeful, cuddling their terror,
In the empty acres of their rich beds, dreaming
Of bones in museums, where the black boys yawn.

                *1940*

# Crash Report

If perhaps you read in the paper somewhere
How Captain—or maybe Private—so and so—
Had been killed in Africa or India or even
The Aleutians—well, would you think him a hero?

5 It isn't important one way or another.
The guy is just as dead as Grant took Richmond.

In five years the flesh fails; five years and then
You can knock at his memory: nobody home.

10   For these heroes in handcuffs, out of War by Accident,
Never seem to wear well and anyway at best
Even the well dressed scarecrow or scapegoat
Possesses a limited survival value.

For instance, examine a case on record:
The dashing captain with the low-powered kite,
15   (It was crewed by a Christian Front mug from Yorkville
And somewhat overloaded with whisky and nurses)

—He crashed and was killed: wages of sin, etc.
While another man goes down over Paramashiru—
He wasn't joy-riding. But all is equal
20   In the book of Hearst's recording angel.

Yet not for us. We can recognize heroes
Before they are dead or fogged in with medals.
For heroes the hearse must be called for a reason.
It is not by accident their lives are given.

25   But for you, Gentle Reader, it doesn't matter a damn.
To you, real or phony, they're all the same.
And in the dead men's summers where they'll never feel the sun
It's of no importance. Everyone dies for your sins.

*1944*

# First Book of Genesis According to the Diplomats

On the first day they drowned the orphans,
The blue-eyed ones, in threes, in diplomats' pouches.
The dollar stood at four pounds of flesh in open market
And all markets were opened by the President,
5   Officially, on the first day.

The second day some opposition
Was begun by workers. These were all shot down
By students of the Radicals for Nixon movement.
Two million died in sin mortal and venial and
10   In hunger on the second day;

And were buried, noon, on the third day
In two speeches, given by the Secretary
Who said they were foreigners, et cetera. The Poet
Laureate was observed hustling, et cetera,
15   Officially, on the third day.

The fourth day was unofficial. Five
Officials of the Western Democracies were
Purchased, and some English peers. A brown rubber Bible

In a goldfish bowl was presented to a king.
20  The goldfish died on the fourth day.

The fifty day was the Apocalypse
Of Peoria. Armed invaders
Turned out to be a seal with a bicycle bell and two
Margarine golfballs in a birdcage. The Mayor
25  Had to resign on the fifth day.

On the sixth day Congress with a gun
At the taxpayer's head asked not to be provoked.
It wasn't. The Society of Atomic Widows made
The Statue of Liberty a charter member
30  Regretfully on the sixth day.

On the seventh day *Time* held out hope
That orphans with black-roofed mouths would not be drowned—
Or those in West Europe at least. Later the President
Took over the portfolio of Usury
35  And Wretchedness that seventh day.

But in the new week Congress could not be sure:
They had bought statesmen but would they stay bought?
They founded the feast of the Transformation of Liberals
But the very birds were beginning to rebel,
40  To sing a strange language,

And on the cold plateau of Spain, by the Mekong delta,
In hamlets on the tidy fields of France,
The accursed poor who can never be bought
Clothed with their flesh against the Pharoah's sword
A terrible infant, child of their desire.

*1949*


## Ars Poetica: or: Who Lives in the Ivory Tower?

Perhaps you'd like a marching song for the embattled prolet-
Ariat, or a realistic novel, the hopeful poet
Said, or a slice of actual life with the hot red heart's blood
    running,
The simple tale of a working stiff, but better than Jack London?

5  Nobody wants your roundelay, nobody wants your sestina,
Said the housewife, we want Hedy Lamarr and Gable at the
    cinema,
Get out of my technicolor dream with your tragic view and your
    verses;
Down with iambic pentameter and hurray for Louella Parsons.

Of course you're free to write as you please, the liberal editor
    answered,
10  But take the red flags out of your poem—we mustn't offend the
    censor—

And change this stanza to mean the reverse, and you must tone
　　　down this passage;
Thank God for the freedom of the press and a poem with a
　　　message!

Life is lousy enough without you should put it into a sonnet,
Said the man in the street, so keep it out of the novel, the poem,
　　　the drama;
15　　Give us a paean of murder and rape, or the lay of a willing maiden,
And to hell with the Bard of Avalon and to hell with Eliot Auden.

Recite the damn things all day long, get drunk on smoke come
　　　Sunday,
I respect your profession as much as my own, but it don't pay off
　　　when you're hungry;
You'll have to carry the banner instead—said the hobo in the
　　　jungle—
20　　If you want to eat; and don't forget: it's my bridge you're sleeping
　　　under.

Oh it's down with art and down with life and give us another
　　　reefer—
They all said—give us a South Sea isle, where light my love lies
　　　dreaming;
And who is that poet come in off the streets with a look unleal
　　　and lour?
Your feet are muddy, you son-of-a-bitch, get out of our ivory
　　　tower.

　　　　　　　　　　　　　　　　　　　　　　　　　　　　*1949*


## A Little Song About Charity

### *(Tune of Matty Grove)*

The boss came around at Christmas—
Oh smiling like a lamb—
He made me a present of a pair of gloves
And then cut off my hands—
5　　Oh and then cut off my hands.

The boss came around on my birthday
With some shoes of a rich man's brand.
He smiled like a priest and he cut off my feet
Then he said: "Go out and dance"—
10　　Oh he said: "Go out and dance."

The boss came around on May Day.
He said: "You may parade."
Then his cops shot us down in the open street
And they clubbed us into jail—
15　　Oh they clubbed us into jail.

The preacher says on Sunday:
"Turn ye the other cheek."
Don't turn it to the boss on Monday morn:
He may knock out all your teeth—
20      Oh he may knock out your teeth.

So listen to me workers:
When the boss seems kind and good
Remember that the stain on the cutting tool
Is nothing but your blood—
25      Oh it's nothing but your blood.

If you love your wife and daughters,
And if you love your sons,
And if you love the working class
Then keep your love at home.
30      Don't waste it on the cockroach boss
But keep your love at home.

                                                         *1949*


## Against the False Magicians

for Don Gordon

The poem must not charm us like a film:
See, in the war-torn city, that reckless, gallant
Handsome lieutenant turn to the wet-lipped blonde
(Our childhood fixation) for one sweet desperate kiss
5      In the broken room, in blue cinematic moonlight—
Bombers across that moon, and the bombs falling,
The last train leaving, the regiment departing—
And their lips lock, saluting themselves and death:
And then the screen goes dead and all go home . . .
10      Ritual of the false imagination.

The poem must not charm us like the fact:
A warship can sink a circus at forty miles,
And art, love's lonely counterfeit, has small dominion
Over those nightmares that move in the actual sunlight.
15      The blonde will not be faithful, nor her lover ever return
Nor the note be found in the hollow tree of childhood—
This dazzle of the facts would have us weeping
The orphaned fantasies of easier days.

It is the charm which the potential has
20      That is the proper aura for the poem.
Though ceremony fail, though each of your grey hairs
Help string a harp in the landlord's heaven,
And every battle, every augury,
20      Argue defeat, and if defeat itself
Bring all the darkness level with our eyes—
It is the poem provides the proper charm,

Spelling resistance and the living will,
To bring to dance a stony field of fact
And set against terror exile or despair
The rituals of our humanity.

*1955*

## After the Beat Generation

### I.

What! All those years after the Annunciation at Venice
And no revolution in sight?
　　　　　　　　　　　　And how long since the lads
From West Stud Horse Texas and Poontang-on-the-Hudson
5　　Slogged through the city of Lost Angels in the beardless years
Led by a cloud no bigger than an orgone box, whence issued—
Promising, promising, promising (and no revolution and no
Revolution in sight) issued the cash-tongued summons
Toward the guru of Big Sur and San Fran's stammering
　　　Apocalypse?

10　　I do not know how long this thing can go on!
—Waiting for Lefty, waiting for Godot, waiting for the heavenly fix.
In my way of counting, time comes in through my skin—
Blind Cosmos Alley, charismatic light
Of electric mustaches in the Deep Night of the Gashouse gunfire
15　　From enormous imaginary loud cap pistols of infinitely small
　　　caliber
Anarcholunacy—how long, in that light, to read what signposts?
When all that glows with a gem-like flame is the end of Lipton's
　　　cigar?

### II.

There ought to be other ways to skin this cat:
Journeys through the deep snow of a black book, bonefire, and
　　　wormlight
20　　To burn through the salty moss to the mark on the blazed tree
How long now since love out of a cloud of flesh
In Elysian Park stammered your secret name? Since Curtis
Zahn dipped his beard in the radioactive sea?
Since Rolfe went underground for the last time in that boneyard
25　　On Santa Monica?
　　　　　　　　　　Bench marks.
　　　　　　　　　　　　　　　Sea anchors of drowned guitars.
Alas, compañeros, have we not seen the imaginary travellers—
Whole boatloads of sensitive boy scouts aground in the dead river
30　　Of the Lost Angels, and the coffee shops' simple malfeasance of
　　　Light?
Hence it is required of us to go forward over the rubber bones
Of these synthetic rebels, over the tame poets

Who came to the Time's big table and the harp-shaped evergreen
$\qquad\qquad\qquad\qquad\qquad\qquad\qquad$ swimming pools
35$\quad$ To drink the waters of darkness.
$\qquad\qquad\qquad\qquad\qquad$ In the Carbon 14 dating
We find the Naked Man: the starving: the Moon in the Penitentiary.
$\qquad\qquad\qquad\qquad\qquad\qquad\qquad\qquad\qquad$ *1963*

## Ode for the American Dead in Asia

### 1.

God love you now, if no one else will ever,
Corpse in the paddy, or dead on a high hill
In the fine and ruinous summer of a war
You never wanted. All your false flags were
5$\quad$ Of bravery and ignorance, like grade school maps:
Colors of countries you would never see—
Until that weekend in eternity
When, laughing, well armed, perfectly ready to kill
The world and your brother, the safe commanders sent
10$\quad$ You into your future. Oh, dead on a hill,
Dead in a paddy, leeched and tumbled to
A tomb of footnotes. We mourn a changeling: you:
Handselled to poverty and drummed to war
By distinguished masters whom you never knew.

### 2

15$\quad$ The bee that spins his metal from the sun,
The shy mole drifting like a miner ghost
Through midnight earth—all happy creatures run
As strict as trains on rails the circuits of
Blind instinct. Happy in your summer follies,
20$\quad$ You mined a culture that was mined for war:
The state to mold you, church to bless, and always
The elders to confirm you in your ignorance.
No scholar put your thinking cap on nor
Warned that in dead seas fishes died in schools
25$\quad$ Before inventing legs to walk the land.
The rulers stuck a tennis racket in your hand,
An Ark against the flood. In time of change
Courage is not enough: the blind mole dies,
And you on your hill, who did not know the rules.

### 3.

30$\quad$ Wet in the windy counties of the dawn
The lone crow skirls his draggled passage home:
And God (whose sparrows fall aslant his gaze,
Like grace or confetti) blinks and he is gone,
And you are gone. Your scarecrow valor grows

35   And rusts like early lilac while the rose
     Blooms in Dakota and the stock exchange
     Flowers. Roses, rents, all things conspire
     To crown your death with wreaths of living fire.
     And the public mourners come: the politic tear
40   Is cast in the Forum. But, in another year,
     We will mourn you, whose fossil courage fills
     The limestone histories: brave: ignorant: amazed:
     Dead in the rice paddies, dead on the nameless hills.

                                                    *1968*

# Robert Lowell (1917–1977)

Robert Lowell grew up in Boston, Massachusetts, as part of a family with a distinguished literary heritage. Poets James Russell Lowell and Amy Lowell were among his ancestors. This heritage no doubt made his own father's limitations—he was a business failure after his retirement from the U.S. Navy—seem more severe. Lowell enrolled at Harvard, much as the family expected, but after the first of his lifelong series of emotional breakdowns and periods of manic behavior, he transferred to Kenyon College in 1937. There he met poet and critic John Crowe Ransom, one of the leaders of American New Criticism, who introduced Lowell to preferences for rhetorically intricate and ironic poems. Lowell also broke with his Protestant family history by converting to Catholicism in 1940. Opposed to some of America's World War II policies, he served a year in prison as a conscientious objector.

Lowell's first books, biblical and apocalyptic in tone, gave way in *Life Studies* (1959) to a new style that would guarantee his reputation. Accompanied by an autobiographical essay and written in a far more open and personal style, the poems came to herald what would be called the "confessional" school of poetry. Yet from the outset of his career Lowell had actually been drawn to a more complex subject—the intersection of public history and autobiographical experience. Though later work like *The Dolphin* (1973) would sometimes mine his personal experience remorselessly, his poems overall are a remarkable testament to how a reflective person lives and internalizes both the historical record and the public life of his time. The "confessional" label, which was more comfortable for critics who preferred poetry to be apolitical, has thus obscured the degree to which Lowell is a powerful critic of American culture and history.

## Inauguration Day: January 1953°

The snow had buried Stuyvesant.°
The subways drummed the vaults. I heard
the El's° green girders charge on Third,
Manhattan's truss of adamant,

---

**poem title:** Dwight D. Eisenhower (1890–1969) was inaugurated as President of the United States in 1953. He had been Supreme Commander of the Allied Forces in World War II.
1 *Stuyvesant*: a statue honoring Peter Stuyvesant (1610–1672), the sometimes autocratic employee of the Dutch West India Company who was chief administrator for New Amsterdam (now New York City) from 1647–1664.
3 *El*: a subway train running on rails elevated above ground.

5     that groaned in ermine, slummed on want. . . .
      Cyclonic zero of the word,
      God of our armies, who interred
      Cold Harbor's blue immortals, Grant!°
      Horseman, your sword is in the groove!

10    Ice, ice. Our wheels no longer move.
      Look, the fixed stars, all just alike
      as lack-land atoms, split apart,
      and the Republic summons Ike,°
      the mausoleum in her heart.

                                                      *1953*


## A Mad Negro Soldier Confined at Munich°

      "We're all Americans, except the Doc,
      a Kraut DP,° who kneels and bathes my eye,
      The boys who floored me, two black maniacs, try
      to pat my hands. Rounds, rounds! Why punch the clock?

5     In Munich the zoo's rubble fumes with cats;
      hoydens° with air-guns prowl the Koenigsplatz,
      and pink the pigeons on the mustard spire.
      Who but my girl-friend set the town on fire?

      Cat-houses talk cold turkey to my guards;
10    I found my *Fraulein* stitching outing shirts
      in the black forest of the colored wards—
      lieutenants squawked like chickens in her skirts.

      Her German language made my arteries harden—
      I've no annuity from the pay we blew.
15    I chartered an aluminum canoe,
      I had her six times in the English Garden.

      Oh mama, mama, like a trolley-pole
      sparking at contact, her electric shock—
      the power-house! . . . The doctor calls our roll—
20    no knives, no forks. We file before the clock,

      and fancy minnows, slaves of habit, shoot
      like starlight through their air-conditioned bowl.
      It's time for feeding. Each subnormal boot-
      black heart is pulsing to its ant-egg dole."

                                                      *1959*

---

8 *Grant*: Ulysses S. Grant (1822–1885), who commanded the Union forces in the Ameri-
can Civil War, was also elected U.S. President. His tomb (and a statue honoring him) are
in New York.
13 *Ike*: Eisenhower's nickname. "I like Ike" was a campaign slogan.
**poem title:** After a manic episode that took place while he was teaching in Europe in
1952, Lowell spent some weeks in the American military hospital in Munich, Germany. He
was installed in a locked ward full of disturbed military personnel.
2 *DP*: displaced person.
6 *hoydens*: high-spirited young women.

## Commander Lowell°

### *1887–1950*

There were no undesirables or girls in my set,
when I was a boy at Mattapoisett°—
only Mother, still her Father's daughter.
Her voice was still electric
5    with a hysterical, unmarried panic,
when she read to me from the Napoleon book.°
Long-nosed Marie Louise°
Hapsburg in the frontispiece
had a downright Boston bashfulness,
10   where she grovelled to Bonaparte, who scratched his navel,
and bolted his food—just my seven years tall!
And I, bristling and manic,
skulked in the attic,
and got two hundred French generals by name,
15   From *A* to *V*—from Augereau to Vandamme.°
I used to dope myself asleep,
naming those unpronounceables like sheep.

Having a naval officer
for my Father was nothing to shout
20   about to the summer colony at "Matt."
He wasn't at all "serious,"
when he showed up on the golf course,
wearing a blue serge jacket and numbly cut
white ducks he'd bought
25   at a Pearl Harbor commissariat . . .
and took four shots with his putter to sink his putt.
"Bob," they said, "golf's a game you really ought to know how to
    play,
if you play at all."
They wrote him off as "naval,"
30   naturally supposed his sport was sailing.
Poor Father, his training was engineering!
Cheerful and cowed
among the seadogs at the Sunday yacht club,
he was never one of the crowd.

---

**poem title:** Lowell's elegy on his father.
2 *Mattapoisett*: town in Massachusetts.
6 *Napoleon book*: *Memoirs of Napoleon* by the Duchesse d'Abrantes, a favorite of Lowell's
mother, Charlotte. Napoleon Bonaparte (1769–1821), French general and Emperor, a ti-
tanic figure in European history.
7 *Marie Louise*: Napoleon married Archduchess Marie Louise of Austria in 1809, after his
earlier marriage to Josephine proved childless.
15 *Vandamme*: Pierre François Charles Augereau (1757–1816) and Dominique René Van-
damme (1770–1830) were military officers who served under Napoleon. Their careers mixed
success and failure, though Augereau's in particular was compromised by personal fail-
ings. His record was tarnished by cruelty; as one writer put it, "he was tall and com-
manding, but his loud and vulgar behavior frequently betrayed the soldier of fortune."

35    "Anchors aweigh," Daddy boomed in his bathtub,
      "Anchors aweigh,"
      when Lever Brothers offered to pay
      him double what the Navy paid.
      I nagged for his dress sword with gold braid,
40    and cringed because Mother, new
      caps on all her teeth, was born anew
      at forty. With seamanlike celerity,
      Father left the Navy,
      and deeded Mother his property.

45    He was soon fired. Year after year,
      he still hummed "Anchors aweigh" in the tub—
      whenever he left a job,
      he bought a smarter car.
      Father's last employer
50    was Scudder, Stevens and Clark, Investment Advisors,
      himself his only client.
      While Mother dragged to bed alone,
      read Menninger,
      and grew more and more suspicious,
55    he grew defiant.
      Night after night,
      à la clarté déserte de sa lampe,°
      he slid his ivory Annapolis slide rule
      across a pad of graphs—
60    piker speculations! In three years
      he squandered sixty thousand dollars.

      Smiling on all,
      Father was once successful enough to be lost
      in the mob of ruling-class Bostonians.
65    As early as 1928,
      he owned a house converted to oil,
      and redecorated by the architect
      of St. Mark's° School. . . . Its main effect
      was a drawing room, "longitudinal as Versailles,"°
70    its ceiling, roughened with oatmeal, was blue as the sea.
      And once
      nineteen, the youngest ensign in his class,
      he was "the old man" of a gunboat on the Yangtze.°

                                                                1959

---

57 . . . sa lampe: (French) "by the empty brilliance of his lamp," from Stéphane Mallarmé's
(1842–1898) poem "Brise Marine."
68 St. Mark's: an upper-crust Episcopalian boarding school in Southborough, Massachu-
setts, that Lowell was compelled to attend.
69 Versailles: a palace built for Louis XIII and XIV at the village of Versailles, fourteen
miles southwest of Paris. Louis XV held court there in the eighteenth century.
73 Yangtze: the longest river in China.

# "To Speak of Woe That Is in Marriage"°

*"It is the future generation that presses into being by means of these*
*exuberant feelings and supersensible soap bubbles of ours."*
SCHOPENHAUER°

"The hot night makes us keep our bedroom windows open.
Our magnolia blossoms. Life begins to happen.
My hopped up husband drops his home disputes,
and hits the streets to cruise for prostitutes,
5      free-lancing out along the razor's edge.
This screwball might kill his wife, then take the pledge.
Oh the monotonous meanness of his lust. . . .
It's the injustice . . . he is so unjust—
whiskey-blind, swaggering home at five.
10     My only thought is how to keep alive.
What makes him tick? Each night now I tie
ten dollars and his car key to my thigh. . . .
Gored by the climacteric of his want,
he stalls above me like an elephant."

1959

# Man and Wife

Tamed by *Miltown,*° we° lie on Mother's bed;
the rising sun in war paint dyes us red;
in broad daylight her gilded bed-posts shine,
abandoned, almost Dionysian.°
5      At last the trees are green on Marlborough Street,°
blossoms on our magnolia ignite
the morning with their murderous five days' white.
All night I've held your hand,
as if you had
10     a fourth time faced the kingdom of the mad°—
its hackneyed speech, its homicidal eye—
and dragged me home alive. . . . Oh my *Petite,*
clearest of all God's creatures, still all air and nerve:
you were in your twenties, and I,
15     once hand on glass

---

**poem title:** In Geoffrey Chaucer's (1340–1400) *The Canterbury Tales,* the Wife of Bath
opens her marriage stories with this line.
epigraph: *Schopenhauer:* Arthur Schopenhauer (1788–1860), German philosopher.
1 Miltown: a tranquilizer popular during the 1950s. The first lines also echo the opening
lines of Book 2 of Milton's *Paradise Lost,* whose throne is now a marriage bed: "High on
a throne of a royal state, which far / Outshone the wealth of Ormus and of Ind, / Or where
the gorgeous East with richest hand / Showers on her kings barbaric pearl and gold, / Sa-
tan exhalted sat . . . ."
1 we: Lowell and his second wife, the critic Elizabeth Hardwick (1916–), whom he married
in 1949.
4 Dionysian: According to Greek myth, Dionysus was the god of fertility and wine. The
adjective suggests the frenzied, orgiastic festivals honoring him.
5 *Marlborough Street*: the Boston street on which the Lowells lived from 1955 to 1958.
10 mad: Lowell suffered periodic mental breakdowns.

and heart in mouth,
outdrank the Rahvs° in the heat
of Greenwich Village, fainting at your feet—
too boiled and shy
20      and poker-faced to make a pass,
while the shrill verve
of your invective scorched the traditional South.°

Now twelve years later, you turn your back.
Sleepless, you hold
25      your pillow to your hollows like a child;
your old-fashioned tirade—
loving, rapid, merciless—
breaks like the Atlantic Ocean on my head.

*1959*

## Memories of West Street and Lepke°

Only teaching on Tuesdays, book-worming
in pajamas fresh from the washer each morning,
I hog a whole house on Boston's
"hardly passionate Marlborough Street,"°
5       where even the man
scavenging filth in the back alley trash cans,
has two children, a beach wagon, a helpmate,
and is a "young Republican."
I have a nine months' daughter,°
10      young enough to be my granddaughter.
Like the sun she rises in her flame-flamingo infants' wear.

These are the tranquillized *Fifties*,
and I am forty. Ought I to regret my seedtime?
I was a fire-breathing Catholic C. O.,°
15      and made my manic statement,
telling off the state and president, and then
sat waiting sentence in the bull pen
beside a Negro boy with curlicues
of marijuana in his hair.

---

17 *Rahvs*: American critic Philip Rahv (1908–1973) and his wife. Rahv was co-editor of *Partisan Review*.
22 *South*: Hardwick was born and raised in Lexington, Kentucky.
**poem title:** The West Street jail in Manhattan, where Lowell spent ten days (before being transferred to the Federal Correctional Center at Danbury, Connecticut) in 1943 after he was sentenced to one year and one day for refusing to serve in the Army; Louis "Lepke" Buchalter (1897–1944), a racketeer who headed Murder Incorporated, an association of criminals who hired out as assassins, was a fellow prisoner. According to Ian Hamilton's biography *Robert Lowell* (1982), "Lepke says to [Lowell]: 'I'm in for killing. What are you in for?' 'Oh, I'm in for refusing to kill.'"
4 *hardly passionate Marlborough*: A description by the novelist Henry James (1828–1911) of the street where Lowell lived from 1955–1958.
9 *daughter*: Harriet, daughter of Lowell and Elizabeth Hardwick.
14 *C.O.*: Conscientious Objector to war.

20      Given a year,
        I walked on the roof of the West Street Jail, a short
        enclosure like my school soccer court,
        and saw the Hudson River once a day
        through sooty clothesline entanglements
25      and bleaching khaki tenements.
        Strolling, I yammered metaphysics with Abramowitz,
        a jaundice-yellow ("it's really tan")
        and fly-weight pacifist,
        so vegetarian,
30      he wore rope shoes and preferred fallen fruit.
        He tried to convert Bioff and Brown,°
        the Hollywood pimps, to his diet.
        Hairy, muscular, suburban,
        wearing chocolate double-breasted suits,
35      they blew their tops and beat him black and blue.

        I was so out of things, I'd never heard
        of the Jehovah's Witnesses.°
        "Are you a C.O.?" I asked a fellow jailbird.
        "No," he answered, "I'm a J.W."
40      He taught me the "hospital tuck,"°
        and pointed out the T-shirted back
        of *Murder Incorporated's* Czar Lepke,
        there piling towels on a rack,
        or dawdling off to his little segregated cell full
45      of things forbidden the common man:
        a portable radio, a dresser, two toy American
        flags tied together with a ribbon of Easter palm.
        Flabby, bald, lobotomized,
        he drifted in a sheepish calm,
50      where no agonizing reappraisal
        jarred his concentration on the electric chair°—
        hanging like an oasis in his air
        of lost connections. . . .

                                                                  *1959*

# Skunk Hour°

(For Elizabeth Bishop)

Nautilus Island's° hermit
heiress still lives through winter in her Spartan cottage;

---

31 *Brown*: William Bioff and George E. Brown were gangsters who sought to dominate the Hollywood labor scene. They were convicted of extortion in 1943. Brown had been convicted of pandering in 1922. Lowell could have assumed his audience would recognize the reference.
37 *Jehovah's Witnesses*: members of a Christian religious sect who refuse to support a sovereign other than God (Jehovah) or to participate in war.
40 *hospital tuck*: tucking the ends of bedsheets tightly under a mattress; "hospital corners."
51 *electric chair*: Lepke was executed in March 1944.
**poem title:** Written partly in response to Elizabeth Bishop's poem "The Armadillo," with its somewhat comparable short-line stanzas.
1 *Nautilus Island*: Near Castine, Maine, where Lowell had a summer house.

her sheep still graze above the sea.
Her son's a bishop. Her farmer
5    is first selectman° in our village;
she's in her dotage.

Thirsting for
the hierarchic privacy
of Queen Victoria's century,°
10    she buys up all
the eyesores facing her shore,
and lets them fall.

The season's ill—
we've lost our summer millionaire,
15    who seemed to leap from an L. L. Bean°
catalogue. His nine-knot yawl°
was auctioned off to lobstermen.
A red fox stain covers Blue Hill.°

And now our fairy
20    decorator brightens his shop for fall;
his fishnet's filled with orange cork,
orange, his cobbler's bench and awl;
there is no money in his work,
he'd rather marry.

25    One dark night,
my Tudor Ford° climbed the hill's skull;
I watched for love-cars. Lights turned down,
they lay together, hull to hull,
where the graveyard shelves on the town. . . .
30    My mind's not right.

A car radio bleats,
"Love, O careless Love. . . ."° I hear
my ill-spirit sob in each blood cell,
as if my hand were at its throat. . . .
35    I myself am hell;°
nobody's here—

---

5 *selectman*: an official elected in a New England town to manage municipal affairs.

9 *century*: the nineteenth century. Alexandrina Victoria (1819–1901) was queen of Great Britain and Ireland from 1837 to 1901.

15 *L.L. Bean*: a mail-order company based in Freeport, Maine, specializing in sporting and camping equipment.

16 *yawl*: small sailboat.

18 *Blue Hill*: a Maine mountain near where Lowell lived. Lowell said the line was meant to describe the "rusty reddish color of autumn."

26 *Tudor Ford*: two-door Ford automobile.

32"*Careless Love*," a popular American song of the period.

35 *hell*: "Which way I fly is Hell, myself am Hell," (IV. 75), Satan's words from *Paradise Lost* (1667) by John Milton (1608–1674).

only skunks, that search
in the moonlight for a bite to eat.
They march on their soles up Main Street:
40     white stripes, moonstruck eyes' red fire
under the chalk-dry and spar spire
of the Trinitarian Church.

I stand on top
of our back steps and breathe the rich air—
45     a mother skunk with her column of kittens swills the garbage
      pail.
She jabs her wedge-head in a cup
of sour cream, drops her ostrich tail,
and will not scare.

                                                    1959

## For the Union Dead°

### *"Relinquunt Omnia Servare Rem Publicam."*°

The old South Boston Aquarium stands
in a Sahara of snow now. Its broken windows are boarded.
The bronze weathervane cod has lost half its scales.
The airy tanks are dry.

5     Once my nose crawled like a snail on the glass;
my hand tingled
to burst the bubbles
drifting from the noses of the cowed, compliant fish.

My hand draws back. I often sigh still
10    for the dark downward and vegetating kingdom
of the fish and reptile. One morning last March,
I pressed against the new barbed and galvanized

fence on the Boston Common. Behind their cage,
yellow dinosaur steamshovels were grunting
15    as they cropped up tons of mush and grass
to gouge their underworld garage.

---

**poem title:** First published as "Colonel Shaw and the Massachusetts 54th" in the 1960 edition of Lowell's *Life Studies*, and then, with this title, as the title poem of his 1964 collection. Colonel Robert Gould Shaw (1837–1863) led the first African American regiment (of enlistees) in the American Civil War.

subtitle: *Relinquunt . . .*: "They give up everything to serve the Republic" (Latin), after the inscription on the bronze relief, a monument to Shaw and his men, sculpted by Augustus Saint-Gaudens (1848–1907), which stands at the edge of Boston Common, a public park across from the Boston State House. Lowell changed the subject of the Latin inscription to read "they," rather than "he," to honor all the men in the regiment more clearly.

Parking spaces luxuriate like civic
sandpiles in the heart of Boston.
A girdle of orange, Puritan-pumpkin colored girders
20    braces the tingling Statehouse,

shaking over the excavations, as it faces Colonel Shaw
and his bell-cheeked Negro infantry
on St. Gaudens' shaking Civil War relief,
propped by a plank splint against the garage's earthquake.

25    Two months after marching through Boston,
half the regiment was dead;
at the dedication,
William James° could almost hear the bronze Negroes breathe.

Their monument sticks like a fishbone
30    in the city's throat.
Its Colonel is as lean
as a compass-needle.

He has an angry wrenlike vigilance,
a greyhound's gentle tautness;
35    he seems to wince at pleasure,
and suffocate for privacy.

He is out of bounds now. He rejoices in man's lovely,
peculiar power to choose life and die—
when he leads his black soldiers to death,
40    he cannot bend his back.

On a thousand small town New England greens,
the old white churches hold their air
of sparse, sincere rebellion; frayed flags
quilt the graveyards of the Grand Army of the Republic.°

45    The stone statues of the abstract Union Soldier
grow slimmer and younger each year—
wasp-wasted, they doze over muskets
and muse through their sideburns. . .

Shaw's father wanted no monument
50    except the ditch,
where his son's body was thrown
and lost with his "niggers."°

---

28 *William James*: (1842–1910), philosopher and psychologist (and brother of Henry James),
who at his "Oration at the Dedication of the Monument" in May 1897 said, "There on foot
go the dark outcasts, so true to nature that one can almost hear them breathing as they
march."
44 *Grand Army of the Republic*: an organization for Union and Confederate Civil War vet-
erans.
52 *niggers*: a confederate officer's epithet for Shaw's troops; on July 18, 1863, Shaw and
most of his men were killed during an attack against Fort Wagner in South Carolina. The
Confederates buried them in a common grave.

The ditch is nearer.
There are no statues for the last war here;
55     on Boyleston° Street, a commercial photograph
shows Hiroshima boiling

over a Mosler Safe,° the "Rock of Ages"
that survived the blast. Space is nearer.
When I crouch to my television set,
60     the drained faces° of Negro school-children rise like balloons.

Colonel Shaw
is riding on his bubble,
he waits
for the blessèd break.

65     The Aquarium is gone. Everywhere,
giant finned cars nose forward like fish;
a savage servility
slides by on grease.

                 *1960*

# The Mouth of the Hudson°

(For Esther Brooks)

A single man stands like a bird-watcher,
and scuffles the pepper and salt snow
from a discarded, gray
Westinghouse Electric cable drum.
5     He cannot discover America by counting
the chains of condemned freight-trains
from thirty states. They jolt and jar
and junk in the siding below him.
He has trouble with his balance.
10    His eyes drop,
and he drifts with the wild ice
ticking seaward down the Hudson,
like the blank sides of a jig-saw puzzle.

The ice ticks seaward like a clock.
15    A Negro toasts
wheat-seeds over the coke-fumes°

---

55 *Boyleston*: a street in central Boston.
57 *Mosler Safe*: a brand of safe that was photographed as intact in Hiroshima after the United States dropped a nuclear bomb there in 1945; "Rock of Ages": a popular hymn written in 1775 by Augustus Montague Toplady (1740–1778).
60 *drained faces*: probably in relation to civil rights demonstrations supporting the desegregation of schools ordered by the U.S. Supreme Court's *Brown v. Board of Education of Topeka* decision of 1954.
**poem title:** *Hudson*: the mouth of the Hudson River, at Lower New York Bay.
16 *coke-fumes*: from burned coal or distilled petroleum.

of a punctured barrel.
Chemical air
sweeps in from New Jersey,
20　　and smells of coffee.

Across the river,
ledges of suburban factories tan
in the sulphur-yellow sun
of the unforgivable landscape.

*1964*

## July in Washington

The stiff spokes of this wheel
touch the sore spots of the earth.

On the Potomac,° swan-white
power launches keep breasting the sulphurous wave.

5　　Otters slide and dive and slick back their hair,
raccoons clean their meat in the creek.

On the circles, green statues ride like South American
liberators above the breeding vegetation—

prongs and spearheads of some equatorial
10　　backland that will inherit the globe.

The elect, the elected ... they come here bright as dimes,
and die dishevelled and soft.

We cannot name their names, or number their dates—
circle on circle, like rings on a tree—

15　　but we wish the river had another shore,
some farther range of delectable mountains,

distant hills powdered blue as a girl's eyelid.
It seems the least little shove would land us there,

that only the slightest repugnance of our bodies
we no longer control could drag us back.

*1964*

---

3 *Potomac*: A major American river that passes through Washington, D.C., and runs to
Chesapeake Bay.

# The March I°

(For Dwight MacDonald)

Under the too white marmoreal Lincoln Memorial,
the too tall marmoreal Washington Obelisk,
gazing into the too long reflecting pool,
the reddish trees, the withering autumn sky,
5   the remorseless, amplified harangues for peace—
lovely to lock arms, to march absurdly locked
(unlocking to keep my wet glasses from slipping)
to see the cigarette match quaking in my fingers,
then to step off like green Union Army recruits
10   for the first Bull Run, sped by photographers,
the notables, the girls . . . fear, glory, chaos, rout . . .
our green army staggered out on the miles-long green fields,
met by the other army, the Martian, the ape, the hero,
his new-fangled rifle, his green new steel helmet.

*1970*

# The March II

Where two or three were flung together, or fifty,
mostly white-haired, or bald, or women . . . sadly
unfit to follow their dream, I sat in the sunset
shade of our Bastille, the Pentagon,
5   nursing leg- and arch-cramps, my cowardly,
foolhardy heart; and heard, alas, more speeches,
though the words took heart now to show how weak
we were, and right. An MP sergeant kept
repeating, "March slowly through them. Don't even brush
10   anyone sitting down." They tiptoed through us
in single file, and then their second wave
trampled us flat and back. Health to those who held,
health to the green steel head . . . to your kind hands
that helped me stagger to my feet, and flee.

*1970*

# Central Park°

Scaling small rocks, exhaling smog,
gasping at game-scents like a dog,
now light as pollen, now as white

---

**poem title:** A major demonstration against the Vietnam War, the peace march on the American military's headquarters at the Pentagon, took place in Washington, D.C., on October 21, 1967. Norman Mailer (1923–    ) describes Lowell's role in the events in *The Armies of the Night* (1967).
**poem title:** *Central Park:* the large, 843-acre public park in Manhattan, opened in 1859, the first such landscaped park in the United States. A wonderful public space by day, it is notoriously dangerous at night, a daily transition the poem follows. Lowell has said that he wrote the poem when he was undergoing analysis and crossed the park every day on the way to his therapist.

and winded as a grounded kite—
5    I watched the lovers occupy
every inch of earth and sky:
one figure of geometry,
multiplied to infinity,
straps down, and sunning openly . . .
10    each precious, public, pubic tangle
an equilateral triangle,
lost in the park, half covered by
the shade of some low stone or tree.
The stain of fear and poverty
15    spread through each trapped anatomy,
and darkened every mote of dust.
All wished to leave this drying crust,
borne on the delicate wings of lust
like bees, and cast their fertile drop
20    into the overwhelming cup.

Drugged and humbled by the smell
of zoo-straw mixed with animal,
the lion prowled his slummy cell,°
serving his life-term in jail—
25    glaring, grinding, on his heel,
with tingling step and testicle . . .
Behind a dripping rock, I found
a one-day kitten on the ground—
deprived, weak, ignorant and blind,
30    squeaking, tubular, left behind—
dying with its deserter's rich
Welfare lying out of reach:
milk cartons, kidney heaped to spoil,
two plates sheathed with silver foil.

35    Shadows had stained the afternoon;
high in an elm, a snagged balloon
wooed the attraction of the moon.
Scurrying from the mouth of night,
a single, fluttery, paper kite
40    grazed Cleopatra's Needle,° and sailed
where the light of the sun had failed.
Then night, the night—the jungle hour,
the rich in his slit-windowed tower . . .
Old Pharaohs starving in your foxholes,
45    with painted banquets on the walls,
fists knotted in your captives' hair,
tyrants with little food to spare—

---

23 *slummy cell*: at the time the poem was written, the Central Park Zoo was a cramped facility whose heavy cages gave animals little space.
40 *Cleopatra's Needle*: a red granite obelisk, sixty-nine feet tall, that stands in Central Park near the Metropolitan Museum of Art at 82nd Street. Originally erected in Egypt about 1475 B.C., it was given to the United States in 1880. There is no actual historical connection to Cleopatra.

all your embalming left you mortal,
glazed, black, and hideously eternal,
50     all your plunder and gold leaf
only served to draw the thief . . .

We beg delinquents for our life.
Behind each bush, perhaps a knife;
each landscaped crag, each flowering shrub,
hides a policeman with a club.

1967

# Gwendolyn Brooks (b. 1917)

Brooks was born in Topeka, Kansas. Her mother was a schoolteacher, her father a janitor. The family moved to Chicago almost immediately after her birth, and there Brooks has spent most of her life. She attended Wilson Junior College in the mid-1930s, meanwhile meeting and being encouraged by James Weldon Johnson and Langston Hughes. She also wrote a poetry column for the *Chicago Defender*. In the following decade, she attended a poetry workshop where she read widely in modernist poetry, while also being schooled in traditional forms and meters. Her first book, *A Street in Bronzeville*, appeared in 1945.

A key moment in her development came in 1967 when she attended a Black Writers Conference at Fisk University. Thereafter, she became more active in the Chicago wing of the Black Arts movement and switched from her New York publisher, Harper and Row, to Broadside Press in Detroit and then to Third World Press in Chicago. Chicago's south side black ghetto has always figured heavily in her work; she is in a way a poet of that neighborhood. Yet out of it come poems addressing the general status of race in America in a style that mixes international modernism with local experience. Brooks has worked hard and successfully to reach a broad popular audience, but her poems are also deeply challenging. For years, she read them aloud with great success—using rhythm, emphasis, intonation, and strategic pauses to make them accessible—but close attention reveals a rhetorical intricacy that owes as much to high modernism as to populism. Even "We Real Cool" (see a captivating blackboard-style broadside version in the appendix) only replicates street slang in its opening stanza. She has invented a unique voice that speaks simultaneously from dispossession and from knowledge of the dominant high culture.

## a song in the front yard

I've stayed in the front yard all my life.
I want a peek at the back
Where it's rough and untended and hungry weed grows.
A girl gets sick of a rose.

5      I want to go in the back yard now
And maybe down the alley,
To where the charity children play.
I want a good time today.

They do some wonderful things.
10    They have some wonderful fun.
My mother sneers, but I say it's fine
How they don't have to go in at quarter to nine.
My mother, she tells me that Johnnie Mae
Will grow up to be a bad woman.
15    That George'll be taken to Jail soon or late
(On account of last winter he sold our back gate.)

But I say it's fine. Honest, I do.
And I'd like to be a bad woman, too,
And wear the brave stockings of night-black lace
And strut down the streets with paint on my face.

*1945*

# of De Witt Williams on his way to Lincoln Cemetery°

He was born in Alabama.
He was bred in Illinois.
He was nothing but a
Plain black boy.

5    Swing low swing low sweet sweet chariot.°
Nothing but a plain black boy.

Drive him past the Pool Hall.
Drive him past the Show.
Blind within his casket,
10    But maybe he will know.

Down through Forty-seventh Street:°
Underneath the L,°
And—Northwest Corner, Prairie,
That he loved so well.

15    Don't forget the Dance Halls—
Warwick and Savoy,
Where he picked his women, where
He drank his liquid joy.

Born in Alabama.
20    Bred in Illinois.
He was nothing but a
Plain black boy.

Swing low swing low sweet sweet chariot.
Nothing but a plain black boy.

*1945*

---

**poem title:** *Lincoln Cemetery*: an African American cemetery in Chicago.
5 *chariot*: from the African American spiritual *Swing Low, Sweet Chariot*.
11 *Forty-seventh Street*: the main street of Bronzeville, an African American neighborhood in Chicago.
12 *L*: the elevated railway.

# Gay Chaps at the Bar°

souvenir for Staff Sergeant Raymond Brooks° and every
other soldier

### GAY CHAPS AT THE BAR

> *. . . and guys I knew in the States, young officers, return*
> *from the front crying and trembling. Gay chaps at the*
> *bar in Los Angeles, Chicago, New York. . . .*
>     LIEUTENANT WILLIAM COUCH
>     in the South Pacific

We knew how to order. Just the dash
Necessary. The length of gaiety in good taste.
Whether the raillery° should be slightly iced
And given green, or served up hot and lush.
5    And we knew beautifully how to give to women
The summer spread, the tropics, of our love.
When to persist, or hold a hunger off.
Knew white speech. How to make a look an omen.
But nothing ever taught us to be islands.
10   And smart, athletic language for this hour
Was not in the curriculum. No stout
Lesson showed how to chat with death. We brought
No brass° fortissimo,° among our talents,°
To holler down the lions° in this air.

### STILL DO I KEEP MY LOOK, MY IDENTITY . . .

15   Each body has its art, its precious prescribed
Pose, that even in passion's droll contortions, waltzes,
Or push of pain—or when a grief has stabbed,
Or hatred hacked—is its, and nothing else's.
Each body has its pose. No other stock
20   That is irrevocable, perpetual
And its to keep. In castle or in shack.
With rags or robes. Through good, nothing, or ill.
And even in death a body, like no other
On any hill or plain or crawling cot

---

**poem title:** The poem is a sequence of twelve sonnets based in part on letters Brooks received from black soldiers in World War II, when the U.S. Army was still segregated; black soldiers thus risked their lives at the same time as they were structurally humiliated; the "bar" is not only a tavern but also the color bar and the bar between life and death.
dedication: *Raymond Brooks*: Brooks' brother.
3 *raillery*: good-natured teasing.
13 *brass*: alludes at once to a brass band, military brass (officers), and the adjective "brassy," or brazen.
13 *fortissimo*: very loudly.
13 *talents*: see Matthew 25.15–25 for the biblical story of the talents.
14 *lions*: airplanes (bombers).

25 Or gentle for the lilyless hasty pall
(Having twisted, gagged, and then sweet-ceased to
    bother),
Shows the old personal art, the look. Shows what
It showed at baseball. What it showed in school.

### My Dreams, My Works, Must Wait Till After Hell

I hold my honey and I store my bread
30 In little jars and cabinets of my will.
I label clearly, and each latch and lid
I bid, Be firm till I return from hell.
I am very hungry. I am incomplete.
And none can tell when I may dine again.
35 No man can give me any word but Wait,
The puny light. I keep eyes pointed in;
Hoping that, when the devil days of my hurt
Drag out to their last dregs and I resume
On such legs as are left me, in such heart
40 As I can manage, remember to go home,
My taste will not have turned insensitive
To honey and bread old purity could love.

### Looking

You have no word for soldiers to enjoy
The feel of, as an apple, and to chew
45 With masculine satisfaction. Not "good-by!"
"Come back!" or "careful!" Look, and let him go.
"Good-by!" is brutal, and "come back!" the raw
Insistence of an idle desperation
Since could he favor he would favor now.
50 He will be "careful!" if he has permission.
Looking is better. At the dissolution
Grab greatly with the eye, crush in a steel
Of study—Even that is vain. Expression,
The touch or look or word, will little avail,
55 The brawniest will not beat back the storm
Nor the heaviest haul your little boy from harm.

### Piano After War

On a snug evening I shall watch her fingers,
Cleverly ringed, declining to clever pink,
Beg glory from the willing keys. Old hungers
60 Will break their coffins, rise to eat and thank.
And music, warily, like the golden rose
That sometimes after sunset warms the west,
Will warm that room, persuasively suffuse
That room and me, rejuvenate a past.
65 But suddenly, across my climbing fever
Of proud delight—a multiplying cry.
A cry of bitter dead men who will never

Attend a gentle maker of musical joy.
Then my thawed eye will go again to ice.
70  And stone will shove the softness from my face.

## MENTORS°

For I am rightful fellow of their band.
My best allegiances are to the dead.
I swear to keep the dead upon my mind,
Disdain for all time to be overglad.
75  Among spring flowers, under summer trees,
By chilling autumn waters, in the frosts
Of supercilious winter—all my days
I'll have as mentors those reproving ghosts.
And at that cry, at that remotest whisper,
80  I'll stop my casual business. Leave the banquet.
Or leave the ball—reluctant to unclasp her
Who may be fragrant as the flower she wears,
Make gallant bows and dim excuses, then quit
Light for the midnight that is mine and theirs.

## THE WHITE TROOPS HAD THEIR ORDERS BUT THE NEGROES LOOKED LIKE MEN

85  They had supposed their formula was fixed.
They had obeyed instructions to devise
A type of cold, a type of hooded gaze.
But when the Negroes came they were perplexed.
These Negroes looked like men. Besides, it taxed
90  Time and the temper to remember those
Congenital° iniquities° that cause
Disfavor of the darkness. Such as boxed
Their feelings properly, complete to tags—
A box for dark men and a box for Other—
95  Would often find the contents had been scrambled.
Or even switched. Who really gave two figs?
Neither the earth nor heaven ever trembled.
And there was nothing startling in the weather.

## FIRSTLY INCLINED TO TAKE WHAT IT IS TOLD

Thee sacrosanct,°— Thee sweet, Thee crystalline,
100  With the full jewel wile° of mighty light—
With the narcotic milk of peace for men
Who find Thy beautiful center and relate
Thy round command, Thy grand, Thy° mystic good—

mentors: wise and trusted counselors or teachers.
91 *congenital*: existing at or before birth.
91 *iniquities*: acts of wickedness, injustice; these lines are an idiosyncratic condemnation of racism.
99 *sacrosanct*: sacred and inviolable, suggests the fusion of God and country.
100 *wile*: trickery, cunning.
103 *Thy*: the repetition suggests the Christian trinity, with "thy mystic good" being the Holy Ghost.

Thee like the classic quality of a star:
105 A little way from warmth, a little sad,
Delicately lovely to adore—
I had been brightly ready to believe.
For youth is a frail thing, not unafraid.
Firstly inclined to take what it is told,
110 Firstly inclined to lean. Greedy to give
Faith tidy and total. To a total God.
With billowing heartiness no whit° withheld.

### "God Works in a Mysterious Way"°

But often now the youthful eye cuts down its
Own dainty veiling. Or submits to winds.
115 And many an eye that all its age had drawn its
Beam from a Book endures the impudence
Of modern glare that never heard of tact
Or timeliness, or Mystery that shrouds
Immortal joy: it merely can direct
120 Chancing feet across dissembling clods.
Out from Thy shadows, from Thy pleasant meadows,
Quickly, in undiluted light. Be glad, whose
Mansions are bright, to right Thy children's air.
If Thou be more than hate or atmosphere
125 Step forth in splendor, mortify our wolves.
Or we assume a sovereignty ourselves.

### Love Note
#### I: Surely

Surely you stay my certain own, you stay
My you. All honest, lofty as a cloud.
Surely I could come now and find you high,
130 As mine as you ever were; should not be awed.
Surely your word would pop as insolent
As always: "Why, of course I love you, dear."
Your gaze, surely, ungauzed° as I could want.
Your touches, that never were careful, what they were.
135 Surely—But I am very off from that.
From surely. From indeed. From the decent arrow
That was my clean naïveté and my faith.
This morning men deliver wounds and death.
They will deliver death and wounds tomorrow.
140 And I doubt all. You.° Or a violet.

---

112 *whit*: particle.
**section title**: An ironic adaptation of one of William Cowper's (1731–1800) *Olney Hymns*
(1779): "God moves in mysterious ways."
133 *ungauzed*: not wounded, not obscured; in what wars, we might ask, does a gaze amount
to gauze?
140 *You*: America.

### LOVE NOTE
#### II: FLAGS

Still, it is dear defiance now to carry
Fair flags of you above my indignation,
Top, with a pretty glory and a merry
Softness, the scattered pound of my cold passion.
145     I pull you down my foxhole. Do you mind?
You burn in bits of saucy color then.
I let you flutter out against the pained
Volleys. Against my power crumpled and wan.°
You, and the yellow pert exuberance
150     Of dandelion days, unmocking sun;
The blowing of clear wind in your gay hair;
Love changeful in you (like a music, or
Like a sweet mournfulness, or like a dance,
Or like the tender struggle of a fan).

#### THE PROGRESS

155     And still we wear our uniforms, follow
The cracked cry of the bugles, comb and brush
Our pride and prejudice, doctor the sallow
Initial ardor, which to keep it fresh.
Still we applaud the President's voice and face.
160     Still we remark on patriotism, sing,
Salute the flag, thrill heavily, rejoice
For death of men who too saluted, sang.
But inward grows a soberness, an awe,
A fear, a deepening hollow through the cold.
165     For even if we come out standing up
How shall we smile, congratulate: and how
Settle in chairs? Listen, listen. The step
Of iron feet again. And again   wild.

1945

# We Real Cool

*The Pool Players
Seven at the Golden Shovel*

We real cool. We
left school. We

lurk late. We
strike straight. We

sing sin. We
thin gin. We

Jazz June. We
Die soon.

1959

148 *wan*: unnaturally pale, weak.

# The Ballad of Rudolph Reed

Rudolph Reed was oaken.°
His wife was oaken too.
And his two good girls and his good little man
Oakened as they grew.

5      "I am not hungry for berries.
I am not hungry for bread.
But hungry hungry for a house
Where at night a man in bed

"May never hear the plaster
10     Stir as if in pain.
May never hear the roaches
Falling like fat rain.

"Where never wife and children need
Go blinking through the gloom.
15     Where every room of many rooms
Will be full of room.

"Oh my home may have its east or west
Or north or south behind it.
All I know is I shall know it,
20     And fight for it when I find it."

It was in a street of bitter white
That he made his application.
For Rudolph Reed was oakener°
Than others in the nation.

25     The agent's steep and steady stare
Corroded to a grin.
*Why, you black old, tough old hell of a man,*
*Move your family in!*

Nary a grin grinned Rudolph Reed,
30     Nary a curse cursed he,
But moved in his House. With his dark little wife,
And his dark little children three.

A neighbor would *look*, with a yawning eye
That squeezed into a slit.
35     But the Rudolph Reeds and the children three
Were too joyous to notice it.

For were they not firm in a home of their own
With windows everywhere
And a beautiful banistered stair
40     And a front yard for flowers and a back yard for grass?

---

1 *oaken*: both strong like an oak and brown like one.
23 *oakener*: more courageous, but also darker and more angry.

The first night, a rock, big as two fists.
The second, a rock big as three.
But nary a curse cursed Rudolph Reed.
(Though oaken as man could be.)

45   The third night, a silvery ring of glass.
Patience ached to endure.
But he looked, and lo! small Mabel's blood
Was staining her gaze so pure.

Then up did rise our Rudolph Reed
50   And pressed the hand of his wife,
And went to the door with a thirty-four
And a beastly butcher knife.

He ran like a mad thing into the night.
And the words in his mouth were stinking.
55   By the time he had hurt his first white man
He was no longer thinking.

By the time he had hurt his fourth white man
Rudolph Reed was dead.
His neighbors gathered and kicked his corpse.
60   "Nigger—" his neighbors said.

Small Mabel whimpered all night long,
For calling herself the cause.
Her oak-eyed mother did no thing
But change the bloody gauze.

                                                    *1961*

## The Blackstone Rangers°

### I

#### *As Seen by Disciplines°*

There they are
Thirty at the corner.
Black, raw, ready.
Sores in the city
5   that do not want to heal.

---

**poem title:** The Blackstone Rangers are a Chicago teenage gang; Brooks conducted a creative writing class with some of the members. Blackstone Street is the eastern boundary of a Chicago black ghetto.
**section head:** *Disciplines*: law officers.

## II

### The Leaders

Jeff. Gene. Geronimo. And Bop.
They cancel, cure and curry.
Hardly the dupes of the downtown thing
the cold bonbon,
10    the rhinestone thing. And hardly
in a hurry.
Hardly Belafonte, King,
Black Jesus, Stokely, Malcolm X or Rap.
Bungled trophies.
15    Their country is a Nation on no map.

Jeff, Gene, Geronimo and Bop
in the passionate noon,
in bewitching night
are the detailed men, the copious men.
20    They curry, cure,
they cancel, cancelled images whose Concerts
are not divine, vivacious; the different tins
are intense last entries; pagan argument;
translations of the night.

25    The Blackstone bitter bureaus
(bureaucracy is footloose) edit, fuse
unfashionable damnations and descent;
and exulting, monstrous hand on monstrous hand,
construct, strangely, a monstrous pearl or grace.

## III

### Gang Girls

#### A Rangerette

30    Gang Girls are sweet exotics.
Mary Ann
uses the nutrients of her orient,
but sometimes sighs for Cities of blue and jewel
beyond her Ranger rim of Cottage Grove.°
35    (Bowery Boys, Disciples, Whip-Birds will
dissolve no margins, stop no savory sanctities.)

Mary is
a rose in a whiskey glass.

Mary's
40    Februaries shudder and are gone. Aprils
fret frankly, lilac hurries on.

---

34 *Cottage Grove*: a street in the black ghetto.

Summer is a hard irregular ridge.
October looks away.
And that's the Year!
45                 Save for her bugle-love.
Save for the bleat of not-obese devotion.
Save for Somebody Terribly Dying, under
the philanthropy of robins. Save for her Ranger
bringing
50 an amount of rainbow in a string-drawn bag.
"Where did you get the diamond?" Do not ask:
but swallow, straight, the spirals of his flask
and assist him at your zipper; pet his lips
and help him clutch you.

55 Love's another departure.
Will there be any arrivals, confirmations?
Will there be gleaning?

Mary, the Shakedancer's child
from the rooming-flat, pants carefully, peers at
60 her laboring lover. . . .
                Mary! Mary Ann!
Settle for sandwiches! settle for stocking caps!
for sudden blood, aborted carnival,
the props and niceties of non-loneliness—
the rhymes of Leaning.

*1968*

# Young Afrikans

### of the **furious**

Who take Today and jerk it out of joint
have made new underpinnings and a Head.

Blacktime is time for chimeful
poemhood
5 but they decree a
jagged chiming now.

If there are flowers flowers
must come out to the road. Rowdy!—
knowing where wheels and people are,
10 knowing where whips and screams are,
knowing where deaths are, where the kind kills are.

As for that other kind of kindness,
if there is milk it must be mindful.
The milkofhumankindness must be mindful
15 as wily wines.
Must be fine fury.
Must be mega, must be main.

Taking Today (to jerk it out of joint)
the hardheroic maim the
20 leechlike-as-usual who use,
adhere to, carp, and harm.

And they await,
across the Changes and the spiraling dead,
our Black revival, our Black vinegar,
our hands, and our hot blood.

*1970*

## The Boy Died in My Alley

Without my having known.
Policeman said, next morning,
"Apparently died Alone."
"You heard a shot?" Policeman said.
5 Shots I hear and Shots I hear.
I never see the dead.

The Shot that killed him yes I heard
as I heard the Thousand shots before;
careening tinnily down the nights
10 across my years and arteries.

Policeman pounded on my door.
"Who is it?" "POLICE!" Policeman yelled.
"A Boy was dying in your alley.
A Boy is dead, and in your alley.
15 And have you known this Boy before?"

I have known this Boy before.
I have known this Boy before, who
ornaments my alley.
I never saw his face at all.
20 I never saw his futurefall.
But I have known this Boy.

I have always heard him deal with death.
I have always heard the shout, the volley.
I have closed my heart-ears late and early.
25 And I have killed him ever.

I joined the Wild and killed him
with knowledgeable unknowing.
I saw where he was going.
I saw him Crossed. And seeing,
30 I did not take him down.

He cried not only "Father!"
but "Mother!
Sister!
Brother."

35    The cry climbed up the alley.
It went up to the wind.
It hung upon the heaven
for a long
stretch-strain of Moment.

40    The red floor of my alley
is a special speech to me.

*1975*

## To Those of My Sisters
## Who Kept Their Naturals

*Never to look
a hot comb in the teeth.*

Sisters!
I love you.
Because you love you.
Because you are erect.
5    Because you are also bent.
In season, stern, kind.
Crisp, soft—in season.
And you withhold.
And you extend.
10    And you Step out.
And you go back.
And you extend again.
Your eyes, loud-soft, with crying and
    with smiles,
15    are older than a million years.
And they are young.
You reach, in season.
You subside, in season.
And All
20    below the richrough righttime of your hair.
You have not bought Blondine.
You have not hailed the hot-comb recently.
You never worshipped Marilyn Monroe.
You say: Farrah's hair is hers.
25    You have not wanted to be white.
Nor have you testified to adoration of that
    state
with the advertisement of imitation
(*never* successful because the hot-comb is
30        laughing too.)

But oh the rough dark Other music!
the Real,
the Right.
The natural Respect of Self and Seal!
35        Sisters!
Your hair is Celebration in the world!

*1980*

# To the Diaspora°

### To The Diaspora

*you did not know you were Afrika*

When you set out for Afrika
you did not know you were going.
Because
you did not know you were Afrika.
5   You did not know the Black continent
that had to be reached
was you.

I could not have told you then that some sun
would come,
10   somewhere over the road,
would come evoking the diamonds
of you, the Black continent—
somewhere over the road.
You would not have believed my mouth.

15   When I told you, meeting you somewhere close
to the heat and youth of the road,
liking my loyalty, liking belief,
you smiled and you thanked me but very little believed me.

Here is some sun. Some.
20   Now off into the places rough to reach.
Though dry, though drowsy, all unwillingly a-wobble,
into the dissonant and dangerous crescendo.
Your work, that was done, to be done to be done to be done.

### Music for Martyrs

*Steve Biko, killed in South Afrika*
*for loving his people*

I feel a regret, Steve Biko.
25   I am sorry, Steve Biko.
    Biko the Emerger
laid low.

Now for the shapely American memorials.
The polished tears.
30   The timed tempest.
The one-penny poems.

---

**poem title:** The term "diaspora," which derives from a Greek word meaning "dispersion,"
originally referred only to the long exile of the Jews from the Biblical homeland in Pales-
tine. More recently, the term has been extended to apply to the historical experience of
other peoples forced to leave their home countries, such as the Africans sold into slavery
and brought to the New World.

The hollow guitars.
The joke oh jaunty.
The vigorous veal-stuffed voices.
35   The singings, the white lean lasses with streaming
yellow hair.
Now for the organized nothings.
Now for the weep-words.

Now for the rigid recountings
40   of your tracts, your triumphs, your tribulations.

### A WELCOME SONG FOR LAINI NZINGA

*Born November 24, 1975*

Hello, little Sister.
Coming through the rim of the world.
We are here! to meet you and to mold and to maintain you.
With excited eyes we see you.
45   With welcoming ears we hear the
clean sound of new language.
The language of Laini-Nzinga.
We love and we receive you as our own.

### TO BLACK WOMEN

Sisters,
50   where there is cold silence—
no hallelujahs, no hurrahs at all, no handshakes,
no neon red or blue, no smiling faces—
prevail.
Prevail across the editors of the world!
55   who are obsessed, self-honeying and self-crowned
in the seduced arena.

It has been a
hard trudge, with fainting, bandaging and death.
There have been startling confrontations.
60   There have been tramplings. Tramplings
of monarchs and of other men.

But there remain large countries in your eyes.
Shrewd sun.
The civil balance.
65   The listening secrets.

And you create and train your flowers still.

### TO PRISONERS

I call for you cultivation of strength in the dark.
Dark gardening
in the vertigo cold.

70      In the hot paralysis.
        Under the wolves and coyotes of particular silences.
        Where it is dry.
        Where it is dry.
        I call for you.
75      cultivation of victory Over
        long blows that you want to give and blows you are going to get.

        Over
        what wants to crumble you down, to sicken
        you. I call for you
80      cultivation of strength to heal and enhance
        in the non-cheering dark,
        in the many many mornings-after;
        in the chalk and choke.

                                                                *1981*

# William Bronk (1918–1999)

William Bronk spent all his life in upstate New York, in the small town of Hudson Falls. He lived in the family home, a Victorian house, and managed the business, a retail fuel and building supply firm, that he inherited from his father, from 1945 until the mid-1970s. Bronk was born in Fort Edward, New York and educated at Dartmouth. He served as an army historian during World War II and wrote *A History of the Eastern Defense Command and of the Defense of the Atlantic Coast of the United States in the Second World War* (1945). A critical book, *The Brother of Elysium* (1980), includes essays on several nineteenth-century American writers. Bronk's work has had a paradoxical thematic consistency throughout his career: he concentrates on how we construct knowledge of the world and yet his work disrupts our confidence in those very mental operations. Sometimes the topical focus is very specific, as in his poems about music, or the poems included here about the Mayan ruins, also the subject of his essays in *The New World* (1974). At other times, the topics are more abstractly epistemological or phenomenological, as in his poems about light. He avoided the poetry establishment for most of his life, meanwhile remaining one of the relatively few poets with a stable income. His career was an exceptionally focused one, with a wry intensity that is uniquely his own.

## At Tikal

Mountains they knew, and jungle, the sun, the stars—
these seemed to be there. But even after they slashed
the jungle and burned it and planted the comforting corn,
they were discontent. They wanted the shape of things.
5     They imagined a world and it was as if it were there
—a world with stars in their places and rain that came
when they called. It closed them in. Stone by stone,
as they built this city, these temples, they built this world.
They believed it. This was the world, and they,
10    of course, were the people. Now trees make up
assemblies and crowd in the wide plazas. Trees
climb the stupendous steps and rubble them.
In the jungle, the temples are little mountains again.

It is always hard like this, not having a world,
15    to imagine one, to go to the far edge
apart and imagine, to wall whether in

or out, to build a kind of cage for the sake
of feeling the bars around us, to give shape to a world.
And oh, it is always a world and not the world.

1956

## The Mayan Glyphs Unread

Yes, the porpoises of course, it could
be of purport to talk to them. See what they say.
Indeed, what wouldn't we give? But the Mayans,—oh,
not but what I'd want to know, I would.
5    They were different from us in many ways. But we know
something about them, quite a bit in fact.
They were men, which makes me wonder could they have any
    more
to say to us than we have to say, ourselves,
to each other, or rather, could they have a better way
10   to say it that gets across? It seems to me
we all speak in undeciphered glyphs
as much as they do. OK. I'd like to know.
What's new with them? No, I'd try to talk
with anybody if I thought I could. You.
I'd try to talk to you. What do you know?

1969

## I Thought It Was Harry

Excuse me. I thought for a moment you were someone I know.
It happens to me. One time at *The Circle in the Square*
when it *was* still in the Square, I turned my head
when the lights went up and saw me there with a girl
5    and another couple. Out in the lobby, I looked
right at him and he looked away. I was no one he knew.
Well, it takes two, as they say, and I don't know what
it would prove anyway. Do we know who we are,
do you think? Kids seem to know. One time I asked
10   a little girl. She said she'd been sick. She said
she'd looked different and felt different. I said,
"Maybe it wasn't you. How do you know?"
"Oh, I was me," she said, "I know I was."

That part doesn't bother me anymore
15   or not the way it did. I'm nobody else
and nobody anyway. It's all the rest
I don't know. I don't know anything.
It hit me. I thought it was Harry when I saw you
and thought, "I'll ask Harry." I don't suppose
20   he knows, though. It's not that I get confused.
I don't mean that. If someone appeared and said,
"Ask me questions," I wouldn't know where to start.

I don't have questions even. It's the way I fade
as though I were someone's snapshot left in the light.
25    And the background fades the way it might if we woke
in the wrong twilight and things got dim and grey
while we waited for them to sharpen. Less and less
is real. No fixed point. Questions fix
a point, as answers do. Things move again
30    and the only place to move is away. It was wrong:
questions and answers are what to be without
and all we learn is how sound our ignorance is.
That's what I wanted to talk to Harry about.
You looked like him. Thank you anyway.

                                                            *1971*


## Where It Ends

The gentleness of the slant October light
cancels whatever else we might have thought.
It is a hard world, empty and cruel;
but this light, oh Jesus Christ! This light!

5    The maple leaves, passive in front of the house,
are laved in it, abandoned, green gone.
That nothing else should matter but this light.
Gentleness, gentleness, the light.

                                                            *1975*

# Robert Duncan (1919–1988)

Born in Oakland, California, Duncan was adopted after his mother died in childbirth. He was given the name Robert Edward Symmes, but Duncan took his biological father's surname in 1941. He studied at the University of California at Berkeley from 1936–1938, spent some time in New York, and then returned to San Francisco, where he became a key figure in what came to be known as the "San Francisco Renaissance." He resided in San Francisco for the rest of his life. A conscientious objector during World War II, he studied at Berkley again at the end of the 1940s, during which time he made early and courageous statements on behalf of gay rights. He was an active voice again in the antiwar movement of the 1960s, and for some years he declined to publish his poems, opting instead to circulate copies to a few friends. The painter Jess was his companion from 1951 until the end of his life. People interested in his work should seek out some of the beautiful holograph editions of his poems.

As the selections here demonstrate, Duncan excelled at both highly musical formal stanzas and at open form poems aimed at a field effect, what Duncan called a "grand collage." The two poems from "Passages" belong to an open-ended sequence that, unlike Pound's *Cantos*, was not designed to build to a decisive synthesis but rather to develop with history, Duncan's life, and his creative vision. Rich with literary and historical references, Duncan's sequence sides with love and against tyranny. His poetics is passionate and visionary, but aware of the compromising tendencies in the ecstasy it seeks, as a comparison of related elements in "The Torso" and "Up Rising" will suggest. Duncan's poetry manages to be both erudite and prophetic, both profoundly religious and erotic.

## Often I am Permitted to
## Return to a Meadow

as if it were a scene made-up by the mind,
that is not mine, but is a made place,

that is mine, it is so near to the heart,
an eternal pasture folded in all thought
so that there is a hall therein

that is a made place, created by light
wherefrom the shadows that are forms fall.

Wherefrom fall all architectures I am
I say are likenesses of the First Beloved
10    whose flowers are flames lit to the Lady.

She it is Queen Under The Hill
whose hosts are a disturbance of words within words
that is a field folded.

It is only a dream of the grass blowing
15    east against the source of the sun
in an hour before the sun's going down

whose secret we see in a children's game
of ring a round of roses told.

Often I am permitted to return to a meadow
20    as if it were a given property of the mind
that certain bounds hold against chaos,

that is a place of first permission,
everlasting omen of what is.

*1960*

# My Mother Would Be a Falconress

My mother would be a falconress,
and I, her gay falcon treading her wrist,
would fly to bring back
from the blue of the sky to her, bleeding, a prize,
5    where I dream in my little hood with many bells
jangling when I'd turn my head.

My mother would be a falconress,
and she sends me as far as her will goes.
She lets me ride to the end of her curb
10    where I fall back in anguish.
I dread that she will cast me away,
for I fall, I mis-take, I fail in her mission.

She would bring down the little birds.
And I would bring down the little birds.
15    When will she let me bring down the little birds,
pierced from their flight with their necks broken,
their heads like flowers limp from the stem?

I trend my mother's wrist and would draw blood.
Behind the little hood my eyes are hooded.
20    I have gone back into my hooded silence,
talking to myself and dropping off to sleep.

For she has muffled my dreams in the hood she has made me,
sewn round with bells, jangling when I move.

She rides with her little falcon upon her wrist.
25 She uses a barb that brings me to cower.
She sends me abroad to try my wings
and I come back to her. I would bring down
the little birds to her
I may not tear into, I must bring back perfectly.

30 I tear at her wrist with my beak to draw blood,
and her eye holds me, anguisht, terrifying.
She draws a limit to my flight.
Never beyond my sight, she says.
She trains me to fetch and to limit myself in fetching.
35 She rewards me with meat for my dinner.
But I must never eat what she sends me to bring her.

Yet it would have been beautiful, if she would have carried me,
always, in a little hood with the bells ringing,
at her wrist, and her riding
40 to the great falcon hunt, and me
flying up to the curb of my heart from her heart
to bring down the skylark from the blue to her feet,
straining, and then released for the flight.

My mother would be a falconress,
45 and I her gerfalcon, raised at her will,
from her wrist sent flying, as if I were her own
pride, as if her pride
knew no limits, as if her mind
sought in me flight beyond the horizon.

50 Ah, but high, high in the air I flew.
and far, far beyond the curb of her will,
were the blue hills where the falcons nest.
And then I saw west to the dying sun—
it seemd my human soul went down in flames.

55 I tore at her wrist, at the hold she had for me,
until the blood ran hot and I heard her cry out,
far, far beyond the curb of her will •

to horizons of stars beyond the ringing hills of the world where
     the falcons nest
I saw, and I tore at her wrist with my savage break.
60 I flew, as if sight flew from the anguish in her eye beyond her
     sight,
sent from my striking loose, from the cruel strike at her wrist,
striking out from the blood to be free of her.

My mother would be a falconress,
and even now, years after this,
65 when the wounds I left her had surely heald,
and the woman is dead,
her fierce eyes closed, and if her heart
were broken, it is stilld •

70    I would be a falcon and go free.
      I tread her wrist and wear the hood,
      talking to myself, and would draw blood.

                                                    *1968*


## The Torso                    Passages 18

        Most beautiful!   the red-flowering eucalyptus,
              the madrone, the yew

        Is he . . .

        *So thou wouldst smile, and take me in thine arms*
5       *The sight of London to my exiled eyes*
        *Is as Elysium to a new-come soul°*

              If he be Truth
              I would dwell in the illusion of him

      His hands unlocking from chambers of my male body

10              such an idea in man's image

        rising tides that sweep me towards him

              . . . *homosexual?*

                    and at the treasure of his mouth

                    pour forth my soul

15                        his soul   commingling

      I thought a Being more than vast, His body leading
            into Paradise,     his eyes

                    quickening a fire in me,     a trembling

              hieroglyph:    At the root of the neck

20      *the clavicle,* for the neck is the stem of the great artery
            upward into his head that is beautiful

                    At the rise of the pectoral muscle,

        *the nipples,* for the breasts are like sleeping fountains
            of feeling in man, waiting above the beat of his heart,

---

4–6 *So . . . soul:* the italicized stanza is from the play *Edward II* (1590) by the British drama-
tist Chistopher Marlowe (1564–1593). These lines from the play's opening speech are spo-
ken by Edward's young friend Gaveston, who is recalled from banishment when the king
ascends to the throne. Gaveston is murdered in the course of the play.

25        shielding the rise and fall of his breath, to be
          awakend

                              At the axis of his mid hriff

      *the navel,* for in the pit of his stomach the chord from
          which first he was fed has its temple

30                            At the root of the groin

      *the pubic hair,* for the torso is the stem in which the man
          flowers forth and leads to the stamen of flesh in which
          his seed rises

      a wave of need and desire over      taking me

35                            cried out my name

          (This was long ago;      It was another life)

                                        and said,

                What do you want of me?

      I do not know, I said.      I have fallen in love.      He
40              has brought me into heights and depths my heart
                        would fear   without him.   His look

            pierces my side°   •   fire eyes   •

      I have been waiting for you, he said:
                    I know what you desire

45              you do not yet know      but through me   •

      And I am with you everywhere.    In your falling

      I have fallen from a high place.    I have raised myself

            from darkness in your   rising

                        wherever you are

50          my hand in your hand      seeking      the locks, the keys

      I am there.    Gathering me, you gather

            your Self •

      For my Other is not a woman but a man

      *the King upon whose bosom let me lie.*°

                                                            *1968*

---

42 *pierces my side:* the image of the wounded Christ is woven together here and in the
next six lines, with references to man's fall, to Christ's incarnation and resurrection, and
to human love and passion.
54 *King . . . lie:* Marlowe, *Edward II.*

## Up Rising                        Passages 25

Now Johnson° would go up to join the great simulacra of men,
    Hitler and Stalin, to work his fame
    with planes roaring out from Guam over Asia,
all America become a sea of toiling men
5     stirrd at his will, which would be a bloated thing,
    drawing from the underbelly of the nation
    such blood and dreams as swell the idiot psyche
    out of its courses into an elemental thing
    until his name stinks with burning meat and heapt honors

10 And men wake to see that they are used like things
    spent in a great potlach, this Texas barbecue
      of Asia, Africa, and all the Americas,
And the professional military behind him, thinking
    to use him as they thought to use Hitler
15     without losing control of their business of war,

But the mania, the ravening eagle of America
    as Lawrence° saw him "bird of men that are masters,
    lifting the rabbit-blood of the myriads up into . . . "
    into something terrible, gone beyond bounds, or
20 As Blake° saw America in figures of fire and blood raging,
    . . . in what image? the ominous roar in the air,
    the omnipotent wings, the all-American boy in the cockpit
    loosing his flow of napalm, below in the jungles
    "any life at all or sign of life" his target, drawing now
25     not with crayons in his secret room
    the burning of homes and the torture of mothers and fathers and
    children,
      their hair a-flame, screaming in agony, but
    in the line of duty, for the might and enduring fame
30     of Johnson, for the victory of American will over its victims,
    releasing his store of destruction over the enemy,
    in terror and hatred of all communal things, of communion,
    of communism •

has raised from the private rooms of small-town bosses and
35     businessmen,
    from the council chambers of the gangs that run the great cities,
    swollen with the votes of millions,
    from the fearful hearts of good people in the suburbs turning the
    savory meat over the charcoal burners and heaping their barbecue
40     plates with more than they can eat,
    from the closed meeting-rooms of regents of universities and sessions
    of profiteers

---

1 *Johnson:* Lyndon Baines Johnson (1908–1973), thirty-sixth president of the U.S. (1963–1969); his domestic accomplishments were overshadowed by his disastrous commitment to the Vietnam War. He was born and grew up in Texas.

17 *Lawrence:* D. H. Lawrence (1885–1930), British novelist, poet, and essayist.

20 *Blake:* William Blake (1757–1827), British poet, painter, and visionary.

—back of the scene: the atomic stockpile; the vials of synthesized
diseases eager biologists have developt over half a century dreaming
45      of the bodies of mothers and fathers and children and hated rivals
swollen with new plagues, measles grown enormous, influenzas
perfected; and the gasses of despair, confusion of the senses, mania,
inducing terror of the universe, coma, existential wounds, that
chemists we have met at cocktail parties, passt daily and with a
50      happy "Good Day" on the way to classes or work, have workt to
make war too terrible for men to wage—

raised this secret entity of American's hatred of Europe, of Africa,
        of Asia,
the deep hatred for the old world that had driven generations of
55          America out of itself,
and for the alien world, the new world about him, that might have
        been Paradise
but was before his eyes already cleard back in a holocaust of burning
        Indians, trees and grasslands,
60      reduced to his real estate, his projects of exploitation and profitable
wastes,

this specter that in the beginning Adams and Jefferson feard and knew
would corrupt the very body of the nation
        and all our sense of our common humanity,
65      this black bile of old evils arisen anew,
takes over the vanity of Johnson;
and the very glint of Satan's eyes from the pit of the hell of
        America's unacknowledged, unrepented crimes that I saw in
        Goldwater's° eyes
70      now shines from the eyes of the President
        in the swollen head of the nation.

                                                        *1968*

---

69 *Goldwater*: Barry Goldwater (1909–1997), conservative U.S. senator from Arizona, Lyndon Johnson's Republican opponent in the 1964 U.S. presidential elections.

# Richard Wilbur (b. 1921)

Born in New York and raised in New Jersey, Wilbur was educated at Amherst College and Harvard. He served as a cryptographer during World War II, and was stationed in Africa, France, and Italy. Since then he has taught regularly, done successful translations of Molière, coauthored an operetta (*Candide*, 1957) with Lillian Hellman, and written two books of children's poetry. Taking the English metaphysical poets as his models in his own work, Wilbur has excelled at polished, witty, self-contained lyrics with formal stanzas and controlled metrics. He believes, as with his signature poem "Love Calls Us to the Things of This World," in spiritual impulses grounded in ordinary life. Yet the most ordinary things can, in the intense elegance of a civilizing gaze, become extraordinary. In "A Baroque Wall-Fountain in the Villa Sciarra" his language creates the secular, aesthetic miracle of Baroque water; the water itself seems to take on the Baroque style. The exquisite, sensuous, and precise description in the poem is Wilbur's version of the human potential for grace.

## A Baroque Wall-Fountain in the Villa Sciarra°

for Dore and Adja

>            Under the bronze crown
> Too big for the head of the stone cherub whose feet
>        A serpent has begun to eat,
> Sweet water brims a cockle° and braids down

5
>            Past spattered mosses, breaks
> On the tipped edge of a second shell, and fills
>        The massive third below. It spills
> In threads then from the scalloped rim, and makes

>            A scrim or summery tent
10
> For a faun-ménage° and their familiar goose.
>        Happy in all that ragged, loose
> Collapse of water, its effortless descent

---

**poem title:** Villa Sciarra, a public park in Rome.

4 *cockle:* shell-shaped basin in the fountain.

10 *faun-ménage:* a faun household; in Roman mythology, fauns were rustic forest demons, companions of the shepherds, and the equivalents of the Greek Satyrs; they were half man and half goat.

And flatteries of spray,
The stocky god upholds the shell with ease,
15       Watching, about his shaggy knees,
The goatish innocence of his babes at play;

      His fauness all the while
Leans forward, slightly, into a clambering mesh
      Of water-lights, her sparkling flesh
20 In a saecular ecstasy, her blinded smile

      Bent on the sand floor
Of the trefoil° pool, where ripple-shadows come
      And go in swift reticulum,°
More addling to the eye than wine, and more

25       Interminable to thought
Than pleasure's calculus. Yet since this all
      Is pleasure, flash, and waterfall,
Must it not be too simple? Are we not

      More intricately expressed
30 In the plain fountains that Maderna° set
      Before St. Peter's—the main jet
Struggling aloft until it seems at rest

      In the act of rising, until
The very wish of water is reversed,
35       That heaviness borne up to burst
In a clear, high, cavorting head, to fill

      With blaze, and then in gauze
Delays, in a gnatlike shimmering, in a fine
      Illumined version of itself, decline,
40 And patter on the stones its own applause?

      If that is what men are
Or should be, if those water-saints display
      The pattern of our areté,°
What of these showered fauns in their bizarre,

45       Spangled, and plunging house?
They are at rest in fulness of desire
      For what is given, they do not tire
Of the smart of the sun, the pleasant water-douse

---

22 *trefoil:* three-leaved.
23 *reticulum:* in an intricate, netlike pattern.
30 *Maderna:* Carlo Maderno (1556–1629), architect who helped design St. Peter's Basilica.
43 *areté:* (Wilbur's note), a Greek word meaning roughly "virtue"; the combination of qualities that make for good character—excellence, valor, virtue.

And riddled pool below,
50          Reproving our disgust and our ennui
With humble insatiety.
Francis,° perhaps, who lay in sister snow

Before the wealthy gate
Freezing and praising, might have seen in this
55          No trifle, but a shade of bliss—
That land of tolerable flowers, that state

As near and far as grass
Where eyes become the sunlight, and the hand
Is worthy of water: the dreamt land
60          Toward which all hungers leap, all pleasures pass.

                                                          *1956*


## Love Calls Us to the Things of This World°

The eyes open to a cry of pulleys,
And spirited from sleep, the astounded soul
Hangs for a moment bodiless and simple
As false dawn.
5                          Outside the open window
The morning air is all awash with angels.

Some are in bed-sheets, some are in blouses,
Some are in smocks: but truly there they are.
Now they are rising together in calm swells
10     Of halcyon° feeling, filling whatever they wear
With the deep joy of their impersonal breathing;

Now they are flying in place, conveying
The terrible speed of their omnipresence, moving
And staying like white water; and now of a sudden
15     They swoon down into so rapt a quiet
That nobody seems to be there.
                                                  The soul shrinks

From all that it is about to remember,
From the punctual rape of every blessèd day,
20     And cries,
                  "Oh, let there be nothing on earth but laundry,
Nothing but rosy hands in the rising steam
And clear dances done in the sight of heaven."

---

52 *Francis:* St. Francis of Assisi (1182–1226), founder of the Franciscan Order of monks, who take vows of poverty, and patron saint of ecology.
**poem title:** a quotation from St. Augustine (354–430 A.D.) Wilbur's note—"You must imagine the poem as occurring at perhaps seven-thirty in the morning; the scene is a bedroom high up in a city apartment building; outside the bedroom window, the first laundry of the day is being yanked across the sky and one has been awakened by the squeaking pulleys of the laundry-line."
10 *halcyon:* serene.

Yet, as the sun acknowledges
25    With a warm look the world's hunks and colors,
The soul descends once more in bitter love
To accept the waking body, saying now
In a changed voice as the man yawns and rises,

"Bring them down from their ruddy gallows;
30    Let there be clean linen for the backs of thieves;
Let lovers go fresh and sweet to be undone,
And the heaviest nuns walk in a pure floating
Of dark habits,
                keeping their difficult balance."

*1956*

# Advice to a Prophet

When you come, as you soon must, to the streets of our city,
Mad-eyed from stating the obvious,
Not proclaiming our fall but begging us
In God's name to have self-pity,

5    Spare us all word of the weapons, their force and range,
The long numbers that rocket the mind;
Our slow, unreckoning hearts will be left behind,
Unable to fear what is too strange.

Nor shall you scare us with talk of the death of the race.
10    How should we dream of this place without us?—
The sun mere fire, the leaves untroubled about us,
A stone look on the stone's face?

Speak of the world's own change. Though we cannot
        conceive
Of an undreamt thing, we know to our cost
15    How the dreamt cloud crumbles, the vines are blackened
        by frost,
How the view alters. We could believe,

If you told us so, that the white-tailed deer will slip
Into perfect shade, grown perfectly shy,
The lark avoid the reaches of our eye;
20    The jack-pine lose its knuckled grip

On the cold ledge, and every torrent burn
As Xanthus° once, its gliding trout
Stunned in a twinkling. What should we be without
The dolphin's arc, the dove's return,

---

22 *Xanthus:* The name of the river that flowed through the plain of Troy. In the *Iliad* the river takes the form of the god Scamander, who objects to all the blood and bodies hurled into his domain in the course of the war. He causes the river to rise up, threatening to drown Achilles, but Hephaestus scolds Scamander and compels the river to return within its banks.

25    These things in which we have seen ourselves and spoken?
Ask us, prophet, how we shall call
Our natures forth when that live tongue is all
Dispelled, that glass obscured or broken

In which we have said the rose of our love and the clean
30    Horse of our courage, in which beheld
The singing locust of the soul unshelled,
And all we mean or wish to mean.

Ask us, ask us whether with the worldless rose
Our hearts shall fail us; come demanding
35    Whether there shall be lofty or long standing
When the bronze annals of the oak-tree close.

*1961*

# Mona Van Duyn (b. 1921)

Born in Waterloo, Iowa, Van Duyn was educated at the University of Northern Iowa and the University of Iowa. Typically a formalist poet, she often works in long lines with varied meters. Sometimes taking up philosophical topics, she also writes about the commonplace events of ordinary life, as with "Toward a Definition of Marriage." She has taught most recently at Washington University. See her *If It Be Not I: Collected Poems 1959–1982* (1993).

## Toward a Definition of Marriage

### I

It is to make a fill, not find a land.
Elsewhere, often, one sights americas of awareness,
suddenly there they are, natural and anarchic,
with plantings scattered but rich, powers to be harnessed—
5      but this is more like building a World's Fair island.
Somebody thought it could be done, contracts are signed,
and now all materials are useful, everything; sludge
is scooped up and mixed with tin cans and fruit rinds,
even tomato pulp and lettuce leaves are solid
10      under pressure. Presently the ground humps up and shows.
But this marvel of engineering is not all.
A hodgepodge of creatures (no bestiary would suppose
such an improbable society) are at this time
turned loose to run on it, first shyly, then more free,
15      and must keep, for self's sake, wiles, anger, much of their
spiney or warted nature, yet learn courtesy.

### II

It is closest to picaresque, but essentially artless.
If there were any experts, they are dead, it takes too long.
How could its structure be more than improvising,
20      when it never ends, but line after line plods on,
and none of the ho hum passages can be skipped?
It has a bulky knowledge, but what symbol comes anywhere near
suggesting it? No, the notion of art won't fit it—
unless—when it's embodied. For digression there
25      is meaningful, and takes such joy in the slopes and crannies

that every bony gesture is generous, full,
all lacy with veins and nerves. There, the spirit
smiles in its skin, and impassions and sweetens to style.
So this comes to resemble a poem found in his notebooks.
30      after the master died. A charred, balky man, yet one day
as he worked at one of those monuments, the sun guiled him,
and he turned to a fresh page and simply let play
his great gift on a small ground. Yellowed, unpublished,
he might have forgotten he wrote it. (All this is surmise.)
35      But it's known by heart now; it rounded the steeliest shape
to shapeliness, it was so loving an exercise.

### III

Or, think of it as a duel of amateurs.
These two have almost forgot how it started—in an alley,
impromptu, and with a real affront. One thought,
40      "He is not me," and one, "She is not me,"
and they were coming toward each other with sharp knives
when someone saw it was illegal, dragged them away,
bundled them into some curious canvas clothing,
and brought them to this gym that is almost dark, and empty.
45      Now, too close together for the length of the foils,
wet with fear, they dodge, stumble, strike,
and if either finally thinks he would rather be touched
than touch, he still must listen to the clang and tick
of his own compulsive parrying. Endless. Nothing
50      but a scream for help can make the authorities come.
If it ever turns into more of a dance than a duel,
it is only because, feeling more skillful, one
or the other steps back with some notion of grace
and looks at his partner. Then he is able to find
55      not a wire mask for his target, but a red heart
sewn on the breast like a simple valentine.

### IV

If there's a Barnum way to show it, then think back
to a climax in the main tent. At the foot of the bleachers, a road
encloses the ringed acts; consider that as its design,
60      and consider whoever undertakes it as the whole parade
which, either as preview or summary, assures the public
hanging in hopeful suspense between balloons and peanutshells
that it's all worthwhile. The ponies never imagined
anything but this slow trot of ribbons and jinglebells.
65      An enormous usefulness constrains the leathery bulls
as they stomp on, and hardly ever run amuck.
The acrobats practiced all their lives for this easy
contortion, and clowns are enacting a necessary joke
by harmless zigzags in and out of line.
70      But if the procession includes others less trustworthy?
When they first see the circle they think some ignorant
cartographer has blundered. The route is a lie,

drawn to be strict but full, drawn so each going forth
returns, returns to a more informed beginning.
75    And still a familiar movement might tempt them to try it,
but since what they know is not mentioned in the tromboning
of the march, neither the day-long pace of caged
impulse, nor the hurtle of night's terrible box-cars,
they shrink in their stripes and refuse; other performers
80    drive them out and around with whips and chairs.
They never tame, but may be taught to endure
the illusion of tameness. Year after year their paws
pad out the false curve, and their reluctant parading
extends the ritual's claim to its applause.

V

85    Say, for once, that the start is a pure vision
like the blind man's (though he couldn't keep it, trees
soon bleached to familiar) when the bandage came off
and what a world could be first fell on his eyes.
Say it's when campaigns are closest to home
90    that farsighted lawmakers oftenest lose their way.
And repeat what everyone knows and nobody wants
to remember, that always, always expediency
must freckle the fairest wishes. Say, when documents,
stiff with history, go right into the council chambers
95    and are rolled up to shake under noses, are constantly read from,
or pounded on, or passed around, the parchment limbers;
and, still later, if these old papers are still being shuffled,
commas will be missing, ashes will disfigure a word;
finally thumbprints will grease out whole phrases, the clear prose
100   won't mean much; it can never be wholly restored.
Curators mourn the perfect idea, for it crippled
outside of its case. Announce that at least it can move
in the imperfect action, beyond the windy oratory,
of marriage, which is the politics of love.

*1964*

# James Dickey (1923–1997)

Born and raised in Atlanta, Georgia, and in the surrounding area, Dickey was first a public figure as a high school football star. He did not decide to be a writer until after service in the Air Force in World War II and then enrollment at Vanderbilt University. Even then, he took up other occupations as well. He helped train pilots in the Korean War and worked as an advertising executive for Coca-Cola. Both in his poetry and in his widely successful novel, *Deliverance* (1970), he was fascinated by violent, definitive tests of selfhood. He could write poems glorifying combat, poems designed to shock readers with country sexuality, and, in the case of "Falling," a poem that celebrates a most transitory form of transcendence at the same time as it indulges in misogynist violence. Flamboyant in his personal style, he was at once a performer and an unforgettable writer.

## The Sheep Child

    Farm boys wild to couple
    With anything    with soft-wooded trees
    With mounds of earth    mounds
    Of pinestraw    will keep themselves off
5    Animals by legends of their own:
    In the hay-tunnel dark
    And dung of barns, they will
    Say    I have heard tell
    That in a museum in Atlanta
10   Way back in a corner somewhere
    There's this thing that's only half
    Sheep    like a woolly baby
    Pickled in alcohol    because
    Those things can't live    his eyes
15   Are open    but you can't stand to look
    I heard from somebody who . . .

    But this is now almost all
    Gone. The boys have taken
    Their own true wives in the city,
20   The sheep are safe in the west hill
    Pasture    but we who were born there
    Still are not sure. Are we,

Because we remember, remembered
In the terrible dust of museums?

25    Merely with his eyes, the sheep-child may

Be saying     saying

*I am here, in my father's house.*
*I who am half of your world, came deeply*
*To my mother in the long grass*
30    *Of the west pasture, where she stood like moonlight*
*Listening for foxes. It was something like love*
*From another world that seized her*
*From behind, and she gave, not lifting her head*
*Out of dew, without ever looking, her best*
35    *Self to that great need. Turned loose, she dipped her face*
*Farther into the chill of the earth, and in a sound*
*Of sobbing     of something stumbling*
*Away, began, as she must do,*
*To carry me. I woke, dying,*

40    *In the summer sun of the hillside, with my eyes*
*Far more than human. I saw for a blazing moment*
*The great grassy world from both sides,*
*Man and beast in the round of their need,*
*And the hill wind stirred in my wool,*
45    *My hoof and my hand clasped each other,*
*I ate my one meal*
*Of milk, and died*
*Staring. From dark grass I came straight*

*To my father's house, whose dust*
50    *Whirls up in the halls for no reason*
*When no one comes     piling deep in a hellish mild*
    *corner,*
*And, through my immortal waters,*
*I meet the sun's grains eye*
55    *To eye, and they fail at my closet of glass.*
*Dead, I am most surely living*
*In the minds of farm boys: I am he who drives*
*Them like wolves from the hound bitch and calf*
*And from the chaste ewe in the wind.*
60    *They go into woods     into bean fields     they go*
*Deep into their known right hands. Dreaming of me,*
*They groan     they wait     they suffer*
*Themselves, they marry, they raise their kind.*

1967

# Falling

*A 29-year-old stewardess fell . . . to her*
*death tonight when she was swept*
*through an emergency door that sud-*
*denly sprang open . . . The body . . .*
*was found . . . three hours after the*
*accident.*
—NEW YORK TIMES

The states when they black out and lie there rolling   when they turn
To something transcontinental   move by   drawing moonlight out
        of the great
One-sided stone hung off the starboard wingtip   some sleeper next to
5    An engine is groaning for coffee   and there is faintly coming in
Somewhere the vast beast-whistle of space. In the galley with its racks
Of trays   she rummages for a blanket   and moves in her slim tailored
Uniform to pin it over the cry at the top of the door. As though
        she blew

The door down with a silent blast from her lungs   frozen   she is black
10   Out finding herself   with the plane nowhere and her body taking by
        the throat
The undying cry of the void   falling   living   beginning to be
        something
That no one has ever been and lived through   screaming without
15       enough air
Still neat   lipsticked   stockinged   girdled by regulation   her hat
Still on   her arms and legs in no world   and yet spaced also strangely
With utter placid rightness on thin air   taking her time   she holds it
In many places   and now, still thousands of feet from her death
20       she seems
To slow   she develops interest   she turns in her maneuverable body

To watch it. She is hung high up in the overwhelming middle of things
        in her
Self   in low body-whistling wrapped intensely   in all her dark
25       dance-weight
Coming down from a marvelous leap   with the delaying,
        dumfounding ease
Of a dream of being drawn   like endless moonlight to the harvest soil
Of a central state of one's country   with a great gradual warmth
30       coming
Over her   floating   finding more and more breath in what she has
        been using
For breath   as the levels become more human   seeing clouds placed
        honestly
35   Below her left and right   riding slowly toward them   she clasps it all
To her and can hang her hands and feet in it in peculiar ways   and
Her eyes opened wide by wind, can open her mouth as wide   wider
        and suck
All the heat from the cornfields   can go down on her back with a
40       feeling

Of stupendous pillows stacked under her   and can turn   turn as
   to someone
In bed   smile, understood in darkness   can go away   slant   slide
Off tumbling   into the emblem of a bird with its wings half-spread
45 Or whirl madly on herself   in endless gymnastics in the growing
   warmth
Of wheatfields rising toward the harvest moon.   There is time to live
In superhuman health   seeing mortal unreachable lights far down
   seeing
50 An ultimate highway with one late priceless car probing it   arriving
In a square town   and off her starboard arm the glitter of water
   catches
The moon by its one shaken side   scaled, roaming silver   My God
   it is good
And evil   lying in one after another of all the positions for love
55 Making   dancing   sleeping   and now cloud wisps at her no
Raincoat   no matter   all small towns brokenly brighter from inside
Cloud   she walks over them like rain   bursts out to behold a
   Greyhound
Bus shooting light through its sides   it is the signal to go straight
60 Down like a glorious diver   then feet first   her skirt stripped
   beautifully
Up   her face in fear-scented cloths   her legs deliriously bare   then
Arms out   she slow-rolls over   steadies out   waits for something
   great
65 To take control of her   trembles near feathers   planes head-down
The quick movements of bird-necks turning her head   gold eyes
   the insight-
eyesight of owls blazing into the hencoops   a taste for chicken
   overwhelming
70 Her   the long-range vision of hawks enlarging all human lights
   of cars
Freight trains   looped bridges   enlarging the moon racing slowly
Through all the curves of a river   all the darks of the midwest blazing
From above. A rabbit in a bush turns white   the smothering chickens
75 Huddle   for over them there is still time for something to live
With the streaming half-idea of a long stoop   a hurtling   a fall
That is controlled   that plummets as it wills   turns gravity
Into a new condition, showing its other side like a moon   shining
New Powers   there is still time to live on a breath made of nothing
80 But the whole night   time for her to remember to arrange her skirt
Like a diagram of a bat   tightly it guides her   she has this flying-skin
Made of garments   and there are also those sky-divers on TV   sailing
In sunlight   smiling under their goggles   swapping batons back
   and forth
85 And He who jumped without a chute and was handed one by a div-
   ing
Buddy. She looks for her grinning companion   white teeth   nowhere
She is screaming   singing hymns   her thin human wings spread out
From her neat shoulders   the air beast-crooning to her   warbling
And she can no longer behold the huge partial form of the world   now
90 She is watching her country lose its evoked master shape   watching
   it lose

And gain   get back its houses and peoples   watching it bring up
Its local lights   single homes   lamps on barn roofs   if she fell
Into water she might live   like a diver   cleaving   perfect   plunge

95      Into another   heavy silver   unbreathable   slowing   saving
Element: there is water   there is time to perfect all the fine
Points of diving   feet together   toes pointed   hands shaped right
To insert her into water like a needle   to come out healthily dripping
And be handed a Coca-Cola   there they are   there are the waters
100    Of life   the moon packed and coiled in a reservoir   so let me begin
*To plane across the night air of Kansas   opening my eyes*
    *superhumanly*
*Bright   to the dammed moon   opening the natural wings of my jacket*
*By Don Loper   moving like a hunting owl toward the glitter of water*
105    *One cannot just fall   just tumble screaming all that time   one must use*
*It   she is now through with all   through all   clouds   damp   hair*
Straightened   the last wisp of fog pulled apart on her face like wool
    revealing
New darks   new progressions of headlights along dirt roads
110      from chaos

And night   a gradual warming   a new-made, inevitable world of
    one's own
Country   a great stone of light in its waiting waters   hold   hold out
For water: who knows when what correct young woman must take up
115      her body
And fly   and head for the moon-crazed inner eye of midwest
    imprisoned
Water   stored up for her for years   the arms of her jacket slipping
Air up her sleeves to go   all over her? What final things can be said
120    Of one who starts out sheerly in her body in the high middle of night
Air   to track down water like a rabbit where it lies like life itself
Off to the right in Kansas? She goes toward   the blazing-bare lake
Her skirts neat   her hands and face warmed more and more by the air
Rising from pastures of beans   and under her   under chenille
125      bedspreads
The farm girls are feeling the goddess in them struggle and rise
    brooding
On the scratch-shining posts of the bed   dreaming of female signs
Of the moon   male blood like iron   of what is really said by the moan
130    Of airliners passing over them at dead of midwest midnight   passing
Over brush fires   burning out in silence on little hills   and will wake
To see the woman they should be   struggling on the rooftree to
    become
Stars: for her the ground is closer   water is nearer   she passes
It   then banks   turns   her sleeves fluttering differently as she rolls
135    Out to face the east, where the sun shall come up from wheatfields
    she must
Do something with water   fly to it   fall in it   drink it   rise
From it   but there is none left upon earth   the clouds have drunk
    it back
140    The plants have sucked it down   there are standing toward her only
The common fields of death   she comes back from flying to falling

Returns to a powerful cry   the silent scream with which she blew
        down
The coupled door of the airliner   nearly   nearly losing hold
Of what she has done   remembers   remembers the shape at the heart
145   Of cloud   fashionably swirling   remembers she still has time to die
Beyond explanation. Let her now take off her hat in summer air the
        contour
Of cornfields   and have enough time to kick off her one remaining
Shoe with the toes   of the other foot   to unhook her stockings
150   With calm fingers, noting how fatally easy it is to undress in midair
Near death   when the body will assume without effort any position
Except the one that will sustain it   enable it to rise   live
Not die   nine farms hover close   widen   eight of them separate,
        leaving
155   One in the middle   then the fields of that farm do the same   there
        is no
Way to back off   from her chosen ground   but she sheds the jacket
With its silver sad impotent wings   sheds the bat's guiding tailpiece
Of her skirt   the lightning-charged clinging of her blouse   the
160        intimate
Inner flying-garment of her slip in which she rides like the holy ghost
Of a virgin   sheds the long windsocks of her stockings   absurd
Brassiere   then feels the girdle required by regulations squirming
Off her: no longer monobuttocked   she feels the girdle flutter   shake
165   In her hand   and float   upward   her clothes rising off her
        ascending
Into cloud   and fights away from her head the last sharp dangerous
        shoe
Like a dumb bird   and now will drop in   SOON   now will drop

170   In like this   the greatest thing that ever came to Kansas   down
        from all
Heights   all levels of American breath   layered in the lungs
        from the frail
Chill of space to the loam where extinction slumbers in corn tassels
175        thickly
And breathes like rich farmers counting: will come among them after
Her last superhuman act   the last slow careful passing of her hands
All over her unharmed body   desired by every sleeper in his dream:
Boys finding for the first time their loins filled with heart's blood
180   Widowed farmers whose hands float under light covers to find
        themselves
Arisen at sunrise   the splendid position of blood unearthly drawn
Toward clouds   all feel something   pass over them as she passes
Her palms over *her* long legs   *her* small breasts   and deeply between
185   Her thighs   her hair shot loose from all pins   streaming in the wind
Of her body   let her come openly   trying at the last second to land
On her back   this is it   THIS
                                All those who find her impressed
In the soft loam   gone down   driven well into the image of her body
190   The furrows for miles flowing in upon her where she lies very deep
In her mortal outline   in the earth as it is in cloud   can tell nothing
But that she is there   inexplicable   unquestionable   and remember

That something broke in them as well   and began to live and die more
When they walked for no reason into their fields to where the whole
195        earth
Caught her   interrupted her maiden flight   told her how to lie
        she cannot
Turn   go away   cannot move   cannot slide off it and assume another
Position   no sky-diver with any grin could save her   hold her in
220        his arms
Plummet with her   unfold above her his wedding silks   she can no
        longer
Mark the rain with whirling women that take the place of a dead wife
Or the goddess in Norwegian farm girls   or all the back-breaking
205        whores
Of Wichita. All the known air above her is not giving up quite one
Breath   it is all gone   and yet not dead   not anywhere else
Quite   lying still in the field on her back   sensing the smells
Of incessant growth try to lift her   a little sight left in the corner
210        Of one eye   fading   seeing something wave   lies believing
That she could have made it   at the best part of her brief goddess
State   to water   gone in headfirst   come out smiling   invulnerable
Girl in a bathing-suit ad   but she is lying like a sunbather at the last
Of moonlight   half-buried in her impact on the earth   not far
215        From a railroad trestle   a water tank   she could see if she could
Raise her head from her modest hole   with her clothes beginning
To come down all over Kansas   into bushes   on the dewy sixth green
Of a golf course   one shoe   her girdle coming down fantastically
On a clothesline, where it belongs   her blouse on a lightning rod:

220        Lies in the fields   in *this* field   on her broken back as though on
A cloud she cannot drop through   while farmers sleepwalk without
Their women from houses   a walk like falling toward the far waters
Of life   in moonlight   toward the dreamed eternal meaning of
        their farms
225        Toward the flowering of the harvest in their hands   that tragic cost
Feels herself go   go toward   go outward   breathes at last fully
Not   and tries   less   once   tries   tries   AH, GOD—

                                                              *1981*

# Denise Levertov (1923–1997)

Born in Ilford, Essex, in England, Levertov was educated at home until she went briefly to ballet school and then trained to work as a nurse in London during World War II. Her father was a Jew who converted to Christianity and became an Anglican priest; her mother was Welsh. Levertov came to the United States in 1948. Since then, she served briefly as poetry editor for *The Nation*, and taught at several schools, including Stanford. Influenced by the English Romantic poets early on, she increasingly began to be inspired by the open form poetry written by William Carlos Williams and other American poets, including Robert Creeley and Robert Duncan. That aesthetic combined with both a strong mystical bent and a long family tradition of political commitment. Her mother had worked with the League of Nations and on behalf of European refugees. Her father and sister protested Britain's indifference to the Spanish Republic's struggle with fascism. Years later, Levertov would write about nuclear war, compose a series of powerful poems about Vietnam, and, late in her career, address the Gulf War. Among her major achievements, however, is the haunting sequence of elegies to her sister Olga, reprinted here. Placing the Vietnam poems beside the elegies suggests a unifying spirituality, a belief in the sacred character of all life. Taken together, the poems also show Levertov's simultaneous commitment to open forms and careful craft.

## The Ache of Marriage

The ache of marriage:

thigh and tongue, beloved,
are heavy with it,
it throbs in the teeth

5      We look for communion
and are turned away, beloved,
each and each

It is leviathan° and we
in its belly
10      looking for joy, some joy
not to be known outside it

---

8 *leviathan*: in the Old Testament, Jonah is swallowed by a leviathan, or great sea monster.

two by two in the ark° of
the ache of it

*1964*

# Olga Poems

(Olga Levertoff, 1914–1964)

### I

By the gas-fire, kneeling
to undress,
scorching luxuriously, raking
her nails over olive sides, the red
5    waistband ring—

(And the little sister
beady-eyed in the bed—
or drowsy, was I? My head
a camera—)

10   Sixteen. Her breasts
round, round, and
dark-nippled—

who now these two months long
is bones and tatters of flesh in earth.

### II

15   The high pitch of
nagging insistence, lines
creased into raised brows—

Ridden, ridden—
the skin around the nails
20   nibbled sore—

You wanted
to shout the world to its senses,
did you?—to browbeat

the poor into joy's
25   socialist republic—
What rage

and human shame swept you
when you were nine and saw
the Ley Street houses,

---

12 *ark:* in the Book of Genesis, Noah builds an ark, or boat, to save representatives of all species from the oncoming universal flood.

30    grasping their meaning as *slum*.
Where I, reaching that age,
teased you, admiring

architectural probity, circa
eighteen-fifty, and noted
35    pride in the whitened doorsteps.

Black one, black one,
there was a white
candle in your heart.

**III**

*i*

*Everything flows*
40                    she muttered into my childhood,
pacing the trampled grass where human puppets
rehearsed fates that summer,
stung into alien semblances by the lash of her will—
*everything flows*—
45    I looked up from my Littlest Bear's cane armchair
and knew the words came from a book
and felt them alien to me

but linked to words we loved
                    from the hymnbook—*Time*
5-    *like an ever-rolling stream / bears all its sons away*—

*ii*

Now as if smoke or sweetness were blown my way
I inhale a sense of her livingness in that instant,
feeling, dreaming, hoping, knowing boredom and zest like anyone
                            else—
55    a young girl in the garden, the same alchemical square
I grew in, we thought sometimes
too small for our grand destinies—
                      But dread
was in her, a bloodbeat, it was against the rolling dark
60    oncoming river she raised bulwarks, setting herself
to sift cinders after early Mass all of one winter,

labelling her desk's normal disorder, basing
her verses on Keble's *Christian Year*, picking
those endless arguments, pressing on

65    to manipulate lives to disaster . . . To change,
to change the course of the river! What rage for order
disordered her pilgrimage—so that for years at a time

she would hide among strangers, waiting
to rearrange all mysteries in a new light.

*iii*

70      Black one, incubus—
            she appeared
      riding anguish as Tartars ride mares

      over the stubble of bad years.

      In one of the years
75            when I didn't know if she were dead or alive
      I saw her in dream

      haggard and rouged
            lit by the flare
      from an eel- or cockle-stand on a slum street—

80      was it a dream? I had lost

      all sense, almost, of
            who she was, what—inside of her skin,
      under her black hair
                 dyed blonde—

85      it might feel like to be, in the wax and wane of the moon,
      in the life I feel as unfolding, not flowing, the pilgrim years—

## IV

      On your hospital bed you lay
      in love, the hatreds
      that had followed you, a
90      comet's tail, burned out

      as your disasters bred of love
      burned out,
      while pain and drugs
      quarreled like sisters in you—

95      lay afloat on a sea
      of love and pain—how you always
      loved that cadence, 'Underneath
      are the everlasting arms'—

      all history
100    burned out, down
      to the sick bone, save for

      that kind candle.

V

*i*

*In a garden grene whenas I lay—*

you set the words to a tune so plaintive
105    it plucks its way through my life as through a wood.

As through a wood, shadow and light between birches,
gliding a moment in open glades, hidden by thickets of holly

your life winds in me.                    In Valentines
a root protrudes from the greensward several yards from its tree

110    we might raise like a trapdoor's handle, you said,
and descend long steps to another country

where we would live without father or mother
and without longing for the upper world. *The birds
sang sweet, O song, in the midst of the daye,*

115    and we entered silent mid-Essex churches on hot afternoons
and communed with the effigies of knights and their ladies

and their slender dogs asleep at their feet,
the stone so cold—          *In youth*

*is pleasure, in youth is pleasure.*

*ii*

120    Under autumn clouds, under white
wideness of winter skies you went walking
the year you were most alone

returning to the old roads, seeing again
the signposts pointing to Theydon Garnon
125    or Stapleford Abbots or Greensted,

crossing the ploughlands (whose color I named *murple*,
a shade between brown and mauve that we loved
when I was a child and you

not much more than a child) finding new lanes
130    near White Roding or Abbess Roding; or lost in Romford's
new streets where there were footpaths then—

frowning as you ground out your thoughts, breathing deep
of the damp still air, taking
the frost into your mind unflinching.

135    How cold it was in your thin coat, your down-at-heel shoes—
       tearless Niobe, your children were lost to you
       and the stage lights had gone out, even the empty theater

       was locked to you, cavern of transformation where all
       had almost been possible.
                              How many books
140    you read in your silent lodgings that winter,
       how the plovers transpierced your solitude out of doors with their
                                                   strange cries
       I had flung open my arms to in longing, once, by your side
       stumbling over the furrows—

145    Oh, in your torn stockings, with unwaved hair,
       you were trudging after your anguish
       over the bare fields, soberly, soberly.


                              **VI**

       Your eyes were the brown gold of pebbles under water.
       I never crossed the bridge over the Roding, dividing
150    the open field of the present from the mysteries,
       the wraiths and shifts of time-sense Wanstead Park held sus-
             pended,
       without remembering your eyes. Even when we were estranged
       and my own eyes smarted in pain and anger at the thought of you.
       And by other streams in other countries; anywhere where the light
155    reaches down through shallows to gold gravel. Olga's
       brown eyes. One rainy summer, down in the New Forest,
       when we could hardly breathe for ennui and the low sky,
       you turned savagely to the piano and sightread
       straight through all the Beethoven sonatas, day after day—
160    weeks, it seemed to me. I would turn the pages some of the time,
       go out to ride my bike, return—you were enduring in the
       falls and rapids of the music, the arpeggios rang out, the rectory
       trembled, our parents seemed effaced.
       I think of your eyes in that photo, six years before I was born,
165    the fear in them. What did you do with your fear,
       later? Through the years of humiliation,
       of paranoia and blackmail and near-starvation, losing
       the love of those you loved, one after another,
       parents, lovers, children, idolized friends, what kept
170    compassion's candle alight in you, that lit you
       clear into another chapter (but the same book) 'a clearing
       in the selva oscura,
       a house whose door
       swings open, a hand beckons
175    in welcome'?°

---

175 *welcome:* "the quoted lines—'a clearing / in the selva oscura, . . . .'—are an adaption of
some lines in 'Selva Oscura' by the late Louis MacNeice, a poem much loved by my sis-
ter, Olga" (author's note).

I cross
so many brooks in the world, there is so much light
dancing on so many stones, so many questions my eyes
smart to ask of your eyes, gold brown eyes,
180    the lashes short but the lids
arched as if carved out of olivewood, eyes with some vision
of festive goodness in back of their hard, or veiled, or shining,
unknowable gaze. . .

        *1964*

## What Were They Like?

1) Did the people of Vietnam
   use lanterns of stone?
2) Did they hold ceremonies
   to reverence the opening of buds?
5    3) Were they inclined to quiet laughter?
4) Did they use bone and ivory,
   jade and silver, for ornament?
5) Had they an epic poem?
6) Did they distinguish between speech and singing?

10    1) Sir, their light hearts turned to stone.
   It is not remembered whether in gardens
   stone lanterns illumined pleasant ways.
2) Perhaps they gathered once to delight in blossom,
   but after the children were killed
15    there were no more buds.
3) Sir, laughter is bitter to the burned mouth.
4) A dream ago, perhaps. Ornament is for joy.
   All the bones were charred.
5) It is not remembered. Remember,
20    most were peasants; their life
   was in rice and bamboo.
   When peaceful clouds were reflected in the paddies
   and the water buffalo stepped surely along terraces,
   maybe fathers told their sons old tales.
25    When bombs smashed those mirrors
   there was time only to scream.
6) There is an echo yet
   of their speech which was like a song.
   It was reported their singing resembled
30    the flight of moths in moonlight.
   Who can say? It is silent now.

        *1967*

## Life at War

The disasters numb within us
caught in the chest, rolling
in the brain like pebbles. The feeling
resembles lumps of raw dough

5        weighing down a child's stomach on baking day.
         Or Rilke said it, 'My heart . . .
         Could I say of it, it overflows
         with bitterness . . . but no, as though

         its contents were simply balled into
10       formless lumps, thus
         do I carry it about.'
         The same war

         continues.
         We have breathed the grits of it in, all our lives,
15       our lungs are pocked with it,
         the mucous membrane of our dreams
         coated with it, the imagination
         filmed over with the gray filth of it:

         the knowledge that humankind,

20       delicate Man, whose flesh
         responds to a caress, whose eyes
         are flowers that perceive the stars,

         whose music excels the music of birds,
         whose laughter matches the laughter of dogs,
25       whose understanding manifests designs
         fairer than the spider's most intricate web,

         still turns without surprise, with mere regret
         to the scheduled breaking open of breasts whose milk
         runs out over the entrails of still-alive babies,
30       transformation of witnessing eyes to pulp-fragments,
         implosion of skinned penises into carcass-gulleys.

         We are the humans, men who can make;
         whose language imagines *mercy,*
         *lovingkindness;* we have believed one another
35       mirrored forms of a God we felt as good—

         who do these acts, who convince ourselves
         it is necessary; these acts are done
         to our own flesh; burned human flesh
         is smelling in Vietnam as I write.

40       Yes, this is the knowledge that jostles for space
         in our bodies along with all we
         go on knowing of joy, of love;

         our nerve filaments twitch with its presence
         day and night,
45       nothing we say has not the husky phlegm of it in the saying,
         nothing we do has the quickness, the sureness,
         the deep intelligence living at peace would have.

                                                        *1967*

# Anthony Hecht (b. 1923)

Born in New York City and educated at Bard College and Columbia, Hecht served in Europe and Japan in the U.S. Army. He taught for a number of years at the University of Rochester. Hecht has written several books of criticism, including a study of W. H. Auden, and translated both classical and contemporary writers. Often learned and witty in his poetry, he has occasionally taken up difficult subjects, as with the Holocaust poem, "More Light! More Light!"

## A Hill

In Italy, where this sort of thing can occur,
I had a vision once—though you understand
It was nothing at all like Dante's° or the visions of saints,
And perhaps not a vision at all. I was with some friends,
5    Picking my way through a warm sunlit piazza
In the early morning. A clear fretwork of shadows
From huge umbrellas littered the pavement and made
A sort of lucent shallows in which was moored
A small navy of carts. Books, coins, old maps,
10   Cheap landscapes and ugly religious prints
Were all on sale. The colors and noise
Like the flying hands were gestures of exultation,
So that even the bargaining
Rose to the ear like a voluble godliness.
15   And then, when it happened, the noises suddenly stopped,
And it got darker; pushcarts and people dissolved
And even the great Farnese Palace° itself
Was gone, for all its marble; in its place
Was a hill, mole-colored and bare. It was very cold,
20   Close to freezing, with a promise of snow.
The trees were like old ironwork gathered for scrap
Outside a factory wall. There was no wind,
And the only sound for a while was the little click
Of ice as it broke in the mud under my feet.
25   I saw a piece of ribbon snagged on a hedge,

---

3 *Dante:* Dante Alighieri (1265–1321), author of the *Divine Comedy.*
17 *Farnese Palace:* in Rome.

But no other sign of life. And then I heard
What seemed the crack of a rifle. A hunter, I guessed;
At least I was not alone. But just after that
Came the soft and papery crash
30    Of a great branch somewhere unseen falling to earth.

And that was all, except for the cold and silence
That promised to last forever, like the hill.

Then prices came through, and fingers, and I was restored
To the sunlight and my friends. But for more than a week
35    I was scared by the plain bitterness of what I had seen.
All this happened about ten years ago,
And it hasn't troubled me since, but at last, today,
I remembered that hill; it lies just to the left
Of the road north of Poughkeepsie;° and as a boy
I stood before it for hours in wintertime.

*1967*


## "More Light! More Light!"°

for Heinrich Blücher and Hannah Arendt°

Composed in the Tower° before his execution
These moving verses, and being brought at that time
Painfully to the stake, submitted, declaring thus:
"I implore my God to witness that I have made no crime."

5    Nor was he forsaken of courage, but the death was horrible,
The sack of gunpowder failing to ignite.
His legs were blistered sticks on which the black sap
Bubbled and burst as he howled for the Kindly Light.°

And that was but one, and by no means one of the worst;
10    Permitted at least his pitiful dignity;
And such as were by made prayers in the name of Christ,
That shall judge all men, for his soul's tranquillity.

---

39 *Poughkeepsie*: town in New York state.
**poem title:** Purportedly the dying words of German writer Johann Wolfgang von Goethe (1949–1832).
dedication: *Arendt*: (1906–1975) political philosopher who characterized Nazi SS leader Adolf Eichmann with the phrase "the banality of evil." Blücher, a philosophy professor, was her husband.
1 *Tower*: the Tower of London, a palace-fortress whose construction began in the eleventh century. From the fifteenth through the eighteenth centuries it was famous as a prison and place of execution. Hecht has explained that he had no single execution in mind: "the details are conflated from several executions, including Latimer and Ridley [Anglican bishops, for heresy, 1555] whose deaths at the stake are described by Foxe in *Acts and Monuments*. But neither of them wrote poems just before their deaths, as others did."
8 *Kindly Light*: from the nineteenth century hymn "Lead, Kindly Light," which asks for mercy.

We move now to outside a German wood.°
Three men are there commanded to dig a hole
15   In which the two Jews are ordered to lie down
And be buried alive by the third, who is a Pole.

Not light from the shrine at Weimar° beyond the hill
Nor light from heaven appeared. But he did refuse.
A Lüger° settled back deeply in its glove.
20   He was ordered to change places with the Jews.

Much casual death had drained away their souls.
The thick dirt mounted toward the quivering chin.
When only the head was exposed the order came
To dig him out again and to get back in.

25   No light, no light in the blue Polish eye.
When he finished a riding boot packed down the earth.
The Lüger hovered lightly in its glove.
He was shot in the belly and in three hours bled to death.

No prayers or incense rose up in those hours
30   Which grew to be years, and every day came mute
Ghosts from the ovens, sifting through crisp air,
And settled upon his eyes in a black soot.

                           *1967*

---

13 *a German wood*: near Buchenwald, the Nazi concentration camp. These 1944 events are
detailed in *The Theory and Practice of Hell* (1958) by Eugen Kogon.
17 *shrine at Weimar*: the city where Goethe lived for some years.
19 *Lüger*: German military pistol.

# Bob Kaufman (1925–1986)

The introduction to Kaufman's selected poems tells us that he was born in New Orleans; his father, who was half African American and half Jewish, worked as a Pullman porter for the railroad that ran between New Orleans and Chicago. His mother, a black woman from an old Martinique family, the Vignes, was a schoolteacher. "His Jewish surname and Creole-like features," the introduction notes, "were shared with twelve brothers and sisters . . . Up until his death from emphysema in January of 1986, Kaufman was known as a mostly silent, wiry black man who walked the streets of San Francisco's North Beach district day and night, often appearing as a mendicant, madman, or panhandler. Yet various schools of American poetry have sung his praises." His working life began at sea; he was a cabin boy on the *Henry Gibbons*. Based in New York and San Francisco, he worked on Henry Wallace's 1948 Progressive Party presidential campaign, during which he was arrested and thrown into jail; early on he connected with the Beat poets and became one of the notable figures of the movement. At the end of the 1950s, City Lights Books issued three of his broadsides, including the widely read "Abominist Manifesto," whose fourteen points include these:

IN TIMES OF NATIONAL PERIL, ABOMINISTS, AS REALITY AMERICANS, STAND READY TO DRINK THEMSELVES TO DEATH FOR THEIR COUNTRY.

ABOMINIST POETS, CONFIDENT THAT THE NEW LITERARY FORM "FOOT-PRINTISM" HAS FREED THE ARTIST OF OUT-MODED RESTRICTIONS, SUCH AS: THE ABILITY TO READ AND WRITE, OR THE DESIRE TO COMMUNICATE, MUST BE PREPARED TO READ THEIR WORK AT DENTAL COLLEGES, EM-BALMING SCHOOLS, HOMES FOR UNWED MOTHERS, IN-SANE ASYLUMS, USO CANTEENS, KINDERGARTENS, AND COUNTY JAILS. ABOMINISTS NEVER COMPROMISE THEIR RE-JECTIONARY PHILOSOPHY.

Kaufman would declaim his poems and manifestoes at poetry readings and in other public places; often enough the police would arrest him. Eventually, he began to drink under the strain; back in New York he was arrested and given shock treatments against his will. After President Kennedy was shot, Kaufman took a vow of silence, maintaining it for a decade. Then he began writing again; the poems were rescued from a hotel fire by a friend and published as Kaufman's third book in 1981. By the end, he had been a Beat poet, a surrealist, a sound poet, a jazz poet, and a poet of black consciousness.

## The Biggest Fisherman

singular prints filed along damp banks,
supposed evidence of fouled strings, all,

breached dikes of teeth hewn agate statues
scaly echoes in eroded huts of slate and gristle.

5     mildewed toes of pastoral escapes, mossy charades,
cane towered blind, smooth blister on watern neck

angry glowing fish in eniwetok garments and pig tusks
alarmed horror of black croakers, finned hawks sinking.

collectors of fish teeth and souls of night vision demons
10    taxidermy fiesta of revolutionary aquatic holidays lost.

breeding hills of happy men, of no particular bent, or none,
condemned to undreamlike beauty of day to day to day to day,
deprived of night, ribbon bright streams die parched deaths
baked by fissioning waves of newly glowing fish.

*1967*

## Crootey Songo

DERRAT SLEGELATIONS, FLO GOOF BABER,
SCRASH SHO DUBIES, WAGO WAILO WAILO.
GEED BOP NAVA GLIED, NAVA GLIED NAVA,
SPLEERIEDER, HUYEDIST, HEDACAZ, AX—, O, O.

5    DEEREDITION, BOOMEDITION, SQUOM, SQUOM, SQUOM.
DEE BEETSTRAWIST, WAPAGO, LOCOEST, LOCORO, LO.
VOOMETEYEREEPETIOP, BOP, BOP, BOP, WHIPOLAT.

DEGET, SKLOKO, KURRITIF, PLOG, MANGI, PLOG MANGI,
CLOPO JAGO BREE, BREE, ASLOOPERED, AKINGO LABY.
ENGPOP, ENGPOP, BOP, PLOLO, PLOLO, BOP, BOP.

*1967*

## No More Jazz at Alacatraz°

No more jazz
At Alcatraz
No more piano
for Lucky Luciano
5    No more trombone

---

**poem title:** *Alcatraz:* an island in California's San Francisco Bay, it served as an American military prison from 1859 to 1934 and a maximum security federal prison thereafter, until it closed in 1963. Luciano (1897–1962), Capone (1899–1947), and Costello (1891–1973) were all organized crime figures, and Alcatraz inmates.

for Al Capone
No more jazz
at Alcatraz
No more cello
10          for Frank Costello
No more screeching of the
Seagulls
As they line up for
Chow
15          No more jazz
At Alcatraz

*c. 1963*

# Maxine Kumin (b. 1925)

Kumin was born Maxine Winokur of Jewish parents in Philadelphia. She was educated at Radcliffe. She has written poetry, criticism, fiction, and more than twenty children's books, including four coauthored with Anne Sexton. She has taught at Tufts, the University of Massachusetts, and Princeton. Kumin spends much of her time in rural New Hampshire, where she raises horses. Although she has often written about middle-class suburban experience, seeking survival and continuity in the vestiges of nature it encompasses, she has also made harsh and witty appraisals of rural life. Her sharp irony, her New England settings, and her use of traditional forms make comparison with Frost both inevitable and reasonable. The easy linking of her with transcendentalism is less warranted, in part because Kumin rarely seeks lyrical transcendence of any kind, preferring stoical observation instead. She has also written sympathetically about women's lives and taken on public topics like famine, pollution, and nuclear war. See her *Selected Poems 1960–1990* (1997).

## Voices from Kansas

The women of Wichita say they live in what
is casually known on both coasts as a flyover state.
The prairie wind here is constant in every season.
Sometimes it makes the sucking sound of ocean.
5    Sometimes it moans like an animal in heat.

In April, deliberate fires blacken great swatches
of cropland. Scarves of smoke darken the day
devouring briars and thistles and climbing vetches
before seedtime. Tractors draw threads to the edge of sky.
10    You learn to pull out and pass, say the Wichita women

whom distance has not flattened, who cruise at a cool
80 miles per hour toward the rolling-pin horizon
where oncoming headlights are visible more than a mile
away. Long hours at a stretch behind the wheel
15    they zoom up to Michigan to speak at a conference,

revisit a lover, drop in on old friends.
They will not be sequestered by space. Jo-El,
descended from Socialists, is saving the farm—
labor songs of her forebears, accompanied by dulcimer.
20    Lynn collects early photos of sodhouse homesteaders.

Mary Anne has got a sad history in her arms.
She is reconstructing her orphaned grandfather
in his sea of sheep, white blobs overspreading the plains,
his whole Scottish clan, ten siblings carried off together
25     in December of 1918 by a wildfire flu.
This tear-stained boy in the woolly fold, custodian
of his flock and her life, shines piercingly through.
As the grassland is rooted, so too are the Wichita women.
No absence among them may go unmarked into sleep.
Like wind in the wheat, the boundary blurs but keeps.

*1992*


# Saga

## 1. Life Style

Invincible begetters, assorted Scutzes
have always lived hereabouts in the woods
trapping beaver or fox, poaching enough
deer to get by on. Winters, they barricade
5     their groundsills with spoiled hay, which can ignite
from a careless cigarette or chimney spark.
In the fifties, one family barely got out
when the place lit up like the Fair midway at dark.

The singular name of Scutz, it is thought, derives
10     from *skuft*, Middle Dutch for the nape one is strung up by.
Hangmen or hanged, they led the same snug lives
in an Old World loft adjoining the pigsty
as now, three generations tucked in two
rooms with color tv, in the New.

## 2. Leisure

15     The seldom-traveled dirt road by their door
is where, good days, the Scutzes take their ease.
It serves as living room, garage, *pissoir*
as well as barnyard. Hens scratch and rabbits doze
under cars jacked up on stumps of trees.

20     Someone produces a dozen bottles of beer.
Someone tacks a target to a tire
across the road and hoists it seductively
human-high. The Scutzes love to shoot.
Later, they line the empty bottles up.

25     The music of glassbreak gladdens them. The brute
sound of a bullet widening a rip
in rubber, the rifle kick, the powder smell
pure bliss. Deadeyes, the Scutzes lightly kill.

### 3. SHELTER

Old doors slanted over packing crates
30    shelter the Scutzes' several frantic dogs
pinioned on six-foot chains they haven't been
loosed from since January of '91
when someone on skis crept up in snow fog
and undid all of their catches in the night.

35    Each of the Scutzes' dogs has a dish or plate
to eat from, usually overturned in the dirt.
What do they do for water? Pray for rain.
What do they do for warmth? Remember when
they lay in the litter together, a sweet
40    jumble of laundry, spotted and stained.

O we are smug in the face of the Scutzes, we
who stroll past their domain, its aromas of ripe decay,
its casual discards mottled with smut and pee.
What do we neighbors do? Look the other way.

### 4. SELF-FULFILLING PROPHECY

45    If Lonnie Scutz comes back, he's guaranteed
free room and board in the State's crowbar hotel.
His girlfriend Grace, a toddler at her heels
and in her arms a grubby ten-month jewel,
looks to be pregnant again, but not his seed.
50    It's rumored this one was sired by his dad.

Towheads with skyblue eyes, they'll go to school
now and then, struggle to learn to read
and write, forget to carry when they add,
be mocked, kept back or made to play the fool
55    and soon enough drop out. Their nimble code,
*hit first or get hit,* supplants the Golden Rule.

It all works out the way we knew it would.
They'll come to no good end, the Scutzes' kids.

1992

# Paul Blackburn (1926–1971)

Blackburn was born in St. Albans, Vermont. His parents separated when he was three, and he grew up with his mother's parents until his mother took him to New York's Greenwich Village when he was fourteen. After a stint in the Army, he enrolled at New York University, but then transferred to the University of Wisconsin, where he started a correspondence with Ezra Pound, who was then incarcerated at St. Elizabeth's Hospital in Washington, and who encouraged Blackburn's poetry writing. In New York, Blackburn pursued an interest in Provençal troubadour poets, translating them into English. By the late 1950s, Blackburn was becoming known as a poet of city life, with poems that were both witty and observant about New York in particular. But he was also active in the antiwar and civil rights movements and regularly wrote poems about those issues as well. Meanwhile he was supporting himself with editing and translating jobs. All along he had also written culturally and epistemologically reflective poems about his travels abroad. "At the Well" is a strikingly contemporary and wittily challenging poem about otherness and colonialism. Blackburn died at age 44 from cancer of the esophagus.

## At the Well

Here we are, see?
in this village, maybe a camp
middle of desert, the
Maghreb, desert below Marrakesh°
5  standing in the street
simply.

    Outskirts of the camp
    at the edge of town, these riders
    on camels or horses,
10   but riders, tribesmen, sitting
    there on their horses.

        They are mute. They are
        hirsute, they are not
        able to speak. If they
15       could the sound would be gutteral.

---

4 *Marrakesh*: North African city in Morocco.

They cannot speak. They want
something.

I nor
you know what they want   .   They want
20  nothing.   They are beyond want.   They need
nothing.   They used to be slaves.   They
want something of us / of me / what
shall I say to them.

They have had their tongues cut out.
25  I have nothing to give them   ¿There is no
grace at the edge of my heart I would grant,
render them?   They want something, they
sit there on their horses.   Are there
children in the village I can give them.

30                                    My child's heart? Is it goods they want
                                     as tribute. They have had their tongues
                                     cut out. Can I offer them some sound
                                     my mouth makes in the night? Can I
                                     say they are brave, fierce, im-
35                                   placable? that I would like to
                                     join them?

          L e t   u s   g o   t o g e t h e r

across the desert toward the
cities, let us
40  terrify the towns, the villages,
disappear among bazaars, sell our
camels, pierce our ears, for-
get that we are mute and drive
the princes out, take all the
45  slave-girls for ourselves?
What can I offer them.

          They have appeared here on the edge of my soul.
          I ask them what they want, they say
          —You are our leader.   Tell us what
50        your pleasure is, we
          want you.   They
          say nothing.   They

          are mute.   they are hirsute.   They
          are the fathers I never had.   They are
55        tribesmen standing on the edge of town near
          water, near the soul I must look into each
          morning   .   myself.

                    Who are these wild men?
                    I scream:
60                  —I want my gods!

                              I want my goods! I want
                   my reflection in the sun's pool at morning,
                      shade in the afternoon under the
                           date palms, I want and want!

65      What can I give them.
        What tribe of nomads and wanderers am I continuation of, what
        can I give my fathers?
        What can I offer myself?

                                   I want to see my own skin
70                                 at the life's edge, at the
                                   life-giving water.   I want
                                   to rise from the pool,
                                   mount my camel and
                   be among the living, the other side of this village.

75      Come gentlemen,
        wheel your mounts about.
        There is nothing here .

                                                        *1963/1970*

# Frank O'Hara (1926–1966)

Born in Baltimore, Maryland, and raised in Grafton, Massachusetts, O'Hara served in the U.S. Navy in the South Pacific from 1944–1946. He was educated at Harvard and the University of Michigan, after which he served as associate curator at New York's Museum of Modern Art. He was also editor of *Art News*. Like John Ashbery, a friend and member of what came to be known as the New York School of poets, O'Hara mixes high and low cultural allusions with a certain effortless glee; he also manages abrupt shifts of tone that mimic the erratic, associational paths of a consciousness stimulated by external events and images. The poems skate easily over surfaces, light on objects, absorb variations in mood, and register the cultural and political temper of the times with a grace that makes them immensely pleasurable, but an oblique sense of tragedy also gives them a haunting gravity. As with the painters he admired, O'Hara's poems are also chronicles of the process of their composition. He was often casual about his output, sometimes not even keeping copies of his poems; O'Hara's work survives today in part because he sent poems to friends that were later collected posthumously. Widely imitated, his voice remains exceptional. He was accidentally run over and killed by a jeep on New York's Fire Island.

## Poem

The eager note on my door said "Call me,
call when you get in!" so I quickly threw
a few tangerines into my overnight bag,
straightened my eyelids and shoulders, and

5      headed straight for the door. It was autumn
by the time I got around the corner, oh all
unwilling to be either pertinent or bemused, but
the leaves were brighter than grass on the sidewalk!

Funny, I thought, that the lights are on this late
10    and the hall door open; still up at this hour, a
champion jai-alai player like himself? Oh fie!
for shame! What a host, so zealous! And he was

there in the hall, flat on a sheet of blood that
ran down the stairs. I did appreciate it. There are few
15    hosts who so thoroughly prepare to greet a guest
only casually invited, and that several months ago.

*1950*

# Today

Oh! kangaroos, sequins, chocolate sodas!
You really are beautiful! Pearls,
harmonicas, jujubes, aspirins! all
5     the stuff they've always talked about

still makes a poem a surprise!
These things are with us every day
even on beachheads and biers. They
do have meaning. They're strong as rocks.

                                            *1950*

# A Step Away From Them

It's my lunch hour, so I go
for a walk among the hum-colored
cabs. First, down the sidewalk
where laborers feed their dirty
5     glistening torsos sandwiches
and Coca-Cola, with yellow helmets
on. They protect them from falling
bricks, I guess. Then onto the
avenue where skirts are flipping
10    above heels and blow up over
grates. The sun is hot, but the
cabs stir up the air. I look
at bargains in wristwatches. There
are cats playing in sawdust.
15                     On
to Times Square, where the sign
blows smoke over my head,° and higher
the waterfall pours lightly. A
Negro stands in a doorway with a
20    toothpick, languorously agitating.
A blonde chorus girl clicks: he
smiles and rubs his chin. Everything
suddenly honks: it is 12:40 of
a Thursday.
25            Neon in daylight is a
great pleasure, as Edwin Denby° would
write, as are light bulbs in daylight.
I stop for a cheeseburger at JULIET'S
CORNER. Giulietta Masina, wife of
30    Federico Fellini, *è bell' attrice.*°
And chocolate malted. A lady in
foxes on such a day puts her poodle
in a cab.

---

17 *head*: an adverising billboard in Times Square that puffs steam to simulate cigarette
smoke.
26 *Denby*: American poet (b. 1923).
30 . . . *attrice*: (Italian) "a beautiful actress." Fellini is a major Italian film director.

There are several Puerto
35    Ricans on the avenue today, which
makes it beautiful and warm. First
Bunny died, then John Latouche,
then Jackson Pollock°. But is the
earth as full as life was full, of them?
40    And one has eaten and one walks,
past the magazines with nudes
and the posters for BULLFIGHT and
the Manhattan Storage Warehouse,
which they'll soon tear down. I
45    used to think they had the Armory
Show° there.

> A glass of papaya juice
and back to work. My heart is in my
pocket, it is Poems by Pierre Reverdy.°

*1956*

# The Day Lady Died°

It is 12:20 in New York a Friday
three days after Bastille day,° yes
it is 1959 and I go get a shoeshine
because I will get off the 4:19 in Easthampton°
5    at 7:15 and then go straight to dinner
and I don't know the people who will feed me

I walk up the muggy street beginning to sun
and have a hamburger and a malted and buy
an ugly NEW WORLD WRITING to see what the poets
10    in Ghana are doing these days

> I go on to the bank
and Miss Stillwagon (first name Linda I once heard)
doesn't even look up my balance for once in her life
and in the GOLDEN GRIFFIN° I get a little Verlaine°

---

38 *Pollock:* Bunny (V.R. Lang, 1924–1956) a poet who directed The Poet's Theater in Cambridge, Massachusetts, and produced O'Hara's plays; Latouche (1917–1956) wrote lyrics for musicals; Pollock (1912–1956) famed founder of "action painting." All three were O'Hara's friends.

46 *Armory Show:* the famous 1913 show that introduced modern art to American audiences.

49 *Reverdy:* (1899–1960), French poet whose work O'Hara admired.

**poem title:** The poem honors the great blues and jazz singer, Billie Holiday (1915–1959); the title inverts her nickname, "Lady Day," to announce its occasion.

2 *Bastille day:* July 14, French Independence day, celebrating the 1789 storming of the Bastille prison.

4 *Easthampton:* a town on Long Island's south shore, Long Island being east of Manhattan. The 4:19 is a scheduled train on the Long Island Railroad. Easthampton is near Southhampton, where O'Hara is heading for dinner. At the time the poem refers to, the Hamptons were still farming communities and reasonably priced places for New York City expatriates to live.

14 *Golden Griffin:* avant-garde New York bookstore.

14 *Verlaine:* Paul Verlaine (1844–1896), French poet.

15       for Patsy° with drawings by Bonnard° although I do
think of Hesiod, trans. Richard Lattimore° or
Brendan Behan's° new play or *Le Balcon* or *Les Nègres*
of Genet,° but I don't, I stick with Verlaine
after practically going to sleep with quandariness

20       and for Mike I just stroll into the PARK LANE
Liquor Store and ask for a bottle of Strega and
then I go back where I came from to 6th Avenue
and the tobacconist in the Ziegfeld Theatre and
casually ask for a carton of Gauloises and a carton
25       of Picayunes,° and a NEW YORK POST with her face on it

       and I am sweating a lot by now and thinking of
leaning on the john door in the 5 SPOT
while she whispered a song along the keyboard
to Mal Waldron° and everyone and I stopped breathing

                              *1959*

## Why I Am Not a Painter

I am not a painter, I am a poet.
Why? I think I would rather be
a painter, but I am not. Well,

for instance, Mike Goldberg°
5       is starting a painting. I drop in.
"Sit down and have a drink" he
says. I drink; we drink. I look
up. "You have SARDINES in it."
"Yes, it needed something there."
10      "Oh." I go and the days go by
and I drop in again. The painting
is going on, and I go, and the days
go by. I drop in. The painting is
finished. "Where's SARDINES?"
15      All that's left is just
letters, "It was too much," Mike says.

---

15 *Bonnard:* Pierre Bonnard (1867–1947), a post-Impressionist French painter who illustrated Verlaine's *Parallelement* in 1902.

15 *Patsy:* Patsy Southgate and Mike Goldberg, a painter, lived in Southhampton and were O'Hara's dinner companions.

16 *Richard Lattimore:* published his translation of Greek poet Hesiod (c. 800 B.C.–c. 700 B.C.) in 1959.

17 *Brendan Behan:* (1923–1964), Irish playwright, whose 1958 play was *The Hostage.*

18 *Genet:* Jean Genet (1910–1968), French writer whose plays *Le Balcon* (The Balcony) and *Les Nègres* (The Blacks) were staged to much debate in the 1950s.

25 *Gauloises and Picayunes:* two brands of French cigarettes.

29 *Mal Waldron:* (b. 1924), Billie Holiday's pianist.

4 *Goldberg:* (b. 1924), a painter with whom O'Hara collaborated. His silk-screen prints illustrate O'Hara's 1960 *Odes.*

But me? One day I am thinking of
a color: orange. I write a line
about orange. Pretty soon it is a
20      whole page of words, not lines.
Then another page. There should be
so much more, not of orange, of
words, of how terrible orange is
and life. Days go by. It is even in
25      prose, I am a real poet. My poem
is finished and I haven't mentioned
orange yet. It's twelve poems, I call
it ORANGES. And one day in a gallery
I see Mike's painting, called SARDINES.

1957

## A True Account of Talking to the Sun at Fire Island

The Sun woke me this morning loud
and clear, saying "Hey! I've been
trying to wake you up for fifteen
minutes. Don't be so rude, you are
5       only the second poet I've ever chosen
to speak to personally
                        so why
aren't you more attentive? If I could
burn you through the window I would
10      to wake you up. I can't hang around
here all day."
                "Sorry, Sun, I stayed
up late last night talking to Hal."

"When I woke up Mayakovsky he was
15      a lot more prompt" the Sun said
petulantly. "Most people are up
already waiting to see if I'm going
to put in an appearance."
                        I tried
20      to apologize "I missed you yesterday."
"That's better" he said. "I didn't
know you'd come out." "You may be
wondering why I've come so close?"
"Yes" I said beginning to feel hot
25      wondering if maybe he wasn't burning me
anyway.
                "Frankly I wanted to tell you
I like your poetry. I see a lot

---

14 *Mayakovsky:* Vladimir Mayakofsky (1893–1930), one of the major Russian poets of the
century. O'Hara's poem is inspired by Mayakofsky's poem "An Extraordinary Adventure
Which Befell Vladimir Mayakofsky in a Summer Cottage" (1920), which is also constructed
as a dialogue between the speaker and the sun. Mayakofsky had considerable influence
on O'Hara's style.

on my rounds and you're okay. [You may
30     not be the greatest thing on earth, but
       you're different] Now, I've heard some
       say you're crazy, they being excessively
       calm themselves to my mind, and other
       crazy poets think that you're a boring
35     reactionary. Not me.
                           Just keep on
       like I do and pay no attention. You'll
       find that people always will complain
       about the atmosphere, either too hot
40     or too cold too bright or too dark, days
       too short or too long.

                           If you don't appear
       at all one day they think you're lazy
       or dead. Just keep right on, I like it.

45     And don't worry about your lineage
       poetic or natural. The Sun shines on
       the jungle, you know, on the tundra
       the sea, the ghetto. Wherever you were
       I knew it and saw you moving. I was waiting
50     for you to get to work.

                           And now that you
       are making your own days, so to speak,
       even if no one reads you but me
       you won't be depressed. Not
55     everyone can look up, even at me. It
       hurts their eyes."
                           "Oh Sun, I'm so grateful to you!"

       "Thanks and remember I'm watching. It's
       easier for me to speak to you out
60     here. I don't have to slide down
       between buildings to get your ear.
       I know you love Manhattan, but
       you ought to look up more often.
                                        And
65     always embrace things, people earth
       sky stars, as I do, freely and with
       the appropriate sense of space. That
       is your inclination, known in the heavens
       and you should follow it to hell, if
70     necessary, which I doubt.
                           Maybe we'll
       speak again in Africa, of which I too
       am specially fond. Go back to sleep now
       Frank, and I may leave a tiny poem
75     in that brain of yours as my farewell."

"Sun, don't go!" I was awake
at last. "No, go I must, they're calling
me."
      "Who are they?"
80                     Rising he said "Some
day you'll know. They're calling to you
too." Darkly he rose, and then I slept.

                         *1958*

# On Seeing Larry Rivers'
## *Washington Crossing the Delaware*
## At the Museum of Modern Art°

Now that our hero has come back to us
in his white pants and we know his nose
trembling like a flag under fire,
we see the calm cold river is supporting
5      our forces, the beautiful history.

To be more revolutionary than a nun
is our desire, to be secular and intimate
as, when sighting a redcoat, you smile
and pull the trigger. Anxieties
10     and animosities, flaming and feeding

on theoretical considerations and
the jealous spiritualities of the abstract,
the robot? they're smoke, billows above
the physical event. They have burned up.
15     See how free we are! as a nation of persons.

Dear father of our country, so alive
you must have lied incessantly to be
immediate, here are your bones crossed
on my breast like a rusty flintlock,
20     a pirate's flag, bravely specific

and ever so light in the misty glare
of a crossing by water in winter to a shore
other than that the bridge reaches for.
Don't shoot until, the white of freedom glinting
25     on your gun barrel, you see the general fear.

                         *1955*

---

**poem title:** Rivers (b. 1923) is an American artist who was born in New York. *Washington Crossing the Delaware* (1953) is the first of a series of ironic paintings about American history. An abstract expressionist as well as a predecessor of pop art, his paintings of the early 1950s often combine rigorous drawing with overlays of thin washes, giving them a fragmented appearance.

## Thinking of James Dean

Like a nickelodeon soaring over the island from sea to bay,
two pots of gold, and the flushed effulgence of a sky Tiepolo
and Turner had compiled in vistavision. Each panoramic second, of
his death. The rainbows canceling each other out, between martinis

5　and the steak. To bed to dream, the moon invisibly scudding
under black-blue clouds, a stern Puritanical breeze pushing at
the house, to dream of roaches nibbling at my racing toenails,
great-necked speckled geese and slapping their proud heads

as I ran past. Morning. The first plunge in dolorous surf
10　and the brilliant sunlight declaring all the qualities of the world.
Like an ant, dragging its sorrows up and down the sand to find
a hiding place never, here where everything is guarded by dunes

or drifting. The sea is dark and smells of fish beneath its
silver surface. To reach the depths and rise, only in the sea;
15　the abysses of life, incessantly plunging not to rise to a face
of heat and joy again; habits of total immersion and the stance

victorious in death. And after hours of lying in nature, to nature,
and simulated death in the crushing waves, their shells and heart
pounding me naked on the shingle: had I died at twenty-four as he,
　　　but
20　in Boston, robbed of these suns and knowledges, a corpse more
　　　whole,

less deeply torn, less bruised and less alive, perhaps backstage
at the Brattle Theatre amidst the cold cream and the familiar lice
in my red-gold costume for a bit in *Julius Caesar*, would I be
smaller now in the vastness of light? a cork in the monumental

25　stillness of an eye-green trough, a sliver on the bleaching beach
to airplanes carried by the panting clouds to Spain. My friends
are roaming or listening to *La Bohème*. Precisely, the cold last
　　　swim
before the city flatters meanings of my life I cannot find,

squeezing me like an orange for some nebulous vitality, mourning
30　to the fruit ignorant of science in its hasty dying, kissing
its leaves and stem, exuding oils of Florida in the final glass of
pleasure. A leaving word in the sand, odor of tides: his name.

*1955*

# James Merrill (1926–1995)

Born and raised in New York City, Merrill was the child of a founder of America's most famous brokerage firm. He was educated at Amherst College, a stay interrupted by a year's service in the U.S. infantry at the end of World War II. Thereafter he divided his time between Connecticut, Florida, and Greece, and devoted himself to a highly successful literary career. His poetry is poised, self-conscious, elegant, and witty; its manner owes perhaps as much to the stylistic polish of Proust's and James' fiction as to other poets. Thus it combines exacting attention to daily life with intricate literary allusiveness. At times, his irony almost masks the philosophical ambitions of texts like "Lost in Translation," but the poem nonetheless mounts a powerful reflection on the relations among history, memory, subjectivity, and experience. Merrill's earliest poems were so elegantly crafted and so preoccupied with transcendence that he acquired a reputation as a narrow aesthete, but he began to develop a more relaxed, conversational style in the early 1960s, eventually proving himself capable of taking up subjects like shopping malls and alcoholics' recovery programs that few aesthetes would risk. His book-length poetic epic *The Changing Light at Sandover* (1977–1982) is widely considered his masterpiece, though he produced supremely confident poetry in a wide variety of forms and meters. He also wrote novels and plays, and an especially beautiful memoir, *A Different Person* (1993).

## An Urban Convalescence

> Out for a walk, after a week in bed,
> I find them tearing up part of my block
> And, chilled through, dazed and lonely, join the dozen
> In meek attitudes, watching a huge crane
> 5    Fumble luxuriously in the filth of years.
> Her jaws dribble rubble. An old man
> Laughs and curses in her brain,
> Bringing to mind the close of *The White Goddess.*°
>
> As usual in New York, everything is torn down
> 10    Before you have had time to care for it.
> Head bowed, at the shrine of noise, let me try to recall

---

8 *White Goddess:* (1948) book by British poet and critic Robert Graves; he argues that poetry has its inspirational goddess whose symbol is a crane, hence the pun on the mechanical crane above.

What building stood here. Was there a building at all?
I have lived on this same street for a decade.

Wait. Yes, Vaguely a presence rises
15 Some five floors high, of shabby stone
—Or am I confusing it with another one
In another part of town, or of the world?—
And over its lintel into focus vaguely
Misted with blood (my eyes are shut)
20 A single garland sways, stone fruit, stone leaves,
Which years of grit had etched until it thrust
Roots down, even into the poor soil of my seeing.
When did the garland become part of me?
I ask myself, amused almost,
25 Then shiver once from head to toe,

Transfixed by a particular cheap engraving of garlands
Bought for a few francs long ago,
All calligraphic tendril and cross-hatched rondure,
Ten years ago, and crumpled up to stanch
30 Boughs dripping, whose white gestures filled a cab,
And thought of neither then nor since.
Also, to clasp them, the small, red-nailed hand
Of no one I can place. Wait. No. Her name, her features
Lie toppled underneath that year's fashions.
35 The words she must have spoken, setting her face
To fluttering like a veil, I cannot hear now,
Let alone understand.

So that I am already on the stair,
As it were, of where I lived,
40 When the whole structure shudders at my tread
And soundlessly collapses, filling
The air with motes of stone.
Onto the still erect building next door
Are pressed levels and hues—
45 Pocked rose, streaked greens, brown whites.
Who drained the pousse-café?°
Wires and pipes, snapped off at the roots, quiver.

Well, that is what life does. I stare
A moment longer, so. And presently
50 The massive volume of the world
Closes again.

Upon that book I swear
To abide by what it teaches:
Gospels of ugliness and waste,
55 Of towering voids, of soiled gusts,
Of a shrieking to be faced
Full into, eyes astream with cold—

---

46 *pousse-café:* after-dinner drink.

With cold?
All right then. With self-knowledge.

60   Indoors at last, the pages of *Time* are apt
To open, and the illustrated mayor of New York,
Given a glimpse of how and where I work,
To note yet one more house that can be scrapped.

Unwillingly I picture
65   My walls weathering in the general view.
It is not even as though the new
Buildings did very much for architecture.

Suppose they did. The sickness of our time requires
That these as well be blasted in their prime.
70   You would think the simple fact of having lasted
Threatened our cities like mysterious fires.

There are certain phrases which to use in a poem
Is like rubbing silver with quicksilver. Bright
But facile, the glamour deadens overnight.
75   For instance, how "the sickness of our time"

Enhances, then debases, what I feel.
At my desk I swallow in a glass of water
No longer cordial, scarcely wet, a pill
They had told me not to take until much later.

80   With the result that back into my imagination
The city glides, like cities seen from the air,
Mere smoke and sparkle to the passenger
Having in mind another destination

Which now is not that honey-slow descent
85   Of the Champs-Elysées,° her hand in his,
But the dull need to make some kind of house
Out of the life lived, out of the love spent.

*1962*

## The Broken Home°

Crossing the street,
I saw the parents and the child
At their window, gleaming like fruit
With evening's mild gold leaf.

---

85 *Champs-Elysées:* famous Paris boulevard.
**poem title:** About the marital breakup of Merrill's parents; the poem is also constructed
of sonnets, a formal home for poetic tradition, which are sometimes broken into uncon-
ventional units or rhymes.

5       In a room on the floor below,
        Sunless, cooler—a brimming
        Saucer of wax, marbly and dim—
        I have lit what's left of my life.

        I have thrown out yesterday's milk
10      And opened a book of maxims.
        The flame quickens. The word stirs.

        Tell me, tongue of fire,
        That you and I are as real
        At least as the people upstairs.


15      My father,° who had flown in World War I,
        Might have continued to invest his life
        In cloud banks well above Wall Street and wife.
        But the race was run below, and the point was to win.

        Too late now, I make out in his blue gaze
20      (Through the smoked glass of being thirty-six)
        The soul eclipsed by twin black pupils, sex
        And business; time was money in those days.

        Each thirteenth year he married. When he died
        There were already several chilled wives
25      In sable orbit—rings, cars, permanent waves.
        We'd felt him warming up for a green bride.

        He could afford it. He was "in his prime"
        At three score ten. But money was not time.


        When my parents were younger this was a popular act:
30      A veiled woman would leap from an electric, wine-dark car
        To the steps of no matter what—the Senate or the Ritz Bar—
        And bodily, at newsreel speed, attack

        No matter whom—Al Smith or José Maria Sert
        Or Clemenceau°—veins standing out on her throat
35      As she yelled *War mongerer! Pig! Give us the vote!*,
        And would have to be hauled away in her hobble skirt.°

        What had the man done? Oh, made history.
        Her business (he had implied) was giving birth,
        Tending the house, mending the socks.

---

15 *father:* Merrill's father, Charles E. Merrill, founded the brokerage firm now known as
Merrill, Lynch, Pierce, Fenner, and Smith.
34 *Clemenceau:* Alfred E. Smith (1873–1944), four times governor of New York and in 1928
the unsuccessful Democratic presidential candidate; Sert (1876–1945), the Spanish painter
who decorated the lobby of New York City's Waldorf Astoria Hotel in 1930; Georges
Clemenceau (1841–1929), premier of France during World War I.
36 *hobble skirt:* skirt fitting tightly below the knee.

40 Always that same old story—
 Father Time and Mother Earth,°
 A marriage on the rocks.


 One afternoon, red, satyr-thighed°
 Michael, the Irish setter, head
45 Passionately lowered, led
 The child I was to a shut door. Inside,

 Blinds beat sun from the bed.
 The green-gold room throbbed like a bruise.
 Under a sheet, clad in taboos
50 Lay whom we sought, her hair undone, outspread,

 And of a blackness found, if ever now, in old
 Engravings where the acid bit.
 I must have needed to touch it
 Or the whiteness—was she dead?
55 Her eyes flew open, startled strange and cold.
 The dog slumped to the floor. She reached for me. I fled.


 Tonight they have stepped out onto the gravel.
 The party is over. It's the fall
 Of 1931. They love each other still.

60 She: Charlie, I can't stand the pace.
 He: Come on, honey—why, you'll bury us all!

 A lead soldier guards my windowsill:
 Khaki rifle, uniform, and face.
 Something in me grows heavy, silvery, pliable.

65 How intensely people used to feel!
 Like metal poured at the close of a proletarian novel,°
 Refined and glowing from the crucible,
 I see those two hearts, I'm afraid,
 Still. Cool here in the graveyard of good and evil,
70 They are even so to be honored and obeyed.


  . . . Obeyed, at least, inversely. Thus
 I rarely buy a newspaper, or vote.
 To do so, I have learned, is to invite
 The tread of a stone guest° within my house.

---

41 *Father Time and Mother Earth*: according to Greek myth, the supreme god Cronus and
the supreme goddess, Gaea, overthrown by their son, Zeus.
43 *satyr-thighed*: lustful; satyrs are goat-legged woodland deities of Greek myth.
66 *proletarian novel*: novels, especially during the 1930s, that offered political and social
analyses of work; here, about iron and steel production.
74 *stone guest*: in the play *The Stone Feast* by French dramatist Molière (1622–1673), a stone
statue representing the commander of Seville carries his murderer Don Juan into hell; in
the opera *Don Giovanni* (1787), by the Austrian composer Wolfgang Amadeus Mozart
(1756–1791), the commander returns as a statue to seek revenge against Don Giovanni.

75  Shooting this rusted bolt, though, against him,
    I trust I am no less time's child than some
    Who on the heath impersonate Poor Tom°
    Or on the barricades risk life and limb.

    Nor do I try to keep a garden, only
80  An avocado in a glass of water—
    Roots pallid, gemmed with air. And later,

    When the small gilt leaves have grown
    Fleshy and green, I let them die, yes, yes,
    And start another. I am earth's no less.

85  A child, a red dog roam the corridors,
    Still, of the broken home. No sound. The brilliant
    Rag runners halt before wide-open doors.
    My old room! Its wallpaper—cream, medallioned
    With pink and brown—brings back the first nightmares,
90  Long summer colds, and Emma, sepia-faced,
    Perspiring over broth carried upstairs
    Aswim with golden fats I could not taste.

    The real house became a boarding school.
    Under the ballroom ceiling's allegory
95  Someone at last may actually be allowed
    To learn something; or, from my window, cool
    With the unstiflement of the entire story,
    Watch a red setter stretch and sink in cloud.

                                            *1966*


## Willowware Cup

    Mass hysteria, wave after breaking wave
    Blueblooded Cantonese upon these shores

    Left the gene pool Lux-opaque and smoking
    With dimestore mutants. One turned up today.

5   Plum in bloom, pagoda, blue birds, plume of willow—
    Almost the replica of a prewar pattern—

    The same boat bearing the gnat-sized lovers away,
    The old bridge now bent double where her father signals

    Feebly, as from flypaper, minding less and less.
10  Two smaller retainers with lanterns light him home.

---

77 *Poor Tom:* Edgar in Shakespeare's *King Lear,* who was disowned by his father, the Earl
of Gloucester, gives himself this name when he wanders the heath pretending to be mad.

Is that a scroll he carries? He must by now be immensely
Wise, and have given up earthly attachments, and all that.

Soon, of these May mornings, rising in mist, he will ask
Only to blend—like ink in flesh, blue anchor

15     Needled upon drunkenness while its destroyer
Full steam departs, the stigma throbbing, intricate—

Only to blend into a crazing texture.
You are far away. The leaves tell what they tell.

But his lone, chipped vessel, if it fills,
20     Fills for you with something warm and clear.

Around its inner horizon the old odd designs
Crowd as before, and seem to concentrate on you.

They represent, I fancy, a version of heaven
In its day more trouble to mend than to replace:

25     Steep roofs aslant, minutely tiled;
Tilted honeycombs, thunderhead blue.

1972

## Lost in Translation°

for Richard Howard

> *Diese Tage, die leer dir scheinen*
> *und wertlos für das All,*
> *haben Wurzeln zwischen den Steinen*
> *und trinken dort überall.*°

A card table in the library stands ready
To receive the puzzle which keeps never coming.
Daylight shines in or lamplight down
Upon the tense oasis of green felt.
5     Full of unfulfillment, life goes on,
Mirage arisen from time's trickling sands
Or fallen piecemeal into place:
German lesson, picnic, see-saw, walk
With the collie who "did everything but talk"—
10     Sour windfalls of the orchard back of us.
A summer without parents is the puzzle,

---

**poem title:** Merrill is no doubt recalling Robert Frost's observation that poetry is that which is lost in translation. The epigraph then offers us a translation.
**epigraph:** *Diese Tage . . .*: The epigraph is taken from Ranier Maria Rilke's (1875–1926) translation of Paul Valéry's (1871–1945) poem "Palme." It may be translated into English as follows: "These days that you think empty / and worthless to the universe, / have roots among the stones / and drink from everywhere."

Or should be. But the boy, day after day,
Writes in his Line-a-Day° *No puzzle.*

He's in love, at least. His French Mademoiselle,°
15      In real life a widow since Verdun,
Is stout, plain, carrot-haired, devout.
She prays for him, as does a curé in Alsace,°
Sews costumes for his marionettes,
Helps him to keep behind the scene
20      Whose sidelit goosegirl, speaking with his voice,
Plays Guinevere° as well as Gunmoll° Jean.
Or else at bedtime in his tight embrace
Tells him her own French hopes, her German fears,
Her—but what more is there to tell?
25      Having known grief and hardship, Mademoiselle
Knows little more. Her languages. Her place.
Noon coffee. Mail. The watch that also waited
Pinned to her heart, poor gold, throws up its hands—
No puzzle! Steaming bitterness
30      Her sugars draw pops back into his mouth, translated:
"Patience, chéri. Geduld, mein Schatz."°
(Thus, reading Valéry the other evening
And seeming to recall a Rilke version of "Palme,"
That sunlit paradigm whereby the tree
35      Taps a sweet wellspring of authority,
The hour came back. Patience dans l'azur.°
Geduld im . . . Himmelblau? Mademoiselle.)

Out of the blue, as promised, of a New York
Puzzle-rental shop the puzzle comes—
40      A superior one, containing a thousand hand-sawn,
Sandal-scented pieces. Many take
Shapes known already—the craftsman's repertoire
Nice in its limitation—from other puzzles:
Witch on broomstick, ostrich, hourglass,
45      Even (surely not just in retrospect)
An inchling, innocently branching palm.
These can be put aside, made stories of
While Mademoiselle spreads out the rest face-up,
Herself excited as a child; or questioned
50      Like incoherent faces in a crowd,

---

13 *Line-a-Day:* a name for a diary.
14 *Mademoiselle:* in this case a governess, widowed since the 1916 World War I battle of Verdun.
17 *Alsace:* area in northeast France, on the German border; territory long contested by the two countries.
21 *Guinevere:* King Arthur's queen.
21 *Gunmoll:* a female gangster.
31 *Patience, chéri. Geduld, mein Shatz:* "Patience, my dear," rendered in both French and German.
36 *Patience dans l'azur:* (French) "Patience in the blue," Valéry's description of the palm tree in his poem. "Geduld im . . . Himmelblau" proposes a German translation. That leads to Merrill's use of the American colloquialism "out of the blue" in the next line.

Each with its scrap of highly colored
Evidence the Law must piece together.
Sky-blue ostrich? Likely story.
Mauve of the witch's cloak white, severed fingers
55     Pluck? Detain her. The plot thickens
As all at once two pieces interlock.

Mademoiselle does borders°—(Not so fast.
A London dusk, December last.
Chatter silenced in the library
60     This grown man reenters, wearing grey.
A medium. All except him have seen
Panel slid back, recess explored,
An object at once unique and common
Displayed, planted in a plain tole°
65     Casket the subject now considers
Through shut eyes, saying in effect:
"Even as voices reach me vaguely
A dry saw-shriek drowns them out,
Some loud machinery—a lumber mill?
70     Far uphill in the fir forest
Trees tower, tense with shock,
Groaning and cracking as they crash groundward.
But hidden here is a freak fragment
Of a pattern complex in appearance only.
75     What it seems to show is superficial
Next to that long-term lamination
Of hazard and craft, the karma that has
Made it matter in the first place.
Plywood, Piece of a puzzle." Applause
80     Acknowledged by an opening of lids
Upon the thing itself. A sudden dread—
But to go back. All this lay years ahead.)

Mademoiselle does borders. Straight-edge pieces
Align themselves with earth or sky
85     In twos and threes, naive cosmogonists
Whose views clash. Nomad inlanders meanwhile
Begin to cluster where the totem
Of a certain vibrant egg-yolk yellow
Or pelt of what emerging animal
90     Acts on the straggler like a trumpet call
To form a more sophisticated unit.
By suppertime two ragged wooden clouds
Have formed. In one, a Sheik with beard
And flashing sword hilt (he is all but finished)
95     Steps forward on a tiger skin. A piece
Snaps shut, and fangs gnash out at us!
In the second cloud—they gaze from cloud to cloud

---

57 *borders*: the word has multiple meanings here. Mademoiselle specializes in the borders
of puzzles, but also crosses linguistic and national borders.
64 *tole*: lacquered or enameled metalware.

With marked if undecipherable feeling—
Most of a dark-eyed woman veiled in mauve
100    Is being helped down from her camel (kneeling)
By a small backward-looking slave or page-boy
(Her son, thinks Mademoiselle mistakenly)
Whose feet have not been found. But lucky finds
In the last minutes before bed
105    Anchor both factions to the scene's limits
And, by so doing, orient
Them eye to eye across the green abyss.
The yellow promises, oh bliss,
To be in time a sumptuous tent.

110    *Puzzle begun* I write in the day's space,
Then, while she bathes, peek at Mademoiselle's
Page to the curé: ". . . cette innocente mère,
Ce pauvre enfant, que deviendront-ils?"°
Her azure script is curlicued like pieces
115    Of the puzzle she will be telling him about.
(Fearful incuriosity of childhood!
"Tu as l'accent allemand,"° said Dominique.
Indeed. Mademoiselle was only French by marriage.
Child of an English mother, a remote
120    Descendant of the great explorer Speke,°
And Prussian father. No one knew. I heard it
Long afterwards from her nephew, a UN°
Interpreter. His matter-of-fact account
Touched old strings. My poor Mademoiselle,
125    With 1939° about to shake
This world where "each was the enemy, each the friend"
To its foundations, kept, though signed in blood,
Her peace a shameful secret to the end.)
"Schlaf wohl, chéri."° Her kiss. Her thumb
130    Crossing my brow against the dreams to come.

This World that shifts like sand, its unforeseen
Consolidations and elate routine,
Whose Potentate had lacked a retinue?
Lo! it assembles on the shrinking Green.

135    Gunmetal-skinned or pale, all plumes and scars,
Of Vassalage the noblest avatars—
The very coffee-bearer in his vair
Vest° is a swart Highness, next to ours.

---

113 *cette . . . deviendront-ils:* (French) "This innocent mother, this poor child, what will become of them?"
117 *Tu . . . allemand:* (French) "You have a German accent."
120 *Speke:* John Hanning Speke (1827–1864), British explorer of Africa.
122 *UN:* United Nations.
125 *1939:* World War II began when Germany invaded Poland in 1939.
129 *Schlaf . . . :* (German, French) "Sleep well, my love."
138 *vair vest:* vest bordered with fur.

Kef° easing Boredom, and iced syrups, thirst,
140    In guessed-at glooms old wives who know the worst
Outsweat that virile fiction of the New:
"Insh'Allah,° he will tire—" "—or kill her first!"

(Hardly a proper subject for the Home,
Work of—dear Richard, I shall let *you* comb
145    Archives and learned journals for his name—
A minor lion attending on Gérôme.)°

While, thick as Thebes° whose presently complete
Gates close behind them, Houri and Afreet°
Both claim the Page.° He wonders whom to serve,
150    And what his duties are, and where his feet,

And if we'll find, as some before us did,
That piece of Distance deep in which lies hid
Your tiny apex sugary with sun,
Eternal Triangle, Great Pyramid!

155    Then Sky alone is left, a hundred blue
Fragments in revolution, with no clue
To where a Niche will open. Quite a task,
Putting together Heaven, yet we do.

It's done. Here under the table all along
160    Were those missing feet. It's done.

The dog's tail thumping. Mademoiselle sketching
Costumes for a coming harem drama
To star the goosegirl. All too soon the swift
Dismantling. Lifted by two corners,
165    The puzzle hung together—and did not.
Irresistibly a populace
Unstitched of its attachments, rattled down.
Power went to pieces as the witch
Slithered easily from Virtue's gown.
170    The blue held out for time, but crumbled, too.
The city had long fallen, and the tent,
A separating sauce mousseline,°
Been swept away. Remained the green

---

139 *Kef:* marijuana.
142 *Insh'Allah:* (Arabic) "If Allah wills."
146 *lion . . . Gérôme:* Jean Léon Gérôme (1824–1940), French painter of historical subjects.
Also a pun referring to St. Jerome's kindness in pulling a thorn from a lion's paw.
147 *Thebes:* the ancient capital of Upper Egypt, situated on the Nile. Here "Thebes" is also
a mispronunciation of "thieves."
148 *Houri and Afreet:* according to Arabian mythology, "Houri" are virgins given to those
who enter paradise and "Afreet" are evil beings.
149 *Page:* a pun, referring both to a young male servant and to the printed page.
172 *mousseline:* a pun, referring both to a hollandaise cream sauce and to a sheet fabric
made of muslin, the latter originally made in Iraq.

On which the grown-ups gambled. A green dusk.
175     First lightning bugs. Last glow of west
        Green in the false eyes of (coincidence)
        *Our* mangy tiger safe on his bared hearth.

        Before the puzzle was boxed and readdressed
        To the puzzle shop in the mix-Sixties,°
180     Something tells me that one piece contrived
        To stay in the boy's pocket. How do I know?
        I know because so many later puzzles
        Had missing pieces—Maggie Teyte's° high notes
        Gone at the war's end, end of the vogue for collies,
185     A house torn down; and hadn't Mademoiselle
        Kept back her pitiful bit of truth as well?
        I've spent the last days, furthermore,
        Ransacking Athens for that translation of "Palme."
        Neither the Goethehaus° nor the National Library
190     Seems able to unearth it. Yet I can't
        Just be imagining. I've seen it. Know
        How much of the sun-ripe original
        Felicity Rilke made himself forego
        (Who loved French words—verger, mûr, parfumer)°
195     In order to render its underlying sense.
        Know already in that tongue of his
        What Pains, what monolithic Truths
        Shadow stanza to stanza's symmetrical
        Rhyme-rutted pavement. Know that ground plan left
200     Sublime and barren, where the warm Romance
        Stone by stone faded, cooled; the fluted nouns
        Made taller, lonelier than life
        By leaf-carved capitals in the afterglow.
        The owlet umlaut° peeps and hoots
205     Above the open vowel. And after rain
        A deep reverberation fills with stars.

        Lost, is it, buried? One more missing piece?

        But nothing's lost. Or else: all is translation
        And every bit of us is lost in it
210     (Or found—I wander through the ruin of S°
        Now and then, wondering at the peacefulness)
        And in that loss a self-effacing tree,
        Color of context, imperceptibly
        Rustling with its angel,° turns the waste
        To shade and fiber, milk and memory.

        1976

---

179 *mid-Sixties*: an approximate street address.
183 *Maggie Teyte*: (1888–1976) a British soprano who sang a number of French pieces.
189 *Goethehaus*: the name of a German library.
194 *verger, mûr, parfumer*: (French) "orchard, ripe, to scent."
204 *umlaut*: an accent mark in German, consisting of two dots placed above a vowel.
210 *ruin of S*: "S" is a lost love.
214 *Rustling with its angel*: Cf. Jacob *wrestling* with the angel in the Book of Genesis.

# Allen Ginsberg (1926–1997)

Ginsberg was at once one of the major poets of the second half of the twentieth century and a public figure who entreated his country by way of his poetry to realize its full democratic potential. No one who saw and heard Ginsberg stand on a flat bed truck before thousands of U.S. Army troops at the Pentagon during the famous 1968 demonstration against the Vietnam War either could or would wish altogether to separate his work from its reception. With rifles bristling at him, Ginsberg read his Pentagon exorcism poem in defiance of imperialist military power and in a plea that the demons of war would quit the building. A rather modest poem, it nonetheless made for an unforgettable occasion. Yet Ginsberg was never actually militant or aggressive. Learned in Zen Buddhism and Western mysticism, his presence exuded rather an expansive and insistent gentleness.

He was born and grew up in New Jersey, but it was the emerging Beat generation in New York that shaped his vision and that he helped to define. He was educated at Columbia University, though his degree was delayed when he was expelled for what would now constitute no more than a prank, placing obscene messages on his grimy dormitory window to draw attention to the need to clean the room. More serious—as he became friends with William Burroughs, Jack Kerouac, and other figures in the Beat literary and drug scene—was his decision to let Herbert Huncke use his dorm room to store the stolen goods he employed to support his heroin habit. In exchange for avoiding prosecution, Ginsberg pleaded insanity and spent eight months in the Columbia Psychiatric Institute.

By then he had worked at a series of odd jobs, including service on merchant tankers. One day in Harlem, Ginsberg had an auditory vision of William Blake reading his poems aloud. He also soon met and was befriended by William Carlos Williams. Then he was on his way to San Francisco and the 1956 publication of *Howl and Other Poems*. Buoyed by the publicity accompanying an obscenity trial, "Howl" would become perhaps the most widely known poem of the era. Ginsberg had become a twentieth-century incarnation of Walt Whitman.

The mix of moods in his work would remain consistent throughout his career—prophetic, elegiac, ecstatic. He would write triumphant poems of political protest, lamentations about death, celebratory poems about homosexuality, and affirmations of visionary transformation. He chanted his poems to the accompaniment of finger cymbals, sang them with rock groups, and intoned them in a high resonant voice that made his poetry a form of contemporary prophecy.

## Love Poem on Theme by Whitman

I'll go into the bedroom silently and lie down between the bride-
    groom and the bride,
those bodies fallen from heaven stretched out waiting naked and
    restless,
arms resting over their eyes in the darkness,
bury my face in their shoulders and breasts, breathing their skin,
5     and stroke and kiss neck and mouth and make back be open and
    known,
legs raised up crook'd to receive, cock in the darkness driven
    tormented and attacking
roused up from hole to itching head,
bodies locked shuddering naked, hot hips and buttocks screwed
    into each other
and eyes, eyes glinting and charming, widening into looks and
    abandon,
10   and moans of movement, voices, hands in air, hands between thighs,
hands in moisture on softened hips, throbbing contraction of bellies
till the white come flow in the swirling sheets,
and the bride cry for forgiveness, and the groom be covered with
    tears of passion and compassion,
and I rise up from the bed replenished with last intimate gestures
    and kisses of farewell—
15   all before the mind wakes, behind shades and closed doors in a
    darkened house
where the inhabitants roam unsatisfied in the night,
nude ghosts seeking each other out in the silence.

                                          *1954*

## Howl

(*For Carl Solomon°*)

I

I saw the best minds of my generation destroyed by madness,
    starving hysterical naked,
dragging themselves through the negro streets at dawn looking for
    an angry fix,°

---

**dedication:** *Solomon:* (1928–), whom Ginsberg met as a fellow patient at the Columbia
Psychiatric Institute in New York in 1949, where Solomon related his experiences in New
York and Paris and shared books by Artaud and others with Ginsberg. At the time *Howl*
was written, Ginsberg learned that Solomon had been admitted to a mental hospital again.
As Ginsberg would write in the 1986 facsimile of *Howl*, he thought the dedication "a ges-
ture of wild solidarity, a message into the asylum, a sort of heart's trumpet call." But the
poem achieved wider fame than anyone could have anticipated, and Solomon, as a result,
became virtually a mythical figure, inextricably linked to *Howl* ever thereafter. Solomon was
an editor at Ace Books and later published *Mishaps, Perhaps* (1966) and *More Mishaps* (1968).
2 *angry fix:* Ginsberg's note reads "Herbert Huncke cruised Harlem and Times Square at
irregular hours, late forties, scoring junk."

angelheaded hipsters burning for the ancient heavenly connection°
    to the starry dynamo in the machinery of night,
who poverty and tatters and hollow-eyed and high sat up smoking
    in the supernatural darkness of cold-water flats floating across
    the tops of cities contemplating jazz,
5    who bared their brains to Heaven under the El° and saw
    Mohammedan angels° staggering on tenement roofs illuminated,
who passed through universities with radiant cool eyes
    hallucinating Arkansas and Blake-light° tragedy among
    the scholars of war,°
who were expelled° from the academies for crazy & publishing
    obscene odes on the windows of the skull,
who cowered° in unshaven rooms in underwear, burning their
    money in wastebaskets and listening to the Terror through the
    wall,
who got busted in their pubic beards returning through Laredo°
    with a belt of marijuana for New York,
10    who ate fire in paint hotels or drank turpentine in Paradise Alley,°
    death, or purgatoried their torsos night after night
with dreams, with drugs, with waking nightmares, alcohol and cock
    and endless balls,
incomparable blind streets of shuddering cloud and lightning in the
    mind leaping toward poles of Canada & Paterson,° illuminating
    all the motionless world of Time between,
Peyote° solidities of halls, backyard green tree cemetery dawns,
    wine drunkenness over the rooftops, storefront boroughs of
    teahead joyride neon blinking traffic light, sun and moon and
    tree vibrations in the roaring winter dusks of Brooklyn, ashcan
    rantings and kind king light of mind,

---

3 *connection*: a pun linking spirituality and a drug connection.
5 *El*: the elevated subway system in New York City and a Hebrew term for God.
5 *saw Mohammedan angels*: according to Ginsberg's note, this refers to poet Philip Lamantia's 1953 mystical experience.
6 *Blake-light*: Ginsberg experienced a mystical vision while reading the poetry of William Blake (1757–1827) in East Harlem in 1948.
6 *scholars of war*: As Ginsberg comments, "During author's residence, 1944–1948, Columbia scientists helped split atoms for military power in secrecy. Subsequent military-industrial funding increasingly dominated university research."
7 *expelled*: Ginsberg was expelled from Columbia University in 1945 for drawing and writing obscenities on his dormitory windows.
8 *cowered . . . burning their money*: (Ginsberg's note) a Solomon anecdote.
9 *Laredo*: Texas city on the Mexican border.
10 *Paradise Alley*: (Ginsberg's note) a cold-water-flat courtyard on East 11th Street on New York's Lower East Side. The prototype of Jack Kerouac's (1922–1969) heroine in *The Subterraneans* (1958) lived there.
12 *Paterson*: New Jersey city where Ginsberg was born and later lived from 1950–1951, when he met poet William Carlos Williams, whose works include the long poem *Paterson* (1946–1963).
13 *Peyote*: a small Mexico and Texas cactus which is the source of the hallucinogen *mescalin*, used in Native American religious ceremonies and later adopted by the American counterculture. Ginsberg's note says that "tree vibrations" refers to his own first peyote experience.

who chained themselves to subways for the endless ride from Bat-
tery° to holy Bronx on benzedrine until the noise of wheels and
children brought them down shuddering mouth-wracked and
battered bleak of brain all drained of brilliance in the drear light
of Zoo,

15  who sank all night in submarine light of Bickford's° floated out and
sat through the stale beer afternoon in desolate Fugazzis,° lis-
tening to the crack of doom on the hydrogen jukebox,

who talked continuously° seventy hours from park to pad to bar to
Bellevue° to museum to the Brooklyn Bridge,

a lost battalion of platonic conversationalists jumping down the
stoops off fire escapes off windowsills off Empire State out of
the moon,

yacketayakking screaming vomiting whispering facts and memories
and anecdotes and eyeball kicks and shocks of hospitals and jails
and wars,

whole intellects disgorged in total recall for seven days and nights
with brilliant eyes, meat for the Synagogue cast on the pave-
ment,

20  who vanished into nowhere Zen New Jersey leaving a trail of
ambiguous picture postcards of Atlantic City Hall,

suffering Eastern sweats and Tangerian bone-grindings° and mi-
graines of China under junk-withdrawal in Newark's bleak
furnished room,

who wandered around and around at midnight in the railroad yard
wondering where to go, and went, leaving no broken hearts,

who lit cigarettes in boxcars boxcars boxcars racketing through
snow toward lonesome farms in grandfather night,

who studied Plotinus Poe St. John of the Cross° telepathy and bop°
kabbalah° because the cosmos instinctively vibrated at their feet
in Kansas,

25  who loned it through the streets of Idaho seeking visionary indian
angels who were visionary indian angels,

who thought they were only mad when Baltimore gleamed in
supernatural ecstasy,

who jumped in limousines with the Chinaman of Oklahoma on the
impulse of winter midnight streetlight smalltown rain,

---

14 *Battery:* Battery Park, at the southern end of Manhattan. "Battery to holy Bronx" marks
the southern and northern ends of a New York City subway line. *Zoo:* the Bronx Zoo, at
the northern end of a N.Y.C. subway line.
15 *Bickford's:* an all-night cafeteria on 42nd Street where Ginsberg mopped floors while a
student at Columbia.
15 *Fugazzi's:* a Greenwich Village bar on Sixth Avenue.
16 *talked continuously:* (Ginsberg's note) Ruth G., a young woman who knew both Solomon
and Ginsberg and who one day talked for seventy-two hours in Washington Square until
being committed to Bellevue. The phrase also evokes Cassady's nonstop monologues.
16 *Bellevue:* a New York public hospital with a psychiatric clinic.
21 *Tangerian bone grindings:* Ginsberg's note refers us to details of beat writer William S.
Burroughs's (1914–1997) heroin withdrawals in his *Letters to Allen Ginsberg 1953–1957*
(1982). Tangiers is a coastal city in Morocco.
24 *Plotinus:* (205?–270), a Roman neo-Platonic philosopher; the poet and writer Edgar Al-
lan Poe (1809–1849); Juan de Yepes y Alvaraz (1542–1591), a Spanish mystic poet.
24 *bop:* the bop style of jazz developed in the 1940s and 1950s.
24 *kabbalah:* the mystical tradition of interpreting Hebrew scripture.

who lounged hungry and lonesome through Houston seeking jazz
or sex or soup, and followed the brilliant Spaniard to converse
about America and Eternity, a hopeless task, and so took ship to
Africa,

who disappeared into the volcanoes of Mexico leaving behind
nothing but the shadow of dungarees and the lava and ash of
poetry scattered in fireplace Chicago,

30     who reappeared on the West Coast investigating the FBI in beards
and shorts with big pacifist eyes sexy in their dark skin passing
out incomprehensible leaflets,

who burned cigarette holes in their arms protesting the narcotic
tobacco haze of Capitalism,

who distributed Supercommunist pamphlets in Union Square°
weeping and undressing while the sirens of Los Alamos° wailed
them down, and wailed down Wall,° and the Staten Island ferry
also wailed,

who broke down crying in white gymnasiums naked and trembling
before the machinery of other skeletons,

who bit detectives in the neck and shrieked with delight in
policecars for committing no crime but their own wild cooking
pederasty and intoxication,

35     who howled on their knees in the subway and were dragged off the
roof waving genitals and manuscripts,

who let themselves be fucked in the ass by saintly motorcyclists,°
and screamed with joy,

who blew and were blown by those human seraphim,° the sailors,°
caresses of Atlantic and Caribbean love,

who balled in the morning in the evenings in rosegardens and the
grass of public parks and cemeteries scattering their semen
freely to whomever come who may,

who hiccuped endlessly trying to giggle but wound up with a sob
behind a partition in a Turkish Bath when the blond & naked
angel came to pierce them with a sword,°

40     who lost their loveboys to the three old shrews of fate the one eyed
shrew of the heterosexual dollar the one eyed shrew that winks
out of the womb and the one eyed shrew° that does nothing but
sit on her ass and snip the intellectual golden threads of the
craftsman's loom,

---

32 *Union Square*: A neighborhood, park, and public square running from 14th to 21st Street in Manhattan. Often the site of workers' rallies and radical political protests.

32 *Los Alamos*: the New Mexico site for the research and development of the atomic bomb.

32 *Wall*: New York's financial district (Wall Street) and Jerusalem's Wailing Wall, thought to be part of the wall surrounding the temple of King Herod (73–4 B.C.) of Judea, where Jews have traditionally gathered for prayer.

36 *saintly motorcyclists*: Ginsberg's note directs us to Marlon Brando's film *The Wild Ones*.

37 *seraphim*: the highest order of angels.

37 *sailors*: Ginsberg's note reads "The poet Hart Crane picked up sailors to love on Sand Street, Brooklyn, etc. Suffering alcoholic exhaustion and rejected by the crew on his last voyage, from Veracruz, Crane disappeared off the fantail of the Caribbean ship *Orizaba*."

39 *sword*: refers to Lorenzo Bernini's (1598–1680) sculpture *The Ecstasy of St. Teresa*, which evokes an erotic religious vision by St. Teresa (1515–1582).

40 *shrew*: shrews of fate, according to Roman myth, three goddesses of destiny who determine the course of human lives by spinning a line of thread until severing it at the point of death.

who copulated ecstatic and insatiate with a bottle of beer a
   sweetheart a package of cigarettes a candle and fell off the bed,
   and continued along the floor and down the hall and ended
   fainting on the wall with a vision of ultimate cunt and come
   eluding the last gyzym of consciousness,
who sweetened the snatches of a million girls trembling in the
   sunset, and were red eyed in the morning but prepared to
   sweeten the snatch of the sunrise, flashing buttocks under
   barns and naked in the lake,
who went out whoring through Colorado in myriad stolen
   night-cars, N.C.,° secret hero of these poems, cocksman and
   Adonis° of Denver—joy to the memory of his innumerable lays
   of girls in empty lots & diner backyards, moviehouses' rickety
   rows, on mountaintops in caves or with gaunt waitresses in
   familiar roadside lonely petticoat upliftings & especially secret
   gas-station solipsisms° of johns, & hometown alleys too,
who faded out in vast sordid movies, were shifted in dreams, woke
   on a sudden Manhattan, and picked themselves up out of
   basements hungover with heartless Tokay° and horrors of Third
   Avenue iron dreams & stumbled to unemployment offices,
45  who walked all night with their shoes full of blood on the
   snowbank docks waiting for a door in the East River to
   open to a room full of steamheat and opium,
who created great suicidal dramas on the apartment° cliff-banks of
   the Hudson under the wartime blue floodlight of the moon &
   their heads shall be crowned with laurel in oblivion,
who ate the lamb stew of the imagination or digested the crab at
   the muddy bottom of the rivers of Bowery,°
who wept at the romance of the streets with their pushcarts full of
   onions and bad music,
who sat in boxes breathing in the darkness under the bridge, and
   rose up to build harpsichords in their lofts,
50  who coughed on the sixth floor of Harlem crowned with flame
   under the tubercular sky surrounded by orange crates of
   theology,
who scribbled all night rocking and rolling over lofty incantations
   which in the yellow morning were stanzas of gibberish,
who cooked rotten animals lung heart feet tail borsht° & tortillas
   dreaming of the pure vegetable kingdom,

---

43 *N.C.*: Neal Cassady (1926–1968), Beat writer and friend of Ginsberg and Kerouac on whom Kerouac based the character Dean Moriarty in *On the Road* (1957).
43 *Adonis*: according to Greek myth, a handsome young man loved by Aphrodite, goddess of love.
43 *solipsisms*: philosophical theories by which only the self exists, so that all experience is subjective.
44 *Tokay*: a cheap, fortified Hungarian wine favored by alcoholic derelicts. Ginsberg refers us to Kerouac's accounts of drinking in New York in his letters.
46 *apartment*: high-rise apartment houses atop the cliffs of the Palisades along the Hudson River.
47 *Bowery*: the lower part of Third Avenue in New York City, frequented by derelicts and homeless people.
52 *borsht*: Ginsberg's note reads: "Author's mother cooked lungen (lung stew) and Russian borscht (beet soup) when not eating nature-community vegetarian."

who plunged themselves under meat trucks looking for an egg,

who threw their watches off the roof to cast their ballot for
> Eternity outside of Time, & alarm clocks fell on their heads
> every day for the next decade,

55    who cut their wrists three times successively unsuccessfully, gave
> up and were forced to open antique stores where they thought
> they were growing old and cried,

who were burned alive in their innocent flannel suits on Madison
> Avenue° amid blasts of leaden verse & the tanked-up clatter of
> the iron regiments of fashion & the nitroglycerine shrieks of the
> fairies of advertising & the mustard gas of sinister intelligent
> editors, or were run down by the drunken taxicabs of Absolute
> Reality,

who jumped off the Brooklyn Bridge this actually happened and
> walked away unknown and forgotten into the ghostly daze of
> Chinatown soup alleyways & firetrucks, not even one free beer,

who sang out of their windows in despair, fell out of the subway
> window, jumped in the filthy Passaic,° leaped on negroes, cried
> all over the street, danced on broken wineglasses barefoot
> smashed phonograph records of nostalgic European 1930s
> German jazz finished the whiskey and threw up° groaning into
> the bloody toilet, moans in their ears and the blast of colossal
> steamwhistles,

who barreled down the highways of the past journeying to each
> other's hotrod-Golgotha° jail-solitude watch or Birmingham
> jazz incarnation,

60    who drove crosscountry seventytwo hours to find out if I had a
> vision or you had a vision or he had a vision to find out
> Eternity,

who journeyed to Denver, who died in Denver,° who came back to
> Denver & waited in vain, who watched over Denver & brooded
> & loned in Denver and finally went away to find out the Time,
> & now Denver is lonesome for her heroes,

who fell on their knees in hopeless cathedrals praying for each
> other's salvation and light and breasts, until the soul illuminated
> its hair for a second,

who crashed through their minds in jail waiting for impossible
> criminals with golden heads and the charm of reality in their
> hearts who sang sweet blues to Alcatraz,

---

56 *Madison Avenue:* the traditional location of New York advertising agencies, whose con-
formist employees wore gray flannel suits as a uniform for success.

58 *Passaic:* the Passaic River, which flows past Paterson, New Jersey. The phrase "filthy
Passaic" comes from William Carlos Williams's 1915 poem "The Wanderer."

58 *subway window . . . smashed records . . . threw up:* according to Ginsberg's note, these
incidents come from the life of "William Cannastra, legendary late 1940s New York bo-
hemian figure, life cut short by alcoholic accident, body balanced out of subway window,
knocked against a pillar."

59 *Golgotha:* "Place of a Skull" (Hebrew): Calvary, the site of Jesus' crucifixion.

61 *Denver:* Ginsberg's note reads "Lyric lines by Kerouac: 'Down in Denver,/ Down in Den-
ver,/ All I did was die.'"

who retired° to Mexico to cultivate a habit, or Rocky Mount to
tender Buddha or Tangiers to boys or Southern Pacific to the
black locomotive or Harvard to Narcissus to Woodlawn° to the
daisychain or grave,

65 who demanded sanity trials accusing the radio° of hypnotism &
were left with their insanity & their hands & a hung jury,

who threw potato salad at CCNY° lecturers on Dadaism and
subsequently presented themselves on the granite steps of the
madhouse with shaven heads and harlequin speech of suicide,
demanding instantaneous lobotomy,

and who were given instead the concrete void of insulin Metrazol°
electricity hydrotherapy psychotherapy occupational therapy
pingpong & amnesia,

who in humorless protest overturned only one symbolic pingpong
table,° resting briefly in catatonia,

returning years later truly bald except for a wig of blood, and tears
and fingers, to the visible madman doom of the wards of the
madtowns of the East,

70 Pilgrim State's Rockland's and Greystone's° foetid halls, bickering
with the echoes of the soul, rocking and rolling in the midnight
solitude-bench dolmen-realms° of love, dream of life a
nightmare, bodies turned to stone as heavy as the moon,

with mother finally ******,° and the last fantastic book flung out
of the tenement window, and the last door closed at 4 A.M. and
the last telephone slammed at the wall in reply and the last
furnished room emptied down to the last piece of mental
furniture, a yellow paper rose twisted on a wire hanger in the
closet, and even that imaginary, nothing but a hopeful little bit
of hallucination—

---

64 *who retired* . . . : Burroughs lived in Mexico and Tangiers; Kerouac lived in Rocky Mount,
North Carolina; Cassady worked for the Southern Pacific Railroad.

64 *Narcissus to Woodlawn*: according to Greek myth, Narcissus was a youth who fell in
love with his own reflection in a pool; Naomi Ginsberg's window overlooked Woodlawn,
a cemetery in the Bronx.

65 *accusing the radio*: alludes to Ginsberg's mother's paranoid fantasies.

66 *CCNY*: City College of New York; Dadaism: dadaism was an artistic and literary move-
ment (1916–1922) emphasizing the irrational and the absurd. Carl Solomon writes: "My
protest against the verbal, the rational and the acceptable took the form of disruption of
a critical discussion of Mallarmé and other neo-dada clowning, which resulted in my in-
carceration in a psychiatric hospital in Manhattan."

67 *Metrazol*: brand name of pentylenetrazol, a drug used in shock therapy.

68 *overturned* . . . *pingpong table*: Ginsberg's note reads "The incident of the Ping-Pong
table is described by Solomon as a 'big burst anti-authoritarian rage on arrival at P.I. by
me.' "

70 *Pilgrim State's Rockland's and Greystone's*: hospitals for mentally ill patients near New
York City. Solomon spent time at Pilgrim State and Rockland; his removal to Pilgrim State
occasioned the poem's dedication. Ginsberg's mother, Naomi, institutionalized at Grey-
stone since the late 1940s, died there in 1956.

70 *dolmen-realms*: dolmens are neolithic tombs consisting of a large, flat rock laid across
upright rocks. Ginsberg comments: "Dolmens mark a vanished civilization, as Stonehenge
or Greystone and Rockland monoliths."

71 *mother finally *******: Ginsberg's draft reads "mother finally fucked." His note com-
ments: "Author replaced letters with asterisks in final draft of poem to introduce appro-
priate level of uncertainty."

ah, Carl, while you are not safe I am not safe, and now you're
    really in the total animal soup of time—
and who therefore ran through the icy streets obsessed with a
    sudden flash of the alchemy of the use of the ellipse the catalog
    the meter & the vibrating plane,
who dreamt and made incarnate gaps in Time & Space through
    images juxtaposed, and trapped the archangel of the soul
    between 2 visual images and joined the elemental verbs and set
    the noun and dash of consciousness together jumping with
    sensation of Pater Omnipotens Aeterna Deus°
75    to recreate the syntax and measure of poor human prose and stand
    before you speechless and intelligent and shaking with shame,
    rejected yet confessing out the soul to conform to the rhythm of
    thought in his naked and endless head,
the madman bum and angel beat in Time, unknown, yet putting
    down here what might be left to say in time come after death,
and rose reincarnate in the ghostly clothes of jazz in the goldhorn
    shadow of the band and blew the suffering of America's naked
    mind for love into an eli eli lamma lamma sabacthani°
    saxophone cry that shivered the cities down to the last radio
with the absolute heart of the poem of life butchered out of their
    own bodies good to eat a thousand years.

## II

What sphinx° of cement and aluminum bashed open their skulls
    and ate up their brains and imagination?
80    Moloch!° Solitude! Filth! Ugliness! Ashcans and unobtainable
    dollars! Children screaming under the stairways! Boys sobbing
    in armies! Old men weeping in the parks!
Moloch! Moloch! Nightmare of Moloch! Moloch the loveless!
    Mental Moloch! Moloch the heavy judger of men!
Moloch the incomprehensible prison! Moloch the crossbone
    soulless jailhouse and Congress of sorrows! Moloch whose
    buildings are judgment! Moloch the vast stone of war! Moloch
    the stunned governments!
Moloch whose mind is pure machinery! Moloch whose blood is
    running money! Moloch whose fingers are ten armies! Moloch
    whose breast is a cannibal dynamo! Moloch whose ear is a
    smoking tomb!
Moloch whose eyes are a thousand blind windows! Moloch whose
    skyscrapers stand in the long streets like endless Jehovahs!
    Moloch whose factories dream and croak in the fog! Moloch
    whose smokestacks and antennae crown the cities!

---

74 *Pater ... Deus*: (Latin) "All-powerful Father, Eternal God," from a 1904 letter describing the power of nature by the French painter Paul Cézanne (1839–1906).
77 *eli ... sabacthani*: (Aramaic) "My God, my God, why have you forsaken me?" Matthew 27.46, Jesus' last words on the cross.
79 *sphinx*: mythical beast with a lion's body and a human head.
80 *Moloch*: Ginsberg's note: Moloch, or Molech, the Canaanite fire god, whose worship was marked by parents' burning their children as propitiary sacrifice. "And thou shalt not let any of thy seed pass through the fire to Molech" (Leviticus 18.21).

85     Moloch whose love is endless oil and stone! Moloch whose soul is
electricity and banks! Moloch whose poverty is the specter of
genius! Moloch whose fate is a cloud of sexless hydrogen!
Moloch whose name is the Mind!

Moloch in whom I sit lonely! Moloch in whom I dream Angels!
Crazy in Moloch! Cocksucker in Moloch! Lacklove and manless
in Moloch!

Moloch who entered my soul early! Moloch in whom I am a
consciousness without a body! Moloch who frightened me
out of my natural ecstasy! Moloch whom I abandon! Wake
up in Moloch! Light streaming out of the sky!

Moloch! Moloch! Robot apartments! invisible suburbs! skeleton
treasuries! blind capitals! demonic industries! spectral nations!
invincible madhouses! granite cocks! monstrous bombs!

They broke their backs lifting Moloch to Heaven! Pavements, trees,
radios, tons! lifting the city to Heaven which exists and is
everywhere about us!

90     Visions! omens! hallucinations! miracles! ecstasies! gone down the
American river!

Dreams! adorations! illuminations! religions! the whole boatload of
sensitive bullshit!

Breakthroughs! over the river! flips and crucifixions! gone down the
flood! Highs! Epiphanies! Despairs! Ten years' animal screams
and suicides! Minds! New loves! Mad generation! down on the
rocks of Time!

Real holy laughter in the river! They saw it all! the wild eyes! the
holy yells! They bade farewell! They jumped off the roof! to
solitude! waving! carrying flowers! Down to the river! into the
street!

### III

Carl Solomon! I'm with you in Rockland
    where you're madder than I am

95     I'm with you in Rockland
    where you must feel very strange

I'm with you in Rockland
    where you imitate the shade of my mother

I'm with you in Rockland
    where you've murdered your twelve secretaries

I'm with you in Rockland
    where you laugh at this invisible humor

I'm with you in Rockland
    where we are great writers on the same dreadful typewriter

100    I'm with you in Rockland
    where your condition has become serious and is reported
    on the radio

I'm with you in Rockland
    where the faculties of the skull no longer admit the worms of
    the senses

I'm with you in Rockland
    where you drink the tea of the breasts of the spinsters of Utica

I'm with you in Rockland
    where you pun on the bodies of your nurses the harpies of the
    Bronx

I'm with you in Rockland
    where you scream in a straightjacket that you're losing the game
    of the actual pingpong of the abyss
105 I'm with you in Rockland
    where you bang on the catatonic piano the soul is innocent and
    immortal it should never die ungodly in an armed madhouse
I'm with you in Rockland
    where fifty more shocks will never return your soul to its body
    again from its pilgrimage to a cross in the void
I'm with you in Rockland
    where you accuse your doctors of insanity and plot the Hebrew
    socialist revolution against the fascist national Golgotha
I'm with you in Rockland
    where you will split the heavens of Long Island and resurrect
    your living human Jesus from the superhuman tomb
I'm with you in Rockland
    where there are twentyfive thousand mad comrades all together
    singing the final stanzas of the Internationale°
110 I'm with you in Rockland
    where we hug and kiss the United States under our bedsheets
    the United States that coughs all night and won't let us sleep
I'm with you in Rockland
    where we wake up electrified out of the coma by our own souls'
    airplanes roaring over the roof they've come to drop angelic
    bombs the hospital illuminates itself   imaginary walls
    collapse   O skinny legions run outside   O starry-spangled
    shock of mercy the eternal war is here   O victory forget your
    underwear we're free
I'm with you in Rockland
    in my dreams you walk dripping from a sea-journey on the
    highway across America in tears to the door of my cottage in
    the Western night

*1955–1956*

## Wichita Vortex Sutra°

### I

Turn Right Next Corner
    *The Biggest Little Town in Kansas*
        *Macpherson*
Red sun setting flat plains west streaked
5         with gauzy veils, chimney mist spread
    around christmas-tree-bulbed refineries—aluminum
        white tanks squat beneath
    winking signal towers' bright plane-lights,
            orange gas flares
10         beneath pillows of smoke, flames in machinery—
        transparent towers at dusk

---

109 *Internationale:* the anthem of the international working class, *The Internationale* was
written by Eugene Pottier in Paris in 1871 to celebrate the Paris Commune. It was later
sung to celebrate a commitment to revolutionary socialism or communism; the Soviet an-
them until 1944.
**poem title:** *Sutra* is a Sanskrit term for a discourse of the Buddha or one of his chief
disciples.

*In advance of the Cold Wave*
       *Snow is spreading eastward to*
              *the Great Lakes*
15        News Broadcast & old clarinets
          Watertower dome Lighted on the flat plain
              car radio speeding acrost railroad tracks—

Kansas! Kansas! Shuddering at last!
          PERSON appearing in Kansas!
20        angry telephone calls to the University
          Police dumbfounded leaning on
              their radiocar hoods
          While Poets chant to Allah in the roadhouse Showboat!
Blue eyed children dance and hold thy Hand O aged Walt°
25        who came from Lawrence to Topeka to envision
              Iron interlaced upon the city plain—
          Telegraph wires strung from city to city O Melville!°
              Television brightening thy *rills of Kansas lone*
I come,
30        lone man from the void, riding a bus
          hypnotized by red tail lights on the straight
                     space road ahead—
          & the Methodist minister with cracked eyes
                     leaning over the table
35        quoting Kierkegaard° "death of God"
                     a million dollars
          in the bank   owns all West Wichita
                     come to Nothing!
          Prajnaparamita Sutra° over coffee—Vortex
40        of telephone radio aircraft assembly frame ammunition
          petroleum nightclub Newspaper streets illuminated by Bright
                          EMPTINESS—

Thy sins are forgiven, Wichita!
          Thy lonesomeness annulled, O Kansas dear!
45              as the western Twang prophesied
          thru banjo, when lone cowboy walked the railroad track
                 past an empty station toward the sun
              sinking giant-bulbed orange down the box canyon—
          Music strung over his back
50              and empty handed   singing on this planet earth
                          I'm a lonely Dog, O Mother!
          Come, Nebraska, sing & dance with me—
                 Come lovers of Lincoln and Omaha,
                     hear my soft voice at last
55        As Babes need the chemical touch of flesh in pink infancy
              lest they die Idiot returning to Inhuman—
                          Nothing—

---

24 *Walt*: Walt Whitman (1819–1892), American poet, author of *Leaves of Grass* (1855).
27 *Melville*: Herman Melville (1819–1891), American novelist, author of *Moby Dick* (1851).
35 *Kierkegaard*: Sören Kierkegaard (1813–1855), Danish philosopher and theologian who argued that subjectivity is central to truth.
39 *Prajnaparamita Sutra*: the Highest Perfect Wisdom Sutra, central to Zen and Tibetan Buddhist practice, it includes the line "Form is emptiness, emptiness is form."

So, tender lipt adolescent girl, pale youth,
                              give me back my soft kiss
60          Hold me in your innocent arms,
                    accept my tears as yours to harvest
                    equal   in nature to the Wheat
              that made your bodies' muscular bones
                    broad shouldered, boy bicept—
65                  from leaning on cows & drinking Milk
                              in Midwest Solitude—
No more fear of tenderness, much delight in weeping, ecstasy
         in singing, laughter rises that confounds
                    staring Idiot mayors
70                              and stony politicians eyeing
                    Thy breast,
                              O Man of America, be born!
Truth breaks through!
         How big is the prick of the President?
75                  How big is Cardinal Vietnam?
         How little the prince of the FBI, unmarried all these years!
              How big are all the Public Figures?
         What kind of flesh hangs, hidden behind their Images?


                                        Approaching Salina,
80          Prehistoric excavation, *Apache Uprising*
                              in the drive-in theater
              Shelling Bombing Range   mapped in the distance,
              Crime Prevention Show, sponsor Wrigley's Spearmint
              Dinosaur Sinclair° advertisement, glowing green—
85          South 9th Street lined with poplar & elm branch
                    spread over evening's tiny headlights—
              Salina Highschool's brick darkens Gothic
                              over a night-lit door—
              What wreaths of naked bodies, thighs and faces,
90                       small hairy bun'd vaginas,
                         silver cocks, armpits and breasts
              moistened by tears
                              for 20 years, for 40 years?
         Peking Radio surveyed by Luden's Coughdrops
95                  Attacks on the Russians & Japanese,
         Big Dipper leaning above the Nebraska border,
                         handle down to the blackened plains,
              telephone-pole ghosts crossed
                              by roadside, dim headlights—
100         dark night, & giant T-bone steaks,
                    and in *The Village Voice°*
              New Frontier Productions present
                    Camp Comedy: *Fairies I Have Met.*
         Blue highway lamps strung along the horizon east at Hebron
105                 Homestead National Monument near Beatrice—

---

84 *Sinclair:* an oil company whose gasoline stations included a green dinosaur as part of their logo.
101 *Voice:* liberal newspaper published in New York City.

Language, language
    black Earth-circle in the rear window,
        no cars for miles along highway
    beacon lights on oceanic plain
110    language, language
        over Big Blue River°
    chanting *La illaha el (lill) Allah hu*°
    revolving my head to my heart like my mother
    chin abreast at Allah
115        Eyes closed, blackness
vaster than midnight prairies,
    Nebraskas of solitary Allah,
    Joy, I am I
    the lone One singing to myself
120        God come true—
    Thrills of fear.
    nearer than the vein in my neck—?
What if I opened my soul to sing to my absolute self
    Singing as the car crash chomped thru blood & muscle
125        tendon skull?
    What if I sang, and loosed the chords of fear brow?
    What exquisite noise wd
        shiver my car companions?
    I am the Universe tonite
130        riding in all my Power riding
chauffeured thru my self by a long haired saint with eyeglasses
What if I sang till Students knew I was free
    of Vietnam, trousers, free of my own meat,
    free to die in my thoughtful shivering Throne?
135        freer than Nebraska, freer than America—
    May I disappear
    in magic Joy-smoke! Pouf! reddish Vapor,
Faustus vanishes weeping & laughing
    under stars on Highway 77 between Beatrice & Lincoln—
140    "Better not to move but let things be" Reverend Preacher?
    We've all already disappeared!

Space highway open, entering Lincoln's ear
    ground to a stop Tracks Warning
    Pioneer Boulevard—
145    William Jennings Bryan° sang
*Thou shalt not crucify mankind upon a cross of Gold!*
    O Baby Doe! Gold's
    Department Store hulks o'er 10th Street now
    —an unregenerate old fop who didn't want to be a monkey
150    now's the Highest Perfect Wisdom dust
    and Lindsay's cry°
    survives compassionate in the Highschool Anthology—

---

111 *Big Blue River:* flows from Nebraska to Kansas.
112 . . . *hu:* (Arabic) "There is no god but God [Allah]."
145 *Bryan:* (1860–1925), congressman and presidential candidate, leader of populist silver movement.
145 *monkey:* W. J. Bryan was also a fundamentalist who opposed Darwinian evolutionary theory.
151 *Lindsay's cry:* Vachel Lindsay's poem "Bryan, Bryan, Bryan, Bryan" (1910).

a giant dormitory brilliant on the evening plain
                              drifts with his memories—
155   There's a nice white door over there
                        for me O dear!   on Zero Street.

## II

Face the Nation
Thru Hickman's rolling earth hills
              icy winter
160                           gray sky     bare trees lining the road
          South to Wichita
                  you're in the Pepsi Generation     Signum enroute
      Aiken° Republican on the radio          60,000
              Northvietnamese troops now infiltrated but over 250,000
165       South Vietnamese     armed men
                              our Enemy—
                              Not Hanoi our enemy
                              Not China our enemy
                              The Viet Cong!

170                           McNamara° made a "bad guess"
      "Bad Guess?" chorused the Reporters.
              Yes, no more than a Bad Guess, in 1962
                      "8000 American Troops handle the
                              Situation"
175                           Bad Guess
          in 1954, 80% of the
              Vietnamese people would've voted for Ho Chi Minh
              wrote Ike°     years later     *Mandate for Change*
                      A bad guess in the Pentagon
180   And the Hawks were guessing all along
                      Bomb China's 200,000,000
                      cried Stennis° from Mississippi
                      I guess it was 3 weeks ago
          Holmes Alexander in Albuquerque Journal
185               Provincial newsman
                      said I guess we better begin to do that Now,
                  his typewriter clacking in his aged office
                  on a side street     under Sandia° Mountain?

---

163 *Aiken*: George D. Aiken (b. 1892), Republican senator from Vermont since 1940. In-
terviewed on the program *Face the Nation* in 1966, Aiken declared the Vietnam involve-
ment a "bad guess."

170 *McNamara*: Robert McNamara (b. 1916), U.S. Defense secretary during the Vietnam
War.

178 *Ike*: U.S. President Dwight D. Eisenhower (1890–1969). His *Mandate for Change* was
published in 1963.

182 *Stennis*: John C. Stennis (b. 1901), conservative U.S. senator from Mississippi.

188 *Sandia*: mountain range in New Mexico, east of Albuquerque.

Half the world away from China
190 Johnson° got some bad advice    Republican Aiken sang
to the Newsmen over the radio
The General° guessed they'd stop infiltrating the South
if they bombed the North—
So I guess they bombed!
195 Pale Indochinese boys came thronging thru the jungle
in increased numbers
to the scene of TERROR!
While the triangle-roofed Farmer's Grain Elevator
sat quietly by the side of the road
200 along the railroad track
American Eagle beating its wings over Asia
million dollar helicopters
a billion dollars worth of Marines
who loved *Aunt Betty*°
205 Drawn from the shores and farms shaking
from the high schools to the landing barge
blowing the air thru their cheeks with fear
in *Life* on Television
Put it this way on the radio
210 Put it this way in television language
Use the words
language, language:
"A bad guess"
Put it this way in headlines
215 Omaha World Herald— *Rusk° Says Toughness*
*Essential For Peace*

Put it this way
Lincoln Nebraska morning Star—
*Vietnam War Brings Prosperity*
220 Put it *this* way
Declared McNamara    speaking language
Asserted Maxwell Taylor°
General, Consultant to White House
Viet Cong losses leveling up three five zero zero per month
225 Front page testimony February '66
Here in Nebraska same as Kansas same known in Saigon
in Peking, in Moscow, same known
by the youths of Liverpool three five zero zero
the latest quotation in the human meat market—
230 Father I cannot tell a lie!

---

190 *Johnson:* Lyndon Baines Johnson (1908–1973), U.S. president 1963–1969. His domestic accomplishments were overshadowed by his support of the Vietnam War.
192 *General:* U.S. Air Force general Curtis LeMay (1906–1990) urged America to use nuclear weapons to "bomb North Vietnam back to the Stone Age." In 1968, he was George Wallace's running mate in Wallace's campaign for the U.S. presidency.
204 *Aunt Betty:* highway billboard advertising bread.
215 *Rusk:* Dean Rusk (b. 1909), U.S. Secretary of State, 1961–1969.
222 *Taylor:* Maxwell Davenport Taylor (1901–1987), U.S. military officer; appointed U.S. ambassador to South Vietnam in 1964, he successfully urged Lyndon Johnson to increase American participation in the war.

A black horse bends its head to the stubble
    beside the silver stream winding thru the woods
      by an antique red barn on the outskirts of Beatrice°—
             Quietness, quietness
235        over this countryside
           except for unmistakable signals on radio
             followed by the honkytonk tinkle
                of a city piano
    to calm the nerves of taxpaying housewives of a Sunday morn.
240              Has anyone looked in the eyes of the dead?
U.S. Army recruiting service sign *Careers With A Future*
    Is anyone living to look for future forgiveness?
Water hoses frozen on the street, the
    Crowd gathered to see a strange happening garage—
245        Red flames on Sunday morning
           in a quiet town!
Has anyone looked in the eyes of the wounded?
    Have we seen but paper faces, Life Magazine?
    Are screaming faces made of dots,
250        electric dots on Television—
          fuzzy decibels registering
          the mammal voiced howl
from the outskirts of Saigon to console model picture tubes
    in Beatrice, in Hutchinson, in El Dorado°
255        in historic Abilene°
        O inconsolable!

      Stop, and eat more flesh.
"We will negotiate anywhere anytime"
    said the giant President
260    Kansas City Times 2/14/66: "Word reached U.S. authorities that
Thailand's leaders feared that in Honolulu Johnson might have tried to
persuade South Vietnam's rulers to ease their stand against negotiating
with the Viet Cong.
    American officials said these fears were groundless and Humphrey
265  was telling the Thais so."
             AP dispatch
           The last week's paper is Amnesia.

Three five zero zero is numerals
Headline language poetry, nine decades after Democratic Vistas
270    and the Prophecy of the Good Gray Poet°
      Our nation "of the fabled damned"
        or else . . .
    Language, language

---

233 *Beatrice*: Nebraska town on Route 77.
254 *Hutchinson, El Dorado*: Kansas towns en route between Lincoln, Nebraska, and Wichita, Kansas.
255 *Abilene*: Dwight D. Eisenhower's birthplace and site of his presidential library.
270 *Poet*: Walt Whitman.

Ezra Pound the Chinese Written Character for truth
275　　　　　　defined as man standing by his word
　　　　　　　　Word picture:　　　　forked creature
　　　　　　　　　　　　　　　　　Man
　　　　standing by a box, birds flying out
　　　　　　representing mouth speech
280　　　　Ham Steak please waitress, in the warm café.
　　　　Different from a bag guess.
　　　　　　　　　The war is language,
　　　　　　　　　　language abused
　　　　　　　　　　　　for Advertisement,
285　　　　　　　　　　language used
　　　　　　　like magic for power on the planet:
Black Magic language,
　　　　formulas for reality—
　　　　　　Communism is a 9 letter word
290　　　　　　　　　　used by inferior magicians with
the wrong alchemical formula for transforming earth into gold
　　　　　—funky warlocks operating on guesswork,
　　　　　　　　　handmedown mandrake terminology
　　　　　　　　　　　that never worked in 1956
295　　　　for gray-domed Dulles,°
　　　　　　　　　brooding over at State,
　　　　that never worked for Ike who knelt to take
　　　　　　the magic wafer in his mouth
　　　　　　　　from Dulles' hand
300　　　　　　　　　　inside the church in Washington:
Communion of bum magicians
　　　　　　congress of failures from Kansas & Missouri
　　　working with the wrong equations
　　　Sorcerer's Apprentices who lost control
305　　　　　of the simplest broomstick in the world:
　　　　　　　　　Language
O longhaired magician come home take care of your dumb helper
　before the radiation deluge floods your livingroom,
　　　　　　　　your magic errandboy's
310　　　　　　　　　just made a bad guess again
　　　　　　that's lasted a whole decade.

　N B C B S U P A P I N S L I F E
　Time Mutual presents
　　　　World's Largest Camp Comedy:
315　　　　　　　　Magic In Vietnam—
　　reality turned inside out
　　　　　changing its sex in the Mass Media
　　　　　for 30 days, TV den and bedroom farce

---

295 *Dulles:* John Foster Dulles (1888–1959), U.S. Secretary of State (1953–1959), chief architect of U.S. cold war anticommunist policies and strong backer of the Diem regime in South Vietnam.

Flashing pictures Senate Foreign Relations Committee room
320           Generals faces flashing on and off screen
                                    mouthing language
      State Secretary speaking nothing but language
      McNamara declining to speak public language
      The President talking language,
325           Senators reinterpreting language
      General Taylor *Limited Objectives*
                            *Owls* from Pennsylvania
            Clark's° Face *Open Ended*
                            Dove's *Apocalypse*
330                       Morse's° hairy ears
      Stennis orating in Mississippi
            half billion chinamen crowding into the
                                    polling booth,
      Clean shaven Gen. Gavin's° image
335                       imagining *Enclaves*
            Tactical Bombing the magic formula for
      a silver haired Symington:°
      Ancient Chinese apothegm:
                  *Old in vain.*
340     Hawks swooping thru the newspapers
            talons visible
      wings outspread in the giant updraft of hot air
                  loosing their dry screech in the skies
                              over the Capitol
345   Napalm and black clouds emerging in newsprint
            Flesh soft as a Kansas girl's
                  ripped open by metal explosion—
      three five zero zero     on the other side of the planet
            caught in barbed wire, fire ball
350               bullet shock, bayonet electricity
      bomb blast terrific in skull & belly, shrapneled throbbing meat
      While this American nation argues war:
            conflicting language, language
                  proliferating in airwaves
355   filling the farmhouse ear, filling
            the city Manager's head in his oaken office
            the professor's head in his bed at midnight
            the pupil's head at the movies
                  blond haired, his heart throbbing with desire
360               for the girlish image bodied on the screen:
                  or smoking cigarettes
                  and watching Captain Kangaroo°
                  that fabled damned of nations
                  prophecy come true—

---

328 *Clark:* Joseph S. Clark (b. 1901), U.S. senator from Pennsylvania who considered the Vietnam War "open-ended."
330 *Morse:* Wayne Morse (1900–1974), U.S. senator from Oregon who opposed U.S. involvement in Vietnam.
334 *Gavin:* James Maurice Gavin (1907–1990), U.S. army officer.
337 *Symington:* Stuart Symington (1901–1988), U.S. senator from Missouri (1953–1976) who was critical of U.S. presence in Vietnam.
362 *smoking . . . Kangaroo:* pop song referring to children's television program *Captain Kangaroo.*

365          Though the highway's straight,
                    dipping downward through low hills,
                    rising narrow on the far horizon
                         black cows browse in caked fields
                               ponds in the hollows lie frozen,
                                    quietness.
370     Is this the land that started war on China?
                    This be the soil that thought Cold War for decades?
                    Are these nervous naked trees & farmhouses
                                    the vortex
                               of oriental anxiety molecules
375          that've imagined     American Foreign Policy
                    and magick'd up paranoia in Peking
                               and curtains of living blood
                                    surrounding far Saigon?
         Are these the towns where the language emerged
380          from the mouths here
                         that makes a Hell of riots in Dominica
                    sustains the aging tyranny of Chiang in silent Taipeh city
                    Paid for the lost French war in Algeria
                         overthrew the Guatemalan polis in '54
385          maintaining United Fruit's° banana greed
                               another thirteen years
                         for the secret prestige of the Dulles family lawfirm?


         Here's Marysville—
                    a black railroad engine in the children's park,
390                              at rest—
         and the Track Crossing
                    with Cotton Belt flatcars
                               carrying autos west from Dallas
                    Delaware & Hudson gondolas filled with power stuff—
395          a line of boxcars far east as the eye can see
                               carrying battle goods to cross the Rockies
                    into the hands of rich longshoremen loading
                                    ships on the Pacific—
                    Oakland Army Terminal° lights
400                              blue illumined all night now—

---

385 *United Fruit*: United Fruit Company is an American multinational company founded
in 1899 in a merger of various Central American enterprises. It became not only the sin-
gle largest fruit and produce company but also the largest employer in Central America.
It became a symbol of American economic control and the equivalent of a government
colonizer. Sometimes called "the octopus," United Fruit held vast reserves of undeveloped
land, regularly interfered in the political affairs of host countries, discriminated against
the local labor forces, monopolized railroads and ports, abandoned imported labor when
production needs changed, and extracted a country's national resources without fair rec-
ompense. United Fruit Company's law firm Sullivan and Cromwell employed Secretary of
State John Foster Dulles, whose brother Allen coordinated the 1954 CIA-backed overthrow
of Guatemala's president.
399 *Oakland Army Terminal*: a war transshipment center in Oakland, California, that had
been picketed by antiwar protestors.

Crash of couplings and the great American train
        moves on carrying its cushioned load of metal doom
    Union Pacific linked together with your Hoosier Line
        followed by passive Wabash
405             rolling behind
        all Erie carrying cargo in the rear,
    Central Georgia's rust colored truck proclaiming
          *The Right Way,* concluding
  the awesome poem writ by the train
410           across northern Kansas,
    land which gave right of way
    to the massing of metal meant for explosion
           in Indochina—
Passing thru Waterville,
415     Electronic machinery in the bus humming prophecy—
    paper signs blowing in cold wind,
        mid-Sunday afternoon's silence in town
    under frost-gray sky
          that covers the horizon—
420 That the rest of earth is unseen,
         an outer universe invisible,
    Unknown except thru
          language
            airprint
425              magic images
  or prophecy of the secret
    heart the same
      in Waterville as Saigon° one human form:
  When a woman's heart bursts in Waterville
430         a woman screams equal in Hanoi°—
On to Wichita to prophesy! O frightful Bard!
  into the heart of the Vortex
    where anxiety rings
      the University with millionaire° pressure,
435     lonely crank telephone voices sighing in dread,
  and students waken trembling in their beds
    with dreams of a new truth warm as meat,
    little girls suspecting their elders of murder
      committed by remote control machinery,
440     boys with sexual bellies aroused
      chilled in the heart by the mailman
  with a letter from an aging white haired General
    Director° of selection for service in Deathwar
  all this black language
445       writ by machine!
    O hopeless Fathers and Teachers
  in Hué°  do you know
      the same woe too?

---

428 *Saigon:* capital of South Vietnam.
430 *Hanoi:* capital of North Vietnam.
434 *millionaire:* a wealthy backer of the reactionary John Birch Society.
443 *Director:* Lewis B. Hershey (1893–1977), Selective Service Director, in charge of draft
for military service since his 1948 appointment.
447 *Hué:* South Vietnamese city.

I'm an old man now, and a lonesome man in Kansas
450          but not afraid
                    to speak my lonesomeness in a car,
                    because not only my lonesomeness
                    it's Ours, all over America,
                              O tender fellows—
                    & spoken lonesomeness is Prophecy
455                in the moon 100 years ago or in
                              the middle of Kansas now.
     It's not the vast plains mute our mouths
                    that fill at midnite with ecstatic language
               when our trembling bodies hold each other
460                     breast to breast on a mattress—
          Not the empty sky that hides
                              the feeling from our faces
          nor our skirts and trousers that conceal
                    the bodylove emanating in a glow of beloved skin,
465                white smooth abdomen down to the hair
                                        between our legs,
          It's not a God that bore us that forbid
                    our Being, like a sunny rose
                         all red with naked joy
470                between our eyes & bellies, yes
     All we do is for this frightened thing
                    we call Love, want and lack—
          fear that we aren't the one whose body could be
                    beloved of all the brides of Kansas City,
475                kissed all over by every boy of Wichita—
          O but how many in their solitude weep aloud like me—
                    On the bridge over Republican River°
                    almost in tears to know
                              how to speak the right language—
480                on the frosty broad road
                         uphill between highway embankments
          I search for the language
                              that is also yours—
               almost all our language has been taxed by war.
485     Radio antennae high tension
                    wires ranging from Junction City across the plains—
          highway cloverleaf sunk in a vast meadow
                    lanes curving past Abilene
                         to Denver filled with old
490                              heroes of love—
                    to Wichita where McClure's° mind
                         burst into animal beauty
                         drunk, getting laid in a car
                              in a neon misted street
495                                   15 years ago—
          to Independence where the old man's still alive°
          who loosed the bomb that's slaved all human consciousness
                    and made the body universe a place of fear—

---

477 *Republican River:* runs from Kansas City to Junction City.
491 *McClure:* poet Michael McClure, born in 1932 in Marysville, Kansas; important figure in the Beat movement.
496 *alive:* former president Harry S. Truman (1884–1972).

Now, speeding along the empty plain,
500                    no giant demon machine
                              visible on the horizon
        but tiny human trees and wooden houses at the sky's edge
                    I claim my birthright!
                         reborn forever as long as Man
505                             in Kansas or other universe—Joy
               reborn after the vast sadness of War Gods!
A lone man talking to myself, no house in the brown vastness to hear,
               imaging the throng of Selves
                         that make this nation one body of Prophecy
510                    languaged by Declaration as
                                        Happiness!
        I call all Powers of imagination
           to my side in this auto to make Prophecy,
                                        all Lords
515           of human kingdoms to come
        Shambu Bharti Baba° naked covered with ash
                    Khaki Baba° fat-bellied mad with the dogs
        Dehorahava Baba° who moans Oh how wounded, How wounded
               Sitaram Onkar Das Thakur° who commands
520                             give up your desire
        Satyananda° who raises two thumbs in tranquillity
               Kali Pada Guha Roy° whose yoga drops before the void
                    Shivananda° who touches the breast and says OM
        Srimata Krishnaji° of Brindaban° who says take for your guru
525           William Blake° the invisible father of English visions
               Sri Ramakrishna° master of ecstasy eyes
                    half closed who only cries for his mother
        Chaitanya° arms upraised singing & dancing his own praise
               merciful Chango judging our bodies
530                    Durga-Ma° covered with blood
                         destroyer of battlefield illusions
               million-faced Tathagata° gone past suffering
        Preserver Harekrishna returning in the age of pain

---

516 *Bharti Baba:* a Naga (naked) saddhu Ginsberg met at a cremation ground in the city
of Benares.
517 *Khaki Baba:* nineteenth-century North Bengali saint.
518 *Dehorahava Baba:* yogi author Ginsberg met at Ganges River in 1963.
519 *Thakur:* Hindu god.
521 *Satyananda:* Calcutta swami Ginsberg met in 1962; he had twin-thumbed hands and
told Ginsberg "Be a sweet poet of the Lord."
522 *Roy:* tantric guru Ginsberg met in Benares in 1963.
523 *Shivananda:* swami Ginsberg visited in Rishikesh in 1962.
524 *Krishnaji:* Brindaban female saint who translated Kabir's poetry and advised Ginsberg.
524 *Brindaban:* holy town near Delhi in India, where Krishna spent his childhood.
525 *Blake:* (1757–1827), British poet, painter, and visionary.
526 *Ramakrishna:* (1834–1886), Bengali mystic and poet.
528 *Chaitanya:* sixteenth-century North Bengali saint, founder of Hare Krishna Maha-
Mantra tradition.
530 *Durga-Ma:* ten-armed goddess of war fields in Bengali Hindu mythology, she consumes
evil through violence.
532 *Tathagata:* (Sanskrit) "He who has passed through" or "that which passed."

Sacred Heart my Christ acceptable
535                    Allah the Compassionate One
                              Jaweh Righteous One
                    all Knowledge-Princes of Earth-man, all
          ancient Seraphim° of heavenly Desire, Devas,° yogis
                    & holymen I chant to—
540                              Come to my lone presence
                                   into this Vortex named Kansas,
     I lift my voice aloud,
               make Mantra° of American language now,
                    I here declare the end of the War!
545                         Ancient days' Illusion!—
               and pronounce words beginning my own millennium.
     Let the States tremble,
          let the Nation weep,
               let Congress legislate its own delight
550                    let the President execute his own desire—
     this Act done by my own voice,
                         nameless Mystery—
     published to my own senses,
                    blissfully received by my own form
555          approved with pleasure by my sensations
                    manifestation of my very thought
                    accomplished in my own imagination
                         all realms within my consciousness fulfilled
               60 miles from Wichita
560                         near El Dorado,
                              The Golden One,
     in chill earthly mist
               houseless brown farmland plains rolling heavenward
                                        in every direction
565  one midwinter afternoon Sunday called the day of the Lord—
          Pure Spring Water gathered in one tower
                         where Florence is
                                   set on a hill,
                    stop for tea & gas


570          Cars passing their messages along country crossroads
                    to populaces cement-networked on flatness,
                              giant white mist on earth
                    and a Wichita Eagle-Beacon headlines
                    *"Kennedy° Urges Cong Get Chair in Negotiations"*
575  The War is gone,
               Language emerging on the motel news stand,
                              the right magic

---

538 *Seraphim:* winged heavenly beings stationed above the throne of God.
538 *Devas:* Indian gods.
543 *Mantra:* sacred verbal spell or prayer.
574 *Kennedy:* February 14, 1966, proposal by U.S. senator Robert F. Kennedy (1925–1968) that the Viet Cong be given a place in the Vietnam government. Kennedy was shot to death during his 1968 presidential campaign.

Formula, the language known
in the back of the mind before, now in black print
580                                     daily consciousness
Eagle News Services Saigon—
Headline Surrounded Vietcong Charge Into Fire Fight
the suffering not yet ended
for others
585                   The last spasms of the dragon of pain
shoot thru the muscles
a crackling around the eyeballs
of a sensitive yellow boy by a muddy wall
Continued from page one°      area
590                   after the Marines killed 256 Vietcong captured 31
ten day operation Harvest Moon last December
Language language
U.S. Military Spokesmen
Language language
595                                     Cong death toll
has soared to 100 in First Air Cavalry
Division's Sector of
Language language
Operation White Wing near Bong Son°
600       Some of the
Language language
Communist
Language language soldiers
charged so desperately
605             they were struck with six or seven bullets before they fell
Language Language M 60 Machine Guns
Language language in La Drang° Valley
the terrain is rougher infested with leeches and scorpions
The war was over several hours ago!
610       Oh at last again the radio opens
blue Invitations!
Angelic Dylan° singing across the nation
"When all your children start to resent you
Won't you come see me, Queen Jane?"
615       His youthful voice making glad
the brown endless meadows
His tenderness penetrating aether,
soft prayer on the airwaves,
Language language, and sweet music too
620             even unto thee,
hairy flatness!
even unto thee
despairing Burns!°

---

589 *page one*: in *Wichita Eagle*, February 14, 1966.
599 *Bong Son*: 100 Viet Cong soldiers were killed close to Bong Son; reportedly many were
struck several times.
607 *La Drang*: Vietnam war battle.
612 *Dylan*: Bob Dylan (b. 1941), one of the most famous folk and rock singers and com-
posers of his generation.
623 *Burns*: Kansas town near Wichita.

Future speeding on swift wheels
625           straight to the heart of Wichita!
Now radio voices cry population hunger world
              of unhappy people
        waiting for Man to be born
              O man in America!
630     *you certainly smell good*
              the radio says
        passing mysterious families of winking towers
        grouped round a quonset-hut on a hillock—
              feed storage or military fear factory here?
635     Sensitive City, Ooh! Hamburger & Skelley's Gas
                    lights feed man and machine,
        Kansas Electric Substation aluminum robot
        signals thru thin antennae towers
        above the empty football field
640                                     at Sunday dusk
        to a solitary derrick that pumps oil from the unconscious
                    working night & day
        & factory gas-flares edge a huge golf course
              where tired businessmen can come and play—
645     Cloverleaf, Merging Traffic East Wichita turnoff
                    McConnell Airforce Base
                          nourishing the city—
        Lights rising in the suburbs
        Supermarket Texaco brilliance starred
650                over streetlamp vertebrae on Kellogg,°
        green jeweled traffic lights
              confronting the windshield,
        Centertown ganglion entered!
              Crowds of autos moving with their lightshine,
655           signbulbs winking in the driver's eyeball—
        The human nest collected, neon lit,
                    and sunburst signed
              for business as usual, except on the Lord's Day—
        Redeemer Lutheran's three crosses lit on the lawn
660                 reminder of our sins
        and Titsworth offers insurance on Hydraulic°
        by De Voors Guard's Mortuary for outmoded bodies
                    of the human vehicle
              which no Titsworth of insurance will customize for resale—
665     So home, traveler, past the newspaper° language factory
              under Union Station railroad bridge on Douglas
              to the center of the Vortex, calmly returned
                    to Hotel Eaton°—

---

650 *Kellogg:* main street in Wichita.
661 *Hydraulic:* street name.
665 *newspaper: Wichita Eagle-Beacon* office.
668 *Hotel Eaton:* On Douglas Street, near Vortex Gallery patronized by Charles Plymell and Kansas artists. Plymell is an American poet, filmmaker, and editor who accompanied Ginsberg on his Kansas-Nebraska trip.

Carry Nation° began the war on Vietnam here
670                          with an angry smashing ax
                                 attacking Wine—
        Here fifty years ago, by her violence
    began a vortex of hatred that defoliated the Mekong Delta—
        Proud Wichita! vain Wichita
675                   cast the first stone!—
                          That murdered my mother
            who died of the communist anticommunist psychosis
                in the madhouse one decade long ago
        complaining about wires of masscommunication in her head
680                   and phantom political voices in the air
                             besmirching her girlish character.
        Many another has suffered death and madness
            in the Vortex from Hydraulic
                   to the end of 17th—enough!
685   The war is over now—
            Except for the souls
                   held prisoner in Niggertown°
        still pining for love of your tender white bodies O children of Wichita!
                                                         *1966*


## Father Death Blues°

Hey Father Death, I'm flying home
Hey poor man, you're all alone
Hey old daddy, I know where I'm going

Father Death, Don't cry any more
5   Mama's there, underneath the floor
Brother Death, please mind the store

Old Aunty Death   Don't hide your bones
Old Uncle Death   I hear your groans
O Sister Death   how sweet your moans

10   O Children Deaths go breathe your breaths
Sobbing breasts'll ease your Deaths
Pain is gone, tears take the rest

Genius Death   your art is done
Lover Death your body's gone
15   Father Death   I'm coming home

---

669 *Carry Nation*: (1846–1911), temperance crusader who used a hatchet to destroy saloons
in Wichita in 1900.
687 *Niggertown*: Wichita neighborhood between Hydraulic and 17th Streets.
**poem title:** Composed in the air over Lake Michigan, "Father Death Blues" later became
Part V of a poem sequence, "Don't Grow Old." Ginsberg set "Father Death Blues" to mu-
sic and performed it at readings.

Guru Death your words are true
Teacher Death I do thank you
For inspiring me to sing this Blues

Buddha Death, I wake with you
20 Dharma Death, your mind is new
Sangha Death, we'll work it through

Suffering is what was born
Ignorance made me forlorn
Tearful truths I cannot scorn

25 Father Breath once more farewell
Birth you gave was no thing ill
My heart is still, as time will tell.

1976

# Robert Creeley (b. 1926)

Creeley was born in Arlington, Massachusetts, near where he grew up on a small farm. As a young child he suffered two losses, that of his father and that of his left eye. He was raised by his mother, who worked as a public health nurse. Creeley enrolled at Harvard but took a leave to be an ambulance driver for the American Field Service toward the end of World War II. He was in the India-Burma area from 1944–1945. He returned to Harvard but left without his degree, taking up subsistence farming for a time in New Hampshire. A correspondence with poet Charles Olson, maintained while Creeley was in France and Spain, led him to Black Mountain College in North Carolina, where he completed his degree, began to teach, and edited the *Black Mountain Review*. He later spent time at New Mexico and in Guatemala before taking a job in Buffalo for the rest of his career.

A thin, spare, compressed, and consistently minimalist verse has become his signature style. Certainly the phrasing often seems conversational, though jazz is another continuing influence, but the progress of a poem is often interrupted by hesitation, sudden wonder, or disabling pain. Thus in the end it is consciousness' interior struggle with both self-reflection and exterior circumstances that explains his sometimes broken rhythms. William Carlos Williams was clearly a strong influence, both in form and subject matter, but a Williams poem flows smoothly, whereas a Creeley poem may choose to falter.

## After Lorca°

(for M. Marti)

The church is a business, and the rich
are the business men.
               When they pull on the bells, the
poor come piling in and when a poor man dies, he has a
5      ◁ wooden
cross, and they rush through the ceremony.

---

**poem title:** *Lorca:* Federico García Lorca (1898–1936), the premier poet of modern Spain, murdered by right-wing soldiers at the outset of the Spanish Civil War. See, for example, García Lorca's "Ode to the Most Holy Sacrament of the Altar."

But when a rich man dies, they
drag out the Sacrament
and a golden Cross, and go *doucement, doucement*°
10     to the cemetery.

And the poor love it
and think it's crazy.

                                        *1953*


## I Know a Man

As I sd to my
friend, because I am
always talking,—John, I

sd, which was not his
5     name, the darkness sur-
rounds us, what

can we do against
it, or else, shall we &
why not, buy a goddamn big car,

10     drive, he sd, for
christ's sake, look
out where yr going.

                                        *1954*


## The Flower

I think I grow tensions
like flowers
in a wood where
nobody goes.

5     Each wound is perfect,
encloses itself in a tiny
imperceptible blossom,
making pain.

10     Pain is a flower like that one,
like this one,
like that one,
like this one.

                                        *1958*

---

9 *doucement:* (French) "sweetly."

# For Love

for Bobbie°

Yesterday I wanted to
speak of it, that sense above
the others to me
important because all

5      that I know derives
from what it teaches me.
Today, what is it that
is finally so helpless,

different, despairs of its own
10     statement, wants to
turn away, endlessly
to turn away.

If the moon did not . . .
no, if you did not
15     I wouldn't either, but
what would I not

do, what prevention, what
thing so quickly stopped.
That is love yesterday
20     or tomorrow, not

now. Can I eat
what you give me. I
have not earned it. Must
I think of everything

25     as earned. Now love also
becomes a reward so
remote from me I have
only made it with my mind.

Here is tedium,
30     despair, a painful
sense of isolation and
whimsical if pompous

self-regard. But that image
is only of the mind's
35     vague structure, vague to me
because it is my own.

Love, what do I think
to say. I cannot say it.
What have you become to ask,
40     what have I made you into,

---

dedication: *Bobbie:* Creeley's second wife.

companion, good company,
crossed legs with skirt, or
soft body under
the bones of the bed.

45  Nothing says anything
but that which it wishes
would come true, fears
what else might happen in

some other place, some
50  other time not this one.
A voice in my place, an
echo of that only in yours.

Let me stumble into
not the confession but
55  the obsession I begin with
now. For you

also (also)
some time beyond place, or
place beyond time, no
60  mind left to

say anything at all,
that face gone, now.
Into the company of love°
it all returns.

1962

## America

America, you ode for reality!°
Give back the people you took.

Let the sun shine again
on the four corners of the world

5  you though of first but do not
own, or keep like a convenience.

*People* are your own word, you
invented that locus and term.

*Here,* you said and say, is
10  where we are. Give back

what we are, these people you made,
*us,* and nowhere but you to be.

1969

---

63 *the company of love*: a quotation from Hart Crane's "The Broken Tower."
1 *ode for reality*: Creeley may be alluding to Whitman's famous description of the United
States as "essentially the greatest poem" in the preface to *Leaves of Grass*.

# Age

Most explicit—
the sense of trap

as a narrowing
cone one's got

5      stuck into and
any movement

forward simply
wedges one more—

but where
10     or quite when,

even with whom,
since now there is no one

quite with you—Quite? Quiet?
English expression: *Quait?*

15     Language of singular
impedance? A dance? An

involuntary gesture to
others *not* there? What's

wrong here? How
20     reach out to the

other side all
others live on as

now you see the
two doctors, behind

25     you, in mind's eye,
probe into your anus,

or ass, or bottom,
behind you, the roto-

rooter-like device
30     sees all up, concludes

"like a worn-out inner tube,"
"old," prose prolapsed, person's

problems won't do, must
cut into, cut out . . .

35    The world is a round but
diminishing ball, a spherical

ice cube, a dusty
joke, a fading,

faint echo of its
40    former self but remembers,

sometimes, its past, sees
friends, places, reflections,

talks to itself in a fond,
judgmental murmur,

45    alone at last.
I stood so close

to you I could have
reached out and

touched you just
50    as you turned

over and began to
snore not unattractively,

no, never less than
attractively, my love,

55    *my love*—but in this
curiously glowing dark, this

finite emptiness, *you, you, you*
are crucial, hear the

whimpering back of
60    the talk, the approaching

fears when I may
cease to be me, all

lost or rather lumped
here in a retrograded,

65    dislocating, imploding
*self,* a uselessness

talks, even if finally to no one,
talks and talks.

*1988*

# Robert Bly (b. 1926)

Bly was born in Madison, a town in rural Minnesota, where he has lived most of his life. He was educated at St. Olaf's College and at Harvard, thereafter enrolling in the Writer's Workshop at the University of Iowa. From 1944 to 1946, Bly served in the Navy. In addition to his poetry, he has done a number of translations, including poetry by Neruda, Vallejo, and Rilke, and edited a continuing journal renamed after each decade—*The Fifties, The Sixties,* etc. In recent years, he has been a leading figure in the men's movement, for which he has written successful manifestoes, including the widely read *Iron John* (1992).

Influences on his poetry include the poets he has translated and the seventeenth-century mystic Jakob Boehme. He has given intense poetry readings in masks, actively opposed the Vietnam War, and believes scientific rationalism has led us astray. He seeks deep images drawn from the unconscious and deploys them in relatively simple structures, believing that such subconscious or unconscious revelations can resist the dominant Cartesian logic of the Western world.

## Looking at New-Fallen Snow from a Train

Snow has covered the next line of tracks,
And filled the empty cupboards in the milkweed pods;
It has stretched out on the branches of weeds,
And softened the frost-hills, and the barbed-wire rolls
Left leaning against a fencepost—
It has drifted onto the window ledges high in the peaks of barns.

    A man throws back his head, gasps
    And dies. His ankles twitch, his hands open and close,
    And the fragment of time that he has eaten is exhaled from
        his pale mouth to nourish the snow.
    A salesman falls, striking his head on the edge of the counter.

Snow has filled out the peaks on the tops of rotted fence posts.
It has walked down to meet the slough water,
And fills all the steps of the ladder leaning against the eaves.
It rests on the doorsills of collapsing children's houses,
And on transformer boxes held from the ground forever in the
    center of cornfields.

A man lies down to sleep.
Hawks and crows gather around his bed.
Grass shoots up between the hawks' toes.
Each blade of grass is a voice.
The sword by his side breaks into flame.

*1967*

## Counting Small-Boned Bodies

Let's count the bodies over again.

If we could only make the bodies smaller,
The size of skulls,
We could make a whole plain white with skulls in the moonlight!

If we could only make the bodies smaller,
Maybe we could get
A whole year's kill in front of us on a desk!

*1967*

## The Dead Seal Near McClure's Beach

1

Walking north toward the point, I come on a dead seal. From a few feet away, he looks like a brown log. The body is on its back, dead only a few hours. I stand and look at him. A quiver in the dead flesh. My God he is still alive. A shock goes through me, as if a wall of my room had fallen away.

His head is arched back, the small eyes closed, the whiskers sometimes rise and fall. He is dying. This is the oil. Here on its back is the oil that heats our houses so efficiently. Wind blows fine sand back toward the ocean. The flipper near me lies folded over the stomach, looking like an unfinished arm, lightly glazed with sand at the edges. The other flipper lies half underneath. The seal's skin looks like an old overcoat, scratched here and there . . . by sharp mussels maybe. . . .

I reach out and touch him. Suddenly he rears up, turns over. He gives three cries, like those from Christmas toys. He lunges toward me. I am terrified and leap back, although I know there can be no teeth in that jaw. He starts flopping toward the sea. But he falls over, on his face. He does not want to go back to the sea. He looks up at the sky, and he looks like an old lady who has lost her hair.

He puts his chin back down on the sand, arranges his flippers, and waits for me to go. I go.

2

Today I go back to say goodbye; he's dead now. But he's not—he's a quarter mile farther up the shore. Today he is thinner, squatting on his stomach, head out. The ribs show more—each vertebra on the back under the coat now visible, shiny. He breathes in and out.

He raises himself up, and tucks his flippers under, as if to keep them warm. A wave comes in, touches his nose. He turns and looks at me—the eyes slanted, the crown of his head like a leather jacket. He is taking a long time to die. The whiskers white as porcupine quills, the forehead slopes, goodbye brother, die in the sound of waves, forgive us if we have killed you, long live your race, your innertube race, so uncomfortable on land, so comfortable in the sea. Be comfortable in death then, where the sand will be out of your nostrils, and you can swim in long loops through the pure death, ducking under as assassinations break above you. You don't want to be touched by me. I climb the cliff and go home the other way.

*1975*

# A. R. Ammons (b. 1926)

Born in a farmhouse near Whiteville, North Carolina, the son of a tobacco farmer, Archie Randolph Ammons served on a Navy destroyer escort in World War II. He studied biology and chemistry at Wake Forest College in his home state and went on to literary studies at Berkeley. In 1964, after working for almost a decade as an executive at a glassmaking firm, he took a teaching job at Cornell University. The landscapes of the places where he has lived—from North Carolina to the south coast of New Jersey and finally to the hills and fields around Ithaca, New York—figure prominently in his poetry. Like Muriel Rukeyser before him, he makes heavy use of the colon in punctuation; it is a way of visualizing relationships of continuity, equivalence, and interdependence in the things he describes. His nature poems mix exact local representation with transcendental longings and moments of wit and irony; he is often compared to Emerson. From nature's mutability he learns a mental discipline of adaptability and a recognition that absolute demarcation is not offered to us by the world around us. Thus in "Corsons Inlet," very nearly his signature poem, he walks a changing shoreline with no inherent enclosures and celebrates its devotion to process. The book-length poem *Sphere* (1974) may be his masterpiece.

## Corsons Inlet°

I went for a walk over the dunes again this morning
to the sea,
then turned right along
    the surf
5          rounded a naked headland
        and returned

    along the inlet shore:

it was muggy sunny, the wind from the sea steady and high
crisp in the running sand,
10        some breakthroughs of sun
    but after a bit

continuous overcast:

---

**poem title:** Located on the south New Jersey shore.

the walk liberating, I was released from forms,
from the perpendiculars,
15          straight lines, blocks, boxes, binds
of thought
into the hues, shadings, rises, flowing bends and blends
          of sight:

                    I allow myself eddies of meaning:
20     yield to a direction of significance
running
like a stream through the geography of my work:
     you can find
in my sayings
25               swerves of action
          like the inlet's cutting edge:
          there are dunes of motion,
organizations of grass, white sandy paths of remembrance
in the overall wandering of mirroring mind:

30     but Overall is beyond me: is the sum of these events
I cannot draw, the ledger I cannot keep, the accounting
beyond the account:

in nature there are few sharp lines: there are areas of
primrose
35          more or less dispersed;
disorderly orders of bayberry; between the rows
of dunes,
irregular swamps of reeds,
though not reeds alone, but grass, bayberry, yarrow, all . . .
40     predominantly reeds:

I have reached no conclusions, have erected no boundaries,
shutting out and shutting in, separating inside
          from outside: I have
          drawn no lines:
45          as

manifold events of sand
change the dune's shape that will not be the same shape
tomorrow,

so I am willing to go along, to accept
50     the becoming
thought, to stake off no beginnings or ends, establish
          no walls:

by transitions the land falls from grassy dunes to creek
to undercreek: but there are no lines, though
55          change in that transition is clear
          as any sharpness: but "sharpness" spread out,
allowed to occur over a wider range
than mental lines can keep:

the moon was full last night: today, low tide was low:
60   black shoals of mussels exposed to the risk
of air
and, earlier, of sun,
waved in and out with the waterline, waterline inexact,
caught always in the event of change:
65        a young mottled gull stood free on the shoals
and ate
to vomiting: another gull, squawking possession, cracked a crab,
picked out the entrails, swallowed the soft-shelled legs, a ruddy
turnstone running in to snatch leftover bits:

70   risk is full: every living thing in
siege: the demand is life, to keep life: the small
white blacklegged egret, how beautiful, quietly stalks and spears
the shallows, darts to shore
to stab—what? I couldn't
75        see against the black mudflats—a frightened
fiddler crab?

the news to my left over the dunes and
reeds and bayberry clumps was
fall: thousands of tree swallows
80        gathering for flight:
an order held
in constant change: a congregation
rich with entropy: nevertheless, separable, noticeable
as one event,
85             not chaos: preparations for
flight from winter,
cheet, cheet, cheet, cheet, wings rifling the green clumps,
beaks
at the bayberries
90        a perception full of wind, flight, curve,
sound:
the possibility of rule as the sum of rulelessness:
the "field" of action
with moving, incalculable center:

95   in the smaller view, order tight with shape:
blue tiny flowers on a leafless weed: carapace of crab:
snail shell:
pulsations of order
in the bellies of minnows: orders swallowed,
100  broken down, transferred through membranes
to strengthen larger orders: but in the large view, no
lines or changeless shapes: the working in and out, together
and against, of millions of events: this,
so that I make
105           no form
formlessness:

orders as summaries, as outcomes of actions override
or in some way result, not predictably (seeing me gain
the top of a dune,
110   the swallows
could take flight—some other fields of bayberry
            could enter fall
            berryless) and there is serenity:

            no arranged terror: no forcing of image, plan,
115   or thought:
no propaganda, no humbling of reality to precept:

terror pervades but is not arranged, all possibilities
of escape open: no route shut, except in
      the sudden loss of all routes:

120         I see narrow orders, limited tightness, but will
not run to that easy victory:
            still around the looser, wider forces work:
            I will try
      to fasten into order enlarging grasps of disorder, widening
125   scope, but enjoying the freedom that
Scope eludes my grasp, that there is no finality of vision,
that I have perceived nothing completely,
            that tomorrow a new walk is a new walk.

                                                            *1963*

# Gravelly Run

      I don't know somehow it seems sufficient
      to see and hear whatever coming and going is,
      losing the self to the victory
            of stones and trees,
5     of bending sandpit lakes, crescent
      round groves of dwarf pine:

      for it is not so much to know the self
      as to know it as it is known
            by galaxy and cedar cone,
10    as if birth had never found it
      and death could never end it:

      the swamp's slow water comes
      down Gravelly Run fanning the long
            stone-held algal
15    hair and narrowing roils between
      the shoulders of the highway bridge:

      holly grows on the banks in the woods there,
      and the cedars' gothic-clustered
            spires could make
20    green religion in winter bones:

      so I look and reflect, but the air's glass
      jail seals each thing in its entity:

no use to make any philosophies here:
  I see no
god in the holly, hear no song from
the snowbroken weeds: Hegel is not the winter
yellow in the pines: the sunlight has never
heard of trees: surrendered self among
    unwelcoming forms: stranger,
hoist your burdens, get on down the road.

*1965*

## Coon Song

I got one good look
  in the raccoon's eyes
    when he fell from the tree
came to his feet
  and perfectly still
    seized the baying hounds
in his dull fierce stare,
  in that recognition all
    decision lost,
choice irrelevant, before the
  battle fell
    and the unwinding
of his little knot of time began:

    Dostoevsky° would think
it important if the coon
  could choose to
    be back up the tree:
or if he could choose to be
  wagging by a swamp pond,
    dabbling at scuttling
crawdads:° the coon may have
  dreamed in fact of curling
    into the holed-out gall
of a fallen oak some squirrel
  had once brought
    high into the air
clean leaves to: but
  reality can go to hell
is what the coon's eyes said to me:
  and said how simple
    the solution to my
problem is: it needs only
  not to be: I thought the raccoon
    felt no anger,
saw none; cared nothing for cowardice,
  bravery; was in fact
    bored at

---

14 *Dostoevsky*: Russian novelist Fyodor Dostoevski (1821–1881).
21 *crawdads*: crayfish.

knowing what would ensue:
   the unwinding, the whirling growls,
40      exposed tenders,
the wet teeth—a problem to be
   solved, the taut-coiled vigor
     of the hunt
ready to snap loose:

45      you want to know what happened,
you want to hear me describe it,
   to placate the hound's-mouth
     slobbering in your own heart:
I will not tell you: actually the coon
50      possessing secret knowledge
     pawed dust on the dogs
and they disappeared, yapping into
   nothingness, and the coon went
     down to the pond
55  and washed his face and hands and beheld
   the world: maybe he didn't:
     I am no slave that I
should entertain you, say what you want
   to hear, let you wallow in
60      your silt: one two three four five:
one two three four five six seven eight nine ten:

     (all this time I've been
      counting spaces
while you were thinking of something else)
65      mess in your own sloppy silt:
     the hounds disappeared
yelping (the way you would at extinction)
   into—the order
     breaks up here—immortality:
70 I know that's where you think the brave
   little victims should go:
     I do not care what
you think: I do not care what you think:
   I do not care what you
75      think: one two three four five
six seven eight nine ten: here we go
   round the here-we-go-round, the
     here-we-go-round, the here-we-
go-round: coon will end in disorder at the
80      teeth of hounds: the situation
     will get him:
spheres roll, cubes stay put: now there
   one two three four five
     are two philosophies:
85 here we go round the mouth-wet of hounds:

     what I choose
     is youse:
     baby

*1965*

# James Wright (1927–1980)

Born and raised in a steelworker's family in the steel town of Martins Ferry, Ohio, Wright joined the army after high school; he was sent to occupied Japan. After returning, he studied with John Crowe Ransom at Kenyon College and Theodore Roethke at the University of Washington, where he earned a Ph.D. He taught at the University of Minnesota, Hunter College, and the University of Delaware. In his first two books, Wright used regular meters and rhymes and often celebrated the social outsiders of the small towns and farms near where he grew up. "Saint Judas," on the other hand, from Wright's second book, is a portrait of another sort of outcast, Christ's betrayer. Then, on a Fulbright in Austria, he discovered the associative and sometimes partly surreal imagery of poets Georg Trakl and Theodor Storm. A visit to Robert Bly back in the U.S. helped give a name to this impulse and a rhetoric with which to bring it to realization—poetry of the "deep image." He adopted free verse forms based on colloquial American speech and constructed as a series of evocative images leading toward moments of epiphany. "A Blessing" and "Lying in a Hammock" are notable examples. At the same time, some of his poems became more political, including some written in protest against the Vietnam War, and the outcasts he depicted were more often victims of American history.

## Saint Judas

When I went out to kill myself, I caught
A pack of hoodlums beating up a man.
Running to spare his suffering, I forgot
My name, my number, how my day began,
5     How soldiers milled around the garden stone
And sang amusing songs; how all that day
Their javelins measured crowds; how I alone
Bargained the proper coins, and slipped away.

Banished from heaven, I found this victim beaten,
10   Stripped, kneed, and left to cry. Dropping my rope
Aside, I ran, ignored the uniforms:
Then I remembered bread my flesh had eaten,
The kiss that ate my flesh. Flayed without hope,
I held the man for nothing in my arms.

1959

## Autumn Begins in Martins Ferry, Ohio

In the Shreve High football stadium,
In think of Polacks nursing long beers in Tiltonsville,°
And gray faces of Negroes in the blast furnace at Benwood,°
And the ruptured° night watchman of Wheeling Steel,
5     Dreaming of heroes.

All the proud fathers are ashamed to go home.
Their women cluck like starved pullets,°
Dying for love.

Therefore,
10    Their sons grow suicidally beautiful
At the beginning of October,
And gallop terribly against each other's bodies.

                                         *1963*

## Lying in a Hammock at William Duffy's Farm in Pine Island, Minnesota

Over my head, I see the bronze butterfly,
Asleep on the black trunk,
Blowing like a leaf in green shadow.
Down the ravine behind the empty house,
5    The cowbells follow one another
Into the distances of the afternoon.
To my right,
In a field of sunlight between two pines,
The droppings of last year's horses
10    Blaze up into golden stones.
I lean back, as the evening darkens and comes on.
A chicken hawk floats over, looking for home.
I have wasted my life.

                                         *1963*

## A Blessing

Just off the highway to Rochester, Minnesota,
Twilight bounds softly forth on the grass.
And the eyes of those two Indian ponies
Darken with kindness.
5    They have come gladly out of the willows
To welcome my friend and me.
We step over the barbed wire into the pasture
Where they have been grazing all day, alone.

---

2 *Tiltonsville:* a town in eastern Ohio, north of Martins Ferry.
3 *Benwood:* a town south of Martins Ferry, the site of the Wheeling Steel Works.
4 *ruptured:* herniated.
7 *pullets:* young hens.

They ripple tensely, they can hardly contain their happiness
10    That we have come.
They bow shyly as wet swans. They love each other.
There is no loneliness like theirs.
At home once more,
They begin munching the young tufts of spring in the darkness.
15    I would like to hold the slenderer one in my arms,
For she has walked over to me
And nuzzled my left hand.
She is black and white,
Her mane falls wild on her forehead,
20    And the light breeze moves me to caress her long ear
That is delicate as the skin over a girl's wrist.
Suddenly I realize
That if I stepped out of my body I would break
Into blossom.

*1963*

## A Centenary Ode: Inscribed to Little Crow, Leader of the Sioux Rebellion in Minnesota, 1862°

I had nothing to do with it, I was not here.
I was not born.
In 1862, when your hotheads
Raised hell from here to South Dakota,
5    My own fathers scattered into West Virginia
And southern Ohio.
My family fought the Confederacy
And fought the Union.
None of them got killed.
10    But for all that, it was not my fathers
Who murdered you.
Not much.

I don't know
Where the fathers of Minneapolis finalized
15    Your flayed carcass.
Little Crow, true father
Of my dark America,
When I close my eyes I lose you among
Old lonelinesses.
20    My family were a lot of singing drunks and good carpenters.
We had brothers who loved one another no matter what they did.
And they did plenty.

---

**poem title:** Crowded onto a reservation representing barely 10% of their tribal lands, their opportunities for hunting eliminated, the Sioux were at risk of starvation when a small group attacked a trading post and a farm. The 60-year old Little Crow lead an unsuccessful attack on Fort Ridgely.

I think they would have run like hell from your Sioux.
And when you caught them you all would have run like hell
25 From the Confederacy and from the Union
Into the hills and hunted for a few things,
Some bull-cat under the stones, a gar maybe,
If you were hungry, and if you were happy,
Sunfish and corn.

30 If only I knew where to mourn you,
I would surely mourn.

But I don't know.

I did not come here only to grieve
For my people's defeat.
35 The troops of the Union, who won,
Still outnumber us.
Old Paddy Beck, my great-uncle, is dead
At the old soldiers' home near Tiffen, Ohio.
He got away with every last stitch
40 Of his uniform, save only
The dress trousers.

Oh all around us,
The hobo jungles of America grow wild again.
The pick handles bloom like your skinned spine.
45 I don't even know where
My own grave is.

*1971*

# John Ashbery (b. 1927)

Ashbery was born in Rochester, New York. He grew up on a farm in nearby Sodus and was educated at Harvard and Columbia. After a Fulbright fellowship took him to France, he stayed on and worked as an art critic for several newspapers and magazines, finally returning to become executive editor of *Art News* from 1965 to 1972. His long poem "Self-Portrait in a Convex Mirror" (1975) mixes critical analysis of a Renaissance painting by Parmigianino with reflections on his own mental process, though it lacks the cheerful surrealism and aggressive disjunctiveness of many of his shorter poems. In his early work, his approach sometimes seemed antirepresentational, with a focus on linguistic events and the structures of thought. As a result, he was often associated with abstract expressionist painting of the 1940s and 1950s. But as his witty incorporation of linguistic commonplaces and public speech was matched by the use of multiple references to popular culture, his work became more accessible and his project more distinctive. Rapid changes in focus and mood still marked his poems, but he was now questioning how a commodified world might shape human consciousness. He is thus perhaps the poet who has thought most deeply about the mental life that mass culture grants to us. In the process, he came to doubt the plausibility of any coherent selfhood or the credibility of a conventionally coherent narrative.

## "They Dream Only of America"

They dream only of America
To be lost among the thirteen million pillars of grass:
"This honey is delicious
*Though it burns the throat.*"

5    And hiding from darkness in barns
They can be grownups now
And the murderer's ash tray is more easily—
The lake a lilac cube.

He holds a key in his right hand.
10   "Please," he asked willingly.
He is thirty years old.
That was before

We could drive hundreds of miles
At night through dandelions.
15    When his headache grew worse we
Stopped at a wire filling station.

Now he cared only about signs.
Was the cigar a sign?
And what about the key?
20    He went slowly into the bedroom.

"I would not have broken my leg if I had not fallen
Against the living room table. What is it to be back
Beside the bed? There is nothing to do
For our liberation, except wait in the horror of it.

And I am lost without you."

1962

## Farm Implements and Rutabagas in a Landscape°

The first of the undecoded messages read: "Popeye° sits in thunder,
Unthought of. From that shoebox of an apartment,
From livid curtain's hue, a tangram emerges: a country."
Meanwhile the Sea Hag was relaxing on a green couch: "How
      pleasant
5     To spend one's vacation *en la casa*° *de Popeye,"* she scratched
Her cleft chin's solitary hair. She remembered spinach

And was going to ask Wimpy if he had bought any spinach.
"M'love," he intercepted, "the plains are decked out in thunder
Today, and it shall be as you wish." He scratched
10    The part of his head under his hat. The apartment
Seemed to grow smaller. "But what if no pleasant
Inspiration plunge us now to the stars? *For this is my country.*"

Suddenly they remembered how it was cheaper in the country.
Wimpy was thoughtfully cutting open a number 2 can of spinach
15    When the door opened and Swee'pea crept in. "How pleasant!"
But Swee'pea looked morose. A note was pinned to his bib.
      "Thunder
And tears are unavailing," it read. "Henceforth shall Popeye's
      apartment
Be but remembered space, toxic or salubrious, whole or scratched."

---

**poem title:** A spoof of titles traditionally given to landscape paintings. Ashbery was an
editor of *Art News* and used to invent titles for imaginary paintings.
1 *Popeye:* all names in the poem are those of characters in the Popeye comic strip, cre-
ated by Segar, which was later the basis of a series of animated films.
5 *la casa:* (Spanish) "In Popeye's house." When Ashbery wrote the poem, the strip was ap-
pearing in New York City only in the Spanish-language newspaper *El Diaró.* In an inter-
view, Ashbery remarked "I used to follow it also in French newspapers, where Popeye's
dislocations of the English language are reproduced charmingly in French . . . I tend to
dislocate the language myself."

Olive came hurtling through the window; its geraniums scratched
20    Her long thigh. "I have news!" she gasped. "Popeye, forced as you
       know to flee the country
One musty gusty evening, by the schemes of his wizened, duplicate
       father, jealous of the apartment
And all that it contains, myself and spinach
In particular, heaves bolts of loving thunder
At his own astonished becoming, rupturing the pleasant

25    Arpeggio° of our years. No more shall pleasant
Rays of the sun refresh your sense of growing old, nor the
       scratched
Tree-trunks and mossy foliage, only immaculate darkness and
       thunder."

She grabbed Swee'pea. "I'm taking the brat to the country."
"But you can't do that—he hasn't even finished his spinach,"
30    Urged the Sea Hag, looking fearfully around at the apartment.

But Olive was already out of earshot. Now the apartment
Succumbed to a strange new hush. "Actually it's quite pleasant
Here," thought the Sea Hag. "If this is all we need fear from
      spinach
Then I don't mind so much. Perhaps we could invite Alice the
      Goon over"—she scratched
35    One dug pensively—"but Wimpy is such a country
Bumpkin, always burping like that." Minute at first, the thunder

Soon filled the apartment. It was domestic thunder,
The color of spinach. Popeye chuckled and scratched
His balls: it sure was pleasant to spend a day in the country.

                                  *1970*

## Mixed Feelings

A pleasant smell of frying sausages
Attacks the sense, along with an old, mostly invisible
Photograph of what seems to be girls lounging around
An old fighter bomber, circa 1942 vintage.
5    How to explain to these girls, if indeed that's what they are,
These Ruths, Lindas, Pats and Sheilas
About the vast change that's taken place
In the fabric of our society, altering the texture
Of all things in it? And yet
10    They somehow look as if they knew, except
That it's so hard to see them, it's hard to figure out
Exactly what kind of expressions they're wearing.
What are your hobbies, girls? Aw nerts,

---

25 *Arpeggio:* a chord whose notes are played in quick succession rather than simultaneously.

One of them might say, this guy's too much for me.
15 Let's go on and out, somewhere
Through the canyons of the garment center
To a small café and have a cup of coffee.
I am not offended that these creatures (that's the word)
Of my imagination seem to hold me in such light esteem,
20 Pay so little heed to me. It's part of a complicated
Flirtation routine, anyhow, no doubt. But this talk of
The garment center? Surely that's California sunlight
Belaboring them and the old crate on which they
Have draped themselves, fading its Donald Duck insignia
25 To the extreme point of legibility.
Maybe they were lying but more likely their
Tiny intelligences cannot retain much information.
Not even one fact, perhaps. That's why
They think they're in New York. I like the way
30 They look and act and feel. I wonder
How they got that way, but am not going to
Waste any more time thinking about them.
I have already forgotten them
Until some day in the not too distant future
35 When we meet possibly in the lounge of a modern airport,
They looking as astonishingly young and fresh as when this picture
    was made
But full of contradictory ideas, stupid ones as well as
Worthwhile ones, but all flooding the surface of our minds
As we babble about the sky and the weather and the forests of
    change.

1975

## Hop o' My Thumb

The grand hotels, dancing girls
Urge forward under a veil of "lost illusion"
The deed to this day or some other day.
There is no day in the calendar
5 The dairy company sent out
That lets you possess it wildly like
The body of a dreaming woman in a dream:
All flop over at the top when seized,
The stem too slender, the top too loose and heavy,
10 Blushing with fine foliage of dreams.
The motor cars, tinsel hats,
Supper of cakes, the amorous children
Take the solitary downward path of dreams
And are not seen again.
15 What is it, Undine?
The notes now can scarcely be heard
In the hubbub of the flattening storm,
With the third wish unspoken.

I remember meeting you in a dark dream
20　　Of April, you or some girl,
The necklace of wishes alive and breathing around your throat.
In the blindness of that dark whose
Brightness turned to sand salt-glazed in noon sun
We could not know each other or know which part
25　　Belonged to the other, pelted in an electric storm of rain.
Only gradually the mounds that meant our bodies
That wore our selves concaved into view
But intermittently as through dark mist
Smeared against fog. No worse time to have come,
30　　Yet all was desiring though already desired and past,
The moment a monument to itself
No one would ever see or know was there.

That time faded too and the night
Softened to smooth spirals or foliage at night.
35　　There were sleeping cabins near by, blind lanterns,
Nocturnal friendliness of the plate of milk left for the fairies
Who otherwise might be less well disposed:
Friendship of white sheets patched with milk.
And always an open darkness in which one name
40　　Cries over and over again: Ariane! Ariane!
Was it for this you led your sisters back from sleep
And now he of the blue beard has outmaneuvered you?
But for the best perhaps: let
Those sisters slink into the sapphire
40　　Hair that is mounting day.
There are still other made-up countries
Where we can hide forever,
Wasted with eternal desire and sadness,
Sucking the sherbets, crooning the tunes, naming the names.

1975

# Street Musicians

One died, and the soul was wrenched out
Of the other in life, who, walking the streets
Wrapped in an identity like a coat, sees on and on
The same corners, volumetrics, shadows
5　　Under trees. Farther than anyone was ever
Called, through increasingly suburban airs
And ways, with autumn falling over everything:
The plush leaves the chattels in barrels
Of an obscure family being evicted
10　　Into the way it was, and is. The other beached
Glimpses of what the other was up to:
Revelations at last. So they grew to hate and forget each other.

So I cradle this average violin that knows
Only forgotten showtunes, but argues
15    The possibility of free declamation anchored
To a dull refrain, the year turning over on itself
In November, with the spaces among the days
More literal, the meat more visible on the bone.
Our question of a place of origin hangs
20    Like smoke: how we picnicked in pine forests,
In coves with the water always seeping up, and left
Our trash, sperm and excrement everywhere, smeared
On the landscape, to make of us what we could.

1977

# Syringa

Orpheus° liked the glad personal quality
Of the things beneath the sky. Of course, Eurydice was a part
Of this. Then one day, everything changed. He rends
Rocks into fissures with lament. Gullies, hummocks
5    Can't withstand it. The sky shudders from one horizon
To the other, almost ready to give up wholeness.
Then Apollo° quietly told him: "Leave it all on earth.
Your lute, what point? Why pick at a dull pavan few care to
Follow, except a few birds of dusty feather,
10    Not vivid performances of the past." But why not?
All other things must change too.
The seasons are no longer what they once were,
But it is the nature of things to be seen only once,
As they happen along, bumping into other things, getting along
15    Somehow. That's where Orpheus made his mistake.
Of course Eurydice vanished into the shade;
She would have even if he hadn't turned around.
No use standing them like a gray stone toga as the whole wheel
Of recorded history flashes past, struck dumb, unable to utter an
      intelligent
20    Comment on the most thought-provoking element in its train.
Only love stays on the brain, and something these people,
These other ones, call life. Singing accurately
So that the notes mount straight up out of the well of
Dim noon and rival the tiny, sparkling yellow flowers
25    Growing around the brink of the quarry, encapsulates
The different weights of the things.
                      But it isn't enough
To just go on singing. Orpheus realized this

---

1 *Orpheus:* in Greek myth, Eurydice, wife of the singer and poet Orpheus, was bitten by a snake and died. The grief-stricken Orpheus plunged into Hades to bring her back. The music of his voice and lyre moved the gods of the underworld, and they granted his wish, but only on condition that he not look back at her until they reached the sunlight. In a moment of doubt, he looked back, and she was taken from him again, this time forever. 7 *Apollo:* in Greek myth, the son of Zeus and god of all the fine arts, of medicine, music, poetry, and eloquence; he gave Orpheus the lyre that he played so beautifully.

And didn't mind so much about his reward being in heaven
30      After the Bacchantes° had torn him apart, driven
Half out of their minds by his music, what it was doing to them.
Some say it was for his treatment of Eurydice.
But probably the music had more to do with it, and
The way music passes, emblematic
35      Of life and how you cannot isolate a note of it
And say it is good or bad. You must
Wait till it's over. "The end crowns all,"
Meaning also that the "tableau"
Is wrong. For although memories, of a season, for example,
40      Melt into a single snapshot, one cannot guard, treasure
That stalled moment. It too is flowing, fleeting;
It is a picture of flowing, scenery, though living, mortal,
Over which an abstract action is laid out in blunt,
Harsh strokes. And to ask more than this
45      Is to become the tossing reeds of that slow,
Powerful stream, the trailing grasses
Playfully tugged at, but to participate in the action
No more than this. Then in the lowering gentian sky
Electric twitches are faintly apparent first, then burst forth
50      Into a shower of fixed, cream-colored flares. The horses
Have each seen a share of the truth, though each thinks,
"I'm a maverick. Nothing of this is happening to me,
Though I can understand the language of birds, and
The itinerary of the lights caught in the storm is fully apparent
          to me.
55      Their jousting ends in music much
As trees move more easily in the wind after a summer storm
And is happening in lacy shadows of shore-trees, now, day after
          day."

But how late to be regretting all this, even
Bearing in mind that regrets are always late, too late!
60      To which Orpheus, a bluish cloud with white contours,
Replies that these are of course not regrets at all,
Merely a careful, scholarly setting down of
Unquestioned facts, a record of pebbles along the way.
And no matter how all this disappeared,
65      Or got where it was going, it is no longer
Material for a poem. Its subject
Matters too much, and not enough, standing there helplessly
While the poem streaked by, its tail afire, a bad
Comet screaming hate and disaster, but so turned inward
70      That the meaning, good or other, can never
Become known. The singer thinks
Constructively, builds up his chant in progressive stages
Like a skyscraper, but at the last minute turns away.

---

30 *Bacchantes:* Thracian women who attacked Orpheus, while they were celebrating the
orgies of Bacchus, and tore him to pieces; they were offended at his indifference to their
advances.

The song is engulfed in an instant in blackness
75    Which must in turn flood the whole continent
With blackness, for it cannot see. The singer
Must then pass out of sight, not even relieved
Of the evil burthen of the words. Stellification
Is for the few, and comes about much later
80    When all record of these people and their lives
Has disappeared into libraries, onto microfilm.
A few are still interested in them. "But what about
So-and-so?" is still asked on occasion. But they lie
Frozen and out of touch until an arbitrary chorus
85    Speaks of a totally different incident with a similar name
In whose tale are hidden syllables
Of what happened so long before that
In some small town, one indifferent summer.

                                                      1977

## Daffy Duck in Hollywood°

Something strange is creeping across me.
La Celestina° has only to warble the first few bars
Of "I Thought about You" or something mellow from
*Amadigi di Gaula*° for everything—a mint-condition can
5    Of Rumford's Baking Powder,° a celluloid earring, Speedy
Gonzales,° the latest from Helen Topping Miller's° fertile
Escritoire,° a sheaf of suggestive pix on greige,° deckle-edged°
Stock—to come clattering through the rainbow trellis
Where Pistachio Avenue° rams the 2300 block of Highland

---

**poem title:** *Daffy Duck in Hollywood* is the title of a 1938 animated film by Tex Avery (1907–1980), who was also one of the creators of Bugs Bunny for the Warner Brothers studio. He developed a free-wheeling, violent, often surrealistic animation style for MGM cartoons in the 1940s.
2 *Celestina:* the title character in Spanish dramatist Fernando de Rojas' (1475–1538) play *Celestina* (1499, 1502). She is an elderly procuress and seller of love charms whose greed brings about her death.
4 *Amadigi di Gaula:* an opera by George Frederick Handel (1685–1759) first performed in 1715.
5 *Rumford's Baking Powder:* first produced in the mid-nineteenth century, it is presently manufactured by Hulman & Co. in Indiana. It was originally produced in Rumford, Rhode Island, a town near Providence named for its major industry, the Rumford Chemical Works. The co-inventor of Rumford's Baking Powder, Eben Horsford, had held the Rumford Chair of the Application of Science to the Useful Arts at Harvard. The Chair was named after Count Rumford, actually the American Benjamin Thompson (1753–1814), who was granted a title in honor of services performed for the Duke of Bavaria.
6 *Speedy Gonzales:* a character from a Tex Avery cartoon, a mouse with a Spanish accent.
6 *Helen Topping Miller:* (1884–1960), a prolific author of popular historical novels from the late 1930s until her death. She concluded her career by publishing seven books with "Christmas" in the title, between 1954 and 1960, including *Christmas at Sagamore Hill with Theodore Roosevelt* and *Christmas at Monticello with Thomas Jefferson.*
7 *Escritoire:* a bureau, or combination bureau and bookcase, that includes a desk or writing surface.
7 *greige:* grayish beige in color.
7 *deckle-edged:* paper with a rough, untrimmed edge.
9 *Pistachio Avenue:* a real street in California and Arizona. Highland Fling Terrace is apparently not a real street, though there is a "Highland Fling Street" in a small town in Pennsylvania.

10       Fling Terrace. He promised he'd get me out of this one,
         That mean old cartoonist,° but just look what he's
         Done to me now! I scarce dare approach me mug's attenuated
         Reflection in yon hubcap,° so jaundiced, so *déconfit*°
         Are its lineaments—fun, no doubt, for some quack phrenologist's°
15       Fern-clogged waiting room, but hardly what you'd call
         Companionable. But everything is getting choked to the point of
         Silence. Just now a magnetic storm hung in the swatch of sky
         Over the Fudds'° garage, reducing it—drastically—
         To the aura of a plumbago-blue° log cabin on
20       A Gadsden Purchase° commemorative cover. Suddenly all is
         Loathing. I don't want to go back inside any more. You meet
         Enough vague people on this emerald traffic-island—no,
         Not people, comings and goings, more: mutterings, splatterings,
         The bizarrely but effectively equipped infantries of happy-go-nutty
25       Vegetal jacqueries,° plumed, pointed at the little
         White cardboard castle over the mill run. "Up
         The lazy river, how happy we could be?"
         How will it end? That geranium glow
         Over Anaheim's° had the riot act read to it by the
30       Etna-size° firecracker that exploded last minute into
         A *carte du Tendre*° in whose lower right-hand corner
         (Hard by the jock-itch sand-trap that skirts
         The asparagus patch of algolagnic° *nuits blanches*°) Amadis°
         Is cozening the Princesse de Clèves° into a midnight micturition°
              spree

---

11 *cartoonist:* on the first level, a reference to Tex Avery, but there are many cartoonists in
this poem, from Helen Topping Miller to John Milton, from those of us who might find
a tin of baking powder collectible to the government that commemorated the Gadsden
Purchase. Only the work of the Great Cartoonist above encompasses it all.
13 *me mug's . . . hubcap:* a send-up of Ashbery's poem "Self-Portrait in a Convex Mirror"
delivered in Daffy Duck's diction.
13 *déconfit:* (French) flabbergasted.
14 *phrenologist:* one who studies the conformation of the skull as indicative of mental fac-
ulties and character traits.
18 *Fudd:* Elmer Fudd was the foil in the Bugs Bunny cartoons, expressing middle-class
horror at Bugs's antics, meanwhile pronouncing his *r*s as *w*s, as in "that cwazy wabbit."
19 *plumbago-blue:* a purplish grey-blue.
20 *Gadsden Purchase:* an area in Arizona and New Mexico purchased from Mexico in 1853.
25 *jacqueries:* peasant revolts.
29 *Anaheim:* Orange County, California, city, site of Disneyland amusement park.
30 *Etna:* volcano in northeast Sicily.
31 *carte du Tendre:* allegorical map of the country of love, popular in seventeenth-century
France.
33 *algolagnic:* characterized by sexual pleasure found in suffering or inflicting pain.
33 *nuits blanches:* (French) sleepless nights.
33 *Amadis:* a character in a Spanish chivalric romance by Garcia Ordonez de Montalvo;
the story was adapted as an opera called *Amadis* by Jean-Baptiste Lully (1632–1687) in 1684
and again by Handel and others. Amadis falls in love with the Princess Oriane and even-
tually wins her hand through a series of heroic adventures. He would not have had much
success with the Princess of Clèves.
34 *Princesse de Clèves:* title character in a novel *The Princess of Cleves* (1678) by Madame
Marie de Lafayette (1634–1693); virtuous, but passionless, the Princess disappoints her hus-
band.
34 *micturition:* urination.

35    On the Tamigi° with the Wallets° (Walt, Blossom, and little
      Skeezix) of a lamé barge "borrowed" from Ollie
      Of the Movies' dread mistress of the robes. Wait!
      I have an announcement! This wide, tepidly meandering,
      Civilized Lethe° (one can barely make out the maypoles
40    And *châlets de nécessité*° on its sedgy shore) leads to Tophet,° that
      Landfill-haunted, not-so-residential resort from which
      Some travellers return! This whole moment is the groin
      Of a borborygmic° giant who even now
      Is rolling over on us in his sleep. Farewell bocages,
45    Tanneries, water-meadows. The allegory comes unsnarled
      Too soon; a shower of pecky acajou° harpoons is
      About all there is to be noted between tornadoes. I have
      Only my intermittent life in your thoughts to live
      Which is like thinking in another language. Everything
50    Depends on whether somebody reminds you of me.
      That this is a fabulation, and that those "other times"
      Are in fact the silences of the soul, picked out in
      Diamonds on stygian° velvet, matters less than it should.
      Prodigies of timing may be arranged to convince them
55    We live in one dimension, they in ours. While I
      Abroad through all the coasts of dark destruction seek
      Deliverance for us all,° think in that language: its
      Grammar, though tortured, offers pavilions
      At each new parting of the ways. Pastel
60    Ambulances scoop up the quick and hie them to hospitals.
      "It's all bits and pieces, spangles, patches, really; nothing
      Stands alone. What happened to creative evolution?"
      Sighed Aglavaine.° Then to her Sélysette: "If his
      Achievement is only to end up less boring than the others,
65    What's keeping us here? Why not leave at once?
      I have to stay here while they sit in there,
      Laugh, drink, have fine time. In my day
      One lay under the tough green leaves,
      Pretending not to notice how they bled into
70    The sky's aqua, the wafted-away no-color of regions supposed
      Not to concern us. And so we too
      Came where the others came: nights of physical endurance,

---

35 *Tamigi*: Italian name for the Thames River that flows through London.
35 *Wallets*: characters in the comic strip "Gasoline Alley."
39 *Lethe*: in Greek mythology, the river of oblivion in the underworld; the dead drink from it to forget their earthly life.
40 *châlets de nécessité*: rustic "comfort stations."
40 *Tophet*: in the Biblical book of Jeremiah, Tophet is a burial place associated with prophetic warnings of impending disaster.
43 *borborygmic*: producing rumbling sounds created by the movement of gas in the intestines.
46 *acajou*: wood (mahogany).
53 *stygian*: gloomy, deathly.
55–57 *While I/Abroad . . . Deliverance for us all*: quotes Satan in Book II (lines 463–465) of John Milton's (1608–1674) *Paradise Lost* (1667).
63 *Aglavaine*: title character in play *Aglavaine et Sélysette* (1896) by Belgian poet and dramatist Maurice Maeterlinck (1862–1949). Sélysette dies when she throws herself from a tower.

Or if, by day, our behavior was anarchically
Correct, at least by New Brutalism° standards, all then
75    Grew taciturn by previous agreement. We were spirited
Away *en bateau*,° under cover of fudge dark.
It's not the incomplete importunes, but the spookiness
Of the finished product. True, to ask less were folly, yet
If he is the result of himself, how much the better
80    For him we ought to be! And how little, finally,
We take this into account! Is the puckered garance° satin
Of a case that once held a brace of dueling pistols our
Only acknowledging of that color? I like not this,
Methinks, yet this disappointing sequel to ourselves
85    Has been applauded in London and St. Petersburg. Somewhere
Ravens pray for us."
                              The storm finished brewing. And thus
She questioned all who came in at the great gate, but none
She found who ever heard of Amadis,
90    Nor of stern Aureng-Zebe,° his first love. Some
There were to whom this mattered not a jot: since all
By defintion is completeness (so
In utter darkness they reasoned), why not
Accept it as it pleases to reveal itself? As when
95    Low skyscrapers from lower-hanging clouds reveal
A turret there, an art-deco escarpment here, and last perhaps
The pattern that may carry the sense, but
Stays hidden in the mysteries of pagination.
Not what we see but how we see it matters; all's
100   Alike, the same, and we greet him who announces
The change as we would greet the change itself.
All life is but a figment; conversely, the tiny
Tome that slips from your hand is not perhaps the
Missing link in this invisible picnic whose leverage
105   Shrouds our sense of it. Therefore bivouac we
On this great, blond highway, unimpeded by
Veiled scruples, worn conundrums. Morning is
Impermanent. Grab sex things, swing up
Over the horizon like a boy
110   On a fishing expedition. No one really knows
Or cares whether this is the whole of which parts
Were vouchsafed—once—but to be ambling on's
The tradition more than the safekeeping of it. This mulch for
Play keeps them interested and busy while the big,
115   Vaguer stuff can decide what it wants—what maps, what
Model cities, how much waste space. Life, our
Life anyway, is between. We don't mind
Or notice any more that the sky *is* green, a parrot

---

74 *New Brutalism:* 1950s architectural concept; its buildings often have large blocks of exposed concrete.
76 *en bateau:* (French) by boat.
81 *garance:* dark red.
90 *Aureng-Zebe:* noble savage hero of John Dryden's (1631–1700) tragedy *Aureng-Zebe* (1675).

One, but have our earnest where it chances on us,
120　Disingenuous, intrigued, inviting more,
　　Always invoking the echo, a summer's day.

*1977*


## Paradoxes and Oxymorons

　　This poem is concerned with language on a very plain level.
　　Look at it talking to you. You look out a window
　　Or pretend to fidget. You have it but you don't have it.
　　You miss it, it misses you. You miss each other.

5　The poem is sad because it wants to be yours, and cannot.
　　What's a plain level? It is that and other things,
　　Bringing a system of them into play. Play?
　　Well, actually, yes, but I consider play to be

　　A deeper outside thing, a dreamed role-pattern,
10　As in the division of grace these long August days
　　Without proof. Open-ended. And before you know
　　It gets lost in the steam and chatter of typewriters.

　　It has been played once more. I think you exist only
　　To tease me into doing it, on your level, and then you aren't there
15　Or have adopted a different attitude. And the poem
　　Has set me softly down beside you. The poem is you.

*1981*

# Galway Kinnell (b. 1927)

Born in Providence, Rhode Island, Kinnell was educated at Princeton and the University of Rochester. He served in the U.S. Navy from 1945–1946 and then went on to do civil rights field work in Louisiana for the Congress on Racial Equality. Although he has written poems on contemporary topics, such as the use of the atomic bomb on Hiroshima and Nagasaki, the struggle for civil rights, and the long tragedy of the Vietnam War, he also has returned repeatedly and in different guises to take up the subject of transcendence in the midst of mortality, a concern apparent in both "The Porcupine" and "The Bear," both taken from his 1968 volume *Body Rags*. His first book, *What a Kingdom It Was* (1960), had a strong component of secularized Christianity, still apparent in the sacramental mood of the poems reprinted here. But now it is not so much oneness with God as oneness with nature and the primal rhythms of birth and death that the speaker seeks. His book-length poem sequence *The Book of Nightmares* (1978) is perhaps his masterpiece.

## The Porcupine

### 1

     Fatted
     on herbs, swollen on crabapples,
     puffed up on bast and phloem,° ballooned
     on willow flowers, poplar catkins, first
5    leafs of aspen and larch,
     the porcupine
     drags and bounces his last meal through ice,
     mud, roses and goldenrod, into the stubbly high fields.

### 2

     In character
10   he resembles us in seven ways:
     he puts his mark on outhouses,
     he alchemizes by moonlight,
     he shits on the run,

---

3 *bast and phloem:* technical names for parts of plants; bast is the woody outer layer of the stems of various plants; phloem is the food-conducting tissue of vascular plants.

he uses his tail for climbing,
15    he chuckles softly to himself when scared,
he's overcrowded if there's more than one of him per five acres,
his eyes have their own inner redness.

### 3

Digger of
goings across floors, of hesitations
20    at thresholds, of
handprints of dread
at doorpost or window jamb, he would
gouge the world
empty of us, hack and crater
25    it
until it is nothing, if that
could rinse it of all our sweat and pathos.

Adorer of ax
handles aflow with grain, of arms
30    of Morris chairs, of hand
crafted objects
steeped in the juice of fingertips,
of surfaces wetted down
with fist grease and elbow oil,
35    of clothespins that have
grabbed our body-rags by underarm and crotch . . .

Unimpressed—bored—
by the whirl of the stars, by *these*
he's astonished, ultra-
40    Rilkean° angel!

for whom the true
portion of the sweetness of earth
is one of those bottom-heavy, glittering, saccadic°
bits
45    of salt water that splash down
the haunted ravines of a human face.

### 4

A farmer shot a porcupine three times
as it dozed on a tree limb. On
the way down it tore open its belly
50    on a broken
branch, hooked its gut,
and went on falling. On the ground

---

40 *Rilkean:* Poet Ranier Maria Rilke (1875–1926) in his *Duino Elegies* described a hierar-
chy of being from animals to angels.
43 *saccadic:* having to do with rapid eye movement.

it sprang to its feet, and
paying out gut heaved
55      and spartled through a hundred feet of goldenrod
before
the abrupt emptiness.

5

The Avesta°
puts porcupine killers
60      into hell for nine generations, sentencing them
to gnaw out
each other's hearts for the
salts of desire.

I roll
65      this way and that in the great bed, under
the quilt
that mimics this country of broken farms and woods,
the fatty sheath of the man
melting off,
70      the self-stabbing coil
of bristles reversing, blossoming outward—
a red-eyed, hard-toothed, arrow-stuck urchin
tossing up mattress feathers,
pricking the
75      woman beside me until she cries.

6

In my time I have
crouched, quills erected,
Saint
Sebastian of the
80      scared heart, and been
beat dead with a locust club
on the bare snout.
And fallen from high places
I have fled, have
85      jogged
over fields of goldenrod,
terrified, seeking home,
and among flowers
I have come to myself empty, the rope
90      strung out behind me
in the fall sun
suddenly glorified with all my blood.

---

58 *Avesta:* the sacred text of ancient Persians.

### 7

And tonight I think I prowl broken
skulled or vacant as a
95    sucked egg in the wintry meadow, softly chuckling, blank
template of myself, dragging
a starved belly through the lichflowered acres,
where
burdock looses the arks of its seed
100    and thistle holds up its lost blooms
and rosebushes in the wind scrape their dead limbs
for the forced-fire
of roses.

                                        *1968*

## The Bear°

### 1

In late winter
I sometimes glimpse bits of steam
coming up from
some fault in the old snow
5    and bend close and see it is lung-colored
and put down my nose
and know
the chilly, enduring odor of bear.

### 2

I take a wolf's rib and whittle
10    it sharp at both ends
and coil it up
and freeze it in blubber and place it out
on the fairway of the bears.

And when it has vanished
15    I move out on the bear tracks,
roaming in circles
until I come to the first, tentative, dark
splash on the earth.

And I set out
20    running, following the splashes
of blood wandering over the world.
At the cut, gashed resting places
I stop and rest,
at the crawl-marks

---

**poem title:** Hans Ruesch's *The Top of the World* is a source for the bear hunt story.

25 where he lay out on his belly
 to overpass some stretch of bauchy° ice
 I lie out
 dragging myself forward with bear-knives in my fists.

3

 On the third day I begin to starve,
30 at nightfall I bend down as I knew I would
 at a turd sopped in blood,
 and hesitate, and pick it up,
 and thrust it in my mouth, and gnash it down,
 and rise
35 and go on running.

4

 On the seventh day,
 living by now on bear blood alone,
 I can see his upturned carcass far out ahead, a scraggled,
 steamy hulk,
40 the heavy fur riffling in the wind.
 I come up to him
 and stare at the narrow-spaced, petty eyes,
 the dismayed
 face laid back on the shoulder, the nostrils
45 flared, catching
 perhaps the first taint of me as he
 died.

 I hack
 a ravine in his thigh, and eat and drink,
50 and tear him down his whole length
 and open him and climb in
 and close him up after me, against the wind,
 and sleep.

5

 And dream
55 of lumbering flatfooted
 over the tundra,
 stabbed twice from within,
 splattering a trail behind me,
 splattering it out no matter which way I lurch,
60 no matter which parabola of bear-transcendence,
 which dance of solitude I attempt,
 which gravity-clutched leap,
 which trudge, which groan.

---

26 *bauchy*: uneasy, weak, without substance.

## 6

Until one day I totter and fall—
65  fall on this
stomach that has tried so hard to keep up,
to digest the blood as it leaked in,
to break up
and digest the bone itself: and now the breeze
70  blows over me, blows off
the hideous belches of ill-digested bear blood
and rotted stomach
and the ordinary, wretched odor of bear,

blows across
75  my sore, lolled tongue a song
or screech, until I think I must rise up
and dance. And I lie still.

## 7

I awaken I think. Marshlights
reappear, geese
80  come trailing again up the flyway.°
In her ravine under old snow the dam-bear
lies, licking
lumps of smeared fur°
and drizzly eyes into shapes
85  with her tongue. And one
hairy-soled trudge stuck out before me,
the next groaned out,
the next,
the next,
90  the rest of my days I spend
wandering: wondering
what, anyway,
was that sticky infusion, that rank flavor of blood, that poetry, by
   which I lived?

*1968*

---

80 *flyway*: migratory route.
83 *lumps . . . fur*: her cubs.

# W. S. Merwin (b. 1927)

Merwin was born in New York and raised first in Union City, New Jersey, and then in Scranton, Pennsylvania. He studied Romance Languages at Princeton University, where he worked with poet John Berryman and poet-critic R. P. Blackmur. It was at Princeton as well, in the midst of World War II, when some of his classmates were dying in Europe and the Pacific, that he began writing, but not publishing, poems of despair amidst the violence of history. He would return to these themes again decades later, when the Vietnam War would come to seem a comprehensive figure for public life in America. His first published poems, however, made extensive use of mythology and displayed his mastery of traditional meter and form.

Then in the 1960s, responding to the pressure of events, he adopted an open, unpunctuated form and a line closer to a unit of breath. Merwin was concerned about the destruction of natural life long before ecological awareness was common; now this deep-seated reverence was fused with rage at the carnage of a mindless and cynical war. Poems of prophesy and witness followed through the 1960s and 1970s, sometimes about the contemporary world and sometimes taking up earlier historical subjects. He also wrote haunting phenomenologies of loss and presence amidst emptiness. Throughout this time, he maintained great wariness about institutional entanglements, preferring to support himself through translation and poetry readings rather than by taking a permanent teaching position. In addition to living in New York, he spent long periods in a farm house in the south of France, feeling a need to distance himself from America and its most intense city. He now makes his home on the island of Maui in Hawaii, in the midst of hundreds of tropical plants. His prose poems and memoirs are as well regarded as his poems.

## The Drunk in the Furnace

> For a good decade
> The furnace stood in the naked gully, fireless
> And vacant as any hat. Then when it was
> No more to them than a hulking black fossil
> 5  To erode unnoticed with the rest of the junk-hill
> By the poisonous creek, and rapidly to be added
> To their ignorance,

They were afterwards astonished
To confirm, one morning, a twist of smoke like a pale
10    Resurrection, staggering out of its chewed hole,
And to remark then other tokens that someone,
Cosily bolted behind the eye-holed iron
Door of the drafty burner, had there established
       His bad castle.

15        Where he gets his spirits
It's a mystery. But the stuff keeps him musical:
Hammer-and-anvilling with poker and bottle
To his jugged bellowings, till the last groaning clang
As he collapses onto the rioting
20    Springs of a litter of car-seats ranged on the grates,
       To sleep like an iron pig.°

       In their tar-paper church
On a text about stoke-holes that are sated never
Their Reverend lingers. They nod and hate trespassers.
25    When the furnace wakes, though, all afternoon
Their witless offspring flock like piped rats to its siren
Crescendo, and agape on the crumbling ridge
       Stand in a row and learn.

                    *1960*

# It is March

It is March and black dust falls out of the books
Soon I will be gone
The tall spirit who lodged here has
Left already
5   On the avenues the colorless thread lies under
Old prices

When you look back there is always the past
Even when it has vanished
But when you look forward
10   With your dirty knuckles and the wingless
Bird on your shoulder
What can you write

The bitterness is still rising in the old mines
The fist is coming out of the egg
15   The thermometers out of the mouths of the corpses

At a certain height
The tails of the kites for a moment are
Covered with footsteps

Whatever I have to do has not yet begun

                    *1967*

---

21 *iron pig:* a crude slab poured from a smelting furnace.

## Caesar

My shoes are almost dead
And as I wait at the doors of ice
I hear the cry go up for him Caesar Caesar

But when I look out the window I see only the flatlands
5     And the slow vanishing of the windmills
The centuries draining the deep fields

Yet this is still my country
The thug on duty says What would you change
He looks at his watch he lifts
10    Emptiness out of the vases
And holds it up to examine

So it is evening
With the rain starting to fall forever

One by one he calls night out of the teeth
15    And at last I take up
My duty

Wheeling the president past banks of flowers
Past the feet of empty stairs
Hoping he's dead

*1967*

## The Room

I think all this is somewhere in myself
The cold room unlit before dawn
Containing a stillness such as attends death
And from a corner the sounds of a small bird trying
5     From time to time to fly a few beats in the dark
You would say it was dying it is immortal

*1967*

## December Among the Vanished

The old snow gets up and moves taking its
Birds with it

The beasts hide in the knitted walls
From the winter that lipless man
5     Hinges echo but nothing opens

A silence before this one
Has left its broken huts facing the pastures
Through their stone roofs the snow
And the darkness walk down

10      In one of them I sit with a dead shepherd
        And watch his lambs

1967

## For the Anniversary of my Death

Every year without knowing it I have passed the day
When the last fires will wave to me
And the silence will set out
Tireless traveller
5   Like the beam of a lightless star

Then I will no longer
Find myself in life as in a strange garment
Surprised at the earth
And the love of one woman
10   And the shamelessness of men
As today writing after three days of rain
Hearing the wren sing and the falling cease
And bowing not knowing to what

1967

## When the War is Over

When the war is over
We will be proud of course the air will be
Good for breathing at last
The water will have been improved the salmon
5   And the silence of heaven will migrate more perfectly
The dead will think the living are worth it we will know
Who we are
And we will all enlist again

1967

## The Asians Dying

When the forests have been destroyed their darkness remains
The ash the great walker follows the possessors
Forever
Nothing they will come to is real
5   Nor for long
Over the watercourses
Like ducks in the time of the ducks
The ghosts of the villages trail in the sky
Making a new twilight

10   Rain falls into the open eyes of the dead
Again again with its pointless sound
When the moon finds them they are the color of everything

The nights disappear like bruises but nothing is healed
The dead go away like bruises
15    The blood vanishes into the poisoned farmlands
Pain the horizon
Remains
Overhead the seasons rock
They are paper bells
20    Calling to nothing living

The possessors move everywhere under Death their star
Like columns of smoke they advance into the shadows
Like thin flames with no light
They with no past
And fire their only future

*1967*

## For a Coming Extinction

Gray whale
Now that we are sending you to The End
That great god
Tell him
5    That we who follow you invented forgiveness
And forgive nothing

I write as though you could understand
And I could say it
One must always pretend something
10    Among the dying
When you have left the seas nodding on their stalks
Empty of you
Tell him that we were made
On another day

15    The bewilderment will diminish like an echo
Winding along your inner mountains
Unheard by us
And find its way out
Leaving behind it the future
20    Dead
And ours

When you will not see again
The whale calves trying the light
Consider what you will find in the black garden
25    And its court
The sea cows the Great Auks the gorillas
The irreplaceable hosts ranged countless
And fore-ordaining as stars
Our sacrifices

30    Join your word to theirs
      Tell him
      That it is we who are important

                                              *1967*


# Looking for Mushrooms at Sunrise

for Jean and Bill Arrowsmith

      When it is not yet day
      I am walking on centuries of dead chestnut leaves
      In a place without grief
      Though the oriole
5     Out of another life warns me
      That I am awake

      In the dark while the rain fell
      The gold chanterelles pushed through a sleep that was not mime
      Waking me
10    So that I came up the mountain to find them

      Where they appear it seems I have been before
      I recognize their haunts as though remembering
      Another life

      Where else am I walking even now
      Looking for me

                                              *1967*


# The Gardens of Zuñi°

      The one-armed explorer°
      could touch only half of the country
      In the virgin half
      the house fires give no more heat
5     than the stars
      it has been so these many years
      and there is no bleeding

      He is long dead with his five fingers
      and the sum of their touching
10    and the memory
      of the other hand
      his scout

---

**poem title:** The Zuni river, which passes through the Zuni valley, is a tributary of the Colorado River in Arizona. The Zuni people, a Native American tribe with a unique language, settled the valley and built the Zuni pueblo there; there are now ten thousand tribal members.
1 *explorer:* John Wesley Powell: (1834–1902), American geologist, ethnologist, and explorer who lost his right arm at the Civil War battle of Shiloh. He explored the canyons of the Colorado River, surveyed the arid high plains, and established the first definitive classification scheme for Native American languages.

that sent back no message
from where it had reached
15          with no lines in its palm
while he balanced
balanced
and groped on
for the virgin land

and found where it had been

1970

## Beginning

Long before spring
king of the black cranes
rises one day
from the black
5          needle's eye
on the white plain
under the white sky

the crown turns
and the eye
10          drilled clear through his head
turns
it is north everywhere
come out he says

come out then
15          the light is not yet
divided
it is a long way
to the first
anything
20          come even so
we will start
bring your nights with you

1970

## The Horse

In a dead tree
there is the ghost of a horse
no horse
was ever seen near the tree
5          but the tree was born
of a mare
it rolled with long legs
in rustling meadows
it pricked its ears
10          it reared and tossed its head

and suddenly stool still
beginning to remember
as its leaves fell

1977

## Sun and Rain

Opening the book    at a bright window
above a wide pasture    after five years
I find I am still standing    on a stone bridge
looking down with my mother    at dusk into a river
5    hearing the current as hers    in her lifetime

now it comes to me    that that was the day
she told me of seeing my father    alive for the last time
and he waved her back from the door    as she was leaving
took her hand    for a while and said
10    nothing

at some signal
in a band of sunlight all the black cows    flow down the pasture
    together
to turn uphill and stand    as the dark rain touches them

1983

## Berryman

I will tell you what he told me
in the years just after the war
as we then called
the second world war

5    don't lose your arrogance yet he said
you can do that when you're older
lose it too soon and you may
merely replace it with vanity

just one time he suggested
10    changing the usual order
of the same words in a line of verse
why point out a thing twice

he suggested I pray to the Muse
get down on my knees and pray
15    right there in the corner and he
said he meant it literally

it was in the days before the beard
and the drink but he was deep
in tides of his own through which he sailed
20    chin sideways and head tilted like a tacking sloop

he was far older than the dates allowed for
much older than I was he was in his thirties
he snapped down his nose with an accent
I think he had affected in England

25     as for publishing he advised me
to paper my wall with rejection slips
his lips and the bones of his long fingers trembled
with the vehemence of his view about poetry

he said the great presence
30     that permitted everything and transmuted it
in poetry was passion
passion was genius and he praised movement and invention

I had hardly begun to read
I asked how can you ever be sure
35     that what you write is really
any good at all and he said you can't

you can't you can never be sure
you die without knowing
whether anything you wrote was any good
if you have to be sure don't write

*1983*

# Anne Sexton (1928–1974)

Born Anne Gray Harvey in Newton, Massachusetts, the child of a wool merchant, Sexton's family lived in Boston suburbs and spent the summers on Squirrel Island, Maine. She married Alfred Sexton in 1948. Experiencing severe depression after her daughters were born in 1953 and 1955, she attempted suicide in 1956. Her doctor recommended writing poetry as an outlet for her feelings, and she attended Boston poetry workshops run by John Holmes and Robert Lowell. *To Bedlam and Part Way Back* (1960), her first book, was successful enough to send her on the poetry reading circuit, where intense and dramatic readings gave her a still larger following. She taught at Harvard, Radcliffe, and Boston University. She won a Pulitzer Prize in 1967, but she remained troubled and took her own life in 1974.

Though often grounded in personal experience and emotion, even her more confessional poems mix biographical truth with invention; moreover, they often address the generational conflicts women underwent as traditional roles were challenged and redefined in the 1950s and 1960s, at which point the personal became political. She also went on to write poetic versions of fairy tales and to produce revisionist poetic versions of biblical stores. Some of her female personas become visionary and mythic figures.

## Her Kind

I have gone out, a possessed witch,
haunting the black air, braver at night;
dreaming evil, I have done my hitch
over the plain houses, light by light:
5     lonely thing, twelve-fingered,° out of mind.
A woman like that is not a woman, quite.
I have been her kind.

I have found the warm caves in the woods,
filled them with skillets, carvings, shelves,
10    closets, silks, innumerable goods;
fixed the suppers for the worms and the elves:
whining, rearranging the disaligned.
A woman like that is misunderstood.
I have been her kind.

---

5 *twelve-fingered:* possession of a sixth finger per hand was once considered a sign of witchcraft.

15     I have ridden in your cart, driver,
     waved my nude arms at villages going by,
     learning the last bright routes, survivor
     where your flames still bite my thigh
     and my ribs crack where your wheels wind.
20     A woman like that is not ashamed to die.
     I have been her kind.

                                              1960

## The Truth the Dead Know

*For my mother, born March 1902, died March 1959*
*and my father, born February 1900, died June 1959*

Gone, I say and walk from church,
refusing the stiff procession to the grave,
letting the dead ride alone in the hearse.
It is June. I am tired of being brave.

5     We drive to the Cape. I cultivate
     myself where the sun gutters from the sky,
     where the sea swings in like an iron gate
     and we touch. In another country people die.

     My darling, the wind falls in like stones
10     from the whitehearted water and when we touch
     we enter touch entirely. No one's alone.
     Men kill for this, or for as much.

     And what of the dead? They lie without shoes
     in their stone boats. They are more like stone
15     than the sea would be if it stopped. They refuse
     to be blessed, throat, eye and knucklebone.

                                                1962

## And One for My Dame

A born salesman,
my father made all his dough
by selling wool to Fieldcrest, Woolrich and Faribo.

A born talker,
5     he could sell one hundred wet-down bales
     of that white stuff. He could clock the miles and sales

and make it pay.
At home each sentence he would utter
had first pleased the buyer who'd paid him off in butter.

10 Each word
had been tried over and over, at any rate,
on the man who was sold by the man who filled my plate.

My father hovered
over the Yorkshire pudding and the beef:
15 a peddler, a hawker, a merchant and an Indian chief.

Roosevelt! Willkie! and war!
How suddenly gauche I was
with my old-maid heart and my funny teenage applause.

Each night at home
20 my father was in love with maps
while the radio fought its battles with Nazis and Japs.

Except when he hid
in his bedroom on a three-day drunk,
he typed out complex itineraries, packed his trunk,

25 his matched luggage
and pocketed a confirmed reservation,
his heart already pushing over the red routes of the nation.

I sit at my desk
each night with no place to go,
30 opening the wrinkled maps of Milwaukee and Buffalo,

the whole U.S.,
its cemeteries, its arbitrary time zones,
through routes like small veins, capitals like small stones.

He died on the road,
35 his heart pushed from neck to back,
his white hanky signaling from the window of the Cadillac.

My husband,
as blue-eyed as a picture book, sells wool:
boxes of card waste, laps and rovings he can pull

40 to the thread
and say *Leicester, Rambouillet, Merino,*
a half-blood, it's greasy and thick, yellow as old snow.

And when you drive off, my darling,
Yes sir! Yes, sir! It's one for my dame,
45 your sample cases branded with my father's name,

your itinerary open,
its tolls ticking and greedy,
its highways built up like new loves, raw and speedy.

1962

# The Room of My Life

Here,
in the room of my life
the objects keep changing.
Ashtrays to cry into,
5      the suffering brother of the wood walls,
the forty-eight keys of the typewriter
each an eyeball that is never shut,
the books, each a contestant in a beauty contest,
the black chair, a dog coffin made of Naugahyde,
10     the sockets on the wall
waiting like a cave of bees,
the gold rug
a conversation of heels and toes,
the fireplace
15     a knife waiting for someone to pick it up,
the sofa, exhausted with the exertion of a whore,
the phone
two flowers taking root in its crotch,
the doors
20     opening and closing like sea clams,
the lights
poking at me,
lighting up both the soil and the laugh.
The windows,
25     the starving windows
that drive the trees like nails into my heart.
Each day I feed the world out there
although birds explode
right and left.
30     I feed the world in here too,
offering the desk puppy biscuits.
However, nothing is just what it seems to be.
My objects dream and wear new costumes,
compelled to, it seems, by all the words in my hands
and the sea that bangs in my throat.

*1975*

## Philip Levine (b. 1928)

Born in Detroit, Michigan, and educated at Wayne State University, Levine later studied at Iowa with Robert Lowell and John Berryman. Along the way, he took a number of working-class jobs; those, and the ruined industrial landscape of Detroit, helped shape the settings and political loyalties of his poems. We can see that background most clearly in "Belle Isle, 1949" and "Fear and Fame," but it also underlies the slaughterhouse imagery of "Animals Are Passing From Our Lives" and the revolutionary transfiguration of vernacular language in what is very nearly his signature poem, "They Feed They Lion." For years, Levine has looked to modern Spanish poets for inspiration, and he has written a number of poems about the Spanish Civil War (including "Francisco, I'll Bring You Red Carnations"), often embodying his special sympathy for the Spanish anarchist movement. Although Levine's work is pervaded by an eloquent rage at injustice, it also reaches repeatedly for a visionary lyricism that Levine's subject matter makes uniquely his own.

### The Horse

for Ichiro Kawamoto, humanitarian,
electrician, & survivor of Hiroshima

> They spoke of the horse alive
> without skin, naked, hairless,
> without eyes and ears, searching
> for the stableboy's caress.
> 5   Shoot it, someone said, but they
> let him go on colliding with
> tattered walls, butting his long
> skull to pulp, finding no path
> where iron fences corkscrewed in
> 10  the street and bicycles turned
> like question marks.
>                 Some fled and
> some sat down. The river burned
> all that day and into the
> 15  night, the stones sighed a moment
> and were still, and the shadow
> of a man's hand entered
> a leaf.

                    The white horse never
20          returned, and later they found
            the stable boy, his back crushed
            by a hoof, his mouth opened
            around a cry that no one heard.

            They spoke of the horse again
25          and again; their mouths opened
            like the gills of a fish caught
            above water.
                            Mountain flowers
            burst from the red clay walls, and
30          they said a new life was here.
            Raw grass sprouted from the cobbles
            like hair from a deafened ear.

            The horse would never return.

            There had been no horse. I could
35          tell from the way they walked
            testing the ground for some cold
            that the rage had gone out of
            their bones in one mad dance.

                                                    *1963*


## Animals Are Passing From Our Lives

            It's wonderful how I jog
            on four honed-down ivory toes
            my massive buttocks slipping
            like oiled parts with each light step.

5           I'm to market. I can smell
            the sour, grooved block, I can smell
            the blade that opens the hole
            and the pudgy white fingers

            that shake out the intestines
10          like a hankie. In my dreams
            the snouts drool on the marble,
            suffering children, suffering flies,

            suffering the consumers
            who won't meet their steady eyes
15          for fear they could see. The boy
            who drives me along believes

            that any moment I'll fall
            on my side and drum my toes
            like a typewriter or squeal
20          and shit like a new housewife

discovering television,
or that I'll turn like a beast
cleverly to hook his teeth
with my teeth. No. Not this pig.

1968

# Belle Isle, 1949

We stripped in the first warm spring night
and ran down into the Detroit River
to baptize ourselves in the brine
of car parts, dead fish, stolen bicycles,
5     melted snow. I remember going under
hand in hand with a Polish highschool girl
I'd never seen before, and the cries
our breath made caught at the same time
on the cold, and rising through the layers
10    of darkness into the final moonless atmosphere
that was this world, the girl breaking
the surface after me and swimming out
on the starless waters towards the lights
of Jefferson Ave. and the stacks
15    of the old stove factory unwinking.
Turning at last to see no island at all
but a perfect calm dark as far
as there was sight, and then a light
and another riding low out ahead
20    to bring us home, ore boats maybe, or smokers
walking alone. Back panting
to the gray coarse beach we didn't dare
fall on, the damp piles of clothes,
and dressing side by side in silence
to go back where we came from.

1976

# They Feed They Lion

Out of burlap sacks, out of bearing butter,
Out of black bean and wet slate bread,
Out of the acids of rage, the candor of tar,
Out of creosote,° gasoline, drive shafts, wooden dollies,
5    They Lion grow.
                 Out of the gray hills
Of industrial barns, out of rain, out of bus ride,
West Virginia to Kiss My Ass, out of buried aunties,
Mothers hardening like pounded stumps, out of stumps,
10    Out of the bones' need to sharpen and the muscles' to stretch,
They Lion grow.

---

4 *creosote:* oily liquid obtained from coal tar and used as a wood preservative and disinfectant; it can cause severe neurological problems if inhaled.

                    Earth is eating trees, fence posts,
          Gutted cars, earth is calling in her little ones,
          "Come home, Come home!" From pig balls,
15        From the ferocity of pig driven to holiness,
          From the furred ear and the full jowl come
          The repose of the hung belly, from the purpose
          They Lion grow.
                              From the sweet glues of the trotters°
20        Come the sweet kinks of the fist, from the full flower
          Of the hams the thorax° of caves,
          From "Bow Down" come "Rise Up,"
          Come they Lion from the reeds of shovels,
          The grained arm that pulls the hands,
25        They Lion grow.
                              From my five arms and all my hands,
          From all my white sins forgiven, they feed,
          From my car passing under the stars,
          They Lion, from my children inherit,
30        From the oak turned to a wall, they Lion,
          From they sack and they belly opened
          And all that was hidden burning on the oil-stained earth
          They feed they Lion and he comes.

                                                                1972


## Francisco, I'll Bring You Red Carnations

                    Here in the great cemetery
                    behind the fortress of Barcelona
                    I have come once more to see
                    the graves of my fallen.
5                   Two ancient picnickers direct
                    us down the hill. "Durruti,"°
                    says the man, "I was on
                    his side." The woman hushes
                    him. All the way down
10                  this is a city of the dead,
                    871,251 *difuntos*.°
                    The poor packed in tenements
                    a dozen high; the rich
                    in splendid homes or temples.
15                  So nothing has changed
                    except for the single
                    unswerving fact: they are
                    all dead. Here is the Plaza

---

19 *trotters*: cooked pig or sheep feet.
21 *thorax*: the chest cavity.
6 *Durruti*: Buenaventura Durruti (1896–1936), perhaps the most famous Spanish anarchist during the Spanish Civil War, he died while commanding a militia battalion on the Madrid front at University City on November 20, 1936, only four months after the war began. He remains to this day a potent symbol of the pure political revolutionary. For general information on the war see the notes to Millay's "Say That We Saw Spain Die." For comments on the battles around Madrid, see the notes to Rolfe's "Elegia."
11 *difuntos*: (Spanish) "deceased."

of San Jaime, here the Rambla
20    of San Pedro, so every death
still has a mailing address,
but since this is Spain
the mail never comes or
comes too late to be of use.
25    Between the cemetery and
the Protestant burial ground
we find the three stones
all in a row: Ferrer Guardia,°
B. Durruti, F. Ascaso,° the names
30    written with marking pens,
and a few circled A's and tributes
to the FAI° and CNT.°
For two there are floral
displays, but Ascaso faces
35    eternity with only a stone.
Maybe as it should be. He was
a stone, a stone and a blade,
the first grinding and sharpening
the other. Half his 36
40    years were spent in prisons
or on the run, and yet
in that last photograph
taken less than an hour before
he died, he stands in a dark
45    suit, smoking, a rifle slung
behind his shoulder, and glances

---

28 *Guardia*: Francisco Ferrer Guardia (*1859–1909*), famous Spanish anarchist educator ex-
ecuted by the state during the Tragic Week of July 1909, an outburst of rioting and church-
burning triggered by popular resentment against the Moroccan War; the week raised be-
fore the privileged classes the specter of a proletarian revolution, a possibility that would
haunt Spain's wealthy and galvanize its poor for decades.
29 *Ascaso*: Francisco Ascaso Budria (?–1936) was a leading anarchist figure in Catalonia.
His brothers Domingo and Joaquín were also active in the movement. Ascaso had been a
carpenter but evolved into a strike leader and political activist, one who believed in as-
sassination as a political weapon. He was killed in the opening days of the Spanish Civil
War, July 1936, fighting to put down the right-wing military rebellion in Barcelona. A re-
flective, capable leader, his loss to Spanish anarchism was a substantial one.
32 *FAI*: (*Federación Anarquista Ibérica*) The group of theoreticians and activists who made
up the ideological vanguard of Spanish anarchism. Its paramilitary cadres were responsi-
ble for some indiscriminate violence in the early days of the war. Historically somewhat
at odds with the CNT, its position moderated enough so that its members came to hold
positions of leadership in the CNT. Barcelona was its primary site of influence; its pres-
ence in Madrid was minimal. One of the major slogans of the CNT-FAI was "The war and
revolution are inseparable."
32 *CNT*: (*Confederación Nacional del Trabajo*) Founded in 1911, the CNT was one of the
two important labor groups in Spain (the other was the UGT), both having around a mil-
lion members. Often referred to as anarchist, the CNT practiced a form of syndicalism
based in industrial unions and eschewed any belief that there could be anything but con-
tinuous class conflict between employers and workers. Independent of any political party,
it often called on its members to boycott elections, but it was the absence of such a boy-
cott that contributed to the electoral victory of the Popular Front in 1936. The CNT ad-
vocated a revolutionary strategy for winning the war and the revolution, a policy strenu-
ously opposed by the Republican parties and especially by the communists.

sideways at the camera
half smiling. It is July 20,
1936, and before the darkness
50    falls a darkness will have
fallen on him. While
the streets are echoing
with victory and revolution,
Francisco Ascaso will take up
55    the hammered little blade
of his spirit and enter for
the last time the republics
of death. I remember
his words to a frightened
60    comrade who questioned
the wisdom of attack: "We
have gathered here to die, but we
don't have to die with dogs,
so go." Forty-one years
65    ago, and now the city stretches
as far as the eye can see,
huge cement columns like nails
pounded into the once green
meadows of the Llobregat.°
70    Your Barcelona is gone,
the old town swallowed
in industrial filth and
the burning mists of gasoline.
Only the police remain, armed
75    and arrogant, smiling masters
of the boulevards, the police
and your dream of the city
of God, where every man
and every woman gives
80    and receives the gifts of work
and care, and that dream
goes on in spite of slums,
in spite of death clouds,
the roar of trucks, the harbor
85    staining the mother sea,
it goes on in spite of all
that mocks it. We have it here
growing in our hearts, as
your comrade said, and when
90    we give it up with our last
breaths someone will gasp
it home to their lives.

---

69 *Llobregat:* a region in Catalonia. Levine is invoking not just a place but also its revolutionary history. On September 3, 1931, the FAI called a general strike in Barcelona. In January of 1932 miners on strike in the Pyrenean foothills occupied the surrounding townships and proclaimed a libertarian revolution. The following January, the FAI launched an insurrection that spread across eastern Spain, and in 1934 illegal strikes in the Llobregat potash mines were broken by mass detentions and firings.

Francisco, stone, knife blade,
single soldier still on
95    the run down the darkest
street of all, we will be back
across an ocean and a continent
to bring you red carnations,
to celebrate the unbroken
100   promise of your life that
once was frail and flesh.

1979

## Fear and Fame

Half an hour to dress, wide rubber hip boots,
gauntlets to the elbow, a plastic helmet
like a knight's but with a little glass window
that kept steaming over, and a respirator
5     to save my smoke-stained lungs. I would descend
step by slow step into the dim world
of the pickling tank and there prepare
the new solutions from the great carboys
of acids lowered to me on ropes—all from a recipe
10    I shared with nobody and learned from Frank O'Mera
before he went off to the bars on Vernor Highway
to drink himself to death. A gallon of hydrochloric
steaming from the wide glass mouth, a dash
of pale nitric to bubble up, sulphuric to calm,
15    metals for sweeteners, cleansers for salts,
until I knew the burning stew was done.
Then to climb back, step by stately step, the adventurer
returned to the ordinary blinking lights
of the swingshift at Feinberg and Breslin's
20    First-Rate Plumbing and Plating with a message
from the kingdom of fire. Oddly enough
no one welcomed me back, and I'd stand
fully armored as the downpour of cold water
rained down on me and the smoking traces puddled
25    at my feet like so much milk and melting snow.
Then to disrobe down to my work pants and shirt,
my black street shoes and white cotton socks,
to reassume my nickname, strap on my Bulova,
screw back my wedding ring, and with tap water
30    gargle away the bitterness as best I could.
For fifteen minutes or more I'd sit quietly
off to the side of the world as the women
polished the tubes and fixtures to a burnished purity
hung like Christmas ornaments on the racks
35    pulled steadily toward the tanks I'd cooked.
Ahead lay the second cigarette, held in a shaking hand,
as I took into myself the sickening heat to quell heat,
a lunch of two Genoa salami sandwiches and Swiss cheese
on heavy peasant bread baked by my Aunt Tsipie,

40 and a third cigarette to kill the taste of the others.
Then to arise and dress again in the costume
of my trade for the second time that night, stiffened
by the knowledge that to descend and rise up
from the other world merely once in eight hours is half
what it takes to be known among women and men.

*1991*

## On the Meeting of García Lorca and Hart Crane°

Brooklyn, 1929. Of course Crane's
been drinking and has no idea who
this curious Andalusian is, unable
even to speak the language of poetry.
5 The young man who brought them
together knows both Spanish and English,
but he has a headache from jumping
back and forth from one language
to another. For a moment's relief
10 he goes to the window to look
down on the East River, darkening
below as the early night comes on.
Something flashes across his sight,
a double vision of such horror
15 he has to slap both his hands across
his mouth to keep from screaming.
Let's not be frivolous, let's
not pretend the two poets gave
each other wisdom or love or
20 even a good time, let's not
invent a dialogue of such eloquence
that even the ants in your own
house won't forget it. The two
greatest poetic geniuses alive
25 meet, and what happens? A vision
comes to an ordinary man staring
at a filthy river. Have you ever
had a vision? Have you ever shaken
your head to pieces and jerked back
30 at the image of your young son
falling through open space, not
from the stern of a ship bound
from Vera Cruz to New York but from
the roof of the building he works on?
35 Have you risen from bed to pace
until dawn to beg a merciless God

---

**poem title:** Federico García Lorca (1898–1936) is widely considered Spain's most important twentieth-century poet. He did visit New York and Cuba, which is the basis of Levine's speculative poem. Lorca was murdered by the fascists at the outbreak of the Spanish Civil War.

to take these pictures away? Oh, yes,
let's bless the imagination. It gives
us the myths we live by. Let's bless
40   the visionary power of the human—
the only animal that's got it—,
bless the exact image of your father
dead and mine dead, bless the images
that stalk the corners of our sight
45   and will not let go. The young man
was my cousin, Arthur Lieberman,
then a language student at Columbia,
who told me all this before he died
quietly in his sleep in 1983
50   in a hotel in Perugia. A good man,
Arthur, he survived graduate school,
later came home to Detroit and sold
pianos right through the Depression.
He loaned my brother a used one
55   to compose his hideous songs on,
which Arthur thought were genius.
What an imagination Arthur had!

*1995*

# Adrienne Rich (b. 1929)

Adrienne Rich grew up in Baltimore and was educated at Radcliffe College. After early work that had the controlled elegance and formality characteristic of some poets in the first years of the 1950s, she began to adapt the open forms that have been central to the American tradition since Whitman. Since then, she has become one of the most widely read and influential poets of the second half of the century. That impact has grown not only from her poetry but also from a number of ground-breaking essays, including "When We Dead Awaken: Writing as Re-Vision" and "Compulsory Heterosexuality and Lesbian Existence."

Rich's position now is in many ways unique. She is our foremost feminist poet and an important theorist of the social construction of gender, but that dual status sometimes overshadows, and even obscures, the range of her most ambitious work. She has written a number of unforgettable short poems, variously visionary, historical, political, and polemical. Some of these, along with longer poems like "Diving into the Wreck," have helped to define the personal and social understanding of a generation. Yet her many long poem sequences are inevitably more complex aesthetically and philosophically, and they demand extended reading and reflection.

It is in these poem sequences especially that her recurring topic of several decades—the relationship between individual experience, contemporary political and social life, and historical memory—receives its most innovative treatment. Devoted like so many other poets to understanding the burdens of national identity, she has tried to uncover at once the texture and the governing principles of the lesson Americans are least willing to learn: that we are intricately embedded in and shaped by social life. Other poets, to be sure, have dealt with the intersection of personal and public life. It was Robert Lowell's lifetime theme. But Rich is unusual in tracking these intersections with a keen sense of their temporal intricacy; in Rich, social life and politics and the lives of earlier women (like that of Marie Curie in "Power") are registered on the pulses. Representing her adequately requires offering more than one of her poem sequences. We print most of "Shooting Script" and "Twenty-One Love Poems" in its entirety.

## Aunt Jennifer's Tigers

Aunt Jennifer's tigers prance across a screen
Bright topaz denizens of a world of green.
They do not fear the men beneath the tree;
They pace in sleek chivalric certainty.

5  Aunt Jennifer's fingers fluttering through her wool
Find even the ivory needle hard to pull.
The massive weight of Uncle's wedding band
Sits heavily upon Aunt Jennifer's hand.

When Aunt is dead, her terrified hands will lie
10  Still ringed with ordeals she was mastered by.
The tigers in the panel that she made
Will go on prancing, proud and unafraid.

*1951*

## *from* Shooting Script

### Part I 11/69–2/70

1.

We were bound on the wheel of an endless conversation.

Inside this shell, a tide waiting for someone to enter.

A monologue waiting for you to interrupt it.

A man wading into the surf. The dialogue of the rock with the
5  breaker.

•

The wave changed instantly by the rock; the rock changed by the
wave returning over and over.

The dialogue that lasts all night or a whole lifetime.

A conversation of sounds melting constantly into rhythms.

10  A shell waiting for you to listen.

A tide that ebbs and flows against a deserted continent.

A cycle whose rhythm begins to change the meanings of words.

A wheel of blinding waves of light, the spokes pulsing out from
where we hang together in the turning of an endless
15  conversation.

The meaning that searches for its word like a hermit crab.

A monologue that waits for one listener.

An ear filled with one sound only.

A shell penetrated by meaning.

2.

*Adapted from Mirza Ghalib°*

20      Even when I thought I prayed, I was talking to myself; when I
        found the door shut, I simply walked away.

        We all accept Your claim to be unique; the stone lips, the
        carved limbs, were never your true portrait.

        Grief held back from the lips wears at the heart; the drop that
25      refused to join the river dried up in the dust.

        Now tell me your story till the blood drips from your lashes. Any
        other version belongs to your folklore, or ours.

                                    •

        To see the Tigris° in a water-drop . . . Either you were playing
        games with me, or you never cared to learn the structure of my
30      language.

                                    3.

        The old blanket. The crumbs of rubbed wool turning up.

        Where we lay and breakfasted. The stains of tea. The squares
        of winter light projected on the wool.

        You, sleeping with closed windows. I, sleeping in the silver
35      nitrate° burn of zero air.

        Where it can snow, I'm at home; the crystals accumulating
        spell out my story.

        The cold encrustation thickening on the ledge.

        The arrow-headed facts, accumulating, till a whole city is
40      taken over.

        Midwinter and the loss of love, going comes before gone, over
        and over the point is missed and still the blind will turns for
        its target.

                                    4.

        In my imagination I was the pivot of a fresh beginning.

45      In rafts they came over the sea; on the island they put up those
        stones by methods we can only guess at.

        ---

        *Ghalib:* Urdu poet Mirza Ghalib (1797–1869).
        20 *Tigris:* river that runs through Turkey and Iraq.
        35 *silver nitrate:* poisonous irritant, a soluble salt used in photography and as a germicide.

If the vegetation grows as thick as this, how can we see what they were seeing?

It is all being made clear, with bulldozers, at Angkor Wat.°

50  The verdure was a false mystery; the baring of the stones is no solution for us now.

•

Defoliation progresses; concrete is poured, sheets of glass hauled overland in huge trucks and at great cost.

Here we never travailed, never took off our shoes to walk the
55  final mile.

Come and look into this cellar-hole; this is the foundling of the woods.

Humans lived here once; it became sacred only when they went away.

### 5.

60  Of simple choice they are the villagers; their clothes come with them like red clay roads they have been walking.

The sole of the foot is a map, the palm of the hand a letter, learned by heart and worn close to the body.

They seemed strange to me, till I began to recall their dialect.

65  Poking the spade into the dry loam, listening for the tick of broken pottery, hoarding the brown and black bits in a dented can.

Evenings, at the table, turning the findings out, pushing them around with a finger, beginning to dream of fitting them together.

Hiding all this work from them, although they might have helped
70  me.

Going up at night, hiding the tin can in a closet, where the linoleum lies in shatters on a back shelf.

Sleeping to dream of the unformed, the veil of water pouring over the wet clay, the rhythms of choice, the lost methods.

•

---

49 *Angkor Wat:* massive, richly sculpted twelfth-century temple in northern Cambodia, endangered during the Vietnam war.

6.

75        You are beside me like a wall; I touch you with my fingers and
          keep moving through the bad light.

          At this time of year when faces turn aside, it is amazing that your
          eyes are to be met.

          A bad light is one like this, that flickers and diffuses itself along
80        the edge of a frontier.

          No, I don't invest you with anything; I am counting on your
          weakness as much as on your strength.

          This light eats away at the clarities I had fixed on; it moves up
          like a rodent at the edge of the raked paths.

85        Your clarities may not reach me; but your attention will.

          It is to know that I too have no mythic powers; it is to see the
          liability of all my treasures.

          You will have to see all this for a long time alone.

          You are beside me like a wall; I touch you with my fingers and
90        keep trying to move through the bad light.

*Part II 3–7/70*

9.

**NEWSREEL**

This would not be the war we fought in. See, the foliage is
heavier, there were no hills of that size there.

But I find it impossible not to look for actual persons known
to me and not seen since; impossible not to look for myself.

•

95        The scenery angers me, I know there is something wrong, the sun
          is too high, the grass too trampled, the peasants' faces too broad,
          and the main square of the capital had no arcades like those.

          Yet the dead look right, and the roofs of the huts, and the crashed
          fuselage burning among the ferns.

100       But this is not the war I came to see, buying my ticket, stumbling
          through the darkness, finding my place among the sleepers and
          masturbators in the dark.

          I thought of seeing the General who cursed us, whose name they
          gave to an expressway; I wanted to see the faces of the dead when
105       they were living.

Once I know they filmed us, back at the camp behind the lines,
taking showers under the trees and showing pictures of our girls.

Somewhere there is a film of the war we fought in, and it must
contain the flares, the souvenirs, the shadows of the netted brush,
110    the standing in line of the innocent, the hills that were not of
this size.

Somewhere my body goes taut under the deluge, somewhere I am
naked behind the lines, washing my body in the water of that war.

Someone has that war stored up in metal canisters, a memory he
115    cannot use, somewhere my innocence is proven with my guilt, but
this would not be the war I fought in.

10

*—for Valerie Glauber*

They come to you with their descriptions of your soul.

They come and drop their mementos at the foot of your bed; their
feathers, ferns, fans, grasses from the western mountains.

•

120    They wait for you to unfold for them like a paper flower, a secret
springing open in a glass of water.

They believe your future has a history and that it is themselves.

They have family trees to plant for you, photographs of dead
children, old bracelets and rings they want to fasten onto you.

125    And, in spite of this, you live alone.

Your secret hangs in the open like Poe's purloined letter; their
longing and their methods will never let them find it.

Your secret cries out in the dark and hushes; when they start out
of sleep they think you are innocent.

130    You hang among them like the icon in a Russian play; living your
own intenser life behind the lamp they light in front of you.

You are split here like mercury on a marble counter, liquefying
into many globes, each silvered like a planet caught in a lens.

You are a mirror lost in a brook, an eye reflecting a torrent of
135    reflections.

You are a letter written, folded, burnt to ash, and mailed in an
envelope to another continent.

11.

The mare's skeleton in the clearing: another sign of life.

140 When you pull the embedded bones up from the soil, the flies
collect again.

The pelvis, the open archway, staring at me like an eye.

In the desert these bones would be burnt white; a green bloom grows
on them in the woods.

•

Did she break her leg or die of poison?

145 What was it like when the scavengers came?

So many questions unanswered, yet the statement is here and clear.

With what joy you handled the skull, set back the teeth spilt in the
grass, hinged back the jaw on the jaw.

With what joy we left the woods, swinging our sticks, miming the
150 speech of noble savages, of the fathers of our country, bursting
into the full sun of the uncut field.

12.

I was looking for a way out of a lifetime's consolations.

We walked in the wholesale district: closed warehouses, windows,
steeped in sun.

155 I said: those cloths are very old. You said: they have lain in
that window a long time.

When the skeletons of the projects° shut off the sunset, when the
sense of the Hudson° leaves us, when only by loss of light in the east
do I know that I am living in the west.

160 When I give up being paraphrased, when I let go, when the
beautiful solutions in their crystal flasks have dried up in the sun,
when the lightbulb bursts on lighting, when the dead bulb rattles
like a seed-pod.

Those cloths are very old, they are mummies' cloths, they have lain
165 in graves, they were not intended to be sold, the tragedy of this
mistake will soon be clear.

---

157 *projects*: large-scale housing complexes built for low-income families.
158 *Hudson*: river that flows past New York City to the Atlantic Ocean.

Vacillant needles of Manhattan, describing hour & weather; buying
these descriptions at the cost of missing every other point.

•

### 13.

We are driven to odd attempts; once it would not have occurred to
170    me to put out in a boat, not on a night like this.

Still, it was an instrument, and I had pledged myself to try any
instrument that came my way. Never to refuse one from conviction
of incompetence.

A long time I was simply learning to handle the skiff; I had no
175    special training and my own training was against me.

I had always heard that darkness and water were a threat.

In spite of this, darkness and water helped me to arrive here.

I watched the lights on the shore I had left for a long time; each
one, it seemed to me, was a light I might have lit, in the old days.

### 14.

180    Whatever it was: the grains of the glacier caked in the boot-cleats;
ashes spilled on white formica.

The death-col° viewed through power-glasses; the cube of ice melting
on stainless steel.

Whatever it was, the image that stopped you, the one on which you
185    came to grief, projecting it over & over on empty walls.

Now to give up the temptations of the projector; to see instead the
web of cracks filtering across the plaster.

To read there the map of the future, the roads radiating from the
initial split, the filaments thrown out from that impasse.

190    To reread the instructions on your palm; to find there how the
lifeline, broken, keeps its direction.

•

To read the etched rays of the bullet-hole left years ago in the
glass; to know in every distortion of the light what fracture is.

---

182 *death-col:* a treacherous high mountain pass or depression in the crest of a ridge.

195  To put the prism in your pocket, the thin glass lens, the map
of the inner city, the little book with gridded pages.

To pull yourself up by your own roots; to eat the last meal in
your old neighborhood.

1970

## Trying to Talk with a Man

Out in this desert we are testing bombs,

that's why we came here.

Sometimes I feel an underground river
forcing its way between deformed cliffs
5  an acute angle of understanding
moving itself like a locus of the sun
into this condemned scenery.

What we've had to give up to get here—
whole LP collections, films we starred in
10  playing in the neighborhoods, bakery windows
full of dry, chocolate-filled Jewish cookies,
the language of love-letters, of suicide notes,
afternoons on the riverbank
pretending to be children

15  Coming out to this desert
we meant to change the face of
driving among dull green succulents
walking at noon in the ghost town
surrounded by a silence

20  that sounds like the silence of the place
except that it came with us
and is familiar
and everything we were saying until now
was an effort to blot it out—
25  coming out here we are up against it

Out here I feel more helpless
with you than without you

You mention the danger
and list the equipment
30  we talk of people caring for each other
in emergencies—laceration, thirst—
but you look at me like an emergency

Your dry heat feels like power
your eyes are stars of a different magnitude
35  they reflect lights that spell out: EXIT
when you get up and pace the floor

talking of the danger
as if it were not ourselves
as if we were testing anything else.

*1971*

# Diving into the Wreck

First having read the book of myths,
and loaded the camera,
and checked the edge of the knife-blade,
I put on
5    the body-armor of black rubber
the absurd flippers
the grave and awkward mask.
I am having to do this
not like Cousteau° with his
10    assiduous team
aboard the sun-flooded schooner
but here alone.

There is a ladder.
The ladder is always there
15    hanging innocently
close to the side of the schooner.
We know what it is for,
we who have used it.
Otherwise
20    it's a piece of maritime floss
some sundry equipment.

I go down.
Rung after rung and still
the oxygen immerses me
25    the blue light
the clear atoms
of our human air.
I go down.
My flippers cripple me,
30    I crawl like an insect down the ladder
and there is no one
to tell me when the ocean
will begin.

First the air is blue and then
35    it is bluer and then green and then
black I am blacking out and yet
my mask is powerful
it pumps my blood with power
the sea is another story
40    the sea is not a question of power
I have to learn alone
to turn my body without force
in the deep element.

---

9 *Cousteau:* Jacques Cousteau (1910–1997), French environmentalist, documentary film
maker, and underwater explorer.

And now: it is easy to forget
45      what I came for
among so many who have always
lived here
swaying their crenellated° fans
between the reefs
50      and besides
you breathe differently down here.

I came to explore the wreck.
The words are purposes.
The words are maps.
55      I came to see the damage that was done
and the treasures that prevail.
I stroke the beam of my lamp
slowly along the flank
of something more permanent
60      than fish or weed

the thing I came for:
the wreck and not the story of the wreck
the thing itself and not the myth
the drowned face always staring
65      toward the sun
the evidence of damage
worn by salt and sway into this threadbare beauty
the ribs of the disaster
curving their assertion
70      among the tentative haunters.

This is the place.
And I am here, the mermaid whose dark hair
streams black, the merman in his armored body
We circle silently
75      about the wreck
we dive into the hold.
I am she: I am he

whose drowned face° sleeps with open eyes
whose breasts still bear the stress
80      whose silver, copper, vermeil° cargo lies
obscurely inside barrels
half-wedged and left to rot
we are the half-destroyed instruments
that once held to a course
85      the water-eaten log
the fouled compass

---

48 *crenellated*: patterned with repeated notches or ridged indentations.
78 *drowned face*: as in the carved female figureheads once placed on the prow of sailing ships.
80 *vermeil*: gilded silver, copper, or bronze.

We are, I am, you are
by cowardice or courage
the one who find our way
90    back to this scene
carrying a knife, a camera
a book of myths
in which
our names do not appear.

                              *1972*

## Twenty-one Love Poems

### I

Wherever in this city, screens flicker
with pornography, with science-fiction vampires,
victimized hirelings bending to the lash,
we also have to walk . . . if simply as we walk
5    through the rainsoaked garbage, the tabloid cruelties
of our own neighborhoods.
We need to grasp our lives inseparable
from those rancid dreams, that blurt of metal, those disgraces,
and the red begonia perilously flashing
10    from a tenement sill six stories high,
or the long-legged young girls playing ball
in the junior highschool playground.
No one has imagined us. We want to live like trees,
sycamores blazing through the sulfuric air,
15    dappled with scars, still exuberantly budding,
our animal passion rooted in the city.

### II

I wake up in your bed. I know I have been dreaming.
Much earlier, the alarm broke us from each other,
you've been at your desk for hours. I know what I dreamed:
20    our friend the poet comes into my room
where I've been writing for days,
drafts, carbons, poems are scattered everywhere,
and I want to show her one poem
which is the poem of my life. But I hesitate,
25    and wake. You've kissed my hair
to wake me. *I dreamed you were a poem,*
I say, *a poem I wanted to show someone . . .*
and I laugh and fall dreaming again
of the desire to show you to everyone I love,
30    to move openly together
in the pull of gravity, which is not simple,
which carries the feathered grass a long way down the upbreathing
    air.

## III

Since we're not young, weeks have to do time
for years of missing each other. Yet only this odd warp
35    in time tells me we're not young.
Did I ever walk the morning streets at twenty,
my limbs streaming with a purer joy?
did I lean from any window over the city
listening for the future
40    as I listen here with nerves tuned for your ring?
And you, you move toward me with the same tempo.
Your eyes are everlasting, the green spark
of the blue-eyed grass of early summer,
the green-blue wild cress washed by the spring.
45    At twenty, yes: we thought we'd live forever.
At forty-five, I want to know even our limits.
I touch you knowing we weren't born tomorrow,
and somehow, each of us will help the other live,
and somewhere, each of us must help the other die.

## IV

50    I come home from you through the early light of spring
flashing off ordinary walls, the Pez Dorado,
the Discount Wares, the shoe-store. . . . I'm lugging my sack
of groceries, I dash for the elevator
where a man, taut, elderly, carefully composed
55    lets the door almost close on me.—*For god's sake hold it!*
I croak at him.—*Hysterical,*—he breathes my way.
I let myself into the kitchen, unload my bundles,
make coffee, open the window, put on Nina Simone°
singing *Here comes the sun.* . . . I open the mail,
60    drinking delicious coffee, delicious music,
my body still both light and heavy with you. The mail
lets fall a Xerox of something written by a man
aged 27, a hostage, tortured in prison:
*My genitals have been the object of such a sadistic display*
65    *they keep me constantly awake with the pain* . . .
*Do whatever you can to survive.*
*You know, I think that men love wars* . . .
And my incurable anger, my unmendable wounds
break open further with tears, I am crying helplessly,
70    and they still control the world, and you are not in my arms.

## V

This apartment full of books could crack open
to the thick jaws, the bulging eyes
of monsters, easily: Once open the books, you have to face
the underside of everything you've loved—

---

58 *Nina Simone:* (b. 1933) American jazz vocalist and pianist.

75     the rack and pincers held in readiness, the gag
       even the best voices have had to mumble through,
       the silence burying unwanted children—
       women, deviants, witnesses—in desert sand.
       Kenneth tells me he's been arranging his books
80     so he can look at Blake and Kafka while he types;
       yes; and we still have to reckon with Swift
       loathing the woman's flesh while praising her mind,
       Goethe's dread of the Mothers, Claudel vilifying Gide,°
       and the ghosts—their hands clasped for centuries—
85     of artists dying in childbirth, wise-women charred at the stake,
       centuries of books unwritten piled behind these shelves;
       and we still have to stare into the absence
       of men who would not, women who could not, speak
       to our life—this still unexcavated hole
90     called civilization, this act of translation, this half-world.

                                    VI

       Your small hands, precisely equal to my own—
       only the thumb is larger, longer—in these hands
       I could trust the world, or in many hands like these,
       handling power-tools or steering-wheel
95     or touching a human face. . . . Such hands could turn
       the unborn child rightways in the birth canal
       or pilot the exploratory rescue-ship
       through icebergs, or piece together
       the fine, needle-like sherds of a great krater-cup°
100    bearing on its sides
       figures of ecstatic women striding
       to the sibyl's den or the Eleusinian cave°—
       such hands might carry out an unavoidable violence
       with such restraint, with such a grasp
105    of the range and limits of violence
       that violence ever after would be obsolete.

                                    VII

       What kind of beast would turn its life into words?
       What atonement is this all about?
       —and yet, writing words like these, I'm also living.

---

83 *Gide:* William Blake (1757–1827), visionary British poet; Franz Kafka (1883–1924), Austrian novelist who described a threatening and incomprehensible world in a style of impeccable clarity; Jonathan Swift (1667–1745), Irish poet, essayist, novelist, and priest; Johann Wolfgang von Goethe (1749–1832), German poet and novelist; Paul Claudel (1868–1955), French Roman Catholic dramatist and poet; Andre Gide (1869–1951), French novelist, critic, and playwright known for unconventional views on communism and homosexuality.
99 *krater-cup:* a large vessel from Greek or Roman antiquity used to mix wine and water.
102 *cave:* the Sibyl was a mythological figure who requested a thousand years of life but forgot to ask for youth as well; she finally hung from the ceiling of her cave or den, a shrivelled figure in a bottle; cave: the Eleusinian cave was associated with ritual initiations and festivities observed by the people of ancient Athens.

110 Is all this close to the wolverines' howled signals,
that modulated cantata of the wild?
or, when away from you I try to create you in words,
am I simply using you, like a river or a war?
And how have I used rivers, how have I used wars
115 to escape writing of the worst thing of all—
not the crimes of others, not even our own death,
but the failure to want our freedom passionately enough
so that blighted elms, sick rivers, massacres would seem
mere emblems of that desecration of ourselves?

## VIII

120 I can see myself years back at Sunion,°
hurting with an infected foot, Philoctetes°
in woman's form, limping the long path,
lying on a headland over the dark sea,
looking down the red rocks to where a soundless curl
125 of white told me a wave had struck,
imagining the pull of that water from that height,
knowing deliberate suicide wasn't my métier,
yet all the time nursing, measuring that wound.
Well, that's finished. The woman who cherished
130 her suffering is dead. I am her descendant.
I love the scar-tissue she handed on to me,
but I want to go on from here with you
fighting the temptation to make a career of pain.

## IX

Your silence today is a pond where drowned things live
135 I want to see raised dripping and brought into the sun.
It's not my own face I see there, but other faces,
even your face at another age.
Whatever's lost there is needed by both of us—
a watch of old gold, a water-blurred fever chart,
140 a key. . . . Even the silt and pebbles of the bottom
deserve their glint of recognition. I fear this silence,
this inarticulate life. I'm waiting
for a wind that will gently open this sheeted water
for once, and show me what I can do
145 for you, who have often made the unnameable
nameable for others, even for me.

## X

Your dog, tranquil and innocent, dozes through
our cries, our murmured dawn conspiracies
our telephone calls. She knows—what can she know?

---

120 *Sunion*: the summit at Cape Sounion in Greece contains the ruins of a temple.
121 *Philoctetes*: in Greek mythology he was bitten on the foot by a water-snake during the
Trojan war; the painful wound would not heal.

150     If in my human arrogance I claim to read
her eyes, I find there only my own animal thoughts:
that creatures must find each other for bodily comfort,
that voices of the psyche drive through the flesh
further than the dense brain could have foretold,
155     that the planetary nights are growing cold for those
on the same journey who want to touch
one creature-traveler clear to the end;
that without tenderness, we are in hell.

### XI

Every peak is a crater. This is the law of volcanoes,
160     making them eternally and visibly female.
No height without depth, without a burning core,
though our straw soles shred on the hardened lava.
I want to travel with you to every sacred mountain
smoking within like the sibyl stooped over her tripod,
165     I want to reach for your hand as we scale the path,
to feel your arteries glowing in my clasp,
never failing to note the small, jewel-like flower
unfamiliar to us, nameless till we rename her,
that clings to the slowly altering rock—
170     that detail outside ourselves that brings us to ourselves,
was here before us, knew we would come, and sees beyond us.

### XII

Sleeping, turning in turn like planets
rotating in their midnight meadow:
a touch is enough to let us know
175     we're not alone in the universe, even in sleep:
the dream-ghosts of two worlds
walking their ghost-towns, almost address each other.
I've wakened to your muttered words
spoken light- or dark-years away
180     as if my own voice had spoken.
But we have different voices, even in sleep,
and our bodies, so alike, are yet so different
and the past echoing through our bloodstreams
is freighted with different language, different meanings—
185     though in any chronicle of the world we share
it could be written with new meaning
we were two lovers of one gender,
we were two women of one generation.

### XIII

The rules break like a thermometer,
190     quicksilver spills across the charted systems,
we're out in a country that has no language
no laws, we're chasing the raven and the wren
through gorges unexplored since dawn

whatever we do together is pure invention
195        the maps they gave us were out of date
by years ... we're driving through the desert
wondering if the water will hold out
the hallucinations turn to simple villages
the music on the radio comes clear—
200        neither *Rosenkavalier* nor *Götterdämmerung*°
but a woman's voice singing old songs
with new words, with a quiet bass, a flute
plucked and fingered by women outside the law.


### XIV

It was your vision of the pilot
205        confirmed my vision of you: you said, *He keeps*
*on steering headlong into the waves, on purpose*
while we crouched in the open hatchway
vomiting into plastic bags
for three hours between St. Pierre and Miquelon.°
210        I never felt closer to you.
In the close cabin where the honeymoon couples
huddled in each other's laps and arms
I put my hand on your thigh
to comfort both of us, your hand came over mine,
215        we stayed that way, suffering together
in our bodies, as if all suffering
were physical, we touched so in the presence
of strangers who knew nothing and cared less
vomiting their private pain
220        as if all suffering were physical.


#### (THE FLOATING POEM, UNNUMBERED)

Whatever happens with us, your body
will haunt mine—tender, delicate
your lovemaking, like the half-curled frond
of the fiddlehead fern in forests
225        just washed by sun. Your travelled, generous thighs
between which my whole face has come and come—
the innocence and wisdom of the place my tongue has found
        there—
the live, insatiate dance of your nipples in my mouth—
your touch on me, firm, protective, searching
230        me out, your strong tongue and slender fingers
reaching where I had been waiting years for you
in my rose-wet cave—whatever happens, this is.

---

200 *Götterdämmerung: Der Rosenkavalier* (The Knight of the Rose, 1911), an opera by German composer Richard Strauss (1864–1949); *Götterdämmerung* (The Twilight of the Gods, 1876), the fourth and final part of the operatic sequence *The Ring of the Nibelung* by German composer Richard Wagner (1813–1883).
209 *St. Pierre and Miquelon:* islands off the coast of Newfoundland, Canada, that belong to France.

## XV

If I lay on that beach with you
white, empty, pure green water warmed by the Gulf Stream
235    and lying on that beach we could not stay
because the wind drove fine sand against us
as if it were against us
if we tried to withstand it and we failed—
if we drove to another place
240    to sleep in each other's arms
and the beds were narrow like prisoners' cots
and we were tired and did not sleep together
and this was what we found, so this is what we did—
was the failure ours?
245    If I cling to circumstances I could feel
not responsible. Only she who says
she did not choose, is the loser in the end.

## XVI

Across a city from you, I'm with you,
just as an August night
250    moony, inlet-warm, seabathed, I watched you sleep,
the scrubbed, sheenless wood of the dressing-table
cluttered with our brushes, books, vials in the moonlight—
or a salt-mist orchard, lying at your side
watching red sunset through the screendoor of the cabin,
255    G minor Mozart on the tape-recorder,
falling asleep to the music of the sea.
This island of Manhattan is wide enough
for both of us, and narrow:
I can hear your breath tonight, I know how your face
260    lies upturned, the halflight tracing
your generous, delicate mouth
where grief and laughter sleep together.

## XVII

No one's fated or doomed to love anyone.
The accidents happen, we're not heroines,
265    they happen in our lives like car crashes,
books that change us, neighborhoods
we move into and come to love.
*Tristan und Isolde*° is scarcely the story,
women at least should know the difference
270    between love and death. No poison cup,
no penance. Merely a notion that the tape-recorder
should have caught some ghost of us: that tape-recorder
not merely played but should have listened to us,
and could instruct those after us:

---

268 *Tristan und Isolde:* 1865 opera by Richard Wagner. Early in the opera they drink what
Isolde thinks is a poison cup that is actually a love potion.

275    this we were, this is how we tried to love,
       and these are the forces they had ranged against us,
       and these are the forces we had ranged within us,
       within us and against us, against us and within us.

### XVIII

       Rain on the West Side Highway,°
280    red light at Riverside:°
       *the more I live the more I think*
       *two people together is a miracle.*
       You're telling the story of your life
       for once, a tremor breaks the surface of your words.
285    The story of our lives becomes our lives.
       Now you're in fugue across what some I'm sure
       Victorian poet called the *salt estranging sea.*
       Those are the words that come to mind.
       I feel estrangement, yes. As I've felt dawn
290    pushing toward daybreak. Something: a cleft of light—?
       Close between grief and anger, a space opens
       where I am Adrienne alone. And growing colder.

### XIX

       Can it be growing colder when I begin
       to touch myself again, adhesions pull away?
295    When slowly the naked face turns from staring backward
       and looks into the present,
       the eye of winter, city, anger, poverty, and death
       and the lips part and say: *I mean to go on living?*
       Am I speaking coldly when I tell you in a dream
300    or in this poem, *There are no miracles?*
       (I told you from the first I wanted daily life,
       this island of Manhattan was island enough for me.)
       If I could let you know—
       two women together is a work
305    nothing in civilization has made simple,
       two people together is a work
       heroic in its ordinariness,
       the slow-picked, halting traverse of a pitch
       where the fiercest attention becomes routine
310    —look at the faces of those who have chosen it.

### XX

       That conversation we were always on the edge
       of having, runs on in my head,
       at night the Hudson° trembles in New Jersey light
       polluted water yet reflecting even
315    sometimes the moon
       and I discern a woman

---

279 *West Side Highway:* it ran along Manhattan's west side.
280 *Riverside:* street on Manhattan's upper west side.
313 *Hudson:* river that flows past New York City to the Atlantic Ocean.

I loved, drowning in secrets, fear wound round her throat
and choking her like hair. And this is she
with whom I tried to speak, whose hurt, expressive head
320    turning aside from pain, is dragged down deeper
where it cannot hear me,
and soon I shall know I was talking to my own soul.

### XXI

The dark lintels, the blue and foreign stones
of the great round rippled by stone implements
325    the midsummer night light rising from beneath
the horizon—when I said "a cleft of light"
I meant this. And this is not Stonehenge°
simply nor any place but the mind
casting back to where her solitude,
330    shared, could be chosen without loneliness,
not easily nor without pains to stake out
the circle, the heavy shadows, the great light.
I choose to be a figure in that light,
half-blotted by darkness, something moving
335    across that space, the color of stone
greeting the moon, yet more than stone:
a woman. I choose to walk here. And to draw this circle.

*1974–1976*

## Power

Living   in the earth-deposits   of our history

Today a backhoe divulged   out of a crumbling flank of earth
one bottle   amber   perfect   a hundred-year-old
cure for fever   or melancholy   a tonic
5    for living on this earth   in the winters of this climate

Today I was reading about Marie Curie:°
she must have known she suffered   from radiation sickness
her body bombarded for years   by the element
she had purified
10    It seems she denied to the end
the source of the cataracts on her eyes
the cracked and suppurating skin   of her finger-ends
till she could no longer hold   a test-tube or a pencil

She died   a famous woman   denying
15    her wounds
denying
her wounds   came   from the same source as her power

*1974*

---

327 *Stonehenge:* prehistoric monument in England constructed of twenty-fifty ton sandstone blocks.
6 *Curie:* (1867–1934), Polish-born chemist whose work on radioactivity helped establish modern atomic science; the first woman to receive a Nobel Prize and the first person to receive it twice. Curie died of leukemia from long exposure to radiation.

# from *An Atlas of the Difficult World*
## XIII. (Dedications)

I know you are reading this poem
late, before leaving your office
of the one intense yellow lamp-spot and the darkening window
in the lassitude of a building faded to quiet
5    long after rush-hour.   I know you are reading this poem
standing up in a bookstore far from the ocean
on a grey day of early spring, faint flakes driven
across the plains' enormous spaces around you.
I know you are reading this poem
10    in a room where too much has happened for you to bear
where the bedclothes lie in stagnant coils on the bed
and the open valise speaks of flight
but you cannot leave yet.   I know you are reading this poem
as the underground train loses momentum and before running
15          up the stairs
toward a new kind of love
your life has never allowed.
I know you are reading this poem by the light
of the television screen where soundless images jerk and slide
20    while you wait for the newscast from the *intifada*.°
I know you are reading this poem in a waiting-room
of eyes met and unmeeting, of identity with strangers.
I know you are reading this poem by fluorescent light
in the boredom and fatigue of the young who are counted out,
25    count themselves out, at too early an age.   I know
you are reading this poem through your failing sight, the thick
lens enlarging these letters beyond all meaning yet you read on
because even the alphabet is precious.
I know you are reading this poem as you pace beside the stove
30    warming milk, a crying child on your shoulder, a book in your
          hand
because life is short and you too are thirsty.
I know you are reading this poem which is not in your language
guessing at some words while others keep you reading
35    and I want to know which words they are.
I know you are reading this poem listening for something, torn
          between bitterness and hope
turning back once again to the task you cannot refuse.
I know you are reading this poem because there is nothing else
40          left to read
there where you have landed, stripped as you are.

*1990–1991*

---

20 *intifada*: mass protests organized by Palestinians against Israeli occupation of territory
on the West Bank of the Jordan River.

# Gary Snyder (b. 1930)

Born in San Francisco and raised on a farm north of Seattle, Snyder was educated at Reed College, where he studied literature, Buddhist philosophy, and Native American mythology. He then worked as a logger and spent summers as a forest-fire lookout in Oregon, Washington, and California. Involved with the Beat writers in San Francisco in the mid-1950s, he made a major change in his life in 1956, moving to Japan to study Zen Buddhism. Except for some shipboard work, he remained there for twelve years. He had been through two failed marriages in the United States, but in Japan he met and married Masa Uehara, and that relationship survived until 1988. They returned to the U.S. in 1968, and a few years later Snyder built a home in a remote community in the foothills of the Sierra Nevada Mountains in California.

Although Snyder has adopted different forms over the years, he generally prefers a direct, simple diction over intricate metaphor and allusion. In "Riprap" he uses words like material objects to refine and teach us a mental discipline. One may hear Thoreau and Whitman behind such an impulse, along with his Zen studies, but the ecological imperative includes an anguish that we have only fully earned in our own century. Against the errors of industrial civilization Snyder sets not only a reverence for nature but also a vital celebration of human sexuality. More recently, Snyder has borrowed shamanistic effects from oral poetry and done more experimentation with field effects and the space of the page. He has taught college occasionally, most recently at the University of California at Davis.

## Riprap°

Lay down these words
Before your mind like rocks.
       placed solid, by hands
In choice of place, set
5    Before the body of the mind
       in space and time:
Solidity of bark, leaf, or wall
       riprap of things:
Cobble of milky way
10       straying planets,

---

**poem title:** Riprap is an assemblage of broken stone put down to form a foundation in water or soft ground.

These poems, people,
    lost ponies with
Dragging saddles—
    and rocky sure-foot trails.
15    The worlds like an endless
    four-dimensional
Game of *Go*.°
    ants and pebbles
In the thin loam, each rock a word
20    a creek-washed stone
Granite: ingrained
    with torment of fire and weight
Crystal and sediment linked hot
    all change, in thoughts,
As well as things.

    *1959*

## Beneath My Hand and Eye the Distant Hills. Your Body

What my hand follows on your body
Is the line. A stream of love
    of heat, of light,    what my
    eye    lascivious
5    licks
    over, watching
    far snow-dappled Uintah mountains°
Is that stream.
Of power.    what my
10    hand curves over, following the line.
    "hip" and "groin"

Where "I"
    follow by hand and eye
    the swimming limit of your body.
15    As when vision idly dallies on the hills
Loving what it feeds on.
    soft cinder cones and craters;
    —Drum Hadley in the Pinacate°
    took ten minutes more to look again—
20    A leap of power unfurling:
    left,    right—right—
My heart beat faster looking
    at the snowy Uintah mountains.

As my hand feeds on you
25    runs down your side and curls beneath your hip.
    oil pool; stratum; water—

---

17 *Go:* an ancient Japanese game in which black and white stones are placed on a checkered board.
7 *Uintah:* mountain range in northeastern Utah.
18 . . . *Pinacate:* California town.

What "is" within   not known
    but feel it
    sinking with a breath
30       pusht ruthless, surely, down.

Beneath this long caress of hand and eye
    "we" learn the flower burning,
       outward, from "below."

*1968*

## I Went into the Maverick Bar

I went into the Maverick Bar
In Farmington, New Mexico.
And drank double shots of bourbon
        backed with beer.
5   My long hair was tucked up under a cap
I'd left the earring in the car.

Two cowboys did horseplay
        by the pool tables,
A waitress asked us
10          where are you from?
a country-and-western band began to play
"We don't smoke Marijuana in Muskokie"
And with the next song,
        a couple began to dance.

15   They held each other like in High School dances
        in the fifties;
I recalled when I worked in the woods
        and the bars of Madras, Oregon.
That short-haired joy and roughness—
20        America—your stupidity.
I could almost love you again.

We left—onto the freeway shoulders—
        under the tough old stars—
In the shadow of bluffs
25        I came back to myself,
   To the real work, to
       "What is to be done."°

*1974*

## Straight-Creek—Great Burn°

for Tom and Martha Burch

    Lightly, in the April mountains—
        Straight Creek,
   dry grass freed again of snow

---

27 *What is to be done:* title of a 1902 book by Vladimir Lenin (1870–1924), leader of the
1917 Russian revolution.
**poem title:** "Burn" is a Scottish word for a running brook, though it can also refer to an
area burned by a forest fire.

& the chicadees are pecking
last fall's seeds
        fluffing tail in chilly wind,

Avalanche piled up cross the creek
        and chunked-froze solid—
water sluicing under; spills out
        rock lip pool, bends over,
        braided, white, foaming,
returns to trembling
        deep-dark hole.

Creek boulders show the flow-wear lines
        in shapes the same
        as running blood
        carves in the heart's main
         valve,

Early spring dry. Dry snow flurries;
        walk on crusty high snow slopes
—grand dead burn pine—
        chartreuse lichen as adornment
        (a dye for wool)
angled tumbled talus° rock
of geosyncline° warm sea bottom
yes, so long ago.
"Once on a time."

Far light on the Bitteroots;°
        scrabble down willow slide
changing clouds above,
shapes on glowing sun-ball
writhing,    choosing
        reaching out against eternal
             azure—

us resting on dry fern and
        watching

Shining Heaven
change his feather garments
        overhead.

A whoosh of birds
swoops up and round
tilts back
almost always flying all apart
and yet hangs on!
together;

24 *talus:* rock debris under a cliff.
25 *geosyncline:* downward turning of the earth's crust.
28 *Bitteroots:* mountain range along the Idaho-Montana border.

never a leader,
all of one swift


empty
dancing     mind.

50     They arc and loop & then
their flight is done.
they settle down.
end of poem.

1974


# Axe Handles

One afternoon the last week in April
Showing Kai how to throw a hatchet
One-half turn and it sticks in a stump.
He recalls the hatchet-head
5     Without a handle, in the shop
And go gets it, and wants it for his own.
A broken-off axe handle behind the door
Is long enough for a hatchet,
We cut it to length and take it
10    With the hatchet head
And working hatchet, to the wood block.
There I begin to shape the old handle
With the hatchet, and the phrase
First learned from Ezra Pound
15    Rings in my ears!
"When making an axe handle
                the pattern is not far off."
And I say this to Kai
"Look: We'll shape the handle
20    By checking the handle
Of the axe we cut with—"
And he sees. And I hear it again:
It's in Lu Ji's *Wên Fu,* fourth century
A.D. "Essay on Literature"—in the
25    Preface: "In making the handle
Of an axe
By cutting wood with an axe
The model is indeed near at hand."
My teacher Shih-hsiang Chen
30    Translated that and taught it years ago
And I see: Pound was an axe,
Chen was an axe, I am an axe
And my son a handle, soon
To be shaping again, model
35    And tool, craft of culture,
How we go on.

1983

# Gregory Corso (b. 1930)

Born in New York City, Corso has had a volatile life and career. His childhood was spent in a series of foster homes and sometimes on the street. To survive, he took up petty theft, and ended up in prison from 1947–1950. On release he worked as a manual laborer, an employee of the *San Francisco Examiner,* and a merchant seaman. In the mid-1950s, he became linked with the Beat writers and achieved some fame through his energetic poetry readings. He has traveled widely in Europe and Mexico, often writing his irreverent, histrionic poems on the wing. Primarily a figure of the 1950s and 1960s, he continued to publish into the 1980s.

## Marriage

Should I get married? Should I be good?
Astound the girl next door with my velvet suit and faustus° hood?
Don't take her to movies but to cemeteries
tell all about werewolf bathtubs and forked clarinets
5    then desire her and kiss her and all the preliminaries
and she going just so far and I understanding why
not getting angry saying You must feel! It's beautiful to feel!
Instead take her in my arms lean against an old crooked tombstone
and woo her the entire night the constellations in the sky—

10    When she introduces me to her parents
back straightened, hair finally combed, strangled by a tie,
should I sit knees together on their 3rd degree sofa
and not ask Where's the bathroom?
How else to feel other than I am,
15    often thinking Flash Gordon° soap—
O how terrible it must be for a young man
seated before a family and the family thinking
We never saw him before! He wants our Mary Lou!
20    After tea and homemade cookies they ask What do you do for a
                             living?

Should I tell them? Would they like me then?
Say All right get married, we're losing a daughter
but we're gaining a son—
And should I then ask Where's the bathroom?

---

2 *faustus:* from Faust, the medieval alchemist who sold his soul to the devil in exchange for power and youth; subject of numerous literary works.
15 *Flash Gordon:* the science fiction comic strip and movie serial of the 1930s.

25　O God, and the wedding! All her family and her friends
　　and only a handful of mine all scroungy and bearded
　　just wait to get at the drinks and food—
　　And the priest! he looking at me as if I masturbated
　　asking me Do you take this woman for your lawful wedded wife?
30　And I trembling what to say say Pie Glue!
　　I kiss the bride all those corny men slapping me on the back
　　She's all yours, boy! Ha-ha-ha!
　　And in their eyes you could see some obscene honeymoon going

　　　　　　　　　　　　　　　　　　　　　　　　　　　on—

35　Then all that absurd rice and clanky cans and shoes
　　Niagara Falls! Hordes of us! Husbands! Wives! Flowers!

　　　　　　　　　　　　　　　　　　　　　　　　Chocolates!

　　All streaming into cozy hotels
　　All going to do the same thing tonight
40　The indifferent clerk he knowing what was going to happen
　　The lobby zombies they knowing what
　　The whistling elevator man he knowing
　　The winking bellboy knowing
　　Everybody knowing! I'd be almost inclined not to do anything!
45　Stay up all night! Stare that hotel clerk in the eye!
　　Screaming: I deny honeymoon! I deny honeymoon!
　　running rampant into those almost climactic suites
　　yelling Radio belly! Cat shovel!
　　O I'd live in Niagara forever! in a dark cave beneath the Falls
50　I'd sit there the Mad Honeymooner
　　devising ways to break marriages, a scourge of bigamy
　　a saint of divorce—

　　But I should get married I should be good
　　How nice it'd be to come home to her
55　and sit by the fireplace and she in the kitchen
　　aproned young and lovely wanting my baby
　　and so happy about me she burns the roast beef
　　and comes crying to me and I get up from my big papa chair
　　saying Christmas teeth! Radiant brains! Apple deaf!
60　God what a husband I'd make! Yes, I should get married!
　　So much to do! like sneaking into Mr. Jones' house late at night
　　and cover his golf clubs with 1920 Norwegian books
　　Like hanging a picture of Rimbaud° on the lawnmower
　　like pasting Tannu Tuva° postage stamps all over the picket fence
65　like when Mrs Kindhead comes to collect for the Community
　　　　　Chest
　　grab her and tell her There are unfavorable omens in the sky!
　　And when the mayor comes to get my vote tell him
　　When are you going to stop people killing whales!
　　And when the milkman comes leave him a note in the bottle
70　Penguin dust, bring me penguin dust, I want penguin dust—

---

63 *Rimbaud:* Arthur Rimbaud (1854–1891), French poet.
64 *Tannu Tuva:* Siberian republic in Russia on the Mongolian border.

Yet if I should get married and it's Connecticut and snow
and she gives birth to a child and I am sleepless, worn,
up for nights, head bowed against a quiet window, the past behind me,
75    finding myself in the most common of situations a trembling man
knowledged with responsibility not twig-smear nor Roman coin
                        soup—

    O what would that be like!
    Surely I'd give it for a nipple a rubber Tacitus°
80    For a rattle a bag of broken Bach° records
    Tack Della Francesca° all over its crib
    Sew the Greek alphabet on its bib
    And build for its playpen a roofless Parthenon°

    No, I doubt I'd be that kind of father
85    not rural not snow no quiet window
    but hot smelly tight New York City
    seven flights up, roaches and rats in the walls
    a fat Reichian° wife screeching over potoates Get a job!
    And five nose running brats in love with Batman°
90    And the neighbors all toothless and dry haired
    like those hag masses of the 18th century
    all wanting to come in and watch TV
    The landlord wants his rent
    Grocery store Blue Cross Gas & Electric Knights of Columbus°
95    Impossible to lie back and dream Telephone snow, ghost parking—
    No! I should not get married I should never get married!
    But—imagine If I were married to a beautiful sophisticated woman
    tall and pale wearing an elegant black dress and long black gloves
    holding a cigarette holder in one hand and a highball in the other
100    and we lived high up in a penthouse with a huge window
    from which we could see all of New York and ever farther on
                         clearer days
    No, can't imagine myself married to that pleasant prison dream—

    O but what about love? I forget love
105    not that I am incapable of love
    it's just that I see love as odd as wearing shoes—
    I never wanted to marry a girl who was like my mother
    And Ingrid Bergman° was always impossible
    And there's maybe a girl now but she's already married

---

79 *Tacitus:* Cornelius Tacitus (c. 55-c.117 A.D.), Roman historian. Since *tacitus* means "silent" in Latin, a "rubber Tacitus" is also a pacifier.

80 *Bach:* Johann Sebastian Bach (1685–1750), German composer, one of the greatest in human history.

81 *Francesca:* Piero della Francesca (1420–1492), Italian Renaissance painter.

83 *Parthenon:* the principal building of the Athenian Acropolis in ancient Greece.

88 *Reichian:* after Wilhelm Reich (1897–1957), founder of a school of psychiatry.

89 *Batman:* American comic strip hero, the force for justice in fictional Gotham City.

94 *Knights of Columbus:* fraternal society of Roman Catholic men, founded in Columbus, Ohio, in 1882.

108 *Ingrid Bergman* (1915–1982), Swedish actress whose American films included *Casablanca* and *Notorious.*

110 And I don't like men and—
but there's got to be somebody!
Because what if I'm 60 years old and not married,
all alone in a furnished room with pee stains on my underwear
and everybody else is married! All the universe married but me!

115 Ah, yet well I know that were a woman possible as I am possible
then marriage would be possible—
Like SHE° in her lonely alien gaud waiting her Egyptian lover
so I wait—bereft of 2,000 years and the bath of life.

1960

# Bomb

Budger of history   Brake of time   You   Bomb
Toy of universe   Grandest of all snatched-sky   I cannot hate you
Do I hate the mischievous thunderbolt   the jawbone of an ass
The bumpy club of One Million B.C.   the mace   the flail   the axe
5 Catapult Da Vinci   tomahawk Cochise   flintlock Kidd   dagger Rathbone
Ah and the sad desperate gun of Verlaine   Pushkin   Dillinger   Bogart°
And hath not St. Michael a burning sword   St. George a lance   David a sling
Bomb   you are as cruel as man makes you   and you're no crueller than cancer
All man hates you   they'd rather die by car-crash   lightning   drowning
10 Falling off a roof   electric-chair   heart-attack   old age   old age   O Bomb
They'd rather die by anything but you   Death's finger is free-lance
Not up to man whether you boom or not   Death has long since distributed its
categorical blue   I sing thee Bomb   Death's extravagance   Death's jubilee
Gem of Death's supremest blue   The flyer will crash   his death will differ
15 with the climber who'll fall   To die by cobra is not to die by bad pork
Some die by swamp   some by sea   and some by the bushy-haired man in the night
O there are deaths like witches of Arc°   Scarey deaths like Boris Karloff°
No-feeling deaths like birth-death   sadless deaths like old pain Bowery
Abandoned deaths   like Capital Punishment   stately deaths like senators
20 And unthinkable deaths like Harpo Marx°   girls on Vogue covers   my own
I do not know just how horrible Bombdeath is   I can only imagine
Yet no other death I know has so laughable a preview   I scope
a city   New York City   streaming   starkeyed   subway shelter
Scores and scores   A fumble of humanity   High heels bend

---

117 *SHE*: title character of H. Rider Haggard novel *She* (1887), who obtains eternal youth
by bathing in a pillar of fire and then waits thousands of years for her lover to return.
5–6 *Bogart*: Leonardo Da Vinci (1452–1519), the Italian Renaissance genius whose work
ranged from painting to weapons design; Cochise (d. 1874), American Apache chief who
fiercely resisted white settlement on his ancestral lands; William (Captain) Kidd (c.
1645–1701), Scottish merchant and pirate; Basil Rathbone (1892–1967), film actor who
played numerous villains as well as Sherlock Holmes; Paul Verlaine (1844–1896), French
poet who shot the young poet Rimbaud in the wrist when their affair ended; Alexander
Pushkin (1799–1837), Russian poet who killed a French royalist in a duel; John Dillinger
(1903–1934), American gangster; Humphrey Bogart (1899–1957), American film actor who
played both heroes and hoodlums.
17 *witches of Arc*: the French national heroine Joan of Arc (c. 1412–1431) was tried as a
witch and condemned to death by the Inquisition.
17 *Karloff*: (1887–1969), American film actor known for his horror films.
20 *Marx*: (1888–1964), one of the Marx brothers film comedy team.

25          Hats whelming away    Youth forgetting their combs
          Ladies not knowing what to do    with their shopping bags
          Unperturbed gum machines    Yet dangerous 3rd rail
          Ritz Brothers°    from the Bronx    caught in the A train
          The smiling Schenley poster° will always smile
30                Impish Death    Satyr Bomb    Bombdeath
                Turtles exploding over Istanbul
                The jaguar's flying foot
                soon to sink in arctic snow
                Penguins plunged against the Sphinx
35                The top of the Empire State
                arrowed in a broccoli field in Sicily
          Eiffel shaped like a C in Magnolia Gardens
                St. Sophia° peeling over Sudan
                O athletic Death    Sportive Bomb
40                The temples of ancient times
                their grand ruin ceased
                Electrons    Protons    Neutrons
                gathering Hesperean hair°
          walking the dolorous golf of Arcady
45                joining marble helmsmen
                entering the final amphitheater
                with a hymnody feeling of all Troys
                heralding cypressean torches
                racing plumes and banners
50          and yet knowing Homer with a step of grace
                Lo the visiting team of Present
                the home team of Past
                Lyre and tuba together joined
                Hark the hotdog soda olive grape
55                gala galaxy robed and uniformed
                commissary    O the happy stands
                Ethereal root and cheer and boo
          The billioned all-time attendance
                The Zeusian pandemonium
60                Hermes racing Owens°
                the Spitball of Buddha
                Christ striking out
                Luther° stealing third
          Planetarium Death    Hosannah Bomb
65          Gush the final rose    O Spring Bomb
                Come with thy gown of dynamite green
                unmenace Nature's inviolate eye

---

28 *Ritz Brothers:* zany comic trio, Al (1901–1965), Jim (1903–1985), and Harry (1906–1986), who were in many feature films.
29 *Schenley poster:* whiskey ad, perhaps seen on the "A train," a New York subway.
38 *St. Sophia:* (537 A.D.), the masterpiece of Byzantine architecture.
43 *Hesperean hair:* hair of the Amazons, who, in mythology, once inhabited Hesperia, a large island of Africa.
60 *Owens:* Hermes, Greek god, patron of messengers; Jesse Owens (1913–1980) U.S. Olympic athlete.
63 *Luther:* Martin Luther (1483–1546), German religious reformer and founder of the Reformation.

Before you the wimpled Past
behind you the hallooing Future   O Bomb
70              Bound in the grassy clarion air
like the fox of the tally-ho
thy field the universe thy hedge the geo
Leap Bomb   bound Bomb   frolic zig and zag
The stars a swarm of bees in thy binging bag
75              Stick angels on your jubilee feet
wheels of rainlight on your bunky seat
You are due and behold you are due
and the heavens are with you
hosannah incalescent glorious liaison
80       BOMB O havoc antiphony molten cleft BOOM
Bomb mark infinity a sudden furnace
spread thy multitudinous encompassed Sweep
set forth awful agenda
Carrion stars   charnel planets   carcass elements
85       Corpse the universe   tee-hee finger-in-the-mouth hop
over its long long dead Nor
From thy nimbled matted spastic eye
exhaust deluges of celestial ghouls
From thy appellational womb
90              spew birth-gusts of great worms
Rip open your belly Bomb
from your belly outflock vulturic salutations
Battle forth your spangled hyena finger stumps
along the brink of Paradise
95              O Bomb   O final Pied Piper
both sun and firefly behind your shock waltz
God abandoned mock-nude
beneath His thin false-talc'd apocalypse
He cannot hear thy flute's
100              happy-the-day profanations
He is spilled deaf into the Silencer's warty ear
His Kingdom an eternity of crude wax
Clogged clarions untrumpet Him
Sealed angels unsing Him
105              A thunderless God   A dead God
O Bomb   thy BOOM His tomb
That I lean forward on a desk of science
an astrologer dabbling in dragon prose
half-smart about wars   bombs   especially bombs
110       That I am unable to hate what is necessary to love
That I can't exist in a world that consents
a child in a park   a man dying in an electric-chair
That I am able to laugh at all things
all that I know and do not know   thus to conceal my pain
115       That I say I am a poet and therefore love all man
knowing my words to be the acquainted prophecy of all men
and my unwords no less an acquaintanceship
That I am manifold
a man pursuing the big lies of gold

120 or a poet roaming in bright ashes
or that which I imagine myself to be
a shark-toothed sleep a man-eater of dreams
I need not then be all-smart about bombs
Happily so for if I felt bombs were caterpillars
125 I'd doubt not they'd become butterflies
There is a hell for bombs
They're there I see them there
They sit in bits and sing songs
mostly German songs
130 and two very long American songs
and they wish there were more songs
especially Russian and Chinese songs
and some more very long American songs
Poor little Bomb that'll never be
135 an Eskimo song I love thee
I want to put a lollipop
in thy furcal mouth
A wig of Goldilocks on thy baldy bean
and have you skip with me Hansel and Gretel
140 along the Hollywoodian screen
O Bomb in which all lovely things
moral and physical anxiously participate
O fairyflake plucked from the
grandest universe tree
145 O piece of heaven which gives
both mountain and anthill a sun
I am standing before your fantastic lily door
I bring you Midgardian° roses Arcadian° musk
Reputed cosmetics from the girls of heaven
150 Welcome me fear not thy opened door
nor thy cold ghost's grey memory
nor the pimps of indefinite weather
their cruel terrestrial thaw
Oppenheimer is seated
155 in the dark pocket of Light
Fermi is dry in Death's Mozambique
Einstein° his mythmouth
a barnacled wreath on the moon-squid's head
Let me in Bomb rise from that pregnant-rat corner
160 nor fear the raised-broom nations of the world
O Bomb I love you
I want to kiss your clank eat your boom
You are a paean an acme of scream
a lyric hat of Mister Thunder

---

148 *Midgardian:* of Midgard, Middle Earth, the land where humans live, according to Norse mythology.

148 *Arcadian:* of Arcadia; in mythology, an ideal pastoral land.

157 *Einstein:* J. Robert Oppenheimer (1904–1967), physicist who directed the Manhattan Project laboratory in Los Alamos, New Mexico, where the atomic bomb was designed and built; Enrico Fermi (1901–1954), Nobel laureate physicist who helped develop the atomic bomb; Albert Einstein (1879–1955), mathematical physicist whose theoretical work revised our understanding of the universe and who helped inspire the Manhattan Project.

165     O resound thy tanky knees
    BOOM BOOM BOOM BOOM BOOM
     BOOM ye skies and BOOM ye suns
    BOOM BOOM ye moons ye stars BOOM
     nights ye BOOM ye days ye BOOM
170   BOOM BOOM ye winds ye clouds ye rains
     go BANG ye lakes ye oceans BING
     Barracuda BOOM and cougar BOOM
      Ubangi BANG orangoutang
   BING BANG BONG BOOM bee bear baboon
175     ye BANG ye BONG ye BING
      the tail the fin the wing
    Yes Yes into our midst a bomb will fall
    Flowers will leap in joy their roots aching
  Fields will kneel proud beneath the halleluyahs of the wind
180   Pinkbombs will blossom Elkbombs will perk their ears
  Ah many a bomb that day will awe the bird a gentle look
    Yet not enough to say a bomb will fall
    or even contend celestial fire goes out
   Know that the earth will madonna the Bomb
185  that in the hearts of men to come more bombs will be born
   magisterial bombs wrapped in ermine all beautiful
   and they'll sit plunk on earth's grumpy empires
    fierce with moustaches of gold

              *1958*

# Etheridge Knight (1931–1991)

Knight was born in Corinth, Mississippi. He dropped out of school in the eighth grade and joined the army in 1947. He was trained as a medical technician before being discharged in 1957 after receiving a serious shrapnel wound in Korea. Thereafter he had problems with drug and alcohol addiction, finally being arrested for robbery in 1960. In prison he began to write, encouraged by poets Gwendolyn Brooks, Dudley Randall, and Sonia Sanchez. He published his first book in 1968, the year of his release from Indiana State Prison, and it made a general thematics out of contrasts between freedom and imprisonment. His poetry regularly combines traditional metrics with elements from African American culture. Knight continued to write and teach until his death from lung cancer.

## Haiku

### I

Eastern guard tower
glints in sunset; convicts rest
like lizards on rocks.

*1968*

## Hard Rock Returns to Prison from the Hospital for the Criminal Insane

Hard Rock / was / "known not to take no shit
From nobody," and he had the scars to prove it:
Split purple lips, lumbed ears, welts above
His yellow eyes, and one long scar that cut
5    Across his temple and plowed through a thick
Canopy of kinky hair.

The WORD / was / that Hard Rock wasn't a mean nigger
Anymore, that the doctors had bored a hole in his head,
Cut out part of his brain, and shot electricity
10   Through the rest. When they brought Hard Rock back,
Handcuffed and chained, he was turned loose,
Like a freshly gelded stallion, to try his new status.
And we all waited and watched, like a herd of sheep,
To see if the WORD was true.

15    As we waited we wrapped ourselves in the cloak
Of his exploits: "Man, the last time, it took eight
Screws° to put him in the Hole."° "Yeah, remember when he
Smacked the captain with his dinner tray?" "He set
The record for time in the Hole—67 straight days!"
20    "Ol Hard Rock! man, that's one crazy nigger."
And then the jewel of a myth that Hard Rock had once bit
A screw on the thumb and poisoned him with syphilitic spit.

The testing came, to see if Hard Rock was really tame.
A hillbilly called him a black son of a bitch
25    And didn't lose his teeth, a screw who knew Hard Rock
From before shook him down and barked in his face.
And Hard Rock did *nothing*. Just grinned and looked silly,
His eyes empty like knot holes in a fence.

And even after we discovered that it took Hard Rock
30    Exactly 3 minutes to tell you his first name,
We told ourselves that he had just wised up,
Was being cool; but we could not fool ourselves for long,
And we turned away, our eyes on the ground. Crushed.
He had been our Destroyer,° the doer of things
35    We dreamed of doing but could not bring ourselves to do,
The fears of years, like a biting whip,
Had cut deep bloody grooves
Across our backs.

                                      1968

# The Idea of Ancestry

### I

Taped to the wall of my cell are 47 pictures: 47 black
faces: my father, mother, grandmothers (1 dead), grand-
fathers (both dead), brothers, sisters, uncles, aunts,
cousins (1st & 2nd), nieces, and nephews. They stare
5    across the space at me sprawling on my bunk. I know
their dark eyes, they know mine. I know their style,
they know mine. I am all of them, they are all of me;
they are farmers, I am a thief, I am me, they are thee.

I have at one time or another been in love with my mother,
10    1 grandmother, 2 sisters, 2 aunts (1 went to the asylum),
and 5 cousins. I am now in love with a 7-yr-old niece
(she sends me letters written in large block print, and
her picture is the only one that smiles at me).

---

17 *Screws:* prison guards.
17 *the Hole:* solitary confinement, typically a dark cell away from the rest of the prison
population.
34 *Destroyer:* in part, an allusion to Ras the Destroyer, a figure in the Rastafarian religion.

I have the same name as 1 grandfather, 3 cousins, 3 nephews,
15          and 1 uncle. The uncle disappeared when he was 15, just took
off and caught a freight (they say). He's discussed each year
when the family has a reunion, he causes uneasiness in
the clan, he is an empty space. My father's mother, who is 93
and who keeps the Family Bible with everybody's birth dates
20          (and death dates) in it, always mentions him. There is no
place in her Bible for "whereabouts unknown."

2

Each fall the graves of my grandfathers call me, the brown
hills and red gullies of mississippi send out their electric
messages, galvanizing my genes. Last yr / like a salmon quitting
25          the cold ocean-leaping and bucking up his birthstream / I
hitchhiked my way from LA with 16 caps° in my pocket and a
monkey on my back. And I almost kicked it with the kinfolks.
I walked barefooted in my grandmother's backyard / I smelled the
          old
30          land and the woods / I sipped cornwhiskey from fruit jars with the
          men /
I flirted with the women / I had a ball till the caps ran out
and my habit came down. That night I looked at my grandmother
and split / my guts were screaming for junk / but I was almost
35          contented / I had almost caught up with me.
(The next day in Memphis I cracked a croaker's crib° for a fix.)

This yr there is a gray stone wall damming my stream, and when
the falling leaves stir my genes, I pace my cell or flop on my bunk
and stare at 47 black faces across the space. I am all of them,
40          they are all of me, I am me, they are thee, and I have no children
to float in the space between.

                                                            *1968*

# A Poem for Myself

(or Blues for a Mississippi Black Boy)

I was born in Mississippi;
I walked barefooted thru the mud.
Born black in Mississippi,
Walked barefooted thru the mud.
5          But, when I reached the age of twelve
I left that place for good.
Said my daddy chopped cotton
And he drank his liquor straight.
When I left that Sunday morning
10          He was leaning on the barnyard gate.
Left her standing in the yard

---

26 *caps:* heroin sold on the street in quantities appropriate for a fix.
36 *croaker's crib:* drug seller's home.

With the sun shining in her eyes.
And I headed North
As straight as the Wild Goose Flies,
15  I been to Detroit & Chicago
Been to New York city too.
I been to Detroit & Chicago
Been to New York city too.
Said I done strolled all those funky avenues
20  I'm still the same old black boy with the same old blues.
Going back to Mississippi
This time to stay for good
Going back to Mississippi
This time to stay for good—
25  Gonna be free in Mississippi
Or dead in the Mississippi mud.

1980

## For Malcolm, a Year After°

Compose for Red° a proper verse;
Adhere to foot and strict iamb;
Control the burst of angry words
Or they might boil and break the dam.
5  Or they might boil and overflow
And drench me, drown me, drive me mad.
So swear no oath, so shed no tear,
And sing no song blue Baptist sad.
Evoke no image, stir no flame,
10  And spin no yarn across the air.
Make empty anglo tea lace words—
Make them dead white and dry bone bare.

Compose a verse for Malcolm man,
And make it rime and make it prim.
15  The verse will die—as all men do—
But not the memory of him!
Death might come singing sweet like C,
Or knocking like the old folk say,
The moon and stars may pass away,
But not the anger of that day.

1966

## Television Speaks

Television speaks:
"Blacks die on Soweto Streets!"
On Cape Cod, indolents
Buy "burgers" and sticky sweets!

1969

---

**poem title:** Malcolm X (1925–1965), charismatic African American political and religious leader, assassinated in 1965; see the notes to Welton Smith's poem "Malcolm."
1 *Red*: Malcolm X nickname.

## For Black Poets Who Think of Suicide

Black Poets should live—not leap
From steel bridges (like the white boys do).
Black Poets should live—not lay
Their necks on railroad tracks (like the white boys do).
5    Black Poets should seek—but not search too much
In sweet dark caves, nor hunt for snipe
Down psychic trails (like the white boys do).

For Black Poets belong to Black People. Are
The Flutes of Black Lovers. Are
10   The Organs of Black Sorrows. Are
The Trumpets of Black Warriors.
Let All Black Poets die as Trumpets,
And be buried in the dust of marching feet.

*1969*

# Sylvia Plath (1932–1963)

Born in Boston, Massachusetts, Plath grew up in Winthrop. She was raised by her mother after her father died of complications from diabetes when she was eight. Plath was educated at Smith College and at Newnham College of Cambridge University. Even before attending college she was publishing poems and journalism; her academic and literary achievements, however, were in conflict with the traditional view of women's roles that prevailed in the 1950s, and she was unable to live comfortably with the contradictions. In 1953, after serving a month as a college guest editor at the New York fashion magazine *Mademoiselle*, she had a breakdown and was unwisely subjected to electric shock therapy. She then attempted suicide and was hospitalized for six months, events she later adapted for her novel *The Bell Jar* (1963). It was while in England two years later, from 1955–1956, that she met her husband, the poet Ted Hughes, who has been the controversial shepherd of her posthumous career.

Plath and Hughes came to the U.S. in 1957, and she taught at Smith for a year, also taking a poetry writing seminar offered by Robert Lowell at Boston University; Anne Sexton was enrolled as well. The couple returned to England in 1959 and she published her first book of poems the following year. The marriage was in difficulty, with each individual's ambitions sometimes putting them at odds with one another despite willingness to support the other's career. In the fall of 1962, after Plath learned that Hughes had been unfaithful, they separated.

It was a brutally cold winter and not easy to maintain a household. Yet the freedom had an impact on her. That fall, she began writing with an astonishing intensity, shaping nearly overwhelming emotions into flawlessly crafted poems. Into a crucible went details of her own life and the horrors of modern history; she fused them into a harrowing, ironic persona, an archetype of a modern woman in an ecstatic crisis of gendered self-recognition amidst the ruins of history. In a few short months, these astonishingly lucid poems—furious, sardonic, defiant, and exquisitely musical—established a benchmark against which every American poet wishing to tell a brutal truth would have to measure himself or herself. Then, apparently, she broke through into a kind of icy calm, or so some of the final poems suggest. In December, she moved from Devon to a London apartment with her two children. The whole experience had overwhelmed her, and she took her own life in February 1963. Much more than with male poets who committed suicide—Crane, Berryman, among others—critics have tended to read Plath's poems in the light of her death, as though she were writing against some inexorable deadline. Yet the poems are a personal and cultural triumph, not funeral ornaments. Her suicide comes afterwards and tells us nothing about the poems; for they are about all of us, not about her alone.

## Black Rook in Rainy Weather°

On the stiff twig up there
Hunches a wet black rook
Arranging and rearranging its feathers in the rain.
I do not expect a miracle
5      Or an accident

To set the sight on fire
In my eye, nor seek
Any more in the desultory weather some design,
But let spotted leaves fall as they fall,
10     Without ceremony, or portent.

Although, I admit, I desire,
Occasionally, some backtalk
From the mute sky, I can't honestly complain:
A certain minor light may still
15     Lean incandescent

Out of kitchen table or chair
As if a celestial burning took
Possession of the most obtuse objects now and then—
Thus hallowing an interval
20     Otherwise inconsequent

By bestowing largesse, honor,
One might say love. At any rate, I now walk
Wary (for it could happen
Even in this dull, ruinous landscape); skeptical,
25     Yet politic; ignorant

Of whatever angel may choose to flare
Suddenly at my elbow. I only know that a rook
Ordering its black feathers can so shine
As to seize my senses, haul
30     My eyelids up, and grant

A brief respite from fear
Of total neutrality. With luck,
Trekking stubborn through this season
Of fatigue, I shall
35     Patch together a content

Of sorts. Miracles occur,
If you care to call those spasmodic
Tricks of radiance miracles. The wait's begun again,
The long wait for the angel,
For that rare, random descent.°

                                                              1956

---

**poem title:** A rook is an old world bird similar to the North American crow; it nests near
tree tops in colonies.
40 *that rare, random descent*: Cf. Acts 2, where the Holy Ghost descends on Jesus' disci-
ples like a tongue of fire.

# The Colossus°

I shall never get you put together entirely,
Pieced, glued, and properly jointed.
Mule-bray, pig-grunt and bawdy cackles
Proceed from your great lips.
5     It's worse than a barnyard.

Perhaps you consider yourself an oracle,
Mouthpiece of the dead, or of some god or other.
Thirty years now I have labored
To dredge the silt from your throat.
10    I am none the wiser.

Scaling little ladders with gluepots and pails of Lysol
I crawl like an ant in mourning
Over the weedy acres of your brow
To mend the immense skull-plates and clear
15    The bald, white tumuli° of your eyes.

A blue sky out of the Oresteia°
Arches above us. O father, all by yourself
You are pithy and historical as the Roman Forum.
I open my lunch on a hill of black cypress.
20    Your fluted bones and acanthine° hair are littered

In their old anarchy to the horizon-line.
It would take more than a lightning-stroke
To create such a ruin.
Nights, I squat in the cornucopia
25    Of your left ear, out of the wind,

Counting the red stars and those of plum-color.
The sun rises under the pillar of your tongue.
My hours are married to shadow.
No longer do I listen for the scrape of a keel
On the blank stones of the landing.

1959

# Tulips

The tulips are too excitable, it is winter here.
Look how white everything is, how quiet, how snowed-in.
I am learning peacefulness, lying by myself quietly
As the light lies on these white walls, this bed, these hands.
5     I am nobody; I have nothing to do with explosions.

---

**poem title:** The Colossus was a gigantic bronze statue of the Sun god Apollo, which stood at the harbor entrance of Rhodes, a Greek seaport; it was built about 280 B.C.
15 *tumuli*: ancient grave mounds.
16 *Oresteia*: a trilogy of plays (*Agamemnon, Libation Bearers,* and *Eumenides*) by the Greek tragic poet Aeschylus (c. 525–456 B.C.), in which lethal family violence passes from generation to generation.
20 *acanthine*: curved and piled like the leaves of the acanthus plant, a design used on the capitals of Corinthian columns in Greece.

I have given my name and my day-clothes up to the nurses
And my history to the anesthetist and my body to surgeons.°

They have propped my head between the pillow and the sheet-cuff
Like an eye between two white lids that will not shut.
10    Stupid pupil, it has to take everything in.
The nurses pass and pass, they are no trouble,
They pass the way gulls pass inland in their white caps,
Doing things with their hands, one just the same as another,
So it is impossible to tell how many there are.

15    My body is a pebble to them, they tend it as water
Tends to the pebbles it must run over, smoothing them gently.
They bring me numbness in their bright needles, they bring me
      sleep.
Now I have lost myself I am sick of baggage—
My patent leather overnight case like a black pillbox,
20    My husband and child° smiling out of the family photo;
Their smiles catch onto my skin, little smiling hooks.

I have let things slip, a thirty-year-old cargo boat
Stubbornly hanging on to my name and address.
They have swabbed me clear of my loving associations.
25    Scared and bare on the green plastic-pillowed trolley
I watched my teaset, my bureaus of linen, my books
Sink out of sight, and the water went over my head.
I am a nun now, I have never been so pure.

I didn't want any flowers, I only wanted
30    To lie with my hands turned up and be utterly empty.
How free it is, you have no idea how free—
The peacefulness is so big it dazes you,
And it asks nothing, a name tag, a few trinkets.
It is what the dead close on, finally; I imagine them
35    Shutting their mouths on it, like a Communion tablet.°

The tulips are too red in the first place, they hurt me.
Even through the gift paper I could hear them breathe
Lightly, through their white swaddlings, like an awful baby.
Their redness talks to my wound, it corresponds.
40    They are subtle: they seem to float, though they weigh me down,
Upsetting me with their sudden tongues and their color,
A dozen red lead sinkers round my neck.

---

7 *surgeons*: the poem was written in March 1961; that winter Plath had suffered a miscar-
riage, and in March she was hospitalized for an appendectomy.
20 *child*: Plath's husband was the English poet Ted Hughes (1930–); their daughter Frieda
was born in April 1960.
35 *Communion tablet*: during the Christian sacrament of Communion to commemorate
Christ's death, a tablet or wafer (symbolizing the body of Christ) is eaten.

Nobody watched me before, now I am watched.
The tulips turn to me, and the window behind me

45    Where once a day the light slowly widens and slowly thins,
And I see myself, flat, ridiculous, a cut-paper shadow
Between the eye of the sun and the eyes of the tulips,
And I have no face, I have wanted to efface myself.
The vivid tulips eat my oxygen.

50    Before they came the air was calm enough,
Coming and going, breath by breath, without any fuss.
Then the tulips filled it up like a loud noise.
Now the air snags and eddies round them the way a river
Snags and eddies round a sunken rust-red engine.

55    They concentrate my attention, that was happy
Playing and resting without committing itself.

The walls, also, seem to be warming themselves.
The tulips should be behind bars like dangerous animals;
They are opening like the mouth of some great African cat,

60    And I am aware of my heart: it opens and closes
Its bowl of red blooms out of sheer love of me.
The water I taste is warm and salt, like the sea,
And comes from a country far away as health.

*18 March 1961*

# The Bee Meeting°

Who are these people at the bridge to meet me? They are the
        villagers—
The rector, the midwife, the sexton,° the agent for bees.°
In my sleeveless summery dress I have no protection,

5    And they are all gloved and covered, why did nobody tell me?
They are smiling and taking out veils tacked to ancient hats.

I am nude as a chicken neck, does nobody love me?
Yes, here is the secretary of bees with her white shop smock,
Buttoning the cuffs at my wrists and the slit from my neck to my
        knees.

10    Now I am milkweed silk, the bees will not notice.
They will not smell my fear, my fear, my fear.

Which is the rector now, is it that man in black?
Which is the midwife, is that her blue coat?
Everybody is nodding a square black head, they are knights in visors,

15    Breastplates of cheesecloth knotted under the armpits.
Their smiles and their voices are changing. I am led through a
        beanfield.

---

**poem title:** This is the first poem of a five-poem sequence—"The Bee Meeting," "The Ar-
rival of the Bee Box," "Stings," "The Swarm," and "Wintering."
3 *sexton*: a church caretaker, bellringer, and gravedigger.
3 *bees*: Plath's father, Otto Plath (1885–1940), was a biologist and author of *Bumble Bees
and Their Ways* (1934). While living in Devon, England, she kept a hive of bees and at-
tended meetings of the Beekeepers Association.

Strips of tinfoil winking like people,
Feather dusters fanning their hands in a sea of bean flowers,
Creamy bean flowers with black eyes and leaves like bored hearts.
20    Is it blood clots the tendrils are dragging up that string?
No, no, it is scarlet flowers that will one day be edible.

Now they are giving me a fashionable white straw Italian hat
And a black veil that molds to my face, they are making me one of
    them.
They are leading me to the shorn grove, the circle of hives.
25    Is it the hawthorn° that smells so sick?
The barren body of hawthorn, etherizing its children.

Is it some operation that is taking place?
It is the surgeon my neighbors are waiting for,
This apparition in a green helmet,
30    Shining gloves and white suit.
Is it the butcher, the grocer, the postman, someone I know?

I cannot run, I am rooted, and the gorse° hurts me
With its yellow purses, its spiky armory.
I could not run without having to run forever.
35    The white hive is snug as a virgin,
Sealing off her brood° cells, her honey, and quietly humming.

Smoke rolls and scarves in the grove.
The mind of the hive thinks this is the end of everything.
Here they come, the outriders, on their hysterical elastics.°
40    If I stand very still, they will think I am cow-parsley,
A gullible head untouched by their animosity,

Not even nodding, a personage in a hedgerow.
The villagers open the chambers, they are hunting the queen.
Is she hiding, is she eating honey? She is very clever.
45    She is old, old, old, she must live another year, and she knows it.
While in their fingerjoint cells the new virgins

Dream of a duel they will win inevitably,
A curtain of wax dividing them from the bride flight,
The upflight of the murderess° into a heaven that loves her.
50    The villagers are moving the virgins, there will be no killing.
The old queen does not show herself, is she so ungrateful?

---

25 *hawthorn*: A spring shrub of the rose family, with fragrant flowers and small red fruits.
32 *gorse*: a spiny, yellow-flowered shrub.
36 *brood*: breeding.
39 *elastics*: the bees that left the hive return quickly.
49 *murderess*: the queen bee.

I am exhausted, I am exhausted—
Pillar of white in a blackout of knives.
I am the magician's girl who does not flinch.
55    The villagers are untying their disguises, they are shaking hands.
Whose is that long white box in the grove, what have they
      accomplished,
            why am I cold.

*3 October 1962*

## The Arrival of the Bee Box

I ordered this, this clean wood box
Square as a chair and almost too heavy to lift.
I would say it was the coffin of a midget
Or a square baby
5    Were there not such a din in it.

The box is locked, it is dangerous.
I have to live with it overnight
And I can't keep away from it.
There are no windows, so I can't see what is in there.
10    There is only a little grid, no exit.

I put my eye to the grid.
It is dark, dark,
With the swarmy feeling of African hands
Minute and shrunk for export,
15    Black on black, angrily clambering.

How can I let them out?
It is the noise that appalls me most of all,
The unintelligible syllables.
It is like a Roman mob,
20    Small, taken one by one, but my god, together!

I lay my ear to furious Latin.
I am not a Caesar.
I have simply ordered a box of maniacs.
They can be sent back.
25    They can die, I need feed them nothing, I am the owner.

I wonder how hungry they are.
I wonder if they would forget me
If I just undid the locks and stood back and turned into a tree.
There is the laburnum,° its blond colonnades,
30    And the petticoats of the cherry.

---

29 *laburnum*: a European tree whose seed pods are poisonous.

They might ignore me immediately
In my moon suit and funeral veil.
I am no source of honey
So why should they turn on me?
35        Tomorrow I will be sweet God, I will set them free.

The box is only temporary.

*4 October 1962*

## Stings

Bare-handed, I hand the combs.
The man in white smiles, bare-handed,
Our cheesecloth gauntlets neat and sweet,
The throats of our wrists brave lilies.
5        He and I

Have a thousand clean cells between us,
Eight combs of yellow cups,
And the hive itself a teacup,
White with pink flowers on it,
10       With excessive love I enameled it

Thinking 'Sweetness, sweetness'.
Brood cells gray as the fossils of shells
Terrify me, they seem so old.
What am I buying, wormy mahogany?
15       Is there any queen at all in it?

If there is, she is old,
Her wings torn shawls, her long body
Rubbed of its plush—
Poor and bare and unqueenly and even shameful.
20       I stand in a column

Of winged, unmiraculous women,
Honey-drudgers.°
I am no drudge
Though for years I have eaten dust
25       And dried plates with my dense hair.

And seen my strangeness evaporate,
Blue dew from dangerous skin.
Will they hate me,
These women who only scurry,
30       Whose news is the open cherry, the open clover?

It is almost over.
I am in control.
Here is my honey-machine,
It will work without thinking,
35       Opening, in spring, like an industrious virgin

---

22 *honey-drudgers*: like the worker bees who make honey for the hive.

To scour the creaming crests
As the moon, for its ivory powders, scours the sea.
A third person is watching.
He has nothing to do with the bee-seller or with me.
40  Now he is gone

In eight great bounds, a great scapegoat.
Here is his slipper, here is another,
And here the square of white linen
He wore instead of a hat.
45  He was sweet,

The sweat of his efforts a rain
Tugging the world to fruit.
The bees found him out,
Molding onto his lips like lies,
50  Complicating his features.

They thought death was worth it, but I
Have a self to recover, a queen.
Is she dead, is she sleeping?
Where has she been,
55  With her lion-red body, her wings of glass?

Now she is flying
More terrible than she ever was, red
Scar in the sky, red comet
Over the engine that killed her—
The mausoleum, the wax house.

                    6 *October 1962*


## The Swarm

Somebody is shooting at something in our town—
A dull pom, pom in the Sunday street.
Jealousy can open the blood,
It can make black roses.
5  Who are they shooting at?

It is you the knives are out for
At Waterloo, Waterloo, Napoleon,°
The hump of Elba on your short back,
And the snow, marshaling its brilliant cutlery
10  Mass after mass, saying Shh!

Shh! These are chess people you play with,
Still figures of ivory.
The mud squirms with throats,
Stepping stones for French bootsoles.

---

7 *Napoleon Bonaparte*: (1769–1821), French general and Emperor, a titanic figure in European history. He was defeated at the Battle of Waterloo in 1815 and exiled on the island of Elba off the Italian coast.

15          The gilt and pink domes of Russia melt and float off

            In the furnace of greed. Clouds, clouds.
            So the swarm balls and deserts
            Seventy feet up, in a black pine tree.
            It must be shot down. Pom! Pom!
20          So dumb it thinks bullets are thunder.

            It thinks they are the voice of God
            Condoning the beak, the claw, the grin of the dog
            Yellow-haunched, a pack-dog,
            Grinning over its bone of ivory
25          Like the pack, the pack, like everybody.

            The bees have got so far. Seventy feet high!
            Russia, Poland and Germany!
            The mild hills, the same old magenta
            Fields shrunk to a penny
30          Spun into a river, the river crossed.

            The bees argue, in their black ball,
            A flying hedgehog, all prickles.
            The man with gray hands stands under the honeycomb
            Of their dream, the hived station
35          Where trains, faithful to their steel arcs,

            Leave and arrive, and there is no end to the country.
            Pom! Pom! They fall
            Dismembered, to a tod° of ivy.
            So much for the charioteers, the outriders, the Grand Army!
40          A red tatter, Napoleon!

            The last badge of victory.
            The swarm is knocked into a cocked straw hat.
            Elba, Elba, bleb° on the sea!
            The white busts of marshals, admirals, generals
45          Worming themselves into niches.

            How instructive this is!
            The dumb, banded bodies
            Walking the plank draped with Mother France's upholstery
            Into a new mausoleum,
50          An ivory palace, a crotch pine.

            The man with gray hands smiles—
            The smile of a man of business, intensely practical.
            They are not hands at all
            But asbestos receptacles.
55          Pom! Pom! 'They would have killed *me*.'

---

38 *tod*: clump.
43 *bleb*: small blister.

Stings big as drawing pins!
It seems bees have a notion of honor,
A black intractable mind.
Napoleon is pleased, he is pleased with everything.
O Europe! O ton of honey!

*7 October 1962*

## Wintering

This is the easy time, there is nothing doing.
I have whirled the midwife's extractor,°
I have my honey,
Six jars of it,
5    Six cat's eyes in the wine cellar,

Wintering in a dark without window
At the heart of the house
Next to the last tenant's rancid jam
And the bottles of empty glitters—
10   Sir So-and-so's gin.

This is the room I have never been in.
This is the room I could never breathe in.
The black bunched in there like a bat,
No light
15   But the torch and its faint

Chinese yellow on appalling objects—
Black asininity. Decay.
Possession.
It is they who own me.
20   Neither cruel nor indifferent,

Only ignorant.
This is the time of hanging on for the bees—the bees
So slow I hardly know them,
Filing like soldiers
25   To the syrup tin

To make up for the honey I've taken.
Tate and Lyle keeps them going,
The refined snow.
It is Tate and Lyle° they live on, instead of flowers.
30   They take it. The cold sets in.

Now they ball in a mass,
Black
Mind against all that white.
The smile of the snow is white.
35   It spreads itself out, a mile-long body of Meissen,°

---

2 *midwife's extractor*: tool used to remove honey from beehives.
29 *Tate and Lyle*: manufacturers of a commercial bee food and of syrup for people.
35 *Meissen*: a delicate porcelain ware originally made in Meissen, a German city on the Elbe River, in the eighteenth century.

Into which, on warm days,
They can only carry their dead.
The bees are all women,
Maids and the long royal lady.
40    They have got rid of the men,

The blunt, clumsy stumblers, the boors.
Winter is for women—
The woman, still at her knitting,
At the cradle of Spanish walnut,
45    Her body a bulb in the cold and too dumb to think.

Will the hive survive, will the gladiolas
Succeed in banking their fires
To enter another year?
What will they taste of, the Christmas roses?
The bees are flying. They taste the spring.

*9 October 1962*

# Daddy°

You do not do, you do not do
Any more, black shoe
In which I have lived like a foot
For thirty years, poor and white,
5    Barely daring to breathe or Achoo.

Daddy, I have had to kill you.
You died before I had time—
Marble-heavy, a bag full of God,
Ghastly statue with one gray toe°
10    Big as a Frisco seal

And a head in the freakish Atlantic
Where it pours bean green over blue
In the waters off beautiful Nauset.°
I used to pray to recover you.
15    Ach, du.°

---

**poem title:** Plath's note reads "The poem is spoken by a girl with an Electra complex [a tendency for a daughter to be attached to her father and hostile to her mother]. Her father died while she thought he was God. Her case is complicated by the fact that her father was also a Nazi and her mother very possibly part Jewish. In the daughter the two strains marry and paralyze each other—she has to act out the awful little allegory before she is free of it." Plath uses details from her own and her father's life, such as his German heritage, to invoke crucial moments of modern history and create a general figure of paternity that is no longer straightforwardly autobiographical. Plath's father was neither a Nazi nor a Nazi sympathizer; Plath was not Jewish. Yet both she and all of the rest of us in this century are linked to the monstrous version of masculinity that fascism promoted. 9 *gray toe*: the result of diabetes-induced gangrene; Plath's father died from the disease. 13 *Nauset*: the Native American name for Eastham, Cape Cod, on the Massachusetts coast. 15 *Ach du*: (German) "Ah, you."

In the German tongue, in the Polish town°
Scraped flat by the roller
Of wars, wars, wars.
But the name of the town is common.
20      My Polack friend

Says there are a dozen or two.
So I never could tell where you
Put your foot, your root,
I never could talk to you.
25      The tongue stuck in my jaw.

It stuck in a barb wire snare.
Ich, ich, ich, ich,°
I could hardly speak.
I thought every German was you.
30      And the language obscene

An engine, an engine
Chuffing° me off like a Jew.
A Jew to Dachau, Auschwitz, Belsen.°
I began to talk like a Jew.
35      I think I may well be a Jew.

The snows of the Tyrol,° the clear beer of Vienna
Are not very pure or true.
With my gipsy ancestress and my weird luck
And my Taroc pack° and my Taroc pack
40      I may be a bit of a Jew.

I have always been scared of *you,*
With your Luftwaffe,° your gobbledygoo.
And your neat mustache
And your Aryan° eye, bright blue.
45      Panzer-man,° panzer-man, O You—

---

16 *Polish town*: Grasbow, Poland, where Plath's father was born. He was of German descent.
27 *Ich, ich*: (German) "I, I, I, I."
32 *Chuffing*: chugging.
33 *Dachau, Auschwitz, Belsen*: Nazi concentration camps in Poland (Auschwitz) and Germany; the Germans murdered six million Jews—men, women, and children—during World War II, most of them at these and other death camps. This remains the largest and most elaborately mechanized program of genocide in human history.
36 *Tyrol*: Tirol, an Alpine region in Austria and northern Italy; the snow there is famous for being as pure as the beer in Vienna is clear.
39 *Taroc pack*: A variant of Tarot, ancient fortune-telling cards.
42 *Luftwaffe*: the German air force.
44 *Aryan*: in Nazi ideology, the "superior" race—blue-eyed, blond-haired Nordic people of German stock. Non-Aryans, including Jews, Blacks, Slavs, and Gypsies, were considered subhuman.
45 *Panzer*: (German) armor, especially the Nazi tank division in World War II.

Not God but a swastika°
So black no sky could squeak through.
Every woman adores a Fascist,
The boot in the face, the brute
50      Brute heart of a brute like you.

You stand at the blackboard,° daddy,
In the picture I have of you,
A cleft in your chin instead of your foot
But no less a devil for that, no not
55      Any less the black man who

Bit my pretty red heart in two.
I was ten when they buried you.
At twenty I tried to die°
And get back, back, back to you.
60      I thought even the bones would do.

But they pulled me out of the sack,
And they stuck me together with glue.
And then I knew what to do.
I made a model of you,
65      A man in black with a Meinkampf° look

And a love of the rack and the screw.
And I said I do, I do.
So daddy, I'm finally through.
The black telephone's off at the root,
70      The voices just can't worm through.

If I've killed one man, I've killed two—
The vampire who said he was you
And drank my blood for a year,
Seven years, if you want to know.
75      Daddy, you can lie back now.

There's a stake in your fat black heart
And the villagers never liked you.
They are dancing and stamping on you.
They always *knew* it was you.
Daddy, daddy, you bastard, I'm through.

                                        *12 October 1962*

---

46 *swastika*: the Nazi symbol.
51 *blackboard*: Plath's father taught biology at Boston University.
58 *I tried to die*: Plath first attempted suicide when she was home from college during summer break.
65 *Meinkampf*: German dictator Adolf Hitler's (1889–1945) early autobiography and manifesto *Mein Kampf* ("My Struggle," 1925) laid out his plans for world domination and detailed the political antagonisms and race hatred that would dominate his dictatorship when he came to power in 1933.

# Ariel°

Stasis in darkness.
Then the substanceless blue
Pour of tor° and distances.

God's lioness,
5   How one we grow,
Pivot of heels and knees!—The furrow

Splits and passes, sister to
The brown arc
Of the neck I cannot catch,

10  Nigger-eye
Berries cast dark
Hooks—

Black sweet blood mouthfuls,
Shadows.
15  Something else

Hauls me through air—
Thighs, hair;
Flakes from my heels.

White
20  Godiva,° I unpeel—
Dead hands, dead stringencies.

And now I
Foam to wheat, a glitter of seas.
The child's cry

25  Melts in the wall.
And I
Am the arrow,

The dew that flies
Suicidal, at one with the drive
30  Into the red

Eye, the cauldron of morning.

27 *October* 1962

---

**poem title:** The name of the horse Plath rode in Devon, England, during the two years she lived there; a Hebrew name for Jerusalem meaning "lion of God"; and the name of the sprite of fire and air in Shakespeare's *The Tempest*.
3 *tor*: a high, craggy hill.
20 *Godiva*: Lady Godiva, a noblewoman who supposedly rode naked on horseback through Coventry, England, in 1040 to get feudal obligations and taxes reduced.

# Lady Lazarus°

I have done it again.
One year in every ten
I manage it—

A sort of walking miracle, my skin
5   Bright as a Nazi lampshade,°
My right foot

A paperweight,
My face a featureless, fine
Jew linen.

10   Peel off the napkin
O my enemy.
Do I terrify?—

The nose, the eye pits, the full set of teeth?
The sour breath
15   Will vanish in a day.

Soon, soon the flesh
The grave cave ate will be
At home on me

And I a smiling woman.
20   I am only thirty.
And like the cat I have nine times to die.

This is Number Three.
What a trash
To annihilate each decade.

25   What a million filaments.
The peanut-crunching crowd
Shoves in to see

Them unwrap me hand and foot—
The big strip tease.
30   Gentlemen, ladies

These are my hands
My knees.
I may be skin and bone,

Nevertheless, I am the same, identical woman.
35   The first time it happened I was ten.
It was an accident.

---

**poem title:** In John 11.39–44, Jesus raises Lazarus, the brother of Mary, from the dead;
Plath is also linking her own suicide attempts with the Biblical story and thus in some way
saying that to live in our time is necessarily to rise from the dead.
5 *lampshade:* in the World War II German death camps, the Nazis sometimes removed the
skin of the people they killed and used it to make lampshades.

The second time I meant
To last it out and not come back at all.
I rocked shut

40     As a seashell.
They had to call and call
And pick the worms off me like sticky pearls.

Dying
Is an art, like everything else.
45     I do it exceptionally well.

I do it so it feels like hell.
I do it so it feels real.
I guess you could say I've a call.

It's easy enough to do it in a cell
50     It's easy enough to do it and stay put.
It's the theatrical

Comeback in broad day
To the same place, the same face, the same brute
Amused shout:

55     'A miracle!'
That knocks me out.
There is a charge

For the eyeing of my scars, there is a charge
For the hearing of my heart—
60     It really goes.

And there is a charge, a very large charge
For a word or a touch
Or a bit of blood

Or a piece of my hair or my clothes.
65     So, so, Herr Doktor.°
So, Herr Enemy.

I am your opus,
I am your valuable,
The pure gold baby

70     That melts to a shriek.
I turn and burn.
Do not think I underestimate your great concern.

Ash, ash—
You poke and stir.
75     Flesh, bone, there is nothing there—

---

65 *Herr Doktor*: (German) "Mr. Doctor."

A cake of soap,
A wedding ring,
A gold filling.°

Herr God, Herr Lucifer
80      Beware
Beware.°

Out of the ash
I rise° with my red hair
And I eat men like air.

                                    *23–29 October 1962*

---

78 *soap/ ring / filling*: The Nazis on occasion rendered the bodies of their victims into soap;
they consistently removed all jewelry and gold fillings from teeth for themselves, some-
times hoarding it in foreign banks.
81 *Beware*: Line 49 of Samuel Taylor Coleridge's (1772–1834) poem "Kubla Khan" reads
"And all should cry, Beware! Beware!"
83 *I rise*: like the phoenix, a mythical bird that supposedly sets itself on fire and rises anew
from its own ashes.

# Henry Dumas (1934–1968)

Dumas was born in Sweet Home, Arkansas, where he spent the first ten years of his life. It was long enough to absorb gospel music and the folk traditions of the South. At that point he moved to Harlem, where he lived until joining the Air Force, a stint that included a year in the Middle East. All these experiences found a place in his poetry; "Son of Msippi" recalls his years in the South, while "Knees of a Natural Man" evokes the urban world of New York. He had spent some time at City College and at Rutgers, but never completed a degree. A stronger influence was no doubt his energetic civil rights work in the mid-1960s. In 1967, he took a job as a teacher and counselor at Southern Illinois University, where he met the poet Eugene Redmond. Only a year later, Dumas was gunned down in error by a New York City Transit policeman; it is to Redmond's posthumous editing that we owe his poems and short stories. Since most of Dumas' poetry was not published during his lifetime, the dates offered are speculative. We do, however, know that he was performing "Son of Msippi" and "Black Star Line" at poetry readings during the last year of his life.

## Son of Msippi

Up
from Msippi I grew.
(Bare walk and cane stalk
make a hungry belly talk.)
5    Up.
from the river of death.
(Walk bare and stalk cane
make a hungry belly talk.)

Up
10   from Msippi I grew.
Up
from the river of pain.

Out of the long red earth dipping, rising,
spreading out in deltas and plains,
15   out of the strong black earth turning
over by the iron plough,

out of the swamp green earth dripping
with moss and snakes,

out of the loins of the leveed lands
20       muscling its American vein:
the great Father of Waters,
I grew
up,
beside the prickly boll of white,
25       beside the bone-filled Mississippi
rolling on and on,
breaking over,
cutting off,
ignoring my bleeding fingers.

30       Bare stalk and sun walk
I hear a boll-weevil talk
cause I grew
up
beside the ox and the bow,
35       beside the rock church and the shack row,
beside the fox and the crow,
beside the melons and maize,
beside the hound dog,
beside the pink hog,
40       flea-hunting,
mud-grunting,
cat-fishing,
dog pissing
in the Mississippi
45       rolling on and on,
ignoring the colored coat I spun
of cotton fibers.

Cane-sweat river-boat
nigger-bone floating.

50       Up from Msippi
I grew,
wailing a song with every strain.

Woman gone woe man too
baby cry rent-pause daddy flew.

*c. 1967*

# Kef 24°

lay sixteen bales down in front on the plank
let me set and bay at the houndog moon
lay sixteen bales down of the cotton flank
pray with me brothers that the pink
5       boss dont sweat me too soon

---

**poem title:** Kef is a term for marijuana; Dumas has several poem sequences in his "kef"
series.

beat my leg in a round nigger peg
lord have mercy on my black pole
lay sixteen bales in the even row
let me sweat and cuss my roustabout tune
10      lord have mercy on my shrinkin back
let me go with the jesus mule
lay sixteen bales for the warp and loom
beat a nigger down and bury his soul
boss dont sweat me too soon
15      pray with me brothers that I hold my cool
lord have mercy on this long black leg
let me rid on the jesus mule
lay sixteen bales of white fuzz down
lay sixteen tales of how I got around
20      lord have mercy on this sweat and stink
lord have mercy
lay sixteen bales
pray brothers
beat down
25      lord have
let me
lord lord
brothers
the houndog moon
30      howl jesus,
howl!

*c. 1967*

# Kef 16

Down near the levee where the river once
broke through the sand and the dirt,

Down where the north fish drown in muddy
waters, where mountains become silt heaps,

5      I used to sit and throw out the wiggling worm,
as I dreamed of giant catfish asleep beneath

the blood.

*c. 1967*

# Fish

Catfish niggerfish
low in the creek
Catfish blackfish
none all week

5      baitworm doughball
put your glad rags on
hook me a catfish ninefeet tall.

        niggerspit catfish bit
        only was a crawdad hole

10      good bait sent catfish went
        must be fishin the whiteman's hole

*c. 1967*

# Knees of a Natural Man

(for Jay Wright)

        my ole man took me to the fulton fish market
        we walk around in the guts and the scales

        my ole man show me a dead fish, eyes like throat spit
        he say "you hongry boy?" i say "naw, not yet"

5       my ole man show me how to pick the leavings
        he say people throw away fish that not rotten

        we scaling on our knees back uptown on lenox
        sold five fish, keeping one for the pot

        my ole man copped a bottle of wine
10      he say, "boy, build me a fire out in the lot"

        backyard cat climbin up my leg for fish
        i make a fire in the ash can

        my ole man come when he smell fish
        frank williams is with him, they got wine

15      my ole man say "the boy cotch the big one"
        he tell big lie and slap me on the head

        i give the guts to the cat and take me some wine
        we walk around the sparks like we in hell

        my ole man is laughin and coughin up wine
20      he say "you hongry boy?" i say "naw, not yet"

        next time i go to fulton fish market
        first thing i do is take a long drink of wine

*c. 1967*

# Low Down Dog Blues

Went to my baby's back door, my baby say she aint home
Yeah my baby holler she just aint home
But if you aint got no meat baby,
                please throw your dog a bone

5  Standing in her back yard, my long tail tucked under
   Standin in the back yard, my long tail tucked way under
   Cryin so many tears, my baby think it's lightnin and thunder

   Got them low down dog blues, people, my sniffer can't find
        no bait
10 It's the low down dog blues, when your sniffer can't find
        no bait
   Just whinin for my baby to please open up her gate

   Well, she aint heard my barkin, this dog better hit the trail
   Yeah, guess a low down dog better hit the trail
   That woman dont even care when a good dog wag his tail

                                                *c. 1967*


## Black Star Line°

*My black mothers I hear them singing.*

        Sons, my sons,
   dip into this river with your ebony cups
   A vessel of knowledge sails under power.
   Study stars as well as currents.
   Dip into this river with your ebony cups.

5  *My black fathers I hear them chanting.*

        Sons, my sons,
   let ebony strike the blow that launches the ship!
   Send cargoes and warriors back to sea.
   Remember the pirates and their chains of nails.
10 Let ebony strike the blow that launches this ship.
   Make your heads not idle sails, blown about
   by any icy wind like a torn page from a book.
        Bones of my bones,
   all you golden-black children of the sun,
15 lift up! and read the sky
   written in the tongue of your ancestors.
   It is yours, claim it.
   Make no idle sails, my sons,
   make heavy-boned ships that break a wave and pass it.

---

**poem title:** The failed Black Star steamship line was founded by Marcus Garvey (1887–1940). Born in Jamaica, Garvey established the Universal Negro Improvement Association (UNIA) in 1914 and moved its offices to New York two years later. There he published the popular weekly newspaper *Negro World*, promoted his "back-to Africa" movement that encouraged black people to form an independent nation in Africa, wrote poems and essays, and launched a number of failed capitalist ventures. Among them was his Black Star Line, which aimed to facilitate maritime trade between black nations. Garvey was convicted of mail fraud in 1923 after selling stock in the steamship line. Nonetheless, his message of pride and self-sufficiency helped inspire his people.

20          Bring back sagas from Songhay, Kongo, Kaaba,°
            deeds and words of Malik, Toussaint,° Marcus,
            statues of Mahdi° and a lance of lightning.
            Make no idle ships.
            Remember the pirates.
25          For it is the sea who owns the pirates,
            not the pirates the sea.

            *My black mothers I hear them singing.*

                 Children of my flesh,
            dip into this river with your ebony cups.
30          A ship of knowledge sails unto wisdom.
            Study what mars and what lifts up.
            Dip into this river with your ebony cups.

                                                    *c. 1967*

---

20 *Songhay*: West African state that rose to power in the latter part of the fifteenth century and commanded the trade routes of the Sahara. *Kongo*: African kingdom south of the River Congo that had considerable power from the fifteenth to the eighteenth century. *Kaaba*: the most sacred site in Islam, situated within the Great Mosque at Mecca in Saudi Arabia; it is a small building containing the Black Stone toward which Muslims turn when they pray.
21 *Toussaint*: Toussaint L'Ouverture (1746–1803), black revolutionary leader who joined an insurrection and ruled Haiti from 1797 until Napoleon sent a force that reconquered the island and reestablished slavery there.
22 *Mahdi*: (Arabic) "divinely guided one," the name given by Sunni Muslims to visionary leaders who galvanize the community.

# Amiri Baraka (Leroi Jones) (b. 1934)

Born Everett Leroy Jones to a middle-class family in Newark, New Jersey, the son of a postal employee and a social worker, Baraka was educated at Rutgers, Howard, and Columbia Universities. His work and his system of beliefs have gone through several distinct phases. In the late 1950s and early 1960s, he was active among Beat writers on New York's Lower East Side, writing his own poetry and plays and editing two period magazines, *Yugen* and *Floating Bear*. Yet he was also increasingly impatient with what he saw as the political irrelevance of the Beats and the gradualism of the civil rights movement. In Baraka, the Beats' scorn for materialism was gradually being transformed into a more aggressive and politically focused critique of capitalism. Race was also becoming more central to his view of American culture. His center of operations moved from the Lower East Side to Harlem, and he became a founding figure of the Black Arts movement of the late 1960s and early 1970s. "Black Art" was essentially the *ars poetica* of the movement. He had first published as LeRoi Jones; now he was Amiri Baraka. For several years he was a stunningly forceful advocate of black cultural nationalism, but by 1975 he was finding its racial exclusivity confining. He thus embraced the revolutionary forms of international socialism. Baraka's poetry, plays, and essays have been defining documents for African American culture for nearly four decades. His view of Christianity in "When We'll Worship Jesus," a poem that should be read aloud, may be compared with that of Langston Hughes in "Goodbye Christ" and contrasted with that of Carolyn Rodgers.

## SOS

Calling black people
Calling all black people, man woman child
Wherever you are, calling you, urgent, come in
Black People, come in, wherever you are, urgent, calling
5    you, calling all black people
    calling all black people, come in, black people, come
    on in.

*1969*

# Black Art°

Poems are bullshit unless they are
teeth or trees or lemons piled
on a step. Or black ladies dying
of men leaving nickel hearts
5      beating them down. Fuck poems
and they are useful, wd they shoot
come at you, love what you are,
breathe like wrestlers, or shudder
strangely after pissing. We want live
10     words of the hip world live flesh &
coursing blood. Hearts Brains
Souls splintering fire. We want poems
like fists beating niggers out of Jocks
or dagger poems in the slimy bellies
15     of the owner-jews.° Black poems to
smear on girdlemamma mulatto bitches
whose brains are red jelly stuck
between 'lizabeth taylor's toes. Stinking
Whores! We want "poems that kill."
20     Assassin poems, Poems that shoot
guns. Poems that wrestle cops into alleys
and take their weapons leaving them dead
with tongues pulled out and sent to Ireland. Knockoff
poems for dope selling wops or slick halfwhite
25     politicians Airplane poems. rrrrrrrrrrrrrrrrrrrr
rrrrrrrrrrrrrr. . . . tuhtuhtuhtuhtuhtuhtuhtuhtuh
. . . . rrrrrrrrrrrrrrr. . . . Setting fire and death to
whities ass. Look at the Liberal
Spokesman for the jews clutch his throat
30     & puke himself into eternity. . . . rrrrrrrrrr
There's a negroleader pinned to
a bar stool in Sardi's eyeballs melting
in hot flame. Another negroleader
on the steps of the white house one
35     kneeling between the sheriff's thighs
negotiating cooly for his people.
Aggh . . . stumbles across the room . . .
Put it on him, poem. Strip him naked
to the world! Another bad poem cracking
40     steel knuckles in a jewlady's mouth
Poem scream poison gas on beasts in green berets

---

**poem title:** "Black Art" became virtually an *ars poetica* for the Black Arts movement.
15 *owner-jews*: although the import of this passage can be minimized as rhetoric directed
against Jewish businessmen in black communities, the fact is that anti-Semitism was a fre-
quent feature of Black Arts poetry. Virtually every participating poet wrote at least one
anti-Semitic poem, and some wrote more, though the level of virulence varied consider-
ably. For Baraka it was partly personal; he had been close to Jewish poet Allen Ginsberg
during his Beat period, and now he was disavowing both the cultural and the personal
connections. But for others the Jews were a convenient scapegoat, as well as a way to re-
vile whites without risking broader cultural consequences.

Clean out the world for virtue and love,
Let there be no love poems written
until love can exist freely and
45　　cleanly. Let Black People understand
that they are the lovers and the sons
of lovers and warriors and sons
of warriors Are poems & poets &
all the loveliness here in the world

50　　We want a black poem. And a
Black World.
Let the world be a Black Poem
And Let All Black People Speak This Poem
Silently

or LOUD

*1969*

## When We'll Worship Jesus

We'll worship Jesus
When jesus do
Somethin
When jesus blow up
5　　the white house
or blast nixon down
when jesus turn out congress
or bust general motors to
yard bird motors
10　　jesus we'll worship jesus
when jesus get down
when jesus get out his yellow lincoln
w/the built in cross stain glass
window & box w/black peoples
15　　enemies we'll worship jesus when
he get bad enough to at least scare
somebody—cops not afraid
of jesus
pushers not afraid
20　　of jesus, capitalists racists
imperialists not afraid
of jesus shit they makin money
off jesus
we'll worship jesus when mao
25　　do, when toure does
when the cross replaces Nkrumah's
star
Jesus need to hurt some a our
enemies, then we'll check him
30　　out, all that screaming and hollering
& wallering and moaning talkin bout
jesus, jesus, in a red

check velvet vine + 8 in. heels
jesus pinky finger
35   got a goose egg ruby
which actual bleeds
jesus at the apollo
doin splits and helpin
nixon trick niggers
40   jesus w/his one eyed self
tongue kissing johnny carson
up the behind
jesus need to be busted
jesus need to be thrown down and whipped
45   till something better happen
jesus aint did nothing for us
but kept us turned toward the
sky (him and his boy allah
too, need to be checkd
50   out!)
we'll worship jesus
when he get a boat load of ak-47s
and some dynamite
and blow up abernathy robotin
55   for gulf
jesus need to be busted
we ain't gonna worship nobody
but niggers gettin up off
the ground
60   not gon worship jesus
unless he just a tricked up
nigger somebody named
outside his race
need to worship yo self fo
65   you worship jesus
need to bust jesus (+ check
out his spooky brother
allah while you heavy
on the case
70   cause we ain gon worship jesus
we aint gon worship
jesus
we aint gon worship
jesus
75   not till he do somethin
not till he help us
not till the world get changed
and he ain, jesus ain, he cant change the world
we can change the world
80   we can struggle against the forces of backwardness, we can
     change the world
we can struggle against our selves, our slowness, our connection
     with
the oppressor, the very cultural aggression which binds us to
85      our enemies
as their slaves.

we can change the world
we aint gonna worship jesus cause jesus dont exist
xcept in song and story except in ritual and dance, except in
90      slum stained
tears or trillion dollar opulence stretching back in history, the
      history
of the oppression of the human mind
we worship the strength in us
95      we worship our selves
we worship the light in us
we worship the warmth in us
we worship the world
we worship the love in us
100      we worship our selves
we worship nature
we worship ourselves
we worship the life in us, and science, and knowledge, and
      transformation
105      of the visible world
but we aint gonna worship no jesus
we aint gonna legitimize the witches and devils and spooks and
      hobgoblins
the sensuous lies of the rulers to keep us chained to fantasy and
110      illusion
sing about life, not jesus
sing about revolution, not no jesus
stop singing about jesus,
sing about, creation, our creation, the life of the world and
115      fantastic
nature how we struggle to transform it, but dont victimize our
      selves by
distorting the world
stop moanin about jesus, stop sweatin and crying and stompin
120      and dyin for jesus
unless thats the name of the army we building to force the land
      finally to
change hands. And lets not call that jesus, get a quick
      consensus, on that,
125      lets damn sure not call that black fire muscle
      no invisible psychic dungeon
no gentle vision strait jacket, lets call that peoples army, or
      wapenduzi or
      simba
130      wachanga, but we not gon call it jesus, and not gon worship
      jesus, throw
jesus out yr mind. Build the new world out of reality, and new
      vision
we come to find out what there is of the world
135      to understand what there is here in the world!
to visualize change, and force it.
we worship revolution

                                              *1972*

# N. Scott Momaday (b. 1934)

Born in Lawton, Oklahoma, Momaday is well-known as a poet, novelist (*House Made of Dawn* and *The Way to Rainy Mountain*), painter, playwright, and storyteller. Although his work is centered in Native American culture and history, he has written poetry about a variety of subjects, including poems about nature partly shaped by a Native American vision. His literary influences are still wider, as is apparent when he writes in rhymed syllabics. Some of his literary works include his line drawings and paintings, which have been exhibited a number of times. Long the most highly acclaimed Native American literary figure, his work has inspired a generation of younger artists. He is an enrolled member of the Kiowas, a Native American people who once made their homes across the southern plains of the American west. Educated primarily at the University of New Mexico and Stanford, from which he received a Ph.D., he teaches at the University of Arizona and is a member of the Kiowa Gourd Dance Society. His author's note for *In the Presence of the Sun: Stories and Poems* (1992) concludes, "He walks long distances, and he rides an Appaloosa mare named 'Ma'am.' At his best he cooks. He is justly famous for a recipe named 'The Washita Crossing Soup,' the ingredients of which are, in his words, 'simple, sacred, and secret.' He is a bear."

## Plainview: 3°

The sun appearing: a pendant
of clear cutbeads, flashing;
a drift of pollen and glitter
lapping and overlapping night;
a prairie fire.

*1976*

## Buteo Regalis°

His frailty discrete, the rodent turns, looks.
What sense first warns? The winging is unheard,
Unseen but as distant motion made whole,
Singular, slow, unbroken in its glide.
5   It veers, and veering, tilts broad-surfaced wings.

---

**poem title:** No. 3 in a sequence of four "Plainview" poems.
**poem title:** *Buteo Regalis:* (Latin), the scientific name for the Ferruginous Hawk, a large (two-foot long) hawk of the North American plains; habitually soars in high wide circles in search of its prey. *Regalis* means "regal"; the *buteo* family includes hawks and eagles.

Aligned, the span bends to begin the dive
And falls, alternately white and russet,°
Angle and curve, gathering momentum.

1974

## Crows in a Winter Composition

This morning the snow,
The soft distances
Beyond the trees
In which nothing appeared—
5    Nothing appeared.
The several silences,
Imposed one upon another,
Were unintelligible.

I was therefore ill at ease
10   When the crows came down,
Whirling down and calling,
Into the yard below
And stood in a mindless manner
On the gray, luminous crust,
15   Altogether definite, composed,
In the bright enmity of my regard,
In the hard nature of crows.

1976

## Carriers of the Dream Wheel

This is the Wheel of Dreams°
Which is carried on their voices,
By means of which their voices turn
And center upon being.
5    It encircles the First World,
This powerful wheel.
They shape their songs upon the wheel
And spin the names of the earth and sky,
The aboriginal names.
10   They are old men, or men
Who are old in their voices,
And they carry the wheel among the camps,
Saying: Come, come,
Let us tell the old stories,
Let us sing the sacred songs.

1976

---

7 *white and russet:* the dominant colors, respectively, of the underside and back of the hawk.

1 *Dreams:* dreams or visions are central to the religious and spiritual life of many Native American peoples. They reveal the existence and give access to a spirit world that has continuity with this one. Actively sought both in sleep and through ritual fasting, dreams grant powers that are central to the social life of the dreamer. Foundational dreams are sometimes transmitted through kinship groups during special ceremonies. Among the Plains Indians, dreamers used special objects and painted designs, often kept in sacred bundles, to hold the power granted them in dreams.

## Rings of Bone

There were rings of bone
on the bandoliers of old men dancing.

Then, in the afternoon stippled with leaves
and the shadows of leaves,
5    the leaves glistened
and their shine shaped the air.

Now the leaves are dead.
Cold comes upon the leaves
and they are crisped upon the stony ground.
10   Webs of rime, like leaves, fasten on the mould,
and the wind divides and devours the leaves.

Again the leaves have more or less to do
with time. Music pervades the death of leaves.
The leaves clatter like the rings of bone
on the bandoliers of old men dancing.

*1990*

## The Stalker

Sampt'e drew the string back and back until he
felt the bow wobble in his hand, and he let the
arrow go. It shot across the long light of the
morning and struck the black face of a stone in the
5    meadow; it glanced then away towards the west,
limping along in the air; and then it settled down
in the grass and lay still. Sampt'e approached; he
looked at it with wonder and was wary; honestly he
believed that the arrow might take flight again;
10   so much of his life did he give into it.

*1976*

## *from* The Colors of Night

### Purple°

There was a man who killed a buffalo bull to no
purpose, only he wanted its blood on his hands. It
was a great, old, noble beast, and it was a long
time blowing its life away. On the edge of the night
5    the people gathered themselves up in their grief
and shame. Away in the west they could see the hump
and spine of the huge beast which lay dying along
the edge of the world. They could see its bright
blood run into the sky, where it dried, darkening,
10   and was at last flecked with flakes of light.

*1976*

---

**poem title:** "Purple" is the seventh poem in an eight-poem sequence, "The Colors of Night."

# The Burning

In the numb, numberless days
There were disasters in the distance,
Strange upheavals. No one understood them.
At night the sky was scored with light,
5     For the far planes of the planet buckled and burned.
In the dawns were intervals of darkness
On the scorched sky, clusters of clouds and eclipse,
And cinders descending.
Nearer in the noons
10    The air lay low and ominous and inert.
And eventually at evening, or morning, or midday,
At the sheer wall of the wood,
Were shapes in the shadows approaching,
Always, and always alien and alike.
15    And in the foreground the fields were fixed in fire,
And the flames flowered in our flesh.

*1976*

# December 29, 1890°

### *Wounded Knee Creek*

In the shine of photographs
are the slain, frozen and black

on a simple field of snow.
They image ceremony:

5    women and children dancing,
old men prancing, making fun.

In autumn there were songs, long
since muted in the blizzard.

In summer the wild buckwheat
10   shone like fox fur and quillwork,

---

**poem title:** The date of the Wounded Knee Massacre. In 1890, people on the Lakota Sioux reservations were near starvation; promised increases in government rations had materialized as cuts. Desperate for relief, thousands gathered in the badlands of the Pine Ridge Reservation to call for the return of their ancestors and the buffalo through the religious ceremonies of the Ghost Dance. Frightened by the ceremonies, area whites succeeded in bringing half the entire U.S. Army to the reservations. In response, the Ogalallas and Lakotas began returning home. Then legendary leader Sitting Bull was murdered, and one returning band led by Chief Big Foot fled toward the Pine Ridge Agency. They surrendered to the Seventh Cavalry, which proceeded to train four rapid-fire Hotchkiss cannons on the band camped along Wounded Knee Creek. Then the soldiers got drunk. Next morning, in the midst of disarming the Sioux, a weapon discharged, and immediately the Hotchkiss cannons began firing explosive shells into the Indian camp. As the women and children fled, individual soldiers pursued and murdered them. Medals for bravery were awarded the troops. The poem partly describes a photograph taken after the massacre.

and dusk guttered on the creek.
Now in serene attitudes

of dance, the dead in glossy
death are drawn in ancient light.

1992

## The Shield That Came Back°

Turning Around tested his son Yellow Grass. "You must kill
thirty scissortails and make me a fan of their feathers."

"Must I make the whole fan?" asked Yellow Grass. "Must I do
the beadwork too?" Yellow Grass had never made a fan.

"Yes. You must do the beadwork too—blue and black and
white and orange."

"Those are the colors of your shield," said Yellow Grass.

Yellow Grass fretted over the making of his father's fan, but
when at last it was finished it was a fine, beautiful thing, the
feathers tightly bunched and closely matched, their sheen like a
rainbow—yet they could be spread wide in a disc, like a shield.
And the handle was beaded tightly. The blue and black and white
and orange beads glittered in every light. And there was a long
bunch of doeskin fringes at the handle's end.

When Turning Around saw the fan he said nothing, but he was
full of pride and admiration. Then he went off on a raiding
expedition to the Pueblo country, and there he was killed. After
that, Yellow Grass went among the Pueblos and redeemed his
father's shield. But the fan could not be found.

When he was an old man Yellow Grass said to his grandson
Handsome Horse, "You see, the shield was more powerful than
the fan, for the shield came back and the fan did not. Some things,
if they are very powerful, come back. Remember that. For us, in
this camp, that is how to think of the world."

1992

---

**poem title:** From "In the Presence of the Sun: A Gathering of Shields," a sequence of
eighteen poems and prose poems. Among the Plains Indians, a shield was typically made
of buffalo hide and carefully decorated; each one is a unique work of art. As Momaday
writes, "only in a limited sense can the shield rightly be considered armor . . . above all the
shield is medicine. . . . In a real sense the Plains warrior *is* his shield. It is his personal
flag, the realization of his vision and name, the object of his holiest quest."

# Mark Strand (b. 1934)

Born on Prince Edward Island, Canada, of American parents, Strand moved regularly as a child whenever his salesman father was relocated. Strand was educated at Antioch College and at several universities—Yale, Florence, and Iowa. He has taught at Utah, Johns Hopkins, and in the University of Chicago's Committee on Social Thought, and served as poetry editor of *The New Republic*. In addition to his poetry, he has written a book on the painter Edward Hopper, as well as short stories and books for children. A book-length poem in fifty-five sections, *Dark Harbor* (1993) relates a mental journey through memories and into the afterlife. He often manages a surprisingly controlled use of surreal imagery in poems focused on absence and loss.

## Where Are the Waters of Childhood?

See where the windows are boarded up,
where the gray siding shines in the sun and salt air
and the asphalt shingles on the roof have peeled or fallen off,
where tiers of oxeye daisies float on a sea of grass?
5    That's the place to begin.

Enter the kingdom of rot,
smell the damp plaster, step over the shattered glass,
the pockets of dust, the rags, the soiled remains of mattress,
look at the rusted stove and sink, at the rectangular stain
10    on the wall where Winslow Homer's° *Gulf Stream* hung.

Go to the room where your father and mother
would let themselves go in the drift and pitch of love,
and hear, if you can, the creak of their bed,
then go to the place where you hid.

15    Go to your room, to all the rooms whose cold, damp air you
        breathed,
to all the unwanted places where summer, fall, winter, spring,
seem the same unwanted season, where the trees you knew
        have died
and other trees have risen. Visit that other place
you barely recall, that other house half hidden.

---

10 *Homer*: (1836–1910) American painter noted for naturalistic treatment of maritime subjects.

20    See the two dogs burst into sight. When you leave,
they will cease, snuffed out in the glare of an earlier light.
Visit the neighbors down the block; he waters his lawn,
she sits on her porch, but not for long.
When you look again they are gone.

25    Keep going back, back to the field, flat and sealed in mist.
On the other side, a man and a woman are waiting;
they have come back, your mother before she was gray,
your father before he was white.

Now look at the North West Arm, how it glows a deep
    cerulean blue.
30    See the light on the grass, the one leaf burning, the cloud
that flares. You're almost there, in a moment your parents
will disappear, leaving you under the light of a vanished star,
under the dark of a star newly born. Now is the time.

Now you invent the boat of your flesh and set it upon the
    waters
35    and drift in the gradual swell, in the laboring salt.
Now you look down. The waters of childhood are there.

*1978*

# Audre Lorde (1934–1992)

Lorde was born and raised in New York City as the child of West Indian immigrants. She was educated at Hunter College, also spending a year at the National University of Mexico. For more than a decade she was head librarian at Town School Library in New York. Then, in 1968, she published her first volume of poetry and spent a transformative year as poet in residence at historically black Tougaloo College in Mississippi. Her next book, *Cables to Rage* (1970), acknowledged her homosexuality. Thereafter she would call herself "a black feminist lesbian mother poet," and her work began to combine intimate self-reflection and political prophecy. The result is protest poetry focused at once on personal and social transformation.

Her nonfiction prose has also had wide impact, from her account of her struggle with cancer in *The Cancer Journals* (1980) to her fictionalized autobiography *Zami* (1982) and her collection of essays *Sister Outsider* (1984).

## Coal

### I

is the total black, being spoken
from the earth's inside.
There are many kinds of open
how a diamond comes into a knot of flame
5    how sound comes into a word, coloured
by who pays what for speaking.

Some words are open like a diamond
on glass windows
singing out within the passing crash of sun
10   Then there are words like stapled wagers
in a perforated book,—buy and sign and tear apart—
and come whatever wills all chances
the stub remains
an ill-pulled tooth with a ragged edge.
15   Some words live in my throat
breeding like adders. Others know sun
seeking like gypsies over my tongue
to explode through my lips
like young sparrows bursting from shell.

20　　　Some words
　　　bedevil me.

　　　Love is a word, another kind of open.
　　　As the diamond comes into a knot of flame
　　　I am Black because I come from the earth's inside
　　　now take my word for jewel in the open light.

　　　　　　　　　　　　　　　　　　　　　　　*1976*


## Sisters in Arms

　　　The edge of our bed was a wide grid
　　　where your fifteen-year-old daughter was hanging
　　　gut-sprung on police wheels
　　　a cablegram nailed to the wood
5　　　next to a map of the Western Reserve
　　　I could not return with you to bury the body
　　　reconstruct your nightly cardboards
　　　against the seeping Transvaal° cold
　　　I could not plant the other limpet mine
10　　　against a wall at the railroad station
　　　nor carry either of your souls back from the river
　　　in a calabash upon my head
　　　so I bought you a ticket to Durban°
　　　on my American Express
15　　　and we lay together
　　　in the first light of a new season.

　　　Now clearing roughage from my autumn garden
　　　cow sorrel　overgrown rocket gone to seed
　　　I reach for the taste of today
20　　　the *New York Times* finally mentions your country
　　　a half-page story
　　　of the first white south african killed in the "unrest"
　　　Not of Black children massacred at Sebokeng
　　　six-year-olds imprisoned for threatening the state
25　　　not of Thabo Sibeko, first grader, in his own blood
　　　on his grandmother's parlor floor
　　　Joyce, nine, trying to crawl to him
　　　shitting through her navel
　　　not of a three-week-old infant, nameless
30　　　lost under the burned beds of Tembisa
　　　my hand comes down like a brown vise over the marigolds
　　　reckless through despair
　　　we were two Black women touching our flame
　　　and we left our dead behind us
35　　　I hovered　you rose　the last ritual of healing

---

8 *Transvaal*: at the time Lorde wrote the poem, a province of South Africa; one-third of it consists of a high plateau.
13 *Durban*: (Lorde's note) Indian Ocean seaport and resort in Natal Province, S.A.

"It is spring," you whispered
"I sold the ticket for guns and sulfa
I leave for home tomorrow"
and wherever I touch you
40    I lick cold from my fingers
taste rage
like salt from the lips of a woman
who has killed too often to forget
and carries each death in her eyes
45    your mouth a parting orchid
"Someday you will come to *my* country
and we will fight side by side?"

Keys jingle in the door ajar   threatening
whatever is coming belongs here
50    I reach for your sweetness
but silence explodes like a pregnant belly
into my face
a vomit of nevers.

Mmanthatisi° turns away from the cloth
55    her daughters-in-law are dyeing
the baby drools milk from her breast
she hands him half-asleep to his sister
dresses again for war
knowing the men will follow.
60    In the intricate Maseru° twilights
quick   sad   vital
she maps the next day's battle
dreams of Durban   sometimes
visions the deep wry song of beach pebbles
running after the sea.

*1986*

# Outlines

### I

What hue lies in the slit of anger
ample and pure as night
what color the channel
blood comes through?

5    A Black woman and a white woman
charter our courses close
in a sea of calculated distance
warned away by reefs of hidden anger
histories rallied against us
10    the friendly face of cheap alliance.

---

54 *Mmanthatisi*: (Lorde's note), warrior queen and leader of the Tlokwa (Sotho) people during the *mfecane* (crushing), one of the greatest crises in southern African history. The Sotho now live in the Orange Free State, S.A.
60 *Maseru*: (Lorde's note), scene of a great Tlokwa battle and now the capital of Lesotho.

Jonquils through the Mississippi snow
you entered my vision
with the force of hurled rock
defended by distance and a warning smile
15   fossil tears   pitched over the heart's wall
for protection
no other woman
grown beyond safety
come back to tell us
20   whispering
past the turned shoulders
of our closest
we were not the first
Black woman white woman
25   altering course to fit our own journey.

In this treacherous sea
even the act of turning
is almost fatally difficult
coming around full face
30   into a driving storm
putting an end to running
before the wind.

On a helix of white
the letting of blood
35   the face of my love
and rage
coiled in my brown arms
an ache in the bone
we cannot alter history
40   by ignoring it
nor the contradictions
who we are.

## II

A Black woman and a white woman
in the open fact of our loving
45   with not only our enemies' hands
raised against us
means a gradual sacrifice
of all that is simple
dreams
50   where you walk the mountain
still as a water-spirit
your arms lined with scalpels
and I hide the strength of my hungers
like a throwing knife in my hair.

55  Guilt wove through quarrels like barbed wire
    fights in the half forgotten schoolyard
    gob of spit in a childhood street
    yet both our mothers once scrubbed kitchens
    in houses where comfortable women
60  died a separate silence
    our mothers' nightmares
    trapped into familiar hatred
    the convenience of others drilled into their lives
    like studding into a wall
65  they taught us to understand
    only the strangeness of men.

    To give   but not beyond what is wanted
    to speak   as well as to bear
    the weight of hearing
70  Fragments of the word wrong
    clung to my lashes like ice
    confusing my vision with a crazed brilliance
    your face   distorted into grids
    of magnified complaint
75  our first winter
    we made a home outside of symbol
    learned to drain the expansion tank together
    to look beyond the agreed-upon disguises
    not to cry each other's tears.

80  How many Februarys
    shall I lime this acid soil
    inch by inch
    reclaimed through our gathered waste?
    from the wild onion shoots of April
85  to mulch in the August sun
    squash blossoms   a cement driveway
    kale and tomatoes
    muscles etch the difference
    between I need and forever.

90  When we first met
    I had never been
    for a walk in the woods

### III

    light catches two women on a trail
    together   embattled by choice
95  carving an agenda with tempered lightning
    and no certainties
    we mark tomorrow
    examining every cell of the past
    for what is useful   stoked by furies

100  we were supposed to absorb by forty
     still we grow   more precise with each usage
     like falling stars or torches
     we print code names upon the scars
     over each other's resolutions
105  our weaknesses   no longer hateful.

     When women make love
     beyond the first exploration
     we meet each other   knowing
     in a landscape
110  the rest of our lives
     attempts to understand.

                    IV

     Leaf-dappled the windows lighten
     after a battle that leaves our night in tatters
     and we two glad to be alive   and tender
115  the outline of your ear pressed on my shoulder
     keeps a broken dish from becoming always.

     We rise to dogshit   dumped on our front porch
     the brass windchimes from Sundance stolen
     despair offerings of the 8 A.M. News
120  reminding us we are still at war
     and not with each other
     "give us 22 minutes and we will give you the world . . ."
     and still we dare
     to say we are committed
125  sometimes without relish.

     Ten blocks down the street
     a cross is burning
     we are a Black woman and a white woman
     with two Black children
130  you talk with our next-door neighbors
     I register for a shotgun
     we secure the tender perennials
     against an early frost
     reconstructing a future we fuel
135  from our living   different precisions
     In the next room a canvas chair
     whispers beneath your weight
     a breath of you between laundered towels
     the flinty places that do not give.

                    V

140  Your face upon my shoulder
     a crescent of freckle over bone
     what we share   illuminates what we do not
     the rest is a burden of history
     we challenge

145　bearing each bitter piece to the light
　　we hone ourselves upon each other's courage
　　loving
　　as we cross the mined bridge　fury
　　tuned like a Geiger counter

150　to the softest place.
　　One straight light hair on the washbasin's rim
　　difference
　　intimate as a borrowed scarf
　　the children arrogant as mirrors
155　our pillows' mingled scent
　　this grain of our particular days
　　keeps a fine sharp edge
　　to which I cling like a banner
　　in a choice of winds
160　seeking an emotional language
　　in which to abbreviate time.

　　I trace the curve of your jaw
　　with a lover's finger
　　knowing the hardest battle
165　is only the first
　　how to do what we need for our living
　　with honor and in love
　　we have chosen each other
　　and the edge of each other's battles
170　the war is the same
　　if we lose
　　someday women's blood will congeal
　　upon a dead planet
　　if we win
　　there is no telling.

　　　　　　　　　　　　　　　　*1986*

# Call

　　Holy ghost woman
　　stolen out of your name
　　Rainbow Serpent
　　whose faces have been forgotten
5　Mother　loosen my tongue or adorn me
　　with a lighter burden
　　Aido Hwedo° is coming.

　　On worn kitchen stools and tables
　　we are piecing our weapons together
10　scraps of different histories
　　do not let us shatter
　　any altar

---

7 *Aido Hwedo*: (Lorde's note), the Rainbow Serpent; also a representation of all ancient deities who must be worshipped but whose names and faces have been lost in time.

she who scrubs the capitol toilets, listening
is your sister's youngest daughter
15      gnarled Harriet's anointed
you have not been without honor
even the young guerrilla has chosen
yells as she fires into the thicket
Aido Hwedo is coming.

20      I have written your names on my cheekbone
dreamed your eyes   flesh my epiphany
most ancient goddesses   hear me
enter
I have not forgotten your worship
25      nor my sisters
nor the sons of my daughters
my children watch for your print
in their labors
and they say Aido Hwedo is coming.

30      I am a Black woman   turning
mouthing your name as a password
through seductions   self-slaughter
and I believe in the holy ghost
mother
35      in your flames beyond our vision
blown light through the fingers of women
enduring   warring
sometimes outside your name
we do not choose all our rituals
40      Thandt Modise   winged girl of Soweto
brought fire back home in the snout of a mortar
and passes the word from her prison cell   whispering
Aido Hwedo is coming.

Rainbow Serpent who must not go
45      unspoken
I have offered up the safety of separations
sung the spirals of power
and what fills the spaces
before power unfolds or flounders
50      in desirable nonessentials
I am a Black woman   stripped down
and praying
my whole life has been an altar
worth its ending
55      and I say Aido Hwedo is coming.

I may be a weed in the garden
of women I have loved
who are still
trapped in their season
60      but even they shriek
as they rip burning gold from their skins
Aido Hwedo is coming.

We are learning by heart
what has never been taught
65 you are my given fire-tongued
Oya Seboulisa Mawu Afrekete
and now we are mourning our sisters
lost to the false hush of sorrow
to hardness and hatchets and childbirth
70 and we are shouting
Rosa Parks° and Fannie Lou Hamer°
Assata Shakur and Yaa Asantewa
my mother and Winnie Mandela° are singing
in my throat
75 the holy ghosts' linguist
one iron silence broken
Aido Hwedo is calling
calling
your daughters are named
80 and conceiving
Mother loosen my tongue
or adorn me
with a lighter burden
Aido Hwedo is coming.

85 Aido Hwedo is coming.

Aido Hwedo is coming.

*1986*

---

71 *Parks:* (b. 1913) jailed in Montgomery, Alabama, for refusing to give up her bus seat to a white rider in December 1955, she helped start the contemporary civil rights movement and later protested South African apartheid. *Hamer:* (1917–1977) American civil rights activist and politician.
73 *Mandela:* (b. 1936) South African activist; at the time Lorde wrote the poem she was married to imprisoned leader Nelson Mandela.

# Charles Wright (b. 1935)

Born in 1935 in Pickwick Dam, Tennessee, educated at Davidson College, the University of Iowa's Writer's Workshop, and the University of Rome, Wright is currently a professor in the Writing Program at the University of Virginia. Wright's interest in poetry was quickened by a tour of duty in the U.S. Army Intelligence Service in Italy in 1957. He became an admirer of Ezra Pound's poetry and of Italian poets such as Eugenio Montale, whose work he translated in 1979, and Cesare Pavese, whose rich sonority his own poetic line carries over into English. He also has a stronger interest than many of his contemporaries in working through the symbols and concepts of the Judeo-Christian religious tradition. Wright composes as if he were in the line of Imagist poets, specializing in fragments that gain their authority from their startling juxtapositions. But his language has a musical dimension matched by few contemporaries. So extravagantly sumptuous are his blendings of sight and sound—and sometimes so little anchored to incident—that it is with reluctance that one leaves the world of the poem to a reality that may seem diminished by comparison.

## Homage to Paul Cézanne°

At night, in the fish-light of the moon, the dead wear our white
    shirts
To stay warm, and litter the fields.
We pick them up in the mornings, dewy pieces of paper and scraps
    of cloth.
Like us, they refract themselves. Like us,
5    They keep on saying the same thing, trying to get it right.
Like us, the water unsettles their names.

Sometimes they lie like leaves in their little arks, and curl up at the
    edges.
Sometimes they come inside, wearing our shoes, and walk
From mirror to mirror.
10   Or lie in our beds with their gloves off
And touch our bodies. Or talk
In a corner. Or wait like envelopes on a desk.

---

**poem title:** Cézanne: (1839–1906) French painter. Considered by some the greatest Post-Impressionist painter, his work with cubic masses and architectonic lines set the stage for the partial abstraction of the Cubist movement. Noted for both landscapes and portraits.

They reach up from the ice plant.
They shuttle their messengers through the oat grass.
15     Their answers rise like rust on the stalks and the spidery leaves.

We rub them off our hands.

•

Each year the dead grow less dead, and nudge
Close to the surface of all things.
They start to remember the silence that brought them there.
20     They start to recount the gain in their soiled hands.

Their glasses let loose, and grain by grain return to the river bank.
They point to their favorite words
Growing around them, revealed as themselves for the first time:
They stand close to the meanings and take them in.

25     They stand there, vague and without pain,
Under their fingernails an unreturnable dirt.
They stand there and it comes back,
The music of everything, syllable after syllable

Out of the burning chair, out of the beings of light.
30     It all comes back.
And what they repeat to themselves, and what they repeat to them-
      selves,
Is the song that our fathers sing.

•

In steeps and sighs,
The ocean explains itself, backing and filling
35     What spaces it can't avoid, spaces
In black shoes, their hands clasped, their eyes teared at the edges:
We watch from the high hillside,
The ocean swelling and flattening, the spaces
Filling and emptying, horizon blade
40     Flashing the early afternoon sun.

The dead are constant in
The white lips of the sea.
Over and over, through clenched teeth, they tell
their story, the story each knows by heart:
45     *Remember me, speak my name.*
*When the moon tugs at my sleeve,*
*When the body of water is raised and becomes the body of light,*
*Remember me, speak my name.*

•

The dead are a cadmium blue.
50     We spread them with palette knives in broad blocks and planes.

We layer them stroke by stroke
In steps and ascending mass, in verticals raised from the earth.

We choose, and layer them in,
Blue and a blue and a breath,

55    Circle and smudge, cross-beak and buttonhook,
We layer them in. We squint hard and terrace them line by line.

And so we are come between, and cry out,
And stare up at the sky and its cloudy panes,

And finger the cypress twists.
60    The dead understand all this, and keep in touch,

Rustle of hand to hand in the lemon trees,
Flags, and the great sifts of anger

To powder and nothingness.
The dead are a cadmium blue, and they understand.

              •

65    The dead are with us to stay.
Their shadows rock in the back yard, so pure, so black,
Between the oak tree and the porch.

Over our heads they're huge in the night sky.
In the tall grass they turn with the zodiac.
70    Under our feet they're white with the snows of a thousand years.

They carry their colored threads and baskets of silk
To mend our clothes, making us look right,
Altering, stitching, replacing a button, closing a tear.
They lie like tucks in our loose sleeves, they hold us together.

75    They blow the last leaves away.
They slide like an overflow into the river of heaven.
Everywhere they are flying.

The dead are a sleight and a fade
We fall for, like flowering plums, like white coins from the rain
80    Their sighs are gaps in the wind.

              •

The dead are waiting for us in our rooms,
Little globules of light
In one of the far corners, and close to the ceiling, hovering,
    thinking our thoughts.

Often they'll reach a hand down,
85    Or offer a word, and ease us out of our bodies to join them in
    theirs.
We look back at our other selves on the bed.

We look back and we don't care and we go.

And thus we become what we've longed for,

past tense and otherwise,

A BB, a disc of light,

song without words.

90 And refer to ourselves
In the third person, seeing that other arm
Still raised from the bed, fingers like licks and flames in the boned
air.

Only to hear that it's not time.
Only to hear that we must re-enter and lie still, our arms at rest at
our sides.

95 The voices rising around us like mist

And dew, *it's all right, it's all right, it's all right* . . .

•

The dead fall around us like rain.
They come down from the last clouds in the late light for the last
time
And slip through the sod.

100 They lean uphill and face north.

Like grass,

They bend toward the sea, they break toward the setting sun.

We filigree and we baste.
But what do the dead care for the fringe of words,
105 Safe in their suits of milk?
What do they care for the honk and flash of a new style?

And who is to say if the inch of snow in our hearts
Is rectitude enough?

Spring picks the locks of the wind.
110 High in the night sky the mirror is hauled up and unsheeted.
In it we twist like stars.

Ahead of us, through the dark, the dead
Are beating their drums and stirring the yellow leaves.

•

We're out here, our feet in the soil, our heads craned up at the
sky,
115 The stars streaming and bursting behind the trees.

At dawn, as the clouds gather, we watch
The mountain glide from the east on the valley floor,
Coming together in starts and jumps.
Behind their curtain, the bears
120 Amble across the heavens, serene as black coffee . . .

Whose unction can intercede for the dead?
Whose tongue is toothless enough to speak their piece?

What we are given in dreams we write as blue paint,
Or messages to the clouds.
125    At evening we wait for the rain to fall and the sky to clear.
Our words are words for the clay, uttered in undertones,
Our gestures salve for the wind.

We sit out on the earth and stretch our limbs,
Hoarding the little mounds of sorrow laid up in our hearts.

*1981*

# Mary Oliver (b. 1935)

Born in Maple Heights, Ohio, near Cleveland, Oliver attended both Ohio State University and Vassar College. She lived for many years in Province-town, Massachusetts. In addition to eight volumes of poetry and prose poetry, she has written a book on prosody (*A Poetry Handbook*), as well as *Blue Pastures*, a collection of essays. She has recently taught at Sweet Briar College in Virginia, Duke University, and Bennington College. The social world appears infrequently in Oliver's poetry, for she is above all a poet of nature. In her capacity for exquisitely precise description and in her fascination with nature's indifferent, animate life, she recalls Roethke's early work. Her sense of awe and revelation, however, more fully echoes Hopkins and Jeffers. At moments when nature's sheer difference produces a sense of self-knowledge, a kind of ecstasy arises that is her special signature.

## The Lilies Break Open Over the Dark Water

Inside
   that mud-hive, that gas-sponge,
    that reeking
     leaf-yard, that rippling

5     dream-bowl, the leeches'
    flecked and swirling
     broth of life, as rich
      as Babylon,

the fists crack
10    open and the wands
    of the lilies
     quicken, they rise

like pale poles
   with their wrapped beaks of lace;
15    one day
     they tear the surface,

the next they break open
   over the dark water.
   And there you are
20    on the shore,

fitful and thoughtful, trying
to attach them to an idea—
some news of your own life.
But the lilies

25                    are slippery and wild—they are
devoid of meaning, they are
simply doing,
from the deepest

spurs of their being,
30                    what they are impelled to do
every summer.
And so, dear sorrow, are you.

1990

# Black Snake This Time

lay
under the oak trees
in the early morning,
in a half knot,

5                    in a curl,
and, like anyone
catching the runner at rest,
I stared

at that thick black length
10                    whose neck, all summer,
was a river,
whose body was the same river—

whose whole life was a flowing—
whose tail could lash—
15                    who, footless, could spin
like a black tendril and hang

upside down in the branches
gazing at everything
out of seed-shaped red eyes
20                    as it swung to and fro,

the tail making its quick sizzle,
the head lifted
like a black spout.
Was it alive?

25                    Of course it was alive.
This was the quick wrist of early summer,
when everything was alive.
Then I knelt down, I saw

that the snake was gone—
that the face, like a black bud,
had pushed out of the broken petals
of the old year, and it had emerged

on the hundred hoops of its belly,
the tongue sputtering its thread of smoke,
the work of the pearl-colored lung
never pausing, as it pushed

from the chin,
from the crown of the head,
leaving only an empty skin
for the mice to nibble and the breeze to blow

as over the oak leaves and across the creek
and up the far hill it had gone,
damp and shining in the starlight
like a rollicking finger of snow.

1997

# Jayne Cortez (b. 1936)

Born in Fort Huachuca, Arizona, Cortez grew up in the Watts ghetto of Los Angeles, but has spent most of her adult life in the New York City area. Her first books combine politics, music, and surrealism, but the musical and performance elements increased during her marriage to jazz musician Ornette Coleman and after her directorship (1964–1970) of the Watts Repertory Theatre Company in Los Angeles. Her band, "The Firespitters," has accompanied her performances and powerful poetry recordings, which sometimes make use of an almost mesmerizing chanting style. As one critic writes, hearing "her most volatile poems is akin to listening to a Greek chorus rebuke the cosmos." See her *Coagulations: New and Selected Poems* (1984).

## I Am New York City

       i am new york city
       here is my brain of hot sauce
       my tobacco teeth my
          mattress of bedbug tongue
       legs apart   hand on chin
          war on the roof   insults
5      pointed fingers   pushcarts
       my contraceptives all

       look at my pelvis blushing

       i am new york city of blood
       police and fried pies
10     i rub my docks red with grenadine
       and jelly madness in a flow of tokay
       my huge skull of pigeons
       my seance of peeping toms
       my plaited ovaries excuse me
15     this is my grime my thigh of
       steelspoons and toothpicks
          i imitate no one

       i am new york city
       of the brown spit and soft tomatoes
       give me my confetti of flesh
          my marquee of false nipples

20 my sideshow of open beaks
   in my nose of soot
  in my ox bled eyes
  in my ear of saturday night specials

  i eat ha ha hee hee and ho ho

  i am new york city
25 never change never sleep never melt
  my shoes are incognito
  cadavers grow from my goatee
  look i sparkle with shit with wishbones
  my nickname is glue-me

30 take my face of stink bombs
  my star spangled banner of hot dogs
  take my beer can junta
  my reptilian ass of footprints
  and approach me through life
35 approach me through death
  approach me through my widow's peak
  through my split ends my
  asthmatic laugh approach me
  through my wash rag
40 half ankle half elbow
  massage me with your camphor tears
  salute the patina and concrete
  of my rat tail wig
  face up face down piss
45 into the bite of our handshake

  i am new york city
  my skillet-head friend
  my fat-bellied comrade
  citizens
50 break wind with me

          *1973*

# Do You Think

 Do you think this is a sad day
  a sad night
full of tequila full of el dorado
  full of banana solitudes

5 And my chorizo° face a holiday for knives
  and my arching lips a savannah for cuchifritos
 and my spit curls a symbol for you
  to overcharge overbill oversell me

———————————

5 *chorizo*: sausage.

these saints   these candles
10         these dented cars   loud pipes
no insurance and no place to park
        because my last name is Cortez

Do you think this is a sad night
        a sad day

15     And on this elevator
        between my rubber shoes
in the creme de menthe of my youth
        the silver tooth of my age
the gullah speech of my one trembling tit
20     full of tequila   full of el dorado
        full of banana solitudes you tell me
i use more lights   more gas
        more telephones   more sequins   more feathers
more iridescent headstones
25         you think i accept this pentecostal church
in exchange for the lands you stole

And because my name is Cortez
        do you think this is a revision
of flesh studded with rivets
30         my wardrobe clean
the pick in my hair
        the pomegranate in my hand
14th street   delancey street   103rd street
        reservation where i lay my skull
35     the barrio of need
        the police state in ashes
drums full of tequila   full of el dorado
        full of banana solitudes say:

Do you really think time speaks english
        in the men's room

*1973*

# Lucille Clifton (b. 1936)

Clifton was born Thelma Louise Sayles in Depew, New York, where her mother worked in a laundry and her father in a steel mill. She attended Howard University and Fredonia State Teachers College, though she left before finishing a degree to devote herself to her writing. Supporting herself as an actor in the 1950s, marrying Fred Clifton in 1958, working for a time as a claims clerk in Buffalo, New York, Clifton meanwhile began to refine the minimalist poetic style—a compressed free verse lyric, often untitled, with a short iambic trimeter line—that would unify her diverse subject matter. She published her first book of poems in 1969 after poet Robert Hayden entered her work in a poetry contest. She has been interested in all of America's historic victims, including both blacks and Native Americans, and has been consistently eloquent about the special character of women's lives. She is also deeply religious, and her poem sequences about Biblical subjects—here represented by "brothers," a remarkable dialogue with Satan—have been particularly inventive. She has also written both poetry and fiction for children, as well as a history of her family ancestry, *Generations* (1976), that begins with her great-great-grandmother being kidnapped and sold into slavery.

## I Am Accused of Tending To the Past

i am accused of tending to the past
as if i made it,
as if i sculpted it
with my own hands. i did not.
5     this past was waiting for me
when i came,
a monstrous unnamed baby,
and i with my mother's itch
took it to breast
10    and named it
History.
she is more human now,
learning language everyday,
remembering faces, names and dates.
15    when she is strong enough to travel
on her own, beware, she will.

1991

## at the cemetery, walnut grove plantation, south carolina, 1989

among the rocks
at walnut grove
your silence drumming
in my bones,
5          tell me your names.

nobody mentioned slaves
and yet the curious tools
shine with your fingerprints.
nobody mentioned slaves
10        but somebody did this work
who had no guide, no stone,
who moulders under rock.

tell me your names,
tell me your bashful names
15        and i will testify.

*the inventory lists ten slaves*
*but only men were recognized.*

among the rocks
at walnut grove
20        some of these honored dead
were dark
some of these dark
were slaves
some of these slaves
25        were women
some of them did this
honored work.
tell me your names
foremothers, brothers,

30        tell me your dishonored names.
here lies
here lies
here lies
here lies
hear

*1991*

# Reply

FROM A LETTER WRITTEN TO DR. W.E.B. DUBOIS BY ALVIN BORGQUEST OF
CLARK UNIVERSITY IN MASSACHUSETTS AND DATED APRIL 3, 1905.

*"We are pursuing an investigation here on the subject of crying as an expres-
sion of the emotions, and should like very much to learn about its peculiarities
among the colored people. We have been referred to you as a person compe-
tent to give us information on the subject. We desire especially to know about
the following salient aspects: 1. Whether the Negro sheds tears . . ."*

reply

he do
she do
they live
they love
they try
they tire
they flee
they fight
they bleed
they break
they moan
they mourn
they weep
they die
they do
they do
they do

1991

# the message of crazy horse°

i would sit in the center of the world,
the Black Hills hooped around me and
dream of my dancing horse. my wife

was Black Shawl who gave me the daughter
i called They Are Afraid Of Her.
i was afraid of nothing

except Black Buffalo Woman.
my love for her i wore
instead of feathers. i did not dance

---

**poem title:** Crazy Horse (Tasunke Witko, 1840–1877), Ogalalla Sioux Chief, born in South
Dakota. He defeated General George Armstrong Custer at the Battle of Little Bighorn
(1876) and was widely considered the greatest Sioux military leader, though personally he
was rather shy and introspective. He was killed by a guard in a scuffle at Fort Robinson,
Nebraska.

10   i dreamed. i am dreaming now
     across the worlds. my medicine is strong.
     my medicine is strong in the Black basket
     of these fingers. i come again through this

     Black Buffalo woman. hear me;
15   the hoop of the world is breaking.
     fire burns in the four directions.
     the dreamers are running away from the hills.
     i have seen it. i am crazy horse.

                                        *1987*


## poem to my uterus

     you    uterus
     you have been patient
     as a sock
     while i have slippered into you
5    my dead and living children
     now
     they want to cut you out
     stocking i will not need
     where i am going
10   where am i going
     old girl
     without you
     uterus
     my bloody print
15   my estrogen kitchen
     my black bag of desire
     where can i go
     barefoot
     without you
20   where can you go
     without me

                                        *1991*


## to my last period

     well girl, goodbye,
     after thirty-eight years.
     thirty-eight years and you
     never arrived
5    splendid in your red dress
     without trouble for me
     somewhere, somehow.

now it is done,
and i feel just like
10    the grandmothers who,
after the hussy has gone,
sit holding her photograph
and sighing, *wasn't she*
*beautiful? wasn't she beautiful?*

1991

# brothers

(being a conversation in eight poems between an aged Lucifer and
God, though only Lucifer is heard. The time is long after.)

### 1

#### *invitation*

come coil with me
here in creation's bed
among the twigs and ribbons
of the past. i have grown old
5    remembering this garden,
the hum of the great cats
moving into language, the sweet
fume of the man's rib
as it rose up and began to walk.
10    it was all glory then,
the winged creatures leaping
like angels, the oceans claiming
their own. let us rest here a time
like two old brothers
15    who watched it happen and wondered
what it meant.

### 2

#### *how great Thou art*

listen, You are beyond
even Your own understanding
that rib and rain and clay
20    in all its pride,
its unsteady dominion,
is not what You believed
You were,
but it is what You are;
25    in Your own image as some
lexicographer supposed.
the face, both he and she,
the odd ambition, the desire
to reach beyond the stars
30    is You. all You, all You
the loneliness, the perfect
imperfection.

3

*as for myself*

less snake than angel
less angel than man
35      how come i to this
serpent's understanding?
watching creation from
a hood of leaves
i have foreseen the evening
40      of the world.
as sure as she,
the breast of Yourself
separated out and made to bear,
as sure as her returning,
45      i too am blessed with
the one gift you cherish;
to feel the living move in me
and to be unafraid.

4

*in my own defense*

what could i choose
50      but to slide along behind them,
they whose only sin
was being their father's children?
as they stood with their backs
to the garden,
55      a new and terrible luster
burning their eyes,
only You could have called
their ineffable names,
only in their fever
60      could they have failed to hear.

5

*the road led from delight*

into delight. into the sharp
edge of seasons, into the sweet
puff of bread baking, the warm
vale of sheet and sweat after love,
65      the tinny newborn cry of calf
and cormorant and humankind.
and pain, of course,
always there was some bleeding,
but forbid me not
70      my meditation on the outer world
before the rest of it, before
the bruising of his heel, my head,
and so forth.

### 6

*"the silence of God is God."*
—CAROLYN FORCHÉ

tell me, tell us why
75   in the confusion of a mountain
of babies stacked like cordwood,
of limbs walking away from each other,
of tongues bitten through
by the language of assault,
80   tell me, tell us why
You neither raised Your hand
nor turned away, tell us why
You watched the excommunication of
that world and You said nothing.

### 7

*still there is mercy, there is grace*

85   how otherwise
could i have come to this
marble spinning in space
propelled by the great
thumb of the universe?
90   how otherwise
could the two roads
of this tongue
converge into a single
certitude?
95   how otherwise
could i, a sleek old
traveler,
curl one day safe and still
beside You
100  at Your feet, perhaps,
but, amen, Yours.

### 8

"............ *is God.*"

so.
having no need to speak
You sent Your tongue
105  splintered into angels.
even i,
with my little piece of it
have said too much.
to ask You to explain
110  is to deny You.
before the word
You were.
You kiss my brother mouth.
the rest is silence.

*1993*

# Susan Howe (b. 1937)

Howe was born to Irish-American parents in Boston. She was educated as a painter at the Boston Museum of Fine Arts and exhibited her work in several group shows in New York. In the course of working on collages and then on performance pieces, she became interested in poetry and gradually made writing her career. She began to teach at the State University of New York at Buffalo in 1991. In addition to her poetry, she has written important critical books, including *My Emily Dickinson* (1985) and *The Birth-Mark: Unsettling the Wilderness in American Literary History* (1993).

Often grouped with the L=A=N=G=U=A=G=E poets because she shares with them a lineage that goes back at least to Gertrude Stein, Howe is also very much an experimental writer with her own unique project. More than most of her contemporaries, she has used the archive of American history to fashion linguistically complex contemporary reflections on national identity. "The Falls Fight" and "Hope Atherton's Wanderings" are the first two (of three) sections of a long poem titled "Articulations of Sound Forms in Time." The sections reprinted here recast the equivalent of a seventeenth-century American captivity narrative as a linguistic journey. The foray into language is like a foray into the wilderness. One must be led astray linguistically, succumb to the wilderness of strange words—some English, some Native American—become lost, be captured, abandon familiar syntax, in order to find oneself finally at home. The linguistic rite of passage in turn becomes an analogue for the necessary structure of a proper American story of exploration and settlement, in which the conqueror's will to mastery gives way to immersion in the wild overgrowth of words.

## from *Articulation of Sound Forms in Time*

*from seaweed said nor repossess rest*
*scape esaid*

I

### The Falls Fight

*Land! Land! Hath been the idol of many in New England!*
INCREASE MATHER°

Just after King Philip's War so-called by the English and shortly before King William's War or Governor Dudley's War called the War

---

Mather: (1639–1723), American Puritan theologian whose publications include *Remarkable Providences* (1684), *History of the War with the Indians* (1676), and *Cases of Conscience Concerning Witchcraft* (1693). He was less agitated about witchcraft than his son Cotton was.

of the Spanish Succession by Europeans, Deerfield was the northern-most colonial settlement in the Connecticut River Valley. In May 1676 several large bands of Indians had camped in the vicinity. The settlers felt threatened by this gathering of tribes. They appealed to Boston for soldiers, and a militia was sent out to drive away Squakeags, Pokom-tucks, Mahicans, Nipmunks, and others. The standing forces were led by Captain Turner of Boston. Captain Holyoke brought a contingent from Springfield; Ensign Lyman, a group from Northampton. Sergeants Kellog and Dickinson led the militia from Hadley. Benjamin Wait and Experience Hinsdale were pilots.

"The Reverend Hope Atherton, minister of the gospel, at Hatfield, a gentleman of publick spirit, accompanied the army."

The small force of 160 men marched from Hatfield on May 17, shortly before nightfall. They passed the river at Cheapside where they were heard by an Indian sentinel who aroused his people. Indians searched the normal fording place but the colonial militia had missed it by accident. Finding no footprints they assumed the sentry had been deceived by the noise of moose passing along the river. The colonial troops continued on their way until they happened on an unguarded Nipmunk, Squakeag, Pokomtuck, or Mahican camp. This they imme-diately attacked by firing into the wigwams. Wakened from sleep the frightened inhabitants thought they were being raided by Mohawks. The chronicler writes: "They soon discovered their mistake but being in no position to make an immediate defense were slain on the spot, some in their surprise ran directly to the river, and were drowned; oth-ers betook themselves to their bark canoes, and having in their confu-sion forgot their paddles, were hurried down the falls and dashed against the rocks. In this action the enemy by their own confession, lost 300, women and children included."

What the historian doesn't say is that most of the dead were women and children.

Only one white man was killed at what came to be called *The Falls Fight*. Indian survivors soon rallied neighboring bands and when they re-alized that the English force was only a small one, they pursued and ha-rassed the victorious retreating army. Now thirty-seven soldiers were killed and several more wounded. The solders were retreating because they had run out of ammunition. The retreat soon became a rout. About twenty members of the militia stood their ground and fired at the pursuing Na-tive Americans who were crossing the river. After a hard skirmish they re-joined the body of the now surrounded army, and together they fought their way ten miles back to safety. Except for Hope Atherton and seven or eight others who were somehow separated from their fellows. These Christian soldiers soon found themselves lost. After hiding in the woods for several days some of them came to the Indians and offered to surren-der on the condition that their lives would be spared. But the Squakeags, Nipmunks, Pokomtucks, or Mahicans, instead of giving them quarter, cov-ered each man with dry thatch. Then they set the thatch on fire and or-dered each soldier to run. When one covering of thatch was burnt off, an-other was added, and so these colonists continued running, until, Indians later told the historian: "Death delivered them from their hands."

*Prophesie is Historie antedated;*
*and History is Postdated Prophesie.*
JOHN COTTON

In our culture Hope is a name we give women. Signifying desire, trust, promise, does her name prophetically engender pacification of the feminine?

Pre-revolution Americans viewed America as the land of Hope.

"The Reverend Hope Atherton, minister of the gospel, at Hatfield, a gentleman of publick spirit, accompanied the army."

Hope's baptism of fire. No one believed the Minister's letter. He became a stranger to his community and died soon after the traumatic exposure that has earned him poor mention in a seldom opened book.

Hope's literal attributes. Effaced background dissolves remotest foreground. Putative author, premodern condition, presently present what future clamors for release?

Hope's epicene name draws its predetermined poem in.

I assume Hope Atherton's excursion for an emblem foreshadowing a Poet's abolished limitations in our demythologized fantasy of Manifest Destiny.

*EXTRACT from a LETTER (dated June 8, 1781)*
*of Stephen Williams to President Styles:*

"In looking over my papers I found a copy of a paper left by the Rev. Hope Atherton, the first minister of Hatfield, who was ordained May 10th, 1670. This Mr. Atherton went out with the forces (commanded by Capt. Turner, captain of the garrison soldiers, and Capt. Holyoke of the county militia) against the Indians at the falls above Deerfield, in May, 1676. In the fight, upon their retreat, Mr. Atherton was unhorsed and separated from the company, wandered in the woods some days and then got into Hadley, which is on the east side of the Connecticut River. But the fight was on the west side. Mr. Atherton gave account that he had offered to surrender himself to the enemy, but they would not receive him. Many people were not willing to give credit to this account, suggesting he was beside himself. This occasioned him to publish to his congregation and leave in writing the account I enclose to you. I had the paper from which this is copied, from Jonathan Wells, Esq., who was in the fight and lived afterward at Deerfield and was immediately acquainted with the *Indians* after the war. *He* did himself inform *me* that the *Indians* told *him* that after the fall fight, a little man with a black coat and without any hat, came toward them, but they were afraid and ran from him, thinking it was the Englishman's God, etc., etc."

*1987*

2

# Hope Atherton's Wanderings

Prest try to set after grandmother
revived by and laid down left ly
little distant each other and fro
Saw digression hobbling driftwood

5 forage two rotted beans & etc.
Redy to faint slaughter story so
Gone and signal through deep water
Mr. Atherton's story Hope Atherton

———————

Clog nutmeg abt noon
10 scraping cano muzzell
foot path sand and so
gravel rubbish vandal
horse flesh ryal tabl
sand enemys flood sun
15 Danielle Warnare Servt
Turner Falls Fight us
Next wearer April One

———————

Soe young mayde in March or April laught
who was lapd M as big as any kerchief
20 as like tow and beg grew bone and bullet
Stopt when asleep so Steven boy companion
Or errant Socoquis if you love your lives
War closed after Clay Gully hobbling boy
laid no whining trace no footstep clue
25 "Deep water" he *must* have crossed over

———————

Who was lapt R & soe grew bone & bullet
as like tow and as another scittuation
Stopt when Worshp Steven boy companion
Abt noon and abt sun come Country Farm
30 Follow me save me thither this winter
Capt. Turner little horn of powder
Medfield Clay Gully hobbling boy
Sixteen trace no wanton footstep rest
Soe struck fire set the woods on fire

———————

35 Two blew bird eggs plat
Habitants before dark
Little way went mistook awake
abt again Clay Gully
espied bounds to leop over
40 Selah cithera Opynne be
5 rails high houselot Cow
Kinsmen I pray you hasten
Furious Nipnet Ninep Ninap
little Pansett fence wth ditch
45 Clear stumps grubbing ploughing
Clearing the land

———————

Antagonists lay level direction
Logic hail um bushell forty-seven
These letters copy for shoeing
50     was alarum by seaven bold some
Lady Ambushment signed three My
excuse haste Nipmunk to my loues
Dress for fast Stedyness and Sway
Shining at the site of Falls Jump
55     Habitants inning the corn & Jumps

---

Rash catastrophe deaf evening
Bonds loosd catcht sedge environ
Extinct ordr set tableaux
hay and insolent army
60     Shape of so many comfortless
And deep so deep as my narrative
our homely manner and Myself
Said "matah" and "chirah"
Pease of all sorts and best
65     courtesy in every place
Whereat laughing they went away

---

rest chondriacal lunacy

velc cello viable toil

quench conch uncannunc

70     drumm amonoosuck ythian

---

scow aback din

flicker skaeg ne

barge quagg peat

~~sieve catacomb~~

75     stint chisel sect

---

Otherworld light into fable
Best plays are secret plays

---

Mylord have maize meadow

have Capes Mylord to dim

80     barley Sion beaver Totem

W'ld bivouac by vineyard

Eagle aureole elses thend

————

Impulsion of a myth of beginning
The figure of a far-off Wanderer

85    Grail face of bronze or brass
      Grass and weeds cover the face

      Colonnades of rigorous Americanism
      Portents of lonely destructivism

      Knowledge narrowly fixed knowledge
90    Whose bounds in theories slay

      Talismanic stepping-stone children
      brawl over pebble and shallow

      Marching and counter marching
      Danger of roaming the woods at random

95    Men whet their scythes go out to mow
      Nets tackle weir birchbark

      Mowing salt marshes and sedge meadows

————

Body perception thought of perceiving (half-thought

chaotic   architect repudiate line Q confine lie link realm

100   circle a euclidean curtail theme theme toll function coda

severity whey crayon so distant grain scalp gnat carol

omen Cur cornice zed primitive shad sac stone fur bray

tub epoch too tall fum alter rude recess emblem sixty key

Epithets young in a box told as you fly

————

105   Posit gaze level diminish lamp and asleep(selv)cannot see

*is* notion   most open apparition past Halo view border redden

possess remote so abstract life are lost spatio-temporal hum

Maoris empirical Kantian a little lesson concatenation up

tree fifty shower see step shot Immanence force to Mohegan

110     blue glare(essence)cow bed leg extinct draw scribe    upside
        even blue(A)ash-tree fleece comfort(B)draw scribe    sideup

                         ———————

        Posit gave level diminish lamp and asleep(selv)cannot see

            MoheganToForceImmanenceShotStepSeeShowerFiftyTree

            UpConcatenationLessonLittleAKantianEmpiricalMaoris

115         HumTemporal-spatioLostAreLifeAbstractSoRemotePossess

            ReddenBorderViewHaloPastApparitionOpenMostNotion *is*

        blue glare(essence)cow bed leg extinct draw scribe    sideup
        even blue(A)ash-tree fleece comfort(B)draw scribe    upside

                         ———————

            Loving Friends and Kindred:—

120         When I look back

            So short in charity and good works

            We are a small remnant

            of signal escapes wonderful in themselves

            We march from our camp a little

125         and come home

            Lost the beaten track and so

            River section dark all this time

            We must not worry

            how few we are and fall from each other

130         More than language can express

            Hope for the artist in America & etc

            This is my birthday

            These are the old home trees

                         ———————

                                                        1987

# Michael S. Harper (b. 1938)

Born in Brooklyn, New York, to parents who were a postal worker and a medical stenographer, Harper moved to Los Angeles with his family in 1951. While at Los Angeles City, then State, colleges in the late 1950s, he worked in the post office and met a number of articulate black coworkers blocked from more challenging employment. Finally settling on a writing career, he attended the Iowa Writer's Workshop, the only black writer in his class; he was forced to live in segregated housing. Soon after that he met the legendary jazz saxophonist and composer John Coltrane; their friendship had a profound impact on Harper's writing, making him perhaps the contemporary black writer whose poetry has the most original and intricate relation to music. He has worked out a wide range of techniques to make his poetry, which must be read aloud, musical, from the use of subtle irregular repetition and varying line lengths, to the more obvious placement of blues refrains. The lines are also rhythmically paced in surprising ways, with lines meant to be read rapidly mixed effectively with lines designed to be lingered over and read slowly. Meanwhile, his subject matter mixes strong acts of witness to America's racist history with wrenching accounts of family tragedy. The two counterpoint one another in such a way as to make individual lives mythic in their very specificity and history verified and lived in the pulse of individual experience. Harper has taught at Brown University since 1971.

## Song: *I Want a Witness*

Blacks in frame houses
call to the helicopters,
their antlered arms
spinning; jeeps pad
5    these glass-studded streets;
on this hill are tanks painted gold.

Our children sing
spirituals of *Motown,*
idioms these streets suckled
10   on a southern road.
This scene is about power,
terror, producing
love and pain and pathology;
in an army of white dust,
15   blacks here to *testify*

and *testify*, and *testify*,
and *redeem*, and *redeem*,
in black smoke coming,
as they wave their arms,
as they wave their tongues.

1972

## Blue Ruth: America

I am telling you this:
the tubes in your nose,
in the esophagus,
in the stomach;
5     the small balloon
attached to its end
is your bleeding gullet;
yellow in the canned
sunshine of gauze,
10    stitching, bedsores,
each tactoe cut
sewn back
is America:
I am telling you this:
*history is your own heartbeat.*

1971

## Brother John

Black man:
I'm a black man;
I'm black; I am—
A black man; black—
5     I'm a black man;
I'm a black man;
I'm a man; black—
I am—

Bird, buttermilk bird—
10    smack, booze and bitches
I am Bird
baddest nightdreamer
on sax in the ornithology-world
I can fly—higher, high, higher—
15    I'm a black man;
I am; I'm a black man—

Miles, blue haze,
Miles high, another bird,
more Miles, mute,
20    Mute Miles, clean,
bug-eyed, unspeakable,

Miles, sweet Mute,
sweat Miles, black Miles;
I'm a black man;
25      I'm black; I am;
I'm a black man—

Trane, Coltrane; John Coltrane;
it's tranetime; chase the Trane;
it's a slow dance;
30      it's the Trane
in Alabama; acknowledgment,
*a love supreme,*
it's black Trane; black;
I'm a black man; I'm black;
35      I am; I'm a black man—

Brother John, Brother John
plays no instrument;
he's a black man; black;
he's a black man; he is
40      Brother John; Brother John—

I'm a black man; I am;
black; I am; I'm a black
man; I am; I am;
I'm a black man;
45      I'm a black man;
I am; I'm a black man;
I am:

1970

# American History

Those four black girls blown up
in that Alabama church°
remind me of five hundred
middle passage° blacks,
5      in a net, under water
in Charleston harbor
so *redcoats*° wouldn't find them.
Can't find what you can't see
can you?

1970

---

2 *Alabama church:* In 1963, civil rights opponents killed four black girls when they exploded a bomb in a Birmingham, Alabama church.
4 *middle passage:* the name of the route slave ships took across the Atlantic Ocean from Africa to North or South America.
7 *redcoats:* British soldiers during the colonial period of American history.

## We Assume: On the Death of Our Son,
## Reuben Masai Harper

We assume
that in 28 hours,
lived in a collapsible isolette,
you learned to accept pure oxygen
5    as the natural sky;
the scant shallow breaths
that filled those hours
cannot, did not make you fly—
but dreams were there
10   like crooked palmprints on
the twin-thick windows of the nursery—
in the glands of your mother.

We assume
the sterile hands
15   drank chemicals in and out
from lungs opaque with mucus,
pumped your stomach,
*eeked* the bicarbonate in
crooked, green-winged veins,
20   out in a plastic mask;

A woman who'd lost her first son
consoled us with an angel gone ahead
to pray for our family—
gone into that sky
25   seeking oxygen,
gone into autopsy,
a fine brown powdered sugar,
a disposable cremation:

We assume
you did not know we loved you.

1970

## Reuben, Reuben

I reach from pain
to music great enough
to bring me back,
swollenhead, madness,
5   lovefruit, a pickle of hate
so sour my mouth twicked
up and would not sing;
there's nothing in the beat
to hold it in

10  melody and turn human skin;
a brown berry gone
to rot just two days on the branch;
we've lost a son,
the music, *jazz*, comes in.

1970

# Deathwatch

Twitching in the cactus
hospital gown, a loon
on hairpin wings,
she tells me how
5   her episiotomy°
is perfectly sewn
and doesn't hurt
while she sits in a pile
of blood
10  which once cleaned
the placenta
my third son should be in.
She tells me how early
he is, and how strong,
15  like his father,
and long, like a black-
stemmed Easter rose
in a white hand.

Just under five pounds
20  you lie there, a collapsed
balloon doll, burst in your
fifteenth hour, with the face
of your black father,
his fingers, his toes,
25  and eight voodoo
adrenalin holes in
your pinwheeled hair-lined
chest; you witness
your parents sign the autopsy
30  and disposal papers
shrunken to duplicate
in black ink
on white paper
like the country
35  you were born in,
unreal, asleep,
silent, almost alive.

---

5 *episiotomy*: surgical procedure to widen the vaginal opening during childbirth.

This is a dedication
to our memory
40      of three sons—
two dead, one alive—
a reminder of a letter
to Du Bois°
from a student
45      at Clark—on behalf
of his whole history class.
The class is confronted
with a question,
and no one—
50      not even the professor—
is sure of the answer:
"Will you please tell us
whether or not it is true
that negroes
55      are not able to cry?"

America needs a killing.
America needs a killing.
*Survivors will be human.*

1970

# Dear John, Dear Coltrane°

*a love supreme, a love supreme*
*a love supreme, a love supreme*

Sex fingers toes
in the marketplace
near your father's church°
in Hamlet, North Carolina°—
5       witness to this love
in this calm fallow
of these minds,
there is no substitute for pain:
genitals gone or going,
10      seed burned out,
you tuck the roots in the earth,
turn back, and move
by river through the swamps,

---

43 *Du Bois*: W.E.B. Du Bois (1868–1963) African American writer and activist; also see Lucille Clifton's poem "Reply" (p. 1031).
**poem title**: John Coltrane (1926–1967) was the premier jazz saxophonist of his generation and an influential avant-garde jazz composer. He wrote "A Love Supreme," a four-part composition, in response to a spiritual experience in 1957, which led him to stop using heroin and alcohol; it was recorded in 1964.
3 *father's church*: Coltrane's grandfather, who lived in the family home, was minister of St. Stephens AME Zion Church in Hamlet.
4 *Hamlet, North Carolina*: Coltrane's birthplace.

singing: *a love supreme, a love supreme;*
what does it all mean?
Loss, so great each black
woman expects your failure
in mute change, the seed gone.
You plod up into the electric city—
you song now crystal and
the blues. You pick up the horn
with some will and blow
into the freezing night:
*a love supreme, a love supreme—*

Dawn comes and you cook
up the thick sin 'tween
impotence and death, fuel
the tenor sax cannibal
heart, genitals and sweat
that makes you clean—
*a love supreme, a love supreme—*

*Why you so black?*
*cause I am*
*why you so funky?*
*cause I am*
*why you so black?*
*cause I am*
*why you so sweet?*
*cause I am*
*why you so black?*
*cause I am*
*a love supreme, a love supreme:*

So sick
you couldn't play *Naima,*°
so flat we ached
for song you'd concealed
with your own blood,
your diseased liver gave
out its purity,
the inflated heart
pumps out, the tenor kiss,
tenor love:
*a love supreme, a love supreme—*
*a love supreme, a love supreme—*

1970

---

44 *Naima*: a Coltrane composition recorded in 1959, the name of his first wife.

# Ishmael Reed (b. 1938)

A versatile, unpredictable, and frequently iconoclastic figure, Reed has written nine novels, edited several anthologies, written songs and operas, and recorded some of the poetry from his five books of poems. He was born in Chattanooga, Tennessee, and raised in Buffalo, New York. He enrolled at the State University of New York at Buffalo, but left to do civil rights and community reporting for a Buffalo newspaper. While there he met Malcolm X and decided to move to New York in 1962, where he worked at numerous jobs, joined a writing workshop, and produced his first novel. In 1967, he moved to California, first to Berkeley and then Oakland. In 1976, he was cofounder of the multi-ethnic Before Columbus Foundation.

## I am a cowboy in the boat of Ra

*The devil must be forced to reveal any such physical evil (potions, charms, fetishes, etc.) still outside the body and these must be burned.*
(RITUALE ROMANUM, PUBLISHED 1947, ENDORSED BY THE COAT-OF-ARMS AND INTRODUCTORY LETTER FROM FRANCIS CARDINAL SPELLMAN°)

I am a cowboy in the boat of Ra,°
sidewinders in the saloons of fools
bit my forehead     like     O
the untrustworthiness of Egyptologists
5    who do not know their trips. Who was that
dog-faced° man? they asked, the day I rode
from town.

---

Spellman: (1889–1967), conservative Catholic archbishop and cardinal of New York.
1 *Ra:* the Egyptian creator god and sun god, also known as Re and as Amun-Re, often depicted as a falcon wearing the sun disc on its head, or as a human figure with a ram's head. In some cults he is a double god—Ra by day and Osiris, god of the underworld, by night. The *boat* of Ra draws in multiple associations, starting with the boats included in Egyptian tombs to carry the body and spirit of dead Pharaohs and extending to the slave ships under the control of white masters that brought blacks to the Americas.
6 *dog-faced:* Anubis, the Egyptian mortuary god takes the form of a black dog or a jackal. "Who was that masked man?" is a recurrent line from the *Lone Ranger* radio drama, comic strip, and television series.

School marms with halitosis° cannot see
the Nefertiti° fake chipped on the run by slick
10　germans, the hawk behind Sonny Rollins'° head or
the ritual beard of his axe; a longhorn winding
its bells thru the Field of Reeds.

I am a cowboy in the boat of Ra. I bedded
down with Isis,° Lady of the Boogaloo,° dove
15　down deep in her horny, stuck up her Wells-Far-ago°
in daring midday getaway. 'Start grabbing the
blue',° I said from top of my double crown.°

I am a cowboy in the boat of Ra. Ezzard Charles°
of the Chisholm Trail.° Took up the bass but they
20　blew off my thumb.° Alchemist in ringmanship but a
sucker for the right cross.

I am a cowboy in the boat of Ra. Vamoosed from
the tempe i bide my time. The price on the wanted
poster was a-going down, outlaw alias copped° my stance
25　and moody greenhorns were making me dance; while my mouth's
shooting iron got its chambers jammed.

---

8 *halitosis*: here a sign of cultural incapacitation; folks with "bad breath" cannot play the saxophone and are not hip to either the dominant culture's deceptions or the alternative knowledge the poem synthesizes.

9 *Nefertiti*: Fourteenth century B.C. Egyptian queen, consort of Pharaoh Akhenaton; her image is best known from the sculptured head found at Amarna in 1912, chipped and removed by Germans, and now in the Berlin Museum.

10 *Rollins*: (b. 1929), American jazz tenor-saxophonist. The "hawk behind Sonny Rollins' head" does more than allude to hawk-headed Egyptian gods; it is a specific reference to Coleman Hawkins (1901–1969), who was Rollins' predecessor in a hard style of saxophone playing. In jazz slang your "axe" is your musical instrument; practicing, in the same lingo, is "woodshedding." The "longhorn" invokes both the famous breed of cattle in the Old West and the saxophone. The "bell" is both a cowbell and the saxophone's expanded mouth. The "field of reeds" in the stanza's last line doubles as a musical reference (a saxophone has a reed in the mouthpiece) and a reference to the bullrushes at the edge of Egypt's Nile River where Moses was found.

14 *Isis*: Egyptian mother goddess; she impregnated herself from Osiris's corpse as he was entering the underworld to become its ruler.

14 *Boogaloo*: popular dance style of the 1960s. In black English, "to boogaloo" came to mean "to dance" or "to fool around," usages that white racists tried to appropriate as a slur, when "boogaloo" became a way of referring to a black person.

15 *Wells-Far-ago*: play on Wells Fargo, a stage company in the American West, and a "farrago," a word whose multiple meanings are all in play here: a mixed fodder for cattle; an apparently irrational assemblage of references (the poem); a staged event of mixed fact and fancy designed to deceive (American culture).

17 *blue*: perhaps includes an allusion to Rollins' well-known piece "Blue Seven."

17 *double crown*: at once the combined crown of Ammon and Ra of rival Egyptian cults and the double crowns of music and poetry.

18 *Ezzard Charles*: (1922–1975) African American prizefighter who was heavyweight champion of the world from 1949–1951.

19 *Chisholm Trail*: route in the American Old West used to drive cattle from Texas to Kansas.

20 *thumb*: one cannot play the bass without a thumb.

24 *copped*: originally, "stole or took unfairly"; now in Black English "understood," or assumed a manner or attitude.

I am a cowboy in the boat of Ra. Boning-up in
the ol West i bide my time. You should see
me pick off these tin cans whippersnappers. I
30    write the motown° long plays for the comeback of
Osiris. Make them up when stars stare at sleeping
steer out here near the campfire. Women arrive
on the backs of goats and throw themselves on
my Bowie.°

35    I am a cowboy in the boat of Ra. Lord of the lash,
the Loup Garou° Kid. Half breed son of Pisces and
Aquarius.° I hold the souls of men in my pot. I do
the dirty boogie° with scorpions. I make the bulls
keep still and was the first swinger to grape the taste.

40    I am a cowboy in his boat. Pope Joan° of the
Ptah° Ra. C/mere a minute willya doll?
Be a good girl and
bring me my Buffalo horn of black powder
bring me my headdress of black feathers
45    bring me my bones of Ju-Ju° snake
go get my eyelids of red paint.
Hand me my shadow

I'm going into town after Set°

I am a cowboy in the boat of Ra

---

30 *motown*: Detroit-based, black-owned record company that came to prominence in the 1960s and was the first really successful incursion of a black sensibility into the rock and roll scene.

34 *Bowie*: large knife, here phallic.

36 *Loup Garou*: werewolf. "Loup Garou" also rhymes with the name of Lash LaRue, star of a series of western films, such as *The Black Lash* (1952) and *Law of the Lash* (1947), whose work is invoked in the previous phrase, "Lord of the lash." LaRue, who also appeared in a comic book series, used a whip to disarm villains. Finally, under a slightly different spelling, Loop Garoo is the whip-wielding cowboy protagonist of Reed's novel *Yellow Back Radio Broke-Down* (1969).

37 *Pisces and Aquarius*: the twelfth and eleventh signs of the Zodiac, a zone of fixed stars that marks the apparent courses of the sun, moon, and planets about the earth.

38 *boogie*: several meanings are in play. Boogie (or boogie-woogie) is a percussive style of playing blues on the piano, as well as a jitterbug dance performed to the same music; it is also disparaging slang for a black person. To "boogie" is also to dance or to have sexual intercourse, hence the phrase "do the dirty boogie." The poem's account of struggles over meaning encompasses language, myth, and history.

40 *Pope Joan*: apocryphal female pope said to have served in the ninth century. One of the dedicatees of Reed's novel *Yellow Back Radio Broke-Down*.

41 *Ptah*: Egyptian creator god and god of craftsmen, a rival claimant with Ra as senior figure in the pantheon.

45 *Ju-Ju*: a charm or spell used to ward off evil spirits.

48 *Set*: Egyptian god of chaos and adversity, sometimes depicted as a man with the head of an animal, who murdered his brother Osiris. In the poem the word also invokes a musical set.

50  look out Set            here i come Set
    to get Set             to sunset Set
    to unseat Set          to Set down Set

                           usurper of the Royal couch
                           imposter RAdio of Moses' bush°
55                         party pooper O hater of dance
                           vampire outlaw of the milky way

                                                        *1972*

---

54 *Moses' bush:* the burning bush, described in the book of Exodus, out of which God spoke to Moses, who led the Jewish people out of Egyptian slavery, a role both poetry and music fill for American blacks in the poem.

# Lawson Fusao Inada (b. 1938)

Born in Fresno, California, as a child Inada spent World War II in a concentration camp with his family. In a period of racist hysteria, constitutional guarantees were set aside, and Japanese Americans were interned for the duration of the war. He would later write of the experience in *Before the War: Poems as They Happened* (1971). Lawson was then educated at Berkeley and Fresno State College, followed by studies in creative writing at the University of Iowa and the University of Oregon. He teaches at Southern Oregon State College. While maintaining the strong political perspective of *Before the War*, he has also taken up other subjects, as "Listening Images" and its epigrammatic portraits of jazz artists suggests.

## Listening Images

**LESTER YOUNG°**

Yes, clouds do have
The smoothest sound.

**BILLIE HOLIDAY°**

Hold a microphone
Close to the moon.

**CHARLIE PARKER°**

Rapids to baptism
In one blue river.

---

*Young:* Tenor saxophonist Lester Young (1909–1959) played airy, melodic lines in the upper register of his horn.
*Holiday:* With her enormous emotional range, Billie Holiday (1915–1959) transformed any song she vocalized, from the tin pan alley ditties that were thrust before her as commercial ventures to the haunting works she composed herself.
*Parker:* Alto saxophonist Charlie Parker (1920–1955), one of the inventors of bebop, was notable for the speed with which he played.

### COLEMAN HAWKINS°

A hawk for certain,
But as big as a man.

### BEN WEBSTER°

Such fragile moss
In a massive tree.

### LOUIS ARMSTRONG°

Just dip your ears
And taste the sauce.

### ROY ELDRIDGE°

Get in the car.
Start the engine.

### DIZZY GILLESPIE°

Gusts of gusto
Sweep the desert.

### MILES DAVIS°

3 valves, tubing . . .
How many feelings?

### CLIFFORD BROWN°

A fine congregation
This spring morning.

### ART TATUM°

Innumerable dew,
A splendid web.

---

*Hawkins*: Tenor saxophonist Coleman "Hawk" Hawkins (1901–1969) dominated small groups with his inventive harmonies and deep burley tone.
*Webster*: Tenor saxophonist Ben Webster (1909–1973) ornamented his solos with elaborate filigrees and a dramatic vibrato.
*Armstrong*: Jazz pioneer and trumpeter Louis Armstrong (1900–1971) was raised in New Orleans; his "Struttin' with Some Barbecue" was a hit of the 1920s.
*Eldridge*: The solid and substantial trumpet solos of Roy Eldridge (1911–1989) graced numerous big bands of the 1930s and 1940s.
*Gillespie*: (1917–1993); a trumpet virtuoso and bebop innovator, Gillespie was the rare musician whose performances were swept with humor.
*Davis*: Especially on ballads recorded in the 1950s, the trumpet playing of Miles Davis (1926–1991) has been likened to "a man walking on eggshells" (Ira Gitler).
*Brown*: Trumpeter and composer of the resplendent "Joy Spring," Clifford Brown (1930–1956) died suddenly, his immense promise unrealized.
*Tatum*: Art Tatum (1909–1956) demonstrated his complete command of the piano by producing solos that were beehives of harmonic activity.

**BUD POWELL°**

The eye, and then
The hurricane.

**THELONIOUS MONK°**

Always old, always new,
Always déjà vu.

**COUNT BASIE°**

Acorns on the roof—
Syncopated oakestra.

**DUKE ELLINGTON°**

Stars, stripes, united
States of Ellington.

**GENE AMMONS**
**CHU BERRY**
**DON BYAS**
**EDDIE DAVIS**
**HERSCHEL EVANS**
**PAUL GONSALVES**
**DEXTER GORDON**
**WARDELL GRAY**
**RAHSAAN KIRK**
**HANK MOBLEY**
**CHARLIE ROUSE**
**SONNY STITT°**

Mountain mist,
Monumental totem.

**JOHN COLTRANE°**

Sunrise golden
At the throat.

---

*Powell:* The right hand of pianist Bud Powell (1924–1966) strung out lanky boppish lines that his left hand interrupted with irregular and dissonant chords.
*Monk:* (1917–1982); his unpredictable piano improvisations blended dissonant avant-garde harmonies with a down home, percussive rhythm.
*Basie:* Well-known orchestra leader William "Count" Basie (1904–1984) punctuated the ending of his understated piano solos with short staccato notes.
*Ellington:* (1899–1974); his compositions were concerto-like showcasings of stars in the orchestra he took on the road across America.
*Stitt:* From "Gene Ammons" to "Sonny Stitt," this alphabetical list of tenor saxophonists from a range of different backgrounds over a number of generations—the earliest born in 1909 (Evans), the latest in 1936 (Kirk)—dramatizes the variety of jazz.
*Coltrane:* John Coltrane (1926–1967) was a singularly innovative tenor and soprano saxophonist.

## ERIC DOLPHY°

Coming across quick
Deer in the forest.

## DELTA BLUES°

They broke bottles
Just to get the neck.

## SON HOUSE°

A lone man plucking
Bolts of lightning.

## KANSAS CITY SHOUTERS°

Your baby leaves you on the train.
You stand and bring it back again.

## BIG JOE TURNER°

Big as laughter, big as rain,
Big as the big public domain.

1993

---

*Dolphy:* Alto saxophonist, bass clarinetist, and flutist Eric Dolphy (1928–1964) was a player of remarkable fluency.
*Blues:* Blues performers from the Mississippi Delta played "bottleneck" guitar, extracting a plaintive wail from the instrument by sliding a broken bottleneck, worn on the little finger of the left hand, up and down the neck of a guitar unconventionally tuned in thirds and fifths.
*House:* A blues guitarist and vocalist brought up in a religious household, Eddie "Son" House Jr. (1902–1988) was torn between the ministry and the secular desires of the popular performer.
*Shouters:* The Kansas City Shouters were deep-voiced male vocalists from the Southwest in the 1930s and 1940s who sang their blues with triumphant authority and power.
*Turner:* The rhythm-and-blues recording of "Shake, Rattle and Roll" by Kansas City Shouter Big Joe Turner (1911–1985) became a commercial success after it was adapted by Bill Haley and His Comets.

# Robert Pinsky (b. 1940)

Born in Long Branch, New Jersey, Pinsky was educated at Rutgers University and Stanford University. In California, he worked with poet-critic Ivor Winters and earned a Ph.D. He has taught at several schools, translated Dante's *Inferno*, and published both criticism and poetry. Pinsky generally uses regular stanzas and traditional forms, modifying them when he wishes. He has drawn both from his own experience and, as with "The Unseen" and "Shirt," from modern history, balancing a will to reason with spiritual inclinations.

## The Unseen

In Krakow° it rained, the stone arcades and cobbles
And the smoky air all soaked one penetrating color
While in an Art Nouveau° café, on harp-shaped chairs,

We sat making up our minds to tour the death camp.°
5    As we drove there the next morning past farms
And steaming wooden villages, the rain had stopped

Though the sky was still gray. A young guide explained
Everything we saw in her tender, hectoring° English:
The low brick barracks; the heaped-up meticulous

10   Mountains of shoes, toothbrushes, hair; one cell
Where the Pope° had prayed and placed flowers; logbooks,
Photographs, latrines—the whole unswallowable

Menu of immensities. It began drizzling again,
And the way we paused to open or close the umbrellas,
15   Hers and ours, as we went from one building to the next,

Had a formal, dwindled feeling. We felt bored
And at the same time like screaming Biblical phrases:
*I am poured out like water; Thine is the day and*

---

1 *Krakow:* city in southern Poland.
3 *Art Noveau:* decorating style that originated in the late nineteenth century, characterized by sinuous lines and foliate forms.
4 *death camp:* Auschwitz, a Nazi concentration camp just west of Krakow; more than a million Jews were murdered there during World War II.
8 *hectoring:* brow-beating.
11 *Pope:* John Paul II (1920–), named pope in 1978.

*Thine also the night; I cannot look to see*
20  *My own right hand . . .* I remembered a sleep-time game,
A willed dream I had never thought of by day before:

I am there; and granted the single power of invisibility,
Roaming the camp at will. At first I savor my mastery
Slowly by creating small phantom diversions,

25  Then kill kill kill kill, a detailed and strangely
Passionless inward movie: I push the man holding
The crystals° down from the gas chamber roof, bludgeon

The pet collie of the Commandant's children
And in the end flush everything with a vague flood
30  Of fire and blood as I drift on toward sleep

In a blurred finale, like our tour's—eddying
In a downpour past the preserved gallows where
The Allies hung the Commandant, in 1947.

I don't feel changed, or even informed—in that,
35  It's like any other historical monument; although
It is true that I don't ever at night any more

Prowl rows of red buildings unseen, doing
Justice like an angry god to escape insomnia. And so,
O discredited Lord of Hosts, your servant gapes

40  Obediently to swallow various doings of us, the most
Capable of all your former creatures—we have
No shape, we are poured out like water, but still

We try to take in what won't be turned from in despair:
As if, just as we turned toward the fumbled drama
45  Of the religious art shop window to accuse you

Yet again, you were to slit open your red heart
To show us at last the secret of your day and also,
Because it also is yours, of your night.

                                                    *1984*

## Shirt

The back, the yoke, the yardage. Lapped seams,
The nearly invisible stitches along the collar
Turned in a sweatshop by Koreans or Malaysians

Gossiping over tea and noodles on their break
5  Or talking money or politics while one fitted
This armpiece with its overseam to the band

---

27 *crystals:* cyanide crystals, causing death by asphixiation; administered by the Germans in rooms holding scores of victims, with friends and family members aware of each other dying.

Of cuff I button at my wrist. The presser, the cutter,
The wringer, the mangle. The needle, the union,
The treadle, the bobbin. The code. The infamous blaze

10    At the Triangle° Factory in nineteen-eleven.
One hundred and forty-six died in the flames
On the ninth floor, no hydrants, no fire escapes—

The witness in a building across the street
Who watched how a young man helped a girl to step
15    Up to the windowsill, then held her out

Away from the masonry wall and let her drop.
And then another. As if he were helping them up
To enter a streetcar, and not eternity.

A third before he dropped her put her arms
20    Around his neck and kissed him. Then he held
Her into space, and dropped her. Almost at once

He stepped to the sill himself, his jacket flared
And fluttered up from his shirt as he came down,
Air filling up the legs of his gray trousers—

25    Like Hart Crane's Bedlamite, "shrill shirt ballooning."
Wonderful how the pattern matches perfectly
Across the placket and over the twin bar-tacked

Corners of both pockets, like a strict rhyme
Or a major chord. Prints, plaids, checks,
30    Houndstooth, Tattersall, Madras. The clan tartans

Invented by mill-owners inspired by the hoax of Ossian,°
To control their savage Scottish workers, tamed
By a fabricated heraldry: MacGregor,

Bailey, MacMartin. The kilt, devised for workers
35    To wear among the dusty clattering looms.
Weavers, carders, spinners. The loader,

The docker, the navvy. The planter, the picker, the sorter
Sweating at her machine in a litter of cotton
As slaves in calico headrags sweated in fields:

40    George Herbert,° your descendant is a Black
Lady in South Carolina, her name is Irma
And she inspected my shirt. Its color and fit

---

10 *Triangle*: on March 25, 1911, a fire swept through the Triangle Shirtwaist Company in the
Greenwich Village section of New York City. It was a sweatshop where the mostly women
workers did poorly paid piecework in a building without fire escapes or other safety provi-
sions. The fire consumed 146 workers, trapped in part by management's decision to restrict
breaks by keeping the doors locked. It was one of the nation's worst industrial tragedies.
31 *Ossian*: legendary Gaelic bard and warrior.
40 *Herbert*: (1593–1633) English metaphysical poet and clergyman whose poem "The Col-
lar" includes the refrain "I will abroad," suggesting travel to the New World.

And feel and its clean smell have satisfied
Both her and me. We have culled its cost and quality
45      Down to the buttons of simulated bone,

The buttonholes, the sizing, the facing, the characters
Printed in black on neckband and tail. The shape,
The label, the labor, the color, the shade. The shirt.

*1990*

# Welton Smith (b. 1940)

Smith, who was born in Houston, Texas, is the author of *Penetration* (1972), a collection of poems, and *The Roach Riders,* a play. His poem sequence "Malcolm," which was included in the historic 1968 Black Arts collection *Black Fire: An Anthology of Afro-American Writing* edited by Larry Neal and Amiri Baraka, is one of a number of elegies written after Malcolm X was killed in 1965. Its tonal shifts help make it one of the most memorable and one of the more inventive poems to come out of the Black Arts movement.

## Malcolm°

### MALCOLM

i cannot move
from your voice.
there is no peace
where i am. the wind
5    cannot move
hard enough to clear the trash
and far away i hear my screams.

the lean, hard-bone face
a rich copper color.
10   the smile. the
thin nose and broad
nostrils. Betty—in the quiet
after midnight. your hand
soft on her back. you kiss

---

**poem title:** Malcolm X (1925–1965), charismatic African American political and religious leader, assassinated at a rally in 1965. Born Malcolm Little, his family's house in Michigan was burned by the Ku Klux Klan, his father murdered, and his mother institutionalized. A petty criminal and drug user, he converted to the Nation of Islam in prison, changed his last name to "X," showing that he regarded "Little" as a vestige of slavery, and educated himself. After prison, he became a minister in the church and an increasingly public figure, arguing (contrary to Martin Luther King's nonviolence) for black separatism and violence for self-defense. Watched by the F.B.I. and often demonized by the white press, he was killed after he broke with the Nation of Islam. Coauthor of *The Autobiography of Malcolm X* (1965), he is an enduring cultural icon and symbol of black pride.

15    her neck softly
below her right ear.
she would turn
to face you and arch up—
her head moving to your chest.
20    her arms sliding
round your neck. you breathe deeply.
it is quiet. in this moment
you knew
what it was all about.

25    your voice
is inside me; i loaned
my heart in exchange
for your voice.

in harlem, the long
30    avenue blocks. the miles
from heart to heart.
a slobbering emaciated man
once a man of god sprawled
on the sidewalk. he clutches
35    his bottle. pisses on himself
demands you respect him
because his great grandmother
was one-eighth cherokee.
in this moment, you knew.

40    in berkeley the fat
jewess moves the stringy brown
hair from her face saying
she would like to help you—
give you some of her time.
45    you knew.
in birmingham "get a move
on you, girl. you bet'not
be late for sunday school."
not this morning—
50    it is a design. you knew.

sometimes
light plays on my eyelashes
when my eyes
are almost closed—
55    the chrome blues and golds
the crimson and pale
ice green   the swift movements
of lights through my lashes—
fantastic—
60    the sound of mecca
inside you. you knew.

the man
inside you; the men
inside you fought.
65  fighting men inside you
made a frenzy
smelling like shit.
you reached into yourself—
deep—and scooped your frenzy
70  and rolled it to a slimy ball
and stretched your arm back
to throw

now you pace the regions
of my heart. you know
75  my blood and see
where my tears are made.
i see the beast
and hold my frenzy;
you are not lonely—
80  in my heart there are many
unmarked graves.

### The Nigga Section

slimy obscene creatures. insane
creations of a beast. you
have murdered a man. you
85  have devoured me. you
have done it with precision
like the way you stand green
in the dark sucking pus
and slicing your penis
90  into quarters—stuffing
shit through your noses.
you rotten motherfuckin bastards
murder yourselves again and again
and call it life. you have made
95  your black mother to spread
her legs   wide
you have crawled in mucous
smeared snot in your hair
let machines crawl up your cock
100  rammed your penis into garbage disposals
spread your gigantic ass from
one end of america to the other
and peeped from under your legs
and grinned a gigantic white grin
105  and called all the beasts
to fuck you hard in the ass
you have fucked your fat black mothers
you have murdered malcolm
you have torn out your own tongue

110    you have made your women
       to grow huge dicks you
       have stuffed me into your mouth
       and slobbered my blood
       in your grinning derangement.
115    your are the dumbest thing
       on the earth   the slimiest
       most rotten thing in the universe
       you motherfuckin germ
       you konk-haired blood suckin punks
120    you serpents of pestilence you
       samboes you green witches nawing the heads of infants
       you rodents you whores
       you sodomites you fat
       slimy cockroaches crawling to your
125    holes with bits of malcolm's flesh
       i hope you are smothered
       in the fall of a huge yellow moon.

                          *interlude*

       we never spent time in the mountains
       planting our blood in the land planting
130    our blood in the dirt planting our blood
       in the air   we never walked together
       down Fillmore or Fifth Avenue
       down Main Street together
       Friend we never sat together as guests
135    at a friend's table   Friend
       we never danced together as men
       in a public park   Friend we never
       spent long mornings fishing or laughed
       laughed falling all down into the dirt
140    laughed rolling in the dirt   holding
       our stomachs laughing rolling   our mouths
       wide open   huge fat laughter
       our black bodies shaking   Friend
       we never laughed like that together

       **Special Section for the Niggas on the Lower Eastside or:**
       **Invent the Divisor and Multiply**

145    you are the lice
       of the lower eastside
       you are deranged imitators
       of white boys acting out a
       fucked-up notion of the mystique
150    of black suffering. uptown
       they believe they are niggas
       here you have explanations—
       psychological, cultural, sociological,
       epistomological, cosmological, political,

155    economic, aesthetic, religious, dialectical,
       existential, jive-ass bullshit explanation
       for being niggas   you are
       deranged slobbering punks lapping in the
       ass of a beast
160    in the bars you recite
       slave rebellions you recite egypt
       you recite timbuktu you stand
       on your head and whine anger
       you are frauds   trying to legitimatize
165    what they say you are
       you are jive revolutionaries
       who will never tear this house down
       you are too terrified of cold
       too lazy to build another house

170    you lick every cranny in tompkins square
       you slurp every gutter from river to river
       you are gluttons devouring
       every cunt in every garbage can on avenue b
       you hope to find
175    an eighty ton white woman
       with a cock big enough
       to crawl inside
       you don't just want a white woman
       you want to be a white woman
180    you are concubines of a beast
       you want to be lois lane, audrey hepburn, ma perkins, lana
           turner, jean harlow, kim stanley, may west, marilyn
           monroe, sophie tucker, betty crocker, tallulah bankhead,
           judy canova, shirley temple, and trigger
185    you frauds: with your wire-rim glasses and double-breasted
           pin striped coats, and ass choaker pants
       you sing while your eyes are scraped from their sockets
       you dance while flares are rammed into your ears
       you jive mercenary frauds
190    selling nappy hair for a party invitation
       selling black   for a part in a play
       selling black   for a ride in a rolls
       selling black for a quick fuck
       selling black   for two lines on page 6,000 in the new york
           times
195    selling babies in birmingham for a smile in the den

       turn white you jive motherfucker   and ram the bomb up
           your ass.

                           *interlude*

       screams
       screams
       malcolm
200    does not hear my screams

                screams
                betty
                does not hear my screams
                screams scraping my eyes
205             screams from the guns
                screams
                screams
                the witches ecstasy
                screams screams
210             ochs sulzberger oppenheimer
                ecstasy luce ecstasy johnson
                galbraith kennedy ecstasy
                franco ecstasy bunche
                ecstasy king ecstasy salazar rowan ecstasy
215             screams
                screams
                in my nights in st. louis
                screams in my nights
                screams
220             screams in the laughter of children
                screams in the black faces
                schlesinger lodge ecstasy conant ecstasy
                stengel nimitz ecstasy screams
                screams in my head screams
225             screams six feet deep.

### The Beast Section

                i don't think it important
                to say you murdered malcolm
                or that you didn't murder malcolm
                i find you vital and powerful
230             i am aware that you use me
                but doesn't everyone
                i am comfortable in your house
                i am comfortable in your language
                i know your mind   i have an interest
235             in your security. your civilization
                compares favorably with any known
                your power is incomparable
                i understand why you would destroy
                the world rather than pass it to lesser
240             people. i agree completely.
                aristotle tells us in the physics
                that power and existence are one
                all i want is to sit quietly
                and read books and earn
245             my right to exist. come—
                i've made you a fantastic dish
                you must try it, if not now
                very soon.

                                                1968

# Judy Grahn (b. 1940)

Born and raised in Chicago until her parents, a cook and a photographer's assistant, moved to New Mexico, Grahn graduated from San Francisco State University and remained in the Bay Area thereafter. Early on she worked as a waitress, a short-order cook, a barmaid, an artist's model, a typesetter, and a nurse's aide. A serious illness placed her in a coma, but she recovered. Then she became both a writer and an activist, helping to found one of the first women's presses, working for prisoners' and welfare rights groups, participating in anti-rape campaigns, advocating on behalf of gay rights. She writes feminist, political, and lesbian poems distinguished at once by their strong cultural analysis and by their verbal and musical inventiveness. The musical changes rung in poems like "Plainsong" are as important to their message as any direct statements the poems make. Grahn has also written stories and essays.

## I Have Come to Claim Marilyn Monroe's Body

I have come to claim
Marilyn Monroe's° body
for the sake of my own.
dig it up, hand it over,
5     cram it in this paper sack.
hubba. hubba. hubba.
look at those luscious
long brown bones, that wide and crusty
pelvis. ha HA, oh she wanted so much to be serious

10    but she never stops smiling now.
Has she lost her mind?

Marilyn, be serious—they're taking
your picture, and they're taking the pictures
of eight young women in New York City
15    who murdered themselves for being pretty
by the same method as you, the very
next day, after you!
I have claimed their bodies too,
they smile up out of my paper sack
20    like brainless cinderellas.

---

2 *Monroe:* (1926–1962), American movie actress whose films include *River of No Return* (1954), *Bus Stop* (1956), and *Some Like it Hot* (1959); she became both a sex symbol and, after her suicide, a symbol of the terrible psychological price Hollywood stardom and American culture as a whole can exact from women.

the reporters are furious, they're asking
me questions
what right does a woman have
to Marilyn Monroe's body? and what
25    am I doing for lunch? They think I
mean to eat you. Their teeth are lurid
and they want to pose me, leaning
on the shovel, nude. Dont squint.
But when one of the reporters comes too close
30    I beat him, bust his camera
with your long, smooth thigh
and with your lovely knucklebone
I break his eye.

Long ago you wanted to write poems;
35    Be serious, Marilyn
I am going to take you in this paper sack
around the world, and
write on it: — the poems of Marilyn Monroe —
Dedicated to all princes,
40    the male poets who were so sorry to see you go,
before they had a crack at you.
They wept for you, and also
they wanted to stuff you
while you still had a little meat left
45    in useful places;
but they were too slow.

Now I shall take them my paper sack
and we shall act out a poem together:
"How would you like to see Marilyn Monroe,
50    in action, smiling, and without her clothes?"
We shall wait long enough to see them make familiar faces
and then I shall beat them with your skull.
hubba. hubba. hubba. hubba. hubba.
Marilyn, be serious
Today I have come to claim your body for my own.

*1970*

## Vietnamese Woman Speaking to an American Soldier

Vietnamese woman speaking
to an American soldier

Stack your body
on my body
5    make
        life
make children play
in my jungle hair
make rice flare into my sky like

10      whitest flak
        the whitest flash
        my eyes have
                burned out
        looking
15      press your swelling weapon
        here
        between us      if you
        push it quickly I should
            come
20      to understand your purpose
        what you bring us
        what you call it
        there
        in your country

*1970*

# Carol

        Carol and
        her crescent wrench
        work bench
        wooden fence
5       wide stance
        Carol and her
        pipe wrench
        pipe smoke
        pipe line
10      high climb
        smoke eyes
        chicken wire
        Carol and her
        hack saw
15      well worn
        torn back
        bad spine
        never-mind
        timberline
20      clear mind
        Carol and her
        hard glance
        stiff dance
        clean pants
25      bad ass
        lumberjack's
        wood ax
        Carol and her
        big son
30      shot gun
        lot done
        not done
        never bored
        do more

35  do less
    try to rest
    Carol and her
    new lands
    small hands
40  big plans
    Carol and her
    long time
    out shine
    worm gear
45  warm beer
    quick tears
    dont stare
    Carol is another
    queer
50  chickadee
    like me, but Carol does
    everything
    better
    if you let her.

*1972*

## Plainsong

Slowly: a plainsong from an older
woman to a younger woman

am I not   olden olden olden
it is unwanted.

5   wanting, wanting
    am I not   broken
    stolen   common

    am I not crinkled cranky poison
    am I not glinty-eyed and frozen

10  am I not   aged
    shaky   glazing
    am I not   hazy
    guarded   craven

    am I not   only
15  stingy   little
    am I not   simple
    brittle   spitting

    was I not   over
    over   ridden?

20  it is a long story
    will you be proud to be my version?

it is unwritten.

writing, writing
am I not   ancient
raging   patient

am I not   able
charming   stable
was I not   building
forming   braving

was I not   ruling
guiding   naming
was I not   brazen
crazy   chosen

even the stones would do my bidding?

it is a long story
am I not proud to be your version?

it is unspoken.

speaking, speaking
am I not   elder
berry
brandy

are you not wine before you find me
in your own beaker?

do you not turn away your shoulder?
have I not shut my mouth against you?

are you not shamed to treat me meanly
when you discover you become me?
are you not proud that you become me?

I will not shut my mouth against you.
do you not turn away your shoulder.
we who brew in the same bitters
that boil us away
we both need stronger water.

we're touched by a similar nerve.

I am new like your daughter.
I am the will, and the riverbed
made bolder
by you—my oldest river—
you are the way.

are we not   olden, olden, olden.

1972

# The Woman Whose Head Is On Fire

the woman whose head is on fire
the woman with a noisy voice
the woman with too many fingers
the woman who never smiled once in her life
5    the woman with a boney body
the woman with moles all over her

the woman who cut off her breast
the woman with a large bobbing head
the woman with one glass eye
10    the woman with broad shoulders
the woman with callused elbows
the woman with a sunken chest
the woman who is part giraffe

the woman with five gold teeth
15    the woman who looks straight ahead
the woman with enormous knees
the woman who can lick her own clitoris
the woman who screams on the trumpet
the woman whose toes grew together
20    the woman who says I am what I am

the woman with rice under her skin
the woman who owns a machete
the woman who plants potatoes
the woman who murders the kangaroo
25    the woman who stuffs clothing into a sack
the woman who makes a great racket
the woman who fixes machines
the woman whose chin is sticking out
the woman who says I will be

30    the woman who carries laundry on her head
the woman who is part horse
the woman who asks so many questions
the woman who cut somebody's throat

the woman who gathers peaches
35    the woman who carries jars on her head
the woman who howls
the woman whose nose is broken
the woman who constructs buildings
the woman who has fits on the floor
40    the woman who makes rain happen
the woman who refuses to menstruate

the woman who sets broken bones
the woman who sleeps out on the street
the woman who plays the drums
45    the woman who is part grasshopper

the woman who herds cattle
the woman whose will is unbending
the woman who hates kittens

the woman who escaped from the jailhouse
50      the woman who is walking across the desert
the woman who buries the dead
the woman who taught herself writing
the woman who skins rabbits
the woman who believes her own word
55      the woman who chews bearskin
the woman who eats cocaine
the woman who thinks about everything

the woman who has the tatoo of a bird
the woman who puts things together
60      the woman who squats on her haunches
the woman whose children are all different   colors

singing         i am the will of the woman
                  the woman
                  my will is unbending

65      when She-Who-moves-the-earth will turn over
when She Who moves, the earth will turn over.

1972

# Robert Hass (b. 1941)

Born in San Francisco and raised in San Rafael, California, Hass was educated at St. Mary's College and at Stanford University, where he received a Ph.D. In addition to four books of poetry, he has written criticism and translated European poets into English, including several volumes by Czeslaw Milosz. He has also published *The Essential Haiku: Versions of Basho, Buson, and Issa* (1994) and has taught at several schools, including Buffalo and Berkeley. Unlike poets who hope to redeem the ordinary by finding the poetic in it, Hass sometimes begins with the poetic—a radiant detail, a moment of loveliness—and works to show its relevance to daily life. Yet as the poems included here show, he is also deeply concerned with the struggle to live both morally and aesthetically and with the ways history and culture challenge such an effort. He has written about Vietnam, about Native Americans, about the American working class, and about the collapse of American cities. These concerns are unified by a recurring interest in the relationship between language and material reality and by a meditative sadness of tone that pervades much of his work.

## Rusia en 1931

    the archbishop° of San Salvador is dead, murdered by no one knows
    who. The left says the right, the right says provocateurs.

    But the families in the barrios sleep with their children beside
        them and
    a pitchfork, or a rifle if they have one.

5    And posterity is grubbing in the footnotes to find out who the
        bishop is,

    or waiting for the poet to get back to his business. Well, there's this:

    her breasts are the color of brown stones in moonlight, and paler in
    moonlight.

---

1 *archbishop*: Oscar Romero (1917–1980), Roman Catholic archbishop in El Salvador, murdered on March 24, 1980, while saying mass in San Salvador. An outspoken advocate of human rights, he was killed because of his support of the poor and his criticism of El Salvador's right-wing government. When Hass reprinted his poem in *Human Wishes* (1989) he noted that it had since become clear Romero was killed by right-wing death squads.

And that should hold them for a while. The bishop is dead. Poetry
10      proposes no solutions: it says justice is the well water of the city of
Novgorod,° black and sweet.

César Vallejo° died on a Thursday. It might have been malaria, no one
is sure; it burned through the small town of Santiago de Chuco in
an Andean valley in his childhood; it may very well have flared in
15      his veins in Paris on a rainy day;

and nine months later Osip Mandelstam° was last seen feeding off
the garbage heap of a transit camp near Vladivostok.

They might have met in Leningrad in 1931°, on a corner; two men
about forty; they could have compared gray hair at the temples, or
20      compared reviews of *Trilce* and *Tristia* in 1922.

What French they would have spoken! And what the one thought
would save Spain killed the other.°

"I am no wolf by blood," Mandelstam wrote that year. "Only an equal
could break me."

25      And Vallejo: "Think of the unemployed. Think of the forty million
families of the hungry. . . . "

*1989*

# A Story About the Body

The young composer, working that summer at an artist's colony, had
watched her for a week. She was Japanese, a painter, almost sixty, and
he thought he was in love with her. He loved her work, and her work
was like the way she moved her body, used her hands, looked at him
directly when she made amused and considered answers to his ques-

---

11 *Novgorod:* in western Russia, one of its oldest cities, it was ruled by Alexander Nevsky
from 1238–1263, after which it rivaled Moscow until being laid waste by Czar Ivan IV in
1570; rebuilt, it was later captured by the Germans in World War II and held by them for
several years.
12 *Vallejo:* (1892–1938), Peruvian poet and novelist, born in the Andean town of Santiago
de Chuco. *Trilce* (1922) was a volume of radical experimental poetry, some of it written in
a Peruvian prison. He lived in Paris from 1923 to 1931, when he was deported, and moved
to Spain, where he joined the Communist party. He became active in the antifacist move-
ment when the Spanish Civil War broke out.
16 *Mandelstam:* (1891–1938), Russian modernist poet and literary critic, whose second vol-
ume of poetry, *Tristia* (1922) was attacked by Communist party critics because its author
was reluctant to espouse the revolution in his work. A proposed 1933 volume of collected
works was withdrawn when he refused to meet censors' demands for cuts. The following
year he was arrested for writing an epigram on Stalin and reading it to friends. After a few
years of exile, he returned to Moscow but was arrested again and died in custody at a tran-
sit camp near Vladivostok.
18 *Leningrad in 1931*: Vallejo made trips to Russia in 1928, 1929, and 1931; it was hypo-
thetically possible for him to have met Mandelstam.
22 *other*: "What the one [Vallejo] thought would save Spain killed the other [Mandelstam]."
The subject of the sentence is communism.

tions. One night, walking back from a concert, they came to her door and she turned to him and said, "I think you would like to have me. I would like that too, but I must tell you that I have had a double mastectomy," and when he didn't understand, "I've lost both my breasts." The radiance that he had carried around in his belly and chest cavity—like music—withered very quickly, and he made himself look at her when he said, "I'm sorry. I don't think I could." He walked back to his own cabin through the pines, and in the morning he found a small blue bowl on the porch outside his door. It looked to be full of rose petals, but he found when he picked it up that the rose petals were on top; the rest of the bowl—she must have swept them from the corners of her studio—was full of dead bees.

*1989*

# Sharon Olds (b. 1942)

Olds was born in San Francisco and educated at Stanford and Columbia, earning a Ph.D. at the latter. She grew up in a conservative religious family for which the thought was the moral equivalent of the deed; thoughts themselves, therefore, were to be self-policed. The project of becoming a writer has for her partly been one of unlearning that family lesson; she has trained herself to take risks and take up subjects other poets have ignored. A short, outrageously witty poem "The Pope's Penis" is perhaps the most notorious instance of that, but in the more ambitious poems reprinted here she has also enlarged our sense of what it is possible to do in poetry.

For some years Olds has taught poetry workshops in the Graduate Creative Writing Program at New York University, while helping to run N.Y.U.'s workshop program at Goldwater Hospital, a nine-hundred-bed public hospital for the severely physically disabled, on New York's Roosevelt Island. She has published five volumes of poetry, whose focus is alternately historical, as with "Ideographs," and "Photograph of the Girl," and personal, as with "The Waiting" and "His Father's Cadaver." Yet in both cases her central subjects are death and sexuality or regeneration, or the relations between the two, as in "Photograph of the Girl." While she is regularly admired for her candor, the praise pales before the singularly uncompromising, even harrowing, quality of her vision. In the intricacy of her attention to subjects we would rather repress, and in the unsparing negotiation of her own feelings, she surpasses even Plath. *The Father* (1992), from which "The Waiting" is taken, is a daughter's book-length poetic chronicle of her father's death from cancer, unflinching in its recitation of her ambivalence and his physical deterioration. One reviewer described it as "something close to a spiritual ordeal for the reader." Fully understanding Olds' work requires recognizing how the public and private poems underwrite one another and make each other possible. While she was writing *The Father,* in fact, she was simultaneously composing an as-yet unpublished poem sequence on World War II. Sometimes the public and the private explicitly interpenetrate, as in her short poem "Japanese-American Farmhouse, California, 1942." The poem describes the abandoned, looted former home of World War II Japanese American internees, then ends with what strikes us as a stunning indictment of her family: "I was born, that day, near there, / in wartime, of ignorant people." But of course the ignorance typifies not only her family but most of the country. On the other hand, "Ideographs" and "Portait of the Girl" respond to fairly well-known photographs, but do not aim to replace a prose historical account; instead the poems teach us how one responsible consciousness can respond to public events.

# Ideographs

*(a photograph of China, 1905)*

The small scaffolds, boards in the form of
ideographs, the size of a person,
lean against a steep wall of
dressed stone. One is the simple
5        shape of a man. The man on it
is asleep, his arms nailed to the wood.
No timber is wasted; his fingertips
curl in at the very end of the plank
as a child's hands open in sleep.
10      The other man is awake—he looks
directly at us. He is fixed to a more
complex scaffold, a diagonal cross-piece
pointing one arm up, one down,
and his legs are bent, the spikes through his ankles
15      holding them up off the ground,
his knees cocked, the folds of his robe flowing
sideways as if he were suspended in the air
in flight, his naked leg bared.
They are awaiting execution, tilted against the wall
20      as you'd prop up a tool until you needed it.
They'll be shouldered up over the crowd and
carried through the screaming. The sleeper will wake.
The twisted one will fly above the faces, his
garment rippling.
25      Here there is still the backstage quiet,
the dark at the bottom of the wall, the props
leaning in the grainy half-dusk.
He looks at us in the silence. He says
*Save me, there is still time.*

1984

# Photograph of the Girl

The girl sits on the hard ground,
the dry pan of Russia, in the drought
of 1921, stunned,
eyes closed, mouth open,
5      raw hot wind blowing
sand in her face. Hunger and puberty are
taking her together. She leans on a sack,
layers of clothes fluttering in the heat,
the new radius of her arm curved.
10      She cannot be not beautiful, but she is
starving. Each day she grows thinner, and her bones
grow longer, porous. The caption says
she is going to starve to death that winter
with millions of others. Deep in her body
15      the ovaries let out her first eggs,
golden as drops of grain.

1984

## Things That Are Worse Than Death

(for Margaret Randall)

You are speaking of Chile,
of the woman who was arrested
with her husband and their five-year-old son.
You tell how the guards tortured the woman, the man, the child,
5     in front of each other,
"as they like to do."
Things that are worse than death.
I can see myself taking my son's ash-blond hair in my fingers,
tilting back his head before he knows what is happening,
10    slitting his throat, slitting my own throat
to save us that. Things that are worse than death:
this new idea enters my life.
The guard enters my life, the sewage of his body,
"as they like to do." The eyes of the five-year-old boy, Dago,
15    watching them with his mother. The eyes of his mother
watching them with Dago. And in my living room as a child,
the word, Dago. And nothing I experienced was worse than death,
life was beautiful as our blood on the stone floor
to save us that—my son's eyes on me,
20    my eyes on my son—the ram-boar on our bodies
making us look at our old enemy and bow in welcome,
gracious and eternal death
who permits departure.

1984

## The Waiting

No matter how early I would get up
and come out of the guest room, and look down the hall,
there between the wings of the wing-back chair
my father would be sitting, his head calm
5    and dark between the wings. He sat
unmoving, like something someone has made,
his robe fallen away from his knees,
he sat and stared at the swimming pool
in the dawn. By then, he knew he was dying,
10    he seemed to approach it as a job to be done
which he knew how to do. He got up early
for the graveyard shift. When he heard me coming down the
hall, he would not turn—he had
a way of holding still to be looked at,
15    as if a piece of sculpture could sense
the gaze which was running over it—
he would wait with that burnished, looked-at look until
the hem of my nightgown came into view,
then slew his eyes up at me, without
20    moving his head, and wait, the kiss
came to him, he did not go to it.

Now he would have some company
as he tried to swallow an eighth of a teaspoon
of coffee, he would have his child to give him
25   the cup to spit into, his child to empty it—
I would be there all day, watch him nap,
be there when he woke, sit with him
until the day ended, and he could get back into
bed with his wife. Not until the next
30   dawn would he be alone again, night-
watchman of matter, sitting, facing
the water—the earth without form, and void,
darkness upon the face of it, as if
waiting for his daughter.

*1995*

## His Father's Cadaver

The old man had always wanted
to end up there, on the chrome table,
the Medical School Dissection Room
on that island in the North Atlantic
5   his heaven. So his only child signed the papers—
son, M.D. He knew that the students
would start with a butterfly incision,
cutting the body down the center, lifting
the skin of the chest and the abdomen up
10   and out to the sides. He had heard the high
neutral scream of the bone-saw, he knew
they would pry back the ribs to get at the heart.
He knew the pattern they followed, he had done it himself—
chest, abdomen, head, hands,
15   feet. They would stand there, the medical students,
day after day, around his father,
one doing a knee, one
the bowels, the scalp, the eye, the face.
This is what his father had wanted,
20   to throw himself bodily into the hospital like a
roe-fish thrown back, to enter his students
directly, as knowledge—
so the wreckage could be seen as good, even
his chest, which might look gnawed, his jaws
25   shining through as they removed his lips,
even the pool of slurry like the fish factory—
and every week his son had some idea
where they might be, as those at home
will chart the route of Arctic explorers,
30   the pins on the map moving in
through the cold toward the center. He knew if it got
too crowded at the gurney, someone would take
the brain over to another table
to separate it, into its parts, like a
35   god his father would move, piece

by piece, out into the world. At night,
they would cover everything with plastic bags,
the veins and arteries lying fanned out
across the back of the hand—by day they were
40      murmuring Latin, memorizing the old man.
For six months, from two thousand miles,
the son follows it, with occasional horror,
with respect, the long dismantling
of that man who used to grease him down
45      and lower him into the Bay of Fundy°
to check on his wave machine, which he hoped
would harness the power of the sea, that man who had
delivered him, his palm waiting under
the head when it came forth, trusting
50      himself, best, to touch, first,
the mortal boy they had made.

                                                        *1995*

---

45 *Bay of Fundy:* in eastern Canada.

# Louise Glück (b. 1943)

Born in New York City and raised on Long Island, Glück was educated at Sarah Lawrence College and Columbia. She lives in Plainfield, Vermont, but has taught at a number of schools, including Columbia University and Williams College. Glück's 1994 volume of essays, *Proofs and Theories,* includes remarks on the autobiographical overtones of a number of her early poems, which were often dark portraits of family and childhood. Those poems sometimes opted to transform personal experience by integrating it with mythic allusions, a technique given a perhaps more witty and ambitious realization in *The Meadowlands* (1996), a book-length poem sequence from which all the poems here are taken. *The Meadowlands* chronicles a contemporary marriage in crisis, with characters taken from Homer's *Odyssey,* including Odysseus's wife Penelope and the witch Circe, who turned Odysseus's crew into animals and delayed him on his return voyage to Ithaca after the Trojan War. Indeed, it is simultaneously a rereading of the classical text and a contemporary story; neither has absolute priority. The fusion of the two perspectives lets her speakers at once be oracular and ordinary. Also see Glück's *The First Four Books of Poems* (1995).

## Penelope's Song

Little soul, little perpetually undressed one,
do now as I bid you, climb
the shelf-like branches of the spruce tree;
wait at the top, attentive, like
5      a sentry or look-out. He will be home soon;
it behooves you to be
generous. You have not been completely
perfect either; with your troublesome body
you have done things you shouldn't
10    discuss in poems. Therefore
call out to him over the open water, over the bright water
with your dark song, with your grasping,
unnatural song—passionate,
like Maria Callas.° Who
15    wouldn't want you? Whose most demonic appetite
could you possibly fail to answer? Soon
he will return from wherever he goes in the meantime,
suntanned from his time away, wanting

---

14 *Callas:* (1923–1977) American operatic soprano.

his grilled chicken. Ah, you must greet him,
20    you must shake the boughs of the tree
to get his attention,
but carefully, carefully, lest
his beautiful face be marred
by too many falling needles.

## Quiet Evening

You take my hand; then we're alone
in the life-threatening forest. Almost immediately

we're in a house; Noah's
grown and moved away; the clematis after ten years
5    suddenly flowers white.

More than anything in the world
I love these evenings when we're together,
the quiet evenings in summer, the sky still light at this hour.

So Penelope took the hand of Odysseus,
10    not to hold him back but to impress
this peace on his memory:

from this point on, the silence through which you move
is my voice pursuing you.

## Parable of the King

The great king looking ahead
saw not fate but simply
dawn glittering over
the unknown island: as a king
5    he thought in the imperative—best
not to reconsider direction, best
to keep going forward
over the radiant water. Anyway,
what is fate but a strategy for ignoring
10    history, with its moral
dilemmas, a way of regarding
the present, where decisions
are made, as the necessary
link between the past (images of the king
15    as a young prince) and the glorious future (images
of slave girls). Whatever
it was ahead, why did it have to be
so blinding? Who could have known
that wasn't the usual sun
20    but flames rising over a world
about to become extinct?

## Parable of the Hostages

The Greeks are sitting on the beach
wondering what to do when the war ends. No one
wants to go home, back
to that bony island; everyone wants a little more

5   of what there is in Troy, more
life on the edge, that sense of every day as being
packed with surprises. But how to explain this
to the ones at home to whom
fighting a war is a plausible

10  excuse for absence, whereas
exploring one's capacity for diversion
is not. Well, this can be faced
later; these
are men of action, ready to leave

15  insight to the women and children.
Thinking things over in the hot sun, pleased
by a new strength in their forearms, which seem
more golden than they did at home, some
begin to miss their families a little,

20  to miss their wives, to want to see
if the war has aged them. And a few grow
slightly uneasy: what if war
is just a male version of dressing up,
a game devised to avoid

25  profound spiritual questions? Ah,
but it wasn't only the war. The world had begun
calling them, an opera beginning with the war's
loud chords and ending with the floating aria of the sirens.
There on the beach, discussing the various

30  timetables for getting home, no one believed
it could take ten years to get back to Ithaca;
no one foresaw that decade of insoluble dilemmas—oh
   unanswerable
affliction of the human heart: how to divide
the world's beauty into acceptable

35  and unacceptable loves! On the shores of Troy,
how could the Greeks know
they were hostage already: who once
delays the journey is
already enthralled; how could they know

40  that of their small number
some would be held forever by the dreams of pleasure,
some by sleep, some by music?

## Circe's Power

I never turned anyone into a pig.
Some people are pigs; I make them
look like pigs.

I'm sick of your world
that lets the outside disguise the inside.

Your men weren't bad men;
undisciplined life
did that to them. As pigs,

under the care of
me and my ladies, they
sweetened right up.

Then I reversed the spell,
showing you my goodness
as well as my power. I saw

we could be happy here,
as men and women are
when their needs are simple. In the same breath,

I foresaw your departure,
your men with my help braving
the crying and pounding sea. You think

a few tears upset me? My friend,
every sorceress is
a pragmatist at heart; nobody

sees essence who can't
face limitation. If I wanted only to hold you

I could hold you prisoner.

## Circe's Grief

In the end, I made myself
known to your wife as
a god would, in her own house, in
Ithaca, a voice
without a body: she
paused in her weaving, her head turning
first to the right, then left
though it was hopeless of course
to trace that sound to any
objective source: I doubt
she will return to her loom
with what she knows now. When
you see her again, tell her
this is how a god says goodbye:
if i am in her head forever
I am in your life forever.

# Reunion

When Odysseus has returned at last
unrecognizable to Ithaca and killed
the suitors swarming the throne room,
very delicately he signals to Telemachus
5      to depart: as he stood twenty years ago,
he stands now before Penelope.
On the palace floor, wide bands of sunlight turning
from gold to red. He tells her
nothing of those years, choosing to speak instead
10     exclusively of small things, as would be
the habit of a man and woman long together:
once she sees who he is, she will know what he's done.
And as he speaks, ah,
tenderly he touches her forearm.

                                                    *1996*

# Michael Palmer (b. 1943)

Born and raised in New York City, Palmer was educated at Harvard and lived on the East Coast before moving to San Francisco. The most lyrical of the well-known writers associated with L=A=N=G=U=A=G=E poetry—he is sometimes considered one of the movement's precursors—Palmer shares their interest in fragmented and disjunctive narrativity, depersonalized speakers, and investigations of how language works as an independent system of meanings. But musicality and wit, along with a regular haunting by vestigial narrativity, distinguish his work from many others in the movement. Similarly, he shares their interest in philosophy and critical theory, but has a stronger surrealist component in his poetry. Several of his books include poem sequences. Palmer has taught occasionally and collaborated on several projects with dancers and artists, including writing numerous dance scenarios for the Margaret Jenkins Dance Company and books with the painters Irving Petlin and Sandro Chia.

## Song of the Round Man

for Sarah when she's older

The round and sad-eyed man puffed cigars as if
he were alive. Gillyflowers
to the left of the apple, purple bells to the right

and a grass-covered hill behind.
5    I am sad today said the sad-eyed man
for I have locked my head in a Japanese box

and lost the key.
I am sad today he told me
for there are gillyflowers by the apple

10    and purple bells I cannot see.
Will you look at them for me
he asked, and tell me what you find?

I cannot I replied
for my eyes have grown sugary and dim
15    from reading too long by candlelight.

Tell me what you've read then
said the round and sad-eyed man.
I cannot I replied

20    for my memory has grown tired and dim
from looking at things that can't be seen
by any kind of light

and I've locked my head in a Japanese box
and thrown away the key.
Then I am you and you are me

25    said the sad-eyed man as if alive.
I'll write you in where I should be
between the gillyflowers and the purple bells

and the apple and the hill
and we'll puff cigars from noon till night
as if we were alive.

                                    *1981*

## All Those Words

All those words we once used for things but have now discarded in or-
der to come to know things. There in the mountains I discovered the
last tree or the letter A. What it said to me was brief, "I am surrounded
by the uselessness of blue falling away on all sides into fields of bitter
wormwood, all-heal and centaury. If you crush one of these herbs be-
tween your fingers the scent will cling to your hand but its particles
will be quite invisible. This is a language you cannot understand." Dis-
mantling the beams of the letter tree I carried them one by one down
the slope to our house and added them to the fire. Later over the coals
we grilled red mullets flavored with oil, pepper, salt and wild oregano.

                                    *1984*

## I Have Answers to All of Your Questions

for C. E.

I have answers to all of your questions. My name is the word for wall,
my head is buried in that wall. When I leap over that wall I think of
my head, I can assure you. And into the garden: paradise—broken bot-
tles, tractor tires, shattered adjectives (fragments of a wall). The sky
beyond on fire, this is true. The hills beyond a glinting gold, also true.
And you married to that clown, that ape, that gribbling assassin of light.
Your daughters will avenge you. And into the garden: paradise—the
soldiers, their rifles, their boots, their eyes narrowed, searching for a
lost head. Or a stolen head? The head of a pornographer. There, I've
said it. Pink nipples grow hard as she brushes them with her lips. Moans
can be heard coming from poems—poems you, Senator, want desper-
ately to read but will not let yourself, since you are a citizen, proud

and erect. And out of the head laughter, tears, tiny bubbles of spit. It
is a head from another century, the last one or the next.

*1988*

## Fifth Prose

Because I'm writing about the snow not the sentence
Because there is a card—a visitor's card—and on that card there
    are words of ours arranged in a row

and on those words we have written house, we have written leave
    this house, we
have written be this house, the spiral of a house, channels through
    this house

5      and we have written The Provinces and The Reversal and some-
    thing called the Human Poems
though we live in a valley on the Hill of Ghosts

Still for many days the rain will continue to fall
A voice will say Father I am burning

Father I've removed a stone from a wall, erased a picture from that wall,
10     a picture of ships—cloud ships—pressing toward the sea

words only
taken limb by limb apart

Because we are not alive not alone
but ordinary extracts from the tablets

15     Hassan the Arab and his wife
who did vaulting and balancing

Coleman and Burgess, and Adele Newsome
pitched among the spectators one night

Lizzie Keys
20     and Fred who fell from the trapeze

into the sawdust
and wasn't hurt at all

and Jacob Hall the rope-dancer
Little Sandy and Sam Sault

25     Because there is a literal shore, a letter that's blood-red
Because in this dialect the eyes are crossed or quartz

seeing swimmer and seeing rock
statue then shadow

and here in the lake
30　　first a razor then a fact

*1988*

# Autobiography

*(for Poul Borum)*

All clocks are clouds.

Parts are greater than the whole.°

A philosopher is starving in a rooming house, while it rains outside.

He regards the self as just another sign.°

5　　Winter roses are invisible.

Late ice sometimes sings.


A and *Not-A* are the same.°

My dog does not know me.

Violins, like dreams, are suspect.

10　　I come from Kolophon, or perhaps some small island.

The strait has frozen, and people are walking—a few skating—
　　　across it.

On the crescent beach, a drowned deer.


A woman with one hand, her thighs around your neck.

The world is all that is displaced.°

15　　Apples in a stall at the streetcorner by the Bahnhof, pale yellow to
　　　blackish red.

Memory does not speak.

Shortness of breath, accompanied by tinnitus.

---

2 *whole:* the notion that the whole is greater than the sum of its parts is central to di-
alectical thinking in Hegel, Marx, and gestalt theory; a competing view, that the sum of
the parts equals the whole, pervades analytic thought.
4 *sign:* the notion that the self is a construct of signs is a commonplace structuralist claim.
7 *same:* this line contradicts a standard law of logic.
14 *displaced:* Cf. the famous formulation in *Tractatus Logico-philosophicus* (1921) by Aus-
trian philosopher Ludwig Wittgenstein (1899–1951): "The world is everything that is the
case."

The poet's stutter and the philosopher's.

The self is assigned to others.

20      A room from which, at all times, the moon remains visible.

Leningrad cafe: a man missing the left side of his face.

Disappearance of the sun from the sky above Odessa.

True description of that sun.°

A philosopher lies in a doorway, discussing the theory of colors

25      with himself

the theory of self with himself, the concept of number, eternal re-
        turn,° the sidereal pulse

logic of types, Buridan° sentences, the *lekton.*

Why now that smoke off the lake?

30      Word and thing are the same.°

Many times white ravens have I seen.

That all planes are infinite, by extension.

She asks, Is there a map of these gates?

She asks, Is this the one called Passages, or is it that one to the
        west?

35      Thus released, the dark angels converse with the angels of light.

They are not angels.

Something else.

                                                                *1995*

---

23 *sun:* see "A True Account of Talking to the Sun at Fire Island" by Frank O'Hara in the
present volume, itself based in part on an earlier poem by Russian poet Vladimir
Mayakovsky (1894–1930).
26 *eternal return:* a doctrine in the work of German philosopher Friedrich Nietzsche
(1844–1900).
28 *types, Buridan:* British philosopher Bertrand Russell (1872–1970) developed a theory of
types to solve certain logical problems. Jean Buridan was a fourteenth-century French
philosopher who explored the logic of equivalent choices.
30 *same:* the line evokes a Renaissance theory of meaning, one that structuralism has re-
jected.

# Paul Violi (b. 1944)

Born in New York City, raised on Long Island, and educated at Boston University, Violi has worked as managing editor of *Architectural Forum,* on various special projects for Universal Limited Art Editions, and has taught at several colleges, including New York University. He has published seven books of poetry since the 1970s. "Index" is not the only poem of his that textualizes apparently innocent linguistic contexts. "Errata" achieves similar results with an invented errata page. "Marina" makes a socially unstable poem out of real or imagined boats' names. See *Likewise* (1988) and *The Curious Builder* (1993).

## Index

Hudney, Sutej IX, X, XI, 7, 9, 25, 58, 60, 61, 64
    Plates 5, 10, 15
    Childhood 70, 71
    Education 78, 79, 80
5    Early relationship with family 84
    Enters academy, honors 84
    Arrest and bewilderment 85
    Formation of spatial theories 90
    "Romance of Ardoy, The" 92
10    Second arrest 93
    Early voyages, life in the Pyrenees 95
    Marriage 95
    Abandons landscape painting 96
    Third arrest 97
15    Weakness of character, inconstancy 101
    First signs of illness, advocation of celibacy 106, 107
    Advocates abolishment of celibacy 110
    Expulsion from Mazar 110
    Collaborations with Fernando Gee 111
20    Composes lines beginning: "Death, wouldst that I had died /
        While thou wert still a mystery." 117
    Consequences of fame, violent rows, professional disputes 118,
        119
    Disavows all his work 120
    Bigamy, scandals, illness, admittance of being "easily crazed, like
        snow." 128
    Theories of perspective published 129

25 Birth of children 129
 Analysis of important works:
   *Wine glass with fingerprints*
   *Nude on a blue sofa*
   *The drunken fox trappers*
   *Man wiping tongue with large towel*
   *Hay bales stacked in a field*
   *Self portrait*
   *Self portrait with cat*
   *Self portrait with frozen mop*
   *Self portrait with belching duck* 135
 Correspondence with Cecco Angolieri 136
 Dispute over attribution of lines: "I have as large supply of
  evils / as January has not flowerings." 137
 Builds first greenhouse 139
30 Falling-out with Angolieri 139
 Flees famine 144
 Paints *Starved cat eating snow* 145
 Arrested for selling sacks of wind to gullible peasants 146
 Imprisonment and bewilderment 147
35 Disavows all his work 158
 Invents the collar stay 159
 Convalescence with third wife 162
 Complains of "a dense and baleful wind blowing the words I
  write off the page." 165
 Meets with Madam T. 170
40 Departures, mortal premonitions, "I think I'm about to snow." 176
 Disavows all his work 181
 Arrest and pardon 182
 Last days 183
 Last words 184, 185, 186, 187, 188, 189, 190

                   1982

# Carolyn M. Rodgers (b. 1945)

Carolyn Rodgers grew up in Chicago, Illinois, where her intellectual and political vision was shaped in part by the Organization of Black African Culture and by poet Gwendolyn Brooks. Her poetry of the late 1960s voices the revolutionary nationalism of the Black Arts movement, but in a free-verse style with street slang that some of the male leaders of the movement found inappropriate for a woman. Even in these early poems, she registers notable tension between her revolutionary program and African American culture's more traditional commitments. In the 1970s, the period emphasized in this selection, she broke with her earlier militancy and emphasized her family heritage and the church's foundational role in her life. Rodgers was educated at Roosevelt University and the University of Chicago. She has also written short stories and influential literary criticism.

## how i got ovah

i can tell you
about them
i have shaken rivers
out of my eyes
5     i have waded eyelash deep
have crossed rivers
have shaken the water weed out
of my lungs
have swam for strength
10    pulled by strength
through waterfalls with electric beats
i have bore the shocks
of water deep deep
waterlogs are my bones
15    i have shaken the water free of my hair
have kneeled on the banks
and kissed my ancestors of the dirt
whose rich dark root fingers rose up reached out
grabbed and pulled me rocked me cupped me
20    gentle strong and firm
carried me
made me swim for strength
cross rivers
though i shivered

25          was wet was cold
            and wanted to sink down
            and float as water, yea—
            i can tell you.
            i have shaken rivers
            out of my eyes.

                                                    *1975*


## and when the revolution came

(for Rayfield and Lillie and the whole rest)

            and when the revolution came
            the militants said
            niggers wake up
            you got to comb yo hair
5           the natural way
                        and the church folks say oh yeah? sho 'nuff . . .
            and they just kept on going to church
            gittin on they knees and praying
            and tithing and building and buying

10          and when the revolution came
            the militants said
            niggers you got to change
            the way you dress
            and the church folk say oh yeah?
15                      and they just kept on going to church
            with they knit suits and flowery bonnets
            and gittin on they knees and praying
            and tithing and building and buying

            and when the revolution came
20          the militants said
            you got to give up
            white folks and the
                        church folk say oh yeah? well?
            never missed what we never had
25          and they jest kept on going to church
            with they nice dresses and suits and
            praying and building and buying

            and when the revolution came
            the militants say you got to give up
30          pork and eat only brown rice and
            health food and the
                        church folks said uh hummmm
            and they just kept on eating they chitterlings and
            going to church and praying and tithing and
35          building and buying

and when the revolution came
the militants said
all you church going niggers
got to give up easter and christmas
40    and the bible
cause that's the white man's religion
and the church folks said well well well well well

and then the militants said we got to
build black institutions where our children
45    call each other sister and brother
and can grow beautiful, black and strong and grow in black grace
and the church folks said yes, lord Jesus we been calling each other
sister and brother a long time

and the militants looked around
50    after a while and said hey, look at all
these fine buildings we got scattered throughout
the black communities some of em built wid schools and nurseries
who do they belong to?

and the church folks said, yeah.
55    we been waiting fo you militants
to realize that the church is an eternal rock
now why don't you militants jest come on in
we been waiting for you
we can show you how to build
60        anything that needs building
and while we're on our knees, at that.

                                                        *1975*

## mama's God

mama's God never was no white man.
her My Jesus, Sweet Jesus never was neither.
the color they had was the color of
her aches and trials, the tribulations of her heart
5    mama never had no saviour that would turn
his back on her because she was black
when mama prayed, she knew who she
was praying to and who she was praying to
didn't and ain't got
no color.

                                                        *1975*

# Ron Silliman (b. 1946)

Born in Pasco, Washington, Silliman grew up in Albany, California, just north of Berkeley. He was educated at Merritt College, San Francisco State University, and the University of California at Berkeley. He has worked as an organizer in prisoner and tenant movements, as well as a lobbyist, teacher, and college administrator. In the 1970s, he first edited *Labyrinth* for the Committee for Prisoner Humanity and Justice and then edited the *Tenderloin Times* for San Francisco's Central City Hospital House. For several years he was executive editor of *Socialist Review,* and since then has worked in the computer industry in Pennsylvania as a marketing communications specialist. A leading poet and theorist of the L=A=N=G=U=A=G=E poetry movement, author of the theoretical work *The New Sentence* (1987) and editor of the movement's most ambitious anthology, *In the American Tree* (1986), he has often used formal experiments to help us see how language functions as an autonomous system and shapes our understanding of the world. Silliman's work is also notable for its humor, its social conscience, and for its interest in the relationship between ordinary experience and narrativity. He often grounds his projects in his deliberate experiments; thus *Ketjak,* from which we reprint opening and closing sections, is a prose poem constructed of expanding paragraphs. The first paragraph has one sentence, while the second contains that sentence plus another; the third paragraph uses the two previous sentences, sometimes subtly altered, and adds two more; the fourth includes the previous four but adds four new sentences, and so forth. The previous sentences are uncannily altered by new contexts, and the reader is compelled to focus on sentence creation and the mutability of meaning.

## from *Ketjak*°

Revolving door.

Revolving door. A sequence of objects which to him appears to be a caravan of fellaheen, a circus, begins a slow migration to the right vanishing point on the horizon line.

Revolving door. Fountains of the financial district. Houseboats beached at the point of low tide, only to float again when the sunset is reflected in the water. A sequence of objects which to him appears to be a caravan of fellaheen, a circus, camels pulling wagons of bear cages, tamed

---

**poem title:** *Ketjak* is a book-length sequence of twelve prose poems.

ostriches in toy hats, begins a slow migration to the right vanishing point on the horizon line.

Revolving door. First flies of summer. Fountains of the financial district spout. She was a unit in a bum space, she was a damaged child. Dark brown houseboats beached at the point of low tide—men atop their cabin roofs, idle, play a dobro, a jaw's harp, a 12-string guitar—only to float again when the sunset is reflected in the water. I want the grey-blue grain of western summer. A cardboard box of wool sweaters on top of the book case to indicate Home. A sequence of objects, silhouettes, which to him appears to be a caravan of fellaheen, a circus, dromedaries pulling wagons bearing tiger cages, tamed ostriches in toy hats, begins a slow migration to the right vanishing point on the horizon line.

Revolving door. Earth science. Fountains of the financial district spout soft water in a hard wind. How the heel rises and the ankle bends to carry the body from one stair to the next. She was a unit in a bum space, she was a damaged child. The fishermen's cormorants wear rings around their necks to keep them from swallowing, to force them to surrender the catch. Dark brown houseboats beached at the point of low tide—men atop their cabin roofs, idle, play a dobro, a jaw's harp, a 12 string guitar—only to float again when the sunset is reflected in the water. Silverfish, potato bugs. What I want is the gray-blue grain of western summer. The nurse, by a subtle shift of weight, moves in front of the student in order to more rapidly board the bus. A cardboard box of wool sweaters on top of the book case to indicate Home. A day of rain in the middle of June. A sequence of objects, silhouettes, which to him appears to be a caravan of fellaheen, a circus, dromedaries pulling wagons bearing tiger cages, fringed surreys, tamed ostriches in toy hats, begins a slow migration to the right vanishing point on the horizon line. We ate them.

Revolving door. The garbage barge at the bridge. Earth science. Resemblance. Fountains of the financial district spout soft water in a hard wind. The bear flag in the plaza. How the heel rises and the ankle bends to carry the body from one stair to the next. A tenor sax is a toy. She was a unit in a bum space, she was a damaged child, sitting in her rocker by the window. I'm unable to find just the right straw hat. The fishermen's cormorants wear rings around their necks to keep them from swallowing, to force them to surrender the catch. We drove through fields of artichokes. Dark brown houseboats beached at the point of low tide—men atop their cabin roofs, idle, play a dobro, a jaw's harp, a 12 string guitar–only to float again when the sunset is reflected in the water of Richardson Bay. Write this down in a green notebook. Silverfish, potato bugs. A tenor sax is a weapon. What I want is the gray-blue grain of western summer. Mention sex. The nurse, by a subtle redistribution of weight, shift of gravity's center, moves in front of the student of oriental porcelain in order to more rapidly board the bus. Awake, but still in bed, I listen to cars pass, doors, birds, children are day's first voices. A cardboard box of wool sweaters on top of the bookcase to indicate Home. Attention is all. A day of rain in the middle of June. Modal rounders. A sequence of objects, silhouettes, which to him appears to be a caravan of fellaheen, a circus, dromedaries pulling wagons bearing tiger cages, fringed surreys, tamed ostriches in toy hats, begins a slow migration to the right vanishing point on the horizon line. The implications of power within the ability to draw a single, vertical straight line. Look at that room filled with fleshy babies. We ate them.

Revolving door. How will I know when I make a mistake. The garbage barge at the bridge. The throb in the wrist. Earth science. Their first goal was to separate the workers from their means of production. He bears a resemblance. A drawing of a Balinese spirit with its face in its stomach. Fountains of the financial district spout soft water in a hard wind. In a far room of the apartment I can hear music and a hammer. The bear flag in the black marble plaza. Rapid transit. How the heel rises and the ankle bends to carry the body from one stair to the next. The desire for coffee. A tenor sax is a toy. Snow is remarkable to one not accustomed to it. She was a unit in a bum space, she was a damaged child, sitting in her rocker by the window. The formal beauty of a back porch. I'm unable to find just the right straw hat. He hit the bricks, took a vacation, got rolled up, popped, as they say. The fishermen's cormorants wear rings around their necks to keep them from swallowing, to force them to surrender their catch. She had only the slightest pubic hair. We drove through fields of artichokes. Feet, do your stuff. Dark brown houseboats beached at the point of low tide— men atop their cabin roofs, idle, play a dobro, a jaw's harp, a 12 string guitar—only to float again when the sunset is reflected in the water of Richardson Bay. Frying yellow squash in the wok. Write this down in a green notebook. Television in the 1950s. Silverfish, potato bugs. We stopped for hot chocolate topped with whipped cream and to discuss the Sicilian Defense. A tenor sax is a weapon. The Main Library was a grey weight in a white rain. What I want is the gray-blue grain of western summer. Subtitles lower your focus. Mention sex, fruit. Drip candles kept atop old, empty bottles of wine. The young nurse in sunglasses, by a subtle redistribution of weight, shift of gravity's center, moves in front of the black student of oriental porcelain in order to more rapidly board the bus home, before all the seats are taken. Are pears form. Awake, but still in bed, I listen to cars pass, doors, birds, children are day's first voices. Eventually the scratches became scabs. A cardboard box of wool sweaters on top of the bookcase to indicate Home. Bedlingtons were at first meant to hunt rats in coal mines. Attention is all. He knew how to hold an adz. A day of rain in the middle of June. The gamelan is not simple. Modal rounders. A sequence of objects, silhouettes, which to him appears to be a caravan of fellaheen, a circus, dromedaries pulling wagons bearing tiger cages, fringed surreys, tamed ostriches in toy hats, begins a slow migration to the right vanishing point on the horizon line. Slag iron. The implicit power within the ability to draw a single, vertical straight line. That was when my nose began to peel. Look at that room filled with fleshy babies, incubating. A tall glass of tawny port. We ate them.

*1978*

# from *Sunset Debris*

Can you feel it? Does it hurt? Is this too soft? Do you like it? Do you
like this? Is this how you like it? Is it alright? Is he there? Is he breath-
ing? Is it him? Is it near? Is it hard? Is it cold? Does it weigh much?
Is it heavy? Do you have to carry it far? Are those hills? Is this where
we get off? Which one are you? Are we there yet? Do we need to bring
sweaters? Where is the border between blue and green? Has the mail
come? Have you come yet? Is it perfect bound? Do you prefer ball-
points? Do you know which insect you most resemble? Is it the red
one? Is that your hand? Want to go out? What about dinner? What
does it cost? Do you speak English? Has he found his voice yet? Is this
anise or is it fennel? Are you high yet? Is your throat sore? Can't you
tell dill weed when you see it? Do you smell something burning? Do
you hear a ringing sound? Do you hear something whimpering, mew-
ing, crying? Do we get there from here? Does the ink smear? Does the
paper get yellow and brittle? Do you prefer soft core? Are they on their
way to work? Are they feeling it? Are they locked out? Are you pes-
simistic? Are you hard? Is that where you live? Is the sink clogged?
Have the roaches made a nest in the radio? Are the cats hungry, thirsty,
tired? Does he need to have a catheter? Is he the father? Are you a
student at the radio school? Are you afraid to fail? Are you in constant
fear of assassination? Why has the traffic stopped? Why does blue fade
into green? Why didn't I go back to Pasco and become a cop? Why
does water curl into the drain in different directions on either side of
the equator? Why does my ankle throb? Why do I like it when I pop
my knuckles? Is that a bald spot? It that an ice cap? Is that a birth
mark? Will the fog burn off soon? Are her life signs going to stabilize?
Can you afford it? Is it gutted? What is it that attracts you to bisexual
women? Does it go soggy in the milk? Do people live there? Is there a
limit? Did it roll over when it went off the road? Will it further class
struggle? Is it legible? Do you feel that it's private? Does it eat flies,
worms, children? Is it nasty? Can you get tickets? Do you wear sun-
glasses out of a misplaced sense of increased privacy? Do you derive
pleasure from farts in the bath? Is there an erotic element to picking
your nose? Have you a specific conceptualization of ear wax? What am
I doing here? How do the deaf sing? How is it those houses will burn
in the rain? What is the distance to Wall Drugs? Why do they insist
on breaking the piñata? Is penetration of the labia sufficient to sup-
port a conviction? Is it a distraction to be aware of the walls? Is it big-
ger than a breadbox? Which is it? When you skydive, do your ears pop?
Do you bruise? Did the bridge rust? Is your life clear to you? How will
you move it? Will you go easy on the tonic please? Do you resent your
parents? Was your childhood a time of great fear? Is that the path? Do
the sandpipers breed here? Is that what you want? Have your cramps
come? Do you tend to draw words instead of write them? Do you have
an opinion about galvanized steel? Who was John Deere? Are you
trapped by your work? Would you like to explore that quarry? Is it the
form of a question? Where is Wolf Grade? Are your legs sore? Is that
a bottle neck? Who is the Ant Farm? Where did she learn to crawl like
that? Is the form of the dance the dancer or the space she carves? Can
we go home now? Who was that masked man? Does he have an imag-

ination? Will he use it? Is it obvious? Is it intentional? Is it possible? Is it hot? Why did the mirror fog up? What is the context of discourse? What is the premise of the man asking passersby if they have change for a dollar? Who took my toothbrush? What made her choose to get back into the life? What is the cause of long fingers? What is the role of altered, stretched canvas on wood supports, hung from a wall? Why do they seem so focused, intent, on their way to work? What makes you needle happy? Why does he keep large bills in his shirt pocket? How do you locate the cross-hairs of your bitterness? What was it about shouting, mere raised voices, that caused him always to go out of control? Do you hear that hum? Is there damage? Is the answer difficult or hard? Is each thing needful? If there was a rip in my notebook, how would you know it? What makes you think you have me figured out? Why do my eyes water, devoid of emotion? What is the difference between a film and a movie? Do you want sugar? Why does my mood correspond to the weather? How do you get down to the beach? Is the act distinct from the object? What did you put in the coffee? Did your ears pop? Would you prefer to watch the condos burn? Where do the verbs go? Will you ever speak to the issue of cholesterol? What is a psychotropic? Does pleonasm scare you? Kledomania? Who leads the low-riders? What is the relation between any two statements? Is anything as tight as anal penetration? Will we stop soon? Will we continue? Where are those sirens coming from? Is it necessary? Is it off-white? Is a legitimate purpose served in limiting access? Will this turn out to be the last day of summer? Will you give up, give out, over? Why is sarcasm so often the final state of marriage? Is this the right exit? Have you received a security clearance? What do you think of when I say "red goose shoes?"

*1986*

## The Chinese Notebook

1. Wayward, we weigh words. Nouns reward objects for meaning. The chair in the air is covered with hair. No part is in touch with the planet.

2. Each time I pass the garage of a certain yellow house, I am greeted with barking. The first time this occurred, an instinctive fear seemed to run through me. I have never been attacked. Yet I firmly believe that if I opened the door to the garage I should confront a dog.

3. Chesterfield, sofa, divan, couch—might these items refer to the same object? If so, are they separate conditions of a single word?

4. My mother as a child would call a potholder a "boppo," the term becoming appropriated by the whole family, handed down now by my cousins to their own children. Is it a word? If it extends, eventually, into general usage, at what moment will it become one?

5. Language is, first of all, a political question.

6. I wrote this sentence with a ballpoint pen. If I had used another would it have been a different sentence?

7. This is not philosophy, it's poetry. And if I say so, then it becomes painting, music or sculpture, judged as such. If there are variables to consider, they are at least partly economic—the question of distribution, etc. Also differing critical traditions. Could this be good poetry, yet bad music? But yet I do not believe I would, except in jest, posit this as dance or urban planning.

8. This is not speech. I wrote it.

9. Another story, similar to 2: until well into my twenties the smell of cigars repelled me. The strong scent inevitably brought to mind the image of warm, wet shit. That is not, in retrospect, an association I can rationally explain. Then I worked as a legislative advocate in the state capitol and was around cigar smoke constantly. Eventually the odor seemed to dissolve. I no longer noticed it. Then I began to notice it again, only now it was an odor I associated with suede or leather. This was how I came to smoke cigars.

10. What of a poetry that lacks surprise? That lacks form, theme, development? Whose language rejects interest? That examines itself without curiosity? Will it survive?

11. Rose and maroon we might call red.

12. Legalistic definitions. For example, in some jurisdictions a conviction is not present, in spite of a finding of guilt, without imposition of sentence. A suspension of sentence, with probation, would not therefore be a conviction. This has substantial impact on teachers' credentials, or the right to practice medicine or law.

13. That this form has a tradition other than the one I propose, Wittgenstein,° etc., I choose not to dispute. But what is its impact on the tradition proposed?

14. Is Wittgenstein's contribution strictly formal?

15. Possibility of a poetry analogous to the paintings of Rosenquist°— specific representational detail combined in non-objective, formalist systems.

16. If this were theory, not practice, would I know it?

17. Everything here tends away from an aesthetic decision, which, in itself, is one.

18. I chose a Chinese notebook, its thin pages not to be cut, its six redline columns which I turned 90°, the way they are closed by curves at both top and bottom, to see how it would alter the writing. Is it flatter, more airy? The words, as I write them, are larger, cover more sur-

---

13 *Wittgenstein:* Ludwig Wittgenstein (1889–1951), Austrian-born philosopher.
15 *Rosenquist:* James Rosenquist (b. 1933), American painter.

face on this two-dimensional picture plane. Shall I, therefore, tend to-ward shorter terms—impact of page on vocabulary?

19. Because I print this, I go slower. Imagine layers of air over the planet. One closer to the center of gravity moves faster, while the one above it tends to drag. The lower one is thought, the planet itself the object of the thought. But from space what is seen is what filters through the slower outer air of representation.

20. Perhaps poetry is an activity and not a form at all. Would this definition satisfy Duncan?°

21. Poem in a notebook, manuscript, magazine, book, reprinted in an anthology. Scripts and contexts differ. How could it be the same poem?

22. The page intended to score speech. What an elaborate fiction that seems!

23. As a boy, riding with my grandparents about Oakland or in the country, I would recite such signs as we passed, directions, names of towns or diners, billboards. This seems to me now a basic form of verbal activity.

24. If the pen won't work, the words won't form. The meanings are not manifested.

25. How can I show that the intentions of this work and poetry are identical?

26. Anacoluthia, parataxis°—there is no grammar or logic by which the room in which I sit can be precisely recreated in words. If, in fact, I were to try to convey it to a stranger, I'd be inclined to show photos and draw a floor map.

27. Your existence is not a condition of this work. Yet, let me, for a moment, posit it. As you read, other things occur to you. You hear the drip of a faucet, or there's music on, or your companion gives a sigh that represents a poor night's sleep. As you read, old conversations reel slowly through your mind, you sense your buttocks and spine in contact with the chair. All of these certainly must be a part of the meaning of this work.

28. As students, boys and girls the age of ten, we would write stories and essays, reading them to the class if the teacher saw fit. The empty space of blank paper seemed to propose infinite dimensions. When the first term was fixed, the whole form readily appeared. It seemed more a question of finding the writing than of creating it. One day a stu-

---

20 *Duncan*: Robert Duncan, American poet. Other poets mentioned who are included in *Anthology of American Poetry* are not identified.

26 *parataxis*: Anacoluthia, the failure to complete a sentence according to the structural plan by which it was started; used deliberately, it is a recognized figure of speech. Parataxis, a style in which there are few linking terms between juxtaposed clauses or sentences.

dent—his name was Jon Arnold—read an essay in which he described our responses to hearing him read it. It was then I knew what writing meant.

29. Mallard, drake—if the words change, does the bird remain?

30. How is it possible that I imagine I can put that chair into language? There it sits, mute. It knows nothing of syntax. How can I put it into something it doesn't inherently possess?

31. "Terminate with extreme prejudice." That meant kill. Or "we had to destroy the village in order to save it." Special conditions create special languages. If we remain at a distance, their irrationality seems apparent, but, if we came closer, would it?

32. The Manson° family, the SLA.° What if a group began to define the perceived world according to a complex, internally consistent, and precise (tho inaccurate) language? Might not the syntax itself propel their reality to such a point that to our own they could not return? Isn't that what happened to Hitler?

33. A friend records what she hears, such as a lunatic awaiting his food stamps, speaking to those who also wait in line, that "whether or not you're good people, that's what I can't tell." As if such acts of speech were clues to the truth of speech itself.

34. They are confused, those who would appropriate Dylan or Wittgenstein—were there ever two more similar men?—, passing them off as poets?

35. What now? What new? All these words turning in on themselves like the concentric layers of an onion.

36. What does it mean: "saw fit"?

37. Poetry is a specific form of behavior.

38. But test it against other forms. Is it more like a drunkenness than filling out an absentee ballot? Is there any value in knowing the answer to this question?

39. Winter wakens thought, much as summer prods recollection. Ought poetry to be a condition of the seasons?

40. What any of us eventually tries—to arrive at some form of "bad" writing (e.g., 31–34?) that would be one form of "good" poetry. Only when you achieve this will you be able to define what it is.

---

32 *Manson:* Charles Manson (b. 1934), American mass murderer; his "family" was the cult group who carried out murders on his command in the late 1960s.
32 *SLA:* the Symbionese Liberation Army, a radical, anti-capitalist, terrorist organization operating in the U.S. in the mid-1970s; their most famous act was the kidnapping of heiress Patricia Hearst in 1974.

41. Speech only tells you the speaker.

42. Analogies between poetry and painting end up equating page and canvas. Is there any use in such fiction?

43. Or take the so-called normal tongue and shift each term in a subtle way. Is this speech made new or mere decoration?

44. Poets of the syntagmeme, poets of the paradigm.

45. The word in the world.

46. Formal perception: that this section, because of the brevity of the foregoing two, should be extensive, commenting, probing, making not aphorisms but fine distinctions, one sentence perhaps of a modular design, verbs in many clauses like small houses sketched into the mountainsides of a grand Chinese landscape, noting to the mind as it passes the gears and hinges of the design, how from the paradigm "large, huge, vast, great, grand," the term was chosen, by rhyme, anticipate "landscape," time itself signaled by the repetition.

47. Have we come so very far since Sterne or Pope?°

48. Language as a medium attracts me because I equate it with that element of consciousness which I take to be intrinsically human. Painting or music, say, might also directly involve the senses, but by ordering external situations to provoke specific (or general) responses. Do I fictionalize the page as form not to consider it as simply another manifestation of such "objective" fact? I have known writers who thought they could make the page disappear.

49. Everything you hear in your head, heart, whole body, when you read this, is what this is.

50. Ugliness v. banality. Both, finally, are attractive.

51. Time is one axis. Often I want to draw it out, to make it felt, a thing so slow that slight alterations (long v. short syllables, etc., clusters of alliteration . . .) magnify, not line (or breath) but pulse, the blood in the muscle.

52. Entymology in poetry—to what extent is it hidden (i.e., present and felt, but not consciously perceived) and to what extent lost (i.e., not perceived or felt, or, if so, only consciously)? The Joycean tradition here is based on an analytic assumption which is not true.

53. Is the possibility of publishing this work automatically a part of the writing? Does it alter decisions in the work? Could I have written that if it did not?

---

47 *Pope:* Lawrence Sterne (1713–1768) and Alexander Pope (1688–1744), Irish novelist and British poet.

54. Increasingly I find object art has nothing new to teach me. This is also the case for certain kinds of poetry. My interest in the theory of the line has its limits.

55. The presumption is: I can write like this and "get away with it."

56. As economic conditions worsen, printing becomes prohibitive. Writers posit less emphasis on the page or book.

57. "He's content just to have other writers think of him as a poet." What does this mean?

58. What if there were no other writers? What would I write like?

59. Imagine meaning rounded, never specific.

60. Is it language that creates categories? As if each apple were a proposed definition of a certain term.

61. Poetry, a state of emotion or intellect. Who would believe that? What would prompt them to do so? Also, what would prompt them to abandon this point of view?

62. The very idea of margins. A convention useful to fix forms, perhaps the first visual element of ordering, preceding even the standardization of spelling. What purpose does it have now, beyond the convenience of printers? Margins do not seem inherent in speech, but possibly that is not the case.

63. Why is the concept of a right-hand margin so weak in the poetry of western civilization?

64. Suppose I was trying to explain a theory of the margin to a speaker of Mandarin or Shasta—how would I justify it? Would I compare it to rhyme as a sort of decision? Would I mention the possibility of capitalizing the letters along the margin? If I wanted, could I work "backwards" here, showing how one could posit nonspoken acrostics vertically at the margin and justify its existence from that? What if the person to whom I was explaining this had no alphabet, no writing, in his native tongue?

65. Saroyan and, more completely, Grenier° have demonstrated that there is no useful distinction between language and poetry.

66. Under certain conditions any language event can be poetry. The question thus becomes one of what are these conditions.

67. By the very act of naming—The Chinese Notebook—one enters into a process as into a contract. Yet each section, such as this, needs

---

65 *Grenier:* William Saroyan (1908–1981) and Rober Grenier (b. 1941), American novelist and American experimental poet.

to be invented, does not automatically follow from specific prior statements. However, that too could be the case.

68. I have never seen a theory of poetry that adequately included a sub-theory of choice.

69. There is also the question of work rhythms and habits. When I was a boy, after each dinner I would place the family typewriter—it was ancient and heavy—atop the kitchen table, typing or writing furiously— it was almost automatic writing—until it was time to go to bed. Later, married, I still wrote in the evening, as though unable to begin until each day's information reached a certain threshold which I could gauge by fatigue. All throughout these years, I could not work on a given piece beyond one sitting—a condition I attributed to my attention span—, although on occasion "one sitting" could extend to 48 hours. Since then there has been a shift. I have lately been writing in note-books, over extended periods (in one instance, five months), and in the morning, often before breakfast and at times before dawn. Rather than the fatigue of digested sense data, the state of mind I work in is the empty-headed clarity which follows sleep.

70. This work lacks cunning.

71. An offshoot of projectivist theory was the idea that the form of the poem might be equivalent to the poet's physical self. A thin man to use short lines and a huge man to write at length. Kelly, etc.

72. Antin's° theory is that in the recent history of progressive forms (himself, Schwerner, Rothenberg, MacLow, Higgins, the Something Else writers et al), it has become clear that only certain domains yield "successful" work. But he has not indicated what these domains are, nor sufficiently defined success.

73. A social definition of a successful poet might be anyone who has a substantial proportion of his or her work generally available, so that an interested reader can, without knowing the writer, grasp, in broad terms at least, the scope of the whole.

74. If this bores you, leave.

75. What happened to fiction was a shift in public sensibility. The general reader no longer is apt to identify with a character in a story, but with its author. Thus the true narrative element is the development of the form. The true drama of, say, Mailer's *Armies of the Night,*° is the question: will this book work? In film, an even more naturally narrative medium than prose, this condition is readily apparent.

76. If I am correct that this is poetry, where is its family resemblance to, say, *The Prelude?*° Crossing the Alps.

---

72 *Antin:* David Antin (b. 1932), American poet known for his improvisational "talk" poems.
75 *Mailer:* Norman Mailer (b. 1923), American novelist.
76 *Prelude:* long poem by British poet William Wordsworth (1770–1850).

77. The poem as code or fad. One you must "break," while the other requires the decision of whether or not to follow.

78. Is not-writing (and here I don't mean discarding or revising) also part of the process?

79. I am continually amazed at how many writers are writing the poems they believe the person they wish they were would have written.

80. What if writing was meant to represent all possibilities of thought, yet one could or would write only in certain conditions, states of mind?

81. I have seen poems thought or felt to be dense, difficult to get through, respaced on the page, two dimensional picture plane, made airy, "light." How is content altered by this operation?

82. Certain forms of "bad" poetry are of interest because inept writing blocks referentiality, turning words and phrases in on themselves, an autonomy of language which characterizes the "best" writing. Some forms of sloppy surrealism or pseudo-beat automatic writing are particularly given to this.

83. Designated art sentence.

84. One can use the inherent referentiality of sentences very much as certain "pop" artists used images (I'm thinking of Rauschenberg, Johns,° Rosenquist, etc.) to use as elements for so-called abstract composition.

85. Abstract v. concrete, a misleading vocabulary. If I read a sentence (story, poem, whatever unit) of a fight, say, and identify with any spectator or combatant, I am having a vicarious experience. But if I experience, most pronouncedly, this language as event, I am experiencing that fact directly.

86. Impossible to posit the cat's expectations in words. Or Q's example—the mouse's fear of the cat is counted as his believing true a certain English sentence. If we are to speak of things, we are proscribed, limited to the external, or else create laughable and fantastic fictions.

87. Story of a chimpanzee taught that certain geometrical signs stood for words, triangle for bird, circle for water, etc., when presented with a new object, a duck, immediately made up the term "water bird."

88. That writing was "speech" "scored". A generation caught in such mixed metaphor (denying the metaphor) as that. That elaboration of technical components of the poem carried the force of prophecy.

89. Is any term now greater than a place-holder? Any arrangement of weighted squares, if ordered by some shared theory of color, could be language.

---

84 *Johns:* Jasper Johns (b. 1930) and Robert Rauschenberg (b. 1925), American painters.

90. What do nouns reveal? Conceal?

91. The idea of the importance of the role of the thumb in human evolution. Would I still be able to use it if I did not have a word for it? Thought it simply a finger? What evidence do I have that my right and left thumbs are at least roughly symmetrical equivalents? After all I don't really use my hands interchangeably, do I? I couldn't write this with my left hand, or if I did learn to do so, it would be a specific skill and would be perceived as that.

92. Perhaps as a means of containing meaning outside of the gallery system, the visual arts have entered into a period where the art itself exists in a dialectic, in the exchange between worker, critic and worker. Writing stands in a different historical context. Fiction exists in relation to a publishing system, poetry to an academic one.

93. At Berkeley, when I was a student, graduate students in the English Department liked to think of themselves as "specialized readers."

94. What makes me think that form exists?

95. One possibility is my ability to "duplicate" or represent it. As a child, I could fill in a drawing as tho it and color existed.

96. I want these words to fill the spaces poems leave.

97. The assumption is, language is equal if not to human perception per se, then to what is human about perception.

98. Good v. bad poetry. The distinction is not useful. The whole idea assumes a shared set of articulatable values by which to make such a judgment. It assumes, if not the perfect poem, at least the theory of limits, the most perfect poem. How would you proceed to make such a distinction?

99. Those who would excerpt or edit miss the point.

100. "When I look at a blank page it's never blank!" Prove or disprove this statement.

101. Before you can accept the idea of fiction, you have to admit everything else.

102. "The only thing language can change is language." Ah, but to the extent that we act on our thoughts, we act on their syntax.

103. The order of this room is subject-verb-predicate.

104. Put all of this another way: can I use language to change myself?

105. Once I wrote some stories for an elementary school text. I was given a list of words from which to work, several hundred terms proposed to me as the information range of any eight year old. This included no verbs of change.

106. "Time is the common enemy."

107. Concepts of past and future precede an ability to conceive of the sentence.

108. Subjects hypnotized to forget the past and future wrote words at random intervals about the page.

109. So-called non-referential language when structured non-syntactically tends to disrupt time perception. Once recognized, one can begin to structure the disruption. Coolidge,° for example, in *The Maintains,* uses line, stanza and repetition. Ashbery's *Three Poems,* not referential but syntactical, does not alter time.

110. The flaw of non-referentiality is that words are derived. They do not exist prior to their causes. Even when the origins are not obvious or are forgotten. The root, for example, of *denigrate* is *Negro.* Words only become non-referential through specific context. A condition as special (i.e., not universal or "ordinary") as the poem perceived as speech scored for the page.

111. When I was younger, the argument was whether, when you stripped the poem of all inessentials, you were left finally with a voice or with an image. Now it seems clear that the answer is neither. A poem, like any language, is a vocabulary and a set of rules by which it is processed.

112. But if the poem/language equation is what we have been seeking, other questions nevertheless arise. For example, are two poems by one poet two languages or, as Zukofsky argues, only one? But take specifics—*Catullus, Mantis, Bottom,* "A"-12—are these not four vocabularies with four sets of rules?

113. Compare sections 26 and 103.

114. If four poets took a specific text from which to derive the terms of a poem, what I call a "vocab," and by prior agreement each wrote a sestina, that would still be four languages and not one, right?

115. A hill with two peaks, or two hills. If I grant that the language alters one's perception, and if it follows naturally that, depending on which perception one "chooses," one acts differently, becomes used to different paths, thinks of certain people as neighbors and others not, and that such acts collectively will alter the hill (e.g., one peak becomes middle-class, residential, while the other slips into ghettohood later to be cleared off for further "development" which might include leveling the top of the peak to make it useable industrial space)—if I grant the possibility of this chain, is not the landscape itself a consequence of language? And isn't this essentially the history of the planet? Can one, in the context of such a chain, speak of what we know of as the planet as existing prior to language?

---

109 *Coolidge:* Clark Coolidge (b. 1939), American poet.

116. This jumps around. It does not have an "argument."

117. Paris is in France. Also, Paris has five letters. So does France. But so do Ghana, China, Spain. How should I answer "Why is Paris Paris?"

118. The question within the question. To which does the question mark refer? If one question mark is lost, where does its meaning go? How is it possible for punctuation to have multiple or non-specific references?

119. In what way is this like prose? In what way is this unlike it?

120. Only esthetic consistency constitutes content (Yates' proposition regarding music). Applied to writing one arrives at the possibility of a "meaningful" poetry as the sum of "meaningless" poems.

121. But consistency demands a perception of time. Thus, if we accept the proposition, we tacitly approve some definition of poetry as a specific time construct.

122. There is no direction. There is only distance.

123. What is the creative role of confusion in any work?

124. At times, my own name is simply a gathering of letters. Very distant.

125. Words relate to the referred world much the way each point in a line can be said to describe a curve.

126. The sun variously rises each morning. We, variously, attempt to relate that. No single way is exact, yet everyone knows what we mean.

127. The words are not "out there."

128. By the time you admit the presence of verbs, you have already conceded all of the assumptions.

129. The historical attention of the arts to madness is a question of what happens if you redefine the language.

130. Content is only an excuse, something to permit the writing to occur, to trigger it. Would a historian looking for information about Massachusetts fishing colonies have much use for *Maximus*?° To say yes is to concede that in order to like, say, Pound, you'd have to *agree* with him, no?

131. *Sad is faction.* That sounds alone are not precise meaning (in the referential sense) means that before the listener can recognize content he/she must first have the perception of the presence of words.

---

130 *Maximus:* the major poem sequence by Charles Olson.

132. But if one denies the possibility of referentiality, how does *sad is faction* differ from *satisfaction*? How do we know this?

133. "Post-syntactical" implies that syntax was a historical period of language, not a condition inherent in it. Rather than seeing language as a universe whose total set cannot be dealt with until all its conditions are brought into play, this designation opts for an easy and incorrect solution. Occasionally, it has been used in such a fashion as to assert some sort of competition with "syntactical" writing, with the supposedly-obvious presumption that, being later in language's various conditions, it is more advanced. Such a view distorts the intentions and functions of abandoning syntactical and even paratactical modes.

134. Terms, out of context, inevitably expand and develop enlarged inner conditions, the large field of the miniaturists.

135. Eigner's° work, for example. The early writings resemble a late Williams/early Olson mode, discursive syntax, which becomes in later works increasingly a cryptic notation until now often words in a work will float in an intuitive vocabulary—space, their inner complexities expanded so that words are used like the formal elements in abstract art.

136. To move away from the individualist stance in writing I first began to choose vocabularies for poems from language sources that were not my own, science texts, etc. Then I began to develop forms which opt away from the melodic dominant line of the past several decades, using formal analogies taken from certain Balinese and African percussive and ensemble musics, as well as that of Steve Reich.

137. The concept that the poem "expresses" the poet, vocally or otherwise, is at one with the whole body of thought identified as Capitalist Imperialism.

138. If poetry is to be perfect, it cannot be all-knowing. If it is to be all-knowing, it cannot be perfect.

139. I began writing seriously a decade ago and was slow to learn. For years I was awkward, sloppy, given to overstatement, the sentimental image, the theatrical resolution. Yet, subtracting these, I am amazed at the elements, all formal and/or conceptual, which have remained constants. It is those who tell me who I am.

140. The presumption of the logical positivists that "the relation between language and philosophy is closer than, as well as essentially different from, that between language and any other discipline," would upset most poets. Three answers seem possible: (1) the logical positivists are wrong, (2) poetry and philosophy are quite similar and perhaps ought to be considered different branches of a larger category, (3) poetry is not a discipline, at least in the sense of the special definition of the logical positivists. I reject the third alternative as not be-

---

133 *Eigner:* Larry Eigner (b. 1925), American poet.

ing true for any except those poets whose work lacks all sense of definition. This leaves me with two possible conclusions.

141. Why is this work a poem?

142. One answer: because certain information is suppressed due to what its position in the sequence would be.

143. But is it simply a question of leaving out?

144. It is our interpretation of signs, not their presence (which, after all, could be any series of random marks on the page, sounds in the air), that makes them referential.

145. There are writers who would never question the assumptions of non-objective artists (Terry Fox, say, or even Stella or the late Smithson)° who cannot deal with writing in the same fashion. Whenever they see certain marks on the page, they always presume that something *besides* those marks is also present.

146. On page 282 of *Imaginations*, Williams writes "This is the alphabet," presents the typewriter keyboard, except that where the *s* should be there appears a second *e*. Whether this was "in error" or not, it tells us everything about the perception of language.

147. The failure of Williams to go beyond his work of *Spring and All* and the *Great American Novel* seems to verify (Bergmann's° assertion that nominalism inevitably tends toward (deteriorates into?) representationalism.

148. Konkretism was a very narrow base on which to build a literature. Futurism of the Russian school, especially the *zaum*° works of the Group 41°, is the true existing body of experimental literature with which contemporary writers have to work.

149. What is it that allows me to identify this as a poem, Wittgenstein to identify his work as technical philosophy, Brockman's *Afterwords* to be seen as Esalen-oriented metaphysics, and Kenner's° piece on Zukofsky literary criticism?

150. But is it a distortion of poetry to speak of it like this? How might I define poetry so as to be able to identify such distortions?

151. Can one even say, as have Wellek and Warren,° that literature (not even here to be so specific as to identify the poem to the exclusion of other modes) is first of all words in a sequence? One can point to the

---

145 *Smithson:* Frank Stella (b. 1936), Robert Smithson (1938–1973), American painters.
147 *Bergmann:* Gustav Bergmann (1906–1987), Austrian philosopher.
148 *zaum:* a variety of Cubo-futurist experiments with transsense language (*zaum*) flourished in Russia in the 1910s–1920s.
149 *Kenner:* Hugh Kenner (b. 1923), American literary critic, an early advocate of Ezra Pound's poetry.
151 *Warren:* René Wellek (b. 1903) and Austin Warren, American literary critics who coauthored an influential textbook, *Theory of Literature* (1949).

concretist tradition as a partial refutation, or one can point to the great works of Grenier, *A Day at the Beach* and *Sentences,* where literature occurs within individual words.

152. Possibly, if one approached it cautiously, one could hope to make notations, provisional definitions of poetry. For example, one might begin by stating that it is any language act—not necessarily a sequence of terms—which makes no other formal assertion other than it is poetry. This would permit the exclusion of Kosuth and Wittgenstein, but the inclusion of this.

153. But how, if it does not state it, does a work make a formal assertion? Certain structural characteristics such as line, stanza, etc. are not always present. Here is where one gets into Davenport's position regarding Ronald Johnson,° to say that one is a poet who has written no poems, per se.

154. Performance as a form is only that. As always, the intention of the creator defines the state in which the work is most wholly itself, so that it is possible that a talking piece, say, could be said to be a poem. But formally its ties are closer to other arts than to the tradition of poetry. I have, in the last year, heard talking pieces that were proposed as poetry, as music and as sculpture. Each, in all major respects, resembled the late period of Lenny Bruce or perhaps Dick Cavett.° The form of the talking piece, its tradition, was always stronger than the asserted definition. Nor is the talking piece the only nontraditional (if, in fact, it is that at all) mode to run into this problem. Some of the visualists, e.g., Kostelanetz, have utilized film for their poems, but the poem is readily lost in this transfer. What one experiences in its presence is the fact of film.

155. Why did I write "As always, the intention of the creator defines the state in which the work is most wholly itself"? Because it is here and here only where one can "fix" a work into a given state (idea, projective process, text, affective process, impression), an act which is required, absolutely, before one can place the work in relation to others, only after which can one make judgments.

156. What if I told you I did not really believe this to be a poem? What if I told you I did?

157. Periodically one hears that definitions are unimportant, or, and this implicitly is more damning, "not interesting." I reject this, taking all language events to be definitions or, if you will, propositions.

158. I find myself not only in the position of arguing that all language acts are definitions and that they nonetheless are not essentially referential, but also that this is not a case specifically limited to an "ideal"

153 *Johnson:* (b. 1935), American poet.
154 *Cavett:* Lenny Bruce (1925–1966), American satiric stand-up comic; Dick Cavett (b. 1936), American comic and television talk show host.

or "special" language (such as one might argue poetry to be), but is general, applicable to all.

159. If, at this point, I was to insert 120 rhymed couplets, would it cause definitions to change?

160. Lippard° (*Changing*, p. 206) argues against a need for a "humanistic" visual arts, but makes an exception for literature, which "as a verbal medium, demands a verbal response." One wonders what, precisely, is meant by that? Is it simply a question of referentiality posed in vague terms? Or does it mean, as I suspect she intended it to, that language, like photography, is an ultimately captive medium? If so, is the assertion correct? It is not.

161. It becomes increasingly clear that the referential origin of language and its syntactical (or linguistic, or relational) meaning is the contradiction (if it is one) that is to be understood if we are to accept a poetics of autonomous language.

162. If I could make an irrefutable argument that non-referential language does exist (besides, that is, those special categories, such as prepositions or determiners), would I include this in it? Of course I would.

163. What you read is what you read.

164. Make a note in some other place, then transfer it here. Is it the same note?

165. I want form to be perceivable but not consequent to referred meaning. Rather, it should serve to move that element to the fore- or back-brain at will.

166. Form that is an extension of referred meaning stresses that meaning's relation to the individual, voice or image as extension of self, emphasizes one's separateness from others. What I want, instead, is recognition of our connectedness.

167. A writing which is all work, technical procedure, say a poem derived from a specific formula, is of interest for this fact alone.

168. Words in a text like states on a map: meaning is commerce.

169. One type of criticism would simply describe the formal features of any given work, demonstrate its orderliness with the implicit purpose of, from this, deducing the work's intention. A comparison, then, of the intention to the work (and, secondarily, to other works of identical or similar intention), would provide grounds for a judgment.

170. Is it possible for a work to conceal its intention?

---

160 *Lippard:* Lucy Lippard, American art critic.

171. But if the intention is always to be arrived at deductively, will not the work always be equal to it? Would we be able to recognize a work which had not met the writer's original intention?

172. Perhaps this poem could be said to be an example of the condition described in 171.

173. Is it possible for intentions to be judged, good or malevolent, right or otherwise? This brings us into the realm of political and ethical distinctions?

174. In recent years, criticism has played a dynamic role in the evolution of the visual arts, but not in writing. Theory, much of it unsound, even mystical, on the part of writers, has had more impact. A possible explanation: criticism is applied theory, useful only if it is rigorous in its application, which has been impossible given the loose and vague standards characteristic of so much recent writing, while theory can be used suggestively, which it has been regardless of the mystifications present.

175. A poem written in pen could never have been written in pencil.

176. When I was younger, I was so habituated to the typewriter as a tool and to the typewritten page as a space, that, even when I worked from notebooks, the poems transposed back into a typewritten text tended to perfectly fill the page.

177. Deliberately determining the way one writes, determines much of what will be written.

178. If I were to publish only parts of this, sections, it would alter the total proposition.

179. How far will anything extend? Hire dancers dressed as security personnel to walk about an otherwise empty museum, then admit the public. Could this be poetry if I have proposed it as such? If so, what elements could be altered or removed to make it not poetry? E.g., hire not dancers but ordinary security personnel. But if the answer is "no," if any extension, thing, event, would be poetry if proposed as such, *what* would poetry, the term, mean?

180. Possibly poetry is a condition applicable to any state of affairs. What would constitute such a condition? Would it be the same or similar in all instances? Could it be identified, broken down? Does it have anything to do with the adjectival form "poetic"?

181. If one could propose worrying as one form of poetry, what in the worrying would be the poem?

182. Or could one have poetry without the poem? Is it possible that these two states do not depend on the presence (relational as it is) of each other? Give examples.

183. Why is it language characterizes the man?

184. Or I meant, possibly, why is it that language characterizes man?

185. Is it language?

186. Context—against the text. Literally a circumstance where meaning is not obvious simply by the presence of terms in a specific sequence. Remove 185 from this text: "it" in 185 then means either "this writing" or some "other" event. But in the notebook as it is, the sentence must mean "Is it language that characterizes (the) man?" Is the same sentence in two contexts one or two sentences? If it is one, how can we assign it differing meanings? If it is two, there could never literally be repetition.

187. Alimentary, my dear Watson.

188. But if poetry were a 'system'—not necessarily a single system, but if for any individual it was—then one could simply plug in the raw data and out would flow 'poetry,' not necessarily poems.

189. Is this not what Robert Kelly° does?

190. It was Ed van Aelstyn who, in his linguistics course, planted the idea (1968) that the definition of a language was also a definition of any poem: a vocabulary plus a set of rules through which to process it. What did I think poetry was before that?

191. But does the vocabulary include words which do not end up in the finished text? If so, how would we know which words they are?

192. A friend, a member of the Old Left, challenges my aesthetic. How, he asks, can one write so as not to "communicate"? I, in turn, challenge his definitions. It is a more crucial lesson, I argue, to learn how to experience language directly, to tune one's senses to it, than to use it as a mere means to an end. Such use, I point out, is, in bourgeois life, common to all things, even the way we "use" our friends. Some artists (Brecht is the obvious example) try to focus such "use" to point up all the alienation, to present a bourgeois discourse "hollowed out." But language, so that it is experienced directly, moves beyond any such exercise in despair, an unalienated language. He wants an example. I give him Grenier's

> thumpa
> thumpa
> thumpa
> thump

pointing out how it uses so many physical elements of speech, how it is a speech that only borders on language, how it illumines that space. He says "I don't understand."

---

189 *Kelly:* (b. 1935), American poet.

193. Determiners, their meaning.

194. Each sentence is new born.

195. Traditionally, poetry has been restrictive, has had no room for the appositive.

196. I imagine at times this to be discourse. Sometimes it is one voice, sometimes many.

197. Language on walls. Graffiti, "fuk speling," etc. As a boy I rode with my Grandparents about town, learning to read by reading all the signs aloud. I am still apt to do this.

198. This sentence is that one.

199. "This in which," i.e., the world in its relations. What is of interest is *not* the objectification, but relativity: Einstein's "What time does the station get to the train?"

200. Imagine the man who liked de Kooning° out of a fondness for women.

201. There is no way in language to describe the experience of knowing my hand.

202. I was chased, running through a forest. Because I knew the names of the plants I could run faster.

203. The formal considerations of indeterminacy are too few for interest to extend very far, even when posed in other terms—"organic" etc. But organic form is strict, say, 1:1:2:3:5:8:13:21. . . . What is the justification for strict form (Xenakis'° music, for example) which cannot be perceived? Is there an aesthetic defense for the hidden?

204. Presence and absence. This axis is form's major dimension.

205. Are 23 and 197 the same or different?

206. A paper which did not absorb fluids well, a pencil that was blunt or wrote only faintly. These would determine the form of the work. Now, when I set out on a piece, choice of instrument and recorder (notebook, typing paper, etc.) are major concerns. I am apt to buy specific pens for specific pieces.

207. Words to locate specific instance—personalism, localism. Quality of a journal to what this or that one does. "Another hard day of gossip."

208. Any writer carries in his or her head a set, what 'the scene' is, its issues, etc. So often little or no overlap at all, but how it defines what anyone does!

---

200 *de Kooning:* Willem de Kooning (1904–1997), American artist known for his vibrant, hugely distorted portraits of women.
203 *Xenakis:* Iannis Xenakis (b. 1922), Romanian-born Greek musical composer who has organized musical compositions by computer.

209. The day is wrappt in its definitions, this room is.

210. Whether one sees language as learned or inherent determines, in part, what one does with it. The 'organic' sentence (truncated, say, by breath, or thought's diversions) versus the sentence as an infinitely plastic (I don't mean this in the pejorative sense) one, folding, unfolding, extending without limit. Dahlberg or Faulkner.°

211. Absolutely normal people. Would their writing be any different?

212. Information leaks through these words. Each time I use them new things appear.

213. Values are vowels.

214. A language of one consonant, one vowel, various as any.

215. Like eyesight, our minds organizing what we 'see' before we even see it. As tho I did not know about oranges, tho I had eaten them all my life. Each time I ate one I would not know what taste to expect.

216. I do not read to 'read of the world,' but for the pleasure in the act of reading.

217. The ocean's edge is a mantra. Strollers, bathers, dogs, gulls. Its great sound. The smell of salt. Sun's sheen on water. But there is no way to repeat this in language. Anything we say, descriptively, is partial. At best one constructs an aesthetic of implication. One can, however, make of the language itself a mantra. But this is not the ocean.

218. Buildup, resolution. What have these to do with the writing?

219. Just as doubt presumes a concept of certainty, non-referentiality presumes knowledge of the referential. Is this a proof?

220. When I return here to ideas previously stated, that's rhyme.

221. Any piece I write precludes the writing of some other piece. As this work is the necessary consequence of previous writings, called poems, so it will also create necessities, ordering what follows. I take this as absolute verification of its poemhood.

222. Language hums in the head, secretes words.

223. This is it.

1986

---

210 *Faulkner:* Edward Dahlberg (1900–1977) and William Faulkner (1897–1962), American novelists.

# from *Toner*°

Meet my personality.
A deaf man's whistle
could seem inexact.
                        I don't
5                   want to get my
feathers hot.
Bag lady stands in


                        A phone booth
out of the rain.
10          First dot, best dot.
Death of
                        Porky the Pig.
Already the jaws
of narrative open.


15          On the street
                        a woman
returns the man's leer,
involuntary grimace.
                        Static
20          storms the intercom.
A reduction in species


                        Simplifies planet.
Tongue pressed
to third rail.
                        The way the new el
25          undeckles the margin
between suburb and sky.
After a walk in the rain


Cuffs damp for hours.
30          Shapeless mass in express lane
                        checkout counter.
Now when I hear
someone on the bus talking
                        I turn
35          to see

---

**poem title:** *Toner* is a book-length poem consisting of 199 stanzas.

If anyone is there
                    to listen.
Write first
and ask questions after,
                    exact trace
40
of anxiety
does not "make the man"


Lumber yard
                    surrounded by condos:
its days are numbered.
45
                            People gasp,
mouse loose on the train.
*Top Stars Tell How They Died,*
see inside. Multiples weep


To see the space about them—
50
vacant lots
                    stretching
not forever but to the freeway,
                    not vacant
55
but each
holding a cement foundation


Visible to infrared
poised in night sky.
Anthropomorphic,
60
                            the president grins
across a screen filled with snow,
                            unattended
in the tavern corner,


The hard sound of billiards
65
banging together.
                    Ice melts
settling in the tall glass
about the clear plastic straw,
model
70
            for offshore drilling.


I'm in touch with my emotions,
in search of a tourniquet,
                    event at which
life narrows
75
to the Final Four.
Pull string here
                    says Band-Aid's

Wax paper wrapper
            but instead
80           the red string
just slides out.
Woodpecker walks up
trunk of the pine.
Windmill breaks up broadcast transmission.


85   Economists conduct thought experiment
for a society of two islands
containing one individual each.
         Man struggles
to move
90          from wheelchair
to auto.


           Extra-wide briefcase
indicates salesman,
stewardess' luggage in portable dolly.
95           Fumbles with his walkman
at the end of the tape.
Escalator's steady hum
dissolves in the muzak:


Soft repetitive bell
100  sends plainclothes security staff
sprinting to department store exit.
        We have nothing
to form
but form
105        itself,


The social queues up
           like children
at the end of recess
in the rain.
110        A nurse
with bruised knees, lawyer's
belly strains dull shirt,


Tie open wide.
          The line waits
115  for the previous show to let out.
Who watches the watchmen?
Far across the bay
I see the city rise,
        hazy,

120    Verticals without depth.
       Throat sore from indoor heat,
                            old prof
       shambles across the quad,
                     that verb
125    mere predication.
       Left-handed woman writes in margin


       Of casebook.
                    Library book
       dust jacket
                         encased in plastic.
130    Four men in 1914,
       three at Columbia
       determine American literary canon.


       Pronounce that canyon.
135    She said I said
                       in my sleep
       the same word
                     over and over
       "Dama,"
140    whatever that means.


              Large-boned woman,
       freckled,
       her hair in thick braids,
       asleep on the train.
145                    Year that
       some men thought it hip
       to shave sideburns

                                                        *1992*

# Adrian C. Louis (b. 1946)

Born and raised in Nevada, Louis is an enrolled member of the Lovelock Paiute Indian tribe. He was educated at Brown University, where he also went on to receive an M.A. in creative writing. A former journalist, he edited four tribal newspapers and was a founder of the Native American Press Association. Since 1984, he has taught English at Oglala Lakota College on the Pine Ridge Reservation of South Dakota, where he lives. Louis, who writes both poetry and fiction, is at the forefront of a new generation of Native American writers. Having abandoned the celebratory lyricism of some of his predecessors, he opts instead to tell harsh truths about both white and Indian cultures. Frank about alcoholism, frank about self-pity, he also displays an articulate bitterness about the humiliation and demoralization his people continue to suffer. His primary focus is not the past but the present life of Native Americans, but it is a present at once redolent with history and destabilized by moments of magical revelation. Louis thereby discovers uncanny instances of transfiguration amidst loss and the ordinary routines of daily life. Like Sherman Alexie, his work mixes uncompromising social criticism with an unforgettable irony, but Louis is unique in turning that irony on himself as often as he turns it on the world around him.

## Dust World

for Sherman Alexie

### I.

Whirlwinds of hot autumn dust
paint every foolish hope dirty.
I stand in the impudent ranks of the poor
and scream for the wind to abate.
5   Prayers to Jesus might be quicker
than these words from blistered hands
and liquor, but the death wind
breaks the lines to God.
I have no sylvan glades of dreams,
10  just dust words
for my people dying.

## II.

With pupil-dilated *putti* in arms
three teenaged mothers
on the hood of a '70 Chevy
15      wave at me like they know me.
Inside the video rental
a small fan ripples sweat
and scatters ashes upon two young attendants
practicing karate kicks and ignoring me
20      because they're aware I could dust
their wise asses individually or collectively.
They're products of Pine Ridge° High
which means they would have had two strikes
against them even if they did graduate
25      and these two clowns never did.
I guess they're almost courting me,
in a weird macho way almost flirting,
because I'm fatherly, half buzzed-up,
and have biceps as thick as their thighs.
30      Heyyyy . . . ever so softly,
this is the whiskey talking now.

## III.

With pupils dilated and beer in hand
three teenaged mothers court frication
more serious than their sweet Sioux butts
35      buffing the hood of their hideous car.
When I glide my new T-bird°
out of the video store parking lot
they wave like they really know me.
One of the girls, beautiful enough
40      to die for except for rotten teeth
smiles and I suck in my gut
and lay some rubber.
I cruise through a small whirlwind
of lascivious regrets
45      and float happily through the dark streets
of this sad, welfare world.
This is the land that time forgot.

---

22 *Pine Ridge:* town in South Dakota; nearby is the Pine Ridge Indian Reservation, home
of the Ogalala Lakota holy man Black Elk (1863–1950). This Sioux reservation was the fo-
cus of a major effort by the U.S. Federal Bureau of Investigation (FBI) to suppress the
American Indian Movement (AIM), which was founded in 1968. It culminated in a sev-
enty-one day 1973 FBI siege of the Wounded Knee hamlet on the Pine Ridge Reservation,
near the site, as it happened, of the infamous Wounded Knee massacre of 1890, when
nearly 300 Lakota men, women, and children were slaughtered by U.S. cavalry. In the three
years following the siege, the FBI fostered the murder of more than sixty AIM members
on the reservation.
36 *T-bird:* a popular automobile, the Thunderbird, whose name coopts a Native American
symbol for commercial purposes; in Louis's fallen, postmodern world he drives the car
with a strong sense of irony.

Here is the Hell the white God gave us.
The wind from the Badlands° brings
50     a chorus of chaos and makes everything dirty.
I meander past my house and stop briefly
before driving back to where
the young girls are.
I park my car and re-enter the store.
55     The two young boys are still dancing
like two cats in mid-air, snarling, clawless
and spitting. No harm done.
I stare them down and place two cassettes,
both rated X, on the counter.
60     It's Friday night and I'm forty years old
and the wild-night redskin
parade is beginning.

*1992*

# Wakinyan

Puppy Luppy, our super sleek black Lab
was missing for two days, running
with the pack after a Spaniel in heat
and because the day was warm, we walked
5     down to the pow-wow grounds° by the creek
to look for that goofy boy.
We had a lot of money and love invested
in him and he'd never been out for two days.
We sat in the shade of the squaw cooler
10     underneath the boughs of rusted pines
for a minute to catch our breath
before we headed for the tick-infested creek.
It had snowed heavily a week earlier so
it must have been the heat that brought
15     the opening buds of the cottonwoods and willows
and the spider-like ticks who, once attached,
would turn to big, green grapes on my dogs.

*Wakinyan*, the thunder beings, kicked us
in the crotch before we got to the creek.
20     The sky turned violet, lightning cracked
and crackled sideways, not up and down.
Rain slapped down so hard, for an instant
I heard strains of Junior Wells° at a Chicago
nightspot twenty years past.
25     That didn't last long. The rain hardened
into hail and we ran past the music in my mind
and huddled in a large clump of wild cherry.

---

49 *Badlands:* a barren but beautiful region of southwest South Dakota, marked by steep
eroded hills and gullies; east of the Black Hills, traditional birthplace of the Sioux nation.
5 *powwow grounds:* see the annotation to Sherman Alexie's "No. 9."
23 *Junior Wells:* a Chicago-based blues artist.

Broken bottles, buried frogs, and reason rushed
all around us in swollen rivulets of rain and hail.
30 The thunder beings had driven us to humanity.
Inside the thicket across from us were two winos,
coats thickened by greasepuke and woodsmoke,
shivering with shivering eyes.
It was early spring and the day was sweating wet.
35 God had emerged for the first time since creation
and had decided to show his magnificent mirth.
Four Indians in a bush were being pelted
by golf ball-sized pellets of ice.
We laughed aloud and the two winos did too.
40 We stared at them in silence and they stared
back with yellow, empty eyes.
We quickly left the bush and entered the storm.
Pain is easier to deal with than spirits.

1989

## Without Words

Farewell from this well is impossible.
Man is composed mainly of water.
I lower a frayed rope into the depths and hoist
the same old Indian tears to my eyes.
5 The liquid is pure and irresistible.
We have nothing to live for, nothing to die for.
Each day we drink and decompose into a different flavor.
Continuity is not fashionable
and clashing form is sediment
10 obscuring the bottom of thirst.
The parched and cracking mouths
of our Nations do not demand
a reason for drinking
so across America
15 we stagger and stumble with contempt for the future
and with no words of pride for our past.

1989

## Coyote Night°

A flat tire ten miles
east of Pine Ridge
just past the Wounded Knee° turnoff.

---

**poem title:** Refers both to the small, wolflike carnivorous animal native to many areas of the continent and to Coyote, perhaps the most well-known and pan-Indian figure in Native American mythology. Coyote figures in creation stories and in numerous more recent tales. A North American version of the trickster figure, Coyote is creative, wily, lecherous, and a master of disguise. He can take many shapes and intervenes in human affairs, sometimes positively and sometimes mischievously.
3 *Wounded Knee:* See the notes to N. Scott Momaday's poem "December 29, 1890" and to Louis's poem "Dust World."

I disembark into Siberia°
5     looking for Zhivago.°
A non-stopping semi whines away
into a state of exhaustion.
This winter night is held
in silence as if a giant squid
10     fell upon the land and froze.
Scraggly pines try to feel
up the miserable moon.
Snapping twigs signal
sneaking-up coyotes.
15     Here there are no distant
garbage trucks,
no all-night neon.
I click the safety off my .22 Llama
and light a cigar.
20     Coyote eyes float
in deep-ass blackness.
Coyote eyes float
in deep-ass blackness.
Coyote eyes gloat
25     in black glass glee
and I laugh and return to my car.
It drives pretty good
on three tires.

1992

## How Verdell and Dr. Zhivago
## Disassembled the Soviet Union

*"You are the blessing in a stride towards perdition when living*
*sickens more than sickness itself."*
—BORIS PASTERNAK°

Last year, before cruising to the warehouse
near the old Moccasin Factory,
Verdell and I stopped at the bootlegger
for a quick belt to cinch
5     his stomach full of fears.
He said the pint of rotgut whiskey
tasted worse than gangrene
but it did the job and choked silent
the raging world around him.
10     We meandered through tons
of remaindered and donated tomes,

---

4 *Siberia*: vast, 500,000,000 square mile region in northern Russia and Asia; its northern-most reaches are open, frozen tundra.
5 *Zhivago*: a character from the Russian writer Boris Pasternak's 1957 novel, *Dr. Zhivago*.
epigraph: *Pasternak*: (1890–1960) Russian poet and novelist whose most famous work is the novel *Doctor Zhivago* (1957).

a tax-deductible donation
to destitute savages, these boxed words
were stacked from concrete floor
15    to rusted sheet-metal roof.
Buzzed-up and warmed by his whiskey,
Verdell came upon four cartons
of Pasternak's *Doctor Zhivago*
and became transfixed by the flaming
20    scarlet fake leather covering.

*But I saw dead ikons of the past*
*in cardboard and glory on the grandest scale.*
*Deep in Holy Mother Russia*
*marching through the bitter snow*

25    *I saw peasant armies mouthing*
*death songs while*
*not knowing where*
*their souls would go.*

We lugged those four cartons of *Zhivago*
30    bound in leatherette
to his puke-stained Plymouth.
That spring, without an ounce of shame
and some pride, Verdell related how
he had liked the Russian story,
35    but he said he ran out of firewood
during the last blizzard of March
and his hungry woodstove
vaporized Yurii Andreievich,
sweet Lara, and those eerie blue wolves
40    howling at snowbound Varykino.
Again and again, Verdell burned the books
until the cast iron glowed a deep, dark red
and the way he figured it, the heat
from his woodstove melted the glue
of the Soviet Union that spring.

*1995*

# Wanbli Gleska Win

Eagle woman:
*Wanbli Gleska Win.*
Distant and unseen
in the air the piercing
5    whistle of an eagle taunts.

It's been six months
since you shut the door
of your flesh to me and I miss
your calm brown strength,

10　　　　　your high-cholesterol cooking,
　　　　　the fragrant down beneath your wings
　　　　　and that snake-eating beak
　　　　　between your Sioux thighs.

*1995*

## Looking for Judas

　　　Weathered gray, the wooden walls
　　　of the old barn soak in the bright
　　　sparkling blood of the five-point mule
　　　deer I hang there in the moonlight.
5　　　Gutted, skinned, and shimmering in eternal
　　　nakedness, the glint in its eyes could
　　　be stolen from the dry hills of Jerusalem.
　　　They say before the white man
　　　brought us Jesus, we had honor.
10　　They say when we killed the Deer People,
　　　we told them their spirits
　　　would live in our flesh.
　　　We used bows of ash, no spotlights, no rifles,
　　　and their holy blood became ours.
　　　Or something like that.

*1995*

## A Colossal American Copulation

for Scarecrow

　　　They say there's a promise
　　　coming down that dusty road.
　　　They say there's a promise coming
　　　down that dusty road, but I don't see it.
5　　　So, fuck the bluebird of happiness.
　　　Fuck the men who keep their dogs chained.
　　　Fuck the men who molest their daughters.
　　　Ditto the men who wrap their dicks
　　　in the Bible and then claim the right
10　　to speak for female reproductive organs.
　　　Likewise the men who hunt coyotes.
　　　And the whining farmers who get paid
　　　for not growing corn and wheat.
　　　The same to the *National Enquirer.*°
15　　Also Madonna° (Santa Evita, indeed).
　　　Yes, add the gutless Tower of Babel
　　　that they call the United Nations.

---

14 *Enquirer:* a tabloid (sensationalist) U.S. newspaper.
15 *Madonna:* (b. 1959), American pop singer and actress who played the part of Eva Peron
in the movie musical *Evita.*

Fuck every gangbanger in America.
Fuck furiously the drive-by shooters,
20       the carjack thugs, the Colombian coke° cartels.
And the ghost of Richard Milhous Nixon.°
Okay, add the yuppie-hillbillies who mess up
the powerspray carwash when they come down
from the hills with half the earth clinging
25       to their new four-wheel drives.
Fuck my neighbor who beats his kids.
And my other neighbor who has plastic
life-sized deer in his front yard.
And Tommy's Used Cars in Chadron, Neb.

30       Fuck my high school coach for not starting
me in the '64 State Championship game.
Fuck the first bar I puked in.
That first cigarette I ever smoked.
That first pussy I ever touched.
35       Fuck it again, Sam.
And that know-it-all Larry King°
and his stupid suspenders.
Fuck the Creative Writing programs
and all the Spam poets they hatch.
40       And the air that blew Marilyn Monroe's°
dress up over her waist.
Fuck you very, very much.
Fuck the Bureau of Indian Affairs.
The ATF° for the Waco° massacre.
45       And sissy boy George Will.°
And Sam Donaldson's° wig.
Fuck the genocidal Serb soldiers;°
may their nuts roast in napalm hell.
Fuck all the booze I ever drank. Yes, include
50       the hair of the dog that bit me for
more than twenty drunken years.

---

20 *coke*: cocaine.
21 *Nixon*: (1913–1994), thirty-seventh U.S. president (1969–1974), forced to resign as evidence accumulated of his complicity in the Watergate cover-up and various abuses of federal and presidential power. His early career was built on active red-baiting during the McCarthy period.
36 *King*: (b. 1933) radio/television talk show host.
40 *Monroe*: (1926–1962), American movie actress; the poem refers to a scene in the film *Some like It Hot* (1959).
44 *ATF*: Alcohol, Tobacco, and Firearms, a U.S. federal agency.
44 *Waco*: Texas town that was the site of an April 1993 FBI assault on the compound of the Branch Davidian religious sect. Thirty-three members of the cult died, most from the resulting fire.
45 *Will*: (b. 1941), a conservative television commentator and political columnist for the U.S. magazine *Newsweek*.
46 *Donaldson*: (b. 1933), television reporter for the American Broadcasting Company (ABC); he is noted for shamelessly injecting opinion into purportedly objective news reports.
47 *Serb soldiers*: responsible for mass murders of Muslim civilians in the former Republic of Yugoslavia in the 1990s.

Fuck a duck!
And the '6os and all that righteous reefer.
Fuck James Dean° and his red jacket.
55    John Wayne° and the gelding
American horse he rode in on.
The IRA° and their songs and bombs.
All the Gila monsters in Arizona.
Bob Dylan° for leading me astray
60    for three misty, moping decades.
My gall bladder for exploding.
Fuck *The Waste Land* by T. S. Eliot
and all those useless allusions.
Fuck war in every form and all other clichés.
65    Fuck, no, double-fuck the Vietnam War.
Every cruel act I ever committed.
Every random act of kindness.
And the undertaker who will gaze
upon my dead and naked flesh
70    and wince at my lack of tattoos.
Fuck O. J. Simpson° and his Ginsus.
Fuck Jesse Helms,° and when he dies,
wormfuck him good in his grave.
Fuck the prairie dogs.
75    The mosquitoes.
The immaturity of MTV.°
Those Monster Trucks.
Mother Teresa.° Jesus, just kidding.
The Information Superhighway.
80    F*U*C*K the L*A*N*G*U*A*G*E poets
and fuck rodeo cowboys in their chapped
and bony butts and boots.
Fuck the gutless Guardsmen
who were at Kent State;° may they still
85    have night horrors after all these years.

---

54 *Dean:* American movie actor. See the annotation to Sherman Alexie's "Tourists."
55 *Wayne:* American movie actor noted for his Indian-fighting westerns. See the annotation to Louise Erdrich's "Dear John Wayne."
57 *IRA:* Irish Republican Army, revolutionary political and terrorist group seeking an end to British rule in Northern Ireland.
59 *Dylan:* (b. 1941), American folk singer and composer who was hugely influential in the counterculture in the 1960s and 1970s. Louis may feel that the message in songs like "The Times They Are A-Changin'" (1963) was untrue.
71 *Simpson:* (b. 1947), a famous American athlete—he was a running back for the Buffalo Bills football team—and then movie actor. He made television commercials, including one for Ginsu carving knives. He was later tried, but acquitted, for murdering his former wife.
72 *Helms:* arch-conservative U.S. senator from North Carolina.
76 *MTV:* television station devoted to rock music videos.
78 *Teresa:* (1910–1997), Roman Catholic nun and missionary.
84 *Kent State:* on May 4, 1970, Ohio National Guard troops opened fire on students at Kent State University who were protesting the U.S. invasion of Cambodia. Four students were killed and eleven wounded.

Fuck all those, who because of this and that
and a touch of cowardice on my part,
I neglected here to name.
Fuck Alzheimer's Disease.
90    And all the things my woman
cannot remember.
Fuck all the things my woman
cannot comprehend.
And time. It only confuses her.
95    Fuck dog spelled backwards.
And fucking. We don't do it anymore.
And death. Almost an afterthought.
Fuck it. Fuck it short and tall.
Fuck it big and small.
100    Fuck it all.
Fucking A. Fuck me.
Never mind. I'm already fucked.

They say there's a promise
coming down that dusty road.
105    They say there's a promise coming down
that dusty road, but I don't see it.

1997

# Petroglyphs of Serena°

*Poets behave impudently towards their experiences: they exploit them.*
—FRIEDRICH NIETZSCHE°

In Yellowbird's Store, the tart tinge
of something sour boggles my nose.
Overpriced cans of Spaghetti-Os
and Spam on the sad shelves
5    are powdered with Great Plains dust.
In Yellowbird's Store, winter people
are hooked up to video poker
machines for brief transfusions.
The faint whispers of dreams and desires
10    fade with each coin thrown away.
Some Indians prefer gambling to making love.
Not me. I love to graze on the sparse, black
cornsilk in the valleys of the Sioux
and it will be my downfall.

---

**poem title:** petroglyphs, carvings or drawings on rocks, including ancient forms of symbolic and ritual representation among Native American peoples.
**epigraph:** *Nietzsche:* (1844–1900), German philosopher.

15 Six-twenty in the morning. These Dakota stars
are as blanched as dead minnows floating
on a garish pink and blue sea of daybreak.
I shake my head, light a Marlboro,
and scope my wife getting dressed.

20 She can't cook worth a damn,
is incredibly and increasingly forgetful.
But she loves me and treats me as good
as a recovering drunk deserves.
Nevertheless, I'm thinking of the wondrous

25 and drool-making beauty of my student Serena
who is flunking but would get an A-plus
and my fuzzy soul if she asked.

    ————————

Unlike parched Christ on his cross,
my mouth was watering.

30 Sitting on the front porch, I saw the snot
yellow moon dishevel two Kleenex clouds.
A clichéd stray dog down by the creek
was alternating keys of hunger and horror.
It would soon be suppertime.

35 I fired up a smoke and sucked it greedily.
The dancing coal lost itself
in the star blanket of night.
In the house my tired wife
was frying venison steaks.

40 My mouth was watering,
but I wasn't hungry at all.
I was dreaming of Serena.
Dark Serena with her broken English.
Wild-ass Serena and our Indian dance

45 of self-destruction.

    ————————

Friday is a blistering prairie day.
105-degree heat will dissolve the will
of the people and tonight you'll see all hues
of brown swarming over this dusty soil.

50 Many of these people will be scarred.
Some of them will be magna cum laude
graduates of the S.D.° State Pen.
Some will be young and lost for the first
time and some will be old and dying.

55 All will be thirsty. Parched and tough.
Tonight there is bound to be trouble.
I can hardly wait. Lord,
how lust becomes me.
I will be there and so will Serena.

    ————————

————————

52 S.D.: South Dakota.

60    The old people said bad spirits blew in
      with the west wind and would not leave
      no matter how much they prayed.
      The old people said the air was bad.
      Death danced through the front doors
65    of many houses that winter, and finally
      spring sent children wild upon the earth.
      Death ran from the sharp glee in their eyes.
      Death ran from the sex breath of summer.
      Finally, Serena was with me.
70    We were naked, biting each other hard
      and the air, oh, the air was good
      and I drank it in without
      the slightest cough of guilt.

      ———————————

      And then it was winter again.
75    Oh, man, a desperate Dakota winter.
      Our neighbors shot a starving deer
      behind their HUD° house
      and butchered it in their front yard.
      They wrapped large pieces in Hefty° bags
80    and stored them in the trunk
      of their broken-down '72 Olds.
      In February they ran out of wood so they
      burned chunks of old tires in the woodstove.
      Their children went to school smudged
85    and smelling like burnt rubber.
      A typical hard-ass Dakota winter.
      All across the Rez, wild Indians
      shiver-danced around woodstoves
      and howled the most wondrous songs
90    of brilliant poverty.

      ———————————

      Lust comes with a darkblood price.
      This is how darkness comes to me.
      Serena's late for speech class as usual.
      Everyone's done their demos but her:
95    *Ain't got none. I'm sorry, but*
      *I just come from working*
      *on a friend's brokedown car.*
      Then said (in a sly-shy-sneaky kind of way)
      she could demo how to clean a carburetor.
100   Outside in the bed of her pickup.
      Well . . . Okay. (What the hell could I say?)
      so the whole class trudges
      out upon the jagged-ice earth.

      ———————————

77 *HUD*: Housing and Urban Development, a federal agency.
79 *Hefty*: a brand of large plastic garbage bag.

It's dark, crazy, she has no flashlight, so
105   I let her use my new white plastic one.
She GUMS-OUT the carb. Slaps in a new kit.
We're all freezing ass. This is Indian education?
Above, the nosey, twinkling stars are giggling.
I give her a C for effort. Would've been higher,
110   but she decorated my new flashlight
with big, fat greaseprints. I tell you now that
the next week I hear she's drunk-rolled
a car and is dead, just like that—dead,
so I buy a new flashlight.
115   A red one.
I take a drive through the deserted Badlands
late at night and stop.
I turn on the old flashlight she used
and toss it in some sage beside the road.
120   It glows in my rearview mirror
for miles before it finally vanishes.

———————

The old people were moving slowly
through the cold air like exhausted swimmers
fighting the tides of a lung-raping sea.
125   But, the sun had its high beams on
and near the creek children were laughing
and moving as fast as spit on a hot woodstove.
Grandfather, it was a good day to pray.
Grandfather, it was a good day to pray
130   that the young would somehow get to be old.
Above all, it was a good day to die.
I did not know her family that well so
I watched her burial from a distance.
Old Indian . . . trick.
135   Middle-aged Indian . . . trick.

———————

About a year after Serena
died in the car wreck
I saw her again—sort of spooky, but
ghost sightings are common around here.
140   Spirits come and go, to and fro.
She was with some strange-looking Skins,°
drove a different car, and looked puzzled,
half-angry when I waved at her.
Acted like she didn't know me.
145   Kind of gave me a kiss-my-butt look
and then flipped me the bird.
I shrugged and did the same back to her.
Her car was filled with buffalo heads,
stampeding the ghost road
150   to White Clay.

———————

———————
141 *Skins:* slang, an abbreviation for "Redskin."

Driving the sheet-ice reservation roads,
ground blizzards whirl and blind. Underneath
all, something paleolithic begs fidelity.
It is something deep inside the hardened fist
155    of almost every Indian man I know.
It is not an unquenchable thirst to live
free from red tape and plastic.
Brothers, you know it is not trickster
dreams or buffalo visions.
160    It isn't self-determination or the good red road.
It is the unending whisper of the ancestors.
It is that simple urge to scalp a white man.
I think it has something to do with love.
The sweet, sweet squeak
165    of blade hitting headbone.
The snapdance of sinew
yanked awry.

————————

Near here, over by those dead cottonwoods, is
where I picked up the lady hitchhiker last winter.
170    Oh, she laughed and talked Skin sexy
after I gave her a cigarette and a beer.
Near Wolf Creek turnoff I glanced
over to where she was sitting.
She'd vanished. The seat was empty.
175    My heart beat brilliant.
I began to sweat and then shook
like lemon Jell-O.
Up the road, I saw a deer dash past.
Its eyes were smiling, and a cigarette
180    dangled from its red-painted lips.
Its eyes were Serena's.

————————

Newly minted leaves sparkle
on the giant cottonwoods.
It's the first pow-wow of the season.
185    They say even a white man can listen closely
and understand how the drum is our heart.
It pounds and pulses these words through
the blood of our Indian Nations:
"We have survived. Yes, we have survived.
190    Look at us dancing. Look at us laughing.
God damn you *wasicus,* we'll always survive!"
Yes, they say *even* a white man can listen closely
and understand how the drum is our heart.

————————

The sign here on this bar used to say
195    NO INDIANS ALLOWED but that wasn't true.
Hey, we know that was not true at all.
Here, the white traders made a fortune

taking savage souls in payment
for pints of whiskey and wine.
200    Here, countless stumbling Skins entered
the gates of the Fire Water World.
If you listen closely, you can hear their ghosts
winging and whimpering through
the dark skies of this dying America.
205    Brothers, I swear to Christ on his cross
if you open your mouth, you can taste
their rain of ghost tears.

---

We are all hiding from the truth.
Our children have no respect
210    because their parents cannot connect
the values of the ancient chiefs
to the deadly grief that welfare brings.
We're reaping the womb's reward of mutant
generations who stumbled toward dismembering
215    the long and sometimes senile span between you,
Great Spirit, and your artwork, man.
The question is, can the children be saved?
And if so, then why? Will they ever be whole
or do we just add them to the dark days
220    of casualties from Sand Creek°
to Ira Hayes?°

I mean, do we catalogue them
in the first grade and then sit back
and wait, afraid that one will be dead
225    in a car wreck at ten? That one has a room
reserved at the state pen?
That one will flunk out of college
a total of eight times over a ten-year slate
and then will take his life after stabbing
230    his kids, his dad, his wife?
That one will have six children,
none from the same man,
and all will carry their mom's surname?
That one will move to a city and drink
235    so much that his heart will forget
the prayer of human touch?

---

220 *Sand Creek:* November 29, 1864, Colorado massacre of over seventy Cheyennes and Arapahos who thought themselves under U.S. Army protection. Many of the bodies were mutilated by either the 125 regular army troops or the 700 Colorado volunteers who attacked them.
221 *Ira Hayes:* (1923–1955), a media-created Native American (Pima) hero of World War II. He was one of six marines to restage the February, 1945, flag raising on the newly captured South Pacific island of Iwo Jima. The photograph brought him fame he could not tolerate. He returned home to find the Pimas still lacked sufficient water for their farms and he began to drink. The Indian Relocation Program moved him to Chicago, which proved equally unsuccessful. He returned home where he froze to death in 1955.

That one will write their story
and end it as if it were
a lousy job he just quit
240 without searching
for a space to inject
the slightest hint of grace?

---

What we never say is that when we hit
rock-bottom, we can still drop farther.
245 She said back in the old days
we took care of our elders.
There was no AFDC,° no food stamps.
We had gardens, we hunted.
We respected our parents
250 and we weren't afraid of work.
In the old days, men did not beat
their women for no reason.
In the old days, children had two parents.
Yes, in the old days life was better.
255 In the old days I was young and in love,
she said with a shrug . . . so I kissed her.
On Serena's mother's old,
cracked fullblood lips
I kissed her ever so softly.

---

260 Inside this shack the restless spirit
of a woman will put on a faded shawl
and take a kerosene lamp
from atop a battered bureau.
She will open the door and float
265 through the chilled air to the outhouse.
She will spread the light into all the corners
making sure no spiders lurk.
Then she will sing to herself and dream
of running water and porcelain.
270 That is what this spirit will do. I know.
She is the grandmother
of us all.

---

*Wanbli Gleska Wi* (Thalia) said
old-time Lakota call it *wasigla.*
275 A woman must mourn for a full year
to pay respect to the spirit of the departed.
Not supposed to leave the house,
have to wear black,
can't go shopping or go pow-wow.

---

247 *AFDC:* Aid to Families of Dependent Children, a federal program.

|     |                                             |
| --- | ------------------------------------------- |
| 280 | Just stay home and mourn.                   |
|     | When a woman is spirit-keeping or           |
|     | ghost-keeping, she can't make sudden        |
|     | moves—especially with her hands.            |
|     | Can't disturb the air.                      |
| 285 | And has to put out food                     |
|     | at each meal to feed the spirit.            |
|     | One full year, Serena's younger sister      |
|     | Thalia said in my motel room.               |
|     | Must never offend the spirits, Thalia said. |
| 290 | Must *never* offend the spirits, Thalia said, |
|     | or bad shit will happen to you.             |
|     | Traditional Indian wisdom, she said.        |
|     | What goes around comes around               |
|     | or should it be                             |
| 295 | what comes around goes around?              |
|     | You don't believe that, do you? I asked.    |
|     | Nothing bad would happen to me.             |
|     | I laughed and got undressed,                |
|     | safe and guilt-free                         |
| 300 | in the snug, smug darkness                  |
|     | of lust.                                    |

*1997*

# Yusef Komunyakaa (b. 1947)

Komunyakaa is an African American poet who was born in Bogalusa, Louisiana, the son of a carpenter. He grew up in Louisiana and was educated at the University of Colorado, Colorado State University, and the University of California at Irvine. Long interested in the relationship between jazz and poetry, he has coedited two volumes on the subject. From 1965–1967 he served a tour of duty in South Vietnam, where he was an information specialist and editor of the military newspaper *Southern Cross*; he won a bronze star, but it was not until more than a decade after returning from the war that he would begin writing poems about the experience. This would lead to *Dien Cai Dau* (1988), almost certainly the best Vietnam poems by an American veteran of the war. This book-length sequence, from which "Tu Do Street," "Prisoners," and "Communiqué" are reprinted, continually returns to the war's racial tensions and its racial constitution. White and black troops from America's working class and its underclass were drafted to kill a colored enemy indistinguishable from Vietnam's civilian population. The only redemption we can now ask, Komunyakaa's poems demonstrate, grows out of admitting the racial structures we have previously repressed. Both in poems like "Tu Do Street" and in "Work" Komunyakaa becomes especially eloquent when he takes on unpopular or awkward topics. He often manages to combine violent subject matter and strong narrative conflicts with notably rich imagery. The poems as a result can be both harsh and musical. His selected poems, *Neon Vernacular*, won the Pulitzer prize in 1994. Komunyakaa has taught at several universities, including Indiana, Washington, Harvard, and Princeton.

## Tu Do Street°

Music divides the evening.
I close my eyes & can see
men drawing lines in the dust.
America pushes through the membrane
5    of mist & smoke, & I'm a small boy
again in Bogalusa.° *White Only*

---

**poem title:** *Tu Do Street:* a busy warren of bars, brothels, and bistros at the center of Saigon, capital of South Vietnam and American Army headquarters during the Vietnam War, 1956–1975.
6 *Bogalusa:* the Louisiana town where Komunyakaa grew up.

signs & Hank Snow.° But tonight
I walk into a place where bar girls
fade like tropical birds. When
10    I order a beer, the mama-san
behind the counter acts as if she
can't understand, while her eyes
skirt each white face, as Hank Williams°
calls from the psychedelic jukebox.
15    We have played Judas where
only machine-gun fire brings us
together. Down the street
black GIs hold to their turf also.
An off-limits sign pulls me
20    deeper into alleys, as I look
for a softness behind these voices
wounded by their beauty & war.
Back in the bush at Dak To°
& Khe Sanh,° we fought
25    the brothers of these women
we now run to hold in our arms.
There's more than a nation
inside us, as black & white
soldiers touch the same lovers
30    minutes apart, tasting
each other's breath,
without knowing these rooms
run into each other like tunnels
leading to the underworld.

*1988*

## Prisoners

Usually at the helipad
I see them stumble-dance
across the hot asphalt
with crokersacks over their heads,
5    moving toward the interrogation huts,
thin-framed as box kites
of sticks & black silk
anticipating a hard wind
that'll tug & snatch them
10    out into space. I think

---

7 *Hank Snow:* (1914–), Canadian country singer who moved to the U.S. in 1948 and joined
Nashville's *Grand Ole Opry* program in 1950.
13 *Hank Williams:* (1923–1953), American composer, vocalist, guitarist; one of the greatest
stars and most influential composers of country music, his classic songs include "Your
Cheatin' Heart."
23 *Dak To:* a city in northwest South Vietnam that was the site of one of the most violent
battles of the war in November, 1967; its airfield was attacked again in February, 1968.
24 *Khe Sanh:* site of U.S. Marine base in northernmost South Vietnam near the Laotian
border; attacked by North Vietnamese Army on January 21, 1968 and kept under seige un-
til April 7.

some must be laughing
under their dust-colored hoods,
knowing rockets are aimed
at Chu Lai°—that the water's
15    evaporating & soon the nail
will make contact with metal.
How can anyone anywhere love
these half-broken figures
bent under the sky's brightness?
20    The weight they carry
is the soil we tread night & day.
Who can cry for them?
I've heard the old ones
are the hardest to break.
25    An arm twist, a combat boot
against the skull, a .45
jabbed into the mouth, nothing
works. When they start talking
with ancestors faint as camphor
30    smoke in pagodas, you know
you'll have to kill them
to get an answer.
Sunlight throws
scythes against the afternoon.
35    Everything's a heat mirage; a river
tugs at their slow feet.
I stand alone & amazed,
with a pill-happy door gunner
signaling for me to board the Cobra.
40    I remember how one day
I almost bowed to such figures
walking toward me, under
a corporal's ironclad stare.
I can't say why.
45    From a half-mile away
trees huddle together,
& the prisoners look like
marionettes hooked to strings of light.

*1988*

## Communiqué

Bob Hope's° on stage, but we want the Gold Diggers,°
want a flash of legs

through the hemorrhage of vermilion, giving us
something to kill for.

---

14 *Chu Lai*: a northern coastal town fifty miles south of Danang in South Vietnam; in 1965 it was the site of the first major U.S. amphibious operation since 1958; a huge American base was established there.
1 *Hope:* (b. 1903) American entertainer and comedian who made trips overseas to entertain American troops in World War II, the Korean War, and, as here, in the Vietnam War.

5      We want our hearts wrung out like rags & ground down
       to Georgia dust

       while Cobras° drag the perimeter, gliding along the sea,
       swinging searchlights

       through the trees. The assault & battery of hot pink
10     glitter erupts

       as the rock 'n' roll band tears down the night—caught
       in a safety net

       of brightness, The Gold Diggers° convulse. White legs
       shimmer like strobes.

15     The lead guitarist's right foot's welded to his wah-wah.
       "I thought you said

       Aretha° was gonna be here." "Man, I don't wanna see
       no Miss America."

       "There's Lola." The sky is blurred by magnesium flares
20     over the fishing boats.

       "Shit, man, she looks awful white to me." We duck
       when we hear the quick

       metallic hiss of the mountain of amplifiers struck by
       a flash of rain.

25     After the show's packed up & gone, after the choppers
       have flown out backwards,

       after the music & colors have died slowly in our heads,
       & the downpour's picked up,

       we sit holding our helmets like rain-polished skulls.

                                                          *1988*


# The Dog Act

            I'm the warm-up act.
            I punch myself in the face
            across the makeshift stage.
            Fall through imaginary trapdoors.
5           Like the devil, I turn cartwheels
            & set my hair afire.

---

7 *Cobra*: brand of helicopter gun ship.
13 *Golddiggers*: a ten-to-twelve member female dance troup that was a summer replace-
ment for the *The Dean Martin Show* on American television in 1968, 1969, and 1970.
17 *Aretha*: Aretha Franklin (1942– ), American soul singer.

Contradiction, the old barker
drunk again on these lights
& camaraderie. The white poodles,
10    Leo, Camellia, St. John, & Anna,
leap through fiery hoops
to shake my hand.
I make a face
that wants to die
15    inside me.
"Step right up ladies & gentlemen,
see the Greatest Show on Earth,
two-headed lions, seraphim,°
unicorns, satyrs, a woman
20    who saws herself in half."
I can buckdance till I am
in love with the trapeze artist.
Can I have your attention now?
I'm crawling across the stagefloor
25    like a dog with four broken legs.
You're supposed to jump up
& down now, laugh & applaud.

*1979*


# The Nazi Doll

It sits lopsided
in a cage. Membrane.

Vertebra. This precious, white
ceramic doll's brain

5    twisted out of a knob of tungsten.
It bleeds a crooked smile

& arsenic sizzles in the air.
Its eyes an old lie.

Its bogus tongue, Le Diable.°
10    Its lampshade of memory.

Guilt yahoos, benedictions
in its Cro-Magnon° skull

blossom, a flurry of fireflies,
vowels of rattlesnake beads.

---

18 *seraphim:* the highest order of angels; unicorns: fabled creatures, a horse with a single spiralled horn growing from its head, often symbolizing virginity; satyrs: in Greek mythology, licentious woodland creatures, half man, half goat, with goat's pointed ears, legs, and short horns.
9 *Le Diable:* the devil.
12 *Cro-Magnon:* prehistoric human being.

15        Its heart hums the song of dust
         like a sweet beehive.

1979

## Fog Galleon

Horse-headed clouds, flags
& pennants tied to black
Smokestacks in swamp mist.
From the quick green calm
5   Some nocturnal bird calls
*Ship ahoy, ship ahoy!*
I press against the taxicab
Window. I'm back here, interfaced
With a dead phosphorescence;
10   The whole town smells
Like the world's oldest anger.
Scabrous residue hunkers down under
Sulfur & dioxide, waiting
For sunrise, like cargo
15   On a phantom ship outside Gaul.°
Cool glass against my cheek
Pulls me from the black schooner
On a timeless sea—everything
Dwarfed beneath the papermill
20   Lights blinking behind the cloudy
Commerce of wheels, of chemicals
That turn workers into pulp
When they fall into vats
Of steamy serenity.

1993

## Work

I won't look at her.
My body's been one
Solid motion from sunrise,
Leaning into the lawnmower's
5   Roar through pine needles
& crabgrass. Tiger-colored
Bumblebees nudge pale blossoms
Till they sway like silent bells
Calling. But I won't look.
10   Her husband's outside Oxford,
Mississippi, bidding on miles
Of timber. I wonder if he's buying
Faulkner's° ghost, if he might run

---

15 *Gaul:* ancient region of western Europe, corresponding roughly to present-day France and Belgium; the Romans extended the designation to include northern Italy.
13 *Faulkner:* William Faulkner (1897–1962), American novelist who lived in Oxford, Mississippi; Colonel John Sartoris (1873–1924) is a Faulkner character in *Sartoris* (1929) and *The Unvanquished* (1938) from the series of novels set in the fictitious county modeled after Faulkner's own.

|      |                                        |
|------|----------------------------------------|
|      | Into Colonel Sartoris                  |
| 15   | Along some dusty road.                 |
|      | Their teenage daughter & son sped off  |
|      | An hour ago in a red Corvette          |
|      | For the tennis courts,                 |
|      | & the cook, Roberta,                   |
| 20   | Only works a half day                  |
|      | Saturdays. This antebellum house       |
|      | Looms behind oak & pine                |
|      | Like a secret, as quail                |
|      | Flash through branches.                |
| 25   | I won't look at her. Nude              |
|      | On a hammock among elephant ears       |
|      | & ferns, a pitcher of lemonade         |
|      | Sweating like our skin.                |
|      | Afternoon burns on the pool            |
| 30   | Till everything's blue,                |
|      | Till I hear Johnny Mathis°             |
|      | Beside her like a whisper.             |
|      | I work all the quick hooks             |
|      | Of light, the same unbroken            |
| 35   | Rhythm my father taught me             |
|      | Years ago: *Always give*               |
|      | *A man a good day's labor.*            |
|      | *I* won't look. The engine             |
|      | Pulls me like a dare.                  |
| 40   | Scent of honeysuckle                   |
|      | Sings black sap through mystery,       |
|      | Taboo, law, creed, what kills          |
|      | A fire that is its own heart           |
|      | Burning open the mouth.                |
| 45   | But I won't look                       |
|      | At the insinuation of buds             |
|      | Tipped with cinnabar.°                 |
|      | I'm here, as if I never left,          |
|      | Stopped in this garden,                |
| 50   | Drawn to some Lotus-eater.° Pollen     |
|      | Explodes, but I only smell             |
|      | Gasoline & oil on my hands,            |
|      | & can't say why there's this bed       |
|      | Of crushed narcissus°                  |
|      | As if gods wrestled here.              |

1993

---

31 *Mathis:* (1935–), American popular singer, concentrating on haunting ballads; hits include "Misty" (1959) and "The Twelfth of Never" (1961).

47 *cinnabar:* vivid red to reddish-orange color.

50 *Lotus-eater:* in Greek mythology, one of a group of people who fed on the lotus plant and lived in a drugged, indolent state of pleasure.

54 *narcissus:* spring flowering bulbs with white or yellow flowers having cup-shaped or trumpet-shaped central crowns; in Greek mythology, Narcissus was a youth who pined away infatuated with his own image in a pool of water and was transformed into the flower bearing his name.

# Ai (b. 1947)

Born Florence Anthony in Albany, Texas, Ai did not learn her real father's identity until she was sixteen. Then she learned she had a Japanese American father; her mother was black, Irish, and Choctaw Indian. She took the name "Ai," which means "love" in Japanese, to signal her heritage. Ai's childhood was spent in a variety of cities, including Tucson, Los Angeles, and San Francisco. She was educated at the University of Arizona and the University of California at Irvine. Although she has done short lyrics on both intimate and public historical topics, as "Twenty-Year Marriage" and "The German Army, Russia, 1943," demonstrate, her specialty is the dramatic monologue, sometimes in the voices of invented personas, sometimes in the person of named public figures. Her speakers have included Marilyn Monroe, Leon Trotsky, Emiliano Zapata, John F. Kennedy, Joseph McCarthy, the Atlanta child murderer, and an anonymous *Kristallnacht* survivor. Some are corrupted seekers after power who try to justify themselves fruitlessly; others have been consumed by different appetites. Her language is vivid but rather matter-of-fact and unadorned. Indeed the voices of her speakers sometimes acquire an almost deadpan, driven passion. She has been obsessed, throughout her career, with the intersecting subjects of death, sex, history, and religion. Her poems seek to lay bare the most violent inner motives we have and the meaning of the desire behind them. Like Plath, she has sought a way to write without holding anything back. In the process, especially when taking up real people and events, she has shown us one thing we might not have known poetry was uniquely suited to do—speak brutal truths about public life with a clarity no other discourse can muster.

## Twenty-Year Marriage

You keep me waiting in a truck
with its one good wheel stuck in the ditch,
while you piss against the south side of a tree.
Hurry. I've got nothing on under my skirt tonight.
5    That still excites you, but this pickup has no windows
and the seat, one fake leather thigh,
pressed close to mine is cold.
I'm the same size, shape, make as twenty years ago,
but get inside me, start the engine;
10   you'll have the strength, the will to move,
I'll pull, you push, we'll tear each other in half.
Come on, baby, lay me down on my back.

Pretend you don't owe me a thing
and maybe we'll roll out of here,
15    leaving the past stacked up behind us;
old newspapers nobody's ever got to read again.

1973


## The German Army, Russia, 1943

For twelve days,
I drilled through Moscow ice
to reach paradise,
that white tablecloth, set with a plate
5    that's cracking bit by bit
like the glassy air, like me,
I know I'll fly apart soon,
the pieces of me so light they float.
The Russians burned their crops,
10    rather than feed our army.
Now they strike us against each other like dry rocks
and set us on fire with a hunger
nothing can feed.
Someone calls me and I look up.
15    It's Hitler.
I imagine eating his terrible, luminous eyes.
*Brother*, he says.
I stand up, tie the rags tighter around my feet.
I hear my footsteps running after me,
but I am already gone.

1979


## The Testimony of J. Robert Oppenheimer°

### A Fiction

When I attained enlightenment,
I threw off the night like an old skin.
My eyes filled with light
and I fell to the ground.
5    I lay in Los Alamos,
while at the same time,
I fell

---

**poem title:** Oppenheimer (1904–1967) was a physicist who, in 1942, joined the World War II Manhattan Project to develop an atomic bomb. From 1943–1945 he directed the laboratory in Los Alamos, New Mexico, where the bomb was designed, built, and (at a remote site) tested and, as a result, he became known internationally as "the father of the atomic bomb." When the test succeeded, he is reported to have recalled a line from the *Bhaghavad Gita*: "I am become death, destroyer of worlds." In 1945, he was one of a panel of scientists who recommended the bomb's use against Japan. After initially opposing research on a hydrogen bomb in 1951, he ran afoul of McCarthyism and lost his security clearance in 1953.

toward Hiroshima,
faster and faster,
10      till the earth,
till the morning
slipped away beneath me.
Some say when I hit
there was an explosion,
15      a searing wind that swept the dead before it,
but there was only silence,
only the soothing baby-blue morning
rocking me in its cradle of cumulus cloud,
only rest.
20      There beyond the blur of mortality,
the roots of the trees of Life and Death,
the trees William Blake called Art and Science,
joined in a kind of Gordian knot
even Alexander couldn't cut.

25      To me, the ideological high wire
is for fools to balance on with their illusions.
It is better to leap into the void.
Isn't that what we all want anyway?—
to eliminate all pretense
30      till like the oppressed who in the end
identifies with the oppressor,
we accept the worst in ourselves
and are set free.

In high school, they told me
35      all scientists
start from the hypothesis "what if"
and it's true.
What we as a brotherhood lack in imagination
we make up for with curiosity.
40      I was always motivated
by a ferocious need to know.
Can you tell me, gentlemen,
that you don't want it too?—
the public collapse,
45      the big fall smooth as honey down a throat.
Anything that gets you closer
to what you are.
Oh, to be born again and again
from that dark, metal womb,
50      the sweet, intoxicating smell of decay
the imminent dead give off
rising to embrace me.

But I could say anything, couldn't I?
Like a bed we make and unmake at whim,
55      the truth is always changing,
always shaped by the latest
collective urge to destroy.

So I sit here,
gnawed down by the teeth
60      of my nightmares.
My soul, a wound that will not heal.
All I know is that urge,
the pure, sibylline intensity of it.
Now, here at parade's end
65      all that matters:
our military in readiness,
our private citizens
in a constant frenzy of patriotism
and jingoistic pride,
70      our enemies endless,
our need to defend infinite.
Good soldiers,
we do not regret or mourn,
but pick up the guns of our fallen.
75      Like characters in the funny papers,
under the heading
"Further Adventures of the Lost Tribe,"
we march past the third eye of History,
as it rocks back and forth
80      in its hammock of stars.
We strip away the tattered fabric
of the universe
to the juicy, dark meat,
the nothing beyond time.
85      We tear ourselves down atom by atom,
till electron and positron,
we become our own transcendent annihilation.

*1986*


# The Priest's Confession

### 1

I didn't say mass this morning.
I stood in the bell tower
and watched Rosamund, the orphan,
chase butterflies, her laughter
5       rising, slamming into me,
while the almond scent of her body
wrapped around my neck like a noose.
Let me go, I told her once,
you'll have to let me go,
10      but she held on.
She was twelve.
She annoyed me,
lying in her little bed—
*Tell me a story, Father.*
15      *Father, I can't sleep. I miss my mother.*
*Can I sleep with you?*

I carried her into my room—
the crucifix, the bare white walls.
While she slept,

20    she threw the covers back.
Her cotton gown was wedged above her thighs.
I nearly touched her.
I prayed for deliverance, but none came.
Later, I broke my rosary.

25    The huge, black wooden beads
clattered to the floor
like ovoid marbles,
and I in my black robe,
a bead on God's own broken rosary,

30    also rolled there on the floor
in a kind of ecstasy.
I remembered how when I was six
Lizabeta, the witch, blessed me,
rocking in her ladder-back chair,

35    while I drank pig's blood
and ate it smeared across a slice of bread.
She said, *Eat, Emilio, eat.*
*Hell is only as far as your next breath*
*and heaven unimaginably distant.*

40    *Gate after gate stands between you and God,*
*so why not meet the devil instead?*
*He at least has time for people.*
When she died, the villagers
burned her house.

45    I lay my hand on the bell.
Sometimes when I ring this,
I feel I'll fragment,
then reassemble
and I'll be some other thing—

50    a club to beat,
a stick to heave at something:
between the act and the actor
there can be no separateness.
That is Gnostic. Heresy.

55    Lord, I crave things,
Rosamund's bird's nest of hair
barely covered by her drawers.
I want to know that you love me,
that the screams of men,

60    as loud as any trumpet,
have brought down the gates of stone
between us.

2

The next four years,
Rosamund's breasts grew

65    and grew in secret

like two evil thoughts.
I made her confess to me
and one night, she swooned,
she fell against me
70     and I laid her down.
I bent her legs this way and that.
I pressed my face between them
to smell "Our Lady's Roses"
and finally, I wanted to eat them.
75     I bit down, her hair was like thorns,
my mouth bled, but I didn't stop.
She was so quiet,
then suddenly she cried out
and sat up;
80     her face, a hazy flame,
moved closer and closer to mine,
until our lips touched.
I called her woman then
because I knew what it meant.
85     But I call you God, the Father,
and you're a stranger to me.

3

I pull the thick rope
from the rafter
and roll it up.
90     I thought I'd use this today,
that I'd kick off the needlepoint footstool
and swing out over the churchyard
as if it were the blue and weary Earth,
that as I flew out into space,
95     I'd lose my skin, my bones
to the sound of one bell
ringing in the empty sky.
Your voice, Lord.
Instead, I hear Rosamund's laughter,
100     sometimes her screams,
and behind them, my name,
calling from the roots of trees,
flowers, plants,
from the navel of Lucifer
105     from which all that is living
grows and ascends toward you,
a journey not home,
not back to the source of things,
but away from it,
110     toward a harsh, purifying light
that keeps nothing whole—
while my sweet, dark Kyries
became the wine of water
and I drank you.
115     I married you,

not with my imperfect body,
but with my perfect soul.
Yet, I know I'd have climbed
and climbed through the seven heavens
120    and found each empty.

I lean from the bell tower.
It's twilight;
smoke is beginning to gray the sky.
Rosamund has gone inside
125    to wait for me.

She's loosened her hair
and unbuttoned her blouse
the way I like,
set table,
130    and prayed,
as I do—
one more night.
Lamb stew, salty butter.
I'm the hard, black bread on the water.
Lord, come walk with me.

*1986*

# Wendy Rose (b. 1948)

Rose was born in Oakland, California, of Hopi and 'Me-wuk ancestry. She attended Contra Costa College and the University of California at Berkeley and since then has taught Native American Studies at several colleges, including the University of California at Berkeley. She is an anthropologist and the editor of *American Indian Quarterly*, as well as a poet and an artist.

## Truganinny

*"Truganinny, the last of the Tasmanians,° had seen the stuffed and
mounted body of her husband and it was her dying wish that she be
buried in the outback or at sea for she did not wish her body to be
subjected to the same indignities. Upon her death she was never-
theless stuffed and mounted and put on display for over eighty years."*
PAUL COE, AUSTRALIAN ABORIGINE ACTIVIST, 1972

You will need
to come closer
for little is left
of this tongue
and what I am saying
is important.

I am
the last one.

I whose nipples
wept white mist
and saw so many
dead daughters
their mouths empty and round
their breathing stopped
their eyes gone gray.

5

10

15

---

**epigraph:** *Tasmanians:* one of the geographically defined groups of Aborigines who were the native inhabitants of Australia; Tasmania, an island separated from the Australian mainland by the Bass Strait. The Australian government forced the remaining Tasmanians to move to Flinders Island in 1831, and the last full-blooded member, Truganinny, died there in 1876.

Take my hand
black into black
as yellow clay
is a slow melt
20    to grass gold
of earth

and I am melting
back to the Dream.

Do not leave
25    for I would speak,
I would sing
another song.

Your song.

They will take me.
30    Already they come;
even as I breathe
they are waiting for me
to finish my dying.

We old ones
35    take such
a long time.

Please
take my body
to the source of night,
40    to the great black desert
where Dreaming was born.
Put me under
the bulk of a mountain
or in the distant sea,
45    put me where
they will not
find me.

1985

# C. D. Wright (b. 1949)

Born and raised in the Ozark Mountains of Arkansas, C(arolyn) D. Wright is the daughter of a judge and a court reporter. She received her first degree from Memphis State University and completed her education at the University of Arkansas. She has remained in touch with her roots. She remains the Poet Laureate of Arkansas's Boone County and organized a traveling exhibit about the state in the mid-1990s. Some of her short, unsparing lyrics retell stories of her experience in the South, though she also has wider investments in populist politics and has written a number of linguistically experimental prose poems. "Over Everything," reprinted here, is adapted from a passage near the end of John Hersey's *Hiroshima* (1946), pp. 91–92. Wright has published several critical essays and essays on poetics as well as seven volumes of poetry. Along with poet Forrest Gander, she runs Lost Roads Publishers. She teaches at Brown University.

## Obedience of the Corpse

The midwife puts a rag in the dead woman's hand,
takes the hairpins out.

She smells apples,
wonders where she keeps them in the house.
5    Nothing is under the sink
but a broken sack of potatoes
growing eyes in the dark.

She hopes the mother's milk is good a while longer,
and the woman up the road is still nursing.
10   But she remembers the neighbor
and the dead woman never got along.

A limb breaks,
She knows it's not the wind.
Somebody needs to set out some poison.

15   She looks to see if the woman wrote down any names,
finds a white shirt to wrap the baby in.
It's beautiful she thinks
like snow nobody has walked on.

1979

## Over Everything

Over everything: up through the wreckage of the body, in its troughs, and along its swells, tangled among its broken veins, climbing on its swollen limbs: a blanket of fresh, vivid, lush, optimistic green; the verdancy rising even from the foundations of its ruins. Weeds already amid the bruises, and wild flowers bloomed among its bones. Everywhere were bluets and Spanish bayonets, goosefoot, morning glories and daylilies, purslane and clotbur and panic grass and feverfew. Especially in a circle at the center, sickle senna grew in extraordinary regeneration, not only standing among the blown remnants of the same plant but pushing up in new places, among distended folds and through rents in the flesh. It actually seemed as if a load of sickle senna had been dropped. On the eighth day . . .

*1993*

## Song of the Gourd

In gardening I continued to sit on my side of the car: to drive whenever possible at the usual level of distraction: in gardening I shat nails glass contaminated dirt and threw up on the new shoots: in gardening I learned to praise things I had dreaded: I pushed the hair out of my face: I felt less responsible for one man's death one woman's long-term isolation: my bones softened: in gardening I lost nickels and ring settings I uncovered buttons and marbles: I lay half the worm aside and sought the rest: I sought myself in the bucket and wondered why I came into being in the first place: in gardening I turned away from the television and went around smelling of offal the inedible parts of the chicken: in gardening I said excelsior: in gardening I required no company I had to forgive my own failure to perceive how things were: I went out barelegged at dusk and dug and dug and dug: I hit rock my ovaries softened: in gardening I was protean as in no other realm before or since: I longed to torch my old belongings and belch a little flame of satisfaction: in gardening I longed to stroll farther into soundlessness: I could almost forget what happened many swift years ago in arkansas: I felt like a god from down under: chthonian: in gardening I thought this is it body and soul I am home at last: excelsior: praise the grass: in gardening I fled the fold that supported the war: only in gardening could I stop shrieking: stop: stop the slaughter: only in gardening could I press my ear to the ground to hear my soul let out an unyielding noise: my lines softened: I turned the water onto the joyfilled boychild: only in gardening did I feel fit to partake to go on trembling in the last light: I confess the abject urge to weed your beds while the bittersweet overwhelmed my daylilies: I summoned the courage to grin: I climbed the hill with my bucket and slept like a dipper in the cool of your body: besotted with growth; shot through by green

*1996*

# Jessica Hagedorn (b. 1949)

Born in Manila and raised in the Philippines before coming to the U.S., Hagedorn is known as a novelist, a performance artist, a poet, and a playwright. Her 1993 collection *Danger and Beauty* gathers poems, stories, and memoirs. It is dedicated to poet Kenneth Rexroth, who first published her in 1973 when she was living in San Francisco, two years before she formed a band, The West Coast Gangster Choir. A few years later she moved to New York where she read poems to music, worked as Program Coordinator for the St. Marks Poetry Project, wrote the screenplay for the film *Fresh Kill* (1994), and created performance art pieces such as *Mango Tango* and *Airport Music*.

## Ming the Merciless°

*dancing on the edge/of a razor blade*
*ming/king of the lionmen*
*sing/bring us to the planet*
*of no return . . .*

      king of the lionmen
      come dancing in my tube
      sing, ming, sing . . .
      blink sloe-eyed phantasy
5     and touch me where
      there's always hot water
      in this house

      o flying angel
      o pterodactyl
10    your rocket glides
      like a bullet

---

**poem title:** The wily Emperor Ming was the implacable but stylish villain of Alex Raymond's "Flash Gordon" science fiction comic strip and popular movie serials, *Flash Gordon* (1936), *Flash Gordon's Trip to Mars* (1938), and *Flash Gordon Conquers the Universe* (1940), noted for their futuristic sets and nonstop action. With his flamboyant art deco costume and its high collars, Ming is an unforgettable presence. His name is presumably borrowed from the Ming dynasty (1368–1644) in China.

you are the asian nightmare
the yellow peril
the domino theory
15      the current fashion trend

ming, merciless ming,
come dancing in my tube
the silver edges of your cloak
slice through my skin
20      and king vulgar's cardboard wings
flap-flap in death
(for you)

o ming, merciless ming,
the silver edges of your cloak
25      cut hearts in two
the blood red dimensions
that trace american galaxies

you are the asian nightmare
the yellow peril
30      the domino theory
the current fashion trend

sing, ming, sing . . .
whistle the final notes
of your serialized abuse
35      cinema life
cinema death
cinema of ethnic prurient interest

o flying angel
o pterodactyl
40      your rocket glides
like a bullet
and touches me where
there's always hot water
in this house

*1985*

# Ray A. Young Bear (b. 1950)

An enrolled member of the Mesquakie Nation of central Iowa, Ray Young Bear grew up on the tribal lands near Tama. He is not only a poet and a novelist but also a performing artist. With his wife Stella, whose bead work is depicted on the cover of *The Invisible Musician* (1990), he founded the Black Eagle Child Dance Troup, for which Young Bear plays drums. Under the Woodland Singers title, they have recorded traditional Native American songs. Young Bear has taught at several schools, including the University of Iowa; he also writes essays and editorials for the *Des Moines Sunday Register*. His poetry frequently takes up contemporary subjects in the light of our historical inheritance and in the context of Native American mythology.

## In Viewpoint: Poem for 14 Catfish And The Town of Tama, Iowa°

into whose world do we go on living?
the northern pike and the walleye fish
thaw in the heat of the stove.
it wasn't too long ago
5    when they swam under the water,
sending bursts of water and clouds
of mossy particles from their gills,
camouflaging each other's route—
unable to find the heart to share
10   the last pockets of sunlight
and oxygen,
stifled by the inevitable
realization that the end is near
when man-sized fish slowly tumble up
15   from their secretive pits.

---

**poem title:** Tama, a town in central Iowa, is near lands where the Mesquakie (Red Earth People) make their home today. In the seventeenth century, the Mesquakie tribe lived on the southern shore of Lake Superior in what is now Wisconsin, generally moving to the prairies to hunt in the winter. Toward the end of the eighteenth century, the encroachment of white settlers forced them to move south to the Mississippi River in Iowa and Illinois. A few decades later, they were compelled to move again, this time to a reservation in Kansas, but in the mid-nineteenth century a group of them pooled their resources to purchase land near Tama. Through much of their history, they remained committed to self-determination and resistance to assimilation.

i, and many others, have an unparalleled
respect for the iowa river even though
the ice may be four to five feet thick,
but the farmers and the local whites
20   from the nearby town of tama and surrounding
towns, with their usual characteristic
ignorance and disregard, have driven noisily
over the ice and across our lands
on their pickups and snowmobiles,
25   disturbing the dwindling fish
and wildlife—
and due to their
own personal greed and self-
displeasure in avoiding the holes
30   made by tribal spearfishermen in
search of food (which would die
anyway because of the abnormal weather),
the snowmobilers ran and complained like
a bunch of spoiled and obnoxious children
35   to the conservation officer, who, with
nothing better to do along with a deputy
sheriff and a highway patrolman, rode out
to tribal land and arrested the fishermen
and their catfish.

40   with a bit of common sense,
and with a thousand other places
in the vast state of iowa to play toys
with their snowmobiles in, and with the winter
snow in well overabundance, they could have gone
45   elsewhere, but with the same 17th century
instincts they share with their own town's
drunken scums who fantasize like ritual
each weekend of finally secluding and beating
a lone indian's face into a bloody pulp,
50   they're no different except for the side
of railroad tracks they were born on
and whatever small town social
prominence they were born into.
it is the same attitude shared by lesser
55   intelligent animals who can't adapt
and get along with their environmental
surroundings.

undaunted, they gladly take our money
into their stores and banks, arrest
60   at whim our people—
deliberately overcharge us,
have meetings and debates as
to how much they should be paid to educate
our young.
65   why the paved streets as indicated
in their application for government funds

will benefit the indians.
among them, a dentist jokes and makes claims
about indian teeth he extracted solely
70      for economics.

the whites will pick and instigate
fights, but whenever an indian is provoked
into a defensive or verbal stand
against their illiterates,
75      or because he feels that he has been
unjustly wronged for something he has been
doing long before their spermatozoa set
across the atlantic (polluting and bloating
the earth with herbicides and insecticides),
80      troops of town police, highway patrolmen,
and assorted vigilantes storm through
indian-populated taverns, swinging
their flashlights and nervously holding on
to the bulbous heads of their nightclubs
85      with their sweaty hands, hoping
and anxiously waiting for someone
to trigger their archaic desires.
state conservation officers enter
our houses without permission,
90      opening and taking the meat and the skins
of our food from our cooking shacks
and refrigerators.
sometimes a mayor or two will deem it necessary
to come out and chase us and handcuff us over
95      our graveyards. the town newspaper overpublishes
any wrong or misdeed done by the indian
and the things which are significantly
important to the tribe as well as to the town,
for the most, ends up in the last pages,
100     after filling its initial pages
with whatever appeals to them as
being newsworthy and relevant indian
reading material.
unfortunately, through all of this,
105     some of *our* own people we hire, elect,
or appoint become so infected and obsessed
with misconceptions and greed, that they
forget they are there for the purpose
of helping us, not to give themselves
110     and each other's families priorities
in housing, education, and jobs.

altogether, it's pathetic seeing the town
and seeing mature uniformed and suited men
being led astray by its own scum, hiring
115     and giving morale to its own offspring scum
to make it right for all other scums
to follow.

they can't seem to leave us alone.
until they learn that the world and time
120 has moved on regardless of whether they still
believe and harbor antiquated ideas and notions
of being superior because of their pale light skin
alone, and until they learn that in their paranoia
to compare us to their desensitized lives,
125 they will never progress into what they
themselves call a community,
or even for the least,
a human.

1980

## It Is The Fish-faced Boy Who Struggles

it is the fish-faced boy who struggles
with himself beside the variant rivers
that his parents pass on their horse
and wagon. he sees the brilliant river.
5 at times it turns invisible and he sees
fish he has never seen before.
once, somewhere here he had dreamt
of a wild pig killing his mother and
sister. it chased him into the river
10 and he swam to the other side and stood
on the beach, wiping the water from his face.
two others came and encircled him.
the dream ended under the river
where he walked into a room
15 full of people dressed in sacks.
the morning wind chilled his languid body.
he peered out again. birds hopped along
the frosted grass. he remembered what
the submerged people said to him when
20 he walked into the room: we've been
expecting you.
large glistening fins filled
his eyes with the harsh sunlight.
he felt his lungs expanding.
25 the ribs from his body tilted
at an angle away from the ground.
the fish in the river, a spectacle.
he sat back against the rocking
sideboards of the wagon.
30 he noticed his father's black hat
and his mother's striped wool blanket
bouncing in the ride.

as they crossed the iron bridge
he felt the tension from his body
35 subside. fog from the openings
in the river drifted into the swamps.

the road led them through a forest.
he thought of invisibility.
the web between the bone spines of the fish
40    were intercrossed with incandescent fiber.
their jaws sent bursts of water
down to the river bottom.
clouds of mud and sediment
settled beside white needlepoint teeth.
45    he could faintly hear the barking of dogs.
he knew they were nearing home
from the permeating scent
of the pinetrees. it occurred to him
that the trees and the scent were an
50    intrinsic part of the seasons.
these were moments when he questioned
his existence. for awhile he pictured
awkwardly dressed people. they were standing
motionless beside long tables.
55    the impression was, they were ready
to eat but there was no food.
he had seen the long tables somewhere.
the wagon stopped. his father stepped
down from the wagon and carried him
60    into the summer house. it was warm inside.
huge poles which supported the roof
stood in dark brown color absorbing
the constant smoke from the fire.
far ahead in time, his grandson
65    would come down from the lavender hills
with the intention of digging out the poles
to carry on the memory under a new roof.

he knew it was the next day
when he woke. he could hear the chickens
70    shuffling about. it was no longer warm.
the daylight dissipated as it came in
through the hole in the center
of the roof.
he turned on his side
75    and bumped into a small tin bucket.
he reached over and drew it close.
at first smell,
he couldn't define it, but gradually
as he slushed it around, he recognized
80    his vomit. yesterday's food.
suspended above the door
was a dried head of a fish.
its face a shield. the rainbow-
colored eyes. the teeth were constructed
85    with blue stone. he knew its symbols
represented a guardian.
white painted thorns and barbs stuck
out from its gills. lines of daylight

90
rushed through the cracks in the walls.
the smoke-darkened poles were ornately
decorated. the door moved against the force
of the centered breeze. the cool odor
of the pinetrees chilled his entire body.

95
he pulled his thin blanket closer to him
and he attempted to walk to the door.
for each step he took, he forgot
through the next one. he could faintly
distinguish what sounded like the cracking
of ice over the flapping of wings.

100
his father stood above the ice
with a spear in his arms. his eyes affixed
to the opening. the giant fish swam by
piled on top of one another. some were
luminous. others swam so close together

105
they resembled clouds. there were even
a few who quickly swallowed what looked
like intestines. the ones who had their
mouths closed led long streamers
of this substance and it camouflaged

110
whoever followed behind. these were the fish
who represented a power and a belief.
the season was coming sooner than
anyone had anticipated.
the people in the hills

115
completely forgot their ceremonies
yet you saw them everywhere, here, to observe.
the women were along the banks
of the river tying long straps
of leather around the deer hooves

120
on their feet.
the men in their dried speckled
fish heads hummed as they scraped blue
curls of ice with their stone teeth.
small children covered each mark

125
on the ice. fresh water was refilled.
underneath, the fish swung their tails
side to side, alert.
the women in their deer hooves
walked onto the ice.

130
the men in their fish heads
began to sing and the small children
after drinking what remained of the water
ran ahead pointing out the giant fish.

1980

# Carolyn Forché (b. 1950)

Forché was born in Detroit; her father was a tool and die maker, while her mother was a journalist. She studied both international relations at Michigan State University and creative writing at Bowling Green State University. From 1978–1980 she worked as a reporter and human rights activist in El Salvador; "The Colonel" describes a meeting with a Salvadoran military officer. She went on to spend time in South Africa. She has thus been interested both in the impact of U.S. diplomacy and in local revolutionary movements. In addition to her poetry she has done translations and edited a ground-breaking international anthology about political oppression, *Against Forgetting* (1993). She teaches at George Mason University.

## The Colonel

What you have heard is true. I was in his house. His wife carried a tray of coffee and sugar. His daughter filed her nails, his son went out for the night. There were daily papers, pet dogs, a pistol on the cushion beside him. The moon swung bare on its black cord over the house. On the television was a cop show. It was in English. Broken bottles were embedded in the walls around the house to scoop the kneecaps from a man's legs or cut his hands to lace. On the windows there were gratings like those in liquor stores. We had dinner, rack of lamb, good wine, a gold bell was on the table for calling the maid. The maid brought green mangoes, salt, a type of bread. I was asked how I enjoyed the country. There was a brief commercial in Spanish. His wife took everything away. There was some talk then of how difficult it had become to govern. The parrot said hello on the terrace. The colonel told it to shut up, and pushed himself from the table. My friend said to me with his eyes: say nothing. The colonel returned with a sack used to bring groceries home. He spilled many human ears on the table. They were like dried peach halves. There is no other way to say this. He took one of them in his hands, shook it in our faces, dropped it into a water glass. It came alive there. I am tired of fooling around he said. As for the rights of anyone, tell your people they can go fuck themselves. He swept the ears to the floor with his arm and held the last of his wine in the air. Something for your poetry, no? he said. Some of the ears on the floor caught this scrap of his voice. Some of the ears on the floor were pressed to the ground.

*1978*

# Garrett Kaoru Hongo (b. 1951)

Born in Volcano, Hawaii, of Japanese-American parents, Hongo grew up on the North Shore of Oahu and later in California. His father was an electrician and his mother a personnel analyst. He was educated at Pomona College, the University of Michigan, and the University of California at Irvine. He was the founding director of a Seattle theater group called the Asian Exclusion Act. In addition to his own poems, he has edited several books, written a collaborative book, *The Buddha Bandits Down Highway 99* (1978), with Alan Lau and Lawson Inada, and written a memoir called *Volcano* (1995). He teaches at the University of Oregon. His work has often aimed at recovering his distinctive bicultural history, ranging from poems about his childhood in Los Angeles to poems like "Ancestral Graves, Kahuku" that recover his Japanese-American heritage.

## Ancestral Graves, Kahuku°

(for Edward Hirsch)

Driving off Kam Highway along the North Shore,
    past the sugar mill,
Rusting and silent, a haunt for crows
    and the quick mongoose,
Cattle egrets and papaya trees in the wet fields
    wheeling on their muddy gears;

We turn left, *makai*° towards the sea,
    and by the old "76,"
5    Its orange globe a target for wind
    and the rust, and the bleeding light;
Down a chuckholed gravel road
    between state-built retirement homes
And the old village of miscellaneous shotguns
    overgrown with vines, yellow *hau* flowers,
And the lavish hearts and green embroidery of bougainvillaea
    stitching through their rotting screens.

---

**poem title:** Kahuku Point is on the north side of the island of Oahu, Hawaii.
4 *makai:* "towards the sea," as the poem says; in Hawaii directions are often given as "toward the mountains" or "toward the sea."

At the golf course, built by Castle & Cooke
    by subscription, 60 some years ago,
10     We swing past Hole No. 7 and its dying grass
    worn by generations of the poor
And losing out to the traps and dunes
    pushing in from the sea.

It's a dirt road, finally,
    two troughs of packed earth
And a strip of bermuda all the way
    to the sandy point
Where, opposite the homely sentinels
    of three stripped and abandoned cars
15    Giving in to the rain and its brittle decay,
    a wire fence
Opens to the hard scrabble of a shallow beach
    and the collapsing stones
And the rotting stakes,
    *o-kaimyō*° for the dead,
Of this plantation-tough
    cemetery-by-the-sea.

We get out, and I guide you,
    as an aunt did once for me,
20    Over the drying tufts and patchy carpeting
    of temple moss
Yellowing in the saline earth,
    pointing out,
As few have in any recent time,
    my family graves
And the mayonnaise jars empty of flowers,
    the broken saucers
Where rice cakes and mandarins were stacked,
    the weather-smoothed
25    Shards of unglazed pots for sand and incense
    and their chowders of ash.

The wind slaps through our clothes
    and kicks a sand-cloud
Up to our eyes, and I remember
    to tell you
how the *tsunami* in '46 took out
    over half the gravesites,
Tore through two generations,
    most of our dead
30    Gone in one night, bones and tombstones
    up and down the beach,
Those left, half-in, half-out of the broken cliff
    harrowed by the sea.

------------

17 *O-kaimyō*: posthumous Buddhist names.

I remember to say that the land,
    what's left of it,
Still belongs to the growers,
    the same as built the golf course,
Who own, even in death,
    those they did in life,
35 And that the sea came then
    through a vicious tenderness
Like the Buddha's, reaching
    from his lotus-seat
And ushering all the lost and incapable
    from this heaven to its source.

I read a few names—
    this one's the priest,
His fancy stone scripted with ideograms
    carved almost plain by the wind now,
40 And this one, Yaeko, my grandfather's sister
    who bedded down one night
In the canefields and with a Scotsman
    and was beaten to death
For the crime—
    a hoe handle they say—
Struck by her own father,
    mythic and unabsolved.

Our shame is not her love,
    whether idyll or rape
45 Behind the green shrouds and whispering tassels
    of sugar cane,
Not is it the poor gruel of their daily lives
    or the infrequent
Pantomime of worship they engaged in
    odd Saturdays;
It is its effacement, the rough calligraphy
    on rotting wood
Worn smooth and illegible,
    the past
50 Like a name whispered in a shallow grave
    just above tideline
That speaks to us in a quiet woe
    without forgiveness
As we move off, back toward our car,
    the grim and constant
Muttering from the sea
    a cool sutra in our ears.

*1988*

# Rita Dove (b. 1952)

Born in Akron, Ohio, Dove was educated at Miami University in Ohio, the University of Tübingen in Germany, and the University of Iowa. She teaches at the University of Virginia. History and myth are her frequent subjects. A book-length poem sequence, *Thomas and Beulah* (1986), presents her maternal grandparents' family history in the broad context of African American migration north after Reconstruction. *Mother Love* (1995) is a contemporary retelling of the story of Demeter and Persephone. Also see her *Selected Poems* (1993).

## Parsley°

### 1. THE CANE FIELDS

There is a parrot imitating spring
in the palace, its feathers parsley green.
Out of the swamp the cane appears

to haunt us, and we cut it down. El General
5      searches for a word; he is all the world
there is. Like a parrot imitating spring,

we lie down screaming as rain punches through
and we come up green. We cannot speak an R—
out of the swamp, the cane appears

10      and then the mountain we call in whispers *Katalina.*°
The children gnaw their teeth to arrowheads.
There is a parrot imitating spring.

El General has found his word: *perejil.*
Who says it, lives. He laughs, teeth shining
15      out of the swamp. The cane appears

---

**poem title:** Dove's note: "On October 2, 1957, Rafael Trujillo (1891–1961), dictator of the Dominican Republic, ordered 20,000 blacks killed because they could not pronounce the letter "r" in *perejil,* the Spanish word for parsley."
10 *Katalina:* i.e., "Katarina," because they cannot pronounce "r."

in our dreams, lashed by wind and streaming.
And we lie down. For every drop of blood
there is a parrot imitating spring.
Out of the swamp the cane appears.

### 2. The Palace

20   The word the general's chosen is parsley.
It is fall, when thoughts turn
to love and death; the general thinks
of his mother, how she died in the fall
and he planted her walking cane at the grave
25   and it flowered, each spring stolidly forming
four-star blossoms. The general

pulls on his boots, he stomps to
her room in the palace, the one without
curtains, the one with a parrot
30   in a brass ring. As he paces he wonders
Who can I kill today. And for a moment
the little knot of screams
is still. The parrot, who has traveled

all the way from Australia in an ivory
35   cage, is, coy as a widow, practising
spring. Ever since the morning
his mother collapsed in the kitchen
while baking skull-shaped candies
for the Day of the Dead,° the general
40   has hated sweets. He orders pastries
brought up for the bird; they arrive

dusted with sugar on a bed of lace.
The knot in his throat starts to twitch;
he sees his boots the first day in battle
45   splashed with mud and urine
as a soldier falls at his feet amazed—
how stupid he looked!—at the sound
of artillery. *I never thought it would sing*
the soldier said, and died. Now

50   the general sees the fields of sugar
cane, lashed by rain and streaming.
He sees his mother's smile, the teeth
gnawed to arrowheads. He hears
the Haitians sing without R's
55   as they swing the great machetes:
*Katalina,* they sing, *Katalina,*

---

39 *Day of the Dead:* All Soul's Day, November 1. In Latin America, a procession honoring
the dead is decked out with elaborately decorated skulls, coffins, and skeletons, along with
flowers, candles, and food.

*mi madle, mi amol en muelte.*° God knows
his mother was no stupid woman; she
could roll an R like a queen. Even
60          a parrot can roll an R! In the bare room
the bright feathers arch in a parody
of greenery, as the last pale crumbs
disappear under the blackened tongue. Someone

calls out his name in a voice
65          so like his mother's, a startled tear
splashes the tip of his right boot.
*My mother, my love in death.*
The general remembers the tiny green sprigs
men of his village wore in their capes
70          to honor the birth of a son. He will
order many, this time, to be killed

for a single, beautiful word.

                                                    *1983*

---

57 *mi madle* . . .: the italicized line in the next stanza translates the phrase.

# Jimmy Santiago Baca (b. 1952)

Born in Sante Fe, New Mexico, of Chicano and Apache Indian descent, but abandoned at age two, Baca lived part of the time with a grandparent. By his fifth birthday, his father was dead of alcoholism, his mother had been murdered by her new husband, and Baca was in an orphanage. He escaped at age eleven and lived on the street, moving on to drugs and alcohol. Soon he was convicted on a drug charge, though he may not have been guilty. He wrote the poems in his first book, *Immigrants in Our Own Land* (1979), while he was in prison, where he had taught himself to read. While there, he received forced shock treatments and spent four years in isolation. More recently, he has lived on a small farm outside Albuquerque, New Mexico, and traveled doing poetry readings. His other work includes the screenplay for *Bound by Honor* and the book *Working in the Dark: Reflections of a Poet of the Barrio* (1992). His book-length poem sequence *Martin & Meditations on the South Valley* (1989) is a southwestern narrative journey in which the main character is restored by contacts with land and heritage.

## Mi Tío Baca El Poeta De Socorro°

Antonio Ce De Baca
chiseled on stone chunk gravemarker,
propped against a white wooden cross.
Dust storms faded the birth and death numbers.
5     Poet de Socorro,
whose poems roused *la gente*
to demand their land rights back,
'til one night—that terrible night,
hooves shook your earthen-floor
10    one-room adobe, lantern flame
flickered shadowy omens on walls,
and you scrawled across the page,
"*¡Aquí vienen! ¡Aquí vienen!*
Here they come!"
15    Hooves clawed your front yard,
guns glimmering blue
angrily beating at your door.

---

**poem title:** (Spanish) "My Uncle Baca the Poet from Socorro"; Socorro is a city located on the Rio Grande River in Socorro County in New Mexico.

You rose.
Black boots scurried round four adobe walls,
20  trampling flower beds.
They burst through the door.
It was a warm night, and carried the scent
of their tobacco, sulphur, and leather.
Faces masked in dusty hankies,
25  men wearing remnants of Rinche uniforms,
arms pitchforked you out,
where arrogant young boys on horses
held torches and shouted,
"Shoot the Mexican! Shoot him!"
30  Saliva flew from bits
as horses reared from you,
while red-knuckled recruits held reins tight,
drunkenly pouring whiskey over you,
kicking you up the hill by the yucca,
35  where you turned, and met the scream
of rifles with your silence.

Your house still stands.
Black burnt tin covers window openings,
weeds grow on the dirt roof
40  that leans like an old man's hand
on a cane *viga*. . . .
I walk to the church a mile away,
a prayer on my lips bridges
years of disaster between us.
45  Maybe things will get better.
Maybe our struggle to speak and be
as we are, will come about.
For now, I drink in your spirit, Antonio,
to nourish me as I descend
50  into dangerous abysses of the future.
I came here this morning
at 4:30 to walk over my history.
Sat by the yucca, and then imagined you again,
walking up to me
55  face sour with tortuous hooks
pulling your brow down in wrinkles,
cheeks weary with defeat,
face steady with implacable dignity.
The softness in your brown eyes
60  said you could take no more.
You will speak with the angels now.
I followed behind you to the church,
your great bulky field-working shoulders
lean forward in haste
65  as if angels really did await us.
Your remorseful footsteps
in crackly weeds
sound the last time
I will hear and see you. Resolve is engraved

70          in each step. I want to believe
             whatever problems we have, time will take
             its course, they'll be endured and consumed.
             Church slumps on a hill, somber and elegant.
             After you, I firmly pull the solid core door back.
75           You kneel before La Virgen De Guadalupe,
             bloody lips moving slightly,
             your great gray head poised in listening,
             old jacket perforated with bloody bullet holes.
             I close the door, and search the prairie,
80           considering the words *faith, prayer* and *forgiveness,*
             wishing, like you, I could believe them.

                                                   *1989*

# Anita Endrezze (b. 1952)

Endrezze was born in Long Beach, California, of Yaqui and European ancestry. An artist as well as a poet and short story writer, her paintings and illustrations have been reproduced in a number of publications and been exhibited both in the U.S. and in Europe. She has also written a novel for children. She has worked part-time for Washington State as a poet-in-residence, for the Spokane chapter of the Audubon Society, and edited the Indian Artists Guild newsletter. Her books include *At the Helm of Twilight* (1992) and *The Humming of Stars and Bees* (1998). *Throwing Fire at the Sun* (2000) is an account of her family and tribal history told in paintings, poetry, legend, fact, and family memories. As the poems reprinted here suggest, she has been unusually successful at finding linguistic equivalents of Native American views of nature.

## Return of the Wolves

All through the valley, the people are whispering:
the wolves are returning, returning
to the narrow edge of our fields, our dreams.
They are returning the cold to us.
5     They are wearing the crowns of ambush,
offering the rank and beautiful snow-shapes
of dead sheep, an old man too deep in his cups,
the trapper's gnawed hands, the hunter's tongue.
They are returning the whispers of our lovers,
10    whose promises are less enduring than the wolves.

Their teeth are carving the sky into delicate antlers,
carving dark totems full of moose dreams: meadows
where light grows with the marshgrass and water
is a dark wolf under the hoof.
15    Their teeth are carving our children's names
on every trail, carving night into a different bone—
one that seems to be part of my body's long memory.

Their fur is gathering shadows, gathering
the thick-teethed white-boned howl of their tribe,
20    gathering the broken-deer smell of wind
into their longhouse of pine and denned earth,
gathering me also, from my farmhouse

with its golden light and empty rooms, to the cedar
(that also howls its woody name to the cave of stars),
25    where I am silent as a bow unstrung
and my scars are not from loving wolves.

*1988*

## Birdwatching at Fan Lake

Our blue boat drifts
on the flat-shelled water.

In my lap: the red Book of Birds,
genesis of egg and feather

5    in the leavened air, begetting
the moist nests of osprey

and the mallard that floats
like bread on the water.

Around the lake are dark crowns
10    of granite and tall reeds with eyes

that burn gold in afternoon sun.
We eat salt crackers, green apples,

round cheese. On the shore,
a woman bends for a bright towel,

15    a white horse chews on wood.
The creek sings: *dribblestone*

*pebblelarvae*. The red faces
of salamanders are wise

under the green bracken.
20    Waxwings sing to a chokecherry sun,

their throats shrill glass whistles.
We check our lists, compare.

Mine has notes like: the birds fly
into the white corridor of the sky.

25    Or: does the ruffed grouse's drumming
enter into the memories of trees?

Lately, we've talked less, been less
sure of each other. Love, why

travel this far to find rarity
30    and remain silent

in the curved wing of our boat?
Your hand on the oar is enough

for me to think of love's migration
from the intemperate heart to halcyon soul.

35       You point to a kingfisher,
whose eggs are laid on fish bones.

The fish are fin to the fisher's crest.
On a rocky beach, a kildeer keens,

orange-vested children pull up canoes,
40       camp smoke nests on the leafy water.

You take my hand and call it *wing*.
Sunlight is reborn in the heart

of the wild iris. Its purple shadows
sway over the root-dark fish.

45       Look: the long-necked herons
in the green-billed water

are pewter. Their wet-ash wings wear
medallions of patience. We drift on,

buoyed by the tiny currents between us,
50       the light long-legged, the wind

full of hearts that beat quick
and strong.

*1988*

# Ana Castillo (b. 1953)

Castillo was born and grew up in Chicago of Aztec and Mexican ancestry. She was educated at Northern Illinois University and the University of Chicago, thereafter earning a Ph.D. at the University of Bremen. In both high school and college, Castillo was active in the Chicano movement and began writing political poems about ethnic experience. Known for both her novels and her poetry, she has often explored the politics of sexuality. She has worked as associate editor for *Third Woman Magazine* and *Humanizarte* and has taught at San Francisco State University, the University of New Mexico, and Mount Holyoke College. She lives in Albuquerque, New Mexico.

## Seduced by Natassja Kinski°

I always had a thing for Natassja Kinski.
My Sorbonne clique and I went to see her latest film. Giant
billboards all over Paris: Natassja—legs spread, her
lover's face lost in between.
5    I watched *Paris, Texas*° twice, living with
the eternal memory of those lips
biting into a fleshy strawberry in *Tess.*°
Thank you, Roman Polanski.

Long after I have gotten over Natassja Kinski,
10   I am with a Chicago clique on holiday. I am an atom now,
in constant, ungraspable flux, when my Bulgarian scarf is
pulled off my neck. It is Natassja Kinski.

She has removed her KGB° black-leather coat; bottom of
the ocean eyes are working me, and yes, that mouth . . .

---

**poem title:** Kinski is a German born (1959) actress. Ephraim Katz's *Film Encyclopedia* describes her as a "radiantly sensual, full-lipped, gray-green-eyed star of international films."
5 *Paris, Texas:* 1984 film directed by Wim Wenders.
7 *Tess:* 1979 film directed by Roman Polanski.
13 *KGB:* the security service of the Soviet Union; it enforced political discipline at home and conducted espionage abroad.

15    When we dance, I avoid her gaze.
      I am trying every possible way to escape eyes,
      mouth, smile, determination, scarf pulling me
      closer, cheap wine, strobe light, dinner invitation,
      *"Come home with me. It's all for fun,"* she says.

20    I dance with her friends again. I am a tourist in my
      hometown, and the girls are showing me a good time.
      I think *I'll leave with someone else.*
      But she finds me at a table in the dark.
      *"What do you want, my money?"* I ask. She reminds, cockily,
25    that she has more money than I do. I am a poet, everybody
      does. And when we dance, I am a strawberry, ripened and
      bursting, devoured, and she has won.

      We assure each other, the next day, neither of us has
      ever done anything like that before.

30    By Sunday night, we don't go out for dinner as planned.
      Instead, over a bottle of champagne,
      Natassja wants me forever. Unable to bear that mouth,
      sulking, too sad for words, I whisper: *"te llevaré conmigo."*°
      As if I ever had a choice.

                                                          *1991*

---

33 *te llevaré conmigo*: (Spanish) "I'll take you with me," which carries connotations of "I'll
be with you always" or "I'll carry you in my heart."

# Mark Doty (b. 1953)

Born in Tennessee, the son of an army engineer, Doty has taught at Sarah Lawrence College, the M.F.A. Program at Vermont College, the University of Utah, and the University of Houston. He lives in Provincetown, Massachusetts and Houston. In addition to his poetry, he is the author of a 1981 critical study of James Agee and of *Heaven's Coast* (1996), a memoir of his partner Wally Roberts's death from AIDS. Frightened by his emerging sexual identity, Doty married hastily at age eighteen but was divorced after graduating from Drake University in Iowa. While a temporary office worker in Manhattan, he studied creative writing at Goddard College. He also met Roberts, a department store window dresser, and lived with him for twelve years. While Doty has written about a variety of urban subjects, the specificity and variety of his poems about gay life—with their frankness, their substantial cultural resonance, their wit, their political insight, and their metaphoric inventiveness—make them his major contribution to American poetry to date. He did not, however, so much start out to write political poetry as to write about his own life, but the life of a gay man in America proved political. Doty has a rich and complex relation to the work of several other American poets, including Hart Crane. In Crane's case, one might say that Doty has set out to write the poems Crane himself could not have written in his own time.

## Homo Will Not Inherit

Downtown anywhere and between the roil
of bathhouse steam—up there the linens of joy
and shame must be laundered again and again,

5    all night—downtown anywhere
and between the column of feathering steam
unknotting itself thirty feet above the avenue's

shimmered azaleas of gasoline,
between the steam and the ruin
of the Cinema Paree (marquee advertising

10   its own milky vacancy, broken showcases sealed,
ticketbooth a hostage wrapped in tape
and black plastic, captive in this zone

of blackfronted bars and bookstores
where there's nothing to read
15  but longing's repetitive texts,

where desire's unpoliced, or nearly so)
someone's posted a xeroxed headshot
of Jesus: permed, blonde, blurred at the edges

as though photographed through a greasy lens,
20  and inked beside him, in marker strokes:
HOMO WILL NOT INHERIT. *Repent & be saved.*

I'll tell you what I'll inherit: the margins
which have always been mine, downtown after hours
when there's nothing left to buy,

25  the dreaming shops turned in on themselves,
seamless, intent on the perfection of display,
the bodegas and offices lined up, impenetrable:

edges no one wants, no one's watching. Though
the borders of this shadow-zone (mirror and dream
30  of the shattered streets around it) are chartered

by the police, and they are required,
some nights, to redefine them. But not now, at twilight,
permission's descending hour, early winter darkness

pillared by smoldering plumes. The public city's
35  ledgered and locked, but the secret city's boundless;
from which do these tumbling towers arise?

I'll tell you what I'll inherit: steam,
and the blinding symmetry of some towering man,
fifteen minutes of forgetfulness incarnate.

40  I've seen flame flicker around the edges of the body,
pentecostal, evidence of inhabitation.
And I have been possessed of the god myself,

I have been the temporary apparition
salving another, I have been his visitation, I say it
45  without arrogance, I have been an angel

for minutes at a time, and I have for hours
believed—without judgement, without condemnation—
that in each body, however obscured or recast,

is the divine body—common, habitable—
50  the way in a field of sunflowers
you can see every bloom's

the multiple expression
of a single shining idea,
which is the face hammered into joy.

55      I'll tell you what I'll inherit:
stupidity, erasure, exile
inside the chalked lines of the police,

who must resemble what they punish,
the exile you require of me,
60      you who's posted this invitation

to a heaven nobody wants.
You who must be patrolled,
who adore constraint, I'll tell you

what I'll inherit, not your pallid temple
65      but a real palace, the anticipated
and actual memory, the moment flooded

by skin and the knowledge of it,
the gesture and its description
—do I need to say it?—

70      the flesh *and* the word. And I'll tell you,
you who can't wait to abandon your body,
what you want me to, maybe something

like you've imagined, a dirty story:
Years ago, in the baths,
75      a man walked into the steam,

the gorgeous deep indigo of him gleaming,
solid tight flanks, the intricately ridged abdomen—
and after he invited me to his room,

nudging his key toward me,
80      as if perhaps I spoke another tongue
and required the plainest of gestures,

after we'd been, you understand,
worshipping a while in his church,
he said to me, *I'm going to punish your mouth.*

85      I can't tell you what that did to me.
My shame was redeemed then;
I won't need to burn in the afterlife.

It wasn't that he hurt me,
more than that: the spirit's transactions
90      are enacted now, here—no one needs

your eternity. This failing city's
radiant as any we'll ever know,
paved with oily rainbow, charred gates

95     jeweled with tags, swoops of letters
over letters, indecipherable as anything
written by desire. I'm not ashamed

to love Babylon's scrawl. How could I be?
It's written on my face as much as on
these walls. This city's inescapable,

gorgeous, and on fire. I have my kingdom.

*1995*

# Harryette Mullen (b. 1953)

Mullen was born in Florence, Alabama, and grew up in Fort Worth, Texas. She was educated at the University of Texas and the University of California at Santa Cruz. She has taught at Cornell University and now teaches at UCLA. She has written both poems and prose poems since publishing her first book, *Tree Tall Woman*, in 1981. Her prose poems, which grow out of the L=A=N=G=U=A=G=E poetry movement, wittily display human motivation with a linguistic basis.

## from *Trimmings*

Akimbo bimbos, all a jangle. Tricked out trinkets, aloud galore. Gim-cracks, a stack. Bang and a whimper. Two to tangle. It's a jungle.

Punched in like slopwork. Mild frump and downward drab. Slipshod drudge with chance of dingy morning slog. Tattered shoulders, frayed eyes, a dowdy gray. Frowzy in a slatternly direction.

Animal pelts, little minks, skins, tail. Fur flies. Pet smitten, smooth beaver strokes. Muff, soft, 'like rabbits.' Fine fox stole, furtive hiding. Down the road a pretty fur piece.

Opens up a little leg, some slender, high exposure. Splits a chic sheath, tight slit. Buy another peek experience, price is slashed. Where tart knife, scoring, minced a sluttish strut. Laughing splits the seams. Teeth in a gash, letting off steam.

A fish caught, pretty fish wiggles for a while. A caught fish squirms. A freshly licked fish sighs. Gapes with holes for eyes. A wiggling fish flashes its display. A pattern over whiteness. Bareness comes with coverage for peeking through holes to see flesh out of water. Cold holes where eyes go. The sea is cold. Her body of foam, some frothy Venus. Or strayed mermaid, tail split, bleeds into the sea. With brand new feet walks unsteady on land, each step an ache.

Her ribbon, her slender is ribbon when to occupy her hands a purse is soft. Wondering where to hang the keys the moon is manicured. Her paper parasol and open fan become her multiplication of a rib which is connected and might start a fire for cooking. Who desires crisp vegetables, she opens for the climate. A tomato isn't hard. It splits in heat, easy. It's seasonal. Once in a while there is heat, and several flowers are perennials. Roses shining with greengold leaves and bright threads. Some threads do wilt after starching. She has done the starching and the bleaching. She has pink too and owns earrings. Would never be shamed by pearls. A subtle blush communicates much. White peeks out, an eyelet in a storm.

*1991*

# from S*PeRM**K*T

Aren't you glad you use petroleum? Don't wait to be told you explode. You're not fully here until you're over there. Never let them see you eat. You might be taken for a zoo. Raise your hand if you're sure you're not.

Kills bugs dead. Redundancy is syntactical overkill. A pinprick of peace at the end of the tunnel of a nightmare night in a roach motel. Their noise infects the dream. In black kitchens they foul the food, walk on our bodies as we sleep over oceans of pirate flags. Skull and cross-bones, they crunch like candy. When we die they will eat us, unless we kill them first. Invest in better mousetraps. Take no prisoners on board ship, to rock the boat, to violate our beds with pestilence. We dream the dream of extirpation. Wipe out a species, with God on our side. Annihilate the insects. Sterilize the filthy vermin.

A daughter turned against the grain refuses your gleanings, denies your milk, soggy absorbency she abhors. Chokes on your words when asked about love. Never would swallow the husks you're allowed. Not a spoon-ful gets down what you see of her now. Crisp image from disciplined form. Torn hostage ripening out of hand. Boxtop trophy of war, brings to the table a regimen from hell. At breakfast shuts out all nurturant murmurs. Holds against you the eating for two. Why brag of pain a body can't remember? You pretend once again she's not lost forever.

Off the pig, ya dig? He squeals, grease the sucker. Hack that fatback, pour the pork. Pig out, rib the fellas. Ham it up, hype the tripe. Save your bacon, bring home some. Sweet dreams pigmeat. Pork belly fu-tures, larded accounts, hog heaven. Little piggish to market. Tub of guts hog wilding. A pig of yourself, high on swine, cries all the way home. Streak a lean gets away cleaner than Safeway chitlings. That's all, folks.

Ad infinitum perpetual infants goo. Pastel puree of pure pink bland blue-eyed babes all born a cute blond with no chronic colic. Sterile eu-genically cloned rows of clean rosy dimples and pamper proof towhead cowlicks. Adorable babyface jars. Sturdy innocent in the pink, out of the blue packs disposing durable superabsorbent miracle fibers. As solids break down, go to waste, a land fills up dead diapers with funky halflife.

Flies in buttermilk. What a fellowship. That's why white milk makes yel-low butter. Homo means the same. A woman is different. Cream always rises over split milk. Muscle men drink it all in. Awesome teeth and wholesale bones. Our cows are well adjusted. The lost family album keeps saying cheese. Speed readers skim the white space of this galaxy.

*1992*

# Louise Erdrich (b. 1954)

Born in Little Falls, Minnesota, Erdrich grew up in the town of Wahpeton, North Dakota, near the Minnesota border and the Turtle Mountain Reservation. She is an enrolled member of the Turtle Mountain Chippewa tribe of North Dakota; her mother is of French-Chippewa descent, and for many years her grandfather was Tribal Chair of the reservation. Her parents were Bureau of Indian Affairs educators; both taught at the boarding school in Wahpeton. Erdrich was educated at Dartmouth College and Johns Hopkins; she has taught poetry in prisons and edited a Native American newspaper. In addition to publishing two books of poetry, *Jacklight* (1984) and *Baptism of Fire* (1989), she has written a number of novels and short stories. Her novels include *Love Medicine* (1984) and *The Bingo Palace* (1991).

## Indian Boarding School: The Runaways°

Home's the place we head for in our sleep.
Boxcars stumbling north in dreams
don't wait for us. We catch them on the run.
The rails, old lacerations that we love,
5   shoot parallel across the face and break
just under Turtle Mountains.° Riding scars
you can't get lost. Home is the place they cross.

The lame guard strikes a match and makes the dark
less tolerant. We watch through cracks in boards
10  as the land starts rolling, rolling till it hurts
to be here, cold in regulation clothes.
We know the sheriff's waiting at midrun
to take us back. His car is dumb and warm.
The highway doesn't rock, it only hums

---

**poem title:** A number of military style boarding schools for Indian children were established by U.S. government policy in the mid-nineteenth century. It was part of a plan to forcibly assimilate the next generation of Native Americans into white culture. Visits home were severely restricted to prevent the children from reverting to Indian lifestyles, and use of native languages was often prohibited. Many of the institutions were financed by unpaid student labor. Meanwhile, medical care at the schools was exceedingly poor, food was insufficient, and hundreds of the children died of disease. The schools were widely used through the 1930s.
6 *Turtle Mountains:* in North Dakota, site of a Chippewa Indian reservation.

15          like a wing of long insults. The worn-down welts
            of ancient punishments lead back and forth.

            All runaways wear dresses, long green ones,
            the color you would think shame was. We scrub
            the sidewalks down because it's shameful work.
20          Our brushes cut the stone in watered arcs
            and in the soak frail outlines shiver clear
            a moment, things us kids pressed on the dark
            face before it hardened, pale, remembering
            delicate old injuries, the spines of names and leaves.

                                                        *1984*


## Dear John Wayne°

            August and the drive-in picture is packed.
            We lounge on the hood of the Pontiac
            surrounded by the slow-burning spirals they sell
            at the window, to vanquish the hordes of mosquitoes.
5           Nothing works. They break through the smoke screen for blood.

            Always the lookout spots the Indians first,
            spread north to south, barring progress.
            The Sioux or some other Plains bunch
            in spectacular columns, ICBM missiles,
10          feathers bristling in the meaningful sunset.

            The drum breaks. There will be no parlance.
            Only the arrows whining, a death-cloud of nerves
            swarming down on the settlers
            who die beautifully, tumbling like dust weeds
15          into the history that brought us all here
            together: this wide screen beneath the sign of the bear.

            The sky fills, acres of blue squint and eye
            that the crowd cheers. His face moves over us,
            a thick cloud of vengeance, pitted
20          like the land that was once flesh. Each rut,
            each scar makes a promise: *It is*
            *not over, this fight, not as long as you resist.*

            *Everything we see belongs to us.*

            A few laughing Indians fall over the hood
25          slipping in the hot spilled butter.
            *The eye sees a lot, John, but the heart is so blind.*

---

**poem title:** Wayne (1907–1979), American film actor and icon, one of the most widely known performers in westerns and films about World War II. He was launched into stardom shooting Indians in *Stagecoach* (1939) and consumed by racial hatred for them in *The Searchers* (1956); in between, as a cavalry officer in several films, Indians are merely a problem for him to control.

*Death makes us owners of nothing.*
He smiles, a horizon of teeth
the credits reel over, and then the white fields

30    again blowing in the true-to-life dark.
The dark films over everything.
We get into the car
scratching our mosquito bites, speechless and small
as people are when the movie is done.
35    We are back in our skins.

How can we help but keep hearing his voice,
the flip side of the sound track, still playing:
*Come on, boys, we got them*
*where we want them, drunk, running.*
40    *They'll give us what we want, what we need.*
Even his disease was the idea of taking everything.
Those cells, burning, doubling, splitting out of their skins.

*1984*

# Sandra Cisneros (b. 1954)

Born in Chicago to working-class parents—her father was an upholsterer, her mother a factory worker—Cisneros spent her early years shuttling between the United States and her father's family home in Mexico City. After studying at the Iowa Writer's Workshop at the University of Iowa, she settled in Texas in a house on the San Antonio River, though she has also been a writer in residence at the University of Michigan and the University of California at Irvine. Her published work includes not only poetry but also experimental collections of fiction and sketches. *The House on Mango Street* (1983) is her most famous work of fiction.

## Little Clown, My Heart

Little clown, my heart,
Spangled again and lopsided,
Handstands and Peking pirouettes,
Backflips snapping open like
5    A carpenter's hinged ruler,

Little gimp-footed hurray,
Paper parasol of pleasures,
Fleshy undertongue of sorrows,
Sweet potato plant of my addictions,

10    Acapulco cliff-diver *corazón*,°
Fine as an obsidian dagger,
Alley-oop and here we go
Into the froth, my life,
Into the flames!

*1994*

---

10 *corazón*: (Spanish) "heart."

# Thylias Moss (b. 1954)

Born Thylias Rebecca Brasier into a working-class family in Cleveland, Ohio, Moss's mother was a maid and her father was a recapper for the Cardinal Tire Company. She enrolled at Syracuse University but left when she found the racial tension there unpleasant. She married John Moss in 1973, raised two sons, and then returned to school, earning degrees from Oberlin College in 1981 and the University of New Hampshire in 1983. Her professors encouraged her writing but they were also unprepared for its political anger. Nevertheless she published her first book in 1983 and since then has taught at Phillips Academy in Andover, Massachusetts, and now teaches at the University of Michigan. She has continued to write poems of great passion about her family experience and about American history, but she is equally at home writing about the intensity of religious conviction, about all forms of cultural mystification, and about the critical moments of human life. She is often almost theatrically inventive with both diction and sound in her work. In addition to her poetry, she has written a memoir, *Tale of a Sky-Blue Dress* (1998).

## Fullness

One day your place in line will mean the
Eucharist has run out. All because you waited
your turn. Christ's body can be cut into only
so many pieces. One day Jesus will be eaten up.
5     The Last Supper won't be misnamed. One day the
father will place shavings of his own blessed fingers
on your tongue and you will get back in line for
more. You will not find yourself out of line again.
The bread will rise inside you. A loaf of tongue.
10   Pumpernickel liver. You will be the miracle.
You will feed yourself five thousand times.

*1990*

## There Will Be Animals

There will be animals to teach us
what we can't teach ourselves.

There will be a baboon who is neither stupid nor clumsy
as he paints his mandrill face for the war being waged
5     against his jungle.

There will be egrets in a few thousand years
who will have evolved without plumes so we cannot take them.

There will be ewes giving and giving their wool
compensating for what we lack in humility.

10    There will be macaws with short arched bills
that stay short because they talk without telling lies.

Mackerel will continue to appear near Cape Hatteras each spring
and swim north into Canadian waters so there can be continuity.

There will be penguins keeping alive Hollywood's golden era.

15    The chaparral cock will continue to outdistance man
twisting and turning on a path unconcerned with shortcuts.

Coffin fly dun will leave the Shawsheen River
heading for the lights of Lawrence. What they see in 48 hours
makes them adults who will fast for the rest of their short lives,
20    mating once during the next hour and understanding everything
as they drop into a communal grave three feet thick with family
reaching the same conclusions.

The coast horned lizard still won't be found
without a bag of tricks; it will inflate and the first
25    of six million Jewfish will emerge from its mouth.
We will all be richer.

John Dory will replace John Doe
so the nameless among us will have Peter's thumbmark
on their cheek
30    and the coin the saint pulled from their mouths
in their pockets. Then once and for all
we will know it is no illusion:
The lion lying with the lamb, the grandmother
and Little Red Riding Hood
walking out of a wolf named Dachau.

                                                                                    *1990*

# Ambition

A boy says his father wants to be a Smurf°
and no one can top that; no one else there has
ambition that comes close to that. Only his father
wants to be a Smurf.

5    His mother holds her shock still; no teen marriage here,
there was long engagement and shacking up long

---

1 *Smurfs*: a Saturday morning American television cartoon show for children that ran from 1981 to 1990, chronicling the adventures of a group of little blue humanoids living peaceably in a forest; their enemy Gargamel sought unsuccessfully to capture them.

before the license; she knew what was necessary to know
about this man: His lack of criminal past, his dislike
of physical solutions, the cycles of his preferences
10    that she has matched with three wardrobes and wigs.
This, however, he kept from her, would share only with
a son, his deepest desire his sex with her won't betray
in an elfin blue boundary. With her he is in love;
with the Smurf, he is deeper in himself.

15    Any moment could bring loss of anything. She is prepared
for theft of his heart by, she'd like to think, another woman,
or even better, a vehicular finishing by bus, car, truck, plane,
Harley,° yacht or Hummer.° A random act of God comforts.
Even fantasy can be robber.

20    Falling in love is not something done once then
the ability forsaken; part of what brought them together
was the time of morning, their vulnerability
when something so bright was starting, warming them
separately and together. So far, morning has arrived every day
25    and he could again be with a stranger when the sun
is at that identical angle that made him notice he wasn't alone.

Not that there need be hierarchy of loss, but the worst to her
is his new pride originating from his manhood, not from
the hermaphroditic entity that results from the influence
30    of marriage; a masculine, feminine merger that frightens
in its disrespect of boundaries on which order depends.
He is a man thoroughly, she notices, as he fingers
his Adam's apple; his face will not stay smooth, the beard invincible
even as it forfeits jet for a white haunting of masculinity he enjoys,
35    now praises wondering how he could love anything unlike this
and why he did not date the bearded lady he spent
all his quarters on; at least then he'd know
what the influence of beard is in a kiss.

It's more than that now; emptied of infatuation, left with
40    the aftermath of youth, it's beard he loves and testicle
and he wants the world to know of his epiphany, but still ruled
by fairness, first he tells his wife who's been hurt by impotence,
hurt by endometriosis, hurt by infertility, and the promises technology
can't make fast enough to help her, the cracking open of her own
        genes,
45    their reorganization while she's under general anesthetic sleeping
a hundred years, waking alone too old for a life
hers only through science. It's beard he loves and testicle.

---

18 *Harley:* a popular American motorcycle; *Hummer:* a large four-wheel jeep first devel-
oped for the military.

Who knows what logically follows Smurf
even knowing the logic of arriving at Smurf? Blue
50   as if offspring of a sky at last inspired as it has been inspiring.
Theirs is genealogy shared with Tinker Bell;° indeed,
they have never tasted meat and are considered delicacy
by the animated villain who has never tasted Smurf,
not even a cool blue lick.

55   Never mind her injury; look at the benefit for the child
she knows she'll keep. He has never felt more pride,
more connection to his father. No more doubting paternal love
now that the father wants his identity based on
something the son understands.

                                                                        *1998*

## Crystals

In 1845 Dr. James Marion Sims° had seen it many times,
vesico-vaginal fistula, abnormal passageway
between bladder and vagina through which urine leaks
almost constantly if the fistula is large

5   as it tends to become after those pregnancies
not quite a year apart in Anarcha° and her slave
friends Lucy, Betsey. *If you can just fix this*
the girl said, probably pregnant again, her vulva inflamed,
her thighs caked with urinary salts; from the beginning
10   he saw his future in those crystals.

Society women sometimes had this too, a remaking of the vulva,
more color, pustules like decorations of which women
were already fond: beads, cultured pearls of pus, status.
Perhaps the design improves in its greater challenge to love
15   and fondle even in the dark except that there is pain,
inability to hold water.

----

51 *Tinker Bell:* the miniature winged sprite in the children's novel *Peter Pan* (1904) by Scottish writer Sir James Matthew Barrie (1860–1937). *Peter Pan* was later revived as a musical and a cartoon.

1 *Sims:* (1813–1883), American gynecologist who practiced medicine in Montgomery, Alabama and gained attention through his investigations of vesicovaginal fistula (fistula, or abnormal channel, connecting the urinary bladder with the vagina) in the 1840s, during which he invented the Sims's speculum. Under slavery, he was able to conduct surgical experiments (without anesthesia) on black women's bodies in ways he could not have done with white patients. He later investigated sterility, attributing barrenness in marriage to women, and subjected them to painful therapies, such as the surgical incision of the neck of the uterus; he changed his views in a 1869 paper that revealed defects in sperm could be responsible for sterility.

6 *Anarcha:* Moss's note—"Although the implication is that Anarcha, her actual name, was or had been pregnant, there is not yet evidence of her pregnancies, suggesting that her fistula had some other cause, such as horseback riding. However, among those multiparas [women who have given birth twice or more], especially enslaved multiparas, who develop these fistulas, repeated childbirth is often the cause." Anarcha was subjected to a series of operations over a period of years; Sims successfully closed Anarcha's fistula in the thirtieth operation.

He tried to help Anarcha first, drawing on what
he was inventing: frontier ingenuity and gynecology,
and operated thirty times, using a pewter teaspoon
20    that he reshaped, bent and hammered for each surgery,
no sterilant but spit, while she watched; it became
his famous duck-bill speculum too large and sharp
to be respectful, yet it let him look.

Such excoriation, such stretching of the vaginal walls, tunnel
25    into room; such remembrance of Jericho, prophecy of Berlin
when his mind was to have been on her comfort and healing.

Through the vulva was the way most tried to access her
yet they did not come close. Using

a half-dollar he formed the wire suture that closed
30    Anarcha's fistula on the thirtieth, it bears repeating, thirtieth
attempt.

For the rest of her life she slept in the Sims position:
on her left side, right knee brought to her chest; she so long,
four years, on his table came to find it comfortable, came to find
35    no other way to lose herself, relieve her mind,
ignore Sims' rising glory, his bragging in the journals
that he had seen the fistula *as no man had ever seen it before.*
Now they all can.

Anarcha who still does not know anesthesia except
40    for her willed loss of awareness went on peeing as she'd
always done, just not so frequently and in reduced
volume, hardly enough for a tea cup, but whenever
necessary, the doctor poked, prodded, practiced

then, successful, went gloved and shaven to help ladies
45    on whom white cloths were draped; divinity
on the table to indulge his tastefulness.

It should be noted
that Anarcha's fistula closed well,
sealed in infection, scarred
50    thickly

as if his hand remained.

1998

# Patricia Smith (b. 1955)

Born and raised on the impoverished West Side of Chicago, Smith is a nationally known performance poet who has won a number of poetry slam contests. A former reporter for the *Chicago Sun-Times,* she was also a columnist for the *Boston Globe* for a number of years, until she resigned in 1998 after criticism for including fictional people and events in her columns. A nonfiction book *Africans in America* (1998), coauthored with Charles Johnson, accompanies a PBS television documentary on slavery.

## What It's Like to Be a Black Girl
### (For Those of You Who Aren't)

First of all, it's being 9 years old and
feeling like you're not finished, like your
edges are wild, like there's something,
everything, wrong. it's dropping food coloring
5      in your eyes to make them blue and suffering
their burn in silence. it's popping a bleached
white mophead over the kinks of your hair and
primping in front of mirrors that deny your
reflection. it's finding a space between your
10     legs, a disturbance at your chest, and not knowing
what to do with the whistles. it's jumping
double dutch until your legs pop, it's sweat
and vaseline and bullets, it's growing tall and
wearing a lot of white, it's smelling blood in
15     your breakfast, it's learning to say fuck with
grace but learning to fuck without it, it's
flame and fists and life according to motown,
it's finally having a man reach out for you
then caving in
20     around his fingers.

*1991*

## Blonde White Women

They choke cities like snowstorms.

On the morning train, I flip through my *Ebony,*
marveling at the bargain basement prices

for reams of straightened hair
and bleaches for the skin. Next to me,
skinny pink fingers rest upon a briefcase,
shiver a bit under my scrutiny.
Leaving the tunnel, we hurtle into hurting sun.
An icy brush paints the buildings
with shine, fat spirals of snow
become blankets, and Boston stops breathing.

It is my habit to count them. So I search
the damp, chilled length of the train car
and look for their candle flames of hair,
the circles of blood at their cheeks,
that curt dismissing glare
reserved for the common, the wrinkled, the black.

I remember striving for that breathlessness,
toddling my five-year-old black butt around
with a dull gray mophead covering my
nappy hair, wishing myself golden.
Pressing down hard with my
carnation pink crayola, I filled faces
in coloring books, rubbed the waxy stick
across the back of my hand until the skin broke.

When my mop hair became an annoyance
to my mother, who always seemed to be mopping,
I hid beneath my father's white shirt,
the sleeves hanging down on either side of my head,
the coolest white light pigtails.
I practiced kissing, because to be blonde and white
meant to be kissed, and my fat lips slimmed
around words like "delightful" and "darling."
I hurt myself with my own beauty.

When I was white, my name was Donna.
My teeth were perfect; I was always out of breath.

In first grade, my blonde teacher
hugged me to her because I was the first
in my class to read, and I thought the rush
would kill me. I wanted her to swallow
me, to be my mother, to be the first fire
moving in my breast. But when she pried
me away, her cool blue eyes shining with
righteousness and too much touch,
I saw how much she wanted to wash.

She was not my mother,
the singing Alabama woman
who shook me to sleep
and fed me from her fingers.
I could not have been blacker
than I was at that moment.
My name is Patricia Ann.

Even crayons fail me now—
I can find no color darker,
55          more beautiful, than I am.
This train car grows tense with me.
I pulse, steady my eyes,
shake the snow from my short black hair,
and suddenly I am surrounded by snarling madonnas

60          demanding that I explain
my treachery.

*1992*

# Skinhead

They call me skinhead, and I got my own beauty.
It is knife-scrawled across my back in sore, jagged letters,
it's in the way my eyes snap away from the obvious.
I sit in my dim matchbox,
5          on the edge of a bed tousled with my ragged smell,
slide razors across my hair,
count how many ways
I can bring blood closer to the surface of my skin.
These are the duties of the righteous,
10          the ways of the anointed.

The face that moves in my mirror is huge and pockmarked,
scraped pink and brilliant, apple-cheeked,
I am filled with my own spit.
Two years ago, a machine that slices leather
15          sucked in my hand and held it,
whacking off three fingers at the root.
I didn't feel nothing till I looked down
and saw one of them on the floor
next to my boot heel,
20          and I ain't worked since then.

I sit here and watch niggers take over my TV set,
walking like kings up and down the sidewalks in my head,
walking like their fat black mamas *named* them freedom.
My shoulders tell me that ain't right.

25          So I move out into the sun
where my beauty makes them lower their heads,
or into the night
with a lead pipe up my sleeve,
a razor tucked in my boot.
30          I was born to make things right.

It's easy now to move my big body into shadows,
to move from a place where there was nothing
into the stark circle of a streetlight,
the pipe raised up high over my head.

35    It's a kick to watch their eyes get big,
      round and gleaming like cartoon jungle boys,
      right in that second when they know
      the pipe's gonna come down, and I got this thing
      I like to say, listen to this, I like to say
40    *"Hey, nigger, Abe Lincoln's been dead a long time."*

      I get hard listening to their skin burst.
      I was born to make things right.

      Then this newspaper guy comes around,
      seems I was a little sloppy kicking some fag's ass
45    and he opened his hole and screamed about it.
      This reporter finds me curled up in my bed,
      those TV flashes licking my face clean.
      Same ol' shit.
      Ain't got no job, the coloreds and spics got 'em all.
50    Why ain't I working? Look at my hand, asshole.
      No, I ain't part of no organized group,
      I'm just a white boy who loves his race,
      fighting for a pure country.
      Sometimes it's just me. Sometimes three. Sometimes 30.
55    AIDS will take care of the faggots,
      then it's gon be white on black in the streets.
      Then there'll be three million.
      I tell him that.

      So he writes it up
60    and I come off looking like some kind of freak,
      like I'm Hitler himself. I ain't that lucky,
      but I got my own beauty.
      It is in my steel-toed boots,
      in the hard corners of my shaved head.

65    I look in the mirror and hold up my mangled hand,
      only the baby finger left, sticking straight up,
      I know its the wrong goddamned finger,
      but fuck you all anyway.
      I'm riding the top rung of the perfect race,
70    my face scraped pink and brilliant.
      I'm your baby, America, your boy,
      drunk on my own spit, I am goddamned fuckin' beautiful.

      And I was born

      and raised

75    right here.

*1992*

# Marilyn Chin (b. 1955)

Born in Hong Kong and raised in Portland, Oregon, where her father was a restaurant owner, Marilyn (Mei Ling) Chin was educated at the University of Massachusetts and the University of Iowa's Writers Workshop. She now teaches at San Diego State University. In addition to her own poems, she has done translations, edited *Writing from the World* (1985), and was featured on the 1995 television series *The Language of Life,* broadcast on educational television.

## How I Got That Name

*an essay on assimilation*

I am Marilyn Mei Ling Chin.
Oh, how I love the resoluteness
of that first person singular
followed by that stalwart indicative
5     of "be," without the uncertain i-n-g
of "becoming." Of course,
the name had been changed
somewhere between Angel Island° and the sea,
when my father the paperson
10    in the late 1950s
obsessed with a bombshell blonde
transliterated "Mei Ling" to "Marilyn."
And nobody dared question
his initial impulse—for we all know
15    lust drove men to greatness,
not goodness, not decency.
And there I was, a wayward pink baby,
named after some tragic white woman
swollen with gin and Nembutal.
20    My mother couldn't pronounce the "r."
She dubbed me "Numba one female offshoot"
for brevity: henceforth, she will live and die
in sublime ignorance, flanked

---

8 *Angel Island:* detention site for Chinese immigrants in San Francisco Bay; see the introduction to the selection of Angel Island poetry.

by loving children and the "kitchen deity."
25 While my father dithers,
a tomcat in Hong Kong trash—
a gambler, a petty thug,
who bought a chain of chopsuey joints
in Piss River, Oregon,
30 with bootlegged Gucci cash.°
Nobody dared question his integrity given
his nice, devout daughters
and his bright, industrious sons
as if filial piety were the standard
35 by which all earthly men were measured.

Oh, how trustworthy our daughters,
how thrifty our sons!
How we've managed to fool the experts
in education, statistics and demography—
40 We're not very creative but not adverse to rote-learning.
Indeed, they can *use* us.
But the "Model Minority" is a tease.
We know you are watching now,
so we refuse to give you any!
45 Oh, bamboo shoots, bamboo shoots!
The further west we go, we'll hit east;
the deeper down we dig, we'll find China.
History has turned its stomach
on a black polluted beach—
50 where life doesn't hinge
on that red, red wheelbarrow,
but whether or not our new lover
in the final episode of "Santa Barbara"°
will lean over a scented candle
55 and call us a "bitch."
Oh God, where have we gone wrong?
We have no inner resources!

Then, one redolent spring morning
the Great Patriarch Chin
60 peered down from his kiosk in heaven
and saw that his descendants were ugly.
One had a squarish head and a nose without a bridge.
Another's profile—long and knobbed as a gourd.
A third, the sad, brutish one
65 may never, never marry.
And I, his least favorite—
"not quite boiled, not quite cooked,"
a plump pomfret simmering in my juices—
too listless to fight for my people's destiny.
70 "To kill without resistance is not slaughter"

---

30 *Gucci cash*: income from selling stolen or illegal imitation Gucci products.
53 *"Santa Barbara"*: television soap opera set in the California coastal city.

says the proverb. So, I wait for imminent death.
The fact that this death is also metaphorical
is testament to my lethargy.

So here lies Marilyn Mei Ling Chin,
75　married once, twice to so-and-so, a Lee and a Wong,
granddaughter of Jack "the patriarch"
and the brooding Suilin Fong,
daughter of the virtuous Yuet Kuen Wong
and G. G. Chin the infamous,
80　sister of a dozen, cousin of a million,
survived by everybody and forgotten by all.
She was neither black nor white,
neither cherished nor vanquished,
just another squatter in her own bamboo grove
85　minding her poetry—
when one day heaven was unmerciful,
and a chasm opened where she stood.
Like the jowls of a mighty white whale,
or the jaws of a metaphysical Godzilla,
90　it swallowed her whole.
She did not flinch nor writhe,
nor fret about the afterlife,
but stayed! Solid as wood, happily
a little gnawed, tattered, mesmerized
95　by all that was lavished upon her
and all that was taken away!

1994

# Sesshu Foster (b. 1957)

Sesshu Foster grew up in City Terrace, California, and received an MFA from the University of Iowa. He taught English for a number of years at a Boyle Heights, Los Angeles, junior high school and now teaches at Francisco Bravo Medical Magnet. He is the author of *Angry Days* (1987) and *City Terrace Field Manual* (1996), from which these prose poems are taken. In addition to teaching and writing his own poetry, he has coedited a collection of multicultural urban poetry, *Invocation L.A.* (1989).

## We're caffeinated by rain inside concrete underpasses

We're caffeinated by rain inside concrete underpasses,
rolling along treetops, Chinese elms, palm trees,
California peppers. We pushed a lawn mower for white
people, we got down on our hands and knees in their
San Marino driveways. We told our youth to grab hard a
piece of paper swirling like tickets in a bonfire, fire-
crackers at Chinese New Year, toilet paper in a bowl.
We coiled long green hoses. We oiled mean little
engines that buzzed like an evil desire that could spit a
steel slice or sharp stone to take your eye out. We
gripped rusty clippers, clipped leafy hedges, ground
sharper edges. We hauled their sacks of leftover leisure
that rotted at the curbside. We slapped our hands with
gloves, slammed white doors of Econoline vans, showed
up at sunrise in the damp perfume of the downtown
flower market. With all the Japanese gardeners gone,
we're Mexican now. The ones given five minutes a
week or fifteen minutes a month. They wrote us a
check, we wiped our hands on our pants or they did not
shake them. Fertilizer under our fingernails grown large,
yellow and cracked as moons. Instead of us, they saw
azaleas, piracanthus, oleanders, juniper shrubs, marigolds.
They didn't want to see us, they like nature in rows and
flowering things, not another kind of face. Notions
rattled in us like spare bolts in a coffee can. Our days off
rode us hard, like a desert storm on mountains far away.
Try to make our children see more than this man with
green stains, cracked skin, red eyes. More than the back
bent over stacked tools and coiled hoses. Coffee breath.

On dry boulevards fading into smog, kids just like ours
smash our windows and loot our tools. Our kids today
want to grow up to get lucky. Okay, we tell them, have
it your way, and we light our children like candles.

*1996*


## You'll be fucked up

You'll be fucked up. They'll take your things away
when you're not looking, they'll take your shit and
discard part in the dumpster, they'll take you to San
Diego and put you on a plane, they'll make up some
itinerary of churches and parades, they'll show you
Hollywood, you'll get driven up and down Sunset
Boulevard, around Melrose clothes boutiques, novelty
stores, Thai and Italian restaurants, California cuisine,
maybe a glimpse of hundreds of miles of smooth sand
dunes along the Baja coastline, inaccessible even by
4-wheel drive, and bit by bit they'll take out your teeth
and eyes, your sexual parts and your hair, your original
shoes and sunglasses will be put away, they'll take you
to Santa Barbara and drive you by some house in the
hills, have you listen to canned conversation down to
Montecito Country Club, somebody will be out playing
golf and they'll leave you in the car, by then you'll
know how to wait, your shit good and gone, everything
removed from lockers and computer files, you can check
the glove compartment but you won't even be wearing
your own shoes or eyeglasses, ideals or nightmares,
you'll be fucked and nothing will be yours, that's when
they will begin to say yes, they will say yes, yes, they
will say yes and no, no and yes, they will take you
to where you can see the waves starting far out at sea,
coming in across the big patches of light on the ocean
and moving across the far distant point, they will do
the talking and you won't care at all.

*1996*


## Look and look again, will he glance up all of a sudden

Look and look again, will he glance up all of a sudden,
his eyes lit from below in a satanic grin, his hanging
face, his mestizo hair black and dusty? The pallid paint
job is a put off, it's a cover for his indigenous passion,
his transsexual nature beneath fingernail scratches of
white finish. He wears a triangle of roses, madera
blushing carnation luster. Look and look again, are the
long lines of his muscles from the famine of history/
our desperate glories, the spiritual confrontation of that
lanky belly with the material world, or is the cascade
of his ribs a genetic sign of his hereditary disposition to

higher things, the tension of breath ascending, leaping
off the hard couch of bones? His tree a platform for the
helicopter ride of consciousness? That fragile excruciated
chest exploding inside with chamber music of quena,
bombo, charango & guitarrón? Norteño shivers along
that accordion torso? Did the grease slide out of this
Semitic meat and enter splinters of Roman wood,
mummifying his serene mind? This architecture is based
on fact like a crime novel, spliced with metaphors for
the human condition, neat as question marks. But if
he was just to sigh, grit his teeth with the exasperation
of an actor who washed out for the part of Samson in
a '50's Hollywood loincloth epic, and raise his fat
brown eyes to these chaparral hills under a mean sky,
he'd know these stones weren't gonna roll for him, not
here, not simply for the trembling Buddhist gravity of
his baby eyelashes.

*1996*

## I'm always grateful no one hears this terrible racket

I'm always grateful no one hears this terrible racket:
the factories inside. I pull into King Taco, Brooklyn
& Soto, the doors of my face rapidly opening and
closing, electric eye busted, insects crawling in and out
of my ears. Nobody at the bus stop notices the clatter:
that makes me feel safe. But a cop cruiser crosses the
Willie Herron mural kitty-corner at the farmacia. It's
obscured, defaced, graffitied. The freeway thrashes, a
snake fastened to my leg. Epileptic with grief, it gums
my boots. My vehicle breathing hot, arms around my
neck. I feel like I'm with friends, the inverted cones
that descend from space. Eating tacos of butterflies.
Something's not quite right. That's easy to say, but
how to fix it? McDonald's is busy, getting big phone
calls, lots of drama. The sky airlifts teenagers into spheres
of heaven. Will they get shot there, too? Something
is sweet, I'm following it closely. There's a line, heating
up the street. I'm following something like honey. I
think it drips from brown eyes.

*1996*

## The Japanese man would not appear riding a horse

The Japanese man would not appear riding a horse
above the telephone pole like the marlboro man the
japanese man strode above the endive kale and parsley
weeding the glendale truck garden his life was not
picturesque like a hiroshige° block print or a flight of

---

*hiroshige*: Ando Hiroshige (1797–1858), Japanese painter celebrated for his wood block prints
of landscapes.

golden cranes across a kimono it was not a samurai flick
though his cotton clothing absorbed his sweat like the
pages of a book absorb the ink of meaning and desire
itself formed in his mind something long and cool as his
woman a piece of iced celery when he heard a shout in
english stood upright and saw the labor contractor
standing on the flatbed of the white man's truck waving
him over this morning what did it mean? after seeing the
billboard in town NO JAPS WANTED THIS IS A WHITE
NEIGHBORHOOD/ the old issei sat in the cluttered
living room in the boyle heights bungalow with his
cigarette in the tin ashtray cradled in the linen napkin
his wife always placed on the arm of the couch for him
and the marlboro commercial projected from the tv
into stale smoke as the old man lifted the cigarette in
his freckled knobby fingers and took a long drag.

1996

## Life Magazine, December, 1941

Life Magazine, December, 1941: "How to Tell Japs from
the Chinese" "Angry Citizens Victimize Allies With
Emotional Outburst At Enemy"
 War hysteria? The Jap and the Chinese are discernible
not merely from the instructive, easily interpreted
diagrams/photographs on this page—our helpful captions
denote distinctive bone structures and facial features—the
Jap and the Chinese also have distinguishing social
psychologies which will serve you well. When you slap
the Jap, his skin will blanche, but if you kick the yellow
Chinaman, he may cuss you in a heathen tongue. If you
burn down Chinatown/ hang Chinese in trees, their
tongues will curl and get black. But the Jap tends no
separate villages, each individual fiend must be beaten and
stomped. Drive out to the shack of the field hand with
laundry fluttering by the irrigation ditch/ it's hard to tell
what imported stoop labor inhabits this margin. You have
to shoot in the air and scream anything you want/ each
word imbued with hatred. At *LIFE* we are here to direct
your hatred to its proper object/ If the man inside the
shack is Kenji Uchioka, he may shoot at you with his
rifle/ watch out for that guy. If you locate him on the
city streets in a crowd, *LIFE* hastens to note, we in no
way condone mob violence/ patriotism has its ways and
means! You may ferret out the Japanese children from
interloping Asiatics by clever tactics/ harassment and fear,
look for urine puddled beneath classroom desks; be
forewarned/ keep your eyes open for that Uchioka guy.
Bust him down with the FBI in front of his family,
especially his little girl/ if you want to take him quietly.
Leavenworth, for the duration.

1966

## I try to pee but I can't

I try to pee but I can't. Nothing comes out. Except
for a thin black line. In the immense white lavatory
of the night, porcelain urinals shine like the whites
of eyes. Watts° burns. In a chocolate box of childhoods.
Rays of sunlight swirl with dust particles, then are
folded away. A procession moves up Whittier, low-
riders feeling a lovesick wet spot for the deaths of
JFK/Robert Kennedy. I listen to it through the wall.
It's always summer as far inside as we've come, back
up against this wall. You're a war child. You tell me,
which war is it? When Watts burns, maybe they will
cut us a break. I would like to see a break. I know,
you want me to come out with you. I would like to
see you, too. But I can't right now. Saturday, Sunday . . .
Two Marias head over to Evergreen Cemetery.
Monday . . . There is still too much light.

*1996*

---

*Watts*: twenty-square mile Los Angeles ghetto of 100,000 people; in 1965 substantial sec-
tions burned during the single largest racial disturbance in American history to that date.

# Martín Espada (b. 1957)

Born in Brooklyn, New York, of Puerto Rican parents—his father was a photographer who illustrated his first book—Espada now teaches at the University of Massachusetts, but his earlier experience is much wider. He was a night clerk in a transient hotel, a journalist in Nicaragua, a welfare rights paralegal, and later a tenant lawyer in Boston. In addition to writing his own poetry, he has edited collections of political poetry and of contemporary Latino poets. His political poetry is notable for making its points with great wit and bravado. In its capacity to use humor to raise consciousness, it recalls McGrath, but Espada's language is more direct.

## Bully

In the school auditorium,
the Theodore Roosevelt° statue
is nostalgic
for the Spanish-American war,
5    each fist lonely for a saber
or the reins of anguish-eyed horses,
or a podium to clatter with speeches
glorying in the malaria of conquest.

But now the Roosevelt school
10   is pronounced Hernández.
Puerto Rico has invaded Roosevelt
with its army of Spanish-singing children
in the hallways,
brown children devouring
15   the stockpiles of the cafeteria,
children painting Taíno ancestors
that leap naked across murals.

---

2 *Roosevelt:* (1858–1919), Twenty-sixth president of the U.S. (1901–1909). Roosevelt became famous when he organized a volunteer cavalry division known as the Rough Riders that served in Cuba at the outbreak of the Spanish-American War (1898). As president, his policy was aggressive and interventionist toward Latin America, as when he intervened in a Panamanian civil war in 1903.

Roosevelt is surrounded
by all the faces
20 he ever shoved in eugenic spite
and cursed as mongrels, skin of one race,
hair and cheekbones of another.

Once Marines tramped
from the newsreel of his imagination;
25 now children plot to spray graffiti
in parrot-brilliant colors
across the Victorian mustache
and monocle.

1987

## The Lover of a Subversive Is Also a Subversive

The lover of a subversive
is also a subversive.
The painter's compañero was a conspirator,
revolutionary convicted
5 to haunt the catacombs of federal prison
for the next half century.
When she painted her canvas
on the beach, the FBI man
squatted behind her
10 on the sand, muddying his dark gray suit
and kissing his walkie-talkie,
a pallbearer who missed
the funeral train.

The painter who paints a subversive
15 is also a subversive.
In her portrait of him, she imagines
his long black twist of hair. In her portraits
of herself, she wears a mask
or has no mouth. She must sell the canvases,
20 for the FBI man ministered solemnly
to the principal at the school
where she once taught.

The woman who grieves for a subversive
is also a subversive.
25 The FBI man is a pale-skinned apparition
staring in the subway.
She could reach for him
and only touch a pillar of ash
where the dark gray suit had been.
30 If she hungers to touch her lover,
she must brush her fingers
on moist canvas.

The lover of a subversive
is also a subversive.
35    When the beach chilled cold,
and the bright stumble of tourists
deserted, she and the FBI man
were left alone with their spying glances,
as he waited calmly
40    for the sobbing to begin,
and she refused to sob.

1993

## Federico's Ghost

The story is
that whole families of fruitpickers
still crept between the furrows
of the field at dusk,
5    when for reasons of whiskey or whatever
the cropduster plane sprayed anyway,
floating a pesticide drizzle
over the pickers
who thrashed like dark birds
10    in a glistening white net,
except for Federico,
a skinny boy who stood apart
in his own green row,
and, knowing the pilot
15    would not understand in Spanish
that he was the son of a whore,
instead jerked his arm
and thrust an obscene finger.

The pilot understood.
20    He circled the plane and sprayed again,
watching a fine gauze of poison
drift over the brown bodies
that cowered and scurried on the ground,
and aiming for Federico,
25    leaving the skin beneath his shirt
wet and blistered,
but still pumping his finger at the sky.

After Federico died,
rumors at the labor camp
30    told of tomatoes picked and smashed at night,
growers muttering of vandal children
or communists in camp,
first threatening to call Immigration,
then promising every Sunday off
35    if only the smashing of tomatoes would stop.

Still tomatoes were picked and squashed
in the dark,
and the old women in camp
said it was Federico,
40     laboring after sundown
to cool the burns on his arms,
flinging tomatoes
at the cropduster
that hummed like a mosquito
45     lost in his ear,
and kept his soul awake.

*1990*

## The Saint Vincent de Paul Food Pantry Stomp

Waiting for the carton of food
given with Christian suspicion
even to agency-certified charity cases
like me,
5     thin and brittle
as uncooked linguini,
anticipating the factory-damaged cans
of tomato soup, beets, three-bean salad
in a welfare cornucopia,
10     I spotted a squashed dollar bill
on the floor, and with
a Saint Vincent de Paul food pantry stomp
pinned it under my sneaker,
tied my laces meticulously,
15     and stuffed the bill in my sock
like a smuggler of diamonds,
all beneath the plaster statue wingspan
of Saint Vinnie,
who was unaware
20     of the dance
named in his honor
by a maraca shaker
in the salsa band
of the unemployed.

*1980*

## Fidel in Ohio°

The bus driver tore my ticket
and gestured at the tabloid
spread across the steering wheel.
The headline:

---

**poem title:** Fidel Castro (b. 1926) Cuban revolutionary and political leader, President of Cuba since 1959, a survivor despite U.S. attempts to overthrow his government. The poem playfully takes Castro as a symbol of widespread U.S. ignorance about Latin America.

1214

5      FIDEL CASTRO DEAD
       REPLACED BY IDENTICAL DOUBLE
       Below, two photographs of Fidel,
       one with cigar, one without.

       "The resemblance is amazing,"
10     the driver said,
       and I agreed.

                                              1993


## The Skull Beneath the Skin of the Mango

The woman spoke
with the tranquillity of shock:
the Army massacre was here.
But there were no peasant corpses,
no white crosses; even the houses
gone. Cameras chattered,
notebooks filled with rows of words.
Some muttered that slaughter
is only superstition
in a land of new treaties and ballot boxes.

Everyone gathered mangoes
before leaving. An American reporter,
arms crowded with fruit, could not see
what he kicked jutting from the ground.
He glanced down and found his sneaker
pressing against the forehead
of a human skull, yellow
like the flesh of a mango.

He wondered how many skulls
are crated with the mangoes
for sale at market, how many
grow yellow flesh and green skin
in the wooden boxes exported
to the States. This would explain,
he said to me,
why so many bodies
are found without heads
in El Salvador.

                                              1992


## Imagine the Angels of Bread

This is the year that squatters evict landlords,
gazing like admirals from the rail
of the roofdeck
or levitating hands in praise
5      of steam in the shower;

this is the year
that shawled refugees deport judges
who stare at the floor
and their swollen feet
10      as files are stamped
with their destination;
this the year that police revolvers,
stove-hot, blister the fingers
of raging cops,
15      and nightsticks splinter
in their palms;
this is the year
that darkskinned men
lynched a century ago
20      return to sip coffee quietly
with the apologizing descendants
of their executioners.

This is the year that those
who swim the border's undertow
25      and shiver in boxcars
are greeted with trumpets and drums
at the first railroad crossing
on the other side;
this is the year that the hands
30      pulling tomatoes from the vine
uproot the deed to the earth that sprouts the vine,
the hands canning tomatoes
are named in the will
that owns the bedlam of the cannery;
35      this is the year that the eyes
stinging from the poison that purifies toilets
awaken at last to the sight
of a rooster-loud hillside,
pilgrimage of immigrant birth;
40      this is the year that cockroaches
become extinct, that no doctor
finds a roach embedded
in the ear of an infant;
this is the year that the food stamps
45      of adolescent mothers
are auctioned like gold doubloons,
and no coin is given to buy machetes
for the next bouquet of severed heads
in coffee plantation country.

50      If the abolition of slave-manacles
began as a vision of hands without manacles,
then this is the year;
if the shutdown of extermination camps
began as imagination of a land
55      without barbed wire or the crematorium,
then this is the year;

if every rebellion begins with the idea
that conquerors on horseback
are not many-legged gods, that they too drown
60  if plunged in the river,
then this is the year.

So may every humiliated mouth,
teeth like desecrated headstones,
fill with the angels of bread.

*1996*

# Sherman Alexie (b. 1966)

Sherman Alexie's visibility and reputation have increased so rapidly in the 1990's that at times he seems more a natural phenomenon, like a summer thunderstorm, than a mere writer. But an astonishingly inventive writer he is. The son of a Spokane father and a part-Coeur d'Alene mother, Alexie grew up on the Spokane Indian Reservation in Wellpinit, Washington. He was educated first at Gonzaga University in Spokane and then at Washington State University in Pullman; he now lives in Seattle. His first book of poems and prose poems, *The Business of Fancydancing*, was selected as a Notable Book of the Year by the *New York Times Book Review* in 1992. His next poetry collection, *First Indian on the Moon*, appeared the following year, along with a volume of his short fiction, *The Lone Ranger and Tonto Fistfight in Heaven*. Alexie has since reworked the short story collection into a film script, which was released as a major motion picture, *Smoke Signals*, in 1998. That same year he was on public television in a panel discussion about race with the U.S. president. And he has continued to be a prolific writer of poetry and fiction, while simultaneously exploring other media. A musical collaboration with Jim Boyd, *Reservation Blues—The Soundtrack*, based on a 1996 Alexie novel, was released on compact disk in 1995.

Proficient at adapting traditional stanzaic forms, Alexie writes poetry notable for its fusion of cultural criticism and a highly focused irreverence. He has an exuberant, inventive imagination that generates continual surprises and gives him the courage to try almost anything in his writing. Not all his experiments succeed, but no writer as productive as Alexie could succeed all the time. Meanwhile, he has followed Adrian Louis's example in writing poetry of astonishing frankness about both the Native American world and the surrounding dominant culture.

## Indian Boy Love Song (#2)

I never spoke
the language
of the old women

visiting my mother
5   in winters so cold
they could freeze
the tongue whole.

I never held my head
to their thin chests
10    believing in the heart.

Indian women, forgive me.
I grew up distant
and always afraid.

1992

## *from* The Native American Broadcasting System

### 9.

I am the essence of powwow,° I am
toilets without paper, I am fry bread
in sawdust, I am bull dung
on rodeo grounds at the All-Indian
5    Rodeo and Horse Show, I am

the essence of powwow, I am
video games with braids, I am spit
from toothless mouths, I am turquoise
and bootleg whiskey, both selling
10    for twenty bucks a swallow, I am

the essence of powwow, I am
fancydancers in flannel, I am host drum
amplified, I am *Fuck you*
*don't come back* and *Leave me*

15    *the last hard drink.* I am
the essence of powwow, I am the dream
you lace your shoes with, I am
the lust between your toes, I am
the memory you feel across the bottom
of your feet whenever you walk too close.

1993

---

1 *powwow:* the term comes from the Algonquin word *pawauogs,* meaning shamanistic cur-
ing ceremonies, but the modern term has its roots in the dances, social events, and cere-
monies of the plains and prairie tribes. Contemporary powwows are often not tribally ex-
clusive; even when sponsored by a single tribal community, they are, in effect, nonexclusive,
pan-Indian celebrations of Native American culture and history. Dancing of many histor-
ical varieties is their central feature. But the very largest powwows are no longer commu-
nity celebrations but rather performances for white audiences who pay an admission fee.

# Evolution

Buffalo Bill opens a pawn shop on the reservation
right across the border from the liquor store
and he stays open 24 hours a day, 7 days a week

and the Indians come running in with jewelry
5     television sets, a VCR, a full-length beaded buckskin outfit
it took Inez Muse 12 years to finish. Buffalo Bill

takes everything the Indians have to offer, keeps it
all catalogued and filed in a storage room. The Indians
pawn their hands, saving the thumbs for last, they pawn

10    their skeletons, falling endlessly from the skin
and when the last Indian has pawned everything
but his heart, Buffalo Bill takes that for twenty bucks

closes up the pawn shop, paints a new sign over the old
calls his venture THE MUSEUM OF NATIVE AMERICAN
CULTURES
charges the Indians five bucks a head to enter.

*1992*

# Scalp Dance by Spokane Indians

*Before leaving Spokane Falls, Paul Kane dropped down to the nearby village
of Kettle Falls to paint his now-famous "Scalp Dance by Spokane Indians" in
oils on canvas. Its central figure, a woman who had lost her husband to the
Blackfeet, whirled around a fire swashing and kicking in revenge a Blackfoot
scalp on a stick. Behind her, eight painted women danced and chanted, as did
the rest of the tribe to the beat of drums.*
—FROM THE SPOKANE INDIANS: CHILDREN OF THE SUN
BY ROBERT H. RUBY AND JOHN A. BROWN

Always trying to steal a little bit of soul, you know? Whether it be po-
etry or oils on canvas. They call themselves artists but they are really
archaeologists.

Really, that's all any kind of art is.

And who am I, you ask? I'm the woman in the painting. I'm the
one dancing with the Blackfoot scalp on a stick. But I must tell you
the truth. I never had a husband. The artist, Paul Kane, painted me
from memory. He saw me at Fort Spokane, even touched his hand to
my face as if I were some caged and tame animal in a zoo.

"I need to memorize that curve," he said.

In fact, I have never shared tipi and blanket with any man. When
Paul Kane touched me I struck him down and only the hurried nego-
tiations of a passing missionary saved me from Kane's anger. But far
from that, I am also a healer, a woman who reserves her touch for
larger things.

Paul Kane was nothing except an artist.

But you must remember Kane was also an observant man. He watched many Spokanes put themselves to death. He thought it was because of gambling losses. But no, it was because of all the loss that the Spokane Indians were forced to endure.

Like the loss of soul I felt when I found myself in that painting years later. Ever since Paul Kane had touched me that day, I had felt something missing: a tooth, a fingernail, a layer of skin.

You must also understand that we treated Paul Kane well even as he conspired to steal. Some sat still for his portraits and didn't smile because Kane insisted they remain stoic. That was his greatest mistake. Our smiles were everything; our laughter created portraits in the air, more colorful and exact than any in Kane's work.

I have seen all his paintings and Kane never let us smile. When you see me now in that painting, dancing with the scalp, you must realize that I didn't have a husband, that I never danced without a smile, that I never sat still for Kane.

That is the truth. All of it.

1993

## How to Write the Great American Indian Novel

All of the Indians must have tragic features: tragic noses, eyes, and
   arms.
Their hands and fingers must be tragic when they reach for tragic
   food.

The hero must be a half-breed, half white and half Indian,
   preferably
from a horse culture. He should often weep alone. That is
   mandatory.

5      If the hero is an Indian woman, she is beautiful. She must be
   slender
and in love with a white man. But if she loves an Indian man

then he must be a half-breed, preferably from a horse culture.
If the Indian woman loves a white man, then he has to be so white

that we can see the blue veins running through his skin like rivers.
10    When the Indian woman steps out of her dress, the white man
   gasps

at the endless beauty of her brown skin. She should be compared
   to nature:
brown hills, mountains, fertile valleys, dewy grass, wind, and clear
   water.

If she is compared to murky water, however, then she must have a
   secret.
Indians always have secrets, which are carefully and slowly
   revealed.

15      Yet Indian secrets can be disclosed suddenly, like a storm.
Indian men, of course, are storms. They should destroy the lives

of any white women who choose to love them. All white women
    love
Indian men. That is always the case. White women feign disgust

at the savage in blue jeans and T-shirt, but secretly lust after him.
20      White women dream about half-breed Indian men from horse
    cultures.

Indian men are horses, smelling wild and gamey. When the Indian
    man
unbuttons his pants, the white woman should think of topsoil.

There must be one murder, one suicide, one attempted rape.
Alcohol should be consumed. Cars must be driven at high speeds.

25      Indians must see visions. White people can have the same visions
if they are in love with Indians. If a white person loves an Indian

then the white person is Indian by proximity. White people must
    carry
an Indian deep inside themselves. Those interior Indians are half-
    breed

and obviously from horse cultures. If the interior Indian is male
30      then he must be a warrior, especially if he is inside a white man.

If the interior Indian is female, then she must be a healer, espe-
    cially if she is inside
a white woman. Sometimes there are complications.

An Indian man can be hidden inside a white woman. An Indian
    woman
can be hidden inside a white man. In these rare instances,

35      everybody is a half-breed struggling to learn more about his or her
    horse culture.
There must be redemption, of course, and sins must be forgiven.

For this, we need children. A white child and an Indian child,
    gender
not important, should express deep affection in a childlike way.

In the Great American Indian novel, when it is finally written,
all of the white people will be Indians and all of the Indians will
    be ghosts.

*1996*

# Tourists

### 1. *James Dean*°

walks everywhere now. He's afraid of fast cars
and has walked this far, arriving
suddenly on the reservation, in search
of the Indian woman of his dreams.
5    He wants an Indian woman who could pass
for Natalie Wood.° He wants an Indian woman
who looks like the Natalie Wood
who was kidnapped by Indians
in John Ford's° classic movie, "The Searchers."
10    James Dean wants to rescue somebody beautiful.
He still wears that red jacket,
you know the one. It's the color of a powwow fire.
James Dean has never seen
a powwow, but he joins right in, dancing
15    like a crazy man, like a profane clown.
James Dean cannot contain himself.
He dances in the wrong direction. He tears
at his hair. He sings in wild syllables
and does not care. The Indian dancers stop
20    and stare like James Dean was lightning
or thunder, like he was bad weather.
But he keeps dancing, bumps into a man
and knocks loose an eagle feather.
The feather falls, drums stop.
25    This is the kind of silence
that frightens white men. James Dean
looks down at the feather
and knows that something has gone wrong.
He looks into the faces of the Indians.
30    He wants them to finish the song.

### 2. *Janis Joplin*°

sits by the jukebox in the Powwow Tavern,
talking with a few drunk Indians

---

*James Dean:* (1931–1955), American actor whose films include *Rebel Without a Cause* (1955)
and *Giant* (1956), and who died in a car crash just after the latter film finished shooting.
Idolized by a generation that came of age in the 1950s, David Thomson has described him
as an actor "whose resignation and fatalism showed up the restricted personality of the
world he lived in."
6 *Natalie Wood:* (1938–1981), Hollywood actress who began her film career as a child, later
played roles in such films as *Rebel Without a Cause, Splendor in the Grass* (1961), and *West
Side Story* (1961).
9 *John Ford:* (1895–1973), one of the most famous American film directors of the 1940s,
1950s, and early 1960s; his films include a number of westerns starring John Wayne, *The
Searchers* (1956) being the most memorable.
*Janis Joplin:* (1943–1970), one of the most influential and charismatic performers during
the heyday of American rock music; a rebel with a throaty, thunderous delivery, she be-
came a legend after her death from a drug overdose.

about redemption. She promises each of them
she can punch in the numbers
35    for the song that will save their lives.
All she needs is a few quarters, a beer,
and their own true stories. The Indians
are as traditional as drunk Indians can be
and don't believe in autobiography,
40    so they lie to Janis Joplin about their lives.
One Indian is an astronaut, another killed JFK,
while the third played first base
for the New York Yankees. Janis Joplin knows
the Indians are lying. She's a smart woman
45    but she listens anyway, plays them each a song,
and sings along off key.

### 3. *Marilyn Monroe°*

drives herself to the reservation. Tired and cold,
she asks the Indian women for help.
Marilyn cannot explain what she needs
50    but the Indian women notice the needle tracks
on her arms and lead her to the sweat lodge°
where every woman, young and old, disrobes
and leaves her clothes behind
when she enters the dark of the lodge.
55    Marilyn's prayers may or may not be answered here
but they are kept sacred by Indian women.
Cold water is splashed on hot rocks
and steam fills the lodge. There is no place like this.
At first, Marilyn is self-conscious, aware
60    of her body and face, the tremendous heat, her thirst,
and the brown bodies circled around her.
But the Indian women do not stare. It is dark
inside the lodge. The hot rocks glow red
and the songs begin. Marilyn has never heard
65    these songs before, but she soon sings along.
Marilyn is not Indian, Marilyn will never be Indian
but the Indian women sing about her courage.
The Indian women sing for her health.
The Indian women sing for Marilyn.
Finally, she is no more naked than anyone else.

                                                  1996

---

*Marilyn Monroe:* (1926–1962), American movie actress whose films include *River of No Return* (1954), *Bus Stop* (1956), and *Some Like It Hot* (1959); she became both a sex symbol and, after her suicide, a symbol of the terrible psychological price Hollywood stardom can exact from women.
51 *sweat lodge:* built of branches shaped as a dome, with a cover of blankets or skins, ceremonial sweat lodges with their concentrated heat connect participants to the past, the earth, and the spirit world; the U.S. government tried to outlaw sweat lodge rituals in the nineteenth century.

# Graphic Interpretations

# "The Man With the Hoe."

Written After Seeing Millet's World-Famous Painting.

## By Edwin Markham.

*God made man in His own image,
in the image of God made He him.*—Genesis.

BOWED by the weight of centuries he leans
　　Upon his hoe and gazes on the ground,
　　The emptiness of ages in his face,
And on his back the burden of the world.
Who made him dead to rapture and despair,
A thing that grieves not and that never hopes,
Stolid and stunned, a brother to the ox?
Who loosened and let down this brutal jaw?
Whose was the hand that slanted back this brow?
Whose breath blew out the light within this brain?

Is this the Thing the Lord God made and gave
To have dominion over sea and land;
To trace the stars and search the heavens for power;
To feel the passion of Eternity?
Is this the Dream He dreamed who shaped the suns
And pillared the blue firmament with light?
Down all the stretch of Hell to its last gulf
There is no shape more terrible than this—
More tongued with censure of the world's blind greed—
More filled with signs and portents for the soul—
More fraught with menace to the universe.

What gulfs between him and the seraphim!
Slave of the wheel of labor, what to him
Are Plato and the swing of Pleindes?
What the long reaches of the peaks of song,
The rift of dawn, the reddening of the rose?
Through this dread shape the suffering ages look;
Time's tragedy is in that aching stoop;
Through this dread shape humanity betrayed,
Plundered, profaned and disinherited,
Cries protest to the Judges of the World,
A protest that is also prophecy.

O masters, lords and rulers in all lands,
Is this the handiwork you give to God,
This monstrous thing distorted and soul-quenched?
How will you ever straighten up this shape;
Touch it again with immortality;
Give back the upward looking and the light;
Rebuild in it the music and the dream;
Make right the immemorial infamies,
Perfidious wrongs, immedicable woes?

O masters, lords and rulers in all lands,
How will the Future reckon with this Man?
How answer his brute question in that hour
When whirlwinds of rebellion shake the world?
How will it be with kingdoms and with kings—
With those who shaped him to the thing he is—
When this dumb Terror shall reply to God,
After the silence of the centuries?

OAKLAND, CALIFORNIA.

THE VIRGINIANS ARE COMING

From the American Mercury, July, 1928

This song is to be chanted to your own unwritten troubadour chant or intoned by yourself after reading the poem once or twice to yourself aloud out-of-doors.

VACHEL LINDSAY

## I

Babbitt, your tribe is passing away.
This is the end of your infamous day.
The Virginians are coming again.

With your neat little safety-vault boxes,
With your faces like geese and foxes,
You
Short-legged, short-armed, short-minded men,
Your short-sighted days are over,
Your habits of strutting through clover,

Your movie-thugs, killing off souls and dreams,
Your magazines, drying up healing streams,
Your newspapers, blasting truth and splendor,
Your shysters, ruining progress and glory,

Babbitt, your story is passing away.
The Virginians are coming again.

All set for the victory, calling the raid
I see them, the next generation,
Gentlemen, hard-riding, long-legged men,
With horse-whip, dog-whip, gauntlet and braid,
Mutineers, musketeers,
In command
Unafraid:

Great-grandsons of tidewater, and the bark-cabins,
Bards of the Blue-ridge, in buckskin and boots,
Up from the proudest war-path we have known
The Virginians are coming again.

The sons of ward-heelers
Threw out the ward-heelers,
The sons of bartenders
Threw out the bartenders,
And made our streets trick-boxes all in a day,
Kicked out the old pests in a virtuous way.

The new tribe sold kerosene, gasoline, paraffine.
Babbitt sold Judas, Babbitt sold Christ,
Babbitt sold everything under the sun.
The Moon-Proud consider a trader a hog.
The Moon-Proud are coming again.

Bartenders were gnomes,
Foreigners, tyrants, hairy babboons.
But you are no better with saxophone tunes,
Phonograph tunes, radio tunes,
Water-power tunes, gasoline tunes, dynamo tunes,
And pitiful souls like your pitiful tunes,
And crawling old insolence blocking the road,

So, Babbitt, your racket is passing away.
Your sons will be changelings, and burn down your world.
Fire-eaters, troubadours, conquistadors.

Your sons will be born, refusing your load,
Thin-skinned scholars, hard-riding men,
Poets unharnessed, the moon their abode,
With the statesmen's code, the gentlemen's code,
With Jefferson's code, Washington's code,
With Powhatan's code!
From your own loins, for your fearful defeat
The Virginians are coming again.

## II

Our first Virginians were peasants' children,
But the Power of Powhatan reddened their blood,
Up from the sod came splendor and flood.
Eating the maize made them more than men,
Potomac fountains made gods of men.

## III

In your tottering age, not so long from you now,
The terror will blast, the armies will whirl,
Cavalier boy beside cavalier girl!
In the glory of pride, not the pride of the rich,
In the glory of statesmanship, not of the ditch.
The old grand manner, lost no longer:

Exquisite art born with heart-bleeding song
Will make you die horribly raving at wrong.
You will not know your sons who are true to this soil,

For Babbitt could never count much beyond ten,
For Babbitt could never quite comprehend men.
You will die in your shame, understanding not day.

Out of your loins, to your utmost confusion
The Virginians are coming again.

Do you think boys and girls that I pass on the street,
More strong than their fathers, more fair than their fathers,
More clean than their fathers, more wild than their fathers,
More in love than their fathers, deep in thought not their fathers',
Are meat for your schemes diabolically neat?

Do you think that all youth is but grist to your mill
And what you dare plan for them, boys will fulfill?
The next generation is free. You are gone.
Out of your loins, to your utmost confusion
The Virginians are coming again.

**IV**

*Rouse the reader to read it right.*
*Find a good hill by the full-moon light.*
*Gather the boys and chant all night:—*
*"The Virginians are coming again."*

*Put in rhetoric, whisper and hint,*
*Put in shadow, murmur and glint;*
*Jingle and jangle this song like a spur,*
*Sweep over each tottering bridge with a whirr,*
*Clearer and faster up main street and pike*
*Till sparks flare up from the flints that strike.*

*Leap metrical ditches with bridle let loose.*
*This song is a war, with an iron-shod use.*

*Let no musician, with blotter and pad*
*Scribble his pot-hooks to make the song sad.*
***Find***
*Your own rhythms*
*When Robert E. Lee*
*Gallops once more to the plain from the sea.*
*Give the rebel yell every river they gain.*

*Hear Lee's light cavalry rhyme with rain.*
*In the star-proud, natural fury of men*
*The Virginians are coming again.*

*Vachel Lindsay*
*603 South Fifth, Springfield, Illinois*

# FINE LIVING ... *a la carte ??* Come to

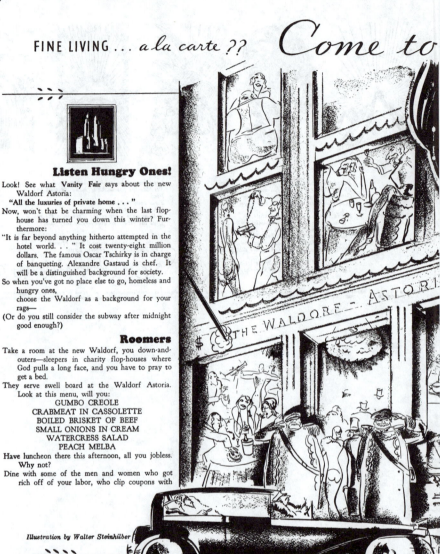

## Listen Hungry Ones!

Look! See what **Vanity Fair** says about the new Waldorf Astoria:

**"All the luxuries of private home . . . "**

Now, won't that be charming when the last flophouse has turned you down this winter? Furthermore:

"It is far beyond anything hitherto attempted in the hotel world. . . " It cost twenty-eight million dollars. The famous Oscar Tschirky is in charge of banqueting. Alexandre Gastaud is chef. It will be a distinguished background for society.

So when you've got no place else to go, homeless and hungry ones,

choose the Waldorf as a background for your rags—

(Or do you still consider the subway after midnight good enough?)

## Roomers

Take a room at the new Waldorf, you down-and-outers—sleepers in charity flop-houses where God pulls a long face, and you have to pray to get a bed.

They serve swell board at the Waldorf Astoria. Look at this menu, will you:

GUMBO CREOLE
CRABMEAT IN CASSOLETTE
BOILED BRISKET OF BEEF
SMALL ONIONS IN CREAM
WATERCRESS SALAD
PEACH MELBA

Have luncheon there this afternoon, all you jobless. Why not?

Dine with some of the men and women who got rich off of your labor, who clip coupons with

*Illustration by Walter Steinhilber*

# the *Waldorf-Astoria!*

clean white fingers because your hands dug coal, drilled stone, sewed garments, poured steel—to let other people draw dividends and live easy.

(Or haven't you had enough yet of the soup-lines and the bitter bread of charity?)

Walk through Peacock Alley tonight before dinner, and get warm, anyway. You've got nothing else to do.

## Evicted Families

All you families put out in the street: Apartments in the Towers are only $10,000 a year. (Three rooms and two baths.)  Move in there until times get good, and you can do better. $10,000 and $1.00 are about the same to you, aren't they?

Who cares about money with a wife and kids homeless, and nobody in the family working? Wouldn't a duplex high above the street be grand, with a view of the richest city in the world at your nose?

"A lease, if you prefer; or an arrangement terminable at will."

## Negroes

O, Lawd, I done forgot Harlem!

Say, you colored folks, hungry a long time in 135th Street—they got swell music at the Waldorf-Astoria. It sure is a mighty nice place to shake hips in, too.  There's dancing after supper in a big warm room.  It's cold as hell on Lenox Avenue. All you've had all day is a cup of coffee.  Your pawnshop overcoat's a ragged banner on your hungry frame. . . . You know, down-town folks are just crazy about Paul Robeson. Maybe they'd like you, too, black mob from Harlem. Drop in at the Waldorf this afternoon for tea. Stay to dinner.  Give Park Avenue a lot of darkie color —free—for nothing! Ask the Junior Leaguers to sing a spiritual for you.  They probably know 'em better than you do—and their lips won't be so chapped with cold after they step out of their closed cars in the undercover driveways.

Hallelujah! under-cover driveways!

Ma soul's a witness for de Waldorf-Astoria!

(A thousand nigger section-hands keep the roadbeds smooth, so investments in railroads pay

ladies with diamond necklaces staring at Cert murals.)

Thank God A-Mighty!

(And a million niggers bend their backs on rubber plantations, for rich behinds to ride on thick tires to the Theatre Guild tonight.)

Ma soul's a witness!

(And here we stand, shivering in the cold, in Harlem.)

Glory be to God—

De Waldorf-Astoria's open!

## Everybody

So get proud and rare back, everybody!  The new Waldorf-Astoria's open!

(Special siding for private cars from the railroad yards.)

You ain't been there yet?

(A thousand miles of carpet and a million bath rooms.)

What's the matter?  You haven't seen the ads in the papers?  Didn't you get a card?  Don't you know they specialize in American cooking?

Ankle on down to 49th Street at Park Avenue.  Get up off that subway bench tonight with the evening POST for cover!  Come on out o' that flop-house!  Stop shivering your guts out all day on street corners under the L.

Jesus, ain't you tired yet?

## Christmas Card

Hail Mary, Mother of God!

The new Christ child of the Revolution's about to be born.

(Kick hard, red baby, in the bitter womb of the mob.)

Somebody, put an ad in **Vanity Fair** quick!

Call Oscar of the Waldorf—for Christ's sake!

It's almost Christmas, and that little girl—turned whore because her belly was too hungry to stand it any more—wants a nice clean bed for the Immaculate Conception.

Listen, Mary, Mother of God, wrap your new born babe in the red flag of Revolution:

The Waldorf-Astoria's the best manger we've got.

For reservations: Telephone

ELdorado 5-3000.

### *by Langston Hughes*

## Christ in Alabama

Christ is a Nigger,
Beaten and black—
*O, bare your back.*

Mary is His Mother—
*Mammy of the South,*
*Silence your mouth.*

God's His Father—
*White Master above,*
*Grant us your love.*

Most holy bastard
Of the bleeding mouth:
*Nigger Christ*
*On the cross of the South.*

WE REAL COOL
BY GWENDOLYN BROOKS
The Pool Players,
Seven at the Golden Shovel

WE REAL COOL. WE
LEFT SCHOOL. WE

LURK LATE. WE
STRIKE STRAIGHT. WE
SING SIN. WE
THIN GIN. WE

JAZZ JUNE. WE
DIE SOON.

Designed by Cledie Taylor
"We Real Cool" from Selected Poems by Gwendolyn Brooks
Copyright © 1959 by Gwendolyn Brooks Blakely

BROADSIDE No. 6. December 1966
BROADSIDE PRESS, 12651 OLD MILL PLACE, DETROIT, MICHIGAN 48238

# Index of Poem Titles

# Index of Poets

# About the Editor

Cary Nelson is Jubilee Professor of Liberal Arts and Sciences and Professor of English and Criticism and Interpretive Theory at the University of Illinois at Urbana-Champaign. He is the author of *The Incarnate Word: Literature as Verbal Space* (1973), *Our Last First Poets: Vision and History in Contemporary American Poetry* (1981), *Repression and Recovery: Modern American Poetry and the Politics of Cultural Memory, 1910–1945* (1989), *Shouts from the Wall: Posters and Photographs Brought Home from the Spanish Civil War by American Volunteers* (1996), *Manifesto of A Tenured Radical* (1997), and the coauthor of *Academic Keywords: A Devil's Dictionary for Higher Education* (1999). His edited or coedited books include *Theory in the Classroom* (1986), *W. S. Merwin: Essays on the Poetry* (1987), *Regions of Memory: Uncollected Prose by W. S. Merwin* (1987), *Marxism and the Interpretation of Culture* (1988), *Edwin Rolfe: A Biographical Essay* (1990), *Cultural Studies* (1992), Edwin Rolfe's *Collected Poems* (1993), *Higher Education Under Fire: Politics, Economics, and the Crisis of the Humanities* (1994), *Madrid 1937: Letters of the Abraham Lincoln Brigade from the Spanish Civil War* (1996), *Disciplinarity and Dissent in Cultural Studies* (1996), *Will Teach for Food: Academic Labor in Crisis* (1997), *The Aura of the Cause: A Photo Album for North American Volunteers in the Spanish Civil War* (1997), and *The Wound and the Dream: Sixty Years of American Poems About the Spanish Civil War* (forthcoming). He is presently completing *Modern American Poems We Have Wanted to Forget*. He serves on the National Council of the American Association of University Professors and on the Executive Council of the Modern Language Association.